FEDERAL INCOME TAXATION OF INDIVIDUALS:

CASES, PROBLEMS & MATERIALS

Second Edition

By

Samuel A. Donaldson
Associate Professor of Law
Director, Graduate Program in Taxation
University of Washington School of Law

AMERICAN CASEBOOK SERIES®

THOMSON
™
WEST

Mat # 40540329

American Casebook Series and West Group are trademarks registered in the U.S. Patent and Trademark Office.

© West, a Thomson business, 2005
© 2007 Thomson/West
      610 Opperman Drive
      P.O. Box 64526
      St. Paul, MN 55164–0526
      1–800–328–9352
Printed in the United States of America

ISBN: 978–0–314–17597–7

 TEXT IS PRINTED ON 10% POST CONSUMER RECYCLED PAPER

Dedication

This casebook is dedicated to Professor Arthur W. Andrews, the Dorothy H. and Lewis Rosenstiel Distinguished Professor of Law at the University of Arizona James E. Rogers College of Law.

In his 36 years of law teaching, Professor Andrews introduced thousands of students, including me, to the wonderful complexity and compelling human drama that is federal income taxation. His superb instructional skills and gregarious manner inspired countless disciples, again including me, to pursue an LL.M. in Taxation and a career as a tax attorney. Professor Andrews possessed all of the qualities of a great lawyer: attention to detail, an inquiring intellect, and most importantly, both a sense of humor and a deep compassion for others. Whether he knew it or not, he was a model of professionalism and excellence for his students, again including me.

If I am fortunate enough to teach for 36 years, I doubt I will have the same influence that Professor Andrews has had. For certain, I will never have his classroom presence. Even now, more than a decade since I sat as a student in his class, I can still remember many of his unique expressions and teaching methods. Every day, students walked into a classroom with a whiteboard *completely* covered with charts, outlines, diagrams, and summaries. (In fact, he usually reserved the classroom for the hour before his classes just to have the time to prepare the board for each class session.) As if by magic, Professor Andrews turned this mountain of information and numbers into something meaningful and useful for students. Upon the conclusion of each class session, Professor Andrews dismissed the class with his trademark signoff, "Peace." By that time, students had ten pages of notes, a better understanding of the material, and writers' cramp.

It seems most fitting, therefore, that a text created to assist in the learning and teaching of federal income taxation be dedicated to one of the premier tax teachers and scholars. Professor Andrews retired from law teaching at the end of 2004. Thanks for all of your support and guidance, Professor Andrews. Peace.

*

Preface

> In my own case the words of such an act as the Income Tax, for example, merely dance before my eyes in a meaningless procession: cross-reference to cross-reference, exception upon exception—couched in abstract terms that offer no handle to seize hold of—leave in my mind only a confused sense of some vitally important, but successfully concealed, purport, which it is my duty to extract, but which is within my power, if at all, only after the most inordinate expenditure of time.
>
> —Judge Learned Hand, *Thomas Walter Swan*,
> 57 Yale L. J. 167, 169 (1947).

The Function and Structure of this Book

The primary texts for any course in federal taxation are the Internal Revenue Code and the corresponding regulations issued by the United States Department of the Treasury. This book serves as a supplement to the Code and regulation provisions applicable to the federal income taxation of individuals. It contains various materials designed to explain and analyze the fundamental interpretive issues, doctrines, and public policies at play in this field.

Perhaps most importantly, this book offers structure, the "handle to seize hold" that Judge Hand so desperately sought. The federal income tax laws are marvelously complex, to be sure, but it is certainly possible to walk away from an introductory course in taxation with a sense of the big picture and an appreciation of some of the finer details required to make that big picture work in a complicated society.

Taxation affects all of us and is often the guiding force behind our personal and business transactions. We hate to pay taxes, but we all benefit from the revenues generated. As Oliver Wendell Holmes observed, "Taxes are what we pay for civilized society." With taxes, we buy infrastructure, protection, maintenance and preservation of national parks, and other benefits we all enjoy. We also use the revenues to provide education, Medicare and Social Security benefits, although some of us get more benefit than others from these programs. We even use the tax receipts to service the national debt. Like them or not, without taxes, we revert back to a state described by Thomas Hobbes as "solitary, poor, nasty, brutish, and short."

The most significant source of revenue for the federal government is also the exclusive focus of this book: the individual income tax. General topics to be discussed include the computation of individual tax liability, the nature of gross income, statutory exclusions from gross income, deductions allowed in the computation of taxable income, basic timing and accounting issues, and characterization of income. Journalists might find this description more helpful: This book is about _what_ items of income are taxed (and what types of expenses are deductible), _when_ such items should be taken into account for tax purposes, _who_ is the proper taxpayer to report a particular income or deduction item, _how_ different types of income are taxed, and _why_ the rules read as they do.

While the hope is that this book facilitates your learning of the fundamental concepts related to the federal income taxation of individuals, this book is no substitute for reading from the Code and regulation provisions themselves. Mere mention of the Internal Revenue Code invokes chills down many spines. Contemporary political rhetoric paints the Internal Revenue Code as something less approachable than the Old English versions of _Beowulf_ and _The Canterbury Tales_. Without ever reading the Code, armchair commentators deem it overly complex and inefficient. Others point to long sentences with technical terms as they decry complexity. These commentators have scared most of us away from trying to understand the basic rules. No doubt several of your peers refuse to enroll in this course because they fear it will be "too technical," "too mathematical," or simply "dull."

There is no denying that the Code contains long sentences, and many sentences do rely upon cross-references for complete understanding. The Code is an intricate set of detailed rules, and we will now shy away from the detail in this text. But like anything in life, one can become proficient with the Code through attentive study and perseverance. By the end of your first tax course, you might even _appreciate_ the Code as generally well-written and devoid of unnecessary clutter. What makes the Code so "technical" is its absence of excessive (or, to be more pejorative, "fluffy") terms that reward casual reading. Densely-packed sentences may not be the easiest to read, but they contain more information in fewer words.

Thus far in law school, you have learned how to read complicated cases, law review articles, and some statutes with an increasing degree of speed. It used to take three or four hours to read 15 pages in a casebook—now you can do it in an hour or less. What makes this subject somewhat different is that you will have to slow back down when you read from the Code or the regulations. You will often need to read a provision twice, three times, maybe more before it makes sense. You will find exceptions to rules, exceptions to the exceptions, and, yes, even exceptions to the exceptions to the exceptions. Then, when you think you have the gist of the statute, you have to apply your understanding to a basic fact pattern. In many cases, this process helps you find the holes in your earlier analysis, and you have to return to the Code (yet _again_) to dig deeper. Reading and applying the Code and Regulations is a difficult exercise, not because of the Code's "technicality," but because of the unique skills required in statutory analysis.

Maybe your fears lie elsewhere. For some, the reluctance associated with this subject stems from a fear of numbers. Liberal arts majors (like me) may shy away from taking a tax course because they think they will have to perform complex tax computations. This is simply not true. Oh sure, we will use numbers to illustrate transactions, and we will perform basic computations from time to time (especially early in the book). If you can add, subtract, multiply, and divide, you can successfully complete a basic income tax course. If use of a calculator gives you an added sense of security, then by all means carry one with you. For our purposes, numbers will be used to *help* illustrate basic concepts—they will not be used to obfuscate concepts. I promise.

Let's assume you are now convinced that the Code is not "too technical," and that the course will not be "too mathematical." You may still be concerned that the course will be dull. Rest assured that nothing could be further from the truth. Professor Martin Ginsburg noted that "[b]asic tax, as everyone knows, is the only genuinely funny subject in law school." We will read funny cases, and some fact patterns will stay with you long after the exam. Beyond humor, the study of taxation involves politics, history, sociology, economics, philosophy, drama, and other disciplines. We will see how taxation intersects with corporate law, family law, health law, property law, constitutional law, and estate planning. This may in fact prove to be one of the most interdisciplinary courses you take in law school.

This text has several instructional goals, but most importantly, this book is intended to improve your ability to comprehend and apply complex statutes and regulations. It would be a mistake simply to discuss the current rules in the Internal Revenue Code. For one thing, you will forget substantially all of the rules you learn in this book within a few months. That's not meant to insult you—it's just true that most of us forget black-letter rules within a relatively short time. Besides, taxation is a highly dynamic field of law. Almost every year, Congress amends the Internal Revenue Code. Sometimes, like in 1998, 1999, 2002, and 2005, the changes are fairly minor. Other times, like in 1986, 1990, 1993, 2001, 2003, 2004, and 2006, Congress changes the playing field dramatically. A book that simply explains the current law would have little long-term value. Regardless of how the law changes, however, a lawyer that possesses the ability to understand and apply the Code and regulations will be better prepared to handle a client's situation. Even if you do not become a tax lawyer (not everyone sees the light!), the ability to read, decipher, and apply complex statutes is an important skill that can be applied in virtually every legal field.

Many aspects of this book are dedicated to the goal of improving your skills in statutory analysis. For example, you will find several **Self-Assessment Questions** throughout the text. These SAQs are designed to measure immediate comprehension of core topics and to let you apply simple Code and regulation provisions outside of class. Answers to SAQs are set forth in Appendix 3, so you can check your answers prior to class and assess whether you need to spend additional time on certain topics. The SAQs also enhance your skills in applying laws to fact patterns.

In addition, each major section of the text contains one or more **Problems** designed for class discussion. The Problems are generally more complicated than the SAQs, and answers to Problems are not contained in the text. Instructors will likely use the Problems as the springboard for classroom discussions, as they help illustrate the Code and regulations in action. Most modern tax casebooks make extensive use of the problem method, and this text intentionally follows that trend.

Finally, the casebook contains a greater share of **diagrams** and flowcharts than what you would find in most other casebooks. These charts help show you how to read carefully and apply a statute or regulation. You can then use the same techniques when reading and applying other Code and regulation provisions assigned elsewhere in the text.

As mentioned above, the other chief goal of this text is to provide you with a sense of the structure of the federal income tax laws. Accordingly, the text is formatted to provide *three* **successive passes through the federal income tax system**, each in somewhat more detail. In addition to building long-term retention, the early runs through the system allow you to see the "big picture" early on.

Part One: A First Glance. The first run through the system introduces the basic tax tables and the fundamental concepts of progressivity, marginal tax rates, and effective tax rates. You will also learn the basic formula for computing the tax liability of individuals. These materials will give you a feel for the concepts of gross income, deductions, and credits that are developed in more detail throughout the text. The materials in the first part of the text will likely take about one week to cover in class, although instructors may spend more or less time on this material.

Part Two: A Closer Look. The second tour through the system explores the meaning of "gross income" and examines the federal income tax treatment of taxpayer costs. Here, you will read many of seminal cases defining gross income and get the chance to analyze and apply several of the principal exclusion provisions. With respect to taxpayer expenditures, the casebook presents a broad overview of the general rules followed by a detailed look at how taxpayers distinguish between business, investment, and personal activities, as well as distinguishing deductible expenses from non-deductible capital expenditures. The materials in this part of the casebook will likely consume about four to five weeks of class.

Part Three: A Hard Stare. The third trip through the system, which consumes the rest of the casebook, contains detailed examination of timing principles, characterization issues, personal deductions, and other more advanced topics. Instructors have the flexibility to mix and match the materials in this part of the casebook to customize their courses as they choose to fill the remaining four to nine weeks of class (depending upon whether the class is taught under a semester or quarter system).

Instructors teaching a very introductory (2 credit) course in federal income taxation can provide a sufficient overview simply by covering Parts One and Two of the book. If the federal income tax course is spread out over more than one term, an instructor can save many of the topics in Part Three for the second course. The text should thus be easily adaptable for all instructors.

Suggested Study Approach

Some of you might be wondering how to approach your study for this course. As a very busy law student, you want the most "bang for your buck," so to speak. You can get the most from your reading time by following this general approach for each assignment:

(1) Skim the assigned readings in the casebook. Try to get a sense of the main topic(s) covered in the assignment. Skimming the assignment lets you judge the time required to complete the assignment and helps you to budget that time effectively.

(2) Read the assigned Code and regulation provisions carefully. Relevant provisions of the Internal Revenue Code and corresponding Treasury regulations are set forth under each major heading in the book. You should read the assigned provisions carefully, except where the book tells you merely to skim the provisions.

(3) Read the materials in the casebook, looking for connections that help explain or develop the assigned Code and regulation provisions. Answer the Self-Assessment Questions as you encounter them in the text, and read the answers in Appendix 3.

(4) Write out complete answers to the "Problems." Be sure to include Code, regulation, case, or other authority for your answers where appropriate. By writing out the answers, you force yourself to articulate the rules as they apply to the fact pattern contained in the Problem. You will also get practice in writing answers to questions, which will be of great help come time for exams.

(5) Go over the answers to the Problems with one or more colleagues before class. This will not only save you from the possible embarrassment of saying something blatantly wrong in class, but will also help you see other perspectives of the Problems that you may have missed.

By following these steps for every assignment, you should be well prepared for class.

Formatting

Deleted material from cases, rulings, and other original sources is replaced with asterisks (* * *). Exceptions to this procedure involve case and statute citations, as well as footnotes. These items were omitted without any specification. Footnote numbers used in cases are retained as they appear in the original opinions. Thus, the footnotes may not run consecutively.

Acknowledgment

Many current and former students at the University of Washington School of Law contributed hours and hours to review and test drive this text, and their comments were especially helpful in reaching this final product. Special thanks go to Shawn Barrett, Audra Dineen, Emily Fountain, Daniel Jenkins, and Ilesa McAuliffe for their help with collecting cases, reviewing problems, checking citations, and endless proofreading. This Second Edition reflects not only important changes to the federal income tax laws since the publication of the First Edition but also the many helpful suggestions received from instructors and their students. Neither edition would have been possible without the support and encouragement of the editorial staff at West Law School, especially Heidi Hellekson.

SAMUEL A. DONALDSON
SEATTLE, WASHINGTON

Summary of Contents

Table of Contents

*

Table of Cases

The principal cases are in bold type. Cases cited or discussed in the text are roman type. References are to pages. Cases cited in principal cases and within other quoted materials are not included.

Table of Internal Revenue Code Sections

*

Table of Revenue Rulings

*

Table of Treasury Regulations

*

FEDERAL INCOME TAXATION OF INDIVIDUALS

CASES, PROBLEMS & MATERIALS

Second Edition

*

Part One

A FIRST GLANCE

Chapter 1

APPLICABLE TAX RATES

It's Time. We can put it off no longer—it is time to open the Internal Revenue Code. Pull out your copy of the Code and have it at your side at all times as we maneuver through this book. Approach it slowly ... carefully. Make sure it sees you coming—you do not want to startle it. Speak to it warmly, but with confidence. Introduce yourself. Don't expect a response (in fact, if you hear one, you should seek professional counseling). Your hands are probably moist; wipe them dry and gently open the Code, just to the Table of Contents.

The Internal Revenue Code is the official name for Title 26 of the United States Code. Notice that Title 26 is broken down into eleven "subtitles," the first of which, subtitle A, deals with "income taxes," our focus in this text. For our immediate purposes, the other ten subtitles are irrelevant, with one exception. We will occasionally look at provisions in subtitle F ("procedure and administration"). As the name implies, the provisions in subtitle F will tell us about various procedural matters: when returns are due, when taxes must be paid, how long the Internal Revenue Service has to "assess" a return and issue a deficiency notice if the taxpayer owes more money, and the like.

For now, though, let us focus on subtitle A, the income taxes. The subtitle is divided into six "chapters," the first of which is "normal taxes and surtaxes." The good news is that we will focus exclusively on chapter 1. The bad news is that chapter 1 is the largest chapter in the Code: it is further divided into 23 "subchapters." We will examine provisions in subchapters A (determination of tax liability), B (computation of taxable income), O (gain or loss on disposition of property), and P (capital gains and losses). The other subchapters are addressed in other, advanced tax courses. Subchapters are divided into "parts," which are sometimes then divided into "subparts." Parts (or subparts, if so divided) contain "sections." By custom, almost all references to Code provisions use the "section" as the starting point. In this book (as is the case in practically every book and article on federal income taxation), any citation with a section symbol, "§," is a reference to a section of the Code unless otherwise provided.

2

Having fun yet? In most cases, even sections are divided into various components: first come subsections, then paragraphs, then subparagraphs, then clauses and subclauses. Thus, "§ 170(e)(6)(B)(i)(II)" is technically "subclause (II) of clause (i) of subparagraph (B) of paragraph (6) of subsection (e) of section 170." No one actually says all that, of course. But it is helpful to know the difference between, for example, a paragraph and a clause. Sometimes a provision will say "solely for purposes of this *paragraph*" or "for purposes of this *subsection*." When you see this language, you always have to keep in mind that the rule only pertains to that particular portion of the Code section and not necessarily some other part of the same section.

Other Sources of Authority. Part of the complexity of this subject stems from the fact that there are so many sources of authority for the federal tax laws. While the Code is easily the most important source, there are others that deserve mention at the outset.

Congress writes the Code, but the United States Treasury Department and the Internal Revenue Service are charged with enforcing it. Section 7805(a) of the Code gives the Secretary of the Treasury the power to "prescribe all needful rules and regulations for the enforcement of this title." Federal tax regulations promulgated by the Treasury Department appear in Title 26 (go figure) of the Code of Federal Regulations. While you might see these regulations cited as "26 C.F.R. __," it is also quite common to see citations like "Treas. Reg. __." Your statutory supplement for this course no doubt includes a selected number of these regulations. Take some time now to flip through these pages in your statutory supplement.

Notice that the regulations are conveniently numbered (most of the time) according to the Code section they interpret. Regulation § 1.61–2, therefore, interprets § 61 of the Code. The "1." prefix before the Code section number refers to the type of tax at issue. As you might have guessed, the "1" stands for income taxes. Other prefixes you might see include "20" (federal estate taxes), "25" (federal gift taxes), and "301" (procedure and administration provisions). The numbering to the right of the Code section—the "–2" in this case—represents the order of the regulations under that Code provision. Thus, Regulation § 1.61–2 is the second income tax regulation related to § 61 of the Code. Like Code sections, individual regulations may then be divided into paragraphs (e.g., Treas. Reg. § 1.61–2(c)), subparagraphs (e.g., Treas. Reg. § 1.61–2(d)(1)), and subdivisions (e.g., Treas. Reg. § 1.61–2(d)(6)(i)). Divisions go even further (yikes!), but they do not have specific names.

Treasury regulations are first drafted by the Internal Revenue Service and then issued as **proposed regulations** (cited as "Prop. Reg."), published as such in the Federal Register. Under the Administrative Procedure Act, taxpayers are entitled to submit written comments or speak at hearings before **final regulations** are published in the Federal Register. This process can take from several months to several years. In those cases where Treasury wants a regulation to become effective more quickly, it will often issue a proposed regulation simultaneously as a **temporary regulation**. Temporary regulations (identified by the use of a "T," as in "Treas. Reg. § 1.469–5T") are effective immediately upon publication in the Federal Register. After publication, temporary regulations undergo the same notice and comment procedures applicable to proposed regulations, and may be published as final regulations (in the same or in a different form, depending upon comments received and intervening changes in the law).

One final preliminary point about Treasury regulations: those regulations promulgated pursuant to the general grant of authority under § 7805(a) are referred to as **interpretive regulations**. In some cases, Congress specifically grants authority to Treasury to write the rules for more technical issues. Regulations issued under such a specific grant of authority are referred to as **legislative regulations**. As a general rule of thumb, when a Code provision contains language along the lines of "under regulations prescribed by the Secretary," the corresponding regulations are most likely legislative regulations. Because legislative regulations are issued under an express grant of authority from Congress, courts tend to give them more weight than they do interpretive regulations. See *Fife v. Commissioner*, 82 T.C. 1 (1984).

Beyond the Code and Treasury regulations, there are still other sources of tax law. Of course, **court cases** help to interpret, supplement, and shape the federal tax laws. In addition, the United States is a party to 50+ bilateral **income tax treaties** with other nations. Administrative **rulings and pronouncements** of the Internal Revenue Service can be binding on taxpayers (as you will see later in the text), and the **legislative history** documenting congressional intent has often been used to answer difficult interpretive issues.

With all of these sources, perhaps it is not surprising to learn that they sometimes conflict. When that happens, one must resort to the "last-in-time rule." It states that if two authorities of equal weight contradict, the one issued later in time is controlling. Thus, the provisions of a 2005 tax treaty generally prevail over contradictory provisions of a Code section enacted in 1986. But what authorities are of equal weight? Very generally, sources of tax laws can be grouped into three tiers:

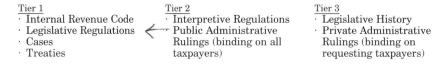

Tier 1	Tier 2	Tier 3
· Internal Revenue Code	· Interpretive Regulations	· Legislative History
· Legislative Regulations	· Public Administrative	· Private Administrative
· Cases	Rulings (binding on all	Rulings (binding on
· Treaties	taxpayers)	requesting taxpayers)

Any authority in Tier 1 outweighs any authority in Tiers 2 and 3, regardless of which is last in time. Likewise, any Tier 2 authority outweighs any Tier 3 authority. The last-in-time rule is applied only where the conflict exists between two authorities in the same tier.

If all of this has you ready to drop the course (after only these few pages, no less), fear not. You will get the hang of it as you work with the

Code over time. We can start to get more comfortable by digging into something substantive.

A. THE IMPACT OF FILING STATUS

Code: IRC §§ 1(a)–(d); 1(f)(8). *Skim* IRC §§ 2; 7703(a).

Regs: None.

Right away you will notice that an individual's tax liability depends upon two variables: the individual's *filing status* (married filing jointly, surviving spouse, head of household, unmarried, or married filing separately) and his or her *taxable income*. We will address the second variable in considerable detail in Chapter 2, but here we will briefly consider a taxpayer's filing status.

Married Filing Jointly. Married couples have been able to file a single return since the 1930s, but the idea of *combining* their incomes on that single return did not emerge until 1948. Allowing married couples to combine their incomes stemmed from a discrepancy between states with community property laws and those without them. In *Poe v. Seaborn*, 282 U.S. 101, 51 S.Ct. 58, 75 L.Ed. 239 (1930), the Supreme Court held that because community property laws considered the earnings of one spouse to belong to the community, it was appropriate for couples in community property states to divide a spouse's earnings equally between them for federal income tax purposes. Thus, half of the income earned by a spouse in a community property state was reportable by the other spouse. If one spouse earned all or most of the couple's income, residents of community property states enjoyed a lower total tax liability than residents of common-law states. To illustrate this, suppose all taxpayers used the following simple rate table:

If taxable income is:	The tax is:
Not over $10,000	10% of taxable income.
Over $10,000 but not over $50,000	$1,000, plus 20% of the excess over $10,000
Over $50,000	$9,000, plus 30% of the excess over $50,000

Now suppose that Roseanne and Tom, a married couple living in a community property state, have taxable income of $100,000, all attributable to Roseanne's earnings. Under *Poe*, Roseanne would report taxable income of $50,000, and Tom would do the same. Each spouse would owe $9,000 in tax, or $18,000 total. If Roseanne and Tom lived in a state without community property laws, however, Roseanne would have taxable income of $100,000 and Tom would have zero taxable income. Roseanne's tax liability (and, thus, the couple's combined tax liability) would be $24,000—a figure $6,000 higher than the one applicable where they live in a community property state! In response to this inequity, Congress permitted spouses filing a joint return to combine their incomes no matter whether they lived in community property states or common-law property states. Accordingly, the tax table in § 1(a) expands the size of each of the lower tax brackets so that couples in all states will be treated more or less equally.

In order to qualify for the § 1(a) tax table, of course, the taxpayers must be married. We can distinguish married and unmarried individuals pretty easily, but with only a little probing, some questions arise. For instance, suppose a couple was married for less than the entire taxable year. Should they be allowed to file a joint return for the entire year, or for only part of the year? Furthermore, what if the couple divorces during the year? And should we care whether the couple gets along, or whether the couple actually shares all items of income, as the § 1(a) tax table implicitly assumes? Section 7703(a) avoids a messy "facts and circumstances" or "intent" rule in favor of a very bright-line rule: if the couple is married on the last day of the taxable year, the couple can file a joint return for the year. Period. That's right—you can get married on December 31 of Year One and file a joint return for *all* of Year One. Likewise, if your first day of legal separation from your spouse is December 31 of Year One, you cannot file a joint return for any portion of Year One. This rule is very arbitrary, but it suggests a preference for avoiding intrusion into the couple's relationship by asking about their intent or their happiness.

Notice, too, that "married filing jointly" status is also available to a "surviving spouse." Section 2(a) defines a "surviving spouse" generally as an individual whose spouse died in either of the two prior years and who maintains a home that is also the principal residence of his or her child or stepchild. This definition raises some interesting points (well, okay, maybe not "interesting," but at least noteworthy), best illustrated by an example. Suppose Fred and Wilma are married with one child, Pebbles. Now suppose that Fred dies in Year One. Wilma can still file a joint return for Year One. (Fred's executor will sign the income tax return after it is prepared—there is no séance.) For Years Two and Three, Wilma may still file as a "surviving spouse" (and thus still compute her tax using the favorable table in § 1(a)) so long as Pebbles also lives with her. If Pebbles is not living with Wilma, Wilma cannot file as a "surviving spouse" for Years Two and Three.

Head of Household. If an individual qualifies as a "head of household," he or she uses the tax table in § 1(b). Section 2(b) defines a head of household as one who both maintains his or her home as the principal residence of a dependent and is neither married nor a surviving spouse. The qualification rules here are somewhat more relaxed than is the case for surviving spouses seeking the continued benefit of the § 1(a) tax table. For instance, a head of household need only maintain his or her home for the dependent for at least one-half of the year (as opposed to the entire year). Furthermore, a "dependent" for these purposes includes grandchildren and step-grandchildren, not just children and stepchildren. Keep in mind that the definitions of both "surviving spouse" and "head of household" contain a host of exceptions and other special rules. If you encounter a situation where filing status is an issue, of course, be sure to read the entire statute carefully.

Unmarried and Not Head of Household. Unmarried individuals who do not qualify as a head of household or a surviving spouse use the tax table contained in § 1(c). It should be no surprise that the tax table in § 1(b) for heads of households is more generous than the table in § 1(c); after all, the incomes of heads of household are by definition supporting more individuals than the incomes of unmarried individuals with no dependents.

Married Filing Separately. Although the joint return often produces a better tax result, married couples may opt to file separate returns for a taxable year. As one would expect, the tax brackets in § 1(d), the table for married couples filing separately, are exactly half the size of the brackets applicable to joint returns in § 1(a). What may be somewhat surprising, however, is the fact that there are different brackets for unmarried taxpayers than for married taxpayers who file separately. Unmarried taxpayers enjoy wider tax brackets, meaning they pay less tax on the same amount of income. This result might be justified on the grounds that married couples enjoy an economy of scale by sharing certain household expenses that unmarried taxpayers also incur. Giving unmarried individuals slightly fatter tax brackets might be a fair accommodation to reflect this economic reality. That assumption might hold less weight today, as more unmarried couples cohabitate and thus share many of the same economies of scale as married couples.

Policy Implications of Filing Status. The joint return and the resulting income-splitting between spouses reflect the social assumption that a husband and wife are one economic unit. In the vast majority of cases, married couples pay less total tax if they file a joint return. There are situations, however, where a joint return will result in a higher income tax liability. In these cases, the spouses could consider filing separate returns, but note again that an unmarried individual often receives more favorable tax treatment than a married individual who files a separate return. You can see this phenomenon for yourself as you work through the Self–Assessment Questions below. As you determine the answers, consider whether the results are acceptable as a matter of public policy.

* * *

Self-Assessment Questions

(Answers to Self–Assessment Questions are set forth in Appendix 3.)

SAQ 1–1. Ralph and Alice are married. Ralph works as a bus driver and Alice is not employed. Ralph's taxable income for the year is $35,000. What is the couple's federal income tax liability if they file a joint return? In making this computation, assume that the taxpayers do not live in a community property state, and use only the relevant rate table in § 1(a)–(d). (Ignore inflation adjustments or other changes to the relevant tax table and also ignore any deductions, credits and exemptions that might be applicable to the taxpayers.)

SAQ 1–2. How would your answer to the previous question change if Ralph and Alice are married but file separate returns?

SAQ 1–3. How would your answer to SAQ 1–1 change if Ralph and Alice were never married but lived together?

SAQ 1–4. Now assume that Alice is employed as a paralegal and that her gross income for the year is $40,000. How would the answers to previous three questions change?

* * *

Adjustments to Basic Rate Tables. In real life, the actual tax tables used to compute an individual's federal income tax liability are different than the basic rate tables set forth in § 1(a)–(d). Consider, for example, the actual rate tables used by taxpayers in 2007 (adapted from *Revenue Procedure 2006–53, 2006–48 I.R.B. 996):*

Married Individuals Filing Joint Returns and Surviving Spouses

If taxable income is:	The tax is:
Not over $15,650	10% of taxable income.
Over $15,650 but not over $63,700	$1,565 + 15% of the excess over $15,650
Over $63,700 but not over $128,500	$8,772.50 + 25% of the excess over $63,700
Over $128,500 but not over $195,850	$24,972.50 + 28% of the excess over $128,500
Over $195,850 but not over $349,700	$43,850.50 + 33% of the excess over $195,850
Over $349,700	$94,601 + 35% of the excess over $349,700

Heads of Households

If taxable income is:	The tax is:
Not over $11,200	10% of taxable income.
Over $11,200 but not over	$42,650 $1,120 + 15% of the excess over $11,200
Over $42,650 but not over $110,100	$5,837.50 + 25% of the excess over $42,650
Over $110,100 but not over $178,350	$22,700 + 28% of the excess over $110,100
Over $178,350 but not over $349,700	$41,810 + 33% of the excess over $178,350
Over $349,700	$98,355.50 + 35% of the excess over $349,700

Unmarried Individuals (other than Surviving Spouses and Heads of Households)

If taxable income is:	The tax is:
Not over $7,825	10% of taxable income.
Over $7,825 but not over $31,850	$782.50 + 15% of the excess over $7,825
Over $31,850 but not over $77,100	$4,386.25 + 25% of the excess over $31,850
Over $77,100 but not over $160,850	$15,698.75 + 28% of the excess over $77,100
Over $160,850 but not over $349,700	$39,148.75 + 33% of the excess over $160,850
Over $349,700	$101,469.25 + 35% of the excess over $349,700

Married Filing Separately

If taxable income is:	The tax is:
Not over $7,825	10% of taxable income.
Over $7,825 but not over $31,850	$782.50 + 15% of the excess over $7,825
Over $31,850 but not over $64,250	$4,386.25 + 25% of the excess over $31,850

Over $64,250 but not over $97,925	$12,486.25 + 28% of the excess over $64,250
Over $97,925 but not over $174,850	$21,925.25 + 33% of the excess over $97,925
Over $174,850	$47,300.50 + 35% of the excess over $174,850

These tables are significantly different from the basic rate tables in § 1, and that is the result of four separate Code provisions. Under these provisions, virtually all taxpayers pay less tax under the adjusted tax tables than they would under the basic rate tables in § 1(a)–(d). First, § 1(f)(1) requires inflation adjustments to the rate tables. Inflation adjustments are well accepted and have been around for several years. The inflation adjustments are made by the Secretary of the Treasury based on changes in the Consumer Price Index over the past year. Various rules for making this adjustment are provided in § 1(f)(2)–(6).

Second, § 1(f)(8) mitigates the "marriage penalty" effect in the lower tax brackets. As illustrated in the Self–Assessment Questions above, two-earner married couples with relatively equal incomes often pay more tax by filing a joint return than they would if they were unmarried. To alleviate the impact of this "marriage penalty," § 1(f)(8) requires that the ceiling of the 15–percent tax bracket for joint return filers be adjusted relative to the ceiling of the 15–percent tax bracket for unmarried taxpayers. Section 1(f)(8) was introduced in the Economic Growth and Tax Relief Reconciliation Act of 2001 (the "2001 Act"), and was originally scheduled to kick in starting in 2005. By 2008, the 15–percent bracket for joint filers would be double the size of the 15–percent bracket for unmarried taxpayers, thus completely eliminating the marriage penalty in that bracket. The Jobs and Growth Tax Relief Reconciliation Act of 2003 (the "2003 Act"), however, accelerated the benefit to joint return filers by completely eliminating the marriage penalty for 2003 and 2004. The Working Families Tax Relief Act of 2004 extended this benefit to 2005–2007. Consequently, the marriage penalty in the lower tax brackets will be eliminated through 2010. It should be noted that § 1(f)(8) is scheduled to terminate altogether in 2011. Absent Congressional action before then, therefore, the marriage penalty will return in full force starting in 2011.

Of course, married couples with disparate incomes enjoy a "marriage benefit" by filing a joint return, as the Self–Assessment Questions above demonstrated. Put differently, unmarried taxpayers suffer a "singles penalty" because they are not married. Yet there are no provisions to mitigate the singles penalty, apparently reflecting the belief that marriage is better than cohabitation. Should the tax laws reflect this policy, or should it be entirely neutral toward marriage?

Third, § 1(i)(1) introduced the 10–percent rate bracket. Thus, there are now six rate brackets instead of five. Section 1(i) was added by the 2001 Act. Section 1(i)(1)(B) sets fixed bracket amounts for this lowest rate, but § 1(i)(1)(C) requires inflation adjustments to those amounts starting in 2004.

Finally, § 1(i)(2) provides for rate reductions applicable to the four highest tax brackets for all taxpayers. The 2001 Act provided that the rate reductions would be phased in from 2001 to 2006, but the 2003 Act accelerated the phase-in to 2003. No other rate reductions are scheduled before 2011, when both the 2001 Act and the 2003 Act expire. At that time, the original rates listed in § 1(a)–(d) will resurface.

One of the signature features of the legislation described in the preceding paragraphs is the use of so many delayed effective dates and temporary rules, making multi-year tax planning a much more difficult undertaking. All of these temporary phase-ins and phase-outs are thought to be necessary because of budget reconciliation laws, but many conclude that the added complexity resulting from the shifting sands represents poor tax policy. Do you agree?

B. TAX RATES AND PROGRESSIVITY

Code: IRC § 1(f)(1)–(2), (i). *Review* IRC § 1(a)–(d).

Regs: None.

As you saw in Part A of this Chapter, individual taxpayers are potentially subject to as many as six different tax rates. Even with all of the recent changes to the basic tax tables, one thing remains the same: the federal income tax is **progressive**, for as a taxpayer's taxable income increases, so too does the rate of tax. Consider Bert and Ernie, two single individuals with 2004 taxable incomes of $7,000 and $70,000, respectively. Bert will pay tax of $700 (ignoring any credits), which represents ten percent of his taxable income. See § 1(i)(1)(B)(iii). Ernie, on the other hand, will pay tax of $14,237.50 in 2004, see § 1(i)(2), which represents about 20.3 percent of taxable income.

We generally use the term **effective tax rate** (or average tax rate) to describe a taxpayer's tax liability as a percentage of taxable income. In the prior examples, then, Bert's effective tax rate was ten percent ($700 tax divided by $7,000 taxable income), while Ernie's effective rate was 20.3 percent ($14,237.50 tax divided by $70,000 taxable income). We sometimes also refer to a taxpayer's **marginal tax rate**, meaning the rate of tax applicable to the taxpayer's last dollar of taxable income. In the prior examples, Bert's marginal tax rate was ten percent because his last dollar of taxable income (the seven thousandth dollar) was taxed at a rate of ten percent. Likewise, Ernie's marginal tax rate was 25 percent.

Because taxpayers always get the benefit of the lower tax rates on the first dollars of taxable income, a taxpayer's effective tax rate will always be less than (or equal to) his or her marginal tax rate. It would be misleading for Ernie to say that he has lost 25 percent of his income to the federal income tax, but it would be perfectly accurate for him to state that another dollar in taxable income would be subject to a 25 percent rate.

Section 1 is not the only source of progressivity in the federal income tax. Certain tax benefits targeted to low-income taxpayers (like the earned income tax credit in § 32) and the denial of benefits for high-income taxpayers (like reduced exemption amounts under § 151) are designed to enhance the progressivity of the federal income tax rates. A number of the provisions designed to enhance progressivity are examined in Chapter 2.

Not all taxes are progressive like the federal income tax. A sales tax, for instance, is labeled a "regressive" tax since all taxpayers, regardless of wealth, pay the same rate of tax. As a result, regressive taxes consume a much smaller percentage of the total assets and income of a wealthier taxpayer.

Section 1 used to have many more tax brackets. As recently as 1985, § 1 contained 15 tax brackets (the highest bracket being 50 percent); in 1978, there were 26 tax brackets (with a high bracket of 70 percent). In recent years, Congress has felt considerable pressure to "flatten" the tax rates even further; some bills introduced in the last Congress called for a single rate of taxation, while others have proposed only two or three tax brackets. Even under the "flatter" system used today, the progressive rate structure works in allocating a larger tax burden to wealthier taxpayers. Consider how the liability for the federal income tax on individuals was distributed among taxpayers in 2001:

INCOME CATEGORY	NUMBER OF RETURNS (%) (in millions)	INCOME (%) (in billions)	INDIVIDUAL INCOME TAX (in billions)	NUMBER OF RETURNS WITH NO OR NEGATIVE TAX LIABILITY (%) (in millions)
Less than $10,000	19.9 (14.0%)	$83 (1.0%)	-$6 (-0.6%)	18.8 (38.7%)
10,000–20,000	23.3 (16.4%)	347 (4.2%)	-10 (-1.0%)	16.2 (33.3%)
20,000–30,000	18.5 (13.0%)	460 (5.6%)	9 (0.9%)	8.1 (16.6%)
30,000–40,000	15.8 (11.1%)	549 (6.7%)	28 (2.8%)	3.2 (6.6%)
40,000–50,000	13.1 (9.2%)	589 (7.2%)	39 (3.9%)	1.4 (3.0%)
50,000–75,000	21.9 (15.4%)	1,337 (16.4%)	112 (11.1%)	0.8 (1.6%)
75,000–100,000	12.9 (9.1%)	1,121 (13.7%)	119 (11.8%)	0.1 (0.1%)
100,000–200,000	12.8 (9.0%)	1,683 (20.6%)	237 (23.6%)	(< 50,000) (< 0.005%)
200,000 and over	3.8 (2.7%)	1,999 (24.5%)	478 (47.5%)	(<50,000) (< 0.005%)
All taxpayers	**142.0 (100%)**	**8,168 (100%)**	**1,006 (100%)**	**48.6 (100%)**

Adapted from Joint Committee on Taxation, *Overview of Present Law and Economic Analysis Relating to Marginal Tax Rates and the President's Individual Income Tax Rate Proposals* (JCX–6–01), March 6, 2001, at 38, Table 16.

Clearly, progressivity is a signature feature of the current federal income tax. But it is not without controversy. The debate over whether the federal income tax should be more or less progressive has continued for decades. Some find progressivity intuitively appealing, while others express distrust or at least skepticism. To understand the debate, it is helpful to consider arguments for and against progressivity.

There are three basic arguments in favor of progressive tax rates. First, they ensure that an individual's tax liability is based on his or her ability to pay. Wealthier individuals are, without doubt, in a better position to pay a greater share of the total tax burden. This is supported by the theory of the declining marginal utility of money. This theory states that as one becomes wealthier, the satisfaction derived from one dollar declines. So if one dollar in the hands of a wealthy taxpayer is worth less (in terms of satisfaction or "utility") than one dollar in the hands of a less affluent taxpayer, then it is fair to tax a greater share of the wealthy person's last dollar than the less affluent person's last dollar. Put another way, suppose you have only $5 in your pockets, with no access to additional funds. A $2 coffee drink at the local espresso shop seems pretty expensive because if you buy it, you have only $3 left for other expenses. But if you have $5,000 in your pockets (just imagine wads of twenty-dollar bills hanging out of each pocket!), spending $2,000 of the $5,000 to enjoy an exceptionally rare bottle of wine is not as painful to purchase, for your pockets will still bulge with $3,000. In both the coffee case and the wine case, you would be spending 40 percent of your stash on something you have just consumed, but the pain of spending 40 percent of $5 feels much sharper than the pain of spending 40 percent of $5,000. Progressive tax rates thus reflect the preference that all taxpayers should feel the same amount of pain. Individuals with incomes of $5x should be taxed at a lower rate than individuals with incomes of $5,000x.

Intuitive though this argument may be, the search for the perfect rate table proves quixotic. One cannot conclude with certainty that a 10–percent tax rate causes the same pain to lower income taxpayers that a 35–percent tax rate causes to more affluent taxpayers. The actual tax rates in § 1 are not the result of empirical research but are instead a product of budget forecasts, past experience, and political compromise. Yet even if the current rate structure is flawed, any progressive tax system will better "spread the pain" than a flat tax system.

The second argument for progressivity is that wealthier individuals should bear a higher percentage of the total tax burden because they receive more benefits from the use of those tax dollars. Congress uses the federal income tax revenues to fund many programs that benefit citizens and residents: national defense, preservation of national parks, and infrastructure to name a few. Arguably, wealthier people receive greater benefits from these appropriations. After all, wealthy folks have more to lose if another country invades the United States and converts a market economy into a socialist economy. More affluent people benefit more from increased government regulation of corporate and securities fraud because they own more stocks and other equities. Wealthy people are in a better position to visit national parks and to have time to care about environmental issues in areas they are unlikely to visit. To the extent they enjoy more benefits from the way tax revenues are spent, therefore, wealthier taxpayers should produce a greater share of those revenues.

The third argument in favor of progressivity is that it accomplishes some degree of wealth redistribution. Just as a society should not allow any member to starve, a society too should not let any one member hoard all of its resources. Redistribution prevents these extremes. To the extent Congress also uses tax revenues to fund health and human service programs, revenues are indirectly redirected to those more needy. Of course, this argument for progressive tax rates contradicts the second argument: how can a progressive tax redistribute wealth if it is also defended as providing more benefits to high-income taxpayers? Proponents of progressivity argue that the benefits to the wealthy *also* benefit those of lower incomes (just not as much because the wealthy have more at stake). National defense benefits everyone. Likewise, redistribution benefits everyone, but it benefits those with lower incomes more than it benefits the wealthy. The benefit to those receiving funds is obvious, but there is also benefit to the affluent taxpayers who lose a portion of their wealth to these efforts. If the redistribution is effective, for example, the society should have less disease, less crime, and fewer individuals without shelter or other basic needs. These advances would free up resources otherwise devoted to fighting these social ills.

There are also three recurring arguments against progressivity. First, progressivity necessarily makes the federal income tax system more complex. The computation of tax liability would be marginally simpler if taxpayers applied a flat percentage rate to taxable income instead of using the tables in § 1, as modified annually. But progressivity triggers additional complexities. We will see in Chapter 2 that the several benefits under the Code are phased-out as one's income increases. These phase-outs trigger additional computations that are more complicated than those required to navigate through the basic tax tables.

Another argument is that progressive tax rates often distort a taxpayer's decisions. Some claim, for example, that progressive tax rates may affect a taxpayer's decision to work. An individual in the ten-percent tax bracket knows that by earning an additional $1,000 of taxable income, he or she will get to keep $900 of the compensation after tax. But an individual in the 35–percent bracket has less incentive to accept additional work, because an additional $1,000 of taxable income will only generate $650 of after-tax income. Taxpayers subject to higher rates are more likely to conclude that the extra work and the opportunity cost of lost relaxation are not worth the after-tax income and thus forego the additional work. If so, the argument goes, society loses the benefit of the taxpayer's extra labor. Critics counter that the decision of whether to accept additional work is based more on the applicable rate of taxation than the progressivity of the rates. A progressive tax system with rates ranging from one percent to ten percent would not create disincentives to work. And a flat tax with a high rate would create disincentives to work. Thus, progressivity does not cause taxpayers to decide not to work.

But taxpayers do alter timing decisions because of progressivity. A taxpayer who is near the top of his or her current tax bracket might choose to postpone additional income until the next year so as to avoid creeping into the next highest tax bracket. Likewise, a taxpayer who just barely creeps into a higher tax bracket might be more willing to incur a deductible expense so as to bring the "taxable income" figure down to within range of the lower bracket. Yet this incentive would exist even under a flat tax system. By deferring additional income until a later year, the taxpayer also defers payment of federal income taxes. Suppose a taxpayer could earn an additional $10,000 in December of Year One but decides to postpone the work (and, thus, the income) until January of Year Two. If the income had been received in Year One, then the taxpayer would owe tax on April 15, Year Two. This gives the taxpayer a little over three months to earn interest on the money used to pay taxes. But if the taxpayer receives the income in Year Two, the tax is not due until April 15, Year Three, giving the taxpayer over 15 months to earn interest or otherwise invest the money used to pay taxes. From a "time value of money" perspective, therefore, there is already an incentive to defer income. Likewise, there is already an incentive to accelerate deductible expenses. And these incentives would persist in a flat tax system, too. While progressivity may enhance these incentives, it does not single-handedly cause them.

Finally, some attack progressive tax rates because they can cause inequities between similarly-situated taxpayers. For instance, suppose Laverne earns a salary of $50,000 in each of Years One and Two, but that Shirley earns $100,000 in Year One and nothing in Year Two. Laverne and Shirley have the same amount of income over the two-year period, but the total tax bills will vary, thanks to progressivity. In addition, Lenny and Squiggy might both have $1,000 deductions, but if Lenny is in a higher tax bracket than Squiggy, Lenny will save more in federal income tax from the deduction than Squiggy will. If there was a single rate of tax, Laverne and Shirley would have equal tax bills, and Lenny and Squiggy would get the same tax savings from their deductions.

Having considered the arguments for and against progressive tax rates, how would you alter the individual income tax rate structure currently in effect? Would you make the system more or less progressive? Why?

C. LIABILITY FOR TAX AND THE INNOCENT SPOUSE RULES

Code: IRC §§ 6013(d); 6015(a)–(c)(3), (f). *Skim* IRC §§ 6012(a); 6072(a); 6151(a).

Regs: *Skim* Treas. Reg. §§ 1.6015–1 through–5.

The United States collects its federal income tax by voluntary assessment. That is, individual taxpayers prepare and file their own reports of federal income tax liability using one of several different forms. We know these forms as "tax returns." Section 6012(a) generally requires taxpayers to prepare and file an income tax return if their "gross incomes" exceed certain minimum levels. Most individuals are required to file a return for any given year by April 15 of the following year. See § 6072(a). If a taxpayer's return shows a tax due, § 6151(a) requires taxpayers to include the tax with the return.

Where spouses file a joint return, § 6013(d)(3) imposes joint and several liability for any deficiency on the return. If the spouses do not include income on the return or mistakenly claim improper deductions on the return (intentionally or unintentionally), either one can be liable to pay the entire tax deficiency resulting from the error. If spouses do not wish to share liability, they can file separately.

In some circumstances, however, it may be difficult for a spouse to insist on separate returns, particularly in abusive marriages. Even in households without abuse, joint and several liability can work unjust results where it is impractical for one spouse to know everything about the activities of the other. Suppose, for example, that one spouse earns income that the other spouse knows nothing about. If the couple files a joint return and fails to pay tax on the undisclosed income, the innocent spouse can be held liable for the resulting tax deficiency.

Concerns for these inequities led to the adoption of relief rules for innocent spouses in 1971. The relief rules, now set forth in § 6015, underwent substantial modification in 1984 and again in 1998. There are three instances in which an ''innocent'' spouse can seek relief from joint and several liability, as explained in the following case.

CHESHIRE v. COMMISSIONER

United States Court of Appeals, Fifth Circuit, 2002.
282 F.3d 326.

KING, CHIEF JUDGE:

The Commissioner of Internal Revenue assessed a tax deficiency and associated penalties against Petitioner-Appellant Kathryn Cheshire. In the United States Tax Court, Cheshire asserted claims for innocent spouse relief from the tax deficiency and penalties under § 6015(b), (c), and (f) of the Internal Revenue Code. * * * The Tax Court denied Cheshire's request for innocent spouse relief, and Cheshire appeals that denial. For the following reasons, we AFFIRM the judgment of the Tax Court.

I. FACTUAL HISTORY

The facts in this case are undisputed. Kathryn Cheshire (''Appellant'') married David Cheshire in 1970. More than twenty years later, Mr. Cheshire retired from Southwestern Bell Telephone Company effective January 1, 1992, and received * * * retirement distributions in 1992 * * *. Of the $229,924 total distribution, $42,183 was rolled over into a qualified account and is not subject to federal income tax. Mr. Cheshire deposited $184,377 of the retirement distributions into the Cheshires' joint checking account, which earned $1168 in interest for 1992.[1] Appel-

---

1. The amounts rolled over into the qualified account ($42,183) and deposited in the joint checking account ($184,377) account for only $226,560 of the retirement

lant knew of Mr. Cheshire's receipt of $229,924 in retirement distributions and of the $1168 in interest earned on the distributions.

The Cheshires made several large disbursements from the retirement distributions in their joint checking account. They withdrew $99,425 from this account to pay off the mortgage on their marital residence, and they withdrew an additional $20,189 to purchase a new family car, a 1992 Ford Explorer. Mr. Cheshire also used the retirement proceeds to provide start-up capital for his new business, to satisfy loans taken out to acquire a family truck and an automobile for the Cheshires' daughter, to pay family expenses, and to establish a college fund for the Cheshires' daughter. Appellant knew of all these expenditures.

Appellant and Mr. Cheshire filed a joint federal income tax return, prepared by Mr. Cheshire, for 1992. On line 17a of this return, they reported the * * * retirement distributions but claimed only $56,150.12 of this amount as taxable. Before signing the return, Appellant questioned Mr. Cheshire about the tax consequences of the retirement distributions. Mr. Cheshire replied that John Daniel Mican, a certified public accountant, advised Mr. Cheshire that retirement proceeds used to pay off a mortgage are nontaxable. Appellant accepted this answer and made no further inquiries prior to signing the return on March 14, 1993. In fact, Mr. Cheshire had not consulted Mican, and all retirement proceeds that are not rolled over into a qualified account are taxable. Because of Mr. Cheshire's persistent problems with alcohol, the Cheshires permanently separated on July 13, 1993, and they divorced seventeen months later. The divorce decree awarded Appellant unencumbered title to the marital residence and to the Ford Explorer.

The Commissioner of Internal Revenue (the "Commissioner") audited the Cheshires' 1992 return and determined that Mr. Cheshire had received taxable retirement distributions of $187,741—the difference between the total distributions ($229,924) and the rollover ($42,183). Thus, the Cheshires had understated the amount of their taxable distributions by $131,591. The Commissioner also determined that the Cheshires had underreported the interest income earned on the retirement distributions by $717. Because of these inaccuracies, the Commissioner imposed a penalty under § 6662(a) of the Internal Revenue Code.

II. Procedural History

Appellant commenced this action in the Tax Court. She conceded that $131,591 of the retirement distributions and the corresponding earned interest were improperly excluded from taxable income. She claimed, however, that she was entitled to relief as an innocent spouse under § 6015(b), § 6015(c), or § 6015(f) of the Internal Revenue Code. * * *

---

distributions. The unaccounted-for remainder ($3364), although mysterious, is not significant enough to affect our analysis of the case.

The Tax Court majority, consisting of twelve judges, denied Appellant relief under § 6015(b), (c), and (f). *Cheshire v. Comm'r*, 115 T.C. 183 (2000). The Tax Court found that Appellant failed to establish that she "did not know, and had no reason to know" of the tax understatement as required for relief under § 6015(b)(1)(C). *Id.* at 193. The Tax Court also found that Appellant was not entitled to relief under § 6015(c) because she had "actual knowledge . . . of any item giving rise to a deficiency" within the meaning of § 6015(c)(3)(C). *Id.* at 197. Finally, the Tax Court held that the Commissioner did not abuse his discretion in denying Appellant equitable relief under § 6015(f) with respect to the retirement distributions and the interest income, as well as the § 6662(a) penalty associated with the interest income. *Id.* at 198.

III. THE STATUTORY SCHEME

Generally, spouses who choose to file a joint return are subject to joint and several liability for tax deficiencies under the Internal Revenue Code. 26 U.S.C. § 6013(d)(3) (Supp. 2001). Recognizing that joint and several liability may be unjust in certain circumstances, Congress authorized relief from such liability under the "innocent spouse" provision, 26 U.S.C. § 6015. Section 6015 provides three distinct types of relief for taxpayers who file joint returns. First, § 6015(b) provides relief for all joint filers who satisfy the five requirements listed in that section. Second, § 6015(c) allows a spouse who filed a joint tax return to elect to limit her income tax liability for that year to her separate liability amount. Section 6015(c) applies only to taxpayers who are no longer married, are legally separated, or do not reside together over a twelve-month period. * * * Furthermore, a spouse who had actual knowledge of an item giving rise to a deficiency at the time that spouse signed the return may not seek relief under § 6015(c). * * *

Finally, a taxpayer may seek relief as an "innocent spouse" under § 6015(f), which authorizes the Secretary of the Treasury (the "Secretary") or his delegate to grant equitable relief from joint and several liability when relief is unavailable under § 6015(b) and (c). Except for the knowledge requirement of § 6015(c)(3)(C) (the provision disallowing election of separate liability to a spouse with actual knowledge of the item giving rise to the deficiency), the taxpayer bears the burden of proving that she has met all the prerequisites for innocent spouse relief. See *Reser v. Comm'r*, 112 F.3d 1258, 1262–63 (5th Cir. 1997). Section 6015(c)(3)(C) explicitly places the burden of proof on the Secretary.

IV. STANDARD OF REVIEW

This court reviews decisions of the Tax Court "in the same manner and to the same extent as decisions of the district courts in civil actions tried without a jury." 26 U.S.C. § 7482(a)(1) (1989 & Supp. 2001). Thus, we review issues of law *de novo* and findings of fact for clear error. *Park v. Comm'r*, 25 F.3d 1289, 1291 (5th Cir. 1994). The Tax Court's determination that a spouse is not entitled to innocent spouse relief is a finding of fact that this court reviews for clear error. *Reser,* 112 F.3d at 1262.

V. SECTION 6015(b) RELIEF

Section 6015(b)(1) provides innocent spouse relief if the taxpayer satisfies all of the five requirements listed in that section. In this case, the parties concede that Appellant satisfied the requirements of subsections (A), (B), and (E) of § 6015(b)(1). Thus, the § 6015(b) issue presented by this case is whether Appellant satisfied the requirements of subsections (C) and (D). We conclude that Appellant has not satisfied the requirement of subsection (C) and thus is not entitled to relief under § 6015(b).

Subsection (C) allows for innocent spouse relief only if the spouse "establishes that in signing the return he or she did not know, and had no reason to know, that there was such understatement." * * * Originally, the innocent spouse provision (formerly codified at § 6013(e)(1)) granted relief only in cases involving omitted income, i.e., cases in which the tax return failed to report taxable income. Since the enactment of the original provision, courts have agreed that in omitted income cases, the spouse's actual knowledge of the underlying transaction that produced the income is sufficient to preclude innocent spouse relief (the "knowledge-of-the-transaction test"). *Reser*, 112 F.3d at 1265[16] In 1984, the innocent spouse provision was expanded to include relief in erroneous deduction cases, i.e., cases in which an incorrect deduction results in an understatement of taxable income. *Park*, 25 F.3d at 1292. The Tax Court applies the knowledge-of-the-transaction test to both types of cases, see *Bokum v. Comm'r*, 94 T.C. 126, 151 (1990), though some circuits have adopted an alternate test for erroneous deduction cases.[17] See, e.g., *Price v. Comm'r*, 887 F.2d 959, 965 (9th Cir. 1989); *Reser*, 112 F.3d at 1267 (Fifth Circuit case).

The Ninth Circuit was the first circuit to adopt an alternative knowledge test for erroneous deduction cases. In *Price*, the Ninth Circuit established that a spouse fails to satisfy the § 6015(b)(1)(C) knowledge requirement in erroneous deduction cases if "a reasonably prudent taxpayer in her position at the time she signed the return could be expected to know that the return contained the substantial understatement." 887 F.2d at 965. The Ninth Circuit reasoned that since erroneous deductions are necessarily reported on a tax return, any spouse who signs the joint return is thereby put on notice that an income-producing transaction occurred. *Id.* at 963 n.9. Thus, in erroneous deduction cases, it would be illogical to bar recovery for spouses with mere knowledge of

---

16. The knowledge-of-the-transaction test conflicts with the plain meaning of § 6015(b)(1)(C), which limits relief to spouses with no knowledge of the understatement. Along with other courts, this court has concluded that this deviation from plain meaning is justified because it avoids "acceptance of an ignorance of the law defense." *Sanders v. United States*, 509 F.2d 162, 169 n.14 (5th Cir. 1975); see also *Price v. Comm'r*, 887 F.2d 959, 963 n.9 (9th Cir. 1989).

17. The Tax Court has suggested that if the case is appealable to a circuit that has adopted a different knowledge test for erroneous deduction cases, it will apply that circuit's knowledge test rather than the knowledge-of-the-transaction test. See *Bokum*, 94 T.C. at 151 (declining to follow the Ninth Circuit's knowledge standard in erroneous deduction cases "except in those instances where appeal lies to that Court of Appeals").

the transaction as this would preclude any spouse from obtaining relief under § 6015(b). *Id.* The Ninth Circuit noted that "adoption of such an interpretation would do violence to the intent Congress clearly expressed when it expanded coverage of the provision to include relief for spouses from deficiencies caused by deductions for which there is no basis in fact or law." *Id.*

Thus, under the *Price* approach, actual knowledge of the underlying transaction, standing alone, is not enough to preclude innocent spouse relief under § 6015(b)(1)(C) in erroneous deduction cases. However, *Price* notes that if the spouse knows "virtually all of the facts pertaining to the transaction which underlies the substantial understatement," then her defense "is premised solely on ignorance of law," and "she is considered as a matter of law to have reason to know of the substantial understatement." *Id.* at 964 * * *.

This court adopted the *Price* approach and reasoning in *Reser.*[18] * * * Accordingly, in erroneous deduction cases, this court questions whether the spouse "knew or had reason to know that the deduction in question would give rise to a substantial understatement of tax on the joint return." *Id.* * * * However, if the spouse knows enough about the underlying transaction that her innocent spouse defense rests entirely upon a mistake of law, she has "reason to know" of the tax understatement as a matter of law. See *Park*, 25 F.3d at 1293–94 (noting that ignorance of the law cannot establish an innocent spouse defense to tax liability); *Sanders v. United States*, 509 F.2d 162, 169 & n.14 (5th Cir. 1975). If "reason to know" cannot be determined as a matter of law, the proper factual inquiry is "whether a reasonably prudent taxpayer in the spouse's position at the time she signed the return could be expected to know that the stated liability was erroneous or that further investigation was warranted." *Reser*, 112 F.3d at 1267.

In this case, the Cheshires reported the receipt of $199,771.05 in retirement distributions on line 17a of their joint tax return. On line 17b, they reported $56,150.12 as the taxable amount of those retirement distributions. Mr. Cheshire led Appellant to believe that he calculated this amount of taxable income by properly deducting the money placed in a qualified account ($42,183) and the money used to pay off the mortgage on their home ($99,425). In fact, only the money placed in a qualified account was properly excludable from the Cheshires' taxable income. Appellant argues that these facts present a case of erroneous deduction and that the knowledge-of-the-incorrect-deduction standard is therefore applicable. The Commissioner argues that this is a case of omitted income and that the knowledge-of-the-transaction test is therefore applicable.

18. The Second, Seventh, Eighth, and Eleventh Circuits have also followed the Ninth Circuit's decision in *Price*. See *Resser v. Comm'r*, 74 F.3d 1528, 1535–36 (7th Cir. 1996); *Bliss v. Comm'r*, 59 F.3d 374, 378 n.1 (2d Cir. 1995); *Kistner v. Comm'r*, 18 F.3d 1521, 1527 (11th Cir. 1994); *Erdahl v. Comm'r*, 930 F.2d 585, 589 (8th Cir. 1991).

This court has not previously determined if such facts present a case of omitted income or of erroneous deduction, and we need not do so here because the outcome under either standard is the same: Appellant knew or had reason to know of the tax understatement. Under the knowledge-of-the-transaction test applied in omitted income cases, Appellant fails to satisfy § 6015(b)(1)(C) because she had actual knowledge of the retirement distributions and of the corresponding earned interest at the time she signed the return. In erroneous deduction cases, this court asks whether Appellant "knew or had reason to know" that the deduction in question would give rise to a tax understatement at the time she signed the return. The parties agree that Appellant did not have actual knowledge that the deduction was improper. However, because Appellant knew all the facts surrounding the transaction that gave rise to the understatement, including the amount of the retirement proceeds, the account where the proceeds were deposited and drawn upon, the amount of interest earned on the proceeds, and the manner in which the proceeds were spent, Appellant had "reason to know" of the improper deduction as a matter of law. Appellant's defense consists only of her mistaken belief that money spent to pay off a mortgage is properly deductible from retirement distributions. Ignorance of the law cannot establish an innocent spouse defense to tax liability. *Park*, 25 F.3d at 1293–94; *Sanders*, 509 F.2d at 169 & n.14.

Because Appellant "knew or had reason to know" of the understatement under both the omitted income standard and the erroneous deduction standard, she fails to establish the requirement of § 6015(b)(1)(C). This conclusion bars relief under § 6015(b)(1), obviating the need for this court to decide whether Appellant satisfied the requirement of § 6015(b)(1)(D). The Tax Court's determination that Appellant is not entitled to innocent spouse relief under § 6015(b)(1) is not clearly erroneous.

VI. SECTION 6015(c) RELIEF

Section 6015(c)(1) allows any divorced (or separated) individual to elect to assume responsibility for only that portion of a joint tax deficiency that is properly allocable to that individual. The parties agree that Appellant falls within the class of taxpayers permitted to make a § 6015(c) election since she and Mr. Cheshire were divorced when she filed her petition with the Tax Court. Moreover, neither party in this case disputes that the deficiency attributable to the retirement distributions is properly allocable to Mr. Cheshire. Thus, if this election is available to Appellant, she can avoid liability for the tax deficiency caused by the retirement distributions. However, the benefit of the § 6015(c) election is not available to an individual with actual knowledge of "any item giving rise to a deficiency." 26 U.S.C. § 6015(c)(3)(C). In order to preclude relief under § 6015(c), the Commissioner must prove by a preponderance of the evidence that Appellant had actual knowledge of "any item giving rise to a deficiency." *Culver v. Comm'r*, 116 T.C. 189,

196 (2001). Whether the Commissioner satisfied this burden is the § 6015(c) issue in this appeal.

The debate between the parties focuses on the meaning of the term "item" in § 6015(c)(3)(C). Appellant argues that "item" means "incorrect tax reporting of an item of income, deduction, or credit" so that § 6015(c)(3)(C) only bars relief for spouses with actual knowledge that an entry on the joint tax return is incorrect. The Commissioner argues that "item" means "an item of income, deduction, or credit" so that § 6015(c)(3)(C) bars relief for all spouses with actual knowledge of the income-producing transaction, even if they lacked knowledge of the incorrect tax reporting of that transaction.

The term "item" appears fifteen times in § 6015. Most of these appearances are uninformative, but the uses of the term "item" in § 6015(b)(1)(B) and (d)(4) support the Commissioner's definition. Section 6015(b)(1)(B) refers to "an understatement of tax attributable to erroneous items of one individual filing the joint return." If "item" refers to the "incorrect tax reporting of an item," as Appellant asserts, then the reference to an "erroneous item" is redundant. Thus, § 6015(b)(1)(B) suggests that "item" means "an item of income, deduction, or credit," as the Commissioner asserts. Furthermore, § 6015(d)(4) refers to "an item of deduction or credit." This use of the term "item" suggests that the term refers to an actual item of income, deduction, or credit, rather than the incorrect reporting of such an item.

Other sections of the Internal Revenue Code define the term "item" without reference to tax consequences. For example, § 61(a) defines "gross income" to include such "items" as compensation for services, interest, rents, and royalties. 26 U.S.C. § 61(a) (1988 & Supp. 2001). Thus, in this context, "item" means an item of income. * * * [This use] of the term "item," as well as those uses appearing in § 6015, suggest that "item" means "an item of income, deduction, or credit." See *Comm'r v. Lundy*, 516 U.S. 235, 250, 116 S.Ct. 647, 133 L.Ed.2d 611 (1996) (stating that "identical words used in different parts of the same act are intended to have the same meaning") (internal citations and quotations omitted). This interpretation supports the Commissioner's position that § 6015(c)(3)(C) bars relief for all spouses with actual knowledge of the income-producing transaction, even if they lacked knowledge of the incorrect tax reporting of that transaction.

Furthermore, Appellant's claim that § 6015(c)(3)(C) precludes relief only if the spouse has knowledge of incorrect tax reporting runs afoul of the general rule that ignorance of the tax laws is not a defense to a tax deficiency. See *Park*, 25 F.3d at 1293–94 (noting that ignorance of the law cannot establish an innocent spouse defense to tax liability). In *Sanders*, a case applying the predecessor innocent spouse statute, we noted that the statute "seemingly makes ignorance of the fact that known receipts constitute taxable income a valid justification for not knowing or having reason to know of omissions from gross income." 509 F.2d at 169 n.14. Rather than establish an ignorance of the law defense, however, in *Sanders* we decided to apply a statutory interpretation that "is difficult to square with a literal reading of the statutory language" because "the practical problems that have always prevented acceptance of an ignorance of the law defense in the criminal law area ... arguably apply just as forcefully here." *Id.* Unlike the court in *Sanders*, we need not overlook the literal meaning of the statute at issue in this case. As the above discussion illustrates, the plain meaning of § 6015(c)(3)(C) suggests that a spouse with actual knowledge of the income-producing transaction cannot receive innocent spouse relief even if she lacks knowledge of the incorrect tax reporting of that transaction. This reading of the plain meaning of § 6015(c)(3)(C) is compelling in light of the general principle that ignorance of the law is not a defense.

To support the theory that "item" means "incorrect tax reporting of an item," Appellant and *amici curiae* point to the legislative history of § 6015(c)(3)(C). We decline to defer to this legislative history for two reasons. First, when interpreting a statute, this court "must presume that a legislature says in a statute what it means and means in a statute what it says there." *Conn. Nat'l Bank v. Germain*, 503 U.S. 249, 253–54, 117 L.Ed.2d 391, 112 S.Ct. 1146 (1992). Unless the text of a statute is ambiguous on its face, this court adheres to that statute's plain meaning. *Id.* As the above analysis demonstrates, the text of § 6015 and other sections of the Internal Revenue Code strongly suggests that "item" refers to "an item of income, deduction, or credit." Section 6015(c)(3)(C) is not facially ambiguous.

Second, the legislative history of § 6015(c)(3)(C) is ambiguous. Some portions of the history appear to support the Commissioner's position. * * * Other parts of the history, however, suggest that the § 6015(c)(3)(C) exception is intended to cover spouses with knowledge of the transaction giving rise to the deficiency in addition to spouses with knowledge that the tax return is incorrect. * * * We decline to allow inconclusive legislative history to affect our interpretation of the plain meaning of § 6015(c)(3)(C). * * * Thus, we conclude that "item" means "an item of income, deduction, or credit," as asserted by the Commissioner.

The Tax Court adopted this definition of "item" and indicated that the knowledge standard under § 6015(c)(3)(C) in an omitted income case is "actual and clear awareness" of an item of income. * * * Since *Cheshire*, the Tax Court has interpreted the knowledge standard in the context of an erroneous deduction to be "actual knowledge of the factual circumstances which made the item unallowable as a deduction." *King v. Comm'r*, 116 T.C. 198, 204 (2001). As Appellant is liable under either standard, we need not determine which standard applies in this case. Appellant had "actual and clear awareness" of Mr. Cheshire's retirement distributions and earned interest. Thus, she satisfies the § 6015(c)(3)(C) knowledge requirement for omitted income cases. Furthermore, Appellant was aware of how the retirement distributions were spent. None of these expenditures qualifies for proper deduction, so Appellant had "actual knowledge of the factual circumstances which made the item unallowable as a deduction.'' In such circumstances, Appellant satisfies the § 6015(c)(3)(C) knowledge requirement for erroneous deduction cases. Thus, § 6015(c)(3)(C) bars relief under either the omitted income or the erroneous deduction knowledge standard, even though Appellant was unaware of the tax consequences of the deduction. The Tax Court's determination that Appellant is not entitled to innocent spouse relief under § 6015(c) is not clearly erroneous.

VII. SECTION 6015(f) RELIEF

Section 6015(f) confers power upon the Secretary and his delegate, the Commissioner, to grant equitable relief where a taxpayer is not entitled to relief under § 6015(b) or (c), but ''taking into account all the facts and circumstances, it is inequitable to hold the individual liable for any unpaid tax or any deficiency (or any portion of either).'' In this case, Appellant argues that the Commissioner improperly denied her equitable relief with respect to the retirement distributions and the interest income. This court reviews the Commissioner's decision to deny equitable relief for abuse of discretion. * * *

This court has stated that ''the most important factor in determining inequity is whether the spouse seeking relief 'significantly benefited' from the understatement of tax.'' *Reser*, 112 F.3d at 1270 (quoting *Buchine v. Comm'r*, 20 F.3d 173, 181 (5th Cir. 1994)). This benefit can be indirect, such as ''a spouse's receipt of more than she otherwise would as part of a divorce settlement.'' *Reser*, 112 F.3d at 1270. In the instant case, Appellant received as part of the divorce settlement the Cheshires' marital residence, the value of which was enhanced by the use of $99,425 in untaxed retirement distributions to pay off the mortgage. Appellant also received the family car, which was purchased with retirement distributions. The Commissioner could have reasonably concluded upon these facts that Appellant received significant benefit from the tax understatement. Thus, the Commissioner's decision to deny equitable relief to Appellant is sufficiently supported and not an abuse of discretion. Accordingly, the Tax Court correctly determined that the Commissioner did not abuse his discretion when he denied equitable relief to Appellant under § 6015(f) with respect to the retirement distributions and the interest income.

VIII. CONCLUSION

For all the foregoing reasons, we AFFIRM the judgment of the Tax Court.

Notes and Questions

1. *The United States Tax Court.* The taxpayer in *Cheshire* commenced litigation in the United States Tax Court, a Federal court established in 1924 by Congress under Article I of the Constitution. The Tax Court allows taxpayers to dispute deficiencies determined by the Service without having to pay the disputed amount in advance. The Tax Court has jurisdiction to

hear a variety of tax disputes, mostly concerning notices of deficiency. It is composed of 19 presidentially-appointed judges selected for their expertise in taxation. Judges serve a renewable term of 15 years. While the Tax Court is physically located in Washington, D.C., the judges travel nationwide to conduct trials in various designated cities.

The typical Tax Court case is commenced by the taxpayer filing a petition. A modest filing fee (currently $60) must be paid when the petition is filed. Once the petition is filed, payment of the underlying tax at issue is usually postponed until the case is resolved. A simplified "small tax case" procedure is available for certain tax disputes involving $50,000 or less. Trials in small tax cases generally are less formal and conclude more quickly; however, decisions in a small tax case may not be appealed.

Most regular Tax Court cases are settled before trial. Trials are conducted before one judge, without a jury. Taxpayers may be represented by counsel admitted to the Tax Court bar, although taxpayers may instead choose to represent themselves. The trial judge submits an opinion to the Tax Court's chief judge, who either refers the decision to the full court for review or allows the decision to stand without a full review. Generally, if the decision breaks new ground or reconsiders an issue on which it has been reversed, the opinions will be circulated for full review.

Regular Tax Court opinions come in two forms: regular opinions (cited as "T.C." and generally viewed as more important and ground-breaking) and memorandum opinions (cited as "T.C. Memo." and given somewhat less weight usually because they typically involve unique facts or the application of well-established rules). Decisions of the Tax Court in a regular case (whether in regular or memorandum opinion form) can be appealed to the United States Court of Appeals. The appropriate circuit for an appeal depends upon the residence of the taxpayer. Thus an appeal of a Tax Court decision involving a Chicago taxpayer would lie in the Seventh Circuit, while an appeal involving a Miami taxpayer would lie in the Eleventh Circuit.

The United States Tax Court is not the only forum available to taxpayers. Taxpayers may also commence actions in United States District Court. While the federal district courts offer the possibility for a jury trial, the courts only have jurisdiction to hear refund cases. Thus, taxpayers seeking to commence litigation in federal district court must first pay the asserted deficiency and sue for refund. Naturally, most taxpayers prefer not to pay the deficiency first, so fewer tax cases begin in federal district court. Of course, the decisions of the federal district court can be appealed to the appropriate United States Court of Appeals.

A third forum is the United States Court of Federal Claims. Like federal district courts, the Court of Federal Claims' jurisdiction is limited to refund cases, so taxpayer must first pay the asserted deficiency. Moreover, the Court of Federal Claims offers only bench trials. It is therefore no surprise that very few tax cases begin in this forum. Appeals from the Court of Federal Claims lie exclusively in the United States Court of Appeals for the Federal Circuit. Can you think of a situation where a taxpayer might choose to commence litigation in the Court of Federal Claims?

2. *Omitted Income or Erroneous Deduction?* The *Cheshire* court punted on the issue of whether the case was one of "omitted income" or an

"erroneous deduction" because the result in the case would, it says, remain the same. How do you think the court would have resolved this issue if the classification of the case would have affected the result? Keep this issue in mind as you work through the next three Chapters.

3. *Statutory Interpretation.* In trying to discern the meaning of the word "item," the *Cheshire* court first considered the context of the statute. The court analyzed how the term is used in other portions of § 6015 and in other provisions of the Code. The court then considered whether its interpretation was consistent with public policy. The court gave little weight to the legislative history because the history could support contrary interpretations of the term. If the legislative history supported only one interpretation, one would apparently give it more weight. These considerations (context, policy, and intent) are relevant in any attempt at statutory interpretation.

4. *Thumbs Up or Thumbs Down?* Speaking of policy, do you think the *Cheshire* court reached the correct result from a fairness perspective? Why or why not?

* * *

Problem 1–1

Curtis and Kathy filed a joint return for 2001 on April 15, 2002. The return claimed bogus deductions related to Curtis' cattle-raising business. After their divorce in 2003, the Internal Revenue Service discovered the bogus deductions and issued a notice of deficiency to both Curtis and Kathy.

While they were married, Kathy often visited Curtis' farmland and on occasion helped out with some chores related to the business. Kathy collected all of Curtis' receipts and sent them to their accountant to prepare their tax returns. Kathy saw that the receipts for 2001 were unusually large, but she did not question Curtis with respect to any of the receipts. Kathy had no other involvement in Curtis' business.

If Kathy files a request for innocent spouse relief under § 6015, how should the Service respond?

* * *

Chapter 2

COMPUTING LIABILITY FOR TAX

We saw in Chapter 1 that an individual's liability for federal income tax is a function of the individual's filing status and his or her "taxable income." Though Chapter 1 tackled the issue of filing status and the policy implications of the progressive rate structure of § 1, we deferred discussion of the meaning of taxable income. Now we can address that concept. Part A of this Chapter presents the "tax ladder," the formula by which one computes federal income tax liability. We will see that part of the tax ladder allows individuals to claim a "personal exemption" for themselves and their dependents. Part B of this Chapter considers the personal exemption in greater detail, with an emphasis on the determination of dependency. Finally, Part C of this Chapter summarizes some of the credits available to taxpayers that can be used to reduce their tax liabilities.

A. DETERMINING "TAXABLE INCOME"

Code: IRC §§ 61(a); 62(a); 63; 67(a)–(b); 68; 151; 161.

Regs: None.

A quick look at § 63 reveals *two* methods for computing "taxable income:" one in § 63(a) and another in § 63(b). Section 63(a) tells us that taxable income means "gross income minus the deductions allowed by this chapter (other than the standard deduction)." Notice that the definition contains three other specific terms: (1) gross income; (2) deductions; and (3) the standard deduction. Only one of these three terms is defined in § 63: the standard deduction. See § 63(c) and discussion below. For definitions of the other two terms, we have to look elsewhere.

Gross Income. Section 61(a) defines gross income as "all income from whatever source derived." It then lists 15 examples of gross income items. As the statute indicates, this list is hardly exhaustive. At first blush, this is a frustrating definition, for it seems to say that gross income is "all income," but then it does not tell us what is meant by "income." Is Congress really so sloppy? Probably not. The language "all

26

income from whatever source derived" parallels the language used in the Sixteenth Amendment to the United States Constitution:

> *The Congress shall have the power to lay and collect taxes on incomes, from whatever source derived, without apportionment among the several States, and without regard to any census or enumeration.*

By providing that gross income is "all income from whatever source derived," Congress clearly intends to exert the full measure of its authority to tax income. Thus, anything that is "income" is potentially subject to taxation. Notice, however, that this broad sweep is limited by exceptions provided elsewhere in the Code. As we will see, certain Code provisions exclude from gross income items that would otherwise constitute income. Thus, with respect to each potential item of income, a taxpayer must first determine whether the item constitutes "income" within the meaning of the Sixteenth Amendment. If so, the taxpayer must treat the item as gross income unless it is specifically excluded from gross income in whole or in part under some other provision of the Code. This two-step analysis, which pops up throughout the text, is the focus of Chapter 3.

Deductions Generally. There is no formal definition of "deductions." The best we can do is the language in § 161, which states that only deductions specifically authorized by the Code may be used to compute taxable income. We can discern from this language that not every taxpayer expenditure is deductible; a taxpayer must have statutory authority for every deduction. Because of the wording of § 161, courts have determined that the deduction provisions are to be construed narrowly, meaning that a taxpayer outlay must clearly meet the requirements of a deduction provision before it can be taken into account in computing taxable income. We will explore the concept of deductions in more detail in Chapter 4.

An Alternative Formula. Things get a little more complicated when we look at § 63(b). This subsection sets forth an alternate definition for taxable income as, in relevant part, "adjusted gross income, minus the standard deduction and the deduction for personal exemptions." Here, in addition to the "standard deduction," we have two more special terms: (1) adjusted gross income; and (2) personal exemptions. Fortunately, there are definitions for those terms in the Code. But before we delve into those terms, consider that every taxpayer can choose between the § 63(a) formula and the § 63(b) formula to compute taxable income. Naturally, taxpayers will probably choose the formula that produces the smaller amount of taxable income. But why are there two different approaches? Congress decided that it would be administratively simpler to offer taxpayers a "standard deduction" that could be claimed in lieu of listing (or "itemizing") all of the individual deductions to which the taxpayer would be entitled. Thus, if a taxpayer's various deduction items for a year do not exceed the standard deduction, the taxpayer will choose to use the standard deduction. If the deductions exceed the standard deduction, the taxpayer should itemize all of the deductions to reduce the tax liability.

Adjusted Gross Income. Congress also decided that even those taxpayers who choose the standard deduction should be entitled to deduct certain items in addition to the standard deduction. In other words, the choice between itemizing and using the standard deduction should be made after certain deductions have already been taken into account. This is the purpose behind the "adjusted gross income" concept. Section 62(a) defines adjusted gross income as gross income minus 18 specifically identified deductions. It is important to note that § 62(a) does not by itself authorize deductions; it merely lists those deductions that are used to compute adjusted gross income. The deductions listed in § 62(a) are sometimes called **above-the-line deductions** because they are used in computing adjusted gross income. (Adjusted gross income is "the line.")

Originally, § 62(a) listed deductions that were related to business and other profit-seeking activities. This is because the standard deduction was seen as a comprehensive substitute for many deductible personal expenses unrelated to business and investment activities. Much of that list remains in tact today. See §§ 62(a)(1)–62(a)(4). Over time, however, Congress has added some personal deductions to the list in § 62(a), deeming in its infinite wisdom that some personal expenses should be allowed on top of the standard deduction. See, e.g., §§ 62(a)(10), 62(a)(15), and 62(a)(17).

At the risk of repetitive redundancy, notice again that *all* taxpayers can claim the deductions listed in § 62(a). Taxpayers using the § 63(a) formula are clearly entitled to these deductions, for they can claim "all deductions" other than the standard deduction. And taxpayers using the § 63(b) formula use "adjusted gross income" as the starting point for the computation of taxable income. As we examine each of the deductions listed in § 62(a), then, it is helpful to think about whether it is good tax policy to make the deduction available to all taxpayers.

Personal Exemptions. Taxpayers who do not itemize get to claim the "personal exemptions" authorized by § 151. Because the personal exemptions are deductions, even taxpayers who do choose to itemize deductions can claim personal exemptions. Thus, the § 151 personal exemptions are also available to all taxpayers. But because the § 151 personal exemptions are not listed in § 62(a), these deductions cannot be taken "above the line;" in other words, they cannot be used to compute adjusted gross income. They must be taken into account *after* a taxpayer has determined adjusted gross income.

The personal exemptions represent Congressional policy that a certain amount of income must be used to meet basic subsistence needs like food, shelter, and clothing. When you look at the exemption amount listed in § 151(d), however, you might be shocked to see the amount Congress thinks we need each year to get by in life. Of course, when the personal exemptions are coupled with the standard deduction, the actual amount of gross income that a taxpayer can have before facing possible liability for federal income taxes is somewhat higher. But even the combined amount is far from abundant. The personal exemptions are considered in more detail later in Part B of this Chapter.

Standard Deduction and Itemized Deductions. As is hopefully clear by now, the decision of whether to itemize all deductions depends upon the amount of the standard deduction. If the standard deduction is roughly equal to the amount of a taxpayer's itemized deductions, the taxpayer might choose to claim the standard deduction simply to avoid the hassle of itemizing each of the deductions. If the standard deduction clearly exceeds the amount of itemized deductions, the choice is easy. As explained in § 63(d), **itemized deductions** are all deductions other than above-the-line deductions and the personal exemptions. Of course, since a taxpayer cannot claim both itemized deductions and the standard deduction, the standard deduction is not an itemized deduction. Itemized deductions are often referred to as "below-the-line deductions," as they are taken into account after the determination of adjusted gross income.

The **standard deduction** amount is set forth in § 63(c). It is comprised of a "basic standard deduction" and, where appropriate, an "additional standard deduction." Like the tax tables in § 1, the amount of the standard deduction is adjusted annually for inflation. See § 63(c)(4). For the last several years, about 70 percent of individual taxpayers claim the standard deduction. The Treasury Department, however, estimates that many taxpayers use the standard deduction even though they have itemized deductions that exceed the standard deduction amount. Is this the result of taxpayer apathy, tax complexity, or both?

The Tax Ladder. We have now looked at all of the components of both the § 63(a) formula for computing taxable income and the § 63(b) formula. Based on our analysis, we can create one comprehensive formula that all taxpayers can use. Because the formula looks like a ladder, it is sometimes referred to as the "tax ladder" (some punsters like to call it the "taxing formula"):

Gross Income [§ 61(a)]
Less: Deductions Listed in § 62(a)
Equals: Adjusted Gross Income
Less: Personal Exemptions
And Less: EITHER the Standard Deduction [§ 63(c)] OR Itemized Deductions [§ 63(d)]
Equals: Taxable Income

* * *

Self-Assessment Questions

(Solutions to Self–Assessment Questions are set forth in Appendix 3.)

SAQ 2–1. As a general rule, does a taxpayer prefer above-the-line deductions or below-the-line deductions? Why?

SAQ 2–2. Ignoring any inflation adjustments to the dollar amounts set forth in the Code, what is the maximum amount of gross income that an unmarried individual with no dependents can have in a taxable year to be assured of no liability for federal income taxes for such year?

* * *

Limitations on Itemized Deductions. Sections 67 and 68 impose separate limitations on the amount of itemized deductions that a taxpayer may claim in a taxable year. Section 67 targets so-called "miscellaneous itemized deductions," effectively reducing the amount of such deductions by two percent of the taxpayer's adjusted gross income. Section 68 gradually phases-out the amount of itemized deductions for the most affluent taxpayers.

"The Two–Percent Haircut." Section 67(a) states that a taxpayer can deduct "miscellaneous itemized deductions" only to the extent that such deductions (in the aggregate) exceed two percent of the taxpayer's adjusted gross income. For example, suppose a taxpayer has miscellaneous itemized deductions totaling $3,000 for Year One and an adjusted gross income for Year One of $100,000. The taxpayer may deduct only $1,000 of the miscellaneous itemized deductions ($3,000 minus $2,000, which is 2% of adjusted gross income). The $2,000 disallowed amount is not preserved for later use and does not carry over to Year Two—it is permanently disallowed. If the same taxpayer had miscellaneous itemized deductions of $500, none of them would be deductible on the Year One tax return.

The big-money issue, therefore, is the definition of "miscellaneous itemized deductions." This is supplied in § 67(b). Notice that the definition is tricky! The casual reader would look at the heading of § 67(b) and assume that the twelve items listed there are the "miscellaneous itemized deductions." But the careful reader sees that "miscellaneous itemized deductions" are all itemized deductions *other than* the twelve deductions listed in § 67(b). Thus, the twelve itemized deductions listed are "regular itemized deductions" not subject to the "two-percent haircut" of § 67(a).

The policy behind the two-percent haircut is difficult to discern. It might help to look at the types of expenses that frequently constitute miscellaneous itemized deductions. The most significant miscellaneous itemized deduction is for unreimbursed business expenses of an employee. As we will see in Chapter 4, only some business expenses incurred by an employee (as opposed to an independent contractor or a self-employed taxpayer) are above-the-line deductions. The rest are miscellaneous itemized deductions, because they are listed in neither § 62(a) nor § 67(b). Perhaps Congress suspects that some of these employee expenses are not purely for business but also personal in nature. By imposing the two-percent haircut, Congress might be weeding out a number of expenses that might otherwise be questionable. After all, if such expenses were really important, the employer would have paid them (or reimbursed the employee for such costs). But this justification for the two-percent haircut rings somewhat hollow when one considers that many expenses that are purely personal are deductible without limitation—even above-the-line. See §§ 62(a)(10) (deduction for alimony payments under § 215); 62(a)(15) (deduction for moving expenses under § 217); and 62(a)(17) (deduction for interest on education loans under § 221).

Another justification for the two-percent haircut might be administrative convenience: by limiting these deductions, the Service will not have to spend as much time and resources on verifying the legitimacy of the claimed amounts. But this assumes that the Internal Revenue Service regularly audits taxpayer returns, when in fact the audit rate (the percentage of tax returns actually audited by the Service) is less than one percent. Although the policy justification for § 67(a) is hard to defend, the Tax Court has held that the two-percent haircut is constitutional. *Lickiss v. Commissioner*, T.C. Memo. 1994–103.

It should be noted that miscellaneous itemized deductions bear another curse: they are not deductible at all for purposes of the "alternative minimum tax," a topic explored in Chapter 11. For now, suffice it to say that an abundance of miscellaneous itemized deductions might increase a taxpayer's chances of facing liability for the alternative minimum tax in addition to the regular federal income tax.

The Phase–Out of Itemized Deductions. Under § 68(a), affluent taxpayers with taxable incomes in excess of an "applicable amount" will lose up to 80 percent of their total itemized deductions (both regular itemized deductions and what is left of the miscellaneous itemized deductions after the two-percent haircut of § 67). This very broad statement of the general rule is subject to some significant exceptions, but first we need to study the mechanics of this "phase-out."

Only taxpayers with adjusted gross incomes in excess of the "applicable amount" are subject to the § 68 limitation. For all individuals except those who are married but filing separate returns, the applicable amount is $100,000. Section 68(b)(1). For those married individuals filing separately, sensibly enough, the applicable amount is $50,000. Notice that these amounts are adjusted annually for inflation (just like the § 1 tax tables and the standard deduction amount), so the actual amounts will be higher. See § 68(b)(2). A taxpayer with an adjusted gross income in excess of the applicable amount must reduce the amount of itemized deductions by three percent of such excess. For example, suppose an unmarried taxpayer has an adjusted gross income of $200,000 for Year One, and that the taxpayer's itemized deductions (after applying the two-percent haircut in § 67) for that year total $10,000. Ignoring any adjustments for inflation, the taxpayer must reduce the total Year One itemized deductions by $3,000, which is three percent of the $100,000 excess of the Year One adjusted gross income over the applicable amount. Thus, the taxpayer can only claim $7,000 of the $10,000 in total itemized deductions. The $3,000 disallowed does not carry over to Year Two. As this example shows, the total itemized deductions are phased out as the taxpayer's adjusted gross income increases. Section 68 is one of many income-based "phase-out" provisions in the Code. We will see others throughout the text.

At no point, however, will the reduction under § 68 ever exceed 80 percent of the total itemized deductions. In other words, the total itemized deductions are never fully phased out. For example, suppose in the prior example that the taxpayer's adjusted gross income for Year One was $1,100,000, which exceeds the "applicable amount" by an even $1,000,000. Three percent of that excess is $30,000, which would appear to wipe out completely the taxpayer's $10,000 in total itemized deductions. But because § 68(a) requires a reduction by the *lesser of* three percent of the excess or 80 percent of the total itemized deductions, the taxpayer need only reduce the total itemized deductions by $8,000 (80 percent of $10,000).

Notice that four itemized deductions are spared from the § 68 phase-out. They are listed in § 68(c). Thus, if a taxpayer has only these four itemized deductions and no others, § 68 will not apply even if the taxpayer's adjusted gross income is well above the regular threshold. Of course, if the taxpayer has itemized deductions in addition to the "fantastic four" listed in § 68(c), the § 68(a) reduction will still apply to those other itemized deductions.

As you might imagine, the § 68 reduction often acts as a trap for the unwary. One could easily become subject to the reduction in a given taxable year without knowing about it until completing the return. Many tax professionals and scholars object to the "surprise" element of § 68, and several of them have argued for repeal. Their cry was heard in 2001, when Congress enacted § 68(f) and § 68(g) as part of the Economic Growth and Tax Relief Reconciliation Act of 2001. Under § 68(f), the § 68(a) phase-out itself will be "phased-out" in upcoming years. For taxable years beginning in 2006 and 2007, taxpayers facing the § 68(a) phase-out need only reduce their total itemized deductions by two-thirds of the normal reduction amount. Then, in taxable years beginning in 2008 and 2009, taxpayers need only reduce total itemized deductions by one-third of the normal reduction amount. Finally, beginning in 2010, § 68(g) provides that the phase-out shall no longer apply. Because of a quirk in the procedure of enacting the Economic Growth and Tax Relief Reconciliation Act of 2001, however, the repeal only lasts for the year 2010—as of 2011, § 68(a) applies as if the provisions of § 68(f) and § 68(g) were never enacted. In other words, the § 68(a) phase-out will spring back to full life in 2011.

* * *

Self-Assessment Questions

(Solutions to Self–Assessment Questions are set forth in Appendix 3.)

SAQ 2–3. Does the overall limitation on itemized deductions in § 68 make the federal income tax more progressive or less progressive? How so?

SAQ 2–4. Does the § 67 limitation on miscellaneous itemized deductions make above-the-line deductions more attractive or less attractive? How so?

Problem 2–1

John and Jane Doe are married. They have no children. John and Jane are both new employees of ACME Corporation, located in City. The Does moved to City to begin work at ACME during the most recent taxable year. To supplement their regular salaries, the Does converted the basement of their home into a one-bedroom apartment that they rent to a struggling student at Law School. For the most recent taxable year, the Does had the following items of income and expense (expense items are marked in parentheses):

Combined Salaries	95,000
Rental Income (home apartment)	5,000
Moving Expenses [amount deductible under § 217]	(8,000)
Medical Expenses [amount deductible under § 213]	(2,000)
Accountant Fees to Prepare Federal Tax Return [deductible under § 212]	(1,000)
Mortgage Interest [deductible under § 163]	(6,000)
Expenses Related to Home Apartment [deductible under § 212]	(2,000)
Charitable Contribution to National Public Radio [amount deductible under § 170]	(500)
Unreimbursed Employee Expenses of Jane [deductible under § 162]	(500)

(a) Determine the Does' "taxable income" for the most recent taxable year, assuming they file a joint return. Ignore any cost-of-living, inflation, or other similar adjustments to tax allowed under the Code.

(b) Same as (a), but assume that the combined salaries of John and Jane for the most recent taxable year was $395,000.

(c) Same as (a), but assume that the combined salaries of John and Jane for the most recent taxable year was $49,000.

B. PERSONAL EXEMPTIONS

Code: IRC § 152. *Review* IRC § 151.

Regs: Treas. Reg. §§ 1.151–1(b); 1.152–1(a)(2)(i).

As stated in Part A of this Chapter, the deduction for personal exemptions reflects the policy that a certain base amount of income should not be subject to federal income tax. Combined with the standard deduction, the deduction for personal exemptions shelters a minimal amount of gross income from the imposition of tax. Section 151(d)(1) states that the exemption amount is a paltry $2,000, but § 151(d)(4) allows that amount to be adjusted annually for inflation. In 2007, for example, the exemption amount was $3,400.

Section 151(a) allows a deduction for all of the personal exemptions provided elsewhere in § 151. There are two sources of personal exemptions within § 151: the exemption for the taxpayer in § 151(b) and exemptions for the taxpayer's dependents in § 151(c). In addition to providing a single exemption for the taxpayer, § 151(b) also gives the taxpayer an exemption for his or her spouse, but only if the couple files separately and the taxpayer's spouse has no gross income and is not the "dependent" of another. What, then, about spouses who file a joint return? Read strictly, one might think § 151(b) would give the couple only one exemption, but the regulations come to rescue. Regulation § 1.151–1(b) makes it clear that spouses filing a joint return may claim two exemptions, as there are two taxpayers on a joint return.

The additional exemptions for dependents under § 151(c) can make things more complicated. Generally speaking, a taxpayer may claim an exemption for an individual who qualifies as the taxpayer's "dependent." That requires close examination of § 152, a provision that underwent substantial revision in the Working Families Tax Relief Act of 2004. Prior to that legislation, a taxpayer could claim an exemption for another individual that met a five-part test for a "dependent." The 2004 Families Act divides exemption-eligible dependents into two groups, **qualifying relatives** and **qualifying children**.

Qualifying relatives are those individuals who meet the same five-part test that was previously used for determining dependent status: (1) the individual must have one of seven listed relationships to the taxpayer or be a member of the taxpayer's household; (2) the taxpayer must provide over half of the individual's total support; (3) the individual's gross income must be less than the exemption amount; (4) the individual must be a citizen or resident of the United States or a resident of Canada or Mexico; and (5) the individual does not file a joint return with a spouse. See § 152(d).

Qualifying children are those individuals who meet a different five-part test: (1) the individual must be the taxpayer's child (biological or adopted son, biological or adopted daughter, stepson, stepdaughter, eligible foster child or any descendent of such a child) or sibling (brother, sister, stepbrother, stepsister, half brother, half sister, or any descendant of such a sibling); (2) the individual must be under the age of 19 (or under the age of 24 and a full-time student); (3) with some exceptions the individual must be a citizen or resident of the United States or a resident of Canada or Mexico who does not file a joint return with a spouse; (4) the individual's principal place of abode for more than half of the year must be the same as the taxpayer's; and (5) the individual must not have provided over half of his or her own support. See § 152(c).

Both classifications require some determination of the level of support furnished by the taxpayer. This can prove to be a difficult task. For one thing, the statute does not define "support," and the Regulations only state that the term includes items like food, shelter, clothing, medical and dental care expenses, education expenses, and similar items.

Reg. § 1.152–1(a)(2)(i). This list implies that support costs are limited to expenses that provide the necessities of life, but in practice, the Internal Revenue Service and the courts have applied a much more liberal standard. In *Revenue Ruling 77–282*, 1977–2 C.B. 52, for example, the Service conceded that the cost of a car given to a child was includible in determining whether the child's parents had furnished over half of the child's total support. The ruling cautions, however, that if title to the car remains with the parents, the cost of the car is not includible in calculating support even if the child is the primary user of the vehicle. In *McKay v. Commissioner*, 34 T.C. 1080 (1960), the Tax Court held that costs to care for an individual's dog are part of the support of that individual. Because of this broad interpretation of support, taxpayers rarely get into too much trouble with the support test. Most cases involving denied dependency exemptions involve either a problem with the relationship test or inadequate proof of support offered by the taxpayer. Only rarely would the issue of whether a cost constitutes "support" come into play.

Special support tests are set forth in §§ 152(f)(5) (for students) and 152(e) (for children of divorced parents). This latter test will be discussed in the context of the tax consequences of divorce and separation in Chapter 9.

What if no one taxpayer furnishes over half of an individual's support? Section 152(d)(3) makes accommodation for so-called "multiple support agreements," wherein those taxpayers who do furnish support to an individual may decide among themselves who gets to claim the dependency exemption. As long as these support providers together furnish over half of the individual's support, and so long as the provider chosen supplied over ten percent of the total support, the decision of the providers will be effective.

If an individual qualifies as both a qualifying relative and a qualifying child, that individual is treated as a qualifying child. This is important because the definition of a qualifying child is also important for other Code provisions, including the definition of a head of household under § 1, the dependent care credit in § 21, the earned income tax credit of § 32, and the statutory fringe benefit rules of § 132, just to name a few.

As illustrated in Part A of this Chapter, the personal exemptions are phased-out if the taxpayer's adjusted gross income exceeds the "threshold amount" listed in the statute. Section 151(d)(3)(C) lists the threshold amounts applicable to each filing status, and those figures are adjusted for inflation. See § 151(d)(4)(B). The policy here is easy to discern: taxpayers with high adjusted gross incomes do not need a minimum amount of income sheltered from tax liability; they will easily be able to meet subsistence needs with after-tax funds even if all of their adjusted gross incomes are subject to taxation.

One last observation about exemptions for dependents: the Tax Reform Act of 1986 (which created the current Internal Revenue Code of

1986) imposed the requirement in § 151(e) that the taxpayer must provide the Taxpayer Identification Number (for United States citizens, that is usually the Social Security Number) of each dependent claimed on the federal income tax return. Individual tax returns filed for 1987 claimed *seven million* fewer dependents than returns filed for 1986. Is there a link? Or was there a massive abduction spree by outer-space aliens that year?

* * *

C. OVERVIEW OF CREDITS

Code: *Skim* IRC §§ 21; 25A; 26; 31(a); 32.

Regs: None.

After computing taxable income, taxpayers consult the § 1 rate tables as adjusted for the year at issue to determine tentative tax liability. Then, taxpayers may claim various credits against this tentative tax liability. Any tax liability remaining after application of the appropriate credits is the taxpayer's final tax liability. This Part considers four of the more significant credits available to individuals.

As an introductory matter, it is important to note that taxpayers generally prefer credits to deductions. A credit reduces tax liability dollar for dollar, while a deduction only produces a tax savings equal to the amount of the deduction multiplied by the taxpayer's marginal tax rate (the rate at which the last dollar of taxable income is taxed). See Chapter 1. So while deductions provide a greater benefit to taxpayers in higher tax brackets, credits benefit all taxpayers equally. That is why, for example, Congress chose to use an earned income credit instead of a deduction for earned income.

(1) HOUSEHOLD AND DEPENDENT CARE CREDIT

We will see in Chapter 4 that taxpayers may generally deduct expenses related to their business activities. It is well settled, however, that costs incurred to provide for babysitting, day care, or similar services while the taxpayer is away at work are not deductible as business expenses. *Smith v. Commissioner*, 113 F.2d 114 (2d Cir. 1940). This rule creates a disparity between single-earner households with one or more dependents and two-earner households with one or more dependents. Because two-earner households have to incur the expense of providing care for the dependents while they are at work, the real net gain from their labors is reduced. Suppose Fred and Wilma, a married couple with one child, earn a total of $55,000 in combined wages but pay $15,000 in day care costs for their child. Their net gain is $40,000. Their neighbors, Barney and Betty, also are married with one child. The gross income for their household is only $40,000 because only one of the spouses works. Barney and Betty do not incur the day care costs because the other spouse stays at home with the child. In terms of real gain from their labors, the couple in each case has $40,000 of income, but for federal income tax purposes, Fred and Wilma will pay tax on $55,000 while Barney and Betty pay tax on $40,000.

To ameliorate this disparity, § 21 offers a limited credit for certain expenses related to the care of a dependent. Generally, a taxpayer can credit anywhere from 20 percent to 35 percent of such costs against the taxpayer's federal income tax liability. The applicable percentage will depend upon the taxpayer's adjusted gross income: the higher the adjusted gross income, the lower the percentage. In any case, the maximum credit amount available under § 21 is $3,000 (or $6,000, if the taxpayer household contains more than one dependent). Creditable expenses include not only those incurred for actual physical care of the dependent but also ancillary "household" services like meal preparation and cleaning.

There are some restrictions on who qualifies as a dependent for purposes of this credit. In fact, § 21 uses the term "qualifying individual," not "dependent," to refer to the types of dependents the care for whom will trigger the credit. Qualifying individuals are one of three types: (1) dependents under age 13; (2) dependents of any age who share the same principal place of abode as the taxpayer and are physically or mentally incapable of caring for themselves; and (3) spouses of any age who share the same principal place of abode as the taxpayer and are physically or mentally incapable of caring for themselves. The taxpayer must also "maintain the household" for these qualifying individuals in order to obtain the credit. This means that the taxpayer must furnish over one-half of the total cost of maintaining the household.

The household and dependent care credit is "nonrefundable." This means that if the amount of the credit, after application of all relevant limitations, exceeds the taxpayer's pre-credit federal income tax liability, the excess is not paid to the taxpayer. Nonrefundable credits can only reduce or eliminate liability for tax; by definition, they cannot create a balance due to the taxpayer.

(2) HOPE SCHOLARSHIP CREDIT AND LIFETIME LEARNING CREDIT

Two nonrefundable credits are available for certain expenses related to higher education. The Hope Scholarship Credit is available for tuition and related expenses incurred during the first two years of postsecondary education. See § 25A(b). The student must go to school on at least a half-time basis, and the credit is lost if the student is convicted of a felony drug offense. If all other requirements are met, the first $1,000 in "qualified tuition and related expenses" (an amount adjusted for inflation) is fully creditable, as are half of such expenses in excess of $1,000. Thus, for example, if the total of such expenses for the year is $4,600, the taxpayer can credit $2,800 (all of the first $1,000 plus half of the remaining $3,600).

"Qualified tuition and related expenses" is defined as the tuition and fees paid at most colleges and universities for the enrollment or attendance of the taxpayer, the taxpayer's spouse, or any dependent of the taxpayer (assuming the taxpayer is eligible to claim the dependency exemption in § 151(c) with respect to that dependent). The term specifically does not include student activity fees, athletic fees, insurance costs, or room and board expenses.

The second credit under § 25A is the Lifetime Learning Credit. See § 25A(c). As its name implies, this credit is not limited to the first two years of college education. Instead, the qualified tuition and related expenses are creditable as long as they relate to any course of instruction (at most colleges and universities) designed to develop or improve the student's job skills. The credit is limited to 20 percent of the first $10,000 in qualified tuition and related expenses, so no taxpayer can claim a credit of more than $2,000 in any one year. Furthermore, if the taxpayer was eligible for the Hope Scholarship Credit with respect to qualified tuition and related expenses, those same expenses may not be used for the Lifetime Learning Credit.

Both the Hope Scholarship Credit and the Lifetime Learning Credit are subject to an income limitation designed to limit the benefit of these credits to low-and moderate-income taxpayers. Very generally, the combined credit amount is phased-out if a taxpayer's adjusted gross income exceeds $40,000 ($80,000 for joint return filers). If the taxpayer's adjusted gross income exceeds $50,000 ($100,000 for joint filers), the credits are phased-out entirely. These thresholds are adjusted for inflation.

Additional aspects of the tax treatment of education expenses await in Chapter 10.

(3) CREDIT FOR INCOME TAXES WITHHELD ON WAGES

With the Current Tax Payment Act of 1943, Congress re-introduced the concept of withholding federal income taxes "at the source"—i.e., requiring employers to withhold and remit a portion of an employee's paycheck directly to the federal government. Income tax withholding was part of the very first federal income tax under the Sixteenth Amendment. Passed in 1913, the authority to withhold was revoked in 1917 due to massive unpopularity. During World War II, however, Congress was able to resurrect the withholding mechanism, touting it as a tool of convenience. The withholding system has remained in place ever since. See Charlotte Twight, *Evolution of Federal Income Tax Withholding: The Machinery of Institutional Change*, 14:3 Cato J. 359 (1995).

Of course, if a taxpayer has already had enough federal income tax withheld from his or her paycheck, there is no need to impose additional tax liability. Amounts withheld from wages thus are credited against the taxpayer's pre-credit tax liability to determine if enough tax was collected through the withholding process. See § 31(a). As you may know from personal experience, this credit is refundable: if the federal income tax withheld from the paychecks exceeds the taxpayer's pre-credit tax liability, the excess tax withheld is refunded to the taxpayer (without interest, alas).

Income tax withholding gives the federal government a steady stream of revenue, which is preferable to a massive one-time deposit of revenue every April 15. Yet to the extent that over-withheld amounts do not earn interest for the taxpayer, taxpayers have an incentive to under-withhold wages as much as possible. Various provisions of the Code discourage excessive under-withholding, and now is not the time to bore you with a recitation of those provisions. What is important at this point is the understanding of why a taxpayer wants as little withheld as possible.

Suppose a taxpayer earns wages of $500 and that $100 of that amount is withheld by the employer and paid to the federal government on behalf of the taxpayer. The taxpayer has $400 to save and/or spend. If the taxpayer saves the $400, he or she might earn interest income on that amount. Assuming the taxpayer earns five percent interest on the $400 savings, then, the taxpayer has an additional $20 of income (five percent of $400 is $20). If the taxpayer has no other income for the year, it is likely that all or a portion of the $100 withheld from the paycheck will be refunded to the taxpayer after he or she files a federal income tax return showing a refund due. If the taxpayer gets all $100 refunded, without interest, then the taxpayer's total income for the year is $520 ($500 in wages and $20 in interest). Had the taxpayer been allowed to keep the $500, he or she could have earned $25 in interest (five percent of $500 is $25). The taxpayer would still have no liability for federal income tax under our assumptions, so the taxpayer would keep all $525. Notice that federal income tax withholding reduced the taxpayer's earning power. The taxpayer could only earn interest on the $400 remaining after withholding and not the $500 gross income even though the withheld tax was refunded to the taxpayer.

This principle arises in contexts beyond income tax withholding. Taxpayers generally seek to defer the inclusion of gross income so they can invest and earn interest on that portion of the gross income that will be used to pay tax. Suppose a taxpayer is about to have gross income in December of Year One. If the taxpayer receives the income in Year One, the tax on that income will be due by April 15, Year Two. If the taxpayer does not receive the income until January of Year Two, however, the tax on that income will not be due until April 15, Year *Three*. That gives the taxpayer nearly twelve more months to invest the money that will be used to pay the tax on the gross income.

For the same reason, taxpayers generally try to accelerate deductions. Deductions usually result in tax savings, and taxpayers can invest that savings and make more interest. If a deduction is deferred until a later year, however, the taxpayer loses a year's worth of interest that could have been made. For example, assume that a taxpayer pays a $1,000 deductible expense at the end of Year One, and that the deduction results in a tax savings of $200. In theory, that $200 in tax savings is available for investing as of the time the tax return for Year One is filed. If the deductible expense does not occur until the beginning of Year

Two, the $200 tax savings from the resulting deduction is not available for investment until sometime in Year Three.

No big deal to lose a year of interest? Think again. In nine years, the $200 tax savings would grow to $310.27, assuming a modest five percent interest. In ten years, the same savings would grow to $325.78 under the same assumptions. Would you rather have $310.27 or $325.78? If you have a preference, then the extra year of earnings matters. It matters even more if the assumed return on the investment is more than five percent (which it usually is) or if the amount at issue is greater.

The timing of income and deductions (and of income tax payments) thus has very great significance. More attention will be devoted to these issues in Chapter 6.

(4) EARNED INCOME CREDIT

Another significant refundable credit is the earned income credit under § 32. Eligible taxpayers can credit from 7.65 percent to 40 percent of their "earned incomes" (all forms of taxable compensation like wages, salaries, and tips, as well as earnings from self-employment) against their pre-credit federal income tax liabilities. The credit is targeted to low-income taxpayers, so the credit amount is phased-out as the taxpayer's adjusted gross income (or earned income, if larger) exceeds $5,280 (or $11,610 if the taxpayer has one or more "qualifying children"). These dollar thresholds are adjusted for inflation. The credit percentage is a function of the number of "qualifying children" the taxpayer has. To be a "qualifying child," the child must share the same principal place of abode with the taxpayer for the majority of the year, must bear a certain relationship to the taxpayer, and must meet certain age requirements.

The central policy of the earned income credit is to provide a work incentive for low-income taxpayers. Since the credit only applies if the taxpayer has earned income, taxpayers who qualify for the credit have an incentive to earn income. The credit is also designed to alleviate poverty. Since the credit amount usually exceeds the tax due on the earned income, the credit typically generates a refund. By limiting the refund to low-income taxpayers, the redistributive feature of the income tax is enhanced. Yet to the extent the credit is conditioned on a taxpayer having earned income, no subsidy is provided to individuals with *no* incomes. The earned income credit is thus not a perfect vehicle for wealth redistribution.

The definitions and computations related to the earned income credit make any other computation we have seen thus far look like a walk in the park. This overview of the earned income credit is necessarily brief, for any explanation beyond the bare surface will engulf the reader into a morass of detail that would chill any further study of federal income tax. Critics lament the complexity of the earned income credit, and some studies suggest that this complexity has deterred eligible taxpayers from claiming it.

* * *

*

Part Two

A CLOSER LOOK

Chapter 3

THE MEANING OF "GROSS INCOME"

A. JUDICIAL AND ADMINISTRATIVE DEFINITIONS OF INCOME

Code: IRC § 61(a).

Regs: Treas. Reg. §§ 1.61–2(d)(1); 1.61–14(a).

As explained in Chapter 2, the starting point for the determination of "taxable income" is the computation of "gross income." Section 61(a) defines gross income as "all income from whatever source derived." The Sixteenth Amendment to the United States Constitution (adopted in 1913) gives Congress the power "to lay and collect taxes on *incomes, from whatever source derived,* without apportionment among the several states and without regard to any census or enumeration" (emphasis added). Apparently, in defining gross income as "all income from whatever source derived," Congress states its intention to exercise the full measure of the power granted to it by the Sixteenth Amendment. See *Glenshaw Glass, infra.*

We are still left, then, with the question of what is meant by "income." Section 61(a) offers fifteen examples of items that are included in gross income, but the list is only representative and not exclusive. The Treasury Department has not offered any regulatory guidance on the general concept of income. Since the Code and the Treasury Regulations offer no help on this issue, we have to look elsewhere for help.

Economists have debated the meaning of "income" and have not reached consensus. The most common definition of income in economic theory states that income is the sum of a taxpayer's consumption plus his or her change in wealth for a particular period. *See* Robert M. Haig, *The Concept of Income—Economic and Legal Aspects*, in THE FEDERAL INCOME TAX 1, 7 (Robert M. Haig, ed. 1921), reprinted in Am. Econ. Ass'n, READINGS IN THE ECONOMICS OF TAXATION 54 (Richard A. Musgrave & Carl Shoup, eds. 1959); Henry C. Simons, PERSONAL INCOME TAXATION 50 (1938). Suppose, for example, that a taxpayer receives wages from employment totaling $50,000. The taxpayer spends $40,000 of the wages on personal living expenses (groceries, apparel, rent, gasoline, and the like) and invests the remaining $10,000 by purchasing stock in a publicly traded corporation. In this simple example, the taxpayer's income is $50,000, for the $40,000 spent on personal expenses represents consumption and the remaining $10,000 represents an increase in the taxpayer's net worth.

The "Haig–Simons definition" is of greater utility in more complex cases. Now suppose that the same taxpayer in the prior example receives another $50,000 in wages in the following taxable year. The taxpayer spends all of these wages on personal expenses, making no additional investments. Yet the value of the corporate stock purchased in the prior year increases from $10,000 to $15,000. Under the Haig–Simons definition of income, the taxpayer's income in this case is $55,000—the $50,000 consumed on personal expenses and the $5,000 growth in the value of the taxpayer's stock investment.

While consumption is fairly easy to measure, imagine the inherent complexities in administering a system where mere fluctuations in value were of significance! In the prior example, the taxpayer has $5,000 of income because the value of the taxpayer's stock increases during the year. If the income from the appreciation in value is subject to taxation, the taxpayer will have to use a portion of the taxpayer's wages to pay that tax. That result may be acceptable, but suppose the taxpayer did not have any wages for the year. The appreciation in the value of the stock would still be subject to tax, but the taxpayer would not have the cash to pay any tax on this increased wealth. Nonetheless, the Haig–Simons definition of income would require the appreciation to be included in gross income. If the Haig–Simons formula was followed, taxpayers would have to value their assets at the end of each year and measure gains and losses. Taxpayers would also have to sell assets to obtain the cash necessary to pay the resulting income tax.

But the fun would not stop there. Presumably, if the stock in the prior example was sold at the beginning of the next year for $15,000, there would be no additional tax on the sale since the $5,000 appreciation was already taken into account in the prior tax year. But what if the value declined in the next year and there was no sale? Would the taxpayer be entitled to a deduction in the amount of the decreased value (an unfortunate result that requires more appraisals)? Or would the taxpayer simply be out of luck (a result that would probably cause a revolt akin to the Boston Tea Party)? If a deduction was allowed, what should happen if the taxpayer has no other income to offset that loss? These additional issues could all be answered, of course, but the very complexities created by these additional issues have precluded the adoption of the Haig–Simons definition for all federal income tax purposes.

The Haig–Simons definition might be helpful from a theoretical perspective, but the practical limitations have forced the courts to find a more suitable definition of income. The United States Supreme Court first tackled the issue in *Eisner v. Macomber*, briefed below. The Court then modified its definition in *Glenshaw Glass*, which follows the *Macomber* brief. As you read these cases, consider the extent to which the definitions adopted by the Court are consistent with the Haig–Simons formula.

EISNER v. MACOMBER, 252 U.S. 189, 40 S.Ct. 189, 64 L.Ed. 521 (1920).

Facts: The Standard Oil Company of California, a publicly traded corporation, declared a 50–percent stock dividend. Myrtle Macomber, the taxpayer in this case, owned 2,200 shares of Standard's stock. She received 1,100 additional shares of stock pursuant to the distribution, bringing her total ownership to 3,300 shares. Because all Standard shareholders participated proportionately in the stock dividend distribution, the receipt of the additional shares did not affect her proportionate interest in Standard's assets or profits.

Issue: Does the taxpayer have gross income from the receipt of 1,100 additional shares of Standard stock pursuant to the distribution?

Holding: No.

Rationale: Although the Income Tax Act of 1916 expressly included stock dividends as part of "net income" (the statutory predecessor of "gross income" set forth in § 61(a) of the modern statute), Justice Pitney, writing for the majority (5–4), relied on other definitions of income from earlier decisions to conclude that a stock dividend was not within the meaning of "income" as used in the Sixteenth Amendment:

> We find little to add to the succinct definition adopted in two cases arising under the Corporation Tax Act of 1909 (*Stratton's Independence v. Howbert*, 231 U.S. 399, 415; *Doyle v. Mitchell Bros. Co.*, 247 U.S. 179, 185—"Income may be defined as the gain derived from capital, from labor, or from both combined," provided it be understood to include profit gained through a sale or conversion of capital assets, to which it was applied in the *Doyle* Case. * * *
>
> Brief as it is, it indicates the characteristic and distinguishing attribute of income essential for a correct solution of the present controversy. The Government, although basing its argument upon the definition as quoted, placed chief emphasis upon the word "gain," which was extended to include a variety of meanings; while the significance of the next three words ["derived from capital"] was either overlooked or misconceived. * * * Here we have the essential matter: *not* a gain *accruing* to capital, not a *growth* or *increment* of value *in* the investment; but a gain, a profit, something of exchangeable value *proceeding from* the property, *severed from* the capital however invested or employed, and *coming in*, being "*derived*," that is, *received* or *drawn by* the recipient (the taxpayer) for his *separate* use, benefit and disposal;—*that* is income derived from property. Nothing else answers the description.
>
> The same fundamental conception is clearly set forth in the Sixteenth Amendment—"incomes from whatever source derived"—

the essential thought being expressed with conciseness and lucidity entirely in harmony with the form and style of the Constitution.

Can a stock dividend, considering its essential character, be brought within the definition? * * * [It] does not alter the pre-existing proportionate interest of any stockholder or increase the intrinsic value of his holding or of the aggregate holdings of the other stockholders as they stood before. The new certificates simply increase the number of the shares, with consequent dilution of the value of each share.

* * *

Far from being a realization of profits of the stockholder, [a stock dividend] tends rather to postpone such realization, in that the fund represented by the new stock has been transferred from surplus to capital, and no longer is available for actual distribution.

The essential and controlling fact is that the stockholder has received nothing out of the company's assets for his separate use and benefit; on the contrary, every dollar of his original investment, together with whatever accretions and accumulations have resulted from employment of his money and that of the other stockholders in the business of the company, still remains the property of the company, and subject to business risks which may result in wiping out the entire investment. Having regard to the very truth of the matter, to substance and not to form, he has received nothing that answers the definition of income within the meaning of the Sixteenth Amendment.

Dissents: Justice Holmes, joined by Justice Day, reasoned in a brief dissent that because the 1916 Act expressly identified stock dividends as income, and since most lay persons would consider such dividends as income, the statutory definition of income should be constitutional. Justice Brandeis, in a lengthy dissent joined by Justice Clarke, analyzed the issue as one of substance versus form. Justice Brandeis argued that the stock dividend was no different than a cash distribution followed by a purchase of additional shares in the corporation. A cash distribution would, of course, be a taxable event; thus, according to Justice Brandeis, the stock dividend should also be taxed.

* * *

Notes and Questions

1. *The Realization Requirement.* The majority distinguished accretion and appreciation on the one hand and income on the other. In order for a taxpayer to have income from property, says the majority, the taxpayer must receive some right or asset that is sufficiently distinct from the property. The Court called this a "realization" of the profits. *Macomber* seemingly makes realization a constitutional prerequisite to income, but in later decisions we will see the Court back down from this position. Yet while

realization may no longer be constitutionally required, the concept remains a helpful guidepost for determining the proper timing of taxation.

The *Macomber* case is like an impressionist painting: easy to comprehend from a distance, but increasingly unclear upon closer examination. We have come to accept without question that the appreciation in value of an asset is not "income" until the asset is sold, exchanged, or otherwise disposed, but the Court never really offers a satisfactory explanation for why this should be the result. It is intuitively appealing to side with the taxpayer because her wealth was not affected by the stock dividend. But in some respects, the *Macomber* facts miss the important issue: can Congress, if it chooses, tax unrealized appreciation under the Sixteenth Amendment? The *Macomber* Court answers this question in the negative, but the issue was not really before the Court. The Court could have concluded that "income," for purposes of the Sixteenth Amendment, includes unrealized appreciation and still hold for the taxpayer; the Court could have ruled that a stock dividend simply does not represent "appreciation" in value. *Macomber* is therefore a troubling case because it pronounces a rule (that realization must occur) that is broader than warranted by the facts.

This is not to say that the *Macomber* Court reached the wrong result. Prior to the enactment of the Sixteenth Amendment, the Court had decided that mere appreciation in value was not income. It is widely accepted that the purpose of the Sixteenth Amendment was only to eliminate the requirement that a federal income tax, like any other direct tax imposed by Congress, be apportioned among the States according to population. The Sixteenth Amendment was not an attempt to supplant prior definitions of income. From the perspective of *stare decisis*, the holding in *Macomber* is correct.

But is there something more to the realization requirement than homage to precedent? Put differently, why hasn't a member of Congress introduced a bill to include unrealized appreciation in gross income? The short answer is that the bill would not get support from Democrats or Republicans. The bill would add to the burden of lower-income taxpayers with few resources to pay taxes on appreciated property. More affluent taxpayers would object to the broadening of the tax base. Taxpayers of all income levels would face an increased compliance burden. Taxpayers would have to value all assets at the end of each taxable year. This is a fairly easy task for assets like marketable securities and savings accounts, but a very difficult one with respect to collectibles, interests in closely-held businesses, and other assets that are hard to value. The valuation methods used by taxpayers would, by necessity, be met with careful scrutiny by the Internal Revenue Service. Realization, then, is justified on two grounds. The rule of realization postpones taxation: (1) until a taxpayer has adequate resources to pay the tax; and (2) until the amount of gain or profit can be measured with reasonable certainty.

2. *The Benefit of a Stock Dividend*. Part of the majority's rationale is based on the assumption that a shareholder participating in a proportionate stock distribution receives nothing of benefit from the distribution. One could argue that a stock dividend does provide a shareholder with at least some benefit. With more shares, the shareholder is able to sell smaller

portions of his or her original interest, and a smaller per share price may attract more buyers. Is that benefit sufficient to warrant the imposition of tax?

* * *

Self-Assessment Question

(Solutions to Self–Assessment Questions are set forth in Appendix 3.)

SAQ 3–1. Would the result in *Macomber* be different if, instead of additional Standard stock, the taxpayer and the other shareholders received:

    (a) cash?

    (b) other corporate assets?

    (c) promissory notes from the corporation?

* * *

COMMISSIONER v. GLENSHAW GLASS COMPANY

United States Supreme Court, 1955.
348 U.S. 426, 75 S.Ct. 473, 99 L.Ed. 483.

Mr. Chief Justice Warren delivered the opinion of the Court.

This litigation involves two cases with independent factual backgrounds yet presenting the identical issue. The two cases were consolidated for argument before the Court of Appeals for the Third Circuit and were heard en banc. The common question is whether money received as exemplary damages for fraud or as the punitive two-thirds portion of a treble-damage antitrust recovery must be reported by a taxpayer as gross income * * *.

The facts of the cases were largely stipulated and are not in dispute. So far as pertinent they are as follows:

Commissioner v. Glenshaw Glass Co. The Glenshaw Glass Company, a Pennsylvania corporation, manufactures glass bottles and containers. It was engaged in protracted litigation with the Hartford–Empire Company, which manufactures machinery of a character used by Glenshaw. Among the claims advanced by Glenshaw were demands for exemplary damages for fraud and treble damages for injury to its business by reason of Hartford's violation of the federal antitrust laws. In December, 1947, the parties concluded a settlement of all pending litigation, by which Hartford paid Glenshaw approximately $800,000. Through a method of allocation which was approved by the Tax Court, and which is no longer in issue, it was ultimately determined that, of the total settlement, $324,529.94 represented payment of punitive damages for fraud and antitrust violations. Glenshaw did not report this portion of the settlement as income for the tax year involved. The Commissioner determined a deficiency claiming as taxable the entire sum less only deductible legal fees. * * *

Commissioner v. William Goldman Theatres, Inc. William Goldman Theatres, Inc., a Delaware corporation operating motion picture houses in Pennsylvania, sued Loew's, Inc., alleging a violation of the federal antitrust laws and seeking treble damages. After a holding that a violation had occurred, the case was remanded to the trial court for a determination of damages. It was found that Goldman had suffered a loss of profits equal to $125,000 and was entitled to treble damages in the sum of $375,000. Goldman reported only $125,000 of the recovery as gross income and claimed that the $250,000 balance constituted punitive damages and as such was not taxable. The Tax Court agreed, and the Court of Appeals, hearing this with the *Glenshaw* case, affirmed.

It is conceded by the respondents that there is no constitutional barrier to the imposition of a tax on punitive damages. Our question is one of statutory construction: are these payments comprehended by § 22(a) [the predecessor of § 61(a)]?

The sweeping scope of the controverted statute is readily apparent:

"§ 22. Gross income

"(a) General definition. 'Gross income' includes gains, profits, and income derived from salaries, wages, or compensation for personal service * * * of whatever kind and in whatever form paid, or from professions, vocations, trades, businesses, commerce, or sales, or dealings in property, whether real or personal, growing out of the ownership or use of or interest in such property; also from interest, rent, dividends, securities, or the transaction of any business carried on for gain or profit, or gains or profits and income derived from any source whatever. * * * "

This Court has frequently stated that this language was used by Congress to exert in this field "the full measure of its taxing power." Respondents contend that punitive damages, characterized as "windfalls" flowing from the culpable conduct of third parties, are not within the scope of the section. But Congress applied no limitations as to the source of taxable receipts, nor restrictive labels as to their nature. And the Court has given a liberal construction to this broad phraseology in recognition of the intention of Congress to tax all gains except those specifically exempted. Thus, the fortuitous gain accruing to a lessor by reason of the forfeiture of a lessee's improvements on the rented property was taxed in *Helvering v. Bruun*, 309 U.S. 461, 60 S.Ct. 631, 84 L.Ed. 864. Such decisions demonstrate that we cannot but ascribe content to the catchall provision of § 22(a), "gains or profits and income derived from any source whatever." * * *

Nor can we accept respondents' contention that a narrower reading of § 22(a) is required by the Court's characterization of income in *Eisner v. Macomber*, 252 U.S. 189, 207, 40 S.Ct. 189, 193, 64 L.Ed. 521, as "the gain derived from capital, from labor, or from both combined." The Court was there endeavoring to determine whether the distribution of a corporate stock dividend constituted a realized gain to the shareholder, or changed "only the form, not the essence," of his capital investment. It was held that the taxpayer had "received nothing out of the company's assets for his separate use and benefit." The distribution, therefore, was held not a taxable event. In that context—distinguishing gain from capital—the definition served a useful purpose. But it was not meant to provide a touchstone to all future gross income questions.

Here we have instances of undeniable accessions to wealth, clearly realized, and over which the taxpayers have complete dominion. The mere fact that the payments were extracted from the wrongdoers as punishment for unlawful conduct cannot detract from their character as taxable income to the recipients. Respondents concede, as they must, that the recoveries are taxable to the extent that they compensate for damages actually incurred. It would be an anomaly that could not be justified in the absence of clear congressional intent to say that a recovery for actual damages is taxable but not the additional amount extracted as punishment for the same conduct which caused the injury. And we find no such evidence of intent to exempt these payments.

It is urged that re-enactment of § 22(a) without change since the Board of Tax Appeals held punitive damages nontaxable in *Highland Farms Corp.*, 42 B.T.A. 1314, indicates congressional satisfaction with that holding. Re-enactment—particularly without the slightest affirmative indication that Congress ever had the Highland Farms decision before it—is an unreliable indicium at best. Moreover, the Commissioner promptly published his non-acquiescence in this portion of the *Highland Farms* holding and has, before and since, consistently maintained the position that these receipts are taxable. It therefore cannot be said with certitude that Congress intended to carve an exception out of § 22(a)'s pervasive coverage. Nor does the 1954 Code's legislative history, with its reiteration of the proposition that statutory gross income is "all-inclusive," give support to respondents' position. The definition of gross income has been simplified, but no effect upon its present broad scope was intended. Certainly punitive damages cannot reasonably be classified as gifts, nor do they come under any other exemption provision in the Code. We would do violence to the plain meaning of the statute and restrict a clear legislative attempt to bring the taxing power to bear upon all receipts constitutionally taxable were we to say that the payments in question here are not gross income.

Reversed.

MR. JUSTICE DOUGLAS dissents.

MR. JUSTICE HARLAN took no part in the consideration or decision of this case.

Note

The *Glenshaw Glass* Court revealed that the definition of income used by the majority in *Eisner v. Macomber* was not the exclusive test for income subject to tax under the Sixteenth Amendment. In its place, the Court indirectly offered a more comprehensive test for income, one broader than that employed by the *Macomber* Court. The *Glenshaw Glass* definition of income has survived for half a century—to this day it is the preferred test for identifying whether a taxpayer has income.

* * *

CESARINI v. UNITED STATES

United States District Court, Northern District of Ohio, 1969.
296 F.Supp. 3.

YOUNG, DISTRICT JUDGE.

This is an action by the plaintiffs as taxpayers for the recovery of income tax payments made in the calendar year 1964. Plaintiffs contend that the amount of $836.51 was erroneously overpaid by them in 1964, and that they are entitled to a refund in that amount, together with the statutory interest from October 13, 1965, the date which they made their claim upon the Internal Revenue Service for the refund.

* * * In 1957, the plaintiffs purchased a used piano at an auction sale for approximately $15.00, and the piano was used by their daughter for piano lessons. In 1964, while cleaning the piano, plaintiffs discovered the sum of $4,467.00 in old currency, and since have retained the piano instead of discarding it as previously planned. Being unable to ascertain who put the money there, plaintiffs exchanged the old currency for new at a bank, and reported the sum of $4,467.00 on their 1964 joint income tax return as ordinary income from other sources. On October 18, 1965, plaintiffs filed an amended return with the District Director of Internal Revenue in Cleveland, Ohio, this second return eliminating the sum of $4,467.00 from the gross income computation, and requesting a refund in the amount of $836.51, the amount allegedly overpaid as a result of the former inclusion of $4,467.00 in the original return for the calendar year of 1964. On January 18, 1966, the Commissioner of Internal Revenue rejected taxpayers' refund claim in its entirety, and plaintiffs filed the instant action in March of 1967.

Plaintiffs make three alternative contentions in support of their claim that the sum of $836.51 should be refunded to them. First, that the $4,467.00 found in the piano is not includable in gross income under Section 61 of the Internal Revenue Code. Secondly, even if the retention of the cash constitutes a realization of ordinary income under Section 61, it was due and owing in the year the piano was purchased, 1957, and by 1964, the statute of limitations provided by § 6501 had elapsed. And thirdly, that if the treasure trove money is gross income for the year 1964, it was entitled to capital gains treatment under Section 1221. The Government, by its answer and its trial brief, asserts that the amount found in the piano is includable in gross income under Section 61(a) of Title 26, U.S.C., that the money is taxable in the year it was actually found, 1964, and that the sum is properly taxable at ordinary income rates, not being entitled to capital gains treatment * * *.

After a consideration of the pertinent provisions of the Internal Revenue Code, Treasury Regulations, Revenue Rulings, and decisional law in the area, this Court has concluded that the taxpayers are not entitled to a refund of the amount requested, nor are they entitled to capital gains treatment on the income item at issue.

The starting point in determining whether an item is to be included in gross income is, of course, Section 61(a) of Title 26 U.S.C., and that section provides in part:

> "Except as otherwise provided in this subtitle, gross income means all income from whatever source derived, including (but not limited to) the following items: * * * "

Subsections (1) through (15) of Section 61(a) then go on to list fifteen items specifically included in the computation of the taxpayer's gross income, and Part II of Subchapter B of the 1954 Code (Sections 71 et seq.) deals with other items expressly included in gross income. While neither of these listings expressly includes the type of income which is at issue in the case at bar, Part III of Subchapter B (Sections 101 et seq.) deals with items specifically excluded from gross income, and found money is not listed in those sections either. This absence of express mention in any of the code sections necessitates a return to the "all income from whatever source" language of Section 61(a) of the code, and the express statement there that gross income is "not limited to" the following fifteen examples. Section 1.61–1(a) of the Treasury Regulations, the corresponding section to Section 61(a) in the 1954 Code, reiterates this board construction of gross income, providing in part:

> "Gross income means all income from whatever source derived, unless excluded by law. Gross income includes income realized in any form, whether in money, property, or services. * * * "

The decisions of the United States Supreme Court have frequently stated that this broad all-inclusive language was used by Congress to exert the full measure of its taxing power under the Sixteenth Amendment to the United States Constitution.

In addition, the Government in the instant case cites and relies upon an I.R.S. Revenue Ruling which is undeniably on point:

> "The finder of treasure-trove is in receipt of taxable income, for Federal income tax purposes, to the extent of its value in United States Currency, for the taxable year in which it is reduced to undisputed possession." *Rev. Rul. 61*, 1953–1, Cum. Bull. 17.

The plaintiffs argue that the above ruling does not control this case for two reasons. The first is that subsequent to the Ruling's pronouncement in 1953, Congress enacted Sections 74 and 102 of the 1954 Code, § 74 expressly including the value of prizes and awards in gross income in most cases, and § 102 specifically exempting the value of gifts received from gross income. From this, it is argued that Section 74 was added because prizes might otherwise be construed as non-taxable gifts, and since no such section was passed expressly taxing treasure-trove, it is therefore a gift which is non-taxable under Section 102. This line of reasoning overlooks the statutory scheme previously alluded to, whereby income from all sources is taxed unless the taxpayer can point to an express exemption. Not only have the taxpayers failed to list a specific exclusion in the instant case, but also the Government has pointed to express language covering the found money, even though it would not be required to do so under the broad language of Section 61(a) and the foregoing Supreme Court decisions interpreting it.

* * *

* * * In addition to the numerous cases in the Supreme Court which uphold the broad sweeping construction of Section 61(a) found in Treas. Reg. § 1.61–1(a), other courts and commentators writing at a point in time before the ruling came down took the position that windfalls, including found monies, were properly includable in gross income under Section 22(a) of the 1939 Code, the predecessor of Section 61(a) in the 1954 Code. While it is generally true that revenue rulings may be disregarded by the courts if in conflict with the code and the regulations, or with other judicial decisions, plaintiffs in the instant case have been unable to point to any inconsistency between the gross income sections of the code, the interpretation of them by the regulations and the Courts, and the revenue ruling which they herein attack as inapplicable. On the other hand, the United States has shown a consistency in letter and spirit between the ruling and the code, regulations, and court decisions.

Although not cited by either party, and noticeably absent from the Government's brief, the following Treasury Regulation appears in the 1964 Regulations, the year of the return in dispute:

"§ 1.61–14 Miscellaneous items of gross income.

"(a) In general. In addition to the items enumerated in section 61(a), there are many other kinds of gross income * * *. Treasure trove, to the extent of its value in United States currency, constitutes gross income for the taxable year in which it is reduced to undisputed possession."

Identical language appears in the 1968 Treasury Regulations, and is found in all previous years back to 1958. This language is the same in all material respects as that found in Rev. Rul. 61, 53–1, Cum. Bull. 17, and is undoubtedly an attempt to codify that ruling into the Regulations which apply to the 1954 Code. This Court is of the opinion that Treas. Reg. § 1.61–14(a) is dispositive of the major issue in this case if the $4,467.00 found in the piano was "reduced to undisputed possession" in the year petitioners reported it, for this Regulation was applicable to returns filed in the calendar year of 1964.

This brings the Court to the second contention of the plaintiffs: that if any tax was due, it was in 1957 when the piano was purchased, and by 1964 the Government was blocked from collecting it by reason of the statute of limitations. Without reaching the question of whether the voluntary payment in 1964 constituted a waiver on the part of the taxpayers, this Court finds that the $4,467.00 sum was properly included in gross income for the calendar year of 1964. Problems of when title vests, or when possession is complete in the field of federal taxation, in the absence of definitive federal legislation on the subject, are ordinarily determined by reference to the law of the state in which the taxpayer resides, or where the property around which the dispute centers is located. Since both the taxpayers and the property in question are found within the State of Ohio, Ohio law must govern as to when the found money was "reduced to undisputed possession" within the meaning of Treas. Reg. § 1.61–14 and *Rev. Rul. 61*, 53–1, Cum. Bull. 17.

In Ohio, there is no statute specifically dealing with the rights of owners and finders of treasure trove, and in the absence of such a statute the common-law rule of England applies, so that "title belongs to the finder as against all the world except the true owner." * * * Therefore, in the instant case if plaintiffs had resold the piano in 1958, not knowing of the money within it, they later would not be able to succeed in an action against the purchaser who did discover it. Under Ohio law, the plaintiffs must have actually found the money to have superior title over all but the true owner, and they did not discover the old currency until 1964. Unless there is present a specific state statute to the contrary, the majority of jurisdictions are in accord with the Ohio rule. Therefore, this Court finds that the $4,467.00 in old currency was not "reduced to undisputed possession" until its actual discovery in 1964, and thus the United States was not barred by the statute of limitations from collecting the $836.51 in tax during that year.

Finally, plaintiffs' contention that they are entitled to capital gains treatment upon the discovered money must be rejected. While the broad definition of "capital asset" in Section 1221 of Title 26 would on its face cover both the piano and the currency, Section 1222(3) defines long-term capital gains as those resulting from the "sale or exchange of a capital asset * * *." Aside from the fact that the piano for which plaintiffs paid $15.00 and the $4,467.00 in currency found within it are economically dissimilar, neither the piano nor the currency have been sold or exchanged. The benefits of capital gains treatment in the taxing statutes are not allowed to flow to every gain growing out of a transaction concerning capital assets, but only to gains from the "sale or exchange" of capital assets, and the terms "sale" and "exchange" are to be given ordinary meaning in determining whether capital gains treatment is proper. It has been held that a "sale" in the ordinary sense of the word is a transfer of property for a fixed price in money or its equivalent. Applying the ordinary meaning of the words sale or exchange to the facts of this case, it is readily apparent that neither transaction has occurred, the plaintiffs not having sold or exchanged the piano or the money. They are therefore not entitled to capital gains treatment on the $4,467.00 found inside the piano, but instead incurred tax liability for the sum at ordinary income rates. Since it appears to the Court that the income tax on these taxpayers' gross income for the calendar year of 1964 has been properly assessed and paid, this taxpayers' suit for a refund in the amount of $836.51 must be dismissed, and judgment entered for the United States. An order will be entered accordingly.

Notes and Questions

1. *Getting Caught.* How did the Service discover that the taxpayers in *Cesarini* had found old currency inside their piano? Were the taxpayers foolish to have included the value of the currency in gross income on their 1964 federal income tax return? Suppose a client informs you of some cash found on the client's property earlier this year, and the client wants to know whether the cash should be included in the client's gross income. How would you advise the client? Would your advice change if you knew that only a little more than one percent of all federal income tax returns are subject to a random audit by the Service?

2. *The Alternative Argument.* Although the taxpayers in *Cesarini* maintained that they had no gross income from the treasure inside the piano, they argued in the alternative that if the treasure was indeed taxable that it should have been included in gross income on the 1957 tax return. Why do they make this argument? See § 6501(a).

* * *

Problem 3–1

For each of the situations described below, determine whether the taxpayer has gross income and, if so, the amount that should be included in gross income on the taxpayer's federal income tax return.

(a) The taxpayer finds $500 cash in an envelope behind an old appliance in the taxpayer's home.

(b) The taxpayer finds a diamond ring in the attic of the taxpayer's home.

(c) The taxpayer purchases a personal residence and finds a valuable painting left behind in the attic.

(d) In the year after the facts in part (c) occur, the artist who created the painting dies, and the painting increases in value by $10,000.

(e) The taxpayer purchases a piano for $15 at a garage sale, but in fact the piano is a rare collectible worth $10,000.

Problem 3–2

On September 8, 1998, Mark McGwire, the first baseman for the St. Louis Cardinals, hit his 62nd home run of the season, surpassing the single-season home run record established by Roger Maris in 1961. The ball was retrieved by Tim Forneris, a 22 year-old grounds crewman at Busch Stadium. In a ceremony following the game, Forneris stepped up to the microphone and said, "Mr. McGwire, I have something here that belongs to you." He then handed the ball to McGwire.

In the days leading up to the game, several sports memorabilia collectors stated that the record-breaking ball would likely fetch at least $1 million if sold at auction. For his actions, Forneris received a souvenir Rawlings bat and a 1999 red minivan (with a license plate that read "NO 62") from his employer. He was presented with a key to his home town of Collinsville, Illinois, a free dinner and souvenir items from the All–Star Café in New York City, a free trip to Disney World in Florida, and hundreds of one-dollar bills by mail from baseball fans from around the world.

(a) Do either McGwire or Forneris have gross income based on these facts? If so, how much?

(b) Suppose Forneris kept the ball and placed it in his dresser drawer, never selling the ball despite firm offers of $1 million for the ball. Does Forneris have gross income?

(c) Would the answer to either (a) or (b) be different if Forneris was not an employee of Busch Stadium but instead a fan who paid admission to sit in the left field bleachers?

Problem 3–3

Seymore Skinner, an elementary school principal, receives free textbooks from publishers. After reviewing the books, Skinner is allowed to keep them for his personal use.

(a) Does Skinner have gross income from the receipt of the books?

(b) How would the answer to (a) change if, upon receipt of the textbooks, Skinner donates them to the school library and claims a charitable contribution deduction on his federal income tax return equal to the value of the books?

* * *

REVENUE RULING 79–24
1979–1 C.B. 60.

FACTS

Situation 1. In return for personal legal services performed by a lawyer for a housepainter, the housepainter painted the lawyer's personal residence. Both the lawyer and the housepainter are members of a barter club, an organization that annually furnishes its members a directory of members and the services they provide. All the members of the club are professional or trades persons. Members contact other members directly and negotiate the value of the services to be performed. *Situation 2.* An individual who owned an apartment building received a work of art created by a professional artist in return for the rent-free use of an apartment for six months by the artist.

LAW

The applicable sections of the Internal Revenue Code of 1954 and the Income Tax Regulations thereunder are 61(a) and 1.61–2, relating to compensation for services.

Section 1.61–2(d)(1) of the regulations provides that if services are paid for other than in money, the fair market value of the property or services taken in payment must be included in income. If the services were rendered at a stipulated price, such price will be presumed to be the fair market value of the compensation received in the absence of evidence to the contrary.

HOLDINGS

Situation 1. The fair market value of the services received by the lawyer and the housepainter are includible in their gross incomes under section 61 of the Code.

Situation 2. The fair market value of the work of art and the six months fair rental value of the apartment are includible in the gross incomes of the apartment-owner and the artist under section 61 of the Code.

Notes and Question

1. *What's a Revenue Ruling?* Taxpayers who seek binding advice from the Internal Revenue Service as to the proper tax treatment of a transaction may, for a fee, request a private ruling from the Service. The ruling binds only the Service and the requesting party; a private ruling may not be cited or relied upon as precedent. The Service may, however, in its discretion, redact the text of a private ruling and issue it as a "revenue ruling," one that is binding on all taxpayers and the Service. The numbering system for revenue rulings corresponds to the year in which they are issued. Thus, for example, *Revenue Ruling 79–24* was the twenty-fourth revenue ruling issued in 1979. Revenue Rulings are published in the weekly *Internal Revenue Bulletin* (cited "I.R.B.") and then again semi-annually in the *Cumulative Bulletin* (cited "C.B."). The *Cumulative Bulletin* is generally the preferred source for citing a revenue ruling.

2. *Distinguishing Imputed Income from Barter Exchanges.* In *Revenue Ruling 79–24*, a lawyer had gross income from a barter exchange where the lawyer received painting services in exchange for legal services. If the lawyer had painted his or her own home, however, no gross income would result. This is because so-called **imputed income**, benefits resulting from a taxpayer's personal efforts, has never been considered part of the federal income tax base. While imputed income would be taxable if the Haig–Simons definition of income were strictly applied to the federal income tax (because imputed income is either consumed or enhances the taxpayer's net worth), Congress and the Service apparently recognize the insurmountable practical obstacles inherent in enforcing its taxation. Thus, benefits from growing one's own garden vegetables, owning one's own home, or (in the case of a lawyer, at least) writing one's own will are not subject to taxation.

If, in Situation 1 of the ruling, the lawyer had performed his or her own legal services, and if the painter had painted his or her own home, each would have non-taxable imputed income. Yet the barter exchange between them is taxable. Why? To the extent you have performed services for others in exchange for their services (child care in exchange for home repair, for instance), have you been a delinquent taxpayer?

* * *

Problem 3–4

Henrietta lives in a small cottage and is an expert quilt-maker. Her next door neighbor, X, works in construction and repair. When Henrietta's roof started leaking, X offered to fix the problem.

(a) Using some basic materials Henrietta already had on hand, X patched the roof. X did not want to charge Henrietta his normal $300 fee for three hours of work, but when she insisted on paying him, X asked for one of Henrietta's special quilts. Henrietta normally sold her quilts for $300, so she happily made the trade. Do either Henrietta or X have gross income on these facts?

(b) Suppose that X's normal fee for the services he performed for Henrietta is $500. How does the answer to (a) change?

(c) Assume instead that Henrietta fixed her own roof. Would she have gross income? From a policy perspective, should the answer here be different than the answer in (a)?

Problem 3–5

On the television show "Trading Spaces," neighbors agree to switch homes for 48 hours and completely redecorate one room in the other's house. They are assisted by a professional designer and a carpenter. The designer and the neighbors are limited to a budget of $1,000, furnished by the producers of the show.

Suppose that Ricky and Lucy Ricardo, a married couple, agree to appear on the show with their neighbors, Fred and Ethel Mertz, also married. Ricky and Lucy remodeled the kitchen in the Mertz home with the assistance of designer Laurie Hickson–Smith. Meanwhile, Fred and Ethel remodeled the living room in the Ricardo home with the idle assistance of designer Doug Wilson. Amy Wynn Pastor served as the carpenter for both projects.

Because of Laurie's expert eye and good taste, and because of the Herculean efforts of Ricky and Lucy, the Mertz home increased in value by $5,000. On the other hand, Doug's awkward sense of style and penchant for clashing colors caused the value of the Ricardo home to increase by only $1,000, the cost of the materials used to make the "improvements." Without the skills of Amy Wynn, the Ricardo home might have even lost value!

Assuming that Laurie and Doug both charge their normal customers $10,000 for two full days of advice and assistance, what are the federal income tax consequences to Ricky, Lucy, Fred, and Ethel?

JAMES v. UNITED STATES

United States Supreme Court, 1961.
366 U.S. 213, 81 S.Ct. 1052, 6 L.Ed.2d 246.

MR. CHIEF JUSTICE WARREN announced the judgment of the Court and an opinion in which MR. JUSTICE BRENNAN, and MR. JUSTICE STEWART concur.

The issue before us in this case is whether embezzled funds are to be included in the "gross income" of the embezzler in the year in which the funds are misappropriated * * *. *issue*

The facts are not in dispute. The petitioner is a union official who, with another person, embezzled in excess of $738,000 during the years 1951 through 1954 from his employer union and from an insurance company with which the union was doing business. Petitioner failed to report these amounts in his gross income in those years and was convicted for willfully attempting to evade the federal income tax due for each of the years 1951 through 1954 in violation of * * * § 7201 of the Internal Revenue Code of 1954. He was sentenced to a total of three years' imprisonment. The Court of Appeals affirmed. Because of a conflict with this Court's decision in *Commissioner of Internal Revenue v. Wilcox*, 327 U.S. 404, 66 S.Ct. 546, 90 L.Ed. 752, a case whose relevant facts are concededly the same as those in the case now before us, we granted certiorari.

In *Wilcox*, the Court held that embezzled money does not constitute taxable income to the embezzler in the year of the embezzlement * * *. Six years later, this Court held, in *Rutkin v. United States*, 343 U.S. 130, 72 S.Ct. 571, 96 L.Ed. 833, that extorted money does constitute taxable income to the extortionist in the year that the money is received * * *. In *Rutkin*, the Court did not overrule *Wilcox*, but stated:

"We do not reach in this case the factual situation involved in *Commissioner of Internal Revenue v. Wilcox*, 327 U.S. 404, 66 S.Ct. 546, 90 L.Ed. 752. We limit that case to its facts. There embezzled funds were held not to constitute taxable income to the embezzler under § 22(a)."

However, examination of the reasoning used in *Rutkin* leads us inescapably to the conclusion that *Wilcox* was thoroughly devitalized.

The basis for the *Wilcox* decision was "that a taxable gain is conditioned upon (1) the presence of a claim of right to the alleged gain and (2) the absence of a definite, unconditional obligation to repay or return that which would otherwise constitute a gain. Without some bona fide legal or equitable claim, even though it be contingent or contested in nature, the taxpayer cannot be said to have received any gain or profit * * *." Since Wilcox embezzled the money, held it "without any semblance of a bona fide claim of right," and therefore "was at all times under an unqualified duty and obligation to repay the money to his employer," the Court found that the money embezzled was not includible within "gross income." But, Rutkin's legal claim was no greater than that of Wilcox. It was specifically found "that petitioner had no basis for his claim * * * and that he obtained it by extortion." Both Wilcox and Rutkin obtained the money by means of a criminal act; neither had a bona fide claim of right to the funds. Nor was Rutkin's obligation to repay the extorted money to the victim any less than that of Wilcox. The victim of an extortion, like the victim of an embezzlement, has a right to restitution. Furthermore, it is inconsequential that an embezzler may lack title to the sums he appropriates while an extortionist may gain a voidable title. Questions of federal income taxation are not determined by such "attenuated subtleties." Thus, the fact that Rutkin secured the money with the consent of his victim * * * is irrelevant. Likewise unimportant is the fact that the sufferer of an extortion is less likely to seek restitution than one whose funds are embezzled. What is important is that the right to recoupment exists in both situations.

Examination of the relevant cases in the courts of appeals lends credence to our conclusion that the *Wilcox* rationale was effectively vitiated by this Court's decision in *Rutkin*. Although this case appears to be the first to arise that is "on all fours" with *Wilcox*, the lower federal courts, in deference to the undisturbed *Wilcox* holding, have earnestly endeavored to find distinguishing facts in the cases before them which would enable them to include sundry unlawful gains within "gross income."

It had been a well-established principle, long before either *Rutkin* or *Wilcox*, that unlawful, as well as lawful, gains are comprehended within the term "gross income." Section II B of the Income Tax Act of 1913 provided that "the net income of a taxable person shall include gains, profits, and income * * * from * * * the transaction of any lawful business carried on for gain or profit, or gains or profits and income derived from any source whatever * * *." When the statute was amended in 1916, the one word "lawful" was omitted. This revealed, we think, the obvious intent of that Congress to tax income derived from both legal and illegal sources, to remove the incongruity of having the gains of the honest laborer taxed and the gains of the dishonest immune. Thereafter, the Court held that gains from illicit traffic in liquor are includible within "gross income." And, the Court has pointed out, with approval, that there "has been a widespread and settled administrative and judicial recognition of the taxability of unlawful gains of many kinds." These include protection payments made to racketeers, ransom payments paid to kidnappers, bribes, money derived from the sale of unlawful insurance policies, graft, black market gains, funds obtained from the operation of lotteries, income from race track bookmaking and illegal prize fight pictures.

The starting point in all cases dealing with the question of the scope of what is included in "gross income" begins with the basic premise that the purpose of Congress was "to use the full measure of its taxing power." And the Court has given a liberal construction to the broad phraseology of the "gross income" definition statutes in recognition of the intention of Congress to tax all gains except those specifically exempted. The language of * * * § 61(a) of the 1954 Code, "all income from whatever source derived," [has] been held to encompass all "accessions to wealth, clearly realized, and over which the taxpayers have complete dominion." *Commissioner of Internal Revenue v. Glenshaw Glass Co.*, 348 U.S. 426, 431, 75 S.Ct. 473, 477, 99 L.Ed. 483. A gain "constitutes taxable income when its recipient has such control over it that, as a practical matter, he derives readily realizable economic value from it." *Rutkin v. United States, supra*, 343 U.S. at page 137, 72 S.Ct. at page 575. Under these broad principles, we believe that petitioner's contention, that all unlawful gains are taxable except those resulting from embezzlement, should fail.

When a taxpayer acquires earnings, lawfully or unlawfully, without the consensual recognition, express or implied, of an obligation to repay and without restriction as to their disposition, "he has received income which he is required to return, even though it may still be claimed that he is not entitled to retain the money, and even though he may still be adjudged liable to restore its equivalent." *North American Oil Consolidated v. Burnet*, 286 U.S. at page 424, 52 S.Ct. at page 615. In such case, the taxpayer has "actual command over the property taxed—the actual benefit for which the tax is paid." This standard brings wrongful appropriations within the broad sweep of "gross income;" it excludes loans. When a law-abiding taxpayer mistakenly receives income in one year, which receipt is assailed and found to be invalid in a subsequent year, the taxpayer must nonetheless report the amount as "gross income" in the year received. We do not believe that Congress intended to treat a law-breaking taxpayer differently. Just as the honest taxpayer may deduct any amount repaid in the year in which the repayment is made, the Government points out that, "If, when, and to the extent that the victim recovers back the misappropriated funds, there is of course a reduction in the embezzler's income." Brief for the United States, p. 24.

Petitioner contends that the *Wilcox* rule has been in existence since 1946; that if Congress had intended to change the rule, it would have done so; that there was a general revision of the income tax laws in 1954 without mention of the rule; that a bill to change it was introduced in the Eighty-sixth Congress but was not acted upon; that, therefore, we may not change the rule now. But the fact that Congress has remained silent or has re-enacted a statute which we have construed, or that congressional attempts to amend a rule announced by this Court have failed, does not necessarily debar us from re-examining and correcting the Court's own errors. There may have been any number of reasons why Congress acted as it did. One of the reasons could well be our subsequent decision in *Rutkin* which has been thought by many to have repudiated *Wilcox*. Particularly might this be true in light of the decisions of the Courts of Appeals which have been riding a narrow rail between the two cases and further distinguishing them to the disparagement of *Wilcox*.

We believe that *Wilcox* was wrongly decided and we find nothing in congressional history since then to persuade us that Congress intended to legislate the rule. Thus, we believe that we should now correct the error and the confusion resulting from it, certainly if we do so in a manner that will not prejudice those who might have relied on it. We should not continue to confound confusion, particularly when the result would be to perpetuate the injustice of relieving embezzlers of the duty of paying income taxes on the money they enrich themselves with through theft while honest people pay their taxes on every conceivable type of income.

But, we are dealing here with a felony conviction under statutes which apply to any person who "willfully" fails to account for his tax or who "willfully" attempts to evade his obligation. Willfulness "involves a specific intent which must be proven by independent evidence and which cannot be inferred from the mere understatement of income." *Holland v. United States*, 348 U.S. 121, 139, 75 S.Ct. 127, 137, 99 L.Ed. 150.

We believe that the element of willfulness could not be proven in a criminal prosecution for failing to include embezzled funds in gross income in the year of misappropriation so long as the statute contained the gloss placed upon it by *Wilcox* at the time the alleged crime was committed. Therefore, we feel that petitioner's conviction may not stand and that the indictment against him must be dismissed.

Since Mr. Justice Harlan, Mr. Justice Frankfurter, and Mr. Justice Clark agree with us concerning *Wilcox*, that case is overruled. Mr. Justice Black, Mr. Justice Douglas, and Mr. Justice Whittaker believe that petitioner's conviction must be reversed and the case dismissed for the reasons stated in their opinions.

Accordingly, the judgment of the Court of Appeals is reversed and the case is remanded to the District Court with directions to dismiss the indictment.

It is so ordered.

Reversed and remanded with directions.

Mr. Justice Black, whom Mr. Justice Douglas joins, concurring in part and dissenting in part.

On February 25, 1946, fifteen years ago, this Court, after mature consideration, and in accordance with what at that time represented the most strongly supported judicial view, held, in an opinion written by Mr. Justice Murphy to which only one Justice dissented, that money secretly taken by an embezzler for his own use did not constitute a taxable gain to him under the federal income tax laws. The Treasury Department promptly accepted this ruling in a bulletin declaring that the "mere act of embezzlement does not of itself in taxable income," although properly urging that "taxable income may result to the embezzler, depending on the facts in the particular case." During the fifteen years since *Wilcox* was decided, both this Court and Congress, although urged to do so, have declined to change the *Wilcox* interpretation of statutory "income" with respect to embezzlement. In this case, however, a majority of the Court overrules *Wilcox*. Only three of the members of the Court who decided the Wilcox case are participating in this case—Mr. Justice Frankfurter, Mr. Justice Douglas, and myself. Mr. Justice Douglas and I dissent from the Court's action in "overruling" *Wilcox* and from the prospective way in which this is done. We think *Wilcox* was sound when written and is sound now.

I.

We dissent from the way the majority of the Court overrules *Wilcox*. If the statutory interpretation of "taxable income" in *Wilcox* is wrong, then James is guilty of violating the tax evasion statute for the trial court's judgment establishes that he embezzled funds and willfully (sic) refrained from reporting them as income. It appears to us that District Courts are bound to be confused as to what they can do hereafter in tax-evasion cases involving "income" from embezzlements committed prior to this day. Three Justices vote to overrule *Wilcox* under what we believe to be a questionable formula, at least a new one in the annals of this Court, and say that although failure to report embezzled funds has, despite *Wilcox*, always been a crime under the statute, people who have violated this law in the past cannot be prosecuted but people who embezzle funds after this opinion is announced can be prosecuted for failing to report these funds as a "taxable gain." Three other Justices who vote to overrule *Wilcox* say that past embezzlers can be prosecuted for the crime of tax evasion although two of those Justices believe the Government must prove that the past embezzler did not commit his crime in reliance on *Wilcox*. Thus, although it was not the law yesterday, it will be the law tomorrow that funds embezzled hereafter are taxable income; and although past embezzlers could not have been prosecuted yesterday, maybe they can and maybe they cannot be prosecuted tomorrow for the crime of tax evasion. (The question of the civil tax liability of past embezzlers is left equally unclear.) We do not challenge the wisdom of those of our Brethren who refuse to make the Court's new tax evasion crime applicable to past conduct. This would be good governmental policy even though the *ex post facto* provision of the Constitution has not ordinarily been thought to apply to judicial legislation. Our trouble with this aspect of the Court's action is that it seems to us to indicate that the Court has passed beyond the interpretation of the tax statute and proceeded substantially to amend it.

* * *

MR. JUSTICE CLARK, concurring in part and dissenting in part as to the opinion of THE CHIEF JUSTICE.

Although I join in the specific overruling of *Commissioner of Internal Revenue v. Wilcox*, in The Chief Justice's opinion, I would affirm this conviction on either of two grounds. I believe that the Court not only devitalized *Wilcox*, by limiting it to its facts in *Rutkin v. United States*, but that in effect the Court overruled that case *sub silentio* in *Commis-*

sioner of Internal Revenue v. Glenshaw Glass Co. Even if that not be true, in my view the proof shows conclusively that petitioner, in willfully failing to correctly report his income, placed no bona fide reliance on *Wilcox*.

MR. JUSTICE HARLAN, whom MR. JUSTICE FRANKFURTER joins, concurring in part and dissenting in part as to the opinion of THE CHIEF JUSTICE.

I fully agree with so much of The Chief Justice's opinion as dispatches *Wilcox* to a final demise. But as to the disposition of this case, I think that rather than an outright reversal, which his opinion proposes, the reversal should be for a new trial.

* * *

MR. JUSTICE WHITTAKER, whom MR. JUSTICE BLACK and MR. JUSTICE DOUGLAS join, concurring in part and dissenting in part.

* * * The language of the Sixteenth Amendment as well as our prior controlling decisions, compels me to conclude that the question now before us—whether an embezzler receives taxable income at the time of his unlawful taking—must be answered negatively. Since the prevailing opinion reaches an opposite conclusion, I must respectfully dissent from that holding, although I concur in the Court's judgment reversing petitioner's conviction. I am convinced that *Commissioner of Internal Revenue v. Wilcox*, which is today overruled, was correctly decided on the basis of every controlling principle used in defining taxable income since the sixteenth Amendment's adoption.

The Chief Justice's opinion, although it correctly recites *Wilcox*'s holding that "embezzled money does not constitute taxable income to the embezzler in the year of the embezzlement," fails to explain or to answer the true basis of that holding. *Wilcox* did not hold that embezzled funds may never constitute taxable income to the embezzler. To the contrary, it expressly recognized that an embezzler may realize a taxable gain to the full extent of the amount taken, if an when it ever becomes his. The applicable test of taxable income, i.e., the "presence of a claim of right to the alleged gain," of which *Wilcox* spoke, was but a correlative statement of the factor upon which the decision placed its whole emphasis throughout, namely, the "absence of a definite, unconditional obligation to repay or return (the money)." In holding that this test was not met at the time of the embezzlement, the *Wilcox* opinion repeatedly stressed that the embezzler had no "bona fide legal or equitable claim" to the embezzled funds; that the victim never "condoned or forgave the taking of the money and still holds him liable to restore it;" and that the "debtor-creditor relationship was definite and unconditional." These statements all express the same basic fact—the fact which is emphasized most strongly in the opinion's conclusion explaining why the embezzler had not yet received taxable income: "Sanctioning a tax under the circumstances before us would serve only to give the United States an unjustified preference as to part of the money which rightfully and completely belongs to the taxpayer's employer."

However, *Wilcox* plainly stated that "if the unconditional indebtedness is cancelled or retired taxable income may adhere, under certain circumstances, to the taxpayer." More specifically, it recognized that had the embezzler's victim "condoned or forgiven any part of the (indebtedness), the (embezzler) might have been subject to tax liability to that extent," in the tax year of such forgiveness.

* * *

An embezzler, like a common thief, acquires not a semblance of right, title, or interest in his plunder, and whether he spends it or not, he is indebted to his victim in the full amount taken as surely as if he had left a signed promissory note at the scene of the crime. Of no consequence from any standpoint is the absence of such formalities as (in the words of the prevailing opinion) "the consensual recognition, express or implied, or an obligation to repay." The law readily implies whatever "consensual recognition" is needed for the rightful owner to assert an immediately ripe and enforceable obligation of repayment against the wrongful taker. These principles are not "attenuated subtleties" but are among the clearest and most easily applied rules of our law. They exist to protect the rights of the innocent victim, and we should accord them full recognition and respect.

The fact that an embezzler's victim may have less chance of success than other creditors in seeking repayment from his debtor is not a valid reason for us further to diminish his prospects by adopting a rule that would allow the Commissioner of Internal Revenue to assert and enforce a prior federal tax lien against that which "rightfully and completely belongs" to the victim. The Chief Justice's opinion quite understandably expresses much concern for "honest taxpayers," but it attempts neither to deny nor justify the manifest injury that its holding will inflict on those honest taxpayers, victimized by embezzlers, who will find their claims for recovery subordinated to federal tax liens. Statutory provisions, by which we are bound, clearly and unequivocally accord priority to federal tax liens over the claims of others, including "judgment creditors."

* * *

B. COMPENSATION FOR SERVICES

(1) PAYMENTS TO THIRD PARTIES

Code: IRC § 61(a)(1). *Skim* IRC § 74(a).

Regs: Treas. Reg. §§ 1.61–2(a)(1); 1.61–2(d)(1)–(2)(i).

Section 61(a)(1) specifically provides that all forms of compensation for services must be included in gross income. In most cases, compensation is received by the taxpayer directly from the party for whom the services were performed. But taxable compensation does not necessarily need to be received directly by the taxpayer, as the following cases illustrate.

OLD COLONY TRUST CO. v. COMMISSIONER

United States Supreme Court, 1929.
279 U.S. 716, 49 S.Ct. 499, 73 L.Ed. 918.

Mr. Chief Justice Taft delivered the opinion of the Court.

* * *

* * * The petitioners are the executors of the will of William M. Wood, deceased. On June 27, 1925, before Mr. Wood's death, the Commissioner of Internal Revenue notified him by registered mail of the determination of a deficiency in income tax against him for the years 1919 and 1920 * * *.

The facts certified to us are substantially as follows:

William M. Wood was president of the American Woolen Company during the years 1918, 1919, and 1920. In 1918 he received as salary and commissions from the company $978,725, which he included in his federal income tax return for 1918. In 1919 he received as salary and commissions from the company $548,132.87, which he included in his return for 1919.

[By] August 3, 1916, the American Woolen Company had adopted the following resolution, which was in effect in 1919 and 1920:

"Voted: That this company pay any and all income taxes, State and Federal, that may hereafter become due and payable upon the salaries of all the officers of the company, including the president, William M. Wood; the comptroller, Parry C. Wiggin; the auditor, George R. Lawton; and the following members of the staff, to wit: Frank H. Carpenter, Edwin L. Heath, Samuel R. Haines, and William M. Lasbury, to the end that said persons and officers shall receive their salaries or other compensation in full without deduction on account of income taxes, State or Federal, which taxes are to be paid out of the treasury of this corporation."

This resolution was amended on March 25, 1918, as follows:

"Voted: That, referring to the vote passed by this board on August 3, 1916, in reference to income taxes, State and Federal, payable upon the salaries or compensation of the officers and certain employees of this company, the method of computing said taxes shall be as follows, viz.:

"The difference between what the total amount of his tax would be, including his income from all sources, and the amount of his tax when computed upon his income excluding such compensation or salaries paid by this company."

Pursuant to these resolutions, the American Woolen Company paid to the collector of internal revenue Mr. Wood's federal income and surtaxes due to salary and commissions paid him by the company, as follows:

Taxes for 1918 paid in 1919 . . . $681,169 88
Taxes for 1919 paid in 1920 . . .   351,179 27

The decision of the Board of Tax Appeals here sought to be reviewed was that the income taxes of $681,169.88 and $351,179.27 paid by the American Woolen Company for Mr. Wood were additional income to him for the years 1919 and 1920.

The question certified by the Circuit Court of Appeals for answer by this Court is: "Did the payment by the employer of the income taxes assessable against the employee constitute additional taxable income to such employee?"

* * *

Coming now to the merits of this case, we think the question presented is whether a taxpayer, having induced a third person to pay his income tax or having acquiesced in such payment as made in discharge of an obligation to him, may avoid the making of a return thereof and the payment of a corresponding tax. We think he may not do so. The payment of the tax by the employers was in consideration of the services rendered by the employee, and was again derived by the employee from his labor. The form of the payment is expressly declared to make no difference. It is therefore immaterial that the taxes were directly paid over to the government. The discharge by a third person of an obligation to him is equivalent to receipt by the person taxed. The certificate shows that the taxes were imposed upon the employee, that the taxes were actually paid by the employer, and that the employee entered upon his duties in the years in question under the express agreement that his income taxes would be paid by his employer. This is evidenced by the terms of the resolution passed August 3, 1916, more than one year prior to the year in which the taxes were imposed. The taxes were paid upon a valuable consideration, namely, the services rendered by the employee and as part of the compensation therefor. We think, therefore, that the payment constituted income to the employee.

* * *

Nor can it be argued that the payment of the tax * * * was a gift. The payment for services, even though entirely voluntary, was nevertheless compensation within the statute. * * *

It is next argued against the payment of this tax that, if these payments by the employer constitute income to the employee, the employee will be called upon to pay the tax imposed upon this additional income, and that the payment of the additional tax will create further income which will in turn be subject to tax, with the result that there would be a tax upon a tax. This, it is urged, is the result of the government's theory, when carried to its logical conclusion, and results in an absurdity which Congress could not have contemplated.

In the first place, no attempt has been made by the Treasury to collect further taxes, upon the theory that the payment of the additional taxes creates further income, and the question of a tax upon a tax was not before the Circuit Court of Appeals, and has not been certified to this Court. We can settle questions of that sort when an attempt to impose a tax upon a tax is undertaken, but not now. It is not, therefore, necessary to answer the argument based upon an algebraic formula to reach the amount of taxes due. The question in this case is, "Did the payment by the employer of the income taxes assessable against the employee constitute additional taxable income to such employee?" The answer must be "Yes."

McCANN v. UNITED STATES

United States Court of Claims, 1981.
81–2 USTC para. 9689.

Per Curiam

Opinion

* * *

* * * Elvia R. McCann and Mrs. Leone A. McCann, who are husband and wife and residents of Shreveport, Louisiana, made a round trip between Shreveport and Las Vegas, Nevada, in 1973 for the purpose of attending a seminar (the term used by the witnesses) that was conducted in Las Vegas by Mrs. McCann's employer, Security Industrial Insurance Company (Security). All the traveling and other expenses of Mr. and Mrs. McCann in connection with attendance at the Las Vegas seminar were paid by Security.

In filing their joint income tax return for 1973, the McCanns did not include in their gross income any amount reflecting the cost to Security of paying the McCanns' expenses on the Las Vegas trip.

The Internal Revenue Service, upon auditing the McCanns' 1973 income tax return, decided that the fair market value of the Las Vegas trip should have been included in the McCanns' gross income, determined the amount of the fair market value of the trip, and issued a deficiency notice.

Mr. and Mrs. McCann paid the deficiency, amounting to $199.16, plus accrued interest of $64.97.

Thereafter, the McCanns filed a claim for refund; and, when relief from the Internal Revenue Service was not forthcoming, the McCanns instituted the present litigation.

Security is engaged in the sale of life, burial, and accident insurance. Security's best-selling policy is a burial policy with a face amount of $600, which provides merchandise and services necessary for a complete funeral at one of the several funeral homes with which Security has contractual relationships. Many of Security's policyholders are religious people who live in rural areas of Louisiana.

* * *

Ever since 1950, Security has sponsored what is commonly referred to as an annual sales seminar at some place outside the State of Louisiana. These seminars have been held in (among other places): Biloxi, Mississippi; Miami Beach, Florida; Washington, D. C.; New York, New York; San Francisco, California; Houston, Texas; Atlanta, Georgia; Las Vegas, Nevada; and Mexico City, Mexico. The purpose and format of the seminars have been the same through the years.

An agent qualifies to attend a seminar if he or she achieved a specified net increase in sales during the preceding calendar year. The required net increase was $600 for a number of years, including the year involved in the *McCann* case, but the qualification standard was later raised, when the inflationary cycle hit the country.

* * *

Each agent, staff manager, or district manager who qualifies to attend a seminar is entitled to take along his or her spouse, or another family member. An employee who doubles the qualification requirement for attendance at a seminar is entitled to take along, in addition to the person mentioned in the preceding sentence, one guest couple; and if the qualification requirement is tripled, the employee is entitled to take along two guest couples. All travel and other expenses of employees and their guests attending seminars are paid by Security.

However, agents and other employees who qualify for seminars are not required to attend; and their promotional opportunities are not adversely affected if they fail to attend.

Security emphasizes the pleasure aspects of seminars. The company schedules sightseeing tours; furnishes participants with lists of tennis courts and golf courses at, and descriptive travel brochures concerning, seminar sites; and chooses locations which (in the opinion of the company) will have "excitement" and "charisma" for qualifying employees. New Orleans, Louisiana, has never been chosen as a seminar site because of the familiarity of company personnel with New Orleans.

* * * A total of 74 of Security's employees qualified to attend the seminar in Las Vegas. This total included 47 agents, or 11.7 percent of the 400 agents employed by the company in 1973. A total of 66 employees, out of the 74 who qualified, actually attended the seminar in Las Vegas; and the number attending included 40 agents, out of the 47 who qualified.

The total cost to Security of the Las Vegas seminar amounted to $68,116.96. This amount included all the expenses (airfare, lodging, meals, cocktail parties, sightseeing tours, shows, local transportation, and gratuities) of each individual who attended the seminar.

As previously indicated, Mr. and Mrs. McCann attended the Las Vegas seminar in 1973. Mrs. McCann qualified for attendance by achieving the required net increase in sales during the calendar year 1972; and Mr. McCann went along as her guest in accordance with Security's policy of permitting a qualifying employee to take along a spouse or other family member. All the travel and other expenses of Mr. and Mrs. McCann were paid by Security.

As the program for the seminar in Las Vegas was typical of the programs at other seminars sponsored by Security, it will be outlined in some detail.

The official program for the Las Vegas seminar began with a cocktail party at 5:00 p.m. on June 17, 1973. Senior officers of Security and their spouses greeted the other participants at the door. The cocktail party was followed by a dinner of prime ribs, served with wine. E. J. Ourso, president and chief executive officer of Security, delivered a welcoming address; and housekeeping announcements were made. The dinner was followed by a show at the Circus Maximus, featuring singer Diana Ross and "topless" dancers. The remainder of the evening was free time. Some of the participants went to a second show, but the younger participants spent the free time in dancing, drinking, and carousing.

On June 18, there was a group breakfast at 8:00 a.m. There was no formal program at the breakfast; and only housekeeping announcements (such as those relating to lost baggage, the location of certain rooms, and the agenda for the day) were made. The breakfast was followed by a business meeting from 9 to 11 a.m. This meeting featured a panel discussion, the panel being composed of leading agents and one spouse and being moderated by a district manager. The panel discussion was followed by a question-and-answer session and concluding remarks by Mr. Ourso. Employees of Security, but not their guests, were required to attend the business meeting. The business meeting was followed by lunch and a trip to Boulder Dam in the afternoon. At 5:30 p.m. there was a cocktail party and group meeting at the Dunes, followed by dinner and a stage show, "Casino de Paris," which featured "topless" dancers. Alcoholic beverages were served at the dinner and show.

On June 19, there was a group meeting and breakfast at 9:00 a.m.; and this was followed by free time until 11:00 a.m. (the program suggested that the free time be spent "sunning in the Garden of the Gods, playing tennis, or just relaxing"). Lunch was held from 11:00 a.m. to 12:00 noon. There was no formal program at either breakfast or lunch; and only housekeeping announcements were made. Lunch was followed by a tour of the Mint Hotel beginning at 2:00 p.m. At 6:00 p.m., there was a "Farewell to Las Vegas" cocktail party and group meeting. There was no formal program at this function. A banquet was held beginning at 7:00 p.m., and wine was served with the dinner. Mr. Ourso made a speech, reviewing the activities of the company during the preceding year, and then he bestowed an award on each agent, staff manager, and district manager in attendance. The banquet concluded with a guest speaker, an attorney for Security, who spoke of his pride in being associated with the company.

The first question to be decided * * * is whether, as determined by the Internal Revenue Service, the McCanns should have included in their 1973 income tax return, as part of their gross income, an amount based upon the cost to Security of defraying their travel and other expenses on the trip to Las Vegas.

issue:

* * *

The all-expenses trip to Las Vegas—with its airfare, lodging, meals, cocktails, sightseeing tours, shows, local transportation, and gratuities—which Mr. and Mrs. McCann received from Security was obviously an economic benefit to them. Moreover, they received this benefit as a reward for Mrs. McCann's good work in increasing her net sales by a specified amount during the preceding calendar year (1972). Only 47 agents, out of 400 agents employed by Security, qualified for the 1973 seminar in Las Vegas by achieving the required net increase in sales during 1972. The 47 agents (or so many of them as wished to make the trip) were rewarded by receiving from Security the all-expenses trip to Las Vegas for themselves and their spouses, or other family members. The 353 agents who failed to achieve the specified net increase in sales during 1972 did not receive the reward.

Therefore, the reward to Mrs. McCann, although not in the form of money, was clearly compensation to her for the services that she had rendered to Security during 1972, and was within the meaning of income, as that term is used in 26 U.S.C. § 61(a).

It should also be noted that 26 U.S.C. § 74(a) specifically provides that "gross income includes amounts received as prizes and awards." It has been concluded previously in the opinion that the Las Vegas trip which Mr. and Mrs. McCann received from Security was a reward to Mrs. McCann for her good work during 1972. In other words, it was an award given by Security to Mrs. McCann for a job well done, and, therefore, constituted part of the McCanns' gross income under 26 U.S.C. § 74(a).

When services are paid for in a form other than in money, it is necessary to determine the fair market value of the thing received. Treas. Reg. § 1.61–2(d)(1).

In the present case, the Internal Revenue Service decided that the fair market value of the Las Vegas trip which Mr. and Mrs. McCann received from Security was equivalent to the cost of the trip to Security. At the trial, the plaintiff did not introduce any evidence challenging the correctness of the administrative determination on this point. Accordingly, in view of the presumption of legality which supports official administrative actions * * *, the determination of the Internal Revenue Service concerning the fair market value of the Las Vegas trip which Mr. and

Mrs. McCann received from Security will be accepted by the court as correct.

* * *

UNITED STATES v. GOTCHER

United States Court of Appeals, Fifth Circuit, 1968.
401 F.2d 118.

THORNBERRY, CIRCUIT JUDGE.

In 1960, Mr. and Mrs. Gotcher took a twelve-day expense-paid trip to Germany to tour the Volkswagen facilities there. The trip cost $1,372.30. His employer, Economy Motors, paid $348.73, and Volkswagen of Germany and Volkswagen of America shared the remaining $1,023.53. Upon returning, Mr. Gotcher bought a twenty-five percent interest in Economy Motors, the Sherman, Texas Volkswagen dealership, that had been offered to him before he left. Today he is President of Economy Motors in Sherman and owns fifty percent of the dealership. Mr. and Mrs. Gotcher did not include any part of the $1,372.30 in their 1960 income. The Commissioner determined that the taxpayers had realized income to the extent of the $1,372.30 for the expense-paid trip and asserted a tax deficiency of $356.79, plus interest. Taxpayers paid the deficiency, plus $82.29 in interest, and thereafter timely filed suit for a refund. The district court, sitting without a jury, held that the cost of the trip was not income or, in the alternative, was income and deductible as an ordinary and necessary business expense. We affirm the district court's determination that the cost of the trip was not income to Mr. Gotcher ($686.15); however, Mrs. Gotcher's expenses ($686.15) constituted income and were not deductible.

Section 61 of the Internal Revenue Code of 1954 (hereinafter referred to by section number only) defines gross income as income from whatever source derived and specifically includes fifteen items within this definition. The court below reasoned that the cost of the trip to the Gotchers was not income because an economic or financial benefit does not constitute income under section 61 unless it is conferred as compensation for services rendered. This conception of gross income is too restrictive since it is well-settled that section 61 should be broadly interpreted and that many items, including noncompensatory gains, constitute gross income.

Sections 101–123 specifically exclude certain items from gross income. Appellant argues that the cost of the trip should be included in income since it is not specifically excluded by sections 101–123, reasoning that Section 61 was drafted broadly to subject all economic gains to tax and any exclusions should be narrowly limited to the specific exclusions. This analysis is too restrictive since it has been generally held that exclusions from gross income are not limited to the enumerated exclusions. * * *

In determining whether the expense-paid trip was income within section 61, we must look to the tests that have been developed under this section. The concept of economic gain to the taxpayer is the key to section 61. H. Simons, PERSONAL INCOME TAXATION 51 (1938); J. Sneed, THE CONFIGURATIONS OF GROSS INCOME 8 (1967). This concept contains two distinct requirements: There must be an economic gain, and this gain must primarily benefit the taxpayer personally. In some cases, as in the case of an expense-paid trip, there is no direct economic gain, but there is an indirect economic gain inasmuch as a benefit has been received without a corresponding diminution in wealth. Yet even if expense-paid items, as meals and lodging, are received by the taxpayer, the value of these items will not be gross income, even though the employee receives some incidental benefit, if the meals and lodging are primarily for the convenience of the employer.

* * *

The trip was made in 1959 when VW was attempting to expand its local dealerships in the United States. The "buy American" campaign and the fact that the VW people felt they had a "very ugly product" prompted them to offer these tours of Germany to prospective dealers. The VW story was related by Mr. Horton, who is Manager of Special Events for VW of America. His testimony was uncontradicted and unimpeached. He stated that VW operations were at first so speculative that cars had to be consigned with a repurchase guarantee. In 1959, when VW began to push for its share of the American market, its officials determined that the best way to remove the apprehension about this foreign product was to take the dealer to Germany and have him see his investment first-hand. It was believed that once the dealer saw the manufacturing facilities and the stability of the "new Germany" he would be convinced that VW was for him. Furthermore, VW considered the expenditure justified because the dealer was being asked to make a substantial investment of his time and money in a comparatively new product. Indeed, after taking the trip, VW required him to acquire first-class facilities. It was hoped that this would be accomplished by following the international architectural plans that VW had for its dealerships. It was also hoped that the dealer would adopt VW's international plan for the sales and services department. Mr. Horton testified that VW could not have asked that this upgrading be done unless it convinced the dealer that VW was here to stay. Apparently these trips have paid off since VW's sales have skyrocketed and the dealers have made their facilities top-rate operations under the VW requirements for a standard dealership.

The activities in Germany support the conclusion that the trip was oriented to business. The Government makes much of the fact that the travel brochure allocated only two of the twelve days to the touring of VW factories. This argument ignores the uncontradicted evidence that not all of the planned activities were in the brochure. There is ample support for the trial judge's finding that a substantial amount of time was spent touring VW facilities and visiting local dealerships. VW had set up these tours with local dealers so that the travelers could discuss how the facilities were operated in Germany. Mr. Gotcher took full advantage of this opportunity and even used some of his "free time" to visit various local dealerships. Moreover, at almost all of the evening meals VW officials gave talks about the organization and passed out literature and brochures on the VW story.

Some of the days were not related to touring VW facilities, but that fact alone cannot be decisive. The dominant purpose of the trip is the critical inquiry and some pleasurable features will not negate the finding of an overall business purpose. Since we are convinced that the agenda related primarily to business and that Mr. Gotcher's attendance was prompted by business considerations, the so-called sightseeing complained of by the Government is inconsequential. Indeed, the district court found that even this touring of the countryside had an indirect relation to business since the tours were not typical sightseeing excursions but were connected to the desire of VW that the dealers be persuaded that the German economy was stable enough to justify investment in a German product. We cannot say that this conclusion is clearly erroneous. Nor can we say that the enthusiastic literary style of the brochures negates a dominant business purpose. It is the business reality of the total situation, not the colorful expressions in the literature, that controls. Considering the record, the circumstances prompting the trip, and the objective achieved, we conclude that the primary purpose of the trip was to induce Mr. Gotcher to take out a VW dealership interest.

The question, therefore, is what tax consequences should follow from an expense-paid trip that primarily benefits the party paying for the trip. In several analogous situations the value of items received by employees has been excluded from gross income when these items were primarily for the benefit of the employer. Section 119 excludes from gross income of an employee the value of meals and lodging furnished to him for the convenience of the employer. Even before these items were excluded by the 1954 Code, the Treasury and the courts recognized that they should be excluded from gross income. Thus it appears that the value of any trip that is paid by the employer or by a businessman primarily for his own benefit should be excluded from gross income of the payee on similar reasoning.

In the recent case of *Allen J. McDonell*, 26 T.C.M. 115, Tax Ct. Mem. 1967–18, a sales supervisor and his wife were chosen by lot to accompany a group of contest winners on an expense-paid trip to Hawaii. In holding that the taxpayer had received no income, the Tax Court noted that he was required by his employer to go and that he was serving a legitimate business purpose though he enjoyed the trip. The decision suggests that in analyzing the tax consequences of an expense-paid trip one important factor is whether the traveler had any choice but to go. Here, although taxpayer was not forced to go, there is no doubt that in the reality of the business world he had no real choice. The trial judge reached the same conclusion. He found that the invitation did not specifically order the dealers to go, but that as a practical matter it was an order or directive that if a person was going to be a VW dealer, sound business judgment necessitated his accepting the offer of corporate hospitality. So far as Economy Motors was concerned, Mr. Gotcher knew that if he was going to be a part-owner of the dealership, he had better do all that was required to foster good business relations with VW. Besides having no choice but to go, he had no control over the schedule or the money spent. VW did all the planning. In cases involving noncompensatory economic gains, courts have emphasized that the taxpayer still had complete dominion and control over the money to use it as he wished to satisfy personal desires or needs. Indeed, the Supreme Court has defined income as accessions of wealth over which the taxpayer has complete control. Clearly, the lack of control works in taxpayer's favor here.

McDonell also suggests that one does not realize taxable income when he is serving a legitimate business purpose of the party paying the expenses. The cases involving corporate officials who have traveled or entertained clients at the company's expense are apposite. Indeed, corporate executives have been furnished yachts, taken safaris as part of an advertising scheme, and investigated business ventures abroad, but have been held accountable for expenses paid only when the court was persuaded that the expenditure was primarily for the officer's personal pleasure. On the other hand, when it has been shown that the expenses were paid to effectuate a legitimate corporate end and not to benefit the officer personally, the officer has not been taxed though he enjoyed and benefited from the activity. Thus, the rule is that the economic benefit will be taxable to the recipient only when the payment of expenses serves no legitimate corporate purpose. The decisions also indicate that the tax consequences are to be determined by looking to the primary purpose of the expenses and that the first consideration is the intention of the payor. The Government in argument before the district court agreed that whether the expenses were income to taxpayers is mainly a question of the motives of the people giving the trip. Since this is a matter of proof, the resolution of the tax question really depends on whether Gotcher showed that his presence served a legitimate corporate purpose and that no appreciable amount of time was spent for his personal benefit and enjoyment. See *United Aniline Co.*, 1962, 21 T.C.M. 327.

Examination of the record convinces us that the personal benefit to Gotcher was clearly subordinate to the concrete benefits to VW. The purpose of the trip was to push VW in America and to get the dealers to invest more money and time in their dealerships. Thus, although Gotcher got some ideas that helped him become a better dealer, there is no evidence that this was the primary purpose of the trip. Put another way, this trip was not given as a pleasurable excursion through Germany or as a means of teaching taxpayer the skills of selling. He had been selling cars since 1949. The personal benefits and pleasure were incidental to the dominant purpose of improving VW's position on the American market and getting people to invest money.

The corporate-executive decisions indicate that some economic gains, though not specifically excluded from section 61, may nevertheless escape taxation. They may be excluded even though the entertainment and travel unquestionably give enjoyment to the taxpayer and produce indirect economic gains. When this indirect economic gain is subordinate to an overall business purpose, the recipient is not taxed. We are convinced that the personal benefit to Mr. Gotcher from the trip was merely incidental to VW's sales campaign.

As for Mrs. Gotcher, the trip was primarily a vacation. She did not make the tours with her husband to see the local dealers or attend discussions about the VW organization. This being so the primary benefit of the expense-paid trip for the wife went to Mr. Gotcher in that he was relieved of her expenses. He should therefore be taxed on the expenses attributable to his wife. Nor are the expenses deductible since the wife's presence served no bona fide business purpose for her husband. Only when the wife's presence is necessary to the conduct of the husband's business are her expenses deductible under section 162. Also, it must be shown that the wife made the trip only to assist her husband in his business. A single trip by a wife with her husband to Europe has been specifically rejected as not being the exceptional type of case justifying a deduction.

Affirmed in part; reversed in part.

JOHN R. BROWN, CHIEF JUDGE (concurring):

I concur in the result and in the opinion. * * *

Attributing income to the little wife who was neither an employee, a prospective employee, nor a dealer, for the value of a trip she neither planned nor chose still bothers me. If her uncle had paid for the trip, would it not have been a pure gift, not income? Or had her husband out of pure separate property given her the trip would the amount over and above the cost of Texas bed and board have been income? I acquiesce now, confident that for others in future cases on a full record the wife, as now does the husband, also will overcome.

* * *

Problem 3–6

Skipper owes Gilligan $2,000 for services Gilligan performed in repairing Skipper's boat, the *S.S. Minnow*. Skipper takes Thurston and Lovey (a married couple) out for a three-hour tour on the *Minnow*. Skipper normally charges $2,000 for a three-hour boat tour, so he asks Thurston and Lovey to pay the $2,000 to Gilligan (and not to Skipper). The couple does so, delighted that they do not have to pay Skipper a tip if the payment is made directly to Gilligan. Who has gross income under these facts, and how much?

(2) MEALS AND LODGING FURNISHED ON EMPLOYER'S PREMISES

Code: IRC § 119(a)–(b)(4), (d).

Regs: Treas. Reg. § 1.119–1.

Some forms of compensation, while generally includible in gross income under § 61(a)(1), are nonetheless excluded from gross income by operation of a specific statutory provision. Most exclusions are set forth in §§ 101–139. Section 119(a), for instance, excludes both meals and lodging furnished to employees (or their spouses or dependents) if certain conditions are met. A careful reading of § 119(a) shows the several elements that must be present for exclusion:

Meals	Lodging
• furnished by employer	• furnished by employer
• for convenience of employer	• for convenience of employer
• on business premises of employer	• on business premises of employer
	• employee required to accept as a condition of employment

Although the individual elements of § 119(a) are easy to tease out of the statute, there are some complicated issues of construction, as the following cases show.

COMMISSIONER v. KOWALSKI

United States Supreme Court, 1977.
434 U.S. 77, 98 S.Ct. 315, 54 L.Ed.2d 252.

Mr. Justice Brennan delivered the opinion of the Court.

This case presents the question whether cash payments to state police troopers, designated as meal allowances, are included in gross income under § 61(a) of the Internal Revenue Code * * * and, if so, are otherwise excludable under § 119 of the Code.

I

The pertinent facts are not in dispute. Respondent is a state police trooper employed by the Division of State Police of the Department of Law and Public Safety of the State of New Jersey. During 1970, the tax year in question, he received a base salary of $8,739.38, and an additional $1,697.54 designated as an allowance for meals.

The State instituted the cash meal allowance for its state police officers in July 1949. Prior to that time, all troopers were provided with mid-shift meals in kind at various meal stations located throughout the State. A trooper unable to eat at an official meal station could, however, eat at a restaurant and obtain reimbursement. The meal-station system proved unsatisfactory to the State because it required troopers to leave their assigned areas of patrol unguarded for extended periods of time. As a result, the State closed its meal stations and instituted a cash-allowance system. Under this system, troopers remain on call in their assigned patrol areas during their mid-shift break. Otherwise, troopers are not restricted in any way with respect to where they may eat in the patrol area and, indeed, may eat at home if it is located within that area. Troopers may also bring their mid-shift meal to the job and eat it in or near their patrol cars.

The meal allowance is paid biweekly in advance and is included, although separately stated, with the trooper's salary. The meal-allowance money is also separately accounted for in the State's accounting system. Funds are never commingled between the salary and meal-allowance accounts. Because of these characteristics of the meal-allowance system, the Tax Court concluded that the "meal allowance was not intended to represent additional compensation."

Notwithstanding this conclusion, it is not disputed that the meal allowance has many features inconsistent with its characterization as a simple reimbursement for meals that would otherwise have been taken at a meal station. For example, troopers are not required to spend their meal allowances on their midshift meals, nor are they required to account for the manner in which the money is spent. With one limited exception not relevant here, no reduction in the meal allowance is made for periods when a trooper is not on patrol because, for example, he is assigned to a headquarters building or is away from active duty on vacation, leave, or sick leave. In addition, the cash allowance for meals is described on a state police recruitment brochure as an item of salary to be received in addition to an officer's base salary and the amount of the meal allowance is a subject of negotiations between the State and the police troopers' union. Finally, the amount of an officer's cash meal allowance varies with his rank and is included in his gross pay for purposes of calculating pension benefits.

On his 1970 income tax return, respondent reported $9,066 in wages. That amount included his salary plus $326.45 which represented cash meal allowances * * *. The remaining amount of meal allowance, $1,371.09, was not reported. On audit, the Commissioner determined that this amount should have been included in respondent's 1970 income and assessed a deficiency.

Respondent sought review in the United States Tax Court, arguing that the cash meal allowance was not compensatory but was furnished for the convenience of the employer and hence was not "income" within the meaning of § 61(a) and that, in any case the allowance could be excluded under § 119. In a reviewed decision, the Tax Court, with six dissents, held that the cash meal payments were income within the meaning of § 61 and, further that such payments were not excludable under § 119. The Court of Appeals for the Third Circuit, in a *per curiam* opinion, held that its earlier decision in *Saunders v. Commissioner of Internal Revenue*, 215 F.2d 768 (1954), which determined that cash payments under the New Jersey meal-allowance program were not taxable, required reversal. We granted certiorari to resolve a conflict among the Courts of Appeals on the question. We reverse.

II

A

The starting point in the determination of the scope of "gross income" is the cardinal principle that Congress in creating the income tax intended "to use the full measure of its taxing power." * * * In the absence of a specific exemption, therefore, respondent's meal-allowance payments are income within the meaning of § 61 since, like the payments involved in *Glenshaw Glass Co.*, the payments are "undeniabl[y] accessions to wealth, clearly realized, and over which the [respondent has] complete dominion."

Respondent contends, however, that § 119 can be construed to be a specific exemption covering the meal-allowance payments to New Jersey troopers. Alternatively, respondent argues that notwithstanding § 119 a specific exemption may be found in a line of lower-court cases and administrative rulings which recognize that benefits conferred by an employer on an employee "for the convenience of the employer"—at least when such benefits are not "compensatory"—are not income within the meaning of the Internal Revenue Code. In responding to these contentions, we turn first to § 119. Since we hold that § 119 does not cover cash payments of any kind, we then trace the development over several decades of the convenience-of-the-employer doctrine as a determinant of the tax status of meals and lodging, turning finally to the question whether the doctrine as applied to meals and lodging survives the enactment of the Internal Revenue Code of 1954.

B

Section 119 provides that an employee may exclude from income "the value of any meals * * * furnished to him by his employer for the convenience of the employer, but only if * * * the meals are furnished on the business premises of the employer * * *." By its terms, § 119 covers *meals* furnished by the employer and not *cash* reimbursements for meals. This is not a mere oversight. As we shall explain at greater length below, the form of § 119 which Congress enacted originated in the Senate and the Report accompanying the Senate bill is very clear: "Section 119 applies only to meals or lodging furnished in kind." S. Rep. No. 1622, 83d Cong., 2d Sess., 190 (1954). See also Treas. Reg. § 1.119–1(c)(2). Accordingly, respondent's meal-allowance payments are not subject to exclusion under § 119.

C

The convenience-of-the-employer doctrine is not a tidy one. * * * [The Court's extended summary of the doctrine is omitted. Ed.]

D

Even if we assume that respondent's meal-allowance payments could have been excluded from income under the [common law "convenience of the employer" doctrine], we must nonetheless inquire whether such an implied exclusion survives the 1954 recodification of the Internal Revenue Code. * * *

In enacting § 119, the Congress was determined to "end the confusion as to the tax status of meals and lodging furnished an employee by his employer." However, the House and Senate initially differed on the significance that should be given the convenience-of-the-employer doctrine for the purposes of § 119. As explained in its Report, the House proposed to exclude meals from gross income "if they [were] furnished at the place of employment and the employee [was] required to accept them at the place of employment as a condition of his employment." Since no reference whatsoever was made to the concept, the House view apparently was that a statute "designed to end the confusion as to the tax status of meals and lodging furnished an employee by his employer" required complete disregard of the convenience-of-the-employer doctrine.

The Senate, however, was of the view that the doctrine had at least a limited role to play. After noting the existence of the doctrine and the Tax Court's reliance on state law to refuse to apply it * * *, the Senate Report states:

"Your committee believes that the House provision is ambiguous in providing that meals or lodging furnished on the employer's premises, which the employee is required to accept as a condition of his employment, are excludable from income whether or not furnished as compensation. Your committee has provided that the basic test of exclusion is to be whether the meals or lodging are furnished primarily for the convenience of the employer (and thus excludable) or whether they were primarily for the convenience of the employee (and therefore taxable). However, in deciding whether they were furnished for the convenience of the employer, the fact that a State statute or an employment contract fixing the terms of the employment indicate the meals or lodging are intended as compensation is not to be determinative. This means that employees of State institutions who are required to live and eat on the premises will not be taxed on the value of the meals and lodging even though the State statute indicates the meals and lodging are part of the employee's compensation." S. Rep. No. 1622, *supra*, at 19.

In a technical appendix, the Senate Report further elaborated:

"Section 119 applies only to meals or lodging furnished in kind. Therefore, any cash allowances for meals or lodging received by an employee will continue to be includible in gross income to the extent that such allowances constitute compensation." *Id.*, at 190–191.

After conference, the House acquiesced in the Senate's version of § 119. Because of this, respondent urges that § 119 as passed did not discard the convenience-of-the-employer doctrine, but indeed endorsed the doctrine * * *. Respondent further argues that, by negative implication, the technical appendix to the Senate Report creates a class of noncompensatory cash meal payments that are to be excluded from income. We disagree.

* * *

As the last step in its restructuring of prior law, the Senate adopted an additional restriction created by the House and not theretofore a part of the law, which required that meals subject to exclusion had to be taken on the business premises of the employer. Thus § 119 comprehensively modified the prior law, both expanding and contracting the exclusion for meals and lodging previously provided, and it must therefore be construed as its draftsmen obviously intended it to be—as a replacement for the prior law, designed to "end [its] confusion."

Because § 119 replaces prior law, respondent's further argument—that the technical appendix in the Senate Report recognized the existence under § 61 of an exclusion for a class of noncompensatory cash payments—is without merit. If cash meal allowances could be excluded on the mere showing that such payments served the convenience of the employer, as respondent suggests, then cash would be more widely excluded from income than meals in kind, an extraordinary result given the presumptively compensatory nature of cash payments and the obvious intent of § 119 to narrow the circumstances in which meals could be excluded. Moreover, there is no reason to suppose that Congress would have wanted to recognize a class of excludable cash meal payments.
* * *

* * *

Finally, respondent argues that it is unfair that members of the military may exclude their subsistence allowances from income while respondent cannot. While this may be so, arguments of equity have little force in construing the boundaries of exclusions and deductions from income many of which, to be administrable, must be arbitrary. In any case, Congress has already considered respondent's equity argument and has rejected it in the repeal of § 120 of the 1954 Code. That provision as enacted allowed state troopers like respondent to exclude from income up to $5 of subsistence allowance per day. Section 120 was repealed after only four years, however, because it was "inequitable since there are many other individual taxpayers whose duties also require them to incur subsistence expenditures regardless of the tax effect. Thus, it appears that certain police officials by reason of this exclusion are placed in a more favorable position tax-wise than the other individual income taxpayers who incur the same types of expense. . . ."

Reversed.

MR. JUSTICE BLACKMUN, with whom THE CHIEF JUSTICE joins, dissenting.

More than a decade ago the United States Court of Appeals for the Eighth Circuit, in *United States v. Morelan*, 356 F.2d 199 (1966), held that the $3–per–day subsistence allowance paid Minnesota state highway patrolmen was excludable from gross income under § 119 * * *. It held, alternatively, that if the allowance were includable in gross income, it was deductible as an ordinary and necessary meal-cost trade or business expense under § 162(a)(2) of the Code. I sat as a Circuit Judge on that case. I was happy to join Chief Judge Vogel's opinion because I then felt, and still do, that it was correct on both grounds. Certainly, despite the usual persistent Government opposition in as many Courts of Appeals as were available, the ruling was in line with other authority at the appellate level at that time. * * *

     * * *

I have no particular quarrel with the conclusion that the payments received by the New Jersey troopers constituted income to them under § 61. I can accept that, but my stance in *Morelan* leads me to disagree with the Court's conclusion that the payments are not excludable under § 119. The Court draws an in-cash or in-kind distinction. This has no appeal or persuasion for me because the statute does not speak specifically in such terms. It does no more than refer to "meals . . . furnished on the business premises of the employer," and from those words the Court draws the in-kind consequence. I am not so sure. In any event, for me, as was the case in *Morelan*, the business premises of the State of New Jersey, the trooper's employer, are wherever the trooper is on duty in that State. The employer's premises are statewide.

The Court in its opinion makes only passing comment, with a general reference to fairness, on the ironical difference in tax treatment it now accords to the paramilitary New Jersey state trooper structure and the federal military. The distinction must be embarrassing to the Government in its position here, for the Internal Revenue Code draws no such distinction. * * *

I fear that state troopers the country over, not handsomely paid to begin with, will never understand today's decision. And I doubt that their reading of the Court's opinion—if, indeed, a layman can be expected to understand its technical wording—will convince them that the situation is as clear as the Court purports to find it.

ADAMS v. UNITED STATES

United States Claims Court, 1978.
585 F.2d 1060.

PER CURIAM:

The issue in this tax refund suit is whether the fair rental value of a Japanese residence furnished the plaintiffs by the employer of plaintiff Faneuil Adams, Jr., is excludable from their gross income under Section 119 of the Internal Revenue Code of 1954.

* * * In 1970 and 1971, Faneuil Adams [hereinafter "plaintiff"] was president of Mobil Sekiyu Kabushiki Kaisha ("Sekiyu"), a Tokyo-based

Japanese corporation which was wholly owned by Mobil Oil Corporation ("Mobil"). During those years, Sekiyu employed about 1,500 persons in Japan with sales between $400–700 million each year. It had several thousand service stations in Japan and was also involved in two joint ventures with Japanese companies which owned and operated four refineries.

In order to attract qualified employees for foreign service and to maintain an equitable relationship between its domestic and American foreign-based employees, thereby preventing any employee from gaining a benefit or suffering a hardship from serving overseas, Mobil maintained a compensation policy for its American employees assigned outside the United States. One of the components of the policy involved the procurement by Mobil of housing for such employees, regardless of their position or duties. Mobil first calculated a "U.S. Housing Element" for each American foreign-based employee, based on a survey of the Bureau of Labor Statistics, which reflected the approximate average housing costs in the United States at various family sizes and income levels. Mobil then subtracted from that employee's salary the amount of his particular U.S. Housing Element. If Mobil provided housing to the employee, the employee would include in his gross income for federal tax purposes the U.S. Housing Element amount. If the employee instead obtained his own housing abroad, Mobil reimbursed him for the full amount, subject to certain predetermined limitations based upon reasonableness, and the employee would then include the full amount reimbursed in his gross income.

Pursuant to the above policy, Mobil provided plaintiff with a residence for the years in question. The three-level house, which was built and owned by Sekiyu, was 3 miles from headquarters and consisted of a large living room, dining room, pantry and kitchen, three bedrooms, a den, two bathrooms, two maid's rooms, two garage areas, and a garden and veranda. By American standards the house was not large, but it was apparently choice. Sekiyu felt that it was important to house its chief executive officer in prestigious surroundings because, particularly in Japan, there is less of a distinction than in the United States between business activities and social activities. The effectiveness of a president of a company in Japan is influenced by the social standing and regard accorded to him by the Japanese business community. If the president of Sekiyu had not resided in a residence equivalent to the type provided the plaintiff, it would appear that he would have been unofficially downgraded and slighted by the business community and his effectiveness for Sekiyu correspondingly impaired. Sekiyu, therefore, provided such a house to plaintiff and required him to reside there as a matter of company policy.

The house was also designed so that it could accommodate the business activities of the plaintiff. The den was built specifically for the conduct of business, and the kitchen and living room were sufficiently large for either business meetings or receptions. Plaintiff worked in the house in the evenings and on weekends and held small meetings there for mixed business and social purposes. He regularly used the telephone for business purposes from his home after regular working hours, both for business emergencies and also for communicating with persons in the United States because of the time difference. In addition, he regularly discharged his business entertainment responsibilities in the residence, generally averaging about 35–40 such occasions in a normal year. In 1970 his entertaining declined considerably because of the absence of his wife from Japan for 10 months, but it resumed again in 1971. Plaintiff was provided with two maids, only one of whom was needed for his family's personal requirements.

Plaintiff included in his gross income for federal tax purposes, as the value of the housing furnished him by his employer, the U.S. Housing Element amounts which had been subtracted from his gross salary. Those amounts which were designed to approximate the average housing costs of a similarly situated person in the United States during 1970 and 1971, totaled $4,439 for 1970 and $4,824 for 1971. However, because the cost of housing in Tokyo in those years was considerably higher than that in the United States, it is agreed by the parties that the fair rental value of the residence furnished plaintiff by Sekiyu was $20,000 in 1970 and $20,599.09 in 1971. Accordingly, upon audit of plaintiff's 1970 and 1971 income tax returns, the Internal Revenue Service, among other adjustments, increased the amounts reported by plaintiff as the value of the housing furnished by Sekiyu to $20,000 in 1970 and $20,599.09 in 1971. Plaintiff has filed suit to recover the sum of $914.24 plus assessed interest as a result of the Internal Revenue Service's inclusion in his gross income of the amounts in excess of the U.S. Housing Element for the 2 years in suit.

Gross income means all income from whatever source derived, including compensation for services. I.R.C. § 61(a). It includes income realized in any form. Section 1.61–2(d)(1) of Treasury Regulations states, "If services are paid for other than in money, the fair market value of the property or services taken in payment must be included in income."

Presumably, then, if the lodging furnished to plaintiff was compensation to him, the fair rental value of the lodging would be includable in his gross income unless excludable under another provision of the Code.

Plaintiff contends that the fair rental value of the residence supplied to him by Sekiyu in 1970 and 1971 is excludable from his gross income because of Section 119. Alternatively, plaintiff asserts that the excess of the fair rental value of the residence over the U.S. Housing Element amount represented a benefit to his employer and not a benefit to him, and therefore is not gross income to him. Finally, plaintiff contends that even if the fair rental value of the residence is income to him, it should be measured by the amount plaintiff would have spent for housing in the United States, rather than the fair rental value in Japan. Because we hold that the conditions of Section 119 * * * and the Regulations promulgated thereunder have been met, we do not address the other arguments of plaintiff.

* * *   *¥ "Condition of Employment" Test:*

It is clear that the first requirement of the statute has been met because the plaintiff was explicitly required to accept the residence provided by Sekiyu as a condition of his employment as president of the company. Sekiyu's goal was twofold: first, it wanted to insure that its president resided in housing of sufficiently dignified surroundings to promote his effectiveness within the Japanese business community. Secondly, Sekiyu wished to provide its president with facilities which were sufficient for the conduct of certain necessary business activities at home. Since at least 1954 Sekiyu had required that its chief executive officer reside in the residence provided to plaintiff, as a condition to appointment as president.

With respect to this first test of Section 119, then, this case is as compelling as *United States Junior Chamber of Commerce v. United States*, 334 F.2d 660, 167 Ct.Cl. 392 (1964). In that case, the court found that it was not necessary for the taxpayer-president to reside in the Chamber's "White House" during his term of office so long as he lived in the Tulsa area. But, as a practical matter, for the convenience of his employer and as a condition of his tenure, the president was required to live there. Therefore, it was held that the "condition of employment" test was met. The court noted that the "condition of employment" test is met if: *test:*

> due to the nature of the employer's business, a certain type of residence for the employee is required and that it would not be reasonable to suppose that the employee would normally have available such lodging for the use of his employer. 334 F.2d at 664, 167 Ct.Cl. at 399.

Here, because the size and style of one's residence had an important effect upon the Japanese business community, a certain type of residence was both required by Mobil and Sekiyu for the plaintiff and necessary for the proper discharge of his duties in Sekiyu's best interests.

* * * In the present case, plaintiff was required to accept the housing, and the residence was directly related to plaintiff's position as president, both in terms of physical facilities and psychic significance. It is held, therefore, that plaintiff was required to accept the lodging in order to enable him properly to perform the duties of his employment.

"convenience of employer test:" As to the "for the convenience of the employer" test, in *United States Junior Chamber of Commerce v. United States*, 334 F.2d at 663, 167 Ct.Cl. at 397, the court stated:

> "There does not appear to be any substantial difference between the * * * 'convenience of the employer' test and the 'required as a condition of his employment' test."

Since it has already been determined that the condition of employment test has been satisfied, on that basis alone it could be held that the convenience of the employer test has also been met.

In *James H. McDonald,* *supra,* 66 T.C. [223 (1976)], the court stated that the convenience of the employer test is satisfied where there is a direct nexus between the housing furnished the employee and the business interests of the employer served thereby. In *McDonald,* the taxpayer was a principal officer of Gulf who was furnished an apartment by his employer which totaled only about 1,500 square feet of living space. The taxpayer was not required to live in the apartment, and it was found that the only benefit Gulf received in maintaining the apartment was the flexibility it afforded Gulf in personnel transfers. There was no prestige consideration. The court held that there was an insufficient nexus between the apartment and the employer's business interests to meet the convenience of the employer test requirements. Moreover, the court further noted that:

> While its practice of maintaining various leasehold interests for assignment to expatriate employees may have accorded Gulf a benefit in terms of flexibility in personnel transfers, that is not to conclude that the assignments of these lodgings to petitioners at a discount similarly served the interests of Gulf; that is, although convenience may have dictated the form in which the leasehold arrangements were structured, the convenience of Gulf did not require it to subsidize the assignments. 66 T.C. at 229.

Here there was a sufficiently direct relationship between the housing furnished the plaintiff by Sekiyu and Sekiyu's business interests to meet the convenience of the employer test. The lodging had been built and was owned by Sekiyu. It was specially identified with the business of Sekiyu, for the house had served as the home of its presidents since at least 1954. If Sekiyu's president had not resided in housing comparable to that supplied plaintiff, Sekiyu's business would have been adversely affected. The house had been designed for this purpose to accommodate substantial business activities, and therefore further served Sekiyu's business interests.

Moreover, the fact that Sekiyu subsidized plaintiff's use of the house was also in its best business interests. Sekiyu was interested in attracting a qualified person as its chief executive officer. Because of the unusual housing situation in Tokyo during the years in question, a person would have had to pay up to four times his U.S. housing costs to obtain comparable housing in Tokyo. Certainly, such a factor would have been a strong deterrent to any qualified person's interest in Sekiyu's presidency, absent a housing subsidy from Sekiyu. Furthermore, it was clearly in Mobil–Sekiyu's best business interests to maintain an equitable compensation relationship between its domestic employees and its American foreign-based ones. The housing subsidy was designed to accomplish that.

* * *

The third and final test is whether the lodging was on the business premises of the employer. Observe first that "[t]he operative framework of [the clause 'on the business premises'] is at best elusive and admittedly incapable of generating any hard and fast line." *Jack B. Lindeman*, 60 T.C. 609, 617 (1973) (Tannenwald, J., concurring). This question is largely a factual one requiring a commonsense approach. The statute should not be read literally. As noted by the Tax Court in *Lindeman*, *supra*, 60 T.C. at 614:

> [T]he statutory language ordinarily would not permit any exclusion for lodging furnished a domestic servant, since a servant's lodging is rarely furnished on "the business premises of his employer"; yet the committee report * * * shows a clear intention to allow the exclusion where the servant's lodging is furnished in the employer's home.

In the original version of the 1954 Code, as enacted in the House, the term that was used in Section 119 was "place of employment." * * * The pertinent Treasury regulation similarly provides that "business premises" generally refers to the place of employment of the employee. Treas. Reg. Sec. 1.119–1(c)(1) (1956). The phrase, then, is not to be limited to the business compound or headquarters of the employer. Rather, the emphasis must be upon the place where the employee's duties are to be performed. * * * The phrase has also been construed to mean either (1) living quarters that constitute an integral part of the business property, or (2) premises on which the company carries on some substantial segment of its business activities. *Gordon S. Dole*, 43 T.C. 697, 707 (1965), aff'd per curiam, 351 F.2d 308 (1st Cir.1965).

* * * In this case plaintiff, although he had an office at the employer's headquarters, worked in his residence in the evenings and on weekends, had business meetings and performed required business telephone calls from there which could not be made during normal business hours, and conducted regular business entertaining in the residence. In this sense plaintiff's residence was a part of the business premises of his employer, for it was a "premises on which the duties of the employee are to be performed," and a "premises on which the company carries on some of its business activities."

Interpretations of the phrase which are limited to the geographic contiguity of the premises or to questions of the quantum of business activities on the premises are too restrictive. Rather, the statutory language "on the business premises of the employer" infers a functional rather than a spatial unity. In *Rev. Rul. 75–540*, 1975–2 Cum. Bull. 53, it was determined that the fair rental value of the official residence furnished a governor by the state is excludable from the governor's gross income under Section 119 of the Code. The Ruling noted that the business premises test was met because the residence provided by the state enabled the governor to carry out efficiently the administrative, ceremonial, and social duties required by his office. The governor's mansion, thus, served an important business function in that it was clearly identified with the business interests of the state. It was, in short, an inseparable adjunct. * * * In the present case, even apart from the strictly business activities which took place in plaintiff's residence, the house was a symbol to the Japanese business community of the status of Sekiyu's chief executive officer and a place where he officially entertained for business purposes. As such, it influenced plaintiff's effectiveness in the business community and directly served a business function for Sekiyu.

* * *

We take cognizance of the admonition of Judge Raum to avoid "strained or eccentric" interpretations of the phrase "on the business premises." *Gordon S. Dole*, 43 T.C. at 708 (Raum, J., concurring), aff'd per curiam, 351 F.2d 308 (1st Cir.1965). However, we are persuaded that where, as here, (1) the residence was built and owned by the employer, (2) it was designed, in part, to accommodate the business activities of the employer, (3) the employee was required to live in the residence, (4) there were many business activities for the employee to perform after normal working hours in his home because of the extensive nature of the employer's business and the high-ranking status of the employee, (5) the employee did perform business activities in the residence, and (6) the residence served an important business function of the employer, then the residence in question is a part of the business premises of the employer.

The three statutory requisites for exclusion are met. Accordingly, pursuant to Section 119 * * *, the fair rental value of the residence is excludable from plaintiff's gross income. Plaintiffs are entitled to recover * * *.

Problem 3–7

Kevin Lomax is an associate at Milton, Chadwick, Waters, a New York City law firm. Because he is expected to work long hours each day, the firm provides Kevin with a daily "meal supplement" of $20 cash. Kevin and his colleagues regularly eat dinner at a restaurant across the street from the firm's building, using the meal supplements to cover the costs.

(a) Must Kevin include the meal supplement in gross income?

(b) Would the answer to (a) change if, instead of paying the meal supplement to Kevin, the firm paid the restaurant directly?

(c) Would the answer to (a) change if, instead of paying the meal supplement to Kevin, the firm provided him with free dinners at its own cafeteria located on the same floor as Kevin's office?

Problem 3–8

Portland University (PU) owns a number of small homes in the blocks surrounding its main campus. PU rents out the homes to students, employees, and even those with no affiliation to the school. Barb Dwyer is a zoology professor at PU who rents a home owned by the school. Barb is not required to live in PU-owned housing, and she performs no official duties in the home. The home Barb rents has a fair market value of $100,000. Although the average annual rent paid for comparable university-owned housing by persons other than students or employees is $8,000, Barb (as an employee of PU) is only required to pay $6,000 annually ($500 per month).

(a) Does Barb have gross income under these facts?

(b) How would the answer to (a) change, if at all, if Barb paid annual rent of $4,000? $1,000

(c) How would the answer to (a) change, if at all, if Barb is a full-time student at PU and not an employee?

* * *

(3) STATUTORY FRINGE BENEFITS

Code: IRC §§ 132(a)–(e)(1); 132(f)(1)–(5), (7); 132(h)–(j)(1); 132(j)(4). *Skim* IRC §§ 104(a)(3); 105; 106; 125; 127; 129; 137.

Regs: Treas. Reg. §§ 1.132–2(a), (c); 1.132–3(a)(1)–(4), (e); 1.132–4(a)(1)(i), (a)(1)(iv); 1.132–5(b)(1); 1.132–6(a)–(c); 1.132–6(e). *Skim* Treas. Reg. § 1.132–5(b)(1).

Section 132(a) lists eight types of employee fringe benefits specifically excluded from gross income. Not all tax-advantaged fringe benefits are listed in § 132. Indeed, the most significant fringe benefit for most employees—participation in a "qualified" retirement plan—is covered elsewhere in the Code. Under a qualified retirement plan, employers pay a set percentage of the employee's compensation to the plan *before* applying the federal wage withholding taxes (thus, amounts passing to qualified plans are referred to as "pre-tax dollars"). The plan trustee(s) then invest the amounts in each employee's individual account. The growth on the account is entirely income-tax-free and remains so until finally distributed to the employee upon retirement. These *deferred compensation* plans are governed by § 401 *et. seq.* and are well beyond the scope of this course.

There are even more statutory fringe benefit provisions beyond § 132, but § 132 is the centerpiece of the statutory fringe benefit provisions. Read through the assigned provisions of the statute and try your hand at the following Problems.

Self-Assessment Question

(Solutions to Self–Assessment Questions are set forth in Appendix 3.)

SAQ 3–2. For many years, Employer (who owns and operates a hardware store) had given her employees a ham, turkey or gift basket in the holiday season. Some employees with dietary or religious restrictions complained about these items, so Employer changed her policy and instead gave employees $35 gift certificates redeemable at various local stores during the holiday season. The certificates could not be converted to cash and expired shortly after the holiday season. Can the employees exclude the value of these gift certificates from their gross incomes under § 132?

✗ *Problem 3–9* ✗

Leona is an employee of Luxury, Inc., a corporation that owns luxury hotels. Luxury also owns and operates massage parlors as a separate line of business. No Luxury hotel is within walking distance of any Luxury massage parlor, and only the highest-ranking executives of Luxury are involved with both divisions of Luxury's business. Leona works as a concierge in Luxury's hotel division. As an employee, Leona is entitled to free use of Luxury hotel rooms anywhere in the world on a "space-available" basis. Leona is also entitled to a 30–percent discount at all Luxury massage parlors.

(a) Assume that Leona spends one night at no charge in Luxury's hotel in Las Vegas. Luxury normally charges $100 nightly for each room. Does Leona have gross income?

(b) How, if at all, would the answer to (a) change if Leona were allowed to reserve the room weeks in advance of her stay?

(c) Now assume that Leona receives a massage on a "space-available" basis at Luxury's New Orleans massage parlor. The parlor normally charges $100 for a one-hour massage, but Leona pays only $70 because she is an employee. Does Leona have gross income?

(d) How, if at all, would the answers to (a), (b), and (c) change if Leona was the CEO of Luxury and thus the only employee entitled to the benefits?

(e) How, if at all, would the answers to (a), (b), and (c) change if the benefits were provided to Leona's daughters, Paris and Nicky, instead of Leona?

✗ *Problem 3–10* ✗

Dilbert is an employee of Company. During the current taxable year, Dilbert receives the following benefits from Company. Determine whether each such benefit is included in Dilbert's gross income.

(a) Company pays round-trip airfare and lodging for Dilbert to attend a work-related conference in Denver.

(b) Company provides Dilbert with a "company car" that Dilbert uses for both business and personal purposes.

(c) Company furnishes all employees, including Dilbert, with a "holiday ham" in December.

(d) Company provides Dilbert with a free bus pass that would normally cost Dilbert $60 per month.

(e) Company reimburses Dilbert for the $200 he pays each month for parking privileges in the private garage located across the street from Company's premises.

(f) Company permits Dilbert free use of a gymnasium located on Company's premises. The gym is operated by Company and is available only to Company employees and their families.

Other Statutory Fringe Benefits. In addition to the exclusions offered under § 132, employees may qualify for a number of other fringe benefit exclusion provisions. Section 74(c), discussed in Part C of this Chapter, excludes so-called "employee achievement awards" given for length of service or safety achievements. Section 79 excludes group term life insurance benefits provided by an employer. Section 106(a) allows an exclusion for employer-provided accident and health insurance coverage. Sections 79 and 106(a) come up again in Chapter 5.

(4) PROPERTY RECEIVED FOR SERVICES

Code: IRC §§ 83(a)–(c).

Regs: Treas. Reg. §§ 1.83–1(a)(1); 1.83–2(a); 1.83–3(c).

Beware of the String Attached. Sometimes employees receive contingent compensation: consideration the full enjoyment of which is conditioned upon the performance of additional services in the future. Employers like to pay this kind of consideration because it gives employees an incentive to continue their productivity. Contingent compensation frequently comes in the form of stock or an equivalent form of equity interest in the employer. When an employee or other service provider receives contingent consideration, does he or she have gross income at the time of receipt? Or should inclusion in gross income wait until all strings attached to the consideration have been severed?

Section 83 offers some guidance on the timing for inclusion in gross income. As you did with the fringe benefit rules of § 132, read through the assigned portions of the statute and apply it to the following Problem.

✱ Problem 3–11 ✱

Corky is the president and sole shareholder of a corporation that manufactures and sells rocking chairs. The corporation employs several workers, including Mr. McFeely and Lady Aberlin.

(a) To reward McFeely for his good work and long service, the corporation awarded McFeely 100 shares of the corporation's stock. McFeely signed a so-called "restrictive stock agreement" that prohibited any transfers of the stock until McFeely's termination or retirement. Does McFeely have gross income upon receipt of the shares?

(b) Lady Aberlin also received 100 shares of the corporation's stock in recognition of her being named "Employee of the Year." Under the terms of her restrictive stock agreement, Aberlin must forfeit her shares (transfer them back to the corporation for no consideration) if she voluntarily terminates her employment with the corporation before reaching age 65. She must also forfeit the shares if she is terminated "for cause" prior to retirement. If Aberlin transfers her shares to any third party, the third party is also subject to the risk of losing the shares if Aberlin voluntarily terminates her employment or is terminated "for cause" before reaching age 65. Does Aberlin have gross income upon receipt of the shares?

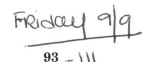

C. GIFTS AND BEQUESTS

Code: IRC §§ 74(a)–(c)(2); 102; 274(j)(3)–(4). *Skim* IRC § 117.

Regs: *Skim* Treas. Reg. §§ 1.74–1(a); 1.102–1. *Skim* Proposed Treas. Reg. §§ 1.74–1(b)–(f); 1.74–2.

Policy Reasons for the Gift Exclusion. Some variation of the § 102(a) exclusion for gifts and bequests has been in every federal income tax act, leading one to think that there is a compelling policy reason for the exclusion. Curiously, there is no consensus among commentators as to why gifts and bequests should be excluded from gross income. Indeed, many commentators conclude that there is no justification for the exclusion. Compare two taxpayers, A and B, each of whom has $50,000 to spend in the taxable year. A derived the $50,000 as wages, and B (who did not work) received the $50,000 as a gift. Under current law, A will pay federal income tax on A's $50,000, but B will pay no federal income tax at all. As this example shows, the gift exclusion violates "horizontal equity," for those with equal amounts of total receipts are not tax equally on those receipts.

Many reasons have been offered to support the § 102(a) gift exclusion. One might conclude that the exclusion is simply a matter of **administrative convenience**, for it would be difficult for taxpayers to track (and for the Service to check) all gift transactions during the year. If gifts were subject to income tax, taxpayers would have to keep a bookkeeping ledger on hand while opening birthday or other holiday gifts. If the value of the gift was not readily apparent, recipients would have to ask their generous donors how much they paid for the gifts, a tacky way to acknowledge receipt of a gift. Since a significant portion of all gifts occur within the family, the taxation of gifts further interposes the government into family affairs. While society might be a little less comfortable if gifts were subject to taxation, a less expansive gift exclusion could address most of these concerns. The gift exclusion, for example, could be structured so that taxpayers could exclude up to a defined dollar amount that would likely cover most of the intra-family gifts one would likely receive. Of course, establishing the proper dollar amount would be no easy task, for any arbitrarily chosen exclusion ceiling will not be perfectly suitable for all situations. Yet the justification of administrative convenience for the § 102(a) exclusion is incomplete at best.

Others might argue that the gift exclusion is appropriate since gifted amounts are **already subject to federal wealth transfer taxes** in the hands of the donor. Section 2001 imposes on the very wealthy a federal estate tax on the privilege of transferring wealth at death. Similarly, § 2501 imposes a federal gift tax on the privilege of making substantial *inter vivos* wealth transfers. To the extent the donor is (or may be) subject to an excise tax for making a gift, perhaps it is too harsh to impose an additional income tax on the recipient of the gift. This too is an incomplete justification for the gift exclusion, as less than two percent of all taxpayers are subject to the federal estate and gift taxes. If concern for excessive taxation was the principal reason for excluding gifts, the exclusion would be limited to situations where the donor incurs liability for estate or gift taxes as a result of the transfer to the recipient.

Maybe the gift exclusion is really a vehicle to **encourage generosity**. A donor might be more willing to effect a gift transfer if the donor knows that the recipient will not also receive a liability for federal income tax on the gift. For example, suppose a donor wants a recipient to receive a gift of $100. If the gift were taxable in the hands of the donor, then the donor would have to transfer something more than $100 so that the recipient would have, after tax, $100. If the recipient had to pay a tax of 20 percent on the gift, then, the donor would have to transfer $125 to the recipient ($125 x 20% = $25 tax) in order to make sure the recipient had $100. The extra gift required to cover the income tax bite might discourage the donor from making the transfer. The disincentive is magnified if the donor transfers property instead of cash. If the recipient is taxed on the value of the gifted property, the recipient might have to sell the property to pay the resulting income tax liability.

But while taxing the recipient might create a disincentive to effect a gift, this rationale is also questionable given that there are much better ways to encourage generosity using the federal tax laws. For example, the donor could be allowed to deduct the cost of a gift, providing a tax benefit directly to the donor. Giving the donor a deduction and making the recipient pay tax on the gift, however, would effectively shift the income tax burden from the donor to the recipient. To the extent the typical recipient is in a lower tax bracket than the typical donor, this alternative would probably cause a drain on federal tax revenues.

Ultimately, then, none of the common justifications for the gift exclusion by itself is persuasive. It is the combination of these factors that probably best accounts for this long-standing benefit to gift recipients.

Tax Consequences to the Donor. The transfer of property by gift is seen as personal consumption by the donor. As a result, there is no deduction for gift transfers. The good news is that the transfer of appreciated property (where the value of the property at the time of the gift exceeds the price the donor paid to acquire the property) by gift will not give rise to any income tax consequences to the donor. For instance, if the donor purchases property for $100 and then gives it to a recipient when the value of the property is $160, the donor could be taxed on the $60 of appreciation that was consumed in the hands of the donor when the gift transfer is completed. The consumption comes in the form of satisfaction to the donor from providing a $160 gift to the recipient at a cost of only $100. While the consumption of appreciation in value could probably be subject to federal income tax under the Sixteenth Amendment, it is well accepted that donors are not taxed on the appreciation in value of gift property.

Gifts of Income. While a gift of property is excluded by § 102(a), § 102(b) makes it clear that income subsequently derived on gifted property is not excludable, nor are gifts of income. Focus on § 102(b) as you answer the following questions.

Self-Assessment Questions

(Solutions to Self–Assessment Questions are set forth in Appendix 3.)

SAQ 3–3. Donor gives all of Donor's right, title and interest in an apartment building worth $300,000 to Recipient. Later in the year, Recipient collects $3,000 in rents from the building's tenants. To what extent can Recipient exclude these amounts from gross income?

SAQ 3–4. Donor gives Recipient a life estate interest in an apartment building worth $300,000. Pursuant to the life estate, Recipient receives rents totaling $3,000 in the year of transfer. To what extent can Recipient exclude these amounts from gross income?

What is a "Gift?" Neither the statute nor the Regulations define what is meant by the term "gift," so the Supreme Court has stepped in to provide guidance.

COMMISSIONER v. DUBERSTEIN

United States Supreme Court, 1960.
363 U.S. 278, 80 S.Ct. 1190, 4 L.Ed.2d 1218.

MR. JUSTICE BRENNAN delivered the opinion of the Court.

These two cases concern the provision of the Internal Revenue Code which excludes from the gross income of an income taxpayer "the value of property acquired by gift." They pose the frequently recurrent question whether a specific transfer to a taxpayer in fact amounted to a "gift" to him within the meaning of the statute. The importance to decision of the facts of the cases requires that we state them in some detail.

No. 376, Commissioner v. Duberstein. The taxpayer, Duberstein, was president of the Duberstein Iron & Metal Company, a corporation with headquarters in Dayton, Ohio. For some years the taxpayer's company had done business with Mohawk Metal Corporation, whose headquarters were in New York City. The president of Mohawk was one Berman. * * * From time to time in their telephone conversations, Berman would ask Duberstein whether the latter knew of potential customers for some of Mohawk's products in which Duberstein's company itself was not interested. Duberstein provided the names of potential customers for these items.

One day in 1951 Berman telephoned Duberstein and said that the information Duberstein had given him had proved so helpful that he wanted to give the latter a present. Duberstein stated that Berman owed him nothing. Berman said that he had a Cadillac as a gift for Duberstein, and that the latter should send to New York for it; Berman insisted that Duberstein accept the car, and the latter finally did so, protesting however that he had not intended to be compensated for the information. At the time Duberstein already had a Cadillac and an Oldsmobile, and felt that he did not need another car. Duberstein testified that he did not think Berman would have sent him the Cadillac if he had not furnished him with information about the customers. It appeared that Mohawk later deducted the value of the Cadillac as a business expense on its corporate income tax return.

Duberstein did not include the value of the Cadillac in gross income for 1951, deeming it a gift. The Commissioner asserted a deficiency for the car's value against him, and in proceedings to review the deficiency the Tax Court affirmed the Commissioner's determination. * * * The Court of Appeals for the Sixth Circuit reversed. 265 F.2d 28, 30.

No. 546, Stanton v. United States. The taxpayer, Stanton, had been for approximately 10 years in the employ of Trinity Church in New York City. He was comptroller of the Church corporation, and president of a corporation, Trinity Operating Company, the church set up as a fully owned subsidiary to manage its real estate holdings, which were more extensive than simply the church property. His salary by the end of his employment there in 1942 amounted to $22,500 a year. Effective November 30, 1942, he resigned from both positions to go into business for himself. The Operating Company's directors, who seem to have included the rector and vestrymen of the church, passed the following resolution upon his resignation: "Be it resolved that in appreciation of the services rendered by Mr. Stanton * * * a gratuity is hereby awarded to him of Twenty Thousand Dollars * * *."

The Operating Company's action was later explained by one of its directors as based on the fact that, "Mr. Stanton was liked by all of the Vestry personally. He had a pleasing personality. He had come in when Trinity's affairs were in a difficult situation. He did a splendid piece of work, we felt. Besides that * * * he was liked by all of the members of the Vestry personally." * * *

  * * *

The "gratuity" was duly paid. * * *

The Commissioner asserted a deficiency against the taxpayer after the latter had failed to include the payments in question in gross income. After payment of the deficiency and administrative rejection of a refund claim, the taxpayer sued the United States for a refund in the District Court for the Eastern District of New York. The trial judge, sitting without a jury, made the simple finding that the payments were a "gift," and judgment was entered for the taxpayer. The Court of Appeals for the Second Circuit reversed. 268 F.2d 727.

The Government, urging that clarification of the problem typified by these two cases was necessary, and that the approaches taken by the Courts of Appeals for the Second and the Sixth Circuits were in conflict, petitioned for certiorari in No. 376, and acquiesced in the taxpayer's petition in No. 546. On this basis, and because of the importance of the question in the administration of the income tax laws, we granted certiorari in both cases.

The exclusion of property acquired by gift from gross income under the federal income tax laws was made in the first income tax statute passed under the authority of the Sixteenth Amendment, and has been a feature of the income tax statutes ever since. The meaning of the term "gift" as applied to particular transfers has always been a matter of contention. Specific and illuminating legislative history on the point does not appear to exist. Analogies and inferences drawn from other revenue provisions, such as the estate and gift taxes, are dubious. The meaning of the statutory term has been shaped largely by the decisional law. With this, we turn to the contentions made by the Government in these cases.

First. The Government suggests that we promulgate a new "test" in this area to serve as a standard to be applied by the lower courts and by the Tax Court in dealing with the numerous cases that arise.[6] We reject this invitation. We are of opinion that the governing principles are necessarily general and have already been spelled out in the opinions of this Court, and that the problem is one which, under the present statutory framework, does not lend itself to any more definitive statement that would produce a talisman for the solution of concrete cases. The cases at bar are fair examples of the settings in which the problem usually arises. They present situations in which payments have been made in a context with business overtones—an employer making a payment to a retiring employee; a businessman giving something of value to another businessman who has been of advantage to him in his business. In this context, we review the law as established by the prior cases here.

The course of decision here makes it plain that the statute does not use the term "gift" in the common-law sense, but in a more colloquial sense. This Court has indicated that a voluntarily executed transfer of his property by one to another, without any consideration or compensation therefor, though a common-law gift, is not necessarily a "gift" within the meaning of the statute. For the Court has shown that the mere absence of a legal or moral obligation to make such a payment does not establish that it is a gift. *Old Colony Trust Co. v. Commissioner*, 279 U.S. 716, 730, 49 S.Ct. 499, 504, 73 L.Ed. 918. And, importantly, if the payment proceeds primarily from "the constraining force of any moral or legal duty," or from "the incentive of anticipated benefit" of an economic nature, it is not a gift. And, conversely, "(w)here the payment is in return for services rendered, it is irrelevant that the donor derives no economic benefit from it." *Robertson v. United States*, 343 U.S. 711, 714, 72 S.Ct. 994, 996, 96 L.Ed. 1237.[7] A gift in the statutory sense, on the other hand, proceeds from a "detached and disinterested generosity," *Commissioner of Internal Revenue v. LoBue*, 351 U.S. 243, 246, 76 S.Ct.

---

6. The Government's proposed test is stated: "Gifts should be defined as transfers of property made for personal as distinguished from business reasons."

7. The cases including "tips" in gross income are classic examples of this. See, e.g., *Roberts v. Commissioner*, 9 Cir., 176 F.2d 221.

800, 803, 100 L.Ed. 1142; "out of affection, respect, admiration, charity or like impulses." *Robertson v. United States, supra*, 343 U.S. at page 714, 72 S.Ct. at page 996. And in this regard, the most critical consideration, as the Court was agreed in the leading case here, is the transferor's "intention." *Bogardus v. Commissioner*, 302 U.S. 34, 43, 58 S.Ct. 61, 65, 82 L.Ed. 32. "What controls is the intention with which payment, however voluntary, has been made." Id., 302 U.S. at page 45, 58 S.Ct. at page 66 (dissenting opinion).

The Government says that this "intention" of the transferor cannot mean what the cases on the common-law concept of gift call "donative intent." With that we are in agreement, for our decisions fully support this. * * * It scarcely needs adding that the parties' expectations or hopes as to the tax treatment of their conduct in themselves have nothing to do with the matter.

> * * *

Second. The Government's proposed "test," while apparently simple and precise in its formulation, depends frankly on a set of "principles" or "presumptions" derived from the decided cases, and concededly subject to various exceptions; and it involves various corollaries, which add to its detail. Were we to promulgate this test as a matter of law, and accept with it its various presuppositions and stated consequences, we would be passing for beyond the requirements of the cases before us, and would be painting on a large canvas with indeed a broad brush. The Government derives its test from such propositions as the following: That payments by an employer to an employee, even though voluntary, ought, by and large, to be taxable; that the concept of a gift is inconsistent with a payment's being a deductible business expense; that a gift involves "personal" elements; that a business corporation cannot properly make a gift of its assets. The Government admits that there are exceptions and qualifications to these propositions. We think, to the extent they are correct, that these propositions are not principles of law but rather maxims of experience that the tribunals which have tried the facts of cases in this area have enunciated in explaining their factual determinations. Some of them simply represent truisms: it doubtless is, statistically speaking, the exceptional payment by an employer to an employee that amounts to a gift. Others are overstatements of possible evidentiary inferences relevant to a factual determination on the totality of circumstances in the case: it is doubtless relevant to the over-all inference that the transferor treats a payment as a business deduction, or that the transferor is a corporate entity. But these inferences cannot be stated in absolute terms. Neither factor is a shibboleth. The taxing statute does not make nondeductibility by the transferor a condition on the "gift" exclusion; nor does it draw and distinction, in terms, between transfers by corporations and individuals, as to the availability of the "gift" exclusion to the transferee. The conclusion whether a transfer amounts to a "gift" is one that must be reached on consideration of all the factors.

> * * *

Third. Decision of the issue presented in these cases must be based ultimately on the application of the fact-finding tribunal's experience with the mainsprings of human conduct to the totality of the facts of each case. The nontechnical nature of the statutory standard, the close relationship of it to the date of practical human experience, and the multiplicity of relevant factual elements, with their various combinations, creating the necessity of ascribing the proper force to each, confirm us in our conclusion that primary weight in this area must be given to the conclusions of the trier of fact.

This conclusion may not satisfy an academic desire for tidiness, symmetry and precision in this area, any more than a system based on the determinations of various fact-finders ordinarily does. But we see it as implicit in the present statutory treatment of the exclusion for gifts, and in the variety of forums in which federal income tax cases can be tried. If there is fear of undue uncertainty or overmuch litigation, Congress may make more precise its treatment of the matter by singling out certain factors and making them determinative of the matters, as it has done in one field of the "gift" exclusion's former application, that of prizes and awards. Doubtless diversity of result will tend to be lessened somewhat since federal income tax decisions, even those in tribunals of first instance turning on issues of fact, tend to be reported, and since there may be a natural tendency of professional triers of fact to follow one another's determinations, even as to factual matters. But the question here remains basically one of fact, for determination on a case-by-case basis.

One consequence of this is that appellate review of determinations in this field must be quite restricted. Where a jury has tried the matter upon correct instructions, the only inquiry is whether it cannot be said that reasonable men could reach differing conclusions on the issue. Where the trial has been by a judge without a jury, the judge's findings must stand unless "clearly erroneous." "A finding is 'clearly erroneous' when although there is evidence to support it, the reviewing court on the entire evidence is left with the definite and firm conviction that a mistake has been committed." *United States v. United States Gypsum Co.*, 333 U.S. 364, 395, 68 S.Ct. 525, 542, 92 L.Ed. 746. * * *

Fourth. A majority of the Court is in accord with the principles just outlined. And, applying them to the *Duberstein* case, we are in agreement, on the evidence we have set forth, that it cannot be said that the conclusion of the Tax Court was "clearly erroneous." It seems to us plain that as trier of the facts it was warranted in concluding that despite the characterization of the transfer of the Cadillac by the parties and the absence of any obligation, even of a moral nature, to make it, it was at bottom a recompense for Duberstein's past services, or an inducement for him to be of further service in the future. We cannot say with the Court of Appeals that such a conclusion was "mere suspicion" on the Tax Court's part. To us it appears based in the sort of informed experience with human affairs that fact-finding tribunals should bring to this task.

As to *Stanton*, we are in disagreement. To four of us, it is critical here that the District Court as trier of fact made only the simple and unelaborated finding that the transfer in question was a "gift." To be sure, conciseness is to be strived for, and prolixity avoided, in findings; but, to the four of us, there comes a point where findings become so sparse and conclusory as to give to revelation of what the District Court's concept of the determining facts and legal standard may be. Such conclusory, general findings do not constitute compliance with Rule 52's direction to "find the facts specially and state separately * * * conclusions of law thereon." While the standard of law in this area is not a complex one, we four think the unelaborated finding of ultimate fact here cannot stand as a fulfillment of these requirements. It affords the reviewing court not the semblance of an indication of the legal standard with which the trier of fact has approached his task. For all that appears, the District Court may have viewed the form of the resolution or the simple absence of legal consideration as conclusive. While the judgment of the Court of Appeals cannot stand, the four of us think there must be further proceedings in the District Court looking toward new and adequate findings of fact. In this, we are joined by Mr. Justice WHITTAKER, who agrees that the findings were inadequate, although he does not concur generally in this opinion.

Accordingly, in No. 376 [*Duberstein*], the judgment of this Court is that the judgment of the Court of Appeals is reversed, and in No. 546 [*Stanton*], that the judgment of the Court of Appeals is vacated, and the case is remanded to the District Court for further proceedings not inconsistent with this opinion. It is so ordered.

MR. JUSTICE HARLAN concurs in the result in No. 376. In No. 546, he would affirm the judgment of the Court of Appeals for the reasons stated by Mr. JUSTICE FRANKFURTER.

MR. JUSTICE WHITTAKER, agreeing * * * that whether a particular transfer is or is not a "gift" may involve "a mixed question of law and fact," concurs only in the result of this opinion.

MR. JUSTICE DOUGLAS dissents, since he is of the view that in each of these two cases there was a gift under the test which the Court fashioned nearly a quarter of a century ago in *Bogardus v. Commissioner*, 302 U.S. 34, 58 S.Ct. 61.

MR. JUSTICE BLACK, concurring and dissenting.

I agree with the Court that it was not clearly erroneous for the Tax Court to find as it did in No. 376 that the automobile transfer to Duberstein was not a gift, and so I agree with the Court's opinion and judgment reversing the judgment of the Court of Appeals in that case.

I dissent in No. 546, *Stanton v. United States*. The District Court found that the $20,000 transferred to Mr. Stanton by his former employer at the end of ten years' service was a gift and therefore exempt from taxation * * *. I think the finding was not clearly erroneous and that the Court of Appeals was therefore wrong in reversing the District

Court's judgment. While conflicting inferences might have been drawn, there was evidence to show that Mr. Stanton's long services had been satisfactory, that he was well liked personally and had given splendid service, that the employer was under no obligation at all to pay any added compensation, but made the $20,000 payment because prompted by a genuine desire to make him a "gift," to award him a "gratuity." The District Court's finding was that the added payment "constituted a gift to the taxpayer, and therefore need not have been reported by him as income * * *." The trial court might have used more words, or discussed the facts set out above in more detail, but I doubt if this would have made its crucial, adequately supported finding any clearer. For this reason I would reinstate the District Court's judgment for petitioner.

MR. JUSTICE FRANKFURTER, concurring in the judgment in No. 376 and dissenting in No. 546.

As the Court's opinion indicates, we brought these two cases here partly because of a claimed difference in the approaches between two Courts of Appeals but primarily on the Government's urging that, in that interest of the better administration of the income tax laws, clarification was desirable for determining when a transfer of property constitutes a "gift" and is not to be included in income for purposes of ascertaining the "gross income" under the Internal Revenue Code. As soon as this problem emerged after the imposition of the first income tax authorized by the Sixteenth Amendment, it became evident that its inherent difficulties and subtleties would not easily yield to the formulation of a general rule or test sufficiently definite to confine within narrow limits the area of judgment in applying it. While at its core the tax conception of a gift no doubt reflected the non-legal, non-technical notion of a benefaction unentangled with any aspect of worldly requital, the diverse blends of personal and pecuniary relationships in our industrial society inevitably presented niceties for adjudication which could not be put to rest by any kind of general formulation.

Despite acute arguments at the bar and a most thorough reexamination of the problem on a full canvass of our prior decisions and an attempted fresh analysis of the nature of the problem, the Court has rejected the invitation of the Government to fashion anything like a litmus paper test for determining what is excludable as a "gift" from gross income. Nor has the Court attempted a clarification of the particular aspects of the problem presented by these two cases, namely, payment by an employer to an employee upon the termination of the employment relation and non-obligatory payment for services rendered in the course of a business relationship. While I agree that experience has shown the futility of attempting to define, by language so circumscribing as to make it easily applicable, what constitutes a gift for every situation where the problem may arise, I do think that greater explicitness is possible in isolating and emphasizing factors which militate against a gift in particular situations.

Thus, regarding the two frequently recurring situations involved in these cases—things of value given to employees by their employers upon the termination of employment and payments entangled in a business relation and occasioned by the performance of some service—the strong implication is that the payment is of a business nature. The problem in these two cases is entirely different from the problem in a case where a payment is made from one member of a family to another, where the implications are directly otherwise. No single general formulation appropriately deals with both types of cases, although both involve the question whether the payment was a "gift." While we should normally suppose that a payment from father to son was a gift, unless the contrary is shown, in the two situations now before us the business implications are so forceful that I would apply a presumptive rule placing the burden upon the beneficiary to prove the payment wholly unrelated to his services to the enterprise. The Court, however, has declined so to analyze the problem and has concluded "that the governing principles are necessarily general and have already been spelled out in the opinions of this Court, and that the problem is one which, under the present statutory framework, does not lend itself to any more definitive statement that would produce a talisman for the solution of concrete cases."

* * *

But I would affirm the decision of the Court of Appeals for the Second Circuit in *Stanton v. United States*. I would do so on the basis of the opinion of Judge Hand and more particularly because the very terms of the resolution by which the $20,000 was awarded to Stanton indicated that it was not a "gratuity" in the sense of sheer benevolence but in the nature of a generous lagniappe, something extra thrown in for services received though not legally nor morally required to be given. * * * The business nature of the payment is confirmed by the words of the resolution, explaining the "gratuity" as "in appreciation of the services rendered by Mr. Stanton as Manager of the Estate and Comptroller of the Corporation of Trinity Church throughout nearly ten years, and as President of Trinity Operating Company, Inc." The force of this document, in light of all the factors to which Judge Hand adverted in his opinion, was not in the least diminished by testimony at the trial. Thus the taxpayer has totally failed to sustain the burden I would place upon him to establish that the payment to him was wholly attributable to generosity unrelated to his performance of his secular business functions as an officer of the corporation of the Trinity Church of New York and the Trinity Operating Co. Since the record totally fails to establish taxpayer's claim, I see no need of specific findings by the trial judge.

⚓ *Note and Question* ⚓

The Court in *Duberstein* expressly refused to adopt a "test" to guide lower courts as to the meaning of a "gift." And yet, in the very next paragraph, a test is unveiled. Oh well—it was a good idea while it lasted.

Is the standard announced in *Duberstein* the same you would use to describe a gift? Why or why not?

* * *

Gifts to Employees. Section 102(c) was added to the Code as part of the Tax Reform Act of 1986. That provision makes it clear that no transfer from an employer to or for the benefit of an employee can be excluded as a gift. Of course, just because the § 102(a) exclusion does not apply, it does not always follow that such a transfer will be included in the employee's gross income. The transfer might qualify as an excludable fringe benefit under § 132, or it might constitute a non-taxable "employee achievement award" under § 74(c).

While the rule contained in § 102(c) is quite broad, there are notable limitations. Section 102(c) does not on its face apply to payments made to *former* employees, non-employees like *independent contractors*, or *survivors* of employees. Transfers to these individuals may still qualify for the § 102(a) exclusion.

Section 102(c) reflects a presumption that payments of a compensatory nature cannot be made with a "detached and disinterested generosity" sufficient to warrant exclusion, as the following cases suggest.

OLK v. UNITED STATES

United States Court of Appeals, Ninth Circuit, 1976.
536 F.2d 876.

Sneed, Circuit Judge:

This is a suit to obtain a refund of federal income taxes. The issue is whether monies, called "tokes" in the relevant trade, received by the taxpayer, a craps dealer employed by Las Vegas casinos, constitute taxable income or gifts within the meaning of section 102(a). The taxpayer insists "tokes" are non-taxable gifts. If he is right, he is entitled to the refund for which this suit was brought. The trial court in a trial without a jury held that "tokes" were gifts. The Government appealed and we reverse and hold that "tokes" are taxable income.

I.

The Facts.

There is no dispute about the basic facts which explain the setting in which "tokes" are paid and received. The district court's finding with respect to such facts which we accept are, in part, as follows:

In 1971 plaintiff was employed as a craps dealer in two Las Vegas gambling casinos, the Horseshoe Club and the Sahara Hotel. The basic services performed by plaintiff and other dealers were described at trial. There are four persons involved in the operation of the game, a boxman and three dealers. One of the three dealers, the stickman, calls the roll of the dice and then collects them for the next shooter. The other two dealers collect losing bets and pay off winning bets under the supervision of the boxman. The boxman is the casino employee charged with direct supervision of the dealers and the play at one particular table. He in turn is supervised by the pit boss who is responsible for several tables. The dealers also make change, advise the boxman when a player would like a drink and answer basic questions about the game for the players.

Dealers are forbidden to fraternize or engage in unnecessary conversation with the casino patrons, and must remain in separate areas while on their breaks. Dealers must treat all patrons equally, and any attempt to provide special service to a patron is grounds for termination.

At times, players will give money to the dealers or place bets for them. The witnesses testified that most casinos do not allow boxmen to receive money from patrons because of their supervisory positions, although some do permit this. The pit bosses are not permitted to receive anything from patrons because they are in a position in which they can insure that a patron receives some special service or treatment.

The money or tokes are combined by the four dealers and split equally at the end of each shift so that a dealer will get his share of the tokes received even while he is taking his break. Uncontradicted testimony indicated that a dealer would be terminated if he kept a toke rather than placed it in the common fund.

Casino management either required the dealers to pool and divide tokes or encouraged them to do so. Although the practice is tolerated by management, it is not encouraged since tokes represent money that players are not wagering and thus cannot be won by the casino. Plaintiff received about $10 per day as his share of tokes at the Horseshoe Club and an average of $20 per day in tokes at the Sahara. (footnotes omitted).

Additional findings of fact by the district court are that the taxpayer worked as a stickman and dealer and at all times was under the supervision of the boxman who in turn was supervised by the pit boss. Also the district court found that patrons sometimes give money to dealers, other players or mere spectators at the game, but that between 90–95% of the patrons give nothing to a dealer. No obligation on the part of the patron exists to give to a dealer and "dealers perform no service for patrons which a patron would normally find compensable." Another finding is that there exists "no direct relation between services performed for management by a dealer and benefit or detriment to the patron."

There then follows two final "findings of fact" which taken together constitute the heart of the controversy before us. These are as follows:

17.   The tokes are given to dealers as a result of impulsive generosity or superstition on the part of players, and not as a form of compensation for services.

18. Tokes are the result of detached and disinterested generosity on the part of a small number of patrons.

These two findings, together with the others set out above, bear the unmistakable imprint of *Commissioner v. Duberstein*, 363 U.S. 278, 80 S.Ct. 1190, 4 L.Ed.2d 1218 (1960) * * *.

II.

Finding Number 18 Is A Conclusion of Law.

The position of the taxpayer is simple. The above findings conform to the meaning of gifts as used in section 102 of the Code. *Duberstein* further teaches, the taxpayer asserts, that whether a receipt qualified as a non-taxable gift is "basically one of fact," and appellate review of such findings is restricted to determining whether they are clearly erroneous. Because none of the recited findings are clearly erroneous, concludes the taxpayer, the judgment of the trial court must be affirmed.

We could not escape this logic were we prepared to accept as a "finding of fact" the trial court's finding number 18. We reject the trial court's characterization. The conclusion that tokes "are the result of detached and disinterested generosity" on the part of those patrons who engage in the practice of toking is a conclusion of law, not a finding of fact. Finding number 17, on the other hand, which establishes that tokes are given as the result of impulsive generosity or superstition on the part of the players is a finding of fact to which we are bound unless it is "clearly erroneous" which it is not.

The distinction is between a finding of the dominant reason that explains the player's action in making the transfer and the determination that such dominant reason requires treatment of the receipt as a gift. Finding number 17 is addressed to the former while number 18 the latter. A finding regarding the basic facts, i.e., the circumstances and setting within which tokes are paid, and the dominant reason for such payments are findings of fact, our review of which is restricted by the clearly erroneous standard. Whether the dominant reason justifies exclusion from gross income under section 102 as interpreted by *Duberstein* is a matter of law. Finding number 18 is a determination that the dominant reason for the player's action, as found in number 17, justifies exclusion. This constitutes an application of the statute to the facts. Whether the application is proper is, of course, a question of law.

* * *

This is a sensible approach. Otherwise an appellate court's inescapable duty of appellate review in this type of case would be all but foreclosed by a finding, such as in number 18, in which the resolution of the ultimate legal issue was disguised as a finding of fact. The error in insisting that findings numbers 17 and 18 are both findings of fact with respect to the "dominant reason" is revealed when the language of finding number 18 is compared with *Duberstein*'s statement, "A gift in the statutory sense, on the other hand, proceeds from a 'detached and disinterested generosity,' 'out of affection, respect, admiration, charity or like impulses.' " Their similarity is not coincidental and demonstrates that finding number 18 is but an application of the statutory definition of a gift to all previous findings of fact including finding number 17. Number 18 merely characterizes all previous findings in a manner that makes classification of the receipt as a gift inevitable. "Detached and disinterested generosity" are, by reason of *Duberstein*, the operative words of the statutory definition of a gift. To apply them to facts, including a finding with respect to "dominant motive" is to apply the statute to such facts. It is a conclusion of law.

III.

FINDING NUMBER 18 AND OTHER CONCLUSIONS OF LAW BASED THEREON ARE ERRONEOUS.

Freed of the restraint of the "clearly erroneous" standard, we are convinced that finding number 18 and all derivative conclusions of law are wrong. "Impulsive generosity or superstition on the part of the players" we accept as the dominant motive. In the context of gambling in casinos open to the public such a motive is quite understandable. However, our understanding also requires us to acknowledge that payments so motivated are not acts of "detached or disinterested generosity." Quite the opposite is true. Tribute to the gods of fortune which it is hoped will be returned bounteously soon can only be described as an "involved and intensely interested" act.

Moreover, in applying the statute to the findings of fact, we are not permitted to ignore those findings which strongly suggest that tokes in the hands of the ultimate recipients are viewed as a receipt indistinguishable, except for erroneously anticipated tax differences, from wages. The regularity of the flow, the equal division of the receipts, and the daily amount received indicate that a dealer acting reasonably would come to regard such receipts as a form of compensation for his services. The manner in which a dealer may regard tokes is, of course, not the touchstone for determining whether the receipt is excludable from gross income. It is, however, a reasonable and relevant inference well-grounded in the findings of fact.

* * * Generalizations are treacherous but not without utility. One such is that receipts by taxpayers engaged in rendering services contributed by those with whom the taxpayers have some personal or functional contact in the course of the performance of the services are taxable income when in conformity with the practices of the area and easily valued. Tokes, like tips, meet these conditions. That is enough.

The taxpayer is not entitled to the refund he seeks.

REVERSED.

* * *

UNITED STATES v. HARRIS, 942 F.2d 1125 (7th Cir. 1991).

Facts: The (married) donor made payments to twin sisters that the sisters excluded from gross income as gifts. The record indicated that the sisters showered the donor with affection, and the Service thought the payments really represented compensation instead of gifts.

Issue: Are the sisters guilty of willfully evading federal income taxes by excluding the payments from gross income?

Holding: No.

Rationale: The payments are close enough to gifts to avoid criminal prosecution.

* * *

Exclusion for Bequests, Devises, and Inheritances. As previously mentioned, the § 102(a) exclusion applies not only to *inter vivos* transfers but also to gifts made at death. Does the same standard of "detached and disinterested generosity" apply to death-time gifts? The following authorities offer an answer to this question.

WOLDER v. COMMISSIONER

United States Court of Appeals, Second Circuit, 1974.
493 F.2d 608.

Oakes, Circuit Judge:

These two cases, involving an appeal and cross-appeal in the individual taxpayers' case and an appeal by the Commissioner in the estate taxpayer's case, essentially turn on one question: whether an attorney contracting to and performing lifetime legal services for a client receives income when the client, pursuant to the contract, bequeaths a substantial sum to the attorney in lieu of the payment of fees during the client's lifetime. In the individual taxpayers' case, the Tax Court held that the fair market value of the stock and cash received under the client's will constituted taxable income under § 61, and was not exempt from taxation as a bequest under § 102 of the Code. From this ruling the individual taxpayers, Victor R. Wolder, the attorney, and his wife, who signed joint returns, appeal. * * *

* * *

There is no basic disagreement as to the facts. On or about October 3, 1947, Victor R. Wolder, as attorney, and Marguerite K. Boyce, as client, entered into a written agreement which, after reciting Mr. Wolder's past services on her behalf in an action against her ex-husband for which he had made no charge, consisted of mutual promises, first on the part of Wolder to render to Mrs. Boyce "such legal services as she shall in her opinion personally require from time to time as long as both ... shall live and not to bill her for such services," and second on the part of Mrs. Boyce to make a codicil to her last will and testament giving and bequeathing to Mr. Wolder or to his estate "my 500 shares of Class B common stock of White Laboratories, Inc." or "such other ... securities" as might go to her in the event of a merger or consolidation of

White Laboratories. Subsequently, in 1957, White Laboratories did merge into Schering Corp. * * *. In a revised will dated April 23, 1965, Mrs. Boyce, true to the agreement with Mr. Wolder, bequeathed to him or his estate the sum of $15,845 and the 750 shares of common stock of Schering Corp. There is no dispute but that Victor R. Wolder had rendered legal services to Mrs. Boyce over her lifetime (though apparently these consisted largely of revising her will) and had not billed her therefor so that he was entitled to performance by her under the agreement, on which she had had a measure of independent legal advice. * * *

* * *

Wolder argues that the legacy he received under Mrs. Boyce's will is specifically excluded from income by virtue of § 102(a) * * *. The individual taxpayer, as did dissenting Judge Quealy below, relies upon *United States v. Merriam*, 263 U.S. 179, 44 S.Ct. 69, 68 L.Ed. 240 (1923), and its progeny for the proposition that the term "bequest" in § 102(a) has not been restricted so as to exclude bequests made on account of some consideration flowing from the beneficiary to the decedent. In *Merriam* the testator made cash bequests to certain persons who were named executors of the estate, and these bequests were "in lieu of all compensation or commissions to which they would otherwise be entitled as executors or trustees." The Court held nevertheless that the legacies were exempt from taxation * * *.

But we think that *Merriam* is inapplicable to the facts of this case, for here there is no dispute but that the parties did contract for services and—while the services were limited in nature—there was also no question but that they were actually rendered. Thus the provisions of Mrs. Boyce's will, at least for federal tax purposes, went to satisfy her obligation under the contract. The contract in effect was one for the postponed payment of legal services, i.e., by a legacy under the will for services rendered during the decedent's life.

Moreover, the Supreme Court itself has taken an entirely different viewpoint from *Merriam* when it comes to interpreting § 102(a) * * *. In *Commissioner v. Duberstein*, the Court held that the true test is whether in actuality the gift is a bona fide gift or simply a method for paying compensation. This question is resolved by an examination of the intent of the parties, the reasons for the transfer, and the parties' performance in accordance with their intentions—"what the basic reason for (the donor's) conduct was in fact—the dominant reason that explains his action in making the transfer." There are other cases holding testamentary transfers to be taxable compensation for services as opposed to tax-free bequests. True, in each of these cases the testator did not fulfill his contractual obligation to provide in his will for payment of services rendered by the taxpayer, forcing the taxpayers to litigate the merits of their claims against the estates, whereas in the case at bar the terms of the contract were carried out. This is a distinction without a difference, and while we could decline to follow them in the case at bar, we see no reason to do so.

Indeed, it is to be recollected that § 102 is, after all, an exception to the basic provision in § 61(a) that "Except as otherwise provided in this subtitle, gross income means all income from whatever source derived, including ... (1) Compensation for services, including fees, commissions and similar items ...." The congressional purpose is to tax income comprehensively. A transfer in the form of a bequest was the method that the parties chose to compensate Mr. Wolder for his legal services, and that transfer is therefore subject to taxation, whatever its label whether by federal or by local law may be.

Taxpayer's argument that he received the stock and cash as a "bequest" under New York law and the decisions of the surrogates is thus beside the point. New York law does, of course, control as to the extent of the taxpayer's legal rights to the property in question, but it does not control as to the characterization of the property for federal income tax purposes. New York law cannot be decisive on the question whether any given transfer is income under § 61(a) or is exempt under § 102(a) of the Code. We repeat, we see no difference between the transfer here made in the form of a bequest and the transfer under *Commissioner v. Duberstein, supra*, which was made without consideration, with no legal or moral obligation, and which was indeed a "common-law gift," but which was nevertheless held not to be a gift excludable under § 102(a).

* * *

REVENUE RULING 67–375, 1967–2 C.B. 60.

Facts: A and B agreed to care for C for the rest of C's life. C agreed to leave all of C's personal property to A and B in exchange for these services.

Issue: Must A and B include the amounts received from C's estate in gross income?

Holding: Yes.

Rationale: C's transfer was specifically made as payment for services and not from "detached and disinterested generosity."

* * *

✗ Problem 3–12 ✗

In Year One, Jerry transferred 100 shares of NBC, Inc., stock to his best friend, George. At the time of the transfer, the stock was worth $5,000. In Year Two, NBC, Inc., declared a cash dividend on its shares. As the owner of the shares, George received a dividend check in the amount of $100 late in Year Two.

(a) Does George have gross income in Year One? In Year Two?

(b) Would the answer to (a) change if, instead of receiving cash, all of the NBC, Inc., shareholders received (in Year Two) two additional shares of NBC, Inc., stock for every share they already own?

Problem 3–13

Pursuant to a trust agreement she created, Elaine transferred title to an apartment building to Cosmo, the trustee. The trust agreement instructed Cosmo to pay the monthly rental income from the apartment building to Susan, Elaine's friend, for Susan's life. At Susan's death, Cosmo is supposed to transfer the apartment building to Elaine's on-again, off-again beau, David.

(a) Does anyone have gross income at the time Elaine transfers the apartment building to Cosmo?

(b) Suppose Cosmo paid the rents to Susan throughout Year One, and that Susan died at the very beginning of Year Two while licking poisoned envelopes. Cosmo then transferred title to the building to David. Does anyone have gross income in Year One or Year Two?

(c) How would the answers to (a) and (b) change if David is Elaine's employee (as well as her one true love)?

Problem 3–14

Newman is an employee of the United States Postal Service. Newman receives the following items from his employer. Determine whether each such item is included in Newman's gross income.

(a) 100 free stamps, worth $40, every month

(b) $50 in flowers upon the death of his father, Paul

(c) A $250 Swatch watch in recognition of completing his first four years at the Postal Service without taking a sick day

(d) Same as (c), except that a watch was given to all employees in recognition of making it through the year without any deaths at any post office branch location in the United States.

Problem 3–15

Late in life, Frank Costanza's health began to deteriorate. Concerned that he would be unable to care for himself, Frank asked his son, George, if he could move into George's apartment. George refused the request. Frank turned to George's childhood friend, Lloyd Braun, for help. Lloyd graciously opened his home to Frank. Until his death, Frank regularly told Lloyd that he would repay Lloyd for Lloyd's kindness and attention. Frank's will left his entire estate to Lloyd.

(a) Does Lloyd have gross income?

(b) Is there a way that Frank could have drafted his bequest so that there would be little or no question that it was a gift?

(c) Suppose George contested the will on the grounds that Frank lacked capacity and was unduly influenced by Lloyd. George argued that he was entitled to the entire estate as Frank's only living heir. If George prevails, does he have gross income when he receives Frank's estate?

———

D. LOANS AND THE CANCELLATION OF DEBT

Code: IRC §§ 61(a)(4), (a)(12); 108(a)–(b)(2), (c)–(d)(3), (e)(5). *Skim* IRC §§ 163; 1017.

Regs: None.

Though we are admonished to be neither borrowers nor lenders, loan transactions are common in our society. Federal income tax laws must account for the fact that taxpayers frequently serve as both lenders and borrowers. The following axioms provide the basic rules, and they are universally accepted. Most are so fundamental that neither Congress nor the Treasury Department has felt compelled to codify them.

Axiom #1. A loan is not gross income to the borrower. In a bona fide loan arrangement, the borrower has the obligation to repay the amount received as a loan. Consequently, the borrower has no accession to wealth from a loan, for while the borrower has received the loan proceeds, the amount of the proceeds are offset by the liability to repay the same amount.

Axiom #2. The lender may not deduct the amount of the loan. Suppose a taxpayer loans $100 to an unrelated party in a bona fide transaction. From the lender's perspective, the loan merely converts one asset (cash) into another asset (a promise of repayment). As Chapter 4 will explain, deductions are typically limited to expenses and are not available when an outlay serves to create a new or different asset.

Axiom #3. The amount paid to satisfy the loan obligation is not deductible by the borrower. Although the outlay made to satisfy a repayment obligation does not serve to create a new or different asset, repayment of a loan does not represent a real "cost" to the borrower, for the repayment of the principal amount represents merely a return of the borrowed amount.

Axiom #4. Repayment of the loan is not gross income to the lender. The repayment represents merely a return of capital to the lender. In effect, the promise of repayment is converted back to cash, with no accession to wealth by the lender. If the lender gets back something less than the entire amount originally loaned, the lender may be able to deduct the amount of the deficiency, as will be discussed in Chapter 9.

Axiom #5. Interest paid to the lender is included in the lender's gross income. Section 61(a)(4) requires this result. Interest paid to a lender is compensation for the use of the lender's money or property and thus represents profit or an accession to wealth in the hands of the lender. Lenders usually cannot avoid gross income simply be charging no interest. Later on, we will see that interest income will even be imputed to the lender in cases where the lender fails to charge a minimum amount of interest on a bona fide loan.

Axiom #6. Interest paid to the lender *may* be deductible by the borrower. Section 163 governs the deductibility of interest payments. Very generally, as we will see later on, interest paid in connection with the borrower's business activity will be deductible, while interest paid on loans used for personal activities or expenses will not be deductible (with the major exception of interest paid on a home mortgage).

Cancellation of Debt. If a lender forgives or cancels an outstanding debt, there may be income tax consequences to the borrower, as the following case illustrates.

UNITED STATES v. KIRBY LUMBER CO.

United States Supreme Court, 1931.
284 U.S. 1, 52 S.Ct. 4, 76 L.Ed. 131.

MR. JUSTICE HOLMES delivered the opinion of the court.

In July, 1923, the plaintiff, the Kirby Lumber Company, issued its own bonds for $12,126,800 for which it received their par value. Later in the same year it purchased in the open market some of the same bonds at less than par, the difference of price being $137,521.30. The question is whether this difference is a taxable gain or income of the plaintiff for the year 1923. * * * [B]y the Treasury Regulations authorized by § 1303, that have been in force through repeated re-enactments, "If the corporation purchases and retires any of such bonds at a price less than the issuing price or face value, the excess of the issuing price or face value over the purchase price is gain or income for the taxable year." We see no reason why the Regulations should not be accepted as a correct statement of the law.

In *Bowers v. Kerbaugh–Empire Co.*, 271 U.S. 170, 46 S.Ct. 449, 70 L.Ed. 886, the defendant in error owned the stock of another company that had borrowed money repayable in marks or their equivalent for an enterprise that failed. At the time of payment the marks had fallen in value, which so far as it went was a gain for the defendant in error, and it was contended by the plaintiff in error that the gain was taxable income. But the transaction as a whole was a loss, and the contention was denied. Here there was no shrinkage of assets and the taxpayer made a clear gain. As a result of its dealings it made available $137,521.30 assets previously offset by the obligation of bonds now extinct. We see nothing to be gained by the discussion of judicial definitions. The defendant in error has realized within the year an accession to income, if we take words in their plain popular meaning, as they should be taken here. *Burnet v. Sanford & Brooks Co.*, 282 U.S. 359, 364, 51 S.Ct. 150, 75 L.Ed. 383.

Judgment reversed.

Notes and Questions

1. What is the rationale for concluding that the Kirby Lumber Company has gross income when the debt to its bondholders is partially discharged? There are two valid theories for requiring inclusion in gross income. First, The Court suggests that the cancellation of debt is a "freeing of assets" to the borrower. To the extent a taxpayer no longer must commit funds to the complete repayment of a debt, the taxpayer is now free to use those previously committed funds to other purposes. Put differently, a cancellation of debt is an accession to wealth. Suppose a taxpayer has $200,000 in total assets and $120,000 in total liabilities. The taxpayer has a "net worth" of $80,000. If one of the taxpayer's creditors forgives a $5,000 loan to the taxpayer, the taxpayer still has $200,000 in assets, but total liabilities amount to only $115,000. The taxpayer's net worth thus increases to $85,000, and that increase in net worth is, in essence, an accession to wealth.

A second theory for inclusion of forgiven debts is based on symmetry. The borrower does not have gross income at the time of the loan because of the obligation of repayment. If some portion of that obligation is subsequently cancelled or forgiven, the rationale for precluding inclusion in gross income disappears, so inclusion should result. If the borrower could exclude both the original loan and the subsequent forgiveness of the liability to repay that amount, the borrower would be receiving a double benefit, and the money was never repaid would never be subject to tax in the taxpayer's hands.

2. Congress codified the result in *Kirby Lumber*. See § 61(a)(12).

Exclusion of COD Income Under § 108. Tax professionals often refer to income from the discharge of indebtedness as "COD" income, standing for "cancellation of debt" income. While § 61(a)(12) generally requires inclusion of COD income, § 108 offers a limited exclusion for certain forms of COD income. Specifically, § 108(a) lists four types of COD income that will qualify for exclusion. The first two types listed in § 108(a) are based on the fact that a bankrupt or insolvent taxpayer has no "freeing of assets" if the taxpayer still has a negative net worth after the discharge. The last two types listed provide special rules for taxpayers engaged in certain activities. Is it good tax policy to provide benefits targeted to these discrete groups?

* * *

Problem 3–16

Determine the federal income tax consequences to Antonio arising from each of the following transactions:

(a) Antonio owed $50,000 to Shylock, an unrelated individual. Antonio, struggling to make a living and feed a family, offered $35,000 cash to Shylock in full satisfaction of the debt. Shylock accepted the cash and retired the debt.

(b) Same as (a), except that at the time Antonio paid $35,000 cash to Shylock, the fair market value of Antonio's assets was $40,000 less than the amount of Antonio's total liabilities.

(c) Same as (a), except that at the time Antonio paid $35,000 cash to Shylock, the fair market value of Antonio's assets was $5,000 less than the amount of Antonio's total liabilities.

(d) Earlier this year, Antonio purchased property from Shylock for $50,000. At closing, Antonio paid $10,000 to Shylock and executed a promissory note payable to "Shylock or order" for $40,000. Following closing, Antonio approached Shylock, upset that the property was in fact worth only $42,000. After a few weeks of negotiations, the parties agreed to reduce the amount of the promissory note to $32,000.

(e) Antonio borrowed $800,000 from Shylock in Year One to purchase a building from another unrelated individual for use in Antonio's trade or business. Assume the loan from Shylock is "qualified real property business indebtedness." In Year Four, the fair market value of the property dropped to $700,000. At that time, Antonio's adjusted basis in the property was $150,000, and the amount due under the loan was $800,000. Later in Year Four, Antonio and Shylock agreed to reduce the amount due under the loan to $600,000. At all times relevant to this Problem, Antonio is solvent and owns no other depreciable real property.

ZARIN v. COMMISSIONER

United States Court of Appeals, Third Circuit, 1990.
916 F.2d 110.

COWEN, CIRCUIT JUDGE.

David Zarin ("Zarin") appeals from a decision of the Tax Court holding that he recognized $2,935,000 of income from discharge of indebtedness resulting from his gambling activities, and that he should be taxed on the income. * * * After considering the issues raised by this appeal, we will reverse.

I.

Zarin was a professional engineer who participated in the development, construction, and management of various housing projects. A resident of Atlantic City, New Jersey, Zarin occasionally gambled, both in his hometown and in other places where gambling was legalized. To facilitate his gaming activities in Atlantic City, Zarin applied to Resorts International Hotel ("Resorts") for a credit line in June, 1978. Following a credit check, Resorts granted Zarin $10,000 of credit. Pursuant to this credit arrangement with Resorts, Zarin could write a check, called a marker,[2] and in return receive chips, which could then be used to gamble at the casino's tables.

Before long, Zarin developed a reputation as an extravagant "high roller" who routinely bet the house maximum while playing craps, his game of choice. Considered a "valued gaming patron" by Resorts, Zarin had his credit limit increased at regular intervals without any further

2. A "marker" is a negotiable draft payable to Resorts and drawn on the maker's bank.

credit checks, and was provided a number of complimentary services and privileges. By November, 1979, Zarin's permanent line of credit had been raised to $200,000. Between June, 1978, and December, 1979, Zarin lost $2,500,000 at the craps table, losses he paid in full.

Responding to allegations of credit abuses, the New Jersey Division of Gaming Enforcement filed with the New Jersey Casino Control Commission a complaint against Resorts. Among the 809 violations of casino regulations alleged in the complaint of October, 1979, were 100 pertaining to Zarin. Subsequently, a Casino Control Commissioner issued an Emergency Order, the effect of which was to make further extensions of credit to Zarin illegal.

Nevertheless, Resorts continued to extend Zarin's credit limit * * *. [These actions] effectively ignored the Emergency Order and were later found to be illegal.

By January, 1980, Zarin was gambling compulsively and uncontrollably at Resorts, spending as many as sixteen hours a day at the craps table.[5] During April, 1980, Resorts again increased Zarin's credit line without further inquiries. That same month, Zarin delivered personal checks and counterchecks to Resorts which were returned as having been drawn against insufficient funds. Those dishonored checks totaled $3,435,000. In late April, Resorts cut off Zarin's credit.

Although Zarin indicated that he would repay those obligations, Resorts filed a New Jersey state court action against Zarin in November, 1980, to collect the $3,435,000. Zarin denied liability on grounds that Resort's claim was unenforceable under New Jersey regulations intended to protect compulsive gamblers. Ten months later, in September, 1981, Resorts and Zarin settled their dispute for a total of $500,000.

The Commissioner of Internal Revenue ("Commissioner") subsequently determined deficiencies in Zarin's federal income taxes for 1980 and 1981, arguing that Zarin recognized $3,435,000 of income in 1980 from larceny by trick and deception. After Zarin challenged that claim by filing a Tax Court petition, the Commissioner abandoned his 1980 claim, and argued instead that Zarin had recognized $2,935,000 of income in 1981 from the cancellation of indebtedness which resulted from the settlement with Resorts.

Agreeing with the Commissioner, the Tax Court decided, eleven judges to eight, that Zarin had indeed recognized $2,935,000 of income from the discharge of indebtedness, namely the difference between the original $3,435,000 "debt" and the $500,000 settlement. *Zarin v. Commissioner,* 92 T.C. 1084 (1989). Since he was in the seventy percent tax bracket, Zarin's deficiency for 1981 was calculated to be $2,047,245. With interest to April 5, 1990, Zarin allegedly owes the Internal Revenue Service $5,209,033.96 in additional taxes. Zarin appeals the order of the Tax Court.

---

5. Zarin claims that at the time he was suffering from a recognized emotional disorder that caused him to gamble compulsively.

II.

The sole issue before this Court is whether the Tax Court correctly held that Zarin had income from discharge of indebtedness.[6] Section 108 and section 61(a)(12) of the Code set forth "the general rule that gross income includes income from the discharge of indebtedness." I.R.C. § 108(e)(1). The Commissioner argues, and the Tax Court agreed, that pursuant to the Code, Zarin did indeed recognize income from discharge of gambling indebtedness.

Under the Commissioner's logic, Resorts advanced Zarin $3,435,000 worth of chips, chips being the functional equivalent of cash. At that time, the chips were not treated as income, since Zarin recognized an obligation of repayment. In other words, Resorts made Zarin a tax-free loan. However, a taxpayer does recognize income if a loan owed to another party is cancelled, in whole or in part. I.R.C. §§ 61(a)(12); 108(e). The settlement between Zarin and Resorts, claims the Commissioner, fits neatly into the cancellation of indebtedness provisions in the Code. Zarin owed $3,435,000, paid $500,000, with the difference constituting income. Although initially persuasive, the Commissioner's position is nonetheless flawed for two reasons.

III.

Initially, we find that sections 108 and 61(a)(12) are inapplicable to the Zarin/Resorts transaction. Section 61 does not define indebtedness. On the other hand, section 108(d)(1), which repeats and further elaborates on the rule in section 61(a)(12), defines the term as any indebtedness "(A) for which the taxpayer is liable, or (B) subject to which the taxpayer holds property." I.R.C. § 108(d)(1). In order to bring the taxpayer within the sweep of the discharge of indebtedness rules, then, the IRS must show that one of the two prongs in the section 108(d)(1) test is satisfied. It has not been demonstrated that Zarin satisfies either.

Because the debt Zarin owed to Resorts was unenforceable as a matter of New Jersey state law, it is clearly not a debt "for which the taxpayer is liable." I.R.C. § 108(d)(1)(A). Liability implies a legally enforceable obligation to repay, and under New Jersey law, Zarin would have no such obligation.

Moreover, Zarin did not have a debt subject to which he held property as required by section 108(d)(1)(B). Zarin's indebtedness arose out of his acquisition of gambling chips. The Tax Court held that gambling chips were not property, but rather, "a medium of exchange within the Resorts casino" and a "substitute for cash." Alternatively, the Tax Court viewed the chips as nothing more than "the opportunity

---

6. Subsequent to the Tax Court's decision, Zarin filed a motion to reconsider, arguing that he was insolvent at the time Resorts forgave his debt, and thus, under I.R.C. section 108(a)(1)(B), could not have income from discharge of indebtedness. He did, not, however, raise that issue before the Tax Court until after it rendered its decision. The Tax Court denied the motion for reconsideration. By reason of our resolution of this case, we do not need to decide whether the Tax Court abused its discretion in denying Zarin's motion.

to gamble and incidental services . . ." *Zarin,* 92 T.C. at 1099. We agree with the gist of these characterizations, and hold that gambling chips are merely an accounting mechanism to evidence debt.

Gaming chips in New Jersey during 1980 were regarded "solely as evidence of a debt owed to their custodian by the casino licensee and shall be considered at no time the property of anyone other than the casino licensee issuing them." N.J. Admin. Code § 19:46–1.5(d) (1990). Thus, under New Jersey state law, gambling chips were Resorts' property until transferred to Zarin in exchange for the markers, at which point the chips became "evidence" of indebtedness (and not the property of Zarin).

Even were there no relevant legislative pronouncement on which to rely, simple common sense would lead to the conclusion that chips were not property in Zarin's hands. Zarin could not do with the chips as he pleased, nor did the chips have any independent economic value beyond the casino. The chips themselves were of little use to Zarin, other than as a means of facilitating gambling. They could not have been used outside the casino. They could have been used to purchase services and privileges within the casino, including food, drink, entertainment, and lodging, but Zarin would not have utilized them as such, since he received those services from Resorts on a complimentary basis. In short, the chips had no economic substance.

Although the Tax Court found that theoretically, Zarin could have redeemed the chips he received on credit for cash and walked out of the casino, *Zarin,* 92 T.C. at 1092, the reality of the situation was quite different. Realistically, before cashing in his chips, Zarin would have been required to pay his outstanding IOUs. New Jersey state law requires casinos to "request patrons to apply any chips or plaques in their possession in reduction of personal checks or Counter Checks exchanged for purposes of gaming prior to exchanging such chips or plaques for cash or prior to departing from the casino area." Since his debt at all times equaled or exceeded the number of chips he possessed, redemption would have left Zarin with no chips, no cash, and certainly nothing which could have been characterized as property.

Not only were the chips non-property in Zarin's hands, but upon transfer to Zarin, the chips also ceased to be the property of Resorts. Since the chips were in the possession of another party, Resorts could no longer do with the chips as it pleased, and could no longer control the chips' use. Generally, at the time of a transfer, the party in possession of the chips can gamble with them, use them for services, cash them in, or walk out of the casino with them as an Atlantic City souvenir. The chips therefore become nothing more than an accounting mechanism, or evidence of a debt, designed to facilitate gambling in casinos where the use of actual money was forbidden. Thus, the chips which Zarin held were not property within the meaning of I.R.C. § 108(d)(1)(B).[9]

---

9. The parties stipulated before the Tax Court that New Jersey casino "chips are property which are not negotiable and may not be used to gamble or for any other

In short, because Zarin was not liable on the debt he allegedly owed Resorts, and because Zarin did not hold "property" subject to that debt, the cancellation of indebtedness provisions of the Code do not apply to the settlement between Resorts and Zarin. As such, Zarin cannot have income from the discharge of his debt.

IV.

Instead of analyzing the transaction at issue as cancelled debt, we believe the proper approach is to view it as disputed debt or contested liability. Under the contested liability doctrine, if a taxpayer, in good faith, disputed the amount of a debt, a subsequent settlement of the dispute would be treated as the amount of debt cognizable for tax purposes. The excess of the original debt over the amount determined to have been due is disregarded for both loss and debt accounting purposes. Thus, if a taxpayer took out a loan for $10,000, refused in good faith to pay the full $10,000 back, and then reached an agreement with the lender that he would pay back only $7,000 in full satisfaction of the debt, the transaction would be treated as if the initial loan was $7,000. When the taxpayer tenders the $7,000 payment, he will have been deemed to have paid the full amount of the initially disputed debt. Accordingly, there is no tax consequence to the taxpayer upon payment.

The seminal "contested liability" case is *N. Sobel, Inc. v. Commissioner*, 40 B.T.A. 1263 (1939). In *Sobel*, the taxpayer exchanged a $21,700 note for 100 shares of stock from a bank. In the following year, the taxpayer sued the bank for rescission, arguing that the bank loan was violative of state law, and moreover, that the bank had failed to perform certain promises. The parties eventually settled the case in 1935, with the taxpayer agreeing to pay half of the face amount of the note. In the year of the settlement, the taxpayer claimed the amount paid as a loss. The Commissioner denied the loss because it had been sustained five years earlier, and further asserted that the taxpayer recognized income from the discharge of half of his indebtedness.

The Board of Tax Appeals held that since the loss was not fixed until the dispute was settled, the loss was recognized in 1935, the year of the settlement, and the deduction was appropriately taken in that year. Additionally, the Board held that the portion of the note forgiven by the bank "was not the occasion for a freeing of assets and that there was no gain ..." *Id.* at 1265. Therefore, the taxpayer did not have any income from cancellation of indebtedness.

There is little difference between the present case and *Sobel*. Zarin incurred a $3,435,000 debt while gambling at Resorts, but in court,

purpose outside the casino where they were issued." It could be argued that we are bound by this stipulation to accept the proposition that chips are property. We do not dispute the notion that chips are property, but as discussed above, they are only property in the hands of the casino. The stipulation is consistent with this idea. In fact, both parties agreed in their briefs that chips are property of the casino. Moreover, during oral arguments, both parties agreed that chips were not property when held by the gambler.

disputed liability on the basis of unenforceability. A settlement of $500,000 was eventually agreed upon. It follows from *Sobel* that the settlement served only to fix the amount of debt. No income was realized or recognized. When Zarin paid the $500,000, any tax consequence dissolved.[10]

* * *

The Commissioner argues that *Sobel* and the contested liability doctrine only apply when there is an unliquidated debt; that is, a debt for which the amount cannot be determined. * * * Since Zarin contested his liability based on the unenforceability of the entire debt, and did not dispute the amount of the debt, the Commissioner would have us adopt the reasoning of the Tax Court, which found that Zarin's debt was liquidated, therefore barring the application of *Sobel* and the contested liability doctrine. *Zarin,* 92 T.C. at 1095 (Zarin's debt "was a liquidated amount" and "[t]here is no dispute about the amount [received].").

We reject the Tax Court's rationale. When a debt is unenforceable, it follows that the amount of the debt, and not just the liability thereon, is in dispute. Although a debt may be unenforceable, there still could be some value attached to its worth. This is especially so with regards to gambling debts. In most states, gambling debts are unenforceable, and have "but slight potential. . . ." Nevertheless, they are often collected, at least in part. For example, Resorts is not a charity; it would not have extended illegal credit to Zarin and others if it did not have some hope of collecting debts incurred pursuant to the grant of credit.

Moreover, the debt is frequently incurred to acquire gambling chips, and not money. Although casinos attach a dollar value to each chip, that value, unlike money's, is not beyond dispute, particularly given the illegality of gambling debts in the first place. This proposition is supported by the facts of the present case. Resorts gave Zarin $3.4 million dollars of chips in exchange for markers evidencing Zarin's debt. If indeed the only issue was the enforceability of the entire debt, there would have been no settlement. Zarin would have owed all or nothing. Instead, the parties attached a value to the debt considerably lower than its face value. In other words, the parties agreed that given the circumstances surrounding Zarin's gambling spree, the chips he acquired might not have been worth $3.4 million dollars, but were worth something. Such a debt cannot be called liquidated, since its exact amount was not fixed until settlement.

To summarize, the transaction between Zarin and Resorts can best be characterized as a disputed debt, or contested liability. Zarin owed an unenforceable debt of $3,435,000 to Resorts. After Zarin in good faith disputed his obligation to repay the debt, the parties settled for $500,000, which Zarin paid. That $500,000 settlement fixed the amount of loss and the amount of debt cognizable for tax purposes. Since Zarin

---

10. Had Zarin not paid the $500,000 dollar settlement, it would be likely that he would have had income from cancellation of indebtedness. The debt at that point would have been fixed, and Zarin would have been legally obligated to pay it.

was deemed to have owed $500,000, and since he paid Resorts $500,000, no adverse tax consequences attached to Zarin as a result.[12]

V.

In conclusion, we hold that Zarin did not have any income from cancellation of indebtedness for two reasons. First, the Code provisions covering discharge of debt are inapplicable since the definitional requirement in I.R.C. section 108(d)(1) was not met. Second, the settlement of Zarin's gambling debts was a contested liability. We reverse the decision of the Tax Court and remand with instructions to enter judgment that Zarin realized no income by reason of his settlement with Resorts.

STAPLETON, CIRCUIT JUDGE, dissenting.

I respectfully dissent because I agree with the Commissioner's appraisal of the economic realities of this matter.

Resorts sells for cash the exhilaration and the potential for profit inherent in games of chance. It does so by selling for cash chips that entitle the holder to gamble at its casino. Zarin, like thousands of others, wished to purchase what Resorts was offering in the marketplace. He chose to make this purchase on credit and executed notes evidencing his obligation to repay the funds that were advanced to him by Resorts. As in most purchase money transactions, Resorts skipped the step of giving Zarin cash that he would only return to it in order to pay for the opportunity to gamble. Resorts provided him instead with chips that entitled him to participate in Resorts' games of chance on the same basis as others who had paid cash for that privilege. Whether viewed as a one or two-step transaction, however, Zarin received either $3.4 million in cash or an entitlement for which others would have had to pay $3.4 million.

Despite the fact that Zarin received in 1980 cash or an entitlement worth $3.4 million, he correctly reported in that year no income from his dealings with Resorts. He did so *solely* because he recognized, as evidenced by his notes, an offsetting obligation to repay Resorts $3.4 million in cash. In 1981, with the delivery of Zarin's promise to pay Resorts $500,000 and the execution of a release by Resorts, Resorts surrendered its claim to repayment of the remaining $2.9 million of the money Zarin had borrowed. As of that time, Zarin's assets were freed of his potential liability for that amount and he recognized gross income in that amount.

The only alternatives I see to this conclusion are to hold either (1) that Zarin realized $3.4 million in income in 1980 at a time when both parties to the transaction thought there was an offsetting obligation to

---

12. The Commissioner argues in the alternative that Zarin recognized $3,435,000 of income in 1980. This claim has no merit. Recognition of income would depend upon a finding that Zarin did not have cancellation of indebtedness income solely because his debt was unenforceable. We do not so hold.

Although unenforceability is a factor in our analysis, our decision ultimately hinges upon the determination that the "disputed debt" rule applied, or alternatively, that chips are not property within the meaning of I.R.C. section 108.

repay or (2) that the $3.4 million benefit sought and received by Zarin is not taxable at all. I find the latter alternative unacceptable as inconsistent with the fundamental principle of the Code that anything of commercial value received by a taxpayer is taxable unless expressly excluded from gross income.[3] I find the former alternative unacceptable as impracticable. In 1980, neither party was maintaining that the debt was unenforceable and, because of the settlement, its unenforceability was not even established in the litigation over the debt in 1981. It was not until 1989 in this litigation over the tax consequences of the transaction that the unenforceability was first judicially declared. Rather than require such tax litigation to resolve the correct treatment of a debt transaction, I regard it as far preferable to have the tax consequences turn on the manner in which the debt is treated by the parties. For present purposes, it will suffice to say that where something that would otherwise be includable in gross income is received on credit in a purchase money transaction, there should be no recognition of income so long as the debtor continues to recognize an obligation to repay the debt. On the other hand, income, if not earlier recognized, should be recognized when the debtor no longer recognizes an obligation to repay and the creditor has released the debt or acknowledged its unenforceability.

In this view, it makes no difference whether the extinguishment of the creditor's claim comes as a part of a compromise. Resorts settled for 14 cents on the dollar presumably because it viewed such a settlement as reflective of the odds that the debt would be held to be enforceable. While Zarin should be given credit for the fact that he had to pay 14 cents for a release, I see no reason why he should not realize gain in the same manner as he would have if Resorts had concluded on its own that the debt was legally unenforceable and had written it off as uncollectible.

I would affirm the judgment of the Tax Court.

Questions

1. Do you agree with the court's holding in *Zarin*? Does it represent good tax policy? In this regard, consider the following observation of Professor Daniel Shaviro with respect to the Tax Court's decision of the case (which held that Zarin had gross income):

> *Zarin* is a perplexing and difficult case, both theoretically and under existing tax law. On the one hand, few would disagree that if Zarin, instead of being able to settle, had been forced to pay Resorts the entire $3,435,000, there would be no good reason to allow him any deduction.

3. As the court's opinion correctly points out, this record will not support an exclusion under § 108(a) which relates to discharge of debt in an insolvency or bankruptcy context. Section 108(e)(5) of the Code, which excludes discharged indebtedness arising from a "purchase price adjustment" is not applicable here. Among other things, § 108(e)(5) necessarily applies only to a situation in which the debtor still holds the property acquired in the purchase money transaction. Equally irrelevant is § 108(d)'s definition of "indebtedness" relied upon heavily by the court. Section 108(d) expressly defines that term solely for the purposes of § 108 and not for the purposes of § 61(a)(12).

This may suggest that he did have income to the extent that he was able to do better than this and escape full liability for the nominal cost of his gambling.

On the other hand, the decision has an undeniable Alice in Wonderland quality. As all three dissenting opinions asked in one way or another, how can a gambler have more pleasure from gambling the more he loses? Was Zarin really $2,935,000 better off at the end than at the beginning, or was he instead, even before being taxed, the hapless victim of a pathological disorder that was hardly less disabling and destructive than, say, an addiction to crack?

Daniel Shaviro, *The Man Who Lost Too Much: Zarin v. Commissioner and the Measurement of Taxable Consumption*, 45 TAX L. REV. 215, 221–222 (1990).

2. As Judge Stapleton's dissent suggests, the *Zarin* court might have strained its interpretation of the Code to reach the result it wanted. Could the majority have used a different approach to justify its holding? For example, could the $2,935,000 difference between the amount extended to Zarin as credit and the amount Zarin paid be viewed as a non-taxable bargain purchase? See Mark J. Marroni, *Zarin v. Commissioner: Does a Gambler Have Gross Income From the Cancellation of a Casino Debt?*, 27 NEW ENG. L. REV. 993 (1993).

Wednesday 9/14
p. 122-132

E.   GAINS FROM DEALINGS IN PROPERTY

(1) THE FORMULA FOR COMPUTING GAIN

Code: IRC §§ 61(a)(3); 109; 1001(a)-(c); 1011(a); 1012; 101*7*. *Skim* IRC § 1016(a). *Review* IRC § 102.

Regs: Treas. Reg. §§ 1.61–6(a); 1.263(a)–2(e); 1.1012–1(c)(1).

Lions and Tigers and Basis—Oh My! Assume you just bought a home for $100,000. If you sold the home a few months later for $125,000, how much should you include in gross income? Section 61(a)(3) clearly states that gross income includes *gains* from dealings in property; accordingly, you would include only the $25,000 of profit in gross income. This intuitive concept, that a taxpayer does not have gross income until after he or she has first recovered his or her capital investment in the property exchanged, was first recognized by the Supreme Court in *Doyle v. Mitchell Bros. Co.*, 247 U.S. 179, 38 S.Ct. 467, 62 L.Ed. 1054 (1918). As the Court stated:

* * * it cannot be said that a conversion of capital assets invariably produces income. If sold at less than cost, it produces rather loss or outgo. Nevertheless, in many if not most cases there results a gain that properly may be accounted as a part of the "gross income" received "from all sources"; * * *. In order to determine whether there has been gain or loss, and the amount of the gain, if any, we must withdraw from the gross proceeds an amount sufficient to

restore the capital value that existed at the commencement of the period under consideration.

Id. at 184–185.

Computation of gain and loss is governed by § 1001(a). That section defines gain as the excess of the **amount realized** over the **adjusted basis** in the property exchanged. Likewise, loss is defined as the excess of the adjusted basis over the amount realized. To perform simple gain and loss computations, then, we need to know what is meant by these two terms. Put in the most pedestrian terms possible, the amount realized is the *value* of what the taxpayer *receives* in the exchange, and the adjusted basis is the *cost* of what the taxpayer *gives up* in the exchange.

	Amount Realized				Adjusted Basis	
minus	Adjusted Basis			minus	Amount Realized	
	Realized Gain				Realized Loss	
		AR	AB			
		-AB	-AR			
		RG	RL			

Amount Realized. Section 1001(b) says that the *amount realized* is "the sum of any money received plus the fair market value of the property (other than money) received." Consider these examples:

- Taxpayer sells a building in exchange for $300,000 cash.

- Taxpayer sells a building in exchange for $250,000 cash and a vehicle worth $50,000.

- Taxpayer sells a building in exchange for $100,000 cash, $100,000 worth of marketable securities, and another building worth $100,000.

In each example, Taxpayer's amount realized is $300,000. If the amount realized exceeds Taxpayer's adjusted basis in the building at the time of sale, Taxpayer will realize a gain from the transaction.

Computing the amount realized is usually the easy part. Knowing when a "realization event" has occurred can be more difficult. Recall that in *Eisner v. Macomber*, Part A, *supra*, Mrs. Macomber did not have gross income even though she received additional shares in Standard Oil Company and even though those additional shares certainly had a value at receipt. Why didn't Mrs. Macomber have gross income under § 1001? Because she did not exchange property to receive the additional shares. Section 1001 only applies when there is an *exchange* and where the taxpayer receives money or other property in the transaction (the "amount realized"). Thus one of the key concepts to understanding a taxpayer's "amount realized" is to identify when an "exchange" has occurred. Maybe the following case will be helpful in that regard.

HELVERING v. BRUUN, 309 U.S. 461, 60 S.Ct. 631, 84 L.Ed. 864 (1940).

Facts: The taxpayer leased improved real property to a tenant for a 99–year term. The lease agreement allowed the tenant to tear down any existing improvements and to construct a new building or other improvements on the property, subject to certain conditions not relevant to the case. In the fourteenth year of the lease term, the tenant removed the existing building and constructed a new one on the property. Four years later, the lease was cancelled due to the tenant's failure to pay rent and taxes according to the lease agreement. Pursuant to the lease agreement, the tenant surrendered the property, including the building and all improvements, to the taxpayer.

The value of the new building as of the date of repossession was $64,245.68. The taxpayer's adjusted basis in the old building removed by the tenant was $12,811.43. The government thus contended that the taxpayer realized a gain of $51,434.25, the difference between these two amounts.

Issue: Did the taxpayer realize a gain upon repossession of the property?

Holding: Yes.

Rationale: "While it is true that economic gain is not always taxable as income, it is settled that the realization of gain need not be in cash derived from the sale of an asset. Gain may occur as a result of exchange of property, payment of the taxpayer's indebtedness, relief from a liability, or other profit realized from the completion of a transaction. The fact that the gain is a portion of the value of property received by the taxpayer in the transaction does not negative (sic) its realization.

"Here, as a result of a business transaction, the respondent received back his land with a new building on it, which added an ascertainable amount to its value. It is not necessary to recognition of taxable gain that he should be able to sever the improvement begetting the gain from his original capital. If that were necessary, no income could arise from the exchange of property; whereas such gain has always been recognized as realized taxable gain."

Notes and Questions

1. The Court's last statement, that gains from property exchanges prove that severability is not a prerequisite to realization, is flawed. In the prototypical property exchange, where two taxpayers exchange assets, severance occurs as each taxpayer surrenders his or her interest in one asset to receive another asset. Indeed, surrender is the ultimate severance. Property exchanges thus bear little resemblance to permanent improvements to capital assets, where a taxpayer does not surrender any interest in the improved asset.

2. Notice that the Court lists four events that trigger realization of gain or loss: (1) a property exchange; (2) relief of a legal obligation owed to a third party; (3) relief of a legal obligation owed to the party receiving

property; and (4) "other" profit transactions. This is helpful guidance going forward, but do the facts of *Bruun* fit snugly within any of these descriptions? The taxpayer in *Bruun* did not surrender any interest by repossessing the leased property, so *Bruun* is not an example of a property exchange.

Nor is *Bruun* an example of a relieved obligation owed to a third party, the second "realization event" listed by the Court. This second event is based upon *Old Colony Trust Co. v. Commissioner*, Part B(1), *supra*, generally cited for the proposition that the discharge by a third person of a taxpayer's obligation to another party is income to the taxpayer. Importantly, the Court in *Old Colony Trust* made no explicit reference to "realization" and only one reference to "gain," stating in its holding that:

> The payment of the (employee-taxpayer's federal income) tax (liability) by the employers was in consideration of the services rendered by the employee and was a gain derived by the employee from his labor.

279 U.S. at 729. The result in *Old Colony Trust* is justified under two alternate theories. First, the employer's payment of the taxpayer's federal income tax liability is in substance, as the Court states, extra compensation to the taxpayer. Since all forms of compensation for services are included in income, *Old Colony Trust* is correct. Second, the taxpayer-employee in *Old Colony Trust* was enriched because he did not have to devote a portion of his cash reserves to pay his federal income tax liability. The employer's satisfaction of his obligation to pay federal income taxes frees assets that would otherwise be paid or sold to meet the obligation.

While *Old Colony Trust* is correct, it hardly controls the result in *Bruun*. For one thing, *Old Colony Trust* was about "gain derived from labor," not "gain derived from property." More significantly, *Old Colony Trust* was really about compensation for services. There is no suggestion in *Bruun* that the new building was additional rent paid by the tenant. Finally, there was no "freeing of assets" in *Bruun*, as the taxpayer was not relieved of any liability by repossessing the improved property.

As there was no indebtedness relieved in *Bruun*, the case cannot be categorized as an example of the third "realization event" described by the Court, relief of debt owed to the party receiving property from the taxpayer. This third event stems from the Court's holding in *United States v. Kirby Lumber Co.*, Part D, *supra*, that a corporate taxpayer realized gain by repurchasing its own bonds for a price less than face value. *Kirby Lumber* articulated the "freeing of assets" justification for realization by explaining that:

> the taxpayer made a clear gain. As a result of its dealings it made available $137,521.30 assets previously offset by the obligation of bonds now extinct.... The (taxpayer) has realized within the year an accession to income, if we take words in their plain popular meaning, as they should be taken here.

284 U.S. at 3. The taxpayer in *Kirby Lumber* clearly realized a gain and has the "freed assets" as resources to pay the tax liability associated with the realization event. *Kirby Lumber* is thus a proper example of realization, and the Court is right to include it in the list of realization events. Again,

though, the taxpayer in *Bruun* did not discharge a liability for less than its full amount.

By elimination, therefore, *Bruun* is the example of an "other profit transaction," the fourth realization event. In essence, *Bruun* stands for the proposition that a taxpayer realizes profit by receiving an asset with a quantifiably enhanced value in a transaction with another party. In one respect, *Bruun* is a narrow holding—only an example of the fourth realization event. On the other hand, *Bruun* could be read as a dramatic departure from the concept of realization first set forth in *Eisner v. Macomber*, Part A, *supra*. No longer is "severance" an element of realization. In substance, this may be the same as saying that Congress has the power to tax appreciation in value even in the absence of any transaction. Yet for the practical reasons identified in Part A of this Chapter, Congress has not yet tried to exert its taxing authority to this extent.

3. In evaluating the correctness and significance of *Bruun*, it is helpful to consider how an economically similar transaction would be treated. Suppose that instead of leasing the improved property to the tenant, the taxpayer hired the tenant to remove the existing building and construct a new building on the property. In consideration of the tenant's performance, the tenant would be permitted to use the building for a stated term of years. The position of the Service is that both parties have income: the tenant has income equal to the fair rental value of the property, and the taxpayer has income equal to the fair market value of the building. See *Rev. Rul. 79–24*, Part A, *supra*. This result is justified on the ground that if barter transactions are not taxed, individuals could easily circumvent the imposition of tax.

When the facts are cast in terms of a transaction, it is easy to conclude that the taxpayer has income. Is the conclusion any different in the absence of a transaction? The *Bruun* Court might say no, but perhaps the answer should be yes. If two parties enter into a formal transaction, the parties should expect that to the extent they are enriched by the transaction, they have "income" for purposes of the Sixteenth Amendment. Knowing this result, the parties can arrange their affairs so as to be able to pay the tax liability resulting from the transaction. But if a party is simply enriched without entering into a formal transaction, and thus has no ability to arrange his or her affairs in anticipation of the tax liability, the party should only have "income" when he or she has the funds to pay the tax liability associated with the enrichment. Realization should be a time when the enriched taxpayer has the means to pay the related tax; it should not force disposition of the received property.

Maybe *Bruun* is just a bad example of a "profit transaction" realization event. Bad because there was no formal transaction between the lessor and lessee vis a vis the improvements, and also because no severance occurred.

4. In response to *Bruun*, Congress enacted sections 109 and 1019. Section 109 allows the lessor of real property to exclude the value of improvements made by a tenant. But § 1019 then prohibits the taxpayer from adding the value of these improvements to the taxpayer's "basis" in the building. The significance of disallowing an adjustment to basis will become clear very soon. Although the result of *Bruun* has been overruled by §§ 109 and 1019, the broader point of the case—that the repossession of an

asset with an enhanced value from a transaction with another party is gross income—is probably still valid. But in what contexts will the *Bruun* rule apply?

* * *

Adjusted Basis. Now that we know what is meant by "amount realized," we must turn our attention to the other variable in the formula for computing gains and losses: "adjusted basis." Section 1011(a) tells us that "adjusted basis" is a taxpayer's "basis" as "adjusted." Thanks for nothing.

"Basis" is defined in § 1012 as a taxpayer's cost in acquiring property, except as provided in §§ 1001–1092. For example, we will see later that where a taxpayer inherits property from another taxpayer, the recipient taxpayer's basis is the fair market value of the property at the date of the deceased taxpayer's death. That rule is an exception to the regular rule that a taxpayer's basis is equal to cost.

The taxpayer's original "cost basis" is then "adjusted" under § 1016. We could spend many weeks just looking at the 27 adjustments to basis listed in § 1016(a). But at this preliminary point, the concept is more important than the details. Generally, a taxpayer **increases** basis for **improvements** to the property and **decreases** basis for **depreciation deductions** allowed with respect to such property.

To understand the general rule, consider a taxpayer who owns a personal residence originally acquired for $200,000 cash. If the taxpayer constructs a deck attached to the residence, the cost of the improvement is added to the taxpayer's basis in the residence. Thus, if the taxpayer spent $25,000 in adding the deck, the taxpayer's basis in the residence becomes $225,000. Notice that the taxpayer cannot deduct the $25,000 expended for materials. We will see later why this is the case (in fact, there are two reasons why a deduction would not be allowed).

Now suppose a taxpayer spends $10,000 for a photocopier that will be used in her business for probably five years before its useful life expires. Assuming for the moment that the taxpayer can deduct the cost of her photocopier (she can, as we will see), the question becomes whether she can deduct the entire cost up front or whether she has to *depreciate* the cost over the expected life of the asset. If she must depreciate the asset, she will be entitled to deduct a portion of the cost over a five-year period. As she does so, she should reduce her basis each year by the amount of the depreciation deduction. This makes sense because she is essentially getting her money back in the form of a deduction.

Notice, then, that a taxpayer's adjusted basis reflects his or her ongoing investment in an asset from a tax perspective. When the asset is sold or exchanged, therefore, the adjusted basis tells us how much unrecovered "cost" the taxpayer continues to have in the property. Only to the extent that the amount realized exceeds the unrecovered cost should the taxpayer have taxable gain.

[handwritten annotation: ONLY if the amount realized exceeds the unrecovered cost should the taxpayer have taxable gain!]

Recognition of Realized Gains. Section 1001(c) finally states that all realized gains shall be "recognized" except as provided elsewhere in the Code. To "recognize" a gain simply means to include it in computing gross income. There are several exceptions (so-called "nonrecognition provisions") scattered throughout the Code. We will study a few of them in Chapter 8. For now, it is important to keep in mind that there is an important difference between *realized* gains and *recognized* gains: not all realized gains are recognized. If a taxpayer has a realized gain, he or she should hunt for a nonrecognition provision.

The Concept of Tax Cost. Section 1012 tells us that a taxpayer's basis in property is his or her "cost." This rule works well enough when a taxpayer acquires property by cash purchase. But what is a taxpayer's basis in property acquired through an exchange? The following case sets forth the only logical answer, albeit cryptically.

PHILADELPHIA PARK AMUSEMENT CO. v. UNITED STATES

United States Court of Claims, 1954.
126 F.Supp. 184.

LARAMORE, JUDGE, delivered the opinion of the court:

[The taxpayer exchanged its title to the Strawberry Bridge to the City of Philadelphia in exchange for a 10–year extension of the taxpayer's railway franchise in Fairmount Park. Because the cost of the railway franchise extension would be deducted over its 10–year life, the taxpayer had to determine its basis in the franchise extension. In a refund action, the taxpayer took the position that the basis of the franchise extension should be the same as its basis in Strawberry Bridge (approximately $230,000). The Internal Revenue Service disagreed, disallowing the taxpayer's claim for a larger depreciation deduction.]

    * * *

This brings us to the question of what is the cost basis of the 10–year extension of taxpayer's franchise. Although defendant contends that Strawberry Bridge was either worthless or not "exchanged" for the 10–year extension of the franchise, we believe that the bridge had some value, and that the contract under which the bridge was transferred to the City clearly indicates that the one was given in consideration of the other. The taxpayer, however, has failed to show that the exchange was one [entitled to] * * * nonrecognition * * * and, therefore, it was a taxable exchange under section 112 (a) of the Code.

The gain or loss, whichever the case may have been, should have been recognized, and the cost basis * * * of the 10–year extension of the franchise was the cost to the taxpayer. The succinct statement in [§ 1012] that "the basis of property shall be the cost of such property," although clear in principle, is frequently difficult in application. One view is that the cost basis of property received in a taxable exchange is the fair market value of the property *given* in the exchange. The other view is that the cost basis of property received in a taxable exchange is the fair market value of the property *received* in the exchange. As will be seen from the cases and some of the Commissioner's rulings the Commissioner's position has not been altogether consistent on this question. The view that "cost" is the fair market value of the property given is predicated on the theory that the cost to the taxpayer is the economic value relinquished. The view that "cost" is the fair market value of the property received is based upon the theory that the term "cost" is a tax concept and must be considered in the light of the * * * prime role that the basis of property plays in determining tax liability. We believe that when the question is considered in the latter context that the cost basis of the property received in a taxable exchange is the fair market value of the property *received* in the exchange.

When property is exchanged for property in a taxable exchange the taxpayer is taxed on the difference between the adjusted basis of the property given in exchange and the fair market value of the property received in exchange. For purposes of determining gain or loss the fair market value of the property received is treated as cash and taxed accordingly. To maintain harmony with the fundamental purpose of these sections, it is necessary to consider the fair market value of the  property received as the cost basis to the taxpayer. The failure to do so would result in allowing the taxpayer a stepped-up basis, without paying a tax therefor, if the fair market value of the property received is less than the fair market value of the property given, and the taxpayer would be subjected to a double tax if the fair market value of the property received is more than the fair market value of the property given. By holding that the fair market value of the property received in a taxable exchange is the cost basis, the above discrepancy is avoided and the basis of the property received will equal the adjusted basis of the property given plus any gain recognized, or that should have been recognized, or minus any loss recognized, or that should have been recognized.

Therefore, the cost basis of the 10–year extension of the franchise was its fair market value on August 3, 1934, the date of the exchange. The determination of whether the cost basis of the property received is its fair market value or the fair market value of the property given in exchange therefor, although necessary to the decision of the case, is generally not of great practical significance because the value of the two properties exchanged in an arms-length transaction are either equal in fact, or are presumed to be equal. The record in this case indicates that the 1934 exchange was an arms-length transaction and, therefore, if the value of the extended franchise cannot be determined with reasonable accuracy, it would be reasonable and fair to assume that the value of Strawberry Bridge was equal to the 10–year extension of the franchise. The fair market value of the 10–year extension of the franchise should be established but, if that value cannot be determined with reasonable certainty, the fair market value of Strawberry Bridge should be established and that will be presumed to be the value of the extended franchise. This value cannot be determined from the facts now before us since the case was prosecuted on a different theory.

The taxpayer contends that the market value of the extended franchise or Strawberry Bridge could not be ascertained and, therefore, it should be entitled to carry over the undepreciated cost basis of the bridge as the cost of the extended franchise * * *. If the value of the extended franchise or bridge cannot be ascertained with a reasonable degree of accuracy, the taxpayer is entitled to carry over the undepreciated cost of the bridge as the cost basis of the extended franchise. *Helvering v. Tex–Penn Oil Co., 300 U. S. 481, 499; Gould Securities Co. v. United States, 96 F. 2d 780.* However, it is only in rare and extraordinary cases that the value of the property exchanged cannot be ascertained with reasonable accuracy. We are presently of the opinion that either the value of the extended franchise or the bridge can be determined with a reasonable degree of accuracy. Although the value of the extended franchise may be difficult or impossible to ascertain because of the nebulous and intangible characteristics inherent in such property, the value of the bridge is subject to more exact measurement. Consideration may be given to expert testimony on the value of comparable bridges, Strawberry Bridge's reproduction cost and its undepreciated cost, as well as other relevant factors.

Therefore, because we deem it equitable, judgment should be suspended and the question of the value of the extended franchise on August 3, 1934, should be remanded to the Commissioner of this court for the taking of evidence and the filing of a report thereon.

     * * *

Note

There are three morals to the *Philadelphia Park* case. First, following a taxable exchange, the taxpayer's basis in property received in the exchange is always equal to the fair market value of the property received. This is because any gain recognized by the taxpayer in the exchange is part of his or her "cost" to acquire the property received in the exchange. Suppose, for example, that a taxpayer sells a painting that cost $20 to an unrelated individual in exchange for a rug worth $100. The taxpayer realizes and recognizes an $80 gain from the exchange ($100 amount realized, less $20 basis in the painting). If the taxpayer sold the rug the next day for its $100 fair market value, should the taxpayer have to recognize another gain? Of course not! Yet if the taxpayer's basis in the rug is his or her "cost" of the rug, how can we ensure that a subsequent sale for $100 will produce no taxable gain? *Philadelphia Park* teaches us that the taxpayer's basis in the rug has to be its fair market value at the time of receipt (here, $100). In effect, the taxpayer's "cost" to acquire the rug is two-fold: (1) giving up a painting that cost $20 (an out-of-pocket cost), and (2) incurring an $80 gain from the exchange of the painting for the rug (a "tax cost"). If we do not reflect the tax cost in the taxpayer's basis, the $80 gain would be taxed a second time when the rug is sold, and that double taxation of the $80 gain would be manifestly unfair.

The second moral is that every taxable year stands alone. The exchange of the bridge and the railway franchise extension at issue in *Philadelphia Park* occurred in a year prior to the year in which the taxpayer sought the depreciation deduction that was the subject of the dispute between the taxpayer and the Service. The court concluded that the taxpayer "should have * * * recognized" a gain on the exchange of the bridge in the prior year. For that reason, the court determined that the taxpayer had a fair market value basis in the franchise extension received in the exchange. In fact, however, the taxpayer did not include the gain in gross income! The court knew this, and yet it still concluded that the proper solution was to pretend as if the taxpayer had correctly included the gain in gross income for the prior year. The idea of basing the current year's tax consequences based upon what *should* have happened in the prior year (and not necessarily what *actually* happened in the prior year) is an accepted tenet of the federal income tax. We will study this "every year stands alone" concept in more detail in Chapter 6.

The third moral is that where the taxpayer does not know and cannot readily ascertain the value of the property received in the exchange, the taxpayer may look to the value of the property surrendered in the exchange. Absent facts to the contrary, we assume that all transactions occur at arms'-length. Thus, if you don't know the value of what you received in the exchange, you can assume that the value of the property is equal to the value of the property you gave in exchange for it. As the *Philadelphia Park* court observes, it will only be in "rare and extraordinary cases" where the value of the property received cannot be determined with reference to the value of the property surrendered in the exchange. In such cases, the taxpayer may use the basis of the surrendered property as the basis of the acquired property.

* * *

✗ **Problem 3–17** ✗

Anne owns a five-acre lot that she purchased several years ago for $15,000. In the current year, Anne sold two acres to an unrelated purchaser for $10,000.

(a) What are the federal income tax consequences of the sale to Anne?

(b) Would your answer to (a) change if the 3 acres retained by Anne were swamp land, worth only one-third of the value of the 5–acre lot?

✗ **Problem 3–18** ✗

In Year One, Bob purchased Boeing stock through a discount brokerage firm. Bob purchased 100 shares at a cost of $40 per share. In addition, Bob paid total commissions of $100 to the brokerage firm on the purchase. In Year Three, Bob sold the Boeing shares for $5,000 (or $50 per share). On the sale, Bob paid another $100 in commissions to the brokerage firm. What are the federal income tax consequences of the Year Three sale to Bob?

Problem 3–19

On January 1, Year One, Connie purchased a small office building for $100,000. Of the total purchase price, $80,000 was allocable to the building and $20,000 was allocable to the land. Connie rented out the office space immediately and properly elected to depreciate the building using a 40–year useful life under § 168(g). Accordingly, she claimed a depreciation deduction of $2,000 attributable to the building in Year One.

In Year Two, however, because of a math error, Connie only deducted $1,500 in depreciation instead of the $2,000 to which she was entitled.

On January 1, Year Three, Connie spent $60,000 to construct an additional building on the same property. Under § 168(g), the annual depreciation deduction attributable to the new building was $1,500, so Connie claimed a total depreciation deduction of $3,500 in Year Three ($2,000 for the old building and $1,500 for the new one).

On January 1, Year Four, Connie sold the entire property (the land plus the two buildings) to an unrelated purchaser for $160,000 cash. What are the federal income tax consequences of this sale to Connie?

Friday - p.132-13↓   * * *

(2) SPECIAL BASIS RULES

Code: IRC §§ 1014(a)(1), (b), (e), (f); 1015(a), (d). *Skim* IRC § 1022.~~~~

Regs: Treas. Reg. §§ 1.1001–1(e); 1.1015–4.

Basis of Property Received by Gift, Bequest, Devise, or Inheritance. We know that a taxpayer's basis in property is his or her cost to acquire such property. See § 1012. Taxpayers who receive property by gift or inheritance have incurred no cost, so their cost basis in such property would be zero. Sections 1014 and 1015 contain exceptions to the cost basis rule for these situations.

Section 1015 applies to *inter vivos* gifts. Generally, the donee takes the donor's adjusted basis in the property. Thus, when Parent gives Child an asset worth $5,000 in which Parent has a basis of $3,000, Child will include nothing in gross income (remember the § 102(a) exclusion) but Child's basis in the asset will be $3,000. This is referred to as a **transferred basis** or, sometimes, as **carryover basis**. Since the donor does not pay income tax upon making a gift with appreciated property, it makes sense to preserve any lurking gain with the donee—and a transferred basis does just that.

The same is not true for lurking losses. Suppose that Parent's basis in the gifted property described above was $8,000. In computing loss from the subsequent sale or exchange of the gifted property, Child's basis is only $5,000. Can you find the authority for this rule? So while untaxed gains are preserved, undeducted losses are not.

The applicable basis rules under § 1015(a) may be summarized as follows:

	Donee's Basis for computing GAIN	Donee's Basis for computing LOSS
FMV > or = to Donor's AB at time of gift	Donor's AB	Donor's AB
FMV < Donor's AB at time of gift	Donor's AB	FMV (loss does not carry over)

Section 1014 applies to property acquired from a decedent. Under § 1014(a), such property shall have a basis to the recipient equal to the value of the property at the date of the decedent's death. This is referred to as a **stepped-up basis**, since in most cases, the property is worth more than the decedent's basis and is certainly worth more than the recipient's cost basis (zero). Of course, it is entirely possible that the fair market value of property at the decedent's death is less than the decedent's basis in such property. In those cases, basis is "stepped-down" to fair market value. For example, if Decedent dies holding an asset worth $20,000, and if Decedent's will bequeaths the asset to Beneficiary, Beneficiary's basis is $20,000, regardless of Decedent's adjusted basis in the asset.

What is the rationale for the stepped-up basis at death? One explanation is that a carryover basis would be hard to administer with respect to gifts from dead people, for evidence of the donor's basis may be known only to the now-deceased donor. As a matter of convenience, then, a fair market value basis gives the asset a fresh start in the recipient's hands. A second justification for a stepped-up basis reflects the thought that the donor is likely not engaging in some notorious form of tax evasion by dying, so there is not a compelling reason to require a carryover basis. A third justification, now fading, is that there is already an excise tax imposed on the transfer of wealth at death—the federal estate tax. To impose an income tax burden in addition to the estate tax might be excessive.

Under current law, the federal estate tax is scheduled to be repealed completely in 2010 (though only for one year, curiously). At the same time, § 1014 will be repealed, and a modified form of carryover basis will be introduced. See §§ 1014(f) and 1022. It is no accident that the § 1014 step-up will be repealed at the same time the federal estate tax is repealed. Interestingly, however, only about one or two percent of all decedents face liability for federal estate taxes. Yet the beneficiaries of *all* decedents get the benefit of a stepped-up basis under § 1014. If the existence of the federal estate tax is a central justification for the § 1014 basis step-up, should the benefit of § 1014 be limited to those who receive bequests and inheritances from estates that actually pay federal estate tax?

* * *

✗ *Problem 3-20* ✗

Jack owns Blackacre, a parcel of real property. Jack purchased Black-acre for $10,000 in 1990. Earlier this year, Jack received an unsolicited offer to purchase Blackacre for $50,000. Jack rejected the offer. Discuss the federal income tax consequences of each of the following transactions.

(a) Jack owns a small business. To reward his assistant, Benny, for his many years of loyalty and hard work to the company, Jack gives Blackacre to Benny. Benny, weary of investments in real estate, immediately sells Black-acre to an unrelated purchaser for $50,000.

(b) Jack falls in love with Rose while on a cruise in the Atlantic Ocean. As a symbol of his love, Jack transfers title in Blackacre to Rose. Rose, unimpressed by the gesture, sells Blackacre for $50,000 to an unrelated purchaser.

(c) Same as (b), except that the value of Blackacre when deeded to Rose was only $7,000. Rose sold the property to an unrelated purchaser for $6,000.

(d) Same as (c), except that Rose held on to the property for several months and then sold it to an unrelated purchaser for $8,500.

(e) Same as (b), except that prior to the transfer to Rose, Jack had utilized all of his "applicable exclusion amount" for federal gift tax purposes. Accordingly, Jack paid $25,000 in federal gift taxes on the transfer to Rose.

(f) Jack wanted to transfer Blackacre to his oldest child, Jill, so that she could build a home. Jill insisted on paying for the property, but Jack did not want to charge his child full price. Accordingly, he sold Blackacre to Jill for $20,000. Jill, in need of cash shortly after the purchase, sold Blackacre to an unrelated purchaser for $50,000.

(g) Jack died. In his will, he left Blackacre to Jill. Three months after his death, Jill took advantages of a surge in the real estate market and sold Blackacre to an unrelated purchaser for $60,000.

(h) Jack transferred Blackacre to a "revocable living trust." Under its terms, Jack received all of the trust income. Jack also retained the right to terminate the trust any time for any reason. Jack died only six months after establishing the trust, and the value of Blackacre at that time was $50,000. As provided in the trust agreement, Blackacre passed to Jill. Jill then sold Blackacre to an unrelated purchaser for $50,000.

(i) Here's a little ditty about Jack and his wife, Diane: upon learning that Diane had a terminal illness, Jack transferred Blackacre to Diane. Diane died eight months later. Under her will, her entire estate (including Blackacre, still worth $50,000) passed to Jack. One month later, Jack sold Blackacre to an unrelated purchaser for $50,000.

* * *

(3) TRANSFERS IN SATISFACTION OF AN OBLIGATION

Code: None.

Regs: None.

We know from § 1001(b) that a taxpayer's "amount realized" includes the amount of cash and the fair market value of any property received in an exchange. But other "accessions to wealth" can constitute part of an "amount realized" as well. In *Kenan v. Commissioner*, 114 F.2d 217 (2d Cir. 1940), the court held that when the trustee of a trust transferred appreciated stock (stock with a value in excess of its cost basis) to a beneficiary in satisfaction of a $5 million pecuniary bequest, the trust had a realized and recognized gain. Notice that the trust did not receive cash or property, but the court still found a "gain." The United States Supreme Court tackled a similar issue in the following case.

UNITED STATES v. DAVIS, 370 U.S. 65, 82 S.Ct. 1190, 8 L.Ed.2d 335 (1962).

Facts: In 1955, the taxpayer, Thomas Crawley Davis, transferred 500 shares of stock in the E.I. du Pont de Nemours & Co. to his spouse pursuant to a separation agreement signed in 1954. In exchange, "the then Mrs. Davis" agreed to relinquish all of her claims and marital rights against the taxpayer's property. The taxpayer's basis in the 500 shares of stock transferred to his spouse was approximately $75,000, and the transferred shares were worth $82,000.

Issues: (1) Was this transfer of stock in exchange for a release of marital rights a taxable event? (2) If so, what is the taxpayer's "amount realized" from the transaction?

Holdings: (1) The transfer is a taxable event. (2) The "amount realized" from the exchange is the fair market value of the released marital rights, which in this case would be equal to the value of the stock transferred.

Rationale: The transfer was a taxable event because the taxpayer received consideration from his spouse in exchange for the stock. Under the separation agreement, the taxpayer was required to make a payment to his spouse in exchange for her release. By choosing to discharge that contractual obligation with appreciated property, the taxpayer realizes the benefit of that appreciation. In this case, he was able to discharge an $82,000 obligation to his spouse by transferring property that only cost him $75,000. He thus realizes the benefit of the $7,000 appreciation in making this transfer.

As to the computation of the "amount realized" from the transfer, the Court concluded that the lower court erred: "[The lower court] found that there was no way to compute the fair market value of these marital rights and that it was thus impossible to determine the taxable gain realized by the taxpayer. We believe this conclusion was erroneous. It must be assumed, we think, that the parties acted at arm's length and that they judged the marital rights to be equal in value to the property for which they were exchanged. There was no evidence to the contrary here. * * * To be sure there is much to be said of the argument that such an assumption is weakened by the emotion, tension and practical necessities involved in divorce negotiations and the property settlements arising therefrom. However, once it is recognized that the transfer was a taxable event, it is more consistent with the general purpose and scheme of the taxing statutes to make a rough approximation of the gain realized thereby than to ignore altogether its tax consequences. Moreover, if the transaction is to be considered a taxable event as to the husband, the [lower court's] position leaves up in the air the wife's basis for the property received. In the context of a taxable transfer by the husband, all indicia point to a 'cost' basis for this property in the hands of the wife. Yet under the [lower court's] position her cost for this property, *i.e.*, the value of the marital rights relinquished therefor, would be indeterminable, and on subsequent disposition of the property she might suffer inordinately over the Commissioner's assessment which she would have the burden of proving erroneous. Our present holding that the value of these rights is ascertainable eliminates this problem; for the same calculation that determines the amount received by the husband fixes the amount given up by the wife, and this figure, *i.e.*, the market value of the property transferred by the husband, will be taken by her as her tax basis for the property received."

Notes and Questions

1. Upset with the result of *Davis*, Congress enacted § 1041. Section 1041 generally provides nonrecognition for all property transfers between spouses (or between former spouses when incident to a divorce, as described in Chapter 9). If § 1041 had been effect during the property transfers in *Davis*, the taxpayer would not have recognized gain upon the transfer of the appreciated stock. Although § 1041 effectively overrules the specific result of *Davis*, the more general principle of the case—that a taxpayer recognizes a gain on the transfer of appreciated property in satisfaction of a legal obligation—is still valid.

2. Notice that the Court assumes that the ex-husband's "amount realized" is equal to the value of the securities he surrendered pursuant to the property settlement. This assumption is based upon one of the morals of the *Philadelphia Park* case.

* * *

⚔ **Self-Assessment Question** ⚔

(Solutions to Self–Assessment Questions are set forth in Appendix 3.)

SAQ 3–5. Consider the facts in *United States v. Davis*. What basis does "the then Mrs. Davis" have in the stock acquired from her ex-husband? The facts state that the value of the securities at the time of the transfer was approximately $82,000 and that the ex-husband's basis was about $75,000. Suppose she sold all of the shares for $85,000 one year following the transfer. How much gain should she include in gross income?

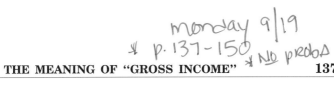
F. AN INTRODUCTION TO THE FLAVOR OF IN-COME

Code: *Skim* IRC §§ 1(h); 1221(a); 1222.

Regs: None.

Although all persons are created equal, not all income is taxed equally. Save for one brief period from 1986 to 1990, Congress has accorded preferential status to so-called "capital gains" since 1921. You probably know from following current events or from your own financial affairs that certain capital gains receive preferential tax treatment. In a very complex way, § 1(h)(1)–(10) sets forth that preference. Very generally, wealthy taxpayers will only pay a tax of 15 percent on net capital gains for the year. Less affluent taxpayers only pay a five percent tax on net capital gains, and, beginning in 2008, that five-percent rate is reduced to zero percent. Since ordinary income is taxed to the wealthiest taxpayers at 35 percent and to less affluent taxpayers at ten percent, the capital gains preference is quite significant. No wonder most individual taxpayers prefer capital gains to ordinary income.

Capital Assets. This, of course, takes us to our first inquiry: what is a "capital gain?" Simply put, a capital gain is the gain from the sale or exchange of a "capital asset." And the definition of a "capital asset" is set forth in § 1221(a). Notice that § 1221(a) is another example of a "negative definition:" it defines capital assets by listing eight types of assets which are *not* capital assets. Anything not described in § 1221(a)(1)–(8) is, therefore, a capital asset. As a general rule, property held for investment or personal-use purposes (and not for the conduct of an active business) usually qualifies as a capital asset.

In order to qualify for the preferential tax rates of § 1(h), an individual must have a "net capital gain," defined in § 1222(11) as the excess of "net long-term capital gains" over "net short-term capital losses." In order to have a net long-term capital gain, the taxpayer must have held the capital asset for more than one year. See § 1222(1)–(4). Thus, the preferential rates will apply only to gains from the sale or exchange of capital assets held for more than one year. If an individual sells a capital asset for a gain but only held the asset for one year or less, the gain will be taxed as ordinary income.

An extended discussion of the preferential treatment for capital gains awaits us in Chapter 7. For now, it is sufficient to note that taxpayers prefer long-term capital gains to other types of gains.

Reasons for the Preference. Because long-term capital gains are taxed at a lower rate, taxpayers often engage in transactions designed to take advantage of this preference. It is therefore appropriate at this point to ask why long-term capital gains deserve special treatment. Historically, preferential rates were justified on the grounds of **inflation**. Because basis is not adjusted to take inflation into account, it was thought that a preferential rate for long-term capital gains was necessary to accommodate for the hardships of taxing gains due to inflation instead of real economic growth. Another rationale for the preferential rate relates to the concept of **bunching**. Very rarely does a capital asset explode in value. In most cases, the gain accrues over the course of the taxpayer's holding period. Yet because of the realization rule, the taxpayer does not recognize this appreciation as it accrues. Instead, when the taxpayer sells the capital asset, all of the gain from the asset is bunched into the year of sale. In a progressive tax system, bunching all of the gain into a single year increases the risk that the gain will be taxed at a higher rate. By limiting the tax rate applicable to long-term capital gains, the rate of tax may better approximate the amount of tax that would have been collected if the gain had been taxed as it accrued. A more modern justification for the preferential tax treatment of long-term capital gains relates to taxpayer behavior. Congress hopes that keeping a low tax rate for capital gains will **stimulate savings and investment activities** by taxpayers. Furthermore, the lower rate might give a taxpayer an incentive to sell the capital asset instead of holding it until death in order to obtain a stepped-up basis for the taxpayer's beneficiary. Curing this **lock-up** problem is thought to benefit the economy.

Not everyone accepts these justifications. Some argue that there are better ways to account for inflation than providing preferential tax treatment at the time of sale. Even if a lower tax rate is the best way to account for inflation, there seems to be no reason to limit the preference to gains from capital assets. And the bunching rationale may not be very persuasive considering that taxpayers generally control the timing of the realization event giving rise to the gain. Others challenge the thought that a lower tax rate for long-term capital gains motivates taxpayers to sell capital assets.

But no matter whether the justifications for preferential tax treatment of long-term capital gains are persuasive, some form of special taxation is probably now a permanent feature of the modern federal income tax. For more on the tax policy aspects of according preferential treatment to capital gains, *see* Noel B. Cunningham & Deborah H. Schenk, *The Case for a Capital Gains Preference*, 48 TAX L. REV. 319 (1993); Daniel Halperin, *A Capital Gains Preference is not EVEN a Second–Best Solution*, 48 TAX L. REV. 381 (1993); Deborah M. Weiss, *Can Capital Tax Policy Be Fair? Stimulating Savings Through Differential Tax Rates*, 78 CORNELL L. REV. 206 (1993); Bonner Menking, Comment, *Making Sense of Capital Gains Taxation*, 39 U. KAN. L. REV. 175 (1990); Charles E. Walker & Mark A. Bloomfield, *The Case for the Restoration of a Capital Gains Tax Differential*, 43 TAX NOTES 1019 (May 22, 1989).

History of the Preferential Treatment of Capital Gains. In 1921, Congress limited the tax rate applicable to capital gains held for more than two years to 12.5 percent. The preferential rate was quite significant because the highest marginal rate applicable to ordinary income was 73 percent. In 1934, Congress adjusted the preference from a lower rate to a deduction: the longer the taxpayer held the capital asset, the less the amount of gain subject to taxation. In fact, if a taxpayer held a capital asset for more than a decade, only 30 percent of the gain was subject to taxation. Given that the highest marginal tax rate at that time was 79 percent, the exclusion of 70 percent of the gain from the sale of a capital asset effectively capped the tax rate applicable to entire capital gain to 23.7 percent (30 percent of 79 percent).

By 1938, Congress reverted to taxing the entire gain at a preferential rate. While the maximum marginal tax rate on ordinary income reached 81.1 percent, long-term capital gains were taxed at a mere 15 percent. In 1942, tax rates were increased. The maximum rate for ordinary income grew to 91 percent, and the preferential rate for capital gains grew to 25 percent.

In 1969, Congress again moved away from a preferential rate for capital gains in favor of a deduction. Congress allowed taxpayers to exclude one-half of their net capital gains. Effectively, then, all taxpayers enjoyed a preferential tax rate on capital gains. Taxpayers in the highest tax bracket (70 percent) were able to limit their tax rate on capital gains to 35 percent. In 1978, Congress increased the deduction from 50 percent to 60 percent (meaning taxpayers in the highest tax bracket incurred tax of 28 percent on their capital gains).

The Tax Reform Act of 1986 repealed all preferences for capital gains. The maximum tax rate applicable to both ordinary income and capital gains was set at 28 percent. The preferential rates for capital gains were restored in 1990 when the maximum tax rate on ordinary income grew to 31 percent (despite the millions who read the first President Bush's lips to say "No new taxes"). Because the 28 percent rate was retained for capital gains, a preference had been reenacted, although it applied only to taxpayers in the highest tax bracket.

The 28 percent preferential rate became even more significant in 1993 when the maximum rate applicable to ordinary income grew to 39.6 percent. By this point, the preference applied to taxpayers in the three highest brackets (31 percent, 36 percent, and 39.6 percent) but not taxpayers in the lower brackets. In 1997, Congress reduced the capital gains tax rate to 20 percent, and it also gave taxpayers in the 15 percent bracket a preferential rate (10 percent).

In the Jobs and Growth Tax Relief Reconciliation Act of 2003, the preferential tax rate applicable to a taxpayer's "net capital gain" was reduced from 20 percent (10 percent in the case of taxpayers in the lower tax brackets) to 15 percent (five percent in the case of taxpayers in the lower brackets). In addition, the five percent rate for taxpayers in the lower brackets will be reduced to zero in 2008. These reduced rates are currently scheduled to remain in place through the end of 2010. Absent further action by Congress, the capital gains rates are set to revert to their pre-2003 levels in 2011. Again, a more detailed analysis of the current preferential rate scheme for capital gains will be presented in Chapter 7.

Extending the Preferential Rates to Dividend Income. As a result of the 2003 Act, the preferential rates for capital gains now also apply to "qualified dividend income," defined as most dividends from domestic corporations and even certain dividends from foreign corporations organized in countries that have income tax treaties with the United States. There is no requirement that the dividends come from earnings that were previously subject to tax or from earnings attributable to dates after the enactment of the 2003 Act—all distributions from current or accumulated earnings and profits will qualify for the reduced rates.

The preferential rate for dividend income is designed to alleviate the "double taxation" of corporate income. As separate legal entities, corporations are also separate taxable entities. Thus, corporations pay federal income on their taxable incomes, just like individuals. See § 11. When a corporation distributes its after-tax income to its shareholders, that distribution is considered a "dividend" to the shareholders that must be included in gross income. See § 61(a)(7). In effect, then, corporate income is taxed twice: once at the corporate level, and again at the shareholder level upon a dividend distribution.

Though double taxation of corporate profits has long been an accepted feature of subchapter C (the Code provisions applicable to most corporations), increasing political pressure to ease double taxation led to the enactment of the preferential rates for dividends in § 1(h)(11). Of course, double taxation is not unique to corporations. When an employer pays taxable wages to an employee who then uses the after-tax income to pay for other services like day care, home repairs, and the like, the wages are being taxed twice: once to the employee and again in the hands of the service-provider. Because the tax is paid by two different parties, however, the double taxation is an acceptable result. Double taxation is improper where the *same* taxpayer pays two taxes on the same income. Yet corporations and shareholders are two distinct taxpayers, so the perils of double taxation are less compelling. Still, to the extent other business forms do not experience double taxation, Congress felt the pressure to provide a similar benefit to those who operate in the corporate form, too.

A New Flavor for a New Millennium: Qualified Production Activities Income. The centerpiece of the American Jobs Creation Act of 2004 was the repeal of the special benefit given to export sales through the exclusion of "extraterritorial income" (ETI) under former § 114. Former § 114 excluded ETI from gross income to the extent it constituted "qualifying foreign trade income." Only two days after the enactment of § 114 in 2000, the European Union complained to the World Trade Organization that the ETI exclusion was a prohibited export subsidy. In August, 2001, a WTO panel concluded that the European Union was correct, and in January, 2002, a WTO Appellate Body affirmed. It took two years, but Congress finally repealed the ETI exclusion with the 2004 Jobs Act. Interestingly, repeal was phased-in over three years. Taxpayers received a full exclusion for ETI in 2004, an 80% exclusion in 2005, and a 60% exclusion in 2006. Complete repeal therefore did not occur until 2007.

Having repealed the exclusion for ETI, Congress felt strong pressure to provide some offsetting benefit for domestic manufacturers. Its solution was the creation of a new deduction related to domestic production that will ultimately allow manufacturers to deduct nine percent of their "qualified production activities income" (QPAI). This deduction, authorized in § 199, effectively reduces the rate of taxation on QPAI, making QPAI another form of income with a special flavor. The phase-in of the full deduction can be summarized as follows:

Year(s)	QPAI Deduction Percentage	Effective Top Tax Rate
2004	None	35%
2005–2006	3%	33.95%
2007–2009	6%	32.9%
2010 and on	9%	31.85%

QPAI is defined as that portion of the taxpayer's taxable income equal to the excess of "domestic production gross receipts" (DPGR) over (i) cost of goods sold, (ii) deductions directly allocable to DPGR, and (iii) a proportionate share of other, general deductions like overhead and administrative expenses. DPGR, in turn, is defined as the taxpayer's gross receipts from (i) any lease, rental, license, sale, exchange or other disposition of tangible personal property, computer software, or sound recording that is produced or grown in whole or in significant part within the United States; (ii) a "qualified film" (a non-sexually explicit film where more than half of the compensation related to its production was paid for services performed within the United States); (iii) electricity, natural gas, or potable water produced by the taxpayer in the United States; (iv) construction performed within the United States; or (v) engineering or architectural services performed in the United States for construction projects within the United States.

G. AN INTRODUCTION TO THE TIMING OF INCOME

Code: None.

Regs: None.

It's About Time. With respect to the concept of "income," we have nearly come full circle. We know generally what is included and excluded from income (including statutory inclusions and exclusions), as well as a little about the different flavors of income. Put another way, we have considered *"what"* is income. Except for the realization rule, we have not, until now, considered *"when"* an item of income arises.

Arguably, the "when" issue is more important than the "what" issue. Although we will cover timing issues in much more detail in Chapter 6, it is appropriate to get a sense of some of the fundamental concepts related to the timing of gross income now. We will consider the claim of right doctrine and the taxation of advance payments. To understand why these concepts are so important, however, we must begin with a basic discussion of the time value of money.

Time Value of Money. Would you rather have one dollar today or one dollar a year from today? Easy—you'll take the dollar now. If you invest the dollar, you can earn interest and have more than one dollar a year from now. If you use the dollar to buy something that will produce more income down the road, having the dollar now will give you an extra year to make that additional income. If you simply consume the dollar, you get the benefit of that consumption now instead of waiting for a year from now to get the same utility. So no matter what you do with the dollar, it makes more sense to take the current dollar instead of the future dollar.

That is the heart of the time value of money: a current dollar is worth more than a future dollar. When it comes to costs, the opposite rule applies: a future cost is better than a current cost. Suppose you owe one dollar to a friend. If you have the choice to repay the dollar today or one year from today, you would prefer to pay one year from today. Your preference is based on the fact that you know you can hold onto the dollar for another year and use that dollar to make more income. If you have to repay the dollar today, you lose the chance to make the additional cash with that dollar.

For this reason, taxpayers prefer to defer the tax on gross income as long as possible. By deferring the tax, taxpayers can use the funds that will pay the tax for a longer period to make more money. Suppose, for example, that a taxpayer performs $500 in services for another in December of Year One. If the taxpayer receives payment in Year One, the $500 payment will be included in gross income on the Year One return, meaning the tax on that payment will be due on April 15, Year Two. Let's assume for purposes of this example that the taxpayer is subject to a flat federal income tax of 30 percent. The $150 tax on the $500 of income would be due and payable on April 15, Year Two.

If the taxpayer delays payment until January of Year Two, however, the $500 of income will be reported on the taxpayer's return for Year Two, meaning the $150 of tax is not paid until April 15 of Year Three. By waiting one more month for the payment, the taxpayer can defer the tax liability for twelve months! The taxpayer has an extra twelve months to invest the $150 that would otherwise be paid to the federal government. If the taxpayer earns a measly five percent interest on the deferred tax liability of $150 over that twelve months, the taxpayer will earn an extra $7.50 by waiting until Year Two for payment. Add a few zeros to the dollar amount in this example (or increase the interest rate to eight or ten percent, the historical average rate of growth for investments in blue-chip companies over the long term), and the wisdom for deferring gross income becomes even more apparent.

As the enforcer of federal income tax laws, the Service must watch for taxpayers who try to manipulate the timing of their incomes in ways that drain the fisc too easily. The claim of right doctrine and the rules for advance payments are two tools that assist the Service in these efforts.

Claim of Right Doctrine. We know that if a taxpayer has an obligation to repay an amount received from another person, the taxpayer does not have gross income. The transaction is properly characterized as a "loan" absent some other facts. What if the obligation to repay is *contingent* on the occurrence of certain events? Just by coincidence, the following case deals with this very issue.

NORTH AMERICAN OIL CONSOLIDATED v. BURNET

United States Supreme Court, 1932.
286 U.S. 417, 52 S.Ct. 613, 76 L.Ed. 1197.

MR. JUSTICE BRANDEIS delivered the opinion of the Court.

The question for decision is whether the sum of $171,979.22, received by the North American Oil Consolidated in 1917, was taxable to it as income of that year.

The money was paid to the company under the following circumstances: Among many properties operated by it in 1916 was a section of oil land, the legal title to which stood in the name of the United States. Prior to that year, the government, claiming also the beneficial ownership, had instituted a suit to oust the company from possession; and on February 2, 1916, it secured the appointment of a receiver to operate the property, or supervise its operations, and to hold the net income thereof. The money paid to the company in 1917 represented the net profits which had been earned from that property in 1916 during the receivership. The money was paid to the receiver as earned. After entry by the District Court in 1917 of the final decree dismissing the bill, the money was paid, in that year, by the receiver to the company. The government took an appeal * * * to the Circuit Court of Appeals. In 1920, that court affirmed the decree. In 1922, a further appeal to this Court was dismissed by stipulation.

The income earned from the property in 1916 had been entered on the books of the company as its income. It had not been included in its original return of income for 1916; but it was included in an amended return for that year which was filed in 1918. Upon auditing the company's income and profits tax returns for 1917, the Commissioner of Internal Revenue determined a deficiency based on other items. The company appealed to the Board of Tax Appeals. There, in 1927, the Commissioner prayed that the deficiency already claimed should be increased so as to include a tax on the amount paid by the receiver to the company in 1917. The Board held that the profits were taxable to the receiver as income of 1916; and hence made no finding whether the company's accounts were kept on the cash receipts and disbursements basis or on the accrual basis. The Circuit Court of Appeals held that the profits were taxable to the company as income of 1917, regardless of whether the company's returns were made on the cash or on the accrual basis. This Court granted a writ of certiorari.

It is conceded that the net profits earned by the property during the receivership constituted income. The company contends that they should have been reported by the receiver for taxation in 1916; that, if not returnable by him, they should have been returned by the company for 1916, because they constitute income of the company accrued in that year; and that, if not taxable as income of the company for 1916, they were taxable to it as income for 1922, since the litigation was not finally terminated in its favor until 1922.

First. The income earned in 1916 and impounded by the receiver in that year was not taxable to him, because he was the receiver * * *. * * *

Second. The net profits were not taxable to the company as income of 1916. For the company was not required in 1916 to report as income an amount which it might never receive. There was no constructive receipt of the profits by the company in that year, because at no time during the year was there a right in the company to demand that the receiver pay over the money. Throughout 1916 it was uncertain who would be declared entitled to the profits. It was not until 1917, when the District Court entered a final decree vacating the receivership and dismissing the bill, that the company became entitled to receive the money. Nor is it material, for the purposes of this case, whether the company's return was filed on the cash receipts and disbursements basis, or on the accrual basis. In neither event was it taxable in 1916 on account of income which it had not yet received and which it might never receive.

Third. The net profits earned by the property in 1916 were not income of the year 1922—the year in which the litigation with the government was finally terminated. They became income of the company in 1917, when it first became entitled to them and when it actually received them. If a taxpayer receives earnings under a claim of right and without restriction as to its disposition, he has received income which he is required to return, even though it may still be claimed that he is not entitled to retain the money, and even though he may still be adjudged liable to restore its equivalent. If in 1922 the government had prevailed, and the company had been obliged to refund the profits received in 1917, it would have been entitled to a deduction from the profits of 1922, not from those of any earlier year.

Affirmed.

Note

The "claim of right" doctrine from *North American Oil* requires, among other things, that a taxpayer receive income "under a claim of right." Yet we learned in *James v. United States*, Part A, *supra*, that a similar result applies to those who obtain income illegally. The *James* Court applied the rule from *North American Oil*, but it had to re-word the rule to make it fit:

When a taxpayer acquires earnings, lawfully or unlawfully, without the consensual recognition, express or implied, of an obligation to repay and without restriction as to their disposition, "he has received income which he is required to return, even though it may still be claimed that he is not entitled to retain the money, and even though he may still be adjudged liable to restore its equivalent. *North American Oil v. Burnet* * * *."

This has to be the result, or else cheaters prosper. But after *James*, is it proper to refer to the rule as the "claim of right" doctrine?

* * *

↓ advance payment = income in year received

Advance Payments and the Issue of Deposits. We will learn in Chapter 6 that advance payments of income are included in gross income even though the payments have not been earned at the time of receipt. For example, if an individual receives an advance payment for services, the full amount of the advance payment is gross income even though the services may extend beyond the year of receipt. This is true even though financial accounting rules may permit or require deferral of income until the services are performed. But as we saw earlier, "loans" are not gross income. So how are *deposits* taxed? Some deposits smell like advance payments, and others smell like loans. Of course, the recipient of the deposit will want to treat the deposit like a loan. But hopes don't always pan out. The following case tackles this tricky issue.

* deposit = not income unless and until the holder has a right to retain it.

COMMISSIONER v. INDIANAPOLIS POWER & LIGHT COMPANY

United States Supreme Court, 1990.
493 U.S. 203, 110 S.Ct. 589, 107 L.Ed.2d 591.

JUSTICE BLACKMAN delivered the opinion of the Court.

Respondent Indianapolis Power & Light Company (IPL) requires certain customers to make deposits with it to assure payment of future bills for electric service. Petitioner Commissioner of Internal Revenue contends that these deposits are advance payments for electricity and therefore constitute taxable income to IPL upon receipt. IPL contends otherwise.

I

IPL is a regulated Indiana corporation that generates and sells electricity in Indianapolis and its environs. It keeps its books on the accrual and calendar year basis. During the years 1974 through 1977, approximately 5% of IPL's residential and commercial customers were required to make deposits "to insure prompt payment," as the customers' receipts stated, of future utility bills. These customers were selected because their credit was suspect. Prior to March 10, 1976, the deposit requirement was imposed on a case-by-case basis. IPL relied on a credit test but employed no fixed formula. The amount of the required deposit ordinarily was twice the customer's estimated monthly bill. IPL paid 3%

accrued basis

interest on a deposit held for six months or more. A customer could obtain a refund of the deposit prior to termination of service by requesting a review and demonstrating acceptable credit. The refund usually was made in cash or by check, but the customer could choose to have the amount applied against future bills.

In March 1976, IPL amended its rules governing the deposit program. Under the amended rules, the residential customers from whom deposits were required were selected on the basis of a fixed formula. The interest rate was raised to 6% but was payable only on deposits held for 12 months or more. A deposit was refunded when the customer made timely payments for either 9 consecutive months, or for 10 out of 12 consecutive months so long as the 2 delinquent months were not themselves consecutive. A customer could obtain a refund prior to that time by satisfying the credit test. As under the previous rules, the refund would be made in cash or by check, or, at the customer's option, applied against future bills. Any deposit unclaimed after seven years was to escheat to the State.

IPL did not treat these deposits as income at the time of receipt. Rather, as required by state administrative regulations, the deposits were carried on its books as current liabilities. Under its accounting system, IPL recognized income when it mailed a monthly bill. If the deposit was used to offset a customer's bill, the utility made the necessary accounting adjustments. Customer deposits were not physically segregated in any way from the company's general funds. They were commingled with other receipts and at all times were subject to IPL's unfettered use and control. It is undisputed that IPL's treatment of the deposits was consistent with accepted accounting practice and applicable state regulations.

Upon audit of respondent's returns for the calendar years 1974 through 1977, the Commissioner asserted deficiencies. * * * The Commissioner took the position that the deposits were advance payments for electricity and therefore were taxable to IPL in the year of receipt. * * * IPL disagreed and filed a petition in the United States Tax Court for redetermination of the asserted deficiencies.

In a reviewed decision, with one judge not participating, a unanimous Tax Court ruled in favor of IPL. 88 T.C. 964 (1987). * * * It noted, among other things, that only 5% of IPL's customers were required to make deposits; that the customer rather than the utility controlled the ultimate disposition of a deposit; and that IPL consistently treated the deposits as belonging to the customers, both by listing them as current liabilities for accounting purposes and by paying interest. *Id.*, at 976–978.

The United States Court of Appeals for the Seventh Circuit affirmed the Tax Court's decision. 857 F.2d 1162 (1988). The court stated that "the proper approach to determining the appropriate tax treatment of a customer deposit is to look at the primary purpose of the deposit based on all the facts and circumstances. . . ." *Id.*, at 1167. The court appeared to place primary reliance, however, on IPL's obligation to pay interest on ~~+ look to primary purpose of the deposit~~ the deposits. It asserted that "as the interest rate paid on a deposit to secure income begins to approximate the return that the recipient would be expected to make from 'the use' of the deposit amount, the deposit begins to serve purposes that comport more squarely with a security deposit." *Id.,* at 1169. Noting that IPL had paid interest on the customer deposits throughout the period in question, the court upheld, as not clearly erroneous, the Tax Court's determination that the principal purpose of these deposits was to serve as security rather than as prepayment of income. *Id.,* at 1170.

　　* * *

II

We begin with the common ground. IPL acknowledges that these customer deposits are taxable as income upon receipt if they constitute *advance payments* for electricity to be supplied.[3] The Commissioner, on his part, concedes that customer deposits that secure the performance of non-income-producing covenants—such as a utility customer's obligation to ensure that meters will not be damaged—are not taxable income. And it is settled that receipt of a loan is not income to the borrower. * * * IPL, stressing its obligation to refund the deposits with interest, asserts that the payments are similar to loans. The Commissioner, however, contends that a deposit which serves to secure the payment of future income is properly analogized to an advance payment for goods or services. See *Rev. Rul. 72–519,* 1972–2 Cum. Bull. 32, 33 ("[W]hen the purpose of the deposit is to guarantee the customer's payment of amounts owed to the creditor, such a deposit is treated as an advance payment, but when the purpose of the deposit is to secure a property interest of the taxpayer the deposit is regarded as a true security deposit").

In economic terms, to be sure, the distinction between a loan and an advance payment is one of degree rather than of kind. A commercial loan, like an advance payment, confers an economic benefit on the recipient: a business presumably does not borrow money unless it believes that the income it can earn from its use of the borrowed funds will be greater than its interest obligation. Even though receipt of the money is subject to a duty to repay, the borrower must regard itself as better off after the loan than it was before. The economic benefit of a loan, however, consists entirely of the opportunity to earn income on the use of the money prior to the time the loan must be repaid. And in that context our system is content to tax these earnings as they are realized.

---

3. This Court has held that an accrual-basis taxpayer is required to treat advance payments as income in the year of receipt. See *Schlude v. Commissioner,* 372 U.S. 128, 83 S.Ct. 601, 9 L.Ed.2d 633 (1963); *American Automobile Assn. v. United States,* 367 U.S. 687, 81 S.Ct. 1727, 6 L.Ed.2d 1109 (1961); *Automobile Club of Michigan v.* *Commissioner,* 353 U.S. 180, 77 S.Ct. 707, 1 L.Ed.2d 746 (1957). These cases concerned payments—nonrefundable fees for services—that indisputably constituted income; the issue was *when* that income was taxable. Here, in contrast, the issue is whether these deposits, as such, are income at all.

The recipient of an advance payment, in contrast, gains both immediate use of the money (with the chance to realize earnings thereon) *and* the opportunity to make a profit by providing goods or services at a cost lower than the amount of the payment.

The question, therefore, cannot be resolved simply by noting that respondent derives some economic benefit from receipt of these deposits. Rather, the issue turns upon the nature of the rights and obligations that IPL assumed when the deposits were made. In determining what sort of economic benefits qualify as income, this Court has invoked various formulations. It has referred, for example, to "undeniable accessions to wealth, clearly realized, and over which the taxpayers have complete dominion." *Commissioner v. Glenshaw Glass Co.,* 348 U.S. 426, 431, 75 S.Ct. 473, 477, 99 L.Ed. 483 (1955). It also has stated: "When a taxpayer acquires earnings, lawfully or unlawfully, without the consensual recognition, express or implied, of an obligation to repay and without restriction as to their disposition, 'he has received income. . . .' " *James v. United States,* 366 U.S., at 219, 81 S.Ct., at 1055, quoting *North American Oil Consolidated v. Burnet,* 286 U.S. 417, 424, 52 S.Ct. 613, 615, 76 L.Ed. 1197 (1932). IPL hardly enjoyed "complete dominion" over the customer deposits entrusted to it. Rather, these deposits were acquired subject to an express "obligation to repay," either at the time service was terminated or at the time a customer established good credit. So long as the customer fulfills his legal obligation to make timely payments, his deposit ultimately is to be refunded, and both the timing and method of that refund are largely within the control of the customer.

The Commissioner stresses the fact that these deposits were not placed in escrow or segregated from IPL's other funds, and that IPL therefore enjoyed unrestricted use of the money. That circumstance, however, cannot be dispositive. After all, the same might be said of a commercial loan; yet the Commissioner does not suggest that a loan is taxable upon receipt simply because the borrower is free to use the funds in whatever fashion he chooses until the time of repayment. In determining whether a taxpayer enjoys "complete dominion" over a given sum, the crucial point is not whether his use of the funds is unconstrained during some interim period. The key is whether the taxpayer has some guarantee that he will be allowed to keep the money. IPL's receipt of these deposits was accompanied by no such guarantee.

Nor is it especially significant that these deposits could be expected to generate income greater than the modest interest IPL was required to pay. Again, the same could be said of a commercial loan, since, as has been noted, a business is unlikely to borrow unless it believes that it can realize benefits that exceed the cost of servicing the debt. A bank could hardly operate profitably if its earnings on deposits did not surpass its interest obligations; but the deposits themselves are not treated as income. Any income that the utility may earn through use of the deposit money of course is taxable, but the prospect that income will be generated provides no ground for taxing the principal.

The Commissioner's advance-payment analogy seems to us to rest upon a misconception of the value of an advance payment to its recipient. An advance payment, like the deposits at issue here, concededly protects the seller against the risk that it would be unable to collect money owed it after it has furnished goods or services. But an advance payment does much more: it protects against the risk that the purchaser will back out of the deal before the seller performs. From the moment an advance payment is made, the seller is assured that, so long as it fulfills its contractual obligation, the money is its to keep. Here, in contrast, a customer submitting a deposit made no commitment to purchase a specified quantity of electricity, or indeed to purchase any electricity at all.[6] IPL's right to keep the money depends upon the customer's purchase of electricity, and upon his later decision to have the deposit applied to future bills, not merely upon the utility's adherence to its contractual duties. Under these circumstances, IPL's dominion over the fund is far less complete than is ordinarily the case in an advance-payment situation.

The Commissioner emphasizes that these deposits frequently will be used to pay for electricity, either because the customer defaults on his obligation or because the customer, having established credit, chooses to apply the deposit to future bills rather than to accept a refund. When this occurs, the Commissioner argues, the transaction, from a cash-flow standpoint, is equivalent to an advance payment. In his view this economic equivalence mandates identical tax treatment.

Whether these payments constitute income when received, however, depends upon the parties' rights and obligations *at the time the payments are made*. The problem with petitioner's argument perhaps can best be understood if we imagine a loan between parties involved in an ongoing commercial relationship. At the time the loan falls due, the lender may decide to apply the money owed him to the purchase of goods or services rather than to accept repayment in cash. But this decision does not mean that the loan, when made, was an advance payment after all. The lender in effect has taken repayment of his money (as was his contractual right) and has chosen to use the proceeds for the purchase of goods or services from the borrower. Although, for the sake of convenience, the parties may combine the two steps, that decision does not blind us to the fact that in substance two transactions are involved. It is this element of choice that distinguishes an advance payment from a loan. Whether these customer deposits are the economic equivalents of advance payments, and therefore taxable upon receipt, must be determined by

6. A customer, for example, might terminate service the day after making the deposit. Also, IPL's dominion over a deposit remains incomplete even after the customer begins buying electricity. As has been noted, the deposit typically is set at twice the customer's estimated monthly bill. So long as the customer pays his bills in a timely fashion, the money he owes the utility (for electricity used but not yet paid for) almost always will be less than the amount of the deposit. If this were not the case, the deposit would provide inadequate protection. Thus, throughout the period the deposit is held, at least a portion is likely to be money that IPL has no real assurance of ever retaining.

examining the relationship between the parties at the time of the deposit. The individual who makes an advance payment retains no right to insist upon the return of the funds; so long as the recipient fulfills the terms of the bargain, the money is its to keep. The customer who submits a deposit to the utility, like the lender in the previous hypothetical, retains the right to insist upon repayment in cash; he may *choose* to apply the money to the purchase of electricity, but he assumes no obligation to do so, and the utility therefore acquires no unfettered "dominion" over the money at the time of receipt.

* * *

We recognize that IPL derives an economic benefit from these deposits. But a taxpayer does not realize taxable income from every event that improves his economic condition. A customer who makes this deposit reflects no commitment to purchase services, and IPL's right to retain the money is contingent upon events outside its control. We hold that such dominion as IPL has over these customer deposits is insufficient for the deposits to qualify as taxable income at the time they are made.

The judgment of the Court of Appeals is affirmed.

It is so ordered.

* * *

Self-Assessment Question

(Solutions to Self–Assessment Questions are set forth in Appendix 3.)

SAQ 3–6. Mr. Roper is a landlord. Mr. Roper requires tenants to pay a "security deposit" in an amount equal to one month of rent. The lease agreement form used by Mr. Roper clearly states that the deposits will be used to pay for any property damage by a tenant and/or to cover unpaid rent. If a tenant makes all payments on time and causes no property damage, the lease agreement requires Mr. Roper to return the deposit with no interest. In most cases, tenants ask Mr. Roper to apply the deposit to the last month's rent (or, without making advance arrangements, they simply fail to pay the last month's rent). As a result, Mr. Roper rarely pays the deposit back to a tenant. Does Mr. Roper have gross income upon receipt of a deposit?

H. ASSIGNMENT OF INCOME

Wednesday
p. 150–169

Code: None.

Regs: None.

Before we leave the concept of income, we must deal with the issue of *who* must pay tax on income. In the usual case, the proper taxpayer for income is easy to identify. We tax the worker on his or her wages, and we tax the owner of income from capital. But taxpayers, often a clever bunch, devise ways to deflect taxable income to another taxpayer (one usually in a lower tax bracket). Sometimes those techniques should work, but in other cases the tax avoidance motive permeates the technique to the extent that the system would lose credibility if it were respected. The "assignment of income" doctrine tries to determine the proper party to tax income.

Income from Services. Generally, income from services is taxed to the party who performed the services. That rule "stems" from the case of *Lucas v. Earl* below (you might appreciate the pun more after you read the case).

LUCAS v. EARL

United States Supreme Court, 1930.
281 U.S. 111, 50 S.Ct. 241, 74 L.Ed. 731.

Mr. Justice Holmes delivered the opinion of the Court.

This case presents the question whether the respondent, Earl, could be taxed for the whole of the salary and attorney's fees earned by him in the years 1920 and 1921, or should be taxed for only a half of them in view of a contract with his wife which we shall mention. The Commissioner of Internal Revenue and the Board of Tax Appeals imposed a tax upon the whole, but their decision was reversed by the Circuit Court of Appeals. A writ of certiorari was granted by this court.

By the contract, made in 1901, Earl and his wife agreed "that any property either of us now has or may hereafter acquire * * * in any way, either by earnings (including salaries, fees, etc.), or any rights by contract or otherwise, during the existence of our marriage, or which we or either of us may receive by gift, bequest, devise, or inheritance, and all the proceeds, issues, and profits of any and all such property shall be treated and considered, and hereby is declared to be received, held, taken, and owned by us as joint tenants, and not otherwise, with the right of survivorship." The validity of the contract is not questioned, and we assume it to be unquestionable under the law of the State of California, in which the parties lived. Nevertheless we are of opinion that the Commissioner and Board of Tax Appeals were right.

* * * A very forcible argument is presented to the effect that the statute seeks to tax only income beneficially received, and that taking the question more technically the salary and fees became the joint property of Earl and his wife on the very first instant on which they were received. We well might hesitate upon the latter proposition, because however the matter might stand between husband and wife he was the only party to the contracts by which the salary and fees were earned, and it is somewhat hard to say that the last step in the performance of those contracts could be taken by anyone but himself alone. But this case is not to be decided by attenuated subtleties. It turns on the import and reasonable construction of the taxing act. There is no doubt that the statute could tax salaries to those who earned them and

provide that the tax could not be escaped by anticipatory arrangements and contracts however skillfully devised to prevent the salary when paid from vesting even for a second in the man who earned it. That seems to us the import of the statute before us and we think that no distinction can be taken according to the motives leading to the arrangement by which the fruits are attributed to a different tree from that on which they grew.

Judgment reversed.

THE CHIEF JUSTICE took no part in this case.

* * *

TESCHNER v. COMMISSIONER, 38 T.C. 1003 (1962).

Facts: The taxpayer entered a contest for an education annuity. The contest rules restricted eligibility for the prize to individuals who were under a stipulated age. Because the taxpayer was too old to be eligible for the prize, the taxpayer listed the taxpayer's daughter as the beneficiary on the contest entry form. Lo and behold, the taxpayer's entry was selected as a winner.

Issue: Who should be taxed on the value of the prize: the taxpayer or the taxpayer's daughter?

Holding: The taxpayer's daughter should be taxed on the value of the prize.

Rationale: The taxpayer should not be taxed on the income because the taxpayer never had the right to claim to the prize according to the rules of the contest. Thus, the taxpayer had not "earned" the income, even though the taxpayer was the individual that performed the services that gave rise to the right to the income.

* * *

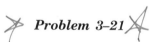

Problem 3–21

Olive Greene–Beane prepares federal income tax returns for her clients. In each of the alternative scenarios described below, determine who should be taxed on the fees received.

(a) Olive performs all of the work on the returns, but she asks her clients to pay one-third of the total fee to Olive's son, Stu. Most of Olive's clients comply with her request.

(b) Same as (a), except that Stu assists Olive in the completion of every client's tax return. Olive reasonably estimates that one-third of the total work on each return is performed by Stu, so she asks clients to pay him one-third of the total fee.

(c) Olive performs all of the work on the returns, but she refuses to bill the clients for her work. Many of Olive's clients feel compelled to pay something for her services, but Olive tells them only to give the money to a good cause. Several of Olive's clients pay reasonable sums directly to Stu.

* * *

Income from Property. The "fruit-and-tree" metaphor established in *Lucas v. Earl* was developed further by the Court in *Helvering v. Horst*, below. *Horst* is the seminal case relating to the application of the assignment of income doctrine to income from property.

HELVERING v. HORST

United States Supreme Court, 1940.
311 U.S. 112, 61 S.Ct. 144, 85 L.Ed. 75.

MR. JUSTICE STONE delivered the opinion of the Court.

The sole question for decision is whether the gift, during the donor's taxable year, of interest coupons detached from the bonds, delivered to the donee and later in the year paid at maturity, is the realization of income taxable to the donor.

In 1934 and 1935 respondent, the owner of negotiable bonds, detached from them negotiable interest coupons shortly before their due date and delivered them as a gift to his son who in the same year collected them at maturity. The Commissioner ruled that * * * the interest payments were taxable, in the years when paid, to the respondent donor who reported his income on the cash receipts basis. The circuit court of appeals reversed the order of the Board of Tax Appeals sustaining the tax. We granted certiorari because of the importance of the question in the administration of the revenue laws and because of an asserted conflict in principle of the decision below with that of *Lucas v. Earl*, 281 U.S. 111, 50 S.Ct. 241, 74 L.Ed. 731, and with that of decisions by other circuit courts of appeals.

The court below thought that as the consideration for the coupons had passed to the obligor, the donor had, by the gift, parted with all control over them and their payment, and for that reason the case was distinguishable from *Lucas v. Earl, supra* * * *.

The holder of a coupon bond is the owner of two independent and separable kinds of right. One is the right to demand and receive at maturity the principal amount of the bond representing capital investment. The other is the right to demand and receive interim payments of interest on the investment in the amounts and on the dates specified by the coupons. Together they are an obligation to pay principal and interest given in exchange for money or property which was presumably the consideration for the obligation of the bond. Here respondent, as owner of the bonds, had acquired the legal right to demand payment at maturity of the interest specified by the coupons and the power to command its payment to others which constituted an economic gain to him.

Admittedly not all economic gain of the taxpayer is taxable income. From the beginning the revenue laws have been interpreted as defining "realization" of income as the taxable event rather than the acquisition of the right to receive it. And "realization" is not deemed to occur until the income is paid. But the decisions and regulations have consistently recognized that receipt in cash or property is not the only characteristic of realization of income to a taxpayer on the cash receipts basis. Where the taxpayer does not receive payment of income in money or property realization may occur when the last step is taken by which he obtains the fruition of the economic gain which has already accrued to him. *Old Colony Trust Co. v. Commissioner,* 279 U.S. 716, 49 S.Ct. 499, 73 L.Ed. 918 * * *.

In the ordinary case the taxpayer who acquires the right to receive income is taxed when he receives it, regardless of the time when his right to receive payment accrued. But the rule that income is not taxable until realized has never been taken to mean that the taxpayer, even on the cash receipts basis, who has fully enjoyed the benefit of the economic gain represented by his right to receive income, can escape taxation because he has not himself received payment of it from his obligor. The rule, founded on administrative convenience, is only one of postponement of the tax to the final event of enjoyment of the income, usually the receipt of it by the taxpayer, and not one of exemption from taxation where the enjoyment is consummated by some event other than the taxpayer's personal receipt of money or property. This may occur when he has made such use or disposition of his power to receive or control the income as to procure in its place other satisfactions which are of economic worth. The question here is, whether because one who in fact receives payment for services or interest payments is taxable only on his receipt of the payments, he can escape all tax by giving away his right to income in advance of payment. If the taxpayer procures payment directly to his creditors of the items of interest or earnings due him, * * * or if he sets up a revocable trust with income payable to the objects of his bounty, * * * he does not escape taxation because he did not actually receive the money.

Underlying the reasoning in these cases is the thought that income is "realized" by the assignor because he, who owns or controls the source of the income, also controls the disposition of that which he could have received himself and diverts the payment from himself to others as the means of procuring the satisfaction of his wants. The taxpayer has equally enjoyed the fruits of his labor or investment and obtained the satisfaction of his desires whether he collects and uses the income to procure those satisfactions, or whether he disposes of his right to collect it as the means of procuring them.

Although the donor here, by the transfer of the coupons, has precluded any possibility of his collecting them himself he has nevertheless, by his act, procured payment of the interest, as a valuable gift to a member of his family. Such a use of his economic gain, the right to receive income, to procure a satisfaction which can be obtained only by the expenditure of money or property, would seem to be the enjoyment of the income whether the satisfaction is the purchase of goods at the corner grocery, the payment of his debt there, or such non-material satisfactions as may result from the payment of a campaign or community chest contribution, or a gift to his favorite son. Even though he never receives the money he derives money's worth from the disposition of the coupons which he has used as money or money's worth in the procuring of a satisfaction which is procurable only by the expenditure of money or money's worth. The enjoyment of the economic benefit accruing to him by virtue of his acquisition of the coupons is realized as completely as it would have been if he had collected the interest in dollars and expended them for any of the purposes named.

In a real sense he has enjoyed compensation for money loaned or services rendered and not any the less so because it is his only reward for them. To say that one who has made a gift thus derived from interest or earnings paid to his donee has never enjoyed or realized the fruits of his investment or labor because he has assigned them instead of collecting them himself and then paying them over to the donee, is to affront common understanding and to deny the facts of common experience. Common understanding and experience are the touchstones for the interpretation of the revenue laws.

The power to dispose of income is the equivalent of ownership of it. The exercise of that power to procure the payment of income to another is the enjoyment and hence the realization of the income by him who exercises it. * * *

power to dispose = ownership

* * *

Reversed.

The separate opinion of Mr. Justice McREYNOLDS.

* * *

The unmatured coupons given to the son were independent negotiable instruments, complete in themselves. Through the gift they became at once the absolute property of the donee, free from the donor's control and in no way dependent upon ownership of the bonds. No question of actual fraud or purpose to defraud the revenue is presented.

* * *

The CHIEF JUSTICE and MR. JUSTICE ROBERTS concur in this opinion.

* * *

Transferring Trees With Ripe Fruit. *Horst* suggests that while transfers of fruit may not be effective to shift the tax on such fruit to another, transfers of the entire tree may be effective to deflect taxation of the fruit to another. The following case reveals that this rule has limitations.

SALVATORE v. COMMISSIONER

United States Tax Court, 1970.
T.C. Memo. 1970–30.

FEATHERSTON, JUDGE:

Respondent determined a deficiency in petitioner's income tax for 1963 in the amount of $31,016.60. The only issue presented for decision is whether petitioner is taxable on all or only one-half of the gain realized on the sale of certain real property in 1963.

FINDINGS OF FACT

* * *

Petitioner's husband operated an oil and gas service station in Greenwich, Connecticut, for a number of years prior to his death on October 7, 1948. His will, dated December 6, 1941, [bequeathed all of his estate, including the service station, to Petitioner.]

* * *

For several years after her husband's death petitioner's three sons, Amedeo, Eugene, and Michael, continued operating the service station with the help of her daughter Irene, who kept the books of the business. Sometime prior to 1958, however, Michael left the service station to undertake other business endeavors; and in 1958 Eugene left to enter the real estate business, leaving Amedeo alone to manage and operate the service station.

* * *

The land on which the service station was located became increasingly valuable. Several major oil companies from time to time made purchase proposals, which were considered by members of the family. Finally, in the early summer of 1963 representatives of Texaco, Inc. (hereinafter Texaco), approached Amedeo regarding the purchase of the service station property. Petitioner called a family conference and asked for advice on whether the property should be sold. Realizing that Amedeo alone could not operate the station at peak efficiency, petitioner and her children decided to sell the property if a reasonable offer could be obtained.

Amedeo continued his negotiations with Texaco and ultimately received an offer of $295,000. During the course of the negotiations Eugene discovered that tax liens in the amount of $8,000 were outstanding against the property. In addition, there was an outstanding mortgage, securing a note held by Texaco, on which approximately $50,000 remained unpaid. The family met again to consider Texaco's offer.

As a result of the family meeting (including consultation with petitioner's daughter Geraldine, who lived in Florida), it was decided that the proposal should be accepted and that the proceeds should be used, first, to satisfy the tax liens and any other outstanding liabilities. Second, petitioner was to receive $100,000, the estimated amount needed to generate income for her life of about $5,000 per year—the approximate equivalent of the $100 per week she previously received out of the service station income. Third, the balance was to be divided equally among the five children. To effectuate this family understanding, it was agreed that petitioner would first convey a one-half interest in the property to the children and that deeds would then be executed by petitioner and the children conveying the property to Texaco.

On July 24, 1963, petitioner formally accepted Texaco's offer by executing an agreement to sell the property to Texaco for $295,000, the latter making a down payment of $29,500. Subsequently, on August 28, 1963, petitioner executed a warranty deed conveying an undivided one-half interest in the property to her five children. This deed was received for record on September 6, 1963. By warranty deeds dated August 28 and 30, 1963, and received for record on September 6, 1963, petitioner and her five children conveyed their interest in the property to Texaco; Texaco thereupon tendered $215,582.12, the remainder of the purchase price less the amount due on the outstanding mortgage.

Petitioner filed a Federal gift tax return for 1963, reporting gifts made to each of her five children on August 1, 1963, of a 1/10 interest in the property and disclosing a gift tax due in the amount of $10,744.35.

After discharge of the mortgage and the tax liens the remaining proceeds of the sale (including the down payment) amounted to $237,082, of which one-half, $118,541, was paid to petitioner. From the other half of the proceeds the gift tax of $10,744.35 was paid and the balance was distributed to the children.

In her income tax return for 1963 petitioner reported as her share of the gain from the sale of the service station property a long-term capital gain of $115,063 plus an ordinary gain of $665. Each of the children reported in his 1963 return a proportionate share of the balance of the gain.

In the notice of deficiency respondent determined that petitioner's gain on the sale of the service station property was $238,856, all of which was taxable as long-term capital gain. Thereafter each of petitioner's children filed protective claims for refund of the taxes which they had paid on their gains from the sale of the service station property.

OPINION

The only question is whether petitioner is taxable on all or only one-half of the gain realized from the sale of the service station property. This issue must be resolved in accordance with the following principle stated by the Supreme Court in *Commissioner v. Court Holding Co.*, 324 U.S. 331, 334 (1945):

> The incidence of taxation depends upon the substance of a transaction. The tax consequences which arise from gains from a sale of property are not finally to be determined solely by the means employed to transfer legal title. Rather, the transaction must be viewed as a whole, and each step, from the commencement of negotiations to the consummation of the sale, is relevant. A sale by one person cannot be transformed for tax purposes into a sale by another by using the latter as a conduit through which to pass title. To permit the true nature of a transaction to be disguised by mere formalisms, which exist solely to alter tax liabilities, would seriously impair the effective administration of the tax policies of Congress.

* * *

The evidence is unmistakably clear that petitioner owned the service station property prior to July 24, 1963, when she contracted to sell it to Texaco. Her children doubtless expected ultimately to receive the property or its proceeds, either through gifts or inheritance, and petitioner may have felt morally obligated to pass it on to them. But at that time the children "held" no property interest therein. Petitioner's subsequent conveyance, unsupported by consideration, of an undivided one-half interest in the property to her children—all of whom were fully aware of her prior agreement to sell the property—was merely an intermediate step in the transfer of legal title from petitioner to Texaco: Petitioner's children were only "conduit(s) through which to pass title." That petitioner's conveyance to the children may have been a bona fide completed gift prior to the transfer of title to Texaco, as she contends, is immaterial in determining the income tax consequences of the sale, for the form of a transaction cannot be permitted to prevail over its substance. In substance, petitioner made an anticipatory assignment to her children of one-half of the income from the sale of the property.

The artificiality of treating the transaction as a sale in part by the children is confirmed by the testimony by petitioner's witnesses that the sum retained by her from the sale was a computed amount—an amount sufficient to assure that she would receive income in the amount of approximately $5,000 annually. If the sales price had been less, petitioner would have retained a larger percentage of the proceeds; if more, we infer, she would have received a smaller percentage. While the children's desire to provide for their mother's care and petitioner's willingness to share the proceeds of her property with her children during her lifetime may be laudable, her tax liabilities cannot be altered by a rearrangement of the legal title after she had already contracted to sell the property to Texaco.

All the gain from sale of the service station property was taxable to petitioner. * * *

Decision will be entered for the respondent.

* * *

Tax Planning Versus Tax Avoidance. We know from *Horst* that transfers of the rights to income may not be effective in shifting the tax burden to the recipient of the income. Should the same rule apply to situations where the transferred income rights are *sold* (not gifted) to the recipient? The following case addresses that issue.

ESTATE OF STRANAHAN v. COMMISSIONER

United States Court of Appeals, Sixth Circuit, 1973.
472 F.2d 867.

PECK, CIRCUIT JUDGE.

This appeal comes from the United States Tax Court, which partially denied appellant estate's petition for a redetermination of a deficiency in the decedent's income tax for the taxable period January 1, 1965 through November 10, 1965, the date of decedent's death.

The facts before us are briefly recounted as follows: On March 11, 1964, the decedent, Frank D. Stranahan, entered into a closing agreement with the Commissioner of Internal Revenue Service (IRS) under which it was agreed that decedent owed the IRS $754,815.72 for interest due to deficiencies in federal income, estate and gift taxes regarding several trusts created in 1932. Decedent, a cash-basis taxpayer, paid the amount during his 1964 tax year. Because his personal income for the 1964 tax year would not normally have been high enough to fully absorb the large interest deduction, decedent accelerated his future income to avoid losing the tax benefit of the interest deduction. To accelerate the income, decedent executed an agreement dated December 22, 1964, under which he assigned to his son, Duane Stranahan, $122,820 in anticipated stock dividends from decedent's Champion Spark Plug Company common stock (12,500 shares). At the time both decedent and his son were employees and shareholders of Champion. As consideration for this assignment of future stock dividends, decedent's son paid the decedent $115,000 by check dated December 22, 1964. The decedent thereafter directed the transfer agent for Champion to issue all future dividend checks to his son, Duane, until the aggregate amount of $122,820 had been paid to him. Decedent reported this $115,000 payment as ordinary income for the 1964 tax year and thus was able to deduct the full interest payment from the sum of this payment and his other income. During decedent's taxable year in question, dividends in the total amount of $40,050 were paid to and received by decedent's son. No part of the $40,050 was reported as income in the return filed by decedent's estate for this period. Decedent's son reported this dividend income on his own return as ordinary income subject to the offset of his basis of $115,000, resulting in a net amount of $7,282 of taxable income.

Subsequently, the Commissioner sent appellant (decedent's estate) a notice of deficiency claiming that the $40,050 received by the decedent's son was actually income attributable to the decedent. After making an adjustment which is not relevant here, the Tax Court upheld the deficiency in the amount of $50,916.78. The Tax Court concluded that decedent's assignment of future dividends in exchange for the present discounted cash value of those dividends "though conducted in the form of an assignment of a property right, was in reality a loan to [decedent] masquerading as a sale and so disguised lacked any business purpose; and, therefore, decedent realized taxable income in the year 1965 when the dividend was declared paid."

As pointed out by the Tax Court, several long-standing principles must be recognized. First, under Section 451(a) * * *, a cash basis taxpayer ordinarily realizes income in the year of receipt rather than the year when earned. Second, a taxpayer who assigns future income for consideration in a bona fide commercial transaction will ordinarily realize ordinary income in the year of receipt. Third, a taxpayer is free to arrange his financial affairs to minimize his tax liability;[2] thus, the presence of tax avoidance motives will not nullify an otherwise bona fide transaction. We also note there are no claims that the transaction was a sham, the purchase price was inadequate or that decedent did not actually receive the full payment of $115,000 in tax year 1964. And it is agreed decedent had the right to enter into a binding contract to sell his right to future dividends.

The Commissioner's view regards the transaction as merely a temporary shift of funds, with an appropriate interest factor, within the family unit. He argues that no change in the beneficial ownership of the stock was effected and no real risks of ownership were assumed by the son. Therefore, the Commissioner concludes, taxable income was realized not on the formal assignment but rather on the actual payment of the dividends.

It is conceded by taxpayer that the sole aim of the assignment was the acceleration of income so as to fully utilize the interest deduction. *Gregory v. Helvering*, 293 U.S. 465, 55 S.Ct. 266, 79 L.Ed. 596 (1935), established the landmark principle that the substance of a transaction, and not the form, determines the taxable consequences of that transaction. * * * In the present transaction, however, it appears that both the form and the substance of the agreement assigned the right to receive future income. What was received by the decedent was the present value of that income the son could expect in the future. On the basis of the stock's past performance, the future income could have been (and was) estimated with reasonable accuracy. Essentially, decedent's son paid consideration to receive future income. Of course, the fact of a family transaction does not vitiate the transaction but merely subjects it to special scrutiny.

We recognize the oft-stated principle that a taxpayer cannot escape taxation by legally assigning or giving away a portion of the income derived from income producing property retained by the taxpayer. *Lucas v. Earl*, 281 U.S. 111, 50 S.Ct. 241, 74 L.Ed. 731 (1930); *Helvering v. Horst*, 311 U.S. 112, 61 S.Ct. 144, 85 L.Ed. 75 (1940); * * *. Here, however, the acceleration of income was not designed to avoid or escape recognition of the dividends but rather to reduce taxation by fully utilizing a substantial interest deduction which was available. As stated previously, tax avoidance motives alone will not serve to obviate the tax benefits of a transaction. Further, the fact that this was a transaction for good and sufficient consideration, and not merely gratuitous, distinguishes the instant case from the line of authority beginning with *Helvering v. Horst, supra.*

* * *

2. "Any one may so arrange his affairs that his taxes shall be as low as possible; he is not bound to choose that pattern which will best pay the Treasury; there is not even a patriotic duty to increase one's taxes." *Helvering v. Gregory*, 69 F.2d 809, 810 (2d Cir. 1934) (Hand, J. Learned), aff'd 293 U.S. 465, 55 S.Ct. 266, 79 L.Ed. 596 (1935).

Hence the fact that valuable consideration was an integral part of the transaction distinguishes this case from those where the simple expedient of drawing up legal papers and assigning income to others is used. The Tax Court uses the celebrated metaphor of Justice Holmes regarding the "fruit" and the "tree," and concludes there has been no effective separation of the fruit from the tree. Judge Cardozo's comment that "[m]etaphors in law are to be narrowly watched, for starting as devices to liberate thought, they end often by enslaving it" (*Berkey v. Third Avenue Railway Co.*, 244 N.Y. 84, 94, 155 N.E. 58, 61 (1926)) is appropriate here, as the genesis of the metaphor lies in a gratuitous transaction, while the instant situation concerns a transaction for a valuable consideration.

[handwritten: fRuit ≠ tRee]

The Commissioner also argues that the possibility of not receiving the dividends was remote, and that since this was particularly known to the parties as shareholders and employees of the corporation, no risks inured to the son. The Commissioner attempts to bolster this argument by pointing out that consideration was computed merely as a discount based on a prevailing interest rate and that the dividends were in fact paid at a rate faster than anticipated. However, it seems clear that risks, however remote, did in fact exist. The fact that the risks did not materialize is irrelevant. Assessment of the risks is a matter of negotiation between the parties and is usually reflected in the terms of the agreement. Since we are not in a position to evaluate those terms, and since we are not aware of any terms which dilute the son's dependence on the dividends alone to return his investment, we cannot say he does not bear the risks of ownership.

Accordingly, we conclude the transaction to be economically realistic, with substance, and therefore should be recognized for tax purposes even though the consequences may be unfavorable to the Commissioner. The facts establish decedent did in fact receive payment. Decedent deposited his son's check for $115,000 to his personal account on December 23, 1964, the day after the agreement was signed. The agreement is unquestionably a complete and valid assignment to decedent's son of all dividends up to $122,820. The son acquired an independent right against the corporation since the latter was notified of the private agreement. Decedent completely divested himself of any interest in the dividends and vested the interest on the day of execution of the agreement with his son.

* * *

The judgment is reversed and the cause remanded for further proceedings consistent with this opinion.

[handwritten: sub over form - when the economic sub does not jive w/ the form of the transaction]

Problem 3–22

[handwritten: Hue ct held there was economic substance]

Johnny Applestein was a shareholder in *X* Inc., a private corporation, for several years prior to Year One. On February 7, Year One, the board of directors of *X* approved a transaction in which all of the shares in *X* would be sold to *Y* Corporation. The stock purchase transaction was scheduled to occur on February 28, Year One. Johnny was pleased to receive news of the proposed stock purchase, for the selling price was substantially in excess of the price he paid for the *X* shares. On February 21, Year One, Johnny transferred all of his *X* stock to his children in a part-gift, part-sale transaction. The stock purchase took place as scheduled on February 28, Year One, and Johnny's children all received cash from the transaction. What are the federal income tax consequences of this sale to Johnny and his children?

* * *

COMMISSIONER v. BANKS
COMMISSIONER v. BANAITIS

United States Supreme Court, 2005.
543 U.S. 426, 125 S.Ct. 826, 160 L.Ed.2d 859.

JUSTICE KENNEDY delivered the opinion of the Court.

The question in these consolidated cases is whether the portion of a money judgment or settlement paid to a plaintiff's attorney under a contingent-fee agreement is income to the plaintiff under the Internal Revenue Code * * *. The issue divides the courts of appeals. In one of the instant cases, *Banks v. Comm'r*, 345 F.3d 373 (2003), the Court of Appeals for the Sixth Circuit held the contingent-fee portion of a litigation recovery is not included in the plaintiff's gross income. The Courts of Appeals for the Fifth and Eleventh Circuits also adhere to this view, relying on the holding, over Judge Wisdom's dissent, in *Cotnam v. Commissioner*, 263 F.2d 119, 125–126 (CA5 1959). In the other case under review, *Banaitis v. Comm'r*, 340 F.3d 1074 (2003), the Court of Appeals for the Ninth Circuit held that the portion of the recovery paid to the attorney as a contingent fee is excluded from the plaintiff's gross income if state law gives the plaintiff's attorney a special property interest in the fee, but not otherwise. Six Courts of Appeals have held the entire litigation recovery, including the portion paid to an attorney as a contingent fee, is income to the plaintiff. Some of these Courts of Appeals discuss state law, but little of their analysis appears to turn on this factor. Other Courts of Appeals have been explicit that the fee portion of the recovery is always income to the plaintiff regardless of the nuances of state law. We granted certiorari to resolve the conflict.

We hold that, as a general rule, when a litigant's recovery constitutes income, the litigant's income includes the portion of the recovery paid to the attorney as a contingent fee. We reverse the decisions of the Courts of Appeals for the Sixth and Ninth Circuits.

I

A. *Commissioner v. Banks*

In 1986, respondent John W. Banks, II, was fired from his job as an educational consultant with the California Department of Education. He retained an attorney on a contingent-fee basis and filed a civil suit against the employer in a United States District Court. The complaint alleged employment discrimination in violation of 42 U.S.C. §§ 1981 and 1983, Title VII of the Civil Rights Act of 1964, as amended, 42 U.S.C. § 2000e, and Cal. Govt. Code Ann. § 12965 (West 1986). The original complaint asserted various additional claims under state law, but Banks later abandoned these. After trial commenced in 1990, the parties settled for $464,000. Banks paid $150,000 of this amount to his attorney pursuant to the fee agreement.

Banks did not include any of the $464,000 in settlement proceeds as gross income in his 1990 federal income tax return. In 1997 the Commissioner of Internal Revenue issued Banks a notice of deficiency for the 1990 tax year. The Tax Court upheld the Commissioner's determination, finding that all the settlement proceeds, including the $150,000 Banks had paid to his attorney, must be included in Banks' gross income.

The Court of Appeals for the Sixth Circuit reversed in part. It agreed the net amount received by Banks was included in gross income but not the amount paid to the attorney. Relying on its prior decision in *Estate of Clarks v. United States*, 202 F.3d 854 (2000), the court held the contingent-fee agreement was not an anticipatory assignment of Banks' income because the litigation recovery was not already earned, vested, or even relatively certain to be paid when the contingent-fee contract was made. A contingent-fee arrangement, the court reasoned, is more like a partial assignment of income-producing property than an assignment of income. The attorney is not the mere beneficiary of the client's largess, but rather earns his fee through skill and diligence. This reasoning, the court held, applies whether or not state law grants the attorney any special property interest (*e.g.,* a superior lien) in part of the judgment or settlement proceeds.

B. *Commissioner v. Banaitis*

After leaving his job as a vice president and loan officer at the Bank of California in 1987, Sigitas J. Banaitis retained an attorney on a contingent-fee basis and brought suit in Oregon state court against the Bank of California and its successor in ownership, the Mitsubishi Bank. The complaint alleged that Mitsubishi Bank willfully interfered with Banaitis' employment contract, and that the Bank of California attempted to induce Banaitis to breach his fiduciary duties to customers and discharged him when he refused. The jury awarded Banaitis compensatory and punitive damages. After resolution of all appeals and post-trial motions, the parties settled. The defendants paid $4,864,547 to Banaitis; and, following the formula set forth in the contingent-fee contract, the defendants paid an additional $3,864,012 directly to Banaitis' attorney.

Banaitis did not include the amount paid to his attorney in gross income on his federal income tax return, and the Commissioner issued a notice of deficiency. The Tax Court upheld the Commissioner's determination, but the Court of Appeals for the Ninth Circuit reversed. In contrast to the Court of Appeals for the Sixth Circuit, the *Banaitis* court viewed state law as pivotal. Where state law confers on the attorney no special property rights in his fee, the court said, the whole amount of the judgment or settlement ordinarily is included in the plaintiff's gross income. Oregon state law, however, like the law of some other States, grants attorneys a superior lien in the contingent-fee portion of any recovery. As a result, the court held, contingent-fee agreements under Oregon law operate not as an anticipatory assignment of the client's income but as a partial transfer to the attorney of some of the client's property in the lawsuit.

II

To clarify why the issue here is of any consequence for tax purposes, two preliminary observations are useful. The first concerns the general issue of deductibility. For the tax years in question the legal expenses in these cases could have been taken as miscellaneous itemized deductions subject to the ordinary requirements, but doing so would have been of no help to respondents because of the operation of the Alternative Minimum Tax (AMT). For noncorporate individual taxpayers, the AMT establishes a tax liability floor equal to 26 percent of the taxpayer's "alternative minimum taxable income" (minus specified exemptions) up to $175,000, plus 28 percent of alternative minimum taxable income over $175,000. Alternative minimum taxable income, unlike ordinary gross income, does not allow any miscellaneous itemized deductions.

Second, after these cases arose Congress enacted the American Jobs Creation Act of 2004. Section 703 of the Act amended the Code by adding § 62(a)[(20)]. The amendment allows a taxpayer, in computing adjusted gross income, to deduct "attorney fees and court costs paid by, or on behalf of, the taxpayer in connection with any action involving a claim of unlawful discrimination." The Act defines "unlawful discrimination" to include a number of specific federal statutes, §§ 62(e)(1) to (16), any federal whistle-blower statute, § 62(e)(17), and any federal, state, or local law "providing for the enforcement of civil rights" or "regulating any aspect of the employment relationship ... or prohibiting the discharge of an employee, the discrimination against an employee, or any other form of retaliation or reprisal against an employee for asserting rights or taking other actions permitted by law," § 62(e)(18). These deductions are permissible even when the AMT applies. Had the Act been in force for the transactions now under review, these cases likely would not have arisen. The Act is not retroactive, however, so while it may cover future taxpayers in respondents' position, it does not pertain here.

III

The Internal Revenue Code defines "gross income" for federal tax purposes as "all income from whatever source derived." The definition extends broadly to all economic gains not otherwise exempted. *Commissioner v. Glenshaw Glass Co.*, 348 U.S. 426, 429–30, 99 L.Ed. 483, 75

S.Ct. 473 (1955); *Commissioner v. Jacobson*, 336 U.S. 28, 49, 93 L.Ed. 477, 69 S.Ct. 358 (1949). A taxpayer cannot exclude an economic gain from gross income by assigning the gain in advance to another party. *Lucas v. Earl*, 281 U.S. 111, 74 L.Ed. 731, 50 S.Ct. 241 (1930); *Comm'r v. Sunnen*, 333 U.S. 591, 604, 92 L.Ed. 898, 68 S.Ct. 715 (1948); *Helvering v. Horst*, 311 U.S. 112, 116–117, 85 L.Ed. 75, 61 S.Ct. 144 (1940). The rationale for the so-called anticipatory assignment of income doctrine is the principle that gains should be taxed "to those who earn them," *Lucas, supra,* at 114, a maxim we have called "the first principle of income taxation," *Comm'r v. Culbertson*, 337 U.S. 733, 739–740, 93 L.Ed. 1659, 69 S.Ct. 1210 (1949). The anticipatory assignment doctrine is meant to prevent taxpayers from avoiding taxation through "arrangements and contracts however skillfully devised to prevent [income] when paid from vesting even for a second in the man who earned it." *Lucas*, 281 U.S. at 115. The rule is preventative and motivated by administrative as well as substantive concerns, so we do not inquire whether any particular assignment has a discernible tax avoidance purpose. As *Lucas* explained, "no distinction can be taken according to the motives leading to the arrangement by which the fruits are attributed to a different tree from that on which they grew." *Ibid.*

Respondents argue that the anticipatory assignment doctrine is a judge-made antifraud rule with no relevance to contingent-fee contracts of the sort at issue here. The Commissioner maintains that a contingent-fee agreement should be viewed as an anticipatory assignment to the attorney of a portion of the client's income from any litigation recovery. We agree with the Commissioner.

In an ordinary case attribution of income is resolved by asking whether a taxpayer exercises complete dominion over the income in question. *Glenshaw Glass Co., supra,* at 431; see also *Commissioner v. Indianapolis Power & Light Co.*, 493 U.S. 203, 209, 107 L.Ed. 2d 591, 110 S.Ct. 589 (1990). In the context of anticipatory assignments, however, the assignor often does not have dominion over the income at the moment of receipt. In that instance the question becomes whether the assignor retains dominion over the income-generating asset, because the taxpayer "who owns or controls the source of the income, also controls the disposition of that which he could have received himself and diverts the payment from himself to others as the means of procuring the satisfaction of his wants." *Horst, supra,* at 116–117. Looking to control over the income-generating asset, then, preserves the principle that income should be taxed to the party who earns the income and enjoys the consequent benefits.

In the case of a litigation recovery the income-generating asset is the cause of action that derives from the plaintiff's legal injury. The plaintiff retains dominion over this asset throughout the litigation. We do not understand respondents to argue otherwise. Rather, respondents advance two counterarguments. First, they say that, in contrast to the bond coupons assigned in *Horst*, the value of a legal claim is speculative at the moment of assignment, and may be worth nothing at all. Second, respondents insist that the claimant's legal injury is not the only source of the ultimate recovery. The attorney, according to respondents, also contributes income-generating assets—effort and expertise—without which the claimant likely could not prevail. On these premises respondents urge us to treat a contingent-fee agreement as establishing, for tax purposes, something like a joint venture or partnership in which the client and attorney combine their respective assets—the client's claim and the attorney's skill—and apportion any resulting profits.

We reject respondents' arguments. Though the value of the plaintiff's claim may be speculative at the moment the fee agreement is signed, the anticipatory assignment doctrine is not limited to instances when the precise dollar value of the assigned income is known in advance. Though *Horst* involved an anticipatory assignment of a predetermined sum to be paid on a specific date, the holding in that case did not depend on ascertaining a liquidated amount at the time of assignment. In the cases before us, as in *Horst*, the taxpayer retained control over the income-generating asset, diverted some of the income produced to another party, and realized a benefit by doing so. * * * That the amount of income the asset would produce was uncertain at the moment of assignment is of no consequence.

We further reject the suggestion to treat the attorney-client relationship as a sort of business partnership or joint venture for tax purposes. The relationship between client and attorney, regardless of the variations in particular compensation agreements or the amount of skill and effort the attorney contributes, is a quintessential principal-agent relationship. The client may rely on the attorney's expertise and special skills to achieve a result the client could not achieve alone. That, however, is true of most principal-agent relationships, and it does not alter the fact that the client retains ultimate dominion and control over the underlying claim. The control is evident when it is noted that, although the attorney can make tactical decisions without consulting the client, the plaintiff still must determine whether to settle or proceed to judgment and make, as well, other critical decisions. Even where the attorney exercises independent judgment without supervision by, or consultation with, the client, the attorney, as an agent, is obligated to act solely on behalf of, and for the exclusive benefit of, the client-principal, rather than for the benefit of the attorney or any other party.

The attorney is an agent who is duty bound to act only in the interests of the principal, and so it is appropriate to treat the full amount of the recovery as income to the principal. In this respect Judge Posner's observation is apt: "[T]he contingent-fee lawyer [is not] a joint owner of his client's claim in the legal sense any more than the commission salesman is a joint owner of his employer's accounts receivable." *Kenseth*, 259 F.3d, at 883. In both cases a principal relies on an agent to realize an economic gain, and the gain realized by the agent's efforts is income to the principal. The portion paid to the agent may be deductible, but absent some other provision of law it is not excludable from the principal's gross income.

This rule applies whether or not the attorney-client contract or state law confers any special rights or protections on the attorney, so long as these protections do not alter the fundamental principal-agent character of the relationship. State laws vary with respect to the strength of an attorney's security interest in a contingent fee and the remedies available to an attorney should the client discharge or attempt to defraud the attorney. No state laws of which we are aware, however, even those that purport to give attorneys an "ownership" interest in their fees, convert the attorney from an agent to a partner.

Respondents and their *amici* propose other theories to exclude fees from income or permit deductibility. These suggestions include: (1) The contingent-fee agreement establishes a Subchapter K partnership * * * ; (2) litigation recoveries are proceeds from disposition of property, so the attorney's fee should be subtracted as a capital expense * * * ; and (3) the fees are deductible reimbursed employee business expenses under § 62(a)(2)(A) * * *. These arguments, it appears, are being presented for the first time to this Court. We are especially reluctant to entertain novel propositions of law with broad implications for the tax system that were not advanced in earlier stages of the litigation and not examined by the Courts of Appeals. We decline comment on these supplementary theories. * * *

IV

The foregoing suffices to dispose of Banaitis' case. Banks' case, however, involves a further consideration. Banks brought his claims under federal statutes that authorize fee awards to prevailing plaintiffs' attorneys. He contends that application of the anticipatory assignment principle would be inconsistent with the purpose of statutory fee shifting provisions. See *Venegas v. Mitchell*, 495 U.S. 82, 86, 109 L.Ed. 2d 74, 110 S.Ct. 1679 (1990) (observing that statutory fees enable "plaintiffs to employ reasonably competent lawyers without cost to themselves if they prevail"). In the federal system statutory fees are typically awarded by the court under the lodestar approach, and the plaintiff usually has little control over the amount awarded. Sometimes, as when the plaintiff seeks only injunctive relief, or when the statute caps plaintiffs' recoveries, or when for other reasons damages are substantially less than attorney's fees, court-awarded attorney's fees can exceed a plaintiff's monetary recovery. See, e.g., *Riverside v. Rivera*, 477 U.S. 561, 564–565, 91 L.Ed. 2d 466, 106 S.Ct. 2686 (1986) (compensatory and punitive damages of $33,350; attorney's fee award of $245,456.25). Treating the fee award as income to the plaintiff in such cases, it is argued, can lead to the perverse result that the plaintiff loses money by winning the suit. Furthermore, it is urged that treating statutory fee awards as income to plaintiffs would undermine the effectiveness of fee-shifting statutes in deputizing plaintiffs and their lawyers to act as private attorneys general.

We need not address these claims. After Banks settled his case, the fee paid to his attorney was calculated solely on the basis of the private contingent-fee contract. There was no court-ordered fee award, nor was there any indication in Banks' contract with his attorney, or in the settlement agreement with the defendant, that the contingent fee paid to Banks' attorney was in lieu of statutory fees Banks might otherwise have been entitled to recover. Also, the amendment added by the American Jobs Creation Act redresses the concern for many, perhaps most, claims governed by fee-shifting statutes.

For the reasons stated, the judgments of the Courts of Appeals for the Sixth and Ninth Circuits are reversed, and the cases are remanded for further proceedings consistent with this opinion.

It is so ordered.

The CHIEF JUSTICE took no part in the decision of these cases.

Notes and Questions

1. As the Court indicates, the facts of the two cases at bar would fit squarely under new § 62(a)(20), enacted as part of the American Jobs Creation Act of 2004. Consequently, the attorney's share of the award would be an above-the-line deduction, sparing it both from the two-percent haircut of § 67 (discussed in Chapter 2) and the alternative minimum tax (a topic explored in Chapter 11). Lest you think § 62(a)(20) renders the issue moot, keep in mind that *Banks* is still precedent for those contingent fee arrangements not eligible for an above-the-line deduction. These would include claims for defamation and invasion of privacy. Perhaps a claim for tortious interference with contract would also present this issue. Section 62(a)(20) does not change the adverse result faced by these (likely few) plaintiffs.

2. The Court expressly refused to comment on the theories advanced for the first time by the parties and by outsiders. Perhaps one or more of these theories would work for parties still affected by the issue. Are any of the "new" theories persuasive?

3. By deciding the issue on the basis of federal law (assignment of income) and not on the interpretation of state attorney lien statutes, the Court provided a uniform answer for all taxpayers regardless of residency. That tactic also allowed the Court to dodge a more direct discussion of why the attorney lien statutes were of no consequence in deciding the case.

* * *

Problem 3–23

Emily Employee was fired by Evil Employer in Year One. Emily believed that she was wrongfully terminated, so she consulted with Laverne Lawyer. Laverne agreed to commence litigation against Evil at no cost to Emily in exchange for a one-third interest in all amounts recovered in the lawsuit or any related settlement. Emily signed a contingent fee agreement consenting to these terms. Laverne filed suit in Year Two, and by the end of the year, the parties settled. Evil agreed to pay $900,000 to Emily, which it did at the beginning of Year Three. Emily then paid $300,000 to Laverne.

(a) Who has gross income, in what amounts, and when?

(b) How would the answer to (a) change if Emily was not fired but was instead injured on the job because of Evil's negligence, and the amount paid in Year Three was in settlement of a physical injury claim? See § 104(a)(2).

Chapter 4

TAX TREATMENT OF TAXPAYER COSTS

Friday 9/23
p. 170 - 180

A. INTRODUCTION

Code: IRC §§ 161; 162(a); 165(c); 212; 262.

Regs: None.

We saw in Chapter 2 that an individual's liability for federal income tax is determined with reference to the taxpayer's "taxable income." We also saw that taxable income is computed by subtracting various deductions from the taxpayer's gross income. Having just concluded our examination of gross income in Chapter 3, we now consider the various deductions available to taxpayers.

Some taxpayers mistakenly believe that all outlays are deductible for federal income tax purposes. In fact, only certain costs are deductible. Section 161 generally requires a taxpayer to have specific authority for a deduction. In the absence of a Code provision authorizing a deduction, then, a taxpayer will not be permitted to take a cost into account when computing taxable income.

What types of costs are deductible? Very generally, the question of whether a cost is deductible depends upon two factors. First, it depends on the *nature* of the cost. Second, it depends upon the type of *activity* to which that cost relates. As to the nature of the cost, deductibility often hinges on whether the cost is a "capital expenditure" or an "expense." Though common usage might equate these terms, they have very different meanings from a tax perspective. **Capital expenditures** are those costs that provide a long-term benefit to the taxpayer, either because they are incurred to acquire a new asset or because they materially add to the value or useful life of some pre-existing asset. We say that such costs must be "capitalized," shorthand for the conclusion that they are capital expenditures. Costs that do not acquire, improve, or prolong the life of an asset are called **expenses**. We shall see that while taxpayers may be able to deduct various *expenses* paid or incurred during a taxable year, taxpayers generally cannot deduct *capital expenditures*. Instead, capital expenditures add to (or create) the taxpayer's basis in property.

170

The distinction between capital expenditures and expenses is thus a very crucial one, and it is the heart of Part B of this Chapter.

Once we know the nature of the cost involved, deductibility also hinges on the activity to which the cost relates. For federal income tax purposes, there are basically three types of activities to which all costs relate: business activities, investment activities, and personal activities. Expenses paid or incurred with respect to **business** and **investment** activities are generally deductible (see §§ 162 and 212, respectively), while expenses related to **personal** activities are generally not deductible (see § 262). The deductions for business and investment expenses are discussed in Part C of this Chapter. Although § 262 generally disallows any deductions for personal, living, or family expenses, Congress has created several exceptions to this rule. The exceptions are so numerous, in fact, that all of Chapter 9 is devoted to them.

But let us return to capital expenditures for a moment. If a taxpayer must capitalize a cost, the taxpayer can recover that cost ultimately upon the sale or disposition of the underlying asset. This is because the capitalized cost makes up all or part of the adjusted basis in the underlying asset. In many cases, however, taxpayers do not have to wait until the disposition of an asset to recover the cost of a capital expenditure. Instead, the cost can be recovered over a period of years roughly equivalent to the useful life of the underlying asset. With respect to tangible property, the applicable cost recovery system is referred to as **depreciation**. In order for the cost of tangible property to be depreciable, the property must (among other things) be subject to wear and tear in the hands of the taxpayer. The general depreciation rules are set forth in the statute at §§ 167 and 168. With respect to intangible property, the applicable cost recovery system is called **amortization**. While "wear and tear" in the hands of the taxpayer is not required for a taxpayer to amortize the cost of intangible property, other statutory requirements for the cost recovery of intangible property are set forth in § 197. The various cost recovery rules (both depreciation and amortization) are discussed in Part D of this Chapter.

Sometimes taxpayers incur "costs" without paying anything currently and without incurring a liability for future payment. Such is the case when a taxpayer disposes of property for an amount less than the taxpayer's adjusted basis in that property. Suppose, for example, that a taxpayer sells an asset with an adjusted basis of $5,000 to an unrelated party for cash in the amount of $2,000. The transaction yields a $3,000 realized loss. Although **losses** are not outlays in the typical sense, they nonetheless represent a cost to the taxpayer, for the amount of the loss represents basis (or cost) that the taxpayer was unable to recover. So losses represent a third type of cost that the federal income tax must consider. The tax treatment of losses is covered in Part E of this Chapter.

The following chart summarizes the general rules described above. You might want to keep this chart handy, not only as you navigate through this Chapter but also as you consider various exceptions to these general rules throughout the rest of the text.

TREATMENT OF TAXPAYER OUTLAYS UNDER THE FEDERAL INCOME TAX

	PERSONAL	**BUSINESS**	**INVESTMENT**
Capital Expenditures (those that: (1) are used to acquire an asset or some other long-lasting benefit; or (2) permanently improve or extend the useful life of that asset or benefit)	**NO DEDUCTION** § 263(a) (but taxpayer gets basis)	**NO DEDUCTION** § 263(a) (but taxpayer gets basis) And the taxpayer may be able to recover the cost over time §§ 167(a); 168; 197	**NO DEDUCTION** § 263(a) (but taxpayer gets basis) And the taxpayer may be able to recover the cost over time §§ 167(a); 168; 197
Expenses (outlays that are not capital expenditures)	Generally, **NO DEDUCTION** § 262 [But see Chapter 9]	**DEDUCTION** § 162(a)	**DEDUCTION** § 212
Realized Losses (loss recognized upon the sale, exchange, or other disposition of an asset)	Generally, **NO DEDUCTION** § 262 [But see § 165(c)(3)]	**DEDUCTION** § 165(c)(1)	**DEDUCTION** § 165(c)(2)

Why all the fuss about the nature of costs and the activities to which they relate? In constructing the "taxable income" base for the federal income tax, remember that Congress seeks to apply the tax to an individual's *income*. We saw in Chapter 1 that income is commonly perceived as the sum of the taxpayer's consumption plus any increase in the taxpayer's net worth. The consumption prong of income measures the extent to which the taxpayer has used receipts for purposes other than the production of additional receipts. For instance, if a taxpayer used $1,000 of gross income to pay for a short vacation, it is said that the taxpayer has consumed that $1,000. The $1,000 of gross income used to provide that consumption should thus be subject to federal income tax. On the other hand, if the taxpayer used the $1,000 to purchase supplies for use in the taxpayer's business activity, the $1,000 has not been "consumed." Instead, the funds have been applied to help the taxpayer generate additional income. Recognizing that "it takes money to make money," Congress appropriately provides that the $1,000 spent on business supplies should be deducted from the federal income tax base. In order to properly track consumption outlays, therefore, the federal income tax must be concerned with the activity to which the cost relates.

The nature of the cost (capital expenditure, expense, or loss) is also important, but not necessarily because the nature of the cost determines whether consumption has occurred. Instead, the nature of the cost relates more to the proper *timing* for deduction. As explained above, capital expenditures are not immediately deductible in full; instead, those costs are either recovered upon disposition of the underlying assets to which they relate or gradually over the useful lives of such assets. Expenses, on the other hand, are deductible right away (assuming, of course, that they are not properly considered consumption expenses by the taxpayer). As for losses, the realization "rule-of-thumb" from Chapter 3 dictates that the deduction awaits sale or disposition of the loss asset.

From all of this, we see that the *nature* of taxpayer outlays determines the proper *timing* of available deductions. The *activity* to which the costs relate are important in determining whether the cost went toward non-deductible *consumption* by the taxpayer.

B. EXPENSES VERSUS CAPITAL EXPENDITURES

As explained in the summary in Part A of this Chapter, only "expenses" are deductible under § 162 (if related to a "trade or business" activity) or § 212 (if related to an "investment" activity—one engaged in for profit that does not quite rise to the level of a trade or business). Expenses are distinct from "capital expenditures." The latter create or add to basis and cannot be deducted in the year paid or incurred. In some cases, capital expenditures are deducted over time in the form of deductions for depreciation and amortization (the subject of Part D of this Chapter). In other cases, capital expenditures are recovered only when the taxpayer disposes of the particular asset created or improved by the capital expenditure. Capitalization is also a timing concept, for a capitalized cost is, effectively, a deferred deduction in some form. From a time value of money perspective, of course, taxpayers want to accelerate deductions; the capitalization rules are thus an impediment to taxpayers seeking to leverage the time value of money.

For such an important everyday concept, it is somewhat surprising (not to mention frustrating) that the Code's treatment of the distinction between expenses and capital expenditures is so sparse. Section 263(a) merely states that no deduction is allowed for amounts "paid out for new buildings or for permanent improvements or betterments made to increase the value of any property," or for amounts "expended in restoring property or in making good the exhaustion thereof for which an allowance is or has been made." The statute therefore contains four types of expenditures that must be capitalized: (1) new buildings; (2) permanent improvements intended to increase value; (3) restoration costs; and (4) expenditures that will give rise to exhaustion deductions (i.e., depreciation and amortization).

The regulations clarify and expand this list considerably. The regulations provide separate rules for the capitalization of costs related to tangible assets and the costs related to intangible assets. Following suit, this Part B considers the capitalization rules first for tangible assets and then for intangible assets.

(1) COSTS RELATED TO TANGIBLE ASSETS

Code: IRC §§ 263(a); 263A. *(omit 263(A) (d),e,f,g) - Read balance.)*

Regs: Treas. Reg. § 1.162–3; ~~Prop. Reg. §§ 1.263(a)–1; 1.263(a)–2;~~ *omit*
~~1.263(a)–3.~~

Regulations proposed in 2006 offer a comprehensive set of rules for the capitalization of costs related to tangible assets. These regulations follow on the heels of the successful implementation of regulations regarding the capitalization of costs related to intangible assets, discussed in Part B(2) below.

New Assets. A taxpayer must capitalize a cost if it results in the acquisition or creation of real or personal property having a useful life substantially beyond the taxable year. Prop. Reg. § 1.263(a)–2(d)(1)(i). This rule makes sense, for if a taxpayer purchases property that will provide a benefit beyond the current taxable year, it is not appropriate to permit a full deduction for the cost in the year of purchase. Suppose, for example, that a taxpayer pays $10,000 in Year One for a photocopier that the taxpayer will use for business purposes. The taxpayer reasonably expects that the copier will last until the end of Year Five. It is not proper to deduct the entire $10,000 cost in Year One because the benefit of the payment (a photocopier) will extend substantially beyond Year One.

A taxpayer must also capitalize the cost of property that the taxpayer intends to sell to another party. Prop. Reg. § 1.263(a)–2(d)(1)(i). This rule applies even if the taxpayer intends to sell the property within a short time following the purchase such that the taxpayer's holding period does not extend substantially beyond the taxable year. Thus, for example, if the taxpayer purchased a parcel of undeveloped real property in December of Year One for $100,000 with the intent to sell the property to an unrelated buyer early in Year Two, the taxpayer must capitalize the cost, meaning the taxpayer's basis in the land will be $100,000. When the taxpayer sells the land for $115,000 in Year Two, the taxpayer will have gross income of $15,000 in Year Two, the extent to which the amount realized from the sale exceeds the taxpayer's adjusted basis. If the taxpayer were allowed to deduct the cost of the land in Year One, the taxpayer's basis would be zero, for there would be no unrecovered cost associated with the asset. The Year Two sale for $115,000 would yield $115,000 of gross income. As between these two options, requiring the cost to be capitalized but taxing only the $15,000 gain in Year Two as opposed to deducting the purchase price in Year One but including the entire $115,000 in gross income in Year Two, the former probably better reflects the real economic consequence of the taxpayer's real estate transaction.

The 12–Month Rule. The proposed regulations make clear that costs producing only a short-term benefit need not be capitalized. This is consistent with the general rule that capitalization is required where the benefit of the cost will extend substantially beyond the end of the taxable year. With some exceptions, amounts paid to buy or make a unit of tangible property with an "economic useful life" of not more than 12 months need not be capitalized. Prop. Reg. § 1.263(a)–2(d)(4)(i). To the extent such assets constitute materials and supplies, the taxpayer can avoid capitalization of the cost under Treas. Reg. § 1.162–3.

* * *

Self-Assessment Question

(Solutions to Self–Assessment Questions are set forth in Appendix 3.)

SAQ 4–1. For each of the following outlays, determine whether the cost should be capitalized or treated as an expense. Do not bother to determine whether the expenses are deductible—this Question asks only whether each cost is properly considered a capital expenditure or an expense.

(a) Automobile

(b) Gasoline for the automobile

(c) Attorney fees to defend against a boundary dispute related to the taxpayer's land

(d) Commissions paid to a real estate broker in purchasing a building

* * *

Costs of Producing Real and Tangible Personal Property: The Uniform Capitalization Rules. We know that when a taxpayer purchases property that will yield benefits substantially beyond the year of purchase, the cost must be capitalized. But suppose a taxpayer constructs the property instead of purchasing it. If we want to treat the purchaser and the builder similarly, construction costs should be capitalized and added to the basis of the constructed property. Thus, wages paid to builders and other construction workers must be capitalized when they relate to the construction of an asset that will provide benefit beyond the taxable year. The authority for this rule in many cases is § 263(a)(1), which disallows deductions for amounts "paid out for new buildings or for permanent improvements or betterments made to increase the value of any property or estate." But this provision does not neatly cover all construction costs that should be subject to capitalization. This is illustrated in the following case.

COMMISSIONER v. IDAHO POWER CO.

United States Supreme Court, 1974.
418 U.S. 1, 94 S.Ct. 2757, 41 L.Ed.2d 535.

Mr. Justice Blackmun delivered the opinion of the Court.

This case presents the sole issue whether, for federal income tax purposes, a taxpayer is entitled to a deduction from gross income, under § 167(a) of the Internal Revenue Code of 1954 * * * for depreciation on equipment the taxpayer owns and uses in the construction of its own capital facilities, or whether the capitalization provision of § 263(a)(1) of the Code * * * bars the deduction.

* * *

I

* * *

For many years, the taxpayer has used its own equipment and employees in the construction of improvements and additions to its capital facilities. The major work has consisted of transmission lines, transmission switching stations, distribution lines, distribution stations, and connecting facilities.

During 1962 and 1963, the tax years in question, taxpayer owned and used in its business a wide variety of automotive transportation equipment, including passenger cars, trucks of all descriptions, power-operated equipment, and trailers. Radio communication devices were affixed to the equipment and were used in its daily operations. The transportation equipment was used in part for operation and maintenance and in part for the construction of capital facilities having a useful life of more than one year.

On its books, the taxpayer used various methods of charging costs incurred in connection with its transportation equipment either to current expense or to capital accounts. To the extent the equipment was used in construction, the taxpayer charged depreciation of the equipment, as well as all operating and maintenance costs (other than pension contributions and social security and motor vehicle taxes) to the capital assets so constructed. This was done either directly or through clearing accounts in accordance with procedures prescribed by the Federal Power Commission and adopted by the Idaho Public Utilities Commission.

For federal income tax purposes, however, the taxpayer treated the depreciation on transportation equipment differently. It claimed as a deduction from gross income all the year's depreciation on such equipment, including that portion attributable to its use in constructing capital facilities. The depreciation was computed on a composite life of 10 years and under straight-line and declining-balance methods. The other operating and maintenance costs the taxpayer had charged on its books to capital were not claimed as current expenses and were not deducted.

To summarize: On its books, in accordance with Federal Power Commission–Idaho Public Utilities Commission prescribed methods, the taxpayer capitalized the construction-related depreciation, but for income tax purposes that depreciation increment was claimed as a deduction under § 167(a).

Upon audit, the Commissioner of Internal Revenue disallowed the deduction for the construction-related depreciation. He ruled that the depreciation was a nondeductible capital expenditure to which § 263(a)(1) had application. * * * A deduction for depreciation of the transportation equipment to the extent of its use in day-to-day operation and maintenance was also allowed. * * *

* * *

II

Our primary concern is with the necessity to treat construction-related depreciation in a manner that comports with accounting and taxation realities. Over a period of time a capital asset is consumed and, correspondingly over that period, its theoretical value and utility are thereby reduced. Depreciation is an accounting device which recognizes that the physical consumption of a capital asset is a true cost, since the asset is being depleted. As the process of consumption continues, and depreciation is claimed and allowed, the asset's adjusted income tax basis is reduced to reflect the distribution of its cost over the accounting periods affected. The Court stated in *Hertz Corp. v. United States*, 364 U.S. 122, 126 (1960): "[The] purpose of depreciation accounting is to allocate the expense of using an asset to the various periods which are benefited by that asset." * * * When the asset is used to further the taxpayer's day-to-day business operations, the periods of benefit usually correlate with the production of income. Thus, to the extent that equipment is used in such operations, a current depreciation deduction is an appropriate offset to gross income currently produced. It is clear, however, that different principles are implicated when the consumption of the asset takes place in the construction of other assets that, in the future, will produce income themselves. In this latter situation, the cost represented by depreciation does not correlate with production of current income. Rather, the cost, although certainly presently incurred, is related to the future and is appropriately allocated as part of the cost of acquiring an income-producing capital asset.

* * *

Accepted accounting practice and established tax principles require the capitalization of the cost of acquiring a capital asset. In *Woodward v. Commissioner*, 397 U.S. 572, 575 (1970), the Court observed: "It has long been recognized, as a general matter, that costs incurred in the acquisition ... of a capital asset are to be treated as capital expenditures." This principle has obvious application to the acquisition of a capital asset by purchase, but it has been applied, as well, to the costs incurred in a taxpayer's construction of capital facilities. * * *

There can be little question that other construction-related expense items, such as tools, materials, and wages paid construction workers, are to be treated as part of the cost of acquisition of a capital asset. The taxpayer does not dispute this. Of course, reasonable wages paid in the carrying on of a trade or business qualify as a deduction from gross income. But when wages are paid in connection with the construction or acquisition of a capital asset, they must be capitalized and are then entitled to be amortized over the life of the capital asset so acquired. * * *

Construction-related depreciation is not unlike expenditures for wages for construction workers. The significant fact is that the exhaustion of construction equipment does not represent the final disposition of the taxpayer's investment in that equipment; rather, the investment in the equipment is assimilated into the cost of the capital asset constructed. Construction-related depreciation on the equipment is not an expense to the taxpayer of its day-to-day business. It is, however, appropriately recognized as a part of the taxpayer's cost or investment in the capital asset. The taxpayer's own accounting procedure reflects this treatment, for on its books the construction-related depreciation was capitalized by a credit to the equipment account and a debit to the capital facility account. By the same token, this capitalization prevents the distortion of income that would otherwise occur if depreciation properly allocable to asset acquisition were deducted from gross income currently realized. * * *

An additional pertinent factor is that capitalization of construction-related depreciation by the taxpayer who does its own construction work maintains tax parity with the taxpayer who has its construction work done by an independent contractor. The depreciation on the contractor's equipment incurred during the performance of the job will be an element of cost charged by the contractor for his construction services, and the entire cost, of course, must be capitalized by the taxpayer having the construction work performed. The Court of Appeals' holding would lead to disparate treatment among taxpayers because it would allow the firm with sufficient resources to construct its own facilities and to obtain a current deduction, whereas another firm without such resources would be required to capitalize its entire cost including depreciation charged to it by the contractor.

           * * *

The presence of § 263(a)(1) in the Code is of significance. Its literal language denies a deduction for "[any] amount paid out" for construction or permanent improvement of facilities. The taxpayer contends, and the Court of Appeals held, that depreciation of construction equipment represents merely a decrease in value and is not an amount "paid out," within the meaning of § 263(a)(1). We disagree.

The purpose of § 263 is to reflect the basic principle that a capital expenditure may not be deducted from current income. It serves to prevent a taxpayer from utilizing currently a deduction properly attributable, through amortization, to later tax years when the capital asset becomes income producing. The regulations state that the capital expenditures to which § 263(a) extends include the "cost of acquisition, construction, or erection of buildings." Treas. Reg. § 1.263(a)–2(a). This manifests an administrative understanding that for purposes of § 263(a)(1), "amount paid out" equates with "cost incurred." The Internal Revenue Service for some time has taken the position that construction-related depreciation is to be capitalized. * * *

There is no question that the cost of the transportation equipment was "paid out" in the same manner as the cost of supplies, materials, and other equipment, and the wages of construction workers. The taxpayer does not question the capitalization of these other items as elements of the cost of acquiring a capital asset. We see no reason to treat construction-related depreciation differently. In acquiring the transportation equipment, taxpayer "paid out" the equipment's purchase price; depreciation is simply the means of allocating the payment over the various accounting periods affected. As the Tax Court stated in *Brooks v. Commissioner*, 50 T.C., at 935, "depreciation—inasmuch as it represents a using up of capital—is as much an 'expenditure' as the using up of labor or other items of direct cost."

Finally, the priority-ordering directive of § 161—or, for that matter, § 261 of the Code, * * *—requires that the capitalization provision of § 263(a) take precedence, on the facts here, over § 167(a). Section 161 provides that deductions specified in Part VI of Subchapter B of the Income Tax Subtitle of the Code are "subject to the exceptions provided in part IX." Part VI includes § 167 and Part IX includes § 263. The clear import of § 161 is that, with stated exceptions set forth either in § 263 itself or provided for elsewhere (as, for example, in § 404 relating to pension contributions), none of which is applicable here, an expenditure incurred in acquiring capital assets must be capitalized even when the expenditure otherwise might be deemed deductible under Part VI.

　　* * *

We hold that the equipment depreciation allocable to taxpayer's construction of capital facilities is to be capitalized.

The judgment of the Court of Appeals is reversed.

It is so ordered.

Notes

1. We cover depreciation deductions in great detail shortly (it is coming up in Part D of this Chapter). *Idaho Power* offers a helpful preview of the concept. Note that the depreciation deduction for an asset in any one taxable year is not based on the actual decline in the asset's value or the actual "wear and tear" suffered by the asset. Instead, the deduction is a simplified estimate of the diminished value. In fact, depreciation deductions rarely match actual decline. In the vast majority of cases, taxpayers are rewarded with greater depreciation deductions in the early years of the asset's useful life. Is there a reason for allowing larger deductions in the early years of an asset's life? We will pick up this question in Part D of this Chapter, too.

2. Congress codified the result of *Idaho Power* in § 263A. Section 263A (known as the "uniform capitalization rules," or "UNICAP rules") generally requires the capitalization of all direct and indirect costs allocable to the construction or production of real property or tangible personal property. It also applies to the acquisition of inventory items held for resale to customers. "Direct" costs include raw materials and wages paid to builders or other production workers. Treas. Reg. § 1.263A–1(e)(2). "Indirect" costs include repairs, depreciation, utilities, rent, sales tax, property tax, insurance, storage, and packaging. Treas. Reg. § 1.263A–1(e)(3). Selling expenses, state

income taxes, and advertising and distribution costs are outside the scope of § 263A. Treas. Reg. § 1.263A–1(e)(3)(iii). The statute contains many exceptions from the UNICAP rules, including: (a) wholesalers and retailers of personal property with average annual gross receipts of $10 million or less [§ 263A(b)(2)(B)]; (b) personal-use property [§ 263A(c)(1)]; and (c) certain animals and plants produced by farmers and ranchers [§ 263A(d)]. Photographers, writers, and artists were subject to the UNICAP rules until 1988, when Congress added § 263A(h), an exemption for these free-lance individuals.

* * *

Problem 4–1

Karen, a professional carpenter, is a sole proprietor who constructs and sells luxury homes to customers. In Year One, Karen paid the following costs in connection with the construction of Blackacre Estates, a luxury home built for sale as part of her construction business:

- $5,000 for temporary scaffolding that will be discarded upon completion of construction

- $5,000 in nuts, bolts, nails, screws, washers, and fasteners

- $10,000 for concrete used to form the home's foundation

- $20,000 in depreciation on Karen's construction equipment (forklift and loader)

- $50,000 for insurance coverage during construction in case of loss or damage resulting from fire, storm, or other casualty

- $150,000 for various appliances and cabinetry installed in the home

- $200,000 in wages paid to Karen's employees who assist in the home's construction

- $400,000 for the land on which the home is constructed

(a) Assuming all of the foregoing costs are ordinary and necessary in the construction of a luxury home, which of the costs may be deducted in Year One?

(b) Assume Karen incurs no additional costs in connection with the construction of Blackacre Estates. If Karen sells Blackacre Estates to a customer in Year Two for $1,500,000, what are the federal income tax consequences to Karen?

* * *

Improvements to Tangible Property. The proposed regulations provide that taxpayers must capitalize costs to improve tangible property if the costs materially add to the property's value or restore the property to a "like-new" condition. Prop. Reg. § 1.263(a)–3(d)(1). Improvement costs are more likely to add substantially to the value of a relatively small asset than a larger one. For instance, suppose a taxpayer pays $20 to install a new air filter hose in a vehicle used in the taxpayer's business. If the unit of property is the vehicle, the cost of the new hose is unlikely to add material value to the car. But if the unit of property is the air filter, then the replacement hose almost certainly adds to its value. Accordingly, in determining whether a cost materially adds to value, one must first determine the unit of property to which the cost relates. This is not always as easy as it may seem, as the following case illustrates.

FEDEX CORP. v. UNITED STATES, 291 F.Supp.2d 699 (W.D. Tenn. 2003), *affirmed*, 412 F.3d 617 (6th Cir. 2005).

Facts: FedEx maintains a fleet of aircraft as part of its overnight delivery business. At scheduled intervals (or when required under Federal Aviation Administration rules), FedEx removes engines from planes and sends the engines out for "engine shop visits" (ESVs) performed by third parties. An ESV involves an initial inspection, after which the engine is disassembled into modules and, where necessary, parts were replaced with new or serviceable used parts. The interval between ESVs for an engine is generally 24 to 60 months. ESV costs typically range from 1–8% of an aircraft's value. FedEx treated these costs as deductible expenses, but the Service disallowed the deductions on the grounds that the ESV costs should be capitalized.

Issue: Must the ESV costs be capitalized?

Holding: No. The costs may be treated as expenses.

Rationale: The court first had to determine whether the appropriate unit of property for ESV costs is the engine or the airplane. In making this determination, the court examined four factors: (1) "whether the taxpayer and the industry treat the component part as part of the larger unit of property for regulatory, market, management, or accounting purposes;" (2) "whether the economic useful life of the component part is coextensive with the economic useful life of the larger unit of property;" (3) "whether the larger unit of property and the smaller unit of property can function without each other;" and (4) "whether the component part can be and is maintained while affixed to the larger unit of property." Using this framework, the court concluded that the appropriate unit of property in this case is the airplane. The facts indicated that the FAA and the taxpayer consistently treated the engine as part of the entire plane. While isolated sales of engines occurred on occasion, it was much more common for engines to be sold as part of the entire plane. Thus the first factor suggested that the proper unit of property was the airplane. The second factor also suggested that the plane was the correct unit of property, for FedEx reasonably expected the engine to last as long as the plane, usually 30 years. The third factor very strongly supports treating the plane as the unit of property, for an engine without a plane does not help FedEx very much (nor does a plane without an engine). The fourth factor, according to the court, weighed in favor of treating the engine as the unit of property, for the engine had to be removed from the plane to perform an ESV. But on balance, the court determined that the unit of property here is the plane. Because an ESV clearly did not adapt the plane to a new or different use, and because an

ESV did not appreciably prolong the life of the plane, and because an ESV did not materially add to the value of the plane, it was proper for FedEx to treat the ESV costs as expenses.

* * *

The proposed regulations provide more detailed guidance in determining the unit of property to which an improvement cost relates. Unless the taxpayer is engaged in a federally-regulated industry subject to uniform systems of accounts, the appropriate unit of tangible personal property is determined with reference to nine exclusive factors, none of which matters more than the others but each of which suggests that the item should be treated as a separate unit of property: (1) whether the item was marketed separately when the taxpayer acquired it; (2) whether the item was acquired or leased separately; (3) whether the item is subject to a separate warranty contract; (4) whether the item is subject to a separate maintenance manual or policy; (5) whether the item is appraised separately; (6) whether the taxpayer sells or leases the item separately to another party; (7) whether industry practice treats the item as a separate unit of property; (8) whether the taxpayer treats the item as something removable and repairable separate from another item; and (9) whether the bigger property of which the item is a part can function on its own without the item in question. Prop. Reg. § 1.263(a)–3(d)(2)(v).

When it comes to real property, a building and its structural components are seen as one unit of property. Prop. Reg. § 1.263(a)–3(d)(2)(iv). Other items of real property are treated as separate units depending upon the facts and circumstances. Prop. Reg. § 1.263(a)–3(d)(2)(vi).

Additions to Value. Once the taxpayer knows the appropriate unit of property, the analysis then shifts to whether the amount paid materially increased the value of such property. Proposed Regulation § 1.263(a)–3(e)(1) identifies the five ways in which costs materially add to value:

(1) PRE–EXISTING DEFECTS. The cost ameliorates a condition or defect that existed prior to the property's acquisition or production by the taxpayer, no matter whether the taxpayer knew of this condition or defect at the time.

(2) PRE–USE COSTS. The cost relates to work performed on the property prior to the date the property is placed in service by the taxpayer.

(3) ADAPTATIONS. The cost adapts the property to a new or different use, no matter whether the cost permanently alters the structural composition of the property.

(4) BETTERMENTS. The cost results in a "betterment" of the property or a material addition to the property. This includes

costs that improve the property's quality or strength, or cause the property to be expanded or enlarged.

(5) INCREASED PRODUCTIVITY. The cost results in a material increase in the property's capacity, productivity, or efficiency.

* * *

REVENUE RULING 2004–62, 2004–25 I.R.B. 1072.

Facts: The taxpayer owns and manages timberland and grows trees for use in its lumber and wood products business. Once the taxpayer's target species establishes dominance in an area and becomes an established timber stand, it incurs costs to perform various "silvicultural practices" to manage, maintain, and protect the stand. These costs include labor and materials for fire, disease, insect, and brush control. In 2004, the taxpayer incurs costs to fertilize a portion of its timberland. This application, known as "post-establishment fertilization," is performed after the target species of timber has established dominance in the stand. The taxpayer generally performs post-establishment fertilization once during the long-term growth cycle of a timber stand. The fertilization supplements nutrients in the soil so as to maintain optimal growing conditions that will promote healthy development and maximize timber volume.

Issue: May the taxpayer deduct the fertilization costs?

Holding: Yes.

Rationale: It is well established that the costs incurred for silvicultural practices performed in established timber stands are deductible business expenses because they do not materially add value to the timber stand, substantially prolong its useful life, or adapt the timber stand to a new or different use. But there is no established rule with respect to fertilization. The Service ruled that a deduction for fertilization costs is proper, for post-establishment fertilization is akin to the deductible post-establishment silvicultural practices in that it does not add to value of the timber or prolong the useful life of any of the taxpayer's assets (the land and the trees).

* * *

Self-Assessment Question

(Solutions to Self–Assessment Questions are set forth in Appendix 3.)

SAQ 4–2. For each of the following outlays, determine whether the cost should be capitalized or treated as an expense. As before, do not bother to determine whether the expenses are deductible—this Question asks only whether each cost is properly considered a capital expenditure or an expense.

(a) Cost to install medical equipment in a vehicle to convert it into an ambulance

(b) Cost to test new machinery before it becomes operational

(c) Costs to prepare a vehicle for sale to an unrelated party, including costs to have the car professionally detailed and have the engine tuned

* * *

Restorations Versus Repairs. Taxpayers must also capitalize costs that "restore" a unit of property, meaning that they "substantially . . . prolong the economic useful life of the unit of property." Prop. Reg. § 1.263(a)–3(f)(1). The restoration of an asset to a "good-as-new" condition certainly constitutes an improvement of the asset, for the restored property will by definition have a longer useful life to the taxpayer than the pre-restoration property. At the same time, however, the regulations provide that "[a]mounts paid or incurred for incidental repairs and maintenance of property are not capital expenditures." Treas. Reg. § 1.263(a)–1(b). As you can imagine, then, taxpayers often claim that costs paid or incurred are merely for "repairs" and do not constitute permanent "restorations" or "improvements." If the costs are deemed "repairs," then the taxpayer gets an immediate deduction under either § 162 or § 212, assuming the costs relate to a business or investment activity. If the costs are "restorations" or "improvements," however, the deduction is deferred because the cost is added to the property's basis. The "repair versus improvement" question is one of the most litigated issues between taxpayers and the government. The following two cases offer some insight into what courts look for in distinguishing repairs and restorations. The results, however, seem to contradict. Is there a way to reconcile them?

MIDLAND EMPIRE PACKING COMPANY
v. COMMISSIONER

United States Tax Court, 1950.
14 T.C. 635 (1950).

ARUNDELL, Judge:

The issue in this case is whether an expenditure for a concrete lining in petitioner's basement to oilproof it against an oil nuisance created by a neighboring refinery is deductible as an ordinary and necessary expense * * * on the theory it was an expenditure for a repair * * *.

The respondent has contended, in part, that the expenditure is for a capital improvement and should be recovered through depreciation charges and is, therefore, not deductible as an ordinary and necessary business expense * * *.

It is none too easy to determine on which side of the line certain expenditures fall so that they may be accorded their proper treatment

for tax purposes. * * * In *Illinois Merchants Trust Co., Executor*, 4
B.T.A. 103, at page 106, we discussed this subject in some detail and in
our opinion said:

> * * * In determining whether an expenditure is a capital one or is
> chargeable against operating income, it is necessary to bear in mind
> that purpose for which the expenditure was made. To repair is to
> restore to a sound state or to mend, while a replacement connotes a
> substitution. A repair is an expenditure for the purpose of keeping
> the property in an ordinarily efficient operating condition. It does
> not add to the value of the property nor does it appreciably prolong
> its life. It merely keeps the property in an operating condition over
> its probable useful life for the uses for which it was acquired.
> Expenditures for that purpose are distinguishable from those for
> replacements, alterations, improvements, or additions which prolong
> the life of the property, increase its value, or make it adaptable to a
> different use. The one is a maintenance charge, while the others are
> additions to capital investment which should not be applied against
> current earnings.

It will be seen from our findings of fact that for some 25 years prior
to the taxable year petitioner had used the basement rooms of its plant
as a place for the curing of hams and bacon and for the storage of meat
and hides. The basement had been entirely satisfactory for this purpose
over the entire period in spite of the fact that there was some seepage of
water into the rooms from time to time. In the taxable year it was found
that not only water, but oil, was seeping through the concrete walls of
the basement of the packing plant and, while the water would soon drain
out, the oil would not, and there was left on the basement floor a thick
scum of oil which gave off a strong odor that permeated the air of the
entire plant, and the fumes from the oil created a fire hazard. It appears
that the oil which came from a nearby refinery had also gotten into the
water wells which served to furnish water for petitioner's plant, and as a
result of this whole condition the Federal meat inspectors advised
petitioner that it must discontinue the use of the water from the wells
and oilproof the basement, or else shut down its plant.

To meet this situation, petitioner during the taxable year undertook
steps to oilproof the basement by adding a concrete lining to the walls
from the floor to a height of about four feet and also added concrete to
the floor of the basement. It is the cost of this work which it seeks to
deduct as a repair. The basement was not enlarged by this work, nor did
the oilproofing serve to make it more desirable for the purpose for which
it had been used through the years prior to the time that the oil
nuisance had occurred. The evidence is that the expenditure did not add
to the value or prolong the expected life of the property over what they
were before the event occurred which made the repairs necessary. It is
true that after the work was done the seepage of water, as well as oil,
was stopped, but, as already stated, the presence of the water had never
been found objectionable. The repairs merely served to keep the property
in an operating condition over its probable useful life for the purpose for
which it was used.

    * * *

In *American Bemberg Corporation*, 10 T.C. 361, we allowed as deductions, on the ground that they were ordinary and necessary expenses, extensive expenditures made to prevent disaster, although the repairs were of a type which had never been needed before and were unlikely to recur. In that case the taxpayer, to stop cave-ins of soil which were threatening destruction of its manufacturing plant, hired an engineering firm which drilled to the bedrock and injected grout to fill the cavities were practicable, and made incidental replacements and repairs, including tightening of the fluid carriers. In two successive years the taxpayer expended $734,316.76 and $199,154.33, respectively, for such drilling and grouting and $153,474.20 and $79,687.29, respectively, for capital replacements. We found that the cost (other than replacement) of this program [was an expense], and stated in our opinion:

> In connection with the purpose of the work, the Proctor program was intended to avert a plant-wide disaster and avoid forced abandonment of the plant. The purpose was not to improve, better, extend, or increase the original plant, nor to prolong its original useful life. Its continued operation was endangered; the purpose of the expenditures was to enable petitioner to continue the plant in operation not on any new or better scale, but on the same scale and, so far as possible, as efficiently as it had operated before. The purpose was not to rebuild or replace the plant in whole or in part, but to keep the same plant as it was and where it was.

The petitioner here made the repairs in question in order that it might continue to operate its plant. Not only was there danger of fire from the oil and fumes, but the presence of the oil led the Federal meat inspectors to declare the basement an unsuitable place for the purpose for which it had been used for a quarter of a century. After the expenditures were made, the plant did not operate on a changed or larger scale, nor was it thereafter suitable for new or additional uses. The expenditure served only to permit petitioner to continue the use of the plant, and particularly the basement for its normal operations.

In our opinion, the expenditure of $4,868.81 for lining the basement walls and floor was essentially a repair and, as such, it is deductible as an ordinary and necessary business expense. * * *

Decision will be entered under Rule 50.

MT. MORRIS DRIVE–IN THEATRE CO. v. COMMISSIONER

United States Tax Court, 1955.
25 T.C. 272.

Kern, Judge:

Findings of Fact

* * *

In 1947 petitioner purchased 13 acres of farm land located on the outskirts of Flint, Michigan, upon which it proceeded to construct a drive-in or outdoor theatre. Prior to its purchase by the petitioner the land on which the theatre was built was farm land and contained vegetation. The slope of the land was such that the natural drainage of water was from the southerly line to the northerly boundary of the property and thence onto the adjacent land, owned by David and Mary D. Nickola, which was used both for farming and as a trailer park. The petitioner's land sloped sharply from south to north and also sloped from the east downward towards the west so that most of the drainage from the petitioner's property was onto the southwest corner of the Nickolas' land. The topography of the land purchased by petitioner was well known to petitioner at the time it was purchased and developed. The petitioner did not change the general slope of its land in constructing the drive-in theatre, but it removed the covering vegetation from the land, slightly increased the grade, and built aisles or ramps which were covered with gravel and were somewhat raised so that the passengers in the automobiles would be able to view the picture on the large outdoor screen.

As a result of petitioner's construction on and use of this land rain water falling upon it drained with an increased flow into and upon the adjacent property of the Nickolas. This result should reasonably have been anticipated by petitioner at the time when the construction work was done.

The Nickolas complained to the petitioner at various times after petitioner began the construction of the theatre that the work resulted in an acceleration and concentration of the flow of water which drained from the petitioner's property onto the Nickolas' land causing damage to their crops and roadways. On or about October 11, 1948, the Nickolas filed a suit against the petitioner in the Circuit Court for the County of Genesee, State of Michigan, asking for an award for damages done to their property by the accelerated and concentrated drainage of the water and for a permanent injunction restraining the defendant from permitting such drainage to continue. Following the filing of an answer by the petitioner and of a reply thereto by the Nickolas, the suit was settled by an agreement dated June 27, 1950. This agreement provided for the construction by the petitioner of a drainage system to carry water from its northern boundary across the Nickolas' property and thence to a public drain. The cost of maintaining the system was to be shared by the petitioner and the Nickolas, and the latter granted the petitioner and its successors an easement across their land for the purpose of constructing and maintaining the drainage system. The construction of the drain was completed in October 1950 under the supervision of engineers employed by the petitioner and the Nickolas at a cost to the petitioner of $8,224, which amount was paid by it in November 1950. The performance by the petitioner on its part of the agreement to construct the drainage system and to maintain the portion for which it was responsible constituted a full release of the Nickolas' claims against it. The petitioner chose to settle the dispute by constructing the drainage system because it did not wish to risk the possibility that continued litigation might result in a permanent injunction against its use of the drive-in theatre and because it wished to eliminate the cause of the friction between it and the adjacent landowners, who were in a position to seriously interfere with the petitioner's use of its property for outdoor theatre purposes. A settlement based on a monetary payment for past damages, the petitioner believed, would not remove the threat of claims for future damages.

On its 1950 income and excess profits tax return the petitioner claimed a deduction of $822.40 for depreciation of the drainage system for the period July 1, 1950, to December 31, 1950. The Commissioner disallowed without itemization $5,514.60 of a total depreciation expense deduction of $19,326.41 claimed by the petitioner. In its petition the petitioner asserted that the entire amount spent to construct the drainage system was fully deductible in 1950 as an ordinary and necessary business expense incurred in the settlement of a lawsuit, or, in the alternative, as a loss, and claimed a refund of part of the $10,591.56 of income and excess profits tax paid by it for that year.

* * *

OPINION

When petitioner purchased, in 1947, the land which it intended to use for a drive-in theatre, its president was thoroughly familiar with the topography of this land which was such that when the covering vegetation was removed and graveled ramps were constructed and used by its patrons, the flow of natural precipitation on the lands of abutting property owners would be materially accelerated. Some provision should have been made to solve this drainage problem in order to avoid annoyance and harassment to its neighbors. If petitioner had included in its original construction plans an expenditure for a proper drainage system no one could doubt that such an expenditure would have been capital in nature.

Within a year after petitioner had finished its inadequate construction of the drive-in theatre, the need of a proper drainage system was forcibly called to its attention by one of the neighboring property owners, and under the threat of a lawsuit filed approximately a year after the theatre was constructed, the drainage system was built by petitioner who now seeks to deduct its cost as an ordinary and necessary business expenses, or as a loss.

We agree with respondent that the cost to petitioner of acquiring and constructing a drainage system in connection with its drive-in theatre was a capital expenditure.

Here was no sudden catastrophic loss caused by a "physical fault" undetected by the taxpayer in spite of due precautions taken by it at the time of its original construction work as in *American Bemberg Corporation*, 10 T.C. 361; no unforeseeable external factor as in *Midland Empire Packing Co.*, 14 T.C. 635; and no change in the cultivation of farm property caused by improvements in technique and made many years after the property in question was put to productive use as in *J. H. Collingwood*, 20 T.C. 937. In the instant case it was obvious at the time when the drive-in theatre was constructed, that a drainage system would be required to properly dispose of the natural precipitation normally to be expected, and that until this was accomplished, petitioner's capital investment was incomplete. In addition, it should be emphasized that here there was no mere restoration or rearrangement of the original capital asset, but there was the acquisition and construction of a capital asset which petitioner had not previously had, namely, a new drainage system.

That this drainage system was acquired and constructed and that payments therefor were made in compromise of a lawsuit is not determinative of whether such payments were ordinary and necessary business expenses or capital expenditures. "The decisive test is still the character of the transaction which gives rise to the payment." *Hales-Mullaly v. Commissioner*, 131 F.2d 509, 511, 512.

In our opinion the character of the transaction in the instant case indicates that the transaction was a capital expenditure.

Reviewed by the Court.

Decision will be entered for the respondent.

* * *

RICE, J. dissenting:

It seems to me that *J.H. Collingwood*, 20 T.C. 937 (1953), *Midland Empire Packing Co.*, 14 T.C. 635 (1950), *American Bemberg Corporation*, 10 T.C. 361 (1948), *aff'd.* 177 F.2d 200 (C.A. 1949), and *Illinois Merchants Trust Co., Executor*, 4 B.T.A. 103 (1926), are ample authority for the conclusion that the expenditure which petitioner made was an ordinary and necessary business expense, which did not improve, better, extend, increase, or prolong the useful life of its property. The expenditure did not cure the original geological defect of the natural drainage onto the Nickolas' land, but only dealt with the intermediate consequence thereof. The majority opinion does not distinguish those cases adequately. And since those cases and the result reached herein do not seem to me to be able to "live together," I cannot agree with the majority that the expenditure here was capital in nature.

OPPER, JOHNSON, BRUCE, and MULRONEY, JJ., agree with this dissent.

Note and Question

On appeal, a divided Sixth Circuit affirmed the Tax Court's decision in *Mt. Morris*, 238 F.2d 85 (6th Cir. 1956). The majority simply affirmed for the reasons stated in the Tax Court's majority opinion, adding only that "[t]here is substantial evidence that [the expenditure] added to the value of the petitioner's land for the use to which it had been put." Judge McAllister, however, reasoned that if the taxpayer paid $8,224 to the Nickolas in settlement of their suit, there would be no question that the settlement payment would be a deductible expense. Finding no substantive difference between a payment to the Nickolas for construction of the drain and the taxpayer's cost in constructing the drain itself, Judge McAllister joined the dissenters of the Tax Court.

Who, in your opinion, has the better argument?

* * *

The Repair Allowance Method. To provide some certainty to taxpayers, the proposed regulations offer the use of a "repair allowance method" to determine whether a particular cost is an improvement that must be capitalized or an expense that might qualify for a current deduction. If a taxpayer elects to use this method, the taxpayer may treat all costs for material and labor paid in any one taxable year to repair or improve the property as expenses (not capital expenditures) up to the "repair allowance amount." Costs in excess of the repair allowance amount in any one taxable year must be capitalized. The repair allowance amount applicable to any one item of property depends upon the recovery period of that property for purposes of depreciation deductions. All assets with the same recovery period are grouped together and a single repair allowance amount for that class of property is determined. The repair allowance amount for any one class of property, in turn, depends generally on the original cost of the property in that classification. An "average unadjusted basis" is computed by averaging the combined original costs of assets in the same class of property at the beginning of the taxable year and the combined original costs of assets in the same class of property at the end of the taxable year. This average unadjusted basis is then multiplied by a fixed percentage amount set forth in the proposed regulations or, if applicable, in future guidance issued by Treasury.

EXAMPLE: At the beginning of Year One, Harvey owns Asset #1 (office furniture), a tangible asset classified as "5–year property" for purposes of depreciation deductions. Harvey uses this asset exclusively in his business. Asset #1 originally cost Harvey $20,000 when he purchased it (some time before the beginning of Year One). During the year, Harvey acquires Asset #2 (automobile), another tangible asset classified as "5–year property" for purposes of depreciation deduction. Harvey pays $10,000 for Asset #2 and uses it exclusively in his business. Harvey also acquires Asset #3 (tug boat), a tangible asset classified as "10–year property" for purposes of depreciation deductions, by paying $500,000. Like the others, Harvey uses Asset #3 exclusively in his business. Harvey still owns Asset #1, Asset #2, and Asset #3 at the end of Year One.

> During Year One, Harvey spends a total of $5,000 in making repairs and improvements to Asset #2. He also spends $20,000 to make repairs and improvements to Asset #3. He incurs no costs with respect to Asset #1.
>
> If Harvey elects to use the repair allowance method, Asset #1 and Asset #2, both classified as 5–year property, will be grouped together. The average original cost of these assets is $15,000 (average of $20,000 for Asset #1 and $10,000 for Asset #2). The "repair allowance percentage" for 5–year property is 10 percent. Prop. Reg. § 1.263(a)–3(g)(8). Thus, the maximum amount of repair and improvement costs with respect to Asset #1 and Asset #2 that can be treated as expenses is $1,500 (10 percent of $15,000). Harvey's total repair and improvement costs with respect to these assets is $5,000. Accordingly, Harvey can expense $1,500 of these costs but he must capitalize the remaining $3,500.
>
> Asset #3 is the only 10–year property described in these facts. Consequently, the repair allowance percentage is applied to the original cost of Asset #3, $500,000. The repair allowance percentage for 10–year property is 5 percent. Prop. Reg. § 1.263(a)–3(g)(8). Thus, the maximum amount of repair and improvement costs with respect to Asset #3 that can be treated as expenses is $25,000 (5 percent of $500,000). Harvey's total repair and improvement costs with respect to Asset #3 in Year One is only $20,000, so Harvey can expense these entire costs even if the other rules in the proposed regulations would treat these costs as improvements or restoration costs.

And the proposed regulations have the nerve to label the repair allowance method a "simplified" method for distinguishing repair costs from improvement costs!

* * *

Problem 4–2

Kermit and Peggy Frogg own a commercial building in Phoenix. They lease space in the building as their sole business activity. In the most recent taxable year, Kermit and Peggy incurred the costs described below, all directly related to the building. For each such item, determine whether the cost gives rise to a current deduction or whether the cost must be capitalized, ignoring any possible election under the repair allowance method.

(a) $50,000 to remove asbestos insulation and replace it with less thermally efficient insulation. The removal and replacement did not affect building operations other than the health and safety of tenants and their employees.

(b) $3,000 to restore an awning that originally cost $1,000 to construct and install. The current cost to construct and install a new awning is $10,000.

(c) $22,000 to repair the driveway providing access from the main road to the building parking lot. The driveway was damaged by a storm that flooded a nearby river. Kermit and Peggy paid to reroute the driveway and raise its elevation at the point of damage in order to prevent damage from future floods.

(d) $5,000 to add safety equipment to the building elevators. The extra equipment was required to bring the building in compliance with the municipal building code.

(e) $2,500 to fix a leak in the building's roof. Does it matter how long Kermit and Peggy have owned the building?

(f) $12,000 in "refurbishing costs." When a tenant vacates space in the building, Kermit and Peggy incur these costs to replace wallpaper and repaint the interior.

(g) $20,000 in "landscaping costs." These costs include trees, shrubs, fertilizer, and water.

* * *

(2) COSTS RELATED TO INTANGIBLE ASSETS

Code: *Review* IRC §§ 263(a); 263A.

Regs: Treas. Reg. §§ 1.263(a)–4; *Skim* Treas. Reg. § 1.263(a)–5.

Perhaps because tangible property can be seen and touched, the capitalization rules for tangible assets are manageable. Costs with respect to intangible assets present more complicated issues. The regulations again offer comprehensive guidance here, but in order to appreciate how the regulations came to be, one must begin with the following case, the Supreme Court's most recent battle with capitalization.

INDOPCO, INC. v. COMMISSIONER

United States Supreme Court, 1992.
503 U.S. 79, 112 S.Ct. 1039, 117 L.Ed.2d 226.

Justice BLACKMUN delivered the opinion of the Court.

In this case we must decide whether certain professional expenses incurred by a target corporation in the course of a friendly takeover are deductible by that corporation as "ordinary and necessary" business expenses under § 162(a) of the Internal Revenue Code.

I

Most of the relevant facts are stipulated. See App. 12, 149. Petitioner INDOPCO, Inc., formerly named National Starch and Chemical Corporation and hereinafter referred to as National Starch, is a Delaware corporation that manufactures and sells adhesives, starches, and specialty chemical products. In October 1977, representatives of Unilever United States, Inc., also a Delaware corporation (Unilever),[1] expressed

1. Unilever is a holding company. Its then principal subsidiaries were Lever Brothers Co. and Thomas J. Lipton, Inc.

interest in acquiring National Starch, which was one of its suppliers, through a friendly transaction. National Starch at the time had outstanding over 6,563,000 common shares held by approximately 3,700 shareholders. The stock was listed on the New York Stock Exchange.

"friendly takeover"

* * *

* * *

In November 1977, National Starch's directors were formally advised of Unilever's interest and the proposed transaction. At that time, Debevoise, Plimpton, Lyons & Gates, National Starch's counsel, told the directors that under Delaware law they had a fiduciary duty to ensure that the proposed transaction would be fair to the shareholders. National Starch thereupon engaged the investment banking firm of Morgan Stanley & Co., Inc., to evaluate its shares, to render a fairness opinion, and generally to assist in the event of the emergence of a hostile tender offer.

Although Unilever originally had suggested a price between $65 and $70 per share, negotiations resulted in a final offer of $73.50 per share, a figure Morgan Stanley found to be fair. Following approval by National Starch's board and the issuance of a favorable private ruling from the Internal Revenue Service that the transaction would be tax free under § 351 for those National Starch shareholders who exchanged their stock * * *, the transaction was consummated in August 1978.

Morgan Stanley charged National Starch a fee of $2,200,000, along with $7,586 for out-of-pocket expenses and $18,000 for legal fees. The Debevoise firm charged National Starch $490,000, along with $15,069 for out-of-pocket expenses. National Starch also incurred expenses aggregating $150,962 for miscellaneous items—such as accounting, printing, proxy solicitation, and Securities and Exchange Commission fees—in connection with the transaction. No issue is raised as to the propriety or reasonableness of these charges.

investment banking fees.

legal fees

misc. items.

On its federal income tax return for its short taxable year ended August 15, 1978, National Starch claimed a deduction for the $2,225,586 paid to Morgan Stanley, but did not deduct the $505,069 paid to Debevoise or the other expenses. Upon audit, the Commissioner of Internal Revenue disallowed the claimed deduction and issued a notice of deficiency. Petitioner sought redetermination in the United States Tax Court, asserting, however, not only the right to deduct the investment banking fees and expenses but, as well, the legal and miscellaneous expenses incurred.

The Tax Court, in an unreviewed decision, ruled that the expenditures were capital in nature and therefore not deductible under § 162(a) in the 1978 return as "ordinary and necessary expenses." The court based its holding primarily on the long-term benefits that accrued to National Starch from the Unilever acquisition. The United States Court of Appeals for the Third Circuit affirmed, upholding the Tax Court's findings that "both Unilever's enormous resources and the possibility of synergy arising from the transaction served the long-term betterment of National Starch." In so doing, the Court of Appeals rejected National Starch's contention that, because the disputed expenses did not "create or enhance ... a separate and distinct additional asset," see *Commissioner v. Lincoln Savings & Loan Assn.,* 403 U.S. 345, 354, 91 S.Ct. 1893, 1899, 29 L.Ed.2d 519 (1971), they could not be capitalized and therefore were deductible under § 162(a). We granted certiorari to resolve a perceived conflict on the issue among the Courts of Appeals.

II

Section 162(a) of the Internal Revenue Code allows the deduction of "all the ordinary and necessary expenses paid or incurred during the taxable year in carrying on any trade or business." In contrast, § 263 of the Code allows no deduction for a capital expenditure—an "amount paid out for new buildings or for permanent improvements or betterments made to increase the value of any property or estate." The primary effect of characterizing a payment as either a business expense or a capital expenditure concerns the timing of the taxpayer's cost recovery: While business expenses are currently deductible, a capital expenditure usually is amortized and depreciated over the life of the relevant asset, or, where no specific asset or useful life can be ascertained, is deducted upon dissolution of the enterprise. Through provisions such as these, the Code endeavors to match expenses with the revenues of the taxable period to which they are properly attributable, thereby resulting in a more accurate calculation of net income for tax purposes.

In exploring the relationship between deductions and capital expenditures, this Court has noted the "familiar rule" that "an income tax deduction is a matter of legislative grace and that the burden of clearly showing the right to the claimed deduction is on the taxpayer." *Interstate Transit Lines v. Commissioner,* 319 U.S. 590, 593, 63 S.Ct. 1279, 1281, 87 L.Ed. 1607 (1943); *Deputy v. Du Pont,* 308 U.S. 488, 493, 60 S.Ct. 363, 366, 84 L.Ed. 416 (1940); *New Colonial Ice Co. v. Helvering,* 292 U.S. 435, 440, 54 S.Ct. 788, 790, 78 L.Ed. 1348 (1934). The notion that deductions are exceptions to the norm of capitalization finds support in various aspects of the Code. Deductions are specifically enumerated and thus are subject to disallowance in favor of capitalization. See §§ 161 and 261. Nondeductible capital expenditures, by contrast, are not exhaustively enumerated in the Code; rather than providing a "complete list of nondeductible expenditures," *Lincoln Savings,* 403 U.S., at 358, 91 S.Ct., at 1901, § 263 serves as a general means of distinguishing capital expenditures from current expenses. For these reasons, deductions are strictly construed and allowed only "as there is a clear provision therefor."

* * * The Court has recognized, however, that the "decisive distinctions" between current expenses and capital expenditures "are those of

degree and not of kind," and that because each case "turns on its special facts," the cases sometimes appear difficult to harmonize.

National Starch contends that the decision in *Lincoln Savings* changed these familiar backdrops and announced an exclusive test for identifying capital expenditures, a test in which "creation or enhancement of an asset" is a prerequisite to capitalization, and deductibility under § 162(a) is the rule rather than the exception. We do not agree, for we conclude that National Starch has overread *Lincoln Savings*.

In *Lincoln Savings,* we were asked to decide whether certain premiums, required by federal statute to be paid by a savings and loan association to the Federal Savings and Loan Insurance Corporation (FSLIC), were ordinary and necessary expenses under § 162(a), as Lincoln Savings argued and the Court of Appeals had held, or capital expenditures under § 263, as the Commissioner contended. We found that the "additional" premiums, the purpose of which was to provide FSLIC with a secondary reserve fund in which each insured institution retained a pro rata interest recoverable in certain situations, "serv[e] to create or enhance for Lincoln what is essentially a separate and distinct additional asset." 403 U.S., at 354, 91 S.Ct., at 1899. "[A]s an inevitable consequence," we concluded, "the payment is capital in nature and not an expense, let alone an ordinary expense, deductible under § 162(a)." *Ibid.*

Lincoln Savings stands for the simple proposition that a taxpayer's expenditure that "serves to create or enhance ... a separate and distinct" asset should be capitalized under § 263. It by no means follows, however, that *only* expenditures that create or enhance separate and distinct assets are to be capitalized under § 263. We had no occasion in *Lincoln Savings* to consider the tax treatment of expenditures that, unlike the additional premiums at issue there, did not create or enhance a specific asset, and thus the case cannot be read to preclude capitalization in other circumstances. In short, *Lincoln Savings* holds that the creation of a separate and distinct asset well may be a sufficient, but not a necessary, condition to classification as a capital expenditure.

Nor does our statement in *Lincoln Savings* that "the presence of an ensuing benefit that may have some future aspect is not controlling" prohibit reliance on future benefit as a means of distinguishing an ordinary business expense from a capital expenditure. Although the mere presence of an incidental future benefit—"*some* future aspect"— may not warrant capitalization, a taxpayer's realization of benefits beyond the year in which the expenditure is incurred is undeniably important in determining whether the appropriate tax treatment is immediate deduction or capitalization. See *United States v. Mississippi Chemical Corp.,* 405 U.S. 298, 310, 92 S.Ct. 908, 915, 31 L.Ed.2d 217 (1972) (expense that "is of value in more than one taxable year" is a nondeductible capital expenditure); *Central Texas Savings & Loan Assn. v. United States,* 731 F.2d 1181, 1183 (CA5 1984) ("While the period of the benefits may not be controlling in all cases, it nonetheless remains a prominent, if not predominant, characteristic of a capital item"). Indeed, the text of the Code's capitalization provision, § 263(a)(1), which refers to "permanent improvements or betterments," itself envisions an inquiry into the duration and extent of the benefits realized by the taxpayer.

III

In applying the foregoing principles to the specific expenditures at issue in this case, we conclude that National Starch has not demonstrated that the investment banking, legal, and other costs it incurred in connection with Unilever's acquisition of its shares are deductible as ordinary and necessary business expenses under § 162(a).

Although petitioner attempts to dismiss the benefits that accrued to National Starch from the Unilever acquisition as "entirely speculative" or "merely incidental," the Tax Court's and the Court of Appeals' findings that the transaction produced significant benefits to National Starch that extended beyond the tax year in question are amply supported by the record. For example, in commenting on the merger with Unilever, National Starch's 1978 "Progress Report" observed that the company would "benefit greatly from the availability of Unilever's enormous resources, especially in the area of basic technology." Morgan Stanley's report to the National Starch board concerning the fairness to shareholders of a possible business combination with Unilever noted that National Starch management "feels that some synergy may exist with the Unilever organization given a) the nature of the Unilever chemical, paper, plastics and packaging operations . . . and b) the strong consumer products orientation of Unilever United States, Inc."

In addition to these anticipated resource-related benefits, National Starch obtained benefits through its transformation from a publicly held, freestanding corporation into a wholly owned subsidiary of Unilever. The Court of Appeals noted that National Starch management viewed the transaction as "swapping approximately 3500 shareholders for one." Following Unilever's acquisition of National Starch's outstanding shares, National Starch was no longer subject to what even it terms the "substantial" shareholder-relations expenses a publicly traded corporation incurs, including reporting and disclosure obligations, proxy battles, and derivative suits. The acquisition also allowed National Starch, in the interests of administrative convenience and simplicity, to eliminate previously authorized but unissued shares of preferred and to reduce the total number of authorized shares of common from 8,000,000 to 1,000.

Courts long have recognized that expenses such as these, "incurred for the purpose of changing the corporate structure for the benefit of future operations are not ordinary and necessary business expenses." *General Bancshares Corp. v. Commissioner,* 326 F.2d, at 715 (quoting *Farmers Union Corp. v. Commissioner,* 300 F.2d 197, 200 (CA9), cert. denied, 371 U.S. 861, 83 S.Ct. 117, 9 L.Ed.2d 99 (1962)). Deductions for professional expenses thus have been disallowed in a wide variety of cases concerning changes in corporate structure. Although support for these decisions can be found in the specific terms of § 162(a), which require that deductible expenses be "ordinary and necessary" and incurred "in carrying on any trade or business," courts more frequently have characterized an expenditure as capital in nature because "the purpose for which the expenditure is made has to do with the corporation's operations and betterment, sometimes with a continuing capital asset, for the duration of its existence or for the indefinite future or for a time somewhat longer than the current taxable year." *General Bancshares Corp. v. Commissioner,* 326 F.2d, at 715. The rationale behind these decisions applies equally to the professional charges at issue in this case.

IV

The expenses that National Starch incurred in Unilever's friendly takeover do not qualify for deduction as "ordinary and necessary" business expenses under § 162(a). The fact that the expenditures do not create or enhance a separate and distinct additional asset is not controlling; the acquisition-related expenses bear the indicia of capital expenditures and are to be treated as such.

The judgment of the Court of Appeals is affirmed.

It is so ordered.

* * *

The Aftermath of INDOPCO. The Service considered *INDOPCO* a tremendous victory. This caused taxpayers to worry that the Service would use the case as authority for requiring taxpayers to capitalize many costs that were traditionally treated as deductible expenses. To its credit, the Service's use of *INDOPCO* was somewhat restrained. In a series of rulings, the Service declared that many previously deductible items remained as such after *INDOPCO*. See, e.g., *Revenue Ruling 92–80* (advertising expenses still deductible); *Revenue Ruling 94–38* (hazardous waste clean-up costs still deductible, except that construction of groundwater treatment facilities would be capitalized); *Revenue Ruling 94–77* (severance benefits still deductible); *Revenue Ruling 95–32* (certain conservation expenditures still deductible); and *Revenue Ruling 96–62* (training costs still deductible).

BLACK HILLS CORP. v. COMMISSIONER, 73 F.3d 799 (8th Cir. 1996).

Facts: The taxpayer, a mining company, paid premiums for insurance covering its miners who suffer from black lung disease. The insurance contract required the taxpayer to pay front-loaded premiums that were used to build a reserve account that would cover the cost of the insurance for later years. The taxpayer deducted the entire cost of the front-loaded premiums, and the Service argued that the cost should be capitalized.

Issue: Must the cost be capitalized?

Holding: The portion of each payment that was credited to the reserve account had to be capitalized.

Rationale: The reserve portion of the premiums represented insurance coverage for future years and not coverage for the present taxable year. "[T]he premiums paid produced significant benefits * * * beyond the tax years in question and [are not] merely incidental or secondary."

REVENUE RULING 2000–4, 2000–1 C.B. 331.

Facts: The International Organization for Standardization issued a set of international standards for quality management systems called "ISO 9000." In order to obtain ISO 9000 certification, a company must "assess its current quality processes, create a quality manual, train its employees, * * * implement the new quality system, * * * [and] obtain formal certification from an independent auditor * * * that its quality management system conforms to a specific ISO 9000 standard." A valid certification of compliance generally lasts from two to four years, and a company may incur additional costs to maintain and renew certification. Many companies and governments require ISO 9000 certification as a condition to doing business. The taxpayer incurred costs in obtaining ISO 9000 certification and sought a current deduction for those costs.

Issue: Are the costs incurred in obtaining ISO 9000 certification deductible as expenses?

Holding: Yes.

Rationale: While the costs to create a quality manual must be capitalized, the remaining costs can be deducted. "ISO 9000 certification does not result in future benefits that are more than incidental."

PNC BANCORP, INC. v. COMMISSIONER, 212 F.3d 822 (3d Cir. 2000).

Facts: The taxpayer, a bank, incurred costs in processing loan applications, obtaining credit reports, getting appraisals on collateral, and recording security interests. In accordance with the Financial Accounting Standards Board's Statement of Financial Accounting Standards No. 91, the bank deferred the costs over the life of a loan. But for federal income tax purposes, the long-accepted practice of the bank was to deduct the origination costs when incurred. In 1998, the Tax Court upheld a deficiency assessment against the bank, concluding that the origination costs must be capitalized.

Issue: Must the loan origination costs be capitalized?

Holding: No. The costs may be treated as expenses.

Rationale: Noting also that financial accounting standards have little relevance to the issue of capitalization for tax purposes, the court faulted the Tax Court's logic. "In the instant case, the Tax Court proceeded from the clearly accurate premise that the expenses in question were associated with the loans, incurred in connection with the acquisition of the loans, * * * to the faulty conclusion that these expenses themselves created the loans. * * * We conclude that the term 'create' does not stretch this far. In *Lincoln Savings*, it was the payments themselves that formed the corpus of the Secondary Reserve; therefore, it naturally follows that these payments 'created' the reserve fund. In [this] case, however, the expenses are merely costs associated with the origination of loans; the expenses themselves do not become part of the balance of the loan.''

WELLS FARGO & CO. v. COMMISSIONER, 224 F.3d 874 (8th Cir. 2000).

Facts: The taxpayer, a bank, merged with another bank in 1991. In the months leading up to the merger, some of the taxpayer's officers spent considerable time exploring the transaction and investigating the other bank. The taxpayer deducted the salaries paid to these officers, but the Tax Court sustained the Service's position that a portion of the salaries must be capitalized under *INDOPCO*. Because the salaries were "connected to an event * * * that produced a significant long-term benefit," the Tax Court determined that capitalization was required.

Issue: Must the officers' salaries attributable to the merger be capitalized?

Holding: Not entirely.

Rationale: The salaries paid to the officers were, at most, *indirectly* related to the merger. However, since the taxpayer made a firm decision to go forward with the merger in July, 1991, salaries attributable to the merger after that date are not "investigatory" costs and must be capitalized.

LYCHUK v. COMMISSIONER, 116 T.C. 374 (2001).

Facts: The taxpayer, whose sole business activity was the procurement and servicing of installment loans made by car dealers to customers with bad credit, deducted various expenses incurred in procurement, including salaries and benefits paid to employees and various overhead expenses like printing, telephone, computer, rent, and utility charges. In deciding whether to purchase a particular contract, the taxpayer conducted a credit check of the customer. The average time to complete a credit check was between three and four hours. The taxpayer deducted the aforementioned expenses, and the Commissioner disallowed the deductions.

Issue: Are these costs incurred in procuring installment contracts deductible?

Holding: The general overhead expenses are deductible but the salaries and benefits paid to the employees must be capitalized.

Rationale: A deduction is proper for the overhead expenses, for these expenses were "not directly related to the anticipated acquisition of any of the installment contracts." But the court, expressly rejecting the analysis of the Third Circuit in *PNC Bancorp*, held that the salaries and benefits allocable to the procurement of the installment contracts had to be capitalized even though such costs were "normal and routine" in the course of the taxpayer's business. The taxpayer in *Lychuk* resided in the Sixth Circuit, so the court was not constrained to follow *PNC Bancorp*.

* * *

The INDOPCO Regulations. In 2004, Treasury issued final regulations generally requiring capitalization of certain amounts paid to acquire, create, or enhance intangible assets. See Treas. Reg. § 1.263(a)–4(b)(1). They also identify specific categories of intangible assets for which capitalization is required even if the taxpayer's cost arguably does not produce a significant future benefit. These identified intangible assets are grouped into categories based on whether the intangible asset is acquired from another party or created by the taxpayer. See Treas. Reg. §§ 1.263(a)–4(c) (for acquired intangibles) and 1.263(a)–4(d) (for created intangibles). For example, an amount paid to acquire another's trademark by purchase must be capitalized. Treas. Reg. § 1.263(a)–4(c)(1)(viii). Likewise, an amount paid to obtain one's own trademark must be capitalized. Treas. Reg. § 1.263(a)–4(d)(5)(i).

The regulations contain a number of conventions designed to simplify the determination of when capitalization is required. For instance, taxpayers may avoid capitalizing amounts paid to induce another to enter into, renew, or renegotiate a contract related to the provision of services if the amount paid does not exceed $5,000. Treas. Reg. §§ 1.263(a)–4(d)(6)(v). Moreover, the regulations contain a special "12–month rule" that allows a current deduction for the amount paid to create or enhance an intangible asset if: (1) the resulting benefit does not last more than 12 months; and (2) the resulting benefit does not extend beyond the end of the taxable year following the taxable year in which the payment is made. Treas. Reg. § 1.263(a)–4(f)(1).

The regulations require capitalization of costs that facilitate the acquisition or creation of an intangible asset. See Treas. Reg. § 1.263(a)–4(e)(1). Here, too, if the costs at issue do not exceed $5,000, a simplifying convention permits the costs to be expensed. Treas. Reg. §§ 1.263(a)–4(e)(4)(i) and 1.263(a)–4(e)(4)(iii).

The regulations also give guidance for determining the extent to which taxpayers must capitalize transaction costs that facilitate the acquisition of a trade or business activity or a change in the capital structure of a business entity. See Treas. Reg. § 1.263(a)–5. These rules for transaction costs, discussed more fully in Part C of this Chapter, are intended to enhance administrability and reduce the cost of compliance to taxpayers.

* * *

Self-Assessment Question

(Solutions to Self–Assessment Questions are set forth in Appendix 3.)

SAQ 4–3. Lucy Van Pelt sells goop, an edible mush, to customers from a sidewalk vending stand. To protect her personal assets from the claims of business creditors, Lucy purchased a general liability insurance policy that protects all aspects of her goop business operations. Lucy purchased the policy for $12,000 on October 1, Year One. Under each of the alternative scenarios described below, determine whether Lucy must capitalize the cost of the policy under Regulation § 1.263(a)–4(f)(1).

(a) The policy's coverage period runs from October 1, Year One, until September 30, Year Two. *Deduct all $12K in Year ~~Two~~ One.*

(b) The policy's coverage period runs from January 1, Year Two, until December 31, Year Two. *Deduct all $12K in Year One.*

(c) The policy's coverage period runs from February 1, Year Two, until January 31, Year Three. *Deduct $11K in Year 2 and $1K in Year 3*

✱ Problem 4-3 ✱

J.K., the author of the bestselling "Larry Kotter" book series, is currently working on her sixth installment, "Larry Kotter and the Internal Revenue Code." Assume she pays the following costs with respect to her work on the book:

- $3,000 for a new laptop computer with a word processing program; – *more than 12 months*
- $300 for several notepads and pens; *less than 12 months necessary ordin.*
- $1,000 for a new computer printer; *more than 12m*
- $500 for toner cartridges and paper, all for the new printer; *less than 12 months*
- $800 for reference books related to the subject of her new book; – *research/experimental except*
- $7,500 for the services of an illustrator; – *capital expend.*
- $5,000 for her attorney to review the publishing contract; and *expense*
- $300 fee for the right to reprint an excerpt from another book. – *capitalized?*

Cost defending or perfecting title to prop. = capital expense

Under the terms of her publishing agreement, J.K. will receive a ten percent royalty from each book sold by the publisher. The contract states that J.K. retains all ownership interests over the work once it is complete, including the illustrations.

(a) To what extent can J.K. treat these costs as expenses deductible under § 162(a)?

(b) Would J.K. have gross income if the publisher paid the $300 reprint fee instead of J.K.? *Yes – but only $30?*

✱ Problem 4-4 ✱

Now assume that J.K. completed the sixth "Larry Kotter" book and that copies again flew off the shelves.

(a) J.K. got upset at her publisher because it paid her ten percent royalty based on net sales, while the contract clearly required the royalty to be based on gross sales. J.K. paid an attorney $10,000 to assist her in collecting the proper amount due under the contract. Can J.K. deduct the fee paid to the attorney? *Yes – litigation about the Right to income from property – are current expenses*

(b) Val DeMort sued J.K. for copyright infringement, claiming that the plot of the sixth "Larry Kotter" book was lifted from a book Val wrote a decade ago. J.K. paid another attorney $5,000 to defend against the lawsuit, and the defense was successful. Can J.K. deduct the fee paid to the attorney?

No. Litigation defending title to prop = capital expense

(c) Would the answer to (b) change if the defense was not successful?

maybe ?

_____

C. DEDUCTION FOR EXPENSES

If a taxpayer's outlay is properly classified an expense and not a capital expenditure, the question becomes whether the expense is deductible. If it is not, then by definition Congress considers the cost to be a consumption expense. In turn, then, the gross income derived to fund that expense should be subject to federal income tax.

Friday Sept. 30th

p. 202-232

omit Rockfeller case

Very generally, expenses are deductible if they relate to a taxpayer's "trade or business" activity, or if the expense is paid or incurred in the production or collection of income from an activity that does not rise to the level of a trade or business (what we earlier classified an "investment" activity). See §§ 162(a) and 212. In this Part, we will look at the deduction provision for business expenses, § 162(a), the deduction provision for investment expenses, § 212, and the special treatment given under § 195 to so-called "start-up expenditures," those that are incurred prior to the commencement of a business or investment activity.

(1) TRADE OR BUSINESS EXPENSES

Code: IRC § 162(a).

Regs: None.

The § 162(a) deduction for business expenses is the most important deduction provision in the Internal Revenue Code. It is, by far, the most widely used authority for deductions. The guts of the deduction are set forth in the first clause of § 162(a)—up to the first comma. This clause contains no less than *six* separate elements required for a deduction:

(1) it must be an **ordinary**

(2) and **necessary**

(3) **expense**

(4) that was **paid or incurred during the taxable year**

(5) **in carrying on**

(6) a **trade or business** activity.

To get an understanding of the § 162(a) deduction, we will examine each of these elements in turn to see how they have been interpreted over the years.

Ordinary and Necessary. The plain connotation here is that an expense should be *routine* and *directly related* to the business activity. As the following case demonstrates, the Supreme Court basically agrees.

WELCH v. HELVERING

United States Supreme Court, 1933.
290 U.S. 111, 54 S.Ct. 8, 78 L.Ed. 212.

MR. JUSTICE CARDOZO delivered the opinion of the Court.

The question to be determined is whether payments by a taxpayer, who is in business as a commission agent, are allowable deductions in the computation of his income if made to the creditors of a bankrupt corporation in an endeavor to strengthen his own standing and credit.

In 1922 petitioner was the secretary of the E. L. Welch Company, a Minnesota corporation, engaged in the grain business. The company was adjudged an involuntary bankrupt, and had a discharge from its debts. Thereafter the petitioner made a contract with the Kellogg Company to purchase grain for it on a commission. In order to re-establish his relations with customers whom he had known when acting for the Welch Company and to solidify his credit and standing, he decided to pay the debts of the Welch business so far as he was able. In fulfillment of that resolve, he made payments of substantial amounts during five successive years. * * * The Commissioner ruled that these payments were not deductible from income as ordinary and necessary expenses, but were rather in the nature of capital expenditures, an outlay for the development of reputation and good will. The Board of Tax Appeals sustained the action of the Commissioner, and the Court of Appeals for the Eighth Circuit affirmed. The case is here on certiorari.

* * *

We may assume that the payments to creditors of the Welch Company were necessary for the development of the petitioner's business, at least in the sense that they were appropriate and helpful. *McCulloch v. Maryland*, 4 Wheat. 316, 4 L.Ed. 579. He certainly thought they were, and we should be slow to override his judgment. But the problem is not solved when the payments are characterized as necessary. Many necessary payments are charges upon capital. There is need to determine whether they are both necessary and ordinary. Now, what is ordinary, though there must always be a strain of constancy within it, is none the less a variable affected by time and place and circumstance. Ordinary in this context does not mean that the payments must be habitual or normal in the sense that the same taxpayer will have to make them often. A lawsuit affecting the safety of a business may happen once in a lifetime. The counsel fees may be so heavy that repetition is unlikely. None the less, the expense is an ordinary one because we know from experience that payments for such a purpose, whether the amount is large or small, are the common and accepted means of defense against attack. * * * The situation is unique in the life of the individual affected, but not in the life of the group, the community, of which he is a part. At such times there are norms of conduct that help to stabilize our judgment, and make it certain and objective. The instance is not erratic, but is brought within a known type.

The line of demarcation is now visible between the case that is here and the one supposed for illustration. We try to classify this act as ordinary or the opposite, and the norms of conduct fail us. No longer can we have recourse to any fund of business experience, to any known business practice. Men do at times pay the debts of others without legal obligation or the lighter obligation imposed by the usages of trade or by neighborly amenities, but they do not do so ordinarily, not even though the result might be to heighten their reputation for generosity and opulence. Indeed, if language is to be read in its natural and common meaning, we should have to say that payment in such circumstances, instead of being ordinary is in a high degree extraordinary. There is nothing ordinary in the stimulus evoking it, and none in the response. Here, indeed, as so often in other branches of the law, the decisive distinctions are those of degree and not of kind. One struggles in vain for any verbal formula that will supply a ready touchstone. The standard set up by the statute is not a rule of law; it is rather a way of life. Life in all its fullness must supply the answer to the riddle.

The Commissioner of Internal Revenue resorted to that standard in assessing the petitioner's income, and found that the payments in controversy came closer to capital outlays than to ordinary and necessary expenses in the operation of a business. His ruling has the support of a presumption of correctness, and the petitioner has the burden of proving it to be wrong. Unless we can say from facts within our knowledge that these are ordinary and necessary expenses according to the ways of conduct and the forms of speech prevailing in the business world, the tax must be confirmed. But nothing told us by this record or within the sphere of our judicial notice permits us to give that extension to what is ordinary and necessary. Indeed, to do so would open the door to many bizarre analogies. One man has a family name that is clouded by thefts committed by an ancestor. To add to this own standing he repays the stolen money, wiping off, it may be, his income for the year. The payments figure in his tax return as ordinary expenses. Another man conceives the notion that he will be able to practice his vocation with greater ease and profit if he has an opportunity to enrich his culture. Forthwith the price of his education becomes an expense of the business, reducing the income subject to taxation. There is little difference between these expenses and those in controversy here. Reputation and learning are akin to capital assets, like the good will of an old partnership. For many, they are the only tools with which to hew a pathway to success. The money spent in acquiring them is well and wisely spent. It is not an ordinary expense of the operation of a business.

      * * *

The decree should be

Affirmed.

JENKINS v. COMMISSIONER

United States Tax Court, 1983.
T.C. Memo. 1983–667.

Irwin, Judge:

Respondent determined deficiencies of $67,141 and $14,226 in petitioners' Federal income taxes for their 1973 and 1974 taxable years, respectively. After concessions by petitioners and respondent, the sole issue for our decision is whether certain payments made by petitioner-husband to investors in a defunct restaurant business known as "Twitty Burger, Inc.," are deductible as ordinary and necessary business expenses of petitioner-husband's business as a country music performer.

Findings of Fact

* * *

* * * At the time the petition in this proceeding was filed, the petitioners resided in Sumner County, Tennessee.[2]

Petitioner is a country music entertainer who for more than 25 years has been more commonly known and referred to by his stage name "Conway Twitty." We will hereinafter refer to him by this name. Since 1964, Conway Twitty has used a logo in connection with his work as an entertainer and in connection with his stage name. The insignia consists of an image of a small yellow bird (i.e., the Twitty Bird) strumming a guitar.

* * *

By 1968, Conway Twitty was firmly rooted in the country music entertainment field. For the 10–year period from January 1968 through December 1977, every title release by Conway Twitty became a Number 1 hit. By mid–1970, considering all popularity charts together, Conway Twitty had earned 43 Number 1 positions for his recordings.[4] He also boasted, in the same period, the largest fan club of any country music entertainer (i.e., over 10,000 members).

* * *

In 1968, Conway Twitty and several of his friends decided to form a restaurant business. In late 1968, Twitty Burger, Inc. (hereinafter referred to as "Twitty Burger"), an Oklahoma corporation, was formed to operate and sell franchises for the operation of Twitty Burger Fast Food Restaurants. A number of Twitty's friends, acquaintances, and business associates were solicited to invest in Twitty Burger. In late 1968 and early 1969, approximately 75 of petitioner's friends and business associ-

---

2. Inasmuch as Temple M. Jenkins is a party to this proceeding solely by reason of her having filed a joint return with her husband for the taxable year 1974, all references hereinafter to the petitioner shall refer to the petitioner-husband.

4. One criteria for a record to became a Number 1 hit is that it must have minimum sales of approximately 150,000 units. Conway Twitty has had more Number 1 hit songs on the country music charts than any other performer.

ates invested money in Twitty Burger by directly remitting a check to Twitty Burger or by sending a check to petitioner on behalf of Twitty Burger, or by sending checks or other money instruments to others in petitioner's employ.

* * *

Conway Twitty became aware of possible violations of the securities laws by Twitty Burger in 1970. * * * During late 1970, Twitty Burger began to encounter financial difficulties. Shortly after the time it was determined that the capital stock could not be registered, it was decided that Twitty Burger should be shut down.

After Twitty Burger ceased operating its restaurants in 1971, petitioner and those in his employ commenced a program of terminating the leases of the restaurant premises and paying the general creditors. The restaurants were in poor financial condition at this time. Thereafter, petitioner had no intention of reopening the Twitty Burger restaurants or attempting to sell the corporation.

The last Twitty Burger restaurant was closed in May 1971, except for one franchise that had been sold to a group of doctors who, as of the date of trial, continue to operate a restaurant in Hemphill, Texas. Subsequently, Conway Twitty decided that the investors should be paid the amount of money that they had invested in Twitty Burger. Although petitioner had not participated in the day-to-day operation of Twitty Burger and had not reviewed many of the documents received by his lawyers and business associates regarding the investments in Twitty Burger and those documents received from the Securities and Exchange Commission, he did participate in the determination that Twitty Burger should be closed down. As Twitty Burger had no assets with which to pay the debentures, Conway Twitty decided that he would repay the investors from his future earnings. After Twitty Burger ceased operations, Conway Twitty repaid the investors in Twitty Burger the amount of their investment and, in some instances, an additional amount representing interest thereon. * * *

On his 1973 and 1974 Federal income tax returns petitioner deducted these total amounts, $92,892.46 and $3,600, respectively, as * * * ordinary and necessary business expenses under section 162. In two separate notices of deficiency mailed to petitioners on December 19, 1978, respondent determined that these total amounts were not deductible * * * but rather were nondeductible personal expenses.

OPINION

The sole issue presented for our decision is whether payments made by petitioner to investors in a failed corporation known as Twitty Burger, Inc., are deductible as ordinary and necessary business expenses of petitioner's business as a country music performer.

The general rule is that a shareholder may not deduct a payment made on behalf of the corporation but rather must treat it as a capital expenditure. However, the payment may be deducted if it is an ordinary and necessary expense of a trade or business of the shareholder. *Lohrke v. Commissioner*, 48 T.C. 679 (1967).

* * *

An exception to the general rule that one person may not deduct the expenses of another person has been recognized in those cases where the expenditures sought to be deducted were made by a taxpayer to protect or promote his own ongoing business, even though the transaction originated with another person.

In *Lohrke*, the taxpayer was allowed a deduction for a payment made on behalf of a corporation in which he had a substantial interest. The corporation had made a shipment of defective fiber produced by a patented process owned by the taxpayer personally and from which he derived significant income. The petitioner believed that if he did not personally reimburse the customers' losses his personal business reputation would be harmed in that the corporation's involvement in the transaction might become known to the entire synthetic fiber industry. The petitioner's surname constituted a portion of the corporation's name and the taxpayer had never attempted to separate his activities as an inventor from his activities as president of the corporation to any member of the industry.

We noted in *Lohrke* that in a number of cases the courts have allowed deductions for expenditures made by a taxpayer to protect or promote his own business even though the transaction originated with another person and that the resulting expenditures would have been deductible by that other person if payment had been made by him. After a fairly exhaustive review of many of the cases dealing with this issue the Court stated as follows:

> The tests as established by all of these cases are that we must first ascertain the purpose or motive which cause the taxpayer to pay the obligations of the other person. Once we have identified that motive, we must then judge whether it is an ordinary and necessary expense of the individual's trade or business; that is, is it an appropriate expenditure for the furtherance or promotion of that trade or business? If so, the expense is deductible by the individual paying it.

Lohrke, supra, at 688.

Applying this test to the facts in *Lohrke*, we found that the taxpayer was of the opinion that his failure to assume the corporate obligation would have adversely affected his licensing business because of the harm that would have resulted to his own reputation. Because we believed that the petitioner's primary motive was the protection of his personal licensing business and that the payment was proximately related to that business, the deduction was allowed as an ordinary and necessary business expense.

Similarly in *Gould v. Commissioner*, 64 T.C. 132 (1975), we allowed the taxpayer a deduction for payments made to debtors of his wholly-owned corporation because we found that the payments were made to preserve his employment at another corporation. We specifically found that petitioner did not make the payments to revitalize the corporation or to enhance the value of his investment. The corporation was defunct and had ceased conducting any activities except those related to terminating its operations.

We turn now to the case at bar. The question presented is whether one person (Conway Twitty) may deduct the expenses of another person (Twitty Burger). In order to determine whether the disallowed expenditures are deductible by petitioner under section 162 we must (1) ascertain the purpose or motive of the taxpayer in making the payments and (2) determine whether there is a sufficient connection between the expenditures and the taxpayer's trade or business. Petitioner bears the burden of proving that respondent's determination was in error.

    * * *

Respondent argues that the payments Conway Twitty made to the investors in Twitty Burger are not deductible by him as ordinary and necessary business expenses under section 162 because there was no business purpose for the payments and, additionally, there was no relationship between his involvement in Twitty Burger and his business of being a country music entertainer. Respondent argues that the payments in question here were made by Conway Twitty gratuitously in that petitioner had no personal liability to the holders of the debentures and made the payments merely out of a sense of moral obligation. Relying on *Welch v. Helvering* and certain of its progeny, respondent concludes that while it was "very nice" of petitioner to reimburse the investors in Twitty Burger, the required nexus between the expenditures and Conway Twitty's career as a country music entertainer does not exist and therefore the payments were not "ordinary and necessary" within the meaning of section 162.

Petitioner argues that the rule of *Welch v. Helvering* is not applicable to the case at bar because petitioner made the payments in question to protect his reputation and earning capacity in his ongoing business of being a country music entertainer whereas in *Welch* the Supreme Court held that the payments made there were capital expenditures of the taxpayer's new business. Petitioner maintains that under the test as formulated by this Court in *Lohrke*, the expenditures in issue here are deductible under section 162 if the payments were made primarily with a business motive and if there is a sufficient connection between the payments and the taxpayer's trade or business.

The question presented for our resolution is purely one of fact. While previously decided cases dealing with this issue are somewhat helpful there is, quite understandably, no case directly on point with the facts before us. * * *

There is no suggestion in the record that any of the payments were made in order to protect petitioner's investment in Twitty Burger or to revitalize the corporation. It is petitioner's contention that Conway

Twitty repaid the investors in Twitty Burger from his personal funds in order to protect his personal business reputation. While it is clear from the facts that Conway was under no legal obligation to make such payments, (at least in the sense that the corporate debentures were not personally guaranteed by him), the law is clear that the absence of such an obligation is not in itself a bar to the deduction of such expenditures under section 162. In addition, the fact that the petitioner also felt a moral obligation to the people who had entrusted him with their funds does not preclude the deductibility of the payments so long as the satisfaction of the moral obligation was not the primary motivation for the expenditures.

After a thorough consideration of the record we are convinced that petitioner Conway Twitty repaid the investors in Twitty Burger with the primary motive of protecting his personal business reputation. There was the obvious similarity of the name of the corporation and petitioner's stage name. There is no doubt that the corporation's name was chosen with the idea of capitalizing on Conway Twitty's fame as a country music performer. Additionally, many of the investors were connected with the country music industry.[13] While there is no doubt that part of petitioner's motivation for making the payments involved his personal sense of morality, we do not believe that this ethical consideration was paramount.

Petitioner testified as follows concerning his motivations for repaying the Twitty Burger investors:

> I'm 99 percent entertainer. That's just about all I know. The name Conway Twitty, and the image that I work so hard for since 1955 and '56 is the foundation that I, my family, and the 30 some odd people that work for me stand on. They depend on it, and they can depend on it.
>
> I handle things the way I did with Shell Oil Company, with Diner's Club, with Gulf Oil Company, with a lot of other things before that and after that other than Twitty Burger. I handled them all the same way for more than one reason. First of all, because of the way I perceive myself and my image. It may not be the same as this guy over here or that one over there, but to me if Conway Twitty does some little old something, it's different than somebody else doing something because everybody has got a different relationship with whoever their fans are.
>
> I handled it that way because of that. Because of the image. And second and very close to it, I handled it that way because I think it is morally right, and if you owe a man something, you pay him. If a man owes you something, he pays you. And if a man is going to pay

---

13. For example, Harlan Howard, Don Davis, Merle Haggard, Steve Lake, and Jimmy Loden, a/k/a/ Sonny James. Petitioner's counsel aptly remarked in his opening statement: "Imagine trying to keep a bank together where somebody has stiffed the drummer's mother." We note, however, that "Pork Chop's" mother, Lucibelle Markham, was repaid in a year not at issue in this case.

you a dollar for an hour's work, you work—you know—it sounds weird to hear myself saying those things. I know they are true. And it's the way I live, but for some reason in this day and time, I feel funny saying that. And I shouldn't because we grew up in a time when that was—that was the way it was.

And I would love to think that that's the way it still is. But when you look around you and you deal with other people, you know it's not true 100 percent of the time anymore, but it's true with Conway Twitty and no matter which way this turns out, I'd do the same thing again tomorrow, if I had to do over.

* * *

The country music fan is different than the people I had dealt with back in the '50's and the kids. They will stay right with you as long as you stay within a certain boundaries. They expect a lot out of you because you—a country singer deals with—they deal with feelings and things inside of people—you know—you can listen to the words in a country song, and you're dealing with emotions and feelings that—it's kind of like a doctor, you know. I'm not comparing myself with a doctor certainly, but when a person gets to trust a doctor, that's all they need is that trust.

Petitioner presented the expert testimony of William Ivey, the Director of Country Music Foundation in Nashville, Tennessee. In his report which was introduced into evidence in lieu of direct testimony he stated as follows:

* * * Though modern country music has developed many new characteristics which separate it from its folk roots, several important elements remain from the folk past. The emphasis on story songs, the use of many stringed instruments in performance, and the close identification of the personality of the performer with the material that is performed are all aspects of folk music which remain a part of modern country music. In the folk communities of the rural South, folk music performers were not viewed as professional entertainers, but were rather seen as friends and neighbors who happened to entertain: Thus the status of a folk musician was based not only upon performing skills but also upon those other traits of personality and character which placed a person in a good or bad light within his community. * * *

Country entertainers go to great lengths to protect their images, for they correctly realize that both business associates and fans judge their artistic efforts in the light of perceptions of the artist's personality, professional conduct, and moral character. The business side of country music is a highly personal activity which depends heavily upon knowledge of reputation and past performance. Throughout the process of recording, touring, and composing, businesses must be established, credit extended, and payments made. The reputation of an entertainer among business associates and within the financial community can have a determinative role in that artist's ability to conduct his affairs.

Reputation can have an even greater effect upon an entertainer as it influences fans. Virtually every article written about Conway Twitty stresses the effort he makes to meet his fans. John Pugh, writing in Country Music Magazine, says "Perhaps there has never been a harder working artist than Conway Twitty.... Or an artist who cared more for his fans." Devotion to fans is a crucial part of Conway's great success, and his scrupulously maintained reputation is one element in maintaining his intense popularity.* * *

* * *

Stories abound of the problems encountered by artists who have not followed Conway's example. George Jones, Waylon Jennings, and Johnny Paycheck are all great entertainers, but each has been plagued by personal problems which have limited the extent of their success. Had, in the matter before this court, Conway Twitty allowed investors to be left dangling with heavy losses following the collapse of the Twitty Burger chain, the multiple lawsuits, unfavorable news stories and disgruntled investors would have all damaged that very reputation which was a key element in Conway's image as an artist. Though he would have continued to perform and record, there exists serious doubt that he would have achieved the unparalleled success he enjoyed during the 1970's had his reputation been so injured. * * *

* * *

As a scholar of country music and an observer of the country music scene, I am convinced that a country entertainer's character, personality, and credit reputation are part and parcel of his role as a singer. This integration of art and the individual existed in the folk communities from which country music grew, and it remains an aspect of country music today. Had Conway Twitty not maintained a flawless financial and personal reputation, he would not have become the most-successful male vocalist within the art form. Had he allowed investors to suffer as a result of Twitty Burger's failure, both his reputation and his career would thus have been damaged.

We conclude that there was a proximate relationship between the payments made to the holders of Twitty Burger debentures and petitioner's trade or business as a country music entertainer so as to render those payments an ordinary and necessary expense of that business. Although, as respondent argues, the chances of a successful lawsuit against Conway Twitty by any of the investors or the Securities and Exchange Commission was remote we agree with petitioner that the possibility of extensive adverse publicity concerning petitioner's involvement with the defunct corporation and the consequent loss of the investors' funds was very real. We do not believe it is necessary for us to find that adverse publicity emanating from Conway Twitty's failure to repay the investors in Twitty Burger would have ruined his career as a country music singer. Rather, we need only find that a proximate relationship existed between the payments and petitioner's business. We find that such relationship exists. It is not necessary that the taxpayer's trade or business be of the same type as that engaged in by the person on whose behalf the payments are made. * * *

In making these payments petitioner was furthering his business as a country music artist and protecting his business reputation for integrity. The mere fact that they were voluntary does not deprive them of their character as ordinary and necessary business expenses. Under the unique circumstances presented in this case, we hold that the payments in issue are deductible as business expenses under section 162.[14]

Decision will be entered under Rule 155.

Notes and Questions

1. Does *Jenkins* contradict *Welch*, or can the cases be reconciled on some principled basis (not on the grounds that the *Jenkins* court was starstruck)?

2. In *Conti v. Commissioner*, 31 T.C.M. 348 (1972), the court allowed the taxpayer, a local business and political figure, to deduct almost $500,000 paid to a struggling savings and loan association of which the taxpayer was a founder. Apparently, the savings and loan suffered in part because of the taxpayer's poor business acumen. The court concluded that the payment served to protect and preserve the taxpayer's present business reputation in the community, so it was an "ordinary" business expense. Do *Conti* and *Jenkins* signal an awareness that payments to protect or enhance a taxpayer's business reputation are indeed "ordinary" in many business circles? If we were writing on a clean slate, should reputation-saving costs be considered "ordinary" in most cases?

* * *

TREBILCOCK v. COMMISSIONER, 64 T.C. 852 (1975), *affd. per curiam*, 557 F.2d 1226 (6th Cir. 1977).

Facts: The taxpayer operated a sole proprietorship that brokered wood products. The taxpayer retained the Reverend James Wardrop for a monthly salary of $585 ($7,020 annually). In exchange, Wardrop

---

14. We close with the following "Ode to Conway Twitty":

Twitty Burger went belly up

But Conway remained true

He repaid his investors, one and all

It was the moral thing to do.

His fans would not have liked it

It could have hurt his fame

Had any investors sued him

Like Merle Haggard or Sonny James.

When it was time to file taxes

Conway thought what he would do

Was deduct those payments as a business expense

Under section one-sixty-two.

In order to allow these deductions

Goes the argument of the Commissioner

The payments must be ordinary and necessary

To a business of the petitioner.

Had Conway not repaid the investors

His career would have been under cloud,

Under the unique facts of this case

Held: The deductions are allowed.

provided four types of services: (1) he provided spiritual ministry to the taxpayer and the taxpayer's employees, mostly through prayer meetings; (2) he counseled the taxpayer and the taxpayer's employees on personal problems; (3) he provided business advice (described more fully below); and (4) he performed various other business tasks including running errands and mailing materials related to the taxpayer's business. "When (Wardrop) offered advice about business problems it was not based on his knowledge of the brokerage business for he had no such knowledge. Rather, he would receive a problem, turn to God in prayer, and then propose an answer resulting from that prayer."

Issue: Are the payments to Rev. Wardrop deductible as "ordinary and necessary" business expenses under § 162(a)?

Holding: To the extent the payments are made for spiritual advice, personal counseling, and business counseling, the payments are not deductible under § 162(a). To the extent the payments are made for the various business tasks, however, like the errands and the mailing, the payments are deductible under § 162(a).

Rationale: The court determined that the benefits derived from ministering services and providing personal counseling "are inherently personal in nature" and thus not deductible under § 162(a). With respect to that portion of the salary paid for business advice, the court disallowed a deduction because the taxpayer failed to prove that the expense was "ordinary." "Petitioner has offered no proof that his payments to Wardrop for solutions to business problems, considering the method Wardrop used, were 'ordinary' in his type of business." As for the salary paid for errands and other assorted business tasks, however, a deduction under § 162(a) was found to be proper. Absent evidence as to the portion of the salary paid for these deductible tasks, the court on its own determined that $1,000 of Wardrop's $7,020 annual salary represented the deductible portion.

HAROLDS CLUB v. COMMISSIONER, 340 F.2d 861 (9th Cir. 1965).

Facts: The taxpayer, a corporation, employed the father of the taxpayer's principal shareholders to work in the taxpayer's casino operations. In the years at issue in the case, the father's annual salary ranged from $350,000 to a cool $500,000. His salary was based on a fixed amount of $10,000 plus 15 percent of the taxpayer's net profits. The taxpayer deducted the compensation paid to the father, and the Service disallowed a portion of the taxpayer's deduction based on its conclusion that the salary was unreasonably high.

Issue: Was the compensation paid to the father "unreasonable" and thus partially in excess of the amount allowable under § 162(a)(1)?

Holding: Yes.

Rationale: The salary agreement was not the result of a "free bargain" between the taxpayer and the father given the familial relationships involved. "The fact that [the principal shareholders] were competent adults at the time they entered into the [employment] contract tends to minimize the significance which should be attached to the fact, standing alone, that they were the sons of [the father]. But that fact did not stand alone. The record fully supports the Tax Court's finding that [the father] dominated the sons, notwithstanding their adulthood and competency. * * * Where there is such domination, lack of ability to bargain freely may exist even as between competent adults." The taxpayer then argued that if it was not entitled to a deduction, then not only must the father pay income tax, so too must the taxpayer. But the court noted that an impermissible "double tax" only arises where the same taxpayer twice pays tax on the same income. The fact that both the casino and the employee will be taxed on the same gross revenues does not give rise to a double tax.

Note

As the *Harolds Club* case illustrates, § 162(a)(1) indeed limits the deduction for compensation for personal services to amounts that are "reasonable." There has been and continues to be much litigation over whether salaries paid in a given situation are reasonable. Of course, the outcome in each case depends upon a number of factors, including: (1) the employee's role in the taxpayer's business (including the employee's position, hours worked, and duties performed); (2) an external comparison with other employers (i.e., salaries paid to comparable employees in similar companies); (3) the character and condition of the taxpayer's business (including the sales, net income, capital value, and general economic fitness of the business); (4) any potential conflicts of interest (the ability to "disguise" dividends from corporate taxpayers as salary, particularly when the employee is the sole or majority shareholder, or where a large percentage of the compensation is paid as a "bonus"); and, (5) the internal consistency of the compensation system throughout the ranks of the taxpayer's business. *Elliotts, Inc. v. Commissioner*, 716 F.2d 1241 (9th Cir. 1983).

As with most multi-factor, fact-intensive tests, no one of these factors is dispositive of the issue. Moreover, if the employer is a corporation, courts often assess the totality of these factors from the perspective of an independent investor. In other words, would an objective shareholder in the employer-corporation approve the compensation paid to the employee, given expected dividends and return on investment? *Rapco, Inc. v. Commissioner*, 85 F.3d 950 (2d Cir. 1996).

Furthermore, it is worth noting that different circuits use different factors, so there is no one magical "test" for excessive compensation. See, e.g., *Eberl's Claim Service, Inc. v. Commissioner*, 249 F.3d 994 (10th Cir. 2001) (using nine factors); *Owensby & Kritikos, Inc. v. Commissioner*, 819 F.2d 1315 (5th Cir. 1987) (using eight factors). The Tax Court even employed 21 factors in *Foos v. Commissioner*, T.C. Memo. 1981–61.

If a portion of the compensation paid to another is "unreasonable," the federal income tax consequences to the service provider may also be affected. If the excessive portion of compensation payable to an employee is deemed to be a gift, can the employee exclude that portion of the compensation from gross income? See § 102(c) and discussion at Chapter 3. If the employer is a corporation, most likely the excessive portion of the compensation will be treated as a dividend. To the extent a dividend is, like compensation, included in gross income, the employee would appear to be indifferent. But see § 1(h)(11).

* * *

Self-Assessment Question

(Solutions to Self–Assessment Questions are set forth in Appendix 3.)

SAQ 4–4. Gary owns and operates a lumber business. Gary hired his son, Ben, to serve on Gary's sales staff. Gary agreed to pay Ben a flat salary of $60,000 regardless of Ben's sales performance. Ben had no prior experience in the lumber business, and he had never been involved previously in sales. All other members of Gary's sales staff are paid on commission, and their total annual compensation ranges from $35,000 to $200,000 per staff member. To what extent can Gary deduct the salary paid to Ben?

* * *

Expenses. The third element of the § 162(a) deduction requires that the cost at issue be an expense, as opposed to a capital expenditure. The distinction between capital expenditures and expenses (discussed *supra* at Part B) should be fresh in your mind. If you are just having an off day, here is a handy summary.

Generally, an expense is any cost paid or incurred to produce a benefit with a useful life of one year or less, while a capital expenditure is a cost paid or incurred to produce a benefit with a useful life of more than one year. While expenses may be deducted in the year of the cost, § 263 generally requires capital expenditures to be added to the basis of the property created or improved. The cost of a capital expenditure, therefore, is not recovered for federal income tax purposes until the property is sold, though in some cases the cost is recovered over the estimated useful life of the property in the form of depreciation and amortization deductions.

Consider these examples: the cost of a new roof for a building is a capital expenditure, while the cost to replace a shingle on the roof is an expense; a vehicle is a capital expenditure, but gasoline to fuel the vehicle is an expense; an x-ray machine is a capital expenditure, but x-ray film (whatever it's called) is an expense. The distinction is based on useful life, not on value. Also, the general distinction is not absolute: wages paid by a taxpayer are almost always expenses, even though they may be substantial and even though they may be paying for services that produce a long-term benefit. Wages are considered capital expenditures under § 263A when paid to create or improve an asset subject to the uniform capitalization rules.

With this general explanation in mind, consider whether the payments in *Welch* and *Jenkins* (payments made to preserve business reputation) were expenses or capital expenditures. What about the payments in *Trebilcock* (compensation paid to Rev. Wardrop)?

Paid or Incurred. The fourth element of the § 162(a) deduction requires that the expense be "paid or incurred" during the taxable year at issue. Although the plain connotation of the statute suggests otherwise, this does *not* mean that a taxpayer may claim a deduction upon the earlier of the date when actual payment is made or the date when liability for the expense first arose. Instead, the language "paid or incurred" is used in recognition of the fact that some taxpayers get deductions when expenses are "paid" while other taxpayers get deductions when expenses are "incurred." As will be seen in Chapter 6, there are generally two accounting methods used by taxpayers. Nearly all individual taxpayers use the "cash method" of accounting, under which a taxpayer has income when items are actually or constructively *received* and a deduction when expenses are actually *paid*. Very few individuals (but most business entities) use the "accrual method" of accounting, whereby a taxpayer has income when receipts are *earned* and a deduction when expenses are *owed*. Since our analysis is limited to individuals, it is sufficient for now to assume that we look to actual payment of the expense as the event giving rise to the deduction, not mere liability for payment.

In Carrying On. Section 162(a) next requires a taxpayer to be "carrying on" a trade or business. Note that the statute does not say "prior to the start of" a trade or business. Nor does it include the words "in creating." This is deliberate. As we soon will see, start-up expenditures (amounts paid in the creation of a new trade or business activity) are not entirely deductible; instead, a portion of such costs may be deducted in the year in which the new business begins and the balance of such costs are to be amortized (deducted on a *pro rata* basis) over 15 years. See § 195. Since a § 162(a) deduction may be taken entirely in the year of expense (and not over time, like start-up expenditures), taxpayers will usually argue that amounts paid were for "carrying on" a trade or business, not "starting" a new trade or business. That argument arose in the following case.

ESTATE OF ROCKEFELLER v. COMMISSIONER

United States Court of Appeals, Second Circuit, 1985.
762 F.2d 264.

FRIENDLY, CIRCUIT JUDGE:

This appeal by the Estate of Nelson A. Rockefeller and his widow[1] from a decision of the Tax Court presents a new variation on the old theme of what constitutes "ordinary and necessary expenses paid or incurred ... in carrying on any trade or business," I.R.C. § 162(a),

1. Mrs. Rockefeller's involvement arises solely because she and Mr. Rockefeller filed a joint return.

which are deductible in determining net income. Appellants contended that expenses incurred by Mr. Rockefeller in connection with the confirmation by the Senate and the House of Representatives, pursuant to the Twenty–Fifth Amendment, of his nomination to be Vice President of the United States were such expenses. The Commissioner of Internal Revenue denied this, the Tax Court agreed, and this appeal followed. We affirm.

The case arises as follows: Mr. Rockefeller incurred expenses of $550,159.78 in connection with the confirmation hearings in 1974, primarily for legal and other professional services. The Commissioner does not contend that the expenses were excessive or unreasonable in relation to the services rendered. In their joint income tax return for 1974, which showed a gross income of $4,479,437, Mr. and Mrs. Rockefeller claimed a deduction of $63,275—an amount of these expenses equal to his salary as Vice President during the year. When the Commissioner of Internal Revenue disallowed this deduction, Mr. Rockefeller's estate and Mrs. Rockefeller petitioned for review by the Tax Court and asserted that the entire amount of $550,159.78 was deductible as expenses of the trade or business of "performing the functions of public office."

The case was submitted on a rather meagre stipulation of facts which cited only Mr. Rockefeller's tenure as Governor of New York State between January 1959 and December 1973, when he resigned to devote his full time to the Commission on Critical Choices for Americans (1973–74) and the National Commission on Water Quality (1973–74), as showing the trade or business in which Mr. Rockefeller had engaged. However, copies of the hearings before and the reports of the Senate and House Committees on his nomination as Vice President were attached to the stipulation, and the Tax Court's opinion lists other positions held by Mr. Rockefeller referred to in these hearings, as follows: Coordinator of Inter–American Affairs (1940–44), Assistant Secretary of State for American Republic Affairs (1944–45), Chairman of the Presidential Advisory Board on International Development (1950–51), Undersecretary of Health, Education and Welfare (1953–54), and Special Assistant to the President for International Affairs (1954–55).

DISCUSSION

* * *

Almost all discussions of the problem here at issue begin, and many of them end, with *McDonald v. C.I.R.*, 323 U.S. 57, 65 S.Ct. 96, 89 L.Ed.2d 68 (1944), although in fact it sheds a most uncertain light. McDonald had been appointed to serve an unexpired term as judge on a Pennsylvania court, carrying an annual salary of $12,000, with the understanding that he would be a contestant in the ensuing primary and general elections for a full term of ten years. To obtain the support of his party organization, he was forced to pay an "assessment" of $8,000, which was to be used for the support of the entire ticket; he spent an additional $5,017.27 for expenses of his own campaign. The Commissioner disallowed the deduction of both amounts. The Tax Court affirmed, as did a sharply divided Supreme Court.[3] The bases for the decision are not altogether clear. At one point Justice Frankfurter emphasized that McDonald's "campaign contributions were not expenses incurred in being a judge but in trying to be a judge for the next ten years." 323 U.S. at 60, 65 S.Ct. at 97. Perhaps fearing that this being-becoming distinction would cut too widely, Justice Frankfurter elaborated other factors. One was that allowance of a deduction for the assessments paid by McDonald would lead to deductions by persons who were not candidates but paid "such 'assessments' out of party allegiance mixed or unmixed by a lively sense of future favors," *id.,* a proposition which would not necessarily follow and which in any event would not explain the disallowance of McDonald's own campaign expenses. * * *

        * * *

Appellants' principal argument is that a post-*McDonald* decision of the Tax Court, in which the Commissioner has acquiesced, *David J. Primuth,* 54 T.C. 374 (1970), has undermined the being-becoming distinction. Primuth, the secretary-treasurer of a small corporation, Foundry Allied Industries, enlisted the aid of a "head-hunter" organization to find him a better job. This work resulted in his employment as "secretary-controller" of a company with greater geographical scope. The Tax Court held that the fees and expenses paid to the head-hunter organization were deductible under I.R.C. § 162.

Judge Sterrett's opinion for a plurality took off from the proposition that "a taxpayer may be in the trade or business of being an employee, such as a corporate executive or manager," 54 T.C. at 377, rather than or in addition to the trade or business of holding a particular job, * * *. With that established, Judge Sterrett believed that "the problem presented ... virtually dissolve[d] for it is difficult to think of a purer business expense than one incurred to permit such an individual to continue to carry on that very trade or business—albeit with a different corporate employer." 54 T.C. at 379. However, he proceeded to emphasize the relatively narrow scope of the decision, *id.*:

> Furthermore, the expense had no personal overtones, led to no position requiring greater or different qualifications than the one given up, and did not result in the acquisition of any asset as that

---

3. Justice Frankfurter delivered a plurality opinion for himself, Chief Justice Stone and Justices Roberts and Jackson. Justice Rutledge concurred in the result. Justice Black dissented for himself and Justices Reed, Douglas and Murphy. It may not be altogether accidental that three of the dissenters had held elective office, an experience not shared by any member of the plurality.

It should be noted that the dissenters did not disagree with the plurality's conclusion that the amounts were not "ordinary and necessary expenses of a trade or business"; they argued rather that the expenses came within what is now § 212(1), adopted in 1942 to overrule *Higgins v. C.I.R.,* 312 U.S. 212, 61 S.Ct. 475, 85 L.Ed. 783 (1941), which allowed deduction of "the ordinary and necessary expenses [of an individual] paid or incurred ... for the production or collection of income."

term has been used in our income tax laws. It was expended for the narrowest and most limited purpose. It was an expense which must be deemed ordinary and necessary from every realistic point of view in today's marketplace where corporate executives change employers with a noticeable degree of frequency. We have said before, and we say again, that the business expenses which an employee can incur in his own business are rare indeed. Virtually all his expenses will be incurred on behalf of, and in furtherance of, his corporate employer's business. What we have here, however, is an exception to that rule.

(footnote omitted). Judge Tannenwald, joined by three other judges, concurred: they were concerned over the "subtle distinctions" which they saw developing in the deduction of employment agency fees and suggested that "everyday meaning" should be the touchstone in interpreting § 162. In a separate concurring opinion, Judge Simpson took issue with language in the plurality opinion which he feared might confine the decision to cases where the taxpayer actually secured a new job. *Id.* at 383. Judge Featherston's concurrence placed greater weight on a Revenue Ruling that explicitly "allow[ed] deductions for fees paid to employment agencies for securing employment." *Id.* at 384. Six judges dissented. The Department of Justice rejected the Commissioner's request for an appeal and the Commissioner acquiesced in the result.

In *Leonard F. Cremona,* 58 T.C. 219 (1972), a majority of the Tax Court rejected an attempt by the Commissioner to contain *Primuth* to cases where the employee had in fact obtained a new position. Again the Department of Justice declined a request to appeal and the Commissioner acquiesced.

However, the erosion of the being-becoming distinction effected by *Primuth* and *Cremona* and the Commissioner's acquiescence in these decisions was partial only. The Tax Court, with the approval of the courts of appeals, has limited deductibility to cases where the taxpayer was seeking employment in the *same* trade or business. Moreover, the courts have insisted on a high degree of identity in deciding the issue of sameness. Thus, in *William D. Glenn,* 62 T.C. 270 (1974), the court found that the broader scope of activities permitted in Tennessee to certified public accountants as compared with public accountants made the former a new trade or business and, in consequence, that the expense of taking a review course designed to assist the taxpayer in qualifying for certification was not deductible. Similarly, being a registered pharmacist constitutes a different trade or business than being an intern pharmacist, so that expenses of attending courses on pharmacology were not deductible. In *Joel A. Sharon,* 66 T.C. 515 (1976), *aff'd,* 591 F.2d 1273 (9 Cir.1978), *cert. denied,* 442 U.S. 941, 99 S.Ct. 2883, 61 L.Ed.2d 311 (1979), the Tax Court disallowed an IRS attorney's deductions for expenses related to taking the California bar examination. The court found that these expenditures would permit the taxpayer to engage in the new "trade or business" of the general practice of law in the State of California. The Ninth Circuit agreed with the Tax Court's reasoning that private practice involved "significantly different tasks and activities" from those required of an IRS lawyer, 591 F.2d at 1275. * * * The Tax Court has also disallowed a deduction for helicopter training expenses by an airline pilot. *Edward C. Lee,* T.C. Memo. 1981–26 (1981), *aff'd on other grounds, Lee v. C.I.R.,* 723 F.2d 1424 (9 Cir.1984). The court found that "a helicopter pilot is in a different trade or business than is an airline pilot" and, since the taxpayer flew only fixed-wing aircraft in his current employment, "the helicopter flight training [led] to Mr. Lee's qualification in a new trade or business." *Joseph Sorin Schneider, supra,* T.C. Memo. 1983–753 (1983), denied a deduction sought by a taxpayer who had resigned from the U.S. Army with a captain's commission and who later, after graduation, entered the business world as a consultant, for amounts spent in applying to graduate schools, in getting the graduate degrees of M.B.A. and M.P.A. at Harvard, and in seeking a summer job in Europe. The court said that the taxpayer's business had been that of an Army officer and rejected his claim that he had been in the business of being a "manager"—a claim strongly resembling the one made here that Mr. Rockefeller was in the business of being "a governmental executive." In *Robert Eugene Evans,* T.C. Memo. 1981–413 (1981), the court denied a deduction for job seeking expenses to a taxpayer who had been in the Air Force for 22 1/2 years and had risen to the rank of Lieutenant Colonel and the post of special assistant to the commander of an Air Force base. The court was convinced that "petitioner's service as an Air Force officer cannot be compared to any employment he might have obtained outside the Air Force" and that while he "undoubtedly sought employment that would utilize the skills he had acquired during his military career, he [had] failed to show that there would not be substantial differences between the employment he sought to obtain in the private sector and his service as an Air Force officer." In sum, the Tax Court's decisions have adopted what Judge Tannenwald, in his concurring opinion in *Primuth,* characterized as "the simple test of comparing the position which the taxpayer occupied before and after the change," and conform to the statement in *Kenneth C. Davis,* 65 T.C. 1014, 1019 (1976), that "[i]f substantial differences exist in the tasks and activities of various occupations or employments, then each such occupation or employment constitutes a separate trade or business."

Appellants' brief uses a number of different phrases to describe Mr. Rockefeller's trade or business at the time of his nomination to be Vice President—"an executive in federal and state governments" (p. 8); "an executive in public office" (p. 8); "an executive in public service" (p. 17); and "a governmental executive" (p. 22). In fact, the only public posts Mr. Rockefeller held at the time of his nomination were the chairmanships of two commissions, posts in which he had no executive duties. One of these, the National Commission on Water Quality was created by the Federal Water Pollution Control Act Amendments of 1972 to review water pollution control methods and issue a report to Congress recommending modifications. Although Mr. Rockefeller was elected chairman by the other members when he joined the Commission while still Governor of New York, the record reveals almost nothing about his activities there. The Commission on Critical Choices for Americans was an idea of Mr. Rockefeller's. It was not a governmental body, although its membership included some members of Congress and of the executive branch. Since federal funding was denied, the Commission was funded from private sources and foundation grants. If only these two activities were to be considered, it would be plain beyond all argument that holding the chairmanship of these Commissions and being Vice President are not the same trade or business but rather separate trades or businesses, if indeed membership on the commissions, particularly the Commission on Critical Choices, was a trade or business at all.

However, a taxpayer who is unemployed when the expenses are incurred is "viewed as still engaged in the business of providing the type of services performed for [his] prior employer, unless 'there is a substantial lack of continuity between the time of [the employee's] past employment and the seeking of the new employment.' " * * * Appellants urge that this principle allows us to look to Mr. Rockefeller's fifteen years of service as Governor of New York in considering whether the confirmation expenses on his nomination to be Vice President were in connection with the continuation of the same trade or business. We disagree, for two reasons. In order to take advantage of what is called the "hiatus" principle, a taxpayer must at least show that during the hiatus he intended to resume the same trade or business. There is no such showing here. Mr. Rockefeller clearly did not intend to run again for Governor after having resigned that office after holding it for fifteen years. Indeed, the stipulation states that Mr. Rockefeller resigned the governorship "to devote his full time to the Chairs" of the two commissions, and there is nothing to suggest that he was contemplating holding executive public office again. The Vice Presidency became available only due to the resignation of President Nixon in the summer of 1974—an event that was not foreseeable until shortly before it occurred. We also cannot fault the Tax Court's holding that being governor of the second most populous state in the union and being Vice President of the United States are not the same trade or business in the narrow sense in which sameness has been consistently characterized. While there are certain areas of overlap, the governorship entails many duties—enforcement of the laws of the state, developing and promoting new laws, supervising a multitude of departments and agencies having thousands of employees and spending billions of dollars, proposing and securing the passage of a budget and the revenues needed to meet it, making appointments, and lobbying for the interests of the state with the Federal Government— which either find no counterparts in the Vice Presidency or find them only to the extent, usually quite limited, which the President has directed. On the other hand, the Vice Presidency involves many duties not found in the governorship of New York—presiding over the Senate, acting on behalf of the President on ceremonial occasions both within and without the United States, and executing special assignments by the

President—not to speak of the Vice President's most important task, readying himself for the possibility of assuming the Presidency on a moment's notice. Although positions with somewhat different duties and responsibilities may be found to be within the same trade or business, whether in public or private employment, the Tax Court's finding that the Vice Presidency involved a trade or business for Mr. Rockefeller different from any in which he was engaged at the time of his nomination is not one that we are free to disturb.

Appellants ask us to take a still broader view and consider Mr. Rockefeller as having been engaged in the same trade or business since his appointment as Coordinator of Inter–American Affairs in 1940. But the cases do not recognize a definition of "trade or business" wide enough to bring all Mr. Rockefeller's various posts within it. While there might be sufficient resemblance and continuity between the posts of Coordinator of Inter–American Affairs which Mr. Rockefeller held between 1940 and 1944 and that of Assistant Secretary of State for American Republic Affairs which he held between 1944 and 1945 to have qualified him as being in the business of being a public servant with special interest and expertise in Latin America, we see little resemblance between these positions and his service as Undersecretary of Health, Education and Welfare in 1953 and 1954 or as Governor of New York between 1959 and 1973. Furthermore there are substantial gaps between Mr. Rockefeller's various posts—five years between 1945 and 1950, one and one-half years between 1951 and 1953, three years between 1955 and 1958—far longer than the "hiatus" theory would recognize. *See, e.g., Canter v. United States,* 354 F.2d 352, 173 Ct.Cl. 723 (1965) (taxpayer who discontinued nursing activities for more than four years held not to retain status of being in the trade or business of nursing); *Peter G. Corbett,* 55 T.C. 884 (1971). *See also Rev. Rul. 68–591,* 1968–2 Cum. Bul. 73 (1968) ("Ordinarily, a suspension [of employment] for a period of a year or less, after which the taxpayer resumes the same ... trade or business, will be considered temporary"). Our reading of the record shows Mr. Rockefeller as a distinguished and public-spirited citizen, ready, for a third of a century, to put his great abilities at the disposal of the government in both appointive and elective office. While he was, of course, entitled to deduct unreimbursed expenses incurred in performing the functions of any of the many offices he held, the Tax Court was warranted in holding that he had not engaged in any trade or business comparable to the Vice Presidency, within the rather narrow sense which the courts have reasonably given to the concept of identity. We therefore have no occasion to decide whether the "policy" reasons underlying the decisions disallowing expenses incurred in elections apply to expenses incurred in seeking confirmation to an appointive office which would seem to be properly regarded as the same trade or business, or whether if they generally do not, there are special considerations for applying them to the unusual bicameral confirmation required by the Twenty–Fifth Amendment which the Commissioner characterizes as the equivalent of an election.

The judgment of the Tax Court is affirmed.

Note

More discussion of the deductibility of job-seeking expenses awaits in Chapter 10. For now, it is sufficient to observe that the expenses at issue in *Estate of Rockefeller* were not deductible because Rockefeller was not yet "carrying on" the business of being Vice President. Where a taxpayer is seeking employment in a new trade or business activity, the § 162(a) deduction is appropriately denied because the taxpayer is not yet carrying on that business.

* * *

Trade or Business. At long last, we come to the requirement in § 162(a) that the expense be paid or incurred in carrying on the taxpayer's "trade or business." It is remarkable to note that the term is not defined in the Code. Perhaps "astounding" is more appropriate than "remarkable," as the phrase "trade or business" is found throughout the Code, not just in § 162(a). See, e.g., §§ 163(h)(2)(A); 165(c)(1); 166(d)(2)(A); 167(a)(1); 174(a)(1); 179(d)(1); 197(c)(1)(B); 198(c)(1)(A). In many cases, the presence of a "trade or business" activity is easy to spot. Presumably, if an activity is not a "trade or business" it is either an "investment" activity (where the deduction is tested under § 212, not § 162) or a "personal" activity (where generally there is no deduction because of § 262). What, then, is required for an activity to rise to the level of a "trade or business?" The following case is helpful on this issue. Even better, it involves gambling!

COMMISSIONER v. GROETZINGER

United States Supreme Court, 1987.
480 U.S. 23, 107 S.Ct. 980, 94 L.Ed.2d 25.

JUSTICE BLACKMUN delivered the opinion of the Court.

The issue in this case is whether a full-time gambler who makes wagers solely for his own account is engaged in a "trade or business" * * *.

I

There is no dispute as to the facts. The critical ones are stipulated. Respondent Robert P. Groetzinger had worked for 20 years in sales and market research for an Illinois manufacturer when his position was terminated in February 1978. During the remainder of that year, respondent busied himself with parimutuel wagering, primarily on greyhound races. He gambled at tracks in Florida and Colorado. He went to the track 6 days a week for 48 weeks in 1978. He spent a substantial amount of time studying racing forms, programs, and other materials. He devoted from 60 to 80 hours each week to these gambling-related endeavors. He never placed bets on behalf of any other person, or sold tips, or collected commissions for placing bets, or functioned as a bookmaker. He gambled solely for his own account. He had no other profession or type of employment.[2]

Respondent kept a detailed accounting of his wagers and every day noted his winnings and losses in a record book. In 1978, he had gross winnings of $70,000, but he bet $72,032; he thus realized a net gambling loss for the year of $2,032.

Respondent received $6,498 in income from other sources in 1978. This came from interest, dividends, capital gains, and salary earned before his job was terminated.

On the federal income tax return he filed for the calendar year 1978 respondent reported as income only the $6,498 realized from nongambling sources. He did not report any gambling winnings or deduct any gambling losses.[3] He did not itemize deductions. Instead, he computed his tax liability from the tax tables.

Upon audit, the Commissioner of Internal Revenue determined that respondent's $70,000 in gambling winnings were to be included in his gross income and that, pursuant to § 165(d) of the Code, a deduction was to be allowed for his gambling losses to the extent of these gambling gains. But the Commissioner further determined that, under the law as it was in 1978, a portion of respondent's $70,000 gambling-loss deduction was an item of tax preference and operated to subject him to the minimum tax under § 56(a) of the Code. At that time, under statutory provisions in effect from 1976 until 1982, "items of tax preference" were lessened by certain deductions, but not by deductions not "attributable to a trade or business carried on by the taxpayer."[4]

These determinations by the Commissioner produced a § 56(a) minimum tax of $2,142 and, with certain other adjustments not now in dispute, resulted in a total asserted tax deficiency of $2,522 for respondent for 1978.

Respondent sought redetermination of the deficiency in the United States Tax Court. That court, in a reviewed decision, with only two judges dissenting, held that respondent was in the trade or business of gambling, and that, as a consequence, no part of his gambling losses constituted an item of tax preference in determining any minimum tax for 1978. In so ruling, the court adhered to its earlier court-reviewed

2. The Tax Court put it this way: "It is not disputed that petitioner during 1978 was engaged fulltime in parimutuel wagering on dog races, had no other employment during that period, gambled solely for his own account, and devoted an extraordinary amount of time and effort to his gambling with a view to earning a living from such activity." 82 T.C. 793, 795 (1984).

3. Respondent, however, did report his net gambling loss of $2,032 in Schedule E (Supplemental Income Schedule) of his return, but he did not utilize that amount in computing his adjusted gross income or claim it as an itemized deduction.

4. This statutory scheme was amended by the Tax Equity and Fiscal Responsibility Act of 1982, § 201(a), 96 Stat. 411. For tax years after 1982, gambling-loss deductions explicitly are excluded from the minimum tax base. The Commissioner acknowledges that a taxpayer like respondent for a year after 1982 would not be subject to minimum tax liability because of his gambling-loss deduction.

decision in *Ditunno v. Commissioner,* 80 T.C. 362 (1983). The court in *Ditunno, id.,* at 371, had overruled *Gentile v. Commissioner,* 65 T.C. 1 (1975), a case where it had rejected the Commissioner's contention (*contrary* to his position here) that a full-time gambler *was* in a trade or business and therefore was subject to self-employment tax.

The United States Court of Appeals for the Seventh Circuit affirmed. Because of a conflict on the issue among Courts of Appeals, we granted certiorari.

II

The phrase "trade or business" has been in § 162(a) and in that section's predecessors for many years. Indeed, the phrase is common in the Code, for it appears in over 50 sections and 800 subsections and in hundreds of places in proposed and final income tax regulations. The slightly longer phrases, "carrying on a trade or business" and "engaging in a trade or business," themselves are used no less than 60 times in the Code. The concept thus has a well-known and almost constant presence on our tax-law terrain. Despite this, the Code has never contained a definition of the words "trade or business" for general application, and no regulation has been issued expounding its meaning for all purposes. Neither has a broadly applicable authoritative judicial definition emerged. Our task in this case is to ascertain the meaning of the phrase as it appears in the sections of the Code with which we are here concerned.[8]

In one of its early tax cases, *Flint v. Stone Tracy Co.,* 220 U.S. 107, 31 S.Ct. 342, 55 L.Ed. 389 (1911), the Court was concerned with the Corporation Tax * * * and the status of being engaged in business. It said: " 'Business' is a very comprehensive term and embraces everything about which a person can be employed." 220 U.S., at 171, 31 S.Ct., at 357. It embraced the Bouvier Dictionary definition: "That which occupies the time, attention and labor of men for the purpose of a livelihood or profit." *Ibid.* And Justice Frankfurter has observed that "we assume that Congress uses common words in their popular meaning, as used in the common speech of men." Frankfurter, *Some Reflections on the Reading of Statutes*, 47 COLUM. L. REV. 527, 536 (1947).

With these general comments as significant background, we turn to pertinent cases decided here. *Snyder v. Commissioner,* 295 U.S. 134, 55 S.Ct. 737, 79 L.Ed. 1351 (1935), had to do with margin trading and capital gains, and held, in that context, that an investor, seeking merely to increase his holdings, was not engaged in a trade or business. Justice Brandeis, in his opinion for the Court, noted that the Board of Tax Appeals theretofore had ruled that a taxpayer who devoted the major portion of his time to transactions on the stock exchange for the purpose of making a livelihood could treat losses incurred as having been sus-

---

8. We caution that in this opinion our interpretation of the phrase "trade or business" is confined to the specific sections of the Code at issue here. We do not purport to construe the phrase where it appears in other places.

tained in the course of a trade or business. He went on to observe that no facts were adduced in *Snyder* to show that the taxpayer "might properly be characterized as a 'trader on an exchange who makes a living in buying and selling securities.' " *Id.,* at 139, 27 S.Ct., at 739. These observations, thus, are dicta, but, by their use, the Court appears to have drawn a distinction between an active trader and an investor.

In *Deputy v. Du Pont,* 308 U.S. 488, 60 S.Ct. 363, 84 L.Ed. 416 (1940), the Court was concerned with what were "ordinary and necessary" expenses of a taxpayer's trade or business, within the meaning of § 23(a) of the Revenue Act of 1928, 45 Stat. 799. In ascertaining whether carrying charges on short sales of stock were deductible as ordinary and necessary expenses of the taxpayer's business, the Court *assumed* that the activities of the taxpayer in conserving and enhancing his estate constituted a trade or business, but nevertheless disallowed the claimed deductions because they were not "ordinary" or "necessary." 308 U.S., at 493–497, 60 S.Ct., at 366–368. Justice Frankfurter, in a concurring opinion joined by Justice Reed, did not join the majority. He took the position that whether the taxpayer's activities constituted a trade or business was "open for determination," *id.,* at 499, 60 S.Ct., at 369, and observed:

> " ' . . . carrying on any trade or business,' within the contemplation of § 23(a), involves holding one's self out to others as engaged in the selling of goods or services. This the taxpayer did not do. . . . Without elaborating the reasons for this construction and not unmindful of opposing considerations, including appropriate regard for administrative practice, I prefer to make the conclusion explicit instead of making the hypothetical litigation-breeding assumption that this taxpayer's activities, for which expenses were sought to be deducted, did constitute a 'trade or business.' " *Ibid.*

Next came *Higgins v. Commissioner,* 312 U.S. 212, 61 S.Ct. 475, 85 L.Ed. 783 (1941). There the Court, in a bare and brief unanimous opinion, ruled that salaries and other expenses incident to looking after one's own investments in bonds and stocks were not deductible under § 23(a) of the Revenue Act of 1932 as expenses paid or incurred in carrying on a trade or business. While surely cutting back on *Flint's* broad approach, the Court seemed to do little more than announce that since 1918 "the present form [of the statute] was fixed and has so continued"; that "[n]o regulation has ever been promulgated which interprets the meaning of 'carrying on a business' "; that the comprehensive definition of "business" in *Flint* was "not controlling in this dissimilar inquiry"; that the facts in each case must be examined; that not all expenses of every business transaction are deductible; and that "[n]o matter how large the estate or how continuous or extended the work required may be, such facts are not sufficient as a matter of law to permit the courts to reverse the decision of the Board." 312 U.S., at 215–218, 61 S.Ct., at 477–478. The opinion, therefore—although devoid of analysis and not setting forth what elements, if any, in addition to profit motive and regularity, were required to render an activity a trade or business—must stand for the propositions that full-time market activity in managing and preserving one's own estate is not embraced within the phrase "carrying on a business," and that salaries and other expenses incident to the operation are not deductible as having been paid or incurred in a trade or business.[9] See also *United States v. Gilmore,* 372 U.S. 39, 44–45, 83 S.Ct. 623, 626–627, 9 L.Ed.2d 570 (1963); *Whipple v. Commissioner,* 373 U.S. 193, 83 S.Ct. 1168, 10 L.Ed.2d 288 (1963). It is of interest to note that, although Justice Frankfurter was on the *Higgins* Court and this time did not write separately, and although Justice Reed, who had joined the concurring opinion in *Du Pont,* was the author of the *Higgins* opinion, the Court in that case did not even cite *Du Pont* and thus paid no heed whatsoever to the content of Justice Frankfurter's pronouncement in his concurring opinion. Adoption of the Frankfurter gloss obviously would have disposed of the case in the Commissioner's favor handily and automatically, but that easy route was not followed.

Less than three months later, the Court considered the issue of the deductibility, as business expenses, of estate and trust fees. In unanimous opinions issued the same day and written by Justice Black, the Court ruled that the efforts of an estate or trust in asset conservation and maintenance did not constitute a trade or business. *City Bank Farmers Trust Co. v. Helvering,* 313 U.S. 121, 61 S.Ct. 896, 85 L.Ed. 1227 (1941); *United States v. Pyne,* 313 U.S. 127, 61 S.Ct. 893, 85 L.Ed. 1231 (1941). The *Higgins* case was deemed to be relevant and controlling. Again, no mention was made of the Frankfurter concurrence in *Du Pont.* Yet Justices Reed and Frankfurter were on the Court.

* * *

From these observations and decisions, we conclude (1) that, to be sure, the statutory words are broad and comprehensive (*Flint*); (2) that, however, expenses incident to caring for one's own investments, even though that endeavor is full time, are not deductible as paid or incurred in carrying on a trade or business (*Higgins; City Bank; Pyne*); (3) that the opposite conclusion may follow for an active trader (*Snyder*); (4) that Justice Frankfurter's attempted gloss upon the decision in *Du Pont* was not adopted by the Court in that case; * * * and (6) that the Frankfurter observation, specifically or by implication, never has been accepted as law by a majority opinion of the Court, and more than once has been totally ignored. We must regard the Frankfurter gloss merely as a two-Justice pronouncement in a passing moment and, while entitled to respect, as never having achieved the status of a Court ruling. One also must acknowledge that *Higgins,* with its stress on examining the facts in each case, affords no readily helpful standard, in the usual sense, with

---

9. See, however, § 212 of the 1954 Code. This section has its roots in § 23(a)(2) of the 1939 Code, as added by § 121 of the Revenue Act of 1942. It allows as a deduction all the ordinary and necessary expenses paid or incurred "for the management, conservation, or maintenance of property held for the production of in-

come," and thus overcame the specific ruling in *Higgins* that expenses of that kind were not deductible. The statutory change, of course, does not read directly on the term "trade or business." Obviously, though, Congress sought to overcome *Higgins* and achieved that end.

which to decide the present case and others similar to it. The Court's cases, thus, give us results, but little general guidance.

III

Federal and state legislation and court decisions, perhaps understandably, until recently have not been noticeably favorable to gambling endeavors and even have been reluctant to treat gambling on a parity with more "legitimate" means of making a living. And the confinement of gambling-loss deductions to the amount of gambling gains, a provision brought into the income tax law as § 23(g) of the Revenue Act of 1934 and carried forward into § 165(d) of the 1954 Code, closed the door on suspected abuses, but served partially to differentiate genuine gambling losses from many other types of adverse financial consequences sustained during the tax year. Gambling winnings, however, have not been isolated from gambling losses. The Congress has been realistic enough to recognize that such losses do exist and do have some effect on income, which is the primary focus of the federal income tax.

The issue this case presents has "been around" for a long time and, as indicated above, has not met with consistent treatment in the Tax Court itself or in the Federal Courts of Appeals. The Seventh Circuit, in the present case, said the issue "has proven to be most difficult and troublesome over the years." The difficulty has not been ameliorated by the persistent absence of an all-purpose definition, by statute or regulation, of the phrase "trade or business" which so frequently appears in the Code. Of course, this very frequency well may be the explanation for legislative and administrative reluctance to take a position as to one use that might affect, with confusion, so many others.

Be that as it may, this taxpayer's case must be decided and, from what we have outlined above, must be decided in the face of a decisional history that is not positive or even fairly indicative, as we read the cases, of what the result should be. There are, however, some helpful indicators.

If a taxpayer, as Groetzinger is stipulated to have done in 1978, devotes his full-time activity to gambling, and it is his intended livelihood source, it would seem that basic concepts of fairness (if there be much of that in the income tax law) demand that his activity be regarded as a trade or business just as any other readily accepted activity, such as being a retail store proprietor or, to come closer categorically, as being a casino operator or as being an active trader on the exchanges.

It is argued, however, that a full-time gambler is not offering goods or his services, within the line of demarcation that Justice Frankfurter would have drawn in *Du Pont*. Respondent replies that he indeed is supplying goods and services, not only to himself but, as well, to the gambling market; thus, he says, he comes within the Frankfurter test even if that were to be imposed as the proper measure. "It takes two to gamble." Surely, one who clearly satisfies the Frankfurter adumbration usually is in a trade or business. But does it necessarily follow that one who does not satisfy the Frankfurter adumbration is not in a trade or business? One might well feel that a full-time gambler ought to qualify as much as a full-time trader, as Justice Brandeis in *Snyder* implied and as courts have held. The Commissioner, indeed, accepts the trader result. In any event, while the offering of goods and services usually would qualify the activity as a trade or business, this factor, it seems to us, is not an absolute prerequisite.

We are not satisfied that the Frankfurter gloss would add any helpful dimension to the resolution of cases such as this one, or that it provides a "sensible test," as the Commissioner urges. It might assist now and then, when the answer is obvious and positive, but it surely is capable of breeding litigation over the meaning of "goods," the meaning of "services," or the meaning of "holding one's self out." And we suspect that—apart from gambling—almost every activity would satisfy the gloss. A test that everyone passes is not a test at all. We therefore now formally reject the Frankfurter gloss which the Court has never adopted anyway.

Of course, not every income-producing and profit-making endeavor constitutes a trade or business. The income tax law, almost from the beginning, has distinguished between a business or trade, on the one hand, and "transactions entered into for profit but not connected with . . . business or trade," on the other. Congress "distinguished the broad range of income or profit producing activities from those satisfying the narrow category of trade or business." *Whipple v. Commissioner,* 373 U.S., at 197, 83 S.Ct., at 1171. We accept the fact that to be engaged in a trade or business, the taxpayer must be involved in the activity with continuity and regularity and that the taxpayer's primary purpose for engaging in the activity must be for income or profit. A sporadic activity, a hobby, or an amusement diversion does not qualify.

     * * *

We do not overrule or cut back on the Court's holding in *Higgins* when we conclude that if one's gambling activity is pursued full time, in good faith, and with regularity, to the production of income for a livelihood, and is not a mere hobby, it is a trade or business within the meaning of the statutes with which we are here concerned. Respondent Groetzinger satisfied that test in 1978. Constant and large-scale effort on his part was made. Skill was required and was applied. He did what he did for a livelihood, though with a less-than-successful result. This was not a hobby or a passing fancy or an occasional bet for amusement.

We therefore adhere to the general position of the *Higgins* Court, taken 46 years ago, that resolution of this issue "requires an examination of the facts in each case." 312 U.S., at 217, 61 S.Ct., at 478. This may be thought by some to be a less-than-satisfactory solution, for facts vary. * * * But the difficulty rests in the Code's wide utilization in various contexts of the term "trade or business," in the absence of an all-purpose definition by statute or regulation, and in our concern that an attempt judicially to formulate and impose a test for all situations would be counterproductive, unhelpful, and even somewhat precarious for the overall integrity of the Code. We leave repair or revision, if any be needed, which we doubt, to the Congress where we feel, at this late date, the ultimate responsibility rests.

The judgment of the Court of Appeals is affirmed.

It is so ordered.

JUSTICE WHITE, with whom THE CHIEF JUSTICE and JUSTICE SCALIA join, dissenting.

The 1982 amendments to the Tax Code made clear that gambling is not a trade or business. Under those amendments, the alternative minimum tax base equals adjusted gross income reduced by specified amounts, including gambling losses, and increased by items not relevant here. If full-time gambling were a trade or business, a full-time gambler's gambling losses would be "deductions ... attributable to a trade or business carried on by the taxpayer," and hence deductible from gross income in computing adjusted gross income, though only to the extent of gambling winnings. To again subtract gambling losses (to the extent of gambling winnings) from adjusted gross income when computing the alternative minimum tax base would be to give the full-time gambler a double deduction for alternative minimum tax purposes, which was certainly not Congress' intent.[2] Thus, when Congress amended the alternative minimum tax provisions in 1982, it implicitly accepted the teaching of *Gentile v. Commissioner,* 65 T.C. 1 (1975), that gambling is not a trade or business. Groetzinger would have had no problem under the 1982 amendments.

One could argue, I suppose, that although gambling is not a trade or business under the 1982 amendments, it was in 1978, the tax year at issue here. But there is certainly no indication that Congress intended in 1982 to alter the status of gambling as a trade or business. Rather, Congress was correcting an inequity that had arisen because gambling is *not* a trade or business, just as 40 years earlier Congress had, by enacting the predecessor to 26 U.S.C. § 212, corrected an inequity that became apparent when this Court held that a full-time investor is not

2. Consider two single individuals filing for the tax year ending December 31, 1986: A has $75,000 in nongambling income, and $75,000 in itemized nongambling deductions; B, a full-time gambler, has $75,000 in gambling winnings, $75,000 in gambling losses, $75,000 in nongambling income, and $75,000 in itemized nongambling deductions. A's gross income and adjusted gross income are both $75,000, and so is his alternative minimum tax base. The alternative minimum tax assessed on A is 20% of the excess of $75,000 over $30,000, or $9,000. Assuming that full-time gambling is a trade or business, B has gross income of $150,000, adjusted gross income of $75,000 (because his gambling losses are attributable to a trade or business), and an alterna- tive minimum tax base of zero (because gambling losses are deducted from adjusted gross income in computing the alternative minimum tax base). Thus, if full-time gam- bling were treated as a trade or business, B's gambling losses would shield him against the $9,000 minimum tax that Con- gress clearly intended him to pay. "The Code should not be interpreted to allow [a taxpayer] 'the practical equivalent of a dou- ble deduction,' *Charles Ilfeld Co. v. Hernan- dez,* 292 U.S. 62, 68, 54 S.Ct. 596, 598, 78 L.Ed. 1127 (1934), absent a clear declara- tion of intent by Congress." *United States v. Skelly Oil Co.,* 394 U.S. 678, 684, 89 S.Ct. 1379, 1383, 22 L.Ed.2d 642 (1969). There is no such clear declaration of intent accompa- nying the 1982 amendments.

engaged in a trade or business. See *Higgins v. Commissioner,* 312 U.S. 212, 61 S.Ct. 475, 85 L.Ed. 783 (1941). In neither case did Congress attempt to alter the then-prevailing definition of trade or business, nor do I think this Court should do so now to avoid a harsh result in this case. In any event, the Court should recognize that its holding is a sport that applies only to a superseded statute and not to the tax years governed by the 1982 amendments. Accordingly, I dissent.

Note

The dissent's beef is with the interpretation of changes to the alternative minimum tax, not with the majority's analysis as to how to determine if an activity rises to the level of a "trade or business." With that there is apparently no dispute. So in deciding whether an activity is a trade or business of a taxpayer, we ask whether the taxpayer has devoted his or her full-time efforts in that activity on a regular, continuous, and substantial basis.

The alternative minimum tax ("AMT") is discussed in summary fashion at Chapter 11. Very generally, the AMT is designed to ensure that affluent taxpayers do not overdose on various deductions and other incentive provisions in the Code so as to reduce their federal income tax liabilities to ridiculously low levels. It does so by re-computing a taxpayer's tax liability by disallowing certain itemized deductions and making other adjustments. This "alternative minimum taxable income" is then applied to a relatively flat rate structure (currently with only two brackets at 26 percent and 28 percent) to determine a taxpayer's "tentative minimum tax." If a taxpayer's tentative minimum tax exceeds his or her regular tax liability for the year as computed under § 1, then the taxpayer must remit the excess in addition to the regular tax liability.

* * *

Problem 4–5

Della Ware is an attorney working as a sole practitioner. Below are listed several expenses Della incurred in the previous taxable year. Identify all of the expenses that may be deducted by Della under § 162(a).

(a) New computer, monitor, and printer, used exclusively in the business.

(b) Repairs to office conference table damaged during client meeting.

(c) Three-week African safari trip to enhance reputation as an international legal expert.

(d) Payment to competitor to refrain from practicing law in Della's home state.

(e) Reimbursement paid to client for loss on an investment recommended by Della.

(f) Cost to keep a jet airplane on 24–hour standby because the timing of business trips is unpredictable and uncontrollable.

(g) Contribution to the "Say No to Anything Government" initiative fund because of Della's political support for libertarian measures. *[handwritten: No personal expense.]*

(h) Annual premium for personal medical insurance. *[handwritten: Yes. Yes under § 162(a) (b)]*

Problem 4–6

Lou Pole is a certified public accountant, licensed in the State of New York, and a member of the New York Bar. As a CPA and lawyer, Lou developed into a tax specialist, but his law practice also includes admiralty and probate work. In Year One, Lou bought a 40–foot boat that he named the *Bar Bill*. In buying the boat, Lou hoped to make contacts among yacht owners and to boost his professional clientele. Lou did not use the boat to entertain or transport existing or prospective clients or business contacts, nor to transport himself on business. To the extent Lou incurs costs to maintain and repair the boat, can he deduct those costs? *[handwritten: No — these costs must be capitalized * ** ** It is only for NEW clientele? maybe]*

Policy Limits on the Deduction for Business Expenses. Should the deduction for business expenses in § 162(a) be limited in any way by concerns for public policy? Both *Estate of Rockefeller* and *Groetzinger* raise the issue, but it appears center stage in the following case.

[handwritten left margin: monday Oct. 3rd p. 232-241]

COMMISSIONER v. TELLIER

United States Supreme Court, 1966.
383 U.S. 687, 86 S.Ct. 1118, 16 L.Ed.2d 185.

Mr. Justice Stewart delivered the opinion of the Court.

The question presented in this case is whether expenses incurred by a taxpayer in the unsuccessful defense of a criminal prosecution may qualify for deduction from taxable income under § 162(a) of the Internal Revenue Code of 1954, which allows a deduction of "all the ordinary and necessary expenses paid or incurred during the taxable year in carrying on any trade or business. . . ." The respondent Walter F. Tellier was engaged in the business of underwriting the public sale of stock offerings and purchasing securities for resale to customers. In 1956 he was brought to trial upon a 36–count indictment that charged him with violating the fraud section of the Securities Act of 1933 and the mail fraud statute, and with conspiring to violate those statutes. He was found guilty on all counts and was sentenced to pay an $18,000 fine and to serve four and a half years in prison. The judgment of conviction was affirmed on appeal. In his unsuccessful defense of this criminal prosecution, the respondent incurred and paid $22,964.20 in legal expenses in 1956. He claimed a deduction for that amount on his federal income tax return for that year. The Commissioner disallowed the deduction and was sustained by the Tax Court. The Court of Appeals for the Second Circuit reversed in a unanimous *en banc* decision, and we granted certiorari. We affirm the judgment of the Court of Appeals.

There can be no serious question that the payments deducted by the respondent were expenses of his securities business under the decisions of this Court, and the Commissioner does not contend otherwise. In *United States v. Gilmore,* 372 U.S. 39, we held that "the origin and character of the claim with respect to which an expense was incurred, rather than its potential consequences upon the fortunes of the taxpayer, is the controlling basic test of whether the expense was 'business' or 'personal'" within the meaning of § 162(a). The criminal charges against the respondent found their source in his business activities as a securities dealer. The respondent's legal fees, paid in defense against those charges, therefore, clearly qualify under *Gilmore* as "expenses paid or incurred ... in carrying on any trade or business" within the meaning of § 162(a). The Commissioner also concedes that the respondent's legal expenses were "ordinary" and "necessary" expenses within the meaning of § 162(a). Our decisions have consistently construed the term "necessary" as imposing only the minimal requirement that the expense be "appropriate and helpful" for "the development of the [taxpayer's] business." *Welch v. Helvering,* 290 U.S. 111, 113. The principal function of the term "ordinary" in § 162(a) is to clarify the distinction, often difficult, between those expenses that are currently deductible and those that are in the nature of capital expenditures, which, if deductible at all, must be amortized over the useful life of the asset. *Welch v. Helvering, supra,* at 113–116. The legal expenses deducted by the respondent were not capital expenditures. They were incurred in his defense against charges of past criminal conduct, not in the acquisition of a capital asset. Our decisions establish that counsel fees comparable to those here involved are ordinary business expenses, even though a "lawsuit affecting the safety of a business may happen once in a lifetime." *Welch v. Helvering, supra,* at 114.

It is therefore clear that the respondent's legal fees were deductible under § 162(a) if the provisions of that section are to be given their normal effect in this case. The Commissioner and the Tax Court determined, however, that even though the expenditures meet the literal requirements of § 162(a), their deduction must nevertheless be disallowed on the ground of public policy. That view finds considerable support in other administrative and judicial decisions. It finds no support, however, in any regulation or statute or in any decision of this Court, and we believe no such "public policy" exception to the plain provisions of § 162(a) is warranted in the circumstances presented by this case.

We start with the proposition that the federal income tax is a tax on net income, not a sanction against wrongdoing. That principle has been firmly imbedded in the tax statute from the beginning. One familiar facet of the principle is the truism that the statute does not concern itself with the lawfulness of the income that it taxes. Income from a criminal enterprise is taxed at a rate no higher and no lower than income from more conventional sources. "The fact that a business is unlawful [does not] exempt it from paying the taxes that if lawful it would have to pay." *United States v. Sullivan,* 274 U.S. 259, 263. See *James v. United States,* 366 U.S. 213.

With respect to deductions, the basic rule, with only a few limited and well-defined exceptions, is the same. During the Senate debate in 1913 on the bill that became the first modern income tax law, amendments were rejected that would have limited deductions for losses to those incurred in a "legitimate" or "lawful" trade or business. Senator Williams, who was in charge of the bill, stated on the floor of the Senate that

"The object of this bill is to tax a man's net income; that is to say, what he has at the end of the year after deducting from his receipts his expenditures or losses. It is not to reform men's moral characters; that is not the object of the bill at all. The tax is not levied for the purpose of restraining people from betting on horse races or upon 'futures,' but the tax is framed for the purpose of making a man pay upon his net income, his actual profit during the year. The law does not care where he got it from, so far as the tax is concerned, although the law may very properly care in another way." 50 Cong. Rec. 3849.

The application of this principle is reflected in several decisions of this Court. As recently as *Commissioner v. Sullivan*, 356 U.S. 27, we sustained the allowance of a deduction for rent and wages paid by the operators of a gambling enterprise, even though both the business itself and the specific rent and wage payments there in question were illegal under state law. In rejecting the Commissioner's contention that the illegality of the enterprise required disallowance of the deduction, we held that, were we to "enforce as federal policy the rule espoused by the Commissioner in this case, we would come close to making this type of business taxable on the basis of its gross receipts, while all other business would be taxable on the basis of net income. If that choice is to be made, Congress should do it." In *Lilly v. Commissioner*, 343 U.S. 90, the Court upheld deductions claimed by opticians for amounts paid to doctors who prescribed the eyeglasses that the opticians sold, although the Court was careful to disavow "approval of the business ethics or public policy involved in the payments...." And in *Commissioner v. Heininger*, 320 U.S. 467, a case akin to the one before us, the Court upheld deductions claimed by a dentist for lawyer's fees and other expenses incurred in unsuccessfully defending against an administrative fraud order issued by the Postmaster General. Deduction of expenses falling within the general definition of § 162(a) may, to be sure, be disallowed by specific legislation, since deductions "are a matter of grace and Congress can, of course, disallow them as it chooses." *Commissioner v. Sullivan*, 356 U.S., at 28. The Court has also given effect to a precise and long-standing Treasury Regulation prohibiting the deduction of a specified category of expenditures; an example is lobbying expenses, whose nondeductibility was supported by considerations not here present. But where Congress has been wholly silent, it is only in extremely limited circumstances that the Court has countenanced exceptions to the general principle reflected in the *Sullivan, Lilly* and *Heininger* decisions. Only where the allowance of a deduction would "frustrate sharply defined national or state policies proscribing particular types of conduct" have we upheld its disallowance. Further, the "policies frustrated must be national or state policies evidenced by some *governmental* declaration of them." *Lilly v. Commissioner*, 343 U.S., at 97. (Emphasis added.) Finally, the "test of nondeductibility always is the severity and immediacy of the frustration resulting from allowance of the deduction." *Tank Truck Rentals v. Commissioner*, 356 U.S. 30, 35. In that case * * *, we upheld the disallowance of deductions claimed by taxpayers for fines and penalties imposed upon them for violating state penal statutes; to allow a deduction in those circumstances would have directly and substantially diluted the actual punishment imposed.

The present case falls far outside that sharply limited and carefully defined category. No public policy is offended when a man faced with serious criminal charges employs a lawyer to help in his defense. That is not "proscribed conduct." It is his constitutional right. *Chandler v. Fretag*, 348 U.S. 3. See *Gideon v. Wainwright*, 372 U.S. 335. In an adversary system of criminal justice, it is a basic of our public policy that a defendant in a criminal case have counsel to represent him.

Congress has authorized the imposition of severe punishment upon those found guilty of the serious criminal offenses with which the respondent was charged and of which he was convicted. But we can find no warrant for attaching to that punishment an additional financial burden that Congress has neither expressly nor implicitly directed. To deny a deduction for expenses incurred in the unsuccessful defense of a criminal prosecution would impose such a burden in a measure dependent not on the seriousness of the offense or the actual sentence imposed by the court, but on the cost of the defense and the defendant's particular tax bracket. We decline to distort the income tax laws to serve a purpose for which they were neither intended nor designed by Congress.

The judgment is

Affirmed.

VITALE v. COMMISSIONER, T.C. Memo. 1999–131 (1999).

Facts: The taxpayer, a former Treasury employee, decided toward the end of his 35 years of service to start work as an author. After completing two manuscripts, he began work on a third, entitled *Searchlight, Nevada*, "a story about the experiences of two men who travel cross-country to patronize a legal brothel in Nevada. * * * In order to authenticate the story and develop characters for the book, petitioner visited numerous legal brothels in Nevada by acting as a customer for prostitutes. In a journal describing his experiences at the brothels, petitioner recorded the brothels he visited, the dates (and sometimes the hours) of his visits, the prostitutes he met, and the amount of cash he paid each one. For each entry, petitioner wrote about his visit with the prostitute and about the happenings at brothels in general. For example, he described the manner in which he selected her, the house rules of the brothel, the manner in which he negotiated a price for her time, their dialogue, and the type of clothing worn by her. He also included personal information on the prostitute, including her age, physical characteristics, city or State of residence, religious background, ethnicity, level of education, and the name and age of her offspring, if any. The journal indicates that, at some point during these meetings, petitioner told the prostitutes that he was writing a book about Nevada's legal brothels and that he wished to use them as characters in his book. The journal shows that, during 1993, petitioner spent, on average, 3 days per month (except during the months of February, May, and December) meeting with prostitutes at the brothels.''

Issue: Are the payments to the brothels deductible under § 162(a)?

Holding: No.

Rationale: "We find that the expenditures incurred by petitioner to visit prostitutes are so personal in nature as to preclude their deductibility."

* * *

Statutory Limits on the Deduction of Business Expenses. Although *Tellier* makes it clear that there is no public policy exception to the § 162(a) deduction at common law, § 162 itself contains a host of policy-based exceptions. Section 162(c)(1) denies a deduction for illegal bribes or kickbacks paid to a domestic government official or agency (as opposed to legal bribes?), and § 162(c)(2) disallows a deduction for any illegal payment made to any person. Section 162(e) generally denies deductions for expenses incurred in certain political lobbying activities and campaigns for public office. Section 162(f) denies a deduction for any fines or penalties paid to a government for violation of any law. Section 162(g) prevents deductions of treble damage payments made by those convicted of (or who pled guilty to) a violation of federal antitrust laws.

Not all of the policy-based exceptions to § 162(a) are contained in § 162. For example, § 280E disallows a deduction for the ordinary and necessary business expenses of a taxpayer engaged in the illegal sale of controlled substances.

* * *

Problem 4–7

Terry Cotta worked as a federal employee. She was indicted on charges of embezzling $156,000 from her employer. Ultimately, Terry avoided prosecution by agreeing to pay a settlement of $250,000 to the federal government.

(a) To what extent can Terry deduct the $250,000 paid to the federal government?

(b) Assuming Terry can deduct at least some portion of the payment to the federal government, what statutory obstacles will preclude Terry from deducting the full amount to which she is entitled?

* * *

(2) INVESTMENT EXPENSES

Code: IRC §§ 212; 265(a)(1); 274(h)(7).

Regs: Treas. Reg. § 1.212–1.

Expenses Incurred in Investment Activities. Section 212 allows a deduction for "ordinary and necessary expenses paid or incurred during the taxable year" for three types of activities, loosely themed "investment" activities because they do not rise to the level of a trade or business. The first is the "production or collection of income." Section 212(1). The second is the "management, conservation, or maintenance of property held for the production of income." Section 212(2). Finally, there is a deduction for expenses "in connection with the determination, collection or refund of any tax." Section 212(3).

As explained in *Groetzinger*, § 212 traces back to the Supreme Court's decision in *Higgins v. Commissioner*, 312 U.S. 212, 61 S.Ct. 475, 85 L.Ed. 783 (1941). The taxpayer in *Higgins* devoted considerable time and effort toward managing his own portfolio of financial investments. When he attempted to deduct various expenses related to his efforts, the Service disallowed the deductions on the grounds that the taxpayer's activity was not a trade or business. The Court ultimately deferred to the Service on the issue and upheld the assessed deficiency.

Yet it was clear to Congress that even if investing activities did not constitute a business, the expenses of investing were indeed costs of earning income. Accordingly, it authorized a deduction by enacting § 212. For over sixty years, then, taxpayers have been able to deduct the various expenses of investment activities.

* * *

Self-Assessment Question

(Solutions to Self–Assessment Questions are set forth in Appendix 3.)

SAQ 4–5. Section 212 contains language very similar to § 162(a), and the terms "ordinary and necessary," "expenses," and "paid or incurred during the taxable year" are assumed to have the same meanings in the context of § 212. Since "trade or business" and "investment" expenses are both deductible, does it matter whether an expense falls under § 162 or § 212? Why or why not?

* * *

⭐ Problem 4–8 ⭐

Jay, a traveling salesman for a laminate company, has a portfolio of stocks and bonds worth about $500,000. During the current year, Jay incurred several expenses related to his portfolio. Which of the following expenses can Jay deduct?

(a) $100 for a subscription to the *Wall Street Journal*.

(b) $25 for the hardcover book "Understanding Tax–Free Bonds."

(c) $500 for investment advice from a financial planner.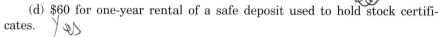

(d) $60 for one-year rental of a safe deposit used to hold stock certificates.

(e) $400 to an accountant for preparation of his federal income tax return.

(f) $1,000 in travel, lodging, and restaurant expenses to attend a shareholder meeting for Microsoft Corporation, in which Jay owns 100 shares.

(g) $250 to an attorney to advise him of the deductibility of the foregoing.

* * *

(3) AMORTIZATION OF START–UP EXPENSES

Code: IRC § 195.

Regs: Treas. Reg. §§ 1.263(a)–5(a)–(b)(1); 1.263(a)–5(d)–(e).

Start-up Expenditures. Taxpayers almost always incur costs to commence a new or different business activity. For example, George Jefferson, a proprietor with a chain of dry cleaning stores, might be thinking about starting a restaurant. George might pay all kinds of expenses in investigating whether to start a restaurant or what kind of restaurant to open (consulting fees, attorney fees, travel expenses, and the like). Because George is not yet "carrying on" the restaurant business when he pays these expenses, however, George is unable to claim a current deduction for these expenses under § 162(a). What, then, does George do with these costs? In *Frank v. Commissioner*, 20 T.C. 511 (1953), the taxpayer incurred travel and legal expenses in searching for and investigating various newspaper and radio properties. The court disallowed the taxpayer's claimed deductions because they were incurred prior to entering into a business activity. The costs were instead capitalized and added to the basis of business assets. Section 195(a) is consistent with *Frank* in that it denies a current deduction for such costs.

Likewise, job training expenses incurred prior to the opening of a business must also be capitalized. This was the holding of *Richmond Television Corp. v. United States*, 345 F.2d 901 (4th Cir. 1965), *vacated and remanded on other grounds*, 382 U.S. 68, 86 S.Ct. 233, 15 L.Ed.2d 143 (1965), where the taxpayer could not deduct job training expenses incurred before it received its operating license from the Federal Communications Commission.

The capitalization of start-up costs is not unique to business activities. Section 212, the deduction provision for expenses related to investment activities, does not contain the same "in carrying on" phrase found in § 162(a). Still, courts have held that start-up expenses related to investment activities must also be capitalized. In *Sorrell v. Commissioner*, 882 F.2d 484 (11th Cir. 1989), for example, investor service fees paid by the taxpayer prior to commencing investment activities had to be capitalized. The service fees were viewed as part of the cost of acquiring the investment assets and thus had to be capitalized and added to the basis of the acquired capital assets.

Not all start-up expenditures must be capitalized. Some Code provisions permit current deductions even though the taxpayer is not yet "carrying on" a business or investment activity. Section 163, for instance, permits a deduction for interest expenses and does not require the taxpayer to be "carrying on" a business or investment activity. See § 163(h) and discussion at Chapter 8. Similarly, certain taxes and research and development costs can be deducted immediately. See §§ 164 and 174.

Yet the lack of a current deduction for most start-up expenses might deter taxpayers like George Jefferson from exploring new business ventures. Accordingly, § 195(b)(1) generally allows taxpayers to *amortize* (that means prorate) "start-up expenditures" over the 180–month period beginning with the month in which the new business activity commences. Thus, for example, if George starts his new restaurant business in October, Year One, after incurring $180,000 in "start-up expenditures," he may deduct $1,000 of these costs each month ($3,000 in Year One, $12,000 in Year Two, and so forth) for the first 15 years of restaurant operations. Should George sell or otherwise dispose of the business before he has completely amortized these costs, any unrecovered costs will likely be deductible as a loss. Section 195(b)(2).

Start-up expenditures are defined in § 195(c) as, generally, investigatory expenses incurred prior to commencing a trade or business activity which would have been deductible had it been paid or incurred when the taxpayer was already engaged in the trade or business activity. So any cost that would be capitalized by a taxpayer already "carrying on" the business activity (a new building, new furnishings, new equipment and the like) is not eligible for § 195(b)(1) amortization.

In this regard, it becomes necessary to distinguish amortizable start-up expenditures from non-amortizable capital expenditures. The differences between these concepts can be quite small. In *Revenue Ruling 99–23*, the Service articulated a standard for ascertaining whether a start-up expenditure was eligible for amortization:

> Expenditures incurred in the course of a general search for, or investigation of, an active trade or business in order to determine *whether* to enter a new business and *which* new business to enter (other than costs incurred to acquire capital assets that are used in the search or investigation) qualify as investigatory costs that are eligible for amortization as start-up expenditures under § 195. However, expenditures incurred in the attempt to *acquire a specific business* do not qualify as start-up expenditures because they are acquisition costs under § 263. The nature of the cost must be analyzed based on all the facts and circumstances of the transaction to determine whether it is an investigatory cost incurred to facilitate the whether and which decisions, or an acquisition cost incurred to facilitate consummation of an acquisition.

(Emphasis added.)

This standard was refined in regulations finalized in 2004. Under Regulation § 1.263(a)–5(a), the main test for capitalization of start-up expenditures is whether such amounts are paid to "facilitate" the acquisition of a new business. The regulations state that an amount is paid to facilitate an acquisition "if the amount is paid in the process of investigating or otherwise pursuing the transaction." Treas. Reg. § 1.263(a)–5(b)(1). While this is generally a fact-intensive test, the regulations offer some "simplifying conventions" for this determination. For example, employee compensation and overhead expenses are treated as amounts that do not facilitate a transaction. Accordingly, these costs may be treated as expenses eligible for amortization under § 195. Treas. Reg. § 1.263(a)–5(d)(1). In addition, if all of the facilitative costs involved with respect to a transaction do not exceed $5,000 in the aggregate, all of the costs can be treated as expenses eligible for § 195 amortization under a special *de minimis* rule. Treas. Reg. § 1.263(a)–5(d)(3).

In the case of an acquisition of the assets of a new trade or business, Regulation § 1.263(a)–5(e) states that investigatory costs paid by the taxpayer "facilitates" the acquisition of a business (and thus must be capitalized) *only* if it is paid *on or after* the earlier of: (1) the date on which a letter of intent, exclusivity agreement, or similar agreement is executed with respect to the acquisition; or (2) the date when the taxpayer "approves" the material terms of the transaction. It is helpful to think of this "earlier of" date as the "go date" for purposes of knowing when the presumption shifts. Investigatory costs paid *before* the "go date," presumably, will qualify for amortization under § 195(b) except to the extent such costs are "inherently facilitative" under Regulation § 1.263(a)–5(e)(2). On and after the "go date," the presumption is for capitalization.

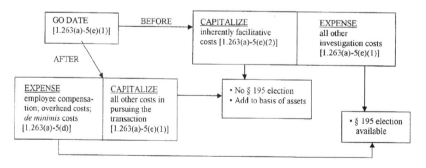

* * *

Problem 4–9

Discuss the federal income tax consequences of the expenditures incurred by the taxpayers described in the following fact patterns.

✦ (a) In April, Year One, *X* hired an investment banker to evaluate the possibility of acquiring a trade or business unrelated to *X*'s existing business. The investment banker conducted research on several industries and evaluated publicly available financial information relating to several businesses. *X* paid $6,000 for these services. By July, Year One, *X* narrowed its focus to one industry. The investment banker then evaluated several businesses within the industry, including *ABC* Corporation and several of *ABC*'s competitors. *X* paid another $6,000 for these services. In September, Year One, *X* decided to make an offer to purchase the assets of *ABC*. The investment banker then commissioned appraisals of *ABC*'s assets and an in-depth review of *ABC*'s books and records in order to determine a fair acquisition price. *X* paid $4,000 for these services. On November, Year One, *X* entered into an acquisition agreement with *ABC* to purchase all of *ABC*'s assets. The acquisition was completed and *X* commenced operation of *ABC*'s business shortly thereafter.

✦ (b) In May, Year One, *Y* began searching for a new business activity to acquire. In anticipation of finding a suitable target to acquire, *Y* hired an investment banker to evaluate three potential business entities: *DEF* Corporation, *GHI* Corporation, and *JKL* Corporation. *Y* also hired a law firm to begin drafting regulatory approval documents for a target. *Y* paid $4,000 to the investment banker and $8,000 to the law firm for these services. In October, Year One, *Y* finally decided to purchase all of the assets of *DEF*. *Y* and *DEF* entered into an acquisition agreement on December 1, Year One. The transaction was completed later that day, and *Y* immediately commenced operation of *DEF*'s business.

(c) In June, Year One, *Z* hired a law firm and an accounting firm to assist in the potential acquisition of *MNO* Corporation—a corporation engaged in a trade or business wholly unrelated to *Z*'s trade or business—by performing certain services labeled by the parties as "preliminary due diligence." These services included conducting research on *MNO*'s industry (including information related to *MNO*'s competitors) and analyzing financial projections for *MNO* for Year One and Year Two. *Z* paid $20,000 total for these "preliminary due diligence" services. In September, Year One, at *Z*'s request, the law firm prepared and submitted a letter of intent to *MNO*. The offer contained in the letter of intent resulted from prior discussions between *Z* and *MNO*, and specifically stated that a binding commitment with respect to the proposed transaction would result only upon execution of an acquisition agreement. *Z* paid $5,000 to the law firm for preparation of the letter of intent. Thereafter, the law firm and accounting firm continued to provide services labeled "due diligence," including a review of *MNO*'s internal documents relating to insurance policies, employment agreements, and lease agreements, as well as an in-depth review of *MNO*'s books and records and preparation of an acquisition agreement. *Z* paid $50,000 for these services. On October 10, Year One, *Z* entered into an acquisition agreement with *MNO* to purchase all of the assets of *MNO*. The transaction was completed on October 15, Year One, and *Z* started conducting *MNO*'s business the same day.

D.   TREATMENT OF CAPITAL EXPENDITURES

    Introduction to Cost Recovery. We know from Part B, *supra*, that capital expenditures create or add to the basis of property. See § 1016(a)(1). Thus a taxpayer generally cannot recover the cost of a capital expenditure for federal income tax purposes until the improved property is sold, exchanged, or otherwise disposed of in some form. For assets that lose value over time, this general rule can create a mismatch between income and expenses.

    Consider a simple example: Moe owns a tavern in Springfield. He purchases a juke box machine in Year One for $5,000. The normal useful life for a juke box machine is five years. Moe expects that the machine will generate annual gross revenues of only $2,000. Assume also that the machine will be worth nothing at the end of its useful life (put another way, the machine will have no "salvage value"). We know that Moe generally cannot deduct the cost of the machine in Year One because the juke box will provide a benefit beyond the current taxable year. If we allowed a deduction, it would be a windfall to Moe. This is easily proved by considering how income and expenses would look over the five-year useful life:

	Year 1	Year 2	Year 3	Year 4	Year 5
Income	2,000	2,000	2,000	2,000	2,000
Deduction	(5,000)				
Net	(3,000)	2,000	2,000	2,000	2,000

Notice that Moe pays less tax at first and more tax in the later years. Moe, naturally, is thrilled. He knows that time value of money principles covet early deductions and deferred incomes. But is it accurate to say Moe has no cost allocable to Years Two through Five?

    If the shoe were on the other foot, Moe would raise that very argument. Consider what happens if Moe is forced to capitalize the cost of the juke box and sell it for zero at the end of its useful life (resulting in a realized and recognized loss of $5,000 under § 1001):

	Year 1	Year 2	Year 3	Year 4	Year 5
Income	2,000	2,000	2,000	2,000	2,000
Deduction					(5,000)
Net	2,000	2,000	2,000	2,000	(3,000)

This is a bad result for Moe, because he pays more tax up front and does not get the deduction until later. This is just as inaccurate as the prior result, for the same reasons.

    A better solution would be to allow Moe to recover the cost of the juke box over its useful life. The income and deduction items would better match, and a truer picture of the real annual profit to Moe would emerge:

	Year 1	Year 2	Year 3	Year 4	Year 5
Income	2,000	2,000	2,000	2,000	2,000
Deduction	(1,000)	(1,000)	(1,000)	(1,000)	(1,000)
Net	1,000	1,000	1,000	1,000	1,000

This is the *theory* behind the cost recovery deductions of "depreciation" and "amortization." "Theory" is emphasized in the prior sentence because you will find that, for various policy reasons, a perfect match of income and deductions in fact does not occur. In most cases, Congress gives taxpayers larger deductions in the early years of an asset's useful life.

The cost recovery system for **tangible** property is referred to as **depreciation** and is governed chiefly by §§ 167 and 168 (although a few other Code sections also come into play). The cost recovery system for **intangible** property is referred to as **amortization**, and is governed mostly by § 197. Of course, not all property is eligible for depreciation or amortization. In the case of depreciation, the tangible property must be described in § 167(a). In the case of amortization, the intangible property must be described in §§ 197(c)(1) and 197(d). Notice that both §§ 167 and 197 require that property be held either for use in a trade or business or for the production of income. Personal-use property, therefore, is not eligible for cost recovery over its useful life.

(1) DEPRECIATION OF TANGIBLE PROPERTY

Code: IRC §§ 167(a)–(c)(1); 168(a)–(e), (g)(1)–(3), (g)(7); 1016(a)(2).

Regs: Treas. Reg. § 1.167(a)–2. *Skim* Prop. Reg. § 1.168–2(d)(2)(ii).

Property Eligible for Depreciation. Notice that § 167(a) permits a deduction for "the exhaustion, wear and tear" and for the "obsolescence" of property used in a trade or business or held for the production of income. Thus, to be eligible for depreciation, an asset must have two features: (1) it has a useful life beyond the taxable year (the reason it was capitalized in the first place); and (2) it wears out, decays, declines in value due to natural causes, or is subject to exhaustion or obsolescence. The first requirement is no sweat—if the cost does not have to be capitalized, the taxpayer can claim a full deduction in the year of acquisition. See §§ 162(a); 212. Cost recovery is only a concern when the cost is capitalized. The second requirement is more problematical.

No depreciation deduction is allowed for inventories or other property held for sale to customers in the ordinary course of business. Treas. Reg. § 1.167(a)–2. Land is also not depreciable. *Id.* These assets are not traditionally subject to wear and tear, exhaustion, or obsolescence. Although land is not depreciable, improvements to land usually are depreciable. For example, a taxpayer cannot depreciate the land on which the taxpayer's factory sits, but the factory building itself is subject to depreciation. If an improvement permanently adds to the value of the land, however, depreciation may be disallowed. In one case, a golf resort could not depreciate the cost of installing tees, greens, and sand traps because those improvements permanently affected the value of the land and had an unlimited useful life. *The Edinboro Co. v. United States*, 224 F.Supp. 301 (W.D. Pa. 1963).

Landscaping costs (costs incurred to plant trees and shrubs on the taxpayer's property), however, are generally depreciable, even though such costs may add to the value of the underlying land. *Revenue Procedure 87–56*, 1987–2 C.B. 674. Maybe this is because landscaping usually accompanies buildings and other depreciable improvements to land. In one case, the taxpayer was allowed to depreciate the costs of clearing, grading and landscaping a mobile home site because these improvements were "directly related to and a necessary part of the construction of depreciable assets, necessary to the operation of the mobile home park * * *." *Trailmont Park, Inc. v. Commissioner*, 30 T.C.M. 871 (1971).

Determining whether an asset has a useful life or whether it is subject to wear and tear is not always an easy inquiry. That issue is presented in the following case, as is a helpful history of the depreciation deduction.

SIMON v. COMMISSIONER

United States Tax Court, 1994.
103 T.C. 247.

LARO, JUDGE:

Richard Simon and Fiona Simon petitioned the Court for a redetermination of respondent's determinations in a notice of deficiency issued to them on December 11, 1991. * * *

Due to concessions by the parties, the sole issue for decision is whether petitioners are entitled to deduct depreciation claimed under the accelerated cost recovery system (ACRS) for the year in issue. Petitioners claimed depreciation on two 19th-century violin bows that they used in their trade or business as full-time professional violinists. As discussed below, we hold that petitioners may depreciate their violin bows during the year in issue.

FINDINGS OF FACT

* * *

Petitioners' Backgrounds

* * *

During the year in issue, petitioners were both full-time performers with the [New York] Philharmonic [Orchestra], playing locally, nationally, and internationally in the finest concert halls in the world. In 1989, petitioners performed four concerts per week with the Philharmonic, playing over 200 different works, and attended many rehearsals with the Philharmonic that were more demanding and more time-consuming than the concerts. Petitioners also carried out the busy schedules connected with their second careers.

Construction of a Violin Bow

A violin bow consists of a flexible wooden stick, horsehair, a frog, and a ferrule (screw). The stick, which varies in thickness, weight, and balance, is the working part of the bow and is an integral part in the production of sound through vibration. It is designed so that horsehair can be stretched between its ends.

The horsehair is a group of single strands of hair that come from the tails of Siberian horses. A hatchet-shaped head holds one end of the horsehair, and the other end is attached to a frog. The frog, which is inserted into the stick, is a movable hollow piece by which the bow is held. The frog has an eyepiece on the end that catches the screw. The screw is the small knob at the end of the bow that is adjusted to tighten or loosen the horsehair in order to change the tension on the horsehair. The horsehair is the part of the bow that touches the violin strings. Rosin is applied to the horsehair to supply the frictional element that is necessary to make the violin strings vibrate.

Old violins played with old bows produce exceptional sounds that are superior to sounds produced by newer violins played with newer bows. The two violin bows in issue were made in the 19th century by François Xavier Tourte (1747–1835). François Tourte is considered the premier violin bow maker. In particular, he is renowned for improving the bow's design. (Hereinafter, the two bows in issue are separately referred to as Bow 1 and Bow 2, and are collectively referred to as the Tourte bows.)

Purchase of the Tourte Bows

On November 13, 1985, petitioners purchased Bow 1 for $30,000; the bow was purchased from Moes & Moes, Ltd., a dealer and restorer of violins and violin bows. On December 3, 1985, petitioners purchased Bow 2 from this dealer for $21,500. The sticks, frogs, and screws were originals of François Tourte at the time of each purchase. No cracks or other defects were apparent in the sticks at the time of each purchase. The frogs and screws, however, were not in playable condition. Therefore, petitioners replaced them.

Petitioners acquired the Tourte bows for regular use in their full-time professional employment as violinists. Petitioners purchased the Tourte bows for their tonal quality, not for their monetary value.[2] In the year of acquisition, petitioners began using the Tourte bows with the original sticks in their trade or business as full-time professional violinists. Petitioners continued to use the Tourte bows with the original sticks during the year in issue.

---

2. Richard Simon plays a violin made by Nicolo Amati in 1660. Fiona Simon plays a violin made circa 1750. The combination of these old violins and the Tourte bows re-sults in a magnificent sound that is superior to the sounds produced by newer instruments.

Depreciation Deductions Claimed for the Tourte Bows

On their 1989 Form 1040, petitioners claimed a depreciation deduction of $6,300 with respect to Bow 1 and $4,515 with respect to Bow 2; these amounts were in accordance with the appropriate ACRS provisions that applied to 5–year property. Respondent disallowed petitioners' depreciation deduction in full and reflected her disallowance in the notice of deficiency at issue here.

Conditions Affecting the Wear and Tear of Violin Bows

Playing with a bow adversely affects the bow's condition; when a musician plays with a bow, the bow vibrates up, down, sideways, and at different angles. In addition, perspiration from a player's hands enters the wood of a bow and ultimately destroys the bow's utility for playing. Cracks and heavy-handed bearing down while playing certain pieces of music also create wear and tear to a bow. A player who has a heavy hand may cause the stick to press against the horsehair; in turn, this may cause the bow to curve and warp. * * * Petitioners' use of the Tourte bows during the year in issue subjected the bows to substantial wear and tear.

Frequent use of a violin bow will cause it to be "played out", meaning that the wood loses it ability to vibrate and produce quality sound from the instrument. From the point of view of a professional musician, a "played out" bow is inferior and of limited use. The Tourte bows were purchased by petitioners, and were playable by them during the year in issue, only because the Tourte bows were relatively unused prior to petitioners' purchase of them; the Tourte bows had been preserved in pristine condition in collections. At the time of trial, the condition of the Tourte bows had deteriorated since the dates of their purchase. Among other things, the sticks on the Tourte bows were worn down.

Value of the Tourte Bows

On November 21, 1985, Bow 1 was appraised for insurance purposes as having a fair market value of $35,000. On December 3, 1985, Bow 2 was appraised for insurance purposes as having a fair market value of $25,000. Petitioners obtained both appraisals from Moes & Moes, Ltd.

In 1994, at the time of trial, the Tourte bows were insured with the Philharmonic for $45,000 and $35,000, respectively. These amounts are based on an appraisal dated May 14, 1990, from Yung Chin Bowmaker, a restorer and dealer of fine bows. The record does not indicate whether these appraised amounts were the fair market values of the Tourte bows or were their replacement values.

An independent market exists for the Tourte bows and other antique bows. Numerous antique bows (including bows made by François Tourte) are regularly bought and sold in this market. The Tourte bows are unadorned; they are not as lavish or decorative as some other bows (including other bows made by François Tourte) that are sold in the independent market. Adornments on other bows include engravings, gold, silver, ivory, and mother of pearl.

One factor that adds value to the Tourte bows is the fact that Pernambuco wood, the wood that was used to make the sticks, is now very scarce. The wood that is currently used to make the sticks of violin bows is inferior to Pernambuco wood.

OPINION

* * *

Taxpayers have long been allowed asset depreciation deductions in order to allow them to allocate their expense of using an income-producing asset to the periods that are benefited by that asset. The primary purpose of allocating depreciation to more than 1 year is to provide a more meaningful matching of the cost of an income-producing asset with the income resulting therefrom; this meaningful match, in turn, bolsters the accounting integrity for tax purposes of the taxpayer's periodic income statements. * * * Such a system of accounting for depreciation for Federal income tax purposes has been recognized with the approval of the Supreme Court for over 65 years; as the Court observed in 1927: "The theory underlying this allowance for depreciation is that by using up the plant, a gradual sale is made of it." *United States v. Ludey,* 274 U.S. 295, 301 (1927); * * *. In this sense, an allocation of depreciation to a given year represents that year's reduction of the underlying asset through wear and tear. Depreciation allocations also represent a return to the taxpayer of his or her investment in the income-producing property over the years in which depreciation is allowed.

Prior to the Economic Recovery Tax Act of 1981 (ERTA), personal property was depreciated pursuant to section 167 of the Internal Revenue Code of 1954 (1954 Code). * * *

* * *

The regulations under this section expanded on the text of section 167 by providing that personal property was only depreciable before ERTA if the taxpayer established the useful life of the property.

The "useful life" of property under pre-ERTA law was the period over which the asset could reasonably be expected to be useful to the taxpayer in his or her trade or business, or in the production of his or her income. This useful life period was not always the physical life or maximum useful life inherent in the asset. A primary factor to consider in determining an asset's useful life was any "wear and tear and decay or decline from natural causes" that was inflicted upon the asset.

Before ERTA, the primary method that was utilized to ascertain the useful life for personal property was the asset depreciation range (ADR) system. Under the ADR system, which was generally effective for assets placed in service after 1970 and before 1981, property was grouped into broad classes of industry assets, and each class was assigned a guideline life. A range of years, i.e., the ADR, was then provided for each class of personal property; the ADR extended from 20 percent below to 20 percent above the guideline class life. For each asset account in the class, the taxpayer selected either a class life or an ADR that was utilized as the useful life for computing depreciation. If an asset was not eligible for ADR treatment, or if the taxpayer did not elect to use the ADR system, the useful life of that asset was generally determined based on either the particular facts and circumstances that applied thereto, or by agreement between the taxpayer and the Commissioner. * * *

In enacting ERTA, the Congress found that the pre-ERTA rules for determining depreciation allowances were unnecessarily complicated and did not generate the investment incentive that was critical for economic expansion. The Congress believed that the high inflation rates prevailing at that time undervalued the true worth of depreciation deductions and, hence, discouraged investment and economic competition. The Congress also believed that the determination of useful lives was "complex" and "inherently uncertain", and "frequently [resulted] in unproductive disagreements between taxpayers and the Internal Revenue Service." Accordingly, the Congress decided that a new capital cost recovery system would have to be structured which, among other things, lessened the importance of the concept of useful life for depreciation purposes. This new system is ACRS. ACRS is mandatory and applies to most tangible depreciable assets placed in service after 1980 and before 1987.

* * *

* * * [T]hrough ERTA, the Congress minimized the importance of useful life by: (1) reducing the number of periods of years over which a taxpayer could depreciate his or her property from the multitudinous far-reaching periods of time listed for the ADR system to the four short periods of time listed in ERTA (i.e., the 3–year, 5–year, 10–year, and 15–year ACRS periods), and (2) basing depreciation on an arbitrary statutory period of years that was unrelated to, and shorter than, an asset's estimated useful life. * * *

* * *

With respect to the pre-ERTA requirement of useful life, the Commissioner had initially taken the position that a taxpayer generally could not deduct depreciation on expensive works of art and curios that he purchased as office furniture. This position was superseded by a similar position that was reflected in *Rev. Rul. 68–232*, 1968–1 C.B. 79. That ruling states:

> A valuable and treasured art piece does not have a determinable useful life. While the actual physical condition of the property may influence the value placed on the object, it will not ordinarily limit or determine the useful life. Accordingly, depreciation of works of art *generally* is not allowable. [Emphasis added.]

In the instant case, respondent determined that petitioners were not entitled to deduct depreciation for the Tourte bows. On brief, respondent supports her disallowance with two primary arguments. First, respondent argues that the useful lives of the Tourte bows are indeterminable because the bows are treasured works of art for which it is impossible to determine useful lives. According to respondent, the Tourte bows are works of art because the Tourte bows have existed for more than 100 years and have increased in value over that time; the presence of an independent market for the Tourte bows also gives them a value independent of their capacity to be used to play music, and serves to extend their useful lives indefinitely.

As an alternative to this first argument, respondent argues that the Tourte bows are depreciable under section 168 only if petitioners first prove that each bow has a determinable useful life within the meaning of section 167. In this regard, respondent contends that petitioners must prove a specific or reasonable estimate of the number of years that the Tourte bows will be useful in order to depreciate them under ACRS. Given that the Tourte bows have existed for more than 100 years, respondent concludes, petitioners may not depreciate the Tourte bows because petitioners cannot determine the number of remaining years during which the Tourte bows will continue to be useful.

Petitioners' argument is more straightforward. According to petitioners, they may claim depreciation on the Tourte bows because the Tourte bows: (1) were necessary to their profession as full-time professional violinists, and (2) suffered wear and tear attributable to their use in that profession. In this regard, petitioners contend, the Tourte bows can be used to produce beautiful sounds superior to those produced by any newer bow, and the Tourte bows harmonize this beautiful music with the reputation of the Philharmonic as one of the most prestigious orchestras in the world.

We agree with petitioners that they may depreciate the Tourte Bows under ACRS. ERTA was enacted partially to address and eliminate the issue that we are faced with today, namely, a disagreement between taxpayers and the Commissioner over the useful life of assets that were used in taxpayers' trades or businesses. With this "elimination of disagreements" purpose in mind, the Congress defined five broad classes of "recovery property", and provided the periods of years over which taxpayers could recover their costs of this "recovery property". Two of these classes, the 3–year and 5–year classes, applied only to personal property; the 3–year class included certain short-lived assets such as automobiles and light-duty trucks, and the 5–year class included all other tangible personal property that was not within the 3–year class. Thus, under section 168 as added to the 1954 Code by ERTA, personal property that is "recovery property" must be either 3–year or 5–year class property. Sec. 168(c)(2) as added to the 1954 Code by ERTA ("Each item of recovery property shall be assigned to one of the following classes of property"). Although "3–year property" requires a taxpayer to determine whether the property had a class life under ADR of 4 years or less, the term "5–year property" is appropriately designed to include all other [depreciable personal] property.

Inasmuch as section 168(a) allows a taxpayer to deduct depreciation with respect to "recovery property", petitioners may deduct depreciation on the Tourte bows if the bows fall within the meaning of that term. The term "recovery property" is defined broadly under ERTA to mean tangible property of a character subject to the allowance for depreciation and placed in service after 1980. Accordingly, property is "recovery property" if it is: (1) tangible, (2) placed in service after 1980, (3) of a character subject to the allowance for depreciation, and (4) used in the trade or business, or held for the production of income.

The Tourte bows fit snugly within the definition of recovery property. First, it is indisputable that the Tourte bows are tangible property, and that they were placed in service after 1980. Thus, the first two prerequisites for ACRS depreciation are met. Second, petitioners regularly used the Tourte bows in their trade or business as professional violinists during the year in issue. Accordingly, we conclude that petitioners have also met this prerequisite for depreciating the Tourte bows.

The last prerequisite for depreciating personal property under section 168 is that the property must be "of a character subject to the allowance for depreciation". The term "of a character subject to the allowance for depreciation" is undefined in the 1954 Code. Comparing the language that the Congress used in section 167(a) of the 1954 Code immediately before its amendment by ERTA with the language that it used in section 168(a) and (c)(1) as added to the 1954 Code by ERTA, we believe that the Congress used the term "depreciation" in section 168(c)(1), to refer to the term "exhaustion, wear and tear (including a reasonable allowance for obsolescence)" that is contained in section 167(a). Accordingly, we conclude that the term "of a character subject to the allowance for depreciation" means that property must suffer exhaustion, wear and tear, or obsolescence in order to be depreciated. Accordingly, petitioners will meet the final requirement under section 168 if the Tourte bows are subject to exhaustion, wear and tear, or obsolescence.

We are convinced that petitioners' frequent use of the Tourte bows subjected them to substantial wear and tear during the year in issue. Petitioners actively played their violins using the Tourte bows, and this active use resulted in substantial wear and tear to the bows.[11] Indeed, respondent's expert witness even acknowledged at trial that the Tourte bows suffered wear and tear stemming from petitioners' business; the witness testified that the Tourte bows had eroded since he had examined them 3 years before, and that wood had come off them. Thus, we

---

11. In this regard, we do not believe that the Tourte bows are so-called works of art. We define a "work of art" as a passive object, such as a painting, sculpture, or carving, that is displayed for admiration of its aesthetic qualities. See Webster's New World Dictionary 1539 (3d coll. ed. 1988). The Tourte bows, by contrast, functioned actively, regularly, and routinely to produce income in petitioners' trade or business.

Although a computer utilized by a child to play games is not a depreciable asset, the same computer becomes a depreciable asset if it is used actively, regularly, and routinely by a data processor in his or her trade or business. By the same token, the Tourte bows could have been a collector's item except for the fact that petitioners used them actively, regularly, and routinely in their full-time business.

conclude that petitioners have satisfied the final prerequisite for depreciating personal property under section 168, and, accordingly, hold that petitioners may depreciate the Tourte bows during the year in issue. Allowing petitioners to depreciate the Tourte bows comports with the text of section 168, and enables them to match their costs for the Tourte bows with the income generated therefrom. Refusing to allow petitioners to deduct depreciation on the Tourte bows, on the other hand, would contradict section 168 and vitiate the accounting principle that allows taxpayers to write off income-producing assets against the income produced by those assets.

With respect to respondent's arguments in support of a contrary holding, we believe that respondent places too much reliance on the fact that the Tourte bows are old and have appreciated in value since petitioners acquired them. Indeed, respondent believes that this appreciation, in and of itself, serves to prevent petitioners from claiming any depreciation on the Tourte bows. We disagree; section 168 does not support her proposition that a taxpayer may not depreciate a business asset due to its age, or due to the fact that the asset may have appreciated in value over time. Respondent incorrectly mixes two well-established, independent concepts of tax accounting, namely, accounting for the physical depreciation of an asset and accounting for changes in the asset's value on account of price fluctuations in the market. Moreover, we find merit in petitioners' claim that they should be able to depreciate an asset that receives substantial wear and tear through frequent use in their trade or business. Simply stated, the concept of depreciation is appropriately designed to allow taxpayers to recover the cost or other basis of a business asset through annual depreciation deductions.

We also reject respondent's contention that the Tourte bows are nondepreciable because they have value as collectibles independent of their use in playing musical instruments, and that this value prolongs the Tourte bows' useful life forever. First, it is firmly established that the term "useful life" under pre-ERTA law refers to the period of time in which a particular asset is *useful to the taxpayer* in his or her trade or business. Thus, the fact that an asset such as the Tourte bows may outlive a taxpayer is not dispositive of the issue of whether that asset has a useful life for depreciation purposes under pre-ERTA law. Second, the same argument concerning a separate, nonbusiness value can be made of many other assets. Such types of assets could include, for example, automobiles, patented property, highly sophisticated machinery, and real property. For the Court to delve into the determination of whether a particular asset has a separate, nonbusiness value would make the concept of depreciation a subjective issue and would be contrary to the Congress' intent to simplify the concept and computation of depreciation.

With respect to respondent's contention that petitioners must prove a definite useful life of the Tourte bows, we acknowledge that the concept of useful life was critical under pre-ERTA law. Indeed, the concept of useful life was necessary and indispensable to the computation of depreciation because taxpayers were required to recover their investments in personal property over the estimated useful life of the property. However, the Congress enacted ERTA, in part, to avoid constant disagreements over the useful lives of assets, to shorten the writeoff periods for assets, and to encourage investment by providing for accelerated cost recovery through the tax law. * * *

Respondent mainly relies on *Clinger v. Commissioner,* T.C.Memo. 1990–459 * * * to support a holding contrary to the one that we reach today. * * * [I]n *Clinger,* the taxpayer was a professional portrait artist who painted in the style of her former teacher and well-known portrait artist, Alvin Gittins. Based on the taxpayer's belief that she could further her studies of Gittins, establish her credentials as a painter, and facilitate the marketing of her paintings, the taxpayer purchased a painting by Gittins and displayed it among her own paintings that she had hanging in her studio. The taxpayer claimed deductions under ACRS with respect to the purchased painting.

We sustained respondent's determination that the taxpayer was not entitled to deductions on the painting under ACRS. In so doing, we rejected the taxpayer's argument that the concept of useful life was eliminated with the enactment of ACRS, and accepted respondent's argument that a taxpayer must prove a determinable useful life. Our holding there, however, is distinguishable from the case at hand; unlike the Tourte bows, the painting in *Clinger* was not an asset that suffered substantial wear and tear through its regular, active, and physical use in the taxpayer's trade or business. To the extent, however, that respondent relies on a broad reading of *Clinger* to support her proposition that petitioners must prove *the* useful life of the Tourte bows in order to depreciate them, respondent misconstrues our holding in *Clinger.* In *Clinger,* the Court merely held that ACRS required that the taxpayer had to prove *a* determinable useful life of her passive business asset that suffered no discernible wear and tear. Determinable means "that can be determined". Webster's New World Dictionary 375 (3d coll. ed. 1988). Accordingly, once a taxpayer establishes that an asset is subject to exhaustion, wear and tear, or obsolescence, we can determine whether its useful life is 3–year or 5–year class property under ACRS. * * *
       * * *

We have considered all other arguments made by respondent and find them to be without merit.

To reflect concessions by the parties,

Decision will be entered under Rule 155.

Reviewed by the Court.

PARKER, SWIFT, WRIGHT, PARR, WELLS, RUWE, and COLVIN, JJ., agree with this majority opinion.

CHIECHI, *J.,* dissents.

RUWE, JUDGE, concurring:

In this case, section 168 is being applied to violin bows used by professional violinists. Everyone would ordinarily agree that such an asset is the "type" of asset that would be subject to an allowance for depreciation.

Under section 167, depreciation was allowed over the useful life of the asset in order to allow taxpayers to deduct the anticipated loss in value attributable to wear and tear. This, in turn, required the often difficult task of proving the useful life and salvage or residual value of the asset. In a significant step in the direction of tax simplification, both of these requirements were eliminated by section 168, which specifies the number of years over which the cost of certain types of assets may be deducted and eliminates the need to calculate salvage or residual value in order to determine the expected economic loss.

Everyone seems to favor tax simplification until the simplified law is actually applied to a real set of facts and produces a less-than-perfect result. The dissenting opinions would resurrect the obligation to establish an asset's actual expected useful life and the actual expected decrease in value over that life, in order to qualify for a section 168 deduction. It is unclear whether the dissenters intend to limit their analyses to assets that are "works of art", whatever that term may mean. However, their legal theories would seem to apply to any case where the Commissioner raises the useful life and value issues.

I can understand the dissenters' concern that section 168 might allow an asset to be written off over a period much shorter than its actual useful life and that the entire cost might be deducted despite the fact that there might be no actual economic decrease in value. However, that is the price of the tax simplification implicit in section 168.

PARKER, COHEN, SWIFT, WRIGHT, PARR, WELLS, and BEGHE, JJ., agree with this concurring opinion.

BEGHE, JUDGE., concurring: [omitted].

HAMBLEN, CHIEF JUDGE, dissenting:

I must disagree with the majority opinion. I respectfully submit that the basis for the majority's allowance of a depreciation deduction in this instance is sophistical and wrong. The majority would create a tax shelter for musicians, which, in my judgment, is based on incorrect legal analysis and some findings of fact that are unsupported by the record. The statutory interpretation of sections 167 and 168 is wrong in this context. Pertinent legislative history regarding determinable useful life is ignored. The antique violin bows are treasured "works of art" that for 71 years the Internal Revenue Service has treated, with congressional acquiescence, as nondepreciable property because as instruments and collectibles they have an indeterminable useful life. * * *

I. *Legal Analysis*

A. *Statutory Construction*

The threshold issue in this case is whether the antique Tourte bows are property "of a character subject to the allowance for depreciation provided in section 167" * * *. The majority opinion concludes, as a matter of law, that if a taxpayer uses in his trade or business tangible personal property which suffers some wear and tear, irrespective of whether the wear and tear can be restored by ordinary maintenance, irrespective of whether it has a determinable useful life, and irrespective of whether it declines in value, the taxpayer is entitled to depreciate the property under ACRS (section 168) by treating it as falling within one of the five broad classes of "recovery property". I cannot agree. That conclusion contradicts the basic underpinnings of the depreciation allowance and the holdings of this Court and other courts. With the exception of the tangibility requirement for ACRS, the definition of "recovery property" is virtually identical to the definition of property eligible for depreciation under the pre-ACRS methods. Because the basic definition resembles the pre-ACRS definition of depreciable property, certain principles and judicial interpretations established thereunder are of value in determining what property meets the basic ACRS "recovery property" definition.

It is true that section 168 represents a restructuring of the concept of depreciation deductions and that Congress has deemphasized the concept of useful life and abandoned the concept of salvage value. But Congress did not release the concept of depreciation from the moorings of useful life. * * *

Although section 168 effects significant changes in the calculation of the depreciation allowance, useful life remains a hallmark of the basic concept of depreciation in both sections 167 and 168. * * *

* * * The premise underlying the depreciation allowance is that wear and tear or obsolescence causes a corresponding *reduction in the value* of an asset and *diminishes its useful life.* The end product of the depreciation allowance is the taxpayer's recovery of capital expenditures (costs) made in acquiring a wasting asset used in a trade or business or held for the production of income. Depreciation is therefore keyed to wear and tear or obsolescence because they generally cause corresponding reductions in the useful life and value of property.

Consequently, sections 167 and 168 are connected or linked so that an asset, such as a Tourte bow, that has an indeterminable useful life is not depreciable. It seems to me that the majority opinion has twisted these depreciation provisions beyond the contours of their clear and unambiguous language so as to defeat the plain purpose of Congress.

B. *Legislative History, Proposed Regulations, and Rulings*

The legislative history of section 168, as revealed in the "Overview" section of the Senate Finance Committee (S.Rept. 97–144 (1981), 1981–2 C.B. 412) and the House Ways and Means Committee (H. Rept. 97–201 (1981), 1981–2 C.B. 352) reports states:

In general, property is depreciable if it is (1) used in a trade or business or for the production of income, and (2) subject to wear and tear, decay or decline from natural causes, exhaustion, or obsolescence. Land, goodwill, stock, and *other assets* that do not have a determinable useful life and that do not decline in value predictably are not depreciable. * * * [S. Rept. 97–144, *supra,* 1981–2 C.B. at 421; emphasis supplied.]

Substantially similar language is used in the conference committee report under the heading "Eligible Property", which states that "ACRS does not apply to (1) property not depreciated in terms of years". Moreover, the Joint Committee on Taxation summary (the so-called Blue Book) states that ACRS "does not change the determination under prior law as to whether property is depreciable or nondepreciable". The majority opinion essentially ignores these statements. The Joint Committee on Taxation summary likewise reiterates the statements made in the committee reports that assets that do not decline in value on a predictable basis or that do not have a determinable useful life are not depreciable.

* * *

Depreciation is defined as a loss in the value of property over the time the property is being used. In *Commissioner v. Idaho Power Co.,* 418 U.S. 1, 10 (1974), the Supreme Court commented as follows:

> Over a period of time a capital asset is consumed and, correspondingly over that period, its theoretical value and utility are thereby reduced. Depreciation is an accounting device which recognizes that the physical consumption of a capital asset is a true cost, since the asset is being depleted. * * *

In 1985, Bow 1 was purchased for $30,000 and appraised at $35,000; Bow 2 was purchased for $21,500 and appraised at $25,000. In 1993, at the time of trial, the bows were insured for $45,000 and $35,000, respectively, based on a 1990 appraisal by Yung Chin, a repairer and dealer of fine bows. Petitioners' costs were simply not used up over the claimed 5–year period. Indeed, Richard Simon could not say how long the bows would be usable.

C.   *Legal Precedent*

The majority opinion has dubiously attempted to distinguish * * * *Clinger v. Commissioner,* T.C.Memo. 1990–459. Candor requires that we not try to discard or overrule [it] sub silentio. * * *

* * *

In *Clinger v. Commissioner, supra,* relating to a Gittins oil painting purchased by a professional artist for use in her studio, this Court specifically held:

> Accordingly, it is our opinion that the concept of useful life was not eliminated by the enactment of ACRS under ERTA; hence, where respondent has determined that a taxpayer's assets have no determinable useful life and consequently are not depreciable, petitioner must establish that an asset used in a trade or business has a

determinable useful life and prove the class of recovery property to which it is assigned. * * *

* * *

The majority opinion relies principally on one case, *Noyce v. Commissioner,* 97 T.C. 670 (1991), which stands in sharp contrast to and is distinguishable from * * * *Clinger.* In *Noyce* we concluded that the taxpayer's use of his private airplane and payment of related expenses in the course of his employment were part of his trade or business of being a corporate official. Thus, it was held that he may deduct depreciation and expenses related to such travel to the extent such amounts exceed amounts reimbursable under his employer's policy. *Noyce* is distinguishable from this case in several respects.

(1) * * * At issue in *Noyce* was the second section 168 requirement—whether the taxpayer used the airplane in his trade or business. It was undisputed that, if properly used, the airplane suffered wear and tear and could be depreciated. Indeed, the Commissioner's *Rev. Proc. 87–56,* 1987–2 C.B. 674 (as clarified and modified by *Rev. Proc. 88–22,* 1988–1 C.B. 785) specifically lists airplanes (except those used in commercial or contract carrying of passengers or freight) as constituting 5–year class property under section 168. The Commissioner did not argue that the airplane was not depreciable property under section 167, but only that the depreciation deduction was dependent on satisfaction of the section 162 requirements. We rejected that argument. By contrast, the key issue in the present case is * * * whether the Tourte bows are the type of property subject to depreciation. Petitioners have not shown that they are.

(2) The majority opinion points out that the taxpayer in *Noyce* was allowed to deduct depreciation on an airplane that appreciated in economic value. Further, it stated that "allowable deductions for depreciation will often not be reflective of economic depreciation." 97 T.C. at 688. Both of these statements are correct, but they cannot be used to wholly disregard the statutory requirement that an asset be a wasting asset. As stated in *Noyce,* "Depreciation is not really an 'expenditure' but an allowance based on a presumed wasting of a previous capital investment." *Id.* While economic and statutory depreciation may not be coincident, they share the factual premise of a wasting asset. Petitioners have not proved the presence of such an asset in this case.

* * *

D. Work of Art Vel Non

The majority opinion characterizes the Tourte bows as not being "works of art" because they are actively and regularly used in petitioners' trade or business as professional musicians. I would not characterize a "work of art" so narrowly. I think the term should be given a broad, expansive meaning. One definition of a "work of art" contained in Webster's New 20th Century Dictionary (unabridged 1983) is "anything beautifully made, played, sung or acted". That definition would certainly include an antique musical instrument or bow, a Shakespearean play, a Verdi opera, or a Navajo rug. And "art" is defined in the same dictionary as "products of creative work". In the final analysis the answer probably lies in the eyes of the beholder or owner. In any event, this Court has rejected the notion that "works of art and commercial equipment necessarily are mutually exclusive concepts." Even if used in a trade or business, a "work of art" retains its character as a work of art because it does not have a determinable useful life and generally does not decline in value over a predictable period. To say the least, I expect the Smithsonian curator of musical instruments would be shocked to learn that a Stradivarius violin or a Tourte bow is not regarded as a treasured "work of art". Consequently, in my view, the Tourte bows in this case should be considered as a type of property which is not subject to depreciation. In cases of this kind it seems that our role should begin and end with assuring that the Commissioner's authority to implement the congressional mandate has been exercised in a reasonable manner. I respectfully submit that the majority has not done so.

E. Matching

The majority opinion focuses on the concept of matching income with the cost of producing that income in allowing the depreciation. The Supreme Court has noted that "it is the primary purpose of depreciation accounting to further the integrity of periodic income statements by making a meaningful allocation of the cost entailed in the use * * * of the asset to the periods to which it contributes." Although the matching concept is perhaps a useful analogy vis-a-vis the depreciation deduction, it is basically an accounting concept and not a concept regarding depreciable property. Moreover, the concept of matching is certainly not a guiding principle of construction of tax statutes or tax policy in every situation. * * *

Even if there were some reassurance to be found in the concept of matching, that reassurance cuts the other way. The concept of matching income and expenses would indicate that when the income-producing asset retains its value, the taxpayer has not expended the purchase price, but rather has merely converted it from cash to an asset of equal value. Depreciation, in a sense, departs from realization principles, allowing a taxpayer to recognize a loss in the value of an asset without the requirement of disposition. But depreciation assumes that the asset will be consumed and decline in value over a predictable period of time. When an asset increases in value, as here, there is no loss or waste to match against income, a circumstance which, to say the least, stands the concept of matching revenue and cost on its head. * * *

  * * *

II. Factual Analysis

There are some intermediate and ultimate findings of fact and conclusions that concern me because they appear to be incorrect or unsupported by the record.

A. Wear and Tear of Violin Bows

The "wear and tear" concept relates to the physical life of tangible property. The physical life must be lessened by wear and tear that cannot be corrected by regular maintenance. See *Lindheimer v. Illinois Bell Tel. Co.,* 292 U.S. 151, 167 (1934) (depreciation represents "the loss, *not restored by current maintenance,* which is due to all the factors causing the ultimate retirement of the property. These facts embrace wear and tear, decay, inadequacy, and obsolescence." (Emphasis added.)).

The majority opinion finds that the "petitioners' frequent use of the Tourte bows subjected them to *substantial* wear and tear during the year in issue." Majority op. p. 21 (emphasis added). While there is obviously some degree of wear and tear to any wood instrument or bow, I doubt whether these particular bows suffered "substantial" wear and tear. Richard Simon, whose testimony was somewhat inconsistent, said the bows were kept in "perfect condition", and that the bows showed "a very minuscule amount of wear". Fiona Simon testified that she avoided "abusive wear and tear to these fine bows" and that "you cannot avoid some wear and tear, but we do try and minimize it by keeping the bows in a good state of repair"; and when asked whether the bows with proper care would last throughout her lifetime, she answered, "I would hope, but who knows?" Yung Chin, the bow repairer, stated that the stick was "worn down somewhat" and that there was "a slight amount of use shown on the handle of the bow". But he said there were no cracks or damage to the bows and that they were fully capable of being used in a professional capacity. Obviously the bows were in excellent condition at the time of trial when Judge Laro permitted both petitioners to play their violins with the two Tourte bows in a courtroom demonstration. That occurred 8 years after they were first used by petitioners.

When asked about the present playability of the bows, Richard Simon testified on cross-examination:

Q. Do both François Tourte bows play as well today as they did when you played them in '85?

A. That's a very interesting question. I can't answer that. I have no idea. For me, they play better, but I—I couldn't tell you. I'd have had to have recorded myself playing them and then have a comparison recording under the same conditions, which—

Q. Do the François Tourte bows produce the same tonal quality today as they did in 1985?

A. I can't answer that question either. I don't know. I hope they do.

Q. When you purchased the bows in 1985, how long did you think you would be playing with them?

A. I didn't. Let me—let me say one thing. You know, there are some people that have really conniving minds and go through all kinds of mental detours. I bought a bow because I bought a bow. I bought a bow because I loved it, and the thing I thought about was living with that bow and that bow living with me. That's all I thought about.

Q. Do you intend to use the François Tourte bows in future performances?

A. As long as I can protect it from anything happening to it, absolutely.

Much of Richard Simon's testimony regarding the "wear and tear" to the bows related to the frog, the ferrule (the screw), and the horsehair. When petitioners acquired the bows, the original frog and ferrule had to be replaced because they were not usable. However, petitioners did not discard them. They put them in a vault for safekeeping so that, as Richard Simon testified, they could protect their investment. Apparently the frog and the ferrule have to be repaired or replaced periodically, and the horsehair is replaced about every 18 months. It is the stick that is most valuable, and as long as it is properly maintained it will be usable for an indefinite period of time. Even assuming the bows may eventually wear out, the unanswered question is how long this would take. They have lasted 175 years so far and may be good for another 175 years, if properly maintained. If ever they do cease to be usable, they may well continue to have independent value as collectibles. * * *

B. *Appendix Photograph*

* * * Exhibit 15 admitted into evidence is a copy of a photograph of a violin bow that appears to have had abusive treatment. Respondent's counsel objected to its admission. The picture, which was admitted into evidence, was taken from a book objected to by respondent's counsel and not admitted into evidence. The photograph is irrelevant. It is not a photograph of either of the François Tourte bows in issue or of another Tourte bow. The maker of the bow is unknown. We do not know when it was made. We do not know its age. We do not know what kind of wood was used to make it. We know nothing about its condition, or how long it was used. * * *

    * * *

In short, it appears that the majority has inferred that this picture of an unidentified and abused bow is similar to the bows owned by petitioners. The picture is, purely and simply, not evidence of wear and tear to petitioners' Tourte bows.

    * * *

D. *Determinable Useful Life*

The record in this case clearly shows that the Tourte bows have no determinable useful life. Nobody knows how long they will last as either usable works of art in petitioners' hands or ultimately as collectibles.

Nowhere in Richard Simon's testimony does he say how many years the bows may last or how long they will be usable if regularly and carefully maintained. His principal comment regarding petitioners' use of the bows was that it is "a very great responsibility for us to preserve the stick for future generations". When Fiona Simon, on cross-examination, was asked how long a bow would last, she responded, "I have no idea."

* * *

Finally, Wiley Grant, respondent's expert, stated in his report that the bows were treasured works of art that had no determinable useful life. Who can say with any degree of certainty how long these bows will last if given reasonable care?

III. Conclusion

The Tourte bows are usable and treasured works of art whose physical life and use to petitioners were not lessened by wear and tear that could not be restored by current maintenance. Their cost was not being consumed or used up over a determinate period. They have inherent and independent value as collectibles that may remain for centuries. Based on the foregoing legal and factual analysis of this case, I would hold that the Tourte bows were not of a character subject to the allowance for depreciation.

CHABOT, JACOBS, WHALEN, and HALPERN, JJ., agree with this dissent.

GERBER, JUDGE, dissenting;

I must, to some extent, agree and disagree with both the majority's view and Chief Judge Hamblen's minority view. Both views are thoughtful, but each approach unnecessarily results in taxpayers' being entitled to all or none of the depreciation claimed. Both positions fail to consider that the bows may have two separate attributes—recoverable or depreciable and intrinsic attributes. If both are considered, the results that the majority and minority views advocate could, to some extent, be achieved. As I see this issue, under either section 167, permitting "a reasonable allowance for the exhaustion, wear and tear", or section 168, permitting depreciation for specific categories of "recovery property", a taxpayer should not be entitled to a depreciation deduction for intrinsic value, which is generally not subject to wear and tear and/or makes the life of the object indeterminable. The facts reveal, and neither viewpoint denies, that the bows are being subjected to wear and tear due to their use by professional musicians. It is also factually indisputable that, in spite of their use, the bows continue to increase in value from the original purchase price because of their unique qualities. The crucial point, which has not been addressed, concerns the effect of the wear and tear upon the intrinsic value inherent in the asset.

The majority reaches the conclusion that each entire bow constitutes recovery property as defined in section 168(c)(1). I agree that the bows are tangible property placed in service after 1980, and that the bows were used in petitioners' trade or business. I do not agree, however, that petitioners have shown that all of the property is of a character subject to the allowance for depreciation. Admittedly, some portion of the bows is subject to wear and tear, but not the intrinsic value that may exist even if the bows can no longer be used as bows. The burden is on petitioners to show which portion of the bows is subject to wear and tear and, therefore, recovery property.

There are numerous situations in the tax law where property is composed of both depreciable and nondepreciable portions. One example of this concept may be found in situations where a business is purchased and some portion of the purchase price may be attributable to goodwill— the nondepreciable intrinsic value of a business. More specifically, our Court has considered the intrinsic value in works of art and musical instruments and not permitted depreciation attributable to that aspect. On several occasions we have delineated the existence of depreciable business use and nondepreciable personal use in the same property. Finally, and by way of analogy, bifurcation of property into depreciable and nondepreciable portions is entrenched in the tax treatment of improvements to realty, which may be depreciable even though the land upon which they rest is not subject to depreciation.

To better illustrate the concept of intrinsic value, let us assume that Elvis Presley had purchased a guitar for $1,000. Due to his fame, however, the value of the guitar immediately increases to $11,000. If Elvis Presley had used the guitar in his business, he would have been entitled to depreciate the $1,000 amount, either over its useful life or in accordance with its section 168 class life, as may have been appropriate. If, however, another musician purchases Elvis' guitar for $11,000, the portion of the guitar which would be subject to wear and tear or be recovery property would be about $1,000, more or less, depending upon how much Elvis had used it and/or the cost of a similar quality guitar at the time of purchase. The fact that it had been Elvis' guitar will sustain a premium value which is attributable to the guitar's intrinsic collector's value. Even if Elvis's guitar became unusable for commercial purposes, collectors would be willing to pay for the intrinsic value because it had belonged to Elvis. Usually, that value increases with time due to increased uniqueness attributable to scarcity or increased popularity. That intrinsic value could be affected by wear and tear, but the wear and tear will not necessarily eliminate the intrinsic value. Accordingly, under section 167 the remaining intrinsic value would be the equivalent of "salvage value". Because section 168 does not consider salvage value, the intrinsic value should not be considered recovery property.

These same principles apply to the bows under consideration. Some portion of the value and purchase price is attributable to the collector's value and is not recovery property within the meaning of section 168. Although Congress, by enacting section 168, intended to simplify the classification of depreciable property and permit shorter periods of writeoff, there was no intent to permit the writeoff of the portion of property attributable to the intrinsic collector's value of unique property. The burden rests with taxpayers to show that portion of the property which is depreciable or recovery property and which portion is intrinsic or investment. Petitioners in this case have not shown the cost portion or value of the bows which is subject to wear and tear and, accordingly, must fail here. Admittedly, it would be unfair to hold that petitioners did not have some depreciation attributable to their use of the bows. It would be equally unfair (to other taxpayers) to permit petitioners to write off the intrinsic value which is unaffected by wear and tear or use.

The majority's holding permits the opportunity for substantial unintended abuse. Taxpayers will be able to depreciate items with current business utility and intrinsic collector's value and, after 3 or 5 years, have the tax benefit of the entire cost, at a time when the value of the item has not decreased or may have increased. The process may be duplicated over and over, providing substantial writeoffs with the cost borne by the public fisc. Ultimately, the taxpayer accumulates numerous of these collector's items which are passed on to future generations because of their intrinsic collector's value, which is likely to have substantially appreciated.

For the reasons expressed, I respectfully dissent.

HALPERN, JUDGE, dissenting:

I agree with Chief Judge Hamblen, and I have joined his dissent. * * * Briefly stated, I believe that, to claim recovery property within the meaning of section 168(c)(1), petitioners would have to show not only that the bows here in question are subject to wear and tear but also that they have determinable useful lives (i.e., useful lives capable of being settled, fixed, or determined). I do not believe that they have done so. I write separately, however, only to address the suggestion of allocation raised by Judge Gerber.

Judge Gerber suggests that the bows are dual use property, having utility both as playables and as collectibles. Judge Gerber recognizes that the utility of the bows as collectibles will not be exhausted in any fixed or determinable period. He assumes that their utility as playables will be exhausted in a fixed period, which can be shown. Judge Gerber would allow a deduction under section 168 with respect to a taxpayer's basis in such dual use property properly allocated to the property's utility as a playable.

* * *

We have allowed less than a full allowance for the exhaustion, wear and tear, and obsolescence of property where only a portion of the property was used in a trade or business or held for the production of income. See, e.g., *International Artists, Ltd. v. Commissioner,* 55 T.C. 94 (1970) (depreciation deduction allowed to the extent premises were used for business purposes and disallowed to the extent used for personal purposes); *Noyce v. Commissioner,* 97 T.C. 670 (1991) (similar allocation under ACRS, with respect to an airplane). It seems to me a different thing, however, to say that property can wear out for one purpose but not another, so that, in effect, we should treat the taxpayer as having purchased two pieces of property rather than one. We have characterized as "bizarre" the suggestion that the owner's life expectancy should determine the depreciable useful life of an asset whose inherent value does not terminate upon the owner's death. Judge Gerber would allow petitioners to carve out of the apparently indeterminable useful lives of the bows as a whole those particular lives that petitioners may (but did not) show to be limited, and get a depreciation deduction for the utility related to those lives. We do not, in general, allow the fee owner of land to fragment the varied utilities inherent in her ownership in order separately to depreciate those with a determinable useful life. I do not see why we should do so with respect to otherwise nondepreciable property, such as the bows.

HAMBLEN, JACOBS, and WHALEN, JJ., agree with this dissent.

SIMON v. COMMISSIONER

United States Court of Appeals, Second Circuit, 1995.
68 F.3d 41.

WINTER, CIRCUIT JUDGE:

This appeal from the Tax Court raises the question whether professional musicians may take a depreciation deduction for wear and tear on antique violin bows under the Accelerated Cost Recovery System ("ACRS") of the Economic Recovery Tax Act of 1981 ("ERTA"), although the taxpayers cannot demonstrate that the bows have a "determinable useful life."

* * *

DISCUSSION

* * *

The parties agree that Section 168's phrase "of a character subject to depreciation" must be interpreted in light of the I.R.C. § 167(a) allowances for "exhaustion, wear and tear, and . . . obsolescence." The Simons and the Tax Court maintain that, when read in conjunction with the plain language of Section 167, Section 168 requires only that the Tourte bows suffer wear and tear in the Simons' trade to qualify as "recovery property." The Commissioner, on the other hand, argues that because all property used in a trade or business is necessarily subject to wear and tear, the Simons' construction of Section 168 would effectively render Section 168's phrase "of a character subject to the allowance for depreciation" superfluous, a result that Congress presumably could not have intended. Therefore, Section 168's requirement that the property be "of a character subject to the allowance for depreciation" must include an element beyond wear and tear, namely the "determinable useful life" requirement * * *.

We do not agree with the Commissioner's premise because some tangible assets used in business are not exhausted, do not suffer wear and tear, or become obsolete. For example, paintings that hang on the wall of a law firm merely to be looked at—to please connoisseur clients or to give the appearance of dignity to combative professionals—do not generally suffer wear or tear. More to the point, the Simons' Tourte bows were playable for a time precisely because they had been kept in a private collection and were relatively unused since their manufacture. Indeed, it appears that one had never been played at all. Had that collection been displayed at a for-profit museum, the museum could not have depreciated the bows under ERTA because, although the bows were being used in a trade or business, they were not subject to wear and tear. The Tourte bows are not unlike numerous kinds of museum pieces or collectors' items. The Commissioner's textual argument thus fails because there are tangible items not subject to wear and tear.

The Commissioner next argues that Congressional intent and the notion of depreciation itself require that Section 168's statutory language be supplemented by reading into the word "character" a requirement that tangible property have a demonstrable useful life. To address that issue, we must briefly examine the history of the depreciation allowance.

The tax laws have long permitted deductions for depreciation on certain income-producing assets used in a trade or business. The original rationale for the depreciation deduction was to allow taxpayers to match accurately, for tax accounting purposes, the cost of an asset to the income stream that the asset produced. * * * In its traditional incarnation, therefore, the pace of depreciation deductions was determined by the period of time that the asset would produce income in the taxpayer's business. As the Supreme Court noted * * *, "Congress intended by the depreciation allowance not to make taxpayers a profit thereby, but merely to protect them from a loss.... Accuracy in accounting requires that correct tabulations, not artificial ones, be used."

To implement this accurate tax accounting, the concept of a determinable useful life was necessary because, without such a determination, one could not calculate the proper annual allowance—"the sum which should be set aside for the taxable year, in order that, at the end of the useful life of the plant in the business, the aggregate of the sums set aside will (with the salvage value) suffice to provide an amount equal to the original cost." *United States v. Ludey,* 274 U.S. 295, 300–01, 47 S.Ct. 608, 610, 71 L.Ed. 1054 (1927). * * *

ERTA, however, altered the depreciation scheme for two reasons other than sound accounting practice that are not consistent with the Commissioner's argument. First, the ACRS introduced accelerated depreciation periods as a stimulus for economic growth. Under ACRS, the cost of an asset is recovered over a predetermined period unrelated to— and usually shorter than—the useful life of the asset. Moreover, the depreciation deductions do not assume consistent use throughout the asset's life, instead assigning inflated deductions to the earlier years of use. Therefore, the purpose served by the determinable useful life requirement of the pre-ERTA scheme—allowing taxpayers to depreciate property over its actual use in the business—no longer exists under the ACRS. * * *

A second congressional purpose embodied in ERTA also militates against reading a determinable useful life prerequisite into Section 168. In addition to stimulating investment, Congress sought to simplify the depreciation rules by eliminating the need to adjudicate matters such as useful life and salvage value, which are inherently uncertain and result in unproductive disagreements between taxpayers and the Internal Revenue Service. Indeed, the legislation specifically sought to "de-emphasize" the concept of useful life. * * *

We also cannot accept the Commissioner's suggestion that her proposed interpretation de-emphasizes useful life by requiring establishment of a demonstrable useful life for only a "narrow category" of property. Insofar as the Commissioner seeks to do this by singling out usable antiques and other business property likely to appreciate in real economic value, she relies on a concept that has nothing whatsoever to do with the useful life of the asset in the business. * * *

The Commissioner's strongest support for her claim that Congress intended to maintain [the] determinable useful life requirement comes from the House Conference Report, which noted that

> Under present law, assets used in a trade or business or for the production of income are depreciable if they are subject to wear and tear, decay or decline from natural causes or obsolescence. Assets that do not decline in value on a predictable basis or that do not have a determinable useful life, such as land, goodwill, and stock, are not depreciable.

H.R. Conf. Rep. No. 215 at 206, U.S.C.C.A.N.1981, p. 296. The Simons unsuccessfully attempt to recharacterize this statement as an inartful catalogue of assets that are not subject to exhaustion, wear and tear, or obsolescence. The House report means what it says but gives us slight pause. In light of the overriding legislative intent to abandon the unnecessarily complicated rules on useful life, we cannot employ two sentences in a legislative report to trump statutory language and a clearly stated legislative purpose. * * * We are thus not persuaded by the Commissioner's call for us to interpret a statute that abrogates a current regulatory regime as in fact incorporating the details of that scheme. In particular, we reject the argument that we should retain regulatory provisions now divorced from their functional purpose.

When a coherent regulatory system has been repudiated by statute—as this one has—it is inappropriate to use a judicial shoehorn to retain an isolated element of the now-dismembered regulation. We thus hold that, for the purposes of the "recovery property" provisions of Section 168, "property subject to the allowance for depreciation" means property that is subject to exhaustion, wear and tear, or obsolescence.

* * *

We acknowledge that the result of our holding may give favorable treatment to past investment decisions that some regard as wasteful, such as a law firm's purchase of expensive antique desks, the cost of which could have been quickly depreciated under our current ruling. However, Congress wanted to stimulate investment in business property generally, and it is not our function to draw subjective lines between the wasteful and the productive. Moreover, courts should take care that the Commissioner's role as revenue maximizer does not vitiate Congress's intent to sacrifice revenue to generate economic activity. If taxpayers cannot trust that such tax measures will be fully honored, some or all of the hoped-for activity will not occur.

One should not exaggerate the extent to which our holding is a license to hoard and depreciate valuable property that a taxpayer expects to appreciate in real economic value. The test is whether property will suffer exhaustion, wear and tear, or obsolescence in its use by a business. Even without a determinable useful life requirement, a business that displayed antique automobiles, for example, and kept them under near-ideal, humidity-controlled conditions, would still have difficulty demonstrating the requisite exhaustion, wear and tear, or obsolescence necessary to depreciate the automobiles as recovery property. Nor is valuable artwork purchased as office ornamentation apt to suffer anything more damaging than occasional criticism from the tutored or untutored, and it too would probably fail to qualify as recovery property. Indeed, even a noted artwork that serves as a day-to-day model for another artist's work cannot be depreciated as recovery property if it does not face exhaustion, wear and tear, or obsolescence in the pertinent business.

For the foregoing reasons, we affirm.

OAKES, SENIOR CIRCUIT JUDGE, dissenting:

I cannot believe that Congress, in changing the depreciation deduction from the Asset Depreciation Range System ("ADRS") for recovery of assets placed in service after December 31, 1980, to the Accelerated Cost Recovery System ("ACRS") whereby the cost of an asset is recovered over a predetermined period shorter than the useful life of the asset or the period the asset is used to produce income, intended to abandon the concept underlying depreciation, namely, that to permit the deduction the property must have a useful life capable of being estimated. I find no indication in either the changes of statutory language or the well-documented legislative history that Congress intended such a radical change as the majority of this panel, the Tax Court majority, and the Third Circuit in *Liddle v. C.I.R.*, 65 F.3d 329 (3d Cir.1995), have held it did. Indeed, it seems to me that the statutory language and the legislative history—consistent with the dual congressional purpose of simplification and stimulating economic growth by permitting accelerated depreciation periods—retained the fundamental principle that, in order to depreciate, the asset involved must have a determinable useful life.

* * *

Under the majority's interpretation, * * * the only criterion necessary to obtain a deduction under section 168(c) is that the property be subject to wear and tear. Thus, a car buff in the trade or business of buying, collecting, and selling antique automobiles, who drives his autos to auto shows may obtain a depreciation deduction, or the law office that buys fine Sheraton or Chippendale desks or chairs for office use can take a deduction, though in each case the auto or furniture is actually appreciating in value and has no determinable useful life.

* * *

The majority of this court joins the Tax Court majority and the Third Circuit in holding that section 168(c)(1) applies to all tangible property that is subject to "wear and tear." I agree with the Commissioner that such an interpretation renders meaningless the phrase in section 168(c)(1) "of a character subject to the allowance for depreciation," since all tangible property used in a trade of business is necessarily subject to wear and tear. * * *

Nor can reliance be placed, as it is by the majority, upon the fact that section 168(f)(9) changed prior law by removing "salvage value" from the depreciation calculus. The fact that Congress eliminated salvage value while simultaneously defining the term "recovery property" as "tangible property of a character subject to the allowance for depreciation," cannot support the conclusion that section 168 eliminated the threshold requirement that taxpayers establish a determinable useful life for their property. * * *

Since, concededly, taxpayers Richard and Fiona Simon have not established that the bows in question have determinable useful lives, the bows do not qualify for the depreciation deduction. It is a long way from the dual purpose of section 168 (to shorten the depreciation periods for property that would have been depreciable under section 167 in order to stimulate investment and to simplify the complex series of rules and regulations pertaining to useful lives by substituting a four-tier system of three-year, five-year, ten-year, and fifteen-year property), to abandonment of the underlying concept of depreciable property altogether. In my view, the decision of the Tax Court should be reversed and accordingly I hereby dissent.

* * *

Self-Assessment Question

(Solutions to Self–Assessment Questions are set forth in Appendix 3.)

SAQ 4–6. Which of the following assets are eligible for depreciation under § 167?

(a) A summer cabin in Maine held by a taxpayer as rental property *Dep. 167(a)*

(b) The right to occupy an office building for five years pursuant to a lease agreement signed by the taxpayer (assuming the taxpayer uses the rented space for business purposes) *No – this is intangible*

(c) A passenger vehicle that the taxpayer uses mostly for business purposes but also for personal purposes *Dep.*

(d) A glass sculpture by Dale Chihuly that hangs in the reception room of the taxpayer's office *No - not subject to wear & tear*

(e) The taxpayer's personal residence NOT

(f) A photocopier used in the taxpayer's business Dep

The Mechanics of Depreciation. After only a quick glance at § 168(a), it is apparent that there are several variables that affect the depreciation deductions that a taxpayer can claim in any one taxable year. In fact, proper computation of the depreciation deduction attributable to a particular asset requires knowledge of <u>five</u> different variables. The first variable is the **depreciation base.** Under ACRS, as noted in *Simon*, the depreciation base for all assets is its cost basis. Because the statute assumes that all depreciable assets have no salvage value, § 168(b)(4), a taxpayer may recover his or her entire basis in the asset. So the first variable is never very difficult to determine.

The second variable is the asset's **class life.** This is the estimated life expectancy of the asset. To prevent taxpayers from making all kinds of far-out arguments as to the useful lives of assets, and to give guidance to taxpayers who would have no clue about the useful lives of their assets, the Service has issued a series of tables that state the class life for many different types of assets. The tables are contained in the following Revenue Procedure, although only the first table is reprinted here.

REVENUE PROCEDURE 87–56

1987–2 C.B. 674.

SECTION 1. PURPOSE

The purpose of this revenue procedure is to set forth the class lives of property that are necessary to compute the depreciation allowances available under section 168 of the Internal Revenue Code, * * *.

SEC. 2. GENERAL RULES OF APPLICATION

.01 In general. This revenue procedure specifies class lives and recovery periods for property subject to depreciation under the general depreciation system provided in section 168(a) of the Code or the alternative depreciation system provided in section 168(g).

* * *

SEC. 5. TABLES OF CLASS LIVES AND RECOVERY PERIODS

.01 Except for property described in section 5.02, below, the class lives (if any) and recovery periods for property subject to depreciation under section 168 of the Code appear in the tables below. These tables are based on the definition of class life in section 2.02 of this revenue procedure and the assigned items described in section 3 of this revenue procedure.

.02 For purposes of depreciation under the general depreciation system, residential rental property has a recovery period of 27.5 years and nonresidential real property has a recovery period of 31.5 years. For purposes of the alternative depreciation system, residential rental and nonresidential real property each has a recovery period of 40 years.

* * *

Asset class	Description of assets included	Class Life (in years)	Recovery Periods (in years) General Depreciation System	Alternative Depreciation System

SPECIFIC DEPRECIABLE ASSETS USED IN ALL BUSINESS ACTIVITIES, EXCEPT AS NOTED:

00.11 Office Furniture, Fixtures, and Equipment:

Includes furniture and fixtures that are not a structural component of a building. Includes such assets as desks, files, safes, and communications equipment. Does not include communications equipment that is included in other classes   10   7   10

00.12 Information Systems:

Includes computers and their peripheral equipment used in administering normal business transactions and the maintenance of business records, their retrieval and analysis. Information systems are defined as:

1) Computers: A computer is a programmable electronically activated device capable of accepting information, applying prescribed processes to the information, and supplying the results of these processes with or without human intervention. It usually consists of a central processing unit containing extensive storage, logic, arithmetic, and control capabilities. Excluded from this category are adding machines, electronic desk calculators, etc., and other equipment described in class 00.13.

2) Peripheral equipment consists of the auxiliary machines which are designed to be placed under control of the central processing unit. Non-limiting examples are: Card readers, card punches, magnetic tape feeds, high speed printers, optical character readers, tape cassettes, mass storage units, paper tape equipment, keypunches, data entry devices, teleprinters, terminals, tape drives, disc drives, disc files, disc packs, vi-

Asset class	Description of assets included	Class Life (in years)	Recovery Periods (in years) General Depreciation System	Alternative Depreciation System
	sual image projector tubes, card sorters, plotters, and collators. Peripheral equipment may be used on-line or off-line. Does not include equipment that is an integral part of other capital equipment that is included in other classes of economic activity, i.e., computers used primarily for process or production control, switching, channeling, and automating distributive trades and services such as point of sale (POS) computer systems. Also, does not include equipment of a kind used primarily for amusement or entertainment of the user	6	5*	5*
00.13	**Data Handling Equipment, except Computers:** Includes only typewriters, calculators, adding and accounting machines, copiers, and duplicating equipment	6	5	6
00.21	**Airplanes (airframes and engines), except those used in commercial or contract carrying of passengers or freight, and all helicopters (airframes and engines)**	6	5	6
00.22	**Automobiles, Taxis**	3	5	5
00.23	**Buses**	9	5	9
00.241	**Light General Purpose Trucks:** Includes trucks for use over the road (actual unloaded weight less than 13,000 pounds)	4	5	5
00.242	**Heavy General Purpose Trucks:** Includes heavy general purpose trucks, concrete ready mix-truckers, and ore trucks, for use over the road (actual unloaded weight 13,000 pounds or more)	6	5	6
00.25	**Railroad Cars and Locomotives, except those owned by railroad transportation companies**	15	7	15
00.26	**Tractor Units For Use Over–The–Road**	4	3	4
00.27	**Trailers and Trailer–Mounted Containers**	6	5	6

Asset class	Description of assets included	Class Life (in years)	Recovery Periods (in years) General Depreciation System	Alternative Depreciation System
00.28	**Vessels, Barges, Tugs, and Similar Water Transportation Equipment, except those used in marine construction**	18	10	18
00.3	**Land Improvements:** Includes improvements directly to or added to land, whether such improvements are section 1245 property or section 1250 property, provided such improvements are depreciable. Examples of such assets might include sidewalks, roads, canals, waterways, drainage facilities, sewers (not including municipal sewers in Class 51), wharves and docks, bridges, fences, landscaping, shrubbery, or radio and television transmitting towers. Does not include land improvements that are explicitly included in any other class, and buildings and structural components as defined in section 1.48–1(e) of the regulations. Excludes public utility initial clearing and grading land improvements as specified in Rev. Rul. 72–403, 1972–2 C.B. 102	20	15	20
00.4	**Industrial Steam and Electric Generation and/or Distribution Systems:** Includes assets, whether such assets are section 1245 property or 1250 property, providing such assets are depreciable, used in the production and/or distribution of electricity with rated total capacity in excess of 500 Kilowatts and/or assets used in the production and/or distribution of steam with rated total capacity in excess of 12,500 pounds per hour for use by the taxpayer in its industrial manufacturing process or plant activity and not ordinarily available for sale to others. Does not include buildings and structural components as defined in section 1.48–1(e) of the regulations. Assets used to generate and/or distribute electricity or steam of the type			

Asset class	Description of assets included	Class Life (in years)	Recovery Periods (in years)	
			General Depreciation System	Alternative Depreciation System
	described above but of lesser-rated capacity are not included, but are included in the appropriate manufacturing equipment classes elsewhere specified. Also includes electric generating and steam distribution assets, which may utilize steam produced by a waste reduction and resource recovery plant, used by the taxpayer in its industrial manufacturing process or plant activity. Steam and chemical recovery boiler systems used for the recovery and regeneration of chemicals used in manufacturing, with rated capacity in excess of that described above, with specifically related distribution and return systems are not included but are included in appropriate manufacturing equipment classes elsewhere specified. An example of an excluded steam and chemical recovery boiler system is that used in the pulp and paper manufacturing industry	22	15	22

* * *

* * *

Once you know the class life of the depreciable property, the next variable is the **applicable recovery period.** Section 168(a)(2). The table in § 168(e)(1) uses the asset's class life to classify it as one of six different types of property (3–year property, 5–year property, 7–year property, and so on). Then, the table in § 168(c) lists the recovery period for each type of property (subject to the four exceptions noted at the end of the § 168(c) table). The recovery period represents the number of taxable years over which the taxpayer may claim depreciation deductions. Taxpayers generally prefer shorter recovery periods, because that means bigger deductions and quicker recovery of the asset's basis. Notice that §§ 168(c) and 168(e) together confer much faster recovery periods than one might expect given an asset's class life.

The fourth variable is the **applicable depreciation method.** The easiest method to understand is the "straight-line" method, where the cost is recovered ratably—one simply divides the depreciation base by the applicable recovery period. Thus, the depreciation deduction for a $5,000 piece of "5–year property" over five years is $1,000 per year. But taxpayers press for bigger, better deductions, and so we also have the "declining balance methods." Section 168(b) lists two declining balance methods—the "200 percent declining balance method" (which is often referred to on the street as the "double declining balance" method) and the "150 percent declining balance method." As you can see from the statute, the double declining balance method is used more frequently than any other method, so we should consider how it works. Go back to the straight-line method example earlier in this paragraph. Notice that the taxpayer recovers 20 percent of the depreciation base each year for five years. Under double declining balance, a taxpayer may claim *double* the percentage (here, 40 percent) of the *declining balance* in the depreciation base. In the first year, for example, the taxpayer can deduct 40 percent of the $5,000 base, or $2,000. The deduction in the first year reduces the depreciation base (and, for that matter, the adjusted basis in the hands of the taxpayer) to $3,000. In the second year, then, the taxpayer can deduct 40 percent of $3,000, or $1,200. This continues over the recovery period. Of course, if the taxpayer can only deduct 40 percent of the declining balance each year, the taxpayer would never fully recover the cost of the asset. That is why the statute says to switch to the straight-line method in the first year when the straight-line method yields a larger result. So each year, the taxpayer must compare the deduction allowed by the double declining balance method with the deduction allowed if the taxpayer converted to the straight-line method for the rest of the asset's useful life. Using our same example, this comparison is shown in the following table:

when straight-line ↗ [handwritten annotation]

Depreciation of 5–year property under double declining
balance method, switching to straight-line method,
assuming $5,000 depreciation base

Year	Declining Balance	40% DDB	Straight–Line	Deduction	Adjusted Basis
1	$5,000	$2,000	$1,000	**$2,000**	$3,000
2	$3,000	$1,200	$ 750*	**$1,200**	$1,800
3	$1,800	$ 720	$ 600**	**$ 720**	$1,080
4	$1,080	$ 432	$ 540***	**$ 540**	$ 540
5	$ 540	$ 216	$ 540	**$ 540**	zero

* = $3,000 balance divided by 4 remaining years = $750 per year
** = $1,800 balance divided by 3 remaining years = $600 per year
*** = $1,080 balance divided by 2 remaining years = $540 per year

Technically, we switched from double declining balance to straight-line in the fourth year, because that was the first year when the straight-line method gave a higher deduction. By switching to the straight-line method, we ensure that the entire depreciation base will be recovered.

The fifth and final variable is the **applicable convention.** Section 168(d)(4) defines three types of conventions: the half-year convention, the mid-month convention, and the mid-quarter convention. Section 168(d)(1)–(3) then tells you which convention to use, depending (again) on the type of asset. The most common convention is the half-year convention. Like the others, the half-year convention affects the depreciation deduction computation in the year which the property is placed in service because the taxpayer can only claim *half* of the deduction to which he or she is otherwise entitled to under the applicable depreciation method (since it is assumed the property was placed in service at the mid-point of the year). Consequently, then, the taxpayer is entitled to another half-year of depreciation at the *end* of the normal recovery period. So a taxpayer with five-year property will have depreciation deductions for *six* taxable years—Year One (which will be limited to half the normal amount), Years Two through Five, and Year Six (when the leftover amount is finally recovered). In other words, for a calendar year taxpayer placing depreciable property in service during Year One, the 5–year recovery period begins on July 1, Year One, and ends on June 30, Year Six—a total of 5 years. In performing your own depreciation computations, keep in mind that the half-year convention and the reduced deduction in the first year will affect the declining balance amount in the later years.

Why is there a half-year convention? Though it has the effect of complicating the computation, it is actually a simplification measure. Taxpayers like the rule because it does not require knowledge or proof of the date on which depreciable property is placed in service. The Service likes the rule because without it, taxpayers would be tempted to buy property in the second half of the year and claim full depreciation deductions as if the property were used for the entire year. The Service's preference also explains the special rule in § 168(d)(3): if a taxpayer buys a lot of depreciable assets in the last three months of the taxable year, the taxpayer will in some cases be forced to use the mid-quarter convention, resulting in an even smaller depreciation deduction in the first year.

Performing depreciation computations can get old after a while. Some never see the fun to begin with. Others just throw up their hands in confusion. For all of these reasons, the Service has issued tables that simplify the calculations significantly. You can check out some of the more common tables in Appendix 2 of this text.

(2) BONUS DEPRECIATION BY ELECTION AND LIMITS ON DEPRECIATION DEDUCTIONS

Code: IRC §§ 179(a)–(d)(4), (d)(10); 280F(a)–(b), (d).

Regs: Treas. Reg. §§ 1.179–1(a)–(f)(1); 1.179–2(a)–(b)(2), (c)(1), (c)(6). *Skim* Treas. Reg. § 1.179–1(e).

Section 179 Expensing. Section 179 is perhaps best described as an annual gift from Congress to taxpayers. Under § 179, a taxpayer may *expense* (i.e., deduct) all or a portion of the cost of depreciable property purchased during the taxable year for use in the active conduct of a trade or business activity, even though normal rules would require capitalization of such costs. This "bonus first-year depreciation" is elective—a taxpayer need not claim the bonus depreciation if he or she does not want it (but in most cases, of course, he or she does indeed want it).

The § 179 election is subject to three limitations. First, there is the **dollar limitation** in § 179(b)(1). Until 2010, the maximum amount of bonus first-year depreciation for any taxpayer is $100,000 (although this amount is adjusted for inflation). Beginning in 2010, the maximum amount is reduced to $25,000. Second, under § 179(b)(1), there is a **phase-out limitation** based on the amount of eligible property placed in service during the year. If the total amount of qualifying property purchased in any year exceeds a certain dollar amount ($400,000 until 2010, $200,000 beginning in 2010), the bonus first-year depreciation deduction is reduced dollar for dollar. These thresholds are also adjusted for inflation. Thus, if a taxpayer purchased qualifying property totaling $413,000 in 2007, only $87,000 of qualifying property can be expensed under § 179, ignoring any adjustment for inflation ($100,000 dollar limitation less the $13,000 excess over the phase-out limitation). Finally, there is a **taxable income limitation** in § 179(b)(3)(A). It generally provides that the amount of bonus first-year depreciation cannot exceed the total taxable income derived by the taxpayer that year from all actively conducted trade or business activities.

If the taxpayer makes a § 179 election, of course, the taxpayer's adjusted basis in the qualifying property will be reduced by the amount expensed. Suppose, for example, that a taxpayer purchased a very expensive piece of "§ 179 property" in 2007 for $150,000. If the taxpayer expenses $100,000 of the cost in 2007 by making a § 179 election, the taxpayer's adjusted basis in the asset would be $50,000. Moreover, the taxpayer's "depreciation base," for purposes of § 168, would be $50,000 as well.

Limits on Depreciation Deductions. Section 280F imposes limits on depreciation deductions claimed with respect to luxury passenger cars and certain "listed property" used for both business and personal purposes. If a passenger car is depreciable, § 280F(a)(1) limits the maximum depreciation deduction that can be claimed to the amounts set forth in the statute. Notice that those amounts are adjusted for inflation based on 1988 dollars. Section 280F(d)(7). In effect, any auto costing more than $12,800 (again, as adjusted for inflation based on 1988 dollars) will be subject to this limitation—because the allowable depreciation deductions on a $12,800 car match the limits contained in § 280F(a)(1). That must be what Congress means by a "luxury" automobile. Notice that the limitation for luxury cars applies regardless of whether the car is used solely for business purposes or for business and personal purposes.

Under § 280F(b), the depreciation deductions attributable to "listed property," defined in § 280F(d)(4), are subject to an additional limitation, but only if the listed property is used for non-business (investment or personal) purposes more often than it is used for business purposes. If the listed property is used predominantly or exclusively for business purposes, the limitation will not apply. If the listed property is used predominantly for other purposes, however, then the depreciation deduction is recomputed using the less generous straight-line method. Moreover, if listed property ceases to be used predominantly for business purposes, any accelerated depreciation deductions (allowed deductions in excess of what the straight line method would allow) will be recaptured in the year in which the taxpayer stops using the listed property predominantly for business purposes. Section 280F(b)(2).

* * *

Problem 4–10

On August 2, Year One, Jane St. Clair purchased a machine for use in her business. The machine has a "class life" of seven years. Jane paid $150,000 for the machine and placed it in service the next day (August 3). The machine was the only item of tangible personal property that Jane acquired for use in her business in Year One. Except as otherwise provided herein, assume that the taxable income Jane derived from her business for Year One totaled $500,000.

(a) How much of the purchase price can Jane deduct in Year One under § 179, assuming she makes the election described therein?

(b) How would the answer to (a) change if the taxable income Jane derived from all of her business activities for Year One totaled only $50,000?

(c) Assume that Jane makes a § 179 election with respect to the machine for Year One. With respect to the remaining purchase price (that portion not already deductible under § 179), the regular "modified accelerated cost recovery system" ("MACRS") of § 168(a) applies. Having fun yet? (That's not the question.) What is "the applicable depreciation method" for the machine under § 168(a)(1), and what (in lay terms) does it mean?

(d) What is "the applicable recovery period" for the machine under § 168(a)(2)?

(e) What is "the applicable convention" for the machine under § 168(a)(3), and what (in lay terms) does that mean?

(f) It turns out that as a result of the variables described in parts (c), (d), and (e) above, the depreciation deductions that Jane can claim for the machine are as follows (assuming a § 168(a) depreciation base of $50,000):

Year	Deduction Amount
Year One	$10,000
Year Two	16,000
Year Three	9,600
Year Four	5,760
Year Five	5,760
Year Six	2,880
TOTAL:	$50,000

Assuming Jane made a full § 179 election, what is Jane's basis in the machine as of January 1, Year Two?

(g) How would the answer to (f) change if Jane made a math error and accidentally deducted only a total of $80,000 with respect to the machine in Year One?

(h) How would the answer to (f) change if Jane deducted the entire cost of the machine ($150,000) in Year One and the Internal Revenue Service, plagued with limited resources and more significant taxpayer mistakes, does not contest the deduction within the statute of limitations?

(i) Given the facts in (f), what are the federal income tax consequences to Jane if she sold the machine to an unrelated purchaser on January 5, Year Two, for $85,000 cash?

Problem 4–11

In the current year, Oscar acquired the following assets:

Date Acquired	Asset	Cost	Purpose
March 28	Equipment	$100,000	Business
June 12	Passenger Car	$20,000	½ Business; ½ Personal
September 25	Computer	$10,000	Business

Oscar placed each of these assets into service in the current year. Oscar purchased no other depreciable assets during the year. The equipment and the computer are used exclusively at Oscar's regular business establishment. Oscar's taxable income from his trade or business activities is $100,000.

(a) To what extent can Oscar deduct the costs described above in the current year? Ignore any inflation adjustments to dollar amounts set forth in the Code.

(b) How does your answer to (a) change if Oscar's taxable income from his trade or business activities is only $20,000?

(c) How does your answer to (a) change if the purchase price of the equipment was $500,000?

(d) If Oscar sells the car on July 1 of next year for $20,000, what are the federal income tax consequences to Oscar?

(e) Suppose that on April 1 of next year, Oscar stops using the computer for business purposes and starts using the computer exclusively for investment purposes unrelated to any business activity. What federal income tax consequences result?

* * *

(3) AMORTIZATION OF INTANGIBLE PROPERTY

Code: IRC §§ 167(f); 197(a)–(e).

Regs: Treas. Reg. §§ 1.167(a)–3; 1.197–2(a)–(d).

The Trouble With Intangibles. Prior to 1993, the Code contained no special rules for the cost recovery of intangible assets. Intangible assets were depreciated under §§ 167 and 168 if they met the requirements imposed by those sections. But meeting those requirements can be quite cumbersome when the asset is intangible. How, exactly, is an

[handwritten: FRI. P277-286 Problem 4.12]

intangible asset subject to "wear and tear?" Proof problems aside, where a taxpayer acquired both intangible assets subject to wear and tear and other intangible assets not so subject (like when a taxpayer acquired all of the assets of another's business), the taxpayer had an incentive to allocate as much of the purchase price as possible to the tangible and intangible assets subject to wear and tear, for at least that portion of the consideration paid could be recovered over time. Any consideration allocated to intangible assets that were *not* subject to wear and tear could not be recovered until such assets were sold, if ever.

The following case is illustrative of the problems that ensued prior to the enactment of § 197 in 1993. To the extent § 197 supercedes the court's discussion, you should not get overly concerned about the technical aspects of the case. Instead, enjoy the case for its elegant prose and insight into the difficulties wrought over a decade ago.

SELIG v. UNITED STATES

United States Court of Appeals, Seventh Circuit, 1984.
740 F.2d 572.

BAUER, CIRCUIT JUDGE.

The government asks this court to overturn the district court's ruling in favor of Plaintiff Allan "Bud" Selig, part owner of the Milwaukee Brewers. The district court held that Selig properly allocated $10.2 million of the $10.8 million purchase price of the Seattle Pilots to the value of the 149 players he bought. We affirm.

I

The theory of the game is that one side takes the field, and the other goes in. The pitcher then delivers the ball to the striker, who endeavors to hit it in such a direction as to elude the fielders, and enable him to run around all the base lines home without being put out. If he succeeds a run is scored.[1]

This year the United States celebrates the centennial of a momentous event in its grand sports history: the introduction of overhand pitching into major league baseball. Although organized baseball and the games from which it derived had been played for many years,[2] overhand pitching and the switch to a cork-center baseball in 1911 were two of the final major steps toward the game as we enjoy it today.

The National Association of Professional Base–Ball Players was born in 1871. In the first recorded professional game, the Kekiongas franchise of Fort Wayne defeated Forest City of Cleveland, 2 to 0. Franchises cost $10. Notably, the White Stockings of Chicago led the league throughout the season and appeared headed for the pennant until an accident in

---

1. 1 Encyclopedia Britannica, 1890.

2. In fact, archeologists have discovered etchings carved almost 4,000 years ago of women playing ball, and one prominent historian believes that all modern ball games evolved from ancient religious rites introduced 5,000 years ago or more. R. Henderson, Ball, Bat and Bishop (1947).

Mrs. O'Leary's barn destroyed their ball yard along with most of the city. Forced to play their remaining games on the road, the White Stockings lost three straight games and the flag to the Athletics of Philadelphia. The birth of the National League in 1876 spelled the end of the National Association. The new Chicago franchise ran away with the pennant in the inaugural season. The American League began in 1901, the result of the nation's yearning for more baseball and the NL's reluctance to expand. Again, a Chicago franchise helped lead the way. The White Sox, headed by AL co-founder Charles Comiskey, won the first-ever AL game and went on to win the league crown. In the first interleague World Series in 1903, Boston, led to the pennant by Denton True "Cy" Young's[3] 32 wins, beat Pittsburgh in a best five-out-of-nine series.[4]

Baseball abounds with legendary players, teams, and events. Some of the greatest memories include Willie Keeler's 44–game hitting streak in 1897; Jack Chesbro's 41 wins in 1904; the 1907 batting title to Ty Cobb—his first of 12; Christy Mathewson's 68 innings without walking a batter in 1913; Babe Ruth hitting 29 home runs in 1919, 54 in 1920, 59 in 1922, and 60 in 1927—all league records; Jim Bottomly hitting in 12 runs in a 9–inning game in 1924; Ruth calling his shot in the 1932 Series; a 1940 Opening Day no-hitter for Bob Feller; Joe DiMaggio's remarkable 1941 season: .357, 30 home runs, 125 RBI, and the 56–game streak; Enos Slaughter scoring from first on a single to break an 8th-inning tie in the seventh game of the 1946 Series; Connie Mack bowing out in 1950 after 50 years as the Athletics field general; "the catch" by Willie Mays robbing Vic Wertz in the 1954 Series; Roger Maris's 61st home run in 1961; the perfect Sandy Koufax on September 9, 1965; Hank Aaron's momentous blast on April 8, 1974; and countless others. And true baseball fans know of the ill-fated careers of Ray Chapman and Wally Pipp.[6]

II

A tonic, an exercise, a safety-valve, baseball is second only to Death as a leveler. So long as it remains our national game, America will abide no monarchy, and anarchy will be too slow.[7]

The first franchise shift of this century occurred when the Boston Braves moved to Milwaukee in 1953. The Braves were a financial success, drawing more than two million fans each year from 1954 to

---

3. Y is for Young The Magnificent Cy;

People batted against him,

But I never knew why.

Ogden Nash.

4. Baseball's first intracity World Series and greatest World Series upset occurred in 1906. The Chicago White Sox, who had strung together 19 victories to steal the AL crown from New York, stunned the mighty Chicago Cubs, who reigned supreme in the NL from 1906 through 1910 behind the tough defense of Steinfeldt, Tinker, Evers, and Chance, and who had won a league-record 116 games in 1906.

6. Ray Chapman, star shortstop of the Cleveland Indians, was killed by a pitch thrown by Carl Mays on August 17, 1920. Wally Pipp, complaining of a headache, was replaced at first base by Lou Gehrig on June 2, 1925. Pipp never again started a game for the Yankees.

7. Allen Sangree, 1907.

1957. This prosperity contributed to the development of baseball on television. The Braves won the World Series in 1957 (defeating the almost invincible New York Yankees), and repeated as pennant winners in 1958.

The Braves' fortunes changed, however, in the early 1960's. Attendance and the team's standings slid. New owners acquired the team in 1962, but, although attendance rose, the team finished in sixth place in 1963 and fifth in 1964. The Braves moved the team to Atlanta, Georgia, in 1966, leaving Milwaukee without a major league franchise. The State of Wisconsin's efforts to stop the move failed. In 1965, Plaintiff Allan Selig and others organized the Milwaukee Brewers Baseball Club, Incorporated in an effort to secure another franchise for the city. The organization negotiated unsuccessfully for the purchase of the Chicago White Sox.

In the meantime, the American League voted to add two expansion teams to begin play in 1969. The league awarded the franchises to organizations in Kansas City and Seattle. Among other expenses, the Seattle Pilots and the Kansas City Royals each paid $5.25 million for thirty players ($175,000 each) acquired from the ten other AL teams through an expansion draft, and $100,000 for their franchises. In anticipation of getting its franchise, the Seattle organization bought the Seattle Angels, a AAA minor league club, and signed a working agreement with another minor league club in Newark, New York.

The Seattle Pilots played ball from April to September 1969, but sunk into financial difficulties with operating expenses of more than $3.7 million. As a result, the Pilots' owners decided to sell the team. Selig learned of the Pilots' financial plight and contacted the team owners. By September 1969, the parties tentatively agreed that Selig would buy the Pilots, including 149 players, for $10.8 million.

The deal was conditioned on Selig's organization (the Brewers) securing league approval to move the team from Seattle to Milwaukee. That approval did not come immediately. Instead, the American League first tried to save the Pilots with league money. The league's efforts failed, and Seattle, at the suggestion of the Brewers' lawyers, petitioned for bankruptcy in March 1970.

Meanwhile, the Brewers and the Pilots on March 8 signed a written contract for the purchase and sale of the Pilots for $10.8 million. The deal was stymied by the league's continued reluctance to approve the move to Milwaukee. The bankruptcy court rescued the deal, however, by ordering the sale of the Pilots by April 1, 1970, and on that day the transaction was completed. The Milwaukee Brewers played their first game six days later.

The contract between the Pilots and the Brewers allocated $100,000 of the purchase price to equipment and supplies, $500,000 to the value of the franchise including league membership, and $10.2 million to the player contracts. The $100,000 allocation is not contested. In the fall of 1970, the Brewers solicited four separate appraisals of their 149-man roster as of April 1, 1970. The appraisals established an average value of $10,043,000, and the Brewers' financial officer decided to retain the $10.2 million allocation. Selig then amortized that cost over the players' five-year useful lives under Section 167(a) of the Internal Revenue Code.[9] The $500,000 allocated to the franchise could not be amortized, because the franchise had no definable limited useful life. Selig thus benefited by allocating as much of the purchase price of the Pilots as possible to the value of the player contracts.

The Internal Revenue Service in 1979 disallowed the entire $10.2 million allocation, attributed zero value to the player contracts, and made the concomitant adjustments in Selig's tax liability for 1967, 1968, and 1970 through 1976. On December 27, 1979, Selig received deficiency notices totaling a little more than $141,000. Selig paid the deficiencies plus interest and applied for a refund in 1980. In March 1981, the refunds were disallowed and this lawsuit was filed.

III

I honestly feel it would be best for the country to keep baseball going. There will be fewer people unemployed and everybody will work longer hours and harder than ever before.[10]

The district court held that Selig's allocation was proper. * * *

* * * The plaintiff offered four appraisals of the Brewers' 149–man roster that the team solicited in the fall of 1970. The first appraisal, prepared by Frank "Trader" Lane, established a roster value of $10.35 million. Lane was a friend of the plaintiff, and later became general manager of the Brewers. The court ruled that this relationship did not taint the appraisal. Cedric Tallis, general manager of the other 1968 expansion club (Kansas City), prepared the second appraisal. He also calculated a value of $10.35 million for the Brewers' player contracts. Tallis relied both on personal observations and on statistics in formulating his appraisal. The court accepted this appraisal, too.

* * *

The government also offered two appraisals. The first was prepared by Dewey Soriano, president of the Seattle organization that secured the Pilots in 1968. Soriano set a value of $3.2 million for the player contracts. The court ruled that Soriano's estimate was unreliable, in part because it was significantly lower than the value Soriano put on the players when he sold the team to the Brewers in 1970. The government's second appraiser, Richard Walsh, was general manager of the California Angels from 1968 to 1971. He calculated the roster value at $5.1 million. The court afforded little weight to Walsh's appraisal, which was based

---

9. The issue whether the Section 167(a) depreciation allowance applies here to intangible assets purchased in a bundle of interrelated assets was settled in *Laird v. United States,* 556 F.2d 1224 (5th Cir.1977), *cert. denied,* 434 U.S. 1014, 98 S.Ct. 729, 54 L.Ed.2d 758 (1978), and is not raised in this appeal.

10. Franklin D. Roosevelt, 1942.

mainly on transactions in the player market and was the product of statistical research rather than first-hand knowledge of the players.

Because the district court concluded that the Brewers' roster could be evaluated properly only with reference to the market in which entire clubs are bought and sold, the court did not accept the government's evidence that was based on transactions in other markets. The court compared the plaintiff's evidence with the remaining government evidence, principally the appraisals. The court concluded that the plaintiff sustained his burden of proving by a preponderance of the evidence that the $10.2 million allocation to player contracts was reasonable.

IV

Show me a good loser, and I'll show you an idiot.[11]

On appeal, the government claims that the $10.2 million allocation to player contracts is "plainly wrong" and "contrary to common sense." The government argues that the fair market value of the franchise is more than five percent of the purchase price of the club. Why would anyone pay more than $10 million, the government asks, for a team when the franchise is "essentially worthless?"[12] Without the right to play baseball in the American League, the government adds, the team could not survive. The government stresses that its evidence at trial established that the franchise constituted most of the $10.8 million value of the Brewers. * * *

A

Time is of the essence. The shadow moves

    From the plate to the box, from the box to second base,

    From second to the outfield, to the bleachers.

Time is of the essence. The crowd and players

    Are the same age always, but the man in the crowd

    Is older every season. Come on, play ball![14]

    * * *

* * * The government argues that it is unrealistic to value the players in the "free" club market when the players will be dealt in the future in a market containing restraints. This argument ignores the reality of the transaction at issue here. The club market is a distinct market. Transactions in the club market take place free of baseball rules, and purchase prices are a result of arms-length negotiations between willing sellers and willing buyers. Here, the Brewers bought a fully staffed baseball enterprise from an organization which desired to sell it. The task of the district court in evaluating this sale for tax

---

11. Leo Durocher.

12. We note that the plaintiff did allocate $500,000 to the franchise. You take $500,000 here and $500,000 there, and

pretty soon you are talking about real money.

14. Rolfe Humphries, from *Polo Grounds*.

purposes was not to assign specific values to individual players, but rather to allocate the purchase price among all the club's assets. In contrast, a sale in the player market or free agent market is a different transaction economically, subject to different restrictions, and may result in attaining values for the players substantially different from those attained in a bulk sale in the club market. Because the transaction here occurred in the club market, we find no error in the district court's decision to rely on data derived from analyses of that market.

* * *

Essentially, the government simply failed to prove its case at trial. It expended a great deal of effort attempting to prove that the players were not worth as much as the plaintiff claimed and that the franchise was worth more than the plaintiff claimed. The district court's ruling does not indicate that the government's evidence was wholly invalid, but rather that the plaintiff carried his burden of proof. For example, the government sharply disagreed with the contention that a franchise in Milwaukee was worthless in 1970. It noted that the Brewers franchise included the right to play other major league teams, the right to eighty percent of gate receipts from home games and twenty percent of gate receipts from games played in other cities, territorial exclusivity, exclusive local broadcasting rights, and the right to sell concessions at home games. Although these rights indeed are worth something, the plaintiff's expert evidence indicated that the franchise in 1970 was not as valuable as the government claimed because of the great risk of failure and the relatively poor commercial-baseball climate in Milwaukee. Moreover, the plaintiff submitted ample evidence of the value of the roster; after all, the players are principally responsible for winning games, drawing fans, and maintaining the financial health of the franchise.

* * *

V

Oh! somewhere in this favored land
   the sun is shining bright;
The band is playing somewhere, and
   somewhere hearts are light.
And somewhere men are laughing, and
   somewhere children shout;
But there is no joy in Mudville—
   mighty Casey has Struck Out.[20]

There should be joy somewhere in Milwaukee—the district court's judgment is affirmed.

20. Ernest L. Thayer, from *Casey at the Bat.*

AFFIRMED.

* * *

In *Selig*, the dispute came down to the allocation of consideration between the cost of the franchise (which had no determinable useful life) and the cost of the player contracts (which did have limited lives that were easily determinable). In other cases, the issue came down to allocating consideration between goodwill (with no determinable useful life, and thus not depreciable) and other, depreciable intangible assets. To end these disputes, Congress in 1993 enacted § 197 to provide clear and uniform rules for the cost recovery of intangible assets. Following is an excerpt from the legislative history to the Revenue Reconciliation Act of 1993.

HOUSE REPORT NO. 103–111

103rd Congress (May 25, 1993).

* * *

F.   Treatment of Intangibles

1.   **Amortization of goodwill** and certain other intangibles
* * *

Present Law

In determining taxable income for Federal income tax purposes, a taxpayer is allowed depreciation or amortization deductions for the cost or other basis of intangible property that is used in a trade or business or held for the production of income if the property has a limited useful life that may be determined with reasonable accuracy. Treas. Reg. § 1.167(a)-(3). These Treasury Regulations also state that no depreciation deductions are allowed with respect to goodwill.

The U.S. Supreme Court recently held that a taxpayer able to prove that a particular asset can be valued, and that the asset has a limited useful life which can be ascertained with reasonable accuracy, may depreciate the value over the useful life regardless of how much the asset appears to reflect the expectancy of continued patronage. However, the Supreme Court also characterized the taxpayers burden of proof as "substantial" and stated that it "often will prove too great to bear." *Newark Morning Ledger Co. v. United States*, * * * (April 20, 1993).

Reasons for Change

The Federal income tax treatment of the costs of acquiring intangible assets is a source of considerable controversy between taxpayers and the Internal Revenue Service. Disputes arise concerning (1) whether an amortizable intangible asset exists; (2) in the case of an acquisition of a trade or business, the portion of the purchase price that is allocable to an amortizable intangible asset; and (3) the proper method and period for recovering the cost of an amortizable intangible asset. These types of disputes can be expected to continue to arise, even after the decision of the U.S. Supreme Court in *Newark Morning Ledger Co. v. United States*, *supra*.

It is believed that much of the controversy that arises under present law with respect to acquired intangible assets could be eliminated by specifying a single method and period for recovering the cost of most acquired intangible assets and by treating acquired goodwill and going concern value as amortizable intangible assets. It is also believed that there is no need at this time to change the Federal income tax treatment of self-created intangible assets, such as goodwill that is created through advertising and other similar expenditures.

Accordingly, the bill requires the cost of most acquired intangible assets, including goodwill and going concern value, to be amortized ratably over a [15]-year period. It is recognized that the useful lives of certain acquired intangible assets to which the bill applies may be shorter than [15] years, while the useful lives of other acquired intangible assets to which the bill applies may be longer than [15] years.

Explanation of Provision

In General

The bill allows an amortization deduction with respect to the capitalized costs of certain intangible property (defined as a "section 197 intangible") that is acquired by a taxpayer and that is held by the taxpayer in connection with the conduct of a trade or business or an activity engaged in for the production of income. The amount of the deduction is determined by amortizing the adjusted basis (for purposes of determining gain) of the intangible ratably over a [15]-year period that begins with the month that the intangible is acquired. No other depreciation or amortization deduction is allowed with respect to a section 197 intangible that is acquired by a taxpayer.

* * *

In general, the bill applies to a section 197 intangible acquired by a taxpayer regardless of whether it is acquired as part of a trade or business. * * * The bill generally does not apply to a section 197 intangible that is created by the taxpayer if the intangible is not created in connection with a transaction (or series of related transactions) that involves the acquisition of a trade or business or a substantial portion thereof.

Except in the case of amounts paid or incurred under certain covenants not to compete (or under certain other arrangements that have substantially the same effect as covenants not to compete) and certain amounts paid or incurred on account of the transfer of a franchise, trademark, or trade name, the bill generally does not apply to any amount that is otherwise currently deductible (i.e., not capitalized) under present law.

No inference is intended as to whether a depreciation or amortization deduction is allowed under present law with respect to any intangible property that is either included in, or excluded from, the definition of a section 197 intangible. In addition, no inference is intended as to whether an asset is to be considered tangible or intangible property for any other purpose of the Internal Revenue Code.

Definition of § 197 Intangible

In General

The term "section 197 intangible" is defined as any property that is included in any one or more of the following categories: (1) goodwill and going concern value; (2) certain specified types of intangible property that generally relate to workforce, information base, know-how, customers, suppliers, or other similar items; (3) any license, permit, or other right granted by a governmental unit or an agency or instrumentality thereof; (4) any covenant not to compete (or other arrangement to the extent that the arrangement has substantially the same effect as a covenant not to compete) entered into in connection with the direct or indirect acquisition of an interest in a trade or business (or a substantial portion thereof); and (5) any franchise, trademark, or trade name.

Certain types of property, however, are specifically excluded from the definition of the term "section 197 intangible." The term "section 197 intangible" does not include: (1) any interest in a corporation, partnership, trust, or estate; (2) any interest under an existing futures contract, foreign currency contract, notional principal contract, interest rate swap, or other similar financial contract; (3) any interest in land; (4) certain computer software; (5) certain interests in films, sound recordings, video tapes, books, or other similar property; (6) certain rights to receive tangible property or services; (7) certain interests in patents or copyrights; (8) any interest under an existing lease of tangible property; (9) any interest under an existing indebtedness (except for the deposit base and similar items of a financial institution); (10) a franchise to engage in any professional sport, and any item acquired in connection with such a franchise; and (11) certain transaction costs.

In addition, the Treasury Department is authorized to issue regulations that exclude certain rights of fixed duration or amount from the definition of a section 197 intangible.

* * *

Section 197 is a bittersweet provision. On the one hand, taxpayers are guaranteed that the cost of many intangibles used in a trade or business can be amortized. But the 15–year straight-line amortization method prescribed by § 197 may be particularly harsh, especially where the actual useful life of the intangible is much shorter. For instance, the cost of a three-year covenant not to compete, if the covenant qualifies as a "§ 197 intangible," must be amortized over 15 years.

If an intangible asset is not eligible for amortization under § 197, the taxpayer can still *depreciate* the cost using the straight-line method if the taxpayer can establish the intangible asset's useful life. See Treas. Reg. § 1.167(a)–3. If no such useful life is determinable, then, no cost recovery is allowed until the asset is sold or otherwise disposed of in a transaction.

✗ *Problem 4–12* ✗

Earlier this year, Enid (an individual engaged in the business of operating fitness studios) acquired all of the assets of Brian Wilson's fitness studio. Some of the assets are described below. For each asset, determine whether the consideration paid for the asset can be: (1) deducted in the year of purchase; (2) depreciated under §§ 167 and 168; (3) amortized under § 197; or (4) none of the above.

(a) Weight-lifting equipment used by studio members.

(b) 350 active memberships.

(c) Goodwill.

(d) Equipment cleaning supplies.

(e) Easement for ingress and egress over adjoining parcel of real property.

(f) Active "Mega–Body Health Club" franchise.

(g) Business licenses and permits.

(h) Brian's agreement not to compete against Enid for five years following the sale.

(i) Microsoft Office Works software program, available to the general public.

(j) Employment agreements with key employees.

E. LOSSES

(1) BUSINESS AND INVESTMENT LOSSES

Code: IRC §§ 62(a)(3); 165(a)–(d). *Review* IRC § 1001(a)–(c).

Regs: Treas. Reg. §§ 1.165–1(a)–(c)(1), –1(d)(1); 1.165–4(a); 1.165–9.

Recall that § 1001(a) defines a loss from the sale or exchange of property as the excess of a taxpayer's adjusted basis over the amount realized. Under § 1001(c) all realized losses are recognized (i.e., deductible) except as provided elsewhere in the Code. For individuals, the major limitation is § 165(c), which only permits the deduction of three types of uncompensated losses: (1) losses incurred in a trade or business; (2) losses incurred in profit-motivated transactions; and (3) casualty and theft losses with respect to personal-use property. In effect, § 165(c) inverts the presumption under § 1001(c) that all realized losses are recognized. If a realized loss is not described in § 165(c), an individual taxpayer cannot deduct the loss.

Section 165(a) itself imposes two additional limitations. First, the loss must be "sustained." This is probably akin to the requirement that gains must be "realized" before they can be taxed. Thus, for example, a decline in the fair market value of an asset cannot be claimed as a loss until the asset is sold or otherwise disposed of in a completed transaction. See Treas. Reg. §§ 1.165–1(d)(1); 1.165–4(a).

Second, the taxpayer must not have been "compensated" for the loss. This rule makes sense: if a taxpayer receives insurance proceeds or other compensation for a loss, it would be a windfall to permit a loss deduction on top of the recovery. For a long time, courts and the Service agreed that if a taxpayer waives a right to compensation, the taxpayer cannot deduct the ensuing loss. In *Revenue Ruling 78–141*, 1978–1 C.B. 58, a lawyer paid money to a client to compensate for giving bad advice to the client. The lawyer tried to claim the amount paid to the client as a loss, but the Service disallowed the loss because the taxpayer did not seek reimbursement from the taxpayer's malpractice insurance carrier. (Can you figure out why the taxpayer did not try to expense the payment under § 162?) Beginning in the mid–1980s, however, courts adopted a different approach.

not necessary and ordinary bus. expense.

MILLER v. COMMISSIONER

United States Court of Appeals, Sixth Circuit, 1984.
733 F.2d 399.

WELLFORD, CIRCUIT JUDGE, delivering the opinion of the Court.

* * *

* * * In June, 1976, a friend of the taxpayer ran the taxpayer's boat aground. The boat was damaged but to an extent less than $1,000. Although the boat was insured, taxpayer did not file a claim for recovery of the damage with his insurance company. The taxpayer's decision not to collect insurance proceeds was motivated by his fear that the submission of another claim would result in the cancellation of his insurance policies. Taxpayer was able to collect $200.00 from his friend, reducing taxpayer's actual loss to $642.55. After taking into account the $100.00 limitation under [§ 165(h)(1)], taxpayer claimed a $542.22 casualty loss deduction on his 1976 return. The Commissioner of Internal Revenue disallowed the deduction and issued a notice of deficiency. Taxpayer filed a timely petition with the United States Tax Court challenging the Commissioner's decision to disallow the deduction. Relying on *Kentucky Utilities Co. v. Glenn*, 394 F.2d 631 (6th Cir. 1968), the Tax Court concluded that the taxpayer's failure to pursue insurance proceeds barred the casualty loss deduction. The Tax Court, however, reconsidered its decision in light of *Hills v. C.I.R.*, 76 T.C. 484 (1981), aff'd., 691 F.2d 997 (11th Cir. 1982), and allowed the deduction.

We are now asked to determine whether a voluntary election not to file an insurance claim for a casualty loss precludes the insured-taxpayer from taking a casualty loss deduction under § 165 of the Internal Revenue Code of 1954. We are not able significantly to distinguish the issue presented in this case from that presented in *Kentucky Utilities*, and, to the extent it is contrary to our holding in this case, we overrule that decision and AFFIRM the holding of the Tax Court below.

In *Kentucky Utilities* (K.U.), a steam generator was damaged in an accident. The generator was originally sold to K.U. by Westinghouse Electric Corporation and was under warranty at the time of the accident. Based on an independent investigation, K.U. concluded that Westinghouse was responsible for the loss. Rather than jeopardize a valued business relationship by pursuing a claim against Westinghouse, K.U. sought indemnification from its insurance company, Lloyds of London. The insurance carrier did not dispute either its liability or the amount necessary to indemnify the loss. In fact, Lloyds offered to indemnify K.U. for the full amount of the damage. Because Lloyds insisted upon its right of subrogation against Westinghouse, however, K.U. refused to accept any insurance proceeds. Instead, K.U., Westinghouse, and Lloyds entered into a settlement agreement whereby Westinghouse and Lloyds agreed to compensate K.U. in the amount of $65,550.93 and $37,500.00, respectively. Pursuant to this settlement, K.U. agreed to absorb the remaining cost of repairs and proceeded to deduct the $44,486.77 on its corporate income tax return, either as a § 165 loss or as [an] "ordinary and necessary" business expense. The district court held that K.U.'s failure reasonably to pursue indemnification from Lloyds barred any casualty loss deduction under § 23(f) of the 1939 I.R.C., except to the extent of the $10,000 deductible provision in its insurance policy. Likewise, the district court held that K.U.'s expenditures did not constitute ordinary or necessary business expenses under * * * § 162 * * *. This Court affirmed.

After our holding in *Kentucky Utilities*, the Eleventh Circuit handed down its decision in *Hills*, *supra*. The *Hills* court attempted to distinguish, rather than to reject, the holding of *Kentucky Utilities*. We have been unable to distinguish, however, *Kentucky Utilities* in any meaningful manner. It is true that *Kentucky Utilities* deals with a corporation and a claimed business loss akin to a § 165(c)(1) loss, while *Hills*, as well as the instant case, deal with subsection 165(c)(3) casualty loss claims by individual taxpayers (theft and shipwreck, respectively). Each situation is subject, nevertheless, to the general overriding requirement of § 165(a), whether business or individual, that a loss be "sustained . . . and not compensated for by insurance or otherwise." An interpretation of the code subsection under consideration, § 165(c)(3), as it pertains to a claimed individual loss, is therefore closely related to the interpretation given in *Kentucky Utilities* to the claimed business loss.

Judges and commentators have given differing interpretations of the holding in *Kentucky Utilities*. Generally speaking, *Kentucky Utilities* is said to set forth a two-part transaction view; it looks to the "sustained loss" clause and the "not compensated" clause of § 165. Thus, *Kentucky Utilities* can be interpreted to hold either (a) that a taxpayer must exhaust all reasonable prospects for insurance indemnification before claiming a "sustained loss," or (b) that the phrase "not compensated by" must be equated with the phrase "not covered by" insurance. We now reject both of these interpretations which would preclude Miller's claim of a loss deduction under the circumstances here present.

The former interpretation must be rejected because it renders the "not compensated by" clause mere surplusage. The question of whether a loss has been sustained depends upon the taxpayer's reasonable expectation of recovery from the wrongdoer. *Alison v. United States*, 344 U.S. 167, 170, 97 L. Ed. 186, 73 S. Ct. 191 (1952). The plain language of § 165(a) supports the proposition that the timing of a loss transaction must be determined *independent* of insurance consequences. Section 165(a) provides that "there shall be allowed as a deduction any *loss sustained* ... *and not compensated* for by insurance...." (emphasis added). To define a sustained loss with reference to potential indemnification by an insurer strips the language of § 165(a), regarding compensation, of its meaning; any time a loss is sustained it, by definition, would not be "compensated for by insurance." In short, we believe that § 165(a) reflects the intent of Congress that the question of whether a loss is sustained should be resolved independently of any insurance consequences involved. This conclusion is bolstered by the rule of statutory construction that requires courts to construe the language of a statute so as to avoid making any word meaningless or superfluous. In the instant case, the parties have stipulated that, at the time of the deduction, there remained no reasonable prospect of recovery from the wrongdoer. Thus, we conclude that the taxpayer has sustained a loss in a "closed transaction" during the taxable year.

We likewise reject *Kentucky Utilities* for the proposition that "not compensated by" means "not covered by." Such an interpretation of the language of § 165 is inconsistent with the plain meaning of the word "compensated." Absent unusual circumstances, we are bound to apply the plain meaning of a statute. Moreover, legislative history, scant though it is, does not support an interpretation of § 165 that equates "not compensated by" with "not covered by." As the court in *Hills* noted:

> The initial House Ways and Means Committee language was "losses ... not covered by insurance or otherwise and compensated for." The Senate Finance Committee amended the language to its final and enacted form of "losses ... not compensated for by insurance or otherwise."
>
> * * *

We agree with the Tax Court's conclusion in *Hills v. Commissioner*, 76 T.C. 484, 487, after its analysis of the legislative history:

> All losses compensated by insurance are also, as a necessary concomitant, covered by insurance; nonetheless, it should be equally obvi-

ous that the converse, i.e. that all losses covered by insurance are also compensated for, is not necessarily true.

See also *Hills*, 691 F.2d at 1006: " 'Compensated' is a word distinct from 'covered'."

* * *

Courts which have held to the contrary generally have reasoned by analogy. See *Jewell v. Commissioner*, 69 T.C. 791 (1978) (where the Tax Court analogized to medical expenses not compensated by insurance or otherwise under 26 U.S.C. § 213(a)); and *Heidt v. Commissioner*, 274 F.2d 25 (7th Cir.) aff'g., 18 T.C.M. (CCH) 149 (1959) (where the Tax Court analogized that no ordinary and necessary business expense can be claimed under § 162(a) for the personal use of an automobile in connection with business when reimbursement is available from the employer).

When the language of a statute is clear, as in this case, one need not resort to analogy. Congress has simply elected to treat seemingly analogous situations differently for underlying policy reasons. We conclude that Congress limited the availability of § 165 deductions to "losses not compensated for by insurance or otherwise" to avoid double compensation for taxpayers who in fact had received indemnification from their insurers. * * *

The plain language of § 165, its legislative history, and the interests of public policy all support the conclusion we reach today. It should be noted that to hold otherwise would unjustifiably work to the disadvantage of taxpayers, not engaged in business, who voluntarily decline insurance indemnification for sound and practical reasons not primarily motivated by tax considerations, such as appellee. To hold otherwise would also work to the indirect advantage of taxpayers who, for whatever reasons, decline to obtain any insurance coverage at all to protect themselves from casualty, and then claim an uncompensated loss as deductible if a casualty occurs.

The Eleventh Circuit's observation in *Hills* that "the disposition the Commissioner favore[d] in this case would deny a section 165 deduction any time a loss is covered by insurance," would apply equally here. Such a disposition, that of the *Kentucky Utilities* case that there was no "insured loss," does not comport with the plain and clear meaning of this section of the Internal Revenue Code in light of the legislative history pointed out. We agree with the *Hills* court in its ultimate holding: Section 165(a) allows a deduction for an economic detriment that (1) is a loss, and (2) is not compensated for by insurance or otherwise.

Accordingly, our prior decision in *Kentucky Utilities* is overruled to the extent it is interpreted as denying any taxpayer in the posture of Miller a deduction under 26 U.S.C. §§ 165(a) and (c)(3), and the judgment of the Tax Court is AFFIRMED.

* * *

If a taxpayer receives no consideration for a realized loss (whether as payment or as compensation), the loss deduction is limited to the taxpayer's basis in the loss property. Section 165(b). Thus, if a taxpayer is unable to collect on an account receivable (in which a taxpayer has a zero basis except in very limited cases), there is no deduction under § 165(a). There is also a special rule for gambling losses: § 165(d) limits the deduction for gambling losses to the amount of the taxpayer's gambling winnings. It does not matter whether gambling is a business, investment, or personal activity of the taxpayer.

Section 165(c)(1) allows individuals a deduction for losses incurred in a trade or business. One might think that § 165(c)(1) is unnecessary given the broad sweep of § 162(a), the deduction for trade or business expenses. But losses and expenses are different animals. Expenses, remember, are costs paid or incurred that provide a short-term benefit to the taxpayer and do not serve to improve permanently the value of some pre-existing asset. Losses, by contrast, represent the culmination of a decline in value that may have accrued over several years. Because realized losses are measured with respect to the taxpayer's adjusted basis in the underlying asset, a loss deduction reflects the taxpayer's failure to recover completely his or her cost that was originally capitalized. Because losses are fundamentally different than expenses, a separate provision for deducting losses is necessary and appropriate.

Likewise, it would be erroneous to claim realized losses from investment activities as expenses under § 212. As § 212 relates only to expenses, § 165(c)(2) is needed to permit a deduction for investment losses. Notice that all recognized losses from the sale or exchange of property, including investment losses, are deductible above the line. Section 62(a)(3). That means all taxpayers can claim these deductions, even those who choose not to itemize deductions. Investment losses thus have preferential status compared to investment expenses, which are miscellaneous itemized deductions available only to those who itemize (and which are never deductible in full because of the two-percent haircut in § 67). Because many investment losses arise from the sale or exchange of a capital asset, however, additional limitations apply, as discussed below in Part E(4)(b).

* * *

Self-Assessment Question

(Solutions to Self–Assessment Questions are set forth in Appendix 3.)

SAQ 4–7. Hiroyuki Sakai purchased a personal residence in Year One for $200,000. On June 23, Year Four, Sakai sold the home for $120,000 to Chen Kenichi, an unrelated individual. Kenichi does not move into the home, but instead rents it to tenants. On November 10, Year Six, Kenichi sold the home to Masahiro Morimoto, another unrelated individual, for $70,000.

(a) What are the federal income tax consequences to Sakai from the Year Four sale?

(b) What are the federal income tax consequences to Kenichi from the Year Six sale?

(c) Do the results in parts (a) and (b) make sense from a policy perspective? Explain.

* * *

Problem 4–13

In Year One, Othello purchased a vacation home in a hamlet. He paid $100,000 for the residence. By the end of Year Two, Othello decided to sell the property, but no one made an offer to purchase it. At the beginning of Year Three, when the property was worth only $70,000, Othello decided to rent out the property to unrelated tenants. Because the property was then held for the production of rental income, Othello validly claimed depreciation deductions of $5,000 with respect to the vacation home in each of Years Three and Four ($10,000 in total deductions). On January 1, Year Five, Othello sold the property to Portia, an unrelated purchaser, for $50,000.

(a) What are the federal income tax consequences of the Year Five sale to Othello, ignoring any depreciation deduction to which Othello may be entitled in Year Five?

(b) How would the answer to (a) change if Othello originally acquired the home as rental property in Year One, claimed $10,000 of depreciation in Years One and Two, and converted the property to his personal vacation home at the beginning of Year Three, when the property was worth $70,000?

* * *

(2) CASUALTY & THEFT LOSSES

Code: IRC § 165(c)(3), (h).

Regs: Treas. Reg. §§ 1.165–1(d)(2)–(3); 1.165–7(a)–(b); 1.165–8(a), (c)–(d).

If a loss is properly classified as a personal loss (one unrelated to business or investment), § 165(c)(3) provides that the loss is deductible only if it qualifies as "casualty" or "theft" loss. The following cases and rulings give you some insight to what is meant by these terms.

MAZZEI v. COMMISSIONER

United States Tax Court, 1974.
61 T.C. 497.

Quealy, J.

Respondent determined a deficiency in income tax against petitioners for the taxable year 1965 in the amount of $7,676.86. As a result of certain concessions by the parties, the sole question presented for

issue :

decision is whether the petitioners are entitled to deduct a loss in the taxable year 1965 on account of being defrauded in a scheme to reproduce United States currency. Petitioners claim the deduction under section 165(c)(2) or section 165(c)(3).

FINDINGS OF FACT

* * *

During the year at issue, and for some time prior thereto, petitioner operated a sheet metal company in Hopewell, Va., in partnership with his brother. Vernon Blick was an employee of the company in 1965 and had been an employee for 4 or 5 years.

In March 1965, Blick was told by a man named Cousins of a scheme for reproducing money. Blick accompanied Cousins to a hotel in Washington, D.C., where Cousins introduced Blick to two other men named Collins and Joe. At that time, Collins and Joe showed Blick a black box which they asserted was capable of reproducing money. The black box was approximately 15 inches long, 8 or 10 inches wide, and 6 inches deep, about the size of a shoebox. It was made of metal and had a handle on it.

Blick gave Collins a $10 bill which Collins took and placed between two pieces of white paper of about the same size. Collins put the money and the paper into the box and connected the box to an electric outlet. The black box began a buzzing sound which continued for about 10 minutes. Then Collins reached into the box and pulled out Blick's $10 bill and what appeared to be a new $10 bill. Collins then told Blick that they could not reproduce any more money at that time because they did not have enough of the type of paper required. In addition, Collins indicated that they would rather not use small denomination bills, but instead they wanted larger denominations such as $100 bills. Blick then returned to Hopewell.

Blick having told Cousins about petitioner, Cousins requested Blick to have petitioner meet with Cousins. In April or May of 1965, Blick recounted the events of the demonstration to petitioner. Thereafter, petitioner and Blick went to see Cousins in Hopewell and discussed a "deal" to reproduce money with Cousins, Collins, and Joe in Washington, D.C., and New York City. Petitioner was to provide money which Cousins, Collins, and Joe would reproduce and then return to petitioner.

After his first meeting with Cousins, petitioner was contacted several times concerning further arrangements for reproducing money.

In May 1965, Cousins took petitioner and Blick to New York City. Petitioner carried $10,000 in cash with him at Cousins' request. They went to a hotel in Brooklyn where Cousins telephoned Collins and Joe who then came over with the black box. Petitioner gave Collins a $100 bill in order to demonstrate the reproduction box. Collins went through the "reproduction" process and returned to petitioner his bill and a new $100 bill. Petitioner requested that they reproduce more money, but was told that there was not enough of the right kind of paper, which was supposed to be a special type used by the Federal Government and obtained through a "friend" in Washington, D.C. Cousins then took petitioner and Blick back to Hopewell that afternoon.

Petitioner continued to inquire of Cousins about reproducing more money but again was told that the difficulty in obtaining the right kind of reproducing paper was holding things up. However, petitioner did give $700 to Cousins who supposedly went to New York and reproduced it. Cousins returned petitioner's $700 plus $300 more, supposedly reproduced. Once again, Cousins said that the reason he did not reproduce more was because of the lack of sufficient paper.

Approximately a week later, Joe telephoned petitioner from New York and stated that they would be ready in a few days to proceed with the deal. Joe requested petitioner to obtain $20,000 in large denominations, preferably $100 bills.

On June 1, 1965, petitioner cashed a check for $20,000 on his company's account at a local bank, taking the proceeds in $100 bills. Blick obtained $5,000, borrowed from petitioner's brother, also through a check on the company account. Several days later, Joe called petitioner, confirmed that petitioner had acquired the cash and requested petitioner and Blick to meet him in New York.

On June 3, 1965, petitioner and Blick flew to New York City with the money. Once in New York, petitioner and Blick went to a designated hotel to meet Cousins, Collins, and Joe. Joe came by the hotel and met petitioner, confirming that petitioner and Blick had the money. The three then went outside where Collins was waiting with a taxicab. They proceeded to an apartment in Brooklyn, stopping on the way for Collins or Joe to purchase some liquor.

Once at the apartment, petitioner and Blick were again shown the black box. Collins then asked petitioner for the money. Petitioner handed Collins a packet of money containing $5,000. Collins removed the wrapper and placed the money into a pan of water. Collins then removed the money from the water and placed each $100 bill between two pieces of white paper which he then set aside. Collins continued the process until he finished with the series of bills in the $5,000 packet. Petitioner then handed Collins another $5,000 packet, and Collins repeated the same process. This continued until petitioner had given Collins the entire $20,000. Petitioner then informed Collins that Blick had $5,000, which Blick then gave to petitioner who in turn gave it to Collins.

Collins then informed petitioner and Blick that the black box was broken and would not work. Collins told them that they would have to use an oven, apparently to complete the reproduction process. Collins then turned on an ordinary electric oven which was in the apartment and put all of the money in the oven. At this point, two armed men broke into the room impersonating law enforcement officers making a counterfeiting raid. Petitioner and Blick were held at gunpoint while one of the men placed handcuffs on Joe. The two men representing themselves to be officers then removed the money from the oven. As the two intruders proceeded to the door of the apartment, petitioner broke away and ran up the street to seek the assistance of a police officer whom he saw. Petitioner reported the incident to the police officer, who told petitioner to wait until a squad car could arrive.

Meanwhile, Blick, who had remained with Collins, Joe, and the two intruders, requested them to return the money. Blick was told he would be shot if he attempted to retrieve the money. Then Collins, Joe, and the two intruders went out of the apartment, got into a taxicab and left with the money.

Petitioner returned with the police and found Blick alone. The black box was examined and found to be nothing more than a tin box with a buzzer. It could not have reproduced any money. Petitioner and Blick accompanied the police to the police station and filed a report of the incident. The next day, petitioner and Blick returned to Hopewell and reported the incident to the police there. The incident was also discussed with the Federal Bureau of Investigation.

On his Federal income tax return for the calendar year 1965, petitioner claimed a theft loss in the amount of $20,000 and took a deduction therefor in the amount of $19,900.

In his statutory notice of deficiency, respondent disallowed the deduction for the loss under section 165(c) (2) or (3) on the grounds of lack of adequate substantiation of the loss and, further, that allowance of the deduction would be contrary to public policy.

OPINION

Petitioner contends that the fact that he incurred a loss is substantiated by the evidence and that such loss is deductible under section 165(c)(2) or section 165(c)(3). Respondent contends initially that petitioner has failed to prove that a loss was in fact suffered, and, further, that even if a loss were proven in fact, a deduction for such loss would not be allowed under section 165(c)(2) or section 165(c)(3) on the grounds that allowance of such a deduction would be contrary to public policy. As our findings of fact indicate, the Court is convinced that petitioner, in fact, incurred a loss in the sum of $20,000, as the result of being defrauded. However, the deductibility of such loss is precluded by our decision in *Luther M. Richey, Jr.*, 33 T.C. 272 (1959).

In the *Richey* case, the taxpayer became involved with two other men in a scheme to counterfeit United States currency. The taxpayer observed a reproduction process involving the bleaching out of $1 bills and the transferring of the excess ink from $100 bills onto the bleached-out bills. Upon observing this demonstration, the taxpayer became convinced that the process could reproduce money. When the taxpayer later met with the other men in a hotel room to carry out the scheme, the taxpayer turned over to one of the other men $15,000 which was to be used in the duplication process. Before the process was completed, one of the other men to whom the taxpayer had given the $15,000 left the room under the pretext of going to get something and never returned. The taxpayer later discovered that his money was gone and was not able to recover it. We disallowed the taxpayer's claimed loss deduction under section 165(c)(2) and section 165(c)(3), on the grounds that to allow the loss deduction would constitute an immediate and severe frustration of the clearly defined policy against counterfeiting obligations of the United States as enunciated by title 18, U.S.C., § 471. This Court said:

> The record establishes that petitioner's conduct constituted an attempt to counterfeit, an actual start in the counterfeiting activity, and overt acts looking to consummation of the counterfeiting scheme. Petitioner actively participated in the venture. He withdrew money from the bank and changed it into high denomination bills with the full knowledge and intention that the money would be used to duplicate other bills. He was physically present at the place of alteration, and assisted in the process by washing the bills and otherwise aiding Randall and Johnson in their chores. He was part and parcel of the attempt to duplicate the money. Petitioner's actions are no less a violation of public policy because there was another scheme involved, namely, that of swindling the petitioner. From the facts, we hold that to allow the loss deduction in the instant case would constitute a severe and immediate frustration of the clearly defined policy against counterfeiting obligations of the United States.

Petitioner would distinguish the *Richey* case on the grounds that there the taxpayer was involved in an actual scheme to duplicate money where the process was actually begun, only to have the taxpayer swindled when his cohorts made off with his money, whereas in the instant case there never was any real plan to counterfeit money, it being impossible to duplicate currency with the black box. Petitioner contends that, from the inception, the only actual illegal scheme was the scheme to relieve petitioner of his money, and petitioner was a victim and not a perpetrator of the scheme.

In our opinion, the fact that the petitioner was victimized in what he thought was a plan or conspiracy to produce counterfeit currency does not make his participation in what he considered to be a criminal act any less violative of a clearly declared public policy. Not only was the result sought by the petitioner contrary to such policy, but the conspiracy itself constituted a violation of law. The petitioner conspired with his co-victim to commit a criminal act, namely, the counterfeiting of United States currency and his theft loss was directly related to that act. If there was a transaction entered into for profit, as petitioner argues, it was a conspiracy to counterfeit.

While it is also recognized that the Supreme Court in *Commissioner v. Tellier*, 383 U.S. 687 (1966), may have redefined the criteria for the disallowance on grounds of public policy of an otherwise deductible business expense under section 162(a), we do not have that type of case.

The loss claimed by the petitioner here had a direct relationship to the purported illegal act which the petitioner conspired to commit.

We also do not feel constrained to follow *Edwards v. Bromberg*, 232 F.2d 107 (C.A. 5, 1956), wherein the court allowed a deduction for a loss incurred by the taxpayer when money, which he thought was being bet on a "fixed" race, was stolen from him. The taxpayer never intended to participate in "fixing" the race.

The ultimate question for decision in this case is whether considerations of public policy should enter into the allowance of a theft loss under section 165(c)(3) where there is a "theft"—and the loss by the petitioner of his money would certainly qualify as such—the statute imposes no limitation on the deductibility of the loss. Nevertheless, in *Luther M. Richey, Jr., supra*, this Court held that the deduction of an admitted theft was properly disallowed on grounds of public policy in a factual situation which we find indistinguishable. We would follow that case.

REVENUE RULING 79–174

1979–1 C.B. 99.

Issue

Under the circumstances described below, is a loss from the death of trees as a result of attack by insects a casualty loss within the meaning of section 165(c) of the Internal Revenue Code of 1954?

Facts

In 1976, a taxpayer owned a residential lot on which 40 ornamental pine trees were growing. The trees were in healthy condition on July 1, 1976. By July 10, 1976, all of the trees were dead. Death was attributable to a mass attack of southern pine beetles. Beetle attacks in epidemic proportions were unknown in the vicinity of the taxpayer's residential lot prior to the attack that killed the trees.

The southern pine beetle is a flying insect that normally attacks living pine trees. The female beetle bores into a tree and enters the cambium tissue beneath the bark. It then emits an attractant that leads other beetles to the tree in a mass attack. The beetles construct tunnels in the cambium tissue and deposit their eggs. These tunnels intersect and in a short time completely girdle the tree. This cuts off the food supply to the higher parts of the tree and kills the tree. In the instant case, the cambium layer of each tree was completely girdled within 5 to 10 days after the arrival of the female beetle.

Law and Analysis

Section 165(a) of the Code provides the general rule that there shall be allowed as a deduction any loss sustained during the taxable year and not compensated for by insurance or otherwise.

Section 165(c) of the Code provides that in the case of an individual, the deduction is limited to (1) losses incurred in a trade or business, (2) losses incurred in any transaction entered into for profit, though not connected with a trade or business, and (3) losses of property not connected with a trade or business, if such losses arise from fire, storm, shipwreck, or other casualty, or from theft. In respect of property not connected with a trade or business, a loss shall be allowed only to the extent that the amount of loss to such individual arising from each casualty, or from each theft, exceeds $100.

Court decisions and revenue rulings have established standards for the application of the above provisions, and have developed the overall concept that the term "casualty" as used in such provisions refers to an identifiable event of a sudden, unexpected, or unusual nature. Damage or loss resulting from progressive deterioration of property through a steadily operating cause would not be a casualty loss.

Revenue Ruling 57–599, 1957–2 C.B. 142, holds in part that a loss arising from the death of trees as a result of an attack by insects does not constitute an allowable deduction as a casualty loss within the meaning of section 165(c)(3) of the Code. The loss was denied on the grounds that the death of the trees resulted from progressive deterioration, and, therefore, the element of suddenness was lacking.

To be sudden, an event must be of a swift and precipitous nature and not gradual or progressive. See *Rev. Rul. 75–592*, 1972–2 C.B. 101. Whether an event is sudden must be determined from all the surrounding facts and circumstances. In the instant case, the cambium layers of the ornamental trees were completely girdled within 5 to 10 days after the arrival of the female beetle. Once the girdling occurred the trees were dead and their value as ornamentals was lost at that point. On the basis of these facts the element of suddenness is satisfied.

In addition to being sudden in nature, the event must also be unusual or unexpected before it can qualify as a casualty within the meaning of section 165(c)(3) of the Code. Since there were no known attacks in epidemic proportions of southern pine beetles in the area of the taxpayer's residence, the event was both unusual and unexpected.

Holding

A casualty loss deduction is allowable to the taxpayer to the extent provided by section 165(c)(3) of the Code and the regulations thereunder.

Effect on Other Revenue Rulings

Rev. Rul. 57–599 is modified to remove any implication that fatal damage to ornamental trees by insect infestation can never be of a sufficiently sudden nature to meet the required elements of a casualty loss under section 165(c)(3) of the Code.

* * *

CARPENTER v. COMMISSIONER

United States Tax Court, 1966.
T.C. Memo 1966–228.

WITHEY, JUDGE: * * *

FINDINGS OF FACT

* * *

During 1962 petitioner Nancy Carpenter owned a diamond engagement ring. At an undisclosed time in 1962 she placed the ring in a waterglass of ammonia for the purpose of cleaning it. The glass containing the ring was left "next" to the kitchen sink. While petitioner William Carpenter was washing dishes, he inadvertently "picked up the glass and emptied its contents down the" sink drain, not realizing the ring was part of such contents. He then activated the garbage disposal unit in the sink damaging the ring. The damaged ring was recovered and taken to a jeweler for appraisal. His appraisal was that the ring was a total loss.

The ring consisted of a platinum mounting, one diamond of .76 carat and four small diamonds of undisclosed weight. Immediately before going into the disposal unit the fair market value of the mounting was $235, that of the large diamond $725, and the aggregate of four small diamonds $50, or an aggregate fair market value of $1,010. This amount was deducted on petitioners' income tax return as a casualty loss.

The fair market value of the mounting immediately after being placed in the disposal unit was $5, that of the large diamond zero, and the aggregate of the small diamonds $25, or a total aggregate fair market value of $30.

Following the above event William purchased and gave Nancy a ring at a purchase price of $169.50.

Nancy had a loss as a result of the above facts in the amount of the difference between the fair market value of her original ring immediately before it was damaged and its fair market value immediately after in the resulting amount of $980.

OPINION

Respondent's position here is that Nancy did not suffer a casualty loss within the meaning of section 165(a) and (c)(3) of the Internal Revenue Code of 1954 in that, by applying the principle of *ejusdem generis*, it cannot be said that the events which gave rise to the ring damage were like or similar to a "fire, storm, [or] shipwreck" and therefore do not amount to "other casualty" under that section. He also takes the position that, should we hold to the contrary on this point, the replacement value of the ring subsequently purchased for Nancy by William and the salvage value of the damaged ring must be offset against the gross loss suffered by Nancy.

* * *

Because William's testimony and his demeanor on the witness stand satisfies us that he is not the type of person who would deliberately and knowingly do so, we have concluded that his placing of the original ring in the disposal unit was inadvertent and accidental. We in turn conclude from this that the damage to the ring resulted from the destructive force of the disposal coupled with the accident or mischance of placing it therein; that, because this is so, the damage must be said to have arisen from fortuitous events over which petitioners had no control.

While the application of the principle of *ejusdem generis* has been consistent in reported cases under this section of the Code and its predecessors, * * * the application has been clearly and consistently broadened. Automobile accidental damage has been likened to shipwreck; earthslide damage to a building, to fire, storm, and shipwreck; and drought damage to buildings, to storm damage. Respondent has gone so far as to allow deduction for damage caused by the sonic boom of a speeding airplane as an "other casualty." See *Rev. Rul. 59–344*, 1959–2 C.B. (Part 2) 74, superseded by *Rev. Rul. 60–329*, 1960–2 C.B. 67, only to clarify the former. This Court has held that "other casualty" includes damage caused by an infestation by termites, *E. G. Kilroe*, 32 T.C. 1304, in no way departing from the principle in doing so.

We think the principle of *ejusdem generis* as now applied fulfills congressional intent in the use of the phrase "other casualty" in that it is being generally held that wherever force is applied to property which the owner-taxpayer is either unaware of because of the hidden nature of such application or is powerless to act to prevent the same because of the suddenness thereof or some other disability and damage results, he has suffered a loss which is, in that sense, like or similar to losses arising from the enumerated causes. Of course, we do not mean to say that one may willfully and knowingly sit by and allow himself to be damaged in his property and still come within the statutory ambit of "other casualty."

Nancy sustained a loss here under circumstances which it is true may be due to her or her husband's negligence, but this has no bearing upon the question whether an "other casualty" has occurred absent any willfulness attributable thereto.

In the circumstances of this case we do not think that the amount of the loss must be reduced by the value of the "replacement" ring. The husband was not an insurer of the ring and it is difficult to conclude that his wife had any claim or measurable right of reimbursement against him for her loss. What he did was simply make another gift to her as an act of repentance or contrition, and not as a compensatory action.

Note

The Seventh Edition of *Black's Law Dictionary* defines *"ejusdem generis"* as follows:

[Latin, "of the same kind or class"] A canon of construction that when a general word or phrase follows a list of specific persons or things, the general word or phrase will be interpreted to include only those persons or things of the same type as those listed. For example, in the phrase, *horses, cattle, sheep, pigs, goats or any other barnyard animal*, the general language *or any other barnyard animal*—despite its seeming breadth—would probably be held to include only four-legged, hoofed mammals (and thus would exclude chickens).

Fortunately for Mary Carpenter, the court decided her husband was more like a pig, not a chicken.

* * *

Self-Assessment Question

(Solutions to Self–Assessment Questions are set forth in Appendix 3.)

SAQ 4–8. Tina Taxpayer has a casualty loss deduction in the amount of $5,900 resulting from a car fire that she did not cause. May she take this deduction into account in computing adjusted gross income (is the deduction above-the-line)?

                         AGI   AB   FMV

* * *   100K   100K   60K

Problem 4–14

Roger Thornhill owned a boat that he used for personal purposes. He purchased the boat in Year One for $100,000.

(a) In Year Three, the boat was stolen. At the time of the theft, the boat was worth $60,000. Roger's adjusted gross income for Year Three was $100,000. The boat was uninsured. If Roger decided to purchase a new boat, it would cost him $200,000. Compute the amount of Roger's deduction from the loss of the boat.

(b) How would the answer to (a) change if the boat was insured, and Roger collected $40,000 in insurance proceeds?

(c) How would the answer to (a) change if, also in Year Three, Roger lost his vacation cabin in a tornado? Assume Roger paid $200,000 for the cabin but that it was worth $300,000 at the time of the loss. Also assume that Roger received $300,000 in insurance proceeds from the cabin loss.

(d) How would the answer to (c) change if the amount of insurance proceeds that Roger received for the cabin totaled $240,000?

(e) How would the answer to (a) change if the boat capsized and was completely destroyed? Assume the boat developed a small leak late in Year Two but Roger never discovered it because he never checked on the boat during the winter months. The boat finally capsized from the leak in March of Year Three.

* * *

(3) NET OPERATING LOSSES

Code: *Skim* IRC § 172.

Regs: None.

Suppose that two proprietors, Bert and Ernie, operate similar businesses. Bert's business income is very steady and reliable. In both Year

One and Year Two, Bert had net business income of $10,000. Ernie's business income, however, is much more volatile. In Year One, Ernie had net business income of $30,000, but he suffered a net loss of $10,000 in Year Two. During the combined two-year operating period, both Bert and Ernie had net income of $20,000. Yet because federal income tax is measured annually, the two taxpayers will not be treated the same.

Bert will pay tax on $10,000 in each of Years One and Two. Ernie will pay tax on $30,000 in Year One. While Ernie pays no tax in Year Two, he is not entitled to a refund, either. Even in a flat tax world, Ernie would pay more tax because his tax base in Year One ($30,000) exceeds the combined tax base of Bert for the two years ($20,000). When you layer in a progressive tax structure and time value of money considerations, the picture gets even more bleak for Ernie.

Section 172 is designed to ameliorate (but not completely cure) the different tax treatments accorded to Bert and Ernie. Under § 172, Ernie can carry his $10,000 "net operating loss" from Year Two *back* to Year One. By doing so, Ernie's Year One taxable income from his business would be reduced to $20,000. If Ernie paid tax on $30,000, therefore, he would be entitled to a refund because of his overpayment. In giving Ernie a refund of his Year One taxes, a rough equity between Bert and Ernie is accomplished. (Ernie still loses the investment power of the refunded taxes for a year, so the net operating loss carryback is not a perfect solution.)

Section 172(b)(1) generally permits taxpayers to carry net operating losses (or "NOLs") *back* for two taxable years and then *forward* for another 20 years. If the NOL remains unused by the end of that time, *c'est la vie*. The remaining net operating loss vanishes. The statute also requires the taxpayer to carry the NOL amount *back* before it can be carried *forward*. Indeed, the taxpayer must apply the NOL to the earliest year available under these rules. So if a taxpayer had a net operating loss in Year Three, the loss must be carried back to Year One first and must set-off any taxable income from Year One before being applied to taxable income from Year Two.

For example, if Kermit has taxable income of $10,000 in Year One, $30,000 in Year Two, and a net operating loss of $20,000 in Year Three, Kermit must first carry the NOL back to Year One. That will reduce the Year One taxable income to zero, and Kermit will receive a refund (without interest) of the amount of tax paid for that year. Kermit may then carry the remaining $10,000 NOL to Year Two, reducing the taxable income that year from $30,000 to $20,000. Kermit may not carry the entire NOL to Year Two, nor may he elect to forego all carrybacks and simply carry the NOL forward to Year Four and beyond.

Under § 172(b)(3) allows the TP to forgo carrying back — and elect a carry-forward only.

Personal losses and deductions cannot give rise to a net operating loss deduction. Section 172(d)(4). A net operating loss only arises if and to the extent business expenses and losses exceed gross income for the taxable year. Thus, if a taxpayer has gross income of $10,000, business expenses of $20,000, and personal deductions of $20,000, the net operating loss amount is $10,000 (not $20,000 or $30,000).

* * *

(4) LOSS LIMITATIONS

In addition to § 165, individuals may be subject to other limitations on the deductibility of losses. This section discusses the loss limitations applicable to transactions between related persons and those arising from the sale or exchange of a capital asset. There are, as one might expect, other limitations as well. First, under § 465, a taxpayer's losses from business and investment activities are limited to the amount that the taxpayer is "at risk" in such activities. Section 465 is the mid–1980s response to "tax shelters," usually partnerships formed by affluent taxpayers designed to generate losses in excess of amounts that partners contribute to the enterprise. In short, if a taxpayer invests $10,000 in an investment activity (like as a limited partner in a real estate limited partnership), the taxpayer can only claim up to $10,000 in losses from the activity, since the taxpayer only has $10,000 "at risk" in the venture. Second, losses from "passive" activities can only be deducted to the extent of income from passive activities. Section 469. This is another anti-tax-shelter provision. Both §§ 465 and 469 are discussed in more detail in Chapter 11. Finally, with respect to sales of marketable securities, taxpayers may face limits from § 1091. Section 1091 disallows losses from so-called "wash sales," where a taxpayer sells shares of stock at a loss and then, within a short period following the sale, purchases shares in the same corporation in anticipation of an upturn in the stock price.

(a) TRANSACTIONS WITH RELATED PERSONS

Code: IRC § 267(a)–(d).

Regs: None.

Suppose a taxpayer holds an asset that originally cost $150 but had declined in value to $100. If the taxpayer believes that the asset will regain its value, there is an incentive to engage in a little chicanery. The taxpayer could sell the asset now, realizing a $50 loss. The loss would be recognized if the asset was held for business or investment purposes. Then, the taxpayer could re-acquire the asset and hold it until the value returned to $150. A subsequent sale at that price would cause the realization (and recognition) of a $50 gain. In the grand scheme of things, it all comes out in the wash: a $50 loss is offset by a $50 gain. But because the taxpayer gets the benefit of a deduction *before* having to include the offsetting gain in gross income, the taxpayer actually comes out ahead.

If we assume that the $50 loss deduction saves the taxpayer $10 in federal income tax (a flat rate of 20 percent just for purposes of this example), the taxpayer has the ability to invest the $10 savings so it can grow. By the time the taxpayer has to pay the $10 additional tax from the subsequent $50 gain (assuming tax rates remained constant), the taxpayer may have grown that $10 into $15 or $20 or perhaps more. Add some zeroes to this example and you can see the tremendous benefits that can result from this plan.

Of course, finding a willing buyer might pose a problem. An unrelated third party has no incentive to buy the taxpayer's asset and then sell the asset back to the taxpayer. Furthermore, if the taxpayer does find such a sucker—um, buyer—the Service might well conclude that the transaction is a sham that should be disregarded for federal income tax purposes. But if the taxpayer sells the asset to a related person (like a corporation that the taxpayer controls or the taxpayer's child), the taxpayer's scheme just might work, provided the related person holds the asset and does not immediately sell it back to the taxpayer. That might be acceptable to the taxpayer since the asset will stay "within the family" under the taxpayer's control. Thus, by manipulating the realization rule, the taxpayer can obtain a very significant benefit that the Service would not be able to attack absent statutory arsenal.

Section 267(a) prevents this easy manipulation by disallowing any otherwise deductible loss if the loss results from the sale or exchange of property to a related person. The key, obviously, is determining whether the buyer is related to the taxpayer. Section 267(b) spells out thirteen specific relationships that will trigger disallowance of the loss.

✗ *Problem 4–15* ✗

Willis owns stock in MBI, a publicly traded corporation, which he purchased in Year One for $5,000. In Year Four, when the value of the stock fell to $2,000, Willis sold the stock to his brother, Arnold, for $2,000 cash. Arnold purchased the stock because he was certain that its value would improve. Indeed it did. In Year Seven, Arnold sold the stock to his sister, Kimberly, for $10,000, its fair market value.

(a) What are the federal income tax consequences to Willis arising out of the Year Four sale to Arnold?

(b) What are the federal income tax consequences to Arnold arising out of the Year Seven sale to Kimberly?

(c) How would the answers to (a) and (b) change if Arnold was Willis' brother-in-law?

(b) LIMITATION ON THE DEDUCTIBILITY OF CAPITAL LOSSES

Code: IRC §§ 1211(b); 1212(b); 1222.

Regs: None.

Deducting Capital Losses: The $3,000 Bonus. In Chapter 3 we saw that preferential treatment is accorded to long-term capital gains. The mechanics of that treatment await in Chapter 7, but it is appropriate here to make some mention of the limitation applicable to the deductibility of capital losses.

Just as there are capital gains, there are capital losses. A "capital loss" is simply a loss arising from the sale or exchange of a capital asset. If the capital asset was held by the taxpayer for more than one year prior to the sale or exchange, the taxpayer has a **long-term capital loss**. If the taxpayer held the asset for one year or less, the taxpayer has a **short-term capital loss**.

In theory, capital losses should be used to offset capital gains and ordinary losses should be used to offset ordinary gains. From a revenue perspective, it is no big deal to allow an ordinary loss to offset net capital gains since the ordinary loss would otherwise offset income taxed as high as 35 percent—by offsetting a capital gain, the loss only reduces the amount taxed at the preferential 15 percent rate. On the other hand, capital losses should not offset ordinary gains (or other types of ordinary income, like wages, rents, dividends, interest, and so on) because in those cases the losses are offsetting 35–percent-rate income, not 15–percent-rate income. Not surprisingly, then, § 1211(b) generally limits the deductibility of capital losses to the extent of capital gains. But § 1211(b) also contains a taxpayer-friendly bonus: if capital losses exceed capital gains (what the statute calls a "net capital loss"), up to $3,000 of the excess can be deducted. In other words, up to $3,000 of net capital loss can be used to offset a taxpayer's ordinary income.

Carryover of Excess Capital Losses. If the taxpayer's net capital loss exceeds the $3,000 bonus amount, then the non-deductible portion carries over to the next taxable year. Section 1212(b)(1). Because capital losses come in two types (long-term capital losses and short-term capital losses), it becomes important to know whether the carryover amount consists entirely of long-term capital loss, entirely of short-term capital loss, or some combination of long-term capital loss and short-term capital loss. Section 1212(b)(2) answers this issue in a rather cryptic way. It generally treats the § 1211(b) bonus amount as a short-term capital gain and then looks to the composition of the carryover amount.

Some examples of the foregoing are necessary for a complete understanding of the limitation and carryover rules.

EXAMPLE (1).

	LONG-TERM	SHORT-TERM
GAINS	5,000	0
LOSSES	(3,000)	0
NET	2,000	0

For Year One, TP, an individual, recognized $5,000 in long-term capital gains and $3,000 in long-term capital losses. TP has no other capital gains or losses. The long-term capital losses are fully deductible and offset the long-term capital gains. TP has a "net capital gain" of $2,000. As we saw briefly in Chapter 3 (and will see again in Chapter 7), the $2,000 net capital gain will be taxed at a preferential rate under § 1(h).

EXAMPLE (2).

	LONG-TERM	SHORT-TERM
GAINS	0	5,000
LOSSES	(3,000)	0
NET	(3,000)	5,000

Same as (1), except the $5,000 in capital gains consists entirely of short-term capital gains. Again, the long-term capital losses are fully deductible and offset the short-term capital gains. The remaining $2,000 of short-term capital gains is *not* eligible for a preferential tax rate, as we saw in Chapter 3 (and will see again in Chapter 7).

EXAMPLE (3).

	LONG-TERM	SHORT-TERM
GAINS	5,000	4,000
LOSSES	(3,000)	(5,000)
NET	2,000	(1,000)

Same as (1), except that TP also recognized $4,000 in short-term capital gains and $5,000 in short-term capital losses in Year One. Because the total capital losses ($8,000) do not exceed the total capital gains ($9,000), all of the capital losses are fully deductible. Furthermore, TP has a "net capital gain" of $1,000, the amount by which the "net long-term capital gain" ($2,000) exceeds the "net short-term capital loss" ($1,000). That $1,000 net capital gain will be taxed at a preferential rate under § 1(h).

EXAMPLE (4).

	LONG-TERM	SHORT-TERM
GAINS	5,000	4,000
LOSSES	(3,000)	(9,000)
NET	2,000	(5,000)

Same as (3), except the amount of recognized short-term capital losses in Year One was $9,000. Here, the total capital losses in Year One ($12,000) exceed the total capital gains ($9,000) by $3,000. Under § 1211(b), however, TP may deduct all of the capital losses in Year One because this excess does not exceed $3,000. The $12,000 deduction will offset all of TP's capital gains ($9,000) and even $3,000 of ordinary income from Year One.

EXAMPLE (5).

	LONG-TERM	SHORT-TERM
GAINS	5,000	4,000
LOSSES	(3,000)	(14,000)
NET	2,000	(10,000)

Same as (3), except the amount of recognized short-term capital losses in Year One was $14,000. This time, the total capital losses in Year One ($17,000) exceed the total capital gains ($9,000) by $8,000. Under § 1211(b), TP can deduct $3,000 of this excess in Year One. The remaining $5,000 comprises TP's "net capital loss." Under § 1212(b), that net capital loss will carry over to Year Two. In order to determine the flavor of that carryover amount, § 1212(b)(2)(A) tells us to treat the $3,000 bonus under § 1211(b) as a short-term capital gain:

	LONG-TERM	SHORT-TERM
GAINS	5,000	4,000 + **3,000** [§ 1211(b)]
LOSSES	(3,000)	(14,000)
NET	2,000	(7,000)

Section 1212(b)(1)(A) says that to the extent the net short-term capital loss (now $7,000, thanks to the modification by § 1212(b)(2)(A) described above) exceeds the net long-term gain ($2,000), the excess shall be treated as a short-term capital loss in Year Two. Thus, the entire $5,000 carryover will be flavored as a short-term capital loss in Year Two. TP can use that carryover amount to offset capital gains (and maybe up to $3,000 of ordinary income) recognized in Year Two.

EXAMPLE (6).

	LONG-TERM	SHORT-TERM
GAINS	5,000	4,000
LOSSES	(13,000)	(14,000)
NET	(8,000)	(10,000)

Same as (5), except that TP recognized long-term capital losses of $13,000 in Year One. Total capital losses ($27,000) exceed total capital gains ($9,000) by a whopping $18,000. We know that TP can use $3,000 of that excess in Year One to offset ordinary income under § 1211(b). The remaining $15,000 excess will be carried over to Year Two. To flavor that carryover, we again account for the $3,000 bonus as short-term capital gain.

	LONG-TERM	SHORT-TERM
GAINS	5,000	4,000 + **3,000** [§ 1211(b)]
LOSSES	(13,000)	(14,000)
NET	(8,000)	(7,000)

Under § 1212(b)(1)(A), the excess of the net short-term capital loss (now $7,000) over the net long-term capital gain (none) carries over as short-term capital loss. Under § 1212(b)(1)(B), the excess of the net long-term capital loss ($8,000) over the net short-term capital gain (none) carries over as long-term capital loss. Thus, the $15,000 carryover to Year Two will consist of $8,000 in long-term capital losses and $7,000 in short-term capital losses.

Riveting, ain't it?

* * *

*

Part Three

A HARD STARE

Chapter 5

STATUTORY EXCLUSIONS FROM GROSS INCOME

Part Two of the text taught us what is meant by "gross income." Recall that under *Glenshaw Glass*, the general test is whether a taxpayer has an *accession to wealth, clearly realized, and over which the taxpayer has complete dominion and control.* Although lots of receipts fall within this very broad definition, Congress has specifically identified receipts that should not be subject to federal income tax even if they meet the *Glenshaw Glass* test for inclusion. Most of the exclusion provisions are grouped together in the Code (§§ 101–139), so it is fairly easy to determine whether an exclusion is available for any given item of income.

We have already encountered several exclusion provisions. We learned that gifts are excluded from gross income under § 102(a), certain forms of income from the discharge of indebtedness are excluded under § 108, meals and lodging furnished to an employee for the convenience of the employer are excluded under § 119, and various statutory fringe benefits received by employees are excluded under § 132. In this Chapter, we study several other exclusions from gross income. As we do so, decide for yourself whether proper tax policy supports each such exclusion.

A. ANNUITY AND LIFE INSURANCE PROCEEDS

Code: IRC §§ 72(a)–(c); 101(a), (c), (d), (g). *Skim* IRC § 79.

Regs: Treas. Reg. §§ 1.72–9, Table V; 1.101–4(c).

Income Taxation of Annuities. An **annuity** is simply a series of cash payments received by a taxpayer. In the most ordinary case, a taxpayer pays a premium to an annuity provider (often an insurance company) in exchange for the right to regular fixed payments later in life. Annuity payments can be fixed for a term of years or can extend for the life of the recipient.

Annuities are an investment, and like any investment, a taxpayer has a basis in the right to future payments. When a taxpayer receives an annuity payment, there is an issue as to how much of the payment represents a return of the taxpayer's basis. For example, assume Myrtle bought an annuity contract for $1,000 in Year One. The contract provides that Myrtle will begin receiving payments of $500 for ten years beginning in Year Sixteen. When Myrtle receives the first $500 payment in Year Sixteen, how should it be characterized for tax purposes?

There are two possible approaches. One approach is to allow Myrtle to recover her basis before taxing any annuity payments as income. Thus, the first two $500 payments would be a return of capital (and thus tax-free) to Myrtle. The remaining eight payments would then be fully taxable, like gain on the annuity. The other approach would be to apportion the basis over the ten-year payout period. Under this model, $400 of each annuity payment would be included in gross income, and the remaining $100 of each payment would represent a return of capital.

Section 72 uses the latter approach. Though it uses other, fancier terms for basis ("investment in the contract") and gain (amounts in excess of the "exclusion ratio"), the statute acts in a fairly straight-forward manner. Although § 72(a) is not technically an exclusion provision (since it requires inclusion in gross income), the application of the "exclusion ratio" in § 72(b) operates to exclude a portion of each annuity payment from gross income. The purpose of the exclusion in this case is easy to spot and well accepted: a taxpayer should be allowed to recover his or her original investment, one likely made with after-tax dollars, without incurring additional tax.

Things get more complicated when the annuity contract provides for payments over the lifetime of the annuitant (the taxpayer receiving the payments). We cannot apportion the taxpayer's basis over ten years, for example, because we do not know for sure that the taxpayer will live that long or that payments will not continue beyond then. In those cases, we have to use life expectancy tables approved by Treasury to determine the "expected return" under the contract. Once we know the annuitant's life expectancy, it's all a matter of applying the statute.

* * *

Self-Assessment Question

(Solutions to Self–Assessment Questions are set forth in Appendix 3.)

SAQ 5–1. Meade, age 59, purchased an annuity contract for $100,000. The contract provides that Meade will receive $10,000 annually for the rest of his life, beginning in the current year.

(a) How much of the first $10,000 payment will be included in Meade's gross income? Consult Treas. Reg. § 1.72–9, Table V, for applicable life expectancy figures.

(b) Suppose Meade dies after having received only four annual payments. What happens to his remaining basis in the contract?

(c) Suppose instead that Meade is still alive in the 26th year of the contract. Going forward, how much of each payment will be included in his gross income?

* * *

The Exclusion for Life Insurance Proceeds. Section 101(a)(1) permits taxpayers to exclude amounts received under a life insurance contract if such amounts were paid because of the death of the insured. In most cases, the death benefit received by a taxpayer exceeds the aggregate premium payments made by the owner of the policy. If, therefore, the death benefit is not excluded as a return of capital, what is the basis for the exclusion? It might be simply that the insurance industry is a powerful force on Capitol Hill. Or maybe Congress thinks that death benefits are often used to pay for subsistence needs of the designated beneficiaries, so taxing those benefits as income would be particularly cruel.

There are two exceptions to the general rule of exclusion. The first is the **transfer-for-value rule** contained in § 101(a)(2). If the owner-beneficiary of the policy acquired the policy for "valuable consideration," the exclusion is limited to the sum of such consideration paid and any amounts (including premiums) paid after the transfer by the owner-beneficiary. This is a very broad exception, and one that, in practice, works as a trap for unsuspecting taxpayers. For that reason, alarm bells should always sound off in one's head whenever an insurance policy is transferred from one owner to another.

The other exception applies to **installment payments after death**. Under § 101(d), to the extent any installment payment of a death benefit represents interest (rent for the use of money), such portion shall be included in gross income. Only the portion representing the death benefit (the principal) should be excluded. In applying this rule, the Code simply divides the gross death benefit by the number of payments to be made. Each payment thus represents an equal portion of the death benefit. Suppose, for example, that a policy pays a death benefit of $45,000 annually for five years. If the lump sum death benefit was $200,000, the portion of each annual payment that would be excluded from gross income would be $40,000 ($200,000 allocated over five annual payments). The extra $5,000 paid each year will be included as ordinary income.

Surrendering a Life Insurance Policy. Section 101(a) generally states that death benefits under a life insurance policy are tax-free to the designated beneficiary. In some cases, however, life insurance is used as an investment vehicle. So-called "whole" life insurance policies feature a constant premium, unlike "term" insurance policies where the premium increases each year to reflect the greater probability of death. In the early years of a "whole" life policy, the excess of the level premium amount over the term premium amount is invested. The policy thus builds what is called a "cash surrender value," the amount that is paid to the owner of the policy if the policy is surrendered, or terminated, before the insured's death. Sometimes the cash surrender value even grows above the death benefit—in those cases, the owners are better off to surrender the policy and take the higher cash value. But since those payments are not paid "by reason of the death of the insured," § 101(a) does not apply.

Instead, § 72 applies, since they are amounts received "under [a] ... life insurance contract." If a policy is surrendered and the owner receives cash, the cash is gross income to the extent it exceeds the aggregate premiums paid by the owner (what you and I would call "basis"). Section 72(a) and (e)(6).

Payments to Terminally Ill and Chronically Ill Insureds. In the past decade, terminally ill individuals have taken to cashing out life insurance policies before death to pay for rising medical care expenses. Section 101(g)(1) now provides an exclusion for these early cash-outs as long as the owner-insured is either "terminally ill" or "chronically ill." These terms are defined in § 101(g)(4). Section 101(g)(2) offers a similar exclusion to taxpayers who sell their insurance policies to "viatical settlement companies" in exchange for a lump sum cash payment—the gain will be excluded from gross income.

A Brief Primer on Life Insurance Policies. New to the concepts of "term insurance" and "whole life insurance?" A brief explanation of the concepts may be helpful in contextualizing the federal income tax issues. As alluded to above, there are two major types of life insurance policies: term insurance and permanent ("whole") insurance.

Term insurance provides the beneficiary with a fixed death benefit if the insured dies within a given period. Typically, the term lasts for one year. At the end of the term, the policy expires. There is no "cash value" or other savings element in a typical term policy. There is such a thing as "renewable term insurance," where the owner pays the premium at regular intervals and, so long as payments continue, the policy remains in force. While the stated death benefit of renewable term insurance remains fixed, the premium increases every year. That is due to the fact that the insured has a greater chance of dying as each year passes. Cheery thought, ay?

But wait—there's more! Individuals can even acquire "level premium term insurance," where the premiums stay level for a period of years (five, 15, even 30 years). The initial premiums with this kind of policy are higher than the premiums for renewable term insurance, but at least the premiums will not increase during the stated period. If the insured survives to the end of the period, he or she must "re-enter" (medically re-qualify) for another period. If the insured does not medically qualify, continuing coverage is usually available but at a much more expensive price.

Employees may also receive so-called "group term insurance" through their employers. Group term insurance is simply renewable term insurance paid for by employers and available to full-time employees on a group basis. In most cases, an employee who retires or otherwise terminates employment may convert the group term coverage to individual coverage without having to undergo new medical tests. In most cases, the conversion must be made within a month after the termination of employment. Under § 79, qualifying group term arrangements confer a special exclusion for employees: they may exclude the first $50,000 of employer-paid group term coverage from gross income.

It is said that **whole life insurance** gets its name from the fact that premiums are payable for the insured's whole life. Thus, the owner pays a fixed premium for the life of the insured (though in some whole life policies, the premium increases by some fixed percentage on certain anniversary dates). Whole life insurance includes not only a death benefit but also a guaranteed cash value. As long as premiums are paid timely, the insurer bears the risk if the guaranteed amounts are not met through investment of the premium payments. Many whole life policies pay dividends. The dividends can be used in many ways, but usually they are used: (1) to purchase additions to the cash value or the death benefit; or (2) to reduce future premium payments.

The key advantage to whole life policies is that once the dividends exceed the premium amount due, they can be used to reduce the premium amount and then buy more cash value and death benefit additions. It can often reach a point where no further premiums are required and yet the cash value and death benefit amounts continue to grow. Moreover, because the policy features a cash value, the policy has an investment aspect separate from the death benefit. Prior to death, the owner-insured can cancel the policy and receive the cash value. The receipt of the cash value is tax-free to the extent of the total premiums paid. If the cash value at termination is less than the total premiums paid, no loss is allowed for federal income tax purposes.

* * *

Self-Assessment Questions

(Solutions to Self–Assessment Questions are set forth in Appendix 3.)

SAQ 5–2. Beverly died in the current year. She owned an insurance policy on her life that would pay $100,000 to her son, Wesley. The policy gave Wesley several options for receipt of the death benefit. What would be the federal income tax consequences in the current year to Wesley if:

(a) Wesley simply accepted the $100,000 death benefit in one lump sum immediately after Beverly's death?

(b) Wesley left all of the proceeds with the insurance company until next year and the insurance company paid him $10,000 interest in the current year?

(c) In lieu of the lump sum, Wesley elected to have the insurance company pay him $12,000 annually for the rest of his life? Assume that Wesley receives the first payment in the current year and that he is expected to live for 25 years. Describe the tax consequences arising only in the current year.

SAQ 5–3. Are premium payments made by a taxpayer with respect to a life insurance contract deductible if the taxpayer is the insured? Would the answer change if someone other than the taxpayer was the insured (assuming the taxpayer has an insurable interest and thus a valid and enforceable contract)?

* * *

Problem 5–1

Mario agreed to play professional hockey for Penguin Corporation. The corporation, afraid that Mario might not survive, acquired a $1,000,000 insurance policy on Mario's life. The corporation paid $20,000 for a two-year term policy.

(a) If Mario dies during the two-year term, what are the federal income tax consequences to the corporation upon receipt of the $1,000,000 death benefit?

(b) How would your answer to (a) change if the policy was originally owned by Mario and he sold the policy to the corporation for $20,000 cash? Assume that after the purchase, the corporation named itself the beneficiary of the policy.

(c) How would your answer to (b) change if Mario was the majority shareholder in Penguin Corporation?

Problem 5–2

Three years ago, Yoko purchased a single-premium life insurance policy that would pay a $100,000 death benefit to her chosen beneficiary. Yoko paid $40,000 for the policy.

(a) In the current year, Yoko sold the policy to her son, Sean, for its $60,000 fair market value. Yoko died later in the current year, and the $100,000 death benefit was paid to Sean. What are the federal income tax consequences of these facts to Yoko and Sean?

(b) Assume instead that Yoko was certified by her physician as "terminally ill." She then sold the policy to a viatical settlement company for $60,000 in the current year. The company collected the $100,000 death benefit upon Yoko's death later in the current year. Describe the tax consequences to Yoko and the viatical settlement company.

B. SCHOLARSHIPS AND FELLOWSHIPS

Code: IRC §§ 74(a); 117. *Skim* IRC §§ 127; 135.

Regs: Treas. Reg. §§ 1.117–3(a)–(c); 1.117–4(c). Proposed Treas. Reg. § 1.117–6(b)–(c)(3)(i), (d).

Under § 74(a), prizes and awards are included in gross income, although the same result would follow even if *Glenshaw Glass* was the only relevant authority. Since scholarships fit within the general framework of a "prize" or "award," they are generally included in gross income. Section 117(a), however, contains two exclusions for certain types of scholarships.

First, § 117(a) excludes **qualified scholarships** received by degree candidates at a nonprofit educational organization, so long as such amounts are not payments for teaching, research, or other services. To be a qualified scholarship, a payment must be used for "qualified tuition" (tuition and certain fees) and "related expenses" (books, supplies, or required equipment) only. Section 117(b). Furthermore, the payment must constitute a "scholarship or fellowship" grant. The *Bingler* case below is instructive as to this requirement.

Second, § 117(d)(1) excludes **qualified tuition reductions**, defined in § 117(d)(2) as tuition reductions given to employees of certain educational organizations for the education of the employee, the employee's spouse, or the employee's children. If such reductions are only available for highly-compensated employees, however, the exclusion is not available. Notice generally that such reductions are excluded only if the student pursues education below the graduate level.

BINGLER v. JOHNSON, 394 U.S. 741, 89 S.Ct. 1439, 22 L.Ed.2d 695 (1969).

Facts: The taxpayers were awarded the Westinghouse Fellowship. The fellowship gave participants a unique opportunity to engage in a combined work-study program conducted in two phases. In the "work-study phase," participants worked on a substantially full-time basis for Westinghouse Corporation, though they were released from work for eight hours each week to attend classes. Participants were paid compensation for their services during this phase. In the "dissertation phase," participants were released from their work duties in order to work on a pre-approved dissertation. During this phase, participants continued to receive between 80 and 90 percent of the pay they received during the first phase.

Issue: Under these terms, is the Westinghouse Fellowship a "scholarship or fellowship" grant eligible for the exclusion in § 117(a)?

Holding: No. The compensation received by the fellowship recipients, together with the fair market value of other benefits provided to the recipients, must be included in gross income.

Rationale: Scholarships and fellowships represent the receipt of "relatively disinterested, 'no-strings' educational grants, with no requirement of any substantial *quid pro quo* from the recipients." Since the Westinghouse Fellowships clearly required the performance of services for the benefit of the grantor, Westinghouse, they do not come within the scope of a scholarship or fellowship for purposes of § 117(a).

* * *

Problem 5–3

To what extent can a law student exclude the following receipts from gross income?

(a) A $10,000 scholarship from The Human Fund, a non-profit organization dedicated to providing educational assistance to those with professional interests in architecture, marine biology, or law. Assume that although The Human Fund directs all scholarship recipients to use awards for tuition, books, and supplies, $7,000 of the scholarship is used to pay tuition to an accredited law school, and that the remaining $3,000 is used to pay for the student's housing costs. Further assume that the student is not required to perform any substantial services as a condition to receiving the award.

(b) Free on-campus housing provided in exchange for the student's services as a residence hall supervisor. To respond to emergencies and disciplinary issues, the student must be present and available in the campus residence halls on all weeknights and every other weekend. In addition to free housing, the student also receives free meals at the campus dining hall.

✗ Problem 5–4 ✗

As an undergraduate student at the University of the Great Lakes at York (UGLY), Stu Dent is required to pay $25,000 tuition. Stu made the tuition payment by obtaining funds from the five different sources described below. Describe the federal income tax consequences of each such receipt.

(a) $5,000 from Stu's summer employer, a fast-food restaurant, in recognition of his superior customer service and deep-fat-frying skills.

(b) $5,000 from Stu's parents, Bucky and Polly. *excluded – this is a gift*

(c) $5,000 tuition waiver from UGLY, a benefit made available to all spouses and children of all UGLY employees (Polly is a professor of dentistry at UGLY and an UGLY alumnus). *excluded*

(d) $5,000 from Bucky's employer, the Union Pacific Railroad, pursuant to a competitive merit scholarship program limited to children of current Union Pacific employees. *included?*

(e) $5,000 stipend to serve as a research assistant for one of Stu's professors in the history department. *Included in gross income b/c payment is for research.*

* * *

Student Athletes. At many major colleges and universities, students recruited to participate in athletic competitions receive "full-ride" scholarships. These awards are clearly compensation for services that would seem to be disqualified for the exclusion under § 117(c), but taxing those awards proves to be quite cumbersome because students lack the funds to pay the federal income tax liability that would result from the inclusion of a full-ride scholarship in gross income. In *Revenue Ruling 77–263*, 1977–2 C.B. 47, the Service concluded that an athletic scholarship qualifies for the § 117(a) exclusion as a "scholarship," but only if the university does *not* require: (1) that the recipient must participate in a particular sport; (2) that the recipient must engage in some particular activity in lieu of participation in a sport; and (3) forfeiture of the award if the student does not participate in a particular sport. Of course, a university will expect the student to participate. But absent some strong-arm requirement of participation, the scholarship can be excluded provided it is used to pay for qualified tuition and related expenses.

Since 2003, the National Collegiate Athletic Association, the governing body for intercollegiate athletics, permits student athletes to accumulate frequent-flier miles earned during travel to and from intercollegiate competitions. The NCAA concluded that conferring this "miscellaneous benefit" to athletes is appropriate as it imposes no cost or burden on the athlete's school. Yet the benefit can be quite significant. In the 2002–03 season, for example, athletes on the University of Hawaii's men's basketball and women's swimming teams each flew approximately 57,400 miles. If the fair market value of a frequent-flier mile is two cents, as estimated by some industry analysts, each Hawaii athlete would have received about $1,150 if the rule had been in effect then. Should this "miscellaneous benefit" be taxed?

Other Education–Related Exclusions. In addition to the exclusion for scholarships in § 117, two other Code provisions grant an exclusion for income items related to education. Section 127 allows employees to exclude up to $5,250 of educational assistance furnished by their employers if such assistance is provided through an "educational assistance program." Qualified educational assistance need not relate to courses at a college or university; the exclusion broadly covers most payments of educational expenses on behalf of an employee, including tuition, fees, books, supplies, and equipment. Three notable exceptions apply: (1) for the payment or provision of tools or supplies that the employee retains after completing the course of study; (2) for the provision of meals, lodging, or transportation costs; and (3) for courses involving sports, games, or hobbies. See § 127(c)(1).

As its title implies, § 135 excludes income from United States savings bonds used to pay higher education tuition and fees. The amount excludable under this section begins to phase out for taxpayers with adjusted gross incomes (subject to certain modifications) in 2007 above $65,600 ($98,400 in the case of married couples filing joint returns). This exclusion completely phases out for taxpayers with adjusted gross incomes (as modified) in 2007 of $80,600 or more ($128,400 or more for joint returns). See § 135(b)(2) and *Revenue Procedure 2006–53*, 2006–48 I.R.B. 996. Interestingly, the exclusion is unavailable to married taxpayers who file separate returns. See § 135(d)(3). The 135 exclusion also does not apply to tuition and fees paid for courses involving sports, games, or hobbies unless such courses are part of a degree program.

C. COMPENSATION FOR PERSONAL INJURIES & SICKNESS

Code: IRC § 104(a). *Skim* IRC §§ 105; 106.

Regs: None.

Personal Injury Lawyers Rejoice! Sections 104–106 all address amounts received by taxpayers as compensation for injuries and sickness. Section 104 gives the general exclusion applicable to all taxpayers, and §§ 105 and 106 contain special provisions for employee-taxpayers. For our purposes, the most important provision at issue is § 104(a)(2), which excludes damages received "on account of personal physical injuries or physical sickness." Section 104(a)(2) has undergone several significant legislative and judicial changes in the past decade—it has had more face lifts than Liz Taylor. Section 104(a)(2) used to exclude all damages received on account of "personal injury or sickness," and the special provision in the flush language to § 104(a) did not exist. The following case describes some of the more significant developments in this regard.

AMOS v. COMMISSIONER

United States Tax Court, 2003.
T.C. Memo. 2003–329.

CHIECHI, JUDGE: * * *

* * *

FINDINGS OF FACT

* * *

During 1997, petitioner was employed as a television cameraman. In that capacity, on January 15, 1997, petitioner was operating a handheld camera during a basketball game between the Minnesota Timberwolves and the Chicago Bulls. At some point during that game, Dennis Keith Rodman (Mr. Rodman), who was playing for the Chicago Bulls, landed on a group of photographers, including petitioner, and twisted his ankle. Mr. Rodman then kicked petitioner. (We shall refer to the foregoing incident involving Mr. Rodman and petitioner as the incident.)

On January 15, 1997, shortly after the incident, petitioner was taken by ambulance for treatment at Hennepin County Medical Center. Petitioner informed the medical personnel at that medical center (Hennepin County medical personnel) that he had experienced shooting pain to his neck immediately after having been kicked in the groin, but that such pain was subsiding. The Hennepin County medical personnel observed that petitioner was able to walk, but that he was limping and complained of experiencing pain. The Hennepin County medical personnel did not observe any other obvious signs of trauma. Petitioner informed the Hennepin County medical personnel that he was currently taking pain medication for a preexisting back condition. The Hennepin

County medical personnel offered additional pain medications to petitioner, but he refused those medications. After a dispute with the Hennepin County medical personnel concerning an unrelated medical issue, petitioner left Hennepin County Medical Center without having been discharged by them.

While petitioner was seeking treatment at Hennepin County Medical Center, he contacted Gale Pearson (Ms. Pearson) about representing him with respect to the incident. Ms. Pearson was an attorney who had experience in representing plaintiffs in personal injury lawsuits. After subsequent conversations and a meeting with petitioner, Ms. Pearson agreed to represent him with respect to the incident.

* * *

Very shortly after the incident on a date not disclosed by the record, Andrew Luger (Mr. Luger), an attorney representing Mr. Rodman with respect to the incident, contacted Ms. Pearson. Several discussions and a few meetings took place between Ms. Pearson and Mr. Luger. Petitioner accompanied Ms. Pearson to one of the meetings between her and Mr. Luger, at which time Mr. Luger noticed that petitioner was limping. Shortly after those discussions and meetings, petitioner and Mr. Rodman reached a settlement.

On January 21, 1997, Mr. Rodman and petitioner executed a document entitled "CONFIDENTIAL SETTLEMENT AGREEMENT AND RELEASE" (settlement agreement). The settlement agreement provided in pertinent part:

> For and in consideration of TWO HUNDRED THOUSAND DOLLARS ($200,000), the mutual waiver of costs, attorneys' fees and legal expenses, if any, and other good and valuable consideration, the receipt and sufficiency of which is hereby acknowledged, Eugene Amos [petitioner], on behalf of himself, his agents, representatives, attorneys, assignees, heirs, executors and administrators, hereby releases and forever discharges Dennis Rodman, the Chicago Bulls, the National Basketball Association and all other persons, firms and corporations together with their subsidiaries, divisions and affiliates, past and present officers, directors, employees, insurers, agents, personal representatives and legal counsel, from any and all claims and causes of action of any type, known and unknown, upon and by reason of any damage, loss or injury which heretofore have been or heretoafter may be sustained by Amos arising, or which could have arisen, out of or in connection with an incident occurring between Rodman and Amos at a game between the Chicago Bulls and the Minnesota Timberwolves on January 15, 1997 during which Rodman allegedly kicked Amos ("the Incident"), including but not limited to any statements made after the Incident or subsequent conduct relating to the Incident by Amos, Rodman, the Chicago Bulls, the National Basketball Association, or any other person, firm or corporation, or any of their subsidiaries, divisions, affiliates, officers, directors, employees, insurers, agents, personal representa-

tives and legal counsel. This Agreement and Release includes, but is not limited to claims, demands, or actions arising under the common law and under any state, federal or local statute, ordinance, regulation or order, including claims known or unknown at this time, concerning any physical, mental or emotional injuries that may arise in the future allegedly resulting from the Incident.

* * *

It is further understood and agreed that the payment of the sum described herein is not to be construed as an admission of liability and is a compromise of a disputed claim. It is further understood that part of the consideration for this Agreement and Release includes an agreement that Rodman and Amos shall not at any time from the date of this Agreement and Release forward disparage or defame each other. It is further understood and agreed that, as part of the consideration for this Agreement and Release, the terms of this Agreement and Release shall forever be kept confidential and not released to any news media personnel or representatives thereof or to any other person, entity, company, government agency, publication or judicial authority for any reason whatsoever except to the extent necessary to report the sum paid to appropriate taxing authorities or in response to any subpoena issued by a state or federal governmental agency or court of competent jurisdiction * * * Any court reviewing a subpoena concerning this Agreement and Release should be aware that part of the consideration for the Agreement and Release is the agreement of Amos and his attorneys not to testify regarding the existence of the Agreement and Release or any of its terms.

* * *

It is further understood and agreed that Amos and his representatives, agents, legal counsel or other advisers shall not, from the date of this Agreement and Release, disclose, disseminate, publicize or instigate or solicit any others to disclose, disseminate or publicize, any of the allegations or facts relating to the Incident, including but not limited to any allegations or facts or opinions relating to Amos' potential claims against Rodman or any allegations, facts or opinions relating to Rodman's conduct on the night of January 15, 1997 or thereafter concerning Amos. In this regard, Amos agrees not to make any further public statement relating to Rodman or the Incident or to grant any interviews relating to Rodman or the Incident. * * *

It is further understood and agreed that any material breach by Amos or his attorney, agent or representative of the terms of this Agreement and Release will result in immediate and irreparable damage to Rodman, and that the extent of such damage would be difficult, if not impossible, to ascertain. To discourage any breach of the terms of this Agreement and Release, and to compensate Rodman should any such breach occur, it is understood and agreed that

Amos shall be liable for liquidated damages in the amount of TWO HUNDRED THOUSAND and No/100 Dollars ($200,000) in the event such a material breach occurs. Amos agrees that this sum constitutes a reasonable calculation of the damages Rodman would incur due to a material breach.

It is further understood and agreed, that, in the event Rodman or Amos claim a material breach of this Agreement and Release has occurred, either party may schedule a confidential hearing before an arbitrator of the American Arbitration Association for a final, binding determination as to whether a material breach has occurred. If, after the hearing, the arbitrator finds that Amos has committed a material breach, the arbitrator shall order that Amos pay the sum of $200,000 in liquidated damages to Rodman. * * *

Amos further represents, promises and agrees that no administrative charge or claim or legal action of any kind has been asserted by him or on his behalf in any way relating to the Incident with the exception of a statement given by Amos to the Minneapolis Police Department. Amos further represents, promises and agrees that, as part of the consideration for this Agreement and Release, he has communicated to the Minneapolis Police Department that he does not wish to pursue a criminal charge against Rodman, and that he has communicated that he will not cooperate in any criminal investigation concerning the Incident. Amos further represents, promises and agrees that he will not pursue any criminal action against Rodman concerning the Incident, that he will not cooperate should any such action or investigation ensue, and that he will not encourage, incite or solicit others to pursue a criminal investigation or charge against Rodman concerning the Incident.

Petitioner filed a tax return (return) for his taxable year 1997. In that return, petitioner excluded from his gross income the $200,000 that he received from Mr. Rodman under the settlement agreement.

       * * *

Opinion

We must determine whether the settlement amount at issue may be excluded from petitioner's gross income for 1997. Petitioner bears the burden of proving that the determination in the notice to include the settlement amount at issue in petitioner's gross income is erroneous.

       * * *

The Supreme Court summarized the requirements of section 104(a)(2) as follows:

In sum, the plain language of section 104(a)(2), the text of the applicable regulation, and our decision in [*United States v.*] *Burke* [504 U.S. 229 (1992)] establish two independent requirements that a taxpayer must meet before a recovery may be excluded under section 104(a)(2). First, the taxpayer must demonstrate that the underlying cause of action giving rise to the recovery is "based upon tort or tort type rights"; and second, the taxpayer must show that the damages were received "on account of personal injuries or sickness." * * * (*Commissioner v. Schleier*, [515 U.S. 323 (1995)] at 336–337.)

When the Supreme Court issued its opinion in *Commissioner v. Schleier*, *supra*, section 104(a)(2), as in effect for the year at issue in *Schleier*, required, *inter alia*, that, in order to be excluded from gross income, an amount of damages had to be received "on account of personal injuries or sickness." After the Supreme Court issued its opinion in *Schleier*, Congress amended (1996 amendment) section 104(a)(2), effective for amounts received after August 20, 1996, by adding the requirement that, in order to be excluded from gross income, any amounts received must be on account of personal injuries that are physical or sickness that is physical. Small Business Job Protection Act of 1996, Pub. L. 104–188, sec. 1605, 110 Stat. 1755, 1838–1839. The 1996 amendment does not otherwise change the requirements of section 104(a)(2) or the analysis set forth in *Commissioner v. Schleier*, *supra*; it imposes an additional requirement for an amount to qualify for exclusion from gross income under that section.

Where damages are received pursuant to a settlement agreement, such as is the case here, the nature of the claim that was the actual basis for settlement controls whether such damages are excludable under section 104(a)(2). *United States v. Burke*, *supra* at 237. The determination of the nature of the claim is factual. *Robinson v. Commissioner*, 102 T.C. 116, 126 (1994), affd. in part, revd. in part, and remanded on another issue 70 F.3d 34 (5th Cir. 1995); *Seay v. Commissioner*, 58 T.C. 32, 37 (1972). Where there is a settlement agreement, that determination is usually made by reference to it. See *Knuckles v. Commissioner*, 349 F.2d 610, 613 (10th Cir. 1965), affg. *T.C. Memo. 1964–33*; *Robinson v. Commissioner*, *supra*. If the settlement agreement lacks express language stating what the amount paid pursuant to that agreement was to settle, the intent of the payor is critical to that determination. *Knuckles v. Commissioner*, *supra*; see also *Agar v. Commissioner*, 290 F.2d 283, 284 (2d Cir. 1961), affg. per curiam *T.C. Memo. 1960–21*. Although the belief of the payee is relevant to that inquiry, the character of the settlement payment hinges ultimately on the dominant reason of the payor in making the payment. *Agar v. Commissioner*, *supra*; *Fono v. Commissioner*, 79 T.C. 680, 696 (1982), affd. without published opinion 749 F.2d 37 (9th Cir. 1984). Whether the settlement payment is excludable from gross income under section 104(a)(2) depends on the nature and character of the claim asserted, and not upon the validity of that claim. See *Bent v. Commissioner*, 87 T.C. 236, 244 (1986), affd. 835 F.2d 67 (3d Cir. 1987); *Glynn v. Commissioner*, 76 T.C. 116, 119 (1981), affd. without published opinion 676 F.2d 682 (1st Cir. 1982); *Seay v. Commissioner*, *supra*.

The dispute between the parties in the instant case relates to how much of the settlement amount at issue Mr. Rodman paid to petitioner on account of physical injuries. It is petitioner's position that the entire $200,000 settlement amount at issue is excludable from his gross income under section 104(a)(2). In support of that position, petitioner contends that Mr. Rodman paid him the entire amount on account of the physical injuries that he claimed he sustained as a result of the incident.

Respondent counters that, except for a nominal amount (i.e., $1), the settlement amount at issue is includable in petitioner's gross income. In support of that position, respondent contends that petitioner has failed to introduce any evidence regarding, and that Mr. Rodman was skeptical about, the extent of petitioner's physical injuries as a result of the incident. Consequently, according to respondent, the Court should infer that petitioner's physical injuries were minimal. In further support of respondent's position to include all but $1 of the settlement amount at issue in petitioner's gross income, respondent contends that, because the amount of any liquidated damages (i.e., $200,000) payable by petitioner to Mr. Rodman under the settlement agreement was equal to the settlement amount (i.e., $200,000) paid to petitioner under that agreement, Mr. Rodman did not intend to pay the settlement amount at issue in order to compensate petitioner for his physical injuries.

On the instant record, we reject respondent's position. With respect to respondent's contentions that petitioner has failed to introduce evidence regarding, and that Mr. Rodman was skeptical about, the extent of petitioner's physical injuries as a result of the incident, those contentions appear to ignore the well-established principle under section 104(a)(2) that it is the nature and character of the claim settled, and not its validity, that determines whether the settlement payment is excludable from gross income under section 104(a)(2). See *Bent v. Commissioner*, *supra*; *Glynn v. Commissioner*, *supra*; *Seay v. Commissioner*, *supra*. In any event, we find below that the record establishes that Mr. Rodman's dominant reason in paying the settlement amount at issue was petitioner's claimed physical injuries as a result of the incident.

With respect to respondent's contention that Mr. Rodman did not intend to pay the settlement amount at issue in order to compensate petitioner for his physical injuries because the amount of liquidated damages (i.e., $200,000) payable by petitioner to Mr. Rodman under the settlement agreement was equal to the settlement amount (i.e., $200,000) paid to petitioner under that agreement, we do not find the amount of liquidated damages payable under the settlement agreement to be determinative of the reason for which Mr. Rodman paid petitioner the settlement amount at issue.

On the record before us, we find that Mr. Rodman's dominant reason in paying the settlement amount at issue was to compensate petitioner for his claimed physical injuries relating to the incident. Our finding is supported by the settlement agreement, a declaration by Mr. Rodman (Mr. Rodman's declaration), and Ms. Pearson's testimony.

The settlement agreement expressly provided that Mr. Rodman's payment of the settlement amount at issue releases and forever discharges * * * [Mr.] Rodman * * * from any and all claims and causes of action of any type, known and unknown, upon and by reason of any damage, loss or injury * * * sustained by Amos [petitioner] arising, or which could have arisen, out of or in connection with * * * [the incident].

Mr. Rodman stated in Mr. Rodman's declaration that he entered into the settlement agreement "to resolve any potential claims" and that the settlement agreement was intended to resolve petitioner's "claim without having to expend additional defense costs." The only potential claims of petitioner that are disclosed by the record are the potential claims that petitioner had for the physical injuries that he claimed he sustained as a result of the incident. Furthermore, Ms. Pearson testified that Mr. Rodman paid the entire settlement amount at issue to petitioner on account of his physical injuries. As discussed below, Ms. Pearson's testimony that Mr. Rodman paid that entire amount on account of petitioner's physical injuries is belied by the terms of the settlement agreement. Nonetheless, her testimony supports our finding that Mr. Rodman's dominant reason in paying petitioner the settlement amount at issue was to compensate him for claimed physical injuries relating to the incident.

We have found that Mr. Rodman's dominant reason in paying petitioner the settlement amount at issue was to compensate him for his claimed physical injuries relating to the incident. However, the settlement agreement expressly provided that Mr. Rodman paid petitioner a portion of the settlement amount at issue in return for petitioner's agreement not to: (1) defame Mr. Rodman, (2) disclose the existence or the terms of the settlement agreement, (3) publicize facts relating to the incident, or (4) assist in any criminal prosecution against Mr. Rodman with respect to the incident (collectively, the nonphysical injury provisions).

The settlement agreement does not specify the portion of the settlement amount at issue that Mr. Rodman paid petitioner on account of his claimed physical injuries and the portion of such amount that Mr. Rodman paid petitioner on account of the nonphysical injury provisions in the settlement agreement. Nonetheless, based upon our review of the entire record before us, and bearing in mind that petitioner has the burden of proving the amount of the settlement amount at issue that Mr. Rodman paid him on account of physical injuries, we find that Mr. Rodman paid petitioner $120,000 of the settlement amount at issue on account of petitioner's claimed physical injuries and $80,000 of that amount on account of the nonphysical injury provisions in the settlement agreement. On that record, we further find that for the year at issue petitioner is entitled under section 104(a)(2) to exclude from his gross income $120,000 of the settlement amount at issue and is required under section 61(a) to include in his gross income $80,000 of that amount.

We have considered all of the contentions and arguments of respondent and of petitioner that are not discussed herein, and we find them to be without merit, irrelevant, and/or moot.

* * *

Notes and Questions

1. By its terms, § 104(a)(2) excludes "any damages" received "on account of" physical injury. There are two ways (perhaps more) to interpret this language. First, the language may mean that all damages are excluded in any case where a physical injury is present. Second, the language may mean that only those damages specifically attributable to a physical injury can be excluded. The *Amos* court clearly applies the latter construction. Writing on a clean slate, would you apply that interpretation as well?

2. In addition to compensation for his physical injury, the taxpayer in *Amos* received compensation for four promises, which the court described as the "non-physical injury provisions" of the settlement agreement: (1) the promise not to defame Dennis Rodman; (2) the promise not to disclose the terms of the settlement agreement; (3) the promise not to publicize facts relating to the "incident;" and (4) the promise not to assist any criminal prosecution against Rodman with respect to the incident. The first promise is a curious one, akin to promising not to commit a tort or promising not to breach a contract. Rodman would be able to recover against the taxpayer even if such a promise was not included in the settlement agreement. The last promise might be unenforceable as a matter of public policy. But the other two promises are likely common provisions in most settlement agreements. Does *Amos* mean that all physical injury plaintiffs who make such promises in a settlement agreement must include at least a portion of the total settlement award in their gross incomes? If so, then the well-advised plaintiff would make sure that the settlement agreement specifically allocates the total settlement award between the damages for physical injury and the consideration paid for these promises.

3. Rodman injured the taxpayer in *Amos* during a professional basketball game in which he was paid to play. Can Rodman rebound from having to pay $200,000 by deducting all or any portion of the amount paid to the taxpayer as a business expense? Is it a slam dunk?

4. The *Amos* court claims it considered all of the facts on record in determining that 60 percent of the total award represented damages for physical injury that were excludable under § 104(a)(2). Yet it is troubling that the court does not explain how it reached this conclusion. If this had been an answer to an essay question on a law school exam, the court would have received a poor grade. Does the lack of an explanation suggest the allocation was arbitrary? Was any satisfactory explanation really possible? Did the court pick 60 percent because it "sensed" that was the right amount? Should judges be held to a higher standard than juries in making these decisions?

 *Problem 5–5*

Paula sued Dennis for injuries stemming from an automobile accident. The accident left Paula unable to maintain full-time employment. The jury determined that Dennis was at fault. The jury awarded Paula total damages of $750,000, broken down by the jury as follows:

Medical Bills	95,000
Lost Wages/Earning Capacity	300,000
Punitive Damages	200,000
Attorney Fees	35,000
Emotional Distress	120,000

Dennis paid the full amount of the judgment later in the same year. To what extent does Paula have gross income?

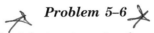 *Problem 5–6*

Peter sued Diane for injuries stemming from a boating accident. Peter recovered $120,000 in compensatory damages and $60,000 in punitive damages from Diane. Pursuant to his contingent fee arrangement with Peter's lawyer, Louise, Peter paid one-third of the total recovery ($60,000) to Louise. What federal income tax consequences arise from these facts?

* * *

JOHNSON v. UNITED STATES, 228 F.Supp.2d 1218 (D. Colo. 2002).

Facts: The taxpayer sued his former employer under the Americans with Disabilities Act (ADA) for failure to make accommodations for his on-the-job injuries and for wrongful termination. The taxpayer recovered a jury award for front and back pay.

Issue: Must the award be included in the taxpayer's gross income?

Holding: Yes.

Rationale: Even though the lawsuit was brought under the ADA and even though the taxpayer's work-related injuries created the condition that required accommodation, the taxpayer's claim was based on discrimination and not on physical injury. The taxpayer argued that but for the physical injuries, the discrimination and wrongful termination would not have occurred, but the court found the connection between the damages and the injuries too remote.

PRIVATE LETTER RULING 200041022 (October 13, 2000).

Facts: Shortly after commencing work as a full-time driver, the taxpayer was the victim of sexual harassment. Her employer made lewd remarks to the taxpayer, and also touched her, though the contact did not leave any "observable bodily harm." On other occasions, however, the taxpayer was the victim of physical and sexual assault by her employer. The taxpayer sued alleging sex discrimination, battery, and intentional infliction of emotional distress. The employer settled the case.

Issue: To what extent must the settlement payment be included in the taxpayer's gross income?

Ruling: The portion of the settlement allocable to the first act of harassment (the remarks and the non-harmful contact) is includible in gross income. The portion of the settlement allocable to the other incidents is excludable under § 104(a)(2).

Rationale: The first act of harassment involved no "observable bodily harm," so these damages are not received on account of physical injury or physical sickness. Observable bodily harm did occur in the other incidents, so the application of the § 104(a)(2) exclusion is proper.

Note and Questions

Private letter rulings are responses issued to requesting taxpayers on issues related to proposed or completed transactions. These rulings bind the Service only with respect to the requesting taxpayer. Indeed, private letter rulings have absolutely no value as precedent. Still, because private rulings are published, practitioners often consult them to discover whether the Service has addressed a certain issue before and whether the Service has ruled consistently on issues that reappear. Understanding that *Private Letter Ruling 200041002* really matters only to the one taxpayer that asked for it, the Service's use of an "observable bodily harm" standard in this ruling is noteworthy. Is the standard useful in other contexts? Was it an appropriate standard to use in the facts at issue?

* * *

Employee Exclusions: §§ 105 and 106. Section 106 contains an exclusion for employer-provided accident and health insurance plans. Without the exclusion, of course, such coverage would be part of the employee's "compensation for services" and would be included in gross income under § 61(a)(1). Of course, once any proceeds from such coverage are paid to the employee, there would be a double benefit to the employee if he or she could also exclude the proceeds. To prevent this double exclusion, Congress provides in § 105 that amounts received under tax-free accident and health insurance plans shall be included in gross income to the extent such amounts do not exceed the amount excluded under § 106.

Suppose, for example, that an employer-provided health insurance plan is worth $2,500 to an employee (measured as the cost to the employee to obtain equivalent coverage on his or her own) and that the employee receives a $10,000 award under the plan in the current year. The $2,500 plan was excluded under § 106, so under § 105, only $7,500 of the $10,000 award will be excluded from gross income.

If the $10,000 award reimburses the taxpayer for expenses incurred in providing medical care to the taxpayer or the taxpayer's family (as specially defined), however, no portion of the award is included in gross income. See § 105(b). Likewise, the award is not subject to inclusion under § 105(a) to the extent it pays for permanent bodily injury or disfigurement, provided the amount of the award is determined with reference to the nature of the injury and not the amount of time away from work. See § 105(c).

Proceeds from accident and health insurance plans not provided by an employer are also excluded from gross income. Section 104(a)(3). Although this exclusion places employees and self-insured individuals on an equal footing, there is nonetheless a preference given to employees who have health coverage under employer-provided plans. A self-employed individual (or an employee whose employer does not provide coverage to employees) must use after-tax dollars to acquire a policy that will pay the same benefits. Although the receipt of benefits will be taxable to an employee participating in an employer-provided plan, such inclusion in gross income will occur (if at all) usually much later. From a time value of money perspective, then, employees participating in an employer-provided plan come out ahead.

Taxation of Non–Injury Damage Awards. If a taxpayer recovers damages *not* on account of physical injury or physical sickness, one might infer from § 104(a)(2) that such damages are included in gross income. But this is not necessarily the case.

It has long been accepted that the receipt of a damage award is taxable if the damages represent lost profits or income. But if damages compensate for loss to capital, the award is included in gross income only to the extent the award exceeds the taxpayer's adjusted basis in the lost capital. *Raytheon Production Corp. v. Commissioner*, 144 F.2d 110 (1st Cir. 1944). In effect, the receipt of damages is akin to a sale or other disposition of the damaged asset.

For instance, suppose a taxpayer owns a widget-making machine with an adjusted basis of $10,000. The machine is damaged by a tortfeasor's negligence. The damage to the machine precludes the taxpayer from producing profitable widgets, so the taxpayer sues the tortfeasor not only for the damage to the machine but also for the taxpayer's lost profits. Now assume that the taxpayer recovers damages from the tortfeasor (whether by judgment, settlement, or otherwise). The taxpayer receives $7,000 compensation for the damage to the machine and $12,000 for lost profits. Because the compensation for the machine does not exceed the taxpayer's adjusted basis in the machine, that portion of the total damages is excluded from gross income (and, naturally, the taxpayer must reduce his or her basis in the machine to $3,000). The $12,000 for lost profits is fully includible in gross income; after all, had there been no damage to the machine, the taxpayer would have included the profits in gross income. If the compensation for the damage to the machine had totaled $11,000, however, then $1,000 of that amount would be included in gross income (and the taxpayer's basis in the machine would be reduced to zero, for all of the taxpayer's remaining cost in the machine has now been recovered).

* * *

Self-Assessment Questions

(Solutions to Self–Assessment Questions are set forth in Appendix 3.)

SAQ 5–4. Old McDonald has a farm. And on that farm, he has some crops. McDonald sued Dale Gribble, an exterminator, for damages to McDonald's crops resulting from Dale's negligent use of insecticide. The parties settled, and Dale paid McDonald a lump sum of $15,000. What are the federal income tax consequences of this payment?

SAQ 5–5. Ten years ago, Lear executed a will that disinherited his daughter, Regan. Five years ago, when Lear was in failing health, he and Regan made amends. Lear promised Regan that he would change his will to make Regan an equal beneficiary with his other daughters, Goneril and Cordelia. Lear died last year without ever changing the will. Regan brought suit against Lear's estate. The suit was settled, and the estate paid $225,000 in one lump sum to Regan. Does Regan have gross income upon receipt of the payment? Why or why not?

* * *

MURPHY v. UNITED STATES

United States Court of Appeals, District of Columbia Circuit, 2006.
460 F.3d 79.

GINSBURG, Chief Judge: Marrita Murphy brought this suit to recover income taxes she paid on the compensatory damages for emotional distress and loss of reputation she was awarded in an administrative action she brought against her former employer. Murphy contends that under § 104(a)(2) of the Internal Revenue Code (IRC) her award should have been excluded from her gross income because it was compensation received "on account of personal physical injuries or physical sickness." In the alternative, she maintains § 104(a)(2) is unconstitutional insofar as it fails to exclude from gross income revenue that is not "income" within the meaning of the Sixteenth Amendment to the Constitution of the United States.

We hold, first, that Murphy's compensation was not "received ... on account of personal physical injuries" excludable from gross income under § 104(a)(2). We agree with the taxpayer, however, that § 104(a)(2) is unconstitutional as applied to her award because compensation for a non-physical personal injury is not income under the Sixteenth Amendment if, as here, it is unrelated to lost wages or earnings.

I. Background

In 1994 Marrita Leveille (now Murphy) filed a complaint with the Department of Labor alleging that her former employer, the New York Air National Guard (NYANG), in violation of various whistle-blower statutes, had "blacklisted" her and provided unfavorable references to potential employers after she had complained to state authorities of environmental hazards on a NYANG airbase. The Secretary of Labor determined the NYANG had unlawfully discriminated and retaliated against Murphy, ordered that any adverse employment references to the taxpayer in Office of Personnel Management files be withdrawn, and remanded her case to an Administrative Law Judge "for findings on compensatory damages."

On remand Murphy submitted evidence that she had suffered both mental and physical injuries as a result of the NYANG's blacklisting her. A physician testified Murphy had sustained "somatic" and "emotional" injuries. One such injury was "bruxism," or teeth grinding often associated with stress, which may cause permanent tooth damage. Upon finding Murphy had also suffered from other "physical manifestations of stress" including "anxiety attacks, shortness of breath, and dizziness," the ALJ recommended compensatory damages totaling $70,000, of which $45,000 was for "emotional distress or mental anguish," and $25,000 was for "injury to professional reputation" from having been blacklisted. None of the award was for lost wages or diminished earning capacity.

In 1999 the Department of Labor Administrative Review Board affirmed the ALJ's findings and recommendations. On her tax return for 2000, Murphy included the $70,000 award in her "gross income" * * *. As a result, she paid $20,665 in taxes on the award.

Murphy later filed an amended return in which she sought a refund of the $20,665 based upon § 104(a)(2) of the IRC, which provides that "gross income does not include . . . damages . . . received . . . on account of personal physical injuries or physical sickness." In support of her amended return, Murphy submitted copies of her dental and medical records. Upon deciding Murphy had failed to demonstrate the compensatory damages were attributable to "physical injury" or "physical sickness," the Internal Revenue Service denied her request for a refund. Murphy thereafter sued the IRS and the United States in the district court.

In her complaint Murphy sought a refund of the $20,665, plus applicable interest * * *. She argued her compensatory award was in fact for "physical personal injuries" and therefore excluded from gross income under § 104(a)(2). In the alternative Murphy asserted § 104(a)(2) as applied to her award was unconstitutional because the award was not "income" within the meaning of the Sixteenth Amendment. The Government moved * * * for summary judgment on all claims.

The district court * * * rejected all Murphy's claims on the merits and granted summary judgment for the Government and the IRS. Murphy now appeals the judgment of the district court with respect to her claims under § 104(a)(2) and the Sixteenth Amendment.

II. ANALYSIS

* * *

B. Section 104(a)(2) of the IRC

Section 104(a) ("Compensation for injuries or sickness") provides that "gross income [under § 61 of the IRC] does not include the amount of any damages (other than punitive damages) received ... on account of personal physical injuries or physical sickness." Since 1996 it has further provided that, for purposes of this exclusion, "emotional distress shall not be treated as a physical injury or physical sickness." The version of § 104(a)(2) in effect prior to 1996 had excluded from gross income monies received in compensation for "personal injuries or sickness," which included both physical and nonphysical injuries such as emotional distress. Id. § 104(a)(2) (1995); see United States v. Burke, 504 U.S. 229, 235 n.6, 112 S. Ct. 1867, 119 L. Ed. 2d 34 (1992) ("§ 104(a)(2) in fact encompasses a broad range of physical and nonphysical injuries to personal interests"). In Commissioner v. Schleier, 515 U.S. 323, 115 S. Ct. 2159, 132 L. Ed. 2d 294 (1995), the Supreme Court held that before a taxpayer may exclude compensatory damages from gross income pursuant to § 104(a)(2), he must first demonstrate that "the underlying cause of action giving rise to the recovery [was] 'based upon tort or tort type rights.' " Id. at 337. The taxpayer has the same burden under the statute as amended. See, e.g., Chamberlain v. United States, 401 F.3d 335, 341 (5th Cir. 2005).

Murphy contends § 104(a)(2), even as amended, excludes her particular award from gross income. First, she asserts her award was "based upon ... tort type rights" in the whistle-blower statutes the NYANG violated—a position the Government does not challenge. Second, she claims she was compensated for "physical" injuries, which claim the Government does dispute.

Murphy points both to her physician's testimony that she had experienced "somatic" and "body" injuries "as a result of NYANG's blacklisting [her]," and to the American Heritage Dictionary, which defines "somatic" as "relating to, or affecting the body, especially as distinguished from a body part, the mind, or the environment." Murphy further argues the dental records she submitted to the IRS proved she has suffered permanent damage to her teeth. Citing Walters v. Mintec/International, 758 F.2d 73, 78 (3d Cir. 1985), and Payne v. General Motors Corp., 731 F. Supp. 1465, 1474–75 (D. Kan. 1990), Murphy contends that "substantial physical problems caused by emotional distress are considered physical injuries or physical sickness."

* * *

For its part, the Government argues Murphy's exclusive focus upon the word "physical" in § 104(a)(2) is misplaced; more important is the phrase "on account of." In O'Gilvie v. United States, 519 U.S. 79, 117 S. Ct. 452, 136 L. Ed. 2d 454 (1996), the Supreme Court read that phrase to require a "strong causal connection," thereby making § 104(a)(2) "applicable only to those personal injury lawsuit damages that were awarded by reason of, or because of, the personal injuries." Id. at 83. The Court specifically rejected a "but-for" formulation in favor of a "stronger causal connection." *Id.* at 82–83. The Government therefore concludes Murphy must demonstrate she was awarded damages "because of" her physical injuries, which the Government claims she has failed to do.

Indeed, as the Government points out, the ALJ expressly recommended, and the Board expressly awarded, compensatory damages "because of" Murphy's nonphysical injuries. The Board analyzed the ALJ's recommendation under the headings "Compensatory damage for emotional distress or mental anguish" and "Compensatory damage award for injury to professional reputation." In describing the ALJ's proposed award as "reasonable," the Board stated Murphy was to receive "$45,000 for mental pain and anguish" and "$25,000 for injury to professional reputation." That Murphy suffered from bruxism or other physical symptoms of stress is of no moment, the Government argues, because "the Board awarded her damages, not to compensate [her for that] particular injur[y], but explicitly with respect to nonphysical injuries."

In reply Murphy merely reiterates that she suffered "physical" injuries. She does not address the Government's point that she received her award "on account of" her mental distress and reputational loss, not her bruxism or other physical symptoms.

Murphy's failure to address the Government's position is telling. Although the pre–1996 version of § 104(a)(2) was at issue in *O'Gilvie*, the Court's analysis of the phrase "on account of," which phrase was unchanged by the 1996 Amendments, remains controlling here. Murphy no doubt suffered from certain physical manifestations of emotional distress, but the record clearly indicates the Board awarded her compensation only "for mental pain and anguish" and "for injury to professional reputation." The Board thus having left no room for doubt about the grounds for her award, we conclude Murphy's damages were not "awarded by reason of, or because of, ... [physical] personal injuries," *O'Gilvie*, 519 U.S. at 83. Therefore, § 104(a)(2) does not permit Murphy to exclude her award from gross income. But is that constitutional?

C. The Sixteenth Amendment

The Government of the United States is a government of limited powers: "Every law enacted by Congress must be based on one or more of its powers enumerated in the Constitution." *United States v. Morrison*, 529 U.S. 598, 607, 120 S. Ct. 1740, 146 L. Ed. 2d 658 (2000). The constitutional power of the Congress to tax income is provided in the Sixteenth Amendment, ratified in 1913:

> The Congress shall have power to lay and collect taxes on incomes, from whatever source derived, without apportionment among the several States, and without regard to any census or enumeration.

The Supreme Court has held the word "incomes" in the Amendment and the phrase "gross income" in § 61(a) of the IRC are coextensive. *See Helvering v. Clifford*, 309 U.S. 331, 334, 60 S. Ct. 554, 84 L. Ed. 788, 1940–1 C.B. 105 (1940) (§ 61 represents the "full measure of [the Congress's] taxing power"). When it first construed those terms in

Eisner v. Macomber, 252 U.S. 189, 207, 40 S. Ct. 189, 64 L. Ed. 521, 1920–3 C.B. 25, T.D. 3010 (1920), the Supreme Court held the taxing power extended to any "gain derived from capital, from labor, or from both combined." Later, after explaining that *Eisner* was not "meant to provide a touchstone to all future gross income questions," the Court added that under the IRC—and, by implication, under the Sixteenth Amendment—the Congress may "tax all gains" or "accessions to wealth." *Commissioner v. Glenshaw Glass Co.*, 348 U.S. 426, 430–31, 75 S. Ct. 473, 99 L. Ed. 483, 1955–1 C.B. 207 (1955).

Murphy argues that, being neither a gain nor an accession to wealth, her award is not income and § 104(a)(2) is therefore unconstitutional insofar as it would make the award taxable as income. Broad though the power granted in the Sixteenth Amendment is, the Supreme Court, as Murphy points out, has long recognized "the principle that a restoration of capital [i]s not income; hence it [falls] outside the definition of 'income' upon which the law impose[s] a tax." *O'Gilvie*, 519 U.S. at 84; *see, e.g., Doyle v. Mitchell Bros. Co.*, 247 U.S. 179, 187–88, 38 S. Ct. 467, 62 L. Ed. 1054, T.D. 2723 (1918); *S. Pac. Co. v. Lowe*, 247 U.S. 330, 335, 38 S. Ct. 540, 62 L. Ed. 1142, T.D. 2730 (1918) (return of capital not income under IRC or Sixteenth Amendment). By analogy, Murphy contends a damage award for personal injuries—including non-physical injuries—is not income but simply a return of capital—"human capital," as it were.

According to Murphy, the Supreme Court read the concept of "human capital" into the IRC in *Glenshaw Glass*. There, in holding that punitive damages for personal injury were "gross income" under the predecessor to § 61, the Court stated:

> The long history of ... holding personal injury recoveries nontaxable on the theory that they roughly correspond to a return of capital cannot support exemption of punitive damages following injury to property ... Damages for personal injury are by definition compensatory only. Punitive damages, on the other hand, cannot be considered a restoration of capital for taxation purposes.

348 U.S. at 432 n.8. In Murphy's view, the Court thereby made clear that the recovery of compensatory damages for a "personal injury"—of whatever type—is analogous to a "return of capital" and therefore is not income under the IRC or the Sixteenth Amendment.

In support of her reading of the case law, Murphy contends the IRC, as drafted shortly after "passage of the [Sixteenth] Amendment demonstrates that compensatory damages designed to make a person whole are excluded from the definition of 'income.' " She focuses upon the three sources the Supreme Court quoted in *O'Gilvie*, to wit, an Opinion of the Attorney General, a Decision of the Department of the Treasury, and a Report issued by the Ways and Means Committee of the House of Representatives—each of which predates the first version of § 104(a)(2), namely, § 213(b)(6) of the Revenue Act of 1918.

In an opinion rendered to the Secretary of the Treasury on the question whether proceeds from an accident insurance policy were income under the IRC as it stood prior to the 1918 Act, the Attorney General stated:

> Without affirming that the human body is in a technical sense the "capital" invested in an accident policy, in a broad, natural sense the proceeds of the policy do but substitute, so far as they go, capital which is the source of future periodical income. They merely take the place of capital in human ability which was destroyed by the accident. They are therefore "capital" as distinguished from "income" receipts.

31 Op. Att'y. Gen. 304, 308 (1918). In a revenue ruling, the Department of the Treasury then reasoned that

> upon similar principles ... an amount received by an individual as the result of a suit or compromise for personal injuries sustained ... through accident is not income [that is] taxable.

T.D. 2747, 20 Treas. Dec. Int. Rev. 457 (1918).

As for the House Report on the bill that became the Revenue Act of 1918, it states:

> Under the present law it is doubtful whether amounts received through accident or health insurance, or under workmen's compensation acts, as compensation for personal injury or sickness, and damages received on account of such injuries or sickness, are required to be included in gross income.

H.R. Rep. No. 65–767, at 9–10 (1918). Thereafter, the Congress passed the Act, § 213(b)(6) of which excluded from gross income "[a]mounts received, through accident or health insurance or under workman's compensation acts, as compensation for personal injuries or sickness, plus the amount of any damages received whether by suit or agreement on account of such injuries or sickness."

Because the 1918 Act followed soon after ratification of the Sixteenth Amendment, Murphy contends that the statute reflects the meaning of the Amendment as it would have been understood by those who framed, adopted, and ratified it. She observes that in *Dotson v. United States*, 87 F.3d 682 (5th Cir. 1996), the court concluded upon the basis of the House Report that the "Congress first enacted the personal injury compensation exclusion ... when such payments were considered the return of human capital, and thus not constitutionally taxable 'income' under the 16th amendment." *Id*. at 685.

The Government attacks Murphy's constitutional argument on all fronts. First, invoking the presumption that the Congress enacts laws within its constitutional limits, *see Rust v. Sullivan*, 500 U.S. 173, 191, 111 S. Ct. 1759, 114 L. Ed. 2d 233 (1991), the Government asserts at the outset that § 104(a)(2) is constitutional even if, as amended in 1996, it does permit the taxation of compensatory damages. Indeed, the Government goes further, contending the Congress could, consistent with the

Sixteenth Amendment, repeal § 104(a)(2) altogether and tax compensation even for physical injuries.

Noting that the power of the Congress to tax income "extends broadly to all economic gains," *Comm'r v. Banks*, 543 U.S. 426, 433, 125 S. Ct. 826, 160 L. Ed. 2d 859 (2005), the Government next maintains that compensatory damages "plainly constitute economic gain, for the taxpayer unquestionably has more money after receiving the damages than she had prior to receipt of the award." On that basis, the Government contends Murphy's reliance upon footnote eight of *Glenshaw Glass* is misplaced; merely because the Congress "has historically excluded personal injury recoveries from gross income, based on the make-whole or restoration-of-human-capital theory, does not mean that such an exclusion is mandated by the Sixteenth Amendment." Because the Supreme Court in *Glenshaw Glass* was construing "gross income" with reference only to the IRC, the Government argues footnote eight addresses only a now abandoned congressional policy, not the outer limit of the Sixteenth Amendment.

According to the Government, the same is true of the 1918 Act and the interpretive rulings that preceded it. Although the Government acknowledges that the dictum in *Dotson* accords with Murphy's position, the Government notes the court there relied solely upon the House Report. Because the House Report merely states "it is doubtful whether . . . compensation for personal injury or sickness . . . [is] required to be included in gross income," H.R. Rep. No. 65–767, at 9–10 (1918), the Government observes that the "report simply does not establish that Congress believed taxing compensatory personal injury damages would be unconstitutional."

In addition, the Government challenges the coherence of Murphy's analogy between a return of "human capital or well-being" and a return of "financial capital," the latter of which it acknowledges does not constitute income under the Sixteenth Amendment. *See Doyle*, 247 U.S. at 187; *S. Pac. Co.*, 247 U.S. at 335. The Government first observes that financial capital, like all property, has a "basis," defined by the IRC as "the cost of such property," adjusted "for expenditures, receipts, losses, or other items, properly chargeable to [a] capital account,"; thus, when a taxpayer sells property, his income is "the excess of the amount realized therefrom over the adjusted basis." The Government then observes that "[b]ecause people do not pay cash or its equivalent to acquire their well-being, they have no basis in it for purposes of measuring a gain (or loss) upon the realization of compensatory damages." Nor is there any corresponding theory of "human depreciation," which would permit "an offsetting deduction for the exhaustion of the taxpayer's physical prowess and mental agility." Boris I. Bittker & Lawrence Lokken, *Federal Taxation of Income, Estates, and Gifts* P 5.6 (2003). Finally, the Government points to the Ninth Circuit's dictum in *Roemer v. Commissioner*, 716 F.2d 693 (1983), suggesting that "[s]ince there is no tax basis in a person's health and other personal interests, money received as compensation for an injury to those interests might be considered a realized accession to wealth." *Id.* at 696 n.2.

At the outset, we reject the Government's breathtakingly expansive claim of congressional power under the Sixteenth Amendment—upon which it founds the more far-reaching arguments it advances here. The Sixteenth Amendment simply does not authorize the Congress to tax as "incomes" every sort of revenue a taxpayer may receive. As the Supreme Court noted long ago, the "Congress cannot make a thing income which is not so in fact." *Burk-Waggoner Oil Ass'n v. Hopkins*, 269 U.S. 110, 114, 46 S. Ct. 48, 70 L. Ed. 183, 1926–1 C.B. 147, T.D. 3790 (1925). Indeed, because the "the power to tax involves the power to destroy," *McCulloch v. Maryland*, 17 U.S. (4 Wheat.) 316, 431, 4 L. Ed. 579 (1819), it would not be consistent with our constitutional government, and the sanctity of property in our system, merely to rely upon the legislature to decide what constitutes income.

Fortunately, we need not rely solely upon the wisdom and beneficence of the Congress for, when the *Sixteenth Amendment* was drafted, the word "incomes" had well understood limits. To be sure, the Supreme Court has broadly construed the phrase "gross income" in the IRC and, by implication, the word "incomes" in the Sixteenth Amendment, but it also has made plain that the power to tax income extends only to "gain[s]" or "accessions to wealth." *Glenshaw Glass*, 348 U.S. at 430–31. That is why, as noted above, the Supreme Court has held a "return of capital" is not income. The question in this case is not, however, about a return of capital—except insofar as Murphy analogizes human capital to physical or financial capital; the question is whether the compensation she received for her injuries is income.*

To determine whether Murphy's compensation is income under the Sixteenth Amendment, we are instructed by the Supreme Court first to consider whether the taxpayer's award of compensatory damages is "a substitute for [a] normally untaxed personal ... quality, good, or 'asset.'" *O'Gilvie*, 519 U.S. at 86. Accordingly, we join our sister circuits by asking: "In lieu of what were the damages awarded"? *Raytheon Prod. Corp. v. Commissioner*, 144 F.2d 110, 113 (1st Cir. 1944); *see Francisco v. United States*, 267 F.3d 303, 319 (3d Cir. 2001) (treating *Raytheon's* "in lieu of" test as authoritative); *Tribune Publ'g Co. v. United States*, 836 F.2d 1176, 1178 (9th Cir. 1988) (applying "in lieu of" test to determine whether settlement proceeds were income); *Gilbertz v. United States*, 808 F.2d 1374, 1378 (10th Cir. 1987) (adopting "in lieu of" test to

---

* In any event, the Government's quarrel with Murphy's analogy, based upon *Glenshaw Glass*, of "human capital" to financial or physical capital is not persuasive. To be sure, the analogy is incomplete; personal injuries do not entail an adjustment to any basis, nor are human resources, such as reputation, depreciable for tax purposes. But nothing in Murphy's argument implies a need to account for the basis in or to depreciate anything. Her point, rather, is that as with compensation for a harm to one's financial or physical capital, the payment of compensation for the diminution of a personal attribute, such as reputation, is but a restoration of the status quo ante, analogous to a "restoration of capital," *Glenshaw Glass*, 348 U.S. at 432 n.8; in neither context does the payment result in a "gain" or "accession to wealth."

determine whether compensatory damages were income). Here, if the $70,000 Murphy received was "in lieu of" something "normally untaxed," *O'Gilvie*, 519 U.S. at 86, then her compensation is not income under the Sixteenth Amendment; it is neither a "gain" nor an "accession to wealth." *Glenshaw Glass*, 348 U.S. at 430–31.

As we have seen, it is clear from the record that the damages were awarded to make Murphy emotionally and reputationally "whole" and not to compensate her for lost wages or taxable earnings of any kind. The emotional well-being and good reputation she enjoyed before they were diminished by her former employer were not taxable as income. Under this analysis, therefore, the compensation she received in lieu of what she lost cannot be considered income and, hence, it would appear the Sixteenth Amendment does not empower the Congress to tax her award.

Our conclusion at this point is tentative because the Supreme Court has also instructed that, in defining "incomes," we should rely upon "the commonly understood meaning of the term which must have been in the minds of the people when they adopted the Sixteenth Amendment." *Merchants' Loan & Trust Co. v. Smietanka*, 255 U.S. 509, 519, 41 S. Ct. 386, 65 L. Ed. 751, T.D. 3173 (1921). And, to discern the original understanding of a provision of the Constitution, we must examine any contemporaneous implementing legislation. *See Myers v. United States*, 272 U.S. 52, 175, 47 S. Ct. 21, 71 L. Ed. 160 (1926) ("This court has repeatedly laid down the principle that a contemporaneous legislative exposition of the Constitution ... , acquiesced in for a long term of years, fixes the construction to be given its provisions"); *see Macomber*, 252 U.S. at 202 (district judge correctly treated "construction of the [Revenue Act of 1913] as inseparable from the interpretation of the Sixteenth Amendment"). Therefore, we must inquire whether "the people when they adopted the Sixteenth Amendment," or the Congress when it implemented the Amendment, would have understood compensatory damages for a nonphysical injury to be "income."

* * * We agree with the Government that the House Report on the 1918 Act is ambiguous and therefore unhelpful on the question before us. We concur in Murphy's view, however, that the Attorney General's 1918 opinion and the Treasury Department's ruling of the same year strongly suggest that the term "incomes" as used in the Sixteenth Amendment does not extend to monies received solely in compensation for a personal injury and unrelated to lost wages or earnings.

That emotional distress and loss of reputation were both actionable in tort when the Sixteenth Amendment was adopted supports the view that compensation for these nonphysical injuries was not regarded differently than was compensation for physical injuries and, therefore, was not considered income by the framers of the Amendment and the state legislatures that ratified it. By 1913, in at least 39 of the then–48 states and in the District of Columbia, the law made compensatory damages for "mental suffering" recoverable in the same matter as compensatory damages for physical harms; indeed, in 34 of those states, there are reported cases involving defamation and other reputational injuries—the very sort of injury Murphy suffered—and at least five more states allowed an action for alienation of affections, also a nonphysical injury. As a result, we see no meaningful distinction between Murphy's award and the kinds of damages recoverable for personal injury when the Sixteenth Amendment was adopted. Because, as we have seen, the term "incomes," as understood in 1913, clearly did not include damages received in compensation for a physical personal injury, we infer that it likewise did not include damages received for a nonphysical injury and unrelated to lost wages or earning capacity.

The IRS itself reached the same conclusion when it first addressed the question, expressly affirming that personal injuries included nonphysical personal injuries:

> [T]here is no gain, and therefore no income, derived from the receipt of damages for alienation of affections or defamation of personal character . . . If an individual is possessed of a personal right that is not assignable and not susceptible of any appraisal in relation to market values, and thereafter receives either damages or payment in compromise for an invasion of that right, it can not be held that he thereby derives any gain or profit.

Sol. Op. 132, I–1 C.B. 82, 93 (1922); *see also Hawkins v. Commissioner*, 6 B.T.A. 1023, 1024–25 (U.S. Bd. of Tax App. 1927) (holding "compensation for injury to [plaintiff's] personal reputation for integrity and fair dealing" was not income because it was "an attempt to make the plaintiff whole as before the injury"). Note that the Service regarded such compensation not merely as excludable under the IRC, but more fundamentally as not being income at all.

In sum, every indication is that damages received solely in compensation for a personal injury are not income within the meaning of that term in the Sixteenth Amendment. First, as compensation for the loss of a personal attribute, such as well-being or a good reputation, the damages are not received in lieu of income. Second, the framers of the Sixteenth Amendment would not have understood compensation for a personal injury—including a nonphysical injury—to be income. Therefore, we hold § 104(a)(2) unconstitutional insofar as it permits the taxation of an award of damages for mental distress and loss of reputation.

III. Conclusion

Albert Einstein may have been correct that "[t]he hardest thing in the world to understand is the income tax," *The Macmillan Book of Business and Economic Quotations* 195 (Michael Jackman ed., 1984), but it is not hard to understand that not all receipts of money are income. Murphy's compensatory award in particular was not received "in lieu of" something normally taxed as income; nor is it within the meaning of the term "incomes" as used in the Sixteenth Amendment. Therefore, insofar as § 104(a)(2) permits the taxation of compensation for a personal injury, which compensation is unrelated to lost wages or earnings, that provision is unconstitutional. Accordingly, we remand this case to the district court to enter an order and judgment instructing the Government to refund the taxes Murphy paid on her award plus applicable interest.

So ordered.

Notes and Questions

1. Is *Murphy* really a case about § 104(a)(2), as the court claims? Consider the court's last statement in Part II of the *Murphy* opinion: "we hold § 104(a)(2) unconstitutional insofar as it permits the taxation of an award of damages for mental distress and loss of reputation." The statement implies, erroneously, that § 104(a)(2) is an inclusion provision. Section 104(a)(2) is an exclusion provision, for it excludes from gross income damages received on account of personal physical injury or physical sickness. Perhaps the court meant to say that damages for personal injury unrelated to lost wages or earnings are not "income" in the constitutional sense. That means, effectively, that such damages are not gross income under § 61(a) in the first place. If the damages are not gross income, there is no need for an exclusion and hence no need to consider § 104(a)(2).

2. The court concludes that Murphy's damage award "is not income under the Sixteenth Amendment; it is neither a 'gain' nor an 'accession to wealth.'" What support does the court offer for this conclusion? Do you agree with the court's conclusion?

3. What support does the court offer for its conclusion that the framers of the Sixteenth Amendment did not intend for damages that compensate for personal injury to be included in gross income? Is the court's conclusion persuasive? Regardless of your answer to that question, should the intent of the Sixteenth Amendment's framers be dispositive of contemporary tax disputes?

4. Notice that the court does not directly adopt the taxpayer's "human capital" theory, that the damages are not income because they represent something akin to a return of capital. The court does not rely on this theory to reach its holding, but in a footnote the court indicates that the taxpayer won this argument. Is this significant? To the extent wages compensate a taxpayer for his or her lost leisure, is it unconstitutional to tax wages? The court does not go this far, expressly limiting its holding to damages that do not compensate for lost wages. But is that a logical implication of the court's implied endorsement of the taxpayer's human capital theory?

D. OTHER EXCLUSION PROVISIONS

Code: *Skim* IRC §§ 103; 107; 109; 111; 121; 139; 1019.

Regs: None.

This Section reviews some other significant exclusion provisions. Some of these exclusions will be addressed in detail later in the text. In other cases, an extended discussion of the exclusion would divert us from more fundamental topics that deserve greater attention.

Section 103: Exclusion for Interest on Certain Municipal Bonds. For as long as there has been an Internal Revenue Code, there has been an exclusion for interest received on municipal bonds. The current version of this exclusion is found in § 103(a). Initially, the exclusion was justified on the grounds that the federal government may face a constitutional barrier to the taxation of interest on state and local bonds. Most scholars agree, however, that the federal government faces no such barrier. Yet the exclusion continues.

Perhaps the exclusion is best explained today as a form of federal assistance to local governments. Because the interest is tax-free, state and local governments can sell their bonds at a lower interest rate, making the bonds less expensive for the governmental units to issue. Suppose, for example, that a taxpayer is choosing between a traditional, taxable corporate bond that will pay interest at the rate of ten percent and a municipal bond that will pay interest at the rate of 7.5 percent. If the taxpayer is in the highest marginal tax bracket, the taxpayer will actually have a greater return, after-tax, if he or she purchases the municipal bond. This is because 35 percent of the interest paid from the corporate bond would be lost to taxes, making the after-tax interest rate on the bond a mere 6.5 percent. To the extent the high-bracket taxpayer in this example "wins" by picking the municipal bond, one can fairly argue that the "subsidy" for local governments is inefficient. If it were a more efficient subsidy, the after-tax return on the corporate bond and the tax-free return on the municipal bond should be the same.

There are several limitations on the exclusion, most attributable to perceived abuses from local governments. For example, a city may issue bonds to finance the development of private businesses, an activity that is, at best, only somewhat public in nature. Accordingly, the Code labels such bonds as "private activity bonds," and unless some discrete exception applies, the interest on private activity bonds will be taxable.

Section 107: The Parsonage Exclusions. Section 107 excludes two items from the gross income of "a minister of the gospel:" (1) the rental value of a home furnished as part of the minister's compensation; and (2) any rental allowance paid as compensation, to the extent such allowance is actually used by the minister to rent or provide for a home. Because the benefit of these exclusions is available only to ministers, there is an on-again, off-again controversy as to the constitutionality of § 107.

This controversy re-emerged recently in a case involving one Reverend Warren, a Baptist minister at a community church he founded. The church paid Reverend Warren a housing allowance instead of providing free housing directly. He excluded these amounts from gross income under § 107(2), even though the allowances he received exceeded the fair rental value of the home. In a 14–3 decision, the Tax Court held that the exclusion should have been allowed, as the record showed the taxpayer actually used the allowance for housing costs. *Warren v. Commissioner*, 114 T.C. 343 (2000). In reaching this holding, the Tax Court grappled with its prior decision in *Reed v. Commissioner*, 82 T.C. 208 (1984), in which the court held that the exclusion was limited to the fair rental value of a minister's housing. This *Warren* court (not the "Warren Court" you are used to reading about) distinguished *Reed* on the grounds that *Reed* dealt with the application of § 107(1), while Reverend Warren's case required application of § 107(2). The dissenting judges in *Warren* observed that the taxpayer's housing allowance comprised 100 percent of his total compensation. Without some limitation on the amount eligible for exclusion under § 107(2), the dissenters believed that ministers and their congregations would have an easy path to avoid inclusion of compensation income.

The Service appealed the Tax Court's decision to the Ninth Circuit. In the early stages of its proceedings, the court (in a 2–1 decision) appointed a noted constitutional law scholar, Professor Erwin Chemerinsky, to provide an *amicus* brief addressing three issues: (1) whether the court had the authority to consider the constitutionality of § 107(2); (2) if so, whether the court should exercise that authority; and (3) if so, whether § 107(2) violates the Establishment Clause. The dissenting judge thought it unnecessary for the court to consider the constitutionality of § 107(2) because neither the parties nor the Tax Court raised the issue.

Professor Chemerinsky filed his brief with the Ninth Circuit about two months later. He concluded that the court did have authority to consider the constitutionality of the parsonage exclusion even though the parties did not raise the issue before the Tax Court. He further concluded that § 107(2) violates the Establishment Clause, both under the *Lemon* test and the neutrality test favored by some Justices. It looked as though the court was getting ready to provide an answer to the issue debated infrequently by scholars for a long time.

That is, until a higher power intervened. On May 20, 2002 (about two weeks after Professor Chemerinsky had filed his *amicus* brief), the parties to the *Warren* case reached a settlement and filed a joint stipulation asking the case to be dismissed. On the same day(!), President George W. Bush signed into law the Clergy Housing Allowance Clarification Act of 2002. The Act limited § 107(2) "to the extent such allowance does not exceed the fair rental value of the home, including furnishings and appurtenances such as a garage, plus the cost of utilities." As a matter of federal tax doctrine, it is now clear that both § 107 exclusions are limited to the fair rental value of the property used by the minister as a home.

But the Establishment Clause issue remained. So Professor Chemerinsky filed a motion opposing dismissal of the *Warren* case and seeking to intervene as a third-party plaintiff. The Ninth Circuit concluded that

Chemerinsky lacked standing to intervene, as he could not show a "significant protectable interest" in the outcome of the *Warren* case. The court noted, however, that Chemerinsky could raise the issue in a separate lawsuit, so his interest as a taxpayer would not be jeopardized. In a concurring opinion, Judge Tallman said that the court should not have considered the motion to intervene, because the motion was moot once the parties stipulated to dismissal. Having rejected Chemerinsky's motion, the court at last dismissed the case. *Warren v. Commissioner*, 302 F.3d 1012 (9th Cir. 2002).

As of this writing, Professor Chemerinsky has not initiated a new suit, nor has any other taxpayer. While the 2002 legislation limited the scope of the § 107(2) exclusion to avoid easy circumvention, it did nothing to address the criticism that the parsonage exclusions violate the Establishment Clause by conferring a benefit only to ministers of the gospel. Are the exclusions constitutional? If not, could they be restructured in some way to pass constitutional muster without depleting federal revenues by extending the free housing exclusion to all taxpayers?

Section 109: Exclusion of Tenant Improvements. In *Helvering v. Bruun*, 309 U.S. 461, 60 S.Ct. 631, 84 L.Ed. 864 (1940), the Supreme Court held that permanent improvements to a landlord's property by a tenant were gross income to the landlord when the landlord reclaimed possession of the premises following the tenant's vacancy. The impact of *Bruun* on the rule of realization was addressed in Chapter 3. Congress reacted to *Bruun* by enacting § 109, which excludes the value of tenant improvements from the landlord's gross income.

Naturally, the landlord should not be able to increase his or her adjusted basis in the property by the value of excluded tenant improvements, else the landlord would have a double benefit (exclusion and an increase to basis). Section 1019 precludes a double benefit by prohibiting any increase to basis for amounts excluded under § 109.

Section 111: The Exclusionary Arm of the Tax Benefit Rule. If a taxpayer recovers a cost or loss that was deducted in a prior taxable year, it would be a double benefit to allow the taxpayer to exclude the recovery from gross income. The prior deduction was premised on a cost or loss to the taxpayer that, ultimately, did not occur. If the recovery is not accounted for, the taxpayer will have received a deduction without actual cost or loss. Because every year stands alone (a mantra you will see oft-repeated in Chapter 6), it is not appropriate for the taxpayer to amend the prior tax return and omit the deduction. Besides, the period for amending the return may have expired by the time the recovery occurs.

To solve this problem, common law required taxpayers to include recoveries in gross income if the year in which the recoveries occur. The doctrine is known as the "tax benefit rule." The theory of the tax benefit rule loses force, however, if the prior deduction did not actually reduce the taxpayer's liability for tax in the prior year. This can happen, for example, where the taxpayer had deductions in excess of gross income in that prior year, or where the taxpayer foregoes an itemized deduction and claims the standard deduction. Section 111 thus excludes recoveries of prior deductions where the prior deduction was of no actual help in reducing the taxpayer's tax liability. This exclusionary aspect of the tax benefit rule is a principal topic in Chapter 6.

Section 121: Exclusion of the Gain From the Sale of a Principal Residence. The current form of § 121 is fairly new to the Code, introduced in 1997. Prior to the current regime, two Code sections potentially applied upon the sale or disposition of a personal residence. First, former § 1034 allowed a taxpayer to defer gain recognition by "rolling over" the basis in the old residence into a new residence. Obviously, the taxpayer had to acquire a new residence to take advantage of the roll-over provision. The statute contained strict timing rules in this regard. Second, taxpayers over age 55 could use a one-time exclusion of up to $125,000 of gain from the sale of a personal residence. This is what *old* § 121 provided.

The new regime greatly simplifies the issue, establishing one exclusionary provision available to all taxpayers on a recurring basis. The current § 121 permits taxpayers to exclude up to $250,000 of realized gain upon a sale of their principal residences. The exclusion grows to $500,000 for married taxpayers filing a joint return. There are only two major requirements for this very generous exclusion. First, the taxpayer must have owned and used the home as the taxpayer's principal residence two of the five years prior to the sale. Second, the taxpayer must not have claimed the § 121 exclusion to any extent in the two years prior to the sale at issue. There is even a partial exclusion available for those who fail to meet these requirements because of certain circumstances beyond the their control. The technical and planning aspects of § 121 are waiting for us in Chapter 8, but even with this brief overview we can appreciate how much simpler the law in this regard has become. But simplicity often comes at the cost of other important objectives. Was the older regime more equitable or more efficient than the current one?

Section 139: Exclusion for Disaster Relief Payments. The Victims of Terrorism Tax Relief Act of 2001 added § 139 to the Code, which provides that gross income does not include any amount received by an individual as a "qualified disaster relief payment." Section 139(b) identifies four receipts eligible for classification as qualified disaster relief payments: (1) payments for "reasonable and necessary" personal expenses resulting from a "qualified disaster;" (2) payments for "reasonable and necessary" repairs made to a personal residence or furnishings within required because of a qualified disaster; (3) payments made by a common carrier by reason of death or physical injury stemming from a qualified disaster (think free bereavement flights offered by airlines); and (4) payments made from a governmental agency as relief from a qualified disaster.

All of the excludable payments depend upon the occurrence of a "qualified disaster." These events include "terroristic or military actions," Presidentially declared disasters, and certain "catastrophic" accidents involving common carriers. Section 139(c). Perpetrators of a disaster are not eligible for the exclusion (so says § 139(e)), but that is probably the least of their concerns.

In *Revenue Ruling 2003–12*, 2003–3 I.R.B. 283, the Service analyzed three situations where this relatively new exclusion comes into play. In the first situation, a state government enacted emergency legislation appropriating funds for grants to pay or reimburse uninsured medical, temporary housing, and transportation expenses individuals incurred as a result of a flood that was a Presidentially declared disaster. Although the state program did not require individuals to provide proof of actual expenses to receive a grant payment, it did contain limitations designed to ensure that the grant amounts were reasonably expected to be commensurate with the amount of unreimbursed expenses individuals incurred as a result of the flood. The Service concluded that while the payments were not gifts because they lacked "detached and disinterested generosity" (the state makes the payments because of its duty to relieve disaster hardship), they qualified for exclusion from gross income under § 139 because of the limitations contained in the state program.

In the second situation, a disaster relief charity also made grants to distressed individuals affected by the flood described in the first situation. The grants paid or reimbursed individuals for uninsured medical, temporary housing, and transportation expenses they incurred as a result of the flood. The Service here concluded that because the charity did not have a moral or legal duty to offer relief, the payments were made out of detached and disinterested generosity. Therefore, the recipients could exclude them as gifts. The Service found it unnecessary to determine whether the charity's payments also met the criteria for exclusion under § 139.

In the third situation, an employer made grants to its employees who were affected by the same flood. Like the other situations, the grants paid or reimbursed employees for uninsured medical, temporary housing, and transportation expenses they incurred as a result of the flood. The employer did not require individuals to provide proof of actual expenses to receive a grant payment. But the employer's offer contained limitations designed to ensure that the grant amounts were reasonably expected to be commensurate with the amount of unreimbursed expenses the employees incurred as a result of the flood. Consequently, the payments (while not gifts) are excludable from gross income under § 139.

In *Revenue Ruling 2003–115*, 2003–2 C.B. 1052, the Service addressed the applicability of § 139 to payments made in connection with the terrorist attacks on September 11, 2001. Congress created the September 11th Victim Compensation Fund to provide relief to individuals physically injured by (and to estates of those killed in) the airline crashes. Individuals seeking payment from the Fund must submit a claim and agree to waive the right to commence or participate in any lawsuit for damages sustained from the terrorist attacks (except to recover damages from one who was a conspirator in the attacks). Claimants generally have the choice to accept a lump sum cash payment or periodic payments over a term of years, with the understanding that if an individual claimant dies before expiration of the term, payments will continue to be made to the claimant's estate. No claimant, however, has the power to transfer or encumber any right to periodic payments, whether by assignment or otherwise. The Service ruled that payments from the Fund are excluded from the gross income of a claimant under both §§ 104(a)(2) and 139(f). Likewise, any payments made to a claimant's estate pursuant to a period payment arrangement are excluded from gross income under the same authorities.

* * *

Chapter 6

TIMING

Timing is everything. What is true of so much in life is certainly true of the federal income tax. In this Chapter, we take a scenic detour away from the issues of *what* and *who* for a moment so that we can appreciate more the critical issue of *when*. We will first look at the two major conventions used to decide when tax items are taken into account (or, in lay terms, when income and gain items are included and when deduction and loss items are deducted). Because both of these conventions are borrowed from financial accounting, they are called "accounting methods." Though that may be a chilling term, the conventions themselves are fairly straight-forward.

Under the **cash method** of accounting, income is included upon receipt, and deductions are claimed when paid. Under the **accrual method** of accounting, income is included when earned, and deductions are claimed when incurred. These simple rules yield the correct answer most of the time, though there are some important limitations and exceptions. In Part A of this Chapter, we will look at the contours of the cash method, and in Part B we will examine the accrual method. For each method, we will examine in turn the timing rules for income inclusion and the timing rules for deductions.

This point may seem obvious (okay, it is), but it is worth stressing: tax accounting does not affect *whether* an item is included in gross income or *whether* an expenditure can be deducted. It only deals with *when* an income or deduction item should be taken into account. This Chapter does not upset the fundamental principles presented in prior Chapters; rather, it adds another layer to the analysis. Indeed, it matters just as much *when* an item must be taken into account as *whether* it can be taken into account in the first place.

Of course, the accounting method used by a taxpayer is relevant only when, for example, an item of income is *earned* in one year but not *received* until the next year. This brings us to the concept of the "taxable year," the subject of Part C. Virtually all individuals use the calendar year as their taxable year, but in some cases a taxpayer can use a "fiscal year" (defined as any one-year period ending on the last day of a month other than December) as the taxable year. Part C will examine the taxable year and the need to preserve the integrity of the taxable year despite matters that arise immediately before or after the year. The mantra here is that "every year stands alone," and we will see why it is so important.

Sometimes taxpayers make mistakes. Dishonest mistakes are outside the scope of this text, but it is appropriate to consider honest mistakes. Suppose, for example, that a taxpayer purchases a toner cartridge for a printer late in Year One. If the printer is used in the taxpayer's trade or business, the taxpayer can deduct the toner expense on the Year One return thanks to § 162(a). Now suppose the toner cartridge turns out to be defective, a fact that the taxpayer discovers in Year Two. Rather than accept a replacement toner cartridge, the taxpayer asks for a cash refund, which is received later in Year Two. Clearly, the Year One deduction is a mistake if, ultimately, the taxpayer incurs no economic outlay. To correct this mistake, we have two choices: amend the tax return for Year One and erase the deduction, or include the cash refund in Year Two's income. If you look again at the mantra in the last paragraph, the fact that our system prefers the latter course should not be a surprise. In addition to this rule, our study in error correction (the topic for Part D of this Chapter) will also include the procedures applicable where it is impossible to correct the mistake in the current year. We will see that in some cases, it is possible for the Service (or the taxpayer) to re-open a year that has already closed under the statute of limitations in order to correct an error.

Throughout this Chapter, the **time value of money** principles are at work. As discussed in Chapter 3, individual taxpayers generally seek to defer the reporting of income as long as possible so that they may invest and make more money with the dollars that will ultimately be used to pay income taxes. Thus, if an individual is offered $1 of gross income on December 31, Year One, or $1 of gross income on January 1, Year Two, the individual should choose to take the income on January 1, Year Two, because the tax on that dollar of gross income will not be due until April 15, Year Three—over 15 months from the time of receipt! If the taxpayer chooses to take the money on December 31, Year One, the tax will be due on April 15, Year Two, only three and one-half months from the time of receipt. With the extra 12 months of time, the taxpayer can obtain more growth on the same dollar.

Just as individual taxpayers like to defer income, they like to accelerate deductions. A deduction claimed on December 31, Year One, saves taxes paid on April 15, Year Two, but a deduction claimed on January 1, Year Two, will not result in a tax savings until April 15, Year Three. Tax savings, then, is like extra tax-free income, and the sooner a taxpayer can get some tax-free income, the bigger the yield on that income can be over time.

Because of these incentives, Congress and the Service must be on the watch for transactions that artificially postpone the inclusion of income or artificially accelerate the reporting of deductions. That explains many of the exceptions and limitations to the basic accounting conventions described in this Chapter, as well as the need for the error correction devices we will study.

While time value of money principles are exceedingly important, there are other reasons why the timing rules matter. A taxpayer's marginal tax rate might change from one year to the next (whether because of changes in the taxpayer's income-producing activities or changes in the tax rates implemented by Congress), making deductions more valuable in the high-tax year and creating a preference to realize income in the low-tax year. Legislation might also tax an item one year but not the next, or vice versa.

In addition, various tax attributes can also be affected by timing. A taxpayer with a carryover loss about to expire wants to realize enough income to fully recoup the loss in the expiration year. And if a taxpayer has miscellaneous itemized deductions during the year, he or she will want to accelerate above-the-line deductions in order to limit the applicability of the two-percent haircut in § 67.

Finally, timing often matters because of the statute of limitations for amending or assessing a deficiency on a tax return. We have already seen taxpayers argue that they realized income in a year then closed under the applicable statute of limitations (recall the *Cesarini* case in Chapter 3). Furthermore, because assessable penalties and interest charges on deficiencies can be a function of when the underlying fault occurred, taxpayers care about when income was supposed to be reported or when deductions should have been taken.

A. THE CASH METHOD

Code: IRC §§ 446(a)–(d); 448.

Regs: Treas. Reg. §§ 1.446–1(a)–(c)(1)(i), –1(c)(2); 1.448–1T(a), (f). (omit)

Who Uses the Cash Method? Virtually all individuals start as cash method taxpayers because their first formal bookkeeping is done by checkbook. Under § 446(a), a taxpayer's accounting method is determined with reference to how the taxpayer keeps his or her books. Because receipts to a checking account are recorded as received (or deposited) and expenditures are recorded as paid, checkbook users start out as cash method taxpayers.

Most businesses, however, start as accrual method taxpayers. This is because the bookkeepers maintaining the business records use different rules in recording receipts and expenditures. We will see just how different that convention is when we study the accrual method in Part B.

Advantages and Disadvantages of the Cash Method. Before we get too far along in analyzing the cash method, it would be useful to consider the pros and cons of being a cash method taxpayer. One important advantage of the cash method is its simplicity. The accrual method requires more technical savvy to apply correctly. While most accrual method taxpayers need trained individuals to keep proper track of receipts and disbursements, most cash method taxpayers do so without professional assistance.

The major advantage of the cash method, though, is the opportunity for tax deferral. Suppose that a cash method taxpayer has the following items at the close of the taxable year:

(1) cash receipts for services performed during the year, $200,000;

(2) accounts receivable from services performed during the year, $300,000;

(3) amounts paid for expenses incurred during the year, $100,000; and

(4) amounts paid for expenses attributable to first month of next year, $200,000.

Under the cash method, the taxpayer has a $100,000 net loss for the year. Gross income includes the $200,000 from item (1) but not the receivables in item (2) because payment has not yet been received. Yet the taxpayer deducts the expenses listed in both items (3) and (4) because they were actually paid in the taxable year. If the taxpayer were on the accrual method, however, there would be taxable income for the year of $400,000! That's because, under a pure accrual method of accounting, both items (1) and (2) would be included in gross income (totaling $500,000) and only item (3) would be allowed as a deduction in the current year. The expenses in item (4) have not yet accrued as of the close of the year.

By being on the cash method, therefore, the taxpayer can defer the income from the accounts receivable to a later year. And your experience with the time value of money suggests (hopefully) that it is much better to defer the taxable income so that the taxpayer can invest the money that would otherwise be used to pay tax. Notice also that the cash method taxpayer accelerates a deduction simply by paying the expense even though the amount is not yet owed. The opportunities for income deferral and accelerating deductions are limited by the doctrines discussed later in this Part. Still, to the extent that the cash method allows this manipulation of timing, the taxpayer has a tremendous advantage.

So why would anyone want to be an accrual method taxpayer? The accrual method might be preferable from a non-tax perspective. After all, there is a reason why most internal financial statements are prepared on an accrual basis: the consensus opinion of accounting gurus is that the accrual method generally gives a better reflection of true economic income over a longer period. This is not to say that the cash method does not produce a "clear" reflection of income, the standard required by § 446(b); rather, the accrual method often paints a "clearer" reflection.

Taxpayers Forbidden From Using the Cash Method. Section 448(a) lists three types of taxpayers that cannot use the cash method: (1) C corporations; (2) partnerships with at least one C corporation partner; and (3) tax shelters. This prohibition is subject to the three exceptions provided in § 448(b). The most significant exception is for taxpayers with average gross receipts not exceeding $5 million. See §§ 448(b)(3) and 448(c). In addition to the limitations spelled-out in the Code, Regulation § 1.446–1(c)(2)(i) requires a taxpayer to use the accrual method if "it is necessary to use an inventory." An inventory is necessary "(i)n all cases in which the production, purchase, or sale of merchandise of any kind is an income-producing factor." Treas. Reg. § 1.446–1(a)(4)(i). In other words, if a taxpayer generates receipts from the production, purchase, or sale of merchandise, that taxpayer cannot use the cash method—even if the taxpayer otherwise qualifies for the cash method.

* * *

(1) INCOME ITEMS

Code: IRC § 451(a).

Regs: Treas. Reg. §§ 1.451–1(a); 1.451–2.

Recall that cash method taxpayers include income items when received, regardless of when the income items are earned. For example, if a cash method taxpayer performs services late in Year One but is not compensated until early in Year Two, the compensation income is reported on the Year Two return. As explained above, this presents significant opportunities for deferral of income, and where there is opportunity, there is often abuse. For this reason, the regulations and the courts have created some limitations on the deferral opportunities by carefully defining when "receipt" occurs. Here we consider those limitations.

The Constructive Receipt Doctrine. The constructive receipt doctrine, set forth in Regulation § 1.451–2, basically means that a taxpayer cannot turn his or her back to income. The following cases give some good examples of its application.

HORNUNG v. COMMISSIONER

United States Tax Court, 1967.
47 T.C. 428.

Hoyt, J.

Respondent determined an income tax deficiency against petitioner in the amount of $3,163.76 for the taxable year 1962. Petitioner having conceded an issue relating to a travel expense deduction, the questions remaining for decision are:

(1) Whether the value of a 1962 Corvette automobile which was won by petitioner for his performance in a professional football game should be included in his gross income for the taxable year 1962.

* * *

FINDINGS OF FACT

* * *

* * * Petitioner is a well-known professional football player who was employed by the Green Bay Packers in 1962. Prior to becoming a professional, petitioner attended the University of Notre Dame and was an All–American quarterback on the university football team.

Issue 1. The Corvette

Sport Magazine is a publication of the McFadden–Bartell Corp., with business offices in New York City. Each year Sport Magazine (hereinafter sometimes referred to as Sport or the magazine) awards a new Corvette automobile to the player selected by its editors (primarily by its editor in chief) as the outstanding player in the National Football League championship game. This award was won by John Unitas of the Baltimore Colts in 1958 and 1959 and by Norm Van Brocklin of the Philadelphia Eagles in 1960. A similar annual award is made to outstanding professional athletes in baseball, hockey, and basketball. The existence of the award is announced several days prior to the sporting event in question, and the selection and announcement of the winner is made immediately following the athletic contest. The Corvette automobiles are generally presented to the recipients at a luncheon or dinner several days subsequent to the sporting event and a photograph of the athlete receiving the car is published in the magazine, together with an article relating to his performance during the particular athletic event. The Corvette awards are intended to promote the sale of Sport Magazine and their cost is deducted by the publisher for Federal income tax purposes as promotion and advertising expense.

The Corvette which is to be awarded to the most valuable player in the National Football League championship game is generally purchased by the magazine several months prior to the date the game is played, and it is held by a New York area Chevrolet dealer until delivered to the recipient of the award. In some years when the game is played in New York the magazine has had the car on display at the stadium on the day of the game.

On December 31, 1961, petitioner played in the National Football League championship game between the Green Bay Packers and the New York Giants. The game was played in Green Bay, Wis. Petitioner scored a total of 19 points during this game and thereby established a new league record. At the end of this game petitioner was selected by the editors of Sport as the most valuable player and winner of the Corvette, and press releases were issued announcing the award. At approximately 4:30 on the afternoon of December 31, 1961, following the game, the editor in chief of Sport informed petitioner that he had been selected as the most valuable player of the game. The editor in chief did not have the key or the title to the Corvette with him in Green Bay and petitioner did not request or demand immediate possession of the car at that time but he accepted the award.

The Corvette which was to be awarded in connection with this 1961 championship game had been purchased by Sport in September of 1961.

However, since the game was played in Green Bay, Wis., the car was not on display at the stadium on the day of the game, but was in New York in the hands of a Chevrolet dealership. As far as Sport was concerned the car was "available" to petitioner on December 31, 1961, as soon as the award was announced. However, December 31, 1961, was a Sunday and the New York dealership at which the car was located was closed. Although the National Football League championship game is always played on a Sunday, Sport is prepared to make prior arrangements to have the car available in New York for the recipient of the award on that Sunday afternoon if the circumstances appear to warrant such arrangements—particularly if the game is played in New York. Such arrangements were not made in 1961 because the game was played in Green Bay, and, in the words of Sport's editor in chief, "it seemed a hundred-to-one that * * * [the recipient of the award] would want to come in [to New York] on New Year's Eve to take possession" of the prize.

On December 31, 1961, when petitioner was informed that he had won the Corvette, he was also informed that a luncheon was to be held for him in New York City on the following Wednesday by the publisher of Sport, at which luncheon his award would be presented. At that time petitioner consented to attend the luncheon in order to receive the Corvette. There was no discussion that he would obtain the car prior to the presentation ceremony previously announced. The lunch was held as scheduled on Wednesday, January 3, 1962, in a New York restaurant. Petitioner attended and was photographed during the course of the presentation of the automobile to him. A photograph of petitioner sitting in the car outside of the restaurant was published in the April 1962 issue of Sport, together with an article regarding his achievements in the championship game and the Corvette prize award. Petitioner was not required to attend the lunch or to pose for photographs or perform any other service for Sport as a condition or as consideration for his receipt of the car.

The fair market value of the Corvette automobile received by petitioner was $3,331.04. Petitioner reported the sale of the Corvette in his 1962 Federal income tax return * * *.

Petitioner did not include the fair market value of this car in his gross income for 1962, or for any other year. McFadden–Bartell Corporation deducted its cost as a promotion and advertising expense.

    * * *

OPINION

Issue 1. The Corvette

Petitioner alleged in his petition that the Corvette was received by him as a gift in 1962. However, at trial and on brief, he argues that the car was constructively received in 1961, prior to the taxable year for which the deficiency is being assessed. If this contention is upheld, the question of whether the car constituted a reportable item of gross income need not be considered. This argument is based upon the assertion that the announcement and acceptance of the award occurred at approximately 4:30 on the afternoon of December 31, 1961, following the game.

It is undisputed that petitioner was selected as the most valuable player of the National Football League championship game in Green Bay on December 31, 1961. It is also undisputed that petitioner actually received the car on January 3, 1962, in New York. Petitioner relies upon the statement at the trial by the editor in chief of Sport that as far as Sport was concerned the car was "available" to petitioner on December 31, 1961, as soon as the award was announced. It is therefore contended that the petitioner should be deemed to have received the value of the award in 1961 under the doctrine of constructive receipt.

The amount of any item of gross income is included in gross income for the taxable year in which received by the taxpayer unless such amount is properly accounted for as of a different period. Sec. 451(a). It is further provided in section 446(c) that the cash receipts method, which the petitioner utilized, is a permissible method of computing taxable income. * * *

The regulations under section 451 elaborate on the meaning of constructive receipt:

> Income although not actually reduced to a taxpayer's possession is constructively received by him in the taxable year during which it is credited to his account, set apart for him, or otherwise made available so that he may draw upon it at any time, or so that he could have drawn upon it during the taxable year if notice of intention to withdraw had been given. However, income is not constructively received if the taxpayer's control of its receipt is subject to substantial limitations or restrictions. * * *

The probable purpose for development of the doctrine of constructive receipt was stated as follows in *Ross v. Commissioner*, 169 F.2d 483, 491 (C.A. 1, 1948):

> The doctrine of constructive receipt was, no doubt, conceived by the Treasury in order to prevent a taxpayer from choosing the year in which to return income merely by choosing the year in which to reduce it to possession. Thereby the Treasury may subject income to taxation when the only thing preventing its reduction to possession is the volition of the taxpayer. * * *

However, it was held in the *Ross* case, at page 496, that the doctrine of constructive receipt could be asserted by a taxpayer as a defense to a deficiency assessment even though the item in controversy had not been reported for the taxable year of the alleged constructive receipt:

> if these items were constructively received when earned they cannot be treated as income in any later year, * * * and, in the absence of misstatement of fact, intentional or otherwise, the petitioner cannot be estopped from asserting that the items were taxable only in the years in which constructively received.

The basis of constructive receipt is essentially unfettered control by the recipient over the date of actual receipt. Petitioner has failed to convince us that he possessed such control on December 31, 1961, over the receipt of the Corvette. The evidence establishes that the Corvette which was presented to petitioner on January 3, 1962, was in the possession of a Chevrolet dealer in New York City on December 31, 1961. At the time the award was announced in Green Bay, the editor in chief of Sport had neither the title nor keys to the car, and nothing was given or presented to petitioner to evidence his ownership or right to possession of the car at that time.

Moreover, since December 31, 1961, was a Sunday, it is doubtful whether the car could have been transferred to petitioner before Monday even with the cooperation of the editor in chief of Sport. The New York dealership at which the car was located was closed. The car had not been set aside for petitioner's use and delivery was not dependent solely upon the volition of petitioner. The doctrine of constructive receipt is therefore inapplicable, and we hold that petitioner received the Corvette for income tax purposes in 1962 as he originally alleged in his petition and as he reported in his 1962 income tax return.

We now must tackle the more basic question involving the Corvette which is whether the value of the car should be included in petitioner's gross income for the taxable year of receipt. Petitioner's offensive strategy on this issue is two-pronged. He contends (1) that the car was received as a gift and therefore properly excluded from gross income under section 102(a), and (2) that the car was received as a nontaxable prize or award under section 74.

It is our opinion that certainly the donor's motive here precludes a determination that Sport made a gift of the Corvette to petitioner in 1962. It is clear that there was no detached and disinterested generosity. It also seems clear that the enactment of section 74 has had the desirable effect of eliminating the theory of gift exclusions from the field of prizes and awards. * * *

Petitioner undeniably received an award for his outstanding performance in the National Football League championship game. Under the provisions of section 74, gross income includes amounts received as prizes and awards unless section 117 (relating to scholarships and fellowship grants), or the exception set forth in subsection (b) is applicable. Therefore, petitioner is precluded from effectively arguing that the award constituted a gift, and he can only hope to score on his argument that the award qualifies as an exception under section 74(b). In making this argument, petitioner shifts into a shotgun formation, contending that his accomplishments in the championship football game constitute educational, artistic, scientific, and civic achievements within the meaning of section 74(b). We believe that petitioner should be caught behind the line of scrimmage on this particular offensive maneuver.

In construing the terms used in section 74(b), we are cognizant of the Supreme Court's recent reaffirmation of the principle that the words of revenue acts should be interpreted in their ordinary, everyday sense unless the internal structure of the statute or the legislative purpose indicates the propriety of a departure from a literal reading. See *Malat v. Riddell*, 383 U.S. 569 (1966). Petitioner relies primarily upon the opinions and beliefs of the editor in chief of Sport to establish the applicability of section 74(b).

In the opinion of this witness, the game of football is educational because it is taught in accredited colleges as part of certain physical education courses. Moreover, being a star football player is said to be an artistic achievement since such status "calls for a degree of artistry." Finally, since the skills of a football player are based upon techniques which encompass certain "scientific" principles,[7] it is contended that petitioner's ability to excel in the execution of these techniques is a scientific achievement worthy of recognition by means of the award presented by Sport. Petitioner also argues that the award was made in recognition of civic achievement due to the alleged interest of the President of the United States in petitioner's application for leave from the Army to allow participation in the championship game.

We believe that the words "educational," "artistic," "scientific," and "civic" as used in section 74(b) should be given their ordinary, everyday meaning in the context of defining certain types of personal achievement. Legislative history supports our belief. For example, the Senate report states that the provisions of section 74(b) are intended to exempt from taxation such awards as the Nobel prize. See S. Rept. No. 1622, to accompany H.R. 8300 (Pub. L. 591), 83d Cong., 2d Sess., p. 178 (1954).

The legislative history of section 74 has been judicially interpreted as indicating that "only awards for genuinely meritorious achievements were to be freed from taxation." *Simmons v. United States*, 308 F.2d 160, 163 (C.A. 4, 1962). It was further stated in *Simmons* that all of the types of achievements singled out in section 74(b) resemble each other in general character since "they all represent activities enhancing in one way or another the public good." This interpretation is consistent with our view that the field of activity here in question, professional football, is not an activity which is "educational," "artistic," "scientific," or

---

7. The record contains the following statements by the editor in chief of Sport describing some of the "scientific" principles of football:

The players have large notebooks that they have at the beginning of the practice season that contain intricate plays. You have to be somewhat of a mathematician to digest them. * * *

* * *

Part of the training, at least related to football, professional football, is that the athlete must know a certain number of plays a year; must know how to play his position in many different ways; must be able to look at a film of another team and decide how to play against his particular opponent; must look at his own films and know what he has done right and what he has done wrong, and whether he has blocked off the wrong shoulder or something like that. He must know what his teammates are doing in relation to a formation, in relation to specific plays.

This is all in the area of technique, and is quite complicated, and in a sense I think scientific.

"civic" in the traditional, ordinarily understood, and intended sense of these words.

We feel confident that Congress had no intention of allowing professional football to constitute a type of activity for which proficiency could be recognized with an exempt award under section 74(b). Professional football cannot be viewed as an "educational," "artistic," "scientific," or "civic" field of endeavor as those terms are used in the statute no matter how fond of the sport we may be. The crucial question for qualification under section 74(b) is the nature of the activity awarded. Had Congress intended to except prizes or awards for recognition of athletic prowess or achievement it could readily and easily have done so; as provided now however, no such exception can be read into the statutory language used. We hold that the value of the Corvette should have been included in petitioner's gross income for 1962. To hold otherwise would be a distortion of the commonly understood meaning of the words in controversy when read in the overall context of section 74.

* * *

start-up

* * *

DAVIS v. COMMISSIONER, T.C. Memo. 1978–12.

Facts: In November, 1974, the taxpayer elected to receive severance pay from her employer, a railroad, when it merged two of its offices and effectively eliminated the taxpayer's position. The taxpayer was told it would take two months to process the necessary paperwork and that she would not receive the payment until sometime early in 1975. In late December, 1974, however, the railroad sent the severance pay by certified mail, return receipt requested, to the taxpayer's home. A mail carrier attempted delivery on December 31, 1974, but the taxpayer was not home. The mail carrier left a notice informing the taxpayer that the letter was available at the local branch of the post office. The taxpayer did not return home until after 5:00 p.m. that day, by which time the post office branch was closed. She obtained the letter containing the check on January 2, 1975. The taxpayer was not expecting the payment so soon; she guessed that the letter was a notice of rent increase. The taxpayer did not include the severance pay in her 1974 gross income, even though the railroad included it in her Form W–2 for the year. The Service concluded that the pay should have been included in income for 1974 because the pay was "unqualifiedly committed" to her by the railroad that year, and the taxpayer fled to Tax Court for resolution of the issue.

Issue: Did the taxpayer constructively receive the severance pay in 1974?

Holding: No.

Rationale: While it is true that the railroad "had unqualifiedly committed the funds to petitioner by December 31, 1974, * * * such a commitment is not sufficient in itself to cause constructive receipt. The funds must be made available to the taxpayer without substantial limitations. Implicit in availability is notice to the taxpayer that the funds are subject to his will and control. Such notice is lacking here." The Service argued that the taxpayer should not be allowed to defer income by choosing not to be at home when the mail carrier attempted delivery, but "[t]he error in respondent's logic lies in equating petitioner's choice to be absent from home with a conscious choice not to receive the severance pay until the following year. In fact, petitioner's absence here was not procured to prevent actual receipt. Under these circumstances application of the doctrine of constructive receipt is inappropriate. [In] general, income should not be construed to have been received prior to the date of actual receipt except where a taxpayer turns his back upon income or does not choose to receive income which he could have if he chose."

VEIT v. COMMISSIONER

United States Tax Court, 1947.
8 T.C. 809.

BLACK, J.

[During 1939 and 1940, the petitioner was an executive vice president of a cotton goods corporation. The petitioner was in charge of sales, production, and styling. Pursuant to the terms of an employment contract entered into in 1939, the petitioner was entitled to a fixed salary plus a bonus equal to ten percent of the corporation's profits in 1939 and 1940. The bonus payment was scheduled to be paid in 1941. In November, 1940, however, the contract was revised to provide that the bonus amount from 1939's profits would be paid in 1941 and that the bonus amount from 1940's profits would be paid in 1942.

The petitioner received the 1941 bonus payment as provided under the revised agreement from November, 1940. But in December, 1941, the corporation and the petitioner agreed to pay the bonus amount from 1940's profits over a five-year period ranging from 1942 to 1946.

In this case, the Service claimed that the petitioner constructively received the bonus amount from 1940's profits in 1941 and that the November, 1940, agreement was ineffective to postpone inclusion in gross income until 1942. The December, 1941, agreement was not before the court.]

    * * *

OPINION

    * * *

    * * * [A]s to petitioner's share of the corporation's profits for the year 1940, this had not yet been determined when the new contract of November 1, 1940, was entered into. However, in the contract and as a part of the consideration for it, it was agreed between the parties that whatever petitioner's share of the profits for 1940 should prove to be, they should not be payable in 1941, as the original contract provided, but

should be payable in 1942 * * *. Petitioner's share of the profits for 1940 was on June 18, 1941, ascertained by agreement of the parties to be $87,076.40 * * *.

Respondent has determined that this $87,076.40 was constructively received by petitioner in 1941 and should have been returned by him for taxation in that year as his separate property. Respondent's action in that respect is the issue we have to determine under the assignment of error we are now discussing. We think it must be determined in favor of petitioner. Respondent, in contending that petitioner constructively received the $87,076.40 in question in 1941, relies on [the doctrine of] constructive receipt * * *.

However, we think that the facts present in the instant case show clearly there was no constructive receipt by the petitioner in 1941 of the $87,076.40 in question * * *. Petitioner, prior to November 1, 1940, had decided that he would move to California and take things easier. He talked things over with Leon Lowenstein, president of the corporation, and it was finally agreed that petitioner would continue in the employment of the corporation, but on a restricted basis. The terms of this new employment were embodied in a contract dated November 1, 1940, which is in evidence. As a part of this new employment contract and as one of the considerations for it, petitioner agreed to defer the receipt of his share of the 1940 profits, at that time undetermined, until 1942 * * *. The whole agreement of November 1, 1940, was an arm's length business transaction entered into by petitioner and the corporation which was regarded as mutually profitable to both. The only way we should be justified in holding that petitioner constructively received the $87,076.40 in 1941 would be to hold that the agreement to defer the payment of such $87,076.40 until 1942 was a mere subterfuge and sham for the purpose of enabling petitioner to postpone his income tax on the amounts involved to another year. The evidence does not justify such a holding, but, on the contrary, seems to establish that the agreement to defer the payments until 1942 was an arm's length contract, arrived at in the ordinary course of business.

As we have already pointed out, in this same agreement it was provided that petitioner should receive the balance of profits for 1939 in 1941, and he did actually receive them as agreed, and he has returned them for taxation. Petitioner testified at the hearing of this proceeding, and in the course of his testimony he was asked why in the contract of November 1, 1940, it was provided that the payment of his share of 1940 profits should be deferred from 1941 to 1942, with an agreement that the corporation should pay him interest on the amount due from October 1, 1941, to the dates payments were made. His answer to this inquiry was:

> It was the habit of Lowenstein to defer payments to me, other employees as well, when they extended employment terms. Accruables that ran from 1931 to 1935 were not paid me until 1937. A profit accruable of 1936 was not paid me until 1939. There was

always a discussion on these payments on my part, that due to the fact that the company charged me interest on capital and surplus before a determination of the profits, that when they deferred payment which I always recorded on a cash basis, in accordance with the law, they should pay me interest. While I was never successful in having them do that—so in this last contract referred to, when Mr. Lowenstein was, as I testified yesterday, anxious to keep me under his thumb, he voluntarily stated that he would make a small token payment in order to make me happy, because I had been contending with him about it for years. It was his proposition.

* * *

* * * In [this case] there was an agreement to pay at a particular time indefinite amounts, and, prior to the date on which those amounts were due or could be determined, payment was deferred. * * *

As we have already stated, we find that the agreement of November 1, 1940, entered into between petitioner and the corporation, by which, among other things, it was provided that payment of petitioner's share of the 1940 profits should be deferred from 1941 to 1942, was bona fide and entered into in a business transaction at arm's length. * * * On this issue we hold for petitioner.

We think we should point out that the evidence shows that in a subsequent contract entered into December 26, 1941, the petitioner and the corporation changed the dates of the payment of the $87,076.40 here in question from * * * 1942 to five equal installments of $17,415.38 each during 1942, 1943, 1944, 1945, and 1946. We do not have the year 1942 before us, and we express no opinion as to whether this contract of December 26, 1941, operates to make inapplicable the doctrine of constructive receipt for the year 1942. In other words, we express no opinion as to the effect of the contract of December 26, 1941.

* * *

* * *

Well, "the contract of December 26, 1941," would come before the Tax Court in a separate action. The following case is thus referred to as "*Veit II.*"

VEIT v. COMMISSIONER

United States Tax Court, 1949.
8 T.C.M. 919.

JOHNSON, JUDGE: * * *

The Commissioner determined deficiencies of $53,625.03 and $18,539.04 in petitioners' respective income and victory taxes for 1943. Petitioners, husband and wife, contend that he erred (1) by including in the husband's 1942 income the full amount due as compensation for services because by contract the amount was payable in five annual installments beginning in 1943; * * *.

OPINION

* * *

Factually the attendant circumstances of the deferments of November 1, 1940, and December 26, 1941, were similar. By each contract the corporation retained petitioner in its employ; by each petitioner procured interest on the amounts due in agreeing to deferred payments and as Leon Lowenstein testified, he, not petitioner, requested the deferments because he wished to retain the money for corporate use. Deferment in the payments of profit percentages due officers as compensation was not new but usual in the corporation's history. Lowenstein and petitioner both testified that each sought his best advantage in making terms, and the record offers no reason to doubt their statements. Petitioner exacted a $15,000 bonus for his 1941 services, and when the United States entered the war after the parties' preliminary negotiations in November, Lowenstein induced him to accept a nominal fixed salary of $2,500 instead of the $15,000 originally contemplated.

Respondent stresses that the amount of petitioner's share of 1940 profits had not been ascertained when the contract of November 1, 1940, was made, while on December 26, 1941, it had been computed, credited on the corporate books, and the full amount deducted on the corporation's 1940 tax return. We do not deem these differences material. Under existing contracts there was never a time when the $87,076.40 was unqualifiedly subject to petitioner's demand or withdrawal. He did not voluntarily refrain from collecting money available for him, nor did he agree to the debtor's deferred payment of money available when the agreements were made. * * *

* * *

We hold that the Commissioner erred in adding to petitioner's 1942 income that part of the $87,076.40 which was payable in future years. * * *

* * *

Note

In *Revenue Procedure 92–65*, 1992–2 C.B. 428, the Service announced that it would not issue a private ruling dealing with the issue of constructive receipt where a taxpayer's election to defer income occurs after the performance of services giving rise to the right to payment but before the originally scheduled date of payment. The taxpayer in *Veit II*, therefore, would not be entitled to the assurance of an advance ruling from the Service if the facts in that case arose today.

But the Service's refusal to issue a ruling should not automatically deter taxpayers from relying on *Veit II* under similar circumstances. While the Service's no-ruling position may indicate its disagreement with the holding in *Veit II*, the case remains reliable authority that taxpayers can use in defense of deferring income.

* * *

The Cash Equivalence Doctrine. When a cash method taxpayer receives cash, there is no question when "receipt" occurs. But what if a taxpayer gets a check? Or a credit card payment? Or a promissory note? When does "receipt" occur in these non-cash payment transactions? The regulations note only that payment may be "in the form of cash, property, or services." Treas. Reg. § 1.446–1(c)(1)(i). From this comes the notion that any benefits that are the equivalent of cash also must be included in gross income when received. It is not necessary that the benefit be transferable. For instance, if an employer provides meals and lodging to a cash method employee, the employee has gross income at the time the free meal or lodging is provided unless the benefit falls within the statutory exclusions under §§ 119 or 132.

The cash equivalence doctrine is harder to apply when the benefit received is in the form of a promise. If a mere promise to pay was considered a cash equivalent, there would effectively be no difference between the cash and accrual methods. Further, the promise may be subject to conditions—perhaps even those outside of the taxpayer's control. On the other hand, when the promise is unconditional, there is a better case for inclusion. The following case wrestles with this important issue.

COWDEN v. COMMISSIONER

United States Court of Appeals, Fifth Circuit, 1961.
289 F.2d 20.

JONES, CIRCUIT JUDGE.

* * * In April 1951, Frank Cowden, Sr. and his wife made an oil, gas and mineral lease for themselves and their children upon described lands in Texas to Stanolind Oil and Gas Company. By related supplemental agreements, Stanolind agreed to make "bonus" or "advance royalty" payments in an aggregate amount of $511,192.50. On execution of the instruments $10,223.85 was payable, the sum of $250,484.31 was due "no earlier than" January 5 "nor later than" January 10, 1952, and $250,484.34 was stipulated to be paid "no earlier than" January 5 "nor later than" January 10, 1953. One-half of the amounts was to be paid to Frank Cowden, Sr. and his wife, and one-sixth was payable to each of their children. In the deferred payments agreements it was provided that:

> This contract evidences the obligation of Stanolind Oil and Gas Company to make the deferred payments referred to in subparagraphs (b) and (c) of the preceding paragraph hereof, and it is understood and agreed that the obligation of Stanolind Oil and Gas Company to make such payments is a firm and absolute personal obligation of said Company, which is not in any manner conditioned upon development or production from the demised premises, nor upon the continued ownership of the leasehold interest in such premises by Stanolind Oil and Gas Company, but that such payments shall be made in all events.

* * * The Commissioner made a determination that the contractual obligations of Stanolind to make payments in future years represented ordinary income * * * to the extent of the fair market value of the obligations at the time they were created. The Commissioner computed the fair market value of the Stanolind obligations, which were not interest bearing, by the deduction of a discount of four per cent, on the deferred payments from the date of the agreements until the respective maturities. Such computation fixed a 1951 equivalent of cash value of $487,647.46 for the bonus payments, paid in 1951 and agreed to be paid thereafter, aggregating $511,192.50. The Commissioner determined that the taxpayers should be taxed in 1951 on $487,647.46, as ordinary income.

A majority of the Tax Court was convinced that, under the particular facts of this case, the bonus payments were not only readily but immediately convertible to cash and were the equivalent of cash, and had a fair market value equal to their face value. The Tax Court decided that the entire amounts of the bonus payments, $511,192.50, were taxable in 1951, as ordinary income. Two judges of the Tax Court dissented.

* * *

It was said in *Gregory v. Helvering*, 293 U.S. 465, 55 S.Ct. 266, 79 L.Ed. 596, 97 A.L.R. 1355, and recently repeated in *Knetsch v. United States*, 364 U.S. 361, 81 S.Ct. 132, 135, 5 L.Ed.2d 128, "The legal right of a taxpayer to decrease the amount of what otherwise would be his taxes, or altogether avoid them, by means which the law permits, cannot be doubted." As a general rule a tax avoidance motive is not to be considered in determining the tax liability resulting from a transaction. The taxpayers had the right to decline to enter into a mineral lease of their lands except upon the condition that the lessee obligate itself for a bonus payable in part in installments in future years, and the doing so would not, of itself, subject the deferred payments to taxation during the year that the lease was made. Nor would a tax liability necessarily arise although the lease contract was made with a solvent lessee who had been willing and able to pay the entire bonus upon the execution of the lease.

While it is true that the parties may enter into any legal arrangement they see fit even though the particular form in which it was cast was selected with the hope of a reduction in taxes, it is also true that if a consideration for which one of the parties bargains is the equivalent of cash it will be subjected to taxation to the extent of its fair market value. Whether the undertaking of the lessee to make future bonus payments was, when made, the equivalent of cash and, as such, taxable as current income is the issue in this case. In a somewhat similar case, decided in 1941, the Board of Tax Appeals stated that "where no notes, bonds, or other evidences of indebtedness other than the contract were given, such contract had no fair market value." *Kleberg v. Commissioner*, 43 B.T.A. 277, quoting from *Titus v. Commissioner*, 33 B.T.A. 928. In 1959 the Tax Court held that where the deferred bonus payments were evidenced by promissory notes the equivalent of cash doctrine might be applicable. *Barnsley v. Commissioner*, 31 T.C. 1260. There the Tax Court said:

> It is, of course, possible under an oil and gas lease containing proper provisions to have a bonus payable and taxable in installments, *Alice K. Kleberg*, 43 B.T.A. 277. The case before us does not constitute such an arrangement. In the Kleberg case the contractual agreement was to pay a named amount in two payments as bonus. It was not a case like the one here where cash and negotiable notes, the latter being the equivalent of cash, representing the bonus were received in the same year by the taxpayer.

The test announced in *Kleberg*, from which *Barnsley* does not depart, seems to be whether the obligation to make the deferred payments is represented by "notes, bonds, or other evidences of indebtedness other than the contract." In this case, the literal test of *Kleberg* is met as the obligation of Stanolind to the Cowdens was evidenced by an instrument other than the contract of lease. This instrument is not, however, one of the kind which fall into the classification of notes or bonds. The taxpayers urge that there can be no "equivalent of cash" obligation unless it is a negotiable instrument. Such a test, to be determined by the form of the obligation, is as unrealistic as it is formalistic. The income tax law deals in economic realities, not legal abstractions, and the reach of the income tax law is not to be delimited by technical refinements or mere formalism.

A promissory note, negotiable in form, is not necessarily the equivalent of cash. Such an instrument may have been issued by a maker of doubtful solvency or for other reasons such paper might be denied a ready acceptance in the market place. We think the converse of this principle ought to be applicable. We are convinced that if a promise to pay of a solvent obligor is unconditional and assignable, not subject to set-offs, and is of a kind that is frequently transferred to lenders or investors at a discount not substantially greater than the generally prevailing premium for the use of money, such promise is the equivalent of cash and taxable in like manner as cash would have been taxable had it been received by the taxpayer rather than the obligation. The principle that negotiability is not the test of taxability in an equivalent of cash case such as is before us, is consistent with the rule that men may, if they can, so order their affairs as to minimize taxes, and points up the doctrine that substance and not from should control in the application of income tax laws.

The Tax Court stressed in its findings that the provisions for deferring a part of the bonus were made solely at the request of and for the benefit of the taxpayers, and that the lessee was willing and able to make the bonus payments in cash upon execution of the agreements. It appears to us that the Tax Court, in reaching its decision that the taxpayers had received equivalent of cash bonuses in the year the leases were executed, gave as much and probably more weight to those findings than to the other facts found by it. We are persuaded of this not only by the language of its opinion but because, in its determination of the cash equivalent, it used the amounts which it determined the taxpayers could have received if they had made a different contract, rather than the fair market value cash equivalent of the obligation for which the taxpayers had bargained in the contracts which they had a lawful right to make. We are unable to say whether or not the Tax Court, if it disregarded, as we think it should have done, the facts as it found them as to the willingness of the lessee to pay and the unwillingness of the taxpayers to receive the full bonus on execution of the leases, would have determined that the equivalent bonus obligations were taxable in the year of the agreements as the equivalent of cash. This question is primarily a fact issue. There should be a remand to the Tax Court for a reconsideration of the question submitted in the light of what has been said here.

* * *

For further proceedings in keeping with the conclusions here expressed, the decision of the Tax Court is reversed and the cause is remanded.

Reversed and remanded.

* * *

Problem 6–1

Helen Back, a cash method individual, paints Natalie Cladd's house on October 20, Year One. The agreed fee for Helen's work is $3,000. In each of the following situations, determine whether Helen, a cash method taxpayer, has gross income in Year One or Year Two.

(a) Natalie gives Helen a check in the amount of $3,000 on December 15, Year One. Helen deposits the check on January 5, Year Two.

(b) Natalie gives Helen a check at 6:00 p.m. on December 31, Year One. At that time, all banks are closed. Helen deposits the check on January 2, Year Two, the next day that banks are open.

(c) On December 31, Year One, Natalie informs Helen that a check in the amount of $3,000 is waiting for Helen at Natalie's office. Natalie's office is 30 miles from Helen's residence. Since December 31 was not a regular business day for Helen, she opted to stay with family and friends. Helen picked up the check on the next business day (January 2, Year Two) and deposited the check that same day.

(d) On October 15, Year One, Natalie gives Helen a promissory note in the amount of $3,000. Under the terms of the note, Natalie will pay Helen the entire principal balance (together with accrued, market-rate interest) on April 15, Year Two. Natalie makes the payment on April 15, Year Two.

(e) Same as (d), except that Natalie is insolvent at the time she delivers the note. On November 1, Year One, Helen exchanges the note for a tractor from Harold, another cash method taxpayer unrelated to Helen. The tractor is worth $2,600, and Harold's adjusted basis in the tractor is $2,000. In addition to Helen, to what extent (and when) does Harold have gross income under these facts?

Problem 6–2

Arnie Becker, an attorney at the law firm of McKenzie, Brackman, Chaney & Kuzak, performed legal services for his client, Belinda Fox, in Year One. Determine when Arnie has gross income in each of the following alternative scenarios.

(a) Arnie sent Belinda a bill for $6,000 at the end of Year One, and Belinda paid the bill in January of Year Two.

(b) Same as (a), except that Belinda paid Arnie's bill with a credit card late in Year One. Belinda timely paid her credit card company's bill in January, Year Two.

(c) Before Arnie commenced work on Belinda's matter, Arnie and Belinda agreed that one-third of Arnie's total fee would be paid in Year One and that the remaining two-thirds of Arnie's total fee would be paid in Year Two. Arnie sent a bill to Belinda for $6,000 near the end of Year One. Belinda paid $2,000 on December 30, Year One, and the remaining $4,000 in March, Year Two.

(d) Same as (c), except that the parties originally agreed that the entire fee would be paid by the end of Year One. It was not until Arnie completed his work (well before the end of Year One) that the parties agreed that one-third of the fee would be payable in Year One and two-thirds of the fee would be payable in Year Two.

* * *

(2) DEDUCTION ITEMS

Code: IRC § 461(a), (g).

Regs: Treas. Reg. §§ 1.263(a)–4(f)(1); 1.461–1(a)(1).

Constructive Payment. We learned that there is a "constructive receipt" doctrine whereby cash method taxpayers may be forced to include an income item in gross income before actual receipt. One would think a cash method taxpayer could claim a deduction item upon "constructive payment." Suppose, for example, that a cash method taxpayer purchases a small amount of supplies for use in a business activity by giving a promissory note for the purchase price payable in the next taxable year. Had the taxpayer paid with cash, check, or credit card, the taxpayer could have claimed a deduction in the year the supplies were purchased. But, alas, there is no "constructive payment" doctrine, so the taxpayer cannot claim that payment was made simply by giving a note in the amount of the purchase price. See, e.g., *Vander Poel v. Commissioner*, 8 T.C. 407 (1947). The taxpayer will get a deduction when the note is paid, because that is when *actual payment* occurs.

Determining Actual Payment. Payment of deductible expenses in cash is the easy case. Payment in other forms can be trickier. Payment also occurs, for example, when the taxpayer transfers property or performs services in lieu of making a cash payment, although these payments may give rise to collateral tax consequences. Thus, where a taxpayer pays a $100 deductible expense by transferring property worth $100 but having a basis to the taxpayer of only $20, the taxpayer has an $80 gain in addition to the $100 deduction. Likewise, where a taxpayer performs $100 worth of services in payment of the expense, the taxpayer has $100 of gross income as compensation for services in addition to the $100 deduction.

Payment by check is deemed to occur when the check is delivered, so long as the check is honored on presentation by the payee. This rule persists even where presentation does not occur until the next taxable year, and even though the taxpayer could stop payment on the check in the meantime. *Estate of Spiegel v. Commissioner*, 12 T.C. 524 (1949). So if a cash method taxpayer delivers a $100 check for a deductible expense on December 31, Year One, the deduction properly belongs on the Year One tax return, even though the payee does not present the check to the bank until Year Two. Postdated checks, however, are not considered payment when delivered; instead, they are treated as a mere promise to pay when delivered. *Griffin v. Commissioner*, 49 T.C. 253 (1967).

Delivery of a promissory note by a cash method taxpayer is not considered "payment" of the expense, even if the note is transferable and even if the note is secured by collateral. The cash method taxpayer claims the deduction only if (and when) the note is paid. *Helvering v. Price*, 309 U.S. 409, 60 S.Ct. 673, 84 L.Ed. 836 (1940). But where a cash method taxpayer borrows funds and uses the proceeds to pay a deductible expense, a deduction is proper. *Granan v. Commissioner*, 55 T.C. 753 (1971). For instance, if a taxpayer borrows $100 and uses the proceeds to pay for a business expense, a $100 deduction is correct unless the taxpayer borrowed the $100 from the party to whom the payment is made.

The Service has generally ruled that payment by credit card occurs at the point of sale, not when the taxpayer is billed by the credit card company or when the taxpayer pays the bill. In *Revenue Ruling 78–38*, 1978–1 C.B. 67, the Service observed that paying with a credit card is similar to using borrowed funds to make a payment. This ruling represented a reversal of the Service's earlier position that analogized payment by credit card to a payment by delivery of a promissory note.

Self-Assessment Question

(Solutions to Self–Assessment Questions are set forth in Appendix 3.)

SAQ 6–1. Recall the facts from Problem 6–2 above (Arnie Becker and Belinda Fox). Assuming the payments to Arnie are deductible expenses, in what year(s) may Belinda claim a deduction in each of the alternative scenarios described in that Problem?

* * *

Deductibility of Advance Payments. A cash method taxpayer can easily exploit the system by pre-paying expenses. Suppose, for example, that a cash method taxpayer leases office space from December 1, Year One, to May 31, Year Two, for $6,000 (or $1,000 per month). If the taxpayer pays the entire $6,000 in Year One, the taxpayer can deduct $6,000 on the Year One tax return. Assuming an applicable tax rate of 35 percent, the deduction saves the taxpayer $2,100 in taxes. If the taxpayer only pays the December rent in Year One, however, the deduction ($1,000) only saves $350 in taxes. By saving the extra $1,750 sooner, the taxpayer can allow the savings to grow for a longer period. Of course, the taxpayer has to be willing to depart with the extra 5 months of rent ($5,000) sooner than required, but over the long term, the benefit might be worthwhile.

Likewise, there could be a benefit to prepaying expenses if the taxpayer expects to be in a lower tax bracket in the next taxable year. If our taxpayer in the last example expected to be taxed at 25 percent in Year Two (as opposed to 35 percent in Year One), there is a greater benefit to claiming the extra $5,000 deduction in Year One. The greater benefit is $500, in this example.

Maybe the taxpayer's deduction of 5 months' rent is not so offensive. But what if the taxpayer pre-pays two full years' worth of rent? Or five years' worth? Is there no limit to the madness?

Regulation § 1.461–1(a)(1) contains a limitation, stating that "if an expenditure results in the creation of an asset having a useful life which extends substantially beyond the close of the taxable year, such an expenditure may not be deductible, or may be deductible only in part, for the taxable year in which made." This is the familiar principle of capitalization, one we already grappled with in Chapter 4. Here again, however, we are faced with trying to discern what is meant by the word "substantially" in the Regulation. The case below discusses the issue in connection with pre-payment of insurance premiums.

COMMISSIONER v. BOYLSTON MARKET ASSOCIATION

United States Court of Appeals, First Circuit, 1942.
131 F.2d 966.

MAHONEY, CIRCUIT JUDGE.

* * *

The taxpayer in the course of its business, which is the management of real estate owned by it, purchased from time to time fire and other insurance policies covering periods of three or more years. It keeps its books and makes its returns on a cash receipts and disbursements basis. The taxpayer has since 1915 deducted each year as insurance expenses the amount of insurance premiums applicable to carrying insurance for that year regardless of the year in which the premium was actually paid.
* * *

We are asked to determine whether a taxpayer who keeps his books and files his returns on a cash basis is limited to the deduction of the insurance premiums actually paid in any year or whether he should deduct for each tax year the pro rata portion of the prepaid insurance applicable to that year. * * *

This court in *Welch v. De Blois*, 1 Cir., 1938, 94 F.2d 842, held that a taxpayer on the cash receipts and disbursements basis who made prepayments of insurance premiums was entitled to take a full deduction for these payments as ordinary and necessary business expenses in the year in which payment was made despite the fact that the insurance covered a three-year period. * * * The Board of Tax Appeals has refused to follow that case in *George S. Jephson v. Com'r*, 37 B.T.A. 1117; *Frank Real Estate & Investment Co.*, 40 B.T.A. 1382, unreported memorandum decision Nov. 15, 1939, and in the instant case. The arguments in that case in favor of treating prepaid insurance as an ordinary and necessary business expense are persuasive. We are, nevertheless, unable to find a real basis for distinguishing between prepayment of rentals, * * * bonuses for the acquisition of leases, * * * bonuses for the cancellation of leases, * * * commissions for negotiating leases, * * * and prepaid insurance. Some distinctions may be drawn in the cases cited on the basis of the facts contained therein, but we are of the opinion that there is no justification for treating them differently insofar as deductions are concerned. All of the cases cited are readily distinguishable from such a clear cut case as a permanent improvement to a building. This latter is clearly a capital expenditure. See *Parkersburg Iron & Steel Co. v. Burnet*, 4 Cir., 1931, 48 F.2d 163, 165. In such a case there is the creation of a capital asset which has a life extending beyond the taxable year and which depreciates over a period of years. The taxpayer regardless of his method of accounting can only take deductions for depreciation over the life of the asset. Advance rentals, payments of bonuses for acquisition and cancellation of leases, and commissions for negotiating leases are all matters which the taxpayer amortizes over the life of the lease. Whether we consider these payments to be the cost of the exhaustible asset, as in the case of advance rentals, or the cost of acquiring the asset, as in the case of bonuses, the payments are prorated primarily because the life of the asset extends beyond the taxable year. To permit the taxpayer to take a full deduction in the year of payment would distort his income. Prepaid insurance presents the same problem and should be solved in the same way. Prepaid insurance for a period of three years may be easily allocated. It is protection for the entire period and the taxpayer may, if he desires, at any time surrender the insurance policy. It thus is clearly an asset having a longer life than a single taxable year. The line to be drawn between capital expenditures and ordinary and necessary business expenses is not always an easy one, but we are satisfied that in treating prepaid insurance as a capital expense we are obtaining some degree of consistency in these matters. We are, therefore, of the opinion that *Welch v. DeBlois*, supra, is incorrect and should be overruled.

The decision of Board of Tax Appeals is affirmed.

* * *

The next two cases discuss the prepayment of rent, although their holdings suggest broader applicability. You will see that the two cases create different tests for deciding whether a current deduction is proper. Keep in mind that the Tax Court would be obligated to follow the Ninth Circuit's test in any case that would be appealed to the Ninth Circuit. See *Golsen v. Commissioner*, 54 T.C. 742 (1970).

ZANINOVICH v. COMMISSIONER

United States Court of Appeals, Ninth Circuit, 1980.
616 F.2d 429.

FERGUSON, CIRCUIT JUDGE:

This case presents the issue of whether a rental payment by a cash basis taxpayer for a lease year that extended eleven months beyond the year of payment is fully deductible in the year of payment as an ordinary and necessary business expense or must be deducted on a prorated basis as a capital expenditure. We hold that the payment in this case was fully deductible in the year of payment.

* * * Martin and Vincent Zaninovich are partners in a farming business in the San Joaquin Valley in California. The partnership used the cash basis method of accounting.

On October 3, 1973, the partnership entered into a lease of farm land for the period December 1, 1973 to November 30, 1993. Yearly rent of $27,000 for the period running from December 1 to November 30 was payable on December 20 of each lease year.[2] On December 20, 1973, the partnership paid $27,000 rent for the lease year running from December 1, 1973 to November 30, 1974. The partnership deducted this entire amount on its return for the taxable year 1973.

The Commissioner disallowed $24,934 of the $27,000 payment, reflecting that portion of the rental allocable to the period January 1 through November 30, 1974, and adjusted each partner's share of income accordingly. The Tax Court sustained the Commissioner's determination in *Zaninovich v. Commissioner*, 69 T.C. 605 (1978). We reverse the holding of the Tax Court.

The Tax Court held, largely on the basis of *University Properties, Inc. v. Commissioner*, 45 T.C. 416 (1966), aff'd, 378 F.2d 83 (9th Cir. 1967), that the partnership had to prorate the 1973 rental payment and therefore could deduct in 1973 only the portion of the rental attributable to that year, i.e., one-twelfth. The court found the following language from University Properties controlling:

2. As the Tax Court noted, leases of farmland for twelve-month periods with rent for the first twelve months payable during the first month of each such period are common in the San Joaquin Valley.

> Rentals may be deducted as such only for the year or years to which they are applied. If they are paid for the continued use of the property beyond the years in which paid they are not deductible in full in the year paid but must be deducted ratably over the years during which the property is so used.

Id. at 421.

The taxpayers here argued that the rule in *University Properties* was inapplicable to their case because the December, 1973 rental payment was allocable to a period of only twelve months. In response to this contention, the Tax Court admitted that many of the cases upon which it relied "involve(d) payments which were properly allocable over a period far in excess of 12 months." *Zaninovich v. Commissioner, supra,* 69 T.C. at 607. The court nonetheless found the taxpayers' attempt to distinguish those cases unpersuasive.

We are persuaded that the cases requiring rental payments to be capitalized are distinguishable from the case before us, and that different treatment is warranted here. * * *

Because the classification of the 1973 rental payment as either a deductible expense in the taxable year 1973 or a capital expenditure depends on whether or not eleven months is "substantially beyond" the taxable year, it is significant that many of the cases requiring capitalization of rent related payments involve payments allocable to periods far in excess of eleven months beyond the year of payment. See, e.g., *Main & McKinney Bldg. Co. v. Commissioner,* 113 F.2d 81 (5th Cir.), cert. denied, 311 U.S. 688, 61 S.Ct. 66, 85 L.Ed. 444 (1940) (payments over 25 year period allocable to 99 year lease term); *University Properties, Inc. v. Commissioner, supra* (payments over three year period allocable to 35 year lease term); *Cartan v. Commissioner,* 30 T.C. 308 (1958) (payment in one year allocable to 20 year term). It is also significant that several of the cases treating payments as capital expenditures have involved not rental payments but rental premiums or payments made as consideration for the lease. See, e.g., *Main & McKinney Bldg. Co. v. Commissioner, supra* (payments in addition to rent of $10,000 a year for the first 25 years of a 99 year lease); *Baton Coal v. Commissioner,* 51 F.2d 469 (3d Cir.), cert. denied, 284 U.S. 674, 52 S.Ct. 129, 76 L.Ed. 570 (1931) (payments totaling $101,250 in the first seven months of a mineral lease of indefinite duration); *University Properties, Inc., supra* (payments of $240,000 in addition to rent in the first three years of a 35 year lease).

The cases involving substantially shorter terms in which taxpayers have been required to amortize have, unlike the case before us, involved advance payments, see, e.g., *Williamson v. Commissioner,* 37 T.C. 941 (1962) (payment on December 27, 1956 for a lease running for one year from March 1, 1957 where payment was not due until beginning of lease); cf. *D.K. Mc Coll v. Commissioner,* para. 41,050 P–H Memo B.T.A. (Vol. 10, 1941) (deduction disallowed where rent paid on December 31 for following year because transaction was a sham but dicta indicated advance payment was deductible in year to which it applied), or accrual basis taxpayers, see, e.g., *Bloedel's Jewelry, Inc. v. Commissioner*, 2 B.T.A. 611 (1925) (payment in May, 1920 of rental due for a lease term running from September 1, 1920 to August 31, 1921).[5]

We recognize that there are cases supporting the result urged here by the Commissioner. * * * Neither * * * the Tax Court here, nor any of the prepaid rent cases cited by the Tax Court, however, discusses the qualification to the general rule for cash basis taxpayers for an expenditure that creates an asset having a useful life which extends "substantially beyond" the close of the taxable year. We feel that these provisions are controlling here, and adopt the "one-year rule" applied by several circuits in distinguishing between currently deductible expenses and capital expenditures having a useful life extending "substantially beyond" the taxable year. See, e.g., *Fall River Gas Appliance Co. v. Commissioner*, 349 F.2d 515 (1st Cir. 1965); *Briarcliff Candy Corp. v. Commissioner*, 475 F.2d 775 (2d Cir. 1973); *Jack's Cookie Co. v. United States*, 597 F.2d 395 (4th Cir.) cert. denied, 444 U.S. 899, 100 S.Ct. 207, 62 L.Ed.2d 134 (1979); *Bilar Tool & Die Corp. v. Commissioner*, 530 F.2d 708 (6th Cir. 1976); *United States v. Akin*, 248 F.2d 742 (10th Cir. 1957), cert. denied, 355 U.S. 956, 78 S.Ct. 542, 2 L.Ed.2d 532 (1958).

Under the "one-year rule" an expenditure is treated as a capital expenditure if it creates an asset, or secures a like advantage to the taxpayer, having a useful life in excess of one year.[6] The rationale behind the rule is as follows:

> The one-year rule is useful because it serves to segregate from all business costs those which cannot possibly be considered capital in nature because of their transitory utility to the taxpayer.

Jack's Cookie Co. v. United States, supra, 597 F.2d at 405.

None of the cases applying the "one-year rule" has involved land rentals. See, e. g., *Jack's Cookie Co. v. United States, supra* (portion of rental payments); *Bilar Tool & Die Corp. v. Commissioner, supra* (attorney's fees); *Colorado Springs Nat'l Bank v. United States*, 505 F.2d 1185 (10th Cir. 1974) (costs incurred in participation in credit card system); *Briarcliff Candy Corp. v. Commissioner, supra* (cost of acquiring business entity); *American Dispenser Co. v. Commissioner*, 396 F.2d 137 (2d Cir. 1968) (payment to competitor in exchange for covenant not to manufacture); *Fall River Gas Appliance Co. v. Commissioner, supra*

---

5. The accrual method of accounting, unlike the cash basis method, aims to allocate to the taxable year expenses attributable to income realized in that year. For this reason, it was appropriate for the lessee in *Bloedel's Jewelry, supra*, to prorate to the next year that portion of the rental payment which could be matched with income realized in the next year. Because the cash basis taxpayer is allowed to deduct items when paid, regardless of when related income is realized, there is no need for a prorated deduction here as a means of matching income and expenses.

6. While the "one-year rule" is strictly applied to allow a full deduction in the year of payment where an expenditure creates an asset having a useful life beyond the taxable year of twelve months or less, it is not applied in the same manner in the other direction. Where an expenditure creates an asset having a useful life beyond the taxable year of more than twelve months, the "one-year rule" has been used as a guidepost only, and not as a rigid rule requiring automatic capitalization of every expenditure which creates an asset having a useful life in excess of one year. * * *

(installation costs for leased gas appliances); *United States v. Akin, supra* (sums paid by farmers to ditch companies). Cf. *Waldheim Realty & Inv. Co. v. Commissioner*, 245 F.2d 823 (8th Cir. 1957) (insurance for one year period is deductible expense even though protection extends into subsequent year); *Bell v. Commissioner*, 13 T.C. 344 (1949) (payment for insurance for period from November, 1946 to August, 1947 is deductible in 1946); *Jephson v. Commissioner*, 37 B.T.A. 117 (1938) (payments in October and November, 1934 for two separate policies, each running one year from time of payment, are deductible in year of payment); *Kauai Terminal, Ltd. v. Commissioner*, 36 B.T.A. 893 (1937) (payment in July, 1933 for insurance covering July, 1933 to July, 1934 is deductible in 1933). Nonetheless, we see no reason why the rule should not apply to land rental cases. * * * The overriding advantage of the "one-year rule" is ease of application. Additionally, the rule eliminates pointless complexity in the calculation of the timing of deductions. This advantage is well illustrated by the instant case.

If the taxpayers here are required to deduct their rental payments on a prorated basis, as the Commissioner urges, the simplicity of the cash basis method of accounting is sacrificed for an inconsequential change in the timing of deductions. Under the prorated deduction system, the taxpayers here could only deduct one-twelfth of their rental payment in 1973. In every year thereafter except for the last year of the lease, however, the taxpayers would be permitted to deduct one-twelfth for the current payment and eleven-twelfths for the preceding year's payment. Consequently, under the prorated system the taxpayers here would end up deducting an amount equal to twelve-twelfths of the amount of the yearly rental payment, precisely as they would have done under the general rule for cash basis taxpayers, in every year of the lease term except the first and last.

A further disadvantage of the rule urged by the Commissioner is that these cash basis taxpayers would be claiming a deduction in the last year of the lease for eleven-twelfths of the prior year's payment despite the fact that they have made no expenditure. A primary principle of the cash basis method is that a deduction is appropriate when an expenditure is made. The inconsistency of the result urged here with that principle is a strong reason, in and of itself, not to require prorated deductions in this case.

* * *

For the foregoing reasons, we apply the "one-year rule" in this case and hold that the December, 1973 payment was fully deductible in the year of payment.

REVERSED.

* * *

GRYNBERG v. COMMISSIONER

United States Tax Court, 1984.
83 T.C. 255.

SWIFT, JUDGE:

* * *

FINDINGS OF FACT

* * *

Prepayments of Delay Rental

During the years 1974 through 1979, petitioners owned several hundred oil and gas leases acquired from the United States government, from various state governments and from private lessors. The properties subject to the leases were located in several states, including Colorado, Michigan, New Mexico, Utah and Wyoming.

Under the lease provisions, petitioners were entitled to search for, extract and sell oil and gas from the properties. Petitioners, however, were also obligated to pay to the lessors a specified annual fee with respect to each lease unless certain conditions enumerated in the various leases were satisfied, such as the commencement of drilling operations or the discovery of specified quantities of oil or gas. This annual fee was referred to as "delay rental." The purpose of delay rental was to compensate the lessor for the delay in the development of drilling or production operations on the properties subject to the leases. Payments of delay rental prevented termination of the leases where drilling or production operations had not commenced. Failure to pay delay rental due on a particular lease would result in automatic termination of the lease.

Depending on the provisions of each lease, delay rental payments were due on the first day of the anniversary month, on the second day of the anniversary month, or on some other day during the anniversary month. From 1971 to the present time, petitioners have paid delay rental due each year during the months of April through December on or about the first day of the month preceding the anniversary month. For example, if a delay rental payment were due sometime in the month of July, petitioners would make payment thereof on or about the first of June. However, from 1971 to the present time, in addition to the delay rental due in the following January, petitioners have prepaid in December of each year delay rental which did not become due until the following February and March.

Petitioners were calendar year taxpayers and utilized the cash receipts and disbursements method of accounting (hereinafter referred to as the "cash method") for Federal income tax purposes. They deducted the delay rental paid in December with respect to lease anniversary dates occurring in February and March of the following year.

* * *

OPINION

* * *

Respondent contends that petitioners' method of accounting with respect to prepayments of delay rental was improper, that petitioners have not been consistent in their treatment of those items, and that as a result there were material distortions of income that violate the clear reflection of income requirement of section 446(b). Additionally, respondent contends that the prepayments of delay rental involved herein were the equivalent of voluntary, nondeductible advance deposits, and that they do not qualify as ordinary and necessary business expenses. The Court agrees with respondent's determination that these prepayments do not satisfy the ordinary and necessary requirements of section 162.

* * *

This case concerns the deductibility of prepaid items solely under the authority of section 162 and section 446(b). Where the deductibility of prepaid items is based on those sections, we believe the test to be applied is clear and relatively straightforward. It is a three-pronged test and is based on well established Federal tax principles which generally are applicable to deductions claimed by cash method taxpayers. Each test is independent and must be satisfied.

The First Requirement

The first requirement is that there must have been an actual payment of the item in question. A mere refundable deposit will not support a current deduction. Section 162(a) allows a deduction for all otherwise qualifying expenses "paid or incurred" during the taxable year. A cash basis taxpayer must actually and irretrievably pay the expense during the taxable year in order to be entitled to a deduction under section 162(a). If the taxpayer retains the unilateral power to require a refund of the money or to redirect its use the transfer is considered a mere deposit and a deduction is not allowed in that year. *Keller v. Commissioner*, 725 F.2d at 1177–1178; *Schenk Commissioner*, 686 F.2d 315, 319 (5th Cir. 1982); *Mann v. Commissioner*, 483 F.2d 673, 678 (8th Cir. 1973), *Ernst v. Commissioner*, 32 T.C. 181, 186 (1959).

The Second Requirement

The second requirement is that there must have been a substantial business reason for making the prepayment in the year in which it was made. If the prepayment occurred simply to accelerate a tax deduction, no deduction will be allowed in the year of prepayment. This requirement is also based on section 162(a). Unless the prepayment of an item is for a valid business purpose, and not solely for a tax reduction, it "cannot fairly be characterized as an ordinary and necessary business expense" of the year of prepayment. *Keller v. Commissioner*, 79 T.C. at 48–50 (no business purpose for prepayment of management fees); *Stice v. United States*, 540 F.2d 1077, 1081 (5th Cir. 1976) (no business purpose in light of slight business benefit received); *Mann v. Commissioner*, *supra* at 680 (business purpose where protection from future price fluctuations was obtained by prepayment); *Bonaire Development Co. v. Commissioner*, 76 T.C. 789, 795 (1981), aff'd 679 F.2d 159 (9th Cir. 1982) (no business purpose for prepayment of management fees); *Williamson v. Commissioner*, 37 T.C. 941 (1962) (no business purpose for prepayment of delay rental).

The Third Requirement

The third requirement is that prepayment of the item in question must not cause a material distortion in the taxpayer's taxable income in the year of prepayment. This requirement is based on section 446(b)[11] which provides that—

> (b) Exceptions.—If no method of accounting has been regularly used by the taxpayer, or if the method used does not clearly reflect income, the computation of taxable income shall be made under such method as, in the opinion of the Secretary, does clearly reflect income.

Respondent's authority under section 446(b) reaches not only taxpayer's overall method of accounting but also taxpayer's treatment of specific items of income and expense * * *, and there is a heavy burden on the taxpayer to overcome respondent's determination under section 446(b) that taxpayer's method of accounting does not clearly reflect income.

The facts in this case must be analyzed in light of the above three requirements. The prepayments by petitioners of delay rental, at the time of prepayment, effected either an extension or renewal of the leases. No provision of the leases entitled petitioners to a refund of the prepaid delay rental. Accordingly, we find that the prepayments did not constitute mere deposits but irretrievable payments which satisfy the first requirement.

The issue of whether the prepayments of delay rental involved herein satisfy the second requirement is controlled by our prior opinion in *Williamson v. Commissioner, supra*. That case involved facts essentially identical to those involved herein and disallowed the deduction of prepaid delay rental on the grounds that the prepayment did not qualify as an ordinary and necessary business expense in the year of prepayment.

The taxpayers therein made a prepayment on December 27, 1956, of delay rental with respect to an oil and gas lease, which delay rental was not due until March 1, 1957. Although the taxpayers offered evidence that similarly situated taxpayers had made delay rental payments from 30 to 60 days in advance to secure their leases, we found that there was an insufficient business reason for the prepayment of delay rental in

---

11. * * * We express no opinion herein as to this Court's acceptance of the Ninth Circuit's recent interpretation of the one-year rule of the above regulation. See *Zani-* *novich v. Commissioner*, 616 F.2d 429 (1980), revg. 69 T.C. 605 (1978) and *Commissioner v. Van Raden*, 650 F.2d 1046, affg. on other grounds 71 T.C. 1083 (1979).

1956 where it was not due until the following year. The Court noted: "The facts in the instant case show no reason for petitioners' payment in 1956 of an obligation which would not arise until 1957 and fail to show that such payment constituted an ordinary and necessary business expense in 1956." *Williamson v. Commissioner, supra* at 945.

Similarly here, while there was a legal obligation to pay the delay rental on a periodic basis in order to obtain renewals of the leases, petitioners had no obligation to make delay rental payments in December when the lease renewal dates did not occur and payment of the delay rental was not due until February or March of the following year. Petitioners argue that the prepayments of delay rental were made in order to secure their rights under the leases. This argument is unpersuasive with respect to the prepayments in issue. The general practice of petitioners for all other months was to make the delay rental payments one month in advance. Such practice with respect to the delay rental due in February or March of each year in issue would have secured petitioners' rights under the leases. No reason or business necessity was offered by petitioners herein to explain why it was necessary to prepay sixty to ninety days in advance the delay rental due in February or March of the following year.

Petitioners argue that *Williamson v. Commissioner, supra*, is distinguishable on the grounds that the taxpayers therein, in years prior to those at issue in that case, had not prepaid delay rental and therefore could not establish a record of consistency. That argument appears to be based on the premise that consistent treatment of prepaid items may override the requirement that the prepayments be ordinary and necessary. We reject this argument because, as previously explained, consistent treatment of an item relates to the third requirement.

Based upon the above authorities, the prepayments of delay rental which are in question herein do not satisfy the ordinary and necessary requirements of section 162.

In light of petitioners' failure to satisfy the second requirement, it is not necessary to apply the third requirement to the facts of this case.

Because of the outstanding issue concerning the proper deduction for depletion allowance,

Decisions will be entered under Rule 155.

* * *

Prepaid Interest. While the rules from *Zaninovich* and *Grynberg* can and do apply to the prepayment of various types of expenses, the prepayment of interest is governed by § 461(g). Section 461(g)(1) generally places cash method taxpayers on the accrual method when it comes to prepaid interest expense. For example, suppose a cash method taxpayer agrees to pay interest at the rate of $1,000 per month for a 3–year period beginning on July 1, Year One. The taxpayer prepays all of the interest on July 1, Year One, paying cash of $36,000. Under § 461(g), the taxpayer can claim an interest deduction of $6,000 for Year One—the amount corresponding to the interest accruing from July 1, Year One, to December 31, Year One. The taxpayer will then claim an interest deduction of $12,000 in Years Two and Three, and a final $6,000 deduction in Year Four. Notice under § 461(g)(2) that this conversion to the accrual method does not apply in some cases to the payment of points in connection with certain mortgage loans. "Points" are extra, up-front fees paid by the borrower in order to obtain the loan.

The One–Year Rule in the Regulations. Regulation § 1.263(a)–4(f)(1) incorporates a *Zaninovich*-like one-year rule to all cash method taxpayers with respect to amounts paid "to create * * * any right or benefit for the taxpayer." Eligible taxpayers can deduct all of such costs in the year of payment so long as the right or benefit does not exceed twelve months total *and* does not extend beyond the end of the taxable year following the year of payment. Examples in the regulation suggest that the one-year rule also applies to legal fees and other costs incurred in creating the benefit. See Treas. Reg. § 1.263(a)–4(f)(8), Ex. (6).

*   *   *

Problem 6–3

For each of the following alternative fact patterns, determine the deduction Tenant, a cash method taxpayer, can claim for Year One under *Commissioner v. Boylston Market, Zaninovich v. Commissioner, Grynberg v. Commissioner*, and Regulation § 1.263(a)–4(f)(1), respectively.

(a) Tenant leases commercial office space from Landlord. The lease term runs from March 1, Year One, to February 28, Year Two, and rent is payable at the rate of $1,000 per month. Tenant pays $12,000 to Landlord on March 1, Year One.

(b) Same as (a), except that the lease term runs from March 1, Year One, to December 31, Year Two, and Tenant pays $22,000 to Landlord on March 1, Year One.

(c) Same as (a), except that the lease term runs for two years, from March 1, Year One, to February 28, Year Three. Tenant pays $24,000 to Landlord on March 1, Year One.

p. 380–391//p. 409–417

――――――

B. THE ACCRUAL METHOD

The very first federal income tax following ratification of the Sixteenth Amendment, the Revenue Act of 1913, required all taxpayers to use the cash method. Income items were to be included only when actually received, and only expenses actually paid during the taxable year could be deducted. It did not take long for business owners and their bookkeepers to object. Since most generally accepted accounting principles ("GAAP") are based on the accrual method, the requirement of the cash method was seen as a severe inconvenience. Within a year, the Service permitted the use of the accrual method for deductions.

Then, in 1915, the Service allowed certain taxpayers to use the accrual method for income items as well. Finally, in the Revenue Act of 1916, the accrual method became a part of the formal tax laws.

Although the general rules of the accrual method have been spelled-out more than once already, it is worth repeating them again here as we commence a more detailed analysis of the accrual method. As a general rule, an accrual method taxpayer includes items in income when they are *earned* and claims deductions when expenses are *owed*. Actual receipt and actual payment, in theory, have no relevance. But we will see that there are occasions when accrual method taxpayers care about actual receipt and actual payment, because in some situations accrual method taxpayers are forced to use cash method conventions.

(1) INCOME ITEMS

Code: IRC § 448(d)(5); 455; 456. *Review* §§ 446(a)–(c); 451(a); 461(a).

Regs: Treas. Reg. § 1.446–1(c)(1)(ii). *Review* Treas. Reg. § 1.451–1(a). *Skim* Treas. Reg. §§ 1.448–2T; 1.451–5. ↳ superceded by final Treas. Reg. §1.448-2

The regulations state that an accrual method taxpayer has income "when all the events have occurred that fix the right to receive the income and the amount of the income can be determined with reasonably accuracy." Treas. Reg. § 1.446–1(c)(1)(ii)(A). This is known as the "all-events test," and, not coincidentally, it complies with GAAP. Notice that the all-events test for income has two prongs (when we cover the accrual of deductions, we will see a similar version of the all-events test with three prongs). First, the right to the income must be fixed. Second, #1 the amount that the taxpayer is to receive is reasonably determinable. #2

While the test is easy to recite, it can prove difficult to apply. To illustrate the application of the all-events test, consider an attorney that agrees to perform work at the rate of $300 per hour for a client. The attorney performs the work in Month One, bills the client in Month Two, and the client pays in Month Three. Of course, we know that a cash method attorney will have income in Month Three. But what about an accrual method attorney? Is the all events test satisfied in Month One, Month Two, or Month Three? The following ruling gives some guidance on this point.

REVENUE RULING 74–607

1974–2 C.B. 149.

Advice has been requested concerning when, under the circumstances described below, points charged by a corporation in connection with making first mortgage and construction loans are to be included in its income.

The taxpayer, a domestic corporation using the accrual method of accounting, is engaged in the business of making first mortgage construction and development loans for periods from eighteen to thirty-six months. The loans are repaid in a single payment upon completion of the project when the borrower obtains permanent financing.

As additional compensation for making the loan, the taxpayer charges the borrower a certain number of points, each point representing one percent of the face amount of the loan. No rebate of points is provided for in case of repayment of the loan prior to the due date.

The term "points" as used in this Revenue Ruling refers to a charge made by the lender (mortgagee) to the borrower (mortgagor) that is in addition to the stated annual interest rate and is paid by the borrower to the lender as an adjustment of the stated interest to reflect the actual cost of borrowing money. The amount of the "points" charged is determined by the lender upon consideration of the factors that usually dictate an acceptable rate of interest and is not paid for specific services performed or to be performed by the lender. Thus, "points" as used in this Revenue Ruling are for the use or forbearance of money and are considered to be interest. See *Rev. Rul. 69–188*, 1969–1 C.B. 54.

In most cases, the taxpayer withholds the entire amount of the points from the initial disbursement of funds to the borrower. However, in some situations the gross amount of the loan funds is disbursed and the taxpayer receives a check for the full amount of the points either at the time the loan is made or at the time the loan is repaid.

As stated in Situation 2 in *Rev. Rul. 70–540*, 1970–2 C.B. 101, the points represent interest that is discounted from the face amount of the loan at the time the loan is made. If the taxpayer uses the accrual method of accounting, *Rev. Rul. 70–540* states that interest in the form of discount is includible in income as payments on the note are due, or as actually received if earlier.

* * * [T]he Income Tax Regulations [provide], in part, that under an accrual method of accounting, income is includible in gross income when all the events have occurred that fix the right to receive such income and the amount thereof can be determined with reasonable accuracy.

All the events that fix the right to receive income occur when (1) the required performance occurs, (2) payment therefor is due, or (3) payment therefor is made, whichever happens earliest.

In applying this rule to the accrual of interest income, performance occurs when the lender allows the borrower to use his money. When he has done this for one day, one day's performance has occurred and one day's interest accrues (assuming the payment has not already been made or come due). Thus, unless interest is paid or such payment is due earlier, interest accrues ratably over the term of the loan.

Accordingly, it is held that when loans are repaid in a single payment at the end of the loan the points that are discounted for the loan proceeds must be reported ratably by the taxpayer on a straight-line basis over the life of the loan. It is further held that in those situations in which the points are not discounted from the loan proceeds, such points are also includible in gross income ratably on a straight-line basis over the life of the loan unless they are received or become due earlier.

* * *

* * *

Notice that *Revenue Ruling 74–607* recites an "earlier-of" test for accruing income. Going back to the hypothetical with the accrual method lawyer, there would be gross income in Month One, because that is when the taxpayer performed the services, and that was the first element of the earlier-of test to occur.

Now see what happens when we consider slightly different facts. Suppose an accrual method painter receives a $1,000 advance payment in Month One based on her reasonable estimation of the time she will spend on the project. The painter performs the work in Month Two and sends a final bill in Month Three (the bill shows she performed $1,000 worth of work, receipt of the Month One payment, and a zero balance). If there was no earlier-of test, a straight-forward application of the "all-events" test would lead to the conclusion that the painter has gross income in Month Two, because that is when all of the events have occurred that fix her right to receive the payment. But under the earlier-of test, the painter has gross income in Month One, because payment occurred first. In effect, accrual method taxpayers are put on the cash method in those instances where payment precedes performance and due date.

Clearly, the receipt of an advance payment in no way means that all events have occurred to establish the taxpayer's right to the payment. But the earlier-of test says that accrual of income happens anyway. It seems fair to conclude, therefore, that the Service's earlier-of test supplants the traditional all-events test. In fact, the traditional all-events test set forth in the regulations is but one prong of the earlier-of test.

* * *

Self-Assessment Question

(Solutions to Self–Assessment Questions are set forth in Appendix 3.)

SAQ 6–2. Sandy Shore is an accrual method taxpayer who provides consulting services to various clients. The arrangements with three of her clients are described below. For each arrangement, determine whether Sandy must include the income in Year One or Year Two.

(a) Sandy performs consulting services for a client in December, Year One. In January, Year Two, she mails a bill to the client for her work in December, Year One. The client pays the bill in February, Year Two.

(b) In December, Year One, Sandy enters into a one-month consulting agreement that requires the client to pay her for services in advance. Although the payment is due when the contract is signed, the client does not make payment. Sandy nevertheless performs her work in January, Year Two, confident that the client will make payment. Indeed, the client pays Sandy in February, Year Two.

(c) In December, Year One, Sandy enters into another one-month consulting agreement, but this agreement does not require the client to pay in advance. Instead, the contract provides that payment will be due when the services are completed (January 31, Year Two). Still, the client pays for Sandy's services when the contract is signed. Sandy performs in January, Year Two, as required.

* * *

Doubts as to Collectibility. Suppose an accrual method taxpayer performs services for a financially-troubled customer. If the taxpayer reasonably believes that the customer will be unable to pay for the taxpayer's services, must the taxpayer still accrue the income when performance is complete? The following two cases address this issue. At first, the results of these cases might seem contradictory, but upon further reflection the cases are consistent (and correct).

SPRING CITY FOUNDRY CO. v. COMMISSIONER, 292 U.S. 182, 54 S.Ct. 644, 78 L.Ed. 1200 (1934).

Facts: From March to September of 1920, the taxpayer sold goods to a customer on account. Toward the end of the year, the taxpayer learned that the customer was "in financial straits." In December, 1920, a receiver was appointed after the customer filed a petition in bankruptcy. The taxpayer originally included the income from the sales to the customer in gross income for 1920 and then on the same return tried to deduct the difference between the amount included and the amount ultimately recovered from the receiver. The Service disallowed the deduction. In contesting that decision, the taxpayer argued that its prior inclusion of the income from sales to the troubled customer in 1920 was wrong because it appeared as of the end of 1920 that the customer would not pay.

Issue: Did the taxpayer have gross income in 1920 from its sales on account to a customer when facts subsequent to the sales but before the end of the year suggest that the taxpayer will not collect payment?

Holding: Yes.

Rationale: At the time of the sales, there was no doubt as to the collectibility of the income. Doubt that arises subsequent to the time when all events have occurred that fix the right to receipt do not change the fact that all events indeed did occur. "Keeping accounts and making returns on the accrual basis, as distinguished from the cash basis, import that it is the right to receive and not the actual receipt that determines the inclusion of the amount in gross income. When the right to receive an amount becomes fixed, the right accrues. * * * On an accrual basis, * * * accounts receivable, less the cost of the goods sold, figure in the statement of gross income. If such accounts receivable become uncollectible, in whole or part, the question is one of the deduction which may be taken according to the applicable statute. That is the question here. It is not altered by the fact that the claim of loss relates to an item of gross income which had accrued in the same year.''

CLIFTON MANUFACTURING CO. v. COMMISSIONER, 137 F.2d 290 (4th Cir. 1943).

Facts: Hunter Manufacturing & Commission Company owed almost $400,000 to the taxpayer, and interest was accruing on this debt. In 1933, Hunter was placed into receivership, and by the end of that year, the taxpayer reasonably figured that it would probably recover about half of the total amount it was owed. Nevertheless, the taxpayer included the interest income that accrued on the debt during 1933. This did not adversely affect the taxpayer, however, because the accrued interest income was completely offset by operating losses from the taxpayer's business. For 1934, the taxpayer did not report any of the interest income that accrued on the Hunter debt. The interest that accrued in 1934 was actually received by the taxpayer in 1937. The taxpayer excluded the 1937 receipt from gross income on the grounds that it properly accrued in 1934 (an argument contradictory to the taxpayer's actions in 1934, but the 1934 year was not susceptible to adjustment thanks to the statute of limitations). The Service argued that the interest received in 1937 was properly includible in 1937 and not in 1934 because in 1934 there was reason to doubt that the interest could be collected from Hunter.

Issue: When was the interest income from Hunter properly accruable by the taxpayer?

Holding: 1936, when the collectibility of the interest income was no longer in doubt.

Rationale: "The parties are in agreement that interest is ordinarily accruable when the right to receive it is fixed, and not when it is actually received; but that it is not accruable as long as reasonable doubt exists as to the amount that is collectible by reason of the financial condition or insolvency of the debtor. Bearing this rule in mind, it seems clear that the interest on the Hunter debt was not accruable in * * * 1933; and while the situation in the year * * * 1934 is not free from doubt, there is evidence to support the [lower court's] conclusion that the collectibility of the item was still open to reasonable question in that year. On the other hand, the collectibility of the item was established beyond all reasonable doubt not later than the fiscal year 1936, as the [lower court] found, for in that year Hunter collected a sufficient sum to pay all of its debts in full. The controversy is therefore reduced to the single question[:] whether a taxpayer on an accrual basis, who does not accrue a debt in the tax year when it is due and owing because of reasonable doubt as to its collectibility, must accrue and report it in a later year as soon as its collectibility is established, or defer its inclusion until the year when it is actually received.

"There are no decisions directly in point, but in our view the debt should be accrued and reported as income when its collectibility is assured. This procedure is in harmony with the principle of accrual accounting which regards the right to receive, accompanied by collectibility, as the criterion; and it accords with the decisions which hold that as soon as the right to receive is fixed, as in cases where the taxpayer's claim is in litigation, the taxpayer must accrue and report the debt as income even though it is not paid until a later date. It may well be that in the general course of events the collectibility of a doubtful item does not become so certain as to require its accrual until collection is made * * *. But, this holding serves merely to accentuate the unusual fact in this case that the complete solvency of the debtor became practically certain at least a year before the debt was paid, so that its accruability was then established."

* * *

Special Rule for Services. Under § 448(d)(5), an accrual method service-provider can defer the accrual of the portion of amounts due for services rendered that, on the basis of past experience, is unlikely to be collected. Temporary Regulation § 1.448–2T (last amended in 1988) provides the only method by which a taxpayer can estimate the "likely uncollectible" portion of an account receivable. Specifically, the regulation defines the uncollectible portion of a receivable as the amount that bears the same ratio to the receivable that total bad debts actually sustained by the taxpayer over the past six years bears to total year-end receivables earned during the same period. Treas. Reg. § 1.448–2T(e)(2). While some commentators have criticized the formula's reference to only year-end receivables (instead of total receivables accrued during the taxable year, regardless of whether they are outstanding at the end of the year), the Tax Court has upheld the validity of Treasury's formula. See *Hospital Corp. of America v. Commissioner*, 107 T.C. 116 (1996).

As the statute states, this special rule for service-providers does not apply if the taxpayer charges interest or a penalty for late payment. If the taxpayer offers an early payment discount, this statutory exception will not apply so long as the taxpayer accrues the full amount due at the time the services are provided and so long as the discount is treated as an adjustment to the taxpayer's income in the year of payment. Treas. Reg. § 1.448–2T(c)(1).

* * *

Problem 6–4

May Ann Naze, an accrual method taxpayer, sells portable restroom units to customers in the ordinary course of her business. In Year One, May Ann sold $50,000 worth of units to ABC Corporation, $100,000 worth of units to DEF Corporation, and $150,000 worth of units to GHI Corporation. All of these sales were on account, meaning that payment was due on delivery. All deliveries were completed in Year One. At the time of the sales, May Ann was concerned only about GHI Corporation, because she knew that GHI was insolvent. Hoping that GHI's new management team would restore GHI's profitability, May Ann filled GHI's order anyway.

In October, Year One, ABC notified May Ann that it was unable to pay her until the beginning of Year Two because of a cash flow shortage that was common at the end of the year. May Ann received full payment from ABC in Year Two.

In December, Year One, May Ann learned that DEF was considering bankruptcy. DEF paid half of May Ann's $100,000 bill later that month, sending written notice along with the partial payment that any additional payment was unlikely. In Year Two, DEF indeed filed for bankruptcy, and DEF's remaining debt to May Ann was discharged.

In November of Year Two, May Ann received a letter from GHI indicating that payment would be forthcoming soon because GHI itself was about to receive a large payment from one of its new customers. May Ann received full payment from GHI in February of Year Three.

When (and to what extent) must May Ann accrue the income from the sales to ABC, DEF, and GHI?

* * *

Contested Income and Unenforceable Claims. The "all-events" test requires an accrual method taxpayer to have a "fixed right" to income before it accrues. Where the taxpayer's right to an amount is contested by another party, the right is hardly "fixed." Thus, income generally does not accrue while the dispute remains. See, e.g., *Lamm v. Commissioner*, 873 F.2d 194 (8th Cir. 1989). The income accrues when a final judgment is rendered or when appeals have been exhausted. *Id.* See also *Schlumberger Technology Corp. v. United States*, 195 F.3d 216 (5th Cir. 1999). If the other party is willing to pay a portion of the contested amount to the taxpayer, the taxpayer does not have to accrue that portion if the taxpayer's acceptance would compromise the taxpayer's claim to the full amount. See *Maryland Shipbuilding and Drydock Co. v. United States*, 409 F.2d 1363 (Ct. Cl. 1969).

One would think the same rules would govern unenforceable obligations. Suppose, for example, that a taxpayer is entitled to payment from a third party under an oral contract that is not enforceable because it does not comply with the state's statute of frauds. The rules for contested income, discussed in the last paragraph, indicate that the taxpayer would not have gross income unless and until actual payment is received. But the following case suggests the opposite.

FLAMINGO RESORT, INC. v. UNITED STATES

United States Court of Appeals, Ninth Circuit, 1982.
664 F.2d 1387.

SNEED, CIRCUIT JUDGE:

* * *

I.

FACTS

* * * Flamingo is a legal, licensed, gambling casino operating in the State of Nevada. The casino, an accrual basis taxpayer, excluded

$676,432.00 of casino receivables in its 1967 tax return. The Commissioner required the accrual of these receivables * * *. He then assessed a tax deficiency in the amount of $261,942.65, plus interest.

The receivables in dispute arose from uncollected loans extended by Flamingo in the course of its business. In order to facilitate its gambling operations, Flamingo extended credit to some of its customers. That line of credit was proffered only after an extensive credit check of the patron was conducted by the casino. The customer would sign a "marker" signifying his liability for the sum loaned.[1] Approximately sixty percent of the casino's total play resulted from such credit extensions.

Extensive collection efforts were undertaken on behalf of Flamingo to receive payment of those outstanding casino receivables not repaid prior to the patron's departure. Flamingo's estimates of collectability of those receivables ranged as high as ninety-six percent. The extension of credit and high incidence of payment occurred despite the fact that Nevada does not recognize the legal enforceability of gambling debts.

II.

ANALYSIS

(1) The time of reporting of income of accrual basis taxpayers is governed by the "all events" test. The origins of this test can be traced to *United States v. Anderson*, 269 U.S. 422, 46 S.Ct. 131, 70 L.Ed. 347 (1926). There the Supreme Court held a tax payment for sale of munitions was deductible only in the year the sale occurred and not the following year in which the tax was paid. The taxpayer had contended the tax could not be accrued as an expense prior to its assessment and due date. The Court, in rejecting that argument, found "that in advance of the assessment of a tax, all the events may occur which fix the amount of the tax and determine the liability of the taxpayer to pay it." *Id.* at 441, 46 S.Ct. at 134. This approach was subsequently adopted by the Treasury Department with respect to the accrual of income. "Under an accrual method of accounting, income is includible in gross income when all the events have occurred which fix the right to receive such income and the amount thereof can be determined with reasonable accuracy." Treas. Reg. § 1.451–1(a). See also Treas. Reg. § 1.446–1(c)(1)(ii).

This case does not involve the question of "reasonable accuracy." Rather the issue is when does the right to receive the income which the "markers" represent become "fixed" for accrual purposes. Commentators and the courts have generally stated that the existence of a definite liability is a prerequisite to the accrual of any obligation. * * * Flamingo, relying on these authorities, contends that because the persons who gave the "markers" for gambling purposes had no legal obligation to repay the casino, the "markers" being void as a matter of law under *Evans v. Cook*, 11 Nev. 69, 75 (1876), the "liability" they represent was not "fixed." Rather discharge of the "liability" was contingent on the

---

1. These markers resemble counter-checks and as such indicate to the maker a definite and binding obligation of repayment.

customer's volition. Therefore, Flamingo should not be required to accrue the "markers."

Flamingo also relies on *H. Liebes & Co. v. Commissioner*, 90 F.2d 932 (9th Cir. 1937). There the issue was when should a debt due an accrual basis taxpayer by the government be accrued. The debt was owed by the government as the result of litigation. This court stated:

> We may conclude that income has not accrued to a taxpayer until there arises to him a fixed or unconditional right to receive it. . . .

> The complete definition would therefore seem to be that income accrues to a taxpayer, when there arises to him a fixed or unconditional right to receive it, if there is a reasonable expectancy that the right will be converted into money or its equivalent.

Id. at 937–38.

The court held that the right was fixed immediately upon expiration of the time for appeal by the government from the judgment in favor of the taxpayer. At that point there was a reasonable expectancy that the claim would be converted into money even if the funds to satisfy the judgment had not been appropriated. Although *Liebes* clearly establishes that an obligation must be "fixed" and that there be a "reasonable expectancy" of the obligation being converted into cash or its equivalent, it did not hold that in all situations the existence of a legal liability to pay is a prerequisite to the existence of a "fixed or unconditional right" to receive payment.

Nor do we believe that this prerequisite universally exists. Support for this position is provided by the line of authority that originates in *Barker v. Magruder*, 95 F.2d 122 (D.C.Cir.1938), a case involving a taxpayer-lender who charged a rate of interest that violated the usury statute of the District of Columbia. The court held that, despite the fact the statute prohibited the taxpayer from legally enforcing the recovery of any interest, the uncollected usurious interest was properly accruable. It stated, "(t)he correct answer, as we think, depends not so much, as appellants urge, upon the legal right to enforce collection as upon the existing probability of its being received." *Id.* at 123.

The taxpayer's course of dealing with its debtor was considered determinative in fashioning the definition of "fixed." In doing so the *Barker* court can be seen as properly avoiding a rigid definition of the term "fixed" in order to be responsive to unique facts and practical considerations.

Barker addresses a problem analogous to that presented in this case. Both involve a taxpayer attempting, as the district court below aptly phrased it, to "shield its unsanctioned operations from the normal incidents of the United States tax laws." Flamingo attacks this characterization as both astonishing and wrong and argues that the casino's operations are sanctioned by law. This is not the point the district court was addressing. Its comments were directed at the unsanctioned activity of gambling debt enforcement, not the day-to-day legally authorized gambling operations of the appellant. Gambling debt enforcement in Nevada in 1967 and usurious interest enforcement in the District of Columbia at the time of *Barker* were each confronted by a bar to the use of the courts. In neither case would the courts have been available to aid enforcement.

(2) Flamingo here, as did the taxpayer in *Barker*, points to certain speculative and potential legal objections to payment available to its debtors. The practical answer emerges from the facts. Few, if any, debtors raise these objections and usually they pay up. Gambling is big business in Nevada. Flamingo and others lawfully engaged in gambling in Nevada who employ the accrual basis in tax accounting should not be permitted to distort that method of accounting merely because the State of Nevada chooses not to permit the use of its courts to collect gambling debts.

Barker does not stand alone. The Court of Claims followed it in a case involving the same taxpayer. See *Barker v. United States*, 26 F.Supp. 1004 (Ct.Cl.1939). The court stated that it was in complete accord with the reasoning of the D. C. Circuit and refused to bar the accrual of income. Another case is *Travis v. Commissioner*, 406 F.2d 987 (6th Cir. 1969). The case involved a statutory prohibition against the collection of monies due under an executory contract for services which have not been rendered. The taxpayer contended such a legal bar should prevent recognition of that income under the accrual basis of accounting prior to the rendition of the services. The court, citing *Barker v. Magruder*, 95 F.2d 122 (D.C.Cir.1938), with approval, noted the Supreme Court in *Commissioner v. Hansen*, 360 U.S. 446, 79 S.Ct. 1270, 3 L.Ed.2d 1360 (1959), had chosen to employ the phrase "fixed right to receive" rather than "enforceable right to recover." It held that accrual was proper when the sums became due and payable even though the service for which the sums were to be paid had not been performed. The *Travis* court believed the practical problems which would arise if legal enforceability were required necessitated such an interpretation.

(3) We agree and, as did the court in *Travis, id.*, emphasize the fact that the taxpayer rarely had to resort to litigation to collect the sums owing to it. Flamingo, as noted earlier, conducted approximately sixty percent of its business through extensions of credit, and its own estimates of collectability on outstanding casino receivables ranged as high as ninety-six percent. The lack of legal liability did not interfere with Flamingo's operation and it is doubtful that legal enforceability of the "markers" would or could increase its recovery rate. Under these circumstances, the obligations of Flamingo's patrons are as "fixed" as it is possible to be and, in fact, no less so than those of other businesses. Flamingo should not be heard to argue that it should be taxed differently from other legitimate businesses. Its inability to enforce its "markers" in court is not a sufficient burden to justify such a differential. The debts which the "markers" represent are, therefore, fixed; there is a reasonable expectancy of collection; and no contention has been made that the amounts cannot be determined with reasonable accuracy.

(4) Flamingo puts forth a plethora of cases in support of its contention that legal enforceability of a debt must exist prior to its accrual. These cases, however, are uniformly inapposite. They involve, as the district court correctly noted, factual circumstances not germane to the instant case. We hasten to add what should be obvious, however. Nothing in this opinion is intended to suggest that legal enforceability is not relevant in determining when a right to income is "fixed" for accrual basis tax accounting purposes. We merely hold that under the circumstances of this case its absence is not controlling.

AFFIRMED.

Note

In *Revenue Ruling 83–106*, 1983–2 C.B. 77, the Service followed *Flamingo Resort*, holding that an accrual method casino must include in income the amount of gambling revenue derived from customers who gamble on credit for the year in which the gambling obligations arise and the gambling occurs. Like the Flamingo Resort, the taxpayer in the ruling extended markers to customers and enjoyed a 95–percent collection rate despite their unenforceability under state law. With respect to accruing unenforceable income, the Service observed:

> In the instant case, the "all events" test is satisfied for the tax year the credit customers wager and lose the credit proceeds (chips or money) at the taxpayer's gambling tables. This is so because (1) the taxpayer's right to receive the income is fixed for this tax year as the required performance has taken place, the customer's use of the taxpayer's gambling tables, and (2) the amount of the obligation is determinable with reasonable accuracy for this tax year as the customer's promissory note (marker) specifies the amount of the credit extension. With respect to the reasonable expectancy of payment exception to the "all events" test, there is no substantial uncertainty that the gambling obligation will be paid at the time the credit customers wager and lose the credit proceeds. This results from the fact that the taxpayer, generally, only authorizes credit to customers that have furnished information enabling taxpayer to verify the particular customer's credit worthiness. Secondly, despite the availability to the customers of a valid defense to the legal enforceability of taxpayer's collection of the gambling obligations, the taxpayer, based on its collection experience, has a reasonable expectancy that these obligations will be paid.

* * *

The Prepayment Issue. For financial accounting purposes, advance payments are generally not included in income when received. This is because of the **matching principle** that is a hallmark of financial accounting. Because the expenses related to advance payments have not yet been incurred, the inclusion of income upon prepayment would cause a "mismatch" of income and expenses.

The "earlier-of" test for federal income tax purposes, clearly, gives little weight to the matching principle. Ever since the Service first argued for the inclusion of prepayments in gross income, accrual method taxpayers have fought to extend the matching principle from financial accounting to the tax laws. Early on, taxpayers met with success. In *Beacon Publishing Co. v. Commissioner*, 218 F.2d 697 (10th Cir. 1955), the court held that a newspaper publishing company could defer amounts received from advance payments for subscriptions until performance. In other words, the income from a prepaid subscription could be allocated over the life of the subscription—it did not have to be accrued immediately upon receipt. Another taxpayer claimed a similar victory in *Schuessler v. Commissioner*, 230 F.2d 722 (5th Cir. 1956).

The Supreme Court Trilogy. Just after *Beacon Publishing* and *Schuessler*, the Supreme Court changed the landscape considerably. Over the course of three opinions, the matching principle was tossed aside in favor of the "earlier-of" test.

Episode One ("The Prepayment Menace"): *Automobile Club of Michigan v. Commissioner*, 353 U.S. 180, 77 S.Ct. 707, 1 L.Ed.2d 746 (1957). In this case, the taxpayer received prepayments of membership dues. Membership in the taxpayer's club entitled members to certain auto services on an "as needed" basis for 12 months. The taxpayer included 1/12 of the annual dues in income each month, but the Service argued that the entire prepayment should have been included in gross income upon receipt. The Supreme Court held for the Service, finding that "[t]he pro rata allocation of the membership dues in monthly amounts is purely artificial and bears no relation to the services which petitioner may in fact be called upon to render for the member." *Id.* at 189. Thus, ruled the Court, the Service did not abuse its discretion in requiring the taxpayer to include the membership prepayments in gross income at receipt.

The Service, armed with the *Automobile Club of Michigan* decision, then asserted that **all** prepayments should be included in income in the year of receipt. But not all of the lower courts agreed. In *Bressner Radio, Inc. v. Commissioner*, 267 F.2d 520 (2d Cir. 1959), the court allowed the taxpayer, a television set dealer, to defer amounts attributable to prepaid service contracts ratably over the one-year service period. The court found the taxpayer's allocation to be reasonable and not artificial, based upon aggregate service contracts. But then in *American Automobile Association v. United States*, 181 F.Supp. 255 (Ct. Cl. 1960), the Court of Claims rejected the taxpayer's pro rata allocation of annual dues paid for certain travel-related services performed at the customer's demand.

Episode Two ("Prepayments Strike Back"): *American Automobile Association v. United States*, 367 U.S. 687, 81 S.Ct. 1727, 6 L.Ed.2d 1109 (1961). The Supreme Court granted certiorari in the Court of Claims case to resolve the apparent conflict with *Bressner Radio*. The Court held once again that the Service was correct because the taxpayer's allocation was too artificial. The Court gave little weight to statistical evidence presented by the taxpayer that suggested, based on aggregate data, that the taxpayer's allocation was appropriate. The Court instead focused on the fact that the taxpayer's performance was rendered only on demand and not on fixed dates.

Episode Three ("Return of the Prepayments"): The last installment of the Supreme Court trilogy is set forth here for your consideration.

SCHLUDE v. COMMISSIONER

United States Supreme Court, 1963.
372 U.S. 128, 83 S.Ct. 601, 9 L.Ed.2d 633.

MR. JUSTICE WHITE delivered the opinion of the Court.

This is still another chapter in the protracted problem of the time certain items are to be recognized as income for the purposes of the federal income tax. The commissioner of Internal Revenue increased the 1952, 1953 and 1954 ordinary income of the taxpayers by including in gross income for those years amounts received or receivable under contracts executed during those years despite the fact that the contracts obligated taxpayers to render performance in subsequent periods. These increases produced tax deficiencies which the taxpayers unsuccessfully challenged in the Tax Court on the ground that the amounts could be deferred under their accounting method. On appeal, the Court of Appeals for the Eighth Circuit agreed with the taxpayers and reversed the Tax Court, the decision having been rendered prior to ours in *American Automobile Ass'n v. United States*, 367 U.S. 687, 81 S.Ct. 1727, 6 L.Ed.2d 1109. Following the *American Automobile Association* case, certiorari in this case was granted, the judgment of the lower court vacated, and the cause remanded for further consideration in light of *American Automobile Association*. In a per curiam opinion, the Court of Appeals held that in view of *American Automobile Association*, the taxpayers' accounting method "does not, for income tax purposes, clearly reflect income" and affirmed the judgment for the Commissioner. We brought the case back once again to consider whether the lower court misapprehended the scope of *American Automobile Association*.

Taxpayers, husband and wife, formed a partnership to operate ballroom dancing studios (collectively referred to as "studio") pursuant to Arthur Murray, Inc., franchise agreements. Dancing lessons were offered under either of two basic contracts. The cash plan contract required the student to pay the entire down payment in cash at the time the contract was executed with the balance due in installments thereafter. The deferred payment contract required only a portion of the down payment to be paid in cash. The remainder of the down payment was due in stated installments and the balance of the contract price was to be paid as designated in a negotiable note signed at the time the contract was executed.

Both types of contracts provided that (1) the student should pay tuition for lessons in a certain amount, (2) the student should not be relieved of his obligation to pay the tuition, (3) no refunds would be made, and (4) the contract was noncancelable. The contracts prescribed a specific number of lesson hours ranging from five to 1,200 hours and some contracts provided lifetime courses entitling the student additionally to two hours of lessons per month plus two parties a year for life. Although the contracts designated the period during which the lessons had to be taken, there was no schedule of specific dates, which were arranged from time to time as lessons were given.

Cash payments received directly from students and amounts received when the negotiable notes were discounted at the bank or fully paid were deposited in the studio's general bank account without segregation from its other funds. The franchise agreements required the studio to pay to Arthur Murray, Inc., on a weekly basis, 10% of these cash receipts as royalty and 5% of the receipts in escrow, the latter to continue until a $20,000 indemnity fund was accumulated. Similarly, sales commissions for lessons sold were paid at the time the sales receipts were deposited in the studio's general bank account.

The studio, since its inception in 1946, has kept its books and reported income for tax purposes on an accrual system of accounting. In addition to the books, individual student record cards were maintained showing the number of hours taught and the number still remaining under the contract. The system, in substance, operated as follows. When a contract was entered into, a "deferred income" account was credited for the total contract price. At the close of each fiscal period, the student record cards were analyzed and the total number of taught hours was multiplied by the designated rate per hour of each contract. The resulting sum was deducted from the deferred income account and reported as earned income on the financial statements and the income tax return. In addition, if there had been no activity in a contract for over a year, or if a course were reduced in amount, an entry would be made canceling the untaught portion of the contract, removing that amount from the deferred income account, and recognizing gain to the extent that the deferred income exceeded the balance due on the contract, i.e., the amounts received in advance. The amounts representing lessons taught and the gains from cancellations constituted the chief sources of the partnership's gross income. The balance of the deferred income account would be carried forward into the next fiscal year to be increased or decreased in accordance with the number of new contracts, lessons taught and cancellations recognized.

Deductions were also reported on the accrual basis except that the royalty payments and the sales commissions were deducted when paid irrespective of the period in which the related receipts were taken into income. Three certified public accountants testified that in their opinion the accounting system employed truly reflected net income in accordance with commercial accrual accounting standards.

The Commissioner included in gross income for the years in question not only advance payments received in cash but the full face amounts of notes and contracts executed during the respective years. The Tax Court and the Court of Appeals upheld the Commissioner, but the United States in this Court has retreated somewhat and does not now claim the includibility in gross income of future payments which were not evidenced by a note and which were neither due by the terms of the contract nor matured by performance of the related services. The question remaining for decision, then, is this: Was it proper for the Commissioner, exercising his discretion under * * * § 446(b) * * * to reject the studio's accounting system as not clearly reflecting income and to include as income in a particular year advance payments by way of cash, negotiable notes and contract installments falling due but remaining unpaid during that year? We hold that it was since we believe the problem is squarely controlled by *American Automobile Association*.

* * *

Plainly, the considerations expressed in *American Automobile Association* are apposite here. We need only add here that since the *American Automobile Association* decision, a specific provision extending the deferral practice to certain membership corporations was enacted, § 456, * * * continuing, at least so far, the congressional policy of treating this problem by precise provisions of narrow applicability. Consequently, as in the *American Automobile Association* case, we invoke the "long-established policy of the Court in deferring, where possible, to congressional procedures in the tax field," and, as in that case, we cannot say that the Commissioner's rejection of the studio's deferral system was unsound.

The *American Automobile Association* case rested upon an additional ground which is also controlling here. Relying upon *Automobile Club of Michigan v. Commissioner*, 353 U.S. 180, 77 S.Ct. 707, 1 L.Ed.2d 746, the Court rejected the taxpayer's system as artificial since the advance payments related to services which were to be performed only upon customers' demands without relation to fixed dates in the future. The system employed here suffers from that very same vice, for the studio sought to defer its cash receipts on the basis of contracts which did not provide for lessons on fixed dates after the taxable year, but left such dates to be arranged from time to time by the instructor and his student. Under the contracts, the student could arrange for some or all of the additional lessons or could simply allow their rights under the contracts to lapse. But even though the student did not demand the remaining lessons, the contracts permitted the studio to insist upon payment in accordance with the obligations undertaken and to retain whatever prepayments were made without restriction as to use and without obligation of refund. At the end of each period, while the number of lessons taught had been meticulously reflected, the studio was uncertain whether none, some or all of the remaining lessons would be rendered. Clearly, services were rendered solely on demand in the fashion of the *American Automobile Association* and *Automobile Club of Michigan* cases.

Moreover, percentage royalties and sales commissions for lessons sold, which were paid as cash was received from students or from its note transactions with the bank, were deducted in the year paid even though the related items of income had been deferred, at least in part, to later periods. In view of all these circumstances, we hold the studio's accrual system vulnerable under * * * § 446(b) with respect to its deferral of prepaid income. Consequently, the Commissioner was fully justified in including payments in cash or by negotiable note in gross income for the year in which such payments were received. If these payments are includible in the year of receipt because their allocation to a later year does not clearly reflect income, the contract installments are likewise includible in gross income, as the United States now claims, in the year they become due and payable. For an accrual basis taxpayer "it is the right to receive and not the actual receipt that determines the inclusion of the amount in gross income," *Spring City Foundry Co. v. Commissioner*, 292 U.S. 182, 184, 54 S.Ct. 644, 645, 78 L.Ed. 1200, and here the right to receive these installments had become fixed at least at the time they were due and payable.

We affirm the Court of Appeals insofar as that court held includible the amounts representing cash receipts, notes received and contract installments due and payable. Because of the Commissioner's concession, we reverse that part of the judgment which included amounts for which services had not yet been performed and which were not due and payable during the respective periods and we remand the case with directions to return the case to the Tax Court for a redetermination of the proper income tax deficiencies now due in light of this opinion. It is so ordered.

Affirmed in part and reversed in part and case remanded with directions.

Mr. Justice Stewart, with whom Mr. Justice Douglas, Mr. Justice Harlan, and Mr. Justice Goldberg join, dissenting.

As the Court notes, this case is but the most recent episode in a protracted dispute concerning the proper income tax treatment of amounts received as advances for services to be performed in a subsequent year by a taxpayer who is on an accrual rather than a cash basis. The Government has consistently argued that such amounts are taxable in the year of receipt, relying upon two alternative arguments: It has claimed that deferral of such payments would violate the "annual accounting" principle which requires that income not be postponed from one year to the next to reflect the long-term economic result of a transaction. Alternatively, the Government has argued that advance payments must be reported as income in the year of receipt under the "claim-of-right doctrine," which requires otherwise reportable income, held under a claim of right without restriction as to use, to be reported when received despite the fact that the taxpayer's claim to the funds may be disputed.[1]

---

1. The Commissioner has sometimes been successful in urging the "claim-of-right doctrine" as a bar to the deferral of advances by accrual-basis taxpayers. See e.g., *Andrews v. Commissioner*, 23 T.C. 1026, 1032–1033; *South Dade Farms v. Commissioner*, 138 F.2d 818 (C.A.5th Cir.); *Clay Sewer Pipe Ass'n v. Commissioner*, 139

As I have elsewhere pointed out, neither of these doctrines has any relevance to the question whether any reportable income at all has been derived when payments are received in advance of performance by an accrual-basis taxpayer. The most elementary principles of accrual accounting require that advances be considered reportable income only in the year they are earned by the taxpayer's rendition of the services for which the payments were made. The Government's theories would force upon an accrual basis taxpayer a cash basis for advance payments in disregard of the federal statute which explicitly authorizes income tax returns to be based upon sound accrual accounting methods.

Apparently the Court agrees that neither the annual accounting requirement nor the claim-of-right doctrine has any relevance or applicability to the question involved in this case. For the Court does not base its decision on either theory, but rather, as in two previous cases,[4] upon the ground that the system of accrual accounting used by these particular taxpayers does not "clearly reflect income" in accord with the statutory command. This result is said to be compelled both by a consideration of legislative history and by an analysis of the particular accounting system which these taxpayers employed.

* * *

The Court's decision can be justified, then, only upon the basis that the system of accrual accounting used by the taxpayers in this case did not "clearly reflect income" * * *. In the *Automobile Club of Michigan* case the taxpayer allocated yearly dues ratably over 12 months, so that only a portion of the dues received during any fiscal year was reported as income for that year. In the absence of any proof that services demanded by the Automobile Club members were distributed in the same proportion over the year, the Court held that the system used by the taxpayer did not clearly reflect income. In the *American Automobile Association* case the taxpayer offered statistical proof to show that its proration of dues reasonably matched the proportion of its yearly costs incurred each month in rendering services attributable to those dues. The Court discounted the validity of this statistical evidence because the amount and timing of the services demanded were wholly within the control of the individual members of the Association, and the Court thought that

F.2d 130 (C.A.3d Cir.); *Automobile Club of Michigan v. Commissioner*, 230 F.2d 585, 591 (C.A.6th Cir.), aff'd on other grounds, 353 U.S. 180, 77 S.Ct. 707, 1 L.Ed.2d 746.

In more recent cases, on the other hand, the Courts of Appeals have held the claim-of-right doctrine irrelevant to this problem. *Bressner Radio, Inc. v. Commissioner*, 267 F.2d 520, 524, 525–528 (C.A.2d Cir.); *Schuessler v. Commissioner*, 230 F.2d 722, 725 (C.A.5th Cir.); *Beacon Publishing Co. v. Commissioner*, 218 F.2d 697, 699–701 (C.A.10th Cir.).

In the present case the Commissioner urged that the "claim-of-right doctrine" was applicable even to advance fees which were due under the contract but not yet paid, a position from which he receded only when the case reached this Court. The Tax Court, at least in one case, has accepted the argument. *Your Health Club, Inc. v. Commissioner*, 4 T.C. 385.

4. *Automobile Club of Michigan v. Commissioner*, 353 U.S. 180, 77 S.Ct. 707, 1 L.Ed.2d 746, and *American Automobile Ass'n v. United States*, 367 U.S. 687, 81 S.Ct. 1727, 6 L.Ed.2d 1109.

the Association could not, therefore, estimate with accuracy the costs attributable to each individual member's demands.

In the present case the difficulties which the Court perceived in *Automobile Club of Michigan* and *American Automobile Association* have been entirely eliminated in the accounting system which these taxpayers have consistently employed. The records kept on individual students accurately measured the amount of services rendered—and therefore the costs incurred by the taxpayer—under each individual contract during each taxable year. But, we are told, there is a fatal flaw in the taxpayers' accounts in this case too: The individual contracts did not provide "for lessons on fixed dates * * *, but left such dates to be arranged from time to time by the instructor and his student." Yet this "fixed date of performance" standard, it turns out, actually has nothing whatever to do with those aspects of the taxpayers' accounting system which the Court ultimately finds objectionable.

There is nothing in the Court's opinion to indicate disapproval of the basic method by which income earned by the rendition of services was recorded. On the contrary, the taxpayers' system was admittedly wholly accurate in recording lessons given under each individual contract. It was only in connection with lessons which had not yet been taught that the taxpayers were "uncertain whether none, some, or all" of the contractual services would be rendered, and the condemned "arbitrariness" therefore is limited solely to the method by which cancellations were recognized. It is, of course, true of all businesses in which services are not rendered simultaneously with payment that the number and amount of cancellations are necessarily unknown at the time advances are received. But surely it cannot be contended that a contract which specified the times at which lessons were to be given would make any more certain how many of the remaining lessons students would in fact demand. Indeed, the Court does not suggest that a schedule fixing the dates of all future lessons would, if embodied in each contract, suffice to make petitioners' accounting system "clearly reflect income."

Instead, the cure suggested by the Court for the defect which it finds in the accounting system used by these taxpayers is that estimated cancellations should be reported as income in the year advance payments are received. I agree that such estimates might more "clearly reflect income" than the system actually used by the taxpayers. But any such estimates would necessarily have to be based on precisely the type of statistical evaluations which the Court struck down in the *American Automobile Association* case. Whatever other artificialities the exigencies of revenue collection may require in the field of tax accounting, it has never before today been suggested that a consistent method of accrual accounting, valid for purposes of recognizing income, is not equally valid for purposes of deferring income. Yet in this case the Court says that the taxpayers, in recognizing income, should have used the very system of statistical estimates which, for income deferral purposes, the *American Automobile* decision held impermissible.

It seems to me that this decision, the third of a trilogy of cases purportedly decided on their own peculiar facts, in truth completes the mutilation of a basic element of the accrual method of reporting income—a method which has been explicitly approved by Congress for almost half a century.

I respectfully dissent.

* * *

ARTNELL COMPANY v. COMMISSIONER, 400 F.2d 981 (7th Cir. 1968).

Facts: The taxpayer operated the Chicago White Sox professional baseball franchise using a fiscal year for federal income tax purposes. In its 1962 taxable year, the taxpayer sold season tickets and single-game admissions to games that would be played in its 1963 taxable year. The taxpayer did not report the income from these sales in its 1962 return. Instead, its practice was to report the income from these sales as the corresponding games were played. Thus, the income from ticket sales to games held in the taxpayer's 1963 taxable year was finally reported as income in 1963. The Commissioner argued that the income should have been reported in the year in which payment was received (the taxpayer's 1962 taxable year).

Issue: Must the taxpayer include in gross income for 1962 the sale proceeds received from tickets allocable to games to be played in 1963?

Holding: No.

Rationale: The court concluded that the Supreme Court trilogy ending with *Schlude* required inclusion of prepayments in gross income because of uncertainties as to when performance would occur, if at all. "The uncertainty stressed in those decisions is not present here. The deferred income was allocable to games which were to be played on a fixed schedule. Except for rain dates, there was certainty. We would have no difficulty distinguishing the instant case in this respect."

The court continued: "It is our best judgment that, although the policy of deferring, where possible, to congressional procedures in the tax field will cause the Supreme Court to accord the widest possible latitude to the commissioner's discretion, there must be situations where the deferral technique will so clearly reflect income that the Court will find an abuse of discretion if the commissioner rejects it."

TAMPA BAY DEVIL RAYS, LTD. v. COMMISSIONER, T.C. Memo. 2002–248.

Facts: The taxpayer is a limited partnership that owns and operates the Tampa Bay Devil Rays baseball franchise (though some might argue that the term "Devil Rays baseball" is an oxymoron). In the taxable years at issue, the taxpayer received deposits from customers on advance season tickets, as well as deposits on reservations for private suites. The accrual method taxpayer treated these receipts as "deposits" and "deferred income," so it did not include them in gross income. The Service argued that the prepaid income should have been included in the year of receipt.

Issue: Must the taxpayer include in gross income the deferred income from tickets and suite rentals allocable to games to be played in a later taxable year?

Holding: No.

Rationale: What is good for the White Sox is good for the Devil Rays. Although the general rule for accrual method taxpayers requires inclusion of advance payments in the year of receipt, there is a narrow exception under *Artnell* where the taxpayer can prove that services will be performed on fixed dates in one or more subsequent taxable years. By deferring income in those limited situations, there is a better matching of income and related expenses.

* * *

REVENUE PROCEDURE 2004–34

2004–1 C.B. 991.

SECTION 1. PURPOSE

This revenue procedure allows taxpayers a limited deferral beyond the taxable year of receipt for certain advance payments. Qualifying taxpayers generally may defer to the next succeeding taxable year the inclusion in gross income for federal income tax purposes of advance payments (as defined in section 4 of this revenue procedure) to the extent the advance payments are not recognized in revenues (or, in certain cases, are not earned) in the taxable year of receipt. Except as provided in section 5.02(2) of this revenue procedure for certain short taxable years, this revenue procedure does not permit deferral to a taxable year later than the next succeeding taxable year. This revenue procedure neither restricts a taxpayer's ability to use the methods provided in § 1.451–5 of the Income Tax Regulations regarding advance payments for goods nor limits the period of deferral available under § 1.451–5.

* * *

SECTION 2. BACKGROUND AND CHANGES

* * *

.03 *Rev. Proc. 71–21*, 1971–2 C.B. 549, was published to implement an administrative decision of the Commissioner in the exercise of his discretion under § 446 to allow accrual method taxpayers in certain specified and limited circumstances to defer the inclusion in gross income for federal income tax purposes of payments received (or amounts due and payable) in one taxable year for services to be performed by the end of the next succeeding taxable year. *Rev. Proc. 71–21* was designed to reconcile the federal income tax and financial accounting treatment of payments received for services to be performed by the end of the next succeeding taxable year without permitting extended deferral of the inclusion of those payments in gross income for federal income tax purposes.

.04 Considerable controversy exists about the scope of *Rev. Proc. 71–21*. In particular, advance payments for non-services (and often, for combinations of services and non-services) do not qualify for deferral under *Rev. Proc. 71–21*, and taxpayers and the Internal Revenue Service frequently disagree about whether advance payments are, in fact, for "services." In addition to the issue of defining "services" for purposes of *Rev. Proc. 71–21*, questions also arise about whether advance payments received under a series of agreements, or under a renewable agreement, are within the scope of *Rev. Proc. 71–21*. In the interest of reducing the controversy surrounding these issues, the Service has determined that it is appropriate to expand the scope of *Rev. Proc. 71–21* to include advance payments for certain non-services and combinations of services and non-services. Additionally, the Service has determined that it is appropriate to expand the scope of *Rev. Proc. 71–21* to include advance payments received in connection with an agreement or series of agreements with a term or terms extending beyond the end of the next succeeding taxable year. The Service has determined, however, that for taxpayers deferring recognition of income under this revenue procedure it is appropriate to retain the limited one-year deferral of *Rev. Proc. 71–21* (except as provided in section 5.02(2) of this revenue procedure for certain short taxable years).

Section 3. Scope

This revenue procedure applies to taxpayers using or changing to an overall accrual method of accounting that receive advance payments as defined in section 4 of this revenue procedure.

Section 4. Definitions

The following definitions apply solely for purposes of this revenue procedure—

.01 *Advance Payment.* Except as provided in section 4.02 of this revenue procedure, a payment received by a taxpayer is an "advance payment" if—

    (1) including the payment in gross income for the taxable year of receipt is a permissible method of accounting for federal income tax purposes (without regard to this revenue procedure);

    (2) the payment is recognized by the taxpayer (in whole or in part) in revenues in * * * a subsequent taxable year (or * * * the payment is earned by the taxpayer (in whole or in part) in a subsequent taxable year); and

    (3) the payment is for—

        (a) services;

(b) the sale of goods (other than for the sale of goods for which the taxpayer uses a method of deferral provided in § 1.451–5(b)(1)(ii));

(c) the use (including by license or lease) of intellectual property as defined in section 4.03 of this revenue procedure;

(d) the occupancy or use of property if the occupancy or use is ancillary to the provision of services (for example, advance payments for the use of rooms or other quarters in a hotel, booth space at a trade show, campsite space at a mobile home park, and recreational or banquet facilities, or other uses of property, so long as the use is ancillary to the provision of services to the property user);

(e) the sale, lease, or license of computer software;

(f) guaranty or warranty contracts ancillary to an item or items described in subparagraph (a), (b), (c), (d), or (e) of this section 4.01(3);

(g) subscriptions (other than subscriptions for which an election under § 455 is in effect), whether or not provided in a tangible or intangible format;

(h) memberships in an organization (other than memberships for which an election under § 456 is in effect); or

(i) any combination of items described in subparagraphs (a) through (h) of this section 4.01(3).

.02 *Exclusions From Advance Payment.* The term "advance payment" does not include—

(1) rent (except for amounts paid with respect to an item or items described in subparagraph (c), (d), or (e) of section 4.01(3));

(2) insurance premiums, to the extent the recognition of those premiums is governed by Subchapter L;

(3) payments with respect to financial instruments (for example, debt instruments, deposits, letters of credit, notional principal contracts, options, forward contracts, futures contracts, foreign currency contracts, credit card agreements, financial derivatives, etc.), including purported prepayments of interest; [or]

* * *

(7) payments in property to which § 83 applies.

* * *

SECTION 5. PERMISSIBLE METHODS OF ACCOUNTING FOR ADVANCE PAYMENTS

.01 *Full Inclusion Method.* A taxpayer within the scope of this revenue procedure that includes the full amount of advance payments in gross income for federal income tax purposes in the taxable year of receipt is using a proper method of accounting under § 1.451–1, regardless of whether the taxpayer recognizes the full amount of advance payments in revenues for that taxable year for financial reporting purposes and regardless of whether the taxpayer earns the full amount of advance payments in that taxable year.

.02 *Deferral Method.*

(1) *In general.*

(a) A taxpayer within the scope of this revenue procedure that chooses to use the Deferral Method described in this section 5.02 is using a proper method of accounting under § 1.451–1. Under the Deferral Method, for federal income tax purposes the taxpayer must—

(i) include the advance payment in gross income for the taxable year of receipt * * * to the extent provided in section 5.02(3) of this revenue procedure, and

(ii) except as provided in section 5.02(2) of this revenue procedure, include the remaining amount of the advance payment in gross income for the next succeeding taxable year.

* * *

(3) *Inclusion of advance payments in gross income.*

(a) Except as provided in paragraph (b) of this section 5.02(3), a taxpayer using the Deferral Method must—

(i) include the advance payment in gross income for the taxable year of receipt * * * to the extent recognized in revenues * * * for that taxable year, and

(ii) include the remaining amount of the advance payment in gross income in accordance with section 5.02(1)(a)(ii) of this revenue procedure.

(b) If the taxpayer * * * is unable to determine * * * the extent to which advance payments are recognized in revenues * * * for the taxable year of receipt * * *, a taxpayer using the Deferral Method must include the advance payment in gross income for the taxable year of receipt * * * to the extent earned in that taxable year and include the remaining amount of the advance payment in gross income in accordance with section 5.02(1)(a)(ii) of this revenue procedure. The determination of whether an amount is earned in a taxable year must be made without regard to whether the taxpayer may be required to refund the advance payment upon the occurrence of a condition subsequent. If the taxpayer is unable to determine the extent to which a payment (such as a payment for contingent goods or services) is earned in the taxable year of receipt (and, if applicable, in a short taxable year described in section 5.02(2)), the taxpayer may determine that amount—

(i) on a statistical basis if adequate data are available to the taxpayer;

(ii) on a straight line ratable basis over the term of the agreement if the taxpayer receives advance payments under a fixed term agreement and if it is not unreasonable to anticipate at the end of the taxable year of receipt that the advance payment will be earned ratably over the term of the agreement; or

(iii) by the use of any other basis that in the opinion of the Commissioner results in a clear reflection of income.

* * *

.03 *Examples*. In each example below, the taxpayer uses an accrual method of accounting for federal income tax purposes and files its returns on a calendar year basis. * * *

Example 1. On November 1, 2004, *A*, in the business of giving dancing lessons, receives an advance payment for a 1–year contract commencing on that date and providing for up to 48 individual, 1–hour lessons. *A* provides eight lessons in 2004 and another 35 lessons in 2005. * * * *A* recognizes 1/6 of the payment in revenues for 2004, and 5/6 of the payment in revenues for 2005. *A* uses the Deferral Method. For federal income tax purposes, *A* must include 1/6 of the payment in gross income for 2004, and the remaining 5/6 of the payment in gross income for 2005.

Example 2. Assume the same facts as in *Example 1*, except that the advance payment is received for a 2–year contract under which up to 96 lessons are provided. *A* provides eight lessons in 2004, 48 lessons in 2005, and 40 lessons in 2006. * * * *A* recognizes 1/12 of the payment in revenues for 2004, 6/12 of the payment in revenues for 2005, and 5/12 of the payment in gross revenues for 2006. For federal income tax purposes, *A* must include 1/12 of the payment in gross income for 2004, and the remaining 11/12 of the payment in gross income for 2005.

Example 3. On June 1, 2004, *B*, a landscape architecture firm, receives an advance payment for goods and services that, under the terms of the agreement, must be provided by December 2005. On December 31, 2004, *B* estimates that 3/4 of the work under the agreement has been completed. * * * *B* recognizes 3/4 of the payment in revenues for 2004 and 1/4 of the payment in revenues for 2005. *B* uses the Deferral Method. For federal income tax purposes, *B* must include 3/4 of the payment in gross income for 2004, and the remaining 1/4 of the payment in gross income for 2005, regardless of whether *B* completes the job in 2005.

Example 4. On July 1, 2004, *C*, in the business of selling and repairing television sets, receives an advance payment for a 2–year contract under which *C* agrees to repair or replace, or authorizes a representative to repair or replace, certain parts in the customer's television set if those parts fail to function properly. * * * *C* recognizes 1/4 of the payment in revenues for 2004, 1/2 of the payment in revenues for 2005, and 1/4 of the payment in revenues for 2006. *C* uses the

Deferral Method. For federal income tax purposes, *C* must include 1/4 of the payment in gross income for 2004 and the remaining 3/4 of the payment in gross income for 2005.

Example 5. On December 2, 2004, *D,* in the business of selling and repairing television sets, sells for $200 a television set with a 90–day warranty on parts and labor (for which *D,* rather than the manufacturer, is the obligor). *D* regularly sells television sets without the warranty for $188. * * * *D* allocates $188 of the sales price to the television set and $12 to the 90–day warranty, recognizes 1/3 of the amount allocable to the warranty ($4) in revenues for 2004, and recognizes the remaining 2/3 of the amount allocable to the warranty ($8) in revenues for 2005. *D* uses the Deferral Method. For federal income tax purposes, *D* must include the $4 allocable to the warranty in gross income for 2004 and the remaining $8 allocable to the warranty in gross income for 2005.

Example 6. *E*, in the business of photographic processing, receives advance payments for mailers and certificates that oblige *E* to process photographic film, prints, or other photographic materials returned in the mailer or with the certificate. *E* tracks each of the mailers and certificates with unique identifying numbers. On July 20, 2004, *E* receives payments for 2 mailers. One of the mailers is submitted and processed on September 1, 2004, and the other is submitted and processed on February 1, 2006. * * * *E* recognizes the payment for the September 1, 2004, processing in revenues for 2004 and the payment for the February 1, 2006, processing in revenues for 2006. *E* uses the Deferral Method. For federal income tax purposes, *E* must include the payment for the September 1, 2004, processing in gross income for 2004 and the payment for the February 1, 2006, processing in gross income for 2005.

Example 7. *F*, a hair styling salon, receives advance payments for gift cards that may later be redeemed at the salon for hair styling services or hair care products at the face value of the gift card. The gift cards look like standard credit cards, and each gift card has a magnetic strip that, in connection with F's computer system, identifies the available balance. The gift cards may not be redeemed for cash, and have no expiration date. * * * *F* recognizes advance payments for gift cards in revenues when redeemed. *F* is not able to determine the extent to which advance payments are recognized in revenues in its applicable financial statement for the taxable year of receipt and therefore does not meet the requirement of section 5.02(1)(b)(i) of this revenue procedure. Further, *F* does not determine under a basis described in section 5.02(3)(b) of this revenue procedure the extent to which payments are earned for the taxable year of receipt. Therefore, *F* may not use the Deferral Method for these advance payments.

Example 8. Assume the same facts as in *Example 7,* except that the gift cards have an expiration date 12 months from the date of sale, *F* does not accept expired gift cards, and *F* recognizes unredeemed gift cards in revenues * * * for the taxable year in which the cards expire.

Because F tracks the sale date and the expiration date of the gift cards * * *, F is able to determine the extent to which advance payments are recognized in revenues for the taxable year of receipt. Therefore, F meets the requirement of section 5.02(1)(b)(i) of this revenue procedure and may use the Deferral Method for these advance payments.

 * * *

Example 11. H is in the business of compiling and providing business information for a particular industry in an online format accessible over the internet. On September 1, 2004, H receives an advance payment from a subscriber for 1 year of access to its online database, beginning on that date. * * * H recognizes 1/3 of the payment in revenues for 2004 and the remaining 2/3 in revenues for 2005. H uses the Deferral Method. For federal income tax purposes, H must include 1/3 of the payment in gross income for 2004 and the remaining 2/3 of the payment in gross income for 2005.

Example 12. On December 1, 2004, I, in the business of operating a chain of "shopping club" retail stores, receives advance payments for membership fees. Upon payment of the fee, a member is allowed access for a 1–year period to I's stores, which offer discounted merchandise and services. * * * I recognizes 1/12 of the payment in revenues for 2004 and 11/12 of the payment in revenues for 2005. I uses the Deferral Method. For federal income tax purposes, I must include 1/12 of the payment in gross income for 2004, and the remaining 11/12 of the payment in gross income for 2005.

Example 13. In 2004, J, in the business of operating tours, receives payments from customers for a 10–day cruise that will take place in April 2005. Under the agreement, J charters a cruise ship, hires a crew and a tour guide, and arranges for entertainment and shore trips for the customers. * * * J recognizes the payments in revenues for 2005. J uses the Deferral Method. For federal income tax purposes, J must include the payments in gross income for 2005.

Example 14. On November 1, 2004, K, a travel agent, receives payment from a customer for an airline flight that will take place in April 2005. K purchases and delivers the airline ticket to the customer on November 14, 2004. K retains a portion of the customer's payment (the excess of the customer's payment over the cost of the airline ticket) as its commission. Because K is not required to provide any services after the ticket is delivered to the customer, K earns its commission when the airline ticket is delivered. The customer may cancel the flight and receive a refund from K only to the extent the airline itself provides refunds. * * * K recognizes its commission in revenues for 2005. The commission is not an advance payment as defined in section 4.01 of this revenue procedure because the payment is not earned by K, in whole or in part, in a subsequent taxable year. Thus, K may not use the Deferral Method for this payment.

 * * *

    * * *

Advance Payments From the Sale of Goods. Another limited exception to the *Schlude* rule applicable to accrual method taxpayers who receive prepayments from the sale of goods in the ordinary course of business is found at Treas. Reg. § 1.451–5. Under this regulation, such prepayments must be included in either the year of receipt or the earlier of: (1) the year when the prepayments would otherwise be reported for tax purposes, or (2) the year when the prepayments would be reported for financial accounting purposes. For example, suppose a taxpayer receives payment in Year One for goods that are shipped in Year Two and received by the purchaser in Year Three. If the taxpayer normally accrues income upon delivery to the purchaser, the taxpayer can defer the prepayment until Year Three, unless, for financial accounting purposes, the taxpayer accrues the income upon shipment (in which case, the taxpayer can only defer the prepayment until Year Two).

Obviously, the regulation presents a significant opportunity for deferral. That's why the regulation contains a limit: generally, if the taxpayer receives "substantial" advance payments and has enough goods on hand in the year of payment to satisfy the orders, then the advance payments must be included in the year of receipt. Advance payments are "substantial," not coincidentally, if all such payments received through the end of the taxable year equal or exceed the taxpayer's aggregate inventory costs. Treas. Reg. § 1.451–5(c).

If a contract for goods also includes a provision for services, deferral under the regulations is still permissible as long as the consideration paid for the services is less than five percent of the total contract price. Treas. Reg. § 1.451–5(a)(3). Thus, for example, if an equipment seller includes training services as part of the total contract price, deferral of an advance payment on the contract is possible so long as the consideration allocable to the training is less than five percent of the total contract price. Do you suppose this rule might affect the price that the equipment seller would charge for training?

The Service has ruled that computer software is generally considered "goods" for purposes of this deferral rule. Moreover, software updates distributed to customers under extended software "maintenance" contracts were also considered "goods." *Technical Advice Memorandum 9231002.*

Prepaid Subscriptions and Dues. Two sections of the Code provide additional exceptions to the general rule in *Schlude.* Under § 455, prepaid subscription income can be recognized over the period covered by the subscription. Notice that this is an elective provision—a taxpayer must take affirmative action to obtain the benefit of deferral. The election is made by attaching a statement to the taxpayer's return. Treas. Reg. § 1.455–6(a)(1). Under § 456, prepaid dues income received by certain taxpayers can be recognized over the dues period. Section 456 is structurally similar to § 455, including the election that must be made to claim the benefit of deferral. Only "membership organizations," entities without capital stock and no part of the net earnings of which is distributable to any member, are entitled to make the election. Section 456(e)(3). Notice, however, that deferral under § 456 is limited to 36 months in all events. Section 456(e)(2).

Warranty Contracts. If you have ever purchased a new automobile, you have no doubt relished the joy of meeting with the "financial manager" at the car dealership. This is the person who prints out all of the paperwork you sign and who tries to get you to pay more for the car by way of various add-ons. The most popular (and profitable) add-on is a service warranty contract. "If there are any problems with the car during the warranty period, just bring the car into our service department and we'll pay for the parts and labor." In most cases, the warranty period extends beyond one taxable year. Absent special provisions, of course, the Supreme Court trilogy would require the seller (the dealership) to include the entire warranty payment in gross income. But this can cause cash flow problems for the dealership (not that car dealers as a class engender much sympathy), because in practice, the dealers turn around and immediately pay a third party to insure the risks of the warranty contract. If the dealers must pay tax on the entire amount of the warranty contract (and not just the net difference between the advance payment and the amount paid to the insurer), the dealer may lack funds to pay the tax. To give dealers some relief, the Service, in *Revenue Procedure 97–38*, 1997–2 C.B. 479, permits accrual method manufacturers, wholesalers and retailers of cars and other durable consumer goods to recognize a portion of the advance payment related to a service warranty contract over the life of the warranty contract (not to exceed six years). Only that portion of the advance payment that is paid to an insurer can be deferred—any immediate net profit from the sale of the of the warranty contract must still be included in gross income in the year of receipt.

* * *

Problem 6–5

Neil Downe, an accrual method individual, provides landscaping services to customers. On October 1, Year One, Neil signed a retainer agreement with Minnie Van Gogh. Under the agreement, Neil will provide landscaping services to Minnie on Minnie's demand during the contract period.

(a) The contract period begins on November 1, Year One, and ends on October 31, Year Two. The contract requires Minnie to pay Neil $1,000 per month, all payable in advance. Accordingly, on October 15, Year One, Minnie paid Neil $12,000. What is the amount of gross income to Neil on these facts and when must this income be included?

(b) How would the answer to (a) change if the contract period begins on November 1, Year One, and ends on December 31, Year Two? Minnie thus paid $14,000 to Neil on October 15, Year One.

(c) How would the answer to (a) change if the contract period begins on November 1, Year One, and ends on January 31, Year Three? Minnie thus paid $15,000 to Neil on October 15, Year One.

(d) How would the answer to (a) change if the contract period begins on November 1, Year One, and ends on October 31, Year Three? Minnie thus paid $24,000 to Neil on October 15, Year One.

(e) How would the answer to (d) change if the retainer agreement stated that Neil was to perform landscaping services only on the 10th and 25th day of each month during the contract period?

(f) How would your answer to (d) change if the retainer agreement also provided that Neil was to deliver and plant several exotic trees and shrubs on Minnie's premises in exchange for an extra $10,000 payable on October 15, Year One? Assume the trees and shrubs were shipped to Minnie's premises in December, Year Two, and arrived in January, Year Three.

* * *

(2) DEDUCTION ITEMS

Code: IRC § 461(f), (h).

Regs: Treas. Reg. §§ 1.461–1(a)(2)(i)–(ii); –1(a)(3); –2; –4(g). *Review* Treas. Reg. § 1.446–1(c)(1)(ii)(A)–(B).

Another All–Events Test. Accrual method taxpayers use a slightly different "all-events test" for deductions. Generally, an accrual method taxpayer can claim a deduction "in the taxable year in which all the events have occurred that establish the fact of the liability, the amount of the liability can be determined with reasonable accuracy, and economic performance has occurred with respect to the liability." Treas. Reg. § 1.461–1(a)(2)(i). Notice that the "all-events test" for deductions has an extra prong. It is not enough that the liability for the payment is established and that the amount that will be paid is reasonably determinable—there must also be "economic performance." This third prong was added in 1984, when Congress became concerned with time value of money principles. Although economic performance is a very important element of the all-events test for deductions (and will be discussed in detail below), we should begin our analysis with the first two prongs of the test. The following case explains how the first two prongs are applied in practice, and deals with the issue of deductions for contingent liabilities.

GOLD COAST HOTEL & CASINO
v. UNITED STATES

United States Court of Appeals, Ninth Circuit, 1998.
158 F.3d 484.

WHALEY, JUDGE:

The United States of America and Commissioner of Internal Revenue appeal the district court's grant of summary judgment in favor of Gold Coast Hotel & Casino, et al. The district court held that a casino using the accrual method of accounting may deduct the value of slot club points won by a slot club member in the tax year in which the member has accumulated the minimum number of points necessary to redeem a prize. We affirm.

FACTUAL BACKGROUND

Gold Coast Hotel & Casino ("Gold Coast") is a Nevada limited partnership formed in 1985 for the purpose of operating a licensed gambling casino in Las Vegas, Nevada. Gold Coast has operated a slot club since March 1987. A slot club is a promotional tool used to attract slot machine players. After filling out the necessary paperwork, slot club members receive a club card, similar to an ATM card. Slot club members insert their club cards into a slot machine and a computer tracks their accumulation of slot club points.

Slot club points can be redeemed for prizes ranging from coffee mugs to Hawaiian vacations. The minimum number of points needed to redeem a prize is 1,200. As stipulated to by the parties, the market value of each club point is $0.0021. Accordingly, 100,000 points have a value of $210. Gold Coast uses a computerized data bank to track each club member's slot club points. The computer credits a member's account for points won and debits the account when points are redeemed for prizes.

Members can redeem slot club points for prizes in two ways. First, members can go to Gold Coast's redemption center and pick their prize. Alternatively, club members can go to the redemption center and get a voucher for a prize from an off-site retailer, such as a travel agency or appliance store. The club member then takes the voucher to the off-site retailer to redeem the prize and the retailer bills Gold Coast a previously agreed upon amount.

At the end of 1988, the difference between the total value of slot club points that had been accumulated by club members and the total value of slot club points that had been redeemed by club members was $1,276,464. In 1989 members accumulated additional slot club points valued at $2,445,780 and redeemed points valued at $1,724,801. Thus, at the end of 1989 there were outstanding slot club points valued at $1,997,443, an increase of $720,979 over the prior year's ending balance. Gold Coast deducted this amount—$720,979—as an expense on its 1989 partnership tax return. In addition, on its 1989 tax return Gold Coast recaptured as income $105,969, representing the value of accumulated slot club points in those accounts in which there had been no activity for over a year, and which had been deducted as an expense in the prior year.

During 1990, club members accumulated additional slot club points valued at $3,076,909 and redeemed points valued at $2,386,216. Thus, at the end of 1990 the value of outstanding slot club points was $2,688,136, an increase of $690,693 over the prior year's ending balance. Gold Coast deducted this amount—$690,693—as an expense on its 1990 partnership tax return. Additionally, on its 1990 tax return Gold Coast recaptured as income $68,910, representing the value of accumulated slot club points in those accounts in which there had been no activity for over a year, and which had been deducted as an expense in the prior year.

On September 26, 1994, the Commissioner * * * proposed that adjustments to income be made in four categories, one of which was accrued slot club points. The [adjustment] for the tax year ending in 1989 proposed to increase income a total of $1,935,469 for adjustments relating to slot club points.[1] While the [adjustment] for the tax year ending in 1990 proposed to increase income a total of $807,330,[2] the parties agree that the proposed increase for 1990 should be $738,420.[3]

* * *

DISCUSSION

* * *

The Commissioner contends that a casino using the accrual method of accounting does not incur the expense of accumulated slot club points until such time as the points are actually redeemed for a prize because until the time of redemption "all events" fixing the casino's liability have not occurred. Whether an expense has been "incurred" is governed by the "all events" test that originated in *United States v. Anderson*, 269 U.S. 422, 441, 70 L. Ed. 347, 46 S. Ct. 131 (1926), now codified at 26 U.S.C. § 461(h)(4).[5] Whether a taxpayer has satisfied the "all events" test is a question of law reviewed de novo. The fundamental premise underlying the "all events" test is that "although expenses may be deductible before they become due and payable, liability must first be firmly established." *United States v. General Dynamics Corp.*, 481 U.S. 239, 243, 95 L. Ed. 2d 226, 107 S. Ct. 1732 (1987). Accordingly, to be deductible the liability must be fixed, absolute, * * * and unconditional * * *. A liability may not be deducted if it is contested or if it is contingent upon the occurrence of a future event.

1. The Commissioner arrived at this figure by disallowing as expenses (1) the value of all outstanding slot club points at the end of 1989 ($1,997,433) and (2) the value of all slot club points redeemed at off-site retailers for which Gold Coast had not been billed at the end of 1989 ($43,995); and crediting Gold Coast for the value of slot club points in accounts for which there had been no activity for over one year, which Gold Coast had already recaptured as income in the tax year 1989 ($105,969).

2. The Commissioner arrived at this figure by disallowing as expenses (1) the value of the increase in outstanding slot club points at the end of 1990 ($752,667) and (2) the value of all slot club points redeemed at off-site retailers for which Gold Coast had not been billed by the end of 1990 ($54,-663).

3. The error in computation was a result of the Commissioner's failure to credit Gold Coast for the value of slot club points

in accounts for which there had been no activity for over one year, which Gold Coast had already recaptured as income for the tax year 1990.

5. The "all events" test was incorporated into the Internal Revenue Code at * * * § 461(h)(4) by the Deficit Reduction Act of 1984 * * *. Section 461(h)(1) further provides that the "all events" test is not satisfied any earlier than when "economic performance" has occurred. However, the parties here agree that the "economic performance" requirement does not apply to the tax years at issue here. See Treas. Reg. § 1.461–4(k)(3) (explaining that, for payment liabilities for which payment is economic performance, the requirement applies to liabilities that would otherwise be deductible or incurred for taxable years beginning after December 31, 1991).

There are two prongs to the "all events" test, both of which must be satisfied before an expense is properly deductible. See *United States v. Hughes Properties, Inc.*, 476 U.S. 593, 600, 90 L. Ed. 2d 569, 106 S. Ct. 2092 (1986). First, all events that establish the fact of the liability must have occurred. Second, the amount of such liability must be capable of being determined with reasonable accuracy. Accordingly, to determine when Gold Coast incurs the expense of the value of accumulated slot club points, it is necessary to determine: first, what event fixes Gold Coast's liability for the value of slot club points; and second, whether the amount of that liability is capable of being determined with reasonable accuracy.

Two leading Supreme Court decisions address the first prong of the "all events" tests, *United States v. General Dynamics Corp.*, 481 U.S. 239, 95 L. Ed. 2d 226, 107 S. Ct. 1732 (1987), and *United States v. Hughes Properties, Inc.*, 476 U.S. 593, 90 L. Ed. 2d 569, 106 S. Ct. 2092 (1986). Gold Coast relies on *Hughes* for its position that the "last event" fixing Gold Coast's liability occurs when the minimum number of club points necessary to earn a prize are accumulated, because at that time liability is fixed pursuant to Nevada gaming regulations.[6] The Commissioner, however, cites *General Dynamics* as support for its position that the "last event" fixing Gold Coast's liability as absolute and unconditional is the redemption of club points by a club member. We agree with the district court that the facts of this case are more analogous to those in Hughes than to those in General Dynamics and, thus, hold that the last event fixing Gold Coast's liability for the value of slot club points is a club member's accumulation of 1,200 slot club points.

In *Hughes*, the Supreme Court held that a casino operator could deduct the amount of money guaranteed for payment on progressive slot machines even though the amount had not been won by the end of the tax year. In doing so, the court in *Hughes* reasoned that although the dollar amount of the jackpot would continue to grow until the winning combination appeared, the obligation to pay the amount that had already accrued on the machine was fixed and irrevocable under state law at any moment. The court recognized that the jackpot may not be won for years or that the casino may go bankrupt before the jackpot was won. Nonetheless, the court noted that:

> the potential nonpayment of an incurred liability exists for every business that uses an accrual method, and it does not prevent accrual.... "The existence of an absolute liability is necessary; absolute certainty that it will be discharged by payment is not."

Id. at 606 (quoting *Helvering v. Russian Fin. & Constr. Corp.*, 77 F.2d 324, 327 (2nd Cir. 1935)). Those liabilities not discharged by payment, the Court noted, can simply be recaptured as income and, thus, subject

---

6. Gold Coast submitted an uncontroverted affidavit from a former Nevada Gaming Control Board member, who states that any attempt by Gold Coast not to redeem points accrued by its customers would have been improper under gaming regulations and would have been grounds for disciplinary action or revocation of Gold Coast's gambling license.

to tax. Accordingly, the court in *Hughes* held that the "last event" fixing the casino's liability was the last play of the slot machine before the end of the casino's fiscal year.

Here, like the guaranteed prize on the jackpot in *Hughes*, Gold Coast's liability to redeem accumulated slot club points is fixed and unconditional under state law once a slot club member accumulates 1,200 points. Moreover, the fact that a club member may choose not to redeem his/her points immediately does not render Gold Coast's otherwise fixed liability conditional. Rather, like the liability of the casino in Hughes, which grew as the jackpot grew, the liability of Gold Coast simply increases when a slot club member elects to let his/her club point total grow. * * *

The Commissioner relies heavily on the fact that not all slot club members will redeem their points for prizes to support its position that Gold Coast's liability is not absolute until a club member actually demands "payment" by redeeming his/her points for a prize. However, the *Hughes* court rejected similar reasoning when it held that a casino's fixed obligation to pay out the amount shown on progressive slot machines was not rendered contingent by the fact that it was possible that the liability would not be paid. Indeed the Court in *Hughes* explicitly noted that potential nonpayment of an incurred liability exists for every business that uses the accrual method of accounting, and that for purposes of the "all events" test, what is critical is the existence of an absolute liability, not an absolute certainty the liability will be discharged by payment.

The Commissioner is correct that in *Hughes* the possibility that the liability represented by the progressive jackpot amount would not eventually be discharged was more remote than the possibility here that a club member who has won 1,200 points will not redeem a prize. Nonetheless, this court has held that where an obligation is "fixed" and there is a "reasonable expectancy" of the obligation being converted into cash or its equivalent, then the obligation satisfies the first prong of the "all events" test, even when less than all of the obligation will eventually be discharged by payment. See *Flamingo Resort, Inc. v. United States*, 664 F.2d 1387, 1389 (9th Cir. 1982) (interpreting the "all events" test for purposes of determining when an accrual-based taxpayer's right to receive income is fixed and unconditional).

Here, Gold Coast's liability to redeem accumulated slot club points is fixed and unavoidable under state law. In addition, the record indicates that there is a reasonable expectancy that members who accumulate more than 1,200 club points redeem those points for prizes. Because the critical factor for purposes of the "all events" test is the existence of an absolute liability, not an absolute certainty that liability will be discharged by payment, Gold Coast's liability is not rendered conditional by the possibility that some of the slot club points accumulated by members may go unredeemed.

The Commissioner's reliance on *General Dynamics* to the contrary is misplaced. The plaintiff in that case, General Dynamics Corporation, was an accrual-basis taxpayer that self-insured its employees' medical plan. Employees seeking reimbursement for medical expenses for services provided by third parties were required to submit properly documented claim forms to employee benefits personnel at General Dynamics. The employee benefits personnel would verify eligibility and forward worthy claims to the plan administrators. The administrators' claim processors would review the claims and approve covered expenses for payment.

Delay by employees in filing claims and the time necessary to process claims resulted in a time lag between when medical services were rendered and when payment was made by General Dynamics. Accordingly, General Dynamics established a reserve account reflecting its estimated liability for medical care received by employees but unpaid by General Dynamics. General Dynamics sought to deduct the amount of its estimated liability in this account at the end of the tax year as an accrued expense.

The Supreme Court in *General Dynamics* held that the estimated liability represented by the reserve account did not satisfy the first prong of the "all events" test because the last event necessary to fix that liability had not occurred by the end of the tax year. The Court held that, as a matter of law, General Dynamics' liability to reimburse its employees was conditioned on the employee's submitting a properly documented claim to General Dynamics. In doing so, the Court reasoned that the employees had been informed that it would be necessary to submit satisfactory proof of the charges claimed in order to obtain payment under the plan. The Court thus found that the filing of such a claim was not a mere technicality but, rather, was a condition precedent to liability on the part of General Dynamics. Since the Court held as a matter of law that General Dynamics was not liable to the employee for payment of covered medical services until the employee filled out and submitted a claim form with satisfactory proof of the charges claimed, it necessarily followed that General Dynamics was not entitled to deduct the amount in the reserve account because the liability it represented was a contingent liability.

Despite the Commissioner's strenuous argument to the contrary, *General Dynamics* is not controlling here. In *General Dynamics*, medical services were provided to General Dynamics' employees by third parties. It follows then that in order to trigger General Dynamics' liability to reimburse its employees for the expenses of covered services rendered by those third parties, an employee was required to file a properly documented claim establishing General Dynamics' obligation. Submitting documented proof of a covered claim, the Court found, was not a technicality.

Here, a slot club member's demand for payment (redemption of points) is a technicality. It is nothing more than making a demand for payment of an uncontested liability. Unlike in *General Dynamics*, there is no involvement of third parties necessitating that slot club members establish or otherwise offer proof of their right to payment. Rather, Gold Coast has a fixed, unavoidable, and uncontested obligation to redeem accumulated slot club points for prizes upon demand. Furthermore, the Commissioner's argument to the contrary, that the liability represented by an uncontested obligation is not unconditional until such time as it is presented for payment, renders the difference between accrual and cash-based accounting methods virtually meaningless. Such a result is inconsistent with the express recognition by the Court in *General Dynamics* that there is a legal difference between a liability being "due and payable" and it being "firmly established." *Id.* at 243 (noting that "although expenses may be deductible before they have become due and payable, liability must first be firmly established"). Accordingly, demand for payment is not a condition precedent to fixing Gold Coast's liability for the value of accumulated slot club points.

Finally, the Commissioner also contends that Gold Coast was not entitled to summary judgment because Gold Coast did not satisfy the second prong of the "all events" test. The second prong of the "all events" test requires that the amount of the liability be capable of being determined with reasonable certainty.

Here, under state law, Gold Coast's liability is fixed for the value of all accumulated club points in accounts with more than 1,200 points. Since the parties have stipulated to the value of each club point, the amount of Gold Coast's liability can be determined by simply multiplying that value by the number of accumulated points in accounts with more than 1,200 points. Thus, Gold Coast's liability is known with reasonable certainty.

The Commissioner contends, however, that Gold Coast has not estimated its liability with reasonable certainty because it deducts the value of all accumulated slot club points in accounts with over 1,200 points. The Commissioner argues that its analysis of the data in the record suggests that only 69% of slot club points are actually redeemed. The Commissioner's argument, however, confuses determining the amount of Gold Coast's liability with determining the percentage of that liability that will be discharged by payment. The second prong of the "all events" test requires only that the amount of the liability be capable of being determined with reasonable certainty. The percentage of that liability that will actually be discharged by payment is simply not relevant to this prong of the "all events" test.

Further, the decision in *Wein Consol. Airlines*, relied on by the Commissioner, is inapposite. In that case, an employer was required to make monthly payments to the children of deceased employees for as long as they remained minors, and to the surviving spouses of deceased employees for as long as they remained single. See *Wien Consol. Airlines, Inc. v. Commissioner*, 528 F.2d 735, 737 (9th Cir. 1976). Thus, the actual amount of the taxpayer's liability, being dependent on the occurrence or nonoccurrence of a future event, could not be calculated, and it was necessary for the taxpayer to use probabilities and actuarial tables to estimate the amount of its liability. The issue faced by the court in *Wein Consol. Airlines* was whether the taxpayer's proposed estimate of its liability was reasonable. Since the court here is not faced with an estimate of Gold Coast's liability, the Commissioner's reliance on *Wein Consol. Airlines* is misplaced.

CONCLUSION

The last event fixing Gold Coast's liability for the value of slot club points is a club member's accumulation of the 1,200th point. Since the parties have stipulated to the value of a slot club point, the amount of Gold Coast's liability is capable of being determined with reasonable certainty. Therefore, Gold Coast has incurred the expense of the value of those slot club points accumulated by members with 1,200 or more points in their slot club accounts and it may properly deduct that expense at the end of Gold Coast's fiscal year pursuant to * * * § 162(a).

AFFIRMED.

* * *

The Concept of "Economic Performance." Now we look at the extra prong of the "all-events" test for deductions—the requirement of **economic performance**. Recall that if an accrual method taxpayer can claim a deduction in Year One but not make actual payment until several years later, the accelerated deduction creates a windfall for the taxpayer. Congress closed the door to such windfalls through the enactment of § 461(h). If you have not done so already, read § 461(h) now and apply it to the following Problem.

Problem 6–6

For each of the fact patterns provided below, determine *when* the taxpayer may deduct the described expenses, assuming in each case that the taxpayer uses the accrual method of accounting.

(a) Chris P. Bacon owns and operates a professional basketball franchise. In June, Year One, he hired Clean Co. to provide custodial services at all of the basketball games for the upcoming season. The games begin on November 1, Year One, and end on April 30, Year Two. Pursuant to their contractual agreement, Chris paid $120,000 to Clean Co. on August 1, Year One.

(b) Candy Kane operates a baseball park. In September, Year One, Candy decided to sponsor a "bobble head" promotional night during the Year Two season. Under this promotion, the first 10,000 fans admitted to the park for a selected game will receive a souvenir bobble head doll designed to look like one of the home team's most popular players. In October, Year One, Candy paid $40,000 to Bobble Co. in exchange for Bobble Co.'s promise to provide 10,000 bobble heads to Candy in time for the promotion. On May 10, Year Two, Bobble Co. provided the bobble heads as agreed.

(c) Bill Foldes leased professional office space in Dallas for a three-year term commencing July 1, Year One. Because of his uncertain credit rating as a new business owner, the lease agreement required Bill to prepay the first two years of rent. The third year of rent was to be paid ratably over the balance of the three-year term. Accordingly, Bill paid $352,800 on July 1, Year One (representing $14,700 per month times 24 months), and $5,040 per month on the first day of each month from August 1, Year One, until June 1, Year Four.

(d) In Year One, Sue Ellen Ewing installed an offshore oil production platform in the Gulf of Mexico as part of her oil extraction business. Under Federal law, Sue Ellen must remove the platform when production ceases. Sue Ellen estimates that oil production will cease in Year Twenty, and that the costs of removal will total $1 million.

(e) In Year One, Employer was sued by Employee for wrongful termination. The parties reached a settlement in Year Two whereby Employer agreed to pay $200,000 to Employee in equal annual installments over ten years, commencing in Year Two. The settlement agreement stated that if Employee died during the 10–year payment period, Employer would continue to make payments to Employee's estate. To satisfy this liability, Employer placed $154,434.70 in reserve in Year One (assuming that if the reserve grew at five percent compounded annually, there would be sufficient funds to pay its liability under the settlement agreement). Employer made all required payments.

(f) Sara Lee bakes breads and various dessert products for customers. Sara conducted a contest that entitled the grand prize winner to $50,000 per year for ten years. On the inside of each frozen dessert wrapper, Sara printed a game piece. One of the wrappers contained the winning game piece. In Year One, Charlie claimed the grand prize, and his wrapper was verified by Sara in the same year. Sara placed $386,086.75 in reserve to pay the liability to Charlie (again, assuming the reserve would grow at five percent compounded annually). Starting in Year Two, Sara paid $50,000 annually from the reserve to Charlie; the last payment was made in Year Eleven.

(g) Henry Ford manufactures and sells automobiles. Henry offers each of his distributors a rebate based on the amount of purchases made by that distributor from Henry during a calendar year. In Year One, Henry became liable to pay a total of $5,000 in rebates to his distributors. He paid the $5,000 on February 1, Year Two.

(h) Ted "Blackjack" McGrath has manufactured and sold fireworks since 1958 (long, long before Year One). Based on his extensive experience, Blackjack knows that he will pay 3.0–3.2 percent of his gross revenues to customers who are injured while using his products. Blackjack's gross revenues for Year One totaled $1 million, and total claims for personal injury totaled $30,000. By June 15, Year Two, Blackjack paid all $30,000 of the claims that arose in Year One.

* * *

U.S. FREIGHTWAYS CORP. v. COMMISSIONER, 270 F.3d 1137 (7th Cir. 2001).

Facts: An accrual method trucking company paid $4.3 million for required licenses, permits and fees in 1993. Some of the licenses and permits had an effective period that extended into 1994. In addition, the taxpayer spent $1 million in 1993 for liability and property insurance, the benefit of which extended into part of 1994. The taxpayer deducted the full $5.3 million on its 1993 return, but the IRS disallowed the deduction, concluding that the expenditures had to be capitalized. The Tax Court agreed that the expenditures had to be capitalized since the benefits of the licenses and the insurance extended substantially beyond 1993. The taxpayer argued that "substantially beyond" meant "more than one year beyond the taxable year," and since no benefit extended beyond the end of 1994, a deduction of the entire amount in 1993 was proper. The Tax Court rejected the taxpayer's interpretation of the one-year rule, stating that the rule asks whether the life of the benefit obtained from the expense "exceeds the tax year in which it is incurred, not whether it endures beyond one 12–month period." But the lower court also observed that even if the taxpayer's version of the one-year rule was correct, the taxpayer could not, as an accrual method taxpayer, claim a deduction for the entire amount in 1993, since a portion of the license and insurance cost did not accrue until 1994. Because the costs at issue arose from the providing of services and/or property to the taxpayer by another person, "economic performance" occurred as the services and/or property were provided (i.e., over the life of the license period and the insurance coverage period).

Issue: May the taxpayer deduct all of the prepaid license and insurance costs it paid in 1993 even though a portion of the benefit of such costs was attributable to 1994?

Holding: Yes.

Rationale: The court concluded that the expenses in question were fixed, one-year items that were ordinary in nature and which would always re-occur "with clockwork regularity." These recurring short-term items should be eligible for expensing, said the court, especially in light of the fact that the Service has not consistently required capitalization of such expenses in the past. As for the Tax Court's decision that a one-year rule was not applicable to accrual method taxpayers, the Seventh Circuit disagreed. "In our view, the decision whether to expense or capitalize a particular item should not turn on whether the taxpayer uses the cash or accrual basis of accounting. As Freightways points out, even the Treasury Regulation on which the Commissioner has relied here, Treas. Reg. § 1.461–1(a), uses identical language in subpart (1) (relating to cash basis taxpayers) and in subpart (2) (relating to accrual basis taxpayers): both must capitalize an expenditure that results in the creation of an asset having a useful life which extends substantially beyond the close of the tax year. The mere fact that Freightways is an accrual method taxpayer thus does not disqualify it from expensing the short-term items at issue here."

Note

U.S. Freightways involved an accrual method taxpayer that sought to deduct certain prepaid expenses. Of course, since economic performance of these expenses did not occur until a later taxable year, our understanding of the accrual method would suggest that a deduction must wait. But the court ultimately finds that a current deduction would *not* violate the accrual method because the expenses should not be capitalized in the first place. Do you agree with the Seventh Circuit's analysis? If the Seventh Circuit is correct in this conclusion, does the economic performance requirement have any independence or significance?

* * *

Contested Liabilities. If a taxpayer contests a liability supposedly owed to another, then of course the liability is not yet established, so the "all-events test" suggests that no deduction is proper while the liability is still contested. The Supreme Court said as much in *Dixie Pine Products Co. v. Commissioner*, 320 U.S. 516, 64 S.Ct. 364, 88 L.Ed. 270 (1944). So what must a taxpayer do to "contest" a liability? Treasury defines a "contest" as follows:

> A contest arises when there is a bona fide dispute as to the proper evaluation of the law or the facts necessary to determine the existence or correctness of the amount of an asserted liability. It is not necessary to institute suit in a court of law in order to contest an asserted liability. An affirmative act denying the validity or accuracy, or both, of an asserted liability to the person who is asserting such liability, such as including a written protest with payment of the asserted liability, is sufficient to commence a contest. Thus, lodging a protest in accordance with local law is sufficient to contest an asserted liability for taxes. It is not necessary that the affirmative act denying the validity or accuracy, or both, of an asserted liability be in writing if, upon examination of all the facts and circumstances, it can be established to the satisfaction of the Commissioner that a liability has been asserted and contested.

Treas. Reg. § 1.461–2(b)(2). As the Regulation implies, the taxpayer must actively assert the dispute. For example, if a taxpayer questions a liability for state taxes, the liability is not contested merely because the taxpayer requests an informal meeting to discuss the liability. *Woodmont Terrace, Inc. v. United States*, 261 F.Supp. 789 (M.D. Tenn. 1966).

Suppose a taxpayer pays a liability while still contesting its validity. A taxpayer might, for example, pay off a disputed debt to stop interest from accruing further. If the taxpayer uses the cash method, the payment gives rise to a deduction. As we will see soon when we cover error correction, if the taxpayer gets the money back, the taxpayer will have gross income to make up for the prior deduction. But if the taxpayer is on the accrual method, is a deduction available for the payment? After all, the liability is still contested at the time of payment. The Supreme Court answered this issue in the following case, but as you will soon see, Congress did not like the answer.

UNITED STATES v. CONSOLIDATED EDISON CO. OF NEW YORK, INC.

United States Supreme Court, 1961.
366 U.S. 380, 81 S.Ct. 1326, 6 L.Ed.2d 356.

Mr. Justice Whittaker delivered the opinion of the Court.

Respondent brought this action in the United States District Court for the Southern District of New York to recover a claimed overpayment of federal income taxes for the year 1951. It keeps its books and files its returns on a calendar-year accrual basis. The case turns on the correct determination of the proper year of accrual and deduction of certain contested real estate taxes. Specifically, the question is whether the contested part of a real estate tax accrued (1) in the year it was assessed and, for the purpose—and as the only mode recognized by the local law—of avoiding seizure and sale of the property for the contested tax while the contest was pending, was "paid" by the taxpayer, or (2) in the year the contest was finally determined.

The District Court, following the holding of the Court of Claims in *Consolidated Edison Co. v. United States*, that such a "payment" of the tax "accrues the item even though payment is made under protest and even though litigation is started within the taxable year to obtain repayment," held, without opinion, that the contested part of the tax accrued in the year of the "payment." On appeal, the Court of Appeals, by a divided court, held that the contested part of the tax accrued in the year the contest was finally determined, and reversed the judgment. It reasoned that inasmuch as respondent was "keeping its books on the accrual basis," the contested part of the tax accrued "only when all events [had] occurred which determine[d] the fact and amount of the tax liability." To resolve the conflict between the decision below and *Consolidated Edison Co. v. United States*, *supra*, we granted certiorari.

During the years involved—1946 through 1950—respondent owned numerous tracts of real estate in New York City which were subject to annual local property taxes. Under the New York law, the City Council annually fixes the tax rate, and the City Tax Commission annually fixes the property valuations. Thus the amount of the tax on each tract is determined by multiplying the valuation by the tax rate. The tax rate is not contestable, but a timely application (commonly called a "protest") may be made to the City Tax Commission to correct an erroneous valuation. Among other things, the protest must state the amount which the taxpayer "consider[s] was the full value of the property on January 25 [of the current] year" thus to establish the amount of the tax that is not contested. Upon exhaustion of this administrative procedure, a review of the Commission's determination may be had by a judicial proceeding, commonly called a certiorari proceeding, in the State Supreme Court, which is the taxpayer's sole and exclusive remedy. But the institution of such a suit does not stay or suspend the maturity of the tax bill, the accrual of 7% interest on it, nor the seizure and sale of the property to satisfy the tax lien. Thus, to obtain review, the taxpayer must either "pay" the tax or suffer the interest penalty and run the risk of seizure and sale of its property.

Though taxes for each of five years on hundreds of tracts are involved and the aggregate amount is very substantial, the parties very commendably stipulated in the District Court that the facts are sufficiently reflected, for the purposes of this suit, in the following simplified example:

In each of the years 1946 through 1950, respondent was notified of a tentative valuation which, at the established tax rate, would produce a tax of $100. Respondent then timely filed a bona fide protest (in respect of many, but not nearly all, of its tracts) stating a valuation which, at the established tax rate, would produce a tax of $85, and asking that the balance of the proposed valuation be stricken as excessive. After hearing, the Commission rejected the protest, and an assessment in the amount of $100 was made. Thereupon respondent, under protest and for the honestly stated purpose of avoiding the interest penalty and the seizure and sale of its property while it was contesting the Commission's valuation by certiorari proceedings in the state court, remitted to the city cash in an amount equal to the tax of $100, and immediately thereafter commenced a certiorari proceeding in the proper court, in which it again admitted liability for a tax in the amount of $85, but denied all liability for any tax in excess of that amount. In December 1951, the court, upon the consent of the parties to the action, entered its order in (each of) the certiorari proceedings fixing respondent's tax liability at $95, and thereupon the city forthwith returned $5 to respondent.

Although it was then engaged in a contest with the Commissioner in the Court of Claims over an identical question, namely, the proper income tax treatment to be accorded the $15 for each of the years 1938, 1939 and 1941—which issue was decided by the Court of Claims in December 1955 in favor of the Government, *Consolidated Edison Co. v. United States, supra*—respondent, in terms of the illustrative example, accrued on its books and deducted on its federal income tax returns, for each of the years 1946 through 1950, the full $100; and in its return for the year 1951—in which year the real estate tax liability was determined to be $95—respondent failed to deduct the $10 from, and included the $5 in, its gross income for that year.

Believing that this treatment of the $15 in 1951 was erroneous and resulted in its paying a lesser amount of federal income taxes in each of the years 1946 through 1950, and more in the year 1951, than it should have paid,[3] respondent filed in February 1955 its claim for refund of so

3. The economic consequences to the parties arise from the fact that corporate income tax rates (normal plus surtax) were increased from 38% in 1946 to 50 3/4% in

much of its 1951 income taxes as resulted (1) from its failure to deduct the $10 of real estate tax that was determined, in that year, to be valid, and (2) from its inclusion in gross income of the $5 returned to it in that year. Upon rejection of that claim, respondent timely brought this action in the District Court to recover the refund claimed, and obtained the result already stated.

It is settled that each "taxable year" must be treated as a separate unit, and all items of gross income and deduction must be reflected in terms of their posture at the close of such year. *Burnet v. Sanford & Brooks Co.*, 282 U.S. 359 * * *. And the parties agree that, under the applicable federal statutes, neither the Government nor an accrual-basis taxpayer may cause an item to be deducted in a year other than the one in which it accrued. *United States v. Anderson*, 269 U.S. 422 * * *. They also agree that the "touchstone" for determining the year in which an item of deduction accrues is the "all events" test established by this Court in *United States v. Anderson, supra,*[5] and since reaffirmed by this Court on numerous occasions, so that it is now a fundamental principle of tax accounting. The parties also recognize that this Court amplified, or as the Government says "added a refinement to," the "all events" test by its holding * * * that an accrual-basis taxpayer could not, while "contesting liability in the courts," deduct "the amount of the tax, on the theory that the state's exaction constituted a fixed and certain liability," but "must, in the circumstances, await the event of the state court litigation and might claim a deduction only for the taxable year in which its liability for the tax was finally adjudicated." * * *

That $85 of the $100 assessment was admitted to be owing and was intended to be paid and satisfied by the remittance, and thus accrued in the year of the remittance, is not in dispute. Respondent's good faith, in contesting $15 of the assessment, is not in dispute, for the Government expressly "disavow[s] any suggestion that the respondent ... filed its claims against the City of New York in bad faith, ... calculatingly inflated those claims, or ... failed to prosecute them with diligence." Nor is it questioned that accrual of such taxes in the proper year accords with "good accounting" principles.

1951, and, in this particular instance, more revenue would be produced by taking the deduction in 1946–1950 than in 1951. The taxpayer recognizes that, if its position be sustained, the Commissioner will have one year after entry of final judgment herein to reaudit the taxpayer's 1946–1950 returns and to assess deficiencies based upon deduction of the $15 in those years, in accordance with the provisions of §§ 1311–1315 of the Internal Revenue Code of 1954.

5. In the *Anderson* case, this Court declared the so-called "all events" test as follows: "In a technical legal sense it may

be argued that a tax does not accrue until it has been assessed and becomes due; but it is also true that in advance of the assessment of a tax, all the events may occur which fix the amount of the tax and determine the liability of the taxpayer to pay it. In this respect, for purposes of accounting and of ascertaining true income for a given accounting period, the munitions tax here in question did not stand on any different footing than other accrued expenses appearing on appellee's books. In the economic and bookkeeping sense with which the statute and Treasury decision were concerned, the taxes had accrued." 269 U.S., at 441.

But concordance of the views of the parties ends at this point. The Government contends that the remittance by respondent to the city, in each of the years in question, of cash in an amount equal to the whole of the assessed tax admitted liability for, and was intended to and did constitute "payment" and "satisfaction" of, both the disputed and undisputed parts of the assessment; and that when "the taxpayer pays the item and thereby discharges its liability, the expense has been incurred and there is no longer any contingency which would prevent its accrual." Respondent, on the other hand, insists that its remittance to the city was not intended to and did not admit liability for, nor constitute "payment" and "satisfaction" of, the contested $15 of the assessment, but was, in effect, a mere deposit, in the nature of a cash bond, required of respondent, in a practical sense, by the local law as the only available mode of avoiding the risk of seizure and sale of the property for the contested tax while its validity was being diligently contested in the only way allowed by the laws of the State.

Thus the very narrow issue here is whether the remittance admitted liability for, and constituted "payment" and "satisfaction" of, the contested part of the assessment and thereby rendered it accruable in the year of the remittance. Like the Court of Appeals, we think the respondent is right in its contention, and that $10 of the contested $15 of the tax accrued when liability in that amount was finally determined by the New York court in 1951, and that the $5, for which respondent was by that judgment held not liable, and which was returned to it by the city, was not income to respondent in 1951.

       * * *

"Payment" is not a talismanic word. It may have many meanings depending on the sense and context in which it is used. As correctly observed by the Court of Appeals, "A payment may constitute a capital expenditure, an exchange of assets, a prepaid expense, a deposit, or a current expense," and "when the exact nature of the payment is not immediately ascertainable because it depends on some future event, such as the outcome of litigation, its treatment for income tax purposes must await that event." 279 F.2d, at 156. * * *

Of course, an unconditional "payment" made by a taxpayer in apparent "satisfaction" of an asserted matured tax liability is, without more, plain and persuasive evidence, at least against the taxpayer, that "all the events [have] occur[red] which fix the amount of the tax and determine the liability of the taxpayer to pay it," *United States v. Anderson, supra,* at 441, and that the item so paid and satisfied has accrued.

But where, as stipulated by the parties in this case, the remittance or "payment" did not admit, but specifically denied, liability for, and was not intended to satisfy, the contested $15 of the assessment, but was, in effect, a mere deposit, "in the nature of a cash bond for the payment of [so much, if any, of the contested] taxes [as might] thereafter [be] found to be due" (*Rosenman v. United States,* 323 U.S. 658, 662 * * *), and was made for the sole purpose of staying—there being no other way to stay—an otherwise possible seizure and sale of the property for the contested tax while its validity was being honestly and diligently contested in the only way allowed by the law of the State, it will not do to say that the taxpayer has made an unconditional "payment" in apparent "satisfaction" of the contested part of an asserted matured tax liability, and thereby rendered it immediately accruable.

We therefore conclude that $10 of the contested $15 tax liability accrued not in the year of the remittance, but in 1951 when the New York court entered its final order determining that liability; and that the $5, for which respondent was held not liable by that judgment and which was returned to it by the city, was not income to respondent in 1951.

Affirmed.

* * *

Congressional Response to <u>Consolidated Edison</u>. Congress enacted § 461(f) to reverse the result in *Consolidated Edison* (and Congress made § 461(f) retroactive to 1953). Under § 461(f), an accrual method taxpayer can claim a deduction for a payment made with respect to a disputed debt even though the dispute survives the payment. Consider the applicability of § 461(f) in the following Problem.

Problem 6–7

Peter Marwick, an accountant, performed services in Year One for Ellie Vader, an accrual method taxpayer. Peter's services related to Ellie's trade or business activity. Peter gave Ellie a bill for $1,000 in Year One, but she disputes any liability for payment in excess of $700. Determine the amount and timing of any deduction to Ellie under each of the following alternatives scenarios.

(a) In Year One, Ellie pays $1,000 to Peter pending the resolution of their dispute. In Year Two, after litigation, the dispute is resolved in Peter's favor.

(b) Same as (a), except that Peter's services related exclusively to Ellie's personal accounting matters; Peter performed no services with respect to Ellie's trade or business activity.

(c) In Year One, Ellie transfers $1,000 to a trustee pursuant to a trust agreement. Under the terms of the trust agreement (signed by Ellie, Peter, and the trustee), the trustee shall pay the entire trust corpus (including any accumulated income) to Peter if Ellie's dispute with Peter is resolved in his favor. If Ellie wins, the funds will be returned to her. The trust is irrevocable. In Year Two, after litigation, the dispute is resolved in Peter's favor, and the trustee pays the entire trust account balance, $1,010, to Peter.

(d) Same as (c), except the trust is revocable, meaning that Ellie retains the power to terminate the trust and reclaim the trust account balance before the dispute with Peter is settled. Ellie never exercised this revocation power, and in Year Two, the trustee pays $1,010 to Peter.

(e) Same as (c), except that Peter was not a party to the trust agreement. In fact, Peter had no knowledge of the trust arrangement until he received payment in Year Two.

(f) Now suppose that Peter was injured while performing services for Ellie, and Peter asserts a $10,000 claim against her for negligence. Ellie disputes liability, but she transfers $10,000 to a trustee pursuant to an irrevocable trust agreement signed by Ellie, Peter, and the trustee. Under the trust agreement, the trustee is required to pay the entire trust account balance to Peter if the dispute over his injuries is resolved in his favor. If Ellie wins, the funds will be returned to her. In Year Two, a court approves a structured settlement that awards Peter $2,000 annually for five years, with interest. Accordingly, the trustee pays $2,000 plus interest to Peter in each of Years Two, Three, Four, Five, and Six.

C. THE TAXABLE YEAR

Code: IRC §§ 441(a)-(g), (i); 442; 444; 644; 706; 1378. *Skim* § 7519.

Regs: None.

Annual Versus Transactional Accounting. We often take for granted that we pay federal income tax once a year. Our tax liabilities are based upon the income and deduction items claimed over a one-year period. This is known as "annual accounting." Some taxes, however, make use of "transactional accounting," where tax is imposed upon the completion of each applicable transaction. For example, state and local sales taxes are imposed upon the completion of every sale subject to the tax. Under transactional accounting, a taxpayer may pay tax several times a year (or maybe no tax at all if the taxpayer defers completion of taxable transactions to a later year).

So why does the federal income tax make use of annual accounting and not transactional accounting? Probably for two reasons: (1) annual accounting ensures a steadier, more predictable stream of revenues to the federal government; and (2) annual accounting requires taxpayers to submit only one return and only pay tax once, thus reducing the overall compliance burden on taxpayers.

The use of annual accounting has profound implications. Suppose a taxpayer is party to a transaction that takes place over two years. The taxpayer receives $100,000 of income from the transaction in the first year but incurs no expenses. All of the expenses, $50,000 in total, occur in the second year, but no additional income is received. Under transactional accounting, the taxpayer would pay tax only on the $50,000 net profit. But under annual accounting, the taxpayer pays tax on $100,000 in the first year and gets a $50,000 deduction in the next year. Assuming equal tax rates in both years, the taxpayer would have preferred transactional accounting. But, alas, such is not the case.

After a brief look at the various taxable years available to taxpayers, we will study the principal rule of annual accounting: that every year stands alone. This means that proper reporting positions are based upon the facts as they existed at the close of the taxable year; events occurring after the close of the taxable year are ignored. Later, we see what happens when amounts included in gross income in one year are subsequently repaid in a different taxable year.

Four Choices. As § 441 indicates, there are four possible taxable years: (1) the calendar year, defined in § 441(d); (2) a fiscal year, defined in § 441(e); (3) a so-called "short taxable year," allowed by § 441(b)(3) and explained more fully in § 443; and (4) a 52–53 week year, described in § 441(f). The last two choices are a little beyond our scope, so we can dispense with them by giving only a very brief description. "Short" years occur when a taxpayer changes accounting periods (like switching from a fiscal year to a calendar year) or when a taxpayer "is in existence during only part of what would otherwise be" the taxable year. Section 443(a). While short years can be quite common with artificial business entities like corporations and partnerships, individuals usually have only one short year: their last one. A "52–53 week year" is used by certain cyclical businesses; by definition, these accounting periods always end on the same day of the week each year (like "the last Saturday in November"). Section 441(f)(1). A taxpayer can elect to use a "52–53 week year" only if the taxpayer regularly maintains its books and records on that same basis. As these brief descriptions suggest, the only practical choice for most taxpayers is between a calendar year and a fiscal year.

Most individuals are required by § 441(g) to use the calendar year. Most of us received some form of gross income (wages from a summer job, interest from a bank account, or the like) before we began keeping formal books. And most of us that keep books do so on an annual basis. Therefore, the only way most individuals can use a fiscal year is to formally request approval from the Treasury Secretary to change from a calendar year. Section 442. And the Treasury Secretary will only give approval upon a showing of a "substantial business purpose" for the change, a standard that is difficult to meet. Treas. Reg. § 1.442–1(b)(1). So while fiscal years are theoretically possible for individuals, you probably will not meet any individuals using a fiscal year at your next party. Fiscal years are much more prevalent for business entities.

Every Year Stands Alone. Now that we know the taxable year of a taxpayer, we can look at just how rigorously we apply the annual accounting concept. Suppose an employee receives a $5,000 bonus from his or her employer at the end of Year One. At the beginning of Year Two, the employee receives a notice from the employer that the correct amount of the Year One bonus (computed according to an objective formula) was only $500, but, due to an internal error, the amount of the bonus check was $5,000. If the employee has not yet filed a federal income tax return for Year One, how should the bonus be treated? Does the employee report $5,000 of income for Year One? $500? Something else? The answer depends upon the credibility of the taxable year concept. If the answer is $500, then the taxable year concept has little real weight. On the other hand, if the answer is $5,000, we are punishing the employee—it wasn't even the employee's fault! The following case suggests which concept wins.

BURNET v. SANFORD & BROOKS CO.

United States Supreme Court, 1931.
282 U.S. 359, 51 S.Ct. 150, 75 L.Ed. 383.

Mr. Justice Stone delivered the opinion of the Court.

* * *

From 1913 to 1915, inclusive, respondent, a Delaware corporation engaged in business for profit, was acting for the Atlantic Dredging Company in carrying out a contract for dredging the Delaware River, entered into by that company with the United States. In making its income tax returns for the years 1913 to 1916, respondent added to gross income for each year the payments made under the contract that year, and deducted its expenses paid that year in performing the contract. The total expenses exceeded the payments received by $176,271.88. The tax returns for 1913, 1915, and 1916 showed net losses. That for 1914 showed net income.

In 1915 work under the contract was abandoned, and in 1916 suit was brought in the Court of Claims to recover for a breach of warranty of the character of the material to be dredged. Judgment for the claimant was affirmed by this Court in 1920. * * * From the total recovery, petitioner received in that year the sum of $192,577.59, which included the $176,271.88 by which its expenses under the contract had exceeded receipts from it, and accrued interest amounting to $16,305.71. Respondent having failed to include these amounts as gross income in its tax returns for 1920, the Commissioner made the deficiency assessment here involved, based on the addition of both items to gross income for that year.

The Court of Appeals ruled that only the item of interest was properly included, holding, erroneously as the government contends, that the item of $176,271.88 was a return of losses suffered by respondent in earlier years and hence was wrongly assessed as income. Notwithstanding this conclusion, its judgment of reversal and the consequent elimination of this item from gross income for 1920 were made contingent upon the filing by respondent of amended returns for the years 1913 to 1916, from which were to be omitted the deductions of the related items of expenses paid in those years. Respondent insists that as the Sixteenth Amendment and the Revenue Act of 1918, which was in force in 1920, plainly contemplate a tax only on net income or profits, any application of the statute which operates to impose a tax with respect to the present transaction, from which respondent received no profit, cannot be upheld.

If respondent's contention that only gain or profit may be taxed under the Sixteenth Amendment be accepted without qualification, see *Eisner v. Macomber*, 252 U. S. 189, 40 S. Ct. 189, 64 L. Ed. 521, 9 A. L. R. 1570 * * *, the question remains whether the gain or profit which is the subject of the tax may be ascertained, as here, on the basis of fixed accounting periods, or whether, as is pressed upon us, it can only be net profit ascertained on the basis of particular transactions of the taxpayer when they are brought to a conclusion.

All the revenue acts which have been enacted since the adoption of the Sixteenth Amendment have uniformly assessed the tax on the basis of annual returns showing the net result of all the taxpayer's transactions during a fixed accounting period, either the calendar year, or, at the option of the taxpayer, the particular fiscal year which he may adopt. * * *

That the recovery made by respondent in 1920 was gross income for that year within the meaning of these sections cannot, we think, be doubted. The money received was derived from a contract entered into in the course of respondent's business operations for profit. While it equaled, and in a loose sense was a return of, expenditures made in performing the contract, still, as the Board of Tax Appeals found, the expenditures were made in defraying the expenses incurred in the prosecution of the work under the contract, for the purpose of earning profits. * * *

* * * Only by including these items of gross income in the 1920 return would it have been possible to ascertain respondent's net income for the period covered by the return, which is what the statute taxes. The excess of gross income over deductions did not any the less constitute net income for the taxable period because respondent, in an earlier period, suffered net losses in the conduct of its business which were in some measure attributable to expenditures made to produce the net income of the later period.

* * *

But respondent insists that if the sum which it recovered is the income defined by the statute, still it is not income, taxation of which without apportionment is permitted by the Sixteenth Amendment, since the particular transaction from which it was derived did not result in any net gain or profit. But we do not think the amendment is to be so narrowly construed. A taxpayer may be in receipt of net income in one year and not in another. The net result of the two years, if combined in a single taxable period, might still be a loss; but it has never been supposed that that fact would relieve him from a tax on the first, or that it affords any reason for postponing the assessment of the tax until the end of a lifetime, or for some other indefinite period, to ascertain more precisely whether the final outcome of the period, or of a given transaction, will be a gain or a loss.

The Sixteenth Amendment was adopted to enable the government to raise revenue by taxation. It is the essence of any system of taxation that it should produce revenue ascertainable, and payable to the government, at regular intervals. Only by such a system is it practicable to produce a regular flow of income and apply methods of accounting, assessment, and collection capable of practical operation. It is not suggested that there has ever been any general scheme for taxing income on any other basis. The computation of income annually as the net result of all transactions within the year was a familiar practice, and taxes upon income so arrived at were not unknown, before the Sixteenth Amendment. It is not to be supposed that the amendment did not contemplate that Congress might make income so ascertained the basis of a scheme of taxation such as had been in actual operation within the United States before its adoption. While, conceivably, a different system might be devised by which the tax could be assessed, wholly or in part, on the basis of the finally ascertained results of particular transactions, Congress is not required by the amendment to adopt such a system in preference to the more familiar method, even if it were practicable. It would not necessarily obviate the kind of inequalities of which respondent complains. If losses from particular transactions were to be set off against gains in others, there would still be the practical necessity of computing the tax on the basis of annual or other fixed taxable periods, which might result in the taxpayer being required to pay a tax on income in one period exceeded by net losses in another.

* * *

The assessment was properly made under the statutes. Relief from their alleged burdensome operation which may not be secured under these provisions, can be afforded only by legislation, not by the courts.

Reversed.

Notes

1. Recall the case of *North American Oil Consolidated v. Burnet* in Chapter 3. In 1916, the taxpayer in that case earned $170,000 in income from its beneficial interest in various oil wells. The United States government asserted beneficial interest in the wells and contested the taxpayer's right to the income, so that year's income was paid to a receiver. In 1917, the receiver paid the profits to the taxpayer although the litigation between the United States and the taxpayer was ongoing. The taxpayer amended its 1916 tax return and reported the income. The dispute between the government and the taxpayer finally resolved in 1920, and the Supreme Court denied cert. in the case in 1922. The issue before the Court in *North American Oil* was the timing of the taxpayer's gross income. Ultimately, the Court determined that the taxpayer should have reported the income in 1917, the year of receipt:

> The net profits earned by the property in 1916 were not income of the year 1922—the year in which the litigation with the Government was finally terminated. They became income of the company in 1917, when it first became entitled to them and when it actually received them. If a taxpayer receives earnings under a claim of right and without restriction as to its disposition, he has received income which he is required to return, even though it may still be claimed that he is not entitled to retain the money, and even though he may still be adjudged liable to restore its equivalent. * * * If in 1922 the Government had prevailed,

and the company had been obliged to refund the profits received in 1917, it would have been entitled to a deduction from the profits of 1922, not from those of any earlier year.

North American Oil is famous for creating the "claim of right" doctrine, and that was our focus when we first read the case in Chapter 3. But together with *Sanford & Brooks*, the case stands for the simple but profound notion that **every year stands alone**. Thus, when the taxpayer received funds in 1917, it was proper to include the funds in gross income because there was no obligation to repay the funds as of the end of that year. According to the last sentence of the Court's opinion, the taxpayer should not amend its 1917 return if the taxpayer repays the funds in 1922—instead, says the Court, the taxpayer should claim a deduction in 1922. The Court further implies (and this is important) that the deduction in 1922 would not be conditioned on the prior inclusion of the money in an earlier year. In other words, the correct treatment of an item in one year does not depend upon the treatment of the same or a related item in another year. Indeed, every year does stand alone.

2. *North American Oil* also illustrates why we need error correction devices, the subject of Part D of this Chapter. Remember that the taxpayer included about $170,000 in gross income in 1916. In 1932, the Supreme Court held that the taxpayer should have included the funds in gross income in 1917. By 1932, however, the statute of limitations on 1916 expired, so the taxpayer could not file an amended return for 1916. Thus the taxpayer included $170,000 in gross income *twice*—in 1916 and in 1917! This illustrates how harsh the concept of "every year stands alone" can be, and why we need the error correction devices described in Part D.

Restatement With a Twist. The following case seems pretty innocent. On its face, it appears simply to be a mere restatement and application of the "claim of right" doctrine. But as you read the case, consider whether it has a deeper meaning.

UNITED STATES v. LEWIS

United States Supreme Court, 1951.
340 U.S. 590, 71 S.Ct. 522, 95 L.Ed. 560.

Mr. Justice Black delivered the opinion of the Court.

* * * In his 1944 income tax return, respondent reported about $22,000 which he had received that year as an employee's bonus. As a result of subsequent litigation in a state court, however, it was decided that respondent's bonus had been improperly computed; under compulsion of the state court's judgment he returned approximately $11,000 to his employer. Until payment of the judgment in 1946, respondent had at all times claimed and used the full $22,000 unconditionally as his own, in the good faith though "mistaken" belief that he was entitled to the whole bonus.

On the foregoing facts the Government's position is that respondent's 1944 tax should not be recomputed, but that respondent should have deducted the $11,000 as a loss in his 1946 tax return. The Court of

Claims, however, relying on its own case, *Greenwald v. United States*, 57 F.Supp. 569, 102 Ct.Cl. 272, held that the excess bonus received "under a mistake of fact" was not income in 1944 and ordered a refund based on a recalculation of that year's tax. We granted certiorari because this holding conflicted with many decisions of the courts of appeals, see, e.g., *Haberkorn v. United States*, 6 Cir., 173 F.2d 587, and with principles announced in *North American Oil Consolidated v. Burnet*, 286 U.S. 417, 52 S.Ct. 613, 76 L.Ed. 1197.

In the *North American Oil* case we said: "If a taxpayer receives earnings under a claim of right and without restriction as to its disposition, he has received income which he is required to return, even though it may still be claimed that he is not entitled to retain the money, and even though he may still be adjudged liable to restore its equivalent." 286 U.S. at 424, 52 S.Ct. at page 615, 76 L.Ed. 1197. Nothing in this language permits an exception merely because a taxpayer is "mistaken" as to the validity of his claim. * * *

Income taxes must be paid on income received (or accrued) during an annual accounting period. The "claim of right" interpretation of the tax laws has long been used to give finality to that period, and is now deeply rooted in the federal tax system. We see no reason why the Court should depart from this well-settled interpretation merely because it results in an advantage or disadvantage to a taxpayer.[1]

Reversed.

Mr. Justice Douglas (dissenting).

The question in this case is not whether the bonus had to be included in 1944 income for purposes of the tax. Plainly it should have been because the taxpayer claimed it as of right. Some years later, however, it was judicially determined that he had no claim to the bonus. The question is whether he may then get back the tax which he paid on the money.

Many inequities are inherent in the income tax. We multiply them needlessly by nice distinctions which have no place in the practical administration of the law. If the refund were allowed, the integrity of the taxable year would not be violated. The tax would be paid when due; but the government would not be permitted to maintain the unconscionable position that it can keep the tax after it is shown that payment was made on money which was not income to the taxpayer.

Note

To uncover the "deeper meaning" of *Lewis*, consider carefully the arguments of the parties. Lewis argued that the proper solution was to amend his 1944 return and exclude the $22,000 bonus. The Service argued

---

1. It has been suggested that it would be more 'equitable' to reopen respondent's 1944 tax return. While the suggestion might work to the advantage of this taxpayer, it could not be adopted as a general solution because, in many cases, the three-year statute of limitations would preclude recovery.

that the 1944 return should be left alone and that Lewis should be able to deduct the $11,000 repayment in 1946. The Service prevailed. (What provokes the strong dissent from Justice Douglas is the fact that 1946 was, by the time the *Lewis* Court rendered judgment in 1951, a closed year, which prevented Lewis from claiming the $11,000 deduction.) By choosing the Service's argument, the Court (maybe unknowingly) created a standard for filing amended returns.

To paraphrase the Court, a taxpayer should include income and claim deductions based upon the information the taxpayer knew or should have known as of the end of the taxable year. An amended return is proper only where the taxpayer knew or should have known of the item (income or deduction) during the taxable year but failed to take the item into account on the taxpayer's original return. If information learned after the close of the taxable year proves that the prior reporting position was incorrect, the taxpayer should account for the subsequent information (and any resulting transactions) in the year such information becomes apparent.

D. ERROR CORRECTION

Introduction. In this Part we study several of the various devices available to taxpayers and to the Service for correcting mistakes: (1) the tax benefit rule, a common law doctrine with a statutory twist; (2) the relief under § 1341 for restoration of a claim of right; (3) the judicial doctrines of res judicata and collateral estoppel; (4) the judicial doctrine of equitable recoupment; and (5) the statutory provisions designed to mitigate the overly harsh (or overly beneficial) effects of the statute of limitations for return assessment. There are several other rules that could legitimately be called "correction devices," but they are best left for other Chapters.

(1) THE TAX BENEFIT RULE

Code: IRC § 111.

Regs: None.

The Rule Has Two Faces. The tax benefit rule is easy to state: if a taxpayer recovers an item that was previously deducted, and if the prior deduction reduced the taxpayer's tax liability in the year of deduction, then the recovery is included in gross income. For example, suppose a taxpayer pays a $5,000 business expense in Year One. Under § 162(a), the taxpayer is entitled to a Year One deduction of $5,000. If the taxpayer is subject to a flat tax rate of 25 percent, the resulting tax savings from the Year One deduction is $1,250. If, in Year Two, the taxpayer receives a $3,000 refund of the Year One business expense, the tax benefit rule requires that the taxpayer include the $3,000 in gross income.

If the taxpayer had no gross income in Year One, however, then the $5,000 deduction would have been meaningless. Accordingly, because the Year One deduction yielded no tax benefit, the Year Two recovery of $3,000 would not be included in gross income.

Notice that the rule has an *inclusionary* aspect and an *exclusionary* aspect. The inclusionary aspect is that the recovery is gross income because the prior deduction was, ultimately, incorrect. The exclusionary aspect is that the recovery is not taxable unless the prior deduction actually yielded a tax savings that year.

The exclusionary aspect of the rule is codified in § 111. Section 111(a) is the taxpayer's authority for excluding the $3,000 refund described in the last example, because the corresponding payment in Year One gave rise to a deduction that did not reduce the taxpayer's tax liability for Year One. Section 111(b) contains a similar rule with respect to credits. Suppose that in Year One, a taxpayer paid $5,000 in child care expenses and thus was entitled to a $1,000 income tax credit (20 percent of the amount paid) for that year under § 21. The taxpayer's tax liability for Year One, however, was only $400, so only $400 of the credit was used. The credit is not refundable, and the $600 excess does not carry over to any other years. Now suppose in Year Two that the taxpayer receives a $500 refund of the child care expenses paid in Year One. Had the taxpayer paid only $4,500 of child care expenses in Year One, the allowable credit amount would have been $900 (again, 20 percent of the amount paid). Again, only $400 of the credit would have been used. Thus, the $100 of credit attributable to the $500 refund did not reduce the taxpayer's income tax liability for Year One. Under § 111(b), therefore, the $500 refund would be excluded from gross income.

The inclusionary aspect of the tax benefit rule is a creature of common law. Arguably, § 61 covers the inclusion of deduction recoveries, because such amounts are, to paraphrase *Glenshaw Glass*, accessions to wealth over which the taxpayer has complete dominion. But there is no specific Code provision related to the inclusionary aspect. Consequently, there are some ambiguities that courts have to resolve from time to time.

One of these ambiguities is whether the tax attributable to the amount included in gross income under the tax benefit rule can exceed the total benefit received by the taxpayer in the year of deduction. Using the business expense recovery example again, suppose that the tax rate applicable to the taxpayer in Year Two was 50 percent. If the taxpayer must include $3,000 in gross income in Year Two under the tax benefit rule, the tax attributable to the inclusion will be $1,500—but that exceeds the $1,250 benefit the taxpayer received from the deduction in Year One. Is that a problem? The following cases addresses this issue, reaching what has to be the right result if "every year stands alone."

ALICE PHELAN SULLIVAN CORPORATION
v. UNITED STATES

United States Court of Claims, 1967.
381 F.2d 399.

COLLINS, JUDGE.

Plaintiff, a California corporation, brings this action to recover an alleged overpayment in its 1957 income tax. During that year, there was returned to taxpayer two parcels of realty, each of which it had previously donated and claimed as a charitable contribution deduction. The first donation had been made in 1939; the second, in 1940. Under the then applicable corporate tax rates, the deductions claimed ($4,243.49 for 1939 and $4,463.44 for 1940) yielded plaintiff an aggregate tax benefit of $1,877.49.[1]

Each conveyance had been made subject to the condition that the property be used either for a religious or for an educational purpose. In 1957, the donee decided not to use the gifts; they were therefore reconveyed to plaintiff. Upon audit of taxpayer's income tax return, it was found that the recovered property was not reflected in its 1957 gross income. The Commissioner of Internal Revenue disagreed with plaintiff's characterization of the recovery as a nontaxable return of capital. He viewed the transaction as giving rise to taxable income and therefore adjusted plaintiff's income by adding to it $8,706.93—the total of the charitable contribution deductions previously claimed and allowed. This addition to income, taxed at the 1957 corporate tax rate of 52 percent, resulted in a deficiency assessment of $4,527.60. After payment of the deficiency, plaintiff filed a claim for the refund of $2,650.11, asserting this amount as overpayment on the theory that a correct assessment could demand no more than the return of the tax benefit originally enjoyed, i.e., $1,877.49. The claim was disallowed.

This court has had prior occasion to consider the question which the present suit presents. In *Perry v. United States*, 160 F.Supp. 270, 142 Ct.Cl. 7 (1958) (Judges Madden and Laramore dissenting), it was recognized that a return to the donor of a prior charitable contribution gave rise to income to the extent of the deduction previously allowed. The court's point of division—which is likewise the division between the instant parties—was whether the "gain" attributable to the recovery was to be taxed at the rate applicable at the time the deduction was first claimed or whether the proper rate was that in effect at the time of recovery. The majority, concluding that the Government should be entitled to recoup no more than that which it lost, held that the tax liability arising upon the return of a charitable gift should equal the tax benefit experienced at time of donation. Taxpayer urges that the *Perry* rationale dictates that a like result be reached in this case.

* * *

---

1. The tax rate in 1939 was 18 percent; in 1940, 24 percent.

A transaction which returns to a taxpayer his own property cannot be considered as giving rise to "income"—at least where that term is confined to its traditional sense of "gain derived from capital, from labor, or from both combined." *Eisner v. Macomber*, 252 U.S. 189, 207, 40 S.Ct. 189, 64 L.Ed. 521 (1920). Yet the principle is well engrained in our tax law that the return or recovery of property that was once the subject of an income tax deduction must be treated as income in the year of its recovery. *Rothensies v. Electric Storage Battery Co.*, 329 U.S. 296, 67 S.Ct. 271, 91 L.Ed. 296 (1946); *Estate of Block v. Commissioner*, 39 B.T.A. 338 (1939), aff'd sub nom. *Union Trust Co. v. Commissioner*, 111 F.2d 60 (7th Cir.), cert. denied, 311 U.S. 658, 61 S.Ct. 12, 85 L.Ed. 421 (1940). The only limitation upon that principle is the so-called "tax-benefit rule." This rule permits exclusion of the recovered item from income so long as its initial use as a deduction did not provide a tax saving. But where full tax use of a deduction was made and a tax saving thereby obtained, then the extent of saving is considered immaterial. The recovery is viewed as income to the full extent of the deduction previously allowed.[2]

Formerly the exclusive province of judge-made law, the tax-benefit concept now finds expression both in statute and administrative regulations. Section 111 of the Internal Revenue Code of 1954 accords tax-benefit treatment * * *.

* * *

Ever since *Burnet v. Sanford & Brooks Co.*, 282 U.S. 359, 51 S.Ct. 150, 75 L.Ed. 383 (1931), the concept of accounting for items of income and expense on an annual basis has been accepted as the basic principle upon which our tax laws are structured. "It is the essence of any system of taxation that it should produce revenue ascertainable, and payable to the government, at regular intervals. Only by such a system is it practicable to produce a regular flow of income and apply methods of accounting, assessment, and collection capable of practical operation." 282 U.S. at 365, 51 S.Ct. at 152. To insure the vitality of the single-year concept, it is essential not only that annual income be ascertained without reference to losses experienced in an earlier accounting period, but also that income be taxed without reference to earlier tax rates. And absent specific statutory authority sanctioning a departure from this principle, it may only be said of *Perry* that it achieved a result which was more equitably just than legally correct.[5]

---

2. The rationale which supports the principle, as well as its limitation, is that the property, having once served to offset taxable income (i.e., as a tax deduction) should be treated, upon its recoupment, as the recovery of that which had been previously deducted. See Plumb, *The Tax Benefit Rule Today*, 57 Harv. L. Rev. 129, 131 n. 10 (1943).

5. This opinion represents the views of the majority and complies with existing law

and decisions. However, in the writer's personal opinion, it produces a harsh and inequitable result. Perhaps, it exemplifies a situation "where the latter of the law killeth; the spirit giveth life." The tax-benefit concept is an equitable doctrine which should be carried to an equitable conclusion. Since it is the declared public policy to encourage contributions to charitable and educational organizations, a donor, whose gift to such organizations is returned, should not be

Since taxpayer in this case did obtain full tax benefit from its earlier deductions, those deductions were properly classified as income upon recoupment and must be taxed as such. This can mean nothing less than the application of that tax rate which is in effect during the year in which the recovered item is recognized as a factor of income. We therefore sustain the Government's position and grant its motion for summary judgment. *Perry v. United States*, *supra*, is hereby overruled, and plaintiff's petition is dismissed.

* * *

Erroneous Deduction Exception. Should the tax benefit rule apply if the prior deduction was improper? For example, Lawyer represents Client in a personal injury action, and Client is unable to pay costs associated with Client's lawsuit. In Year One, Lawyer advances the costs, reserving the right to reimbursement from the proceeds of any amounts recovered in the lawsuit. In Year Two, the lawsuit is successful, and Lawyer's advances are reimbursed. If Lawyer deducted the costs paid in Year One, does Lawyer have gross income in Year Two?

The answer of the Tax Court, on these facts, is no. *Canelo v. Commissioner*, 53 T.C. 217 (1969). Keep in mind that the deduction in Year One is improper—the advances are loans, not expenses, because of the right to reimbursement. Even if the advances are characterized as gifts from Lawyer to Client, there is no deduction for Lawyer. Thus, the amount received by Lawyer in Year Two was judged on its own merits. Ultimately, the court held that Lawyer had no gross income in Year Two—the amount received was a repayment of the loan. Notice that the ultimate result here is a windfall for Lawyer, assuming Year One is closed (although the mitigation rules discussed later in this Part may come into play). Lawyer got a deduction *and* an exclusion. The deduction was wrong, but the court thought that the need to preserve the "every year stands alone" principle outweighed the windfall resulting from these facts. If the Year Two analysis is independent of what happened in Year One (because every year stands alone), then the court was right to exclude the recovered advances as loan repayments.

Canelo and some other Tax Court cases are credited with creating an **erroneous deduction exception** to the tax benefit rule. Not all appellate courts buy into the exception, however.

UNVERT v. COMMISSIONER, 656 F.2d 483 (9th Cir. 1981).

Facts: The taxpayer paid $54,500 in 1969 as prepaid interest expense related to the purchase of various condominiums. The taxpayer deducted the interest payment on his 1969 income tax return, although that deduction was not proper. In 1972, the prepaid interest was refund-

required to refund to the Government a greater amount than the tax benefit received when the deduction was made for the gift. Such a rule would avoid a penalty to the taxpayer and an unjust enrichment to the Government. However, the court cannot legislate and any change in the existing law rests within the wisdom and discretion of the Congress.

ed to the taxpayer. When the taxpayer did not include the refunded interest in gross income for 1972, the Service came knocking.

Issue: Must the taxpayer include the recovery of the prepaid interest expense even though the taxpayer erroneously deducted the expense in a prior year?

Holding: Yes.

Rationale: "The logic of the erroneous deduction exception is that an improper deduction should be corrected by assessing a deficiency before the statute of limitations has run, not by treating recovery of the expenditure as income. * * * We find this unpersuasive. Prior decisions under the tax benefit rule state clearly that inclusion of the recovery as income does not reopen the tax liability for the prior year and does not implicate the statute of limitations. * * * 'Income tax liability must be determined for annual periods on the basis of facts as they existed in each period. When recovery or some other event which is inconsistent with what has been done in the past occurs, adjustment must be made in reporting income for the year in which the change occurs. No other system would be practical in view of the statute of limitations, the obvious administrative difficulties involved, and the lack of finality in income tax liability, which would result.' *First Trust & Savings Bank v. United States*, 614 F.2d 1142, 1145 (7th Cir. 1980) (quoting *Block v. Commissioner*, 39 B.T.A. 338 (1939) (emphasis omitted)). * * *

"Unvert attempts to provide a more fully reasoned justification for this exception. He argues that whether the recovery of a previous expenditure is taxable depends on its character as income or a return of capital. This character, he contends, is determined from the inherent characteristics of the transaction, not whether the taxpayer originally deducted the expenditure. The Commissioner does not contest that the 1969 deduction was improper because the expenditure was capital. Unvert argues that the Commissioner has attempted to recoup the 1969 deduction by improperly recharacterizing the recovery as income rather than correctly treating it as a nontaxable return of capital.

"This argument is unpersuasive. The decisions creating and applying the tax benefit rule make clear that the recovery must be taxed because it previously created a tax benefit, not because of the inherent characteristic of the recovery. * * *

"The erroneous deduction exception is also poor public policy. A taxpayer who properly claims a deduction for an expenditure that is recovered in a later year must treat the recovery as income, while one who claims an improper deduction may not be required to include the recovery as income only because of the impropriety of the deduction. We agree with the Second Circuit that improperly taken tax deductions should not be rewarded.

"We need in this case to concern ourselves with the theory advanced that when * * * a deduction has improperly been claimed and allowed, no part of such deduction when collected can be included in income. It is obvious that if this is so a taxpayer who gets an unlawful deduction in this way not only cuts down his taxable income in the year the deduction is taken, but gets immunity from income taxation on the account receivable which was deducted whenever it, or any part of it, is received. A result so unjust is not to be reached unless plainly required by law. * * *

"At least three circuits have implicitly rejected or criticized the erroneous deduction exception. See *Union Trust Co. v. Commissioner*, 111 F.2d 60, 61 (7th Cir.), cert. denied, 311 U.S. 658, 61 S. Ct. 12, 85 L. Ed. 421 (1940); *Kahn v. Commissioner*, 108 F.2d 748, 749 (2d Cir. 1940); *Askin & Marine Co. v. Commissioner*, 66 F.2d 776, 778 (2d Cir. 1933); *Commissioner v. Liberty Bank & Trust Co.*, 59 F.2d 320, 325 (6th Cir. 1932)."

* * *

Expansion of the Rule. The following case is quite controversial. It is also quite long, largely because it involves two separate sets of facts and because of the extensive bickering between the majority and the dissenters. As you will see, the inclusionary aspect of the tax benefit rule now reaches not only recoveries of amounts previously deducted, but also events that are fundamentally inconsistent with a prior deduction or exclusion.

HILLSBORO NATIONAL BANK v. COMMISSIONER
UNITED STATES v. BLISS DAIRY, INC.

United States Supreme Court, 1983.
460 U.S. 370, 103 S.Ct. 1134, 75 L.Ed.2d 130.

JUSTICE O'CONNOR delivered the opinion of the Court.

These consolidated cases present the question of the applicability of the tax benefit rule to two corporate tax situations: the repayment to the shareholders of taxes for which they were liable but that were originally paid by the corporation; and the distribution of expensed assets in a corporate liquidation. We conclude that, unless a nonrecognition provision of the Internal Revenue Code prevents it, the tax benefit rule ordinarily applies to require the inclusion of income when events occur that are fundamentally inconsistent with an earlier deduction. Our examination of the provisions granting the deductions and governing the liquidation in these cases lead us to hold that the rule requires the recognition of income in the case of the liquidation but not in the case of the tax refund.

I

In No. 81–485, *Hillsboro National Bank v. Commissioner,* the petitioner, Hillsboro National Bank, is an incorporated bank doing business in Illinois. Until 1970, Illinois imposed a property tax on shares held in incorporated banks. Ill. Rev. Stat., ch. 120, § 557 (1971). Banks, required to retain earnings sufficient to cover the taxes, § 558, customarily paid the taxes for the shareholders. Under § 164(e) of the Internal Revenue Code of 1954 * * *, the bank was allowed a deduction for the amount of the tax, but the shareholders were not. [Hillsboro paid such taxes in 1972 even though Illinois' state constitution had been amended to preclude the imposition of ad valorem personal property taxes. Collection of the tax continued because a lawsuit contesting the validity of the amendment was pending. The collected taxes were thus held in escrow. Still, because the bank had paid the taxes in 1972, Hillsboro deducted the payments on its 1972 tax return. The litigation ended in 1973, when the Court upheld the validity of the state constitutional amendment. The State Treasurer thus refunded all of the taxes collected in 1972. The taxes paid by Hillsboro, however, were paid directly to Hillsboro's shareholders; Hillsboro did not collect any portion of the refund. Hillsboro included no portion of the refund in its gross income for 1973, and the Commissioner assessed a deficiency.] Hillsboro sought a redetermination in the Tax Court, which held that the refund of the taxes, but not the payment of accrued interest, was includible in Hillsboro's income. On appeal, relying on its earlier decision in *First Trust and Savings Bank v. United States,* 614 F.2d 1142 (CA7 1980), the Court of Appeals for the Seventh Circuit affirmed.

In No. 81–930, *United States v. Bliss Dairy, Inc.,* the respondent, Bliss Dairy, Inc., was a closely held corporation engaged in the business of operating a dairy. As a cash basis taxpayer, in the taxable year ending June 30, 1973, it deducted upon purchase the full cost of the cattle feed purchased for use in its operations, as permitted by § 162 of the Internal Revenue Code * * *. A substantial portion of the feed was still on hand at the end of the taxable year. On July 2, 1973, two days into the next taxable year, Bliss adopted a plan of liquidation, and, during the month of July, it distributed its assets, including the remaining cattle feed, to the shareholders. [At that time, the liquidation of a corporation like Bliss was not a taxable event to either Bliss or its shareholders. Instead, the shareholders took the corporation's assets (including the feed) with a basis equal to their total basis in the Bliss stock. A portion of the total basis was allocable to the cattle feed, so the shareholders deducted the cost of the feed in their hands as a business expense. The Service objected on the grounds that the shareholders were deducting the cost of an asset that had been completely deducted by Bliss in a prior year.] On audit, the Commissioner challenged the corporation's treatment of the transaction, asserting that Bliss should have taken into income the value of the grain distributed to the shareholders. He therefore increased Bliss's income by $60,000. Bliss paid the resulting assessment and sued for a refund in the district court for the District of Arizona, [which] rendered a judgment in favor of Bliss. While recognizing authority to the contrary, the Court of Appeals * * * affirmed.

II

The Government in each case relies solely on the tax benefit rule—a judicially developed principle that allays some of the inflexibilities of the annual accounting system. An annual accounting system is a practical necessity if the federal income tax is to produce revenue ascertainable and payable at regular intervals. *Burnet v. Sanford & Brooks Co.,* 282 U.S. 359, 365, 51 S.Ct. 150, 152, 75 L.Ed. 383 (1931). Nevertheless, strict adherence to an annual accounting system would create transactional inequities. Often an apparently completed transaction will reopen unexpectedly in a subsequent tax year, rendering the initial reporting improper. * * * Recognizing and seeking to avoid the possible distortions of income, the courts have long required the taxpayer to recognize the repayment in the second year as income. * * *

The taxpayers and the Government in these cases propose different formulations of the tax benefit rule. The taxpayers contend that the rule requires the inclusion of amounts *recovered* in later years, and they do not view the events in these cases as "recoveries." The Government, on the other hand, urges that the tax benefit rule requires the inclusion of amounts previously deducted if later events are inconsistent with the deductions; it insists that no "recovery" is necessary to the application of the rule. Further, it asserts that the events in these cases are inconsistent with the deductions taken by the taxpayers. We are not in complete agreement with either view.

An examination of the purpose and accepted applications of the tax benefit rule reveals that a "recovery" will not always be necessary to invoke the tax benefit rule. The purpose of the rule is not simply to tax "recoveries." On the contrary, it is to approximate the results produced by a tax system based on transactional rather than annual accounting. * * * It has long been accepted that a taxpayer using accrual accounting who accrues and deducts an expense in a tax year before it becomes payable and who for some reason eventually does not have to pay the liability must then take into income the amount of the expense earlier deducted. * * * The bookkeeping entry canceling the liability, though it increases the balance sheet net worth of the taxpayer, does not fit within any ordinary definition of "recovery." Thus, the taxpayers' formulation of the rule neither serves the purposes of the rule nor accurately reflects the cases that establish the rule. Further, the taxpayers' proposal would introduce an undesirable formalism into the application of the tax benefit rule. Lower courts have been able to stretch the definition of "recovery" to include a great variety of events. For instance, in cases of corporate liquidations, courts have viewed the corporation's receipt of its own stock as a "recovery," reasoning that, even though the instant that the corporation receives the stock it becomes worthless, the stock has value as it is turned over to the corporation, and that ephemeral value represents a recovery for the corporation. * * * Or, payment to another party may be imputed to the taxpayer, giving rise to a recovery. Imposition of a requirement that there be a recovery would, in many cases, simply require the Government to cast its argument in different and unnatural terminology, without adding anything to the analysis.

The basic purpose of the tax benefit rule is to achieve rough transactional parity in tax * * * and to protect the Government and the taxpayer from the adverse effects of reporting a transaction on the basis of assumptions that an event in a subsequent year proves to have been erroneous. Such an event, unforeseen at the time of an earlier deduction, may in many cases require the application of the tax benefit rule. We do not, however, agree that this consequence invariably follows. Not every unforeseen event will require the taxpayer to report income in the amount of his earlier deduction. On the contrary, the tax benefit rule will "cancel out" an earlier deduction only when a careful examination shows that the later event is indeed fundamentally inconsistent with the premise on which the deduction was initially based. That is, if that event had occurred within the same taxable year, it would have foreclosed the deduction. In some cases, a subsequent recovery by the taxpayer will be the only event that would be fundamentally inconsistent with the provision granting the deduction. In such a case, only actual recovery by the taxpayer would justify application of the tax benefit rule. For example, if a calendar-year taxpayer made a rental payment on December 15 for a 30–day lease deductible in the current year under § 162(a)(3), see Treas. Reg. § 1.461–1(a)(1) * * *; *e.g., Zaninovich v. Commissioner,* 616 F.2d 429 (CA9 1980), the tax benefit rule would not require the recognition of income if the leased premises were destroyed by fire on January 10. The resulting inability of the taxpayer to occupy the building would be an event not fundamentally inconsistent with his prior deduction as an ordinary and necessary business expense under § 162(a). The loss is attributable to the business and therefore is consistent with the deduction of the rental payment as an ordinary and necessary business expense. On the other hand, had the premises not burned and, in January, the taxpayer decided to use them to house his family rather than to continue the operation of his business, he would have converted the leasehold to personal use. This would be an event fundamentally inconsistent with the business use on which the deduction was based. In the case of the fire, only if the lessor—by virtue of some provision in the lease—had refunded the rental payment would the taxpayer be required under the tax benefit rule to recognize income on the subsequent destruction of the building. In other words, the subsequent recovery of the previously deducted rental payment would be the only event inconsistent with the provision allowing the deduction. It therefore is evident that the tax benefit rule must be applied on a case-by-case basis. A court must consider the facts and circumstances of each case in the light of the purpose and function of the provisions granting the deductions.

* * *

The formulation that we endorse today follows clearly from the long development of the tax benefit rule. Justice STEVENS' assertion that there is no suggestion in the early cases or from the early commentators that the rule could ever be applied in any case that did not involve a physical recovery * * * is incorrect. The early cases frequently framed the rule in terms consistent with our view and irreconcilable with that of the dissent. See *Barnett v. Commissioner,* 39 B.T.A. 864, 867 (1939) ("Finally, the present case is analogous to a number of others, where … [w]hen some event occurs which is *inconsistent* with a deduction taken in a prior year, adjustment may have to be made by reporting a balancing item in income for the year in which the change occurs.'') (emphasis added); *Estate of Block v. Commissioner,* 39 B.T.A. 338 (1939) (''When recovery *or some other event which is inconsistent* with what has been done in the past occurs, adjustment must be made in reporting income for the year in which the change occurs.'') (emphasis added); *South Dakota Concrete Products Co. v. Commissioner,* 26 B.T.A. 1429, 1432 (1932) (''[W]hen an *adjustment* occurs which is *inconsistent* with what has been done in the past in the determination of tax liability, the adjustment should be reflected in reporting income for the year in which it occurs.'') (emphasis added). The reliance of the dissent on the early commentators is equally misplaced, for the articles cited in the dissent, like the early cases, often stated the rule in terms of inconsistent events.

* * *

Justice STEVENS also suggests that we err in recognizing transactional equity as the reason for the tax benefit rule. It is difficult to understand why even the clearest recovery should be taxed if not for the concern with transactional equity * * *. Nor does the concern with transactional equity entail a change in our approach to the annual accounting system. Although the tax system relies basically on annual accounting, see *Burnet v. Sanford & Brooks Co.,* 282 U.S. 359, 365, 51 S.Ct. 150, 152, 75 L.Ed. 383 (1931), the tax benefit rule eliminates some of the distortions that would otherwise arise from such a system. * * * The limited nature of the rule and its effect on the annual accounting principle bears repetition: *only* if the occurrence of the event in the earlier year would have resulted in the disallowance of the deduction can the Commissioner require a compensating recognition of income when the event occurs in the later year.

* * *

In the cases currently before us, then, we must undertake an examination of the particular provisions of the Code that govern these transactions to determine whether the deductions taken by the taxpayers were actually inconsistent with later events and whether specific nonrecognition provisions prevail over the principle of the tax benefit rule.

* * *

In *Hillsboro,* the key provision is § 164(e). That section grants the corporation a deduction for taxes imposed on its shareholders but paid by the corporation. It also denies the shareholders any deduction for the tax. In this case, the Commissioner has argued that the refund of the taxes by the state to the shareholders is the equivalent of the payment of a dividend from Hillsboro to its shareholders. If Hillsboro does not recognize income in the amount of the earlier deduction, it will have deducted a dividend. Since the general structure of the corporate tax provisions does not permit deduction of dividends, the Commissioner concludes that the payment to the shareholders must be inconsistent with the original deduction and therefore requires the inclusion of the amount of the taxes as income under the tax benefit rule.

In evaluating this argument, it is instructive to consider what the tax consequences of the payment of a shareholder tax by the corporation would be without § 164(e) and compare them to the consequences under § 164(e). Without § 164(e), the corporation would not be entitled to a deduction, for the tax is not imposed on it. * * * If the corporation has earnings and profits, the shareholder would have to recognize income in the amount of the taxes, because a payment by a corporation for the benefit of its shareholders is a constructive dividend. * * * The shareholder, however, would be entitled to a deduction since the constructive dividend is used to satisfy his tax liability. Section 164(a)(2). Thus, for the shareholder, the transaction would be a wash: he would recognize the amount of the tax as income, but he would have an offsetting deduction for the tax. For the corporation, there would be no tax consequences, for the payment of a dividend gives rise to neither income nor a deduction.

Under § 164(e), the economics of the transaction of course remain unchanged: the corporation is still satisfying a liability of the shareholder and is therefore paying a constructive dividend. The tax consequences are, however, significantly different, at least for the corporation. The transaction is still a wash for the shareholder; although § 164(e) denies him the deduction to which he would otherwise be entitled, he need not recognize income on the constructive dividend * * *. But the corporation is entitled to a deduction that would not otherwise be available. In other words, the only effect of § 164(e) is to permit the corporation to deduct a dividend. Thus, we cannot agree with the Commissioner that, simply because the events here give rise to a deductible dividend, they cannot be consistent with the deduction. In at least some circumstances, a deductible dividend is within the contemplation of the Code. The question we must answer is whether § 164(e) permits a deductible dividend in these circumstances—when, the money, though initially paid into the state treasury, ultimately reaches the shareholder—or whether the deductible dividend is available, as the Commissioner urges, only when the money remains in the state treasury, as properly assessed and collected tax revenue.

Rephrased, our question now is whether Congress, in granting this special favor to corporations that paid dividends by satisfying the liability of their shareholders, was concerned with the *reason* the money was paid out by the corporation or with the *use* to which it was ultimately put. Since § 164(e) represents a break with the usual rules governing corporate distributions, the structure of the Code does not provide any guidance on the reach of the provision. This Court has described the provision as "prompted by the plight of various banking corporations which paid and voluntarily absorbed the burden of certain local taxes imposed upon their shareholders, but were not permitted to deduct those payments from gross income." *Wisconsin Gas & Electric Co. v. United States,* 322 U.S., at 531, 64 S.Ct., at 1109 (footnote omitted). The section, in substantially similar form, has been part of the Code since the Revenue Act of 1921 * * *. The provision was added by the Senate, but its Committee Report merely mentions the deduction without discussing it, see S. Rep. No. 275, 67th Cong., 1st Sess. 19 (1921). The only discussion of the provision appears to be that between Dr. T.S. Adams and Senator Smoot at the Senate Hearings. Dr. Adams's statement explains why the states imposed the property tax on the shareholders and collected it from the banks, but it does not cast much light on the reason for the deduction. * * * Senator Smoot's response, however, is more revealing:

> I have been a director of a bank ... for over 20 years. They have paid that tax ever since I have owned a share of stock in the bank.... I know nothing about it. I do not take 1 cent of credit for deductions, and the banks are entitled to it. *They pay it out. Id.,* at 251 (emphasis added).

The *payment* by the corporations of a liability that Congress knew was not a tax imposed on them gave rise to the entitlement to a deduction; Congress was unconcerned that the corporations took a deduction for amounts that did not satisfy their tax liability. It apparently perceived the shareholders and the corporations as independent of one another, each "know[ing] nothing about" the payments by the other. In those circumstances, it is difficult to conclude that Congress intended that the corporation have no deduction if the state turned the tax revenues over to these independent parties. We conclude that the purpose of § 164(e) was to provide relief for corporations making these payments, and the focus of Congress was on the act of payment rather than on the ultimate use of the funds by the state. As long as the payment itself was not negated by a refund to the corporation, the change in character of the funds in the hands of the state does not require the corporation to recognize income, and we reverse the judgment below.

IV

The problem in *Bliss* is more complicated. Bliss took a deduction under § 162(a), so we must begin by examining that provision. Section 162(a) permits a deduction for the "ordinary and necessary expenses" of carrying on a trade or business. The deduction is predicated on the consumption of the asset in the trade or business. * * * If the taxpayer later sells the asset rather than consuming it in furtherance of his trade or business, it is quite clear that he would lose his deduction, for the basis of the asset would be zero, see, *e.g., Spitalny v. United States,* 430 F.2d 195 (CA9 1970), so he would recognize the full amount of the proceeds on sale as gain. See § 1001(a), (c). In general, if the taxpayer converts the expensed asset to some other, non-business use, that action is inconsistent with his earlier deduction, and the tax benefit rule would require inclusion in income of the amount of the unwarranted deduction.

That non-business use is inconsistent with a deduction for an ordinary and necessary business expense is clear from an examination of the Code. While § 162(a) permits a deduction for ordinary and necessary business expenses, § 262 explicitly denies a deduction for personal expenses. * * * Thus, if a corporation turns expensed assets to the analog of personal consumption, as Bliss did here—distribution to shareholders—it would seem that it should take into income the amount of the earlier deduction.

That conclusion, however, does not resolve this case, for the distribution by Bliss to its shareholders is governed by a provision of the Code that specifically shields the taxpayer from recognition of gain—§ 336. We must therefore proceed to inquire whether this is the sort of gain that goes unrecognized under § 336. Our examination of the background of § 336 and its place within the framework of tax law convinces us that it does not prevent the application of the tax benefit rule.

* * *

* * * Consequently, we reverse the judgment of the Court of Appeals and hold that, on liquidation, Bliss must include in income the amount of the unwarranted deduction.

V

Bliss paid the assessment on an increase of $60,000 in its taxable income. In the District Court, the parties stipulated that the value of the grain was $56,565, but the record does not show what the original cost of the grain was or what portion of it remained at the time of liquidation. The proper increase in taxable income is the portion of the cost of the grain attributable to the amount on hand at the time of liquidation. In *Bliss*, then, we remand for a determination of that amount. In *Hillsboro*, the taxpayer sought a redetermination in the Tax Court rather than paying the tax, so no further proceedings are necessary, and the judgment of the Court of Appeals is reversed.

It is so ordered.

JUSTICE BRENNAN, dissenting in No. 81–485.

I join Parts I, II, and IV of the Court's opinion. For the reasons expressed in Part I of Justice BLACKMUN's dissenting opinion, however, I believe that a proper application of the principles set out in Part II of the Court's opinion would require an affirmance rather than a reversal in No. 81–485.

JUSTICE STEVENS, with whom JUSTICE MARSHALL joins, concurring in the judgment in No. 81–485 and dissenting in No. 81–930.

These two cases should be decided in the same way. The taxpayer in each case is a corporation. In 1972 each taxpayer made a deductible expenditure, and in 1973 its shareholders received an economic benefit. Neither corporate taxpayer ever recovered any part of its 1972 expenditure. In my opinion, the benefits received by the shareholders in 1973 are matters that should affect their returns; those benefits should not give rise to income on the 1973 return of the taxpayer in either case.

Both cases require us to apply the tax benefit rule. This rule has always had a limited, but important office: it determines whether certain events that enrich the taxpayer—recoveries of past expenditures—should be characterized as income. It does not create income out of events that do not enhance the taxpayer's wealth.

Today the Court declares that the purpose of the tax benefit rule is "to approximate the results produced by a tax system based on transactional rather than annual accounting." Whereas the rule has previously been used to determine the character of a current wealth-enhancing event, when viewed in the light of past deductions, the Court now suggests that the rule requires a study of the propriety of earlier deductions, when viewed in the light of later events. The Court states that the rule operates to "cancel out" an earlier deduction if the premise on which it is based is "fundamentally inconsistent" with an event in a later year.

The Court's reformulation of the tax benefit rule constitutes an extremely significant enlargement of the tax collector's powers. In order to identify the groundbreaking character of the decision, I shall review the history of the tax benefit rule. I shall then discuss the *Bliss Dairy* case in some detail, to demonstrate that it fits comfortably within the class of cases to which the tax benefit rule has not been applied in the past. Finally, I shall explain why the Court's adventure in lawmaking is not only misguided but does not even explain its inconsistent disposition of these two similar cases.

I

What is today called the "tax benefit rule" evolved in two stages, reflecting the rule's two components. The "inclusionary" component requires that the recovery within a taxable year of an item previously deducted be included in gross income. The "exclusionary component," which gives the rule its name, allows the inclusionary component to operate only to the extent that the prior deduction benefited the taxpayer.

The inclusionary component of the rule originated in the Bureau of Internal Revenue in the context of recoveries of debts that had previously been deducted as uncollectible. The Bureau sensed that it was inequitable to permit a taxpayer to characterize the recovery of such a debt as "return of capital" when in a prior year he had been allowed to reduce his taxable income to compensate for the loss of that capital. * * * This principle was quickly endorsed by the Board of Tax Appeals and the courts. * * *

The exclusionary component was not so readily accepted. The Bureau first incorporated it during the Great Depression as the natural equitable counterweight to the inclusionary component. It soon retreated, however, insisting that a recovery could be treated as income even if the prior deduction had not benefited the taxpayer. The Board of Tax Appeals protested, but the Circuit Courts of Appeals sided with the Bureau. * * * At that point, Congress intervened for the first and only time. It enacted the forerunner of § 111 of the present Code, * * * using language that by implication acknowledges the propriety of the inclusionary component by explicitly mandating the exclusionary component.

The most striking feature of the rule's history is that from its early formative years, through codification, until the 1960's, Congress, the Internal Revenue Service, courts, and commentators, understood it in essentially the same way. They all saw it as a theory that appropriately characterized certain recoveries of capital as income. Although the rule undeniably helped to accommodate the annual accounting system to multi-year transactions, I have found no suggestion that it was regarded as a generalized method of approximating a transactional accounting system through the fabrication of income at the drop of a fundamentally inconsistent event. An inconsistent event was always a necessary condition, but with the possible exception of the discussion of the Board of Tax Appeals in *Barnett v. Commissioner*, 39 B.T.A. 864, 867 (1939), inconsistency was never by itself a sufficient reason for applying the rule. Significantly, the first case from this Court dealing with the tax benefit rule emphasized the role of a recovery. And when litigants in this Court suggested that a transactional accounting system would be more equitable, we expressly declined to impose one, stressing the importance of finality and practicability in a tax system.

In the 1960's, the Commissioner, with the support of some commentators and the Tax Court, began to urge that the Tax Benefit Rule be given a more ambitious office. In *Nash v. United States*, 398 U.S. 1, 90 S.Ct. 1550, 26 L.Ed.2d 1 (1970), the Commissioner argued that the rule should not be limited to cases in which the taxpayer had made an economic recovery, but rather should operate to cancel out an earlier deduction whenever later events demonstrate that the taxpayer is no longer entitled to it. The arguments advanced, and rejected, in that case were remarkably similar to those found in the Court's opinion today.

     * * *

Today, the Court again has before it a case in which the Commissioner, with the endorsement of some commentators and a closely divided Tax Court, is pushing for a more ambitious tax benefit rule. This time, the Court accepts the invitation. Since there has been no legislation since *Nash* suggesting that our approach over the past half-century has been wrong-headed, the new doctrine that emerges from today's decision is of the Court's own making.

II

In the *Bliss Dairy* case, the Court today reaches a result contrary to that dictated by a recovery theory. One would not expect such a break with the past unless it were apparent that prior law would produce a palpable inequity—a clear windfall for the taxpayer. Yet that is not the case in *Bliss Dairy.* * * *

* * *

III

Because tax considerations play such an important role in decisions relating to the investment of capital, the transfer of operating businesses, and the management of going concerns, there is a special interest in the orderly, certain and consistent interpretation of the Internal Revenue Code. Today's decision seriously compromises that interest. It will engender uncertainty, it will enlarge the tax gatherer's discretionary power to reexamine past transactions, and it will produce controversy and litigation.

Any inconsistent event theory of the tax benefit rule would make the tax system more complicated than it has been under the recovery theory. Inconsistent event analysis forces a deviation from the traditional pattern of calculating income during a given year: identify the transactions in which the taxpayer was made wealthier, determine from the history of those transactions which apparent sources of enrichment should be characterized as income, and then determine how much of that income must be recognized. Of course, in several specific contexts, Congress has already mandated deviations from that traditional pattern, and the additional complications are often deemed an appropriate price for enhanced tax equity. But to my knowledge Congress has never even considered so sweeping a deviation as a general inconsistent events theory.

Nonetheless, a general inconsistent events theory would surely give more guidance than the vague hybrid established by the Court today. The dimensions of the Court's newly fashioned "fundamentally inconsistent event" version of the tax benefit rule are by no means clear. It obviously differs from both the Government's "inconsistent event" theory and the familiar "recovery" theory, either of which would require these two cases to be decided in the same way. I do not understand, however, precisely why the Court's theory distinguishes between these cases, or how it is to be applied in computing the 1973 taxes of Bliss Dairy, Inc.

* * *

The Court's opinion also leaves unclear the amount of income that is realized in the year in which the fundamentally inconsistent event occurs. In most of its opinion, the Court indicates that the taxpayer is deemed to realize "the amount of his earlier deduction," but from time to time the Court equivocates, and at least once suggests that when an expensed asset is sold, only the "amount of the proceeds on sale" is income. Even in *Bliss Dairy,* which involves a revolving inventory of a fungible commodity, I am not sure how the Court requires the "cost" of the grain to be computed. If the corporation's 1972 consumption matched its 1972 purchases, one might think that the relevant cost was that in the prior years when the surplus was built up. * * *

IV

Neither history nor sound tax policy supports the Court's abandonment of its interpretation of the tax benefit rule as a tool for characterizing certain recoveries as income. If Congress were dissatisfied with the tax treatment that I believe *Bliss Dairy* should be accorded under current law, it could respond by changing any of the three provisions that bear on this case. It could modify the manner in which deductions are authorized under § 162. It could legislate another statutory exception to the annual accounting system * * *. But in the absence of legislative action, I cannot join in the Court's attempt to achieve similar results by distorting the tax benefit rule.

Accordingly, I concur in the Court's judgment in No. 81–485 and respectfully dissent in No. 81–930.

Justice Blackmun, dissenting.

These consolidated cases present issues concerning the so-called "tax benefit rule" that has been developed in federal income tax law. In No. 81–485, the Court concludes that the rule has no application to the situation presented. In No. 81–930, it concludes that the rule operates to the detriment of the taxpayer with respect to its *later* tax year. I disagree with both conclusions.

I

In No. 81–485, the Court interprets § 164(e) of the Internal Revenue Code of 1954. It seems to me that the propriety of a 1972 deduction by the Bank under § 164(e) depended upon the payment by the Bank of a state tax on its shares. This Court's decision in *Lehnhausen v. Lake Shore Auto Parts Co.*, 410 U.S. 356, 93 S.Ct. 1001, 35 L.Ed.2d 351 (1973), rendered any such tax nonexistent and any deduction therefore unavailable. I sense no "focus of Congress ... on the act of payment rather than on the ultimate use of the funds by the State." The focus, instead, is on the payment of a *tax*. Events proved that there was no tax. The situation, thus, is one for the application, not the nonapplication, of some tax benefit rule.

I therefore turn to the question of the application of a proper rule in each of these cases.

II

The usual rule, as applied to a deduction, appears to be this: Whenever a deduction is claimed, with tax benefit, in a taxpayer's federal return for a particular tax year, but factual developments in a later tax year prove the deduction to have been asserted mistakenly in whole or in part, the deduction, or that part of it which the emerging facts demonstrate as excessive, is to be regarded as income to the taxpayer in the later tax year. With that general concept (despite occasionally expressed theoretical differences between "transactional parity" or "transactional inconsistency," on the one hand, and, on the other, a need for a "recovery") I have no basic disagreement.

Regardless of the presence of § 111 in the Internal Revenue Code of 1954, it is acknowledged that the tax benefit rule is judge-made. It came into being, apparently, because of two concerns: 1) a natural reaction against an undeserved and otherwise unrecoverable (by the Government) tax benefit, and 2) a perceived need, because income taxes are payable at regular intervals, to promote the integrity of the annual tax return. Under this approach, if a deduction is claimed, with some justification, in an earlier tax year, it is to be allowed in that year, even though developments in a later year show that the deduction in the earlier year was undeserved in whole or in part. This impropriety is then counterbalanced (concededly in an imprecise manner * * *) by the inclusion of a reparative item in gross income in the later year. * * *

I have no problem with the rule with respect to its first underlying concern (the rectification of an undeserved tax benefit). When a taxpayer has received an income tax benefit by claiming a deduction that later proves to be incorrect or, in other words, when the *premise* for the deduction is destroyed, it is only right that the situation be corrected so far as is reasonably possible, and that the taxpayer not profit by the improper deduction. I am troubled, however, by the tendency to carry out the second concern (the integrity of the annual return) to unnecessary and undesirable limits. The rule is not that sacrosanct.

In No. 81–485, Hillsboro National Bank, in its 1972 return, took as a deduction the amount of assessed state property taxes the Bank paid that year on its stock held by its shareholders; this deduction, were there such a tax, was authorized by the unusual, but nevertheless specific, provisions of § 164(e) of the Code. The Bank received a benefit by the deduction, for its net income and federal income tax were reduced accordingly. Similarly, in No. 81–930, Bliss Dairy, Inc., which kept its books and filed its returns on the cash receipts and disbursements method, took a deduction in its return for its fiscal year ended June 30, 1973, for cattle feed it had purchased that year. That deduction was claimed as a business expense under § 162(a) of the Code. The Dairy received a tax benefit, for its net income and federal income tax for fiscal 1973 were reduced by the deduction. Thus far, everything is clear and there is no problem.

In the Bank's case, however, a subsequent development, namely, the final determination by this Court in 1973 in *Lehnhausen, supra,* that the 1970 amendment of the Illinois Constitution, prohibiting the imposition of the state property taxes in question, was valid, eliminated any factual justification for the 1972 deduction. And, in the Dairy's case, a post-fiscal year 1973 development, namely, the liquidation of the corporation and the distribution of such feed as was unconsumed on June 30, 1973, to its shareholders, with their consequent ability to deduct, when the feed thereafter was consumed, the amount of their adjusted basis in that feed, similarly demonstrated the impropriety of the Dairy's full-cost deduction in fiscal 1973.

I have no difficulty in favoring some kind of "tax benefit" adjustment in favor of the Government for each of these situations. An adjustment should be made, for in each case the beneficial deduction turned out to be improper and undeserved because its factual premise proved to be incorrect. Each taxpayer thus was not entitled to the claimed deduction, or a portion of it, and this nonentitlement should be reflected among its tax obligations.

This takes me, however, to the difficulty I encounter with the second concern, that is, the unraveling or rectification of the situation. The Commissioner and the United States in these respective cases insist that the Bank and the Dairy should be regarded as receiving income in the very next tax year when the factual premise for the prior year's deduction proved to be incorrect. I could understand that position, if, in the interim, the bar of a statute of limitations had become effective or if there were some other valid reason why the preceding year's return could not be corrected and additional tax collected. But it seems to me that the better resolution of these two particular cases and others like them—and a resolution that should produce little complaint from the taxpayer—is to make the necessary adjustment, whenever it can be made, in the tax year for which the deduction was originally claimed. This makes the correction where the correction is due and it makes the amount of net income for each year a true amount and one that accords with the facts, not one that is structured, imprecise, and fictional. This normally would be accomplished either by the taxpayer's filing an amended return for the earlier year, with payment of the resulting additional tax, or by the Commissioner's assertion of a deficiency followed by collection. This actually is the kind of thing that is done all the time, for when a taxpayer's return is audited and a deficiency is asserted due to an overstated deduction, the process equates with the filing of an amended return.

The Dairy's case is particularly acute. On July 2, 1973, on the second day after the end of its fiscal year, the Dairy adopted a plan of liquidation * * *. It seems obvious that the Dairy, its management, and its shareholders, by the end of the Dairy's 1973 fiscal year on June 30, and certainly well before the filing of its tax return for that fiscal year, all had conceived and developed the July 2, 1973, plan of liquidation and were resolved to carry out that plan with the benefits that they felt would be afforded by it. Under these circumstances, we carry the tax benefit rule too far and apply it too strictly when we utilize the unconsumed feed to create income for the Dairy for fiscal 1974 (the month of July 1973), instead of decreasing the deduction for the same feed in fiscal 1973. Any concern for the integrity of annual tax reporting should not demand that much. I thus would have the Dairy's returns adjusted in a realistic and factually true manner, rather than in accord with an inflexibly-administered tax benefit rule.

Much the same is to be said about the Bank's case. The decisive event, this Court's decision in *Lehnhausen,* occurred on Feb. 22, 1973, within the second month of the Bank's 1973 tax year. Indeed, it took place before the Bank's calendar year 1972 return would be overdue. Here again, an accurate return for 1972 should be preferred over inaccurate returns for both 1972 and 1973.

This, in my view, is the way these two particular tax controversies should be resolved. I see no need for anything more complex in their resolution than what I have outlined. Of course, if a statute of limitations problem existed, or if the facts in some other way prevented reparation to the Government, the cases and their resolution might well be different.

I realize that my position is simplistic, but I doubt if the judge-made tax benefit rule really was intended, at its origin, to be regarded as applicable in simple situations of the kind presented in these successive-tax-year cases. So often a judge-made rule, understandably conceived, ultimately is used to carry us farther than it should.

I would vacate the judgment in each of these cases and remand each case for further proceedings consistent with this analysis.

Notes

1. *You Can't Tell the Players Without a Scorecard.* The Court ultimately held that Bliss Dairy had gross income by operation of the tax benefit rule and that the rule did not apply to Hillsboro National Bank. The alignment of the Justices on these cases can be summarized as follows:

	DAIRY HAS GROSS INCOME	DAIRY HAS NO GROSS INCOME
BANK HAS GROSS INCOME	Brennan	Blackmun*
BANK HAS NO GROSS INCOME	O'Connor, White, Powell, Rehnquist, & Burger	Stevens & Marshall

* Blackmun would have vacated the lower court judgments in both cases and thus dissents from the majority in both cases. Substantively, however, he sides with Brennan in believing that both taxpayers have gross income.

2. *Start with Stevens.* Justice Stevens argues that there must be a **recovery** in order to trigger the tax benefit rule. In the garden-variety tax benefit case, a taxpayer deducts a cost in one year and then is refunded that cost in a later year. Justice Stevens reasons that the dairy never recovered any amount (nor received any benefit) from the shareholders' deduction of the feed. While it may be inconsistent for the feed to be deducted twice— once in the hands of the dairy and again in the hands of the shareholders— the tax benefit rule cannot apply because the taxpayer claiming the first deduction (the dairy) did not receive a recovery of the deducted amount.

Likewise, according to Justice Stevens, the bank never recovered its deduction for state taxes because the refund was paid to the bank's shareholders, not to the bank itself. Here too, says Stevens, the benefit of the "recovery" went to someone other than the taxpayer that claimed the deduction.

3. *Now Look Again at the Majority.* The majority does not see direct "recovery" as a requirement for imposing the tax benefit rule. In the case of the dairy, it is enough that the deduction of the feed cost by the shareholders is *fundamentally inconsistent* with the complete deduction of the feed by the dairy, for a deduction by the dairy is premised on the notion that the feed was completely consumed. The majority's approach with respect to the dairy clearly demonstrates that the tax benefit rule applies to more than just recoveries of prior deductions. It is the majority's broad reading of the rule in this case that generated the controversy that surrounds this decision.

As for the bank, the majority did not apply the tax benefit rule because the refund paid to the shareholders was not fundamentally inconsistent with the bank's prior deduction. The bank's deduction was premised on its obligation to pay the tax on behalf of its shareholders, and no refund of the tax to the shareholders would make this obligation illusory or improper to any extent. If the refund had been paid to the bank itself instead of its shareholders, of course, then the tax benefit rule would apply, for the bank, ultimately, would have received a deduction with no permanent outlay.

4. *There's Something About Harry.* Justice Blackmun believes that the proper solution in both cases would be to amend the returns for those years in which the deductions were claimed, since the deductions in both cases ultimately proved to be incorrect. He admits his position is "simplistic," and his assessment is probably spot on. Blackmun seemed to forget that every year stands alone. Since the errors in both cases were not known until after the close of the taxable years in which the deductions were claimed, *Lewis* would insist that amended returns would be improper.

* * *

Self-Assessment Questions

(Solutions to Self–Assessment Questions are set forth in Appendix 3.)

SAQ 6–3. Sam Malone, a cash method taxpayer, is the owner and operator of a downtown Boston bar. In Year One, Sam's gross income from the bar business totaled $100,000. His business expenses that year totaled $130,000. One of the most significant expenses that year was a $20,000 business bad debt, which arose when Sam finally wrote off a loan to one of his largest customers, Norm Peterson. Sam had no other income or deduction items in Year One. In Years Two through Five, Sam's expenses exactly matched his gross income each year. In Year Six, Norm collected a substantial sum in death benefits on the passing of his spouse, Vera. Norm paid $20,000 to Sam to compensate for the old bar tab.

(a) Even without regard to the business bad debt, Sam's expenses in Year One exceeded his gross income in Year One. Will Sam get some benefit from the deduction in Year One? If so, what?

(b) Does Sam have gross income in Year Six when Norm pays him $20,000?

SAQ 6–4. Diane Chambers, a cash method taxpayer, is a server at Sam Malone's Boston bar. When not partaking in witty rapport with the customers at Sam's bar, Diane enjoys playing cello in the local chamber orchestra. In Year Six, Diane loaned $10,000 cash to the conductor, who later that year fled from the United States, never to be seen again. Diane claimed a $10,000 bad debt deduction on her federal income tax return, but her gross income for the year ($25,000) was completely offset by her $25,000 in alimony payments to her ex-husband, Frasier Crane. In Year Eleven, Diane received an envelope sent from Rome. Inside she found $5,000 cash and a note from the conductor apologizing for his misdeed.

(a) Without regard to her bad debt deduction, Diane's expenses in Year Six exactly match her gross income for that year. Will Diane get some benefit from the deduction in Year Six? If so, what?

(b) Does Diane have gross income in Year Eleven?

SAQ 6–5. Carla Tortelli LeBec, a cash method taxpayer, is also a server at Sam Malone's Boston bar. In addition to working for Sam, Carla is a sole proprietor, owning and operating a small bakery business. In Year Eight, Carla purchased some supplies for her bakery business and properly deducted the expense on her Year Eight federal income tax return. In Year Nine, Carla took the supplies home and used them for personal purposes. Does Carla have gross income in Year Nine?

Problem 6–8

O'Hara owns real property located in Georgia. In Year One, O'Hara paid $1,000 in ad valorem real property taxes to the state. Although the property tax payment entitled O'Hara to an itemized deduction on her Year One return, she claimed the standard deduction instead because her total itemized deductions did not exceed the standard deduction amount. In Year Two, the Georgia legislature distributed a budget surplus in the form of property tax rebates to those who paid real property taxes in Year One. O'Hara received $1,200 from the state in Year Two. How much of the $1,200 rebate must O'Hara include in gross income?

Problem 6–9

Suppose, in Problem 6–8, that O'Hara paid $5,000 in ad valorem property taxes in Year One. Combined with other proper itemized deductions of $1,000 for the year, O'Hara's total itemized deductions for Year One ($6,000) exceeded the standard deduction that year ($3,000), so she elected to claim the itemized deductions. Unfortunately, her adjusted gross income exceeded the "applicable amount" in § 68(b) by $30,000, so under § 68(a), O'Hara was required to reduce her total itemized deductions by $900 (3% of the $30,000 excess). Thus, her itemized deductions for Year One totaled $5,100. Suppose further that the amount of the property tax rebate in Year

Two was $4,000. To what extent must O'Hara include the $4,000 rebate in gross income for Year Two?

* * *

(2) RESTORATION OF A CLAIM OF RIGHT

Code: IRC § 1341.

Regs: None.

Toward a More Perfect Union. Recall that the taxpayer in *United States v. Lewis* was required to include his entire $22,000 bonus in gross income in the year of receipt even though he learned after the end of the year that he was entitled to keep only half of that amount. There is a potential problem that stems from the *Lewis* result, one easily illustrated if we modify the facts of *Lewis* slightly. Suppose that Lewis got his $22,000 bonus in Year One and that the state court litigation concluded in Year Two, at which time Lewis repaid the $11,000 amount he was obligated to restore. Now suppose that Lewis paid a flat 40 percent tax in Year One and a flat 30 percent tax in Year Two. The reduced tax rate could be attributable to Congressional action (tax cut legislation) or to a reduction in Lewis' taxable income (placing him in a lower tax bracket). Because Lewis had to include $22,000 in gross income in Year One, he paid an extra $8,800 in taxes (40 percent of $22,000 = $8,800). He later had to restore half of the amount included in income, so the tax attributable to the subsequently restored amount is $4,400 (half of the extra $8,800 in taxes). But the tax benefit of Lewis' Year Two deduction is only $3,300 (a deduction of $11,000 saves $3,300 in taxes when the tax rate is 30%). Ignoring time value of money considerations (blasphemous though it is), Lewis comes out $1,100 short. He paid an extra $4,400 in taxes but gets a deduction that saves only $3,300 in taxes. In a perfect world, Lewis would come out even.

Section 1341 tries to make the world more perfect. In fact, Congress specifically enacted § 1341 in response to *Lewis*. We can use the *Lewis* case to illustrate how the statute works. Notice that we have to meet all three conditions in § 1341(a)(1) through (3) before we can claim the benefit of the "lesser of" computation described in § 1341(a)(4) and (5).

Under § 1341(a)(1), we ask whether Lewis included the full $22,000 in gross income because it appeared he had an unrestricted right to such item. Indeed that is the case. If the facts in Year One showed that Lewis did not have an unrestricted right to the full $22,000, then § 1341 would not apply. Instead, the proper course of action would be to amend the Year One return (if still open, which we can assume it is) because the mistake (including the full $22,000 in gross income) was knowable at the end of Year One.

Under § 1341(a)(2), we must decide whether Lewis is allowed a deduction in Year Two because it was established *after* Year One that Lewis in fact did not have an unrestricted right to the full amount. Clearly, the "error" in Year One was not knowable until Year Two when the state court litigation ended. But Lewis must also be entitled to a deduction for the $11,000 repayment. Notice that § 1341 does not itself grant Lewis a deduction. So is there authority for a deduction—apart from "restoration of a claim of right" notions? The answer, probably, is yes. The most likely authority for the deduction is § 162. It is probably "ordinary" for employees to repay an employer those amounts incorrectly paid to the employees.

Next, under § 1341(a)(3), the amount of Lewis' deduction must exceed $3,000. That's not an issue here, as the amount of the deduction is $11,000. Apparently the benefit of § 1341 is only supposed to apply when the benefit would be significant. That Congress imposed a threshold deduction amount is acceptable, but the fact that Congress chose $3,000 may present some problems, as we shall see.

So it appears that Lewis would meet all three tests. Under §§ 1341(a)(4) and (5), Lewis' income tax liability **for Year Two** is equal to the lesser of the § 1341(a)(4) amount or the § 1341(a)(5) amount. The § 1341(a)(4) amount is simply Lewis' normal Year Two tax, computed by allowing the $11,000 deduction. The § 1341(a)(5) amount is Lewis' Year Two tax liability *without* the $11,000 deduction but *with* a credit for the increased tax from Year One attributable to including the extra $11,000 of the bonus in gross income that year. If we assume that Year One is not between 1939 and 1954, we can dispense with the flush language to § 1341(a).

In order to know which amount (the (a)(4) amount or the (a)(5) amount) is lower, we have to bring in some additional facts. For this purpose, assume that Lewis had $50,000 in income apart from the bonus in both Year One and Year Two. Also assume that Lewis had $10,000 in deductions apart from the repayment in both Year One and Year Two. Next, assume that Lewis paid a flat tax of 40 percent on taxable income in Year One and a flat tax of 30 percent on taxable income in Year Two. Finally, assume away complicating factors like personal exemptions and any applicable phase-outs for deductions. Under these assumptions, the (a)(4) amount is $8,700. That's because Lewis' gross income for Year Two is $50,000, and his deductions total $21,000 ($10,000 plus the $11,000 repayment deduction), producing taxable income of $29,000. Thirty percent of $29,000 is $8,700.

To compute the (a)(5) amount, we start by computing Lewis' tax for Year Two ignoring the $11,000 deduction. That produces a tax of $12,000 (gross income of $50,000 less $10,000 in deductions produces taxable income of $40,000, 30 percent of which is $12,000). We must then subtract from the $12,000 figure the amount described in § 1341(a)(5)(B)—what we can call the "credit amount" for shorthand purposes. The "credit amount" represents the decrease in Year One tax that would result if Lewis only included $11,000 of the $22,000 bonus in gross income that year. To know the amount of the decrease, of course, we must first determine Lewis' Year One tax liability as reported on his return. In Year One, Lewis claimed the entire bonus in gross income, so gross income totaled $72,000 (the bonus plus the $50,000 in other income). Thus, his taxable income, after $10,000 in deductions, was $62,000. The tax on that amount (assuming a 40 percent flat tax) was $24,800. Now we re-compute the Year One tax assuming Lewis included only that portion of the bonus he did not have to repay in Year Two. Thus, his gross income would have been only $61,000, and his taxable income would have been only $51,000. The tax on $51,000 (at a 40 percent flat rate) would have been $20,400. In other words, if Lewis had not included the full bonus in gross income—but only the $11,000 he ultimately kept—he would have saved $4,400 in taxes ($24,800 minus $20,400). By the way, we already knew that including the full bonus cost Lewis an extra $4,400—go back to the first paragraph of this discussion and see how smart we were.

So the (a)(5) amount is $12,000 minus the credit amount of $4,400, or $7,600. Recall that the (a)(4) amount was $8,700. The lesser of these two amounts is $7,600. So Lewis will only pay $7,600 in taxes in Year Two. In effect, the statute says that giving Lewis a deduction in Year Two would not have been enough. In order to make Lewis come out even, the statute gives him a credit in Year Two that accounts for the difference in tax rates. Notice, and this is important, that the statute does NOT cause Lewis to amend his Year One return. Thus § 1341 is somewhat consistent with the notion that "every year stands alone." We say "somewhat" because the computation of Year Two's tax liability is affected by what happened in Year One, even though we do not change the Year One return.

Section 1341 cures Lewis' woes, but it is not a perfect correction device, as the following Problem will show.

Problem 6–10

In Year One, Dolly received $90,000 in salary and a $10,000 cash bonus from her employer. Dolly had no deduction items for Year One, and the tax rate applicable in Year One was 25 percent. In Year Two, Dolly's employer discovered that a computational error accidentally inflated the amount of Dolly's Year One bonus. Dolly learned that the Year One bonus should have been $4,000. In Year Two, she repaid the $6,000 overpayment to the employer. Dolly received $90,000 in salary in Year Two and, again, had no other deductions for the year. The tax rate applicable in Year Two was 30 percent.

(a) Ignoring the standard deduction and personal exemptions, what is Dolly's federal income tax liability for Year Two?

(b) How would your answer to (a) change if the applicable tax rate in Year One was 30 percent and the applicable tax rate in Year Two was 25 percent?

(c) How would your answer to (a) change if, instead of accepting repayment from Dolly, her employer simply withheld $6,000 from Dolly's Year Two salary?

* * *

REYNOLDS METALS CO. v. UNITED STATES, 389 F. Supp. 2d 692 (2005).

Facts: The taxpayer's metal-manufacturing operations generate waste byproducts. For a period of 47 years, the taxpayer disposed of the waste in accordance with industry standards and applicable law. Then, from 1992–1995, the taxpayer incurred substantial environmental remediation costs to re-dispose of the waste and to remediate contaminated areas in compliance with the Comprehensive Environmental Response, Compensation, and Liability Act (CERCLA). The total tab exceeded $110 million. The taxpayer claimed that the costs were allocable to the income generated during the 47 years. Since those costs were not reflected on the tax returns for those years, the taxpayer claimed it had overstated its income and thus overpaid its taxes. Of course, it was too late to make a refund claim for those years under the applicable statute of limitations. The taxpayer could claim the costs as deductions in the years paid, but that would not be a perfect remedy for the taxpayer because tax rates in the 47–year period were higher (usually about 46 percent) than the rates from 1992–1995 (35 percent). So the taxpayer argued that § 1341 should apply to give the taxpayer the functional equivalent of a refund for the claimed overpayments in the now-closed years.

Issue: Does the taxpayer qualify for the benefit of § 1341?

Holding: No.

Rationale: Although the taxpayer reported its income for the 47–year period because it had an unrestricted right to the income it received from its customers during those years, the taxpayer "cannot reasonably argue that it restored those amounts previously received to its customers or to a connected third party. CERCLA forced [the taxpayer] to expend money to remediate past environmental contamination in amounts sufficient to curtail the damage; [the taxpayer] cannot argue that its remediation costs were related to or in proportion to its past sales." Moreover, said the court, the taxpayer "has not repaid any funds to anyone. [The taxpayer] was charged, or more accurately held liable, for additional environmental clean-up costs in the face of more stringent standards as a result of its prior manufacturing activities. [The taxpayer] cannot seriously argue that it is restoring its overstated income to any person or entity in the sense contemplated by § 1341." Accordingly, the court rejected the taxpayer's motion for summary judgment on the applicability of § 1341 and granted the government's motion to dismiss.

* * *

The Arrowsmith Doctrine. Suppose that a taxpayer includes a long-term capital gain in gross income for Year One but learns in Year Two that he or she must repay that amount. Assuming the repayment is deductible, pause for a moment to consider the *flavor* of the deduction. Should the fact that the income at issue in Year One was long-term capital gain, taxed at a preferential rate, affect the flavor of the Year Two deduction? Remember: every year stands alone.

In *Arrowsmith v. Commissioner*, 344 U.S. 6, 73 S.Ct. 71, 97 L.Ed. 6 (1952), the Supreme Court faced this very issue. In 1937, the taxpayers liquidated a corporation. They properly reported their profits from the liquidation as long-term capital gains. But in 1944, creditors of the old corporation successfully obtained a judgment against the taxpayers, and the taxpayers paid off the judgment that year. The taxpayers treated the repayments as ordinary expenses, but the Commissioner argued they should be treated as long-term capital losses. Why? Because the 1944 payments were part of the original liquidation transaction. If the payments were treated as ordinary expenses, the taxpayers would have a huge windfall (the income was taxed at a low rate but the deduction offsets high-rate income). The Court agreed with the Commissioner, holding that the payments had to be treated as long-term capital losses. Thus comes the so-called *"Arrowsmith* doctrine:" restorations associated with prior income items take the same tax flavor as the prior income items.

Section 1341 was not in the Code at the time of *Arrowsmith*. Would it have helped the taxpayers in that case? The answer is no. The taxpayers meet the § 1341(a)(1) test—they received liquidation proceeds from the corporation because they had an unrestricted right to them. The § 1341(a)(2) test, however, requires an establishment sometime after 1937 that the taxpayers "did not have an unrestricted right *to such item* or to a *portion of such item*." The 1944 payments were not, in other words, *restorations* of the liquidation proceeds. They were payments to corporate creditors that shareholders are sometimes called upon to make when the old corporation has liquidated. If the taxpayers in *Arrowsmith* had made their payments back to the corporation (and if § 1341 had been around then), then the second test would be met.

So does the *Arrowsmith* doctrine have relevance in the § 1341 context? (It better, otherwise most of this discussion is pretty much useless.) Fortunately, the following case involves both *Arrowsmith* and § 1341 issues.

UNITED STATES v. SKELLY OIL CO.

United States Supreme Court, 1969.
394 U.S. 678, 89 S.Ct. 1379, 22 L.Ed.2d 642.

Mr. Justice Marshall delivered the opinion of the Court.

During its tax year ending December 31, 1958, respondent refunded $505,536.54 to two of its customers for overcharges during the six preceding years. Respondent, an Oklahoma producer of natural gas, had set its prices during the earlier years in accordance with a minimum price order of the Oklahoma Corporation Commission. After that order was vacated as a result of a decision of this Court, *Michigan Wisconsin Pipe Line Co. v. Corporation Comm'n of Oklahoma*, 355 U.S. 425 (1958), respondent found it necessary to settle a number of claims filed by its customers; the repayments in question represent settlements of two of those claims. Since respondent had claimed an unrestricted right to its sales receipts during the years 1952 through 1957, it had included the $505,536.54 in its gross income in those years. The amount was also included in respondent's "gross income from the property" as defined in § 613 of the Internal Revenue Code of 1954, the section which allows taxpayers to deduct a fixed percentage of certain receipts to compensate for the depletion of natural resources from which they derive income. Allowable percentage depletion for receipts from oil and gas wells is fixed at 27 1/2% of the "gross income from the property." Since respondent claimed and the Commissioner allowed percentage depletion deductions during these years, 27 1/2% of the receipts in question was added to the depletion allowances to which respondent would otherwise have been entitled. Accordingly, the actual increase in respondent's taxable income attributable to the receipts in question was not $505,536.54, but only $366,513.99. Yet, when respondent made its refunds in 1958, it attempted to deduct the full $505,536.54. The Commissioner objected and assessed a deficiency. Respondent paid and, after its claim for a refund had been disallowed, began the present suit. The Government won in the District Court, but the Court of Appeals for the Tenth Circuit reversed. Upon petition by the Government, we granted certiorari to consider whether the Court of Appeals decision had allowed respondent "the practical equivalent of double deduction," in conflict with past decisions of this Court and sound principles of tax law. We reverse.

I.

The present problem is an outgrowth of the so-called "claim-of-right" doctrine. Mr. Justice Brandeis, speaking for a unanimous Court in *North American Oil Consolidated v. Burnet*, 286 U.S. 417, 424 (1932), gave that doctrine its classic formulation. "If a taxpayer receives earnings under a claim of right and without restriction as to its disposition, he has received income which he is required to return, even though it may still be claimed that he is not entitled to retain the money, and even though he may still be adjudged liable to restore its equivalent." Should it later appear that the taxpayer was not entitled to keep the money, Mr. Justice Brandeis explained, he would be entitled to a deduction in the year of repayment; the taxes due for the year of receipt would not be affected. This approach was dictated by Congress' adoption of an annual accounting system as an integral part of the tax code. See *Burnet v. Sanford & Brooks Co.*, 282 U.S. 359, 365–366 (1931). Of course, the tax benefit from the deduction in the year of repayment might differ from the increase in taxes attributable to the receipt; for example, tax rates might have changed, or the taxpayer might be in a different tax "bracket." But as the doctrine was originally formulated, these discrepancies were accepted as an unavoidable consequence of the annual accounting system.

Section 1341 of the 1954 Code was enacted to alleviate some of the inequities which Congress felt existed in this area. As an alternative to the deduction in the year of repayment which prior law allowed, § 1341(a)(5) permits certain taxpayers to recompute their taxes for the year of receipt. Whenever § 1341(a)(5) applies, taxes for the current year are to be reduced by the amount taxes were increased in the year or years of receipt because the disputed items were included in gross income. Nevertheless, it is clear that Congress did not intend to tamper with the underlying claim-of-right doctrine; it only provided an alternative for certain cases in which the new approach favored the taxpayer. When the new approach was not advantageous to the taxpayer, the old law was to apply under § 1341(a)(4).

In this case, the parties have stipulated that § 1341(a)(5) does not apply. Accordingly, as the courts below recognized, respondent's taxes must be computed under § 1341(a)(4) and thus, in effect, without regard to the special relief Congress provided through the enactment of § 1341. Nevertheless, respondent argues, and the Court of Appeals seems to have held, that the language used in § 1341 requires that respondent be allowed a deduction for the full amount it refunded to its customers. We think the section has no such significance.

In describing the situations in which the section applies, § 1341(a)(2) talks of cases in which "a deduction is allowable for the taxable year because it was established after the close of [the year or years of receipt] that the taxpayer did not have an unrestricted right to such item...." The "item" referred to is first mentioned in § 1341(a)(1); it is the item included in gross income in the year of receipt. The section does not imply in any way that the "deduction" and the "item" must necessarily be equal in amount. In fact, the use of the words "a deduction" and the placement of § 1341 in subchapter Q—the subchapter dealing largely with side effects of the annual accounting system—make it clear that it is necessary to refer to other portions of the Code to discover how much of a deduction is allowable. The regulations promulgated under the section make the necessity for such a cross-reference clear. * * * Therefore, when § 1341(a)(4)—the subsection applicable here—speaks of "the tax ... computed with such deduction," it is referring to the deduction mentioned in § 1341(a)(2); and that deduction must be determined, not by any mechanical equation with the "item" originally included in gross income, but by reference to the applicable sections of the Code and the case law developed under those sections.

II.

There is some dispute between the parties about whether the refunds in question are deductible as losses under § 165 of the 1954 Code or as business expenses under § 162. Although in some situations the distinction may have relevance, we do not think it makes any difference here. In either case, the Code should not be interpreted to allow respondent "the practical equivalent of double deduction," *Charles*

Ilfeld Co. v. Hernandez, 292 U.S. 62, 68 (1934), absent a clear declaration of intent by Congress. See *United States v. Ludey*, 274 U.S. 295 (1927). Accordingly, to avoid that result in this case, the deduction allowable in the year of repayment must be reduced by the percentage depletion allowance which respondent claimed and the Commissioner allowed in the years of receipt as a result of the inclusion of the later-refunded items in respondent's "gross income from the property" in those years. Any other approach would allow respondent a total of $1.27½ in deductions for every $1 refunded to its customers.

Under the annual accounting system dictated by the Code, each year's tax must be definitively calculable at the end of the tax year. "It is the essence of any system of taxation that it should produce revenue ascertainable, and payable to the government, at regular intervals." *Burnet v. Sanford & Brooks Co., supra,* at 365. In cases arising under the claim-of-right doctrine, this emphasis on the annual accounting period normally requires that the tax consequences of a receipt should not determine the size of the deduction allowable in the year of repayment. There is no requirement that the deduction save the taxpayer the exact amount of taxes he paid because of the inclusion of the item in income for a prior year.

Nevertheless, the annual accounting concept does not require us to close our eyes to what happened in prior years. For instance, it is well settled that the prior year may be examined to determine whether the repayment gives rise to a regular loss or a capital loss. *Arrowsmith v. Commissioner*, 344 U.S. 6 (1952). The rationale for the *Arrowsmith* rule is easy to see; if money was taxed at a special lower rate when received, the taxpayer would be accorded an unfair tax windfall if repayments were generally deductible from receipts taxable at the higher rate applicable to ordinary income. The Court in *Arrowsmith* was unwilling to infer that Congress intended such a result.

This case is really no different. In essence, oil and gas producers are taxed on only 72½% of their "gross income from the property" whenever they claim percentage depletion. The remainder of their oil and gas receipts is in reality tax exempt. We cannot believe that Congress intended to give taxpayers a deduction for refunding money that was not taxed when received. Accordingly, *Arrowsmith* teaches that the full amount of the repayment cannot, in the circumstances of this case, be allowed as a deduction.

This result does no violence to the annual accounting system. Here, as in *Arrowsmith*, the earlier returns are not being reopened. And no attempt is being made to require the tax savings from the deduction to equal the tax consequences of the receipts in prior years. In addition, the approach here adopted will affect only a few cases. The percentage depletion allowance is quite unusual; unlike most other deductions provided by the Code, it allows a fixed portion of gross income to go untaxed. As a result, the depletion allowance increases in years when disputed amounts are received under claim of right; there is no corresponding decrease in the allowance because of later deductions for repayments. Therefore, if a deduction for 100% of the repayments were allowed, every time money is received and later repaid the taxpayer would make a profit equivalent to the taxes on 27½% of the amount refunded. In other situations when the taxes on a receipt do not equal the tax benefits of a repayment, either the taxpayer or the Government may, depending on circumstances, be the beneficiary. Here, the taxpayer always wins and the Government always loses. We cannot believe that Congress would have intended such an inequitable result.

* * *

Reversed and remanded.

Mr. Justice Douglas, dissenting.

I share Mr. Justice Stewart's views as to this case and add only a word.

* * *

The search for equity in the tax laws is wondrous and elusive. As Edmond Cahn said: "Those only are equal whom the law has elected to equalize." E. Cahn, *The Sense of Injustice* 14 (1949).

Percentage depletion had its roots in granting a reward to men who go into undeveloped territory in search of oil and gas. But today it is granted anyone who has an interest in oil or gas; the beneficiary need not live the life of the oil wildcatter or bear his risks to obtain the benefits of percentage depletion.

When it comes to capital gains what "equities" are to be applied? Is it fair that earned income pay a heavier tax?

A son who spends $1,000 on his destitute father does not get the same tax benefit as he who pays a like sum to his alma mater. Louis Eisenstein pursues example after example of so-called inequities in tax laws in his book *The Ideologies of Taxation* (1961). For example, the profits on the sale of unbred pigs are taxable as ordinary income, while the profits on the sale of pigs once bred are taxable as capital gains. *Id.*, 174. The same is true of turkeys but not of chickens, even though "a bred chicken and a bred turkey are similarly situated. Each has feathers and two legs." *Ibid.*

* * *

Tax laws are indeed arbitrary; the lines they draw are the products of pressures inside the Congress with compromises carrying the day.

The Court of Appeals held that the "item" here in question was properly included in "gross income" prior to 1958 and was an allowable "deduction" in 1958 because the taxpayer did not have "an unrestricted right" to a "portion of such item," and that the amount of such deduction exceeds $3,000—all as provided in § 1341. * * *

There is no irregularity on the face of the return. There is no conflict with any decision of any other Court of Appeals. We are asked, however, to put a gloss on the statute that Treasury desires. I would adhere to the construction given by the Court of Appeals leaving to Congress the correction of any inequities in the tax scheme.

* * *

Treasury unhappily has developed the habit of jockeying in the courts, testing one theory against another. In California, it may take one position and in Massachusetts the opposite position, the issue in each being the same. The hope is that conflicts over litigious and important issues will develop and the case will be brought here.

If we were trained in the art and science of taxation, we might serve a useful function. But taxation is a specialty in which we have only sporadic and no continuous experience. It has been said that one of our decisions is like a "lightning bolt" that "illuminates only a very small portion of the landscape," leaving a darkness that later decisions do not remove. R. Paul, *Studies in Federal Taxation* 249–250 (3d series 1940). Our contributions, if such they can be called, are dubious indeed, for the [Congress] can and does rewrite the Code frequently.

It is therefore the rare tax case we should consider, except the even rarer constitutional case. The present case has no constitutional overtones; the taxpayer followed the words of the tax law literally, using no new or strained construction of words to find a tax advantage; there is no conflict between this case and any other decision. The Solicitor General only claims that the result reached by the Court of Appeals does not fit the neat logic which he finds in a group of related tax cases.

* * *

In absence of an unmistakably clear conflict among the Circuits, I would abide by the opinions of the Courts of Appeals in tax cases and leave to the Joint Committee whether the gloss which Treasury now tries to put on the statute is or is not desirable.

MR. JUSTICE STEWART, with whom MR. JUSTICE DOUGLAS and MR. JUSTICE HARLAN join, dissenting.

The Court today denies the respondent a tax benefit fairly provided by the Code for no other discernible reasons than that, under the statute as written, "the taxpayer always wins and the Government always loses,"[1] and that "the approach here adopted will affect only a few cases." But we are not free, even in a few cases, to abandon settled principles of annual accounting and statutory construction merely to avoid what the Court thinks Congress might consider an "inequitable result."

---

1. Section 1341, of course, is designed precisely to create a situation where "the taxpayer always wins and the Government always loses." Strict adherence to annual accounting and the claim-of-right doctrine before 1954 sometimes benefited the tax- payer, sometimes the Government. Section 1341 retains those principles where they benefit the taxpayer but allows recomputation of the taxes of a prior year if that method would result in a greater tax saving.

From any natural reading of § 1341, it is apparent that Congress believed the "deduction" in § 1341(a)(2) would be in the amount of the "item" described in § 1341(a)(1). If that understanding is not manifest from the face of the statute and the legislative history, it is the unavoidable inference from a study of the pre–1954 law which the Court concedes § 1341(a)(4) was intended to codify. In every case in this area previously decided by the Court the amount deductible in the year of repayment was considered to be exactly the same as the amount of the previously included item. In two of the cases most sharply in congressional focus in 1954, the Government had conceded without hesitation that the taxpayers were "entitled to a deduction for a loss in the year of repayment of the amount earlier included in income." That has been the express position of the Treasury since at least 1936, and the Court today has not cited a single instance of deviation from that understanding.

The Court says that § 1341 is not alone controlling and that "it is necessary to refer to other portions of the Code to discover how much of a deduction is allowable." I agree that § 1341 must be considered in the context of the Internal Revenue Code as an "organic whole." But no other provisions of the Code in any manner bolster the Court's argument. The Court assumes, quite correctly, that either § 162 or § 165 does permit a deduction for the refund. But it does not, and cannot, suggest that either of those sections—or any other statutory provision—limits the amount of the deduction for the undeniable loss of profits in the full amount of the repayment. Instead the Court assumes a broad equitable authority to weed out tax benefits which it calls "double deductions"—a characterization wholly inapposite to the facts of this case.

In prior decisions disallowing what truly were "double deductions," the Court has relied on evident statutory indications, not just its own view of the equities, that Congress intended to preclude the second deduction. In those cases the taxpayers sought to benefit twice from the same statutory deduction. In this case, by contrast, the respondent has taken two different deductions accorded by Congress for distinct purposes. In the years 1952 through 1957 it deducted the proper amounts for depletion—a deduction which is allowed by Congress "on the theory that the extraction of minerals gradually exhausts the capital investment in the mineral deposit," and which is "designed to permit a recoupment of the owner's capital investment in the minerals so that when the minerals are exhausted, the owner's capital is unimpaired." *Commissioner v. Southwest Exploration Co.*, 350 U.S. 308, 312. The respondent's 1958 deduction was granted by Congress for the entirely different reason that the refund of previously reported income constituted a loss, or business expense. In purpose and effect the deductions are wholly unrelated, and each is sustainable on its own merits. Certainly it cannot be said either that the respondent did not in fact exhaust the capital assets for which the deductions were allowed in 1952 through 1957 or that it did not suffer a business loss by the 1958 repayment.

The sole nexus between these distinct transactions on which the Court constructs its "double deduction" theory is that the depletion deductions were computed as a percentage of gross income from the property. But this fact cannot distinguish percentage depletion from any other deduction. If the respondent had elected to take cost depletion in 1952 through 1957, for example, there would also have been a portion of the gross income in those years—perhaps less than 27½%, perhaps more—which was not included in taxable income. Whether a deduction is computed as a fixed percentage of income or in some other manner, it always reduces by some percentage the income which is ultimately taxed. There are other deductions, of course, whose amount is a function of a certain percentage of the taxpayer's income. With respect to the individual taxpayer, the standard * * * deduction, * * * and those for charitable contributions, § 170, and medical expenses, § 213, are doubtless the most frequent. Under the Court's ruling today, any taxpayer who repays money included in gross income in a prior year in which he also took one of the above mentioned deductions will have to reduce his refund deduction by that portion of the previous year's deduction attributable to the included income. Surely this result contravenes the purpose of the annual accounting concept to prevent recomputations of the prior year's tax.

The Court says today that there can be no deduction "for refunding money that was not taxed when received." This means nothing less than that, whenever a taxpayer seeks to deduct a refund of money received as income under a claim of right in a prior year, the deduction must be reduced by the percentage of gross income in that prior year which, for whatever reason, was not also taxable income. Otherwise there will be precisely the same kind of so-called "double deduction" as the Court finds in this case.

It is clear that the Court has wrought a major transformation of the deduction which has heretofore been allowed and which Congress recognized in § 1341(a)(4). That deduction is permitted because, in the words of § 1341, the item "was included in gross income for a prior taxable year" * * *, not because it was included in taxable income. It is no answer to say that the "annual accounting concept does not require us to close our eyes to what happened in prior years." Of course we must look to the prior years to ascertain the amounts included in gross income and the nature of that income as it bears on the provision under which it is deductible in the year of repayment. *Arrowsmith v. Commissioner*, 344 U.S. 6. But the very purpose of the annual accounting concept is to preclude adjustments in the amount of the deduction to reflect the tax consequences of the item's inclusion in the prior year.

One of the major factors, in addition to changes in tax rates and brackets, that determine who will benefit from adherence to the annual accounting principles embodied in § 1341(a)(4) is the extent to which the taxpayer had deductions in the prior or subsequent taxable years to offset gross income. And it is no less inconsistent with annual accounting principles to pare down the allowable loss deduction in the year of repayment because of other deductions in the year of inclusion than because of a lower tax rate or bracket in that year.

Because I cannot agree that the Court's equitable sensibilities empower it to depart from the sound principles of tax accounting specifically endorsed by Congress in § 1341, I respectfully dissent.

* * *

The Problem With $3,000. Recall that § 1341(a)(3) requires that the amount of the deduction must exceed $3,000. Suppose the *Arrowsmith* doctrine requires that a repayment be treated as a capital loss, and suppose further that the taxpayer has no capital gains for the year of restoration. Under § 1211(b), the taxpayer can deduct only $3,000 of the capital loss in the year of repayment. See discussion at Chapter 4. In this example, therefore, the taxpayer could not make use of § 1341 because the deduction would only *equal* $3,000—it would not *exceed* $3,000. Under § 1212(b), the non-deductible portion of the capital loss carries over to the next year as a capital loss. So unless the taxpayer has some capital gains to absorb the loss, § 1341 will never apply. It is doubtful that Congress intended this possible result; it illustrates that the choice of $3,000 as a limit is unfortunate.

* * *

(3) OTHER CORRECTION DEVICES

Code: IRC §§ 1311–1314.

Regs: None.

Res judicata and Collateral Estoppel. Ah, the days of Civil Procedure. Bet you never thought you would see the terms "res judicata" and "collateral estoppel" in a tax book. Well, relax, because we are not going to dwell for very long here. Both of these preclusion doctrines are error correction devices only in a very broad sense: **res judicata** (claim preclusion) preserves the original (litigated) treatment of an item, while **collateral estoppel** (issue preclusion) prevents the admission of additional evidence that might affect the original treatment of the item.

These doctrines, difficult enough in first-year civil procedure courses, are complicated by the use of annual accounting. Briefly, the issue is whether moving from Year One to Year Two creates a new cause of action, thus precluding the use of these doctrines. To understand why this might be the result, we should take a brief detour to consider the statutes of limitation.

Section 6501 generally provides that the Treasury Secretary must assess a deficiency on a tax return within three years of the date of the return. Unless the taxpayer agrees to extend the time limit or one of the few exceptions to the 3–year rule applies, this requirement is almost absolute (we say "almost" because of the mitigation provisions described later in this Part). Likewise, under § 6511, a taxpayer must file refund claims within three years of the return or within two years of payment, whichever is later. If the taxpayer does not timely file the refund claim, it is almost forever barred (again, "almost" is necessary because of the mitigation provisions).

The doctrines of res judicata and collateral estoppel are generally unhelpful to either the government or the taxpayer if the applicable statute of limitations has passed. The treatment in the closed year was, in most cases, never litigated, so res judicata cannot apply. Even where the treatment of the closed year was fixed by litigation, the existence of a new taxable year may be a different fact, which thus prevents applicability of both preclusion doctrines. The Supreme Court dealt with this difficulty in the following case.

COMMISSIONER v. SUNNEN, 333 U.S. 591, 68 S.Ct. 715, 92 L.Ed. 898 (1948).

Facts: The taxpayer assigned his royalty rights under various licenses to a family member by two agreements, one executed in 1928 and another in 1931. In a prior proceedings before the Board of Tax Appeals, the court determined that the assignment of income under the 1928 agreement was effective to prevent inclusion of the corresponding royalties in the taxpayer's gross income. At issue in this case were the royalties paid in 1937 pursuant to the same 1928 agreement, as well as the royalties paid from 1937 to 1941 under the 1931 agreement. The taxpayer argued that the decision of the Board of Tax Appeals precluded a holding that would tax him on the royalties received by the related person.

Issue: Is the government precluded from arguing that the royalties paid to a related person were gross income to the taxpayer?

Holding: No.

Rationale: The 1931 agreement was not before the Board of Tax Appeals in its earlier proceeding, and while the 1928 agreement was at issue in the earlier case, the development of the "assignment of income" doctrine since the time of that decision warranted re-examination of the 1928 agreement.

In reaching this decision, the Court first reviewed the role of res judicata and collateral estoppel in tax cases. "Each year is the origin of a new liability and of a separate cause of action. Thus if a claim of liability or non-liability relating to a particular tax year is litigated, a judgment on the merits is res judicata as to any subsequent proceeding involving the same claim and the same tax year. But if the later proceeding is concerned with a similar or unlike claim relating to a different tax year, the prior judgment acts as a collateral estoppel only as to those matters in the second proceeding which were actually presented and determined in the first suit. Collateral estoppel operates, in other words, to relieve the government and the taxpayer of 'redundant litigation of the identical question of the statute's application to the taxpayer's status.' *Tait v. Western Md. R. Co.*, 289 U.S. 620, 624.

"But collateral estoppel is a doctrine capable of being applied so as to avoid an undue disparity in the impact of income tax liability. A taxpayer may secure a judicial determination of a particular tax matter, a matter which may recur without substantial variation for some years thereafter. But a subsequent modification of the significant facts or a change or development in the controlling legal principles may make that determination obsolete or erroneous, at least for future purposes. If such a determination is then perpetuated each succeeding year as to the taxpayer involved in the original litigation, he is accorded a tax treatment different from that given to other taxpayers of the same class. As a result, there are inequalities in the administration of the revenue laws, discriminatory distinctions in tax liability, and a fertile basis for litigious confusion. Such consequences, however, are neither necessitated nor justified by the principle of collateral estoppel. That principle is designed to prevent repetitious lawsuits over matters which have once been decided and which have remained substantially static, factually and legally. It is not meant to create vested rights in decisions that have become obsolete or erroneous with time, thereby causing inequities among taxpayers.

"And so where two cases involve income taxes in different taxable years, collateral estoppel must be used with its limitations carefully in mind so as to avoid injustice. It must be confined to situations where the matter raised in the second suit is identical in all respects with that decided in the first proceeding and where the controlling facts and applicable legal rules remain unchanged. If the legal matters determined in the earlier case differ from those raised in the second case, collateral estoppel has no bearing on the situation. And where the situation is vitally altered between the time of the first judgment and the second, the prior determination is not conclusive."

As to the 1931 agreement, the Court quickly determined that neither preclusion rule applied. "That is true even though those contracts are identical in all important respects with the 1928 contract, the only one that was before the Board, and even though the issue as to those contracts is the same as that raised by the 1928 contract. For income tax purposes, what is decided as to one contract is not conclusive as to any other contract which is not then in issue, however similar or identical it may be."

With respect to the 1928 agreement, the Court conceded that there was "complete identity of facts, issues and parties as between the Board proceeding and the instant one." Yet if the Board's decision had become erroneous because of subsequent Supreme Court decisions, preclusion rules should not apply. The Court reviewed its cases dealing with the assignment of income doctrine, including *Helvering v. Clifford*, 309 U.S. 331, 60 S.Ct. 554, 84 L.Ed. 788 (1940) and *Helvering v. Horst*, 311 U.S. 112, 61 S.Ct. 144, 85 L.Ed. 75 (1940). "[T]he clarification and growth of these principles through the *Clifford-Horst* line of cases constitute, in our opinion, a sufficient change in the legal climate to render inapplicable, in the instant proceeding, the doctrine of collateral estoppel relative to the assignment of the 1928 contract. True, these cases did not originate the concept that an assignor is taxable if he retains control over the assigned property or power to defeat the receipt of income by the assignee. But they gave much added emphasis and substance to that concept, making it more suited to meet the 'attenuated subtleties' created by taxpayers. So substantial was the amplification of this concept as to justify a reconsideration of earlier Tax Court decisions reached without the benefit of the expanded notions, decisions which are now sought to be perpetuated regardless of their present correctness. Thus in the earlier litigation in 1935, the Board of Tax Appeals was unable to bring to bear on the assignment of the 1928 contract the full breadth of the ideas enunciated in the *Clifford-Horst* series of cases. And, as we shall see, a proper application of the principles as there developed might well have produced a different result, such as was reached by the Tax Court in this case in regard to the assignments of the other contracts. Under those circumstances collateral estoppel should not have been used by the Tax Court in the instant proceeding to perpetuate the 1935 viewpoint of the assignment.''

* * *

Equitable Recoupment: Two Wrongs Make a Right. When a taxpayer makes a mistake on a tax return for a prior year, there are, as we have seen, a host of correction devices that can be applied to make things right. But in some rare cases, none of the correction devices will apply. In those cases, taxpayers have at times asked the courts to permit a second mistake that is designed to cure the first mistake. And believe it or not, taxpayers have succeeded. The following case gives the Supreme Court's most recent spin on the doctrine of "equitable recoupment."

UNITED STATES v. DALM

United States Supreme Court, 1990.
494 U.S. 596, 110 S.Ct. 1361, 108 L.Ed.2d 548.

JUSTICE KENNEDY delivered the opinion of the Court.

Single transactions, it is well known, may be susceptible to different, and inconsistent, theories of taxation. In the case before us, the taxpayer treated moneys derived from her deceased employer's estate as a gift and paid gift tax on the transfer. Some years later, the Government contended that the money the taxpayer had received from the transaction was income. The taxpayer disagreed, and the Government's assertion of an income tax deficiency was the subject of proceedings in the United States Tax Court. The question presented is whether, the statute of limitations long since having run, the doctrine of equitable recoupment supports a separate suit for refund of the earlier paid gift tax after the taxpayer settled the Tax Court deficiency proceeding and agreed to pay income tax on the transaction. We hold that it does not.

I

The taxpayer, Frances Dalm, is the respondent here. Dalm was appointed administratrix of the estate of Harold Schrier in May 1975, at the request of Schrier's surviving brother, Clarence. It appears Dalm had been the decedent's loyal secretary for many years and that Clarence wanted her to take charge of the affairs of the estate and receive some of the moneys that otherwise would belong to him.

Dalm received fees from the estate, approved by the probate court, of $30,000 in 1976 and $7,000 in 1977. She also received from Clarence two payments, $180,000 in 1976 and $133,813 in 1977. Clarence and his wife filed a gift tax return in December 1976 reporting the $180,000 payment as a gift to Dalm, and in that same month Dalm paid the gift tax of $18,675. The Internal Revenue Service (IRS) later assessed an additional $1,587 in penalties and interest with respect to the transfer. The Schriers paid the penalties and interest in 1977, and were reimbursed by Dalm. But no gift tax return was filed with respect to the 1977 payment of $133,813.

After auditing Dalm's 1976 and 1977 income tax returns, the IRS determined that the payments from Clarence represented additional fees for Dalm's services as administratix of the estate and should have been reported as income. The IRS asserted deficiencies in her income tax of $91,471 in 1976, and $70,639 in 1977 * * *.

Dalm petitioned the Tax Court for a redetermination of the asserted deficiencies, as was her right under § 6213(a). In her petition, she argued that the 1976 and 1977 payments from Clarence were gifts to carry out the wish of the decedent that she share in the estate. After two days of trial, Dalm and the IRS settled the case, with the parties agreeing to a stipulated decision that respondent owed income tax deficiencies of $10,416 for 1976 and $70,639 for 1977. No claim for a credit or recoupment of the gift tax paid by Dalm was raised in the Tax Court proceedings, although there is some dispute whether the gift tax was one of the factors considered in arriving at the terms of the settlement.

Immediately after agreeing to the settlement, Dalm filed an administrative claim for refund of the $20,262 in gift tax, interest, and penalties paid with respect to the $180,000 transfer in 1976. The claim was filed in November 1984, even though the [Code] required Dalm to file any claim for a refund of the gift tax by December 1979. See § 6511(a). When the IRS failed to act upon her claim within six months, Dalm filed suit in the United States District Court for the Western District of Michigan, seeking what in her complaint she denominated a refund of "overpaid gift tax." * * *

The Government moved to dismiss the suit for lack of jurisdiction and for summary judgment, arguing that the suit was untimely under the applicable statute of limitations. The District Court granted the Government's motions, rejecting Dalm's contention that her suit was timely under the doctrine of equitable recoupment as set forth in our opinion in *Bull v. United States*, 295 U.S. 247 (1935), a case we shall discuss. The court held that equitable recoupment did not authorize it to exercise jurisdiction over "an independent lawsuit, such as this suit, . . .

maintained for a refund for a year in which the statute of limitations has expired."

On appeal, the Court of Appeals for the Sixth Circuit reversed. * * * The court found Dalm's claim satisfied all of the requirements for equitable recoupment expressed in our cases. It rejected the District Court's characterization of Dalm's action as an independent lawsuit barred by the statute of limitations, reasoning that she could maintain an otherwise barred action for refund of gift tax because the Government had made a timely claim of a deficiency in her income tax based upon an inconsistent legal theory * * *.

Because the approach taken by the Sixth and Ninth Circuits is in conflict with that adopted by Seventh Circuit, we granted certiorari and now reverse.

II

The ultimate question in the case is whether the District Court had jurisdiction over Dalm's suit seeking a refund of the gift tax, interest, and penalties paid on the 1976 transfer. We hold that it did not.

A

In her complaint, Dalm invoked 28 U.S.C. § 1346(a)(1) (1982 ed.), under which a district court has jurisdiction over a "civil action against the United States for the recovery of any internal-revenue tax alleged to have been erroneously or illegally assessed or collected, or any penalty claimed to have been collected without authority or any sum alleged to have been excessive or in any manner wrongfully collected under the internal-revenue laws." Despite its spacious terms, § 1346(a)(1) must be read in conformity with other statutory provisions which qualify a taxpayer's right to bring a refund suit upon compliance with certain conditions. The first is § 7422(a), which, tracking the language of § 1346(a)(1), limits a taxpayer's right to bring a refund suit by providing that

> "[n]o suit or proceeding shall be maintained in any court for the recovery of any internal revenue tax alleged to have been erroneously or illegally assessed or collected, or of any penalty claimed to have been collected without authority, or of any sum alleged to have been excessive or in any manner wrongfully collected, until a claim for refund or credit has been duly filed with the Secretary, according to the provisions of law in that regard, and the regulations of the Secretary established in pursuance thereof."

Second, § 6511(a) provides that if a taxpayer is required to file a return with respect to a tax, such as the gift tax, the taxpayer must file any claim for refund within three years from the time the return was filed or two years from the time the tax was paid, whichever period expires later. Read together, the import of these sections is clear: unless a claim for refund of a tax has been filed within the time limits imposed by § 6511(a), a suit for refund, regardless of whether the tax is alleged to have been "erroneously," "illegally," or "wrongfully collected," §§ 1346(a)(1), 7422(a), may not be maintained in any court.

There is no doubt that Dalm failed to comply with these statutory requirements. The Schriers filed their gift tax return and Dalm paid the gift tax on the 1976 transfer in December 1976. She paid the penalties and interest on that tax in March 1977. Dalm did not file her claim for refund of the gift tax until November 1984, long after the limitations period expired. Under the plain language of §§ 6511(a) and 7422(a), the District Court was barred from entertaining her suit for a refund of the tax.

B

The Court of Appeals did not contest this analysis; indeed, it recognized that "[t]here is no statutory basis for permitting the recovery of a tax overpayment after the statute of limitations has expired." Despite the lack of a statutory basis for recovery, the court concluded that the doctrine of equitable recoupment permits Dalm to maintain an action to recover the overpaid gift tax. We disagree.

The doctrine of equitable recoupment was first addressed by us in our opinion in *Bull v. United States, supra.* There, the dispute centered on whether partnership distributions received by a decedent's estate after his death were subject to estate tax or income tax. After an audit, the executor of the estate included the sums in the estate tax return and paid the estate tax in 1920 and 1921. In 1925, the Commissioner of Internal Revenue notified the estate of a deficiency in the estate's income tax for the 1920 tax year, contending that the same distributions upon which estate tax had been paid should have been treated as income. The Commissioner, however, did not give credit for the estate tax earlier paid on the value of the distributions.

That same year, the estate petitioned to the Board of Tax Appeals for a redetermination of the deficiency. After the Board sustained the Commissioner's deficiency determination, the estate paid the additional income tax and filed a claim for refund of the income tax paid. The Commissioner rejected the claim, and, in September 1930, the executor sued in the Court of Claims for a refund of the income tax. In his petition to the Court of Claims, the executor argued (1) that the amount taxed was not income, so that the estate was entitled to a refund of the entire amount of income tax paid; and (2) alternatively, if the amount taxed was income, the Government should credit against the income tax due the overpayment of estate tax, plus interest, attributable to the inclusion of the amount in the taxable estate. The Court of Claims rejected both arguments.

We reversed, holding that the executor was entitled to a credit against the income tax deficiency in the amount of the overpayment of estate tax, with interest. We began by acknowledging that the executor had not filed a claim for refund of the estate tax within the limitations period, and that any action for refund of the tax was now barred. "If nothing further had occurred Congressional action would have been the sole avenue of redress."

What did occur, however, was that after the limitations period on the estate tax had run, the Government assessed a deficiency in the estate's income tax based upon the same taxable event, and the deficiency became the subject of litigation between the estate and the Government. We reasoned that a tax assessment is in essence an assertion by the sovereign that the taxpayer owes a debt to it; but that, because "taxes are the life-blood of government," it was necessary for the tax assessed to be collected prior to adjudication of whether the assessment was erroneous or unlawful. As a result,

> "the usual procedure for the recovery of debts is reversed in the field of taxation. Payment precedes defense, and the burden of proof, normally on the claimant, is shifted to the taxpayer.... But these reversals of the normal process of collecting a claim cannot obscure the fact that after all what is being accomplished is the recovery of a just debt owed the sovereign." *Id.*, at 260.

Under our reasoning, the proceeding between the executor and the Government was in substance an attempt by the Government to recover a debt from the estate. The debt was the income tax that was owed, even though in fact it already had been paid. Had the Government followed the "usual procedure" of recovering debts by instituting an action at law for the income tax owed, the executor would have been able to defend against the suit by "demanding recoupment of the amount mistakenly collected as estate tax and wrongfully retained."

> "If the claim for income tax deficiency had been the subject of a suit, any counter demand for recoupment of the overpayment of estate tax could have been asserted by way of defense and credit obtained notwithstanding the statute of limitations had barred an independent suit against the Government therefor. This is because recoupment is in the nature of a defense arising out of some feature of the transaction upon which the plaintiff's action is grounded. Such a defense is never barred by the statute of limitations so long as the main action itself is timely." 295 U.S., at 262.

We found it immaterial that, rather than the Government having to sue to collect the income tax, the executor was required first to pay it and then seek a refund. "This procedural requirement does not obliterate his substantial right to rely on his cross-demand for credit of the amount which if the United States had sued him for income tax he could have recouped against his liability on that score." *Id.*, at 263.

Dalm contends that the only distinction between her case and *Bull* is the "meaningless procedural distinction" that her claim of equitable recoupment is raised in a separate suit for refund of gift tax, after she had litigated the income tax deficiency, while in *Bull* the claim of equitable recoupment of the estate tax was litigated as part of a suit for refund of that tax alleged to be inconsistent with the estate tax. A distinction that has jurisdiction as its central concept is not meaningless.

In *Bull*, the executor sought equitable recoupment of the estate tax in an action for refund of income tax, over which it was undisputed that the Court of Claims had jurisdiction. All that was at issue was whether the Court of Claims, in the interests of equity, could adjust the income tax owed to the Government to take account of an estate tax paid in error but which the executor could not recover in a separate refund action. Here, Dalm does not seek to invoke equitable recoupment in determining her income tax liability; she has already litigated that liability without raising a claim of equitable recoupment and is foreclosed from relitigating it now. See § 6512(a). She seeks to invoke equitable recoupment only in a separate action for refund of gift tax, an action for which there is no statutory authorization by reason of the bar of the limitations statute.

It is instructive to consider what the facts in *Bull* would have to be if Dalm's contention is correct that her case is identical to *Bull* in all material respects. The executor in *Bull* would have litigated the income tax liability, without raising a claim of equitable recoupment, in the Board of Tax Appeals and/or in the Court of Claims, with the Government winning in each forum. Then, having exhausted his avenues of litigating the income tax liability and paid the tax, the executor would have filed a claim for refund of the estate tax with the Commissioner, asserting equitable recoupment as the basis for the refund, with the Commissioner rejecting it as untimely. At that point, the executor would have brought suit for refund of the estate tax in the Court of Claims after the statute of limitations had run. Had the case come to us with those facts, we would have faced the issue presented here: whether the court in which the taxpayer was seeking a refund was barred from entertaining the suit. We can say with assurance that we were not presented with this issue in *Bull* and did not consider it. Even had the issue been raised, *Bull* itself suggests that we would have rejected Dalm's argument out of hand. See *Bull*, 295 U.S., at 259 ("The fact that the petitioner relied on the Commissioner's assessment for estate tax, and believed the inconsistent claim of deficiency of income tax was of no force, cannot avail to toll the statute of limitations, which forbade the bringing of any action in 1930 for refund of estate tax payments made in 1921").

The only other decision in which we have upheld a claim or defense premised upon the doctrine of equitable recoupment is consistent with our analysis today. In *Stone v. White*, 301 U.S. 532 (1937), a trust had paid the income it received from the corpus to its sole beneficiary and also paid the tax due on the income. After the statute of limitations governing the Government's right to collect the income tax from the beneficiary had run, the trust filed a timely suit seeking a refund of the income tax paid on the theory that the beneficiary, not the trust, was liable for the tax. We held that, given the identity of interest between the beneficiary and the trust, the Government could invoke equitable recoupment to assert its now-barred claim against the beneficiary as a defense to the trust's timely claim for a refund. As in *Bull*, there was no dispute that the court in which we allowed the doctrine of equitable recoupment to be raised had jurisdiction over the underlying action: the trust's timely action for a refund of income tax.

In sum, our decisions in *Bull* and *Stone* stand only for the proposition that a party litigating a tax claim in a timely proceeding may, in that proceeding, seek recoupment of a related, and inconsistent, but now time-barred tax claim relating to the same transaction. In both cases, there was no question but that the courts in which the refund actions were brought had jurisdiction. To date, we have not allowed equitable recoupment to be the sole basis for jurisdiction.

C

* * *

As we have determined, our previous equitable recoupment cases have not suspended rules of jurisdiction * * *. We likewise refuse Dalm's invitation to do so here. She seeks a refund not of income tax but of gift tax on which the return was filed and the tax paid in December 1976. For the District Court to have jurisdiction over her suit for refund, Dalm was required to file a claim for refund of the tax within three years of the time the gift tax return was filed or two years of the time the tax was paid, whichever period expires later. See §§ 6511(a), 7422(a). There is no question but that she failed to do so. Having failed to comply with the statutory requirements for seeking a refund, she asks us to go beyond the authority Congress has given us in permitting suits against the Government. If any principle is central to our understanding of sovereign immunity, it is that the power to consent to such suits is reserved to Congress.

Our conclusion is reinforced by the fact that Congress has legislated a set of exceptions to the limitations period prescribed by §§ 7422 and 6511(a). In 1938, Congress adopted what are known as the mitigation provisions, now codified at §§ 1311–1314. These statutes, in specified circumstances, permit a taxpayer who has been required to pay inconsistent taxes to seek a refund of a tax the recovery of which is otherwise barred by §§ 7422(a) and 6511(a). It is undisputed that Dalm's action does not come within these provisions; were we to allow her to maintain a suit for refund on the basis of equitable recoupment, we would be doing little more than overriding Congress' judgment as to when equity requires that there be an exception to the limitations bar.

Our holding today does not leave taxpayers in Dalm's position powerless to invoke the doctrine of equitable recoupment. Both the Secretary, at the administrative level, * * * and a court which has jurisdiction over a timely suit for refund may consider an equitable recoupment claim for an earlier tax paid under an inconsistent theory on the same transaction.

III

The Court of Appeals reasoned that recoupment should be permitted because it effected, with respect to a single transaction, the recovery of a tax based upon a theory inconsistent with the theory upon which a later tax was paid. But to permit an independent action for recoupment because there is but one transaction is to mistake the threshold requirement for its rationale. It is true that our precedents allowing recoupment pertain to cases where a single transaction is subjected to inconsistent taxation, but the reason the statute of limitations is not a bar in those cases is that the court has uncontested jurisdiction to adjudicate one of the taxes in question. In such cases, a court has the equitable power to examine and consider the entire transaction:

> "The essence of the doctrine of recoupment is stated in the *Bull* case: 'recoupment is in the nature of a defense arising out of some feature of the transaction upon which the plaintiff's action is grounded.' 295 U.S. 247, 262. It has never been thought to allow one transaction to be offset against another, but only to permit a transaction which is made the subject of suit by plaintiff to be examined in all its aspects, and judgment to be rendered that does justice in view of the one transaction as a whole." *Rothensies v. Electric Storage Battery Co.*, 329 U.S. 296, 299 (1946).

Here the Government asserted an income tax deficiency on a theory inconsistent with the theory upon which Dalm relied in paying gift tax. She chose to litigate the deficiency in the Tax Court, where she did not attempt to raise a recoupment claim. She cannot choose this avenue to adjudicate the income tax consequences of the transaction, and then seek to reopen the matter and override the statute of limitations for the sole purpose of seeking recoupment. The controlling jurisdictional statutes do not permit her to do so.

The judgment of the Court of Appeals is therefore reversed.

It is so ordered.

JUSTICE STEVENS, with whom JUSTICE BRENNAN and JUSTICE MARSHALL join, dissenting.

This is not a decision that will be much celebrated or often cited. Few cases are affected, and not a single brief amicus curiae was filed. * * * The case casts a shadow on the Executive—and on this Court—but otherwise has no apparent importance.

Indeed, the Court's opinion is remarkable not at all for what it says but rather for what it leaves unsaid. The majority's parsing of sovereign immunity and jurisdiction masks what is the ultimate question before us: whether a statute of limitations otherwise barring a refund of federal income tax is tolled by Government conduct that this Court has censured as "immoral" and tantamount to "a fraud on the taxpayer's rights." The Court today offers a jurisdictional apology when it could—and should—follow the just rule of the *Bull* case.

I

This case is remarkably similar to its 55–year-old precursor. The *Bull* case involved an attempt by the Government to collect income tax on partnership distributions received by the estate of a deceased partner. The Commissioner of Internal Revenue had already collected an estate tax on the distributions on the assumption that they constituted part of the estate corpus. The Commissioner contended, first, that the same transactions could constitute both corpus and income and thus be subject to both an estate tax and an income tax, and, second, that, in any event, the statute of limitations barred a recovery of the estate tax. This Court rejected the Commissioner's first argument, and characterized as follows his claim that the Government could retain the estate tax while collecting a second tax on the same transaction pursuant to an inconsistent theory:

> "The United States, we have held, cannot, as against the claim of an innocent party, hold his money which has gone into its treasury by means of the fraud of its agent. *United States v. State Bank*, 96 U.S. 30. While here the money was taken through mistake without any element of fraud, the unjust retention is immoral and amounts in law to a fraud on the taxpayer's rights." 295 U.S., at 261.

This case involves an equally unjust retention of a previously paid tax. The Government has collected an income tax on a transfer of $180,000 to respondent while retaining the gift tax previously paid on the same transfer. The Court's decision assumes, as the summary judgment record requires, that when the Government compromised its claim for an income tax deficiency, it allowed respondent no credit for the gift tax that had previously been paid. Thus, the critical fact that made the Government's position in *Bull* immoral is present here: a single taxable event has been subjected to two taxes on mutually inconsistent theories.

II

Even with the parallel between *Bull* and this case clearly in mind, most readers of the majority's opinion must wonder how this case ever came before our Court, and why the majority must recite so much law to decide it. According to the majority, respondent chose to litigate in the Tax Court the deficiency assessed against her, and, having made this choice, cannot "then seek to reopen the matter and override the statute of limitations for the sole purpose of seeking recoupment." This may seem fair enough, but also plain enough: A legal claim that might have been settled in an earlier proceeding is usually barred by rules of claim preclusion. If the claim is not barred by the settlement agreement in this case, then surely the Government can—without any help from this Court—avoid such problems in the future by drafting its settlement agreements more carefully. There is accordingly no justification for the Court's exercise of certiorari jurisdiction in this case, a discretionary act which has done nothing more useful than deprive the twice-taxed respondent in this case of a remedy for a wrong done by the Government.

Two facts explain why the Government does not rely on principles of claim preclusion as a defense in this case. The first is this: It is undisputed by the parties to this case that the Tax Court lacked jurisdiction to consider recoupment of the gift tax payment against the income tax deficiency. According to the Government, respondent cannot, and for that reason did not, raise her equitable recoupment claim in the Tax Court: "respondent's choice of the Tax Court forum precluded her from claiming equitable recoupment against the income tax deficiency." The Government acknowledges that respondent may have had a sound claim for recoupment, but insists that to pursue this claim she should have "paid the 1976 and 1977 income tax deficiencies and then brought a timely refund suit in district court or the Claims Court."

The second fact is this: an affluent taxpayer, but not a less fortunate one, can pay a deficiency assessment and file suit for a refund. It is undisputed that if respondent had the means to do so, she could have recovered the gift tax that had been paid in 1976 by a refund action filed after she received the notice of income tax deficiency in 1983, even though the statute of limitations had long since run. One might infer from the posture of this case—as respondent's counsel represented to the Court—that respondent's limited means foreclosed this avenue of relief for her. She therefore challenged the deficiency in the Tax Court.

These two facts explain what the majority does not: why we are not addressing a simple case of res judicata. It is clear that the basis for respondent's equitable recoupment claim did not exist until it was determined that the payment made in 1976 was taxable as income. Thus, respondent could apparently obtain a forum to hear her equitable recoupment claim only by seeking a refund of the previously paid gift tax—an action which all agree was barred by limitations when respondent received the notice of deficiency in 1983.

When that determination was made—that is to say, when the income tax case was settled—respondent promptly asserted her recoupment claim in the only forum available. Indeed, she filed her claim for a gift tax refund even before the settlement agreement was consummated. In view of the fact that the character of the 1976 transaction remained in dispute until the claim was filed, none of the policy reasons that normally support the application of a statute of limitations is implicated by this case.

III

The Court nevertheless denies respondent the relief devised by the *Bull* Court. Ignoring both the policies underlying the statute of limitations and the principles of just conduct underlying *Bull*, the Court confronts respondent with the majestic voices of "jurisdiction" and "sovereign immunity"—voices that seem to have a haunting charm for this Court's current majority.

The Court that decided the *Bull* case reasoned not in obeisance to these siren-like voices but rather under the reliable guidance of a bright star in our jurisprudence: the presumption that for every right there should be a remedy. See *Marbury v. Madison*, 1 Cranch 137, 162–163

(1803). Without any sacrifice of technical propriety, the *Bull* Court could have found that the lapse of time had divested the Court of Claims of jurisdiction to allow the taxpayer credit for the previously paid estate tax. It easily avoided that unjust result, however, by relying on the special features of the tax collection procedures that impose burdens on the taxpayer unlike those imposed on ordinary litigants. The net effect of its analysis was to hold that in a refund action based on the multiple and inconsistent taxation of a single transaction, the taxpayer is to be treated as though she were the defendant even though she is actually the plaintiff.

I would adopt the same course in this case. By initiating a proceeding to recover income tax based on the 1976 payment, the Government waived the time bar that would otherwise have precluded a claim for refund of the gift tax. Had respondent paid the deficiency and asserted the claim for a gift tax refund as a second count in one action, even this Court would agree that the claim was timely. If we adopt the Court's reasoning in *Bull*, it is proper to treat the second count of the refund action as timely even when the income tax issues are litigated before the Tax Court, because the deficiency assessment was sufficient to put in issue the right to recoupment and to justify treating the taxpayer as a defendant, rather than a plaintiff. If it was not too late for the Government to litigate the tax consequences of the 1976 payment, it should not be too late for the taxpayer to do so. * * *

IV

It may reasonably be said that the disposition in *Bull* involved an unusually flexible treatment of legal categories. The rights of a plaintiff are construed by reference to the status of a defendant so as to permit, in effect, the equitable tolling of a limitations period. A doctrinal innovation that appears imaginative may, however, be nothing more than the necessary expression of an exception to a generally appropriate definition. This particular exception deserves the status of a legal rule by virtue of our decision in *Bull*. There is no reason to retreat from the direction of that precedent today.

There is, moreover, nothing especially sober or unflinching about the majority's disposition of this case. Quite the contrary is true. The majority's approach depends upon showing that this Court is constrained by tightly drawn jurisdictional boundaries, but, as the majority concedes, the relevant jurisdictional statute speaks in "spacious terms." Indeed, the statute confers jurisdiction not only over any "civil action against the United States for the recovery of any internal-revenue tax alleged to have been erroneously or illegally assessed or collected," but also over any such action to recover "any sum alleged to have been excessive or in any manner wrongfully collected under the internal revenue laws." 28 U.S.C. § 1346(a)(1) (1982 ed.).

The majority correctly recognizes that this blanket waiver of immunity can be converted into a jurisdictional straitjacket only by recourse to limitations spelled out elsewhere. The majority would find these limitations in § 7422 and § 6511(a) of the Internal Revenue Code. The first of these provisions stipulates that no tax refund suit "shall be maintained ... until a claim for refund or credit has been duly filed with the Secretary, according to the provisions of law in that regard, and the regulations of the Secretary established in pursuance thereof." 26 U.S.C. § 7422(a) (1982 ed.). The second provision establishes a statute of limitations applicable to actions for refund of taxes paid by filing a return or by means of a stamp. 26 U.S.C. § 6511(a) (1982 ed.). It is the latter of these two provisions which gives the majority the shackles it seeks: the statute of limitations in § 6511(a) is a provision of law that, under § 7422(a), restricts the capacity of taxpayers to maintain suits. Denominating respondent's suit an action for refund of overpaid gift tax, the majority declares there can be "no doubt" that the combined operation of § 7422(a) and § 6511(a) strips the federal courts of the jurisdiction otherwise accorded by 28 U.S.C. § 1346(a)(1) (1982 ed.) over the recoupment suit.

I have no doubt that § 6511 prescribes the statute of limitations applicable to actions for the refund of overpaid gift tax, and that, if this were such an action, the section would at least support the majority's argument. This suit is not, however, technically a suit for the refund of overpaid gift tax within the meaning of § 6511(a). The gravamen of respondent's claim is not that the gift tax was overpaid, but that it was unjustly retained. According to the *Bull* Court, "[w]hile here the money was taken through mistake without any element of fraud, the unjust retention is immoral and amounts in law to a fraud on the taxpayer's rights." 295 U.S., at 261. In my opinion, a sum fraudulently retained under the internal revenue laws is an amount included within § 1346(a)(1)'s provision for recovery of "any sum ... in any manner wrongfully collected under the internal-revenue laws." The jurisdictional grant expressly distinguishes such wrongfully collected sums from those sums which are simply "excessive," and from taxes "erroneously or illegally assessed or collected." These latter phrases would appear to cover actions for refund of an overpaid gift tax, but the payment fraudulently retained in this case is better characterized as a "sum ... wrongfully collected." Likewise, § 6511(a) by its express terms applies only to actions for refund of an "overpayment of any tax" paid by means of a return or a stamp. It is odd to speak of the overpayment of a fraud, and one is not ordinarily required to file a return in order to be defrauded—even when the sovereign is the malefactor. I conclude that, technically speaking, this action is one for the recoupment of tax wrongfully collected because fraudulently retained, and not for the refund of tax overpaid. The plain language of § 1346(a)(1) accords jurisdiction over respondent's suit, and the terms of § 6511(a) do not divest it. The majority's affection for plain language seems to end where its devotion to sovereign immunity begins.

The majority is able to complete its argument only by inventing a small, but blatant, fiction: that respondent is bringing a suit for the refund of overpaid gift tax within the meaning of 26 U.S.C. § 6511(a) (1982 ed.). This minor fiction is then conscripted by the majority's strategy to serve the vainest of all legal fictions, the doctrine of sovereign immunity. The doctrine has its origin in the ancient myth that the "[K]ing can do no wrong." Whatever might be said in favor of this polite falsehood in English law, the doctrine is an anomalous import within our own. * * * Its persistence cannot be denied but ought not to be celebrated. Nor should its fictive origin ever be forgotten. There is no cause to expand the doctrine, and we do better to interpret § 1346(a)(1) by the light of equity and with due regard for the practicalities of revenue collection discussed in *Bull*.

To be useful, legal concepts must accommodate most disputes without the dissonance accompanying blended categories, but must also permit such flexibility when judgment demands it. It is not surprising that our concepts should be stressed when the Government taxes a citizen twice upon inconsistent theories and then subjects the citizen to a choice among competing fora, each of which provides only half a remedy. It is equally unsurprising, and in fact encouraging, that such problems occur so rarely that Congress has not made any explicit provision for them.

What is surprising is that this Court believes the equitable decision of the Court of Appeals in need of correction. The Court today has taken discretionary jurisdiction over a case of no broad import, and has undone equity by rendering an opinion true to neither the spirit nor the letter of American law. The Court takes its stand upon the grave declaration that a "distinction that has jurisdiction as its central concept is not meaningless." I am not sure what this solemn truism means, but I do know that it does not decide this case.

Because I am unable to discover any just reason for distinguishing this case from *Bull*, I respectfully dissent.

* * *

The Mitigation Provisions. As the *Dalm* Court noted, Congress has provided for exceptions to the statutes of limitation where deference to such rules would produce anomalous results. These exceptions, known collectively as the "mitigation provisions," are found in §§ 1311–1314. As § 1311(a) indicates, there are four prerequisites to get an "adjustment" for a prior, closed year: (1) a "determination" under § 1313; (2) a "circumstance of adjustment" under § 1312; (3) correction of the error must now be barred by law (like the statute of limitations provisions in §§ 6501 (for deficiencies) or 6511 (for refunds)); and (4) a "condition of adjustment" under § 1311(b). If these requirements are met, the necessary adjustment to the closed year can be made pursuant to § 1314.

* * *

Self-Assessment Question

(Solutions to Self–Assessment Questions are set forth in Appendix 3.)

SAQ 6–6. For each of the following fact patterns, determine whether a "circumstance of adjustment" exists under § 1312. Be sure to cite the applicable paragraph of § 1312 that applies.

(a) In Year One, Alice claimed a deduction for a business expense. The Service did not challenge the deduction. In Year Seven, Alice again claimed a deduction for the same expense. The Service challenged her Year Seven return in Year Eight, but Alice prevailed in the Tax Court in a decision made final late in Year Eight.

(b) In Year One, Benny claimed a depreciation deduction for property owned by a trust under which Benny was a beneficiary. The Service did not challenge Benny's Year One deduction. In Year Three, the trustee of the trust filed a timely claim for refund for Year One, arguing that the trust (not Benny) was entitled to the depreciation deduction. When the Service denied the claim, the trustee commenced litigation. In Year Seven, the court sustained the refund claim.

(c) In October, Year One, Charlotte signed an employment contract under which she agreed to perform services in December, Year One, for which she would receive compensation in January, Year Two. Charlotte performed the services on schedule and received payment in Year Two. She included the payment in gross income on her return for Year Two, filed on April 15, Year Three. On September 1, Year Five, the Service issued a notice of deficiency with respect to other items on Charlotte's Year Two return. In her petition to the Tax Court, Charlotte maintained that she was on the accrual method and thus the compensation included in the Year Two return was properly taxable in Year One. The Tax Court issued a final decision in Year Six that sustained Charlotte's argument with respect to the taxation of the compensation received under the employment contract.

(d) Same as (c), except that Charlotte did not include the compensation in the Year Two return. The Service's deficiency notice included the failure to include the compensation in Year Two's gross income. Charlotte paid the entire Year Two deficiency in November, Year Five, and then sued for refund in federal district court, again arguing that the compensation was properly includible in Year One. Charlotte prevailed in a final decision rendered in Year Six.

(e) Same as (d), except that Charlotte did not pay the deficiency; instead, she filed a petition in Tax Court and prevailed in that forum. [Bonus question: assuming there is a "circumstance of adjustment" here, is the Service entitled to an adjustment under § 1314?]

(f) Dwight could have taken a charitable contribution deduction in Year One but, because he was unaware that such a deduction was available, he did not do so. In Year Five, Dwight realized for the first time that his Year One contribution was deductible, so he claimed a deduction in Year Five. The IRS disallowed the Year Five deduction and issued a deficiency notice. The Tax Court's final decision for the IRS was rendered in Year Seven.

(g) Ernestine received ten shares of common stock in *X Corporation* worth $2,000 from her father. Ernestine took the position that the value of the stock was excluded from income under § 102(a). Accordingly, under § 1015(a), she concluded that her basis in the stock was $500, her father's basis. In Year Two, Ernestine gave all of the X shares to Frank, her unrelated lover. (The fact that Frank is unrelated is of no tax significance, but it makes the relationship a lot less questionable.) Frank sold the stock to an unrelated buyer in Year Four for $2,000. On his Year Four return, Frank took the position that his basis in the preferred stock was $2,000 because the Year One transfer to Ernestine was taxable to Ernestine as compensation for services (Ernestine was an employee of her father's business). In a § 7121 closing agreement executed in Year Six, the Service and Frank agree to the $2,000 basis. The Service now wants to re-open Year One for Ernestine and assess a deficiency for her failure to treat the stock transfer as a taxable event.

* * *

Problem 6–11

Lionel Hutz, a cash method tax attorney, performed services for a client in Year One. On December 31, Year One, the client offered to pay Hutz by check. Hutz advised the client to mail the check that afternoon, for that would give the client a deduction for Year One but would postpone Hutz's income inclusion until Year Two. The client followed Hutz's advice, and Hutz received the check in the mail on January 3, Year Two.

Hutz reported the income on his timely filed federal income tax return for Year Two. In December of Year Four, the Service asserted that the income was properly includible in Hutz's gross income for Year One. In January of Year Five, Hutz petitioned the Tax Court for a redetermination of the deficiency. The Tax Court ruled for the Service in a decision that became final on July 15, Year Seven.

It is now September 10, Year Seven. Can Hutz now obtain a refund of the tax erroneously paid in Year Two?

* * *

Chapter 7

FLAVOR

We saw in Chapter 3 that taxpayers with "net capital gains" are entitled to preferential tax rates on such gains, and we learned in Chapter 4 that "capital losses" otherwise deductible under § 165 are subject to an additional limitation: they are deductible only to the extent of "capital gains" plus up to $3,000 in ordinary income. In this Chapter, we consider more carefully what it means to have a "capital gain" and a "capital loss."

Simply enough, a **capital gain** is a recognized gain from the "sale or exchange" of a "capital asset." Likewise, a **capital loss** is a recognized loss from the sale or exchange of a capital asset. In Part A of this Chapter, we parse through the statutory definition of a "capital asset" and get guidance as to how strictly the statutory definition should be construed. In Part B, we consider the "sale or exchange" requirement. Part C then explains exactly how the preferential tax rates for capital gains are derived. In Part D, we discover yet another flavor of gains and losses that applies to certain property held for use in a business activity for more than one year. Part E then discusses depreciation recapture, a concept necessitated by the third flavor of gains and losses at issue in Part D.

A. CAPITAL ASSETS

Code: IRC § 1221(a); 1222; 1223.

Regs: Treas. Reg. §§ 1.1221–1(a)–(d); 1.1223–1(a)–(b).

The definition of a "capital asset" is set forth in § 1221(a). Notice that § 1221(a) is an example of a "negative definition:" it defines capital assets by listing eight types of assets which are *not* capital assets. Anything not described in § 1221(a)(1)-(8) is, therefore, a capital asset.

Is there a common bond among the eight classes of assets listed in § 1221(a)? Yes, in fact there are *two* overarching themes. First, assets that are held to produce ordinary income are generally not capital assets.

485

This includes inventory and other property held for sale to customers, *ORdiNaRy* *income* buildings and equipment used in a business activity, certain intellectual property rights that generate royalties, and supplies consumed in the ordinary course of business. Second, assets where gain results from the *#2* efforts of the taxpayer and not from the mere passage of time are likely not capital assets. Works of art created by the taxpayer appreciate in value mostly because of the taxpayer's efforts in creating the work of art. Likewise, accounts and notes receivable held by a taxpayer typically represent compensation for the taxpayer's services or payment for goods created, distributed, marketed, or sold by the taxpayer. Recall that part of the justification for preferential tax rates on long-term capital gains relates to the belief that one should not be taxed fully on gain that accrued simply from the passage of time. Because the gains from assets listed in § 1221(a) are often attributable to the taxpayer's efforts and not just the passage of time, these assets are rightly excluded from the definition of a capital asset.

Congress does not always adhere to these themes. For example, consider the advantage of being a musical composer instead of a novelist. A novel in the hands of its author is not a capital asset, either because the work is held for sale to customers in the ordinary course of the author's business (rendering the work "inventory" under § 1221(a)(1)) or because of the general rule in § 1221(a)(3) that treats self-created copyrights and literary compositions as ordinary assets. But under § 1221(b)(3), added to the Code by the Tax Increase Prevention and Reconciliation Act of 2006, a musical composition in the hands of its composer can qualify for treatment as a capital asset if the composer so elects. Thus, gain from the sale or exchange of a musical composition can qualify as long-term capital gain eligible for preferential tax rates, while loss from such a sale or exchange can still be treated as ordinary loss. Section 1221(b)(3) apparently intends to eliminate the distinction between songwriters (who would have ordinary income from sales of their works under the general rules in § 1221(a)) and music publishers (who usually hold songs as investments and thus would qualify for capital asset treatment). See Bunning Statement on Senate Passage of the Tax Relief Extension Reconciliation Act (May 11, 2006). In curing one disparity, however, § 1221(b)(3) seemingly creates another—that between composers and novelists. There does not appear to be a compelling reason to limit the benefit of the § 1221(b)(3) election to musical composers, but then again there may not be a compelling reason to confer the benefit in the first place. The gain to the composer effectively represents gain from labor that is normally taxed as ordinary income, while the gain to an investor comes not from labor but from the mere passage of time.

* * *

Self-Assessment Question

(Solutions to Self–Assessment Questions are set forth in Appendix 3.)

SAQ 7–1. Which of the following are capital assets?

(a) Machine used in a trade or business activity

(b) Accounts receivable

(c) Cash

(d) Patent

(e) Personal residence

(f) Artwork purchased from an unrelated party

(g) Artwork created by the taxpayer

(h) Artwork received from a related party as a gift

* * *

Section 1221(a)(1) lists three assets that do not qualify as capital assets: (1) stock in trade; (2) inventory property; and (3) property held primarily for sale to customers in the ordinary course of business. "Stock in trade" refers to the raw materials a taxpayer uses to manufacture or produce his or her inventory property. Of these three items, the last one has given the Service and the courts the most problems. Whether property is held "primarily for sale to customers" or primarily for investment purposes is a fact-intensive inquiry that invites dispute and, ultimately, litigation.

Most often, this dispute is raised with respect to real estate. A taxpayer selling a parcel of land for a gain might argue that the land was held for investment purposes and thus the resulting gain should be treated as a capital gain. The Service might counter that the taxpayer's efforts in developing and selling the parcel suggest that the property was held primarily for sale and not for investment. The following case illustrates how courts handle these disputes.

BYRAM v. UNITED STATES

United States Court of Appeals, Fifth Circuit, 1983.
705 F.2d 1418.

GEE, CIRCUIT JUDGE.

"If a client asks you in any but an extreme case whether, in your opinion, his sale will result in capital gain, your answer should probably be, 'I don't know, and no one else in town can tell you.'"

Sadly, the above wry comment on federal taxation of real estate transfers has, in the twenty-five years or so since it was penned, passed from the status of half-serious aside to that of hackneyed truism. Hackneyed or not, it is the primary attribute of truisms to be true, and this one is: in that field of the law—real property tenure—where the stability of rule and precedent has been exalted above all others, it seems ironic that one of its attributes, the tax incident upon disposition of such property, should be one of the most uncertain in the entire field of litigation. But so it is, and we are called on again today to decide a close case in which almost a million dollars in claimed refunds are at stake.
* * *

FACTS

* * *

During 1973, John D. Byram, the taxpayer, sold seven pieces of real property. Mr. Byram was not a licensed real estate broker, was not associated with a real estate company which advertised itself, and did not maintain a separate real estate office. He advertised none of the seven properties for sale, nor did he list any of them with real estate brokers. To the contrary, all of the transactions were initiated either by the purchaser or by someone acting in the purchaser's behalf.

None of the properties sold was platted or subdivided. Byram devoted minimal time and effort to the sales in question, occupying himself chiefly with his rental properties. Byram's income for 1972 and 1973 included substantial amounts of rental income and interest income.

The district court's findings do not reflect the following additional facts, which apparently are not disputed by the parties. From 1971 through 1973, Byram sold 22 parcels of real property for a total gross return of over $9 million and a net profit of approximately $3.4 million. The seven properties at issue in this case sold for approximately $6.6 million gross, resulting in a profit of approximately $2.5 million. Six of the seven properties were held by Byram for periods ranging from six to nine months, intervals just exceeding the then-applicable holding periods for long-term capital gains. The seventh property had been held for two years and six months.

Although, as noted above, Mr. Byram received substantial rent and interest income in 1973, nevertheless his rental activities for that year resulted in a net tax loss of approximately $186,000. He received rental income from only one of the seven properties sold in 1973. The record does not reflect the exact relative amounts of income attributable to the sales in question and Byram's other activities.

Certain facts are disputed by the parties. The government asserts in its brief that Byram had entered into contracts to sell at least three of the seven properties in issue before he actually acquired them. Byram first responds that the record reflects only two such instances, not three; and at oral argument the government appeared to concede the point. As to those two transactions, Byram asserts that he acquired the right to purchase the properties by executing a contract before he entered into a contract to sell them; it was only closing on the purchases that postdated his contracts to sell. Finally, the government asserts, and Byram denies, that by virtue of Byram's civic activities in Austin, Texas, Byram's business of selling real estate was well-known in the community.

Based on its subsidiary findings indicated, the district court made ultimate findings that Byram held each of the seven properties for investment purposes and not primarily for sale to customers in the ordinary course of his trade or business. Judgment was therefore entered granting Byram the capital gains treatment that he sought. The government brought this appeal.

I.

Profits derived from the sale of "capital assets," known as "capital gains," are entitled to favorable tax treatment under the Internal Revenue Code (the "Code"). * * * The term "capital asset" is defined in relevant part as "property held by the taxpayer," not including property held "primarily for sale to customers in the ordinary course of [the taxpayer's] trade or business." The district court found that Byram "was not engaged in the real estate business" during the relevant years and that each of the seven properties in issue was held "for investment purposes and not primarily for sale to customers in the ordinary course of [Byram's] trade or business." Accordingly, the district court held that Byram was entitled to treat the profits from his 1973 sales as capital gains and ordered an appropriate refund. Our first task is to decide the correct standard by which to review the district court's principal finding[3] that Byram's holding purpose was for investment rather than for sale. The choice of a standard will determine the outcome of many cases; if the issue is treated as factual, the district court's decision is final unless clearly erroneous but if a question of law is presented, we may decide it *de novo*.

The question whether the characterization of property as "primarily held for sale to customers in the ordinary course of [a taxpayer's] trade or business" is an issue of fact or one of law has engendered tremendous controversy and conflict both in this and in other circuits. Recognizing the conflict in our own cases, a panel recently attempted to resolve it by breaking the statutory test down into its component parts, *see* note 3, *supra*, some of which we held "are predominantly legal conclusions or are 'mixed questions of fact and law,' whereas others are essentially questions of fact." *Suburban Realty*, 615 F.2d at 180 (footnote omitted). As we shall see, it must now be admitted that, because we were forced to struggle with this circuit's long-standing distinction between "subsidiary facts" and "ultimate facts," this attempt to clarify the law was not entirely successful.

3. In *Suburban Realty Co. v. United States*, 615 F.2d 171 (5th Cir.), *cert. denied*, 449 U.S. 920, 101 S. Ct. 318, 66 L. Ed. 2d 147 (1980), we recognized that the Code definition of "capital asset" gives rise to at least three inquiries:

(1) was taxpayer engaged in a trade or business, and, if so, what business?

(2) was taxpayer holding the property primarily for sale in that business?

(3) were the sales contemplated by taxpayer "ordinary" in the course of that business?

Id. at 178 (footnote omitted).

In many situations, these questions are analytically independent. For example, it will oftentimes be beyond dispute that a taxpayer is engaged in the real estate business with respect to certain properties, yet other properties may not be held primarily for sale in that business, or *particular sales* may be outside its ordinary scope. *See, e.g., Wood v. Commissioner*, 276 F.2d 586 (5th Cir.1960); *Maddux Construction Co. v. Commissioner*, 54 T.C. 1278 (1970). However, in the present case the three statutory questions tend to merge into one, because the existence of a business, Byram's holding purpose, and the "ordinariness" of sales must all be determined by characterization of the same transactions. Moreover, because we decide below that Byram's holding purpose must be treated as an issue of fact, and that the district court's finding is not clearly erroneous, the holding below must be left undisturbed and we need not address related questions arguably posed by the statute.

The ultimate fact doctrine, first embraced by our court in *Galena Oaks Corp. v. Scofield*, 218 F.2d 217 (5th Cir.1954), posits that review of ultimate facts is not constrained by the clearly erroneous rule since though factual in nature, these issues are also the ultimate ones for resolution in a case and must be determined by a process of legal reasoning from subsidiary facts. Accordingly, in *Suburban Realty* we observed that a taxpayer's holding purpose is "primarily factual," but that it is not a "pure" question of fact. Though we stated that a lower court's finding of holding purpose must be followed unless clearly erroneous, we also maintained that our review of the "ultimate conclusion" in such cases is plenary. Thus, although *Suburban Realty* purported to clarify our role in capital gains cases, the actual dynamics of appellate review remained unclear.

Fortunately, it is unnecessary once again to traverse the conceptual thicket of ultimate and subsidiary facts so carefully husbanded by this court through the years. The Supreme Court has leveled it. *Pullman-Standard v. Swint*, 456 U.S. 273, 102 S. Ct. 1781, 72 L. Ed. 2d 66 (1982).

In *Swint*, the Court reviewed a decision of this court holding that by setting up and perpetuating a particular seniority system, an employer and two unions had discriminated against black employees in violation of Title VII of the Civil Rights Act. In order to establish discrimination in the operation of a seniority system, it is necessary to prove discriminatory intent. Analyzing the issue in the manner suggested by this court, the district court found that the seniority system did not result from an intention to discriminate. Treating the issue of discriminatory purpose as one of ultimate fact, this court independently reviewed the record and made its own finding of discrimination.

Reversing that decision and rejecting our authorities on which it rested, the Supreme Court held that our accepted rule allowing *de novo* review of ultimate facts is incompatible with the dictates of Rule 52, Federal Rules of Civil Procedure. The Court emphasized that Rule 52 "broadly requires" that findings of fact be accepted unless clearly erroneous, and that it does not divide findings of fact into categories.

The Court recognized the "vexing nature of the distinction between questions of fact and questions of law," and noted that Rule 52 provides little guidance in drawing the line. Indeed, the ultimate fact doctrine itself probably can be understood best as an abortive attempt to resolve the law/fact dilemma by making that elusive distinction less determinative. Elusive or not, *Swint* tells us that it is a distinction Rule 52 requires us to draw.

Though the characterization of issues as ones of law or fact may be difficult in some cases, the present case is not one of them. The issue of holding purpose under the Code, like the issue of discriminatory purpose under Title VII, is a pure question of fact. That this is so was made clear by the Court in *Swint*:

> Treating issues of intent as factual matters for the trier of fact is common-place. In *Dayton Board of Education v. Brinkman*, 443 U.S.

526, 534, 61 L.Ed.2d 720, 99 S.Ct. 2971 [2977] (1979), the principal question was whether the defendants had intentionally maintained a racially segregated school system at a specified time in the past. We recognized that issue as essentially factual, subject to the clearly erroneous rule. In *Comm'r v. Duberstein*, 363 U.S. 278, 4 L.Ed.2d 1218, 80 S.Ct. 1190 (1960), the Court held that the principal criterion for identifying a gift under the applicable provision of the Internal Revenue Code was the intent or motive of the donor—"one that inquires what the basic reason for his conduct was in fact." Resolution of that issue determined the ultimate issue of whether a gift had been made. Both issues were held to be questions of fact subject to the clearly erroneous rule. In *United States v. Yellow Cab*, 338 U.S. 338, 341, 94 L.Ed. 150, 70 S.Ct. 177 [179] (1949), an antitrust case, the Court referred to "findings as to the design, motive and intent with which men act" as peculiarly factual issues for the trier of fact and therefore subject to appellate review under Rule 52.

Swint, 456 U.S. at 287–288, 102 S.Ct. at 1789–1790, 72 L.Ed.2d at 79–80.

The purpose for holding property, like the purpose for maintaining a seniority system at issue in *Swint*, is a question of intent and motive.[9] As such, it is a question of pure fact, and is neither a question of law nor a mixed question of law and fact. The factors usually cited to justify plenary review of holding purpose are the same factors that the Court found unpersuasive in determining the proper standard of review in *Swint*. For example, both issues involve a consideration of all facts and circumstances, with emphasis on particular significant factors. * * * Similarly, both issues require the district court to use a reasoning process in analyzing the facts and to apply certain legal standards in making its finding. Resolution of either issue can determine the outcome of a case. None of those considerations affected the *Swint* Court's conclusion that the issue of discriminatory intent is neither a question of law nor a mixed question of law and fact, but is a pure question of fact. We see no reason to subject a district court's determination of holding purpose to a different standard of review than that applied to a district court's finding of discriminatory intent. The district court's finding in the present case that Byram held his property for investment rather than for sale to customers in the ordinary course of his business must be accepted unless it is clearly erroneous.

The record and the district court's findings of fact indicate that in determining Byram's holding purpose, the court considered all the

---

9. We have uniformly held that the statutory exception for property "held" for sale to customers requires an inquiry into a taxpayer's intent. *See, e.g., Suburban Realty*, 615 F.2d at 182–85; *Biedenharn Realty Co. v. United States*, 526 F.2d 409, 422–23 (5th Cir.) (en banc), *cert. denied*, 429 U.S. 819, 97 S.Ct. 64, 50 L.Ed.2d 79 (1976). Moreover, the fact that the taxpayer's subjective state of mind is not controlling and an objective inquiry must be made by the court does not render the issue any less one of intent or any less factual. *See Commissioner v. Duberstein*, 363 U.S. 278, 286, 290–91, 80 S.Ct. 1190, 1199, 4 L.Ed.2d 1218, 1225, 1228 (1960).

factors this court has called "the seven pillars of capital gains treatment":[10]

> (1) the nature and purpose of the acquisition of the property and the duration of the ownership; (2) the extent and nature of the taxpayer's efforts to sell the property; (3) the number, extent, continuity and substantiality of the sales; (4) the extent of subdividing, developing, and advertising to increase sales; (5) the use of a business office for the sale of the property; (6) the character and degree of supervision or control exercised by the taxpayer over any representative selling the property; and (7) the time and effort the taxpayer habitually devoted to the sales.

United States v. Winthrop, 417 F.2d 905, 910 (5th Cir.1969). Recent cases have placed particular emphasis on four of these factors, noting that frequency and substantiality of sales is the most important factor, and that improvements to the property, solicitation and advertising efforts, and brokerage activities are also especially relevant considerations. *Biedenharn Realty*, 526 F.2d at 415–16; *Suburban Realty*, 615 F.2d at 176. At the same time, it has been repeatedly emphasized that these factors should not be treated as talismans. Rather, "each case must be decided on its own peculiar facts.... Specific factors, or combinations of them, are not necessarily controlling." *Biedenharn Realty*, 526 F.2d at 415 (quoting *Thompson v. Commissioner*, 322 F.2d 122, 127 (5th Cir.1963)).

The district court found most of the *Winthrop* factors absent in Byram's case. Byram made no personal effort to initiate the sales; buyers came to him. He did not advertise, he did not have a sales office, nor did he enlist the aid of brokers. The properties at issue were not improved or developed by him. The district court found that Byram devoted minimal time and effort to the transactions.[11] The government does not contend that any of these findings are clearly erroneous. Rather, the government argues that the frequency and substantiality of Byram's sales, together with the relatively short duration of his ownership of most of the

---

10. In application, these "pillars" have come more nearly to resemble the walls of a maze. *See, e.g., Suburban Realty*, 615 F.2d 171; *Biedenharn Realty*, 526 F.2d 409.

11. This factor has been slighted in recent cases, not because it is unimportant, but because it was irrelevant to our consideration of the activities of large corporate organizations. *See e.g. Suburban Realty*, 615 F.2d 171; *Houston Endowment*, 606 F.2d 77; *Biedenharn Realty*, 526 F.2d 409. However, in a case like the present one, where the government seeks to show that an individual taxpayer is holding property for sale in a certain business, the quantum of that individual's activity becomes very relevant. Long before the proliferation of tests and factors engulfed the capital gains field, this court made the common sense observation that the word "business" means "busyness; it implies that one is kept more or less busy, that the activity is an occupation." *Snell v. Commissioner*, 97 F.2d 891, 892, 21 A.F.T.R. (P–H) 608 (5th Cir.1938); *see also Stern v. United States*, 164 F. Supp. 847, 851 (E.D.La.1958) ("[A] court should not be quick to put a man in business ... simply because he has been successful in earning extra income through a hobby or some other endeavor which takes relatively small part of his time.") *aff'd* 262 F.2d 957 (5th Cir.), *cert. denied*, 359 U.S. 969, 79 S. Ct. 880, 3 L. Ed. 2d 836 (1959). The district court was entitled to give great weight to Byram's time and effort devoted to sales in determining whether he held his property for sale in the ordinary course of his business.

properties, establishes that Byram intended to hold the properties for sale in the ordinary course of his business. In light of our decision regarding the standard of review, the government's argument must be that the district court clearly erred in finding these factors outweighed by the other relevant evidence. We cannot reasonably say that the district court's finding that Byram held his properties for investment was clearly erroneous.

The record reveals that during a three-year period, Byram sold 22 parcels of real estate for over $9 million, netting approximately $3.4 million profit. Though these amounts are substantial by anyone's yard-stick, the district court did not clearly err in determining that 22 such sales in three years were not sufficiently frequent or continuous to compel an inference of intent to hold the property for sale rather than investment. Compare *Suburban Realty*, 615 F.2d at 174 (244 sales over 32–year period); *Biedenharn Realty*, 526 F.2d at 411–12 (during 31–year period, taxpayer sold 208 lots and twelve individual parcels from subdivision in question; 477 lots were sold from other properties). This is particularly true in a case where the other relevant factors weigh so heavily in favor of the taxpayer. "Substantial and frequent sales activity, standing alone, has never been held to be automatically sufficient to trigger ordinary income treatment." *Suburban Realty*, 615 F.2d at 176. Moreover, Byram's relatively short holding periods for some of the properties do not tip the balance in favor of the government. Ranging from six to nine months, these periods exceeded the then-applicable threshold for long-term capital gain treatment. In establishing those thresholds, Congress clearly expressed its intent that sales of otherwise qualified capital assets held for six to nine months be accorded capital gains treatment. To avoid frustration of that intent, a court should avoid placing too much weight on duration of ownership where other indicia of intent to hold the property for sale are minimal.

Mr. Byram has presented us with a close case. Had we been called upon to try or retry the facts, perhaps we would have drawn different inferences than did the district court. However, *Swint* has relieved us of that duty. Our review of the evidence convinces us that the district court was not clearly erroneous in finding that Byram held his properties for investment and not for sale in the ordinary course of his trade or business.

* * *

The judgment of the district court is

AFFIRMED.

* * *

Problem 7–1

Margaret Hancock and her husband, J.W., operated Hancock Enterprises, a business that purchased large tracts of land that were then subdivided, rezoned, and improved. Single-family homes were constructed on most of the lots and then sold to customers. The business began in Year One, and enjoyed considerable success until Year Sixteen, when the local housing market slumped and J.W. died.

At the time of J.W.'s death, the business had 48 parcels of real property that had been acquired in Year Ten. Margaret continued her efforts at selling these lots, but she ceased any development activities on these properties. Because of poor market conditions, she reported tax losses from the sale of the lots for several years, as shown below:

Year	Lots Sold	Total Gain (Loss)
Seventeen	7	($231,000)
Eighteen	0	
Nineteen	2	($133,000)
Twenty	3	($166,000)
Twenty-one	13	($248,000)
Twenty-two	11	($300,000)
Twenty-three	4	($208,000)
Twenty-four	4	($167,000)
Twenty-five	2	($125,000)
Twenty-six	1	($ 48,000)

During these years, Margaret paid all expenses related to the lots, including property taxes and insurance costs. She occasionally met with prospective buyers, hung "for sale" signs on several properties, and attended various homebuilders' meetings to solicit potential buyers. Margaret sometimes listed various lots with local real estate agents, but did not do so in Years Twenty-two through Twenty-four.

Margaret reported all of the losses listed above as ordinary losses. The Service challenged her claimed losses for Year Twenty-three and Year Twenty-four, concluding that the eight lots were capital assets in Margaret's hands. Margaret contested the resulting deficiency by filing a petition in the United States Tax Court. How should the court rule in this case?

* * *

Should § 1221(a) be construed strictly? In other words, are the assets listed in § 1221(a) the *only* assets excluded from capital asset status? Or should any asset that fits within the general themes of § 1221(a) be excluded as well? The Supreme Court answered these questions in the following case. As you will see, the answer came as something of a surprise to those who thought the Court had answered otherwise in a prior case.

ARKANSAS BEST CORPORATION
v. COMMISSIONER

United States Supreme Court, 1988.
485 U.S. 212, 108 S.Ct. 971, 99 L.Ed.2d 183.

JUSTICE MARSHALL delivered the opinion of the Court.

The issue presented in this case is whether capital stock held by petitioner Arkansas Best Corporation (Arkansas Best) is a "capital asset" as defined in § 1221 of the Internal Revenue Code regardless of whether the stock was purchased and held for a business purpose or for an investment purpose.

I

Arkansas Best is a diversified holding company. In 1968 it acquired approximately 65% of the stock of the National Bank of Commerce (Bank) in Dallas, Texas. Between 1969 and 1974, Arkansas Best more than tripled the number of shares it owned in the Bank, although its percentage interest in the Bank remained relatively stable. These acquisitions were prompted principally by the Bank's need for added capital. Until 1972, the Bank appeared to be prosperous and growing, and the added capital was necessary to accommodate this growth. As the Dallas real estate market declined, however, so too did the financial health of the Bank, which had a heavy concentration of loans in the local real estate industry. In 1972, federal examiners classified the Bank as a problem bank. The infusion of capital after 1972 was prompted by the loan portfolio problems of the bank.

Petitioner sold the bulk of its Bank stock on June 30, 1975, leaving it with only a 14.7% stake in the Bank. On its federal income tax return for 1975, petitioner claimed a deduction for an ordinary loss of $9,995,688 resulting from the sale of the stock. The Commissioner of Internal Revenue disallowed the deduction, finding that the loss from the sale of stock was a capital loss, rather than an ordinary loss, and that it therefore was subject to the capital loss limitations in the Internal Revenue Code.

Arkansas Best challenged the Commissioner's determination in the United States Tax Court. The Tax Court, relying on cases interpreting *Corn Products Refining Co. v. Commissioner*, 350 U.S. 46, 76 S.Ct. 20, 100 L.Ed. 29 (1955), held that stock purchased with a substantial investment purpose is a capital asset which, when sold, gives rise to a capital gain or loss, whereas stock purchased and held for a business purpose, without any substantial investment motive, is an ordinary asset whose sale gives rise to ordinary gains or losses. The court characterized Arkansas Best's acquisitions through 1972 as occurring during the Bank's " 'growth' phase," and found that these acquisitions "were motivated primarily by investment purpose and only incidentally by some business purpose." The stock acquired during this period therefore constituted a capital asset, which gave rise to a capital loss when sold in 1975. The court determined, however, that the acquisitions after 1972 occurred during the Bank's " 'problem' phase," and, except for certain minor exceptions, "were made exclusively for business purposes and subsequently held for the same reasons." These acquisitions, the court found, were designed to preserve petitioner's business reputation, because without the added capital the Bank probably would have failed. The loss realized on the sale of this stock was thus held to be an ordinary loss.

The Court of Appeals for the Eighth Circuit reversed the Tax Court's determination that the loss realized on stock purchased after 1972 was subject to ordinary-loss treatment, holding that all of the Bank stock sold in 1975 was subject to capital-loss treatment. The court reasoned that the Bank stock clearly fell within the general definition of "capital asset" in Internal Revenue Code § 1221, and that the stock did not fall within any of the specific statutory exceptions to this definition. The court concluded that Arkansas Best's purpose in acquiring and holding the stock was irrelevant to the determination whether the stock was a capital asset. We granted certiorari and now affirm.

II

Section 1221 of the Internal Revenue Code defines "capital asset" broadly as "property held by the taxpayer (whether or not connected with his trade or business)," and then excludes * * * specific classes of property from capital-asset status. * * * Arkansas Best acknowledges that the Bank stock falls within the literal definition of "capital asset" in § 1221, and is outside of the statutory exclusions. It asserts, however, that this determination does not end the inquiry. Petitioner argues that in *Corn Products Refining Co. v. Commissioner, supra,* this Court rejected a literal reading of § 1221, and concluded that assets acquired and sold for ordinary business purposes rather than for investment purposes should be given ordinary-asset treatment. Petitioner's reading of *Corn Products* finds much support in the academic literature and in the courts. Unfortunately for petitioner, this broad reading finds no support in the language of § 1221.

In essence, petitioner argues that "property held by the taxpayer (whether or not connected with his trade or business)" does not include property that is acquired and held for a business purpose. In petitioner's view an asset's status as "property" thus turns on the motivation behind its acquisition. This motive test, however, is not only nowhere mentioned in § 1221, but it is also in direct conflict with the parenthetical phrase "whether or not connected with his trade or business." The broad definition of the term "capital asset" explicitly makes irrelevant any consideration of the property's connection with the taxpayer's business, whereas petitioner's rule would make this factor dispositive.[5]

---

5. Petitioner mistakenly relies on cases in which this Court, in narrowly applying the general definition of "capital asset," has "construed 'capital asset' to exclude property representing income items or accretions to the value of a capital asset themselves properly attributable to income," even though these items are property in the broad sense of the word. *United States v. Midland–Ross Corp.,* 381 U.S. 54, 57, 85 S.Ct. 1308, 1310, 14 L.Ed.2d 214 (1965). See, *e.g., Commissioner v. Gillette Motor Co.,* 364 U.S. 130, 80 S.Ct. 1497, 4 L.Ed.2d 1617 (1960) ("capital asset" does not include compensation awarded taxpayer that represented fair rental value of its facilities); *Commissioner v. P.G. Lake, Inc.,* 356 U.S. 260, 78 S.Ct. 691, 2 L.Ed.2d 243 (1958) ("capital asset" does not include proceeds from sale of oil payment rights); *Hort v. Commissioner,* 313 U.S. 28, 61 S.Ct. 757, 85 L.Ed. 1168 (1941) ("capital asset" does not include payment to lessor for cancellation of unexpired portion of a lease). This line of cases, based on the premise that § 1221 "property" does not include claims or rights to ordinary income, has no application in the present context. Petitioner sold capital stock, not a claim to ordinary income.

In a related argument, petitioner contends that the * * * exceptions listed in § 1221 for certain kinds of property are illustrative, rather than exhaustive, and that courts are therefore free to fashion additional exceptions in order to further the general purposes of the capital-asset provisions. The language of the statute refutes petitioner's construction. Section 1221 provides that "capital asset" means "property held by the taxpayer[,] . . . but does not include" the * * * classes of property listed as exceptions. We believe this locution signifies that the listed exceptions are exclusive. The body of § 1221 establishes a general definition of the term "capital asset," and the phrase "does not include" takes out of that broad definition only the classes of property that are specifically mentioned. The legislative history of the capital-asset definition supports this interpretation, see H.R.Rep. No. 704, 73d Cong., 2d Sess., 31 (1934) ("[T]he definition includes all property, except as specifically excluded"); H.R.Rep. No. 1337, 83d Cong., 2d Sess., A273 (1954), U.S. Code Cong. & Admin. News 1954, pp. 4017, 4415 ("[A] capital asset is property held by the taxpayer with certain exceptions"), as does the applicable Treasury regulation, see 26 CFR § 1.1221–1(a) (1987) ("The term 'capital assets' includes all classes of property not specifically excluded by section 1221").

Petitioner's reading of the statute is also in tension with the exceptions listed in § 1221. These exclusions would be largely superfluous if assets acquired primarily or exclusively for business purposes were not capital assets. Inventory, real or depreciable property used in the taxpayer's trade or business, and accounts or notes receivable acquired in the ordinary course of business, would undoubtedly satisfy such a business-motive test. Yet these exceptions were created by Congress in separate enactments spanning 30 years. Without any express direction from Congress, we are unwilling to read § 1221 in a manner that makes surplusage of these statutory exclusions.

In the end, petitioner places all reliance on its reading of *Corn Products Refining Co. v. Commissioner*—a reading we believe is too expansive. In *Corn Products,* the Court considered whether income arising from a taxpayer's dealings in corn futures was entitled to capital-gains treatment. The taxpayer was a company that converted corn into starches, sugars, and other products. After droughts in the 1930's caused sharp increases in corn prices, the company began a program of buying corn futures to assure itself an adequate supply of corn and protect against price increases. The company "would take delivery on such contracts as it found necessary to its manufacturing operations and sell the remainder in early summer if no shortage was imminent. If shortages appeared, however, it sold futures only as it bought spot corn for grinding." The Court characterized the company's dealing in corn futures as "hedging." As explained by the Court of Appeals in *Corn Products,* "[h]edging is a method of dealing in commodity futures whereby a person or business protects itself against price fluctuations at the time of delivery of the product which it sells or buys." In evaluating the company's claim that the sales of corn futures resulted in capital gains and losses, this Court stated:

> "Nor can we find support for petitioner's contention that hedging is not within the exclusions of [§ 1221]. Admittedly, petitioner's corn futures do not come within the literal language of the exclusions set out in that section. They were not stock in trade, actual inventory, property held for sale to customers or depreciable property used in a trade or business. But the capital-asset provision of [§ 1221] must not be so broadly applied as to defeat rather than further the purpose of Congress. Congress intended that profits and losses arising from the everyday operation of a business be considered as ordinary income or loss rather than capital gain or loss. Since this section is an exception from the normal tax requirements of the Internal Revenue Code, the definition of a capital asset must be narrowly applied and its exclusions interpreted broadly." 350 U.S., at 51–52, 76 S.Ct., at 23–24 (citations omitted).

The Court went on to note that hedging transactions consistently had been considered to give rise to ordinary gains and losses, and then concluded that the corn futures were subject to ordinary-asset treatment.

The Court in *Corn Products* proffered the oft-quoted rule of construction that the definition of "capital asset" must be narrowly applied and its exclusions interpreted broadly, but it did not state explicitly whether the holding was based on a narrow reading of the phrase "property held by the taxpayer," or on a broad reading of the inventory exclusion of § 1221. In light of the stark language of § 1221, however, we believe that *Corn Products* is properly interpreted as involving an application of § 1221's inventory exception. Such a reading is consistent both with the Court's reasoning in that case and with § 1221. The Court stated in *Corn Products* that the company's futures transactions were "an integral part of its business designed to protect its manufacturing operations against a price increase in its principal raw material and to assure a ready supply for future manufacturing requirements." The company bought, sold, and took delivery under the futures contracts as required by the company's manufacturing needs. As Professor Bittker notes, under these circumstances, the futures can "easily be viewed as surrogates for the raw material itself." The Court of Appeals for the Second Circuit in *Corn Products* clearly took this approach. That court stated that when commodity futures are "utilized solely for the purpose of stabilizing inventory cost[,] ... [they] cannot reasonably be separated from the inventory items," and concluded that "property used in hedging transactions properly comes within the exclusions of [§ 1221]." This Court indicated its acceptance of the Second Circuit's reasoning when it began the central paragraph of its opinion: "Nor can we find support for petitioner's contention that hedging is not within the exclusions of [§ 1221]." In the following paragraph, the Court argued that the Treasury had consistently viewed such hedging transactions as a form of insurance to stabilize the cost of inventory, and cited a Treasury ruling which concluded that the value of a manufacturer's raw-material inventory should be adjusted to take into account hedging transactions in futures contracts. This discussion, read in light of the Second Circuit's holding and the plain language of § 1221, convinces us that although the corn futures were not "actual inventory," their use as an integral part of the taxpayer's inventory-purchase system led the Court to treat them as substitutes for the corn inventory such that they came within a broad reading of "property of a kind which would properly be included in the inventory of the taxpayer" in § 1221.

Petitioner argues that by focusing attention on whether the asset was acquired and sold as an integral part of the taxpayer's everyday business operations, the Court in *Corn Products* intended to create a general exemption from capital-asset status for assets acquired for business purposes. We believe petitioner misunderstands the relevance of the Court's inquiry. A business connection, although irrelevant to the initial determination whether an item is a capital asset, is relevant in determining the applicability of certain of the statutory exceptions, including the inventory exception. The close connection between the futures transactions and the taxpayer's business in *Corn Products* was crucial to whether the corn futures could be considered surrogates for the stored inventory of raw corn. For if the futures dealings were not part of the company's inventory-purchase system, and instead amounted simply to speculation in corn futures, they could not be considered substitutes for the company's corn inventory, and would fall outside even a broad reading of the inventory exclusion. We conclude that *Corn Products* is properly interpreted as standing for the narrow proposition that hedging transactions that are an integral part of a business' inventory-purchase system fall within the inventory exclusion of § 1221. Arkansas Best, which is not a dealer in securities, has never suggested that the Bank stock falls within the inventory exclusion. *Corn Products* thus has no application to this case.

It is also important to note that the business-motive test advocated by petitioner is subject to the same kind of abuse that the Court condemned in *Corn Products*. The Court explained in *Corn Products* that unless hedging transactions were subject to ordinary gain and loss treatment, taxpayers engaged in such transactions could "transmute ordinary income into capital gain at will." 350 U.S., at 53–54, 76 S.Ct., at 24–25. The hedger could garner capital-asset treatment by selling the future and purchasing the commodity on the spot market, or ordinary-asset treatment by taking delivery under the future contract. In a similar vein, if capital stock purchased and held for a business purpose is an ordinary asset, whereas the same stock purchased and held with an investment motive is a capital asset, a taxpayer such as Arkansas Best could have significant influence over whether the asset would receive capital or ordinary treatment. Because stock is most naturally viewed as a capital asset, the Internal Revenue Service would be hard pressed to challenge a taxpayer's claim that stock was acquired as an investment, and that a gain arising from the sale of such stock was therefore a capital gain. Indeed, we are unaware of a single decision that has applied the business-motive test so as to require a taxpayer to report a gain from the sale of stock as an ordinary gain. If the same stock is sold at a loss, however, the taxpayer may be able to garner ordinary-loss treatment by emphasizing the business purpose behind the stock's acquisition. The potential for such abuse was evidenced in this case by the fact that as late as 1974, when Arkansas Best still hoped to sell the Bank stock at a profit, Arkansas Best apparently expected to report the gain as a capital gain.

III

We conclude that a taxpayer's motivation in purchasing an asset is irrelevant to the question whether the asset is "property held by a taxpayer (whether or not connected with his business)" and is thus within § 1221's general definition of "capital asset." Because the capital stock held by petitioner falls within the broad definition of the term "capital asset" in § 1221 and is outside the classes of property excluded from capital-asset status, the loss arising from the sale of the stock is a capital loss. *Corn Products Refining Co. v. Commissioner, supra,* which we interpret as involving a broad reading of the inventory exclusion of § 1221, has no application in the present context. Accordingly, the judgment of the Court of Appeals is affirmed.

It is so ordered.

JUSTICE KENNEDY took no part in the consideration or decision of this case.

DAVIS v. COMMISSIONER

United States Tax Court, 2002.
119 T.C. 1.

CHIECHI, JUDGE: * * *

We must determine whether the amount that petitioners received in exchange for the assignment of their right to receive a portion of certain future annual lottery payments is ordinary income or capital gain. We hold that that amount is ordinary income.

BACKGROUND

* * *

On July 10, 1991, petitioner James F. Davis (Mr. Davis) won $13,580,000 in the California State Lottery's On–Line LOTTO game (lottery). Pursuant to certain rules and regulations governing the California State Lottery (CSL) in effect during 1991, Mr. Davis became entitled upon winning the lottery to receive the $13,580,000 in 20 equal annual payments of $679,000 (annual lottery payments), less certain tax withholding. At the time that Mr. Davis won the lottery, CSL did not offer to any lottery winner the option to elect to receive a single lump-sum payment of the lottery prize.

On December 13, 1991, CSL sent Mr. Davis a letter which stated, inter alia:

> This letter certifies that on July 10, 1991 you won $13,580,000 [sic] the California State Lottery's OnLine LOTTO game. You have already received your first payment of $679,000, less 20% for Federal tax withholding. In addition, you will receive nineteen (19) subsequent annual payments of $679,000 each, as near as possible to the anniversary of the day on which you won your prize, $13,580,000. Please maintain this letter for your permanent record. In accordance with Internal Revenue Service regulations, all payments are subject to appropriate Federal tax withholdings. Deductions authorized by California statutes, if such are appropriate, will also be made.

> Your rights under this agreement cannot be assigned, but all remaining rights do become a part of your estate. This document is not negotiable.

On June 16, 1997, at a time when petitioners were entitled to receive 14 future annual lottery payments of $679,000 (less certain tax withholding) during the years 1997 through 2010, petitioners and Singer Asset Finance Company, LLC (Singer), entered into an agreement pursuant to which, in exchange for a lump-sum payment to petitioners by Singer of $1,040,000, petitioners assigned to Singer their right to receive a portion (i.e., $165,000 less certain tax withholding) of each of 11 of the future annual lottery payments that they were entitled to receive during the years 1997 through 2007. (We shall refer to the foregoing assignment as petitioners' assignment.) Petitioners thus assigned to Singer the portions of those future annual lottery payments at a discount of $775,000 (i.e., $1,815,000 (total of 11 future annual payments of $165,000) less $1,040,000 (total of the amount that Singer paid to petitioners)). After petitioners' assignment, petitioners were entitled to receive from CSL for each of the years 1997 through 2007 only $514,000 (less certain tax withholding) of each of the $679,000 future annual lottery payments (less certain tax withholding) to which they had been entitled prior to that assignment. After that assignment, CSL was to pay the balance of each of those future annual lottery payments (i.e., $165,000 (less certain tax withholding)) to Singer.

At all relevant times, the laws of the State of California precluded a lottery winner from assigning such person's right to receive future annual lottery payments without obtaining California Superior Court approval. * * * On August 1, 1997, Sacramento County Superior Court issued an order approving petitioners' assignment.

Singer issued to petitioners Form 1099–B, Proceeds From Broker and Barter Exchange Transactions (Form 1099–B), for 1997. That Form 1099–B showed gross proceeds from the sale of "Stocks, bonds, etc." in the amount of $1,040,000.

CSL issued to petitioners Form W–2G, Certain Gambling Winnings (Form W–2G), for 1997. That Form W–2G showed "Gross winnings" from "STATE LOTTERY" of $514,000 and tax withheld of $143,920.

On March 13, 1998, petitioners signed Form 1040, U.S. Individual Income Tax Return, for their taxable year 1997 (petitioners' 1997 joint return). In petitioners' 1997 joint return, they reported petitioners' assignment as a sale of a capital asset held for more than 1 year, a sale price of $1,040,000, a cost basis of $7,009 [representing attorney fees paid in connection with the assignment—Ed.], and long-term capital gain of $1,032,991. In that return, petitioners also reported as ordinary income the $514,000 payment that they received in 1997 from CSL.

In the notice that respondent issued to petitioners with respect to their taxable year 1997, respondent determined, inter alia, the following:

> b) It is determined that you [petitioners] received the amount of $1,040,000.00 from Singer Asset Finance Company, for the tax year ended December 31, 1997, in payment of assignment of rights to future lottery payments from the State of California. This amount is determined to be ordinary income because rights to future annual lottery payments do not meet the definition of a capital asset according to the provisions of the Internal Revenue Code. Therefore, income is increased $1,040,000.00 for the year 1997.

Discussion

The parties agree that an amount received as a lottery prize constitutes ordinary income. The parties' dispute is over whether the $1,040,000 that petitioners received in exchange for petitioners' assignment is ordinary income or capital gain. Resolution of that dispute depends on whether petitioners' right to receive future annual lottery payments constitutes a capital asset within the meaning of section 1221.

* * *

Petitioners contend that their right to receive future annual lottery payments constitutes property held by them and that such property meets the definition of the term "capital asset" in section 1221. Respondent acknowledges that petitioners' right to receive future annual lottery payments is property in the ordinary sense of the word. However, respondent contends that such right does not qualify as a capital asset within the meaning of section 1221. According to respondent, the $1,040,000 that petitioners received from Singer constitutes ordinary income because petitioners received that amount in exchange for their future right to receive ordinary income.

In support of petitioners' position that the $1,040,000 that they received from Singer constitutes capital gain, petitioners rely on *Ark. Best Corp. v. Commissioner*, 485 U.S. 212, 99 L.Ed.2d 183, 108 S.Ct. 971 (1988). In support of respondent's position that that amount constitutes ordinary income, respondent relies on the principle established in the following cases: *Hort v. Commissioner*, 313 U.S. 28, 85 L.Ed. 1168, 61

S.Ct. 757 (1941); *Commissioner v. P. G. Lake, Inc.*, 356 U.S. 260, 2 L.Ed.2d 743, 78 S.Ct. 691 (1958); *Commissioner v. Gillette Motor Transp., Inc.*, 364 U.S. 130, 4 L.Ed.2d 1617, 80 S.Ct. 1497 (1960); and *United States v. Midland–Ross Corp.*, 381 U.S. 54, 14 L.Ed.2d 214, 85 S.Ct. 1308 (1965).

Petitioners concede that, before the Supreme Court of the United States (Supreme Court) decided *Ark. Best Corp. v. Commissioner, supra,* the line of cases on which respondent relies would have precluded characterizing petitioners' right to receive future annual lottery payments as a capital asset within the meaning of section 1221. However, according to petitioners, *Ark. Best Corp.* effectively overruled that line of cases and requires the result in the instant case that they advocate. Respondent disputes petitioners' reading of *Ark. Best Corp. v. Commissioner, supra.*

We agree with respondent's reading of *Ark. Best Corp. v. Commissioner, supra.* In fact, we have previously concluded that *Ark. Best Corp.* in no way affected the viability of the principle established in the line of cases on which respondent relies. See *Gladden v. Commissioner*, 112 T.C. 209, 221 (1999), revd. on another issue 262 F.3d 851 (9th Cir. 2001); *FNMA v. Commissioner*, 100 T.C. 541, 573 n. 30 (1993). We based that conclusion on footnote 5 of the Supreme Court's opinion in *Ark. Best Corp.*, which states:

> Petitioner [Ark. Best Corp.] mistakenly relies on cases in which this Court, in narrowly applying the general definition of "capital asset," has "construed 'capital asset' to exclude property representing income items or accretions to the value of a capital asset themselves properly attributable to income," even though these items are property in the broad sense of the word. *United States v. Midland–Ross Corp.*, 381 U.S. 54, 57, 85 S.Ct. 1308, 14 L.Ed.2d 214 (1965). See, e.g., *Commissioner v. Gillette Motor Co.*, 364 U.S. 130, 4 L.Ed.2d 1617, 80 S.Ct. 1497 (1960) ("capital asset" does not include compensation awarded taxpayer that represented fair rental value of its facilities); *Commissioner v. P.G. Lake, Inc.*, 356 U.S. 260, 2 L.Ed.2d 743, 78 S.Ct. 691 (1958) ("capital asset" does not include proceeds from sale of oil payment rights); *Hort v. Commissioner*, 313 U.S. 28, 85 L.Ed. 1168, 61 S.Ct. 757 (1941) ("capital asset" does not include payment to lessor for cancellation of unexpired portion of a lease). This line of cases, based on the premise that § 1221 "property" does not include claims or rights to ordinary income, has no application in the present context. Petitioner sold capital stock, not a claim to ordinary income. [*Ark. Best Corp. v. Commissioner, supra* at 217 n. 5.]

We have reviewed *Hort v. Commissioner, supra; Commissioner v. P.G. Lake, Inc., supra; Commissioner v. Gillette Motor Transp., Inc., supra;* and *United States v. Midland–Ross Corp., supra,* and certain of their progeny on which respondent relies. As the Supreme Court stated in *Commissioner v. Gillette Motor Transp., Inc., supra* at 134:

While a capital asset is defined in § 117(a)(1) [of the Internal Revenue Code of 1939] as "property held by the taxpayer," it is evident that not everything which can be called property in the ordinary sense and which is outside the statutory exclusions qualifies as a capital asset. * * *

Petitioners assigned to Singer their right to receive a portion of certain future annual lottery payments. In exchange for petitioners' assignment, petitioners received the discounted value (i.e., $1,040,000) of certain ordinary income which they otherwise would have received during the years 1997 through 2007. We hold that Singer paid petitioners $1,040,000 for the right to receive such future ordinary income, and not for an increase in the value of income-producing property.[9] We further hold that petitioners' right to receive future annual lottery payments does not constitute a capital asset within the meaning of section 1221 and that the $1,040,000 that petitioners received from Singer is ordinary income, and not capital gain. * * *

We have considered all of petitioners' arguments and contentions that are not discussed herein, and we find them to be without merit and/or irrelevant.

To reflect the foregoing,

Decision will be entered for respondent.

* * *

Problem 7–2

For each situation described below, determine whether the taxpayer's sale gives rise to a capital gain.

(a) Vincent Barbarino created an irrevocable trust that paid income to Freddie Washington for his life, remainder to Juan Epstein or his estate. The trust owned various rental properties and corporate bonds that generated a steady and predictable stream of ordinary income. Washington sold his interest in Barbarino's trust to Julie Kotter for cash, producing a realized gain.

(b) Arnold Horshack held a 40 percent interest in Sweathog LLC, a limited liability company. The remaining 60 percent interest in the LLC was owned by various individuals unrelated to Horshack. The LLC did not operate an active business; instead, it managed various investment assets that generated a steady and predictable stream of ordinary income. Hor-

---

9. It is well established that the purpose for capital-gains treatment is

to afford capital-gains treatment only in situations typically involving the realization of appreciation in value accrued over a substantial period of time, and thus to ameliorate the hardship of taxation of the entire gain in one year. * * *

[*Commissioner v. Gillette Motor Transp., Inc.*, 364 U.S. 130, 134, 4 L.Ed.2d 1617, 80 S.Ct. 1497 (1960) (citing *Burnet v. Harmel*, 287 U.S. 103, 106, 77 L.Ed. 199, 53 S.Ct. 74 (1932)).]

shack sold his interest in the LLC to Michael Woodman for cash. The sale produced a realized gain for Horshack.

* * *

Holding Periods. Notice that § 1222 requires netting of "long-term" and "short-term" capital gains and losses. A capital gain or loss is a "long-term" capital gain or loss if the taxpayer held the capital asset for *more* than one year. Obviously, then, if a taxpayer holds a capital asset for exactly one year, the resulting gain or loss will be "short-term."

In certain situations, a taxpayer may add the holding period of another owner or add the holding period from another asset. Section 1223 lists various situations where "tacking" of holding periods is allowed. Unless one of these situations is present, a taxpayer's holding period begins upon acquisition. For example, if a taxpayer exchanges one capital asset for another in a transaction in which the taxpayer does not recognize gain or loss (a so-called nonrecognition transaction, a major topic coming up in Chapter 8), the taxpayer usually takes the new asset with a basis equal to the taxpayer's basis in the property surrendered. In other words, the gain or loss from the surrendered asset is preserved in the acquired asset. Under § 1223(1), the taxpayer's holding period in the surrendered asset also carries over to the acquired asset. Thus, if a taxpayer exchanges one capital asset held for five years for another capital asset in a nonrecognition transaction, the newly-acquired asset is deemed to have been held for five years. An immediate sale of the acquired asset for cash would thus produce long-term capital gain or loss, as the case may be.

* * *

Self-Assessment Question

(Solutions to Self–Assessment Questions are set forth in Appendix 3.)

SAQ 7–2. Determine the character of the gain or loss recognized by the taxpayers in each of the following alternative scenarios.

(a) Jack Tripper received an antique guitar from his father as a birthday present in February, Year One. Jack's father purchased the guitar for $500 12 years prior to the gift. In April, Year One, Jack sold the guitar for $5,000 cash. *[handwritten margin note: long-term cap. gain — as a gift, he can "track" on his dad's holding period]*

(b) Janet Wood received a coin collection in June, Year One, as a bequest from the estate of her deceased sister, Jenny. The coin collection was worth $1,000 at Jenny's death. Janet sold the coin collection to an unrelated purchaser for $800 cash in September, Year One. *[handwritten margin note: long-term cap. loss. — $200 death — always make the holding "long term". and would get her basis of $1k]*

(c) Chrissy Snow purchased a boat for investment purposes in October, Year One. She paid $30,000 for the boat, but quickly suffered buyer's remorse. In November, Year One, she sold the boat to her friend, Larry Dallas. Larry was low on cash, so he transferred to Chrissy marketable securities worth $10,000 that he had purchased three years earlier for $25,000. Chrissy sold the marketable securities in December, Year One, to an unrelated party for $12,000 cash. *a short-term cap. loss of $20k Chrissy and a short-term cap. gain of $2k*

Larry = a long-term cap. loss of $15k

B. THE "SALE OR EXCHANGE" REQUIREMENT

Code: *Review* IRC § 1222.

Regs: None.

Section 1222 states that a capital gain or capital loss arises only upon the "sale or exchange" of a capital asset. Thus, if a taxpayer disposes of a capital asset in a transaction that is not properly characterized as a sale or exchange, any resulting gain would be ordinary income (bad news) and any realized loss would be ordinary loss (good news). The phrase "sale or exchange" might suggest that some kind of bilateral transaction must take place, but courts have defined the term fairly broadly. See for yourself.

KENAN v. COMMISSIONER

United States Court of Appeals, Second Circuit, 1940.
114 F.2d 217.

AUGUSTUS N. HAND, CIRCUIT JUDGE.

The testatrix, Mrs. Bingham, died on July 27, 1917, leaving a will under which she placed her residuary estate in trust and provided in item "Seventh" that her trustees should pay a certain amount annually to her niece, Louise Clisby Wise, until the latter reached the age of forty, "at which time or as soon thereafter as compatible with the interests of my estate they shall pay to her the sum of Five Million ($5,000,000.00) Dollars." The will provided in item "Eleventh" that the trustees, in the case of certain payments including that of the $5,000,000 under item "Seventh", should have the right "to substitute for the payment in money, payment in marketable securities of a value equal to the sum to be paid, the selection of the securities to be substituted in any instance, and the valuation of such securities to be done by the Trustees and their selection and valuation to be final."

Louise Clisby Wise became forty years of age on July 28, 1935. The trustees decided to pay her the $5,000,000 partly in cash and partly in securities. The greater part of the securities had been owned by the testator and transferred as part of her estate to the trustees; others had been purchased by the trustees. All had appreciated in value during the period for which they were held by the trustees, and the Commissioner determined that the distribution of the securities to the niece resulted in capital gains which were taxable to the trustees under the rates specified in Section 117 of the Revenue Act of 1934, which limits the percentage of gain to be treated as taxable income on the "sale or exchange" of capital assets. On this basis, the Commissioner determined a deficiency of $367,687.12 in the income tax for the year 1935.

The Board overruled the objections of the trustees to the imposition of any tax and denied a motion of the Commissioner to amend his answer in order to claim the full amount of the appreciation in value as ordinary income rather than a percentage of it as a capital gain, and confirmed the original deficiency determination. The taxpayers contend that the decision of the Board was erroneous because they realized neither gain from the sale or exchange of capital assets nor income of any character by delivering the securities to the legatee pursuant to the permissive terms of the will. The Commissioner contends that gain was realized by the delivery of the securities but that such gain was ordinary income not derived from a sale or exchange and therefore taxable in its entirety. * * *

* * *

The Taxpayer's Appeal.

In support of their petition the taxpayers contend that the delivery of the securities of the trust estate to the legatee was a donative disposition of property pursuant to the terms of the will, and that no gain was thereby realized. They argue that when they determined that the legacy should be one of securities, it became for all purposes a bequest of property, just as if the cash alternative had not been provided, and not taxable for the reason that no gain is realized on the transfer by a testamentary trustee of specific securities or other property bequeathed by will to a legatee.

We do not think that the situation here is the same as that of legacy of specific property. The legatee was never in the position occupied by the recipient of specific securities under a will. She had a claim against the estate for $5,000,000, payable either in cash or securities of that value, but had no title or right to the securities, legal or equitable, until they were delivered to her by the trustees after the exercise of their option. She took none of the chances of a legatee of specific securities or of a share of a residue that the securities might appreciate or decline in value between the time of the death of the testator and the transfer to her by the trustees, but instead had at all times a claim for an unvarying amount in money or its equivalent.

* * *

In the present case, the legatee had a claim which was a charge against the trust estate for $5,000,000 in cash or securities and the trustees had the power to determine whether the claim should be satisfied in one form or the other. The claim, though enforceable only in the alternative, was * * * a charge against the entire trust estate. If it were satisfied by a cash payment securities might have to be sold on which (if those actually delivered in specie were selected) a taxable gain would necessarily have been realized. Instead of making such a sale the trustees delivered the securities and exchanged them pro tanto for the general claim of the legatee, which was thereby satisfied.

* * * The word "exchange" does not necessarily have the connotation of a bilateral agreement which may be said to attach to the word "sale." Thus, should a person set up a trust and reserve to himself the power to substitute for the securities placed in trust other securities of equal value, there would seem no doubt that the exercise of this reserved power would be an "exchange" within the common meaning of the word, even though the settlor consulted no will other than his own, although, of course, we do not here advert to the problems of taxability in such a situation.

The Board alluded to the fact that * * * the bequest was fixed at a definite amount in money, that * * * there was no bequest of specific securities (nor of a share in the residue which might vary in value), that the rights of the legatee * * * were a charge upon the corpus of the trust, and that the trustees had to part either with $5,000,000 in cash or with securities worth that amount at the time of the transfer. It added that the increase in value of the securities was realized by the trust and benefited it to the full extent, since, except for the increase, it would have had to part with other property, and it cited in further support of its position *United States v. Kirby Lumber Co.*, 284 U.S. 1, 52 S.Ct. 4, 76 L.Ed. 131. Under circumstances like those here, where the legatee did not take securities designated by the will or an interest in the corpus which might be more or less at the time of the transfer than at the time of decedent's death, it seems to us that the trustees realized a gain by using these securities to settle a claim worth $5,000,000 * * *.

> * * *

The Commissioner's Appeal.

We have already held that a taxable gain was realized by the delivery of the securities. It follows from the reasons that support that conclusion that the appreciation was a capital gain, taxable at the rates specified in Section 117. * * *

There can be no doubt that from an accounting standpoint the trustees realized a gain in the capital of their trust when they disposed of securities worth far more at the time of disposition than at the time of acquisition in order to settle (pro tanto) a claim of $5,000,000. It would seem to us a strange anomaly if a disposition of securities which were in fact a "capital asset" should not be taxed at the rates afforded by Section 117 to individuals who have sold or exchanged property which they had held for the specified periods. It is not without significance that the appeal of the Commissioner was plainly an afterthought. The original deficiency was determined on the theory that the capital gains rates were applicable and the Commissioner sought to amend his answer so as to claim that ordinary rates should be applied only after the case had been orally argued before the Board, The Board denied his motion to reopen the case for the consideration of this contention. Since we find that the Commissioner's cross-petition is unfounded on the merits, we have no reason to consider the technical question whether the denial of the motion to amend the answer was an abuse of discretion.

The purpose of the capital gains provision of the Revenue Act of 1934 is so to treat an appreciation in value, arising over a period of years but realized in one year, that the tax thereon will roughly approximate what it would have been had a tax been paid each year upon the appreciation in value for that year. The appreciation in value in the present case took place between 1917 and 1935, whereas the Commissioner's theory would tax it as though it had all taken place in 1935. If the trustees had sold the securities, they would be taxed at capital gain rates. Both the trustees and the Commissioner, in their arguments as respondent and cross-respondents, draw the analogy between the transaction here and a sale, and no injustice is done to either by taxing the gain at the rates which would apply had a sale actually been made and the proceeds delivered to the legatee. It seems to us extraordinary that the exercise by the trustees of the option to deliver to the legatee securities, rather than cash, should be thought to result in an increased deficiency of enormous proportions.

Orders affirmed.

Note

The requirement of a "sale or exchange" in § 1222 must be narrower than the requirement of a "sale or other disposition of property" under § 1001(a), the provision providing the basic formula for computing realized gains and losses. This is because there are ways to dispose of property other than by sale or exchange (abandonment, forfeiture, and the like). Yet there seems to be no overt rationale for limiting capital gain or loss characterization only to property dispositions that constitute a sale or exchange.

* * *

Self-Assessment Question

(Solutions to Self–Assessment Questions are set forth in Appendix 3.)

SAQ 7–3. To what extent does a "sale or exchange" occur in each of the following alternative scenarios?

(a) A taxpayer's capital asset is destroyed by fire and the taxpayer collects insurance as compensation for the loss. *NOT a "sale or exchange" the resulting gain or loss = ordinary*

(b) A parcel of real property held by the taxpayer for investment purposes is taken by eminent domain and the taxpayer receives "just" compensation from the government. *this is considered a "sale or exchange" even though it is not voluntary.*

(c) A professor resigns a tenured position at a university in return for a series of monthly cash payments over two years. *NOT a "sale or exchange"*

* * * *the cash payments are compensation for loss of employment.*

✕ *Problem 7–3* ✕

Sharon Hoarde hired an attorney to draft various legal documents on her behalf. When Sharon received a bill for $5,000 from her attorney, Sharon indicated that she lacked the cash to pay the bill in full. She offered to transfer 100 shares of stock in Bloated Corporation, a publicly-traded company, to the attorney in full satisfaction of the bill. Since the Bloated shares were worth $5,000, the attorney accepted Sharon's offer. Sharon then conveyed the shares to the attorney. What are the federal income tax consequences of this transfer to Sharon, assuming that Sharon's basis in the stock (which she acquired three years before the transfer) was $1,500?

S had a long-term capital gain of $3,500.

Problem 7–4

In Year One, Haywood Jugo transferred 1,000 shares of stock in Bloated Corporation to his sister, Judy Mann. The stock was worth $50,000 at the time of the transfer, although Haywood purchased the shares many years ago for $10,000. As part of the transfer, Judy agreed to pay any federal gift tax liability Haywood incurred in effecting the transfer. In February of Year Two, Haywood prepared a federal gift tax return showing a $15,000 federal gift tax liability from his gift to Judy. Judy wrote a check for $15,000 and Haywood enclosed the check with his return. What are the federal *income* tax consequences to Haywood and Judy?

C. THE PREFERENTIAL RATES FOR LONG–TERM CAPITAL GAINS (AND QUALIFIED DIVIDEND INCOME)

Friday 510–519

Code: IRC § 1(h). *Review* IRC §§ 1221(a); 1222; 1223. *Skim* IRC § 1202.

Regs: None.

Understanding the Big Picture. Recall from Chapter 3 that a taxpayer's "net capital gain" will be taxed at a preferential rate. The preferential rates for capital gains are contained (cryptically, to say the least) in § 1(h). In order to qualify for the preferential tax rates of § 1(h), an individual must have a "net capital gain," defined in § 1222(11) as the excess of "net long-term capital gain" over "net short-term capital loss." In order to have a net long-term capital gain, the taxpayer must have held the capital asset for more than one year. Section 1222(1)–(4). Thus, the preferential rates will apply only to gains from the sale or exchange of capital assets held for more than one year. If an individual sells a capital asset held for one year or less, any gain will be taxed as ordinary income.

In Chapter 4, we learned that capital losses are deductible only to the extent of capital gains, plus (in the case of individuals) up to $3,000. Section 1211(b). Any capital losses in excess of the allowed amount will be carried over to the next taxable year. Section 1212(b). The limitation on capital losses stems from the idea that capital losses should be used generally to offset capital gains and not ordinary income. From a revenue perspective, it is no big deal to allow an ordinary loss to offset net capital gains since the ordinary loss would otherwise offset income taxed at a higher rate—by offsetting a capital gain, the loss only reduces the amount taxed at the preferential rate. On the other hand, capital losses should not offset ordinary gains (or other types of ordinary income, like wages, rents, interest, royalties and so on) because in those cases the losses are offsetting high-tax income, not low-tax income. In this regard, § 1211(b) is a taxpayer-friendly provision: if capital losses exceed capital gains, up to $3,000 of net capital loss can be used to offset a taxpayer's ordinary income.

Consider this example: a taxpayer has capital gains (all long-term) totaling $5,000, and capital losses (again, all long-term) totaling $10,000. For the year, the taxpayer will include the $5,000 in gains and can deduct $8,000 of the losses. The $2,000 disallowed loss is carried over to the next year as a long-term capital loss, as if it arose then. See § 1212(b).

Use the following question to confirm your understanding of the basic concepts at play here.

* * *

Self-Assessment Question

(Solutions to Self–Assessment Questions are set forth in Appendix 3.)

SAQ 7–4. Describe *generally* how each of the following taxpayers will be taxed on his or her capital gains and losses.

(a) John had the following capital gains and losses in Year One:

Long-term capital gains	$10,000
Long-term capital losses	$ 3,000
Short-term capital gains	$ 5,000
Short-term capital losses	$ 7,000

(b) Paul had the following capital gains and losses in Year One:

Long-term capital gains	$10,000
Long-term capital losses	$ 3,000
Short-term capital gains	$15,000
Short-term capital losses	$ 7,000

(c) George had the following capital gains and losses in Year One:

Long-term capital gains	$10,000
Long-term capital losses	$13,000
Short-term capital gains	$15,000
Short-term capital losses	$ 7,000

(d)   Ringo had the following capital gains and losses in Year One:

Long-term capital gains	$10,000
Long-term capital losses	$13,000
Short-term capital gains	$ 5,000
Short-term capital losses	$ 7,000

(e)   Yoko had the following capital gains and losses in Year One:

Long-term capital gains	$10,000
Long-term capital losses	$13,000
Short-term capital gains	$ 5,000
Short-term capital losses	$17,000

* * *

Enter the Labyrinth. Section 1(h) is, far and away, the most difficult provision of the Code discussed in this book—maybe the most difficult provision of the Code period. Even after several readings, the operation of the statute remains elusive. In order to understand how § 1(h) functions, it is helpful to think about its purpose conceptually.

We know from prior study that § 1(h) is designed to confer a preferential rate of tax to a taxpayer's "net capital gain," defined in § 1222(11) as the excess of the taxpayer's net long-term capital gain over the taxpayer's net short-term capital loss. The exact rate to apply to the net capital gain depends upon the marginal rate applicable to the taxpayer's last dollar of ordinary income. As the following scale shows, the preferential rate applied to a net capital gain changes as the taxpayer's marginal tax rate increases.

ORDINARY INCOME   NET CAPITAL GAIN

Thus, if the tax rate applicable to the taxpayer's last dollar of ordinary income (the taxpayer's "marginal tax rate") is 28 percent, the preferential tax rate for the taxpayer's net capital gain is 15 percent. Likewise, if the taxpayer's marginal rate on ordinary income is 15 percent, the first dollar of the net capital gain will be taxed at the rate of five percent (or at zero percent in 2008–2010). If the taxpayer's net capital gain exceeds what is left of the taxpayer's 15 percent bracket, the excess net capital gain will be taxed at 15 percent.

Section 1(h) requires taxpayers to compute their tax on ordinary income and then layer in the tax on the net capital gain. Suppose, for example, that an unmarried taxpayer with a net capital gain of $10,000 in 2007 had ordinary income that year of $100,000, an amount that is $60,850 less than the ceiling of the 28–percent bracket. Ignoring all deductions, the taxpayer's marginal tax rate on ordinary income is 28 percent. The taxpayer's net capital gain is then layered on top of the ordinary income. Since the taxpayer's marginal tax rate exceeds 15 percent, the applicable tax rate on the net capital gain is 15 percent, as shown below.

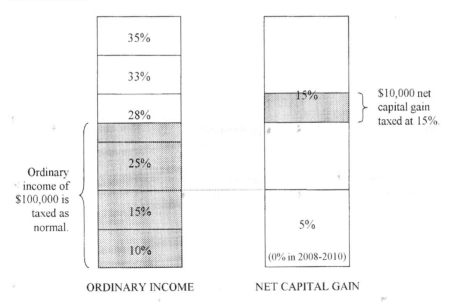

Now suppose that an unmarried taxpayer with a net capital gain of $10,000 in 2007 had ordinary income that year of only $28,850, an amount that is $3,000 less than the ceiling of the 15–percent tax bracket. Assuming away all deductions, the taxpayer's marginal tax rate on ordinary income is 15 percent. The taxpayer's $10,000 net capital gain is then layered on top of the ordinary income. With total income of $38,850, the taxpayer's marginal tax rate would increase to 25 percent absent the preferential rate accorded to the net capital gain. Under § 1(h), however, the first $3,000 of the net capital gain will be taxed at the five-percent rate, and only the remaining $7,000 of net capital gain will be taxed at 15 percent. The layering of the net capital gain and the resulting preferential rate is illustrated below.

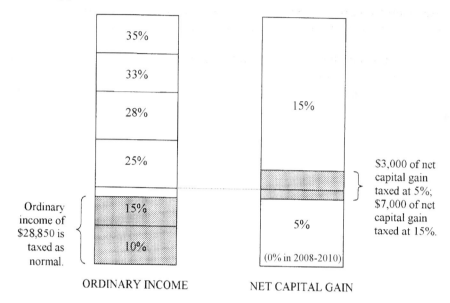

ORDINARY INCOME   NET CAPITAL GAIN

But wait, there is more! The Code taxes some capital gains at slightly higher rates, though these rates are still lower than the highest rates applicable to ordinary income. These special items are gains from sales and exchanges of **collectibles** (taxed at 28 percent under § 1(h)(1)(E)) and gain attributable to **unrecaptured depreciation deductions on real property** (taxed at 25 percent under § 1(h)(1)(D)).

"Collectibles" include artwork, rugs, antiques, metals, gems, stamps, coins, alcoholic (hiccup) beverages, and other assets specifically identified as collectibles by the Treasury Department. See §§ 1(h)(6); 408(m)(2). Why are collectibles subject to a less preferential tax rate? The answer requires a short historical detour. When all capital gains were subject to a partial exclusion instead of a preferential tax rate, commentators argued that an exclusion for collectibles represented poor tax policy. They argued that investments in collectibles were entirely speculative and were economically inefficient because they restricted capital mobility and did not promote growth or employment. This sentiment proved lasting: when Congress reduced the capital gains rate from 28 percent to 20 percent in 1997, it deliberately retained the 28 percent rate for collectibles in light of these criticisms. Even with continued lowering of the basic capital gains tax rate, the rate for collectibles has been stuck at 28 percent. The reason for a less preferential rate on unrecaptured depreciation deductions is set forth in Part E of this Chapter.

In addition to preferential tax rates, an individual can sometimes exclude all or a portion of the gain realized upon the sale or exchange of

[handwritten margin notes: exclude ½ > 5 yrs; 60% empowerment zone]

a capital asset. For instance, a shareholder can exclude half of the gain from the sale or exchange of original issue "qualified small business stock" that he or she has held for more than five years. See § 1202. The exclusion rate grows to 60 percent in the case of qualified small business stock in a corporation doing business within an "empowerment zone" identified by the Secretary of Housing and Urban Development. A "qualified small business" is any regularly taxable corporation with aggregate gross assets of $50 million or less. Section 1202(d). Moreover, some capital gains are excluded entirely, meaning that the effective tax rate on such gains is zero. These gains include sales of capital assets representing stock, partnership interests, or tangible property used in a business operated in the District of Columbia Enterprise Zone and, with respect to assets acquired after 2001, those related to a business operated in a "renewal community" as identified by the Secretary of Housing and Urban Development.

So how exactly does one compute the tax on net capital gain? Section 1(h) states that if a taxpayer has a net capital gain, then the tax imposed under § 1(a)–(d) cannot exceed the sum of the amounts computed in § 1(h)(1)(A)–(E). Thus, taxpayers need to compute separately the amounts described in § 1(h)(1)(A), § 1(h)(1)(B), § 1(h)(1)(C), § 1(h)(1)(D), and § 1(h)(1)(E). Then the taxpayer must add up all of these separate amounts to determine the taxpayer's maximum § 1 tax liability. Very generally, the following table describes what each of these five components is taxing:

Section	Tax Base	Rate
1(h)(1)(A)	Ordinary income (and net short-term capital gain)	Regular
1(h)(1)(B)	Adjusted net capital gain up to what is left of the taxpayer's 15% bracket, if any	5% (0% from 2008–2010)
1(h)(1)(C)	Remaining adjusted net capital gain	15%
1(h)(1)(D)	That portion of net capital gain consisting of unrecaptured depreciation on depreciable real property	25%
1(h)(1)(E)	That portion of net capital gain consisting of collectibles	28%

Example of the § 1(h) Computation. Maybe the best way to get a handle on § 1(h) is to work through a fairly simple example. Suppose Simon realizes and recognizes the following gains and losses in Year One:

(1) Gain from Sale of Stock Purchased 5 Years Before Sale: $20,000

(2) Loss from Sale of Stock Purchased 3 Months Before Sale: ($ 5,000)

(3) Gain from Sale of Stock Purchased 9 Months Before Sale: $ 3,000

Assume that Simon's salary income for Year One is $500,000 and that he has no other items of income or deduction in Year One. We must first assess whether Simon has a "net capital gain" for Year One. If not, then we avoid § 1(h) entirely. The gain in item (1) is a long-term capital gain, for it represents the gain from the sale or exchange of a capital asset held for more than one year. The loss in item (2) is a short-term capital loss, and the gain in item (3) is a short-term capital gain. Simon's net long-term capital gain is $20,000, and his net short-term capital loss is $2,000. Therefore, Simon has a net capital gain of $18,000. Section 1222(11). Because he has a net capital gain, Simon's tax liability under § 1 will be limited to the amount determined under § 1(h)(1).

Section 1(h)(1)(A): The Tax on Ordinary Income. Under § 1(h)(1)(A), we first compute the § 1 tax owing on the *greater* of two numbers. The first number, contained in § 1(h)(1)(A)(i), is Simon's "taxable income reduced by the net capital gain." In other words, we are looking for Simon's ordinary income and net short-term capital gain. Here, Simon's taxable income is $518,000 ($500,000 salary income plus $18,000 net capital gain, with no deductions), and his net capital gain is $18,000. The § 1(h)(1)(A)(i) amount, therefore, is $500,000.

The second number, contained in § 1(h)(1)(A)(ii), is the *lesser* of two other figures. The first figure is the amount of Simon's taxable income taxed at a rate below 25 percent. Section 1(h)(1)(A)(ii)(I). If Simon is unmarried without dependents, and if the applicable tax table in Year One is identical the applicable tax table in 2007, then the portion of his $518,000 of taxable income that is taxed at a rate below 25 percent is $31,850. The second figure is Simon's taxable income reduced by the *adjusted* net capital gain. Section 1(h)(1)(A)(ii)(II). Section 1(h)(3) defines **adjusted net capital gain** as Simon's net capital gain less his "unrecaptured section 1250 gain" and his "28–percent rate gain." (His adjusted net capital gain also includes any qualified dividend income, but we will defer discussion of this wrinkle for now.) In this very simple example, there is no unrecaptured section 1250 gain nor any 28–percent rate gain. Thus, Simon's adjusted net capital gain happens to be the same as his net capital gain, $18,000. The § 1(h)(1)(A)(ii)(II) figure, therefore, is $500,000 ($518,000 taxable income less $18,000 adjusted net capital gain). The lesser of $31,850 and $500,000 is (. . . the suspense is a killer, huh? . . .) $31,850.

Remember that we are supposed to compute the § 1 tax on the *greater* of the § 1(h)(1)(A)(i) amount ($500,000) or the § 1(h)(1)(A)(ii) amount ($29,050). Using the 2007 tax table once again, the tax on $500,000 would be $154,074.25. This figure represents the tax on Simon's ordinary income. So why did we go through the whole "lesser of" exercise in § 1(h)(1)(A)(ii)? Because in some rare cases, a taxpayer may have very little ordinary income and short-term capital gain but a large amount of long-term capital gain. To the extent that long-term capital gain consists of collectibles or other long-term capital gains that are entitled to less favoritism, Congress has determined that a portion of those less-favored long-term capital gains should be taxed in the 10– and 15–percent brackets. The § 1(h)(1)(A)(ii) computation ensures that result. But in most cases, the § 1(h)(1)(A)(i) amount will be the greater number.

Section 1(h)(1)(B): The 5% Rate for Adjusted Net Capital Gain of Lower–Income Taxpayers. As we saw in the conceptual overview to § 1(h), a taxpayer who has not fully utilized his or her 15–percent tax bracket may apply the balance of that bracket to his or her net capital gain. That portion of the net capital gain equal to the unused portion of the 15–percent bracket will be taxed at a preferential rate of five percent. Notice that the five percent rate is scheduled to drop to zero beginning in 2008.

In this example, Simon completely utilized his 10–and 15–percent brackets on his $500,000 of salary income. So in his case, no portion of the adjusted net capital gain will be taxed at five percent. The computations in the statute bear this out:

Excess of—

	Taxable income that would be taxed at a rate less than 25% [§ 1(h)(1)(B)(i)]	$ 31,850
over	*Taxable income minus adjusted net capital gain* [§ 1(h)(1)(B)(ii)]	($500,000)
		no excess

Section 1(h)(1)(C): The 15% Rate for Remaining Adjusted Net Capital Gain. The remaining adjusted net capital gain (or taxable income, if less) is then taxed at a flat rate of 15 percent. Here, because no portion of the adjusted net capital gain was taxed at five percent under § 1(h)(1)(B), the entire $18,000 adjusted net capital gain is utilized here. The tax on the $18,000 adjusted net capital gain is, therefore, $2,700.

Section 1(h)(1)(D): The 25% Rate for Unrecaptured § 1250 Gain. Section 1(h)(1)(D) basically imposes a flat 25 percent rate on so-called "unrecaptured § 1250 gain," a concept described in Part E of this Chapter. For our immediate purposes, it is sufficient to note that unrecaptured § 1250 gain arises only where net capital gain consists in part of gain from the sale or exchange of depreciable real property (like buildings) used in the taxpayer's business or held for investment. In Simon's case, § 1(h)(1)(D) does not apply.

Section 1(h)(1)(E): The 28% Rate for Collectibles and § 1202 Gains. To the extent that a portion of the taxpayer's net capital gain consists of gain from the sale or exchange of collectibles and/or § 1202 stock, such portion is to be taxed at 28 percent under § 1(h)(1)(E). Here, too, Simon's simple situation does not raise this issue.

Having worked through each of the five components of § 1(h)(1), Simon's maximum income tax liability for Year One can thus be determined:

1(h)(1)(A):	$154,074.25
1(h)(1)(B):	0.00
1(h)(1)(C):	$ 2,700.00
1(h)(1)(D):	0.00
1(h)(1)(E):	0.00
	$156,774.25 ← total § 1 tax liability

If there had been no preferential rate applicable to Simon's net capital gain, his total tax liability for Year One would have been $160,374.25 (again, using the 2007 tax table).

* * *

Self-Assessment Question

(Solutions to Self–Assessment Questions are set forth in Appendix 3.)

SAQ 7–5. Simon's unmarried sister, Sally, enjoyed a Year One remarkably similar to her brother: she realized and recognized a $20,000 long-term capital gain, a $5,000 short-term capital loss, and a $3,000 short-term capital gain. Sally's salary for Year One, however, was only $15,000. Assuming Sally has no other items of income or deduction in Year One (and ignoring both the standard deduction and personal exemption), determine Sally's federal income tax liability for Year One. Use tax tables from 2007 (as set forth in Chapter 1) where needed.

* * *

Problem 7–5

In Year One, Polly Ester Coates, an unmarried individual, recognized the following gains and losses:

(1) $12,000 gain on the sale of stock in Disney Corporation held for five years;

(2) $10,000 gain on the sale of investment real property held for eight months;

(3) $8,000 gain on the sale of a stamp collection held for 15 years;

(4) $5,000 loss on the sale of stock in Southland Corporation held for three months; and

(5) $5,000 loss on the sale of stock in Petco Corporation held for two years.

In addition to these items, Polly had salary income of $90,000 in Year One. Assuming the tax tables for Year One are the same as those for 2007 (as set forth in Chapter 1), compute Polly's federal income tax liability for Year One. Ignore the standard deduction, the personal exemption, and any other deductions not specifically described in this Problem to which Polly may be entitled.

* * *

The Preferential Rates for Dividends. Perhaps the centerpiece of the Jobs and Growth Tax Relief Reconciliation Act of 2003 was the application of the preferential tax rates for capital gains to "qualified dividend income." Prior to the 2003 Act, all "dividends," a term of art defined in § 316, were taxed as ordinary income, just like wages, interest, royalties, and rents. Because corporations are separate taxable entities, corporate income distributed to shareholders was effectively taxed twice: once to the corporation as taxable earnings, and again to the shareholders as dividends. Congress apparently decided that the "double taxation" of corporate profits was excessive, so it extended the preferential tax rates to shareholders receiving qualified dividend income. Most every dividend paid by a domestic corporation will qualify for the lower tax rates, though not when the shareholder has held the stock for only a brief period of time. Even dividends paid from corporations organized in a United States possession or in a country that has an income tax treaty with the United States will qualify for the lower tax rates. The policy implications of § 1(h)(11) cannot be overstated, but a detailed examination of these implications is better suited to texts related to corporate taxation.

―――――――

p.458 ‹‹
mon: 519·527
prob: 7-7

D.   SECTION 1231 GAINS AND LOSSES

Code: IRC § 1231.

Regs: None.

A Third Flavor? Section 1221(a)(2) provides that depreciable personal property used in a taxpayer's trade or business is not a capital asset. Likewise, real property used in a trade or business (land and buildings) is not a capital asset. Gains and losses from the sale or exchange of these assets, therefore, produce ordinary income and losses, respectively.

Where business-use property is involuntarily converted into cash by reason of casualty, theft, condemnation or exercise of eminent domain, the resulting gain or loss would not qualify as a capital gain or loss even if the business-use property was not described in § 1221(a)(2). This is because there is no "sale or exchange" of the business-use property. See Part B, *supra*.

In World War II, these rules had a particularly harsh impact on the shipping industry. The federal income tax rates in those years were quite high. When ships were requisitioned by the government for use in battle, or when ships were destroyed and the owners collected insurance, the owners frequently realized substantial gains that forced them into the very high tax brackets. Congress, realizing that many in shipping business were sinking financially, decided to offer relief. By enacting § 1231, Congress allowed shippers to treat the net gains from these involuntary conversions of business-use property as long-term capital gains. That was certainly good news. But the good news did not end there: if taxpayers realized more losses than gains, § 1231 provided that the net loss would still be treated as an ordinary loss. Because ordinary losses are not subject to the same limitation as capital losses, see § 1211(b), this, too, was a favorable result. The benefit was not limited to taxpayers in the shipping industry, but clearly they were the targeted beneficiaries of § 1231.

While § 1231 originally applied only to gains and losses from involuntary conversions of business-use property, it was not long before the "best-of-both-worlds" rule was expanded to include all sales and exchanges of business-use property. And while § 1231 was originally conceived as a provision to help the shipping industry through the crisis of wartime, it remains available to taxpayers 60 years later.

In order to effect the "best-of-both-worlds" result, § 1231 creates a third (though temporary) flavor of gains and losses: so-called **§ 1231 gains and losses**. The formal definition is presented in § 1231(a)(3). Notice that § 1231 treatment is conditioned on the underlying property having been "used in the trade or business." Solely for purposes of § 1231, this term has a special meaning. Section 1231(b)(1) generally provides that property is "used in the trade or business" if it meets three requirements:

- The property was either depreciable personal property used in a trade or business or real property used in a trade or business (§ 1221(a)(2) property);

- The property was held by the taxpayer for more than one year; and

- The property is not described in § 1221(a)(1) (inventory and property held for sale to customers), § 1221(a)(3) (certain created property), or § 1221(a)(5) (government publications).

Section 1231(b) also contains some special rules of inclusion and exclusion. For instance, timber and coal are typically treated as "property used in the trade or business" without regard to the taxpayer's holding period. Section 1231(b)(2). Various livestock also qualifies, but in the case of cattle and horses the requisite holding period is increased to two years. Section 1231(b)(3). Chickens, however, can never qualify as "property used in the trade or business." *Id.* Was Congress in a fowl mood that day?

The Hotchpot. Section 1231(a)(1) states that if a taxpayer's § 1231 gains for a year exceed the § 1231 losses for the same year, then *all* of the § 1231 gains and losses will be treated as long-term capital gains and losses. Again, this is good news: because the excess produces a net capital gain, the net gain will be subject to tax at preferential rates. If, however, § 1231 losses equal or exceed § 1231 gains in any given year, *all* of such gains and losses will be treated as ordinary gains and losses. Section 1231(a)(2). Here again, this is good news: the excess ordinary loss can be used to offset other ordinary income. Accordingly, § 1231 gains and losses are the best types of gains and losses, because the most preferential result will always come to pass.

Netting the § 1231 gains and the § 1231 losses is akin to throwing all such items into a pot during the year and determining their ultimate flavor at the end of the year. In fact, practitioners refer to § 1231 gains and § 1231 losses as "hotchpot" gains and losses. Most likely, they borrowed this term from estate planners, who use it to describe how gifts *causa mortis* (those made in contemplation of death) are added back to the decedent's estate for purposes of computing a beneficiary's intestate share. In any case, the term has stuck. Thus, it is proper to speak of placing § 1231 gains and § 1231 losses into "the hotchpot" for netting at the end of the year.

The Firepot. Section 1231(a)(4)(C) contains a special rule for purposes of determining whether a § 1231 gain or § 1231 loss enters the hotchpot. It states that if the recognized losses from casualties and thefts of either "property used in the trade or business" or certain capital assets exceed the recognized gains from such casualties and thefts, such losses and gains do not enter the hotchpot. It is therefore necessary at the end of the year to net the gains and losses from casualty and theft conversions to determine if such gains and losses pour-over into the hotchpot. Because casualty losses include losses from fires, among other things, practitioners have taken to calling this pre-netting the "firepot" (though some call it the "sub-hotchpot").

The following illustration summarizes the application of § 1231 to qualifying gains and losses:

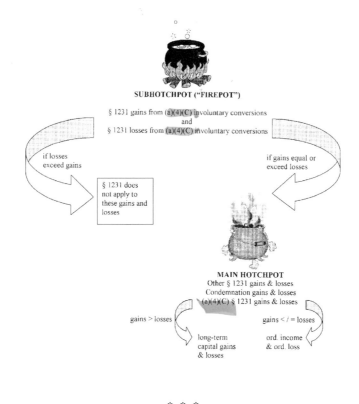

SUBHOTCHPOT ("FIREPOT")

§ 1231 gains from (a)(4)(C) involuntary conversions
and
§ 1231 losses from (a)(4)(C) involuntary conversions

if losses
exceed gains

if gains equal or
exceed losses

§ 1231 does
not apply to
these gains and
losses

MAIN HOTCHPOT
Other § 1231 gains & losses
Condemnation gains & losses
(a)(4)(C) § 1231 gains & losses

gains > losses

gains < / = losses

long-term
capital gains
& losses

ord. income
& ord. loss

* * *

Recapture of Net Ordinary Losses. Suppose a taxpayer intends to sell two assets at the end of Year One. The first asset would produce a $5,000 § 1231 gain, and the second asset would produce a $5,000 § 1231 loss. If the taxpayer follows through with his or her objective and sells both assets at the end of Year One, the two items would cancel each other out in the hotchpot.

Upon reflection, however, the taxpayer might choose a slightly different approach: sell the § 1231 loss asset at the end of Year One and then sell the § 1231 gain asset at the beginning of Year Two. By straddling the two sales over two different taxable years, a better result ensues. Assuming no other § 1231 gain or loss items, the Year One loss would be treated as ordinary loss and the Year Two gain would be treated as long-term capital gain. The loss can offset ordinary income taxed at the maximum marginal tax rate under § 1(a)–(d), and the gain will be taxed at a preferential rate under § 1(h).

This would be smart tax planning, but it would also, apparently, extend the benefit of § 1231 beyond what Congress is willing to provide. Under § 1231(c), the § 1231 gain in Year Two will be recharacterized as ordinary income to compensate for the fact that the Year One loss was an ordinary loss. This recharacterization will occur if the § 1231 gain asset is disposed of anytime after Year One but before Year Seven. In order to avoid the application of § 1231(c), therefore, the taxpayer in this hypothetical situation must either: (a) sell the § 1231 gain asset in Year One and then sell the § 1231 loss asset in Year Two (a less-appealing result because tax is paid earlier and the deduction is deferred); or (b) wait until Year Seven to sell the § 1231 gain asset, at which point the risk of recharacterization based on the net § 1231 loss from Year One will have passed.

§1231 gain will be recharacterized as ordinary unless you wait 5 yrs.

* * *

Self-Assessment Question

(Solutions to Self–Assessment Questions are set forth in Appendix 3.)

SAQ 7–6. In the current year, Samantha Stephens incurred the gains and losses described below. Determine how such gains and losses will be taxed.

• Samantha sold two parcels of real estate which she had owned and used in her business. Blackacre, the first parcel, sold for a gain of $5,000. Samantha had owned Blackacre for two years. Whiteacre, the second parcel, sold for a gain of only $3,000, largely because she had only owned the land for eight months.

• Samantha realized a $15,000 loss from the sale of United Airlines stock she had owned for several years.

• Samantha sustained an uninsured loss on the theft of computer equipment purchased three months before the theft and used in her business. Her adjusted basis in the computer equipment was $10,000 and its value was $11,000.

• Samantha sold several shares of Google stock at a $5,000 gain. She had held the shares for three years.

* * *

Problem 7–6

In Year One, Endora, an individual, recognized a $30,000 § 1231 loss on the sale of an apartment building. She also recognized a $2,000 § 1231 gain on the receipt of insurance proceeds from the loss of a painting used as an office decoration.

In Year Two, Endora had no § 1231 gains or losses.

In Year Three, Endora had $10,000 of § 1231 gain and a $6,000 § 1231 loss.

In Year Four, Endora had no § 1231 gains or losses.

In Year Five, Endora had no § 1231 gains or losses.

In Year Six, Endora had a $42,000 § 1231 gain and no § 1231 losses.

Determine the federal income tax consequences to Endora in Years One through Six.

E. DEPRECIATION RECAPTURE

Code: IRC §§ 1245(a)(1)–(3), (b)(1)–(4). *Skim* § 1250(a)(1)(A), (b)(1).

Regs: None.

All is Fair in Love, War, and Flavor. Like many of the provisions at issue in this Chapter, § 1245 is not an easy read at first blush. A fairly complex statute, the rule is easy to illustrate. Suppose an individual acquires depreciable equipment for use in his or her business at a cost of $100,000, makes no § 179 election, and properly plans to claim straight-line depreciation deductions of $10,000 each year for ten years. After three years of depreciation deductions, and ignoring the half-year convention, the taxpayer's basis in the equipment is $70,000. *See* § 1016(a)(2).

If the taxpayer sells the equipment to an unrelated purchaser for $80,000 cash, we know the taxpayer realizes and recognizes $10,000 of gain, but what is the flavor of the gain? We know the equipment is not a capital asset, § 1221(a)(2), but because the taxpayer held the equipment for more than one year, the gain is properly treated as "§ 1231 gain." That means there is a chance the gain could be treated as long-term capital gain. See § 1231(a)(1).

But notice that the $10,000 gain is entirely due to the fact that the taxpayer received a $10,000 deduction that offset *ordinary* income. To the extent the depreciation deduction was used to offset ordinary income, fairness (as reflected in the *Arrowsmith* doctrine in Chapter 6) dictates that gain attributable solely to depreciation should be treated as ordinary income, not long-term capital gain. In this example, § 1245 would recharacterize the flavor of the gain as ordinary income. Under § 1245(a)(1), gain attributable to depreciation deductions (and not economic appreciation) must be taxed as ordinary income. This recharacterization of the gain is known as "depreciation recapture," for it is triggered by the need to account for the fact that prior depreciation deductions offset ordinary income. In some ways, § 1245 is a form of error correction, as it corrects for the inconsistency that would occur if a taxpayer was entitled to long-term capital gain treatment where the gain was entirely attributable to depreciation.

Depreciation recapture under § 1245 is limited to "section 1245 property." This term is defined in § 1245(a)(3). Easily the broadest category here is in § 1245(a)(3)(A), which snags all depreciable personal property. Only a very few types of real property are subject to § 1245. Most depreciable real property is subject to recapture, if at all, under § 1250, as discussed below.

The Mechanics of § 1245. In order to determine the portion of a realized gain that is attributable to prior depreciation deductions, the statute creates a device called **recomputed basis**. Recomputed basis is generally equal to the original, pre-depreciation cost of the property. It is determined by adding to the adjusted basis all "deductions * * * allowed or allowable to the taxpayer or to any other person for depreciation or amortization." In cases where the taxpayer erred and claimed as depreciation less than the amount allowable under the Code, the taxpayer may be able to add only the amount actually taken as depreciation if the taxpayer can prove that the amount actually claimed was less than the amount allowable. Section 1245(a)(2)(B).

The recomputed basis is then compared to the amount realized (in the case of a sale, exchange, or involuntary conversion of the property) or the fair market value of the property (in the case of any other disposition). The smaller number is then applied against the taxpayer's adjusted basis to determine that recapture amount, the portion of the gain that must be treated as ordinary income.

Notice that § 1245 does not apply where the taxpayer has a realized loss. This is appropriate, for a realized loss on depreciable property means that the asset declined in value much more dramatically than the depreciation computation assumed (a rare event). There is no double benefit to the taxpayer in this situation—because the § 1231 loss on the sale of the depreciable asset might qualify for ordinary loss treatment anyway, there is no inconsistency in flavor.

Notice, too, that § 1245 requires the recognition of ordinary income even where the transaction would not otherwise be taxable. This is because the last sentence of § 1245(a)(1) requires this recognition "notwithstanding any other provision of this subtitle." This trump card will come into play in Chapter 8, when we take up property transactions in more detail.

* * *

Self-Assessment Question

(Solutions to Self–Assessment Questions are set forth in Appendix 3.)

SAQ 7–7. On January 1, Year One, Kelly purchased depreciable personal property for use in her business. The property cost $100,000. Kelly did not make a § 179 election. In addition, she elected to depreciate the cost of the property using the straight-line method over the property's 20–year recovery period ($5,000 annually for 20 years). For purposes of this question, ignore any applicable "conventions" in § 168(d).

On December 31, Year Three, Kelly sold the property to an unrelated purchaser for $110,000 cash.

(a) What is the amount and flavor of gain or loss realized and recognized from the Year Three disposition of the depreciable property?

(b) How would the answer to (a) change if the sale price was $95,000?

(c) How would the answer to (a) change if Kelly had validly elected to expense $20,000 of the original cost in Year One under § 179? Assume that the property had a recovery period of 16 years so that the straight-line depreciation deduction amount for each year was still $5,000.

* * *

Depreciation Recapture for Real Property: Section 1250. Recall that taxpayers can depreciate the cost of real property used in a trade or business activity or held for investment. While the underlying land is not depreciable, structures on the land are subject to "exhaustion" or "wear and tear" and thus qualify for depreciation deductions. The depreciation deductions offset ordinary income and reduce the taxpayer's basis in the subject property. Accordingly, when the taxpayer sells the real property, at least some portion of any resulting gain will be attributable to the prior depreciation deductions. Fairness (again, as underscored by the *Arrowsmith* doctrine) dictates that the portion of the realized gain attributable to prior depreciation deductions should be treated as ordinary income. Although real property used in a trade or business activity is not a capital asset, see § 1221(a)(2), gain from the sale of such property qualifies as "section 1231 gain" if the taxpayer held the property for more than one year. See § 1231(b). If the taxpayer's "section 1231 gains" exceed the taxpayer's "section 1231 losses" for the taxable year, the gains and losses are treated as long-term capital gains and losses, meaning any net gain will qualify for preferential tax treatment. See § 1231(a)(1).

If the subject real property is held as investment property, however, it is a capital asset to begin with, and the resulting gain is automatically eligible for the preferential tax rates if the subject property was held for more than one year—even though the property was depreciable in the hands of the taxpayer. To permit preferential tax treatment to a gain caused only by the taxpayer's taking depreciation deductions to offset ordinary income is an unjustified double benefit. But § 1245 recapture does not apply to most depreciable real property, like buildings and their permanent fixtures.

Section 1250 appears to provide a recapture mechanism, but as a practical matter it does not. In order to trigger § 1250 recapture, the taxpayer must have taken "additional depreciation" on depreciable real property. See § 1250(a)(1)(A). Additional depreciation is generally defined as the excess of the amount of accelerated depreciation deductions allowed to the taxpayer over the amount that would have been allowed had the property been depreciated using the straight-line method. See § 1250(b)(1). Yet since 1986, taxpayers with depreciable real property are required to use the straight-line method. See § 168(b)(3). In modern terms, then, § 1250 is a dinosaur.

While § 1250 is no longer effective to provide recapture for depreciable real property sold at a gain, an indirect form of recapture sits in (of all places) § 1(h). Recall that § 1(h)(1)(D) generally subjects "unrecaptured section 1250 gain" to a preferential tax rate of only 25 percent, not the 15–percent rate normally applicable to a net capital gain. By providing a less preferential rate for that portion of a net capital gain attributable to unrecaptured gain on depreciable real property, an indirect (and certainly imperfect) form of recapture exists.

* * *

Problem 7–7

Willy Wonka owns and operates a candy factory. In Year Three, many exciting things happened to Willy:

- In January, Willy sold a parcel of commercial real property used in his business for $350,000 cash to an unrelated party. Willy purchased the land for $300,000 in Year One.

- In March, a tornado completely destroyed an apartment building that Willy held for rental purposes. Willy originally paid $530,000 for the building in Year One, but because of straight-line depreciation deductions his adjusted basis in the building at the time of the storm was $500,000. Willy recovered $570,000 from his insurer to compensate for the loss in the building's value. Willy was not heavily involved in the management of the rental property, so the rental activity did not rise to the level of a trade or business. Willy decided to keep the cash proceeds instead of using them to acquire new rental property.

- The same tornado destroyed Willy's vacation home. Willy recovered $100,000 from an insurance policy covering the vacation home. The good news is that Willy paid only $80,000 for the property nine months before the storm. The bad news is that the property was worth $110,000 at the time of the storm. Though Willy spent several weekends at the vacation home, it was never his principal residence.

- In June, Willy discovered that a visitor to his candy factory stole a glass elevator that was used in the factory. The elevator, which had been installed in Year One, was worth $90,000 at the time the theft was discovered, but Willy's adjusted basis in the elevator at that time was $120,000. The insurance company paid $90,000 cash to Willy to compensate for the theft.

- In September, the county condemned a portion of real property owned by Willy and used in his candy factory business. Willy received $220,000 from the county as compensation for the taking, but Willy had paid $300,000 for the land in Year One.

- In November, Willy sold a gobstopper machine that had been used in his business to an unrelated purchaser for $120,000 cash. Willy paid $100,000 for the machine in Year One, and correctly claimed depreciation deductions totaling $35,000 in Years One, Two, and Three.

What are the federal income tax consequences of these gains and losses to Willy in Year Three?

* * *

Chapter 8

TRANSACTIONS IN PROPERTY

Wednesday
11/2:
p. 528-552
prob. 8-1

In this Chapter, we return to the basic formula for computing gains and losses in § 1001(a), as first discussed in Chapter 3:

	Amount Realized		Adjusted Basis
minus	Adjusted Basis	minus	Amount Realized
	Realized Gain		Realized Loss

$$\begin{array}{cc} AR & AB \\ -AB & -AR \\ \hline RG & RL \end{array}$$

Specifically, we consider some more advanced issues with respect to this formula. In Part A, we consider how to account for debt secured by the property transferred by a taxpayer. Ultimately, we will see that the amount of any debt encumbering the property is added to the taxpayer's amount realized on a sale or disposition of the property. Though the rule is easy to state, the rationale for the rule and its implications in property transactions is much more complex.

Part B of this Chapter considers the tax aspects of home ownership, with a focus on the deduction for qualified residence interest and the special exclusion provisions for gain on the sale of a principal residence. In Part C, we see that taxpayers do not recognize realized gains or realized losses upon a transfer of property in exchange for property of "like kind." Like-kind exchanges are very popular transactions for obvious reasons, so we should consider the basic application of the statute in this context. Part D of this Chapter examines involuntary conversions of property, another event that can defer recognition of gain.

In a typical property disposition for substantial consideration, the selling taxpayer will receive the purchase price in several installments that may span several taxable years. Part E of this Chapter looks at the tax consequences of the so-called "installment sales." We will see that selling taxpayers can coordinate the reporting of gain from an installment sale with the receipt of payments. Thus, where a taxpayer will receive one-third of the total consideration in each of Years One, Two, and Three, the taxpayer can report one-third of the total recognized gain from the sale in each of those years.

A. THE IMPACT OF DEBT RELIEF ON AMOUNT REALIZED

Code: *Review* IRC §§ 1001; 1012; 1014(a); 1016(a).

Regs: Treas. Reg. § 1.1001–2.

Although Shakespeare counseled against borrowing and lending activities, debt financing is a very common component of contemporary property transactions. Taxpayers routinely sell assets that secure their debts to creditors. Accordingly, these transactions introduce additional complexities to the traditional framework for computing gains and losses from the sale or exchange of property under § 1001(a). Even very simple transactions involving debts can raise a number of issues. For example, assume that Mariam borrows $200 from Bank and uses the loan proceeds, together with $300 of her own funds, to purchase a capital asset for $500. Pursuant to standard Bank policy, Mariam agrees to be personally liable for repayment of the $200 loan. This means that if Mariam defaults on her obligation to repay the loan, Bank can force a sale of the purchased asset. If the forced sale does not generate sufficient funds to repay Bank fully, Bank can require Mariam to pay the difference (or force a sale of other assets held by Mariam until Bank is fully repaid). Because Bank can pursue Mariam's other assets to obtain repayment of the loan if necessary, Mariam's obligation to Bank is said to be a **recourse** loan (because Bank has "recourse" against Mariam's other assets to be made whole in the event of default). As we saw in Chapter 3, borrowing $200 from Bank does not give rise to gross income because Mariam's repayment obligation offsets any "accession to wealth" from receipt of the loan proceeds. Furthermore, because Mariam's repayment obligation to Bank is part of her "cost" in acquiring the purchased asset, Mariam's basis in the asset is $500.

Now, suppose Mariam sells the purchased asset thirteen months later to an unrelated buyer. The fair market value of the asset at the time of the sale is $900. This simple sale offers a number of questions (okay, only three) with federal income tax implications.

1. How much will the buyer pay for the asset? Since the asset still secures Mariam's repayment obligation, the buyer will not pay $900 cash to Mariam. After all, if Mariam defaults on the loan from Bank, Bank's first stop for satisfaction is to foreclose on the purchased asset. The buyer might lose $200 in the asset's value to Bank. In every arms'-length transaction, the buyer will agree to one of two payment routes: either the buyer will *assume* the seller's obligation to the lender and pay to the seller an amount of cash equal to the excess of the asset's value over the

assume obligation

amount of the debt (the seller's "equity" in the property), or the buyer will simply take the property *subject to* the seller's liability and pay to the seller an amount of cash equal to the seller's equity. In this example, therefore, the buyer will pay only $700 to Mariam (the difference between the $900 value of the asset and the $200 owed to Bank that is secured by the asset) and will either assume her liability to Bank or take the property subject to the risk that Mariam may default and the Bank will collect $200 from a forced sale of the asset.

2. *What is the amount realized by Mariam?* Section 1001(b) defines the amount realized on a sale or other disposition of property as the sum of the amount of cash plus the fair market value of any property received in exchange. Mariam receives $700 cash from the buyer but no other property. Yet Mariam receives an additional benefit in this transaction: to the extent Bank will first go after the transferred asset for satisfaction of any default by Mariam, the risk of failing to repay Bank (loss of the transferred asset) has also passed to the buyer. Clearly, where the buyer affirmatively assumes Mariam's obligation to Bank, Mariam's relief from liability should be treated as additional consideration received by her in the sale transaction. And where the buyer simply takes the property subject to the liability and does not affirmatively take over responsibility for repayment, the foregoing analysis suggests that Mariam also enjoys relief from the obligation to repay Bank. Thus, it is well accepted that the amount of a recourse liability secured by transferred property is included in the seller's amount realized. Mariam's amount realized, therefore, is $900 ($700 cash + $200 debt relief), no matter whether the buyer assumes the debt or takes the asset subject to the debt.

3. *What is the flavor of Mariam's gain?* With an amount realized of $900, Mariam realizes a gain of $400 on the sale (amount realized of $900 less adjusted basis of $500). Because the transferred property is a capital asset in Mariam's hands, and because Mariam held the asset for more than one year, the $400 gain will be treated as a long-term capital gain eligible for a preferential tax rate under § 1(h). See Chapter 7. Notice that the entire gain is eligible for taxation at a reduced rate even though a portion of the gain is allocable to Mariam's debt relief. This is a different result from what would happen if Bank simply cancelled or discharged Mariam's debt. Although forgiveness of the debt would give rise to cancellation-of-debt (COD) income (potentially excludable under § 108), such income arises without a "sale or exchange" of a "capital asset." Thus, the COD income would be treated as ordinary income subject to tax at the regular rates of § 1.

By effectively disposing of the debt in the same transaction as the underlying capital asset, therefore, the gain allocable to the debt relief piggybacks onto the flavor of the transferred asset. Although this flavor shift is beneficial to Mariam, there is little potential for abuse here. The transaction is economically the same as if the buyer paid $900 to Mariam and then Mariam paid $200 to Bank in full satisfaction of the debt. If that had occurred, there is no question that all of Mariam's gain would be eligible for taxation at preferential rates. Thus it is fitting that all of

Mariam's gain in the real transaction be treated as long-term capital gain.

We will see that a different result occurs if the outstanding amount of the debt exceeds the value of the underlying property. In such a case, the buyer is assuming (or taking the property subject to) a debt obligation that is greater than the value of the underlying property. If the lender agrees not to pursue a claim for the difference against the seller, the lender is effectively discharging the seller from the obligation to pay the excess debt amount. That represents COD income and will be taxed accordingly (as ordinary income). Thus, for example, if Mariam fully depreciated the asset so that it had a zero basis at the time of the sale, and if the value of the asset had declined to $150, the transfer of the asset to the buyer (who would pay no cash, by the way, because the $200 debt exceeded the $150 value of the property) would give rise to a $150 gain ($150 amount realized less zero basis) and $50 of COD income. While the $150 gain might qualify as something other than ordinary income (unlikely because of § 1245 recapture, but still possible if the asset is not subject to § 1245), the $50 COD income amount would be treated as ordinary income.

The results described in all of the variations of Mariam's sale make sense where the loan is a recourse loan. But what if the loan is a **nonrecourse** loan? In a nonrecourse loan, the lender's recourse for default is limited only to assets that specifically secure the loan and no other assets. Of course, the name "nonrecourse" is somewhat misleading, for the lender *will* have recourse against assets specifically pledged by the borrower, and very few lenders would make loans on a nonrecourse basis without requiring security with a value at least equal to the amount loaned. In Mariam's case, if the Bank loan was nonrecourse, Bank could only force a sale of the transferred asset—Bank could not foreclose on any of Mariam's other assets. When Mariam sells the securing asset to the buyer, does it make sense to include the outstanding amount of the debt in her amount realized? Unlike the recourse liability examples, Mariam is not being relieved of ongoing personal liability by transferring the asset.

The treatment of nonrecourse debt under current law is set forth in the following cases. *Crane* provides the general rule for nonrecourse debt, and *Tufts* examines whether that general rule remains in force where the outstanding amount of the debt exceeds the value of the securing property.

CRANE v. COMMISSIONER

United States Supreme Court, 1947.
331 U.S. 1, 67 S.Ct. 1047, 91 L.Ed. 1301.

Mr. Chief Justice Vinson delivered the opinion of the Court.

The question here is how a taxpayer who acquires depreciable property subject to an unassumed mortgage, holds it for a period, and finally sells it still so encumbered, must compute her taxable gain.

Petitioner was the sole beneficiary and the executrix of the will of her husband, who died January 11, 1932. He then owned an apartment building and lot subject to a mortgage, which secured a principal debt of $255,000.00 and interest in default of $7,042.50. As of that date, the property was appraised for federal estate tax purposes at a value exactly equal to the total amount of this encumbrance. * * * On November 29, 1938, with the mortgagee threatening foreclosure, petitioner sold to a third party for $3,000.00 cash, subject to the mortgage, and paid $500.00 expenses of sale.

Petitioner reported a taxable gain of $1,250.00. Her theory was that the "property" which she had acquired in 1932 and sold in 1938 was only the equity, or the excess in the value of the apartment building and lot over the amount of the mortgage. This equity was of zero value when she acquired it. No depreciation could be taken on a zero value.[2] Neither she nor her vendee ever assumed the mortgage, so, when she sold the equity, the amount she realized on the sale was the net cash received, or $2,500.00. This sum less the zero basis constituted her gain, of which she reported half as taxable on the assumption that the entire property was a "capital asset."[3]

The Commissioner, however, determined that petitioner realized a net taxable gain of $23,767.03. His theory was that the "property" acquired and sold was not the equity, as petitioner claimed, but rather the physical property itself, or the owner's rights to possess, use, and dispose of it, undiminished by the mortgage. The original basis thereof was $262,042.50, its appraised value in 1932. Of this value $55,000.00 was allocable to land and $207,042.50 to building. During the period that petitioner held the property, there was an allowable depreciation of $28,045.10 on the building, so that the adjusted basis of the building at the time of sale was $178,997.40. The amount realized on the sale was said to include not only the $2,500.00 net cash receipts, but also the principal amount[6] of the mortgage subject to which the property was sold, both totaling $257,500.00. The selling price was allocable in the proportion, $54,471.15 to the land and $203,028.85 to the building. The Commissioner agreed that the land was a "capital asset", but thought that the building was not. Thus, he determined that petitioner sustained a capital loss of $528.85 on the land, of which 50% or $264.42 was taken into account, and an ordinary gain of $24.031.45 on the building, or a net taxable gain as indicated.

2. This position is, of course, inconsistent with her practice in claiming such deductions in each of the years the property was held. The deductions so claimed and allowed by the Commissioner were in the total amount of $25,500.00.

3. See § 117(a)(b), Revenue Act of 1938, c. 289, 52 Stat. 447, 26 U.S.C.A. Int. Rev. Code, § 117. Under this provision only 50% of the gain realized on the sale of a "capital asset" need be taken into account, if the property had been held more than two years.

6. The Commissioner explains that only the principal amount, rather than the total present debt secured by the mortgage, was deemed to be a measure of the amount realized, because the difference was attributable to interest due, a deductible item.

The Tax Court agreed with the Commissioner that the building was not a "capital asset." In all other respects it adopted petitioner's contentions, and expunged the deficiency. Petitioner did not appeal from the part of the ruling adverse to her, and these questions are no longer at issue. On the Commissioner's appeal, the Circuit Court of Appeals reversed, one judge dissenting. We granted certiorari because of the importance of the questions raised as to the proper construction of the gain and loss provisions of the Internal Revenue Code.

* * *

Logically, the first step under this scheme is to determine the unadjusted basis of the property, under [§ 1014(a)], and the dispute in this case is as to the construction to be given the term "property". If "property", as used in that provision, means the same thing as "equity", it would necessarily follow that the basis of petitioner's property was zero, as she contends. If, on the contrary, it means the land and building themselves, or the owner's legal rights in them, undiminished by the mortgage, the basis was $262,042.50.

We think that the reasons for favoring one of the latter constructions are of overwhelming weight. In the first place, the words of statutes—including revenue acts—should be interpreted where possible in their ordinary, everyday senses. The only relevant definitions of "property" to be found in the principal standard dictionaries are the two favored by the Commissioner, i.e., either that "property" is the physical thing which is a subject of ownership, or that it is the aggregate of the owner's rights to control and dispose of that thing. "Equity" is not given as a synonym, nor do either of the foregoing definitions suggest that it could be correctly so used. Indeed, "equity" is defined as "the value of a property * * * above the total of the liens. * * * " The contradistinction could hardly be more pointed. Strong countervailing considerations would be required to support a contention that Congress, in using the word "property", meant "equity", or that we should impute to it the intent to convey that meaning.

In the second place, the Commission's position has the approval of the administrative construction of [§ 1014(a)]. With respect to the valuation of property under that section, [Regulations], promulgated under the 1938 Act, provided that "the value of property as of the date of the death of the decedent as appraised for the purpose of the federal estate tax * * * shall be deemed to be its fair market value. * * * " The land and building here involved were so appraised in 1932, and their appraised value—$262,042.50—was reported by petitioner as part of the gross estate. This was in accordance with the estate tax law and regulations, which had always required that the value of decedent's property, undiminished by liens, be so appraised and returned, and that mortgages be separately deducted in computing the net estate. As the quoted provision of the Regulations has been in effect since 1918, and as the relevant statutory provision has been repeatedly reenacted since then in substantially the same form, the former may itself now be considered to have the force of law.

Moreover, in the many instances in other parts of the Act in which Congress has used the word "property", or expressed the idea of "property" or "equity", we find no instances of a misuse of either word or of a confusion of the ideas. In some parts of the Act other than the gain and loss sections, we find "property" where it is unmistakably used in its ordinary sense. On the other hand, where either Congress or the Treasury intended to convey the meaning of "equity," it did so by the use of appropriate language.

A further reason why the word "property" in [§ 1014(a)] should not be construed to mean "equity" is the bearing such construction would have on the allowance of deductions for depreciation and on the collateral adjustments of basis.

* * *

Under these provisions, if the mortgagor's equity were the [§ 1014(a)] basis, it would also be the original basis from which depreciation allowances are deducted. If it is, and if the amount of the annual allowances were to be computed on that value, as would then seem to be required, they will represent only a fraction of the cost of the corresponding physical exhaustion, and any recoupment by the mortgagor of the remainder of that cost can be effected only by the reduction of his taxable gain in the year of sale. If, however, the amount of the annual allowances were to be computed on the value of the property, and then deducted from an equity basis, we would in some instances have to accept deductions from a minus basis or deny deductions altogether. The Commissioner also argues that taking the mortgagor's equity as the [§ 1014(a)] basis would require the basis to be changed with each payment on the mortgage, and that the attendant problem of repeatedly recomputing basis and annual allowances would be a tremendous accounting burden on both the Commissioner and the taxpayer. Moreover, the mortgagor would acquire control over the timing of his depreciation allowances.

Thus it appears that the applicable provisions of the Act expressly preclude an equity basis, and the use of it is contrary to certain implicit principles of income tax depreciation, and entails very great administrative difficulties. It may be added that the Treasury has never furnished a guide through the maze of problems that arise in connection with depreciating an equity basis, but, on the contrary, has consistently permitted the amount of depreciation allowances to be computed on the full value of the property, and subtracted from it as a basis. Surely, Congress' long-continued acceptance of this situation gives it full legislative endorsement.

We conclude that the proper basis under [§ 1014(a)] is the value of the property, undiminished by mortgages thereon, and that the correct basis here was $262,042.50. The next step is to ascertain what adjustments are required under [§ 1016]. As the depreciation rate was stipulated, the only question at this point is whether the Commissioner was warranted in making any depreciation adjustments whatsoever.

Section [1016(a)(2)] provides that "proper adjustment in respect of the property shall in all cases be made * * * for exhaustion, wear and tear * * * to the extent allowed (but not less than the amount allowable * * *." The Tax Court found on adequate evidence that the apartment house was property of a kind subject to physical exhaustion, that it was used in taxpayer's trade or business, and consequently that the taxpayer would have been entitled to a depreciation allowance * * *), except that, in the opinion of that Court, the basis of the property was zero, and it was thought that depreciation could not be taken on a zero basis. As we have just decided that the correct basis of the property was not zero, but $262,042.50, we avoid this difficulty, and conclude that an adjustment should be made as the Commissioner determined.

Petitioner urges to the contrary that she was not entitled to depreciation deductions, whatever the basis of the property, because the law allows them only to one who actually bears the capital loss, and here the loss was not hers but the mortgagee's. We do not see, however, that she has established her factual premise. There was no finding of the Tax Court to that effect, nor to the effect that the value of the property was ever less than the amount of the lien. Nor was there evidence in the record, or any indication that petitioner could produce evidence, that this was so. The facts that the value of the property was only equal to the lien in 1932 and that during the next six and one-half years the physical condition of the building deteriorated and the amount of the lien increased, are entirely inconclusive, particularly in the light of the buyer's willingness in 1938 to take subject to the increased lien and pay a substantial amount of cash to boot. Whatever may be the rule as to allowing depreciation to a mortgagor on property in his possession which is subject to an unassumed mortgage and clearly worth less than the lien, we are not faced with that problem and see no reason to decide it now.

At last we come to the problem of determining the "amount realized" on the 1938 sale. Section [1001(b)], it will be recalled, defines the "amount realized" from "the sale * * * of property" as "the sum of any money received plus the fair market value of the property (other than money) received," and [§ 1001(a)] defines the gain on "the sale * * * of property" as the excess of the amount realized over the basis. Quite obviously, the word "property", used here with reference to a sale, must mean "property" in the same ordinary sense intended by the use of the word with reference to acquisition and depreciation * * *, both for certain of the reasons stated heretofore in discussing its meaning * * *, and also because the functional relation of the two sections requires that the word mean the same in one section that it does in the other. If the "property" to be valued on the date of acquisition is the property free of liens, the "property" to be priced on a subsequent sale must be the same thing.

Starting from this point, we could not accept petitioner's contention that the $2,500.00 net cash was all she realized on the sale except on the absurdity that she sold a quarter-of-a-million dollar property for roughly one per cent of its value, and took a 99 per cent loss. Actually, petitioner does not urge this. She argues, conversely, that because only $2,500.00 was realized on the sale, the "property" sold must have been the equity only, and that consequently we are forced to accept her contention as to the meaning of "property" * * *. We adhere, however, to what we have already said on the meaning of "property", and we find that the absurdity is avoided by our conclusion that the amount of the mortgage is properly included in the "amount realized" on the sale.

Petitioner concedes that if she had been personally liable on the mortgage and the purchaser had either paid or assumed it, the amount so paid or assumed would be considered a part of the "amount realized" * * *. The cases so deciding have already repudiated the notion that there must be an actual receipt by the seller himself of "money" or "other property", in their narrowest senses. It was thought to be decisive that one section of the Act must be construed so as not to defeat the intention of another or to frustrate the Act as a whole, and that the taxpayer was the "beneficiary" of the payment in "as real and substantial (a sense) as if the money had been paid it and then paid over by it to its creditors."

Both these points apply to this case. The first has been mentioned already. As for the second, we think that a mortgagor, not personally liable on the debt, who sells the property subject to the mortgage and for additional consideration, realizes a benefit in the amount of the mortgage as well as the boot.[37] If a purchaser pays boot, it is immaterial as to our problem whether the mortgagor is also to receive money from the purchaser to discharge the mortgage prior to sale, or whether he is merely to transfer subject to the mortgage—it may make a difference to the purchaser and to the mortgagee, but not to the mortgagor. Or put in another way, we are no more concerned with whether the mortgagor is, strictly speaking, a debtor on the mortgage, than we are with whether the benefit to him is, strictly speaking, a receipt of money or property. We are rather concerned with the reality that an owner of property, mortgaged at a figure less than that at which the property will sell, must and will treat the conditions of the mortgage exactly as if they were his personal obligations. If he transfers subject to the mortgage, the benefit to him is as real and substantial as if the mortgage were discharged, or as if a personal debt in an equal amount had been assumed by another.

Therefore we conclude that the Commissioner was right in determining that petitioner realized $257,500.00 on the sale of this property.

* * *

37. Obviously, if the value of the property is less than the amount of the mortgage, a mortgagor who is not personally liable cannot realize a benefit equal to the mortgage. Consequently, a different problem might be encountered where a mortgagor abandoned the property or transferred it subject to the mortgage without receiving boot. That is not this case.

Petitioner contends that the result we have reached taxes her on what is not income within the meaning of the Sixteenth Amendment. If this is because only the direct receipt of cash is thought to be income in the constitutional sense, her contention is wholly without merit. If it is because the entire transaction is thought to have been "by all dictates of common-sense * * * a ruinous disaster", as it was termed in her brief, we disagree with her premise. She was entitled to depreciation deductions for a period of nearly seven years, and she actually took them in almost the allowable amount. The crux of this case, really, is whether the law permits her to exclude allowable deductions from consideration in computing gain.[42] We have already showed that, if it does, the taxpayer can enjoy a double deduction, in effect, on the same loss of assets. The Sixteenth Amendment does not require that result any more than does the Act itself.

Affirmed.

MR. JUSTICE JACKSON [joined by MR. JUSTICE FRANKFURTER and MR. JUSTICE DOUGLAS], dissenting. [omitted]

COMMISSIONER v. TUFTS

United States Supreme Court, 1983.
461 U.S. 300, 103 S.Ct. 1826, 75 L.Ed.2d 863.

JUSTICE BLACKMUN delivered the opinion of the Court.

Over 35 years ago, in *Crane v. Commissioner,* 331 U.S. 1, 67 S.Ct. 1047, 91 L.Ed. 1301 (1947), this Court ruled that a taxpayer, who sold property encumbered by a nonrecourse mortgage (the amount of the mortgage being less than the property's value), must include the unpaid balance of the mortgage in the computation of the amount the taxpayer realized on the sale. The case now before us presents the question whether the same rule applies when the unpaid amount of the nonrecourse mortgage exceeds the fair market value of the property sold.

I

[In 1970, the taxpayers borrowed $1,851,500 on a nonrecourse basis to construct a 120–unit apartment complex in a suburb of Dallas. The taxpayers completed construction but the units did not rent out as hoped due to massive employee layoffs in the area. In 1972, when their basis in the property was $1,455,740, the taxpayers sold the property to one Fred Bayles for no consideration other than his assumption of the nonrecourse liability. The fair market value of the apartment building at the time of the sale was $1,400,000, so the taxpayers claimed a loss of

---

42. In the course of the argument some reference was made, as by analogy, to a situation in which a taxpayer acquired by devise property subject to a mortgage in an amount greater than the then value of the property, and later transferred it to a third person, still subject to the mortgage, and for a cash boot. Whether or not the differ-ence between the value of the property on acquisition and the amount of the mortgage would in that situation constitute either statutory or constitutional income is a question which is different from the one before us, and which we need not presently answer.

$55,740. The Service argued that the taxpayers in fact realized a gain of about $400,000, the difference between the principal amount of the debt and their basis.]

* * *

Relying on *Millar v. Commissioner,* 577 F.2d 212, 215 (CA3), cert. denied, 439 U.S. 1046, 99 S.Ct. 721, 58 L.Ed.2d 704 (1978), the United States Tax Court, in an unreviewed decision, upheld the asserted deficiencies. 70 T.C. 756 (1978). The United States Court of Appeals for the Fifth Circuit reversed. 651 F.2d 1058 (1981). That court expressly disagreed with the *Millar* analysis, and, in limiting *Crane v. Commissioner, supra,* to its facts, questioned the theoretical underpinnings of the *Crane* decision. We granted certiorari to resolve the conflict.

II

* * * Section 1001 governs the determination of gains and losses on the disposition of property. Under § 1001(a), the gain or loss from a sale or other disposition of property is defined as the difference between "the amount realized" on the disposition and the property's adjusted basis. Subsection (b) of § 1001 defines "amount realized": "The amount realized from the sale or other disposition of property shall be the sum of any money received plus the fair market value of the property (other than money) received." At issue is the application of the latter provision to the disposition of property encumbered by a nonrecourse mortgage of an amount in excess of the property's fair market value.

A

In *Crane v. Commissioner, supra,* this Court took the first and controlling step toward the resolution of this issue. Beulah B. Crane was the sole beneficiary under the will of her deceased husband. At his death in January 1932, he owned an apartment building that was then mortgaged for an amount which proved to be equal to its fair market value, as determined for federal estate tax purposes. The widow, of course, was not personally liable on the mortgage. She operated the building for nearly seven years, hoping to turn it into a profitable venture; during that period, she claimed income tax deductions for depreciation, property taxes, interest, and operating expenses, but did not make payments upon the mortgage principal. In computing her basis for the depreciation deductions, she included the full amount of the mortgage debt. In November 1938, with her hopes unfulfilled and the mortgagee threatening foreclosure, Mrs. Crane sold the building. The purchaser took the property subject to the mortgage and paid Crane $3,000; of that amount, $500 went for the expenses of the sale.

Crane reported a gain of $2,500 on the transaction. She reasoned that her basis in the property was zero (despite her earlier depreciation deductions based on including the amount of the mortgage) and that the amount she realized from the sale was simply the cash she received. The Commissioner disputed this claim. He asserted that Crane's basis in the property * * * was the property's fair market value at the time of her husband's death, adjusted for depreciation in the interim, and that the amount realized was the net cash received plus the amount of the outstanding mortgage assumed by the purchaser.

In upholding the Commissioner's interpretation * * *, the Court observed that to regard merely the taxpayer's equity in the property as her basis would lead to depreciation deductions less than the actual physical deterioration of the property, and would require the basis to be recomputed with each payment on the mortgage. The Court rejected Crane's claim that any loss due to depreciation belonged to the mortgagee. The effect of the Court's ruling was that the taxpayer's basis was the value of the property undiminished by the mortgage.

The Court next proceeded to determine the amount realized * * *. In order to avoid the "absurdity," see 331 U.S., at 13, 67 S.Ct., at 1054, of Crane's realizing only $2,500 on the sale of property worth over a quarter of a million dollars, the Court treated the amount realized as it had treated basis, that is, by including the outstanding value of the mortgage. To do otherwise would have permitted Crane to recognize a tax loss unconnected with any actual economic loss. The Court refused to construe one section of the Revenue Act so as "to frustrate the Act as a whole." *Ibid.*

Crane, however, insisted that the nonrecourse nature of the mortgage required different treatment. The Court, for two reasons, disagreed. First, excluding the nonrecourse debt from the amount realized would result in the same absurdity and frustration of the Code. Second, the Court concluded that Crane obtained an economic benefit from the purchaser's assumption of the mortgage identical to the benefit conferred by the cancellation of personal debt. Because the value of the property in that case exceeded the amount of the mortgage, it was in Crane's economic interest to treat the mortgage as a personal obligation; only by so doing could she realize upon sale the appreciation in her equity represented by the $2,500 boot. The purchaser's assumption of the liability thus resulted in a taxable economic benefit to her, just as if she had been given, in addition to the boot, a sum of cash sufficient to satisfy the mortgage.

In a footnote, pertinent to the present case, the Court observed:

"Obviously, if the value of the property is less than the amount of the mortgage, a mortgagor who is not personally liable cannot realize a benefit equal to the mortgage. Consequently, a different problem might be encountered where a mortgagor abandoned the property or transferred it subject to the mortgage without receiving boot. That is not this case." *Id.,* at 14, n. 37, 67 S.Ct., at 1054–55, n. 37.

B

This case presents that unresolved issue. We are disinclined to overrule *Crane,* and we conclude that the same rule applies when the unpaid amount of the nonrecourse mortgage exceeds the value of the property transferred. *Crane* ultimately does not rest on its limited theory of economic benefit; instead, we read *Crane* to have approved the Commissioner's decision to treat a nonrecourse mortgage in this context as a true loan. This approval underlies *Crane's* holdings that the amount of the nonrecourse liability is to be included in calculating both the basis and the amount realized on disposition. That the amount of the loan exceeds the fair market value of the property thus becomes irrelevant.

When a taxpayer receives a loan, he incurs an obligation to repay that loan at some future date. Because of this obligation, the loan proceeds do not qualify as income to the taxpayer. When he fulfills the obligation, the repayment of the loan likewise has no effect on his tax liability.

Another consequence to the taxpayer from this obligation occurs when the taxpayer applies the loan proceeds to the purchase price of property used to secure the loan. Because of the obligation to repay, the taxpayer is entitled to include the amount of the loan in computing his basis in the property; the loan, under § 1012, is part of the taxpayer's cost of the property. Although a different approach might have been taken with respect to a nonrecourse mortgage loan,[5] the Commissioner has chosen to accord it the same treatment he gives to a recourse mortgage loan. The Court approved that choice in *Crane,* and the respondents do not challenge it here. The choice and its resultant benefits to the taxpayer are predicated on the assumption that the mortgage will be repaid in full.

When encumbered property is sold or otherwise disposed of and the purchaser assumes the mortgage, the associated extinguishment of the mortgagor's obligation to repay is accounted for in the computation of the amount realized. See *United States v. Hendler,* 303 U.S. 564, 566–567, 58 S.Ct. 655, 656, 82 L.Ed. 1018 (1938). Because no difference between recourse and nonrecourse obligations is recognized in calculat-

---

5. The Commissioner might have adopted the theory, implicit in Crane's contentions, that a nonrecourse mortgage is not true debt, but, instead, is a form of joint investment by the mortgagor and the mortgagee. On this approach, nonrecourse debt would be considered a contingent liability, under which the mortgagor's payments on the debt gradually increase his interest in the property while decreasing that of the mortgagee. * * * Because the taxpayer's investment in the property would not include the nonrecourse debt, the taxpayer would not be permitted to include that debt in basis. * * * cf. *Gibson Products Co. v. United States,* 637 F.2d 1041, 1047–1048 (CA5 1981) (contingent nature of obligation prevents inclusion in basis of oil and gas leases of nonrecourse debt secured by leases, drill-

ing equipment, and percentage of future production).

We express no view as to whether such an approach would be consistent with the statutory structure and, if so, and *Crane* were not on the books, whether that approach would be preferred over *Crane's* analysis. We note only that the *Crane* Court's resolution of the basis issue presumed that when property is purchased with proceeds from a nonrecourse mortgage, the purchaser becomes the sole owner of the property. Under the *Crane* approach, the mortgagee is entitled to no portion of the basis. The nonrecourse mortgage is part of the mortgagor's investment in the property, and does not constitute a coinvestment by the mortgagee. * * *

ing basis,[7] *Crane* teaches that the Commissioner may ignore the nonrecourse nature of the obligation in determining the amount realized upon disposition of the encumbered property. He thus may include in the amount realized the amount of the nonrecourse mortgage assumed by the purchaser. The rationale for this treatment is that the original inclusion of the amount of the mortgage in basis rested on the assumption that the mortgagor incurred an obligation to repay. Moreover, this treatment balances the fact that the mortgagor originally received the proceeds of the nonrecourse loan tax-free on the same assumption. Unless the outstanding amount of the mortgage is deemed to be realized, the mortgagor effectively will have received untaxed income at the time the loan was extended and will have received an unwarranted increase in the basis of his property. The Commissioner's interpretation of § 1001(b) in this fashion cannot be said to be unreasonable.

C

The Commissioner in fact has applied this rule even when the fair market value of the property falls below the amount of the nonrecourse obligation. Treas. Reg. § 1.1001–2(b), 26 CFR § 1.1001–2(b) (1982); *Rev. Rul. 76–111*, 1976–1 Cum. Bull. 214. Because the theory on which the rule is based applies equally in this situation, * * * we have no reason, after *Crane,* to question this treatment.[11]

---

7. The Commissioner's choice in *Crane* "laid the foundation stone of most tax shelters," Bittker, *Tax Shelters, Nonrecourse Debt, and the* Crane *Case*, 33 Tax. L. Rev. 277, 283 (1978), by permitting taxpayers who bear no risk to take deductions on depreciable property. Congress recently has acted to curb this avoidance device by forbidding a taxpayer to take depreciation deductions in excess of amounts he has at risk in the investment. Pub. L. 94–455, § 204(a), 90 Stat. 1531 (1976), 26 U.S.C. § 465; * * *. Real estate investments, however, are exempt from this prohibition. § 465(c)(3)(D) * * *. Although this congressional action may foreshadow a day when nonrecourse and recourse debts will be treated differently, neither Congress nor the Commissioner has sought to alter *Crane's* rule of including nonrecourse liability in both basis and the amount realized.

11. Professor Wayne G. Barnett, as *amicus* in the present case, argues that the liability and property portions of the transaction should be accounted for separately. Under his view, there was a transfer of the property for $1.4 million, and there was a cancellation of the $1.85 million obligation for a payment of $1.4 million. The former resulted in a capital loss of $50,000, and the latter in the realization of $450,000 of ordinary income. Taxation of the ordinary income might be deferred under § 108 by a

reduction of respondents' bases in their partnership interests.

Although this indeed could be a justifiable mode of analysis, it has not been adopted by the Commissioner. Nor is there anything to indicate that the Code requires the Commissioner to adopt it. We note that Professor Barnett's approach does assume that recourse and nonrecourse debt may be treated identically.

The Commissioner also has chosen not to characterize the transaction as cancellation of indebtedness. We are not presented with and do not decide the contours of the cancellation-of-indebtedness doctrine. We note only that our approach does not fall within certain prior interpretations of that doctrine. In one view, the doctrine rests on the same initial premise as our analysis here— an obligation to repay—but the doctrine relies on a freeing-of-assets theory to attribute ordinary income to the debtor upon cancellation. According to that view, when nonrecourse debt is forgiven, the debtor's basis in the securing property is reduced by the amount of debt canceled, and realization of income is deferred until the sale of the property. Because that interpretation attributes income only when assets are freed, however, an insolvent debtor realizes income just to the extent his assets exceed his liabilities after the cancellation. Similar-

Respondents received a mortgage loan with the concomitant obligation to repay by the year 2012. The only difference between that mortgage and one on which the borrower is personally liable is that the mortgagee's remedy is limited to foreclosing on the securing property. This difference does not alter the nature of the obligation; its only effect is to shift from the borrower to the lender any potential loss caused by devaluation of the property. If the fair market value of the property falls below the amount of the outstanding obligation, the mortgagee's ability to protect its interests is impaired, for the mortgagor is free to abandon the property to the mortgagee and be relieved of his obligation.

This, however, does not erase the fact that the mortgagor received the loan proceeds tax-free and included them in his basis on the understanding that he had an obligation to repay the full amount. See *Woodsam Associates, Inc. v. Commissioner,* 198 F.2d 357, 359 (CA2 1952); Bittker, 33 TAX. L. REV., at 284. When the obligation is canceled, the mortgagor is relieved of his responsibility to repay the sum he originally received and thus realizes value to that extent within the meaning of § 1001(b). From the mortgagor's point of view, when his obligation is assumed by a third party who purchases the encumbered property, it is as if the mortgagor first had been paid with cash borrowed by the third party from the mortgagee on a nonrecourse basis, and then had used the cash to satisfy his obligation to the mortgagee.

Moreover, this approach avoids the absurdity the Court recognized in *Crane.* Because of the remedy accompanying the mortgage in the nonrecourse situation, the depreciation in the fair market value of the property is relevant economically only to the mortgagee, who by lending on a nonrecourse basis remains at risk. To permit the taxpayer to limit his realization to the fair market value of the property would be to recognize a tax loss for which he has suffered no corresponding economic loss. Such a result would be to construe "one section of the Act ... so as ... to defeat the intention of another or to frustrate the Act as a whole." 331 U.S., at 13, 67 S.Ct., at 1054.

In the specific circumstances of *Crane,* the economic benefit theory did support the Commissioner's treatment of the nonrecourse mortgage as a personal obligation. The footnote in *Crane* acknowledged the limitations of that theory when applied to a different set of facts. *Crane* also stands for the broader proposition, however, that a nonrecourse loan should be treated as a true loan. We therefore hold that a taxpayer must

---

ly, if the nonrecourse indebtedness exceeds the value of the securing property, the taxpayer never realizes the full amount of the obligation canceled because the tax law has not recognized negative basis.

Although the economic benefit prong of *Crane* also relies on a freeing-of-assets theory, that theory is irrelevant to our broader approach. In the context of a sale or disposition of property under § 1001, the extinguishment of the obligation to repay is not ordinary income; instead, the amount of the canceled debt is included in the amount realized, and enters into the computation of gain or loss on the disposition of property. According to *Crane,* this treatment is no different when the obligation is nonrecourse: the basis is not reduced as in the cancellation-of-indebtedness context, and the full value of the outstanding liability is included in the amount realized. Thus, the problem of negative basis is avoided.

account for the proceeds of obligations he has received tax-free and included in basis. Nothing in either § 1001(b) or in the Court's prior decisions requires the Commissioner to permit a taxpayer to treat a sale of encumbered property asymmetrically, by including the proceeds of the nonrecourse obligation in basis but not accounting for the proceeds upon transfer of the encumbered property.

* * *

IV

When a taxpayer sells or disposes of property encumbered by a nonrecourse obligation, the Commissioner properly requires him to include among the assets realized the outstanding amount of the obligation. The fair market value of the property is irrelevant to this calculation. We find this interpretation to be consistent with *Crane v. Commissioner,* 331 U.S. 1, 67 S.Ct. 1047, 91 L.Ed. 1301 (1947), and to implement the statutory mandate in a reasonable manner.

The judgment of the Court of Appeals is therefore reversed.

It is so ordered.

JUSTICE O'CONNOR, concurring.

I concur in the opinion of the Court, accepting the view of the Commissioner. I do not, however, endorse the Commissioner's view. Indeed, were we writing on a slate clean except for the *Crane* decision, I would take quite a different approach—that urged upon us by Professor Barnett as *amicus.*

Crane established that a taxpayer could treat property as entirely his own, in spite of the "coinvestment" provided by his mortgagee in the form of a nonrecourse loan. That is, the full basis of the property, with all its tax consequences, belongs to the mortgagor. That rule alone, though, does not in any way tie nonrecourse debt to the cost of property or to the proceeds upon disposition. I see no reason to treat the purchase, ownership, and eventual disposition of property differently because the taxpayer also takes out a mortgage, an independent transaction. In this case, the taxpayer purchased property, using nonrecourse financing, and sold it after it declined in value to a buyer who assumed the mortgage. There is no economic difference between the events in this case and a case in which the taxpayer buys property with cash; later obtains a nonrecourse loan by pledging the property as security; still later, using cash on hand, buys off the mortgage for the market value of the devalued property; and finally sells the property to a third party for its market value.

The logical way to treat both this case and the hypothesized case is to separate the two aspects of these events and to consider, first, the ownership and sale of the property, and, second, the arrangement and retirement of the loan. Under *Crane,* the fair market value of the property on the date of acquisition—the purchase price—represents the taxpayer's basis in the property, and the fair market value on the date of disposition represents the proceeds on sale. The benefit received by the taxpayer in return for the property is the cancellation of a mortgage that is worth no more than the fair market value of the property, for that is all the mortgagee can expect to collect on the mortgage. His gain or loss on the disposition of the property equals the difference between the proceeds and the cost of acquisition. Thus, the taxation of the transaction *in property* reflects the economic fate of the *property*. If the property has declined in value, as was the case here, the taxpayer recognizes a loss on the disposition of the property. The new purchaser then takes as his basis the fair market value as of the date of the sale.

In the separate borrowing transaction, the taxpayer acquires cash from the mortgagee. He need not recognize income at that time, of course, because he also incurs an obligation to repay the money. Later, though, when he is able to satisfy the debt by surrendering property that is worth less than the face amount of the debt, we have a classic situation of cancellation of indebtedness, requiring the taxpayer to recognize income in the amount of the difference between the proceeds of the loan and the amount for which he is able to satisfy his creditor. 26 U.S.C. § 61(a)(12). The taxation of the financing transaction then reflects the economic fate of the loan.

The reason that separation of the two aspects of the events in this case is important is, of course, that the Code treats different sorts of income differently. A gain on the sale of the property may qualify for capital gains treatment, * * * while the cancellation of indebtedness is ordinary income, but income that the taxpayer may be able to defer. Not only does Professor Barnett's theory permit us to accord appropriate treatment to each of the two types of income or loss present in these sorts of transactions, it also restores continuity to the system by making the taxpayer-seller's proceeds on the disposition of property equal to the purchaser's basis in the property. Further, and most important, it allows us to tax the events in this case in the same way that we tax the economically identical hypothesized transaction.

Persuaded though I am by the logical coherence and internal consistency of this approach, I agree with the Court's decision not to adopt it judicially. We do not write on a slate marked only by *Crane*. The Commissioner's longstanding position * * * is now reflected in the regulations. Treas. Reg. § 1.1001–2, 26 CFR § 1.1001–2 (1982). In the light of the numerous cases in the lower courts including the amount of the unrepaid proceeds of the mortgage in the proceeds on sale or disposition, * * * it is difficult to conclude that the Commissioner's interpretation of the statute exceeds the bounds of his discretion. As the Court's opinion demonstrates, his interpretation is defensible. One can reasonably read § 1001(b)'s reference to "the amount realized *from* the sale or other disposition of property" (emphasis added) to permit the Commissioner to collapse the two aspects of the transaction. As long as his view is a reasonable reading of § 1001(b), we should defer to the regulations promulgated by the agency charged with interpretation of the statute. Accordingly, I concur.

Notes

1. *Crane and* Tufts *as Error Correction Devices.* The *Tufts* majority makes it clear that the *Crane* rule ultimately serves as an error correction device. In *Crane*, the Court held as a preliminary matter that a taxpayer's basis in property includes the amount of nonrecourse debt secured by the property. If the taxpayer's basis includes nonrecourse debt, then notions of symmetry require that the amount realized by the taxpayer include relief from nonrecourse debt, even though (because the amount of the debt exceeds the property's value) the taxpayer has no incentive to pay off the debt and does not experience an "accession to wealth" in the traditional sense. If the nonrecourse debt were not included in the amount realized, the taxpayer would have a windfall—either in the form of less gain or higher loss—because the remaining debt is still incorporated into the taxpayer's basis.

2. *More on Basis Symmetry.* The *Crane* and *Tufts* Courts conclude that the outstanding amount of nonrecourse debt must be included in the amount realized in order to account for the fact that the debt was included in the cost basis of the property. If debt that was included in basis was not added to the amount realized, taxpayers would most likely realize losses from transactions where no real loss occurred. In Beulah Crane's case, for example, there would be a realized loss of about $230,000 if the balance of the nonrecourse debt was not included in the amount realized. That result would be silly, for in no sense did Beulah Crane suffer any loss upon disposition of the property. Only by including the debt in the amount realized can a true measure of economic gain be achieved.

But *Crane* and *Tufts* are not limited to situations where the nonrecourse debt is included in basis. Inclusion of debt (recourse or nonrecourse) in the amount realized is required even where the debt proceeds were not used to acquire or improve the encumbered property. Thus, if a taxpayer borrowed cash from a bank on a nonrecourse basis and pledged as security an asset worth more than the amount borrowed, the outstanding principal amount of the debt is still included in the taxpayer's amount realized even if the taxpayer uses no portion of the loan proceeds to purchase or make improvements to the property. Given that *Crane* and *Tufts* are premised on notions of basis symmetry, one might question this result.

But from another perspective, the rule is right. Suppose Woody owns a capital asset worth $100,000 with a basis of $30,000. Woody borrows $50,000 from Mia on a nonrecourse basis and offers the capital asset as security for the loan. Woody uses the loan proceeds to pay various expenses (business and personal in nature, but unrelated to the capital asset). Since no portion of the loan is used to acquire or improve the securing property, no portion of the loan is added to Woody's basis in the capital asset. See §§ 1012 and 1016(a)(1). If Woody sells the asset to an unrelated buyer, subject to the liability, the buyer will pay $50,000 cash to Woody (the difference between the value of the asset and the amount of the debt), assuming no portion of the debt has been repaid. Still, Woody's amount realized from the sale would be $100,000 ($50,000 cash + $50,000 debt relief), giving rise to a $70,000 gain. Basis symmetry does not compel this result, but a cost-benefit analysis does. Woody's total cost in this example is $30,000, his basis in the property transferred. Because Woody paid no portion of the debt, his obligation to repay never represented an actual cost to him. On the benefit side, Woody got $50,000 cash from the buyer and the use of $50,000 to pay various business and personal expenses. (The fact that some portion of these expenses are deductible is not considered here in determining the income from the sale of encumbered property—the deductions will be accounted for in computing adjusted gross income or taxable income.) A comparison of the costs and benefits justifies a $70,000 gain:

Costs	Benefits
Basis $30,000	Cash at sale $50,000
	Use of $50,000 to pay expenses

If Woody had repaid $10,000 of the loan balance prior to the sale, the outstanding amount of the loan at the time of sale would have been $40,000. Under *Crane* and *Tufts*, then, the resulting gain would have been $60,000 ($90,000 amount realized less $30,000 basis). A cost-benefit analysis proves this is the correct result:

Costs	Benefits
Basis $30,000	Cash at sale $50,000
Loan repayment $10,000	Use of $50,000 to pay expenses

If Woody used the loan to improve the encumbered capital asset, his basis in the asset would have increased to $80,000 ($30,000 original basis plus $50,000 improvement). Here, basis symmetry as well as cost-benefit notions require inclusion of the unpaid debt in the amount realized. If Woody repaid $20,000 of the debt prior to sale, his basis would be unchanged (instead of having an $80,000 basis consisting of $30,000 cost plus $50,000 of debt, the basis now consists of $50,000 cost plus $30,000 of debt). In either case, the cash sale would yield a $20,000 gain ($100,000 amount realized less $80,000 basis):

AR	$100,000	[cash + debt relief]
AB	$ 80,000	
RG	$ 20,000	

The result makes sense from a cost-benefit perspective:

Costs	Benefits
Basis $80,000	Cash at sale $50,000
	Use of $50,000 to pay expenses

Here is the funny part: *Tufts* says that *Crane* really rests on the basis symmetry rationale and not its "incentive-to-pay" theory, yet both *Tufts* and *Crane* really rest on the cost-benefit rationale. At least the *Tufts* Court got the right result, assuming *Crane's* conclusion that nonrecourse debt can be added to basis is correct.

3. *The Legacy of Crane.* The holding in *Crane* is credited as giving birth to the "tax shelter" real estate activity of the 1960s, 1970s and 1980s. The tax shelters took many forms, but most involved a variation of a simple

scheme. For example, a taxpayer would pay $100,000 and borrow $4,900,000 on a nonrecourse basis to purchase a $5 million building to be held for rental purposes. Under *Crane*, the taxpayer's basis in the building would be $5 million. Because the building was subject to wear and tear and was held by the taxpayer for investment purposes, the building gave rise to depreciation deductions. See § 167. Assuming straight-line depreciation over 20 years, and ignoring the applicable convention, the taxpayer in this example would be entitled to annual depreciation deductions of $250,000. If the taxpayer was subject to federal and state income taxes at a flat rate of 40 percent, the taxpayer would save $100,000 in taxes each year as a result of the deduction (40% of $250,000). Notice that the taxpayer's savings in the first year completely offsets the taxpayer's initial out-of-pocket investment in the building. All future depreciation deductions would be gravy to the taxpayer, for these deductions would be based on a cost that the taxpayer may never incur (the nonrecourse debt). It was the pursuit of these "deductions-for-nothing" that made tax shelters so popular.

In 1986, Congress implemented a three-pronged attack to thwart real estate tax shelter activity. First, it substantially lengthened the recovery periods for residential and commercial real estate (to 27.5 years and 39 years, respectively). By lengthening the recovery periods, the annual depreciation deductions were less, thus diminishing a tax shelter's profitability. Second, Congress extended the "at-risk" requirements in § 465 to real estate. Section 465 is discussed more fully in Chapter 11. Finally, Congress enacted the "passive activity loss" limitation rules in § 469, another topic awaiting examination in Chapter 11. Both §§ 465 and 469 curb tax shelter activity not by limiting the *amount* of the deductions generated by the tax shelter activity but by limiting the *current deductibility* of such expenses and losses.

* * *

WOODSAM ASSOCIATES, INC. v. COMMISSIONER, 198 F.2d 357 (2d Cir. 1952).

Facts: The taxpayer refinanced a parcel of real property by giving the bank a nonrecourse mortgage in the amount of $400,000. The taxpayer's basis in the property at the time of this transaction was about $300,000. The taxpayer argued that this transaction gave rise to about $100,000 of gain. (Why, you ask? Because that transaction occurred in a year long since closed under the statute of limitations.) Consequently, the $100,000 of gain that should have been recognized would be considered part of the "tax cost" of the property, so when the taxpayer sold the property for a little over $436,000 in the year at issue in the case, the proper basis to be used in computing gain should have been $400,000 instead of $300,000. The Service argued that the refinancing transaction did not give rise to taxable gain, so the taxpayer's basis was properly kept at $300,000.

Issue: When property is mortgaged as security for a nonrecourse loan in excess of the basis of the property, does a taxable gain result?

Holding: No.

Rationale: The refinancing transaction is not a realization event because no sale, exchange, or other disposition of the property has occurred. The taxpayer "merely augmented the existing mortgage indebtedness [by the refinancing transaction] and, far from closing the venture, remained in a position to borrow more if and when circumstances permitted and [it] so desired. And so, [the taxpayer] never 'disposed' of the property to create a taxable event which [§ 1001] makes a condition precedent to the taxation of gain."

ESTATE OF FRANKLIN v. COMMISSIONER, 544 F.2d 1045 (9th Cir. 1976).

Facts: The taxpayer acquired a parcel of improved real property by giving the seller a nonrecourse mortgage in the amount of $1,224,000 and no other consideration (no cash down payment at closing). The principal amount of the promissory note was substantially greater than the fair market value of the purchased property. (Why? Because the taxpayer wanted a higher basis in the property in order to increase the annual depreciation deductions with respect to the property. By borrowing more on a nonrecourse basis, the taxpayer could inflate the basis of the property at no risk.)

The taxpayer then leased the property back to the seller for a ten-year term. The lease agreement required rental payments roughly equal to the taxpayer's payments on the mortgage. At the end of the lease term, the taxpayer was required to pay the remaining principal amount of the mortgage (which at that time would be $975,000). The Service disallowed the depreciation deductions claimed by the taxpayer with respect to the property. The Tax Court upheld the disallowance, concluding that the transaction was, in substance, an option to purchase the property at the end of the ten-year lease term.

Issue: Was it proper for the Service to disallow the taxpayer's depreciation deductions with respect to the property?

Holding: Yes.

Rationale: The Ninth Circuit decided that the Tax Court reached the right result (no depreciation deductions) but for the wrong reason. It was not necessary to cast the transaction as a disguised option. On these facts, the nonrecourse debt had no economic reality unless and until the property substantially appreciated in value. Thus, no portion of the nonrecourse debt should have been added to the taxpayer's basis. "An acquisition * * * at a price approximately equal to the fair market value of the property under ordinary circumstances would rather quickly yield an equity in the property which the purchaser could not prudently abandon. This is the stuff of substance. It meshes with the form of the transaction and constitutes a sale.

"No such meshing occurs when the purchase price exceeds a demonstrably reasonable estimate of the fair market value. Payments on the principal of the purchase price yield no equity so long as the unpaid balance of the purchase price exceeds the then existing fair market value. Under these circumstances the purchaser by abandoning the transaction can lose no more than a mere chance to acquire an equity in the future should the value of the acquired property increase. While this chance undoubtedly influenced the Tax Court's determination that the transaction before us constitutes an option, we need only point out that its existence fails to supply the substance necessary to justify treating the transaction as a sale *ab initio*. It is not necessary to the disposition of this case to decide the tax consequences of a transaction such as that before us if in a subsequent year the fair market value of the property increases to an extent that permits the purchaser to acquire an equity.

"Authority also supports our perception. It is fundamental that 'depreciation is not predicated upon ownership of property *but rather upon an investment in property* * * *.' No such investment exists when payments of the purchase price in accordance with the design of the parties yield no equity to the purchaser. In the transaction before us and during the taxable years in question the purchase price payments by [the taxpayer] have not been shown to constitute an *investment in the property*. Depreciation was properly disallowed. * * *

"Authority also supports disallowance of the interest deductions. This is said even though it has long been recognized that the absence of personal liability for the purchase money debt secured by a mortgage on the acquired property does not deprive the debt of its character as a bona fide debt obligation able to support an interest deduction. * * * However, this is no longer true when it appears that the debt has economic significance only if the property substantially appreciates in value prior to the date at which a very large portion of the purchase price is to be discharged. * * * To justify the deduction the debt must exist; potential existence will not do. For debt to exist, the purchaser, in the absence of personal liability, must confront a situation in which it is presently reasonable from an economic point of view for him to make a capital investment in the amount of the unpaid purchase price.

"Our focus on the relationship of the fair market value of the property to the unpaid purchase price should not be read as premised upon the belief that a sale is not a sale if the purchaser pays too much. Bad bargains from the buyer's point of view—as well as sensible bargains from buyer's, but exceptionally good from the seller's point of view—do not thereby cease to be sales. We intend our holding and explanation thereof to be understood as limited to transactions substantially similar to that now before us."

PLEASANT SUMMIT LAND CORP. v. COMMISSIONER, 863 F.2d 263 (3d Cir. 1988).

Facts: The taxpayer acquired an apartment complex by giving the seller a nonrecourse mortgage in an amount in excess of the property's $4.2 million fair market value. As in *Estate of Franklin*, the Service disallowed the taxpayer's depreciation deductions that were computed with reference to the full amount of the nonrecourse note.

Issue: Was it proper for the Service to disallow the taxpayer's depreciation deductions with respect to the property?

Holding: Not entirely.

Rationale: The court disagreed with the conclusion of *Estate of Franklin* that the taxpayer receives no basis credit for nonrecourse debt in excess of the securing property's value. The court determined that the basis should reflect the debt, but only to the extent of the property's fair market value. "While we realize that a taxpayer holding property subject to a nonrecourse debt in excess of the market value of the property may have no incentive to pay off any portion of the debt, including the amount not exceeding the fair market value of the property, it is equally logical to recognize that the creditor holding the debt has no incentive to take back the property if the taxpayer offers to pay the debt up to the value of the property. For example, if a creditor held a nonrecourse debt for $1,500,000 on a property with a fair market value of $1,000,000, he would have a disincentive to foreclose if his defaulting debtor offered to settle the debt for not less than $1,000,000. Thus, it is appropriate to disregard only the portion of nonrecourse debt in excess of the fair market value of the property when it was acquired for purposes of calculations of the depreciation and interest deductions and to regard the nonrecourse debt as genuine indebtedness to the extent it is not disregarded."

REVENUE RULING 90–16, 1990–1 C.B. 12.

Facts: The taxpayer owned a residential subdivision with a fair market value of $10,000x and a basis of $8,000x. The property was subject to a recourse debt in the amount of $12,000x when the taxpayer defaulted on the debt. The taxpayer negotiated an agreement with the bank whereby the bank foreclosed on (and took possession of) the property and the bank released the taxpayer from all liability on any amounts due on the debt.

Issue: What are the federal income tax consequences of this transfer in satisfaction of a recourse debt?

Holding: The taxpayer has $2,000x of gain from the sale of the property under §§ 61(a)(3) and 1001, as well as $2,000x of income from the discharge of indebtedness under § 61(a)(12).

Rationale: "To the extent of the fair market value of the property transferred to the creditor, the transfer of the subdivision is treated as a sale or disposition upon which gain is recognized under section 1001(c) of the Code. To the extent the fair market value of the subdivision, 10,000x dollars, exceeds its adjusted basis, 8,000x dollars, [the taxpayer] realizes and recognizes gain on the transfer. [The taxpayer] thus recognizes 2,000x dollars of gain.

"To the extent the amount of debt, 12,000x dollars, exceeds the fair market value of the subdivision, 10,000x dollars, [the taxpayer] realizes income from the discharge of indebtedness. However, under section 108(a)(1)(B) of the Code, the full amount of [the taxpayer's] discharge of indebtedness income is excluded from gross income because that amount does not exceed the amount by which [the taxpayer] was insolvent."

* * *

Self-Assessment Questions

(Solutions to Self–Assessment Questions are set forth in Appendix 3.)

SAQ 8–1. In Year One, Sally took out a $250,000 recourse loan from Bank to purchase a piece of commercial real estate (land and building). She used all of the loan proceeds, together with $50,000 of her own funds ($300,000 total) to buy the building. The Bank loan was secured by the property.

(a) What is Sally's basis in the building? *$300k*

(b) Would the answer to (a) change if the Bank loan was not secured by the building? *No*

(c) Would the answer to (a) change if the loan was nonrecourse? *No.*

SAQ 8–2. Assume the same facts in SAQ 8–1. In Year Six, when the property was worth $500,000 (and the balance owing to Bank was $200,000 and Sally's adjusted basis in the property was $250,000), Sally borrowed an additional $150,000 from Bank (again on a recourse basis), giving Bank a second mortgage on the property. Sally used the loan proceeds for personal purposes.

(a) Does Sally have gross income from the receipt of the second loan? *No.*

(b) Would the answer to (a) change if her adjusted basis in the property was only $100,000? *No. a loan is never a realization event (woodsam)*

(c) Would the answers to (a) or (b) change if the loan was nonrecourse? *No.*

(d) What is Sally's basis in the property after she takes out the second Bank loan? *Sally's basis is still $250k. Because she did not use the $ from 2nd mort.*

(e) Would the answer to (d) change if Sally used $50,000 of the proceeds from the second Bank loan to add additional restrooms to the building? *Yes, Sally's basis would increase $50k for a basis total of $300k. to improve the property.*

Problem 8–1

Assume the same facts in SAQ 8–2. In Year Eight, when local economy went sour, Sally's business fell on hard times and the value of her building declined to $220,000. Sally transferred the property, subject to the recourse liabilities, to Linus (an unrelated individual who enjoys making speculative investments) for $10,000 cash. At the time, her adjusted basis in the property was $200,000 and total balance due to Bank was $300,000. As part of the transaction, Bank agreed to hold Sally harmless from repayment of the loans in exchange for Linus' agreement to be personally liable for the recourse loans incurred by Sally.

(a) What gain or loss does Sally realize on the exchange with Linus?

(b) Would the answer to (a) change if the loans were nonrecourse and Linus was not required to give a personal guarantee for the Bank loans?

(c) What is Linus' basis in the property?

(d) How would the answer to (c) change if the loans were nonrecourse?

B.   TAX ASPECTS OF HOME OWNERSHIP

Code: IRC §§ 121(a)–(d)(3); 163(a), (h)(1)–(4).

Regs: Treas. Reg. §§ 1.121–1; 1.121–2; 1.121–3.

Welcome Home! In this Part we consider two important tax benefits from home ownership: the deduction for "qualified residence interest," and the limited exclusion of gain from the sale of a "principal" residence. In tandem, these benefits make home ownership much more attractive than renting, at least from a tax perspective. Home ownership has its headaches, certainly, but the doldrums of constant repairs and landscaping work are usually more than offset by the joys of tax breaks.

The Interest Deduction Generally. In order to appreciate the significance of the deduction for qualified residence interest, it is helpful to understand first the § 163 deduction for interest more generally. Since we have not addressed § 163 in a prior Chapter, let us do so here. Section 163(a) generally permits a deduction for interest paid or accrued during the taxable year. Prior to 1986 that general rule carried much more weight, as most any payment of interest generated a deduction. The Tax Reform Act of 1986 sharply curtailed the scope of the interest deduction. While the general rule in § 163(a) remains, the limitation imposed by § 163(h) renders all but six forms of interest non-deductible. In effect, then, the real general rule is one of non-deduction with six discreet exceptions.

The first exception is for **active business interest**, interest paid or incurred with respect to a trade or business activity in which the taxpayer materially participates. Section 163(h)(2)(A). To the extent interest expense is deductible under § 162(a) already, § 163(h)(2)(A) is seemingly superfluous. Most likely, it is listed again in § 163(h)(2)(A) to confirm that the general rule of disallowance in § 163(h)(1) does not trump the general deduction under § 162(a).

> EXAMPLE OF § 163(h)(2)(A): Gloria obtains a loan to purchase or improve an office building used in her full-time business activity. Interest paid on this loan would be deductible as "active business interest."

The second exception is for **taxable investment interest**, interest paid to finance investment activities that will yield income subject to

amount realized = $300K + $10K = $310K
adjusted basis = $200K
$110K Realized gain

Ch. 8   TRANSACTIONS IN PROPERTY   553

federal income tax. Section 163(h)(2)(B). This form of interest is deductible to the extent of the taxpayer's "net investment income." Section 163(d). Of course, such interest expense would also be deductible under § 212(1). Here again, § 163(h)(2)(B) serves notice that the § 212(1) deduction will not be trumped by the general rule of disallowance.

> EXAMPLE OF § 163(h)(2)(B): Gloria borrows money from Bank to purchase shares of stock in Texas Utilities Corporation. If Gloria's interest expense on the Bank loan is $500 and her net investment income for the year of payment is $200, she can deduct $200 of the interest expense in the year of payment. If Gloria borrows money to purchase municipal bonds, however, no portion of the interest is deductible if the income generated by the bonds is excluded from gross income under § 103. See also § 265(a)(2).

The third exception is for **passive activity business interest**. Section 163(h)(2)(C). To the extent a taxpayer incurs debt for a business activity in which the taxpayer does not materially participate (a "passive activity"), a deduction for the resulting interest expense is allowed, but only to the extent that the income from all passive activities of the taxpayer during the year exceeds the taxpayer's *other* losses and deductions from his or her passive activities. While active business interest is not subject to any such limitation on deductibility, a more restrictive deduction is consistent with the theme of § 469, which limits deductions from passive activities to the taxpayer's gross income from passive activities. The § 469 limitation (and the definition of material participation) is discussed at Chapter 11.

> EXAMPLE OF § 163(h)(2)(C): Gloria borrows money to purchase rental property. Although she rents out the property, she does not "materially participate" in the rental activity. If Gloria's interest expense on this debt is $500 and her gross income from all passive activities for the year of payment is $200, Gloria may deduct $200 of the interest expense in the year of payment.

The fourth exception relates to certain **estate tax interest**. Section 163(h)(2)(E). The Code currently imposes an excise tax on the transfer of wealth at death by individuals with very substantial estates. See § 2001. The excise tax is due nine months after the decedent's death. Sometimes, however, the estate may be unable to pay this tax when due because a significant portion of the estate may include illiquid, unassignable assets that the estate cannot sell to pay the corresponding tax. In such cases, § 6163 permits the estate to defer the estate tax attributable to such illiquid and unassignable assets until such time as the estate is able to finally collect or sell such assets. Of course, interest on this deferral must be paid by the estate. See § 6601. Section 163(h)(2)(E) provides the estate a federal income tax deduction for this interest expense.

> EXAMPLE OF § 163(h)(2)(E): Gloria's estate includes a substantial vested remainder interest that is not assignable. The estate and the Service have agreed to the late payment of that portion of the federal estate tax attributable to the remainder interest. The interest paid by the estate is deductible for federal income tax purposes.

The fifth exception is for **education loan interest**. Section 163(h)(2)(F). Section 221 contains a special deduction for interest paid on certain education loans, and § 163(h)(2)(F) confirms that nothing in § 163 trumps the allowance of this deduction. The § 221 deduction is discussed at Chapter 9.

> EXAMPLE OF § 163(a)(2)(F): Gloria borrows money to attend law school. Subject to certain income-based limitations described in Chapter 9, the interest expense on this loan is deductible for federal income tax purposes.

Qualified Residence Interest. The sixth exception is also the most significant one (not to mention the one relevant to a discussion of the tax aspects of home ownership). The deduction for **qualified residence interest** in § 163(h)(2)(D) is perhaps a principal reason many renters become homeowners. Although interest paid on a home mortgage is a quintessentially personal expense, Congress nonetheless confers a deduction, obviously with the intent of encouraging home ownership. Congress has no vendetta against landlords—it simply recognizes that increased home ownership provides more jobs and other positive externalities for the economy. Absent a deduction for mortgage interest, most renters have little financial incentive (or means) to purchase a home. One can rightly question whether Congress ought to be encouraging home ownership and even, if so, whether tax deductions are the most equitable and efficient means of doing so. But as a matter of political reality, the deduction for qualified residence interest is a sacred cow.

No one questions that federal revenues are weakened when a deduction for a personal expense like home mortgage interest is allowed. The Joint Committee on Taxation estimates that, in 2004 alone, Congress left $61.4 billion (that's "billion," with a "b") on the table by allowing the deduction for qualified residence interest. See Appendix 1 and the discussion of tax expenditures at Chapter 9. Apparently, the economic benefits of the deduction (together with obvious political pressure to retain the deduction) outweigh this cost. As Chapter 9 will demonstrate many times over, deductions for personal expenses are sometimes allowed, even though they are inconsistent the general contours of an income tax as set out in Chapter 4. The § 163(h)(2)(D) deduction just happens to be one of the most significant inconsistencies, at least in terms of lost revenues.

The mechanics of the qualified residence interest deduction are set forth at § 163(h)(3). In order to invoke the qualified residence interest deduction, the interest paid by the taxpayer must be attributable to either **acquisition indebtedness** or **home equity indebtedness**. The deduction for interest on acquisition indebtedness is consistent with the policy of encouraging home ownership, for obvious reasons. But a deduction for interest on home equity indebtedness has little to do with encouraging new home ownership or substantial improvements to existing homes. Perhaps the disconnect between the policy objectives of § 163(h)(2)(D) and the nature of home equity indebtedness helps explain the relatively lower dollar limitation ($100,000 for home equity indebtedness versus $1,000,000 for acquisition indebtedness). Could there be another policy justification in permitting a deduction for interest attributable to home equity indebtedness?

* * *

Problem 8–2

In Year One, George Bailey purchased his Bedford Falls residence for $350,000. He paid $50,000 cash and took out a $300,000 mortgage from Potter Bank. As of January 1, Year Ten, the principal balance on the mortgage was $250,000, and the home was worth $500,000.

On January 1, Year Ten, George borrowed $200,000 from Bailey Brothers Building & Loan, an unrelated party. The loan was secured by a second lien on George's residence. George used $50,000 of the loan proceeds to remodel the residence. He used the remainder of the loan proceeds for personal purposes, including a vacation.

In Year Ten, George paid a total of $45,000 in interest: $25,000 on the Potter Bank loan and $20,000 on the Bailey Brothers loan. To what extent can George deduct the interest payments?

* * *

Exclusion of Gain on Sale of Residence. Section 1001(c) requires all realized gains to be recognized "except as provided" elsewhere in the Code. One such exception rests in § 121, which allows unmarried taxpayers meeting certain ownership and use requirements to exclude up to $250,000 of realized gain on the sale or exchange of a principal residence. Married taxpayers meeting certain ownership and use requirements may exclude up to $500,000 of realized gain. To qualify for the exclusion, selling taxpayers must meet three basic requirements:

(1) the taxpayer must have owned the residence for a total period of 2 years (730 days) in the 5–year period prior to the date of the sale (1,825 days) (the "**ownership test**");

(2) the taxpayer must have used the residence as his or her principal residence for a total period of 2 years (730 days) in the 5–year period prior to the date of the sale (1,825 days) (the "**use test**"); and

(3) the taxpayer must not have made prior use of the § 121 exclusion within the 2–year period (730 days) prior to the date of the sale (the "**once-every-two-years test**").

With the occasional exception of determining whether a taxpayer sold his or her "principal residence," these requirements present only a few technical difficulties. This simple set of rules was introduced in 1997; it replaced a much more complicated set of rules spanning two Code sections. In old § 1034, taxpayers could avoid recognizing gain realized from the sale of a residence as long as they acquired a new residence within two years of the sale. The catch was that the taxpayer's basis in the new home had to reflect the unrecognized gain from the sale of the old home. For example, if a taxpayer sold a residence with a basis of $200,000 for $300,000 and used the proceeds (along with $50,000 sitting under the taxpayer's mattress) to buy a new home for $350,000, the $100,000 gain from the sale of the old home was not recognized, and the taxpayer's basis in the new home was set at $250,000 (preserving the $100,000 gain from the old house in the new house).

In addition, old § 121 gave taxpayers age 55 or over a one-time exclusion of up to $125,000 of gain from the sale of a residence. This added benefit helped taxpayers who sought to "buy down" to a less expensive home once their children had grown and left home. Under the regime of old §§ 1034 and 121, then, taxpayers who did not buy new homes that were at least as expensive as their old homes had to recognize at least a portion of their realized gains unless they qualified for the one-time exclusion under old § 121.

As the brief summary above indicates, the current regime is much simpler. We no longer care what the taxpayer does with the sale proceeds, and we no longer force deferral of unrecognized gains into the basis of any subsequently acquired residence. Only taxpayers with extraordinary gains and those who flunk the statutory requirements of § 121 will face taxation of gains from home sales. Even then, the resulting gain will be treated as a long-term capital gain if the taxpayer held the residence for more than one year.

* * *

Self-Assessment Question

(Solutions to Self–Assessment Questions are set forth in Appendix 3.)

SAQ 8–3. Bill and Whoopi, a married couple, purchased a personal residence in Wisconsin in March of Year One and sold it on September

15, Year Six. In the five-year period prior to the sale of the Wisconsin home, the couple (both retired) also owned homes in Arizona and Georgia. The Georgia home (which they bought long before the Wisconsin residence) was sold early in Year Four, and at that time they bought the Arizona home.

Generally, the couple lived in the Wisconsin home during the summer and at the Georgia or Arizona homes during the rest of the year. In the five-year period prior to the sale of the Wisconsin home, the couple occupied the Wisconsin home for 847 days, the Georgia home for 563 days, and the Arizona home for 375 days, as the following table shows:

Year	Wisconsin	Georgia	Arizona
Sept. Year Five–Sept. Year Six	172	0	189
Sept. Year Four–Sept. Year Five	172	0	186
Sept. Year Three–Sept. Year Four	157	194	0
Sept. Year Two–Sept. Year Three	162	197	0
Sept. Year One–Sept. Year Two	184	172	0
	847	563	375

The couple were active members of the community in all three states. For instance, Bill served on the board of their Wisconsin homeowners' association, and both he and Whoopi returned to Wisconsin during the winter months for major holidays and to attend Green Bay Packers games. Both were active in tennis circles in Georgia, and Bill lectured at local Georgia colleges. The couple received their mail and had bank accounts at each residence. They kept one car and two boats in Wisconsin, and they kept two cars at their Georgia house and then at their Arizona house.

Neither Bill nor Whoopi filed state income tax returns for Wisconsin during the five years prior to the Year Six sale, but they both filed Georgia and/or Arizona state returns. Moreover, neither Bill nor Whoopi was registered to vote in Wisconsin, but both were registered in Georgia and then in Arizona. Neither had a Wisconsin driver's license but both had a Georgia license and then an Arizona license.

The sale of the Wisconsin home yielded a realized gain that Bill and Whoopi seek to exclude from gross income on their joint return. Do they qualify for the § 121 exclusion? Why or why not?

* * *

Problem 8–3

Ross and Rachel, married individuals, file joint federal income tax returns. They are both United States citizens and residents. On December 31, Year Six, Ross and Rachel sold their personal residence in New York to an unrelated purchaser for $500,000. Ross and Rachel purchased the residence for $200,000. Determine the federal income tax consequences of the sale under each of the following additional fact scenarios.

(a) Ross and Rachel purchased the residence on July 1, Year One, and lived in the residence at all times until the Year Six sale. Title to the residence was in both spouses' names.

(b) Same as (a), except that title to the residence was in Ross' name only.

(c) Same as (a), except that Ross and Rachel purchased the residence on December 31, Year Five.

(d) Same as (c), except that Ross and Rachel sold the residence because the noise in their neighborhood far exceeded their expectations and tolerance.

(e) Same as (a), except that Ross and Rachel purchased another residence in Maine on July 1, Year Two. Ross and Rachel immediately moved to the Maine residence but did not sell the New York residence. On July 1, Year Five, Ross and Rachel sold the Maine residence and immediately moved back to the New York residence. Ross and Rachel properly excluded their gain on the sale of the Maine residence under § 121.

(f) Same as (e), except that Ross and Rachel sold the New York residence in Year Six so that the couple could move to Nebraska, where Rachel's place of employment had been relocated.

(g) Same as (b), except that the residence was purchased on December 31, Year Four. On May 1, Year Five, Ross and Rachel separated. Rachel moved out of the house and Ross continued to reside in the home. On July 1, Year Five, Ross decided to move in with his new girlfriend, Phoebe, at her home in New Jersey. Ross agreed to let Rachel stay in the New York residence rent-free. In the final divorce decree, Rachel was awarded the residence. Title was changed to her name on October 1, Year Six. Rachel sold the home to an unrelated purchaser on December 31, Year Six.

C. LIKE–KIND EXCHANGES

Code: IRC § 1031(a)–(d).

Regs: Treas. Reg. §§ 1.1031(a)–1(b)–(c); –2; 1.1031(d)–1(e); 1.1031(d)–2.

The Concept of Nonrecognition. Section 1001(c) provides that all realized gains and losses must be recognized "except as otherwise provided in this subtitle." While the general rule of recognition applies in most cases, there are actually several exceptions sprinkled throughout the Code. Practitioners refer to these exceptions as **nonrecognition provisions**. For convenient reference, many of the nonrecognition provisions are set forth in part III of subchapter O (§§ 1031 through 1045). The three most significant nonrecognition provisions contained in this collection are like-kind exchanges in § 1031 (the topic for this Part C), involuntary conversions in § 1033 (the topic for Part D of this Chapter), and transfers between spouses and certain former spouses in § 1041 (one of the topics addressed in Chapter 9). There are, of course, nonrecognition provisions elsewhere in the Code. For example, realized gain or loss from the transfer of property to a corporation controlled by the transferor in exchange for a controlling interest in the corporation's stock will not give rise to recognized gain or loss thanks to § 351.

Likewise, realized gains and losses from transfers of property to a partnership in exchange for an interest in the partnership will qualify for nonrecognition under § 721.

Nonrecognition provisions generally have two common themes. First, nonrecognition is conferred because it is said that the sale or exchange at issue usually involves a mere change in the form of an investment and not a change in the substance of that investment. For example, suppose a taxpayer owns a parcel of unimproved real property called Blackacre. Naturally, if the taxpayer exchanged Blackacre for cash, for General Motors stock, for services, or for most any other asset or benefit, it would be proper to conclude that the taxpayer has realized the benefit of Blackacre—any realized gain or loss would (and should) be recognized. But if the taxpayer exchanges Blackacre for another parcel of unimproved real property (Whiteacre), arguably the benefit of holding Blackacre has not been realized. After the exchange, the taxpayer is still the owner of unimproved land, albeit a different parcel than the one he or she held before the exchange. Thus, it might be fair to conclude that while the *form* of the taxpayer's investment has changed (from Blackacre to Whiteacre), the *substance* of the investment (land ownership) has not. When you see a mere change in form and not a change in substance, you should dig into the Code to see if there is a nonrecognition provision on point—often there is.

The second common theme to the nonrecognition provisions is that the realized gain or loss usually never disappears: the unrecognized gain or loss typically carries over into the new asset. When the new asset is sold or exchanged in a taxable transaction, the realized gain or loss from the first transaction will then be recognized. Preservation of the unrecognized gain or loss is accomplished by giving the new asset a cost basis equal to the adjusted basis of the old asset. Thus, whenever you see a nonrecognition provision, you should expect to see some basis mechanism within that provision that preserves the unrecognized gain or loss.

In the eyes of some commentators, if a Code section excluding gain or loss does not fit within these two common themes, then that section is not a pure "nonrecognition provision." Others take a more liberal view, defining nonrecognition provisions to include any Code section that excludes gain or loss, no matter whether the "mere change in form" rationale applies and no matter whether the excluded gain or loss is deferred to another day. The § 121 exclusion of gain from the sale of a principal residence, for example, would not constitute a "nonrecognition provision" to a purist because the exclusion is not premised on a "mere change in form," and the exclusion does not require the taxpayer to adjust the basis of other assets to preserve the unrecognized gain. Yet for others (impurists?), § 121 would qualify as a nonrecognition provision simply because it excludes realized gains from sales of principal residences. Whether § 121 is properly labeled as a nonrecognition provision is a meaningless debate. The key for now is to recognize a traditional nonrecognition provision when you see it, and § 1031 is the prototypical nonrecognition provision.

Elements of § 1031. Section 1031(a)(1) requires nonrecognition of gain or loss when three requirements are met:

(1) The taxpayer must have exchanged property that was held either for a productive use in the taxpayer's business or as an investment (the "old property");

(2) The old property must be exchanged *solely* for "property of like kind" (the "new property"); and

(3) The new property must be held either for a productive use in the taxpayer's business or as an investment.

Section 1031(a)(2) enumerates six types of property ineligible for nonrecognition. Notice that nonrecognition is not elective—if the three requirements are met, then the taxpayer cannot avoid nonrecognition and no special election must be filed. Curiously, there has been no significant litigation over the requirement that business property be held for a "productive use." While the statute clearly states that "unproductive use" of the old property or the new property is not enough, the Service apparently has not used this requirement to police like-kind exchanges.

The heart of nonrecognition under § 1031, then, lies in defining "property of like kind." The statute lets us down in this regard, for it contains no such definition. Fortunately, the regulations offer some guidance. Regulation § 1.1031(a)–1(b) begins by observing that the term "like kind" refers to "the nature or character of the property and not to its grade or quality." Now if the regulation defined a property's nature, character, grade, and quality, we might be onto something. But it does not. Instead, we are told only that "[o]ne kind or class of property may not * * * be exchanged for property of a different kind or class." So at this point, we know only that properties are of like kind if they are of the same class, determined with reference to the nature or character of the property. Yeesh.

While the regulations that define like-kind property are not the most descriptive, they do offer some interesting and useful examples of exchanges that do (and do not) qualify as like-kind. These general rules and examples are essentially all one needs for exchanges involving real property. Exchanges of personal property (vehicles, equipment, intellectual property rights, and so forth) are subject to much more restrictive rules set forth at Regulation § 1.1031(a)–2. Generally, *depreciable* personal property will be considered like-kind to other depreciable personal property that has the same "General Asset Class" used in assigning class lives for purposes of depreciation. For *intangible* property (and personal property not subject to depreciation), the more general test of "nature or character" applies.

* * *

Self-Assessment Question

(Solutions to Self–Assessment Questions are set forth in Appendix 3.)

SAQ 8–4. Determine whether the following transactions involve exchanges of "property of like kind." In all cases, assume that the property exchanged was held for a productive use in the taxpayer's trade or business and that the property acquired will likewise be so held.

(a) A five-acre farm is exchanged for a quarter-acre urban lot with an apartment building on it. *Yes. The exchange of unimproved property for improved land is a "like-kind" exchange.* [same kind and class]

(b) A leasehold interest in an oil well is exchanged for a fee simple interest in a ranch. *Yes. This is a "like-kind" exchange.*

(c) A passenger automobile is exchanged for a heavy general purpose truck. *No. While both are depreciable personal property vehicles, they are NOT in the same General Asset class.*

(d) A computer is exchanged for a printer. *Yes. They are in the same General Asset class.*

(e) All rights to a patent on the "E–Z–Zip" zipper are exchanged for all rights to a patent on the "Fro–Do" automatic hair cutter. *No. The nature and character of the underlying property (zippers and haircutters) are NOT the same.*

Basis of Property Acquired in a Like–Kind Exchange. The unrecognized gain or loss from a like-kind exchange is preserved in the new property received in the exchange using the basis mechanism in § 1031(d). Notice that the taxpayer's basis in the new property is determined with reference to the taxpayer's basis in the old property exchanged. Adjustments are then made as needed to account for other property that may be received in the exchange. By using the taxpayer's basis in the old property as the reference point for the new property's basis, unrecognized gain or loss is preserved. Take the case where a taxpayer exchanges an old asset worth $10,000 in which the taxpayer had a basis of $7,000 for a like-kind asset. The transaction can be diagrammed as follows:

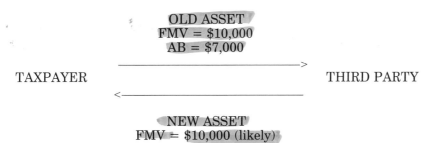

Assuming the exchange qualifies for nonrecognition (based on how the taxpayer held the old property and how the taxpayer intends to hold the new property), the $3,000 realized gain is not recognized, § 1031(a), but the taxpayer's basis in the new asset will be $7,000. Section 1031(d). Because the new asset likely has a value of $10,000 (in an arms'-length transaction the two assets would be deemed to have equal values), the $3,000 unrecognized gain is preserved in the new asset. Thus, in any like-kind exchange, you should expect to see the exact amount of any unrecognized gain or loss preserved in the basis of the asset acquired in the exchange.

Boot. As the preceding paragraph implies, sometimes taxpayers participating in a like-kind exchange receive cash or other property in addition to the like-kind property. Practitioners refer to any additional, non-like-kind property or cash as "boot" (from the phrase "to boot," as in "I got like-kind property and other property *to boot*.") When that occurs, § 1031(a) cannot apply because the taxpayer has not received *solely* like-kind property. But § 1031(b) comes to the rescue: it provides that gain or loss is recognized, but only to the extent of the amount of boot received. For instance, suppose the taxpayer in the last example with an asset worth $10,000, which has a $7,000 basis, exchanges the asset for like-kind property worth $9,000 and $1,000 in cash. The cash payment is required to make the transaction equal (both parties get $10,000 worth of stuff). The transaction now looks like this:

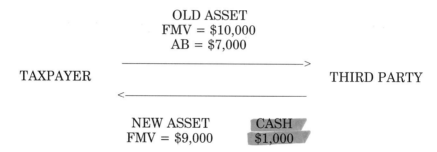

OLD ASSET
FMV = $10,000
AB = $7,000

TAXPAYER   THIRD PARTY

NEW ASSET   CASH
FMV = $9,000 $1,000

Under § 1031(b), the taxpayer recognizes $1,000 of the $3,000 realized gain because the taxpayer received $1,000 in "boot." If the taxpayer had received like-kind property worth $6,000 and cash of $4,000, the entire $3,000 realized gain would be recognized because there is at least $3,000 of "boot." Notice that boot in excess of the realized gain does not serve to increase the realized gain from the transaction. Accordingly, § 1031(b) is best characterized as a "ceiling rule:" gain is recognized, but not in excess of the amount of boot received in the exchange.

The adjustments to basis in § 1031(d) come into play when boot is involved in a like-kind transaction. Consider the example above where the taxpayer receives like-kind property worth $9,000 and $1,000 in cash in exchange for an asset with a basis of $7,000. Under § 1031(d), the taxpayer's basis in the new property is computed as follows:

Basis in Old Property	$7,000
Less Cash Received	($1,000)
Plus Gain Recognized	$1,000
Basis in New Property	$7,000

Notice that if the taxpayer completes a cash sale of the new asset for its fair market value ($9,000), the transaction will give rise to a gain of $2,000. That is exactly the amount of realized gain that was not recognized in the like-kind exchange (of the $3,000 realized gain in the like-kind exchange, only $1,000 was recognized). Conceptually, that is the correct result, so the basis formula in § 1031(d) works.

Consider now the example where the like-kind property received in the exchange is worth $6,000 and the taxpayer also received $4,000 in cash. We saw above that the taxpayer recognizes the entire $3,000 realized gain. Since all of the realized gain is recognized, there is no gain or loss to preserve in the new asset; consequently, the new asset should have a basis equal to its fair market value. Like magic, the basis formula in § 1031(d) achieves that result:

Basis in Old Property	$7,000
Less Cash Received	($4,000)
Plus Gain Recognized	$3,000
Basis in New Property	$6,000

Upon a cash sale of the new property for its fair market value ($6,000), no gain or loss would result!

Liabilities. Debt complicates everything. Unfortunately, property transferred in like-kind exchanges is often encumbered by liabilities, especially where the exchanged asset is real estate. How does the presence of debt affect the tax consequences of a like-kind exchange? The very last sentence of § 1031(d) treats the assumption of a taxpayer's liability as the receipt of cash by that taxpayer. In other words, relief from indebtedness is treated as additional cash boot in a like-kind exchange.

The operation of this rule is perhaps best understood in context. Using our same taxpayer with the $10,000 asset that has a basis of $7,000, suppose the asset also secures a liability in the amount of $2,000. The taxpayer trades the asset in exchange for like-kind property worth $8,000, and the other party to the exchange expressly assumes the $2,000 liability. Notice that the other party will be unwilling to pay any extra consideration in this transaction, for the taxpayer is receiving $8,000 of equity (property worth $10,000 but subject to a liability of $2,000) in exchange for property worth $8,000. No extra consideration should be paid. Here is how the transaction looks under these modified facts:

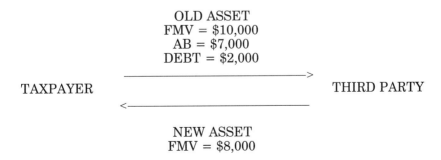

```
                        OLD ASSET
                      FMV = $10,000
                        AB = $7,000
                      DEBT = $2,000
                  ─────────────────────>
TAXPAYER                                      THIRD PARTY
              <─────────────────────

                        NEW ASSET
                       FMV = $8,000
```

What is our taxpayer's realized gain? To answer this question, we must recall the rule from _Crane_ and _Tufts_ in Part A of this Chapter: the debt relief must be included in computing the taxpayer's amount realized. Thus, the amount realized in this transaction is $10,000 ($8,000 worth of property plus $2,000 of debt relief). The amount realized exceeds the taxpayer's basis ($7,000) by $3,000, so the realized gain is $3,000. The last sentence of § 1031(d) says that the other party's assumption of the liability will be treated as cash received by our taxpayer. That means, therefore, that our taxpayer will have to recognize $2,000 of the $3,000 realized gain on the transaction, for our taxpayer is treated as having received $2,000 of "boot."

As for the taxpayer's basis in the new property, keep in mind that the debt relief is treated as cash for all purposes. In this simple example, the deemed cash and the recognized gain cancel each other out when computing the taxpayer's basis in the new property:

Basis in Old Property	$7,000	
Less Cash Received	($2,000)	← liability relief is deemed cash
Plus Gain Recognized	$2,000	
Basis in New Property	$7,000	

Notice that if the taxpayer sells the new asset for its fair market value ($8,000), the taxpayer will realize (and recognize) a $1,000 gain. Not coincidentally, that $1,000 represents the portion of the realized gain in the like-kind exchange that went unrecognized. Once again, we see that the basis mechanism in § 1031(d) reaches the right result.

* * *

Problem 8–4

Monty owns Blackacre, a parcel of real property located in Truth or Consequences, New Mexico. Monty purchased the property several years ago for $20,000. Monty is willing to make a deal involving Blackacre if the price is right, but he does not want to be in jeopardy of recognizing gain from an all-cash deal. To tell the truth, Monty would like to defer the recognition of gain as long as possible. Monty has received a number of proposals from various unrelated parties, and these offers are described below. For each proposed transaction, determine: (i) the realized gain or loss to each party; (ii) the recognized gain or loss to each party; and (iii) the adjusted basis each party would have in the property received in the proposed exchange. Assume that the parties to the exchange in each scenario will hold the acquired property as an investment, just as they held the exchanged property.

(a) Monty transfers Blackacre to Wink in exchange for Whiteacre, a parcel of real property worth $100,000. Wink's basis in Whiteacre is $160,000.

(b) Monty transfers Blackacre to Alex in exchange for Wiseacre, a parcel of real property worth $50,000, and $50,000 cash. Alex's basis in Wiseacre is $20,000.

(c) Monty transfers Blackacre to Vanna in exchange for Peroxideacre, a parcel of real property worth $10,000, and $90,000 cash. Vanna's basis in Peroxideacre is $5,000.

(d) Monty transfers Blackacre to Regis in exchange for Greyacre, a parcel of real property worth $60,000, and stock in XYZ Corporation worth $40,000. Regis' basis in Greyacre is $10,000 and his basis in the XYZ stock is $30,000.

(e) Beginning now and throughout the balance of this Problem, assume that Blackacre secures a $10,000 mortgage that Monty owes to the First National Bank. Monty transfers Blackacre subject to the mortgage to Bob in exchange for Blueacre, a parcel of real property worth $90,000. Bob's basis in Blueacre is $30,000.

(f) Monty transfers Blackacre subject to the mortgage to Chuck in exchange for Greenacre, a parcel of real property worth $60,000, and $30,000 cash. Chuck's basis in Greenacre is $40,000.

(g) Monty transfers Blackacre subject to the First National Bank mortgage to Kennedy in exchange for Redacre, a parcel of real property worth $120,000. Kennedy's basis in Redacre, which secures a $30,000 mortgage Kennedy owes to the Second National Bank, is $80,000. Monty receives Redacre subject to the Second National Bank mortgage.

* * *

Like-Kind Exchanges of Loss Property. Section 1031(a) applies to realized losses just as it does to realized gains. While taxpayers generally prefer nonrecognition for realized gains (so they do not have to recognize the gain currently and pay the resulting federal income tax currently), they generally prefer to recognize realized losses currently in order to obtain the tax benefit of the resulting deduction sooner. So while § 1031(a) is good news in the case of realized gains, it is often bad news in the case of realized losses.

Where a taxpayer realizes loss in a transaction involving boot, nonrecognition still prevails. Section 1031(c). Suppose, for example, that a taxpayer exchanges an old asset worth $7,000 in which the taxpayer has a $10,000 basis for a new, like-kind asset worth $5,000 and $2,000 cash. Here is how the transaction would be diagrammed:

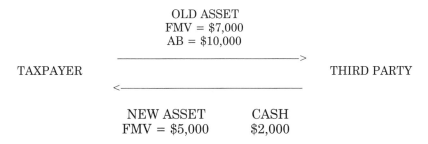

OLD ASSET
FMV = $7,000
AB = $10,000

TAXPAYER   THIRD PARTY

NEW ASSET   CASH
FMV = $5,000 $2,000

In this case, the taxpayer realizes a loss of $3,000 (the taxpayer's $10,000 basis in the old asset exceeds the $7,000 amount realized in the transaction by $3,000). Although the taxpayer receives boot in this transaction, no portion of the loss is recognized. Section 1031(c). Not surprisingly, however, the loss is preserved in the basis of the new asset under the § 1031(d) formula:

Basis in Old Property	$10,000
Less Cash Received	($ 2,000)
Plus Gain Recognized	$ 0
Basis in New Property	$ 8,000

If the taxpayer sold the new asset for cash at its fair market value, the sale would generate a realized (and recognized) loss of $3,000, which is exactly the amount of unrecognized loss from the like-kind exchange.

Should the result in this example change if the other party to the transaction is related to the taxpayer? Recall from Chapter 4 that § 267(a) disallows deductions for losses resulting from sales to related persons. If the realized loss from the like-kind exchange is preserved in the basis of the new asset, then that loss would seemingly be allowable upon a cash sale of the new asset to an unrelated person. Does the taint of disallowance under § 267 carry over to the new asset? Or does the loss preservation under § 1031(d) prevail? In *Revenue Ruling 72–151*, 1972–1 C.B. 225, the Service concluded that "[t]he basis of the property received by the taxpayer in the exchange is governed by section 1031(d) of the Code." In other words, the taint of disallowance under § 267 will *not* carry over to the new asset.

Simultaneous Three–Party Exchanges. In many cases, two parties are unable to complete a like-kind exchange. This can happen when one of the parties to the transaction does not wish to receive like-kind property or wishes to recognize loss on property that has declined in value. Take the case of Sarah, who owns an apartment building with a value far in excess of her basis. Sarah would like to effect a like-kind exchange with Jessica, who owns an orchard. But Jessica does not want to own an apartment building. Meanwhile, Parker, another individual, has his eyes on Sarah's building, and he is willing to pay cash for the property. Can Sarah design a series of transactions that leaves everyone happy?

One option would be for Sarah to sell the apartment building to Jessica in exchange for the orchard. This would be a like-kind exchange that would allow Sarah to avoid recognition of any realized gain. The fact that Jessica does not want to own the building is easily addressed: after the exchange is completed, Jessica could then sell the apartment building for cash to Parker. Since Jessica is unconcerned with the applicability of § 1031 (perhaps because the orchard has a value less than her basis or because her desire for cash exceeds her desire to minimize liability for federal income taxes), the second transaction does not create an undesirable result to any party.

Another possibility is for Sarah to sell the apartment building to Parker and then use the cash proceeds to buy the orchard from Jessica. But the problem with this plan is that Sarah receives cash in the first transaction with Parker and not like-kind property. Even though Sarah might purchase the orchard from Jessica immediately after concluding the cash sale to Parker, there is no denying that Sarah has cash in hand, the hallmark of a taxable exchange. The receipt of cash at any point in the plan, therefore, is fatal to achieving nonrecognition under § 1031.

Now suppose that Sarah seeks to acquire an orchard in exchange for her apartment building, but she has not yet "picked" a specific orchard. Parker might be willing to help Sarah find suitable property (like the orchard owned by Jessica) and then purchase it with his cash. Parker would then exchange his newly-acquired orchard for Sarah's apartment building. Would this plan allow Sarah to avoid recognizing gain on the exchange of her apartment building? The following ruling addresses this plan.

REVENUE RULING 77–297

1977–2 C.B. 304.

Advice is requested whether the transaction described below is an exchange of property in which no gain or loss is recognized pursuant to section 1031(a) of the Internal Revenue Code of 1954.

A entered into a written agreement with B to sell B for 1,000x dollars a ranch (the "first ranch") consisting of land and certain buildings used by A in the business of raising livestock. Pursuant to the agreement, B placed 100x dollars into escrow and agreed to pay at closing an additional 200x dollars in cash, to assume a 160x dollar liability of A, and to execute a note for 540x dollars. The agreement also provided that B would cooperate with A to effectuate an exchange of properties should A locate suitable property. No personal property was involved in the transaction. A and B are not dealers in real estate.

A located another ranch (the "second ranch") consisting of land and certain buildings suitable for raising livestock. The second ranch was owned by C. B entered into an agreement with C to purchase the second ranch for 2,000x dollars. Pursuant to this agreement, B placed 40x dollars into escrow, agreed to pay at closing an additional 800x dollars, assume 400x dollars liability of C and execute a note for 760x dollars. No personal property was involved in the transaction. C could not look to A for specific performance on the contract, thus, B was not acting as A's agent in the purchase of the second parcel of property.

At closing, B purchased the second ranch as agreed. After the purchase, B exchanged the second ranch with A for the first ranch and assumed A's liability of 160x dollars. With C's concurrence, A assumed C's 400x dollar liability and B's note for 760x dollars. C released B from liability on the note. The escrow agent returned the 100x dollars to B that B had initially placed in escrow. This sum had never been available to A, since the conditions of the escrow were never satisfied.

* * *

Section 1.1031(b)–1(c) of the Income Tax Regulations states that consideration received in the form of an assumption of liabilities is to be treated as "other property or money" for the purpose of section 1031(b) of the Code. However, if, on an exchange described in section 1031(b), each party to the exchange assumes a liability of the other party, then, in determining the amount of "other property or money" for purposes of section 1031(b), consideration given in the form of an assumption of liabilities shall be offset against consideration received in the form of an assumption of liabilities.

Ordinarily, to constitute an exchange, the transaction must be a reciprocal transfer of property, as distinguished from a transfer of property for a money consideration only.

In the instant case A and B entered into a sales agreement with an exchange option if suitable property were found. Before the sale was consummated, the parties effectuated an exchange. Thus, for purposes of section 1031 of the Code, the parties entered into an exchange of property. See *Alderson v. Commissioner*, 317 F.2d 790 (9th Cir. 1963), in which a similar transaction was treated as a like-kind exchange of property even though the original agreement called for a sale of the property. In addition, A's 160x dollar liability assumed by B was offset by B's liabilities assumed by A, pursuant to section 1.1031(b)–1(c) of the regulations.

Accordingly, as to A, the exchange of ranches qualifies for nonrecognition of gain or loss under section 1031 of the Code. As to B, the exchange of ranches does not qualify for nonrecognition of gain or loss under section 1031 because B did not hold the second ranch for productive use in a trade or business or for investment. See *Rev. Rul. 75–291*, 1975–2 C.B. 332, in which it is held that the nonrecognition provisions of section 1031 do not apply to a taxpayer who acquired property solely for the purpose of exchanging it for like-kind property.

However, in the instant case, B did not realize gain or loss as a result of the exchange since the total consideration received by B of 2,160x dollars (fair market value of first ranch of 1,000x dollars plus B's liabilities assumed by A of 1,160x dollars) is equal to B's basis in the property given up of 2,000x dollars plus A's liability assumed by B of 160x dollars. * * *

* * *

Deferred Exchanges. *Revenue Ruling 77–297* allowed nonrecognition in part because no binding contract between A and B existed (and thus no final sale occurred) until suitable replacement property was located. Would the result change if A had transferred the first ranch to B prior to the identification of the second ranch? Put differently, suppose A and B had agreed that A had 30 days from the date of transfer to locate suitable replacement property. If A did so, then B would be required to buy the replacement property with the escrowed cash and then transfer it to A. If A did not do so, then A would receive the cash in escrow. Should this plan qualify for nonrecognition under § 1031? On the one hand, there is nothing in § 1031(a)(1) that requires the transactions to be simultaneous. Yet on the other hand, something would be rotten (and not just in Denmark) if A could keep the cash in escrow for years and years until replacement property is found, if ever. A could, for example, wait until a year when the tax rate applicable to A's gain from the sale to B was sufficiently low, or until A had other losses to offset the gain for tax purposes.

In *Starker v. United States*, 602 F.2d 1341 (9th Cir. 1979), the court held that the taxpayer was entitled to § 1031 nonrecognition upon the ultimate receipt of like-kind property, even though the taxpayer in that case had already transferred the property to the buyer and even though the taxpayer had up to five years to identify the replacement property. Congress responded to *Starker* by enacting § 1031(a)(3), which imposes time limits on the identification and receipt of replacement property.

Under § 1031(a)(3)(A), the taxpayer must *identify* the replacement property within 45 days of the transfer of like-kind property, and under § 1031(a)(3)(B), the taxpayer must *receive* the replacement property within 180 days of the transfer of like-kind property. The timing rules contained in § 1031(a)(3) have spawned very detailed regulations that contain a number of technical requirements and even some planning opportunities. See Treas. Reg. § 1.1031(k)–1. For example, the regulations allow taxpayers to identify up to three different replacement properties, regardless of value, or any number of properties with an aggregate value of no more than twice the value of the transferred property. Treas. Reg. § 1.1031(k)–1(c)(4)(i). Even where the taxpayer violates these rules, however, the regulations still allow nonrecognition so long as the actual replacement property has a value equal to at least 95 percent of the value of the property originally transferred. Treas. Reg. § 1.1031(k)–1(c)(4)(ii)(B).

A key hurdle to clear in the successful deferred exchange is the actual or constructive receipt of cash or other property that is not like-kind. Using the modified facts from *Revenue Ruling 77–297* to illustrate, what if A has the option at any time during the identification period to end the search for replacement property and take the cash out of escrow? The regulations (correctly) provide that A has constructive receipt of the escrowed cash, and therefore cannot qualify for nonrecognition. Treas. Reg. § 1.1031(k)–1(f)(2). The regulations then offer four "safe harbors" the use of which precludes the application of the constructive receipt doctrine. Treas. Reg. § 1.1031(k)–1(g). The most significant of these safe harbors relates to the use of "qualified intermediaries," those who serve as conduits on behalf of the taxpayer in locating and acquiring replacement property. If the intermediary meets all of the requirements in the regulations, it will not be considered an agent of the taxpayer, thus ensuring that that the taxpayer is never in actual or constructive receipt of anything other than like-kind property.

The use of a qualified intermediary might be helpful to Sarah, our apartment building owner who seeks an orchard. Sarah could hire an unrelated third party, Carrie Bradshaw, to sell the apartment building to Parker for cash, use the sale proceeds to buy replacement property identified by Sarah (Jessica's orchard), and then transfer that property to Sarah. The fact that Carrie received cash from Parker will not be attributed to Sarah, even though Carrie is, in fact, acting under Sarah's direction and control. In effect, then, the use of a qualified intermediary would allow Sarah to sell the apartment building to Parker and use the cash to buy Jessica's orchard in a tax-free exchange under § 1031! It's a great country, no?

Like-Kind Exchanges of Depreciable Property. In 2004, Treasury issued Temporary Regulation § 1.168(i)–6T. It provides rules for determining the applicable recovery period, depreciation method, and convention used to determine the depreciation allowances for property received in a like-kind exchange or involuntary conversion transaction. Generally, to the extent the taxpayer's basis in the replacement property does not exceed the taxpayer's basis in the relinquished property (the "exchanged basis"), such exchanged basis is depreciated over the remaining recovery period of (and using the depreciation method and convention of) the relinquished property. Thus, if the replacement property has the same or a shorter recovery period than the relinquished property, the taxpayer must still use whatever is left of the longer recovery period, even if the taxpayer could have recovered the cost of the replacement property more quickly by treating it as if was property newly acquired by purchase. To alleviate the hardships of this rule, the regulations contain an election that allows taxpayers to treat the replacement property as if it was purchased for cash in the year in which the replacement property is placed in service.

If the replacement property has a longer recovery period than the relinquished property, however, the exchanged basis is depreciated beginning in the year of replacement over the remainder of the recovery period applicable to the replacement property as if the replacement property had been placed in service in the year in which the relinquished property was placed in service. Any basis in excess of the exchanged basis ("excess basis") is treated as property placed in service in the year in which the replacement property is placed in service. Accordingly, depreciation deductions with respect to the excess basis are computed by using the recovery period, method and convention applicable to the replacement property. The excess basis is also eligible for expensing under § 179.

Like-Kind Exchanges Involving a Principal Residence. Where a taxpayer transfers property used first as a home and then for business purposes in exchange for like-kind property, the taxpayer may qualify both for the § 121 exclusion and for § 1031 nonrecognition. The same result could occur where a taxpayer uses the property concurrently for home and business purposes (using a portion of the property as a residence and the rest of the property for business). In *Revenue Procedure 2005–14*, 2005–1 C.B. 528, Treasury offers guidance for applying both benefits. The Revenue Procedure states that § 121 is applied before § 1031. Although the § 121 exclusion does not apply to gain attributable to depreciation deductions claimed with respect to the business or investment portion of a residence, § 1031 may apply to such gain. In applying § 1031, any boot received in the exchange is taken into account only to the extent the boot exceeds the gain excluded under § 121. In determining the basis of the replacement property, any gain excluded under § 121 is treated as gain recognized by the taxpayer. Thus, the basis of the replacement business property is increased by any gain attributable to the relinquished business property that is excluded under § 121.

In one of the examples from the guidance, a taxpayer buys a residence for $210,000. From 2001–2006, the taxpayer uses 2/3 of the house (by square footage) as the taxpayer's principal residence and uses 1/3 of the house as an office in the taxpayer's business. In 2006, the taxpayer exchanges the entire property for a residence and a separate property that the taxpayer intends to use as an office in the taxpayer's business. The total fair market value of the replacement properties is $360,000, with $240,000 allocable to the replacement residence and $120,000 allocable to the replacement business property. From 2001–2006, the taxpayer claims depreciation deductions of $30,000 for the business use of the surrendered property. The taxpayer realizes gain of $180,000 on the exchange. Under § 121, the taxpayer excludes the $100,000 gain allocable to the residential portion of the house (2/3 of $360,000 amount realized, or $240,000, minus 2/3 of $210,000 basis, or $140,000) because the taxpayer meets the ownership and use requirements of § 121 for that portion of the property. The remaining gain of $80,000 (1/3 of $360,000 amount realized, or $120,000, minus $40,000 adjusted basis—which is 1/3 of $210,000 basis, or $70,000, adjusted by $30,000 depreciation) is allocable to the business portion of the house (the office). The taxpayer applies § 121 before applying § 1031. Accordingly, the taxpayer may exclude $50,000 of the gain allocable to the office because the office and residence are part of a single dwelling unit. The taxpayer may not exclude that portion of the gain ($30,000) attributable to depreciation deductions, but may defer the remaining gain of $30,000 under § 1031. The results are illustrated in the guidance as follows:

	Total property	2/3 residential property	1/3 business property
Amount realized	$360,000	$240,000	$120,000
Basis	$210,000	$140,000	$ 70,000
Depreciation adjustment	$ 30,000		$ 30,000
Adjusted basis	$180,000	$140,000	$ 40,000
Realized gain	$180,000	$100,000	$ 80,000
Gain excluded under § 121	$150,000	$100,000	$ 50,000
Gain deferred under § 1031	$ 30,000		$ 30,000

The taxpayer's basis in the replacement residential property is its fair market value at the time of the exchange ($240,000). The taxpayer's basis in the replacement business property is $90,000, equal to the taxpayer's basis in the relinquished business property at the time of the exchange ($40,000) plus the gain excluded under § 121 attributable to the relinquished business property ($50,000).

D. INVOLUNTARY CONVERSIONS

Code: IRC § 1033(a)–(b)(2), (g).

Regs: None.

Another significant nonrecognition provision applies where a taxpayer's property is involuntarily converted into other property. Absent such a provision, significant hardship could result. Suppose an earthquake destroys a taxpayer's business property and the taxpayer receives insurance proceeds equal to the value of the building immediately before the disaster. If the property had a low basis, the receipt of cash compensation would cause the taxpayer to realize a substantial gain. Because the taxpayer receives cash, § 1031 would be of no avail even if the taxpayer used the proceeds to purchase property of like kind. If the gain is recognized, the taxpayer might be unable to purchase similar property of equivalent value because a portion of the proceeds will pass to Uncle Sam. Section 1033 is thus required to avoid recognition of gain in this and similar cases.

Involuntary Conversions. Even a casual reading of § 1033(a) yields a useful framework for analysis. First, of course, there must be an involuntary conversion of the taxpayer's property. Section 1033(a) identifies four events that give rise to an involuntary conversion: (1) destruction in whole or in part; (2) theft; (3) seizure; and (4) requisition or condemnation (or threat or imminence thereof). Instinctively, one might liken the "destruction" of property to a casualty, defined in Chapter 4 as a sudden, unusual, and unexpected event. While that notion is helpful in identifying events that give rise to destruction, there is no requirement that the destruction be "sudden." See *Revenue Ruling 89–2*, 1989–1 C.B. 259 (property deemed unsafe to occupy because of chemical contamination is "destroyed" and thus involuntarily converted); *Revenue Ruling 59–102*, 1959–1 C.B. 200 ("[s]o long as the causes of destruction otherwise fall within the general concept of a casualty, it is accordingly considered that the taxpayer need not satisfy also the test of "suddenness" which must be met for casualty loss deduction purposes in order to qualify under § 1033).

Note, too, that complete destruction of the property is not required, as the statute expressly allows nonrecognition where the property is destroyed "in part." The following ruling presents an example of partial destruction of property.

REVENUE RULING 96–32

1996–1 C.B. 177.

* * *

ISSUES

(1) If the dwelling portion of the taxpayer's principal residence is destroyed and the remaining land portion of the principal residence is

subsequently sold within the period described in § 1033(a)(2)(B) of the Internal Revenue Code, is the sale treated as part of the involuntary conversion of the principal residence to which § 1033(a) may apply to defer recognition of gain realized on the sale?

(2) If the taxpayer subsequently sells the remaining land portion of the principal residence described above or reconstructs the destroyed dwelling and reoccupies it as the taxpayer's principal residence within a reasonable period of time after the destruction, is the property treated as a qualified residence under § 163(h) during the period between the destruction of the dwelling and the sale or reoccupancy?

Facts

Situation (1)—A's principal residence (within the meaning of [§] 163(h)(4)(A)(i)(I)) was destroyed in September 1991 by a tornado that was subsequently declared a disaster by the President. In the same year, A received insurance proceeds of $120x for the destruction of the dwelling. A's adjusted basis in the property (land and improvements) was $100x. A did not rebuild the dwelling, but instead sold the land for $10x in November 1993. In March 1995, A purchased another home for $130x and used it as A's principal residence.

Situation (2)—B's principal residence (within the meaning of [§] 163(h)(4)(A)(i)(I)) was destroyed in December 1991 by an earthquake that was subsequently declared a disaster by the President. Because the widespread destruction in the region resulted in a severe shortage of available equipment, materials, and skilled labor, B was not able to begin reconstruction of the dwelling until June 1993. Upon its completion in October 1994, B reoccupied the reconstructed dwelling and used it as B's principal residence. During the period from the earthquake until B reoccupied the reconstructed dwelling, B lived in rental housing.

In *Situations (1)* and *(2)*, the residences were encumbered by mortgages securing debts the interest on which was qualified residence interest under § 163(h)(3)(A) prior to the disaster. Had the residences not been destroyed, they would have continued to qualify as principal residences under § 163(h)(4)(A)(i)(I). After the destruction of their principal residences, A and B continued to make payments of principal and interest on their mortgage debts.

Law and Analysis—Issue (1)

Section 1033(a)(2)(A) provides, in part, that if property (as a result of its destruction in whole or in part, theft, seizure, or requisition or condemnation or threat or imminence thereof) is compulsorily or involuntarily converted into money, which in turn is used to purchase (within the period specified in § 1033(a)(2)(B)) property similar or related in service or use to the converted property, gain will be recognized only to the extent that the amount realized upon the conversion exceeds the cost of the replacement property.

Section 1033(a)(2)(B) provides that the period for replacing converted property generally shall be the period beginning on the date of the disposition of the converted property and ending 2 years after the close of the taxable year in which any part of the gain is realized. However, § 1033(h)(1)(B), added by § 13431 of the Omnibus Budget Reconciliation Act of 1993, provides that if a principal residence is compulsorily or involuntarily converted as a result of a Presidentially declared disaster, § 1033(a)(2)(B) shall be applied by substituting "4 years" for "2 years." For this purpose, § 1033(h)(3) generally provides that the term "principal residence" has the same meaning as when used in § [121]. * * *

Section 1033(b) provides that the basis of property acquired in a transaction that resulted in nonrecognition of gain under § 1033(a)(2) shall be the cost of the property acquired reduced by the amount of the gain not so recognized.

* * *

In *Rev. Rul. 76–541*, 1976–2 C.B. 246, a taxpayer owned and resided in a house situated on an undivided parcel of land containing 10 acres, all of which the taxpayer used as the principal residence. During a particular year, the taxpayer sold the dwelling and three immediately surrounding acres at a gain. Later in the same year, the taxpayer sold two more acres at a gain. * * * *Rev. Rul. 76–541* treats the dwelling and the ten acres of surrounding land as the taxpayer's principal residence. The sale of the first three acres and the dwelling did not alter the "principal residence" character of the two-acre portion of land that was later sold * * *.

* * *

In *Situation (1)*, A realized $120x of insurance proceeds upon the 1991 conversion of the dwelling. A may offset the entire $100x basis in the property against the amount realized, consistent with the nonapportionment of basis for the computation of casualty loss deductions on residential real property under § 1.165–7(b)(2)(ii). Thus, A realized a gain from the insurance proceeds of $20x and A's basis in the property is reduced to $0x.

A thereafter realized an additional $10x of gain on the 1993 sale of the land, for a total gain of $30x on the property. Because the principal residence of A before the disaster consisted of both the dwelling and the land that was later sold by A after the destruction of the dwelling, A's sale of that land will be treated as part of a single involuntary conversion of A's principal residence that occurred on the date the dwelling was destroyed. Thus, § 1033, and not § [121], will apply to defer recognition of A's $30x gain.

For purposes of this § 1033 deferral, A's period for purchasing replacement property under § 1033(a)(2)(B) and (h)(1)(B) begins on the date that the dwelling is destroyed and ends 4 years after the close of the taxable year in which gain is first realized. Because A purchased a new principal residence within this period at a cost ($130x) that was not less than the sum of the insurance proceeds ($120x) and the sales proceeds ($10x), A may defer recognition of the entire $30x gain. A's basis in the new principal residence is $100x ($130x cost less $30x unrecognized gain).

LAW AND ANALYSIS—ISSUE (2)

Section 163(a) allows a deduction for all interest paid or accrued within the taxable year on indebtedness. Section 163(h)(1) generally provides that, in the case of taxpayers other than a corporation, no deduction is allowed for personal interest. Section 163(h)(2)(D) specifically excludes from the definition of the term "personal interest" any qualified residence interest.

Section 163(h)(3)(A) provides that the term "qualified residence interest" means any interest paid or accrued during the taxable year on acquisition or home equity indebtedness with respect to any qualified residence of the taxpayer. Section 163(h)(4)(A)(i) defines the term "qualified residence" to mean (I) the taxpayer's principal residence, within the meaning of § [121], and (II) one other residence of the taxpayer selected by the taxpayer for purposes of § 163(h) for the taxable year and used by the taxpayer as a residence.

In *Situation (1)*, A's property will continue to be treated as a qualified residence under § 163(h) for purposes of A's deduction of the interest that A paid on the mortgage debt until the date on which A sold the property.

In *Situation (2)*, B began and completed reconstruction of the dwelling, and reoccupied it as B's principal residence, all within a reasonable period of time after it was destroyed. Accordingly, B's property will continue to be treated as a qualified residence under § 163(h) for purposes of B's deduction for the interest that B paid on the mortgage debt during that period. * * *

HOLDINGS

(1) If the dwelling portion of the taxpayer's principal residence is destroyed and the remaining land portion of the principal residence is subsequently sold within the period described in § 1033(a)(2)(B), the sale is treated as part of the involuntary conversion of the principal residence to which § 1033(a) applies to defer recognition of gain realized on the sale if the requirements of that section are met.

(2) If the taxpayer subsequently sells the land portion of the principal residence described above within a reasonable period of time after the destruction, the property will continue to be treated as a qualified residence under § 163(h) during the period between the destruction of the dwelling and the sale of land. Likewise, if the taxpayer reconstructs the destroyed dwelling and reoccupies it as the taxpayer's principal residence within a reasonable period of time after the destruction, the property will continue to be treated as a qualified residence under § 163(h) during that period.

Holdings (1) and (2) apply whether or not the destruction occurred in connection with a Presidentially declared disaster. These holdings also apply if the property is a second residence within the meaning of § 163(h)(4)(A)(i)(II).

* * *

In addition to destruction, other enumerated events qualify as involuntary conversions. Thefts are easy to spot, but one might wonder about the distinction between "seizures" and "requisitions or condemnations." Seizure likely means the confiscation of property by the government (federal, state, or local) without the payment of compensation, while a requisition or condemnation specifically refers to "the taking or the threat of taking property by some public or quasi-public corporation—by some instrumentality that has the power to do so against the will of the owner, and for the use of the taker." *American Natural Gas Co. v. United States*, 279 F.2d 220, 225 (Ct. Cl. 1960). Thus, the exercise of eminent domain by the government would be considered a requisition or condemnation, while the impoundment of a vehicle used in a drug trafficking scheme likely would qualify as a seizure. Query whether a seizure would routinely give rise to a realized gain, particularly since (by definition) no compensation is paid to the taxpayer.

Conversion into Other Property. If an involuntary conversion has occurred, the second step in the analysis is to determine whether the property was converted into property "similar or related in service or use" to the converted property or into money or other property. If the property is converted into similar-use property (a rare event), then § 1033(a)(1) provides for complete nonrecognition of gain. If the property is converted into money or other, dissimilar property, then the taxpayer may still be able to avoid recognizing all or a portion of the realized gain under § 1033(a)(2), so long as the taxpayer purchases similar-use property within the prescribed time period. Since the key to nonrecognition in both §§ 1033(a)(1) and 1033(a)(2) is a determination of whether the taxpayer acquired similar-use property, it is necessary to consider what it means to have similar-use property.

Oddly enough, the Code does not define property "similar or related in service or use," and the regulations offer little guidance, listing merely three transactions where similar-use property is not acquired by a taxpayer. See Treas. Reg. § 1.1033(a)–2(c)(9). About the most we can glean from the statute is that there is no requirement that similar-use property be held for business or investment purposes. Thus, the involuntary conversion of personal-use property can also qualify for nonrecognition under § 1033 if the taxpayer acquires similar-use property. The Service's position as to what qualifies as similar-use property is set forth in the following ruling.

REVENUE RULING 64-237

1964-2 C.B. 319.

The Internal Revenue Service has reconsidered its position with respect to replacement property that is "similar or related in service or use" to involuntarily converted property within the meaning of * * * section 1033(a) of the Internal Revenue Code of 1954 in light of the decision of the United States Court of Appeals for the Second Circuit in the case of *Liant Record, Inc.* v. *Commissioner,* 303 Fed. (2d) 326 (1962), and other appellate court decisions.

In previous litigation, the Service has taken the position that the statutory phrase, "similar or related in service or use," means that the property acquired must have a close "functional" similarity to the property converted. Under this test, property was not considered similar or related in service or use to the converted property unless the physical characteristics and end uses of the converted and replacement properties were closely similar. Although this "functional use test" has been upheld in the lower courts, it has not been sustained in the appellate courts with respect to investors in property, such as lessors.

In conformity with the appellate court decisions, in considering whether replacement property acquired by an investor is similar in service or use to the converted property, attention will be directed primarily to the similarity in the relationship of the services or uses which the original and replacement properties have to the taxpayer-owner. In applying this test, a determination will be made as to whether the properties are of a similar service to the taxpayer, the nature of the business risks connected with the properties, and what such properties demand of the taxpayer in the way of management, services and relations to his tenants.

For example, where the taxpayer is a lessor, who rented out the converted property for a light manufacturing plant and then rents out the replacement property for a wholesale grocery warehouse, the nature of the taxpayer-owner's service or use of the properties may be similar although that of the end users change. The two properties will be considered as similar or related in service or use where, for example, both are rented and where there is a similarity in the extent and type of the taxpayer's management activities, the amount and kind of services rendered by him to his tenants, and the nature of his business risks connected with the properties.

In modifying its position with respect to the involuntary conversion of property held for investment, the Service will continue to adhere to the functional test in the case of owner-users of property. Thus, if the taxpayer-owner operates a light manufacturing plant on the converted property and then operates a wholesale grocery warehouse on the replacement property, by changing his end use he has so changed the nature of his relationship to the property as to be outside the nonrecognition of gain provisions.

* * *

Finally, if a taxpayer's property has been involuntarily converted into money or dissimilar property but the taxpayer has acquired similar-use property, nonrecognition is conditioned upon the taxpayer acquiring the similar-use property within the applicable time period. For most involuntary conversions, the time period generally begins with the date of the involuntary conversion and ends two full taxable years after the date upon which gain is first realized. Section 1033(a)(2)(B). This time period is expanded to three full taxable years where real property held for business or investment purposes is seized, requisitioned, or condemned and the taxpayer acquires property of like kind. Section 1033(g). Furthermore, the time period is expanded to four full taxable years where the taxpayer's principal residence is involuntarily converted as a result of a Presidentially declared disaster. Section 1033(h).

Basis in Acquired Property. Not surprisingly, any unrecognized gain upon an involuntary conversion is preserved in the basis of the acquired property. If a taxpayer receives similar-use property upon the conversion and gain is nor recognized under § 1033(a)(1), then the taxpayer's basis in the similar-use property is generally the same as the taxpayer's basis in the converted property. Section 1033(b)(1). If the taxpayer purchases similar-use property and the realized gain from the converted property is not recognized (in whole or in part) under § 1033(a)(2), then the taxpayer's basis is the cost of the similar-use property reduced by the amount of unrecognized gain. Section 1033(b)(2).

* * *

Self-Assessment Question

(Solutions to Self–Assessment Questions are set forth in Appendix 3.)

SAQ 8–5. Determine whether the following transactions will qualify for nonrecognition to any extent under § 1033.

(a) The taxpayer owned a shopping center with a basis of $400,000 that was leased out to customers. When the shopping center was condemned, the taxpayer received $1,000,000 from the government and used all of the proceeds to purchase a new shopping center three months later.

(b) Same as (a), except that the original shopping center was destroyed by fire.

(c) Same as (a), except that the taxpayer used all of the proceeds to purchase a tavern that the taxpayer operated as a business.

(d) Same as (b), except that the taxpayer used all of the proceeds to purchase a tavern that the taxpayer operated as a business.

(e) Same as (a), except that the taxpayer's basis in the shopping center was $1,300,000.

(f) The taxpayer owned and operated a retail grocery store with a basis of $400,000. When the store was condemned, the taxpayer received $1,000,000 from the government and used all of the proceeds to purchase a bookstore that the taxpayer then operated as a business.

* * *

Problem 8–5

Stanley and Helen Roper, married individuals, own the Highland Apartments building. Their adjusted basis in the building is $75,000 and the building secures a mortgage in the amount of $120,000. The building was condemned by the state to make room for a new thoroughfare. Stanley and Helen received $225,000 from the state as just compensation, with $120,000 of that amount payable directly to the mortgagee. Within a year of having the Highland Apartments condemned, Stanley and Helen purchased another apartment building, the Mindure Manor, worth $210,000. The couple paid $60,000 cash and assumed an existing mortgage of $150,000 to finance the purchase.

(a) What are the federal income tax consequences of these events to Stanley and Helen?

(b) How would the answer to (a) change if the Mindure Manner was a nursing home facility and not an apartment building?

E.   INSTALLMENT SALE METHOD

Code: IRC §§ 453(a)–(g), (i), (j), (*l*); 453A; 453B(a)–(c), (f), (g); 1239(b).

Regs: Treas. Reg. § 15A.453–1(a), (b), (c).

In many property transactions, the buyer agrees to pay the purchase price to the seller in installments rather than a single lump sum. In computing the gain realized from the sale, however, the seller includes the entire purchase price in the amount realized. If the seller is forced to recognize the entire gain from the sale in the year of the sale, the seller may lack the funds to pay the corresponding tax, especially if only a tiny fraction of the purchase price is paid in the year of sale. Section 453 permits sellers to recognize the gain over the period in which payments will be received.

OVERVIEW OF ISSUES RELATING TO THE MODIFICATION OF THE INSTALLMENT SALES RULES BY THE TICKET TO WORK AND WORK INCENTIVES IMPROVEMENT ACT OF 1999

Joint Committee on Taxation (JCX–15–00), February 28, 2000.

I. BACKGROUND AND PRESENT LAW

A. *Methods of Accounting*

The amount of any item of gross income is required to be included in the gross income of the taxable year in which it is received by the taxpayer, unless, under the method of accounting used in computing taxable income, such amount is to be properly accounted for as of a different period.

Cash method

Under the cash receipts and disbursements method of accounting, an amount is includible in gross income when it is actually or constructively received. An amount does not have to be received in cash in order to be includible in the gross income of a cash method taxpayer. For example, the receipt of a negotiable note requires the value of the note to be included in gross income when the note is received, even if the note does not require payment in cash until some future time. Similarly, the receipt of other types of property or benefits may require their value to be included in income at the time they are received without regard to when, or if, they are ultimately converted to cash.

A cash method taxpayer must also include an item in gross income if it is constructively received, even if the taxpayer has not reduced it to possession. An amount is constructively received if it is credited to the taxpayer's account, set apart for the taxpayer, or otherwise made available so that the taxpayer may draw on it.

Accrual method

Under the accrual method of accounting an amount generally is includible in gross income when all the events have occurred which fix the right to receive such income and the amount thereof can be determined with reasonable accuracy. There is no requirement that cash, a note, or other property be received by the taxpayer. Under the accrual method of accounting, the item is includible in gross income because the right to receive the income is fixed, not because the income has actually been received.

B. *The Installment Method*

In general

The installment method provides an exception to the general principles of income recognition by allowing a taxpayer to defer the inclusion in income of amounts that are to be received from the disposition of certain types of property until payment in cash or cash equivalents is received. In general, a taxpayer using the installment method recognizes gain equal to the amount of payments received during the taxable year times the ratio the profit on the disposition bears to the total contract price. For this purpose, payments do not include the receipt of evidences of indebtedness of the person acquiring the property, unless such evidences of indebtedness are payable on demand, or are issued by a corporation or governmental entity and are readily tradable.

For example, in 2000, an individual taxpayer (who is not in the trade or business of selling real estate) sells non-farm real property with a basis of $100,000 for $1,000,000, realizing a gain of $900,000 and establishing a profit ratio of 90%. At closing, the taxpayer receives $200,000 in cash and an $800,000 note bearing adequate interest that is due in 2002. The taxpayer would recognize gain of $180,000 ($200,000 received times the profit ratio of 90%) in 2000 and an additional gain of $720,000 ($800,000 received on payment of the note times the profit ratio of 90%) in 2002. The interest on the note would be included in gross income by the taxpayer according to the taxpayer's normal method of accounting.

The installment method defers the recognition of income compared to both the cash and accrual methods. Compared to the cash method, the installment method permits additional deferral when payment is received in the form of a negotiable note. The deferral is more pronounced when the installment method is compared to the accrual method, since the accrual method requires income to be recognized as soon as the taxpayer has a right to the income, without regard to when payment is received. For most dispositions, the accrual method requires income to be recognized when title to the property passes, which may substantially precede the time payment is received.

* * *

Self-Assessment Question

(Solutions to Self–Assessment Questions are set forth in Appendix 3.)

SAQ 8–6. On July 1, Year Three, Thurston sold his boat (which he had used solely for personal purposes) for $50,000 to Gilligan. Thurston had purchased the boat in Year One for $29,000. Gilligan paid $10,000 cash at the time of the sale and gave Thurston his promissory note for $40,000, payable in eight annual installments of $5,000 each commencing on October 1, Year Three. Thurston incurred selling expenses totaling $1,000 in the transaction. If Thurston does not elect out of the installment method, how much of his gain must Thurston include in gross income for Year Three?

* * *

Problem 8–6

Randy Poffo sold Blackacre, a parcel of real property, in Year One to Amy Dumas for $200,000, consisting of Amy's assumption of a $100,000 mortgage incurred by Randy to acquire Blackacre and $100,000 in cash ($20,000 payable at closing and $80,000 in four equal annual installments commencing one year after closing). Randy acquired Blackacre three years ago, and his adjusted basis in Blackacre is $130,000. The mortgage is not specifically secured by the property. Amy's obligation to make the remaining cash payments is set forth in a promissory note. Randy, who is not a "dealer" in real property, incurred $10,000 of selling expenses on the sale.

(a) How much gross income does Randy have to report from the sale in Year One?

(b) How would your answer to (a) change if the total consideration paid by Amy consisted of the following: (i) Amy's assumption of a $150,000 mortgage incurred by Randy to acquire Blackacre; and (ii) $50,000 cash ($10,000 payable at closing and $40,000 in four equal annual installments commencing one year after closing)?

(c) How would your answer to (a) change if Randy incurred the $100,000 mortgage to finance a vacation cruise around the world?

* * *

Contingent Payment Sales. Ever since the Installment Sales Revision Act of 1980, the installment method has applied to contingent payment sales—those in which the total selling price cannot be determined as of the end of the taxable year of the sale. Because the sales price is not known, the usual gross profit percentage formula does not apply to a contingent payment sale. Instead, the regulations permit the seller to recover basis ratably over the payment period. Section 453(j)(2); Treas. Reg. § 15A.453–1(c). The exact treatment depends upon whether the maximum price payable to the seller is definite and whether the payment period is definite. The treatment given to contingent payment sales can be summarized generally as follows:

	If there is a stated maximum price payable to the seller...	If there is no stated maximum price ...
... **And if payments are only due for a specified period**	Compute gross profit assuming the maximum price is paid. If the seller recovers less than the full price, seller gets a loss in the final year of payment. *Treas. Reg. § 15A.453–1(c)(2).*	Recover basis ratably over the specified payment period. *Treas. Reg. § 15A.453–1(c)(3).*
... **And if the payment period is indefinite**	Compute gross profit assuming the maximum price is paid. *Treas. Reg. § 15A.453–1(c)(2).*	Recover basis ratably over 15 years unless that period "substantially and inappropriately" defers basis recovery. *Treas. Reg. § 15A.453–1(c)(4).*

These general rules are raised in the following Problem.

Problem 8–7

Stephanie Levesque owns all of the stock of *ABC* Corporation with a basis of $200,000. In Year One, Stephanie sold all of the *ABC* stock to an unrelated buyer in exchange for $100,000 cash at closing plus five percent of *ABC*'s net profits for five years. The sale agreement states that the maximum amount payable to Stephanie, including the down payment, is $2,000,000.

(a) Explain the consequences in Years One through Six if Stephanie receives the following payments in Years One through Five:

Year	Down Payment	Net Profits Payment
One	$100,000	$100,000
Two		$150,000
Three		$200,000
Four		$250,000
Five		$300,000

(b) How would the answer to (a) change if the sale agreement did not contain a maximum selling price?

(c) How would the answer to (b) change if the net profits payment received in Year Two was only $30,000?

(d) How would the answer to (b) change if the sale agreement did not limit the payment of net profits to five years (i.e., net profit payments would continue for the remainder of Stephanie's life and would then be payable to her heirs)?

* * *

Like-Kind Exchanges and Installment Sales. According to § 453(f)(6), when property is exchanged for like-kind property plus an installment note, the like-kind property is ignored in computing the "total contract price" and the receipt of the like-kind property is not considered a "payment." These rules are illustrated in the following example.

> EXAMPLE: Dwayne Johnson owns Blackacre with a basis of $400,000. Blackacre is worth $1 million. Dwayne exchanges Blackacre for Whiteacre, another parcel of real property worth $200,000, $100,000 cash, and an installment obligation for $700,000, payable starting in the next year and bearing adequate interest. The gross selling price is $1 million, producing a gross profit of $600,000. The contract price is initially $1 million, but under § 453(f)(6)(A), Whiteacre is ignored in computing the contract price, so the contract price

slips to \$800,000 (\$1 million minus the \$200,000 value of Whiteacre). The gross profit percentage is thus 75 percent (\$600,000 divided by \$800,000), so \$75,000 of the \$100,000 cash received at closing is included in gross income, and 75 percent of all remaining payments under the installment note will also be included in Dwayne's gross income when received.

Resales by Related Persons. Section 453(e) generally states that if a taxpayer sells property to a related person and uses the installment method to report the gain, the deferred gain will be accelerated if the related person sells the acquired property within two years of the original sale and before final payment has been made on the original installment sale. The amount realized by the related person on the second sale is treated as a payment to the taxpayer. The two-year cutoff for the sale by the related party does not apply to installment sales of marketable securities—in those cases, the § 453(e) taint survives the two-year limitation and will haunt any dispositions made by the related party prior to the full payment of the original installment obligation. The two-year clock is tolled for any number of events described in § 453(e)(2)(B) that have the effect of substantially diminishing the related party's risk of loss.

The definition of a related person is set forth at § 453(f)(1). It includes any person who constructively owns stock owned by the taxpayer under *either* section 267(b) or section 318(a). Notice that § 453(e)(6) excludes a number of specific transactions from the reach of § 453(e)(1). There is also a general exception in § 453(e)(7) for those situations where neither the original installment sale nor the disposition by the related party has an income tax avoidance purpose. There are no regulations offering guidance on the application of § 453(e)(7), so this is still uncharted territory, even though the rule has been in the Code since the Installment Sales Revision Act of 1980.

* * *

Self-Assessment Question

(Solutions to Self–Assessment Questions are set forth in Appendix 3.)

SAQ 8–7. Mother owns 50 percent of the stock of *XYZ* Corporation with a basis of \$10,000. Mother seeks to transfer a portion of her wealth to Son and Daughter, both adults. Mother consults with Lawyer, an estate planning attorney. Lawyer advises Mother to give all or a portion of the *XYZ* stock to Son and Daughter.

A subsequent appraisal of the stock indicates that Mother's shares are worth about \$2 million. Hesitant to incur federal gift tax liability on the proposed transfer, Mother rejects Lawyer's proposal. Lawyer then advises Mother to sell the stock to Son and Daughter in exchange for installment obligations from each of them. Each installment obligation would bear a face amount of $1 million and would be payable (with interest at a rate equal to prevailing market interest rates) in full on the ninth anniversary of the sale. Lawyer indicates that the amount subject to federal estate tax at Mother's death would thus be frozen at the value of the installment obligations, and that no federal wealth transfer taxes would be paid on any appreciation in the value of the shares following the sale. Mother also likes the fact that her capital gain from the sale will be deferred for nine years. Accordingly, Mother sells the *XYZ* shares to Son and Daughter on the terms described above.

Nine months after the sale, Son and Daughter (along with the other *XYZ* shareholders) sell the stock to an unrelated purchaser for cash. Son and Daughter receive $4 million from the sale ($2 million each). What are the income tax consequences to Mother, Son, and Daughter?

* * *

Pledging Installment Notes as Collateral. One of the drawbacks of the installment method is that sellers must wait to get their hands on the loot. Although deferral of tax is generally desirable, deferral in the receipt of payments is certainly less than optimal. Sellers invoking the installment sale method soon discovered an end-run around the deferral of payments: a seller could borrow an amount equal to the principal balance of his or her installment obligation and pledge the installment note as collateral for the loan. Then, the seller could use the installment sale proceeds to pay off the loan. In the end, the seller gets the money (the loan proceeds) well ahead of the scheduled payment date and the seller's tax obligation from the original sale is still deferred.

Section 453A(d) prevents this neat trick from working. It requires the seller to treat the loan proceeds as a payment of the installment obligation, thus accelerating the gain recognition to match the receipt of cash. The application and scope of § 453A(d) is illustrated in the following Problem.

Problem 8–8

In Year One, George Bailey sold a parking garage to Mary Hatch (an unrelated purchaser) in exchange for her promise to pay $100,000 in each of Years Two through Six (total payments of $500,000), together with interest at a rate sufficient to avoid application of the imputed interest rules. Mary's promise was evidenced by a note. George's basis in the garage was $100,000. At the end of Year One, George obtained a $300,000 loan from Mr. Potter, secured by the note from Mary.

(a) How much gross income does George have in Year One?

(b) How much gross income does George have in Year Two?

(c) How would your answer to (a) change if the property sold to Mary was George's vacation home?

(d) How would your answer to (a) change if Mary was only obligated to pay $25,000 in each of Years Two through Six (total payments of $125,000)?

(e) Suppose that George did not obtain the Potter loan until the beginning of Year Five, after Mary had made the payments for Years Two, Three, and Four. How much gross income will George have in Year Five under these revised facts?

* * *

Interest on Deferred Tax Liability. The chief advantage of the installment method is the deferral of gain until payments are received. This deferral is available to taxpayers on both the cash and accrual methods, and generally the taxpayer is not required to pay interest to the government in exchange for the deferral. This makes most installment sales better than a conventional loan. When taxpayers defer very large amounts, however, Congress feels somewhat abused. While Congress is willing to grant deferral to folks like you and me, it has reservations about extending deferral to taxpayers who stand to make gains in the millions of dollars. This is the reason why §§ 453A(a)(1) and 453A(c) contain the interest payment requirements. The operation of the interest requirement is set forth in the following example.

> EXAMPLE: Mark Callaway sells a building on July 1, Year One, to an unrelated purchaser for $8 million, $1 million payable on July 1, Year Two, and $7 million payable on July 1, Year Three. Mark's basis in the building is $2 million. His gross profit from the sale is $6 million, and the gross profit percentage is thus 75 percent ($6 million $8 million). Assume that Mark holds no other installment obligations in Years One through Three and that the "underpayment rate" in effect under § 6621(a)(2) in December of each of Years One through Three is nine percent.
>
> For Year One, Mark received no payments from the buyer, but under § 453A(a)(1) and (c)(1), he will have to pay interest on the deferred tax liability. This is because the installment obligation exceeds $150,000 [§ 453A(b)(1)] and because the face amount of this obligation which arose during Year One and which was still outstanding as of the end of Year One (the only such obligation *T* has at that time) exceeds $5 million [§ 453A(b)(2)]. The interest Mark must pay is added to his regular tax liability for the year [§ 453A(c)(1)]. The interest is computed by applying the underpayment rate (here, nine percent) to "the applicable percentage" of the "deferred tax liability" [§ 453A(c)(2)]. The "applicable percentage" is determined by dividing the amount of the installment obligation in excess of $5 million (here, $3 million) by the total amount of installment obligations subject to the interest requirement (here, $8 million) [§ 453A(c)(4)]. Thus, the applicable

percentage for Mark is 37.5 percent. The "deferred tax liability" is the maximum tax rate times the amount of gain that has not yet been recognized as of the close of Year One [§ 453A(c)(3)]. Assuming the building is a capital asset in Mark's hands, the maximum tax rate is 15 percent per § 1(h). Thus the deferred tax liability here is $900,000 (15 percent x $6 million gain not yet recognized). The applicable percentage of the deferred tax liability is therefore $337,500 (37.5 percent x $900,000). Mark must add $30,375 (9 percent of $337,500) to his tax liability for Year One.

In Year Two, Mark gets $1 million from the buyer, and must therefore include $750,000 in gross income (the gross profit percentage, recall, was 75 percent). The required interest payment is still due, even though he has not made any other high-end installment sales. This is because the determination in § 453A(b)(2) is made on an obligation-by-obligation basis, not on a year-by-year basis. In other words, once an installment obligation bears the interest taint, the taint continues for the duration of the installment note. The "applicable percentage" remains constant at 37.5 percent. But the deferred tax liability drops to $1,050,000 because Mark has now recognized $750,000 of the $6 million realized gain from the sale. The remaining unrecognized gain is thus $5,250,000, and the deferred tax liability is 15 percent of that amount, or $787,500. The applicable percentage of the deferred tax liability is thus 37.5 percent of $787,500, or $295,313. Mark must pay nine percent interest on that figure, or $26,578, in addition to his regular tax.

In Year Three, Mark gets the remaining $7 million from the installment obligation. The gross profit percentage is still 75 percent, so $5,250,000 must be included in gross income. There is no more interest obligation because the installment obligation is not outstanding as of the end of Year Three. Whew!

* * *

Dispositions of Installment Obligations. The privilege of deferring gain from an installment sale is a generally viewed as a personal one. Thus, when a taxpayer transfers an installment obligation owed to the taxpayer to another person, one of two things will happen: (1) the taxpayer must recognize the remaining gain as of the date of disposition; or (2) the transferee will step into the taxpayer's shoes and recognize the deferred gain only as payments are received. As you might have guessed, sometimes the first result occurs and sometimes the second result occurs. The rules applicable to any disposition (sale, gift, bequest, or other transfer) of an installment obligation are set forth in § 453B, and are sufficiently self-explanatory that you can navigate through the following Self–Assessment Question and Problem.

Self-Assessment Question

(Solutions to Self–Assessment Questions are set forth in Appendix 3.)

SAQ 8–8. In Year One, T sold investment property with a basis of $100,000 and a fair market value of $200,000 to X, an unrelated buyer, in exchange for a $50,000 cash down payment and a note whereby the buyer agreed to pay $50,000 in each of Years Three, Five, and Seven, together with interest at a rate sufficient to avoid application of the imputed interest rules. In Year Two, T sold the note to Z, another unrelated individual for $130,000 cash. What are the federal income tax consequences to T arising from the Year Two sale to Z?

* * *

Problem 8–9

T sold property on an installment basis to X in Year One. For each of the situations described below (all of which are assumed to occur in Year Two), determine whether T will have to recognize gain or loss under § 453B.

(a) T sells a one-half interest in the installment obligation to Z, an unrelated buyer.

(b) T gives the note to T's niece as a birthday present.

(c) T exchanges the X note for a different installment obligation issued by Q and owned by A. Assume Q and A are unrelated to T and that the Q note contains a shorter payment period and a different interest rate.

(d) T and X agree to extend the payment dates by five years and to raise the interest rate on the note from nine percent to ten percent.

(e) Assume that X is a corporation. T and X agree to increase the principal balance of the note by 20 percent in exchange for T's waiver of T's right to convert the obligation into common stock of X.

(f) T forgives the note.

(g) T transfers the note to a "revocable living trust." Under the terms of the trust instrument, T receives all of the trust's income for life and retains the power to revoke the trust at any time before T's death. Because of these powers, T considered the owner of the trust for federal income tax purposes under §§ 671–677.

(h) Same as (g), except the trust is irrevocable and T names T's sibling as the income and remainder beneficiary of the trust.

(i) T transfers the note to T's ex-spouse within one year after the date on which their marriage ceases.

(j) Assume once again that X is a corporation. X liquidates, and X's shareholders become the new obligors under the note.

(k) *T* dies, and *T*'s will bequeaths the note to *T*'s son.

(l) *T* dies, and *T*'s will bequeaths the note to *X*.

* * *

Election Out of Installment Method. The installment method applies to any installment sale transaction unless the taxpayer "elects out" of the installment method. Section 453(d)(1). The election must be made on or before the deadline date for filing income tax returns for the year of the installment sale. Section 453(d)(2). The election can be revoked only with the consent of the Secretary of the Treasury. Section 453(d)(3). By electing out, a taxpayer generally agrees to report the gain from the transaction in the year of sale, with the amount realized in all cases including the principal amount (or "face value") of the installment note. Thus, for example, if a taxpayer sells property with a basis of $100 to an unrelated buyer in exchange for $50 at closing and a note obligating the buyer to pay $50 plus interest each year for three years, the amount realized is $200 and the gain of $100 is reported in the year of sale.

Determining the correct amount of gain in a transaction to which the installment method does not apply can sometimes prove quite difficult. As a result, courts have sanctioned the use of alternative reporting methods from time to time. The following case authorizes the use of the so-called "open transaction doctrine." Its applicability to installment sales where the taxpayer elects out of § 453 is discussed afterward.

BURNET v. LOGAN

United States Supreme Court, 1931.
283 U.S. 404, 51 S.Ct. 550, 75 L.Ed. 1143.

Mr. Justice McReynolds delivered the opinion of the Court.

* * *

Prior to March, 1913, and until March 11, 1916, respondent, Mrs. Logan, owned 250 of the 4,000 capital shares issued by the Andrews & Hitchcock Iron Company. It held 12% of the stock of the Mahoning Ore & Steel Company, an operating concern. In 1895 the latter corporation procured a lease for 97 years upon the "Mahoning" mine and since then has regularly taken therefrom large, but varying, quantities of iron ore— in 1913, 1,515,428 tons; in 1914, 1,212,287 tons; in 1915, 2,311,940 tons; in 1919, 1,217,167 tons; in 1921, 303,020 tons; in 1923, 3,029,865 tons. The lease contract did not require production of either maximum or minimum tonnage or any definite payments. Through an agreement of stockholders (steel manufacturers) the Mahoning Company is obligated to apportion extracted ore among them according to their holdings.

On March 11, 1916, the owners of all the shares in Andrews & Hitchcock Company sold them to Youngstown Sheet & Tube Company, which thus acquired, among other things, 12% of the Mahoning Company's stock and the right to receive the same percentage of ore thereafter taken from the leased mine.

For the shares so acquired the Youngstown Company paid the holders $2,200,000 in money and agreed to pay annually thereafter for distribution among them 60 cents for each ton of ore apportioned to it. Of this cash Mrs. Logan received 250/4000ths—$137,500; and she became entitled to the same fraction of any annual payment thereafter made by the purchaser under the terms of sale.

Mrs. Logan's mother had long owned 1100 shares of the Andrews & Hitchcock Company. She died in 1917, leaving to the daughter one-half of her interest in payments thereafter made by the Youngstown Company. This bequest was appraised for federal estate tax purposes at $277,164.50.

During 1917, 1918, 1919 and 1920 the Youngstown Company paid large sums under the agreement. Out of these respondent received on account of her 250 shares $9,900.00 in 1917, $11,250.00 in 1918, $8,995.50 in 1919, $5,444.30 in 1920—$35,589.80. By reason of the interest from her mother's estate she received $19,790.10 in 1919, and $11,977.49 in 1920.

Reports of income for 1918, 1919 and 1920 were made by Mrs. Logan upon the basis of cash receipts and disbursements. They included no part of what she had obtained from annual payments by the Youngstown Company. She maintains that until the total amount actually received by her from the sale of her shares equals their value on March 1, 1913, no taxable income will arise from the transaction. Also that until she actually receives by reason of the right bequeathed to her a sum equal to its appraised value, there will be no taxable income therefrom.

On March 1, 1913, the value of the 250 shares then held by Mrs. Logan exceeded $173,089.80—the total of all sums actually received by her prior to 1921 from their sale ($137,500.00 cash in 1916 plus four annual payments amounting to $35,589.80). That value also exceeded original cost of the shares. The amount received on the interest devised by her mother was less than its valuation for estate taxation; also less than the value when acquired by Mrs. Logan.

The Commissioner ruled that the obligation of the Youngstown Company to pay 60 cents per ton had a fair market value of $1,942,111.46 on March 11, 1916; that this value should be treated as so much cash and the sale of the stock regarded as a closed transaction with no profit in 1916. He also used this valuation as the basis for apportioning subsequent annual receipts between income and return of capital. His calculations, based upon estimates and assumptions, are too intricate for brief statement. He made deficiency assessments according to the view just stated and the Board of Tax Appeals approved the result.

The Circuit Court of Appeals held that, in the circumstances, it was impossible to determine with fair certainty the market value of the agreement by the Youngstown Company to pay 60 cents per ton. Also, that respondent was entitled to the return of her capital—the value of 250 shares on March 1, 1913, and the assessed value of the interest derived from her mother—before she could be charged with any taxable income. As this had not in fact been returned, there was no taxable income.

We agree with the result reached by the Circuit Court of Appeals.

The 1916 transaction was a sale of stock—not an exchange of property. We are not dealing with royalties or deductions from gross income because of depletion of mining property. Nor does the situation demand that an effort be made to place according to the best available data some approximate value upon the contract for future payments. This probably was necessary in order to assess the mother's estate. As annual payments on account of extracted ore come in they can be readily apportioned first as return of capital and later as profit. The liability for income tax ultimately can be fairly determined without resort to mere estimates, assumptions and speculation. When the profit, if any, is actually realized, the taxpayer will be required to respond. The consideration for the sale was $2,200,000.00 in cash and the promise of future money payments wholly contingent upon facts and circumstances not possible to foretell with anything like fair certainty. The promise was in no proper sense equivalent to cash. It had no ascertainable fair market value. The transaction was not a closed one. Respondent might never recoup her capital investment from payments only conditionally promised. Prior to 1921 all receipts from the sale of her shares amounted to less than their value on March 1, 1913. She properly demanded the return of her capital investment before assessment of any taxable profit based on conjecture.

"In order to determine whether there has been gain or loss, and the amount of the gain, if any, we must withdraw from the gross proceeds an amount sufficient to restore the capital value that existed at the commencement of the period under consideration." *Doyle v. Mitchell Bros. Co.*, 247 U.S. 179, 184, 185. * * * Ordinarily, at least, a taxpayer may not deduct from gross receipts a supposed loss which in fact is represented by his outstanding note. *Eckert v. Commissioner of Internal Revenue*, ante, p. 140. And, conversely, a promise to pay indeterminate sums of money is not necessarily taxable income. "Generally speaking, the income tax law is concerned only with realized losses, as with realized gains." *Lucas v. American Code Co.*, 280 U.S. 445, 449.

From her mother's estate Mrs. Logan obtained the right to share in possible proceeds of a contract thereafter to pay indefinite sums. The value of this was assumed to be $277,164.50 and its transfer was so taxed. Some valuation—speculative or otherwise—was necessary in order to close the estate. It may never yield as much, it may yield more. If a sum equal to the value thus ascertained had been invested in an annuity contract, payments thereunder would have been free from income tax until the owner had recouped his capital investment. We think a like rule should be applied here. The statute definitely excepts bequests from receipts which go to make up taxable income. * * *

The judgments below are

Affirmed.

Note

So the question becomes whether a taxpayer who elects out of the installment method can still defer the recognition of gain by using the open transaction doctrine approved in *Burnet v. Logan*. The legislative history suggests that Congress would preclude use of the open transaction doctrine:

... it is the Committee's intent that the cost-recovery [or "open transaction"] method not be available in the case of sales for a fixed price (whether the seller's obligation is evidenced by a note, contractual promise, or otherwise), and that its use be limited to those rare and extraordinary cases involving sales for a contingent price where the fair market value of the purchaser's obligation cannot be reasonably ascertained.

S. Rep. No. 1000, 96th Cong., 2d Sess., reprinted in 1980–2 CB 494, 506–507. Treas. Reg. § 15A.453–1(d)(2)(iii) follows this intent by stating that a taxpayer can use the "open transaction" doctrine only in the rare case in which the fair market value of a contingent payment obligation cannot be reasonably ascertained.

What, then, if the amount realized from a deferred payment sale *can* be reasonably ascertained but the taxpayer nonetheless elects out of § 453? Presumably, the entire amount realized must be taken into account in the year of sale. For a cash method taxpayer, the amount realized would be the fair market value of the installment obligation. *Warren Jones Co. v. Commissioner*, 524 F.2d 788 (9th Cir. 1975). For an accrual method taxpayer, the amount realized would be the *face* value of the installment obligation (i.e., the total principal amount to be paid pursuant to the terms of the promissory note issued by the buyer).

* * *

Chapter 9

PERSONAL MATTERS

Getting Personal. This Chapter examines several deduction and nonrecognition provisions that relate to personal matters, activities unrelated to a taxpayer's business or investment activities. Section 262(a) generally disallows deductions for personal expenses, but several of the provisions at issue in this Chapter deviate from that general rule. The general rule is based mainly on the theory that income is measured in part by *consumption*, which represents (in part) expenditures made for a taxpayer's personal use. As a result, income would not accurately be measured if the taxpayer were allowed to deduct personal expenditures. The deductions discussed in this Chapter, therefore, are inconsistent with a "pure" income tax measured in part by consumption and are viewed by some as improper.

Whether you knew it or not, we have previously examined other deductions for personal expenses. These include the home mortgage interest deduction (Chapter 8) and the casualty loss deduction (Chapter 4). By permitting these and other personal deductions, Congress is foregoing revenues. But how much? If we want to answer the question of whether deductions for personal expenses accord with good tax policy, we must first get a handle of how much revenue Congress is leaving on the table. That brings us to the concept of "tax expenditures" and the tax expenditure budget, an estimation of the dollars lost to the federal government from deductions and other provisions inconsistent with a pure income tax.

ESTIMATES OF FEDERAL TAX EXPENDITURES FOR FISCAL YEARS 2006–2010

Joint Committee on Taxation (JCS–2–06), April 25, 2006.

I. The Concept of Tax Expenditures

Overview

"Tax expenditures" are defined under the Congressional Budget and Impoundment Control Act of 1974 ("the Budget Act") as "revenue losses attributable to provisions of the Federal tax laws which allow a special exclusion, exemption, or deduction from gross income or which provide a special credit, a preferential rate of tax, or a deferral of tax liability." Thus, tax expenditures include any reductions in income tax liabilities that result from special tax provisions or regulations that provide tax benefits to particular taxpayers.

Special income tax provisions are referred to as tax expenditures because they may be considered to be analogous to direct outlay programs, and the two can be considered as alternative means of accomplishing similar budget policy objectives. Tax expenditures are most similar to those direct spending programs that have no spending limits, and that are available as entitlements to those who meet the statutory criteria established for the programs.

Estimates of tax expenditures are prepared for use in budget analysis. They are a measure of the economic benefits that are provided through the tax laws to various groups of taxpayers and sectors of the economy. The estimates also may be useful in determining the relative merits of achieving specified public goals through tax benefits or direct outlays.

The legislative history of the Budget Act indicates that tax expenditures are to be defined with reference to a normal income tax structure (referred to here as "normal income tax law"). The determination of whether a provision is a tax expenditure is made on the basis of a broad concept of income that is larger in scope than "income" as defined under general U.S. income tax principles. The Joint Committee staff has used its judgment in distinguishing between those income tax provisions (and regulations) that can be viewed as a part of normal income tax law and those special provisions that result in tax expenditures. A provision traditionally has been listed as a tax expenditure by the Joint Committee staff if there is a reasonable basis for such classification and the provision results in more than a *de minimis* revenue loss, which solely for this purpose means a total revenue loss of at least $50 million over * * * five fiscal years * * *. The Joint Committee staff emphasizes, however, that in the process of listing tax expenditures, no judgment is made, nor any implication intended, about the desirability of any special tax provision as a matter of public policy.

If a tax expenditure provision were eliminated, Congress might choose to continue financial assistance through other means rather than terminate all Federal assistance for the activity. If a replacement spending program were enacted, the higher revenues received as a result of the elimination of a tax expenditure might not represent a net budget gain. A replacement program could involve direct expenditures, direct loans or loan guarantees, regulatory activity, a different form of tax expenditure, or a general reduction in tax rates. Joint Committee staff estimates of tax expenditures do not anticipate such policy responses.

The Budget Act uses the term tax expenditure to refer to the special tax provisions that are contained in the Federal income taxes on individuals and corporations. Other Federal taxes such as excise taxes, employment taxes, and estate and gift taxes may also have exceptions, exclusions, and credits, but those special tax provisions are not included in this report because they are not part of the income tax. Thus, for example, the income tax exclusion for employer-paid health insurance is included, but the Federal Insurance Contributions Act ("FICA") tax exclusion for employer-paid health insurance is not treated as a tax expenditure. * * *

Some provisions in the Internal Revenue Code provide for special tax treatment that is less favorable than normal income tax law. Examples of such provisions include (1) the denial of deductions for certain lobbying expenses, (2) the denial of deductions for certain executive compensation, and (3) the two–percent floor on itemized deductions for unreimbursed employee expenses. Tax provisions that provide treatment less favorable than normal income tax law are not shown in this report because they are not included in the statutory definition of a tax expenditure.

Individual Income Tax

Under the Joint Committee staff methodology, the normal structure of the individual income tax includes the following major components: one personal exemption for each taxpayer and one for each dependent, the standard deduction, the existing tax rate schedule, and deductions for investment and employee business expenses. Most other tax benefits to individual taxpayers can be classified as exceptions to normal income tax law.

The Joint Committee staff views the personal exemptions and the standard deduction as defining the zero-rate bracket that is a part of normal tax law. An itemized deduction that is not necessary for the generation of income is classified as a tax expenditure, but only to the extent that it, when added to a taxpayer's other itemized deductions, exceeds the standard deduction.

All employee compensation is subject to tax unless the tax code contains a specific exclusion for the income. Specific exclusions for employer-provided benefits include the following: coverage under accident and health plans, accident and disability insurance, group term life insurance, educational assistance, tuition reduction benefits, transportation benefits (parking, van pools, and transit passes), dependent care assistance, adoption assistance, meals and lodging furnished for the convenience of the employer, employee awards, and other miscellaneous fringe benefits (e.g., employee discounts, services provided to employees at no additional cost to employers, and de minimis fringe benefits). Each of these exclusions is classified as a tax expenditure in this report.

Under normal income tax law, employer contributions to pension plans and income earned on pension assets would be taxable to employees as the contributions are made and as the income is earned, and employees would not receive any deduction or exclusion for their pension contributions. Under present law, employer contributions to qualified pension plans and employee contributions made at the election of the employee through salary reduction are not taxed until distributed to the employee, and income earned on pension assets is not taxed until distributed. The tax expenditure for "net exclusion of pension contributions and earnings" is computed as the income taxes forgone on current tax-excluded pension contributions and earnings less the income taxes paid on current pension distributions (including the 10–percent additional tax paid on early withdrawals from pension plans).

Under present law, social security and tier 1 railroad retirement benefits are partially excluded or fully excluded from gross income. Under normal income tax law, retirees would be entitled to an exclusion for only the portion of social security retirement benefits that represents a return of the payroll taxes that they paid during their working years. Thus, the exclusion of social security and railroad retirement benefits in excess of payroll tax payments is classified as a tax expenditure.

* * *

The individual income tax does not include in gross income the imputed income that individuals receive from the services provided by owner-occupied homes and durable goods. However, the Joint Committee staff does not classify this exclusion as a tax expenditure. The measurement of imputed income for tax purposes presents administrative problems and its exclusion from taxable income may be regarded as an administrative necessity. Under normal income tax law, individuals would be allowed to deduct only the interest on indebtedness incurred in connection with a trade or business or an investment. Thus, the deduction for mortgage interest on a principal or second residence is classified as a tax expenditure.

The Joint Committee staff assumes that, for administrative feasibility, normal income tax law would tax capital gains in full in the year the gains are realized through sale, exchange, gift, or transfer at death. Thus, the deferral of tax until realization is not classified as a tax expenditure, but reduced rates of tax, further deferrals of tax (beyond the year of sale or exchange), and exclusions of certain capital gains are classified as tax expenditures. It also is assumed that normal income tax law would not provide for any indexing of the basis of capital assets for changes in the general price level. Thus, under normal income tax law (as under present law), the income tax would be levied on nominal gains as opposed to real gains in asset values.

* * *

One of the most difficult issues in defining tax expenditures for business income relates to the tax treatment of capital costs. Under present law, capital costs may be recovered under a variety of alternative methods, depending upon the nature of the costs and the status of the taxpayer. For example, investments in equipment and structures may qualify for tax credits, expensing, accelerated depreciation, or straight-line depreciation. The Joint Committee staff generally classifies as tax expenditures cost recovery allowances that are more favorable than those provided under the alternative depreciation system (sec. 168(g)), which provides for straight-line recovery over tax lives that are longer than those permitted under the accelerated system. As indicated above, the Joint Committee staff assumes that normal income tax law would not provide for any indexing of the basis of capital assets. Thus, normal income tax law would not take into account the effects of inflation on tax depreciation.

* * *

Comparisons with Treasury Department

The Joint Committee staff and Treasury lists of tax expenditures differ in three respects. First, the Treasury uses a different classification of those provisions that can be considered a part of normal income tax law under both the individual and business income taxes. In general, the Joint Committee staff methodology involves a broader definition of the normal income tax base. Thus, the Joint Committee list of tax expenditures includes some provisions that are not contained in the Treasury list. The cash method of accounting by certain businesses provides an example. The Treasury considers the cash accounting option for certain businesses to be a part of normal income tax law, but the Joint Committee staff methodology treats it as a departure from normal income tax law that constitutes a tax expenditure.

* * *

Third, the Joint Committee staff list excludes those provisions that are estimated to result in revenue losses below the *de minimis* amount, i.e., less than $50 million over * * * five fiscal years * * *. The Treasury rounds all yearly estimates to the nearest $10 million and excludes those provisions with estimates that round to zero in each year, *i.e.*, provisions that result in less than $5 million in revenue loss in each of the years * * *.

* * *

II. MEASUREMENT OF TAX EXPENDITURES

Tax Expenditure Estimates Generally

A tax expenditure is measured by the difference between tax liability under present law and the tax liability that would result from a recomputation of tax without benefit of the tax expenditure provision. Taxpayer behavior is assumed to remain unchanged for tax expenditure estimate purposes.[15]

---

15. An alternative way to measure tax expenditures is to express their values in terms of "outlay equivalents." An outlay equivalent is the dollar size of a direct spending program that would provide taxpayers with net benefits that would equal what they now receive from a tax expenditure. The Treasury Department presents estimates of outlay equivalents in the President's budget in addition to presenting estimates in the same manner as the Joint Committee staff.

The tax expenditure estimates in this report are based on the January 2006 Congressional Budget Office revenue baseline and Joint Committee staff projections of the gross income, deductions, and expenditures of individuals and corporations * * *. These projections are used to compute tax liabilities for the present-law revenue baseline and tax liabilities for the alternative baseline that assumes that the tax expenditure provision does not exist.

Internal Revenue Service ("IRS") statistics from recent tax returns are used to develop projections of the tax credits, deductions, and exclusions that will be claimed under the present-law baseline. These IRS statistics show the actual usage of the various tax expenditure provisions. In the case of some tax expenditures, such as the earned income tax credit, there is evidence that some taxpayers are not claiming all of the benefits to which they are entitled, while others are filing claims that exceed their entitlements. The tax expenditure estimates in this report are based on projections of actual claims under the various tax provisions, not the tax benefits to which taxpayers are entitled.

Some tax expenditure estimates are based partly on statistics for income, deductions, and expenses for prior years. Accelerated depreciation is an example. Estimates for this tax expenditure are based on the difference between tax depreciation deductions under present law and the deductions that would have been claimed in the current year if investments in the current year and all prior years had been depreciated using the alternative (normal income tax law) depreciation system.

Each tax expenditure is estimated separately, under the assumption that all other tax expenditures remain in the tax code. If two or more tax expenditures were estimated simultaneously, the total change in tax liability could be smaller or larger than the sum of the amounts shown for each item separately, as a result of interactions among the tax expenditure provisions.

Year-to-year differences in the estimates for each tax expenditure reflect changes in tax law, including phaseouts of tax expenditure provisions and changes that alter the definition of the normal income tax structure, such as the tax rate schedule, the personal exemption amount, and the standard deduction. Some of the estimates for this tax expenditure report may differ from estimates made in previous years because of changes in law and economic conditions, the availability of better data, and improved estimating techniques.

Tax Expenditures versus Revenue Estimates

A tax expenditure estimate is not the same as a revenue estimate for the repeal of the tax expenditure provision for three reasons. First, unlike revenue estimates, tax expenditure estimates do not incorporate the effects of the behavioral changes that are anticipated to occur in response to the repeal of a tax expenditure provision. Second, tax expenditure estimates are concerned with changes in the tax liabilities of taxpayers. Because the tax expenditure focus is on tax liabilities as opposed to Federal government tax receipts, there is no concern for the timing of tax payments. Revenue estimates are concerned with changes in Federal tax receipts that are affected by the timing of tax payments. Third, some of the tax provisions that provide an exclusion from income also apply to the FICA tax base, and the repeal of the income tax provision would automatically increase FICA tax revenues as well as income tax revenues. There may also be interactions between income tax provisions and other Federal taxes such as excise taxes and the estate and gift tax.

If a tax expenditure provision were repealed, it is likely that the repeal would be made effective for taxable years beginning after a certain date. Because most individual taxpayers have taxable years that coincide with the calendar year, the repeal of a provision affecting the individual income tax most likely would be effective for taxable years beginning after December 31 of a certain year. However, the Federal government's fiscal year begins October 1. Thus, the revenue estimate for repeal of a provision would show a smaller revenue gain in the first fiscal year than in subsequent years. This is due to the fact that the repeal would be effective after the start of the Federal government's fiscal year. The revenue estimate might also reflect some delay in the timing of the revenue gains as a result of the taxpayer tendency to postpone or forgo changes in tax withholding and estimated tax payments.

* * *

* * *

Tax Expenditure Estimates. Table 1 from the Joint Committee on Taxation's report is set forth in Appendix 1 of this book. Notice that the deduction for qualified residence interest is estimated to cost the federal government over $402 billion in lost revenues from 2006 to 2010. By contrast, the deduction for casualty and theft losses is estimated to cost only $2.4 billion in lost revenues over the same period. While both deductions represent a departure from the general rule that personal expenses and losses should not be deductible under an income tax based in part on consumption, the deduction for casualty and theft losses is a much less significant exception than the deduction for qualified residence interest, at least from a revenue perspective. Does that mean the deduction for qualified residence interest should be subject to more scrutiny from commentators and policymakers?

Regardless of your answer to that question, consider the estimated revenue loss from each of the tax expenditure provisions presented in this Chapter. (And if you have some spare time on your hands, consider the estimated losses from various other tax expenditure items we have covered up to this point.) Do the numbers in Appendix 1 influence your view of the merits of each such expenditure?

In the interest of full disclosure, you should know that the tax expenditure concept is not without controversy. Professor Bittker argued that identifying and measuring tax expenditures is a process filled with problems. Boris I. Bittker, *Accounting for Federal "Tax Subsidies" in the National Budget*, 22 NATIONAL TAX JOURNAL 244 (1969). For starters, there is no consensus as to what a "correct" tax structure would look like. Some might argue that several of the items listed as "tax expenditures" in Appendix 1 are in fact significant components of a true income tax. The reliability of tax expenditure estimates is further undermined by the fact that it is often difficult to identify the proper taxpayer (recall the assignment of income doctrine in Chapter 3) and to choose the proper measurement period (i.e., should foregone revenues be based on a taxpayer's lifetime, or, as is currently the case, on the basis of a calendar year).

Professor Bittker and others have also argued that tax expenditure estimates are flawed in that they assume no effect on taxpayer behavior. As one author observed:

> One cannot simply recompute an individual's tax liability with and without the tax expenditure, Bittker argued, because we cannot know what the taxpayer would have done in its absence. If a tax provision caused a taxpayer's behavior to change, then eliminating the provision may only cause him to change back again. This makes any measurement of how much revenue the government would gain from repealing a tax provision almost impossible to calculate accurately. It also means that we cannot know the distributional consequences of many tax provisions, even though distributional considerations now dominate the tax policymaking process.

Bruce Bartlett, *The End of Tax Expenditures As We Know Them?*, 92 TAX NOTES 413 (2001). Even the excerpt from the Joint Committee on Taxation's report concedes that the process of measuring foregone revenues from tax expenditures is an inexact science. Do the estimates have value despite the imprecision?

---

p. 600–609
problem 9–1

A. EXTRAORDINARY MEDICAL EXPENSES

Code: IRC § 213(a)–(b), (d)(1)–(2), (d)(9). *Skim* IRC § 223.

Regs: Treas. Reg. § 1.213–1(a); –1(e)(1)–(2).

Expenses paid for medical care clearly represent personal consumption. In an ideal income tax system, therefore, no deduction should be allowed for such costs. For those taxpayers covered by insurance, the lack of a deduction is not a hardship since those taxpayers incur little or no out-of-pocket expenses for medical care in the first place. Uninsured taxpayers, however, may incur substantial medical costs with no hope of reimbursement. The ideal income tax system would have little sympathy for those who incur substantial medical costs. The message would be clear: get insured!

But not all taxpayers can afford insurance, and others might not be eligible for coverage. Where an uninsured taxpayer pays extraordinarily high costs for medical care in a single year, fortunately, Congress has a heart. Section 213 allows a deduction for uncompensated medical expenses, but only to the extent such costs exceed 7.5 percent of the taxpayer's adjusted gross income. Thus, if a taxpayer has an adjusted gross income of $50,000 and qualifying medical expenses of $10,000, the taxpayer can only deduct $6,250 in medical expenses ($10,000 minus $3,750, which is 7.5 percent of $50,000). Because of the high "co-payment," most taxpayers do not get any benefit from § 213; instead, the section is helpful only to those who pay excessive health care costs in the taxable year.

Note that if the taxpayer in the last example had an adjusted gross income of only $20,000, medical expenses in excess of $1,500 could be deducted. This emphasizes the value of above-the-line deductions, for a smaller adjusted gross income figure increases the chances (and amount) of a deduction under § 213.

* * *

Self-Assessment Question

(Solutions to Self–Assessment Questions are set forth in Appendix 3.)

SAQ 9–1. Because the § 213 deduction amount is computed with reference to a taxpayer's adjusted gross income, the deduction is taken "below the line." In other words, the deduction is available only to those taxpayers who itemize their deductions. Is the § 213 deduction for medical expenses also subject to the two-percent "haircut" in § 67? Is it subject to the overall limitation on itemized deductions in § 68?

[handwritten: ✱ No, not subject to the 2% "haircut" b/c §67(b) specifically states that.]

[handwritten: ✝ No, not subject to the overall limitation b/c it is one of 3 excluded under §68(c)]

* * *

The hot issue in § 213 is the definition of "medical care" set forth in § 213(d). The definition appears to be broad, but there are certainly limits, as the assigned regulations and the following rulings show.

REVENUE RULING 75–187

1975–1 C.B. 92.

[handwritten: ✱partially overturned w/ §213(d)(2) in 1983. (1)involved lodging expenses are now deductible up to $50 per night/per person.]

Advice has been requested whether, under the circumstances described below, the amounts paid for treatment for sexual inadequacy and incompatibility and for meals and lodging are deductible under section 213 of the Internal Revenue Code of 1954.

The taxpayers, husband and wife, underwent treatment for sexual inadequacy and incompatibility. The treatment was conducted by psychiatrists at a hospital and was based on a program of treatment developed by researchers at a biological research foundation. In the opinion of the psychiatrists the probability of successful treatment was greater if their patients resided at a hotel in the vicinity of the hospital during the two-week duration of the treatment.

The taxpayers followed their psychiatrists' recommendation and resided at a hotel near the hospital. Each morning they attended consultation sessions conducted by their psychiatrists at the hospital. The taxpayers' expenditure for their meals and lodging during the period of the treatment was not included in the amount they paid for the treatment.

Section 213(a) of the Code provides, in part, that there shall be allowed as a deduction, subject to specified limitations, the expenses paid for medical care of the taxpayer.

Section [213(d)(1)] of the Code provides, in part, that the term "medical care" means amounts paid (A) for the diagnosis, cure, mitigation, treatment, or prevention of disease, or for the purpose of affecting any structure or function of the body, or (B) for transportation primarily for and essential to medical care referred to in subparagraph (A).

Section 1.213–1(e)(1)(iv) of the Income Tax Regulations provides that although expenses paid for transportation primarily for and essential to the rendition of medical care are expenses paid for medical care, such deductible transportation expenses shall not include the cost of any meals and lodging while away from home receiving medical treatment.

Section 1.213–1(e)(1)(v) of the regulations provides that the cost of in-patient hospital care (including the cost of meals and lodging therein) is an expenditure for medical care. The extent to which expenses for care in an institution other than a hospital shall constitute medical care is primarily a question of fact that depends upon the condition of the individual and the nature of the services he receives.

Section 262 of the Code provides that, except as otherwise expressly provided, no deduction is allowable for personal, living, or family expenses.

In *Commissioner v. Bilder*, 369 U.S. 499 (1962), Ct. D. 1871, 1962–1 C.B. 38, the Supreme Court of the United States held that a taxpayer, who had been ordered by his physician to spend the winter months in Florida as part of a regimen of medical treatment, was not entitled to deduct the rental payments for an apartment in Florida as medical care expenses under section 213 of the Code.

In *Wade Volwiler*, 57 T.C. 367 (1971), an individual resided in a rooming house and in an apartment as part of her overall therapy while under the care of a psychiatrist. Neither the rooming house nor the apartment was specially equipped or furnished, and neither was engaged regularly in providing medical care. In denying the deduction sought under section 213 of the Code for the cost of the lodging, the United States Tax Court stated that although living in the facilities might have been beneficial to the individual, such benefit was not sufficient to make the lodging part of institutional medical care.

In the instant case the hotel in which the taxpayers resided was not engaged in providing medical care, and their room was not specially equipped or furnished. Thus, the taxpayers' stay in the hotel is not distinguishable from a stay in any other personal residence.

Accordingly, since the taxpayers' meals and lodging were not part of institutional medical care, the amount paid for such meals and lodging is not deductible as an amount paid for medical care under section 213 of the Code. However, the amount paid to the psychiatrists for the treatment for sexual inadequacy and incompatibility is deductible under section 213(e)(1)(A), subject to the limitations prescribed therein.

REVENUE RULING 75-319

1975–2 C.B. 88.

Advice has been requested concerning the deductibility, for Federal income tax purposes, of certain counseling fees under the circumstances described below.

The taxpayers, husband and wife, have been consulting with a clergyman associated with a counseling center for several months. The center is a nonprofit organization funded by several religious organizations. The taxpayers went to the center for marriage counseling. As a result of the counseling, the taxpayers feel they are healthier persons and are enjoying a more meaningful relationship.

Section 262 of the Internal Revenue Code of 1954 provides that except as otherwise expressly provided, no deduction shall be allowed for personal, living, or family expenses.

Section 213 of the Code allows a deduction, in computing taxable income, for amounts paid during the taxable year, not compensated for by insurance or otherwise, for medical care of the taxpayer, his spouse, and dependents, subject to certain limitations.

Section [213(d)] of the Code defines the term "medical care" as amounts paid for the diagnosis, cure, mitigation, treatment or prevention of disease, or for the purpose of affecting any structure or function of the body, or for transportation primarily for and essential to medical care.

Section 1.213–1(e) of the Income Tax Regulations provides, in part, that deductions for expenditures for medical care will be confined strictly to expenses incurred primarily for the prevention or alleviation of a physical or mental defect or illness.

In the instant case, the counseling was not for the prevention or alleviation of a physical or mental defect or illness, but rather to help improve the taxpayers' marriage.

Accordingly, the counseling fees paid by the taxpayers are not medical expenses within the meaning of section 213 of the Code, but are personal expenses within the meaning of section 262 and, therefore, nondeductible.

REVENUE RULING 97–9

1997–1 C.B. 77.

ISSUE

Is an amount paid to obtain a controlled substance (such as marijuana) for medical purposes, in violation of federal law, a deductible expense for medical care under § 213 of the Internal Revenue Code?

FACTS

Based on the recommendation of a physician, A purchased marijuana and used it to treat A's disease in a state whose laws permit such purchase and use.

LAW AND ANALYSIS

Section 213(a) allows a deduction for uncompensated expenses of an individual for medical care to the extent such expenses exceed 7.5 percent of adjusted gross income. Section 213(d)(1) provides, in part, that "medical care" means amounts paid for the cure, mitigation, and treatment of disease. However, under § 213(b) an amount paid for medicine or a drug is an expense for medical care under § 213(a) only if the medicine or drug is a prescribed drug or insulin. Section 213(d)(3) provides that a "prescribed drug" is a drug or biological that requires a prescription of a physician for its use by an individual.

Section 1.213–1(e)(2) of the Income Tax Regulations provides, in part, that the term "medicine and drugs" includes only items that are "legally procured." Section 1.213–1(e)(1)(ii) provides that amounts expended for illegal operations or treatments are not deductible.

Rev. Rul. 78–325, 1978–2 C.B. 124, holds that amounts paid by a taxpayer for laetrile, prescribed by a physician for the medical treatment of the taxpayer's illness, are expenses for medicine and drugs that are deductible under § 213. The revenue ruling states that the laetrile was purchased and used in a locality where its sale and use were legal.

Rev. Rul. 73–201, 1973–1 C.B. 140, holds that amounts paid for a vasectomy and an abortion are expenses for medical care that are deductible under § 213. The revenue ruling states that neither procedure was illegal under state law.

A's purchase and use of marijuana were permitted under the laws of A's state. However, marijuana is listed as a controlled substance on Schedule I of the Controlled Substances Act (CSA), 21 U.S.C. §§ 801–971. 21 U.S.C. § 812(c). Except as authorized by the CSA, it is unlawful for any person to manufacture, distribute, or dispense, or possess with intent to manufacture, distribute, or dispense, a controlled substance. 21 U.S.C. § 841(a). Further, it is unlawful for any person knowingly or intentionally to possess a controlled substance except as authorized by the CSA. 21 U.S.C. § 844(a). Generally, the CSA does not permit the possession of controlled substances listed on Schedule I, even for medical purposes, and even with a physician's prescription.

Notwithstanding state law, a controlled substance (such as marijuana), obtained in violation of the CSA, is not "legally procured" within the meaning of § 1.213–1(e)(2). Further, an amount expended to obtain a controlled substance (such as marijuana) in violation of the CSA is an amount expended for an illegal treatment within the meaning of § 1.213–1(e)(1)(ii). Accordingly, A may not deduct under § 213 the amount A paid to purchase marijuana.

HOLDING

An amount paid to obtain a controlled substance (such as marijuana) for medical purposes, in violation of federal law, is not a deductible expense for medical care under § 213. This holding applies even if the state law requires a prescription of a physician to obtain and use the controlled substance and the taxpayer obtains a prescription.

EFFECT ON OTHER DOCUMENTS

Rev. Rul. 78–325 is obsoleted. Subsequent to the issuance of *Rev. Rul. 78–325,* the courts have upheld the Food and Drug Administration determination that generally prohibits interstate commerce in laetrile under the Food, Drug, and Cosmetic Act, 21 U.S.C. §§ 331 and 355(a). See *United States v. Rutherford,* 442 U.S. 544 (1979); *Rutherford v. United States,* 806 F.2d 1455 (10th Cir. 1986). Thus, notwithstanding state and local law, laetrile cannot be legally procured within the meaning of § 1.213–1(e)(2). Accordingly, amounts paid to obtain laetrile are not deductible under § 213.

Rev. Rul. 73–201 is clarified to reflect that the medical procedures at issue in that revenue ruling are not illegal under federal law.

* * *

REVENUE RULING 2003–57

2003–22 I.R.B. 959.

ISSUE

Are amounts paid by individuals for breast reconstruction surgery, vision correction surgery, and teeth whitening medical care expenses within the meaning of § 213(d) and deductible under § 213 of the Internal Revenue Code?

FACTS

Taxpayer *A* undergoes mastectomy surgery that removes a breast as part of treatment for cancer and pays a surgeon to reconstruct the breast. Taxpayer *B* wears glasses to correct myopia and pays a doctor to perform laser eye surgery to correct the myopia. Taxpayer *C*'s teeth are discolored as a result of age. *C* pays a dentist to perform a teeth-whitening procedure. *A*, *B*, and *C* are not compensated for their expenses by insurance or otherwise.

LAW AND ANALYSIS

Section 213(a) allows a deduction for expenses paid during the taxable year, not compensated for by insurance or otherwise, for medical care of the taxpayer, spouse, or dependent, to the extent the expenses exceed 7.5 percent of adjusted gross income. Under § 213(d)(1)(A), medical care includes amounts paid for the diagnosis, cure, mitigation, treatment, or prevention of disease, or for the purpose of affecting any structure or function of the body.

Medical care does not include cosmetic surgery or other similar procedures, unless the surgery or procedure is necessary to ameliorate a deformity arising from, or directly related to, a congenital abnormality, a personal injury resulting from an accident or trauma, or a disfiguring disease. Section 213(d)(9)(A). Cosmetic surgery means any procedure that is directed at improving the patient's appearance and does not meaningfully promote the proper function of the body or prevent or treat illness or disease. Section 213(d)(9)(B).

A's cancer is a disfiguring disease because the treatment results in the loss of *A*'s breast. Accordingly, the breast reconstruction surgery ameliorates a deformity directly related to a disease and the cost is an expense for medical care within the meaning of § 213(d) that *A* may deduct under § 213 (subject to the limitations of that section).

The cost of *B*'s laser eye surgery is allowed under § 213(d)(9) because the surgery is a procedure that meaningfully promotes the proper function of the body. Vision correction with eyeglasses or contact lenses qualifies as medical care. See *Rev. Rul. 74–429*, 1974–2 C.B. 83. Eye surgery to correct defective vision, including laser procedures such as LASIK and radial keratotomy, corrects a dysfunction of the body. Accordingly, the cost of the laser eye surgery is an expense for medical care within the meaning of § 213(d) that *B* may deduct under § 213 (subject to the limitations of that section).

In contrast, the teeth-whitening procedure does not treat a physical or mental disease or promote the proper function of the body, but is directed at improving *C*'s appearance. The discoloration is not a deformity and is not caused by a disfiguring disease or treatment. Accordingly, *C* may not deduct the cost of whitening teeth as an expense for medical care.

HOLDING

Amounts paid by individuals for breast reconstruction surgery following a mastectomy for cancer and for vision correction surgery are medical care expenses under § 213(d) and are deductible under § 213 (subject to the limitations of that section). Amounts paid by individuals to whiten teeth discolored as a result of age are not medical care expenses under § 213(d) and are not deductible.

    * * *

REVENUE RULING 2003–58

2003–22 I.R.B. 959.

ISSUES

(1) Are amounts paid by an individual for medicines that may be purchased without a prescription of a physician deductible under § 213 of the Internal Revenue Code?

(2) Are amounts paid by an individual for equipment, supplies, or diagnostic devices that may be purchased without a prescription of a physician deductible under § 213?

FACTS

Taxpayer *A* has an injured leg and uses crutches to enhance mobility while the leg is healing. *A* uses bandages to cover torn skin on the leg. *A*'s physician recommends that *A* take aspirin to treat pain in the leg. *A* also has diabetes and uses a blood sugar test kit to monitor *A*'s blood sugar level. *A* is not compensated for these expenses by insurance or otherwise.

LAW AND ANALYSIS

Section 213(a) allows a deduction for expenses paid during the taxable year, not compensated for by insurance or otherwise, for medical care of the taxpayer, spouse, or dependent, to the extent the expenses exceed 7.5 percent of adjusted gross income. Under § 213(d)(1), medical care includes amounts paid for the diagnosis, cure, mitigation, treatment, or prevention of disease, or for the purpose of affecting any structure or function of the body.

Section 213(b) permits an amount paid for a medicine or drug to be taken into account for purposes of the § 213 deduction for medical care expenses only if the medicine or drug is a prescribed drug or insulin. Section 213(d)(3) defines a prescribed drug as a drug or biological that requires a prescription of a physician for its use by an individual. Because aspirin is a drug and does not require a physician's prescription for use by an individual, pursuant to § 213(b), its cost may not be taken into account under § 213, even if a physician recommends its use to a patient. Accordingly, A may not deduct the cost of the aspirin under § 213.

However, § 213(b) does not apply to items that are not medicines or drugs, including equipment such as crutches, supplies such as bandages, and diagnostic devices such as blood sugar test kits. Such items may qualify as medical care if they otherwise meet the definition in § 213(d)(1). In this case, the crutches and bandages mitigate the effect of

A's injured leg and the blood sugar test kit monitors and assists in treating *A*'s diabetes. Therefore, the costs of these items are amounts paid for medical care under § 213(d)(1) and are deductible, subject to the limitations of § 213.

HOLDINGS

(1) Amounts paid by an individual for medicines or drugs that may be purchased without a prescription of a physician are not taken into account pursuant to § 213(b) and are not deductible under § 213.

(2) Amounts paid by an individual for equipment, supplies, or diagnostic devices may be expenses for medical care deductible under § 213 (subject to the other limitations of that section).

* * *

Note

If the couple in *Revenue Ruling 75–187* had defined their problem as "marital difficulty" instead of the more revealing "sexual inadequacy," *Revenue Ruling 75–319* suggests the expenses may not have been deductible. Still, the couple in *Revenue Ruling 75–187* had a better case than the couple in *Revenue Ruling 75–319* because the treatment for the taxpayers in the former ruling was provided by psychiatrists at a hospital and not by a member of the clergy.

* * *

✶ ***Problem 9–1*** ✶

Anita Schott, a professional actress, paid the following expenses in Year One:

(i) $500 to Dr. Winchester to diagnose and treat a severe flu.

(ii) $500 to Drug Store for birth control medication.

(iii) $200 to Grocery Store for over-the-counter vitamins recommended to Anita by Dr. Winchester as part of a general fitness regime.

(iv) $10,000 to Dr. Hibbert for breast augmentation surgery, undertaken at the advice of Anita's agent to land better movie roles.

(v) $2,000 to the Snick Clinic for a "stop-smoking" program that included no medication.

(vi) $5,000 to the Snick Clinic for a weight loss program designed to alleviate Anita's stress and clinical obesity.

(vii) $4,000 to attend an educational conference sponsored by the Muscular Dystrophy Association. Anita's son suffers from muscular dystrophy. The costs consisted of transportation expenses ($1,000), the conference registration fee ($2,000), and meals and lodging ($1,000).

(viii) $30,000 for a van that Anita uses for commuting and other personal purposes. The van cost $26,000, but Anita had to spend an additional $4,000 to install a wheelchair lift on the van for the benefit of her son. *modification of a motoR vehicle for a medical reason*

yes   (ix) $5,000 to Dr. Winchester for an abortion.

Determine the extent to which Anita can deduct these expenses, assuming that her adjusted gross income for Year One is $50,000. *7.5% = $3,750*

*$18,000 − $3,750** = $14,250 deduction*

if $20K
then $20 − 3,750
= $16,250

Health Savings Accounts. The Medicare Prescription Drug and Modernization Act of 2003 created the "health savings account" (HSA), a new tax-exempt vehicle to which tax-deductible contributions can be made (under certain circumstances) to pay the "qualified medical expenses" of "eligible individuals." Earnings on contributions made to an HSA are not taxed currently, and distributions from an HSA are tax-free to the extent used to pay for qualified medical expenses. An HSA is a United States trust set up exclusively to pay the account beneficiary's qualified medical expenses (expenses for "medical care" as defined in § 213(d) for the HSA beneficiary, his or her spouse, or a dependent, but only to the extent not compensated for by insurance or otherwise). Generally, contributions to an HSA must be in cash and cannot exceed the annual contribution amounts (in most cases, $2,250 for individual health coverage and $4,500 for family health coverage). Such amounts are deductible in determining adjusted gross income. Individuals age 55 and older may make larger deductible contributions to an HSA. Generally, an "eligible individual" is someone who, with respect to any month is covered under a high-deductible health plan as of the first day of the month and, while covered by a high-deductible plan, is *not* covered under any non-high-deductible health plan that provides coverage for any benefit covered under the high-deductible health plan. A "high-deductible health plan" is one that has an annual deductible of at least $1,000 ($2,000, if the plan covers an entire family) and limits annual expenses (the sum of the annual deductible plus other annual out-of-pocket expenses) required to be paid under the plan (other than for premiums) to $5,000 ($10,000 in the case of family coverage). For all its complexity, the HSA looks to be a significant savings device for medical expenses. Treasury has issued helpful guidance on HSAs in a question-and-answer format. See *Notice 2004–50*, 2004–33 I.R.B. 196.

B.   CHARITABLE CONTRIBUTIONS *skim*

p. 609-625
Prob. 9-2

Code: IRC §§ 170(a)(1), (b)(1), (c), (d)(1)(A), (e)(1), (e)(5), (f)(8), (j), (*l*); 1011(b). *Skim* IRC §§ 170(f)(11)–(12).

Regs: Treas. Reg. § 1.170A–1(c)(1); –1(e); –1(g); –1(h)(1)–(2).

An Incentive to Do Good. The central policy objective for the charitable contribution deduction in § 170 is clear: Congress wants to encourage charitable gifts. Charitable giving not only benefits the recipient organization directly, it also relieves the government's welfare bur-

den. Taxpayers, too, like the deduction because it allows them greater
control over the use of dollars that will otherwise be paid to the federal
government. For instance, a taxpayer in the 25 percent tax bracket who
makes a $1,000 gift to charity is effectively diverting $250 of tax from
the federal government to the charitable organization.

There is some disagreement as to whether the § 170 deduction
really affects the amount of charitable giving by taxpayers. On the one
hand, many taxpayers do not get a tax benefit from their charitable gifts
because the § 170 deduction is an *itemized* deduction. About 70 percent
of taxpayers claim the standard deduction in lieu of itemizing deductions, so charitable contributions by those taxpayers result in no tax
savings. Moreover, many individuals make charitable contributions without any regard to tax savings. On the other hand, it probably is true that
some significant contributions are made with the knowledge that a tax
deduction will defray the out-of-pocket costs to the donors. In soliciting
donations, charities often call attention to the fact that contributions
may be deductible. If such appeals had no effect on contribution levels,
and if charities were not asked about the deductibility of contributions
regularly, charities probably would not market the deduction in their
solicitations. From time to time, charities urge Congress to make the
§ 170 deduction available to all taxpayers whether or not they itemize.
In other words, they lobby Congress to make the charitable contribution
deduction "above the line." If Congress did so, do you think the amount
of gifts would increase? Or would the revenue loss exceed any increased
gifting to charities?

In determining the applicable deduction amount under § 170,
§ 170(a) suggests a three-step framework:

STEP ONE: Determine whether the recipient is a
qualified recipient. Section 170(c) lists the donees a
gift to which will qualify for a deduction. If the recipient is not listed in § 170(c), no deduction may be
claimed for the gift.

STEP TWO: Determine whether the donor made a
contribution to the qualified recipient. The Code offers no help in this regard, but the *Hernandez* case
below explains what it means to make a deductible
contribution to a qualified recipient.

STEP THREE: Determine the **amount** of the deduction and the portion of such amount that is deductible
in the year of contribution. Sections 170(b) and 170(e)
impose several limits on the deductibility of charitable
contributions. In some cases, the deduction amount is
limited to the taxpayer's basis in contributed property.
Moreover, the total amount of charitable deductions
allowed in any single year is limited to a percentage of
the taxpayer's adjusted gross income. Any deduction

amount in excess of the limitation based on adjusted gross income will carry over to the next taxable year.

HERNANDEZ v. COMMISSIONER

United States Supreme Court, 1989.
490 U.S. 680, 109 S.Ct. 2136, 104 L.Ed.2d 766.

JUSTICE MARSHALL delivered the opinion of the Court.

Section 170 of the Internal Revenue Code of 1954 (Code), 26 U.S.C. § 170, permits a taxpayer to deduct from gross income the amount of a "charitable contribution." The Code defines that term as a "contribution or gift" to certain eligible donees, including entities organized and operated exclusively for religious purposes. We granted certiorari to determine whether taxpayers may deduct as charitable contributions payments made to branch churches of the Church of Scientology (Church) in order to receive services known as "auditing" and "training." We hold that such payments are not deductible.

I

Scientology was founded in the 1950's by L. Ron Hubbard. It is propagated today by a "mother church" in California and by numerous branch churches around the world. The mother Church instructs laity, trains and ordains ministers, and creates new congregations. Branch churches, known as "franchises" or "missions," provide Scientology services at the local level, under the supervision of the mother Church.

Scientologists believe that an immortal spiritual being exists in every person. A person becomes aware of this spiritual dimension through a process known as "auditing." Auditing involves a one-to-one encounter between a participant (known as a "preclear") and a Church official (known as an "auditor"). An electronic device, the E-meter, helps the auditor identify the preclear's areas of spiritual difficulty by measuring skin responses during a question and answer session. Although auditing sessions are conducted one on one, the content of each session is not individually tailored. The preclear gains spiritual awareness by progressing through sequential levels of auditing, provided in short blocks of time known as "intensives."

The Church also offers members doctrinal courses known as "training." Participants in these sessions study the tenets of Scientology and seek to attain the qualifications necessary to serve as auditors. Training courses, like auditing sessions, are provided in sequential levels. Scientologists are taught that spiritual gains result from participation in such courses.

The Church charges a "fixed donation," also known as a "price" or a "fixed contribution," for participants to gain access to auditing and training sessions. These charges are set forth in schedules, and prices vary with a session's length and level of sophistication. In 1972, for example, the general rates for auditing ranged from $625 for a 12 1/2–hour auditing intensive, the shortest available, to $4,250 for a 100–hour intensive, the longest available. Specialized types of auditing required higher fixed donations: a 12 1/2–hour "Integrity Processing" auditing intensive cost $750; a 12 1/2–hour "Expanded Dianetics" auditing intensive cost $950. This system of mandatory fixed charges is based on a central tenet of Scientology known as the "doctrine of exchange," according to which any time a person receives something he must pay something back. In so doing, a Scientologist maintains "inflow" and "outflow" and avoids spiritual decline.

The proceeds generated from auditing and training sessions are the Church's primary source of income. The Church promotes these sessions not only through newspaper, magazine, and radio advertisements, but also through free lectures, free personality tests, and leaflets. The Church also encourages, and indeed rewards with a 5% discount, advance payment for these sessions. The Church often refunds unused portions of prepaid auditing or training fees, less an administrative charge.

Petitioners in these consolidated cases each made payments to a branch church for auditing or training sessions. They sought to deduct these payments on their federal income tax returns as charitable contributions under § 170. Respondent Commissioner, the head of the Internal Revenue Service (IRS), disallowed these deductions, finding that the payments were not charitable contributions within the meaning of § 170.

Petitioners sought review of these determinations in the Tax Court. * * * Before trial, the Commissioner stipulated that the branch churches of Scientology are religious organizations entitled to receive tax-deductible charitable contributions under the relevant sections of the Code. This stipulation isolated as the sole statutory issue whether payments for auditing or training sessions constitute "contribution[s] or gift[s]" under § 170.

The Tax Court held a 3–day bench trial during which the taxpayers and others testified and submitted documentary exhibits describing the terms under which the Church promotes and provides auditing and training sessions. Based on this record, the court upheld the Commissioner's decision. 83 T.C. 575 (1984). It observed first that the term "charitable contribution" in § 170 is synonymous with the word "gift," which case law had defined "as a *voluntary transfer* of property by the owner to another *without consideration* therefor." *Id.,* at 580, quoting *DeJong v. Commissioner,* 36 T.C. 896, 899 (1961) (emphasis in original), aff'd, 309 F.2d 373 (CA9 1962). It then determined that petitioners had received consideration for their payments, namely, "the benefit of various religious services provided by the Church of Scientology." The Tax Court also rejected the taxpayers' constitutional challenges based on the Establishment and Free Exercise Clauses of the First Amendment.

The Courts of Appeals for the First Circuit * * * affirmed. The First Circuit rejected Hernandez's argument that under § 170, the IRS' ordinary inquiry into whether the taxpayer received consideration for his payment should not apply to "the return of a commensurate *religious* benefit, as opposed to an *economic or financial* benefit." 819 F.2d, at 1217 (emphasis in original). The court found "no indication that Congress intended to distinguish the religious benefits sought by Hernandez from the medical, educational, scientific, literary, or other benefits that could likewise provide the *quid* for the *quo* of a nondeductible payment to a charitable organization." *Ibid.* The court also rejected Hernandez's argument that it was impracticable to put a value on the services he had purchased, noting that the Church itself had "established and advertised monetary prices" for auditing and training sessions, and that Hernandez had not claimed that these prices misstated the cost of providing these sessions.

Hernandez's constitutional claims also failed. Because § 170 created no denominational preference on its face, Hernandez had shown no Establishment Clause violation. As for the Free Exercise Clause challenge, the court determined that denying the deduction did not prevent Hernandez from paying for auditing and training sessions and thereby observing Scientology's doctrine of exchange. Moreover, granting a tax exemption would compromise the integrity and fairness of the tax system.

* * *

We granted certiorari * * * to resolve a Circuit conflict concerning the validity of charitable deductions for auditing and training payments. We now affirm.

II

For over 70 years, federal taxpayers have been allowed to deduct the amount of contributions or gifts to charitable, religious, and other eleemosynary institutions. Section 170, the present provision, was enacted in 1954; it requires a taxpayer claiming the deduction to satisfy a number of conditions. The Commissioner's stipulation in this case, however, has narrowed the statutory inquiry to one such condition: whether petitioners' payments for auditing and training sessions are "contribution[s] or gift[s]" within the meaning of § 170.

The legislative history of the "contribution or gift" limitation, though sparse, reveals that Congress intended to differentiate between unrequited payments to qualified recipients and payments made to such recipients in return for goods or services. Only the former were deemed deductible. The House and Senate Reports on the 1954 tax bill, for example, both define "gifts" as payments "made with no expectation of a financial return commensurate with the amount of the gift." Using payments to hospitals as an example, both Reports state that the gift characterization should not apply to "a payment by an individual to a hospital *in consideration of* a binding obligation to provide medical treatment for the individual's employees. It would apply only if there were no expectation of any quid pro quo from the hospital."

In ascertaining whether a given payment was made with "the expectation of any quid pro quo," the IRS has customarily examined the external features of the transaction in question. This practice has the advantage of obviating the need for the IRS to conduct imprecise inquiries into the motivations of individual taxpayers. The lower courts have generally embraced this structural analysis. We likewise focused on external features in *United States v. American Bar Endowment*, [477 U.S. 105 (1986)], to resolve the taxpayers' claims that they were entitled to partial deductions for premiums paid to a charitable organization for insurance coverage; the taxpayers contended that they had paid unusually high premiums in an effort to make a contribution along with their purchase of insurance. We upheld the Commissioner's disallowance of the partial deductions because the taxpayers had failed to demonstrate, at a minimum, the existence of comparable insurance policies with prices lower than those of the policy they had each purchased. In so doing, we stressed that "[t]he *sine qua non* of a charitable contribution is a transfer of money or property *without adequate consideration.*" *Id.*, at 118, 106 S.Ct., at 2434 (emphasis added in part).

In light of this understanding of § 170, it is readily apparent that petitioners' payments to the Church do not qualify as "contribution[s] or gift[s]." As the Tax Court found, these payments were part of a quintessential *quid pro quo* exchange: in return for their money, petitioners received an identifiable benefit, namely, auditing and training sessions. The Church established fixed price schedules for auditing and training sessions in each branch church; it calibrated particular prices to auditing or training sessions of particular lengths and levels of sophistication; it returned a refund if auditing and training services went unperformed; it distributed "account cards" on which persons who had paid money to the Church could monitor what prepaid services they had not yet claimed; and it categorically barred provision of auditing or training sessions for free. Each of these practices reveals the inherently reciprocal nature of the exchange.

Petitioners do not argue that such a structural analysis is inappropriate under § 170, or that the external features of the auditing and training transactions do not strongly suggest a *quid pro quo* exchange. * * * Petitioners argue instead that they are entitled to deductions because a *quid pro quo* analysis is inappropriate under § 170 when the benefit a taxpayer receives is purely religious in nature. Along the same lines, petitioners claim that payments made for the right to participate in a religious service should be automatically deductible under § 170.

We cannot accept this statutory argument for several reasons. First, it finds no support in the language of § 170. Whether or not Congress could, consistent with the Establishment Clause, provide for the automatic deductibility of a payment made to a church that either generates religious benefits or guarantees access to a religious service, that is a choice Congress has thus far declined to make. Instead, Congress has specified that a payment to an organization operated exclusively for religious (or other eleemosynary) purposes is deductible *only* if such a payment is a "contribution or gift." 26 U.S.C. § 170(c). The Code makes no special preference for payments made in the expectation of gaining religious benefits or access to a religious service. The House and Senate Reports on § 170, and the other legislative history of that provision, offer no indication that Congress' failure to enact such a preference was an oversight.

Second, petitioners' deductibility proposal would expand the charitable contribution deduction far beyond what Congress has provided. Numerous forms of payments to eligible donees plausibly could be categorized as providing a religious benefit or as securing access to a religious service. For example, some taxpayers might regard their tuition payments to parochial schools as generating a religious benefit or as securing access to a religious service; such payments, however, have long been held not to be charitable contributions under § 170. * * * Taxpayers might make similar claims about payments for church-sponsored counseling sessions or for medical care at church-affiliated hospitals that otherwise might not be deductible. Given that, under the First Amendment, the IRS can reject otherwise valid claims of religious benefit only on the ground that a taxpayers' alleged beliefs are not sincerely held, but not on the ground that such beliefs are inherently irreligious, the resulting tax deductions would likely expand the charitable contribution provision far beyond its present size. We are loath to effect this result in the absence of supportive congressional intent.

Finally, the deduction petitioners seek might raise problems of entanglement between church and state. If framed as a deduction for those payments generating benefits of a religious nature for the payor, petitioners' proposal would inexorably force the IRS and reviewing courts to differentiate "religious" benefits from "secular" ones. If framed as a deduction for those payments made in connection with a religious service, petitioners' proposal would force the IRS and the judiciary into differentiating "religious" services from "secular" ones. We need pass no judgment now on the constitutionality of such hypothetical inquiries, but we do note that "pervasive monitoring" for "the subtle or overt presence of religious matter" is a central danger against which we have held the Establishment Clause guards. * * *

Accordingly, we conclude that petitioners' payments to the Church for auditing and training sessions are not "contribution[s] or gift[s]" within the meaning of that statutory expression.

* * *

IV

We turn, finally, to petitioners' assertion that disallowing their claimed deduction is at odds with the IRS' longstanding practice of permitting taxpayers to deduct payments made to other religious institutions in connection with certain religious practices. Through the appellate stages of this litigation, this claim was framed essentially as one of selective prosecution. * * *

In their arguments to this Court, petitioners have shifted emphasis. They now make two closely related claims. First, the IRS has accorded payments for auditing and training disparately harsh treatment compared to payments to other churches and synagogues for their religious services: Recognition of a comparable deduction for auditing and training payments is necessary to cure this administrative inconsistency. Second, Congress, in modifying § 170 over the years, has impliedly acquiesced in the deductibility of payments to these other faiths; because payments for auditing and training are indistinguishable from these other payments, they fall within the principle acquiesced in by Congress that payments for religious services are deductible under § 170.

Although the Commission[er] demurred at oral argument as to whether the IRS, in fact, permits taxpayers to deduct payments made to purchase services from other churches and synagogues, the Commissioner's periodic revenue rulings have stated the IRS' position rather clearly. A 1971 ruling, still in effect, states: "Pew rents, building fund assessments, and periodic dues paid to a church ... are all methods of making contributions to the church, and such payments are deductible as charitable contributions within the limitations set out in section 170 of the Code." *Rev. Rul. 70–47*, 1970–1 Cum. Bull. 49 (superseding A.R.M. 2, Cum. Bull. 150 (1919)). We also assume for purposes of argument that the IRS also allows taxpayers to deduct "specified payments for attendance at High Holy Day services, for tithes, for torah readings and for memorial plaques."

The development of the present litigation, however, makes it impossible for us to resolve petitioners' claim that they have received unjustifiably harsh treatment compared to adherents of other religions. The relevant inquiry in determining whether a payment is a "contribution or gift" under § 170 is, as we have noted, not whether the payment secures religious benefits or access to religious services, but whether the transaction in which the payment is involved is structured as a *quid pro quo* exchange. To make such a determination in this case, the Tax Court heard testimony and received documentary proof as to the terms and structure of the auditing and training transactions; from this evidence it made factual findings upon which it based its conclusion of nondeductibility, a conclusion we have held consonant with § 170 and with the First Amendment.

Perhaps because the theory of administrative inconsistency emerged only on appeal, petitioners did not endeavor at trial to adduce from the IRS or other sources any specific evidence about other religious faiths' transactions. The IRS' revenue rulings, which merely state the agency's conclusions as to deductibility and which have apparently never been reviewed by the Tax Court or any other judicial body, also provide no specific facts about the nature of these other faiths' transactions. In the absence of such facts, we simply have no way (other than the wholly illegitimate one of relying on our personal experiences and observations) to appraise accurately whether the IRS' revenue rulings have correctly applied a *quid pro quo* analysis with respect to any or all of the religious practices in question. We do not know, for example, whether payments for other faiths' services are truly obligatory or whether any or all of these services are generally provided whether or not the encouraged "mandatory" payment is made.

The IRS' application of the "contribution or gift" standard may be right or wrong with respect to these other faiths, or it may be right with respect to some religious practices and wrong with respect to others. It may also be that some of these payments are appropriately classified as partially deductible "dual payments." With respect to those religions where the structure of transactions involving religious services is established not centrally but by individual congregations, the proper point of reference for a *quid pro quo* analysis might be the individual congregation, not the religion as a whole. Only upon a proper factual record could we make these determinations. Absent such a record, we must reject petitioners' administrative consistency argument.

Petitioners' congressional acquiescence claim fails for similar reasons. Even if one assumes that Congress has acquiesced in the IRS' ruling with respect to "[p]ew rents, building fund assessments, and periodic dues," *Rev. Rul. 70–47,* 1970–1 Cum. Bull. 49, the fact is that the IRS' 1971 ruling articulates no broad principle of deductibility, but instead merely identifies as deductible three discrete types of payments. Having before us no information about the nature or structure of these three payments, we have no way of discerning any possible unifying principle, let alone whether such a principle would embrace payments for auditing and training sessions.

V

For the reasons stated herein, the judgments of the Courts of Appeals are hereby

Affirmed.

JUSTICE BRENNAN and JUSTICE KENNEDY took no part in the consideration or decision of these cases.

JUSTICE O'CONNOR, with whom JUSTICE SCALIA joins, dissenting.

The Court today acquiesces in the decision of the Internal Revenue Service (IRS) to manufacture a singular exception to its 70–year practice of allowing fixed payments indistinguishable from those made by petitioners to be deducted as charitable contributions. Because the IRS cannot constitutionally be allowed to select which religions will receive the benefit of its past rulings, I respectfully dissent.

* * *

It must be emphasized that the IRS' position here is *not* based upon the contention that a portion of the knowledge received from auditing or training is of secular, commercial, nonreligious value. Thus, the denial of a deduction in these cases bears no resemblance to the denial of a deduction for religious-school tuition up to the market value of the secularly useful education received. Here the IRS denies deductibility solely on the basis that the exchange is a *quid pro quo,* even though the *quid* is exclusively of spiritual or religious worth. Respondent cites no instances in which this has been done before, and there are good reasons why.

When a taxpayer claims as a charitable deduction part of a fixed amount given to a charitable organization in exchange for benefits that have a commercial value, the allowable portion of that claim is computed by subtracting from the total amount paid the value of the physical benefit received. If at a charity sale one purchases for $1,000 a painting whose market value is demonstrably no more than $50, there has been a contribution of $950. The same would be true if one purchases a $1,000 seat at a charitable dinner where the food is worth $50. An identical calculation can be made where the *quid* received is not a painting or a meal, but an intangible such as entertainment, so long as that intangible has some market value established in a noncontributory context. Hence, one who purchases a ticket to a concert, at the going rate for concerts by the particular performers, makes a charitable contribution of zero even if it is announced in advance that all proceeds from the ticket sales will go to charity. The performers may have made a charitable contribution, but the audience has paid the going rate for a show.

It becomes impossible, however, to compute the "contribution" portion of a payment to a charity where what is received in return is not merely an intangible, but an intangible (or, for that matter a tangible) that is not bought and sold except in donative contexts so that the only "market" price against which it can be evaluated is a market price that always includes donations. Suppose, for example, that the charitable organization that traditionally solicits donations on Veterans Day, in exchange for which it gives the donor an imitation poppy bearing its name, were to establish a flat rule that no one gets a poppy without a donation of at least $10. One would have to say that the "market" rate for such poppies was $10, but it would assuredly not be true that everyone who "bought" a poppy for $10 made no contribution. Similarly, if one buys a $100 seat at a prayer breakfast receiving as the *quid pro quo* food for both body and soul—it would make no sense to say that no charitable contribution whatever has occurred simply because the "going rate" for all prayer breakfasts (with equivalent bodily food) is $100. The latter may well be true, but that "going rate" *includes* a contribution.

Confronted with this difficulty, and with the constitutional necessity of not making irrational distinctions among taxpayers, and with the even higher standard of equality of treatment among *religions* that the First Amendment imposes, the Government has only two practicable options with regard to distinctively religious *quids pro quo:* to disregard them all, or to tax them all. Over the years it has chosen the former course.

* * *

There can be no doubt that at least some of the fixed payments which the IRS has treated as charitable deductions, or which the Court assumes the IRS would allow taxpayers to deduct are as "inherently reciprocal" as the payments for auditing at issue here. In exchange for their payment of pew rents, Christians receive particular seats during worship services. Similarly, in some synagogues attendance at the worship services for Jewish High Holy Days is often predicated upon the purchase of a general admission ticket or a reserved seat ticket. Religious honors such as publicly reading from Scripture are purchased or auctioned periodically in some synagogues of Jews from Morocco and Syria. Mormons must tithe their income as a necessary but not sufficient condition to obtaining a "temple recommend," *i.e.,* the right to be admitted into the temple. A Mass stipend—a fixed payment given to a Catholic priest, in consideration of which he is obliged to apply the fruits of the Mass for the intention of the donor—has similar overtones of exchange. According to some Catholic theologians, the nature of the pact between a priest and a donor who pays a Mass stipend is "a bilateral contract known as *do ut facias*. One person agrees to give while the other party agrees to do something in return." A finer example of a *quid pro quo* exchange would be hard to formulate.

* * *

Note

Section 170(f)(8) (added to the Code in 1993) disallows any deduction for a charitable contribution of $250 or more unless the taxpayer substantiates the payment "by a contemporaneous written acknowledgment of the contribution by the donee organization." The purpose of the substantiation requirement for larger contributions is obvious, but § 170(f)(8) contains a more subtle statement related to *Hernandez*. Section 170(f)(8)(B) sets forth the required content of the charity's acknowledgment. As part of the document, the charity must provide a "description and good faith estimate of the value of any goods or services" given by the charity in consideration for the taxpayer's contribution. But "if such goods or services consist solely of intangible religious benefits, a statement to that effect" is sufficient. Section 170(f)(8)(B)(iii).

A possible implication of this language is that a contribution of money or property to a religious organization in exchange for "intangible religious benefits" is to be treated as something other than a *quid pro quo* exchange. Yet while § 170(f)(8) was enacted after the Court's decision in *Hernandez*, the statute should not be read as overruling the Court's definition of the term "contribution or gift." Instead, the statute simply eases the reporting requirements in connection with the value of intangible religious benefits received in exchange for payments.

Nonetheless, the Service, after winning the battle in *Hernandez*, apparently surrendered in the war against Scientology. In *Revenue Ruling 93–73*, 1993–2 C.B. 75, the Service obsoleted an earlier ruling that declared the fees paid by Scientology members to be non-deductible. This one-sentence ruling suggests that the Service will no longer challenge the deductibility under

§ 170 of payments for auditing and training services by Scientology members. Why would the Service voluntarily change its position after winning at the Supreme Court? Some have suggested that because the majority in *Hernandez* expressly left open the question of whether the Service's treatment of Scientology was inconsistent with its treatment of other religions, the Service retreated from its position of denying deductions because it determined that it could not prevail if the question was litigated.

SKLAR v. COMMISSIONER

United States Court of Appeals, Ninth Circuit, 2002.
282 F.3d 610.

REINHARDT, CIRCUIT JUDGE:

The taxpayer-petitioners in this action, Michael and Marla Sklar, challenge the Internal Revenue Service's ("IRS") disallowance of their deductions, as charitable contributions, of part of the tuition payments made to their children's religious schools. In the notice of deficiency sent to the Sklars, the IRS explained that "since these costs are personal tuition expenses, they are not deductible." Specifically, the Sklars sought to deduct 55% of the tuition, on the basis that this represented the proportion of the school day allocated to religious education. The Sklars contend that these costs are deductible under section 170 of the Internal Revenue Code, as payments for which they have received "solely intangible religious benefits." They also argue that they should receive this deduction because the IRS permits similar deductions to the Church of Scientology, and it is a violation of administrative consistency and of the Establishment Clause to deny them, as Orthodox Jews, the same deduction. The Tax Court found that under *DeJong v. Commissioner*, 309 F.2d 373, 376 (9th Cir. 1962), tuition paid for the education of a taxpayer's children is a personal expense which is non-deductible under § 170. The Tax Court also rejected the administrative inconsistency argument and the Establishment Clause claim, and ruled inadmissible several documents supporting the Sklars' contentions with respect to the Church of Scientology on the ground that the Sklars are not similarly situated to the members of the Church of Scientology. The Sklars filed this timely appeal.

* * *

I. THE PROVISIONS OF THE TAX CODE GOVERNING CHARITABLE CONTRIBUTION DEDUCTIONS DO NOT APPEAR TO PERMIT THE DEDUCTION CLAIMED BY THE SKLARS

The Sklars assert that the deduction they claimed is allowable under section 170 of the Internal Revenue Code which permits taxpayers to deduct, as a charitable contribution, a "contribution or gift" to certain tax-exempt organizations. Not only has the Supreme Court held that, generally, a payment for which one receives consideration does not constitute a "contribution or gift" for purposes of § 170, see *United States v. American Bar Endowment*, 477 U.S. 105, 118, 91 L. Ed. 2d 89,

106 S. Ct. 2426 (1986) (stressing that "the sine qua non of a charitable contribution is a transfer of money or property without adequate consideration"), but it has explicitly rejected the contention made here by the Sklars: that there is an exception in the Code for payments for which one receives only religious benefits in return. *Hernandez v. Commissioner*, 490 U.S. 680, 104 L. Ed. 2d 766, 109 S. Ct. 2136 (1989). The taxpayers in *Hernandez*, members of the Church of Scientology, sought to deduct, as charitable contributions under § 170(c), payments made by them to the Church of Scientology in exchange for the religious exercises of "auditing" and "training." The Court affirmed the Tax Court's reading of the statute disallowing the deductions on the following three grounds: (1) Congress had shown no preference in the Internal Revenue Code for payments made in exchange for religious benefits as opposed to other benefits * * *; (2) to permit the deductions the taxpayers demanded would begin a slippery slope of expansion of the charitable contribution deduction beyond what Congress intended * * *; and (3) to permit these deductions could entangle the IRS and the government in the affairs and beliefs of various religious faiths and organizations in violation of the constitutional principle of the separation of church and state * * *. Specifically, the Supreme Court stated that to permit these deductions might force the IRS to engage in a searching inquiry of whether a particular benefit received was "religious" or "secular" in order to determine its deductibility, a process which, the Court said, might violate the Establishment Clause.

Despite the clear statutory holding of *Hernandez*, the Sklars contend that recent changes to the Internal Revenue Code have clarified Congressional intent with respect to the deductibility of these payments. We seriously doubt the validity of this argument. The amendments to the Code appear not to have changed the substantive definition of a deductible charitable contribution, but only to have enacted additional documentation requirements for claimed deductions. Section 170(f) of the Code adds a new requirement that taxpayers claiming a charitable contribution deduction obtain from the donee an estimate of the value of any goods and services received in return for the donation, and exempts from that new estimate requirement contributions for which solely intangible religious benefits are received. Similarly, § 6115 requires that tax-exempt organizations inform taxpayer-donors that they will receive a tax deduction only for the amount of their donation above the value of any goods or services received in return for the donation and requires donee organizations to give donors an estimate of this value, exempting from this estimate requirement contributions for which solely intangible religious benefits are received.

Given the clear holding of *Hernandez* and the absence of any direct evidence of Congressional intent to overrule the Supreme Court on this issue, we would be extremely reluctant to read an additional and significant substantive deduction into the statute based on what are clearly procedural provisions regarding the documentation of tax return information, particularly where the deduction would be of doubtful constitutional validity. * * * We need not, however, decide this issue definitively in this case.

II. The IRS Policy Regarding the Church of Scientology May Not Be Withheld from Public Scrutiny and Appears to Violate the Establishment Clause; Further, It Appears That the Sklars Have Not Made Out a Claim of Administrative Inconsistency

Additionally, the Sklars claim that the IRS engages in a "policy" of permitting members of the Church of Scientology to deduct as charitable contributions, payments made for "auditing," "training," and other qualified religious services, and that the agency's refusal to grant similar religious deductions to members of other faiths violates the Establishment Clause and is administratively inconsistent. They assert that the "policy" is contained in a "closing agreement" that the IRS signed with the Church of Scientology in 1993, shortly after the *Hernandez* decision and the 1993 changes to § 170 of the Internal Revenue Code. Because the IRS erroneously asserted that it is prohibited from disclosing all or any part of the closing agreement, we assume, for purposes of resolving this case, the truthfulness of the Sklars' allegations regarding the terms of that agreement. However, rather than concluding that the IRS's pro-Scientology policy would require it to adopt similar provisions for all other religions, we would likely conclude, were we to reach the issue, that the policy must be invalidated on the ground that it violates either the Internal Revenue Code or the Establishment Clause.

    * * *

III. The Sklars' Tuition Payments Do Not Constitute Partially Deductible "Dual Payments" Under the Tax Code

A "dual payment" (or "quid pro quo payment") under the Tax Code is a payment made in part in consideration for goods and services, and in part as a charitable contribution. I.R.C. § 6115. For example, the purchase, for seventy-five dollars, of an item worth five dollars at a charity auction would constitute a dual payment: five dollars in consideration for goods, and seventy dollars as a charitable contribution. The IRS permits a deduction under § 170 for the portion of a dual payment that consists of a charitable contribution, but not for the portion for which the taxpayer receives a benefit in return. Although the Sklars concede that they received a benefit for their tuition payments, in that their children received a secular education, they claim that part of the payment—the part attributable to their children's religious education—should be regarded as a charitable contribution because they received only an "intangible religious benefit" in return. Leaving aside both the issue, discussed in section I, of whether the tax code does indeed treat payments for which a taxpayer receives an "intangible religious benefit" as a charitable contribution, as well as any constitutional considerations, we are left with the Sklars' contention that their tuition payment was a dual one: in part in consideration for secular education, and in part as a charitable contribution. The Sklars assert that because 45% of their children's school day was spent on secular education, and 55% on religious education, they should receive a deduction for 55% of their tuition payments.

On the record before this court, the Sklars failed to satisfy the requirements for deducting part of a "dual payment" under the Tax Code. The Supreme Court discussed the deductibility of such payments in *United States v. American Bar Endowment*, 477 U.S. 105, 91 L. Ed. 2d 89, 106 S. Ct. 2426 (1986), and held that the taxpayer must establish that the dual payment exceeds the market value of the goods received in return. The facts of that case were as follows: The American Bar Endowment ("ABE"), a tax-exempt corporation organized for charitable purposes and associated with the American Bar Association ("ABA"), raised money for its charitable work by providing group insurance policies to its members, all of whom were also members of the ABA. ABE negotiated premium rates with insurers, collected premiums from its members and passed those premiums on to the insurers. Because the group policies purchased by ABE were "experience rated," the group members were entitled to receive, each year, a refund of the portion of their premiums paid above the actual cost to the insurer of providing insurance to the group. Although normally these refunds, called "dividends," would be distributed to individual policyholders, ABE required its members to agree to turn the dividends over to ABE for use in its charitable work. ABE members sought to deduct the dividends as charitable contributions to ABE, claiming that the premiums paid constituted partially deductible "dual payments." The Supreme Court held that the ABE members could not deduct the dividends as charitable contributions because they had not shown that the premiums they paid to ABE exceeded the market value of the insurance they purchased, or that the "excess payment," if any, was made with the intention of making a gift. Because the ABE insurance was no more costly to its members than other policies that were available to them, the taxpayers could not prove that they "purposely contributed money or property in excess of the value of any benefit [they] received in return."

Similarly, the Sklars have not shown that any dual tuition payments they may have made exceeded the market value of the secular education their children received. They urge that the market value of the secular portion of their children's education is the cost of a public school education. That cost, of course, is nothing. The Sklars are in error. The market value is the cost of a comparable secular education offered by private schools. The Sklars do not present any evidence even suggesting that their total payments exceeded that cost. There is no evidence in the record of the tuition private schools charge for a comparable secular education, and thus no evidence showing that the Sklars made an "excess payment" that might qualify for a tax deduction. This appears to be not simply an inadvertent evidentiary omission, but rather a reflection of the practical realities of the high costs of private education. The Sklars also failed to show that they intended to make a gift by contributing any such "excess payment." Therefore, under the clear holding of *American Bar Endowment*, the Sklars cannot prevail on this appeal.[15]

IV. CONCLUSION

We hold that because the Sklars have not shown that their "dual payment" tuition payments are partially deductible under the Tax Code, and, specifically, that the total payments they made for both the secular and religious private school education their children received exceeded the market value of other secular private school education available to those children, the IRS did not err in disallowing their deductions, and the Tax Court did not err in affirming the IRS's decision. We affirm the decision of the Tax Court on that ground.

AFFIRMED.

SILVERMAN, CIRCUIT JUDGE, concurring:

Why is Scientology training different from all other religious training? We should decline the invitation to answer that question. The sole issue before us is whether the Sklars' claimed deduction is valid, not whether members of the Church of Scientology have become the IRS's chosen people.

The majority states that the Church of Scientology's closing agreement is not relevant because "the Sklars are not similarly situated to the members of the Church of Scientology...." That may or may not be true, but it has no bearing on whether the tax code permits the Sklars to deduct the costs of their children's religious education as a charitable contribution. Whether the Sklars are entitled to the deduction they claim is governed by 26 U.S.C. § 170, *Hernandez v. Commissioner*, 490 U.S. 680, 104 L. Ed. 2d 766, 109 S. Ct. 2136 (1989), and *United States v. American Bar Endowment*, 477 U.S. 105, 91 L. Ed. 2d 89, 106 S. Ct. 2426 (1986), not by the Church of Scientology closing agreement.

Section 170 states that quid pro quo donations, for which a taxpayer receives something in return, are not deductible.

Hernandez holds that § 170 applies to religious quid pro quo donations.

American Bar Endowment holds that charitable donations are deductible only to the extent that they exceed the fair market value of what is received in exchange.

The Sklars receive something in return for their tuition payments— the education of their children. Thus, they are not entitled to a charitable deduction under § 170, as Judge Reinhardt carefully shows. *Hernan-*

---

15. Moreover, as the IRS argues in its brief, the Sklars' deduction was properly denied on the alternative ground that they failed to meet the contemporaneous substantiation requirement of § 170(f)(8)(A), (B) & (C). The Sklars did not present, prior to filing their tax return, a letter from the schools acknowledging their "contribution" and estimating the value of the benefit they received, as is required under the statute. As noted earlier, certain reporting requirements are not applicable where intangible religious benefits are received in exchange, but such exemptions apply only where the consideration consists solely of such benefits.

dez clearly forecloses the argument that § 170 should not apply because the tuition payments are for religious education. Finally, the Sklars have not demonstrated that what they pay for their children's education exceeds the fair market value of what they receive in return; therefore, they have not shown that they are entitled to a deduction under *American Bar Endowment*. It is as simple as that.

Accordingly, under both the tax code and Supreme Court precedent, the Sklars are not entitled to the charitable deduction they claimed. The Church of Scientology's closing agreement is irrelevant, not because the Sklars are not "similarly situated" to Scientologists, but because the closing agreement does not enter into the equation by which the deductibility of the Sklars' payments is determined. An IRS closing agreement cannot overrule Congress and the Supreme Court.

If the IRS does, in fact, give preferential treatment to members of the Church of Scientology—allowing them a special right to claim deductions that are contrary to law and rightly disallowed to everybody else—then the proper course of action is a lawsuit to stop to that policy. The remedy is not to require the IRS to let others claim the improper deduction, too.

* * *

✕ *Problem 9–2* ✕

In each of the situations described below, determine whether the donor has made a "charitable contribution" that is eligible for a deduction under § 170(a), assuming in all cases that the recipient organization is described in § 170(c).

(a) Anna donates $5,000 cash to St. Helen's Preparatory Academy, a private religious school that Anna's daughter currently attends. *Yes, as long as it is not part of the tuition.*

(b) Boris donates $5,000 cash to St. Helen's Preparatory Academy. Boris' daughter will be applying for admission at the school in a few months.

(c) Conchita donates $1,000 to a local homeless shelter. The shelter uses the contribution to provide meals to homeless individuals. *Yes.*

(d) Dominic spends $1,000 to purchase all of the ingredients required to make 500 gallons of clam chowder. He spends a Saturday making the chowder and traveling around the city in his van, handing chowder out to homeless people. *Yes. The $1,000 in food and ⸿ for gas milage.*

(e) Elena donates a pint of blood to the American Red Cross. *NO.*

(f) Frederick donates $50 million to University Law School, and University Law School renames itself "Frederick University Law School." *Was this in full consid? If so = NO.*

(g) Gabriela purchases a glass sculpture at an auction benefiting the National Public Radio. Gabriela paid $800 for the sculpture, although its appraised value is only $500. *$300*

* * *

p. 626 - 633

Probs: 9.4/9-5

Deduction Limits for Charitable Contributions. Having determined that a taxpayer has made a "contribution or gift" to a qualified charitable organization, the next steps require us to determine: (1) the amount of the deduction; and (2) the portion of such amount that is deductible in the current year. In order to determine the amount of the deduction, we must consider the nature of the contribution. Cash contributions are the easy case—the deduction is equal to the amount of the cash contributed (less, of course, any consideration received in exchange for the contribution, as discussed above). Property contributions present a more difficult issue. While generally the deduction for contributions of property is equal to the value of such property at the time of the contribution, Treas. Reg. § 1.170A–1(c)(1), there are some important exceptions.

First, consider § 170(e)(1)(A). It requires a reduction to the amount of any charitable contribution of property by the "amount of gain which would not have been long-term capital gain if the property contributed had been sold by the taxpayer at its fair market value." Therefore, if the taxpayer donates ordinary income property or short-term capital gain property, the amount of the contribution must be reduced by the amount of unrealized appreciation at the time of the contribution. By definition, reducing the amount of the deduction by the amount of unrealized appreciation is the same thing as saying that the amount of the deduction is limited to the taxpayer's adjusted basis in the property. Thus, where a taxpayer contributes ordinary income property with unrealized appreciation or short-term capital gain property with unrealized appreciation, the amount of the deduction is limited to the taxpayer's adjusted basis in the property at the time of the contribution.

Under § 170(e)(1)(B), even the deduction amounts for contributions of long-term capital gain property can sometimes be reduced to basis. This happens when the taxpayer contributes tangible personal property that qualifies as long-term capital gain property in the hands of the taxpayer but will be used by the donee in a manner that is unrelated to its charitable purpose. See § 170(e)(1)(B)(i). It also happens when long-term capital gain property of any kind is contributed to most private foundations, see § 170(e)(1)(B)(ii), unless the property in question is "qualified appreciated stock" (generally defined as publicly-traded shares that are a capital asset in the hands of the taxpayer). See § 170(e)(5).

Once the amount of the deduction has been determined, the analysis shifts to determining how much of that deduction amount may be claimed in the year of contribution. Here we begin with § 170(b)(1), an intimidating statute at the first reading. As always, though, we can make some headway if we break down the various subparagraphs.

Section 170(b)(1)(A) generally states that contributions made to the listed recipients will be deductible in the year of contribution "to the extent that the aggregate of such contributions does not exceed 50 percent of the taxpayer's contribution base for the taxable year." Section

170(b)(1)(F) generally equates the taxpayer's contribution base to his or her adjusted gross income, just without regard to any net operating loss carryback to the year at issue. Because such carrybacks are not the norm, it is acceptable conceptually to equate the contribution base to the taxpayer's adjusted gross income. Thus, for example, if a taxpayer with an adjusted gross income of $100,000 in Year One made $80,000 in allowable contributions to organizations described in § 170(b)(1)(A) in Year One, the taxpayer could deduct only $50,000 in Year One.

What happens to the remaining $30,000? Under § 170(d)(1)(A), that excess will carry over to the next taxable year (here, Year Two) as if the taxpayer had made that contribution then. Notice, however, that any such carryover only lasts for five years. So if the taxpayer in this example makes no more charitable contributions and has an adjusted gross income of only $10,000 in each of Years Two through Six, only $25,000 of the $30,000 will ever be deducted—the remaining $5,000 will be forever lost:

Year	Carryover Amount	Deduction Allowed	Remaining Carryover
Two	$30,000	$5,000 (1/2 of $10,000)	$25,000
Three	$25,000	$5,000	$20,000
Four	$20,000	$5,000	$15,000
Five	$15,000	$5,000	$10,000
Six	$10,000	$5,000	$ 5,000
Seven	$ 5,000	zero (carryover expired at end of Year Six)	

The 50–percent limitation on deductibility in the year of contribution indicates Congressional policy that a taxpayer may not avoid tax altogether by contributing everything (well, at least an amount equal to adjusted gross income) to charity. Under § 170(b)(1)(B), the annual limitation is further reduced to 30 percent of adjusted gross income in the case of contributions to charities *other than* those listed in § 170(b)(1)(A). Here too, if the deduction amount exceeds the annual limitation, the excess will carry over for up to five taxable years.

The following chart summarizes the foregoing discussion of the deduction limitations applicable to charitable contributions.

DEDUCTION LIMITATIONS FOR CHARITABLE CONTRIBUTIONS

Type of Contribution	Amount of Deduction	% Limit if Contributed to a § 170(b)(1)(A) Charity	% Limit if Contributed to Something Other Than a § 170(b)(1)(A) Charity
Cash	FMV	50% of AGI* [170(b)(1)(A)]	30% of AGI* [170(b)(1)(B)]
Loss Property (basis exceeds value)	FMV [1.170A–1(c)(1)]	50% of AGI* [170(b)(1)(A)]	30% of AGI* [170(b)(1)(B)]

Type of Contribution	Amount of Deduction	% Limit if Contributed to a § 170(b)(1)(A) Charity	% Limit if Contributed to Something Other Than a § 170(b)(1)(A) Charity
Ordinary Income Property (value exceeds basis, but it's not a capital asset)	AB [170(e)(1)(A)]	50% of AGI* [170(b)(1)(A)]	30% of AGI* [170(b)(1)(B)]
Short-Term Capital Gain Property (value exceeds basis in capital asset, but donor held for 1 year or less)	AB [170(e)(1)(A)]	50% of AGI* [170(b)(1)(A)]	20% of AGI* [170(b)(1)(D)(i)]
Long-Term Capital Gain Real Property (value exceeds basis in real property held for more than 1 year that is a capital asset)	FMV [1.170A–1(c)(1)] AB, if to a private foundation [170(e)(1)(B)(ii)]	30% of AGI* [170(b)(1)(C)(i)]	20% of AGI* [170(b)(1)(D)(i)]
Long-Term Capital Gain Intellectual Property (value exceeds basis in certain intellectual property held for more than 1 year that is a capital asset)	AB [170(e)(1)(B)(iii)]	50% of AGI* [170(b)(1)(A)]	20% of AGI* [170(b)(1)(D)(i)]
Other Intangible Long–Term Capital Gain Property (value exceeds basis in an intangible capital asset held for more than 1 year)	FMV [1.170A–1(c)(1)] AB, if to a private foundation [170(e)(1)(B)(ii)], unless "qualified appreciated stock" [170(e)(5)]	30% of AGI* [170(b)(1)(C)(i)]	20% of AGI* [170(b)(1)(D)(i)]
Long-Term Capital Gain Related Tangible Property (value exceeds basis in a tangible capital asset that is related to the charity's purpose)	FMV [1.170A–1(c)(1)] AB, if to a private foundation [170(e)(1)(B)(ii)]	30% of AGI* [170(b)(1)(C)(i)] 50% of AGI*, if to a private foundation [170(b)(1)(A)]	20% of AGI* [170(b)(1)(D)(i)]
Long-Term Capital Gain Unrelated Tangible Property (value exceeds basis in a tangible capital asset that is unrelated to charity's purpose)	AB [170(e)(1)(B)(i)]	50% of AGI* [170(b)(1)(A)]	20% of AGI* [170(b)(1)(D)(i)]

FMV = fair market value   AB = adjusted basis

* = this is shorthand for the taxpayer's *contribution base*, defined as adjusted gross income as computed without regard to net operating loss carrybacks

Contributions to Both § 170(b)(1)(A) and Other Charities. To understand how the annual limitations in § 170(b)(1) apply when a taxpayer contributes both to charities described in § 170(b)(1)(A) and other charities, take this example:

> EXAMPLE: In Year One, Ward Hussey contributes $40,000 cash to a charity described in § 170(b)(1)(A) and $20,000 cash to a charity not described in § 170(b)(1)(A). Ward's adjusted gross income for all years relevant to this example is $100,000.
>
> ANALYSIS: Under § 170(b)(1)(A), the entire $40,000 contributed to the § 170(b)(1)(A) charity is deductible in Year One, as the total contributions to such charities that year ($40,000) is less than 50 percent of Ward's adjusted gross income ($50,000 is half of $100,000). Under § 170(b)(1)(B), however, only half of the $20,000 contribution to the other charity is deductible in Year One. Although the $20,000 does not exceed the 30 percent limitation in § 170(b)(1)(B)(i), § 170(b)(1)(B)(ii) limits the total § 170 deduction in Year One to 50 percent of Ward's contribution base, or $50,000. Because $40,000 of that $50,000 was used in making the gift to the § 170(b)(1)(A) charity, only $10,000 is left for all other deductible contributions. The other half of the $20,000 contribution will carry over to Year Two as a deduction, again subject to the limitations of § 170(b)(1)(B).

Problem 9–3

Determine the amount of the taxpayer's deduction under § 170 (and the portion of that deduction that may be taken in the year of contribution) in each of the following scenarios. Except as specifically provided to the contrary, assume in all cases that the taxpayer's adjusted gross income (without regard to any "net operating loss carryback") is $50,000, and that the recipient organization is described in § 170(c) and § 170(b)(1)(A).

(a) Helena contributes $30,000 cash to the American Cancer Society.

(b) Ivan contributes his entire interest in a copyright he created to his alma mater, Stanvard University. The copyright has a fair market value of $10,000.

(c) Jimmy contributes supplies he purchased earlier in the year for use in his business to the Salvation Army. Jimmy paid $10,000 for the supplies but they are worth $20,000 at the time of his contribution.

(d) Kim contributes stock in Starbucks Corporation to the Boys & Girls Clubs of America. Kim purchased the stock eight months before the contribution for $7,000, but the value of the stock at the time of contribution is $10,000.

(e) Lindsay contributes stock in Microsoft Corporation to the United Way. Lindsay purchased the stock six years ago for $12,000, but the value of the stock at the time of contribution is $20,000.

(f) Same as (e), except that Lindsay contributes the stock to a private foundation not described in § 170(b)(1)(A).

(g) Martina contributes a painting she purchased five years ago for $10,000 to the City Museum. The painting, now worth $25,000, is displayed to the public at the City Museum.

(h) Same as (g), except that Martina contributes the painting to the Easter Seals Society, which sells the painting for cash shortly after Martina's contribution.

⤧ *Problem 9–4* ⤧

Lovey Howell, your client, has pledged $3,000 to a charitable organization described in § 170(b)(1)(A). To fulfill her pledge, Lovey is contemplating the transfer of shares in Minnow Corporation (a publicly traded stock) that she purchased several years ago for $20,000. Sadly, the weather started getting rough for the company soon after her investment, and the stock is now worth only $3,000. Lovey likes the idea of purging the Minnow stock from her portfolio and meeting her pledge to the charity in one simple move. Do you have any advice for Lovey with respect to her plan to use the Minnow stock to fulfill her pledge?

* * *

Bargain Sales to Charities. When a taxpayer sells property for less than its fair market value, we saw in Chapter 3 that if the discount stems from "detached and disinterested generosity" on the part of the seller, the transaction will be treated as a part-gift, part-sale for federal income tax purposes. Regulations permit a taxpayer to recover all of his or her basis in the transferred property if the sales price is sufficiently high. On its face, a bargain sale of property to a charity is identical to a part-gift, part-sale transaction. Curiously, however, the transaction is treated differently for tax purposes. Under § 1011(b), the seller must apportion his or her basis in the transferred property between the sale portion and the contribution portion.

The results of such an allocation can be demonstrated by an example. Suppose Mia Mohr owns an asset worth $100 in which she has a basis of $20. If she sells the asset for $70 to her son, Ken, and if the reason for the discount is detached and disinterested generosity, Mia will realize and recognize a $50 gain and will be considered to have made a $30 gift to Ken.

Sale Portion	Gift Portion
AR 70	gift of $30
AB 20	(difference between
RG 50	FMV and Mia's AR)

But if Mia sold the same property to a charity (an organization described in § 170(c), presumably) for $70, Mia would realize and recognize a $56 gain and will be considered to have made a gift of property worth $30 in which she has a basis of $6:

Sale Portion	Gift Portion
AR 70	gift of property worth $30,
AB 14 (70% of $20)	in which Mia's basis is $6
RG 56	(30% of $20)

Since Mia sold the property to the charity for 70 percent of its fair market value, she is allowed under § 1011(b) to recover 70 percent of her basis against the amount realized.

Notice that if the property sold to the charity is ordinary income property, short-term capital gain property, or tangible long-term capital gain property unrelated to the charity's purpose, Mia's § 170 deduction from this transaction will be limited to $6, her basis in the gift portion of the transaction. Although at first glance this result may seem less favorable to Mia than the results of the part-gift, part-sale to her son, the apportionment of basis required for bargain sales to charities can yield more favorable results. Suppose, for instance, that the property transferred is tangible long-term capital gain property and that the charity uses the property in a manner unrelated to its charitable purpose. Under § 170(e)(1)(B)(i), Mia's charitable deduction is limited to her basis in the gift portion of the transaction. While Mia's deduction is limited to $6, it is an itemized deduction that will offset ordinary income. Assuming Mia's marginal tax rate is 25 percent, the deduction saves her $1.50 in tax. If Mia had been allowed to apply this $6 of basis against her amount realized from the sale portion of the transaction, her long-term capital gain from the sale would have been reduced from $56 to $50, but that would result in a tax savings of only 90 cents (15 percent rate for long-term capital gains times the $6 in reduced gain). In this case, the basis apportionment rule of § 1011(b) helps Mia.

Where the transferred property is ordinary income property or short-term capital gain property, however, the result is less favorable but still not a bad deal. The $6 deduction under § 170 still offsets ordinary income, but Mia has $6 of additional ordinary gain from the sale portion of the transaction. The income from the sale portion of the transaction exactly offsets the deduction from the gift portion of the transaction, and the two items have the same flavor. So just as the part-gift, part-sale rules are favorable to taxpayers, the rules applicable to bargain sales to charities are also favorable to taxpayers.

The following ruling explains how to handle bargain sales of encumbered property to charities.

REVENUE RULING 81–163

1981–1 C.B. 433.

ISSUE

What is the amount of gain recognized by an individual on the bargain sale of real property to a charitable organization under the circumstances described below?

amount of gain realized for TP

FACTS

During the taxable year, an individual taxpayer transferred unimproved real property subject to an outstanding mortgage of $10x$ dollars to an organization described in section 170(c) of the Internal Revenue Code. On the date of transfer the fair market value of the property was $25x$ dollars, and the taxpayer's adjusted basis in the property was $15x$ dollars. The taxpayer had held the property for more than one year and made no other charitable contributions during the taxable year. The property was a capital asset in the taxpayer's hands. Thus, under the provisions of section 170 the taxpayer made a charitable contribution to the organization of $15x$ dollars ($25x$ dollars fair market value less $10x$ dollars mortgage).

FMV = 25
AB = 15
mort = 10

LAW AND ANALYSIS

Section 1011(b) of the Code and section 1.1011–2(b) of the Income Tax Regulations provide that, if a deduction is allowable under section 170 (relating to charitable contributions) by reason of a sale, the adjusted basis for determining the gain from the sale is the portion of the adjusted basis of the entire property that bears the same ratio to the adjusted basis as the amount realized bears to the fair market value of the entire property.

Section 1.1011–2(a)(3) of the regulations provides that, if property is transferred subject to an indebtedness, the amount of the indebtedness must be treated as an amount realized for purposes of determining whether there is a sale or exchange to which section 1011(b) of the Code and section 1.1011–2 apply, even though the transferee does not agree to assume or pay the indebtedness.

Because the outstanding mortgage of $10x$ dollars is treated as an amount realized, the taxpayer's adjusted basis for determining gain on the bargain sale is $6x$ dollars ($15x$ dollars adjusted basis of the entire property X [$10x$ dollars amount realized ÷ $25x$ dollars fair market value of the entire property]).

10/25 =
0.4

HOLDING

The taxpayer recognizes long-term capital gain of $4x$ dollars ($10x$ dollars amount realized less $6x$ dollars adjusted basis) on the bargain sale of the property to the charitable organization.

LTCG = 4x

* * *

handwritten: 30/50 = 0.6
0.6 × 10 = $6K   = $24K realized gain   FMV $50K
AB = $10K

handwritten: 30K - 6K   encumb = $30K

Problem 9–5

Thornton Mellon donated real property worth $50,000 to University. Thornton's basis in the property at the time of the transaction was $10,000, but the property was encumbered by a mortgage in the amount of $30,000. *— "sale price"* What are the federal income tax consequences to Thornton?

handwritten: 30/50 = 0.6   0.6 × 10 (AB) = $6K

* * *

Substantiating Certain Contributions of Property. The American Jobs Creation Act of 2004 made the reporting and substantiation requirements for charitable contributions of property somewhat more rigorous. Generally, for any contribution of property for which a deduction of more than $500 is claimed, some form of substantiation is required unless the property is readily traded or unless the taxpayer was unable to meet the required substantiation for good cause. See § 170(f)(11). The level of substantiation required varies according to the claimed amount of the deduction:

handwritten: Gift   Sale
$20K gift   A/R 30K
4K   AB   6K
gain 24K

Contribution level	Required substantiation
more than $500	Taxpayer must attach to the return a description of the property.
more than $5,000	Taxpayer must obtain a qualified appraisal of the property and attach to the return such information as the Secretary may require.
more than $500,000	Taxpayer must attach to the return a qualified appraisal of the property.

With respect to contributions of used vehicles, moreover, the taxpayer must substantiate any claimed contribution in excess of $500 by a "contemporaneous written acknowledgment" from the charity. A copy of the acknowledgment must be furnished to the Service. Finally, if the charity sells the donated vehicle without any significant intervening use or material improvement to the vehicle, the amount of the deduction cannot exceed the charity's gross proceeds from the sale. See § 170(f)(12).

C. TAXES

Code: IRC §§ 164(a)–(d)(2)(A); 275; 1001(b).

Regs: None.

Paying federal income tax on dollars used to pay other taxes may seem on its face to be a harsh rule, but an ideal income tax would not allow a deduction for such expenses to the extent they relate to personal consumption or personal-use activities. Yet Congress generally permits a deduction for various tax expenses, most likely because exempting from the federal income tax the dollars used to pay taxes to other governmental bodies acts as an indirect subsidy to such bodies. If the taxes were not deductible, taxpayers might pressure state and local governments into lowering the amount of taxes imposed (more so than they do already). For a taxpayer in the 25 percent tax bracket, for example, a $100 tax payment to a state or local government saves $25 in federal income taxes, so the ultimate out-of-pocket cost of the state or local tax payment is $75. If the tax payment is not deductible, the taxpayer's out-of-pocket cost is $100. With a higher out-of-pocket cost, the taxpayer is more likely to complain about the tax imposed. Get enough taxpayers in a similar situation, and the political pressure on state and local governments can be quite real. So in the name of complicity, Congress grants a federal income tax deduction for many state and local tax payments, effectively ceding revenues to those other governments.

There are a number of Code provisions related to the tax treatment of tax payments. First and foremost is § 164(a), which permits a deduction for certain state and local (and foreign) taxes and for two federal taxes. Notice that § 164 generally makes no distinction between taxes related to business matters, investment activities, or personal activities—all are deductible if listed in § 164(a). The two federal taxes are quite minor: both the generation-skipping transfer tax imposed on income distributions and the environmental tax imposed on certain corporations under § 59A are well outside the scope of this book and do not represent very significant tax expenditures as measured by the Joint Committee on Taxation. See Appendix 1. The deductions for certain state, local, and foreign taxes, however, are quite significant from the standpoint of estimated revenue loss to the federal government.

Section 275 specifically disallows a deduction for most federal taxes paid—a sensible provision given there is no need for the federal government to subsidize itself. With respect to foreign taxes paid, one should also consider the availability of the foreign tax credit under § 901. Taxpayers who pay taxes to foreign governments thus have a choice between deducting such payments under § 164(a) or claiming the credit under § 901. In most cases, the credit is the better option, for it reduces tax liability dollar-for-dollar, while a deduction reduces tax liability only by that proportion equal to the taxpayer's marginal tax rate. The deduction is the better option in those cases where the various limitations on the credit (most notably in § 904) reduce the amount of the credit to a point below the tax savings from the deduction.

Beyond the deduction and credit provisions, the Code also addresses other important aspects of tax payments. Most importantly for individuals, § 212(3) permits a deduction for expenses paid or incurred in the determination, collection, or refund of any tax. Deductible expenses under § 212(3), therefore, include fees paid for tax return preparation, fees paid to a lawyer in seeking a refund of taxes paid, and fees paid to a lawyer to defend against an action to collect additional taxes. Is there a reason to permit a deduction for legal fees paid for tax advice or tax representation but disallow a deduction for legal fees paid with respect to other personal matters?

* * *

Self-Assessment Question

(Solutions to Self–Assessment Questions are set forth in Appendix 3.)

SAQ 9–2. Determine how an individual should treat the following taxes paid during the taxable year for federal income tax purposes:

(a) Federal income taxes paid.

(b) State income taxes paid.

(c) Real property taxes paid annually with respect to a personal residence.

(d) Excise tax for motor vehicle license tabs.

(e) State sales taxes paid to purchase an asset for use in the taxpayer's business.

(f) Special assessment paid to a municipality for new street lighting on the road in front of the taxpayer's residence.

(g) State "intangibles tax" paid (imposed annually on the value of the taxpayer's investment portfolio as of December 31).

* * *

Problem 9–6

On June 16, Year One, Opus sold his personal residence to Bill. The residence is located in Bloom County, which imposes real property taxes on a calendar year basis. The real property taxes for Year One became a lien on all properties within Bloom County on July 1, Year One, and all taxes for Year One had to be paid by December 31, Year One. Bill paid the $12,000 real property tax bill in December of Year One. To what extent can the parties deduct the $12,000 in real property taxes paid?

D. TAX ASPECTS OF SUPPORTING A FAMILY

Code: *Review* IRC §§ 151; 152(a)–(c). *Skim* IRC §§ 21; 22; 23; 24; 45F; 129; 137.

Regs: None.

Procreation: The Last Great Tax Shelter? Perhaps no other joy in life can match that of having a child, but all of that happiness and love comes at a substantial economic cost. A number of Code provisions offer targeted relief to parents and others furnishing support for a child. Some we have seen previously, but many are new. To place these costs and the resulting federal income tax issues in context, let's watch Merlin and Susan Olsen, a married couple, as they raise their twin daughters, Mary–Kate and Ashley.

Medical Expenses. First, by the time the twins are born, Merlin and Susan may have incurred a substantial amount of medical expenses. Assuming these expenses are not reimbursed by insurance or otherwise, they would be deductible to the extent they exceed 7.5 percent of adjusted gross income, as explained in Part A of this Chapter. See § 213.

Adoption Expenses. If Merlin and Susan adopted the twins, the medical costs would be much less but they would incur substantial costs in completing the adoption. Section 23 offers a credit for "qualified adoption expenses" paid or incurred by individual taxpayers. The credit is nonrefundable, meaning that if the credit amount exceeds a taxpayer's total liability for tax, the credit will reduce the taxpayer's liability to zero but the excess credit will not be refunded to the taxpayer. The excess credit, however, can carry over and be added to other credit amounts claimed under § 23 for up to five succeeding taxable years. See § 23(c). The credit is generally claimed in the year in which the adoption is finalized. See § 23(a)(2)(A).

The credit is subject to two additional limitations. First, under § 23(b)(1), the total credit amount in any one year may not exceed $10,000 (an amount that is adjusted for inflation). Prior to 2001, the Code contained two separate credit amounts, with a higher allowance for taxpayers who adopted children with special needs. Now, instead of different credit amounts, one credit ceiling ($10,000) applies to all adoptions. But in the case of special needs children, the taxpayer need not have paid or incurred the "qualified adoption expenses"—the full $10,000 credit is available in the year in which the adoption becomes final even where the taxpayer spent less than that amount in qualified adoption expenses. Section 23(a)(3).

The second limitation is based on the taxpayer's adjusted gross income. If the taxpayer's adjusted gross income exceeds $150,000 (an amount that is adjusted for inflation), the amount of the credit is gradually reduced under § 23(b)(2), eventually reaching zero for taxpayers with adjusted gross incomes of $190,000 or more.

Section 23(d)(1) defines qualified adoption expenses as "reasonable and necessary adoption fees, court costs, attorney fees, and other expenses" directly related to the adoption, provided (among other things) that such payments are not in violation of law, do not relate to the adoption of a child who is also the child of the taxpayer's spouse, and are not reimbursed from any other party.

Should Merlin or Susan persuade his or her employer to pay the costs of adopting the twins, the employer's payments would be compensation includible in gross income. From the perspective of the federal income tax, it is as if the couple received cash compensation from the employer and used the cash to pay the adoption expenses. If that is the case, then the couple should be able to claim the § 23 credit. To save taxpayers from the uncertainty of this approach, § 137 excludes from gross income the amount of qualified adoption expenses paid by a taxpayer's employer. As you would expect, a taxpayer that can exclude the adoption costs paid by his or her employer may not also claim the § 23 credit, for that would be a double benefit (an exclusion and a credit for the same amount). Sure enough, § 23(b)(3)(A) prohibits use of the credit for amounts excluded under § 137.

Support Costs. Now that Mary–Kate and Ashley are finally home from the hospital (and given the size of their modest home, it is a "full house" to say the least), Merlin and Susan will soon see their bank accounts dip further as they provide the twins with food, shelter and clothing. Naturally, these costs are not deductible as they constitute "personal, living, or *family* expenses." Section 262(a) (emphasis added). These costs may force Merlin and Susan to take jobs outside the home, meaning that the couple will have to pay for someone to care for the twins while they are away at work.

Child Care Expenses. Section 21 offers a credit equal to a certain percentage of a taxpayer's "employment-related expenses" in providing the principal place of abode for certain dependents and incapacitated spouses. The amount of the credit varies from 20 percent to 35 percent of such expenses. Not surprisingly, the higher one's adjusted gross income goes, the lower the applicable percentage gets (although the applicable percentage never gets lower than 20 percent). Section 21(a)(2). In any case, the total amount of the credit cannot exceed $3,000 ($6,000 if the taxpayer has two or more dependents for the year, which would be the case for Merlin and Susan). Section 21(c). Furthermore, because the credit is designed to assist those taxpayers who need to hire caretakers while away at work, the amount of the credit generally cannot exceed the taxpayer's earned income for the year. See § 21(d).

The "employment-related expenses" eligible for the credit are limited to payments for household services and for care of a qualifying dependent. See § 21(b)(2). A qualifying dependent is defined as any dependent of the taxpayer who is either age 12 or under or unable to care for himself or herself because of a physical or mental incapacity. As inferred above, the term also includes the taxpayer's spouse if he or she in unable to care for himself or herself because of such incapacity. See § 21(b)(1). Furthermore, in the case of an incapacitated dependent, the dependent must also share the same principal place of abode as the taxpayer for more than half of the taxable year. In our example, the child care expenses incurred by Merlin and Susan would qualify for the credit until the twins reach age 13 (but by that time, the twins should be enjoying their own lucrative careers).

Sometimes employers provide on-site child care services for their employees. They do so, of course, not from "detached and disinterested generosity" but to compensate those employees with dependent children. Employers can claim a credit for the costs of furnishing such services to their employees in an amount determined under § 45F, and employees can exclude all or a part of the value of free child care services from their employers under § 129.

For more details on the § 21 credit, see the discussion at Chapter 2.

* * *

Self-Assessment Question

(Solutions to Self–Assessment Questions are set forth in Appendix 3.)

SAQ 9–3. Alice Hyatt lives with her son, Tommy, in Phoenix. Because Alice works full-time at Mel's Diner, she must arrange babysitting services for Tommy.

(a) Can Alice deduct the amounts paid to the babysitter? If not, does the Code make any accommodation for Alice in this regard?

(b) Suppose Mel Sharples, Alice's employer, provides all employees with a free day-care service on the business premises. Can Mel deduct the costs? Does Alice have gross income?

* * *

The support costs that Merlin and Susan incur to raise Mary–Kate and Ashley will become more significant over the years. Fortunately, the couple can probably count on the § 151 personal exemptions and the § 24 child tax credit to provide them with a tax break that will help them make ends meet.

Dependency Exemptions. Chapter 2 contains a discussion of the personal exemption deduction under § 151 and the additional exemptions given to a taxpayer for his or her dependents as defined in § 152. Recall that a taxpayer's child (and stepchild) will be considered his or her dependent if the taxpayer furnishes over half of the child's support during the calendar year. In the case of children of divorced parents, special support tests are employed, as discussed in Part E of this Chapter.

Keep in mind that the purpose of the § 151 deduction is to work in tandem with the standard deduction to exempt a certain amount of income from any liability for federal income tax. That income is presumably needed to meet basic subsistence needs, and because it would be used entirely for these needs, there would be nothing left of this income to pay any tax that would be levied against it. Of course, this argument is less persuasive with respect to taxpayers in the higher tax brackets, for they have no problems meeting subsistence needs even if the income sheltered by the § 151 deduction was subject to tax. For that reason, § 151(d) phases out the exemption amount for taxpayers with sufficiently high adjusted gross incomes.

Child Tax Credit. Section 24 provides a partially refundable credit equal to a fixed amount for each "qualifying child" of the taxpayer's that is under the age of 17. In general, a qualifying child is any individual for whom the taxpayer can claim a dependency exemption and who is the taxpayer's son or daughter (or descendent of either), stepson or stepdaughter (or descendent of either), or eligible foster child.

The "per child amount" of the credit was originally set at $400 when the credit was first enacted in 1998. In 1999 and 2000, the amount increased to $500. The Economic Growth and Tax Relief Reconciliation Act of 2001 increased the amount to $600 for 2001 through 2004, with gradual increases to $1,000 by 2010. In 2003, the Jobs and Growth Tax Relief Reconciliation Act accelerated the $1,000 amount to taxpayers with qualifying children in 2003 and 2004. The $1,000 amount was fixed for 2005–2010 by the Working Families Tax Relief Act of 2004. Under the sunset provisions of the 2001 Act (described in Chapter 1), the credit amount will go back to $500 beginning in 2011.

The child tax credit is phased-out for taxpayers with income above certain thresholds. Specifically, § 24(b)(1) lowers the total credit amount otherwise allowable by $50 for each $1,000 (or fraction thereof) of "modified adjusted gross income" over the taxpayer's "threshold amount" as defined in § 24(b)(2), which is $75,000 in cases of unmarried taxpayers and heads of households. The modified adjusted gross income threshold for married taxpayers filing a joint return is $110,000, and (logically) the threshold for married taxpayers filing separately is $55,000. Both the per child amount and the income thresholds are not adjusted annually for inflation.

For 2003 and 2004, a taxpayer's total child tax credit was refundable to the extent of ten percent of the taxpayer's earned income in excess of $10,000 (a dollar figure that *is* adjusted for inflation). For 2005 and after, the credit remains partially refundable, and the percentage is increased to 15 percent. Thus, if a taxpayer with one qualifying child has earned income of $15,000 in 2007 (when the inflation-adjusted threshold is $11,750), up to $487.50 (15% times $3,250) of the $1,000 child tax credit for that year may be refunded to the taxpayer.

Education Costs. Of course, Mary–Kate and Ashley have to attend school, and that will not come cheap. Various tax provisions for education expenses are presented in Chapter 10. To help defray the costs of higher education, however, Merlin and Susan might start savings accounts, one for each child. They could then use the account proceeds to make various investments that would generate additional growth and income. Because the accounts belong to Mary–Kate and Ashley, any taxable income attributable to the accounts would be taxable to the twins.

The Kiddie Tax. But wait! If the twins are in a lower tax bracket (which is probably the case, putting movie careers to the side for a moment), titling some investments that generate ordinary gross income in the names of Mary–Kate and Ashley looks to be a brilliant strategy for tax savings—instead of the interest and other income from the accounts being subject to tax at the parents' rate if the investments were held in their names, the income can be taxed to the twins at a lower rate. Unfortunately for Merlin and Susan, § 1(g) applies a special rule in the case of unearned income of children under age 18. This rule, known as the "kiddie tax," taxes certain unearned income of a child at the *parent's* marginal rate, no matter whether the child can be claimed as a dependent on the parent's return.

The kiddie tax applies if: (1) the child has not reached age 18 by the end of the taxable year; (2) the child's investment income was more than

$1,700 (for 2007); (3) the child is required to file a return for the year; (4) the child has at least one parent alive at the close of the taxable year; and (5) the child will not file a joint return with the child's spouse for the taxable year. The kiddie tax applies to all unearned income of a child, no matter how the underlying property got into the child's hands. For example, the kiddie tax would apply to Mary–Kate's unearned income even if it came from property she acquired with compensation derived from her own labor. In addition, the kiddie tax would apply to Ashley's unearned income even if it came from property given to her by an aunt, a neighbor, or anyone other than Merlin and Susan.

The kiddie tax is computed by determining the "allocable parental tax." This determination first requires adding the net unearned income of the child to the parent's income and then applying the parent's tax rate. Under § 1(g)(4)(A), a child's "net unearned income" is the child's unearned income minus the larger of these two amounts:

Option 1:	Option 2:
Twice the minimum standard deduction allowed to dependents ($1,700 in 2007)	• the minimum standard deduction allowed to dependents ($850 in 2007) -plus- • the itemized deductions directly connected with the production of the unearned income

In no case can a child's net unearned income exceed his or her taxable income. See § 1(g)(4)(B).

The allocable parental tax equals the increase in tax to a parent that would result if the child's net unearned income was added to the parent's taxable income. See § 1(g)(3)(A). If a parent has more than one child subject to the kiddie tax, the net unearned income of all of his or her children is combined and a single kiddie tax amount is computed. Each child is then allocated a proportionate share of that hypothetical increase. So while the tax liability is computed with reference to the hypothetical effects on the parent's return, it is really a tax owed by the child and reported on the child's return.

Suppose, for example, that Mary–Kate had unearned income of $11,700 for 2007 and that Ashley had unearned income of $9,700 in the same year. Also assume that neither twin had any itemized deductions attributable to the unearned income. Accordingly, Mary–Kate's net unearned income for the year was $10,000 and Ashley's net unearned income for the year was $8,000.

Suppose further that Merlin and Susan are in the 33 percent marginal tax bracket. If the extra $18,000 of net unearned income was taxed to Merlin and Susan, the couple would owe extra taxes of $6,000 (33% times $18,000). Of the $6,000 in total kiddie tax, $3,333 is to be reported by Mary–Kate and $2,667 is to be reported by Ashley. This allocation is proportionate to the relative net unearned incomes of the twins (55.55 percent of the net unearned income was from Mary–Kate, and 44.45 percent of the net unearned income came from Ashley).

If Merlin and Susan did not file a joint return for 2007, then the kiddie tax is to be computed by using the income of the parent with the greater amount of taxable income. If the couple was unmarried, the custodial parent's taxable income is used in determining the child's liability under § 1(g). If Merlin and Susan were unmarried but lived together throughout 2007, then the return of the parent with the higher taxable income is used.

If Merlin and Susan did not want Mary–Kate and Ashley to be liable for the extra tax owed under § 1(g), they could elect to report the twins' unearned income on their own return. If such an election is made, the twins would be treated as if they had no income for the year; thus they would not have to file a return. This election is available only where the requirements of § 1(g)(7)(A) are met.

Elder Care Issues. Let us briefly turn the tables by supposing that Mary–Kate and Ashley are now adults who must provide care for their parents. Just as Merlin and Susan could avail themselves of special tax provisions in raising their children, Mary–Kate and Ashley may be eligible for other special tax provisions in caring for their dependent parents. For example, the § 21 credit applies not only to child care expenses but also to expenses paid to a "dependent care center" and expenses paid to care for any dependent of the taxpayer residing in the taxpayer's home. If Mary–Kate and Ashley pay costs to care for their parents at their own homes or at a dependent care center, the credit is available. The credit is subject to the same income and per-dependent limitations applicable in the child care context, as described above.

If Mary–Kate and Ashley each provides exactly one-half of the support costs for a parent, then neither would be eligible to claim the parent as her dependent for purposes of the § 151 exemption. This is because § 152 requires the taxpayer to furnish *over half* of the total support of one who the taxpayer seeks to claim as a dependent. Fortunately in this case, a special rule in § 152(c) allows Mary–Kate and Ashley to decide who gets to claim the dependency exemption for the parent. Under this rule, if more than one person collectively provides over half of the support of another individual, and if each such provider pays at least ten percent (but no more than half) of the total support costs, then one of the providers may claim the dependency exemption as long as the other providers all declare in writing that they will not claim the dependency exemption. This written declaration is made on IRS Form 2120. Thus, Mary–Kate and Ashley may agree, for instance, that Mary–Kate will claim the dependency exemption this year and that Ashley will claim the dependency exemption the next year. Or they might agree that Mary–Kate gets the exemption every year. What is interesting, however, is that only one of them may claim the entire exemption; they cannot split the exemption amount between them in any way.

E.   TAX ASPECTS OF DIVORCE AND SEPARATION

p.1092-1096

Prob. 9-7

Code: IRC §§ 71; 215(a)–(c); 1041(a)–(c). *Skim* IRC § 152(e).

Regs: Treas. Reg. §§ 1.71–1T; 1.215–1T; 1.1041–1T. *Skim* Treas. Reg. § 1.1041–2.

Tax issues may not be foremost in the minds of a married couple undergoing separation or dissolution, but practitioners should be very sensitive to the various planning opportunities and traps that often appear in these settings. This Part of the Chapter considers the federal income tax aspects of alimony and child support payments as well as property transfers between spouses that are incident to a divorce. This Part also examines the deductibility of attorney fees paid with respect to a divorce proceeding as well as other significant tax issues. Most of the tax rules related to divorce give significant deference to the arrangements negotiated between the parties. Accordingly, the practitioner simply cannot wait until the end of the negotiations to consider tax issues. While tax implications may not necessarily steer the negotiations, they can and do play a significant role throughout the process.

Alimony and Separate Maintenance Payments. To the extent a divorce decree or other enforceable agreement between the parties requires one spouse to make alimony or separate maintenance payments to the other spouse, may the payor spouse claim a deduction? Are the payments includible in the income of the recipient spouse? The following case supplied an early (but ultimately rejected) answer.

GOULD v. GOULD

United States Supreme Court, 1917.
245 U.S. 151, 38 S.Ct. 53, 62 L.Ed. 211.

MR. JUSTICE McREYNOLDS delivered the opinion of the court.

A decree of the Supreme Court for New York County entered in 1909 forever separated the parties to this proceeding, then and now citizens of the United States, from bed and board; and further ordered that plaintiff in error pay to Katherine C. Gould during her life the sum of three thousand dollars ($3,000.00) every month for her support and maintenance. The question presented is whether such monthly payments during the years 1913 and 1914 constituted parts of Mrs. Gould's income within the intendment of the Act of Congress approved October 3, 1913, *issue* 38 Stat. 114, 166, and were subject as such to the tax prescribed therein. The court below answered in the negative; and we think it reached the proper conclusion.

Pertinent portions of the act follow:

"SECTION II. A. Subdivision 1. That there shall be levied, assessed, collected and paid annually upon the entire net income arising or accruing from all sources in the preceding calendar year to every citizen of the United States, whether residing at home or abroad, and to every person residing in the United States, though not a citizen thereof, a tax of 1 per centum per annum upon such income, except as hereinafter provided; . . .

"B. That, subject only to such exemptions and deductions as are hereinafter allowed, the net income of a taxable person shall include gains, profits, and income derived from salaries, wages, or compensation for personal service of whatever kind and in whatever form paid, or from professions, vocations, businesses, trade, commerce, or sales, or dealings in property, whether real or personal, growing out of the ownership or use of or interest in real or personal property, also from interest, rent, dividends, securities, or the transaction of any lawful business carried on for gain or profit, or gains or profits and income derived from any source whatever, including the income from but not the value of property acquired by gift, bequest, devise, or descent: . . . "

In the interpretation of statutes levying taxes it is the established rule not to extend their provisions, by implication, beyond the clear import of the language used, or to enlarge their operations so as to embrace matters not specifically pointed out. In case of doubt they are construed most strongly against the Government, and in favor of the citizen.

As appears from the above quotations, the new income upon which subdivision 1 directs that an annual tax shall be assessed, levied, collected and paid is defined in division B. The use of the word itself in the definition of "income" causes some obscurity, but we are unable to assert that alimony paid to a divorced wife under a decree of court falls fairly within any of the terms employed.

In *Audubon v. Shufeldt*, 181 U.S. 575, 577, 578, we said: "Alimony does not arise from any business transaction, but from the relation of marriage. It is not founded on contract, express or implied, but on the natural and legal duty of the husband to support the wife. The general obligation to support is made specific by the decree of the court of appropriate jurisdiction. . . . Permanent alimony is regarded rather as a portion of the husband's estate to which the wife is equitably entitled, than as strictly a debt; alimony from time to time may be regarded as a portion of his current income or earnings; . . . "

The net income of the divorced husband subject to taxation was not decreased by payment of alimony under the court's order; and, on the other hand, the sum received by the wife on account thereof cannot be regarded as income arising or accruing to her within the enactment.

The judgment of the court below is

Affirmed.

* * *

Congress changed the result in *Gould* by enacting §§ 71 and 215. Under § 71, payments that qualify as "alimony," defined in § 71(b), are included in the gross income of the recipient spouse. Such payments are deductible by the payor spouse under § 215, and the deduction is taken above the line. See § 62(a)(10). The payor spouse who seeks a deduction must provide the social security number of the recipient spouse on the payor spouse's return, and if the recipient spouse is a nonresident alien individual, the payor must even withhold a percentage of the payment for federal income taxes.

The enactment of §§ 71 and 215 does not completely eradicate the applicability of *Gould*. Clearly, the Code provisions supercede *Gould* in the divorce or separation context, but any cash transfers between spouses in an intact marriage would be subject to *Gould*. Such payments would thus be excludable by the recipient spouse and not deductible by the payor spouse. Obviously, this only matters if the spouses do not file a joint return. *Gould* probably does not apply, however, to payments between unmarried cohabitants or domestic partners. This is because the *Gould* result is premised on a payment made by the "natural and legal duty" of marriage, a concept not yet applicable to unmarried cohabitants and (as of this writing) only inconsistently applicable to domestic partners.

Coming back to the statute, the most significant aspect to its application is the definition of an "alimony" payment in § 71(b). Notice that §§ 71 and 215 apply only to cash payments and not to any transfers of property. Property transfers are handled under a completely different scheme (discussed later in this Part) so the rules in §§ 71 and 215 are specifically limited to cash transfers. The requirements imposed by the definition of alimony in § 71(b) can prove to be a trap for the unwary.

OKERSON v. COMMISSIONER, 123 T.C. No. 14 (2004).

Facts: In 1995, a state court decreed that the taxpayer pay to his former spouse in connection with their divorce 113 monthly payments of alimony totaling $117,000. The 1995 decree stated that this alimony would terminate if the former spouse died before the $117,000 was paid in full but that the taxpayer would then be required to continue making the monthly payments towards the education of the children of the taxpayer and the former spouse until the children completed four years of college. In 1997, the court issued a second decree requiring the taxpayer to make 42 additional monthly payments totaling $33,500 to the former spouse's attorney as additional alimony to the former spouse and that this additional alimony was deductible by the taxpayer and taxable income to the former spouse. The 1997 decree also stated that this additional alimony would terminate if the former spouse died before the $33,500 was paid in full but that the taxpayer would then be required to continue making the monthly payments to the former spouse's attorney until the $33,500 was paid in full. During 2000, the year at issue, the taxpayer paid $12,600 pursuant to the 1995 decree and $9,000 pursuant to the 1997 decree. He deducted these amounts as alimony, but the Service denied the deductions.

Issue: Were the payments deductible as alimony?

Holding: No.

Rationale: Although the state court reaffirmed its decree that the payments were intended to qualify as alimony, and although the former spouse was alive throughout the year at issue, the Tax Court held that none of the payments were deductible because there would have been liability to make the payments to others as a substitute for payments to the former spouse if she had died. Because this arrangement did not meet the requirement of § 71(b)(1)(D), the payments could not qualify as alimony.

* * *

Another Potential Trap. Spouses who seek to transfer extra cash in lieu of property in order to avoid the rules applicable to property transfers will run into the "recapture" trap of § 71(f). If the divorce or separation instrument requires excessively high cash payments in the early years relative to the payments in later years, § 71(f) will determine that the excessive payments are really disguised property settlements. Accordingly, the payor spouse will be required to include as income an amount equal to amounts that the statute identifies as "excess payments," and the recipient spouse will be allowed to deduct that same amount as if he or she repaid it to the payor spouse.

Child Support. Section 71(c) specifically provides that payments made or received for the support of a child do not qualify as alimony. Consequently, the payor spouse may not deduct child support payments and the recipient spouse need not include such payments in gross income. Even if payments are not specifically designated as child support, it is possible under § 71(c)(2) for alimony payments to be treated as child support if such payments will be reduced upon the occurrence of a contingency that is related to the child. Thus, where the payor spouse must pay monthly "alimony" of $5,000 until Junior graduates from college, at which point monthly payments will be reduced to $2,000, § 71(c)(2) will treat the $5,000 payments as consisting of $2,000 of alimony and $3,000 of child support.

* * *

Problem 9–7

Britney and Kevin divorced in Year One and are no longer members of the same household. The divorce decree requires Britney to make monthly cash payments of $4,500 to Kevin until the earlier of: (i) the end of Year Seven; or (ii) Kevin's death.

(a) What are the federal income tax consequences of the monthly payments to Britney and Kevin?

then none of these payments will be deductible or included as income

(b) How would the answer to (a) change if Britney is required to make the monthly cash payments until the end of Year Seven regardless of whether Kevin is alive? Assume the divorce decree provides that the monthly payments are due to Kevin while he is alive, but that if he dies prior to the end of Year Seven, Britney must make the payments to Kevin's estate.

(c) Britney runs low on cash in the middle of Year Six. In August of that year, she gives Kevin a promissory note in the principal amount of $4,500, payable with accrued interest on Kevin's demand. What are the federal income tax consequences of this transaction?

must actually be paid — a debt instrument is NOT cash. cash rule app pretty strictly

(d) Assume for purposes of this part only that you represent Britney in the divorce proceedings. Kevin's counsel insists that he receive monthly cash payments of $4,500 until his death or remarriage and that the parties include a provision in their divorce decree providing that all such payments shall not be included in Kevin's gross income. You know that the payments will be Kevin's only source of income, which would place him in the 25 percent tax bracket if they were taxable. Britney, on the other hand, has substantial income, and she is in the 35 percent tax bracket. How might you negotiate a better deal for Britney that Kevin's counsel might also find appealing? *take the opt out provision out, and increase monthly payments to $6,000*

(e) How would the answer to (a) change if the divorce decree specifies that $3,000 of the $4,500 monthly payment is for Kevin's support and maintenance and the remaining $1,500 is for the support and maintenance of their minor son, Sean? *$3K would be ded/include and the $1.5k would not*

(f) How would the answer to (e) change if the divorce decree simply provided that Britney was to pay $4,500 cash monthly to Kevin until his death, but that the monthly payment amount will be reduced to $3,000 as of November, Year Five? Coincidentally, Sean will reach age 21 in November, Year Five. *under the rebuttable presumption — then the $1. will be viewed as child sup.*

(g) Assume the same facts from part (e). In March of Year Three, Britney is unable to make the entire $4,500 monthly payment, but she does pay $3,000 to Kevin. What are the tax consequences of this payment? *$1.5k chld | $1.5 alimony*

Problem 9–8

Ryan and Trista divorced in Year One. In a written separation agreement executed shortly before the divorce, Trista agreed to make support and maintenance payments to Ryan in cash according to the following schedule:

Year	Cash Payment
Two	$100,000
Three	$ 50,000
Four	$ 20,000
Five	$ 10,000
Six	$ 10,000
Seven	$ 10,000

The agreement provided that Trista had no liability to make payments following Ryan's death or remarriage, whichever occurs first. Assuming Ryan and Trista are not members of the same household at any time in

Years Two through Seven, what are the federal income tax consequences of this arrangement to the parties?

*   *   *

Property Transfers. Not surprisingly, property settlements are a major component of divorce and separation proceedings. What happens, then, when one spouse transfers property with a fair market value substantially in excess of his or her basis to the other (perhaps now former) spouse? To the extent that the transfer effects a division of assets in which both spouses have interests, one could argue that the transfer should not be considered a realization event. On the other hand, if the transferor spouse makes the transfer in satisfaction of a legal obligation to provide the recipient spouse with a certain amount of assets, there is clearly a gain to the transferor spouse because the obligation was satisfied with property in which the transferor spouse had a small basis. Put another way, there is no question that if the transferor spouse sold the transferred property to an unrelated person for cash and then transferred the cash to the spouse, the disposition of the transferred property would result in realized (and recognized) gain.

The Supreme Court provided a temporary answer to this issue in the following case. You might remember it from Chapter 3, but it is provided here again as a refresher.

UNITED STATES v. DAVIS, 370 U.S. 65, 82 S.Ct. 1190, 8 L.Ed.2d 335 (1962).

Facts: In 1955, the taxpayer, Thomas Crawley Davis, transferred 500 shares of stock in the E.I. du Pont de Nemours & Co. to his spouse pursuant to a separation agreement signed in 1954. In exchange, "the then Mrs. Davis" agreed to relinquish all of her claims and marital rights against the taxpayer's property. The taxpayer's basis in the 500 shares of stock transferred to his spouse was approximately $75,000, and the transferred shares were worth $82,000.

Issues: (1) Was this transfer of stock in exchange for a release of marital rights a taxable event? (2) If so, what is the taxpayer's "amount realized" from the transaction?

Holdings: (1) The transfer is a taxable event. (2) The "amount realized" from the exchange is the fair market value of the released marital rights, which in this case would be equal to the value of the stock transferred.

Rationale: The transfer was a taxable event because the taxpayer received consideration from his spouse in exchange for the stock. Under the separation agreement, the taxpayer was required to make a payment to his spouse in exchange for her release. By choosing to discharge that contractual obligation with appreciated property, the taxpayer realizes the benefit of that appreciation. In this case, he was able to discharge an $82,000 obligation to his spouse by transferring property that only cost him $75,000. He thus realizes the benefit of the $7,000 appreciation in making this transfer.

As to the computation of the "amount realized" from the transfer, the Court concluded that the lower court erred. "[The lower court] found that there was no way to compute the fair market value of these marital rights and that it was thus impossible to determine the taxable gain realized by the taxpayer. We believe this conclusion was erroneous. It must be assumed, we think, that the parties acted at arm's length and that they judged the marital rights to be equal in value to the property for which they were exchanged. There was no evidence to the contrary here. * * * To be sure there is much to be said of the argument that such an assumption is weakened by the emotion, tension and practical necessities involved in divorce negotiations and the property settlements arising therefrom. However, once it is recognized that the transfer was a taxable event, it is more consistent with the general purpose and scheme of the taxing statutes to make a rough approximation of the gain realized thereby than to ignore altogether its tax consequences. Moreover, if the transaction is to be considered a taxable event as to the husband, the [lower court's] position leaves up in the air the wife's basis for the property received. In the context of a taxable transfer by the husband, all indicia point to a "cost" basis for this property in the hands of the wife. Yet under the [lower court's] position her cost for this property, *i.e.,* the value of the marital rights relinquished therefor, would be indeterminable, and on subsequent disposition of the property she might suffer inordinately over the Commissioner's assessment which she would have the burden of proving erroneous. Our present holding that the value of these rights is ascertainable eliminates this problem; for the same calculation that determines the amount received by the husband fixes the amount given up by the wife, and this figure, *i.e.,* the market value of the property transferred by the husband, will be taken by her as her tax basis for the property received."

Note

Congress felt a different answer was in order, and ultimately enacted legislation overruling *Davis* in the context of inter-spousal transfers. Under § 1041(a), no gain or loss is recognized on a transfer of property to a spouse. The nonrecognition rule also applies to transfer between former spouses if they are "incident to a divorce." Section 1041(c)(1) automatically deems all transfers within one year of the divorce to be "incident to the divorce," and § 1041(c)(2) includes all transfers "related to the cessation of the marriage" (a term explored to some extent in the Regulations) as being incident to the divorce. Just like other nonrecognition transactions, § 1041(b) preserves the gain or loss in the hands of the recipient spouse by giving the recipient spouse a basis in the transferred property equal to the transferor spouse's basis. Consequently, the transferor spouse's holding period is tacked to the holding period of the recipient spouse. See § 1223(2).

* * *

✳ *Problem 9–9* ✳

Billy Bob and Angelina finalized their divorce on January 1, Year One. During their marriage, Billy Bob and Angelina owned Blackacre, a parcel of real property that they used as their personal residence. Billy Bob and Angelina each paid $40,000 of their personal funds to buy Blackacre. In addition to this property, Billy Bob also owned Whiteacre, a parcel of unimproved real property, as an investment. Angelina owned shares of stock in Croft Corporation, a publicly traded entity.

(a) The final divorce decree awarded title to Blackacre to Angelina. In February of Year One, Billy Bob conveyed his one-half interest in Blackacre to Angelina. The fair market value of Billy Bob's interest was $100,000, and his basis in that interest was $40,000. What are the federal income tax consequences of this transaction to Billy Bob and Angelina?

(b) Assume instead that the divorce decree did not affect ownership of the Blackacre residence, but it allowed Angelina the right to occupy the residence and required Billy Bob to pay the entire monthly mortgage payments with respect to the property until Angelina dies or remarries, whichever occurs first. Also assume that each monthly mortgage payment consisted of $500 in principal and $400 in interest. What are the federal income tax consequences of this arrangement?

(c) The divorce decree required Billy Bob to transfer Whiteacre to Angelina. Billy Bob effected the conveyance in Year Three, at which time his basis in the property was $50,000 and its fair market value was $130,000. What are the federal income tax consequences of this transfer?

(d) The divorce decree required Angelina to transfer all of her shares in Croft Corporation to Billy Bob. Angelina conveyed title to Billy Bob late in Year One. At the time of the transfer, Angelina's basis in the stock was $100,000, but the shares were only worth $80,000. What are the federal income tax consequences of this transaction?

(e) Suppose you represented Angelina in the divorce proceedings. Would you have made any recommendations to Angelina with respect to the Croft Corporation shares?

* * *

Transfers on Behalf of a Spouse. Regulation § 1.1041–1T, Q. & A. 9, provides that property transfers to a third party "on behalf of" a spouse or former spouse are to be treated as if made directly to the spouse. Thus, where a divorce decree requires Wife to transfer property to a third party in satisfaction of a debt Husband owes to that third party, Wife's transfer will be treated as a transfer directly to Husband for purposes of § 1041. A similar rule applies to cash payments made by a former spouse on behalf of the other. See Treas. Reg. § 1.71–1T(b), Q. & A. 6.

Regulations finalized in 2003 provide additional guidance with respect to corporate stock redemptions incident to a divorce. Suppose Fred and Wilma, married for several years, each own 50 shares in X Corporation. Fred and Wilma divorce, and X Corporation repurchases Wilma's shares for cash, leaving Fred as the corporation's sole shareholder. Under prior case law, there was uncertainty as to whether Wilma's redemption qualified for nonrecognition under § 1041 since there was no direct transfer from Wilma to Fred. To provide a clear rule, the regulations generally provide that if Wilma's redemption is treated as a constructive distribution to Fred under corporate tax principles, then the transaction will be treated as if Wilma transferred her shares to Fred (which qualifies for nonrecognition under § 1041) and then Fred had the shares redeemed for the cash used to pay Wilma (a dividend includible in Fred's gross income, assuming sufficient earnings and profits). If, on the other hand, Wilma's redemption is not a constructive distribution to Fred, then § 1041 will not apply to the redemption and Wilma will be taxed on any resulting gain. See Treas. Reg. § 1.1041–2.

So when is a stock redemption treated as a constructive distribution to Fred under current law? The regulations say it is when Fred has the primary and unconditional obligation to buy Wilma's shares. So if the divorce agreement imposes an obligation on Fred to buy Wilma's shares, then the corporation's satisfaction of Fred's obligation via the redemption is a constructive distribution to him. If the divorce agreement states only that Wilma shall sell her shares to the corporation, then the redemption is not a constructive distribution to Fred because he is not primarily and unconditionally obligated to purchase the shares. The regulations, however, specifically allow Fred and Wilma to insert a clause in their divorce agreement whereby the parties agree to treat a corporate redemption as though there had been a transfer first to Fred followed by a corporate redemption. In other words, the parties can determine who should bear the tax bite and structure the divorce agreement accordingly.

When the regulations were first proposed, commentators expressed concern that the regulations contained no provision addressing the situation where (using the example above) the redemption results in a constructive distribution to Fred under applicable tax law, but the spouses nevertheless would like to agree that the redemption will be treated as a redemption distribution to Wilma. They suggested that the final regulations allow the spouses to agree in writing that the redemption will be taxable to Wilma notwithstanding that the redemption might otherwise result in a constructive distribution to Fred. Treasury acquiesced to this request. Consequently, the regulations offer tremendous flexibility in planning the income tax consequences of stock redemptions in the divorce context.

Interaction Between § 1041 and the Assignment of Income Doctrine. In Chapter 3, we learned that where a taxpayer assigns the right to receive accrued but unpaid income to another taxpayer, the assignment of income doctrine may require the taxpayer to pay the tax on the income once it is paid to the assignee. Even where a taxpayer transfers an interest in property, the taxpayer may be subject to tax on any "ripe fruit" associated with the property at the time of the transfer.

How does this work in the context of inter-spousal transfers under § 1041? The ruling and case below grappled with this issue.

REVENUE RULING 87–112, 1987–2 C.B. 207.

Facts: The taxpayer owned Series E and EE bonds set to mature after 1985. In 1985, the taxpayer divorced. As part of a property settlement that year, the taxpayer transferred the bonds to the taxpayer's former spouse. The former spouse then redeemed the bonds in 1986.

Issues: (1) Must the taxpayer include the deferred, accrued interest on the bonds in gross income in 1985, the year of the transfer? (2) What is the former spouse's basis in the bonds immediately after the 1985 transfer?

Holdings: (1) The deferred, accrued interest from the date of original issuance of the bonds to the date of transfer of the bonds to the former spouse is includible in the taxpayer's gross income. (2) The former spouse's basis in the bonds immediately after the transfer is equal to the taxpayer's basis in the bonds increased by the interest income includible by the taxpayer as a result of the transfer of the bonds.

Rationale: "Although section 1041(a) of the Code shields from recognition gain that would ordinarily be recognized on a sale or exchange of property, it does not shield from recognition income that is ordinarily recognized upon the assignment of that income to another taxpayer. Because the income at issue here is accrued but unrecognized interest, rather than gain, section 1041(a) does not shield that income from recognition. The transferred bonds in the present situation contain an interest element that has not been included in income. Accordingly, the specific rule of section 1.454–1(a) of the regulations for dispositions of interest-deferred obligations applies to require that the transferor include the accrued interest in income in the year of the transfer."

KOCHANSKY v. COMMISSIONER, 92 F.3d 957 (9th Cir. 1996).

Facts: The husband, an attorney, commenced medical malpractice litigation on behalf of a client in 1983. Under the contingent fee arrangement with the client, the husband was entitled to a percentage of any amount recovered in the litigation. In 1985, husband and wife divorced. Pursuant to their property settlement agreement, husband transferred a one-half interest in the husband's rights under the contingent fee agreement to the wife. In 1987, husband received payment of his fee under the contingent fee arrangement; he then transferred half of the fee to the wife.

Issue: To what extent (and when) is the husband taxed on the income from the contingent fee arrangement?

Holding: The husband is taxed on the entire fee amount in 1987.

Rationale: The taxpayer "did not own, and could not transfer, the [client's] claim that was producing the contingency. Nor did he transfer himself or his law practice. He continued to render and control the personal services that produced the fee. He transferred only the right to receive the income. In terms of the tree-fruit analogy, 'there was no tree other than [the taxpayer] himself.' *Hall v. United States,* 242 F.2d 412, 413 (7th Cir.), *cert. denied,* 355 U.S. 821, 2 L.Ed.2d 36, 78 S.Ct. 27 (1957). That [the taxpayer's] fee was contingent upon the successful outcome of the [client's] litigation does not change the fact that, when the fee materialized, it was undisputed compensation for [the taxpayer's] personal services. Under *Lucas v. Earl* * * *, it was taxable to [the taxpayer]."

Note

In *Revenue Ruling 87–112,* the taxpayer was taxed in the year of the transfer to the former spouse, but in *Kochansky,* the taxpayer was not taxed until the year the contingent fee was actually received. Perhaps this discrepancy can be reconciled by the fact that the accrued interest in the ruling was more certain to be paid and capable of easy valuation, while the contingent right to payment in *Kochansky* was much less certain and certainly harder to value. Interestingly, the *Kochansky* court makes no mention of the ruling. Even more interestingly, the *Kochansky* court makes no mention of § 1041—even to say that the statute does not apply in this context.

So what conclusions can we draw about the applicability of the assignment of income doctrine in property settlements? The revenue ruling indicates that the assignment of income doctrine trumps the application of § 1041, at least in the context of Series E and EE bonds and perhaps more broadly in any situation where the accrued but unpaid income (the "ripe fruit" on the tree) on the transferred property is easily capable of valuation. And maybe § 1041 has no applicability at all in transfers of naked rights to future payments, as in *Kochansky,* for § 1041 only applies to transfers of *property* and not to transfers of income.

* * *

Effect of Separation or Divorce on Dependency Exemption and Filing Status. One child, one exemption, two parents—during a separation or following a divorce, who gets to claim the § 151 dependency exemption for the child? Section 152(e)(1) generally provides that the "custodial parent" (the one having custody of the child for "a greater portion of the calendar year") gets the full dependency exemption if four factors are present: (1) the child receives over half of his or her support from the parents or stepparents; (2) the parents are divorced or separated under a written separation agreement; (3) the parents live apart for the last six months of the year; and (4) the child is in the custody of one or both parents for more than half of the year. Notice that if these requirements are met, the custodial parent gets the exemption even if the other parent furnishes over half of the child's support.

Under § 152(e)(2), however, the custodial parent may release his or her claim to the exemption to the other parent by signing a written declaration avowing that he or she will not claim the child as a dependent. This declaration may be made on IRS Form 8332. The other parent must then attach this form to his or her own tax return in order to claim the child as a dependent. There is considerable flexibility with respect to this release—the custodial parent may waive the exemption for one year, for multiple years, for alternate years, or any other number of specified years. See Treas. Reg. § 1.152–4T(a), Q. & A. 4. Effectively, then, the dependency exemption is up for negotiation between the spouses. Where the custodial parent is in a lower tax bracket than the other parent but is worried about the other parent making timely support payments, the custodial parent might agree to release his or her claim to the dependency exemption so long as payments from the other parent remain timely. This acts as cheap insurance for the timely payment of support.

Separation and divorce can also affect a taxpayer's filing status. Often spouses who are separated but still married choose to file separate returns. While filing separately can avoid joint liability with the estranged spouse, it also places the taxpayers into the least favorable filing status. Recall from Chapter 1 that married filing separately is generally unappealing, for not only are the tax brackets cut in half, but so are many benefits like the standard deduction. Following a divorce, custodial parents may file as heads of households, while noncustodial parents usually file as "unmarried" taxpayers. Because the brackets for heads of households are slightly fatter than the brackets for unmarried taxpayers, custodial parents have an advantage in this respect.

Attorney Fees in Dissolution Proceedings. Should fees paid to an attorney for representation in a divorce proceeding be deductible? One argument in favor of a deduction is that the property divided in a divorce may consist of business and investment assets. To the extent that divisions at divorce are, unfortunately, ordinary and necessary, and because fees paid to an attorney hardly improve the assets or extend their useful lives, a deduction seems proper. The contrary view holds that while divorce proceedings may involve business or investment assets, they are inherently personal proceedings, no different than seeing a lawyer for a will. These arguments went head-to-head before the Supreme Court in the following case.

UNITED STATES v. GILMORE, 372 U.S. 39, 83 S.Ct. 623, 9 L.Ed.2d 570 (1963).

Facts: The taxpayer divorced his wife in 1954. At the time of the divorce, his gross income consisted almost entirely of his salary as president of three corporations, which were franchised automobile dealers, and from dividends from his controlling stock interests in those corporations. The taxpayer spent a total of $40,611.36 in legal expenses in the divorce proceeding, but the result was a complete victory for the taxpayer—all of his spouse's claims to community property and alimony were defeated. Prevailing in the divorce proceedings was very important to the taxpayer, for he reasonably feared that if his ex-wife obtained control over the three auto dealerships his positions within those companies would be lost and his rights to dividend income would be substantially curtailed. The taxpayer deducted the legal expenses under the precursor to § 212(2) on the theory that the expenses were incurred in the conservation of property held for the production of income. The Service disallowed the deduction on the grounds that legal expenses arising from a divorce proceeding are non-deductible personal expenses.

Issue: May the taxpayer deduct the legal fees paid pursuant to a divorce proceeding where the proceeding serves to preserve the taxpayer's interest in property held for the production of income?

Holding: No.

Rationale: "[T]he characterization, as 'business' or 'personal,' of the litigation costs of resisting a claim depends on whether or not the claim *arises in connection with* the taxpayer's profit-seeking activities. It does not depend on the *consequences* that might result to a taxpayer's income-producing property from a failure to defeat the claim, for * * * that * * * would not be compatible with the basic lines of expense deductibility drawn by Congress. Moreover, such a rule would lead to capricious results. If two taxpayers are each sued for an automobile accident while driving for pleasure, deductibility of their litigation costs would turn on the mere circumstance of the character of the assets each happened to possess, that is, whether the judgments against them stood to be satisfied out of income-or non-income-producing property. We should be slow to attribute to Congress a purpose producing such unequal treatment among taxpayers, resting on no rational foundation. * * *

"[T]he origin and character of the claim with respect to which an expense was incurred, rather than its potential consequences upon the fortunes of the taxpayer, is the controlling basic test of whether the expense was 'business' or 'personal' and hence whether it is deductible or not under [§ 212.] We find the reasoning underlying the cases taking the 'consequences' view unpersuasive.

"In classifying respondent's legal expenses the court below did not distinguish between those relating to the claims of the wife with respect to the *existence* of community property and those involving the *division* of any such property. Nor is such a breakdown necessary for a disposition of the present case. It is enough to say that in both aspects the wife's claims stemmed entirely from the marital relationship, and not, under any tenable view of things, from income-producing activity. This is obviously so as regards the claim to more than an equal division of any community property found to exist. For any such right depended entirely on the wife's making good her charges of marital infidelity on the part of the husband. The same conclusion is no less true respecting the claim relating to the existence of community property. For no such property could have existed but for the marriage relationship."

* * *

Self-Assessment Question

(Solutions to Self–Assessment Questions are set forth in Appendix 3.)

SAQ 9–4. Pam and Tommy divorced. The final divorce decree requires Pam to pay $10,000 monthly to Tommy until he dies or remarries. In consideration of the monthly cash payments, Tommy agrees to relinquish any interest he has in the couple's home video distribution business.

(a) Are Tommy's attorney fees deductible?

(b) Pam's attorney billed her separately for any tax advice given during the course of representation. Are any of Pam's attorney fees deductible?

(c) Suppose the decree requires Pam to pay Tommy's attorney fees. May Pam deduct the payment?

F.   BAD DEBTS AND WORTHLESS SECURITIES

Code: IRC §§ 165(g); 166(a)–(e). *Review* IRC § 165(a), (c).

Regs: Treas. Reg. §§ 1.165–4(a), –5(f); 1.166–2(a)–(c).

When Good Debts Go Bad. If a person owes a debt to a taxpayer and the taxpayer is unable to collect the debt, the taxpayer has undoubtedly suffered a loss in the colloquial sense—funds extended by the taxpayer will not be recovered, so the money is forever lost. But the taxpayer would be entitled to a loss deduction under § 165 only if he or she could prove that the loss was "sustained" in the taxable year. Even where the taxpayer can show that the loss from a bad debt has been sustained, a deduction would only be available if the debt related to the taxpayer's business activities or arose from a transaction entered into for profit. See §§ 165(c)(1)–(2) and discussion at Chapter 4.

Because losses from bad debts are real economic losses to a taxpayer, there is no compelling reason to disallow a deduction, for lending is rarely an act of consumption. Accordingly, § 166 permits a deduction for bad debts, and the deduction is made available to debts arising from business, investment, *and personal* activities. Under § 166, there are two types of bad debts: **business bad debts** (those connected to the taxpayer's trade or business) and **nonbusiness bad debts** (all other debts). Both can be deducted in the year in which they become worthless, but there are two significant limitations with respect to nonbusiness bad debts. First, individual taxpayers can only deduct nonbusiness bad debts where they have become entirely (as opposed to partially) worthless. If a borrower is able to pay a portion (but less than all) of the debt, the taxpayer-lender cannot deduct the worthless portion if the loan is properly classified as a nonbusiness bad debt. This limitation may stem from the premise that if all partially bad debts were deductible, taxpayers might make loans that they do not reasonably expect to be repaid in full.

Second, individual taxpayers must treat losses from entirely worthless nonbusiness bad debts as short-term capital losses. As we saw in Chapter 4, capital losses are less favorable than ordinary losses because capital losses are currently deductible only to the extent of a taxpayer's capital gains plus up to $3,000 of ordinary income. See § 1211(b). By giving the deduction for nonbusiness bad debts a less palatable flavor, perhaps taxpayers will be less likely to loan funds outside of the business context unless they are assured of repayment.

In all cases where a deduction is available for a bad debt, § 166(b) limits the deduction to the taxpayer's basis in the debt. In most cases, that means the deduction is limited to the outstanding amount of the loan. It also means a taxpayer cannot deduct the interest payments that the taxpayer will no longer receive; while there is a deduction for bad debts, no deduction is available for "bad interest."

The foregoing discussion suggests a basic framework for approaching a bad debt deduction under § 166:

(1) Is there a **debt**?

(2) Is it a **bad debt**?

(3) Is it a **business bad debt**?

The first issue is not a significant problem analytically, at least in most cases. Once in a while, however, the issue of whether a taxpayer in fact made a bona fide loan or performed services that created a debt can be tricky.

BUGBEE v. COMMISSIONER

United States Tax Court, 1975.
T.C. Memo. 1975–45.

STERRETT, JUDGE: The respondent determined a deficiency in petitioner's federal income tax for the taxable year 1966 in the amount of $7,242.68. Other issues having been conceded, the sole remaining issue is whether petitioner has established the existence of a debtor-creditor relationship with respect to funds advanced by petitioner to one Paul Billings and thereby validated his claim to a short-term capital loss under sections 166(a) and 166(d), Internal Revenue Code of 1954.

FINDINGS OF FACT

* * *

At all relevant times herein, petitioner was president and majority stockholder of Poop Deck, Inc., a California corporation operating a beer parlor in Hermosa Beach, California. The corporation's other shareholders were petitioner's then spouse Nancy Bugbee and William G. Garbade.

Petitioner first met Paul Billings (hereinafter Billings) at his beer parlor in 1957. Their relationship was first that of proprietor and customer. Over a period of time their friendship grew and they talked of business ventures that Billings might pursue. Billings became godfather to one of petitioner's children.

As a result of their conversations petitioner was impressed with Billings' abilities and thought he could turn his ideas into successful business ventures. Based on this impression, petitioner began to advance money to Billings. These advances were first evidenced by informal notes which were periodically consolidated into larger, more formal notes. There were 11 notes in all representing $19,750 advanced by petitioner to Billings.

These notes were all unconditional, unsecured demand notes signed by Billings between September, 1958 and December, 1960, and evidenced money actually received by Billings from petitioner. The notes provided for interest at a rate of at least 6 percent, however no interest was ever actually paid. Billings has never repaid any part of the principal represented by these notes, although at trial he acknowledged these advances were still outstanding and evidenced an intention to repay them if possible.

During this period when the advances were made Billings was unemployed and he was basically unemployed between 1960 and 1966. Although petitioner knew Billings was unemployed between 1958 and 1960, petitioner neither investigated nor did he have any personal knowledge of Billings' financial position.

Billings used the funds received from the petitioner to investigate various business ventures, although in fact much of the money was used by Billings for personal living expenses.

Petitioner was aware of Billings' activities with respect to these ventures, but he did not participate in them. Petitioner's then spouse, Nancy Bugbee, was also aware that petitioner had advanced funds to Billings. Some of her personal funds represented the source of some of these advances. In 1966 petitioner and his spouse were divorced. In the interlocutory judgment of divorce entered June 23, 1966, by which the rights of the parties were established, no mention of the funds advanced by Nancy Bugbee was made.

Petitioner expected to be repaid after Billings established one of these ventures, but such repayment was not conditioned on the success of any of these ventures. Through 1967 petitioner had periodic personal contact with Billings and requested repayment of the notes without success.

Petitioner, on his 1966 tax return, reported a "Personal Bad Debt– Paul Billings" and claimed a $19,750 short-term capital loss. This loss was used in its entirety to offset long-term capital gain recognized that year from other sources. Respondent disallowed this loss * * *.

　　* * *

OPINION

The case at bar presents for our determination the sole issue of whether petitioner is entitled to claim a short-term capital loss within the terms of sections 166(a) and 166(d) and the accompanying regulations as a result of Billings' failure to repay the funds he had advanced him. Other requirements of these provisions having been previously disposed of, the only remaining factual issue is whether a debtor-creditor relationship existed between Billings and petitioner at the time these advances were made.

To qualify under section 166 there first must exist a bona fide debt which arises from a debtor-creditor relationship based upon a valid and enforceable obligation to pay a fixed and determinable sum of money. Section 1.166–1(c), Income Tax Regs. "Whether a transfer of money creates a bona fide debt depends upon the existence of an intent by both parties, substantially contemporaneous to the time of such transfer, to establish an enforceable obligation of repayment". *Delta Plastics Corp.*, 54 T.C. 1287, 1291 (1970). This determination then is a question of fact to which the substance and not the form of the relationship between petitioner and Billings must be applied. *Delta Plastics Corp., supra.*

Looking beyond the formal relationship between the petitioner and Billings, respondent has pointed out several factors that he believes amply illustrate his position. Respondent first argues that in reality these advances represented the money necessary to investigate prospective business ventures in which both men would share in the potential profits and as such do not represent loans.

Petitioner's testimony with respect to this matter is not entirely clear. At one point he stated that, if any of these ventures materialized, he "would be a part of it." Later, he stated that, although he expected to be repaid after one of these ventures was established, these advances were personal loans to Billings and that they were to be repaid from whatever sources Billings might have. Billings' testimony is more direct. He clearly stated that these advances were for his personal business ventures and that petitioner was not involved in them. Billings also acknowledged liability for these advances and evidenced an intention to repay if possible. There is also no indication in the record of an agreement under which petitioner would be entitled to share in the profits of any of these ventures. We reject this contention of the respondent.

Respondent next argues that bona fide debts never existed since these advances were worthless when made and petitioner did not have a reasonable expectation that they would be repaid. In support respondent points out that during this period Billings was unemployed and had no independent means of support, that the loans were unsecured, that despite the failure of Billings to make interest payments on the first notes additional funds were advanced, that the nature of Billings' proposed ventures was purely speculative, and that petitioner never sought repayment in court.

Respondent does not question the wisdom of these advances. Anyway that determination could only be made with the use of hindsight, which in this instance is not an appropriate tool. As noted earlier our task is to determine the intent of the parties as it existed when the advances were made.

The record in this case does indicate that Billings was in poor financial condition when these advances were made. However this Court has said that this factor does not preclude a finding of the existence of a bona fide debt. The use of unsecured notes reflects the nature of the risk involved that petitioner accepted. Any unsecured debt involves some risk, however this factor is not determinative.

This Court has said, "For the advance to be a loan, it is not necessary that there be an unqualified expectation of repayment." In the final analysis the repayment of any loan depends on the success of the borrower. "The real differences lie in the debt-creating intention of the parties, and the genuineness of repayment prospects in the light of economic realities[.]"

We have found that petitioner made these advances because he believed Billings could be successful and that he would be subsequently repaid. After a careful review of the record, we believe petitioner's motives were genuine and that they existed throughout the period during which these advances were made.

Respondent maintains that, since Billings was in poor financial condition, in reality any repayment was conditioned on Billings' business success and, since that condition was never fulfilled, there never was an enforceable repayment obligation. For support respondent cites *Zimmerman v. United States*, 318 F. 2d 611 (9th Cir. 1963). In that case the taxpayer advanced money to an organization he was initiating. Repayment was to be made out of the dues collected from the members of this new organization. The organization faltered and the taxpayer was not repaid. The court held that the contingent nature of the repayment obligation alone precluded the finding of a bona fide debt. * * *

The facts in the case at bar do not reveal that any repayments by Billings were conditioned on his ultimate success. Although petitioner expected to be repaid after Billings had established one of his ventures, we have found that petitioner was to be repaid from any assets that Billings might have. Billings himself testified that these advances were personal, unconditional loans for which he was liable.

Respondent finally argues that, since petitioner and Billings were close personal friends, these advances might be classified as gifts. Although the parties were friends, their relationship did not have a long history. There also was no blood relationship, although Billings was named godfather to one of the Bugbee children.

Although the record does not indicate petitioner's financial condition during the period 1958–1960, the divorce decree issued in 1966 only describes assets of moderate value. We do not believe that petitioner's financial condition was such that he could make these advances without expectation of repayment. The facts do not support respondent's contention that these advances were gifts. *Commissioner v. Duberstein, 363 U.S. 278 (1960).*

We believe that petitioner has established the existence of a debtor-creditor relationship and that respondent's determination must be denied.

Decision will be entered under Rule 155.

* * *

If there is a bona fide debt, the next issue is whether the debt has become worthless. The regulations give some guidance on this issue, stating that "all pertinent evidence" will be considered. Treas. Reg. § 1.166–2(a). Logically, when a debtor goes bankrupt, such bankruptcy "is an indication of the worthlessness of at least a part of an unsecured and unpreferred debt." Treas. Reg. § 1.166–2(c)(1). Fortunately, the taxpayer need not commence litigation against the debtor, obtain a judgment, and then fail to collect on the judgment in order to claim the § 166 deduction. If the taxpayer can show (if asked) that such action would be futile because the debt is uncollectible, the deduction may be claimed. Treas. Reg. § 1.166–2(b).

Finally, assuming a bona fide debt has become worthless, the taxpayer must determine whether he or she is entitled to an ordinary deduction for a business bad debt or a short-term capital loss for a nonbusiness bad debt. Of course, taxpayers want the debt to be classified as a business bad debt in order to secure the better flavor for the deduction (to say nothing of the ability to deduct a debt that is only partially worthless), just like the taxpayer in the following case.

WHIPPLE v. COMMISSIONER

United States Supreme Court, 1963.
373 U.S. 193, 83 S.Ct. 1168, 10 L.Ed.2d 288.

MR. JUSTICE WHITE delivered the opinion of the Court.

* * * The question before us is whether petitioner's activities in connection with several corporations in which he holds controlling interests can themselves be characterized as a trade or business so as to permit a debt owed by one of the corporations to him to be treated * * * as a "business" rather than a "nonbusiness" bad debt.

Prior to 1941 petitioner was a construction superintendent and an estimator for a lumber company but during that year and over the next several ones he was instrumental in forming and was a member of a series of partnerships engaged in the construction or construction supply business. In 1949 and 1950 he was an original incorporator of seven corporations, some of which were successors to the partnerships, and in 1951 he sold his interest in the corporations along with his equity in five others in the rental and construction business, the profit on the sales being reported as long-term capital gains. In 1951 and 1952 he formed eight new corporations, one of which was Mission Orange Bottling Co. of Lubbock, Inc. * * *.

On April 25, 1951, petitioner secured a franchise from Mission Dry Corporation entitling him to produce, bottle, distribute and sell Mission beverages in various counties in Texas. Two days later he purchased the assets of a sole proprietorship in the bottling business and conducted that business pursuant to his franchise as a sole proprietorship. On July 1, 1951, though retaining the franchise in his own name, he sold the bottling equipment to Mission Orange Bottling Co. of Lubbock, Inc., a corporation organized by petitioner as mentioned, of which he owned approximately 80% of the shares outstanding. In 1952 he purchased land in Lubbock and erected a bottling plant thereon at a cost of $43,601 and then leased the plant to Mission Orange for a 10–year term at a prescribed rental. Depreciation was taken on the new bottling plant on petitioner's individual tax returns for 1952 and 1953.

Petitioner made sizable cash advances to Mission Orange in 1952 and 1953, and on December 1, 1953, the balance due him, including $25,502.50 still owing from his sale of the bottling assets to the corporation in July 1951, totaled $79,489.76. On December 15, 1953, petitioner advanced to Mission Orange an additional $48,000 to pay general creditors and on the same day received a transfer of the assets of the corporation with a book value of $70,414.66. The net amount owing to petitioner ultimately totaled $56,975.10, which debt became worthless in 1953 and is in issue here. During 1951, 1952 and 1953 Mission Orange made no payments of interest, rent or salary to petitioner although he did receive such income from some of his other corporations.

Petitioner deducted the $56,975.10 debt due from Mission Orange as a business bad debt in computing his 1953 taxable income. The Commissioner, claiming the debt was a nonbusiness bad debt, assessed deficiencies. The Tax Court, after determining that petitioner in 1953 was not in the business of organizing, promoting, managing or financing corporations, of bottling soft drinks or of general financing and money lending, sustained the deficiencies. A divided Court of Appeals affirmed, and upon a claim of conflict among the Courts of Appeals, we granted certiorari.

I.

The concept of engaging in a trade or business as distinguished from other activities pursued for profit is not new to the tax laws. As early as 1916, Congress, by providing for the deduction of losses incurred in a trade or business separately from those sustained in other transactions entered into for profit, distinguished the broad range of income or profit producing activities from those satisfying the narrow category of trade or business. This pattern has been followed elsewhere in the Code. * * * It is not surprising, therefore, that we approach the problem of applying that term here with much writing upon the slate.

* * *

* * * [T]o remedy what it deemed the abuses of permitting any worthless debt to be fully deducted, as was the case prior to this time, see H. R. Rep. No. 2333, 77th Cong., 2d Sess. 45, Congress restricted the

full deduction under [§ 166] to bad debts incurred in the taxpayer's trade or business and provided that "nonbusiness" bad debts were to be deducted as short-term capital losses. Congress deliberately used the words "trade or business," terminology familiar to the tax laws, and the respective committees made it clear that the test of whether a debt is incurred in a trade or business "is substantially the same as that which is made for the purpose of ascertaining whether a loss from the type of transaction covered by section [165(c)] is 'incurred in trade or business' under paragraph (1) of that section." H. R. Rep. No. 2333, 77th Cong., 2d Sess. 76–77; S. Rep. No. 1631, 77th Cong., 2d Sess. 90. * * *

The 1942 amendment of [§ 166], therefore, as the Court has already noted, *Putnam v. Commissioner*, 352 U.S. 82, 90–92, was intended to accomplish far more than to deny full deductibility to the worthless debts of family and friends. It was designed to make full deductibility of a bad debt turn upon its proximate connection with activities which the tax laws recognized as a trade or business, a concept which falls far short of reaching every income or profit making activity.

II.

Petitioner, therefore, must demonstrate that he is engaged in a trade or business, and lying at the heart of his claim is the issue upon which the lower courts have divided and which brought the case here: That where a taxpayer furnishes regular services to one or many corporations, an independent trade or business of the taxpayer has been shown. But against the background of the 1942 amendments and the decisions of this Court * * *, petitioner's claim must be rejected. Devoting one's time and energies to the affairs of a corporation is not of itself, and without more, a trade or business of the person so engaged. Though such activities may produce income, profit or gain in the form of dividends or enhancement in the value of an investment, this return is distinctive to the process of investing and is generated by the successful operation of the corporation's business as distinguished from the trade or business of the taxpayer himself. When the only return is that of an investor, the taxpayer has not satisfied his burden of demonstrating that he is engaged in a trade or business since investing is not a trade or business and the return to the taxpayer, though substantially the product of his services, legally arises not from his own trade or business but from that of the corporation. Even if the taxpayer demonstrates an independent trade or business of his own, care must be taken to distinguish bad debt losses arising from his own business and those actually arising from activities peculiar to an investor concerned with, and participating in, the conduct of the corporate business. If full-time service to one corporation does not alone amount to a trade or business, which it does not, it is difficult to understand how the same service to many corporations would suffice. To be sure, the presence of more than one corporation might lend support to a finding that the taxpayer was engaged in a regular course of promoting corporations for a fee or commission or for a profit on their sale, but in such cases there is compensation other than the normal investor's return, income received directly for his own services rather than indirectly through the corporate enterprise * * *. On the other hand, since the Tax Court found, and the petitioner does not dispute, that there was no intention here of developing the corporations as going businesses for sale to customers in the ordinary course, the case before us inexorably rests upon the claim that one who actively engages in serving his own corporations for the purpose of creating future income through those enterprises is in a trade or business. That argument is untenable * * * and we reject it. Absent substantial additional evidence, furnishing management and other services to corporations for a reward not different from that flowing to an investor in those corporations is not a trade or business * * *. We are, therefore, fully in agreement with this aspect of the decision below.

III.

With respect to the other claims by petitioner, we are unwilling to disturb the determinations of the Tax Court, affirmed by the Court of Appeals, that petitioner was not engaged in the business of money lending, of financing corporations, of bottling soft drinks or of any combination of these since we cannot say they are clearly erroneous. Nor need we consider or deal with those cases which hold that working as a corporate executive for a salary may be a trade or business. Petitioner made no such claim in either the Tax Court or the Court of Appeals and, in any event, the contention would be groundless on this record since it was not shown that he has collected a salary from Mission Orange or that he was owed one. Moreover, there is no proof (which might be difficult to furnish where the taxpayer is the sole or dominant stockholder) that the loan was necessary to keep his job or was otherwise proximately related to maintaining his trade or business as an employee.

We are more concerned, however, with the evidence as to petitioner's position as the owner and lessor of the real estate and bottling plant in which Mission Orange did business. The United States does not dispute the fact that in this regard petitioner was engaged in a trade or business but argues that the loss from the worthless debt was not proximately related to petitioner's real estate business. While the Tax Court and the Court of Appeals dealt separately with assertions relating to other phases of petitioner's case, we do not find that either court disposed of the possibility that the loan to Mission Orange, a tenant of petitioner, was incurred in petitioner's business of being a landlord. We take no position whatsoever on the merits of this matter but remand the case for further proceedings in the Tax Court.

Vacated and remanded.

Mr. Justice Douglas dissents.

* * *

Worthless Securities. Acting on a stock tip from Slim Shady, John Q. Taxpayer purchased 100 shares of stock in a new public corporation.

In just a few short months, the stock became completely worthless as the corporation dissolved. Because John Q. Taxpayer never sold or otherwise disposed of the stock, however, a deduction under § 165(c)(2) would probably not be proper because John Q. Taxpayer never "sustained" a loss. The stock is not a "debt," so § 166 would not apply either.

In this case, § 165(g)(1) would permit a loss deduction because the corporation's stock had become completely worthless, but the deduction would be flavored as a capital loss if John Q. Taxpayer had held the stock as a capital asset. This is because § 165(g)(1) creates a deemed sale or exchange of the worthless stock for no consideration. If the stock had merely declined in value but was not worthless, John Q. Taxpayer would not be entitled to any deduction—no taxpayer gets a deduction when a stock (or any other asset) simply declines in value. See Treas. Reg. §§ 1.165–4(a) and 1.165–5(f).

The § 165(g)(1) deduction applies not only to stocks that become worthless but also to rights to subscribe for or to receive shares of stock. It also applies to "a bond, debenture, note, or certificate, *or other evidence of indebtedness*, issued by a corporation or by a government or political subdivision thereof. ..." Section 165(g)(2)(C) (emphasis added). So if a corporate debt instrument becomes worthless, § 165(g)(1) can apply. But a taxpayer's basis in worthless corporate debt instruments would also be deductible under § 166. It might make a difference whether the taxpayer uses § 165(g)(1) or § 166 for the deduction. If the taxpayer held the corporate debt as an investment for more than one year before it became worthless, § 165(g)(1) would authorize a long-term capital loss and § 166 would authorize a short-term capital loss. Where both § 165 and § 166 apply to authorize a deduction for a bad debt, the Supreme Court has stated that § 166 should govern, given it is specifically targeted at bad debts. See *Spring City Foundry Co. v. Commissioner*, 292 U.S. 182 (1934).

* * *

Self-Assessment Question

(Solutions to Self–Assessment Questions are set forth in Appendix 3.)

SAQ 9–5. Ben Dover loaned $10,000 to his sister, Eileen Dover, in Year One. In Year Two, Eileen declared bankruptcy, leaving Ben unable to collect the debt.

(a) What are the federal income tax consequences to Ben?

(b) What are the federal income tax consequences to Eileen?

* * *

Problem 9–10

Late in Year One, Carrie Doff, a consultant, performed services worth $5,000 for a client. Carrie sent the client a bill for $5,000 at the end of Year

One. The client never paid for the services, and in Year Two Carrie reasonably concluded that the client would never pay for the services Carrie provided. May Carrie claim a deduction under § 166 in Year Two?

Problem 9–11

Sam Malone owns and operates a local tavern. In Year One, Sam extended $10,000 in credit to one of his best customers, Norm Peterson. In Year Two, Norm's debt to Sam became wholly worthless, so Sam claimed a $10,000 deduction under § 166 in Year Two. In Year Three, Norm inherited a substantial amount from his spouse's estate. Norm paid $10,000 to Sam later that year. What are the tax consequences of the Year Three payment to Sam?

* * *

Chapter 10

DUAL-PURPOSE EXPENSES

---

p. 686-689
Prob. 10-1

This Chapter concerns a number of expenses that transcend the usual boundaries between business, investment, and personal activities. Suppose a taxpayer travels to Las Vegas. If the trip is treated as purely a business venture because the taxpayer attends a business convention there, then the expenses incurred in attending the convention (transportation, lodging, meals, conference fees, and the like) probably would be deductible at least to some extent under § 162(a) as ordinary and necessary business expenses. But if the trip is purely for personal pleasure, the costs would be considered non-deductible personal expenses. See § 262. Yet it is just as likely that the trip involves both business and pleasure activities. How should such dual-purpose expenses be treated for federal income tax purposes?

Theoretically, there are a number of possibilities. A deduction for the expenses could be disallowed entirely on the grounds that the pleasure element of the trip outweighs any business element. We will see in Part F of this Chapter that this approach is used to deny deductions for clothing expenses under § 162(a) where the clothing is suitable for ordinary wear.

Alternatively, the taxpayer could be allowed to deduct all of the expenses provided the primary purpose of the trip was for business and not for pleasure. We will see that this is in fact the standard used for determining the deductibility of transportation expenses where both business and pleasure elements are present. Where the primary purpose of the trip is for business and not for pleasure, all of a taxpayer's costs for airfare and other transportation expenses are deductible.

A third approach would be to allocate the costs between the business and pleasure elements of the trip, providing a deduction for costs allocated to the business elements and denying a deduction for costs allocated to the pleasure elements. We will see that this approach is used with respect to lodging and meal expenses, for instance.

Finally, a taxpayer could be allowed to deduct a cost only to the extent it exceeds what a taxpayer would normally pay when business elements are not present. While this approach may be the most logically consistent with a pure income tax, it often proves difficult to administer in practice. We will see instances where judges and commentators argue for a deduction to the extent the taxpayer suffers an excessive cost, but more often these arguments get lost in the wind.

What makes this Chapter somewhat complex is that all of the first three theories (disallowance, allowance, and partial allowance) are employed, and one cannot always predict which theory will be employed for a given expense item. Part A of this Chapter considers travel costs, including commuting expenses as well as transportation expenses incurred while away from home in pursuit of business. In Part B we consider the deductibility of entertainment costs and business meals (or, more rhythmically, the costs to wine, dine, and show a good time). Part C of this Chapter considers the deductibility of job-seeking expenses and the costs to move to a new location to commence work. In Part D, we look at the deductibility of education costs (including law school costs!) as business expenses under § 162(a) (but don't get your hopes up). Finally, Part E briefly examines costs related to maintaining a home office or a vacation home, and Part F considers the deduction for clothing expenses required as part of a taxpayer's employment.

A. TRAVEL

Code: IRC §§ 162(a)(2); 274(c), (m)(3)–(n). *Skim* IRC § 274(d).

Regs: Treas. Reg. §§ 1.162–2(b), –2(e).

Section 162(a)(2) permits a deduction for "traveling expenses" so long as the taxpayer is "away from home" and "in the pursuit of a trade or business." Traveling expenses typically include costs for transportation, lodging and meals. Thus, in seeking to deduct these costs, taxpayers must first determine whether they were incurred "away from home." If so, then § 162(a)(2) provides specific authority for the deduction. If not, then a deduction is unlikely.

Commuting Expenses. The most common transportation expense for most taxpayers is the cost to commute from home to work and back again, whether by car, train, bus, taxi, or covered wagon. But is a taxpayer "away from home" when commuting to and from work? The Supreme Court considered this issue in the following case.

COMMISSIONER v. FLOWERS, 326 U.S. 465, 66 S.Ct. 250, 90 L.Ed. 203 (1946).

Facts: The taxpayer resided in Jackson, Mississippi. When he was offered a job by a company whose main office was in Mobile, Alabama (185 miles from Jackson), he wanted to accept but was unwilling to move to Mobile. The taxpayer arranged with his employer to stay in Jackson on the condition that he pay his own traveling expenses between Mobile and Jackson and his own living expenses in both places. The taxpayer deducted amounts incurred to travel between Jackson and Mobile as traveling expenses under the predecessor to § 162(a)(2).

Issue: May the taxpayer deduct the costs incurred to travel between Jackson and Mobile?

Holding: No.

Rationale: "The facts demonstrate clearly that the expenses were not incurred in the pursuit of the business of the taxpayer's employer * * *. Jackson was his regular home. Had his post of duty been in that city the cost of maintaining his home there and of commuting or driving to work concededly would be non-deductible living and personal expenses lacking the necessary direct relation to the prosecution of the business. The character of such expenses is unaltered by the circumstance that the taxpayer's post of duty was in Mobile, thereby increasing the costs of transportation, food and lodging. Whether he maintained one abode or two, whether he traveled three blocks or three hundred miles to work, the nature of these expenditures remained the same.

"The added costs in issue, moreover, were as unnecessary and inappropriate to the development of the [employer's] business as were his personal and living costs in Jackson. They were incurred solely as the result of the taxpayer's desire to maintain a home in Jackson while working in Mobile, a factor irrelevant to the maintenance and prosecution of the [employer's] legal business. The [employer] did not require him to travel on business from Jackson to Mobile or to maintain living quarters in both cities. Nor did it compel him, save in one instance, to perform tasks for it in Jackson. It simply asked him to be at his principal post in Mobile as business demanded and as his personal convenience was served, allowing him to divide his business time between Mobile and Jackson as he saw fit. * * * The fact that he traveled frequently between the two cities and incurred extra living expenses in Mobile, while doing much of his work in Jackson, was occasioned solely by his personal propensities. The [employer] gained nothing from this arrangement except the personal satisfaction of the taxpayer.

"Travel expenses in pursuit of business within the meaning of § [162(a)(2)] could arise only when the [employer's] business forced the taxpayer to travel and to live temporarily at some place other than Mobile, thereby advancing the interests of the [employer]. Business trips are to be identified in relation to business demands and the traveler's business headquarters. The exigencies of business rather than the personal conveniences and necessities of the traveler must be the motivating factors. Such was not the case here."

* * *

Regulations confirm the rule from *Flowers*. See Treas. Reg. §§ 1.162–2(e) and 1.262–1(b)(5). The theory is that commuting is necessarily a personal expense, as one chooses where to live in relation to work. That theory does not hold true for all taxpayers, of course, but courts are generally unwilling to permit a deduction even where a taxpayer has little choice but to commute great distances. In *Sanders v. Commissioner*, 439 F.2d 296 (9th Cir. 1971), for instance, civilian employees of contractors with work sites on an Air Force base were not allowed to deduct their commuting costs even though only military personnel could reside on the base. The Ninth Circuit specifically noted its agreement with the Tax Court by quoting language from the lower court's opinion:

> There is no convincing way to distinguish the expenses here from those of suburban commuters. Petitioner's hardships are no different than those confronting the many taxpayers who cannot find suitable housing close to their urban place of employment and must daily commute to work. We see no reason why petitioners in the case at bar should receive more favored tax treatment than their urban counterparts who also cannot live near their worksites.

439 F.2d at 299.

Though the law on this point is clear, taxpayers routinely try to deduct commuting costs and will even undergo litigation to make their cases. In *Knelman v. Commissioner*, T.C. Memo. 2000–268, the taxpayers operated a landscaping business as sole proprietors in Southern California in the 1980s. In 1991, they decided to move to Ohio, but they also decided to keep operating the California landscaping business. Every month, one of the taxpayers traveled to California to work on the business. On average, each trip to California lasted 14 days. The taxpayers deducted (among other things) the costs of commuting from Ohio to California and back as business expenses. The Service disallowed the deduction and both the Tax Court and Ninth Circuit agreed with the disallowance. The fact that the taxpayers traveled two time zones from home to work did not change the fact that the costs were non-deductible commuting expenses.

While commuting costs are not deductible, transportation costs to travel between work locations is clearly deductible, as there is no element of personal pleasure or choice in traveling between work sites. And it almost always has been the case that travel costs from a taxpayer's residence to a *temporary* work location can be deductible. In the following ruling, the Service attempts to furnish comprehensive guidance by distinguishing non-deductible commuting expenses from deductible travel expenses involving temporary work locations and travel between job sites.

REVENUE RULING 99–7

1999–1 C.B. 361.

ISSUE

Under what circumstances are daily transportation expenses incurred by a taxpayer in going between the taxpayer's residence and a work location deductible under § 162(a) of the Internal Revenue Code?

LAW AND ANALYSIS

Section 162(a) allows a deduction for all the ordinary and necessary expenses paid or incurred during the taxable year in carrying on any trade or business. Section 262, however, provides that no deduction is allowed for personal, living, or family expenses.

A taxpayer's costs of commuting between the taxpayer's residence and the taxpayer's place of business or employment generally are nondeductible personal expenses under §§ 1.162–2(e) and 1.262–1(b)(5) of the Income Tax Regulations. However, the costs of going between one business location and another business location generally are deductible under § 162(a). *Rev. Rul. 55–109*, 1955–1 C.B. 261.

Section 280A(c)(1)(A) (as amended by § 932 of the Taxpayer Relief Act of 1997, Pub. L. No. 105–34, 111 Stat. 881, effective for taxable years beginning after December 31, 1998) provides, in part, that a taxpayer may deduct expenses for the business use of the portion of the taxpayer's personal residence that is exclusively used on a regular basis as the principal place of business for any trade or business of the taxpayer. (In the case of an employee, however, such expenses are deductible only if the exclusive and regular use of the portion of the residence is for the convenience of the employer.) In *Curphey v. Commissioner*, 73 T.C. 766 (1980), the Tax Court held that daily transportation expenses incurred in going between an office in a taxpayer's residence and other work locations were deductible where the home office was the taxpayer's principal place of business within the meaning of § 280A(c)(1)(A) for the trade or business conducted by the taxpayer at those other work locations. The court stated that "we see no reason why the rule that local transportation expenses incurred in travel between one business location and another are deductible should not be equally applicable where the taxpayer's principal place of business with respect to the activities involved is his residence." Implicit in the court's analysis in *Curphey* is that the deductibility of daily transportation expenses is determined on a business-by-business basis.

Rev. Rul. 190, 1953–2 C.B. 303, provides a limited exception to the general rule that the expenses of going between a taxpayer's residence and a work location are nondeductible commuting expenses. *Rev. Rul. 190* deals with a taxpayer who lives and ordinarily works in a particular metropolitan area but who is not regularly employed at any specific work location. In such a case, the general rule is that daily transportation expenses are not deductible when paid or incurred by the taxpayer in going between the taxpayer's residence and a temporary work site inside that metropolitan area because that area is considered the taxpayer's regular place of business. However, *Rev. Rul. 190* holds that daily transportation expenses are deductible business expenses when paid or incurred in going between the taxpayer's residence and a temporary work site outside that metropolitan area.

Rev. Rul. 90–23, 1990–1 C.B. 28, distinguishes *Rev. Rul. 190* and holds, in part, that, for a taxpayer who has one or more regular places of business, daily transportation expenses paid or incurred in going between the taxpayer's residence and temporary work locations are deductible business expenses under § 162(a), regardless of the distance.

Rev. Rul. 94–47, 1994–2 C.B. 18, amplifies and clarifies *Rev. Rul. 190* and *Rev. Rul. 90–23*, and provides several rules for determining whether daily transportation expenses are deductible business expenses under § 162(a). Under *Rev. Rul. 94–47*, a taxpayer generally may not deduct daily transportation expenses incurred in going between the taxpayer's residence and a work location. A taxpayer, however, may deduct daily transportation expenses incurred in going between the taxpayer's residence and a temporary work location outside the metropolitan area where the taxpayer lives and normally works. In addition, *Rev. Rul. 94–47* clarifies *Rev. Rul. 90–23* to provide that a taxpayer must have at least one regular place of business located "away from the taxpayer's residence" in order to deduct daily transportation expenses incurred in going between the taxpayer's residence and a temporary work location in the same trade or business, regardless of the distance. In this regard, *Rev. Rul. 94–47* also states that the Service will not follow the decision in *Walker v. Commissioner*, 101 T.C. 537 (1993). Finally, *Rev. Rul. 94–47* amplifies *Rev. Rul. 190* and *Rev. Rul. 90–23* to provide that, if the taxpayer's residence is the taxpayer's principal place of business within the meaning of § 280A(c)(1)(A), the taxpayer may deduct daily transportation expenses incurred in going between the taxpayer's residence and another work location in the same trade or business, regardless of whether the other work location is regular or temporary and regardless of the distance.

For purposes of both *Rev. Rul. 90–23* and *Rev. Rul. 94–47*, a temporary work location is defined as any location at which the taxpayer performs services on an irregular or short-term (i.e., generally a matter of days or weeks) basis. However, for purposes of determining whether daily transportation expense allowances and per diem travel allowances for meal and lodging expenses are subject to income tax withholding under § 3402, *Rev. Rul. 59–371*, 1959–2 C.B. 236, provides a 1–year standard to determine whether a work location is temporary. Similarly, for purposes of determining the deductibility of travel away-from-home expenses under § 162(a)(2), *Rev. Rul. 93–86*, 1993–2 C.B. 71, generally provides a 1–year standard to determine whether a work location will be treated as temporary.

The Service has reconsidered the definition of a temporary work location in *Rev. Rul. 90–23* and *Rev. Rul. 94–47*, and will replace the "irregular or short-term (i.e., generally a matter of days or weeks) basis" standard in those rulings with a 1–year standard similar to the rules set forth in *Rev. Rul. 59–371* and *Rev. Rul. 93–86*.

If an office in the taxpayer's residence satisfies the principal place of business requirements of § 280A(c)(1)(A), then the residence is considered a business location for purposes of *Rev. Rul. 90–23* or *Rev. Rul. 94–47*. In these circumstances, the daily transportation expenses incurred in going between the residence and other work locations in the same trade or business are ordinary and necessary business expenses (deductible under § 162(a)). See *Curphey*; see also *Wisconsin Psychiatric Services v. Commissioner*, 76 T.C. 839 (1981). In contrast, if an office in the taxpayer's residence does not satisfy the principal place of business requirements of § 280A(c)(1)(A), then the business activity there (if any) is not sufficient to overcome the inherently personal nature of the residence and the daily transportation expenses incurred in going between the residence and regular work locations. In these circumstances, the residence is not considered a business location for purposes of *Rev. Rul. 90–23* or *Rev. Rul. 94–47*, and the daily transportation expenses incurred in going between the residence and regular work locations are personal expenses (nondeductible under §§ 1.162–2(e) and 1.262–1(b)(5)). See *Green v. Commissioner*, 59 T.C. 456 (1972); *Fryer v. Commissioner*, T.C. M. 1974–77.

For purposes of determining the deductibility of travel-away-from-home expenses under § 162(a)(2), *Rev. Rul. 93–86* defines "home" as the "taxpayer's regular or principal (if more than one regular) place of business." See *Daly v. Commissioner*, 72 T.C. 190 (1979), aff'd, 662 F.2d 253 (4th Cir. 1981); *Commissioner v. Flowers*, 326 U.S. 465 (1946), 1946–1 C.B. 57.

Holding

In general, daily transportation expenses incurred in going between a taxpayer's residence and a work location are nondeductible commuting expenses. However, such expenses are deductible under the circumstances described in paragraph (1), (2), or (3) below.

(1) A taxpayer may deduct daily transportation expenses incurred in going between the taxpayer's residence and a temporary work location outside the metropolitan area where the taxpayer lives and normally works. However, unless paragraph (2) or (3) below applies, daily transportation expenses incurred in going between the taxpayer's residence and a temporary work location within that metropolitan area are nondeductible commuting expenses.

(2) If a taxpayer has one or more regular work locations away from the taxpayer's residence, the taxpayer may deduct daily transportation expenses incurred in going between the taxpayer's residence and a temporary work location in the same trade or business, regardless of the distance. (The Service will continue not to follow the *Walker* decision.)

(3) If a taxpayer's residence is the taxpayer's principal place of business within the meaning of § 280A(c)(1)(A), the taxpayer may deduct daily transportation expenses incurred in going between the residence and another work location in the same trade or business, regardless of whether the other work location is regular or temporary and regardless of the distance.

For purposes of paragraphs (1), (2), and (3), the following rules apply in determining whether a work location is temporary. If employment at a work location is realistically expected to last (and does in fact last) for 1 year or less, the employment is temporary in the absence of facts and circumstances indicating otherwise. If employment at a work location is realistically expected to last for more than 1 year or there is no realistic expectation that the employment will last for 1 year or less, the employment is not temporary, regardless of whether it actually exceeds 1 year. If employment at a work location initially is realistically expected to last for 1 year or less, but at some later date the employment is realistically expected to exceed 1 year, that employment will be treated as temporary (in the absence of facts and circumstances indicating otherwise) until the date that the taxpayer's realistic expectation changes, and will be treated as not temporary after that date.

The determination that a taxpayer's residence is the taxpayer's principal place of business within the meaning of § 280A(c)(1)(A) is not necessarily determinative of whether the residence is the taxpayer's tax home for other purposes, including the travel-away-from-home deduction under § 162(a)(2).

* * *

* * *

Self-Assessment Question

(Solutions to Self–Assessment Questions are set forth in Appendix 3.)

SAQ 10–1. Tom Tuttle is a lawyer who lives in Tacoma, Washington. Tom is a partner at a Seattle, Washington, law firm located 30 miles from Tacoma.

(a) Last Monday, Tom left his house at 6:00 a.m. and drove directly to the courthouse in Olympia, Washington, to argue a case. Olympia is located 25 miles south of Tacoma. At noon, Tom drove from the courthouse to his office in Seattle (a total of 55 miles) to work on other client files. At 10:00 p.m., Tom finally drove home. Ah, the life of a litigator. To what extent can Tom deduct these transportation expenses?

(b) Last Thursday, Tom left his house at 5:00 a.m. and drove 120 miles to Portland, Oregon, to meet with a client at the client's office. At 10:00 a.m., Tom then drove 150 miles to his Seattle office to work on other client files. At 2:30 p.m., Tom drove 55 miles to Olympia to file documents at the courthouse. At 4:00 p.m., Tom drove 25 miles back to his Tacoma home. To what extent can Tom deduct these transportation expenses?

* * *

Flowers makes clear that § 162(a)(2) does not allow a deduction for commuting expenses, but other traveling expenses incurred "away from home" are deductible if the taxpayer is in pursuit of a trade or business. Again, traveling expenses deductible under § 162(a)(2) include transportation, lodging, and even meals, subject to limitations discussed below.

The "away from home" element contains two definitional issues: the meaning of "away" and the meaning of "home." Now everyone knows where his or her home is, and everyone also knows when her or she is away from it. But the tax definitions of these terms are slightly different than the colloquial definitions. The following cases explain the tax meaning of these terms. Logically enough, the first case explains what the Code means by "away," and the second case gives insight into the construction of "home."

UNITED STATES v. CORRELL

United States Supreme Court, 1967.
389 U.S. 299, 88 S.Ct. 445, 19 L.Ed.2d 537.

Mr. Justice Stewart delivered the opinion of the Court.

The Commissioner of Internal Revenue has long maintained that a taxpayer traveling on business may deduct the cost of his meals only if his trip requires him to stop for sleep or rest. The question presented here is the validity of that rule.

The respondent in this case was a traveling salesman for a wholesale grocery company in Tennessee. He customarily left home early in the morning, ate breakfast and lunch on the road, and returned home in time for dinner. In his income tax returns for 1960 and 1961, he deducted the cost of his morning and noon meals as "traveling expenses" incurred in the pursuit of his business "while away from home" under § 162(a)(2) of the Internal Revenue Code of 1954. Because the respondent's daily trips required neither sleep nor rest, the Commissioner disallowed the deductions, ruling that the cost of the respondent's meals was a "personal, living" expense under 262 rather than a travel expense under § 162(a)(2). The respondent paid the tax, sued for a refund in the District Court, and there received a favorable jury verdict. The Court of Appeals for the Sixth Circuit affirmed, holding that the Commissioner's sleep or rest rule is not "a valid regulation under the present statute." In order to resolve a conflict among the circuits on this recurring question of federal income tax administration, we granted certiorari.

Under § 162(a)(2), taxpayers "traveling * * * away from home in the pursuit of a trade or business" may deduct the total amount "expended for meals and lodging."[6] As a result, even the taxpayer who incurs substantial hotel and restaurant expenses because of the special demands of business travel receives something of a windfall, for at least part of what he spends on meals represents a personal living expense that other taxpayers must bear without receiving any deduction at all.[7]

---

6. Prior to the enactment in 1921 of what is now § 162(a)(2), the Commissioner had promulgated a regulation allowing a deduction for the cost of meals and lodging away from home, but only to the extent that this cost exceeded "any expenditures ordinarily required for such purposes when at home." Treas. Reg. 45 (1920 ed.), Art. 292, 4 Cum. Bull. 209 (1921). Despite its logical appeal, the regulation proved so difficult to administer that the Treasury Department asked Congress to grant a deduction for the "entire amount" of such meal

and lodging expenditures. See Statement of Dr. T. S. Adams, Tax Adviser, Treasury Department, in Hearings on H.R. 8245 before the Senate Committee on Finance, 67th Cong., 1st Sess., at 50, 234–235 (1921). Accordingly, § 214(a)(1) of the Revenue Act of 1921, c. 136, 42 Stat. 239, for the first time included the language that later became § 162(a)(2). The section was amended in a respect not here relevant by the Revenue Act of 1962, s 4(b), 76 Stat. 976.

7. Because § 262 makes "personal, living, or family expenses" nondeductible, the

Not surprisingly, therefore, Congress did not extend the special benefits of § 162(a)(2) to every conceivable situation involving business travel. It made the total cost of meals and lodging deductible only if incurred in the course of travel that takes the taxpayer "away from home." The problem before us involves the meaning of that limiting phrase.

In resolving that problem, the Commissioner has avoided the wasteful litigation and continuing uncertainty that would inevitably accompany any purely case-by-case approach to the question of whether a particular taxpayer was "away from home" on a particular day. Rather than requiring "every meal-purchasing taxpayer to take pot luck in the courts," the Commissioner has consistently construed travel "away from home" to exclude all trips requiring neither sleep nor rest, regardless of how many cities a given trip may have touched, how many miles it may have covered, or how many hours it may have consumed. By so interpreting the statutory phrase, the Commissioner has achieved not only ease and certainty of application but also substantial fairness, for the sleep or rest rule places all one-day travelers on a similar tax footing, rather than discriminating against intra-city travelers and commuters, who of course cannot deduct the cost of the meals they eat on the road. See *Commissioner of Internal Revenue v. Flowers*, 326 U.S. 465, 66 S.Ct. 250, 90 L.Ed. 203.

Any rule in this area must make some rather arbitrary distinctions, but at least the sleep or rest rule avoids the obvious inequity of permitting the New Yorker who makes a quick trip to Washington and back, missing neither his breakfast nor his dinner at home, to deduct the cost of his lunch merely because he covers more miles than the salesman who travels locally and must finance all his meals without the help of the Federal Treasury. And the Commissioner's rule surely makes more sense than one which would allow the respondent in this case to deduct the cost of his breakfast and lunch simply because he spends a greater percentage of his time at the wheel than the commuter who eats breakfast on his way to work and lunch a block from his office.

The Court of Appeals nonetheless found in the "plain language of the statute" an insuperable obstacle to the Commissioner's construction. We disagree. The language of the statute—"meals and lodging * * * away from home"—is obviously not self-defining.[16] And to the extent

---

taxpayer whose business requires no travel cannot ordinarily deduct the cost of the lunch he eats away from home. But the taxpayer who can bring himself within the reach of § 162(a)(2) may deduct what he spends on his noontime meal although it costs him no more, and relates no more closely to his business, than does the lunch consumed by his less mobile counterpart.

16. The statute applies to the meal and lodging expenses of taxpayers "traveling * * * away from home." The very concept of "traveling" obviously requires a physical separation from one's house. To read the phrase "away from home" as broadly as a completely literal approach might permit would thus render the phrase completely redundant. But of course the words of the statute have never been so woodenly construed. The commuter, for example, has never been regarded as "away from home" within the meaning of § 162(a)(2) simply because he has traveled from his residence to his place of business. See *Commissioner v. Flowers*, 326 U.S. 465, 473, 66 S.Ct. 250, 254, 90 L.Ed. 203. More than a dictionary is thus required to understand the provision

that the words chosen by Congress cut in either direction, they tend to support rather than defeat the Commissioner's position, for the statute speaks of "meals and lodging" as a unit, suggesting—at least arguably— that Congress contemplated a deduction for the cost of meals only where the travel in question involves lodging as well. Ordinarily, at least, only the taxpayer who finds it necessary to stop for sleep or rest incurs significantly higher living expenses as a direct result of his business travel, and Congress might well have thought that only taxpayer in that category should be permitted to deduct their living expenses while on the road.[19] In any event, Congress certainly recognized, when it promulgated § 162(a)(2), that the Commissioner had so understood its statutory predecessor. This case thus comes within the settled principle that "Treasury regulations and interpretations long continued without substantial change, applying to unamended or substantially reenacted statutes, are deemed to have received congressional approval and have the effect of law." *Helvering v. Winmill*, 305 U.S. 79, 83, 59 S.Ct. 45, 47, 83 L.Ed. 52; *Fribourg Nav. Co. v. Commissioner*, 383 U.S. 272, 283, 86 S.Ct. 862, 869, 15 L.Ed.2d 751.

Alternatives to the Commissioner's sleep or rest rule are of course available. Improvements might be imagined. But we do not sit as a committee of revision to perfect the administration of the tax laws. Congress has delegated to the Commissioner, not to the courts, the task of prescribing "all needful rules and regulations for the enforcement" of the Internal Revenue Code. 26 U.S.C. § 7805(a). In this area of limitless factual variations "it is the province of Congress and the Commissioner, not the courts, to make the appropriate adjustments." *Commissioner v. Stidger*, 386 U.S. 287, 296, 87 S.Ct. 1065, 1071, 18 L.Ed.2d 53. The rule of the judiciary in cases of this sort begins and ends with assuring that the Commissioner's regulations fall within his authority to implement the congressional mandate in some reasonable manner. Because the rule challenged here has not been shown deficient on that score, the Court of Appeals should have sustained its validity. The judgment is therefore reversed.

Reversed.

MR. JUSTICE MARSHALL took no part in the consideration or decision of this case.

MR. JUSTICE DOUGLAS, with whom MR. JUSTICE BLACK and MR. JUSTICE FORTAS, concur, dissenting.

here involved, and no appeal to the "plain language" of the section can obviate the need for further statutory construction.

19. The court below thought that "(i)n an era of supersonic travel, the time factor is hardly relevant to the question of whether or not * * * meal expenses are related to the taxpayer's business * * *." But that completely misses the point. The benefits of § 162(a)(2) are limited to business travel "away from home," and all meal expenses incurred in the course of such travel are deductible, however unrelated they may be to the taxpayer's income-producing activity. To ask that the definition of "away from home" be responsive to the business necessity of the taxpayer's meals is to demand the impossible.

The statutory words "while away from home," 26 U.S.C. § 162(a)(2), may not in my view be shrunken to "overnight" by administrative construction or regulations. "Overnight" injects a time element in testing deductibility, while the statute speaks only in terms of geography. As stated by the Court of Appeals:

> "In an era of supersonic travel, the time factor is hardly relevant to the question of whether or not travel and meal expenses are related to the taxpayer's business and cannot be the basis of a valid regulation under the present statute." *Correll v. United States*, 369 F.2d 87, 89–90.

I would affirm the judgment below.

HANTZIS v. COMMISSIONER

United States Court of Appeals, First Circuit, 1981.
638 F.2d 248.

LEVIN H. CAMPBELL, CIRCUIT JUDGE.

The Commissioner of Internal Revenue (Commissioner) appeals a decision of the United States Tax Court that allowed a deduction under 26 U.S.C. § 162(a)(2) (1976) for expenses incurred by a law student in the course of her summer employment. The facts in the case are straightforward and undisputed.

In the fall of 1973 Catharine Hantzis (taxpayer), formerly a candidate for an advanced degree in philosophy at the University of California at Berkeley, entered Harvard Law School in Cambridge, Massachusetts, as a full-time student. During her second year of law school she sought unsuccessfully to obtain employment for the summer of 1975 with a Boston law firm. She did, however, find a job as a legal assistant with a law firm in New York City, where she worked for ten weeks beginning in June 1975. Her husband, then a member of the faculty of Northeastern University with a teaching schedule for that summer, remained in Boston and lived at the couple's home there. At the time of the Tax Court's decision in this case, Mr. and Mrs. Hantzis still resided in Boston.

On their joint income tax return for 1975, Mr. and Mrs. Hantzis reported the earnings from taxpayer's summer employment ($3,750) and deducted the cost of transportation between Boston and New York, the cost of a small apartment rented by Mrs. Hantzis in New York and the cost of her meals in New York ($3,204). * * *

The Commissioner disallowed the deduction on the ground that taxpayer's home for purposes of section 162(a)(2) was her place of employment and the cost of traveling to and living in New York was therefore not "incurred . . . while away from home." The Commissioner also argued that the expenses were not incurred "in the pursuit of a trade or business." Both positions were rejected by the Tax Court, which found that Boston was Mrs. Hantzis' home because her employment in New York was only temporary and that her expenses in New York were "necessitated" by her employment there. The court thus held the expenses to be deductible under section 162(a)(2).

In asking this court to reverse the Tax Court's allowance of the deduction, the Commissioner has contended that the expenses were not incurred "in the pursuit of a trade or business." We do not accept this argument; nonetheless, we sustain the Commissioner and deny the deduction, on the basis that the expenses were not incurred "while away from home."

I.

Section 262 of the Code declares that "except as otherwise provided in this chapter, no deductions shall be allowed for personal, living, or family expenses." Section 162 provides less of an exception to this rule than it creates a separate category of deductible business expenses. This category manifests a fundamental principle of taxation: that a person's taxable income should not include the cost of producing that income.

The test by which "personal" travel expenses subject to tax under section 262 are distinguished from those costs of travel necessarily incurred to generate income is embodied in the requirement that, to be deductible under section 162(a)(2), an expense must be "incurred ... in the pursuit of a trade or business." In *Flowers* the Supreme Court read this phrase to mean that "(t)he exigencies of business rather than the personal conveniences and necessities of the traveler must be the motivating factors."[2] Of course, not every travel expense resulting from business exigencies rather than personal choice is deductible; an expense must also be "ordinary and necessary" and incurred "while away from home." But the latter limitations draw also upon the basic concept that only expenses necessitated by business, as opposed to personal, demands may be excluded from the calculation of taxable income.

With these fundamentals in mind, we proceed to ask whether the cost of taxpayer's transportation to and from New York, and of her meals and lodging while in New York, was incurred "while away from home in the pursuit of a trade or business."

II.

The Commissioner has directed his argument at the meaning of "in pursuit of a trade or business." He interprets this phrase as requiring that a deductible traveling expense be incurred under the demands of a trade or business which predates the expense, i.e., an "already existing" trade or business. Under this theory, section 162(a)(2) would invalidate the deduction taken by the taxpayer because she was a full-time student

---

2. *Flowers* denied a deduction claimed by the taxpayer as not involving expenses required by the taxpayer's employer's business. It is now established, however, that a taxpayer may be in the trade or business of being an employee. See, e.g., *Primuth v. Commissioner*, 54 T.C. 374, 377–78 (1970) (citing cases); *Rev. Rul. 77–16*, 1977–1 C.B. 37; *Rev. Rul.* 60–16, 1960–1 C.B. 58. Thus, expenses necessitated by the exigencies of an employee's occupation, without regard to the demands of the employer's business, are also deductible.

before commencing her summer work at a New York law firm in 1975 and so was not continuing in a trade or business when she incurred the expenses of traveling to New York and living there while her job lasted. The Commissioner's proposed interpretation erects at the threshold of deductibility under section 162(a)(2) the requirement that a taxpayer be engaged in a trade or business before incurring a travel expense. Only if that requirement is satisfied would an inquiry into the deductibility of an expense proceed to ask whether the expense was a result of business exigencies, incurred while away from home, and reasonable and necessary.

Such a reading of the statute is semantically possible and would perhaps expedite the disposition of certain cases. Nevertheless, we reject it as unsupported by case law and inappropriate to the policies behind section 162(a) (2).

The two cases relied on by the Commissioner do not appear to us to establish that traveling expenses are deductible only if incurred in connection with a preexisting trade or business. The seminal interpretation of section 162(a)(2), *Flowers v. Commissioner, supra*, is as equivocal upon that point as the statutory language it construes. *Commissioner v. Janss*, 260 F.2d 99 (8th Cir. 1958), a case with facts somewhat akin to the present, did not articulate any such theory. In *Janss*, a college student from Des Moines, Iowa, worked in Alaska during the summer between his freshman and sophomore years of school and sought to deduct from his taxable income the cost of transportation to and from Alaska as well as the cost of meals and lodging while there. Despite testimony from the personnel manager of the construction company for which Janss worked indicating that workers were available in Alaska and that Janss had been employed there largely as a personal favor, the Tax Court allowed the deduction. The Eighth Circuit reversed. It held, under *Flowers*, that Janss' travel to Alaska was not motivated by the exigencies of the employer's business. The Eighth Circuit placed no emphasis on the fact that Janss had no previously existing trade or business.

Nor would the Commissioner's theory mesh with the policy behind section 162(a)(2). As discussed, the travel expense deduction is intended to exclude from taxable income a necessary cost of producing that income. Yet the recency of entry into a trade or business does not indicate that travel expenses are not a cost of producing income. To be sure, the costs incurred by a taxpayer who leaves his usual residence to begin a trade or business at another location may not be truly travel expenses, i.e., expenses incurred while "away from home," but practically, they are as much incurred "in the pursuit of a trade or business" when the occupation is new as when it is old.

An example drawn from the Commissioner's argument illustrates the point. The Commissioner notes that "if a construction worker, who normally works in Boston for Corp. A, travels to New York to work for Corp. B for six months, he is traveling ... in the pursuit of his own trade as a construction worker." Accordingly, the requirement that travel expenses be a result of business exigencies is satisfied. Had a construction worker just entering the labor market followed the same course his expenses under the Commissioner's reasoning would not satisfy the business exigencies requirement. Yet in each case, the taxpayer's travel expenses would be costs of earning an income and not merely incidents of personal lifestyle. Requiring that the finding of business exigency necessary to deductibility under section 162(a)(2) be predicated upon the prior existence of a trade or business would thus captiously restrict the meaning of "in pursuit of a trade or business."

Insofar as any cases bear on the issue, they seem to support this conclusion. In *United States v. LeBlanc*, 278 F.2d 571 (5th Cir. 1960), a justice of the Louisiana supreme court who resided in Napoleanville sought to deduct as a travel expense the cost of an apartment in New Orleans, where the court sat. Because Louisiana law required justices both to maintain a residence in their home districts and be present at court functions, the cost of the apartment was found to have been necessitated by business exigencies. Such a result is inconsistent with the rule proposed by the Commissioner. The taxpayer in LeBlanc was not previously engaged in the trade or business which he began upon arriving in New Orleans. At least for the period of his first term on the court, therefore, the taxpayer's expenses in New Orleans were not incurred in connection with an already existing occupation and so, by the Commissioner's reasoning, should have been disallowed. In another case, *Kroll v. Commissioner*, 49 T.C. 557 (1968), the court expressly found that the taxpayer, an eight-year-old actor, was not engaged in an already existing trade or business. Indeed, before coming to New York to begin acting, he "had never engaged in a trade or business." That this fact might have been dispositive was never mentioned by the court, which noted that the expenses in question were incurred in connection with an ongoing trade or business, and so went on to address the requirement that they have arisen while away from home.

In other contexts the phrase "in the pursuit of a trade or business" may permit the interpretation urged upon us by the Commissioner, but to require under section 162(a)(2) that a travel expense be incurred in connection with a preexisting trade or business is neither necessary nor appropriate to effectuating the purpose behind the use of that phrase in the provision. Accordingly, we turn to the question whether, in the absence of the Commissioner's proposed threshold limit on deductibility, the expenses at issue here satisfy the requirements of section 162(a)(2) as interpreted in *Flowers v. Commissioner*.

III.

As already noted, *Flowers* construed section 162(a)(2) to mean that a traveling expense is deductible only if it is (1) reasonable and necessary, (2) incurred while away from home, and (3) necessitated by the exigencies of business. Because the Commissioner does not suggest that Mrs. Hantzis' expenses were unreasonable or unnecessary, we may pass directly to the remaining requirements. Of these, we find dispositive the requirement that an expense be incurred while away from home. As we think Mrs. Hantzis' expenses were not so incurred, we hold the deduction to be improper.

The meaning of the term "home" in the travel expense provision is far from clear. When Congress enacted the travel expense deduction now codified as section 162(a)(2), it apparently was unsure whether, to be deductible, an expense must be incurred away from a person's residence or away from his principal place of business. This ambiguity persists and courts, sometimes within a single circuit, have divided over the issue. Compare *Six v. United States*, 450 F.2d 66 (2d Cir. 1971) (home held to be residence) and *Rosenspan v. United States*, 438 F.2d 905 (2d Cir.), cert. denied, 404 U.S. 864, 92 S.Ct. 54, 30 L.Ed.2d 108 (1971) and *Burns v. Gray*, 287 F.2d 698 (6th Cir. 1961) and *Wallace v. Commissioner*, 144 F.2d 407 (9th Cir. 1944) with *Markey v. Commissioner*, 490 F.2d 1249 (6th Cir. 1974) (home held to be principal place of business) and *Curtis v. Commissioner*, 449 F.2d 225 (5th Cir. 1971) and *Wills v. Commissioner*, 411 F.2d 537 (9th Cir. 1969).[10] It has been suggested that these conflicting definitions are due to the enormous factual variety in the cases. * * * We find this observation instructive, for if the cases that discuss the meaning of the term "home" in section 162(a)(2) are interpreted on the basis of their unique facts as well as the fundamental purposes of the travel expense provision, and not simply pinioned to one of two competing definitions of home, much of the seeming confusion and contradiction on this issue disappears and a functional definition of the term emerges.

We begin by recognizing that the location of a person's home for purposes of section 162(a)(2) becomes problematic only when the person lives one place and works another. Where a taxpayer resides and works at a single location, he is always home, however defined; and where a taxpayer is constantly on the move due to his work, he is never "away" from home. (In the latter situation, it may be said either that he has no residence to be away from, or else that his residence is always at his place of employment. See *Rev. Rul. 60–16*, 1960–1 C.B. 58, 62.) However, in the present case, the need to determine "home" is plainly before us, since the taxpayer resided in Boston and worked, albeit briefly, in New York.

We think the critical step in defining "home" in these situations is to recognize that the "while away from home" requirement has to be construed in light of the further requirement that the expense be the result of business exigencies. The traveling expense deduction obviously is not intended to exclude from taxation every expense incurred by a taxpayer who, in the course of business, maintains two homes. Section

---

10. The Tax Court has, with a notable exception, consistently held that a taxpayer's home is his place of business. See *Daly v. Commissioner*, 72 T.C. 190 (1979); *Foote v. Commissioner*, 67 T.C. 1 (1976); *Mont-gomery v. Commissioner*, 64 T.C. 175 (1975), aff'd, 532 F.2d 1088 (6th Cir. 1976); *Blatnick v. Commissioner*, 56 T.C. 1344 (1971). The exception, of course, is the present case.

162(a)(2) seeks rather "to mitigate the burden of the taxpayer who, because of the exigencies of his trade or business, must maintain two places of abode and thereby incur additional and duplicate living expenses." Consciously or unconsciously, courts have effectuated this policy in part through their interpretation of the term "home" in section 162(a)(2). Whether it is held in a particular decision that a taxpayer's home is his residence or his principal place of business, the ultimate allowance or disallowance of a deduction is a function of the court's assessment of the reason for a taxpayer's maintenance of two homes. If the reason is perceived to be personal, the taxpayer's home will generally be held to be his place of employment rather than his residence and the deduction will be denied. If the reason is felt to be business exigencies, the person's home will usually be held to be his residence and the deduction will be allowed. We understand the concern of the concurrence that such an operational interpretation of the term "home" is somewhat technical and perhaps untidy, in that it will not always afford bright line answers, but we doubt the ability of either the Commissioner or the courts to invent an unyielding formula that will make sense in all cases. The line between personal and business expenses winds through infinite factual permutations; effectuation of the travel expense provision requires that any principle of decision be flexible and sensitive to statutory policy.

Construing in the manner just described the requirement that an expense be incurred "while away from home," we do not believe this requirement was satisfied in this case. Mrs. Hantzis' trade or business did not require that she maintain a home in Boston as well as one in New York. Though she returned to Boston at various times during the period of her employment in New York, her visits were all for personal reasons. It is not contended that she had a business connection in Boston that necessitated her keeping a home there; no professional interest was served by maintenance of the Boston home as would have been the case, for example, if Mrs. Hantzis had been a lawyer based in Boston with a New York client whom she was temporarily serving. The home in Boston was kept up for reasons involving Mr. Hantzis, but those reasons cannot substitute for a showing by Mrs. Hantzis that the exigencies of her trade or business required her to maintain two homes. Mrs. Hantzis' decision to keep two homes must be seen as a choice dictated by personal, albeit wholly reasonable, considerations and not a business or occupational necessity. We therefore hold that her home for purposes of section 162(a)(2) was New York and that the expenses at issue in this case were not incurred "while away from home."[12]

12. The concurrence reaches the same result on essentially the same reasoning, but under what we take to be an interpretation of the "in pursuit of business" requirement. We differ from our colleague, it would seem, only on the question of which precondition to deductibility best accommodates the statutory concern for "the taxpayer who, because of the exigencies of his trade or business, must maintain two places of abode and thereby incur additional and duplicate living expenses." Neither the phrase "away from home" nor "in pursuit of business" effectuates this concern without interpretation that to some degree removes it from "the ordinary meaning of the

We are not dissuaded from this conclusion by the temporary nature of Mrs. Hantzis' employment in New York. Mrs. Hantzis argues that the brevity of her stay in New York excepts her from the business exigencies requirement of section 162(a)(2) * * *. The Tax Court here held that Boston was the taxpayer's home because it would have been unreasonable for her to move her residence to New York for only ten weeks. At first glance these contentions may seem to find support in the court decisions holding that, when a taxpayer works for a limited time away from his usual home, section 162(a)(2) allows a deduction for the expense of maintaining a second home so long as the employment is "temporary" and not "indefinite" or "permanent." This test is an elaboration of the requirements under section 162(a)(2) that an expense be incurred due to business exigencies and while away from home. See note 12, supra. Thus it has been said,

> "Where a taxpayer reasonably expects to be employed in a location for a substantial or indefinite period of time, the reasonable inference is that his choice of a residence is a personal decision, unrelated to any business necessity. Thus, it is irrelevant how far he travels to work. The normal expectation, however, is that the taxpayer will choose to live near his place of employment. Consequently, when a taxpayer reasonable (sic) expects to be employed in a location for only a short or temporary period of time and travels a considerable distance to the location from his residence, it is unreasonable to assume that his choice of a residence is dictated by personal convenience. The reasonable inference is that he is temporarily making these travels because of a business necessity."

Frederick [*v. United States*], 603 F.2d at 1294–95 [(8th Cir. 1979)] (citations omitted).

The temporary employment doctrine does not, however, purport to eliminate any requirement that continued maintenance of a first home have a business justification. We think the rule has no application where the taxpayer has no business connection with his usual place of residence. If no business exigency dictates the location of the taxpayer's usual residence, then the mere fact of his taking temporary employment elsewhere cannot supply a compelling business reason for continuing to maintain that residence. Only a taxpayer who lives one place, works another and has business ties to both is in the ambiguous situation that the temporary employment doctrine is designed to resolve. In such circumstances, unless his employment away from his usual home is temporary, a court can reasonably assume that the taxpayer has abandoned his business ties to that location and is left with only personal reasons for maintaining a residence there. Where only personal needs require that a travel expense be incurred, however, a taxpayer's home is defined so as to leave the expense subject to taxation. Thus, a taxpayer who pursues temporary employment away from the location of his usual

term." (Keeton, J., concurring). However, of the two approaches, we find that of the concurrence more problematic than that adopted here.

residence, but has no business connection with that location, is not "away from home" for purposes of section 162(a)(2).

On this reasoning, the temporary nature of Mrs. Hantzis' employment in New York does not affect the outcome of her case. She had no business ties to Boston that would bring her within the temporary employment doctrine. By this holding, we do not adopt a rule that "home" in section 162(a)(2) is the equivalent of a taxpayer's place of business. Nor do we mean to imply that a taxpayer has a "home" for tax purposes only if he is already engaged in a trade or business at a particular location. Though both rules are alluringly determinate, we have already discussed why they offer inadequate expressions of the purposes behind the travel expense deduction. We hold merely that for a taxpayer in Mrs. Hantzis' circumstances to be "away from home in the pursuit of a trade or business," she must establish the existence of some sort of business relation both to the location she claims as "home" and to the location of her temporary employment sufficient to support a finding that her duplicative expenses are necessitated by business exigencies. This, we believe, is the meaning of the statement in *Flowers* that "(b)usiness trips are to be identified in relation to business demands and the traveler's business headquarters." On the uncontested facts before us, Mrs. Hantzis had no business relation to Boston; we therefore leave to cases in which the issue is squarely presented the task of elaborating what relation to a place is required under section 162(a)(2) for duplicative living expenses to be deductible.

Reversed.

KEETON, DISTRICT JUDGE, concurring in the result.

Although I agree with the result reached in the court's opinion, and with much of its underlying analysis, I write separately because I cannot join in the court's determination that New York was the taxpayer's home for purposes of 26 U.S.C. § 162(a)(2). In so holding, the court adopts a definition of "home" that differs from the ordinary meaning of the term and therefore unduly risks causing confusion and misinterpretation of the important principle articulated in this case.

In adopting section 162(a)(2), Congress sought "to mitigate the burden of the taxpayer who, because of the exigencies of his trade or business, must maintain two places of abode and thereby incur additional and duplicate living expenses." In the present case, the taxpayer does not contend that she maintained her residence in Boston for business reasons. Before working in New York, she had attended school near her home in Boston, and she continued to do so after she finished her summer job. In addition, her husband lived and worked in Boston. Thus, on the facts in this case, I am in agreement with the court that the taxpayer's deductions must be disallowed because she was not required by her trade or business to maintain both places of residence. However rather than resting its conclusion on an interpretation of the language of section 162(a)(2) taken as a whole, which allows a deduction for ordinary and necessary expenses incurred "while away from home in the pursuit of trade or business," the court reaches the same result by incorporating the concept of business-related residence into the definition of "home," thereby producing sometimes, but not always, a meaning of "home" quite different from ordinary usage.

The Supreme Court has noted that "(t)he meaning of the word 'home' in (the predecessor of s 162(a)(2)) with reference to a taxpayer residing in one city and working in another has engendered much difficulty and litigation." *Commissioner v. Flowers*, 326 U.S. 465, 471, 66 S.Ct. 250, 253, 90 L.Ed. 203 (1946). The Court has twice rejected opportunities to adopt definitive constructions of the term. Moreover, as the court's opinion in the present case points out, the courts of appeals have split on whether a taxpayer's "home" is her (or his) principal residence or principal place of business.

The court enters this conflict among circuits with a "functional" definition of home not yet adopted by any other circuit. I read the opinion as indicating that in a dual residence case, the Commissioner must determine whether the exigencies of the taxpayer's trade or business require her to maintain both residences. If so, the Commissioner must decide that the taxpayer's principal residence is her "home" and must conclude that expenses associated with the secondary residence were incurred "while away from home," and are deductible. If not, as in the instant case, the Commissioner must find that the taxpayer's principal place of business is her "home" and must conclude that the expenses in question were not incurred "while away from home." The conclusory nature of these determinations as to which residence is her "home" reveals the potentially confusing effect of adopting an extraordinary definition of "home."

A word used in a statute can mean, among the cognoscenti, whatever authoritative sources define it to mean. Nevertheless, it is a distinct disadvantage of a body of law that it can be understood only by those who are expert in its terminology. Moreover, needless risks of misunderstanding and confusion arise, not only among members of the public but also among professionals who must interpret and apply a statute in their day-to-day work, when a word is given an extraordinary meaning that is contrary to its everyday usage.

The result reached by the court can easily be expressed while also giving "home" its ordinary meaning, and neither Congress nor the Supreme Court has directed that "home" be given an extraordinary meaning in the present context. In *Rosenspan v. United States*, *supra*, Judge Friendly, writing for the court, rejected the Commissioner's proposed definition of home as the taxpayer's business headquarters, concluding that in section 162(a)(2) " 'home' means 'home.' " Id. at 912.

> When Congress uses a non-technical word in a tax statute, presumably it wants administrators and courts to read it in the way that ordinary people would understand, and not "to draw on some unexpressed spirit outside the bounds of the normal meaning of

words." *Addison v. Holly Hill Fruit Prods., Inc.*, 322 U.S. 607, 617, 64 S.Ct. 1215, 1221, 88 L.Ed. 1488 (1944).

Id. at 911. Cf. *United States v. New England Coal and Coke Co.*, 318 F.2d 138, 142 (1st Cir. 1963) ("Unless the contrary appears, it is presumed that statutory words were used in their ordinary sense").

In analyzing dual residence cases, the court's opinion advances compelling reasons that the first step must be to determine whether the taxpayer has business as opposed to purely personal reasons for maintaining both residences. This must be done in order to determine whether the expenses of maintaining a second residence were, "necessitated by business, as opposed to personal, demands" and were in this sense incurred by the taxpayer "while away from home in pursuit of trade or business." Necessarily implicit in this proposition is a more limited corollary that is sufficient to decide the present case: When the taxpayer has a business relationship to only one location, no traveling expenses the taxpayer incurs are "necessitated by business, as opposed to personal demands," regardless of how many residences the taxpayer has, where they are located, or which one is "home."

In the present case, although the taxpayer argues that her employment required her to reside in New York, that contention is insufficient to compel a determination that it was the nature of her trade or business that required her to incur the additional expense of maintaining a second residence, the burden that section 162(a)(2) was intended to mitigate. Her expenses associated with maintaining her New York residence arose from personal interests that led her to maintain two residences rather than a single residence close to her work. While traveling from her principal residence to a second place of residence closer to her business, even though "away from home," she was not "away from home in pursuit of business." Thus, the expenses at issue in this case were not incurred by the taxpayer "while away from home in pursuit of trade or business."

In the contrasting case in which a taxpayer has established that both residences were maintained for business reasons, section 162(a)(2) allows the deduction of expenses associated with travel to, and maintenance of, one of the residences if they are incurred for business reasons and that abode is not the taxpayer's home. A common sense meaning of "home" works well to achieve the purpose of this provision.

In summary, the court announces a sound principle that, in dual residence cases, deductibility of traveling expenses depends upon a showing that both residences were maintained for business reasons. If that principle is understood to be derived from the language of section 162(a)(2) taken as a whole, "home" retains operative significance for determining which of the business-related residences is the one the expense of which can be treated as deductible. In this context, "home" should be given its ordinary meaning to allow a deduction only for expenses relating to an abode that is not the taxpayer's principal place of residence. On the undisputed facts in this case, the Tax Court found that

Boston was the taxpayer's "home" in the everyday sense, i.e., her principal place of residence. Were the issue relevant to disposition of the case, I would uphold the Tax Court's quite reasonable determination on the evidence before it. However, because the taxpayer had no business reason for maintaining both residences, her deduction for expenses associated with maintaining a second residence closer than her principal residence to her place of employment must be disallowed without regard to which of her two residences was her "home" under section 162(a)(2).

* * *

Mixing Business and Pleasure. When a taxpayer attends a business conference "away from home," we know that the taxpayer may deduct travel expenses under § 162(a)(2). Should the amount the taxpayer can deduct be limited if the conference is held in a city known for nice weather and abundant tourist diversions and the taxpayer opts to stay for a few days to enjoy the comfortable surroundings? The regulations allow taxpayers to deduct traveling expenses so long as the primary purpose of their trip is for business. Treas. Reg. § 1.162–2(b)(1). In order to determine a taxpayer's primary purpose for travel, all facts and circumstances are considered, but usually the taxpayer is safe if the number of "business days" exceeds the number of "pleasure days." See Treas. Reg. § 1.162–2(b)(2).

The distinction between business days and pleasure days is even more important with respect to *lodging* and *meal* costs. Lodging on business days is deductible under § 162(a)(2), but lodging on personal days is not. Thus, for example, if a taxpayer's conference ends at noon on Friday but the taxpayer elects to stay at the conference hotel on Friday night, the Friday night hotel cost will not be deductible unless the taxpayer can show that he or she had no meaningful choice but to stay at the hotel another night. The same rule applies for meals: meals on business days are deductible, but meals on personal days are not.

No Full Meal Deals. Section 274(n) limits any deduction for meals to 50 percent of the taxpayer's cost. Thus, if a taxpayer pays $10 for lunch at a business conference away from home, the taxpayer's deduction is limited to $5. More limitations with respect to deducting meal costs will be explored in Part B of this Chapter.

Other Limits on Travel Deductions. Section 274 contains two additional (though comparatively minor) limits on the travel deduction authorized by § 162(a)(2). First, § 274(c) disallows a deduction for that portion of international travel expenses not allocable to a trade or business or investment activity. In other words, a taxpayer must apportion all travel expenses between deductible business and investment pursuits and non-deductible personal excursions. All international travel expenses may be deducted, however, if the total travel time is one week or less or if the pleasure component of the overall travel is less than 25 percent of the total travel time.

Second, § 274(m)(3) disallows a deduction for the travel expenses of a spouse or dependent accompanying the taxpayer unless there is a business purpose for the spouse or dependent's attendance. This is similar to the result in *Gotcher*, discussed in Chapter 3 (do you remember back that far?).

Substantiation. Section 274(d) generally requires taxpayers seeking to deduct travel expenses to substantiate the expenses through "adequate records" or "sufficient evidence." The statute, supplemented in significant detail by regulations, supplanted an established common law doctrine that allowed courts to approximate the amount of a taxpayer's deduction where the taxpayer lacked proof of the exact amount of expenses. With respect to travel expenses specifically, a taxpayer must be able to substantiate three things: (1) the amount of the expenses; (2) the time and place of travel; and (3) the business purpose of the trip. See Temp. Reg. § 1.274–5T(b).

Adequate records is the preferred method of substantiation. A taxpayer is considered to have maintained adequate records if he or she keeps an account book, diary, expense statement, or similar record where expenses are entered "at or near the time of the expenditure." Temp. Reg. § 1.274–5T(c)(2)(ii). Furthermore, the taxpayer must keep documentary evidence for away-from-home lodging expenses (like receipts, paid bills, or similar evidence) and for any other travel costs of $75 or more. Treas. Reg. § 1.274–5(c)(2)(iii).

Taxpayers who do not maintain adequate records can only secure a deduction upon other "sufficient evidence" of an expense. This involves submission of the taxpayer's own statement containing "specific information in detail" as to the expense, and this statement must be supported by "other corroborative evidence." Temp. Reg. § 1.274–5T(c)(3)(i). With respect to travel expenses, the regulations offer no guidance as to how a taxpayer can supply corroborative evidence that would not constitute "adequate records." Perhaps, then, the moral of the story here is to maintain adequate records of all travel expenses in order to satisfy the substantiation requirement of § 274(d).

* * *

✳ *Problem 10–1* ✳

Ophelia Paine is a business consultant who works and resides in San Francisco. Ophelia flew to Los Angeles to meet with one of her clients on business matters. In addition to the $150 round-trip airfare, Ophelia paid $50 for meals per day in each of the alternative situations described below. For each such situation, determine the extent to which Ophelia may deduct her travel expenses (airfare, meals, and where relevant, lodging).

(a) Ophelia flies to Los Angeles and returns to San Francisco on the same day.

(b) Ophelia flies to Los Angeles on Monday and returns to San Francisco on Tuesday, spending an additional $200 for lodging on Monday night.

(c) Same as (b), except that Ophelia does not fly back to San Francisco until Sunday. Assume Ophelia spent $200 in lodging for each night (six nights total), and that Ophelia spent eight hours each day Monday through Friday with her client on business matters. She spent Saturday and most of Sunday frolicking in Hollywood.

(d) Same as (c), except that business meetings with the client concluded on Tuesday night, and Ophelia frolicked from Wednesday through Sunday.

(e) Same as (c), except that Ophelia flew to (and the business meetings took place in) Ixtapa, Mexico.

(f) Same as (c), except that Ophelia's spouse, Thomas, accompanied her on the trip. Thomas did not participate in any of the business meetings. Assume that Thomas' airfare and meal costs were the same as those for Ophelia ($150 airfare and $50 daily for meals) and that the couple shared lodging.

Problem 10–2

Bjornstad is a musician and member of the band "Dr. Bop and the Headliners." Bjornstad resided in Madison, Wisconsin, with his parents, but the band performed mostly in Chicago. The taxpayer lived with his parents because the cost of living in Chicago was too high (uh-huh).

On most weekends, Bjornstad left Madison on Thursday or Friday night, played in Chicago and other mid-western cities on Friday and Saturday, and played most every Sunday night at Andy's Night Club in Chicago. Bjornstad usually returned home to the folks in Madison on Mondays. He incurred various travel and lodging expenses on these weekends, but he did not deduct the costs because he never filed federal income tax returns. When the Service issued a deficiency for the years in which Bjornstad did not file, Bjornstad claimed he should be allowed to deduct the travel and lodging costs as business expenses.

Should Bjornstad be allowed to deduct his travel and lodging costs under § 162? Why or why not?

Problem 10–3

Johnson works as a merchant seaman. The nature of his employment requires Johnson to spend about half of every year at sea. When he is not working on board his employer's vessel, he resides at his home in Whidby Island, Washington.

Johnson's employer furnishes meals and lodging while the taxpayer works on the vessel. Johnson also incurs incidental travel expenses that are not reimbursed by his employer, including the purchase of hygiene products, bottled water, and laundry service.

(a) May Johnson deduct the unreimbursed travel expenses under § 162?

(b) Must Johnson include the value of the meals and lodging in his gross income?

B. ENTERTAINMENT EXPENSES AND BUSINESS MEALS

p.690-701

prob 10-4

Code: IRC §§ 274(a), (e), (k), (n). *Skim* IRC § 274(d).

Regs: Treas. Reg. §§ 1.274–2(a) through –2(d).

That's Entertainment! Gary operates a lumber wholesale business in a major metropolitan city. He purchases raw lumber from suppliers and sells it to building contractors. On occasion, Gary entertains suppliers and customers by taking them to professional baseball games at the local ballpark. At the game, Gary and his guest talk about business matters while root, root, rooting for the home team. Gary has secured several good business deals as a result of these entertainment events. But Gary is also a huge baseball fan (like any right-thinking American), and he derives personal pleasure from attending as many games as he can. Can Gary deduct the cost of the baseball tickets? What rules or limitations are proper in this context?

First, of course, Gary must conclude that the cost of the tickets is an ordinary and necessary expense paid or incurred in carrying on his trade or business. These conditions are required to secure a deduction under § 162(a). See Chapter 4. The cost to take a client or a vendor to a baseball game would probably qualify for a deduction under § 162(a), assuming such a cost is "ordinary" within the wholesale lumber industry.

Even if the expense qualifies for a deduction under § 162(a), however, it must also survive the limitations set forth in § 274. Section 274(a)(1)(A) disallows a deduction for entertainment expenses unless the entertainment is **directly related** to a trade or business or, in the case of entertainment before or after a business discussion, **associated with** a trade or business. These fuzzy standards are explained in Regulation §§ 1.274–2(c) (the "directly related" test) and 1.274–2(d) (the "associated with" test). In this case, Gary's baseball tickets would likely be deductible under the "directly related" test if Gary actively engaged in a business discussion during the game with more than a general expectation of deriving some specific business benefit as a result. See Treas. Reg. § 1.274–2(c)(3). If the cost of the tickets meets the "directly related" test (or the "associated with" test), note that Gary can deduct the cost of his own ticket in addition to the guest's ticket. *Revenue Ruling 63–144*, 1963–2 C.B. 129.

But wait, there is more! Deductible entertainment expenses are limited to the same substantiation requirements as meals. Section 274(d). Also, like meals, the 50–percent limitation of § 274(n) limits the amount that can be deducted for entertainment expenses.

Business Meals. Although § 162(a)(2) permits deduction of "reasonable allowances" for meals while traveling away from home, § 274(k) provides more detailed requirements for a deduction. First, the meals must not be "lavish or extravagant under the circumstances." Second, the taxpayer who claims the deduction must be present when the meals are served.

Even if these requirements are met, there are two other limits on deductibility. Section 274(d) requires a taxpayer to substantiate the expenses claimed as a deduction. Generally, as with transportation, lodging and entertainment expenses, the taxpayer must have a receipt that indicates the date, the cost, the business purpose of the meal, and the attendees. Finally, as we have already seen, § 274(n) limits the deduction to 50 percent of the total expense. So if a meal is ever deductible, only half of the cost is deductible.

Deducting the cost of a customer's meal (or a vendor's meal or a business colleague's meal) would seem to be an easier task than trying to deduct the cost of the taxpayer's own meal. Yet there is an argument for deducting (half of) the cost of a taxpayer's own meal, as the following case suggests.

MOSS v. COMMISSIONER

United States Court of Appeals, Seventh Circuit, 1985.
758 F.2d 211.

POSNER, CIRCUIT JUDGE.

The taxpayers, a lawyer named Moss and his wife, appeal from a decision of the Tax Court disallowing federal income tax deductions of a little more than $1,000 in each of two years, representing Moss's share of his law firm's lunch expense at the Cafe Angelo in Chicago. The Tax Court's decision in this case has attracted some attention in tax circles because of its implications for the general problem of the deductibility of business meals.

Moss was a partner in a small trial firm specializing in defense work, mostly for one insurance company. Each of the firm's lawyers carried a tremendous litigation caseload, averaging more than 300 cases, and spent most of every working day in courts in Chicago and its suburbs. The members of the firm met for lunch daily at the Cafe Angelo near their office. At lunch the lawyers would discuss their cases with the head of the firm, whose approval was required for most settlements, and they would decide which lawyer would meet which court call that afternoon or the next morning. Lunchtime was chosen for the daily meeting because the courts were in recess then. The alternatives were to meet at 7:00 a.m. or 6:00 p.m., and these were less convenient times. There is no suggestion that the lawyers dawdled over lunch, or that the Cafe Angelo is luxurious.

The framework of statutes and regulations for deciding this case is simple, but not clear. Section 262 of the Internal Revenue Code (Title 26) disallows, "except as otherwise expressly provided in this chapter," the deduction of "personal, family, or living expenses." Section 119 excludes from income the value of meals provided by an employer to his employees for his convenience, but only if they are provided on the employer's premises; and section 162(a) allows the deduction of "all the ordinary and necessary expenses paid or incurred during the taxable year in carrying on any trade or business, including— ... (2) traveling expenses (including amounts expended for meals ...) while away from home...." Since Moss was not an employee but a partner in a partnership not taxed as an entity, since the meals were not served on the employer's premises, and since he was not away from home (that is, on an overnight trip away from his place of work, see *United States v. Correll*, 389 U.S. 299, 19 L. Ed. 2d 537, 88 S. Ct. 445 (1967)), neither section 119 nor section 162(a)(2) applies to this case. The Internal Revenue Service concedes, however, that meals are deductible under section 162(a) when they are ordinary and necessary business expenses (provided the expense is substantiated with adequate records, see section 274(d)) even if they are not within the express permission of any other provision and even though the expense of commuting to and from work, a traveling expense but not one incurred away from home, is not deductible.

The problem is that many expenses are simultaneously business expenses in the sense that they conduce to the production of business income and personal expenses in the sense that they raise personal welfare. This is plain enough with regard to lunch; most people would eat lunch even if they didn't work. Commuting may seem a pure business expense, but is not; it reflects the choice of where to live, as well as where to work. Read literally, section 262 would make irrelevant whether a business expense is also a personal expense; so long as it is ordinary and necessary in the taxpayer's business, thus bringing section 162(a) into play, an expense is (the statute seems to say) deductible from his income tax. But the statute has not been read literally. There is a natural reluctance, most clearly manifested in the regulation disallowing deduction of the expense of commuting, to lighten the tax burden of people who have the good fortune to interweave work with consumption. To allow a deduction for commuting would confer a windfall on people who live in the suburbs and commute to work in the cities; to allow a deduction for all business-related meals would confer a windfall on people who can arrange their work schedules so they do some of their work at lunch.

Although an argument can thus be made for disallowing *any* deduction for business meals, on the theory that people have to eat whether they work or not, the result would be excessive taxation of people who spend more money on business meals because they are business meals than they would spend on their meals if they were not working. Suppose a theatrical agent takes his clients out to lunch at the expensive restaurants that the clients demand. Of course he can deduct the expense of their meals, from which he derives no pleasure or sustenance, but can he also deduct the expense of his own? He can, because he cannot eat more cheaply; he cannot munch surreptitiously on a peanut butter and jelly sandwich brought from home while his client is wolfing down tournedos Rossini followed by souffle au grand marnier. No doubt our theatrical agent, unless concerned for his longevity, derives personal utility from his fancy meal, but probably less than the price of the meal. He would not pay for it if it were not for the business benefit; he would get more value from using the same money to buy something else; hence the meal confers on him less utility than the cash equivalent would. The law could require him to pay tax on the fair value of the meal to him; this would be (were it not for costs of administration) the economically correct solution. But the government does not attempt this difficult measurement; it once did, but gave up the attempt as not worth the cost, see *United States v. Correll, supra*, 389 U.S. at 301 n.6. The taxpayer is permitted to deduct the whole price, provided the expense is "different from or in excess of that which would have been made for the taxpayer's personal purposes." *Sutter v. Commissioner*, 21 T.C. 170, 173 (1953).

Because the law allows this generous deduction, which tempts people to have more (and costlier) business meals than are necessary, the Internal Revenue Service has every right to insist that the meal be shown to be a real business necessity. This condition is most easily satisfied when a client or customer or supplier or other outsider to the business is a guest. Even if Sydney Smith was wrong that "soup and fish explain half the emotions of life," it is undeniable that eating together fosters camaraderie and makes business dealings friendlier and easier. It thus reduces the costs of transacting business, for these costs include the frictions and the failures of communication that are produced by suspicion and mutual misunderstanding, by differences in tastes and manners, and by lack of rapport. A meeting with a client or customer in an office is therefore not a perfect substitute for a lunch with him in a restaurant. But it is different when all the participants in the meal are coworkers, as essentially was the case here (clients occasionally were invited to the firm's daily luncheon, but Moss has made no attempt to identify the occasions). They know each other well already; they don't need the social lubrication that a meal with an outsider provides—at least don't need it daily. If a large firm had a monthly lunch to allow partners to get to know associates, the expense of the meal might well be necessary, and would be allowed by the Internal Revenue Service. See *Wells v. Commissioner*, T.C. Memo 1977–419, 1977 T.C. Memo 419, 36 T.C.M. (CCH) 1698, 1699 (1977), aff'd without opinion, 626 F.2d 868 (9th Cir. 1980). But Moss's firm never had more than eight lawyers (partners and associates), and did not need a daily lunch to cement relationships among them.

It is all a matter of degree and circumstance (the expense of a testimonial dinner, for example, would be deductible on a morale-building rationale); and particularly of frequency. Daily—for a full year—is too often, perhaps even for entertainment of clients, as implied by *Hankenson v. Commissioner*, T.C. Memo 1984–200, 1984 T.C. Memo 200, 47 T.C.M. 1567, 1569 (1984), where the Tax Court held nondeductible the cost of lunches consumed three or four days a week, 52 weeks a year, by a doctor who entertained other doctors who he hoped would refer patients to him, and other medical personnel.

We may assume it was necessary for Moss's firm to meet daily to coordinate the work of the firm, and also, as the Tax Court found, that lunch was the most convenient time. But it does not follow that the expense of the lunch was a necessary business expense. The members of the firm had to eat somewhere, and the Cafe Angelo was both convenient and not too expensive. They do not claim to have incurred a greater daily lunch expense than they would have incurred if there had been no lunch meetings. Although it saved time to combine lunch with work, the meal itself was not an organic part of the meeting, as in the examples we gave earlier where the business objective, to be fully achieved, required sharing a meal.

The case might be different if the location of the courts required the firm's members to eat each day either in a disagreeable restaurant, so that they derived less value from the meal than it cost them to buy it, cf. *Sibla v. Commissioner*, 611 F.2d 1260, 1262 (9th Cir. 1980); or in a restaurant too expensive for their personal tastes, so that, again, they would have gotten less value than the cash equivalent. But so far as appears, they picked the restaurant they liked most. Although it must be pretty monotonous to eat lunch the same place every working day of the year, not all the lawyers attended all the lunch meetings and there was nothing to stop the firm from meeting occasionally at another restaurant proximate to their office in downtown Chicago; there are hundreds.

An argument can be made that the price of lunch at the Cafe Angelo included rental of the space that the lawyers used for what was a meeting as well as a meal. There was evidence that the firm's conference room was otherwise occupied throughout the working day, so as a matter of logic Moss might be able to claim a part of the price of lunch as an ordinary and necessary expense for work space. But this is cutting things awfully fine; in any event Moss made no effort to apportion his lunch expense in this way.

AFFIRMED.

Problem 10–4

Elle Woods is an attorney fortunate to enjoy a thriving practice representing high-profile clients. One night, Elle accompanied one of her best clients to dinner at the Café Du Jour, an elegant restaurant. Elle and the client discussed their case during the meal. Elle paid the $300 dinner tab. Following dinner, Elle and the client attended the opera. Elle dropped another $400 for the two tickets.

(a) To what extent can Elle deduct the costs of the dinner and the opera tickets?

(b) How would the answer to (a) change if Elle's dinner and opera companion was not an existing client but a prospective client? Assume Elle and the prospective client discussed Elle's practice in considerable detail during the dinner.

(c) How would the answer to (a) change if Elle and the client met at Elle's office earlier in the day to discuss their case and then met for dinner and the opera?

(d) How would the answer to (a) change if Elle did not attend the opera with the client but instead gave two tickets to the client?

(e) To what extent does the prospective client have gross income from the general fact pattern above?

CHURCHILL DOWNS v. COMMISSIONER

United States Court of Appeals, Sixth Circuit, 2002.
307 F.3d 423.

SILER, CIRCUIT JUDGE. Petitioner Churchill Downs, Incorporated and its subsidiaries (together "Churchill Downs") appeal the United States Tax Court's judgment that they were entitled to deduct only 50% of certain expenses they incurred in 1994 and 1995 because the expenses qualified as "entertainment" for purposes of Internal Revenue Code ("I.R.C.") § 274(n)(1)(B). For the reasons stated below, we **AFFIRM**.

I.

The facts of this case are not in dispute. Churchill Downs owns and operates the Churchill Downs race track in Louisville, Kentucky, and three other race tracks. Churchill Downs conducts horse races at these tracks, and earns revenues from wagering, admissions and seating charges, concession commissions, sponsorship revenues, licensing rights, and broadcast fees. Although Churchill Downs does not compete directly with other race tracks due to differences in the timing of race events, it competes for patrons with other sports, entertainment, and gaming operations.

Churchill Downs' biggest race is the Kentucky Derby, held each year on the first Saturday in May. Churchill Downs hosts the following events in connection with the race: (1) a "Sport of Kings" gala, (2) a brunch following the post position drawing for the race, (3) a week-long hospitality tent offering coffee, juice, and donuts to the press, and (4) the Kentucky Derby Winner's Party. The Sport of Kings Gala includes a press reception/cocktail party, dinner, and entertainment. The Kentucky Derby items and amounts at issue in this case are:

Item	1994 Expenditure	1995 Expenditure
Sport of Kings Gala	$114,375	$85,571
Press Hospitality Tent	–0–	$7,803
Derby Winner's Party	$17,500	–0–
Total	$131,875	$93,374

In 1994, Churchill Downs also agreed to host another race, the Breeders' Cup, at the Churchill Downs racetrack. Its contract with Breeders' Cup Limited ("BCL") obligated it to host certain promotional events designed to enhance the significance of the Breeders' Cup races as a national and international horse racing event. These events included: (1) a press reception cocktail party and dinner, (2) a brunch, and (3) a press breakfast. The Breeders' Cup items and amounts at issue in this case are:

Item	1994 Expenditure
Breeders' Cup Dinner	$116,000
Breeders' Cup Brunch	$21,885
Press Breakfast	$7,500
Total	$131,875

Finally, Churchill Downs hosted a number of miscellaneous dinners, receptions, cocktail parties and other events indirectly associated with one or both of these races, at an expense of $4,940 in 1994 and $21,619 in 1995.

Churchill Downs deducted the full amount of these Kentucky Derby and Breeders' Cup expenses on its 1994 and 1995 federal income tax returns as "ordinary and necessary business expenses" pursuant to I.R.C. § 162, 26 U.S.C. § 162(a). In a notice of tax deficiency, Respondent, the Commissioner of Internal Revenue ("Commissioner"), rejected this treatment and concluded that Churchill Downs was entitled to deduct only 50% of these expenses. The Tax Court agreed with the Commissioner, and Churchill Downs now appeals the Tax Court's rejection of its petition for a redetermination of the deficiency.

II.

This court reviews the Tax Court's factual findings for clear error and its conclusions of law *de novo*. In particular, this court reviews the Tax Court's interpretation of Internal Revenue Code provisions and related Treasury regulations *de novo*.

* * *

* * * The Commissioner does not dispute that all of the expenses at issue qualify as "ordinary and necessary" business expenses "directly related" to the "active conduct" of Churchill Downs' business, and thus that some deduction of these expenses is allowed. However, he argues that § 274(n)(1) applies to limit deduction of these expenses because they qualify as items associated with activity generally considered entertainment.

I.R.C. § 274(*o*) gives the Commissioner the power to promulgate "such regulations as he may deem necessary" to enforce § 274. Here the Commissioner has promulgated a regulation in connection with § 274(n), which provides that:

> An objective test shall be used to determine whether an activity is of a type generally considered to constitute entertainment. Thus, if an activity is generally considered to be entertainment, it will constitute entertainment for purposes of this section and section 274(a) regardless of whether the expenditure can also be described otherwise, and even though the expenditure relates to the taxpayer alone. This objective test precludes arguments such as that entertainment means only entertainment of others or that an expenditure for entertainment should be characterized as an expenditure for adver-

tising or public relations. However, in applying this test the taxpayer's trade or business shall be considered. Thus, although attending a theatrical performance would generally be considered entertainment, it would not be so considered in the case of a professional theater critic, attending in his professional capacity. Similarly, if a manufacturer of dresses conducts a fashion show to introduce his products to a group of store buyers, the show would not be generally considered to constitute entertainment. However, if an appliance distributor conducts a fashion show for the wives of his retailers, the fashion show would be generally considered to constitute entertainment.

26 C.F.R. § 1.274–2(b)(1)(ii). Each party relies on this language as support for its position. Churchill Downs argues that the Derby and Breeders' Cup expenses at issue should not be considered entertainment expenses because these pre-and post-race events "showcased" its "entertainment product." Specifically, it contends that the Sport of Kings Gala and the other invitation-only events generated publicity and media attention which introduced its races to the public in the same manner that a dress designer's fashion show introduces its product to clothing buyers. In response, the Commissioner relies on § 1.274–2(b)(1)(ii)'s statement that an item generally considered to be entertainment is subject to the 50% limitation even where it may be otherwise characterized as an advertising or public relations expense. The Commissioner argues that the brunches, dinners, galas, and parties at issue qualify on their face as items "generally considered entertainment" and, following § 1.274–2(b)(1)(ii), that they are not saved from this classification by the fact that these amounts were spent to publicize Churchill Downs' racing events.

These arguments expose an inherent tension in § 1.274–2(b)(1)(ii). On the one hand, § 1.274–2(b)(1)(ii) states that an item generally considered to be entertainment is subject to the 50% limitation even if it may be described otherwise, in particular as advertising or public relations. At the same time, the regulation suggests that certain expenses generally considered entertainment but somehow instrumental to the conduct of a taxpayer's business do not qualify as "entertainment" for purposes of § 274(n). The regulation draws the line between pure publicity and entertainment events integral to the conduct of the taxpayer's business by providing the contrasting examples of a fashion show offered by a dress designer to store buyers (not entertainment) and a fashion show offered by an appliance manufacturer to the spouses of its buyers (entertainment). In the first example, the event is attended by the taxpayer's primary customers, and the taxpayer's product is present at the event and is the focus of it. In contrast, the second example reflects a purely social event focused on something unrelated to the taxpayer's product, held to generate good will among selected third parties with the expectation that they will influence the taxpayer's primary customers into buying its product.

Here, as the Tax Court found, Churchill Downs is in the business of staging horse races and makes its money primarily from selling admission to the races and accepting wagers on them. However, no horse racing was conducted at the dinners and other events at issue. Nor did the events, held away from the track at rented facilities, provide attendees with an opportunity to learn more about the races—for example, the horses that would appear, the odds associated with each horse, the types of wagers available, track conditions, etc.—similar to the product information store buyers might acquire at a fashion show. Rather, Churchill Downs concedes that the events were planned simply as social occasions. Nor were the events open to the gaming public that attends Churchill Downs races and wagers on them. Instead, Churchill Downs invited selected dignitaries and members of the media to these private receptions, not with the expectation that they would later consume significant amounts of its product, but rather in the hopes that they would influence its primary customer base, the general public, to do so, either through the example of their attendance or through favorable reporting. As Churchill Downs explained, the attendance of the celebrities at these pre-race events was "essential" because "the presence of those individuals in Louisville for two or more days before the races gave rise to related publicity and media attention that helped sustain and advance the glamour and prestige of the races." In other words, the purpose of the galas and dinners was not to make Churchill Downs' product directly available to its customers or to provide them with specific information about it, but rather to create an aura of glamour in connection with the upcoming races and generally to arouse public interest in them. In this regard, the dinners, brunches, and receptions at issue most closely resemble the example given above of a fashion show held for the wives of appliance retailers, and are best characterized not as a product introduction event used to conduct the taxpayer's business, but as pure advertising or public relations expenses. Accordingly, we conclude that the Kentucky Derby and Breeders' Cup expenses at issue qualify as "entertainment" under § 1.274–2(b)(1)(ii)'s objective standard.

As an alternative argument, Churchill Downs contends that, under the objective test, an event generally considered entertainment should not be deemed "entertainment" for purposes of § 274 where the event itself is the product the taxpayer is selling. In support of this position, it relies on a statement in the legislative history of § 274(n)(1) that:

> The trade or business of the taxpayer will determine whether an activity is of the type generally considered to constitute entertainment. . . . For example, with respect to a taxpayer who is a professional hunter, a hunting trip would not generally be considered a recreation-type activity.

S. Rep. No. 87–1881 (1962), 1962 WL 4862, at *3330. Churchill Downs argues that its entertainment products, the Kentucky Derby and the Breeders' Cup, necessarily include the Sport of Kings Gala and the other brunches, dinners and receptions at issue as integral parts of a unified entertainment experience.

We disagree. Unlike the hunter in the example above, who earns his money by hosting recreational hunting trips, Churchill Downs did not make any money from hosting the Sport of Kings Gala or the other events for which it seeks a deduction. Indeed, these events are easily separable from Churchill Downs' business because its primary customers, the gaming public, were not permitted to attend them, either by purchasing tickets or otherwise. Instead, Churchill Downs offered the tickets free of charge to a select few it describes as "members of the media, members of the horse industry, dignitaries, and celebrities" in order to raise public awareness of a later event (the races) which the public could attend and from which Churchill Downs made its money. Although Churchill Downs argues, as any business that depends on advertising may, that it made money as a result of these publicity events, this does not change their nature as something distinct from what was actually sold. The Commissioner puts it succinctly: "taxpayers were in the horse racing business, not the business of throwing parties." Accordingly, it is inappropriate to characterize these non-race events as Churchill Downs' "product." Thus, even if § 274(n)(1)'s limitation could be read not to apply where an entertainment event is itself the product sold by the taxpayer, there is no reason to apply such an exception here. We therefore reject Churchill Downs' "entertainment product" argument.

Finally, Churchill Downs offers two additional rationales for allowing a full deduction of these items. I.R.C. § 274(e) provides that:

[I.R.C. § 274(a)] shall not apply to–

* * *

(7) **Items available to public.**—Expenses for goods, services, and facilities made available by the taxpayer to the general public.

(8) **Entertainment sold to customers.**—Expenses for goods or services (including the use of facilities) which are sold by the taxpayer in a bona fide transaction for an adequate and full consideration in money or money's worth.

Churchill Downs argues that the Gala expenses and other items at issue are exempt from § 274(a) pursuant to this section either because these events were available to the general public or because they qualify as entertainment sold to customers.

Churchill Downs does not dispute that these events were by invitation only, or that such invitations were offered only to a small number of individuals. However, it argues that amounts spent on these events meet the requirements of § 274(e)(7) because the expenditures were incurred to promote other events, the Kentucky Derby and Breeders' Cup races, which were open to the general public. We reject this argument. Regardless of whether Churchill Downs incurred these expenses in order to promote an upcoming event open to the public, the goods and services purchased with these expenditures were not "made available" to the general public, as § 274(e)(7) requires, but rather only to a few invited guests at pre-and post-race dining events and the Sport of Kings Gala.

Churchill Downs also relies on an Internal Revenue Service ("IRS") technical advice memorandum holding that food, beverages, lodging, and entertainment offered free by a casino to "high rollers" qualified as "items available to the public" for purposes of I.R.C. § 274(e)(7). See *Tech. Advice Mem. 9641005*, 1996 WL 584428 (July 27, 1996) ("TAM"). The IRS reasoned that all of the benefits provided were items the casino routinely offered to the paying public as part of its stock in trade. As such, the IRS concluded, this practice of "comping" favored customers was akin to providing free product samples, a practice Congress previously had characterized as making goods available to the general public. The agency also concluded that the fact that a customer was required to engage in some amount of gaming activity in order to receive this benefit did not prevent it from being "available to the public" for purposes of § 274(e)(7). However, the IRS concluded that "outside comps"—benefits offered to customers but produced by third parties and provided outside the taxpayer's premises—did not fall within this product sample rationale, and were not exempt under § 274(e)(7). Here Churchill Downs argues that invitations to the Sport of Kings Gala and the other non-race events were akin to the "comps" provided to favored customers at a casino.

We reject this argument. As an initial matter, written determinations like the TAM have no precedential value to parties other than the taxpayer they are issued to, and I.R.C. § 6110(k)(3) prohibits taxpayers from relying on them in proceedings before the agency. Furthermore, unlike the "comps" offered to casino patrons, the dinners and galas at issue here are not the products that members of the general public routinely purchase from Churchill Downs, namely, admission to horse races or wagers. Indeed, Churchill Downs does not sell admission to these non-race dining events at all. Nor does the provision of these benefits appear to have been based on the recipient's attendance at the races, or as an inducement for future attendance. Rather, Churchill Downs acknowledges that the recipients were selectively chosen based on their ability to generate publicity for its races. Finally, as the Commissioner points out, the food, drink, and entertainment appear to have been provided largely by third parties at offsite locations, and thus more closely resemble the "outside comping" example which the agency concluded fell outside of § 274(e)(7). For all these reasons, the TAM does not support Churchill Downs' argument that these items should be exempted under § 274(e)(7) as "items available to the public."

In regards to its "entertainment sold to customers" argument, Churchill Downs concedes that those invited to the Sport of Kings Gala and the other occasions did not pay for the privilege of attending these events. Nevertheless, Churchill Downs once again argues that these dinners and brunches were integral parts of an encompassing entertainment event—the races—which members of the public did in fact pay to attend. For the reasons already discussed above, this argument is unpersuasive.

As a final matter, it would seem that, even if these events were deemed not to constitute "entertainment" for purposes of §§ 274(a) and (n)(1)(B), § 274(n)(1)(A) would preclude full deduction of many of the expenses at issue here. That section, read in conjunction with the rest of § 274(n)(1), provides that "the amount allowable as a deduction under this chapter for ... any expense for food or beverages ... shall not exceed 50 percent of the amount of such expense or item which would (but for this paragraph) be allowable as a deduction under this chapter." This limitation does not appear to be contingent on a classification of the expenses as "entertainment." Given that the events at issue are mainly dinners, brunches, breakfasts, and receptions, it seems likely that a significant portion of the expenses for which Churchill Downs seeks deduction are for food and beverages. However, we need not resolve this issue, which the parties have not briefed, because we conclude that the expenses associated with these events already are subject to the 50% limitation as items "generally considered entertainment."

AFFIRMED.

C. JOB–SEEKING EXPENSES AND MOVING EXPENSES

Code: IRC §§ 82; 132(a)(6), (g); 217(a)–(f). *Review* IRC § 162(a).

Regs: Treas. Reg. § 1.217–2(a), (b)(2)–(4), (b)(8), (d).

The Costs of Obtaining Employment. There is no question that an individual can be in the business of being an employee. See *Primuth v. Commissioner*, 54 T.C. 374 (1970). Thus, ordinary and necessary expenses paid or incurred in carrying on the business of being an employee are deductible under § 162(a). Most employees also incur expenses in seeking employment, as most law students know all too well. Should those expenses qualify for deduction under § 162(a)? The following ruling addresses this issue.

REVENUE RULING 75–120

1975–1 C.B. 55.

The Internal Revenue Service has reconsidered its position whether amounts paid by an employee in seeking new employment are deductible under section 162 or 212 of the Internal Revenue Code of 1954.

* * *

Rev. Rul. 71–308, 1971–2 C.B. 167, holds that fees paid by the taxpayer to a psychological study organization that helped secure him a job are deductible under section 162 of the Code.

Rev. Rul. 70–396, 1970–2 C.B. 68, holds that expenses incurred in making a trip in search of employment are personal and are not deductible.

Rev. Rul. 60–223, 1960–1 C.B. 57, holds that fees paid to employment agencies for securing employment are deductible.

Thus, the longstanding position of the Service has been that expenses incurred by employees in seeking and actually securing new employment are deductible as ordinary and necessary business expenses, but that expenses incurred in seeking but not securing new employment are not deductible.

This distinction between expenses for unsuccessfully and successfully seeking new employment has been rejected by the United States Tax Court.

See, for example, *Leonard F. Cremona*, 58 T.C. 219 (1972), and *David J. Primuth*, 54 T.C. 374 (1970). The *Primuth* opinion concluded that an employee is engaged in the trade or business of performing services as an employee separate and apart from the performance of those services for his existing employer. The court held in *Cremona* that expenses incurred in seeking new employment in the employee's present trade or business are deductible under section 162 of the Code even though new employment was not secured.

In *McDonald v. Commissioner*, 323 U.S. 57 (1944), 1944 C.B. 94, the Supreme Court of the United States held that the campaign expenses of a judge seeking election to the same position that he was filling on an interim basis were not deductible as ordinary and necessary expenses. The court stated that the disallowance of campaign expenses has been consistently reflected by legislative history, court decision, Treasury practice, and Treasury regulations. See section 162(e)(2)(A) of the Code and section 1.162–20(c)(1) of the regulations which disallow the deduction of political campaign expenditures. *McDonald* is therefore distinguishable from *Cremona* and *Primuth*.

In view of the above, it is now the position of the Service that expenses incurred in seeking new employment in the same trade or business are deductible under section 162 of the Code if directly connected with such trade or business as determined by all the objective facts and circumstances.

However, such expenses are not deductible if an individual is seeking employment in a new trade or business even if employment is secured. If the individual is presently unemployed, his trade or business would consist of the services previously performed for his past employer if no substantial lack of continuity occurred between the time of the past employment and the seeking of the new employment. Such expenses are not deductible by an individual where there is a substantial lack of continuity between the time of his past employment and the seeking of the new employment, or by an individual seeking employment for the first time. Such expenses are not deductible under section 212(1) of the

Code which applies only to expenses incurred with respect to an existing profit-seeking endeavor not qualifying as a trade or business.

If a taxpayer travels to a destination and while at such destination seeks new employment in his present trade or business and also engages in personal activities, traveling expenses to and from such destination are deductible only if the trip is related primarily to seeking such new employment. The amount of time during the period of the trip that is spent on personal activity compared to the amount of time spent on seeking such new employment is important in determining whether the trip is primarily personal. Section 1.162–2(b) of the regulations. See *Patterson v. Thomas*, 289 F.2d 108 (5th Cir. 1961).

Expenses while at the destination that are properly allocable to seeking new employment in the taxpayer's present trade or business are deductible even though the traveling expenses to and from the destination are not deductible. Section 1.162–2(b)(1) of the regulations.

Rev. Rul. 71–308, Rev. Rul. 60–223, and *Rev. Rul. 70–396* are hereby revoked. * * *

* * *

Self-Assessment Questions

(Solutions to Self–Assessment Questions are set forth in Appendix 3.)

SAQ 10–2. Peggy Hill worked for many years as a grocery bagger. In Year One, Peggy was fired for cause when she bagged a customer's watermelon on top of a fresh loaf of wheat bread. Peggy has incurred various expenses in seeking a new job, including postage costs, travel costs, and long-distance telephone charges. Determine whether such expenses are deductible in each of the following alternative situations.

(a) Peggy incurred the expenses in Year One, shortly after she was sacked from her first job. She sought employment as a bagger at other grocery stores in the area, and eventually found a new bagging position.

(b) Same as (a), except that Peggy's search for new employment proved unsuccessful.

(c) Same as (a), except that Peggy waited until Year Two to find new employment as a bagger.

(d) Same as (a), except that Peggy sought employment as a substitute middle school Spanish instructor.

SAQ 10–3. *Revenue Ruling 75–120* permits a taxpayer to deduct job-seeking expenses under certain conditions.

(a) Assuming a taxpayer is entitled to a deduction under this ruling, will the deduction be taken above the line?

(b) Assuming a taxpayer is not entitled to a deduction under this ruling, what happens to the job-seeking costs paid by the taxpayer?

* * *

Moving Expenses. Section 217(a) authorizes a deduction for moving expenses "in connection with the commencement of work...at a new principal place of work." Beyond the fact that the taxpayer must be starting a new job, there are two conditions for the deduction. The first condition is that the distance between his or her old residence and the new job location must be at least 50 miles further than the distance between the old residence and the old job location. This is the **geographical condition**. See § 217(c)(1). We can call the second condition the **time condition**. Under § 217(c)(2), the taxpayer must be employed at the new work location (though not necessarily in the same job or even with same employer) for at least 39 weeks of the 12–month period following the move. If the taxpayer cannot meet this test, there is an alternate test using 78 weeks over 24 months. Notice that self-employed taxpayers may only use this second test to meet the time condition.

If all conditions are present, the taxpayer gets to deduct the "reasonable" expenses of moving items from the old residence to the new residence, along with the expenses of traveling from the old residence to the new residence. Section 217(b)(1). The moving and traveling expenses of the taxpayer's spouse and dependents are also deductible if the spouse and dependents lived in the old residence before the move and will live with the taxpayer in the new residence following the move.

* * *

Problem 10–5

Early in Year One, Dr. Frasier Crane quit his job as a therapist and moved from his residence in Boston, Massachusetts, to become a radio talk show host in Seattle, Washington. In making the move, he incurred the following costs: (1) $2,000 to ship his personal possessions; (2) $1,500 airfare for himself and his son, Frederick; (3) $300 in lodging; and (4) $500 in meals. Dr. Crane commenced work at the Seattle radio station immediately after his arrival in town, and he stayed in the employ of the station for 11 years (about six too many).

(a) To what extent may Dr. Crane deduct his moving expenses?

(b) If the Seattle radio station paid $5,000 to Dr. Crane in Year One to cover his moving expenses, to what extent does Dr. Crane have income?

(c) How would the answer to (a) change if Dr. Crane lost his job after only six months (24 weeks)?

(d) Suppose Dr. Crane made the move to Seattle late in Year One. Although he has worked in Seattle since his arrival, he has not met the time condition of § 217(c)(2) by April 15, Year Two, the deadline for filing his Year One return. May Dr. Crane deduct any portion of his moving expenses on his Year One return?

(e) Now assume that Dr. Crane was hired by a Boston radio station only five miles away from his former place of employment in Boston. Since he could finally afford a nicer home, Dr. Crane moved to a country estate 50 miles away from his old residence in Boston, incurring the same expenses described above.

D. EDUCATION EXPENSES

Code: IRC §§ 62(a)(17)–(18); 221; 222. *Review* IRC §§ 162(a)(2); 195. *Skim* IRC §§ 25A; 274(m)(2); 529.

Regs: Treas. Reg. §§ 1.162–5(a)–(c)(2), (e); 1.221–1(a)(1), (b)–(e).

Deductible Education Costs. Education expenses can certainly serve a dual purpose. They can help improve skills required for use in a trade or business, and they can broaden personal horizons. Service professionals (including attorneys, of course) are required to take continuing education courses to maintain their licenses or certifications. There is no doubt that those expenses should be deductible. But what if the educational expenses qualify a taxpayer for a new occupation? Is a deduction proper?

The Code contains no direct answer. Section 274(m)(2) disallows a deduction for travel as a form of education, like when a junior high social studies teacher travels to Egypt in the summer to learn more about pyramids for a unit she will teach her students. The regulations filled the gap by imposing a two-part, two-part test (that's not a typo). In order to be deductible, education expenses must *either*: (1) maintain or improve skills required in the taxpayer's trade or business; or (2) be incurred by the taxpayer's employer as a condition to maintaining employment. Treas. Reg. § 1.162–5(c). Furthermore, if the expenses fall into one of these two categories, they must *neither*: (1) constitute the minimum educational requirements for qualifying the taxpayer for his or her current trade or business; nor (2) be related to a course of study that will qualify the taxpayer for a new trade or business. Treas. Reg. § 1.162–5(b).

Graphically, the requirements of the Regulations may be summarized as follows:

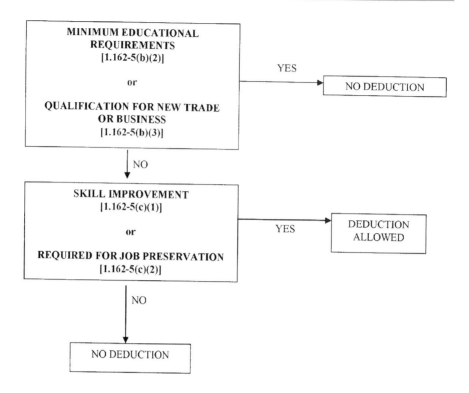

Sound complex? It is. Here are some cases that explain the requirements, some in a context you might appreciate.

WASSENAAR v. COMMISSIONER

United States Tax Court, 1979.
72 T.C. 1195.

Simpson, Judge:

The Commissioner determined a deficiency of $521 in the petitioner's Federal income tax for 1973. The issues for decision are: (1) Whether the petitioner may deduct as an ordinary and necessary business expense the cost of his masters of law degree in taxation; (2) whether such expenses are deductible under section 212(3) of the Internal Revenue Code of 1954, as ordinary and necessary expenses paid in connection with the determination of tax liability; and (3) whether the expenses the petitioner incurred in moving from New York to Detroit to commence employment are deductible under section 217 as a moving expense.

Findings of Fact

* * *

The petitioner graduated from Wayne State University Law School (Wayne State) in Detroit, Mich., in June 1972. He served on law review while at Wayne State in both 1971 and 1972, and although he was a member of the board of editors, his services were no different from those of any other law review member. His duties included editing legal material, checking sources of legal articles, and writing legal articles. He received compensation for such services from Wayne State in the amounts of $845 in 1971 and $1,314 in 1972.

From June to September 1971, the petitioner worked for the law firm of Warner, Norcross & Judd (Warner firm). He prepared legal memorandums, drafted legal documents, and consulted with clients in the presence of an attorney from the firm. He received $2,920 from the Warner firm as compensation for his services that summer.

The petitioner was not employed during the summer following his graduation from law school; instead, he prepared for the Michigan bar, which he took in July 1972. However, he continued to search for employment with a law firm during such period. In October 1972, he passed the bar exam, but he was not formally admitted to the Michigan bar until May of 1973.

In September 1972, the petitioner began courses in the graduate law program in taxation at New York University (NYU), and he graduated with a masters degree in taxation in May 1973. During 1973, he incurred the following expenses in connection with his studies at NYU:

Travel	$96
Meals and lodging	1,075
Auto expenses	64
Tuition and books	1,450
Miscellaneous expenses	96
Total	2,781

The petitioner's principal residence was Holland, Mich., while he lived in New York to attend NYU during the year in issue. Following his graduation from NYU, the petitioner returned to Detroit to commence employment with the law firm of Miller, Canfield, Paddock & Stone (Miller firm).

＊ ＊ ＊

On his Federal income tax return for 1973, the petitioner deducted the expenses he incurred while attending NYU as an employee business expense. In his notice of deficiency, the Commissioner disallowed the deduction on the ground that such expenses were not ordinary and necessary expenses paid or incurred in connection with any trade or business. In his petition, the petitioner has set forth a claim that he is entitled to deduct $919 as the cost of his moving from New York to Detroit to begin working with the Miller firm.

OPINION

The first issue for decision is whether the petitioner may deduct as an ordinary and necessary expense incurred in his trade or business the expense for tuition, books, meals, lodging, and other miscellaneous items paid by him while he obtained his masters degree in taxation.

The petitioner contends that for more than 10 years prior to 1973, he was in a trade or business of "rendering his services to employers for compensation." He contends that he was engaged in the trade or business of "analyzing and solving legal problems for compensation" while he worked on the law review at Wayne State, while he worked for the Warner firm, and later while he worked for the Miller firm. He maintains that the graduate courses in taxation helped maintain and improve his skills in that work. On the other hand, the Commissioner takes the position that the petitioner never began the practice of law until the summer of 1973 and that his attendance at NYU was merely the completion of his program of education preparatory to the practice of law. In the alternative, the Commissioner argues that the petitioner's expenses for travel and meals and lodging are not deductible since he was not "away from home" while attending NYU.

Section 162(a) allows a deduction for all the ordinary and necessary expenses of carrying on a trade or business, including amounts expended for education. Deductible educational expenses under section 162(a) may include expenditures for tuition and books as well as amounts for travel and meals and lodging while the taxpayer is away from home. Section 1.162–5(a)(1), Income Tax Regs., expressly allows a deduction for those educational expenditures which maintain or improve skills "required by the individual in his employment or other trade or business." Whether education maintains or improves skills required by the taxpayer in his trade or business is a question of fact and the burden of proof is on the petitioner. Moreover, the taxpayer must be established in the trade or business at the time he incurs an educational expense to be able to deduct such expense under section 162.

The petitioner artfully attempts to characterize his trade or business as "analyzing and solving legal problems for compensation," and he received compensation for the performance of such services. Nevertheless, it is clear that the petitioner's intended trade or business at the time he attended NYU was that of an attorney, with an emphasis on the law of taxation. We observe that he enrolled in the masters in taxation program at NYU directly from law school, and there was thus an uninterrupted continuity in his legal education. Although the work the petitioner performed before his graduation from law school and NYU was admittedly of a legal nature, such work in no way constituted his being engaged in the practice of law. Before his admission to the bar in May of 1973, he was not authorized to practice law as an attorney. Therefore, his expenses at NYU were not incident to the trade or business of practicing law, and thus, he was not maintaining or improving the skills of that profession within the purview of section 1.162–5(a)(1), Income Tax Regs. See, e.g., *Fielding v. Commissioner*, 57 T.C. 761 (1972) (medical school graduate was denied a business expense deduction for tuition cost of his residency since expenses were not incident to any profession that he previously practiced); *Horodysky v.*

Commissioner, 54 T.C. 490 (1970) (taxpayer who had been a lawyer in Poland was denied a business expense deduction for cost of obtaining an American law school degree since he had no previous employment as a lawyer in this country).

Moreover, although the petitioner completed the requirements for admission to the bar in 1972, he was not formally admitted until May of 1973, and until that time, he could not engage in the practice of law. It is a well-established principle that being a member in good standing of a profession is not tantamount to *carrying on* that profession for the purpose of section 162(a).

Because the petitioner had not practiced law as an attorney before his attendance at NYU, his situation is not analogous to that of other professionals who have been allowed educational expense deductions under section 162(a). In such cases, the taxpayer was already firmly established in his profession and was truly taking courses or attending a seminar for the purpose of maintaining or improving the skills of his profession. See *Coughlin v. Commissioner*, 203 F.2d 307 (2d Cir. 1953), revg. and remanding 18 T.C. 528 (1952) (attorney allowed business deduction for expenses incurred in attending NYU Tax Institute seminar); *Bistline v. United States*, 145 F.Supp. 802 (E.D. Idaho 1956), affd. per curiam on another issue 260 F.2d 80 (9th Cir. 1958) (attorney allowed a business deduction for expenses incurred in attending 2–week course in Federal taxation at the Practicing Law Institute); *Watson v. Commissioner*, 31 T.C. 1014 (1959) (doctor specializing in internal medicine allowed deduction under earlier regulations for courses in psychiatry since such courses helped him to better understand psychosomatic illnesses); *Furner v. Commissioner*, 393 F.2d 292 (7th Cir. 1968), revg. 47 T.C. 165 (1966) (teacher who took year off to secure masters degree was still carrying on a trade or business and allowed to deduct educational expenses); see also sec. 1.162–5(c), Income Tax Regs.

In addition, the petitioner is also denied a deduction for his expenses at NYU by section 1.162–5(b)(3), Income Tax Regs., which provides that educational expenses are not deductible if the education "is part of a program of study being pursued by him which will lead to qualifying him in a new trade or business." The petitioner's attendance at NYU was part of his "program of study" of becoming a lawyer, a trade or business in which he was not previously engaged before his attendance there. After his admission to the bar in May of 1973 and his completion of the program at NYU, he was authorized to and began the practice of law, a wholly different trade or business from any in which he had been previously engaged.

The petitioner is also not entitled to an educational expense deduction on the theory that he was engaged in the trade or business of "rendering his services to employers for compensation." It is a well-established principle that educational expenses must bear a direct and proximate relation to the taxpayer's trade or business. In *Carroll v. Commissioner*, 51 T.C. at 215, this Court stated that it is not sufficient that "the petitioner's education is helpful to him in the performance of his employment." The education must be more than tenuously related to the skills required in the taxpayer's occupation; it must be proximately related to such skills. We cannot accept the petitioner's argument that courses in the more advanced fields of tax law have any proximate relation to his past employment with the Sunday School Guide Publishing Co., Fleetwood Furniture, or the Capital Park Motel—some of his employers as many as 7 years before his attendance at NYU.

In support of his position, the petitioner cites the case of *Primuth v. Commissioner*, 54 T.C. 374, 377 (1970), in which this Court recognized "that a taxpayer may be in the trade or business of being an employee." However, *Primuth* simply held that a fee expended to secure employment is deductible as a business expense under section 162. The case did not involve a claim for an educational expense deduction, and thus, it offers no support for the petitioner's position. Accordingly, we hold that the petitioner's expenses in obtaining a masters of law degree in taxation are not deductible as an ordinary and necessary business expense since he was not engaged in the trade or business of being an attorney at the time such expenses were incurred and since, therefore, he was not maintaining or improving the skills of such trade or business. Such expenses are nondeductible personal expenses. Therefore, it is unnecessary to consider the Commissioner's alternative argument that the petitioner's expenses for travel and meals and lodging are not deductible since he was not "away from home" while attending NYU.

The second issue for consideration is whether the petitioner's expenses of attending NYU are deductible under section 212 as [ordinary and necessary expenses paid in connection with the determination, collection, or refund of any tax.] The petitioner contends that the expenses he incurred at NYU in obtaining a masters degree in taxation are deductible under such section because the courses he took assisted him in preparing his Federal income tax return. Although the Commissioner admits that the petitioner's courses in taxation at NYU assisted him in preparing his tax return and determining the amount due, he contends that the petitioner's expenses in this regard were not "ordinary and necessary." We must agree with the Commissioner.

To be deductible under section 212, any expenses must meet the ordinary and necessary test. Thus, the expenses "must be reasonable in amount and must bear a reasonable and proximate relation" to the purpose for the expenditure. Sec. 1.212–1(d), Income Tax Regs.; see, e.g., *Commissioner v. Flowers*, 326 U.S. 465 (1946); *Limericks, Inc. v. Commissioner*, 165 F.2d 483, 484 (5th Cir. 1948), affg. 7 T.C. 1129 (1946). It strains our credulity to conclude that the petitioner's total expenses of $2,781 incurred while attending NYU are reasonable in amount or bear any reasonable relationship to the preparation of his tax return. Moreover, section 1.212–1(f), Income Tax Regs., provides: "Among expenditures not allowable as deductions under section 212 are the following: * * * expenses of taking special courses or training." The petitioner's expenditures at NYU clearly constitute "special courses" and are nondeductible pursuant to section 1.212–1(f), Income Tax Regs., as well. Accordingly, we hold that the petitioner's educational expenses are not deductible under section 212(3).

The last issue for consideration is whether the expenses incurred by the petitioner in moving from New York to Detroit to commence employment are deductible under section 217 as a moving expense. * * *

Section 1.217–2(b)(8), Income Tax Regs., provides in part:

(8) *Residence.* The term "former residence" refers to *the taxpayer's principal residence* before his departure for his new principal place of work. The term "new residence" refers to the taxpayer's principal residence within the general location of his new principal place of work. * * * [Emphasis supplied.]

The petitioner contends that the expenses he incurred in moving from New York to Detroit are deductible under section 217 because he moved more than 35 miles from his former residence and because he was a full-time employee following such move. However, he conceded on brief that "prior to his move to Detroit, Michigan, Taxpayer's principal residence was Holland, Michigan and Petitioner's temporary residence away from home was New York, New York." Therefore, pursuant to section 1.217–2(b)(8), Income Tax Regs., the petitioner's expenses of moving from New York City to Detroit are not deductible since he conceded that New York was not his *principal residence.*

In conclusion, we hold that the petitioner's educational expenses are not deductible under section 162 since he was not engaged in a trade or business of being an attorney at the time he incurred such expenses, that his educational expenses are not deductible under section 212(3) since such expenses were not reasonable in amount and did not bear a reasonable relationship to the alleged purpose for the expenditure, and that the petitioner may not deduct his moving expenses from New York to Detroit since he admitted that New York was not his principal residence before the move.

Decision will be entered for the respondent.

* * *

GALLIGAN v. COMMISSIONER, T.C. Memo. 2002–150.

Facts: The taxpayer has been a law librarian for 25 years. She worked full-time as a law librarian while attending law school from 1994 to 1998. Her current position did not require that she earn a law degree, but she expensed the costs of attending law school as improving or maintaining her skills as a law librarian. The Service disallowed the deduction on the grounds that the costs qualified her for a new trade or business.

Issue: May the taxpayer deduct the costs of attending law school as a business expense?

Holding: No.

Rationale: "We do not dispute that Mrs. Galligan was an outstanding law librarian and that the legal education was helpful in her profession as a law librarian. However, by attending law school and obtaining her law degree, Mrs. Galligan became entitled to seek admission to the bar, as she did, and to enter the general practice of law if she should choose. * * * Mrs. Galligan's pursuit of a law degree qualified her for the practice of law. Thus, Mrs. Galligan's law school education was part of a program which qualified her for a new trade or business. Accordingly, we sustain [the] determination that Mrs. Galligan's legal education expenses are not deductible."

WARREN v. COMMISSIONER, T.C. Memo. 2003–175.

Facts: The taxpayer, a Methodist minister, decided that he needed to improve his ministry skills, including interpersonal communication, relationship building, sermon writing, leadership, and management. In 1994, he took courses at the University of Great Falls. The classes were not required for him to continue as a local pastor. By the end of 1995, the taxpayer earned a bachelor's degree in human services. On the 1994 tax return, the taxpayer claimed a deduction of $9,698 for "Continuing Education" expenses. The amount claimed represented tuition, books, and course-related fees incurred and paid by the taxpayer for the courses taken at the University of Great Falls.

Issue: May the taxpayer deduct the costs of these courses?

Holding: No.

Rationale: The court held that the courses, which ultimately led to a bachelor's degree, qualified the taxpayer in a new trade or business. "The courses provided him with a background in a variety of social issues that could have prepared him for employment with several public agencies and private non-profit organizations outside of the ministry. Whether or not petitioner remains in the ministry is irrelevant; what is important under the regulations is that the degree 'will lead' petitioner to qualify for a new trade or business." The court conceded that "[i]t may be all but impossible for a taxpayer to establish that a bachelor's degree program does not qualify the taxpayer in a new trade or business."

* * *

Amortization of Education Costs. If a taxpayer is unable to deduct education expenses because they qualify the taxpayer for a new trade or business activity, can the taxpayer instead recover the expenses in another manner? Recall from Chapter 4 that § 195 generally permits taxpayers to amortize the cost of "start-up expenditures" (expenses incurred in investigating and/or creating a new business activity) over a period of 15 years. So can the taxpayer amortize the expenses for education under § 195 once the taxpayer commences work in the new business activity? The following case addresses the issue indirectly, for it involves a taxpayer that tried to apply a different form of cost recovery— depreciation deductions—to education costs.

SHARON v. COMMISSIONER, 66 T.C. 515 (1976), aff'd, 591 F.2d 1273 (9th Cir. 1978).

Facts: The taxpayer attended Brandeis University from 1957–1961, where he earned a Bachelor of Arts degree. He then attended Columbia University School of Law, completing his law degree in 1964. He then sat for the New York bar, incurring a $25 examination fee and another $175 for a bar review course. He passed the bar exam and worked for three years as an attorney at a New York City law firm. In 1967, the taxpayer accepted a position in the Service's Office of Regional Counsel in California. Although the Service did not require the taxpayer to become a member of the California bar, the taxpayer decided to sit for the California bar exam. He spent about $800 to obtain his license to practice in California, including $230 for a bar review course and about $550 in various bar exam and admittance fees. The taxpayer also incurred fees to be admitted to practice before the Ninth Circuit Court of Appeals and the Northern District of California.

The taxpayer argued that he could amortize the costs of obtaining his license to practice in New York over the period beginning with the date of his admission to the New York bar and ending with the date on which he attains age 65, his expected retirement date. In computing these costs, he included the cost of his undergraduate and law degrees in addition to the bar review course and the bar exam fee.

The taxpayer also argued that he could amortize the costs of getting licensed in California, including his bar review course fees, the bar exam fees, and the fees paid to be admitted to practice in two federal courts there. Here, said the taxpayer, an argument for cost recovery was especially strong, for he was already carrying on the business of being an attorney when he incurred the costs he seeks to amortize.

Issues: (1) May the taxpayer amortize the cost of obtaining the license to practice in New York?

(2) May the taxpayer amortize the cost of obtaining the license to practice in California and the licenses to practice in two federal courts there?

Holdings: (1) He may amortize the bar exam fee, but not the costs of his college and law school education and not the cost of the bar review course.

(2) He may amortize the bar exam fee and the fees paid to be licensed in the two federal courts, but not the cost of the bar review course.

Rationale: (1) "There is no merit in the petitioner's claim to an amortization deduction for the cost of his education and related expenses in qualifying himself for the legal profession. His college and law school expenses provided him with a general education which will be beneficial to him in a wide variety of ways. The costs and responsibility for obtaining such education are personal. * * * In the words of [Regulation] section 1.162–5(b), all costs of 'minimum educational requirements for qualification in * * * employment' are 'personal expenditures or constitute an inseparable aggregate of personal and capital expenditures.' There is no 'rational' or workable basis for any allocation of this inseparable aggregate between the nondeductible personal component and a deductible component of the total expense. Such expenses are not made any less personal or any more separable from the aggregate by attempting to capitalize them for amortization purposes. Since the inseparable aggregate includes personal expenditures, the preeminence of section 262 over section 167 precludes any amortization deduction. The same reasoning applies to the costs of review courses and related expenses taken to qualify for the practice of a profession.

"In his brief, the petitioner * * * [asserts] that he is not attempting to capitalize his educational costs, but rather, the cost of his license to practice law. Despite the label which the petitioner would apply to such costs, they nonetheless constitute the costs of his education, which are personal and nondeductible. Moreover, in his petition, he alleged that the capital asset he was seeking to amortize was his education.

"There remains the $25 fee paid for the petitioner's license to practice in New York. This was not an educational expense but was a fee paid for the privilege of practicing law in New York, a nontransferable license which has value beyond the taxable years, and such fee is a capital expenditure. The Commissioner has limited his argument to the educational expenses and apparently concedes that the fee may be amortized."

(2) "In connection with his alternative claim that he be allowed to amortize the costs of acquiring his license to practice law in California, the petitioner asserts that such costs [include] the cost of a California bar review course, registration fees, and other items * * *. However, the petitioner is in error in including the cost of his bar review course, $230, in the capital cost of his license to practice in California.

"It is clear that the amount the petitioner paid for the bar review course was an expenditure 'made by an individual for education' within the meaning of section 1.162–5(a) of the Income Tax Regulations. Although the petitioner was authorized to practice law in some jurisdictions when he took the California bar review course, such course was nevertheless educational in the same sense as the first bar review course. The deductibility of such educational expenses is governed by the rules of section 1.162–5 of the regulations. * * *

"Nor may the petitioner treat the payment for the California bar review course as a part of the costs of acquiring his license to practice in California. Educational expenses which are incurred to meet the minimum educational requirements for qualification in a taxpayer's trade or business or which qualify him for a new trade or business are 'personal expenditures or constitute an inseparable aggregate of personal and capital expenditures.' Sec. 1.162–5(b), Income Tax Regs. We find that the bar review course helped to qualify the petitioner for a new trade or business so that its costs are personal expenses.

"We have previously adopted a 'commonsense approach' in determining whether an educational expenditure qualifies a taxpayer for a 'new trade or business.' If the education qualifies the taxpayer to perform significantly different tasks and activities than he could perform prior to the education, then the education qualifies him for a new trade or business. Thus, we have held that a professor of social work is in a different trade or business than a social caseworker. A licensed public accountant is in a different trade or business than a certified public accountant. A registered pharmacist is in a different trade or business than an intern pharmacist, even though an intern performs many of the same tasks as a registered pharmacist, but under supervision.

"Before taking the bar review course and passing the attorney's bar examination, the petitioner was an attorney licensed to practice law in New York. As an attorney for the Regional Counsel, he could represent the Commissioner in this Court. However, he could not appear in either the State courts of California, the Federal District Courts located there, nor otherwise act as an attorney outside the scope of his employment with the IRS. If he had done so, he would have been guilty of a misdemeanor. Yet, after receiving his license to practice law in California, he became a member of the State bar with all its accompanying privileges and obligations. He could appear and represent clients in all the courts of California. By comparing the tasks and activities that the petitioner was qualified to perform prior to receiving his license to practice in California with the tasks and activities he was able to perform after receiving such license, it is clear that he has qualified for a new trade or business. Consequently, the expenses of his bar review course were personal and are not includable in the cost of his license to practice law in California.

"It is true that even before he became a member of the bar of California, the petitioner was engaged in the business of practicing law. However, in applying the provisions of section 1.162–5 of the regulations to determine whether educational expenses are personal or business in nature, it is not enough to find that the petitioner was already engaged in some business—we must ascertain the particular business in which he was previously engaged and whether the education qualified him to engage in a different business. Before taking the bar review course and becoming a member of the bar of California, the petitioner could not generally engage in the practice of law in that State, but the bar review course helped to qualify him to engage in such business.

"The Commissioner does not argue that the capital expenditures incurred in obtaining his license to practice law in California may not be amortized. In a series of cases, the courts have held that the fees paid by physicians to acquire hospital privileges are not current business expenses but are capital expenditures amortizable over the doctor's life expectancy. * * * We hold that the petitioner may treat the costs of acquiring his license to practice in California in a similar manner." The court thus permitted amortization of the bar exam fees, the admittance fee, the United States District Court fee, and the United States Court of Appeals fee.

Question

The *Sharon* court permitted amortization of certain costs over the taxpayer's life expectancy. But *Sharon* was decided prior to the enactment of § 197, the provision permitting 15–year amortization of certain intangible assets. See Chapter 4. If the *Sharon* case arose today, could the taxpayer amortize the costs over 15 years under § 197?

* * *

The Deduction for Qualified Tuition and Related Expenses. In 2001, Congress created a new, above-the-line deduction for "qualified tuition and related expenses." The deduction, authorized by § 222, uses the same definition of "qualified tuition and related expenses" found in § 25A, the education credit provisions previewed in Chapter 2 and discussed later in this Part. The § 222 deduction is set to expire at the end of 2007, but there is always a chance that the deduction could be extended. In 2002 and 2003, the maximum deduction available under § 222 was $3,000, and the deduction was available only to those taxpayers with adjusted gross incomes of $65,000 or less (or $130,000 for married taxpayers filing jointly). For 2004 and subsequent years, the deduction limit grows to $4,000, as do the adjusted gross income thresholds—$80,000 for single taxpayers and $160,000 for couples filing jointly. A taxpayer may not claim both the deduction and the § 25A credits. Not surprisingly, most taxpayers eligible for the credit would forego the § 222 deduction, as the dollar-for-dollar savings from a credit usually, but not always, yields a better result.

The § 222 deduction is available for education costs that are purely personal in nature. Deductible education costs under § 162(a) and Regulation § 1.162–5 are not affected or in any way limited by § 222. If a taxpayer's education costs qualify for deduction under § 162(a) and Regulation § 1.162–5, therefore, a deduction is allowed for such costs without regard to any limitations imposed by § 222. Section 222 comes into play with respect to education costs that do not qualify for deduction under § 162(a) and Regulation § 1.162–5.

* * *

Problem 10–6

Dewey Cheatham is a third-year student at Law School in Metropolis. Like many of his colleagues, Dewey is anxious to graduate from law school, pass the bar exam, and get a job. Last summer, Dewey worked as a summer associate at a downtown Metropolis law firm. Though chagrined to be selling out to The Man, Dewey hopes to return to a private law firm for permanent employment. In Year One, Dewey incurred all of the costs described below. Determine the extent to which Dewey can deduct these costs, ignoring the possible application of § 222 in each case.

(a) In January, Dewey paid $10,000 tuition for his final semester at Law School.

(b) In February, he paid $500 to photocopy and mail his resume to prospective employers.

(c) In March, he paid $200 for a round-trip ticket to Gotham City to interview with a law firm. The firm paid for his hotel expenses. Dewey paid a total of $100 for his meals away from home.

(d) In April, Dewey received a job offer from the firm. Realizing his business wardrobe consisted entirely of one suit used in several interviews, Dewey spent $2,000 on new professional attire (suits, dress shoes, ties, and such) that he would never, ever wear outside of work.

(e) In May, Dewey paid $2,000 for a bar review course.

(f) In early August, Dewey learned that he passed the bar exam, and he began working in the Gotham City firm's litigation department. By mid-September, Dewey realized his mistake. He asked for a leave of absence from the firm so he could work toward an LL.M. in Taxation at Law School back in Metropolis. The firm granted his request, and Dewey paid $10,000 tuition to Law School for his semester in the graduate tax program.

(g) In December, Dewey paid $500 to photocopy and mail his resume to prospective employers at other firms who were keenly interested (logically) in applicants with LL.M.s in Taxation.

* * *

Self-Assessment Question

(Solutions to Self–Assessment Questions are set forth in Appendix 3.)

SAQ 10–4. Now consider the deduction offered by § 222. If the deduction were in effect during Year One, how would your answers to parts (a) and (f) of Problem 10–6 immediately above change assuming:

(a) That Dewey's adjusted gross income for Year One is $30,000?

(b) That Dewey's adjusted gross income for Year One is $70,000?

* * *

The Education Credits. As discussed briefly in Chapter 2, two nonrefundable credits are available for certain expenses related to higher education. The Hope Scholarship Credit is available for tuition and related expenses incurred during the first two years of postsecondary education. See § 25A(b). The student must be going to school on at least a half-time basis, and the credit is lost if the student is convicted of a felony drug offense. If all other requirements are met, the first $1,000 in "qualified tuition and related expenses" (an amount adjusted for inflation) is fully creditable, as are half of such expenses in excess of $1,000. Thus, for example, if the total of such expenses for the year is $4,600, the taxpayer can credit $2,800 (all of the first $1,000 plus half of the remaining $3,600).

"Qualified tuition and related expenses" is defined as the tuition and fees paid at most colleges and universities for the enrollment or attendance of the taxpayer, the taxpayer's spouse, or any dependent of the taxpayer (assuming the taxpayer is eligible to claim the dependency exemption in § 151(c) with respect to that dependent). The term specifically does not include student activity fees, athletic fees, insurance costs, or room and board expenses.

The second credit under § 25A is the Lifetime Learning Credit. See § 25A(c). As its name implies, this credit is not limited to the first two years of college education. Instead, the qualified tuition and related expenses are creditable as long as they relate to any course of instruction (at most colleges and universities) designed to develop or improve the student's job skills. The credit is limited to 20 percent of the first $10,000 in qualified tuition and related expenses, so no taxpayer can claim a credit of more than $2,000 in any one year. Furthermore, if the taxpayer was eligible for the Hope Scholarship Credit with respect to qualified tuition and related expenses, those same expenses may not be used for the Lifetime Learning Credit.

Both the Hope Scholarship Credit and the Lifetime Learning Credit are subject to an income limitation designed to limit the benefit of these credits to low-and moderate-income taxpayers. Very generally, the combined credit amount is phased-out if a taxpayer's adjusted gross income exceeds $40,000 ($80,000 for joint return filers). If the taxpayer's adjusted gross income exceeds $50,000 ($100,000 for joint filers), the credits are phased-out entirely. These threshold amounts are adjusted for inflation.

Analysts at the Tax Policy Center, a joint venture of the Urban Institute and the Brookings Institution, observed that the § 25A credits have, thus far, been under-utilized:

> The Joint Committee on Taxation first estimated that the credits would cost $25.8 billion over the first four years. IRS data show that the actual cost of the credit for this same period was only $18.3 billion, approximately 71 percent of the initial estimate. The low utilization may be due to lack of knowledge. A 2001 survey of students at the University of California (UC) by Hoblitzell and Smith found that 70 percent of main campus students did not claim either credit—29 percent of them reported they were unaware of the credits and 58 percent reported they were ineligible for the credits. Fewer undergraduates claimed an educational credit (27 percent) than graduate students (32 percent).

Fitzpatrick and Maag, *Subsidizing Higher Education Through the Federal Income Tax Code*, 100 Tax Notes 95 (2003). Going forward, the Joint Committee on Taxation estimates that the credits in § 25A will cost $25.2 billion over the five-year period beginning in 2006. See Appendix 1.

Interest on Education Loans. As you may know all too well, education loans are an important vehicle for financing the rising costs of higher education. Like any borrowing arrangement at arms'-length, however, student loans require the payment of interest. Recall from Chapter 8 that § 163(h)(1) disallows any deduction for "personal interest," defined in § 163(h)(2) as all but six specified forms of interest payments. Fortunately, §§ 163(h)(2)(F) and 221 permit a deduction for interest paid with respect to a "qualified education loan." The deduction is limited to $2,500 annually, and this limitation is reduced for taxpayers with adjusted gross incomes (as modified) in excess of $50,000 ($100,000 for joint filers). No deduction at all is available to taxpayers with modified adjusted gross incomes in excess of $65,000 (or $130,000 for joint filers). These dollar amounts are adjusted for inflation.

The deduction is also denied to those who can be claimed as a dependent on another's tax return, even if that other person did not pay or incur the interest expense and even if that person was not legally obligated to make the interest payment. Regulations issued in May, 2004, confirm that interest payments by third parties on behalf of the taxpayer will be treated as payments made by the taxpayer for purposes of the deduction. See Treas. Reg. § 1.221–1(b)(4).

In order to determine whether the loan is a "qualified education loan," the taxpayer must refer to other Code provisions and even to other federal statutes. Generally speaking, a qualified education loan is one that meets the following four requirements:

(1) it was taken out *solely* to pay "qualified higher education expenses" (the costs of attending a post-secondary educational institution described in § 481 of the Higher Education Act of 1965 that has been certified by the United States Department of Education to be eligible to participate in federal financial aid programs, including tuition, fees, books, supplies, transportation, room and board, and other expenses—all as determined by the educational institution);

(2) it was incurred for the benefit of the taxpayer, the taxpayer's spouse, or anyone who was a dependent of the taxpayer when the loan was incurred;

(3) the qualified higher education expenses were paid or incurred within a reasonable time before or after the loan was incurred; and

(4) the qualified higher education expenses are attributable to education furnished to the person described in (2), above, during the period in which such person was in attendance as a degree candidate on at least a half-time basis.

Naturally, if the amount loaned exceeds the amount of qualified higher education expenses, then the loan proceeds were not used *solely* for paying qualified higher education expenses, meaning no portion of the interest paid on such loan will be deductible under § 221. Importantly, then, the statute reduces the amount of qualified higher education expenses by any qualified scholarships, employer-provided educational assistance, distributions from qualified tuition programs, and other amounts received by the student that are excluded from gross income.

Section 221 used to limit the student loan interest deduction to payments made in the first five years that interest payments were required. Legislation in 2001 repealed this limitation, but when the 2001 legislation sunsets in 2011, the limitation will come back into play.

* * *

Self-Assessment Question

(Solutions to Self–Assessment Questions are set forth in Appendix 3.)

SAQ 10–5. In Year One, Ed Jukayshun borrowed $10,000 from Bank (an unrelated party) to pay tuition and fees as a full-time student at the University of Florida at Orlando (UFO), an educational institution described in § 481 of the Higher Education Act of 1965 that has been certified by the United States Department of Education to be eligible to participate in federal financial aid programs. In Year Two, Ed graduated and secured productive employment. Pursuant to the terms of his loan arrangement, Ed paid $500 interest to Bank in Year Two.

(a) To what extent may Ed deduct the interest paid to Bank in Year Two?

(b) How would the answer to (a) change if Ed borrowed $60,000 in Year One and therefore paid $3,000 interest to Bank in Year Two?

(c) How would the answer to (a) change if Ed's adjusted gross income for Year Two was $100,000?

(d) How would the answer to (a) change if Ed's adjusted gross income for Year Two was $63,500?

(e) How would the answer to (a) change if Ed had borrowed the $10,000 from his parents instead of Bank?

(f) How would the answer to (a) change if Ed's parents made the interest payment to Bank on his behalf?

(g) How would the answer to (a) change if Ed used only half of the loan proceeds to pay tuition to UFO in Year One and used the other half of the loan proceeds to purchase a car?

(h) Now assume that Ed borrowed the money in Year One but did not enroll at UFO until Year Two, at which time he used the loan proceeds to pay the tuition and fees. To what extent can Ed deduct a $500 interest payment made to Bank in Year Three?

E. HOME OFFICE AND VACATION HOME EXPENSES

Code: IRC §§ 280A(a)–(e), (g).

Regs: None.

Home Office Expenses. Recent estimates claim that nearly 20 million Americans operate a business activity from their homes. Of that number, 12 million derive the majority of their household incomes from home business activities. Another 20 million American employees perform a substantial amount of their duties at home. With 40 million taxpayers making both business and personal use of a dwelling, important questions about the deductibility of expenses related to the dwelling arise.

In some cases, taxpayers who work from home devote one or more rooms in the dwelling exclusively to the business activity. Examples include spare bedrooms converted into home offices, garages converted into clinics or studios, and basements converted into day care facilities. While § 280A(a) generally disallows any deductions related to the use of a dwelling that also serves as the taxpayer's residence, § 280A(c) generally restores those deductions to the extent they are allocable to a portion of the dwelling used **regularly** and **exclusively** as the principal place of business for any business activity of the taxpayer. Notice, however, that if the taxpayer's business activity is the performance of services as an employee, the taxpayer may only claim these restored deductions if he or she can prove that the business use of the taxpayer's dwelling is for the convenience of the employer. This limitation, combined with the general requirements in § 280A(c), effectively preclude a deduction for those who perform only occasional work at home on behalf of an employer.

Home office expenses potentially deductible under § 280A include direct costs like depreciation on equipment and improvements used exclusively in the business (shelving, carpeting, and the like), as well as the office's share of indirect costs such as utilities, repair and maintenance costs, and property insurance. Subject to the deduction limitation set forth in § 280A(c)(5), discussed below, the direct costs may be deductible in full. On the other hand, only the "business percentage" (the portion of the home used regularly and exclusively for business) of the indirect costs are potentially deductible. For example, if a taxpayer uses 500 square feet in a 2,000 square-foot home for a home office, then the taxpayer can deduct up to 25 percent of the indirect expenses related to the home (500 is 25 percent of 2,000).

Determining the maximum amount deductible with respect to home office expenses under § 280A(c) can prove cumbersome. Under § 280A(c)(5), potentially deductible home office expenses are limited to an amount equal to the excess of the gross income derived from the home office ("GI" in the formula below, for "gross income") over the sum of: (1) the business percentage portion of the expenses deductible even if the home was not used for a home office ("OAD," for "otherwise allowable deductions"), and (2) other deductions related to the same business activity but not attributable to the use of the home itself ("SBD," for "same business deductions").

> [GI]–[(OAD) + (SBD)] = maximum home office deductions under § 280A(c)

Any potentially deductible expenses in excess of this limitation may be carried over to the next taxable year.

* * *

Self-Assessment Question

(Solutions to Self–Assessment Questions are set forth in Appendix 3.)

SAQ 10–6. Hedra Carlson is a self-employed sales representative who recently converted the 200 square-foot basement of her 2,000 square-foot home into an office. Hedra uses the basement office exclusively and regularly to make appointments, write up orders, file reports with suppliers, and communicate with customers. For Year One, Hedra's gross income from her basement business activity was $5,000. She incurred the following expenses in Year One:

Expenses Related to Business	
Business supplies	$2,000
Interest on bank loan (proceeds used in business)	$1,000

Expenses Related to Home	
Property taxes	$2,000
Mortgage interest	$10,000
Utilities (electricity, sewer, gas, water)	$1,000
Depreciation	$7,500

To what extent may Hedra deduct these expenses on her Year One tax return?

* * *

Vacation Home Expenses. A lakefront cabin set within a remote forest. An oceanfront condominium. A "getaway" home in Aspen. If your view of "the good life" includes a second home in your favorite locale, you need to find a way to afford it. For most, even affluent taxpayers, the answer is to rent the property to others when not enjoying it themselves. But rentals present new and different headaches—not all renters treat the property nicely, and even the most considerate and tidy guests will subject the home to wear and tear.

From a tax perspective, holding a vacation home out for rental may present some benefits. Because the vacation home is rental property held for investment purposes (not just a personal-use residence), the cost of the vacation home can be depreciated. See § 167(a). In addition, expenses attributable to the property might prove deductible under § 212(2) (maintenance of property held for the production of income).

As with home offices, § 280A(a) generally disallows any deduction with respect to a vacation home if the property is used by the taxpayer as a residence. Section 280A(d) generally provides that a taxpayer will be considered to use a dwelling as his or her residence if the taxpayer's personal use of the property exceeds 14 days in the taxable year. But if the taxpayer rents the dwelling to others for more than 140 days in the taxable year, the taxpayer is considered to use the property as a residence only if he or she makes personal use of the property more than ten percent of the number of days it is rented to others at a fair rental value. As you would expect by now, § 280A(d) contains some anti-avoidance rules that prevent easy manipulation of this objective test. For example, where two taxpayers each own a vacation home in Palm Springs, California, and each agrees to use the other's vacation home so as to avoid the use of his or her own home for more than 14 days, § 280A(d)(2)(B) will deem each taxpayer to have used his or her own vacation home as a residence.

If a vacation home is used by the taxpayer both as a residence and as a rental property, then § 280A(e) provides that expenses related to the property that would not be deductible but for the fact that the property is rented to others will only be allowed in part. The amount allowable is to be determined by multiplying such expenses by the following fraction:

$$\frac{\#\text{days the property is rented at fair rental value}}{\text{total }\#\text{days the property is used}}$$

For instance, if a taxpayer rents out her vacation home for 30 days at a fair rental value in the current year and lives in the vacation home for 60 days in the current year, then one-third of the expenses that would be deductible solely because of the rental activity may be deducted on the taxpayer's return. So if the taxpayer spent $3,000 on maintenance and $900 on property insurance for the vacation home, he or she could deduct a total of $1,300. The extra $2,600 is considered allocable to the taxpayer's personal use and thus represents consumption; the excess does not carry over to future taxable years. If an expense would be deductible even if the property was not held for rental (like property taxes), the expense is allowed in full. See § 280A(e)(2).

If a taxpayer's vacation home is actually rented for less than 15 days during the year, however, a different rule applies. Under § 280A(g), *none* of the expenses that would be deductible solely because of the rental activity may be deducted on the taxpayer's return, but the taxpayer may also *exclude* from gross income any "income derived from such use." Interestingly, this provision is apparently being used by some home-owners who have appeared on home improvement television programs to exclude the value of improvements made to their homes as part of the television show. Producers, it seems, lease a home for up to ten days and the owners receive the improvements as "rent." Because the home is rented out for less than 15 days, the homeowners in some cases have been advised to exclude the value of the improvements from gross income using § 280A(g) as authority. See *Tax Trouble for ABC's "Extreme" Winners?*, NEWSWEEK (May 17, 2004). Since § 280A(g) is not limited by its terms to vacation homes, using the exclusion with respect to the taxpayer's principal residence in this context is arguably workable. But Congress clearly did not anticipate that the benefit of § 280A(g) would be utilized in this context. If you had a client who appeared on one of these home improvement programs, would you advise him or her to exclude the value of the improvements under § 280A(g)?

* * *

F. CLOTHING EXPENSES

Code: *Review* IRC §§ 162(a); 262.

Regs: *Skim* Treas. Reg. § 1.262–1(b)(8).

A Clothes Call for a Deduction. In all but a very few places, clothing is one of the basic necessities of life. Just as a taxpayer generally cannot deduct the cost of food, water, or shelter, a taxpayer generally may not deduct the cost of clothing. All of these costs represent nondeductible personal expenses under § 262.

The Service has historically taken a lenient approach with respect to the costs to acquire and maintain uniforms required for the taxpayer's employment. As long as such uniforms are not suitable for ordinary wear and "distinctive" of the related business activity, the Service generally permits employees to treat such costs as deductible business expenses. See, e.g., *Revenue Ruling 70–474*, 1970–2 C.B. 34 (uniform costs of police officers, firefighters, postal carriers, nurses, bus drivers, and railroad employees deductible as business expenses). Curiously, however, the regulations state that the cost of a military uniform is a nondeductible personal expense unless the taxpayer is a reservist. Treas. Reg. § 1.262–1(b)(8).

The key to a deduction for clothing expense is to prove that the apparel is not suitable for ordinary wear. Such proof indicates that the clothing is predominately used for business, not personal purposes. As fashion trends change, then, so too might the eligibility for a deduction. For example, *Revenue Ruling 70–474* indicates that a nurse may deduct the cost of a uniform. More recently, however, nursing uniforms have become more ordinary in appearance, rendering the cost of such clothing nondeductible. *See Bradley v. Commissioner*, T.C. Memo. 1996–461 (nurse denied deduction for cost of uniform absent proof that uniform was not suitable for ordinary wear).

Could an attorney deduct the cost of a new suit if he or she could prove that the suit is worn only when making court appearances and not at any other time? The following case is instructive on this issue.

PEVSNER v. COMMISSIONER

United States Court of Appeals, Fifth Circuit, 1980.
628 F.2d 467.

JOHNSON, Judge:

This is an appeal by the Commissioner of Internal Revenue from a decision of the United States Tax Court. The tax court upheld taxpayer's business expense deduction for clothing expenditures in the amount of $1,621.91 for the taxable year 1975. We reverse.

Since June 1973 Sandra J. Pevsner, taxpayer, has been employed as the manager of the Sakowitz Yves St. Laurent Rive Gauche Boutique located in Dallas, Texas. The boutique sells only women's clothes and accessories designed by Yves St. Laurent (YSL), one of the leading designers of women's apparel. Although the clothing is ready to wear, it is highly fashionable and expensively priced. Some customers of the boutique purchase and wear the YSL apparel for their daily activities and spend as much as $20,000 per year for such apparel.

As manager of the boutique, the taxpayer is expected by her employer to wear YSL clothes while at work. In her appearance, she is expected to project the image of an exclusive lifestyle and to demonstrate to her customers that she is aware of the YSL current fashion trends as well as trends generally. Because the boutique sells YSL clothes exclusively, taxpayer must be able, when a customer compliments her on her clothes, to say that they are designed by YSL. In addition to wearing YSL apparel while at the boutique, she wears them while commuting to and from work, to fashion shows sponsored by the boutique, and to business luncheons at which she represents the boutique. During 1975, the taxpayer bought, at an employee's discount, the following items: four blouses, three skirts, one pair of slacks, one trench coat, two sweaters, one jacket, one tunic, five scarves, six belts, two pairs of shoes and four necklaces. The total cost of this apparel was $1,381.91. In addition, the sum of $240 was expended for maintenance of these items.

Although the clothing and accessories purchased by the taxpayer were the type used for general purposes by the regular customers of the boutique, the taxpayer is not a normal purchaser of these clothes. The taxpayer and her husband, who is partially disabled because of a severe heart attack suffered in 1971, lead a simple life and their social activities are very limited and informal. Although taxpayer's employer has no objection to her wearing the apparel away from work, taxpayer stated that she did not wear the clothes during off-work hours because she felt that they were too expensive for her simple everyday lifestyle. Another reason why she did not wear the YSL clothes apart from work was to make them last longer. Taxpayer did admit at trial, however, that a number of the articles were things she could have worn off the job and in which she would have looked "nice."

On her joint federal income tax return for 1975, taxpayer deducted $990 as an ordinary and necessary business expense with respect to her purchase of the YSL clothing and accessories. However, in the tax court, taxpayer claimed a deduction for the full $1,381.91 cost of the apparel and for the $240 cost of maintaining the apparel. The tax court allowed the taxpayer to deduct both expenses in the total amount of $1,621.91. The tax court reasoned that the apparel was not suitable to the private lifestyle maintained by the taxpayer. This appeal by the Commissioner followed.

The principal issue on appeal is whether the taxpayer is entitled to deduct as an ordinary and necessary business expense the cost of purchasing and maintaining the YSL clothes and accessories worn by the taxpayer in her employment as the manager of the boutique. This determination requires an examination of the relationship between Section 162(a) of the Internal Revenue Code of 1954, which allows a deduction for ordinary and necessary expenses incurred in the conduct of a trade or business, and Section 262 of the Code, which bars a deduction for all "personal, living, or family expenses." Although many expenses are helpful or essential to one's business activities—such as commuting expenses and the cost of meals while at work—these expenditures are considered inherently personal and are disallowed under Section 262.

The generally accepted rule governing the deductibility of clothing expenses is that the cost of clothing is deductible as a business expense only if: (1) the clothing is of a type specifically required as a condition of employment, (2) it is not adaptable to general usage as ordinary clothing, and (3) it is not so worn. *Donnelly v. Commissioner*, 262 F.2d 411, 412 (2d Cir. 1959).

In the present case, the Commissioner stipulated that the taxpayer was required by her employer to wear YSL clothing and that she did not wear such apparel apart from work. The Commissioner maintained, however, that a deduction should be denied because the YSL clothes and accessories purchased by the taxpayer were adaptable for general usage as ordinary clothing and she was not prohibited from using them as such. The tax court, in rejecting the Commissioner's argument for the application of an objective test, recognized that the test for deductibility was whether the clothing was "suitable for general or personal wear" but determined that the matter of suitability was to be judged subjectively, in light of the taxpayer's lifestyle. Although the court recognized that the YSL apparel "might be used by some members of society for general purposes," it felt that because the "wearing of YSL apparel outside work would be inconsistent with ... (taxpayer's) lifestyle," sufficient reason was shown for allowing a deduction for the clothing expenditures.

In reaching its decision, the tax court relied heavily upon *Yeomans v. Commissioner*, 30 T.C. 757 (1958). In *Yeomans*, the taxpayer was employed as fashion coordinator for a shoe manufacturing company. Her employment necessitated her attendance at meetings of fashion experts and at fashion shows sponsored by her employer. On these occasions, she was expected to wear clothing that was new, highly styled, and such as "might be sought after and worn for personal use by women who make it a practice to dress according to the most advanced or extreme fashions." 30 T.C. at 768. However, for her personal wear, Ms. Yeomans preferred a plainer and more conservative style of dress. As a consequence, some of the items she purchased were not suitable for her private and personal wear and were not so worn. The tax court allowed a deduction for the cost of the items that were not suitable for her personal wear. Although the basis for the decision in *Yeomans* is not clearly stated, the tax court in the case *sub judice* determined that

> (a) careful reading of *Yeomans* shows that, without a doubt, the Court based its decision on a determination of Ms. Yeomans' lifestyle and that the clothes were not suitable for her use in such lifestyle. Furthermore, the Court recognized that the clothes Ms. Yeomans purchased were suitable for wear by women who customarily wore such highly styled apparel, but such fact did not cause the court to decide the issue against her. Thus, *Yeomans* clearly decides the issue before us in favor of the petitioner.

T.C. Memo 1979–311 at 9–10.

Notwithstanding the tax court's decision in *Yeomans*, the Circuits that have addressed the issue have taken an objective, rather than subjective, approach. *Stiner v. United States*, 524 F.2d 640, 641 (10th Cir. 1975); *Donnelly v. Commissioner*, 262 F.2d 411, 412 (2d Cir. 1959). An objective approach was also taken by the tax court in *Drill v. Commissioner*, 8 T.C. 902 (1947). Under an objective test, no reference is made to the individual taxpayer's lifestyle or personal taste. Instead, adaptability for personal or general use depends upon what is generally accepted for ordinary street wear.

The principal argument in support of an objective test is, of course, administrative necessity. The Commissioner argues that, as a practical matter, it is virtually impossible to determine at what point either price or style makes clothing inconsistent with or inappropriate to a taxpayer's lifestyle. Moreover, the Commissioner argues that the price one pays and the styles one selects are inherently personal choices governed by taste, fashion, and other unmeasurable values. Indeed, the tax court has rejected the argument that a taxpayer's personal taste can dictate whether clothing is appropriate for general use. See *Drill v. Commissioner*, 8 T.C. 902 (1947). An objective test, although not perfect, provides a practical administrative approach that allows a taxpayer or revenue agent to look only to objective facts in determining whether clothing required as a condition of employment is adaptable to general use as ordinary streetwear. Conversely, the tax court's reliance on subjective factors provides no concrete guidelines in determining the deductibility of clothing purchased as a condition of employment.

In addition to achieving a practical administrative result, an objective test also tends to promote substantial fairness among the greatest number of taxpayers. As the Commissioner suggests, it apparently would be the tax court's position that two similarly situated YSL boutique managers with identical wardrobes would be subject to disparate tax consequences depending upon the particular manager's lifestyle and "socio-economic level." This result, however, is not consonant with a reasonable interpretation of Sections 162 and 262.

For the reasons stated above, the decision of the tax court upholding the deduction for taxpayer's purchase of YSL clothing is reversed. Consequently, the portion of the tax court's decision upholding the deduction for maintenance costs for the clothing is also

REVERSED.

* * *

NICELY v. COMMISSIONER, T.C. Memo. 2006–172.

Facts: The taxpayer is a welder for a pipeline company. On his 2002 return, the taxpayer claimed a number of deductions related to his job, including $600 in clothes, Rocky Wolverine boots, and gloves. The Service disallowed this deduction in its notice of deficiency. The taxpayer appeared *pro se* before the Tax Court to contest this assessment.

Issue: May the taxpayer deduct the claimed clothing costs as a business expense?

Holding: No.

Rationale: The court rejected the taxpayer's claimed deduction for the clothing expense, and not just because the taxpayer lacked receipts for these items: "The record is devoid of evidence that the unidentified clothes and gloves and the Rocky Wolverine boots were required in petitioner's employment, were not suitable for general or personal wear, and were not worn for general or personal purposes. In fact, petitioner acknowledged at trial that he was wearing Rocky Wolverine boots."

* * *

Chapter 11

TAX SHELTER AND TAX AVOIDANCE LIMITATIONS

Gimme Shelter. This Chapter concerns some of the methods by which Congress has addressed the problem of **tax shelters**, activities that comply with the literal requirements of the Internal Revenue Code but produce benefits to taxpayers that are antithetical to the underlying policies of the provisions at issue. In the typical tax shelter transaction, a taxpayer enters into an activity with the hope of using losses and deductions from that activity to offset ordinary income from other sources. The taxpayer often *wants* the shelter activity to be a loser precisely because the value of the transaction comes from the resulting deductions and losses. As one commentator so accurately quipped, a tax shelter transaction is "a deal done by very smart people that, absent tax considerations, would be very stupid." Tom Herman, *Tax Report*, WALL ST. J. at A–1 (Feb. 10, 1999) (quoting Professor Michael J. Graetz).

Part A of this Chapter considers the use of hobby activities to generate deductions. By definition, hobbies are not designed to be profitable ventures. But very often, hobby activities can generate numerous and substantial expenses. While the Code generally disallows deductions related to hobby activities as personal expenses, Congress does (generously) allow a limited amount of deductions allocable to hobbies. While hobbies are not the prototypical tax shelter transaction (taxpayers would engage in hobbies even absent tax considerations), taxpayer attempts to qualify a hobby activity as a business or an investment activity often involve the same tax avoidance impulses that motivate traditional tax shelters.

Part B of this Chapter examines the at-risk limitations in § 465. Here the concern relates to a taxpayer's use of nonrecourse financing to invest in activities designed to be losers. Recall that if the taxpayer defaults on a nonrecourse debt, the taxpayer loses only the assets that specifically secure the debt. If the debt is secured by assets related to the loss-laden activity, foreclosure upon default is hardly a tear-jerking event for the taxpayer. Thus, the taxpayer can reap the losses from an activity funded exclusively (or nearly exclusively) with nonrecourse debt and

729

bear none of the risk of loss normally associated with the obligation of repayment.

Part C of this Chapter looks at the passive activity loss limitation rules in § 469. Recall that taxpayers can generally offset losses from business activities against income from other activities, including employment and investment. An affluent taxpayer with lots of salary or investment income might want to invest in business activities that generate substantial losses to take advantage of this rule. We will see, however, that unless the taxpayer "materially participates" in that business activity, deductions and losses from the "passive activity" will be deductible only to the extent that the taxpayer has gross income in the same year from that or other passive activities.

Finally, Part D of this Chapter offers an introductory overview of the alternative minimum tax, a backstop measure designed to ensure that affluent taxpayers making extensive use of certain deduction and credit provisions pay at least a *minimum* amount of tax on their real incomes. This Part only presents an overview of a richly complex statutory scheme, with an emphasis on the tax policy implications of a separate tax regime designed to enhance the fairness of the tax laws.

Judicial Doctrines to Combat Tax Shelter Activities. Beyond the statutory provisions discussed in this Chapter, courts have developed a number of doctrines to block tax-motivated transactions. Often, a single transaction may trigger more than one doctrine. Indeed, the distinctions between these various doctrines are not altogether clear. They do share a common theme—when a transaction manipulates the provisions of the Code to achieve a result that contradicts the basic structure of the federal tax laws or violates the intent of the specific Code provisions at issue, courts can ignore or invalidate the transaction. Let's briefly consider five doctrines that courts have used to give transactions their "proper" tax treatment.

(1) THE DOCTRINE OF SUBSTANCE OVER FORM. This doctrine holds that the tax results of a transaction are best determined with reference to its underlying substance instead of the formal steps taken to implement it. The basic premise is that if two transactions have the same economic result to the parties involved, they should have the same tax result, too. We have seen examples of this doctrine throughout the text, most notably in *Old Colony Trust Co. v. Commissioner* in Chapter 3. Recall that an employer's payment of an employee's federal income tax liability was taxed as if the employer had paid the same amount as compensation to the employee, who then used those funds to pay the tax liability. Because those two transactions had the same economic effect, the employer's payment to the government was treated as compensation (and thus as gross income) to the employee.

While the government can assert the doctrine of substance over form against a taxpayer, a taxpayer may not use the doctrine to recharacterize the tax treatment of a transaction he or she undertakes. As the Supreme Court observed:

[W]hile a taxpayer is free to organize his affairs as he chooses, nevertheless, once having done so, he must accept the tax consequences of his choice, whether contemplated or not, and may not enjoy the benefit of some other route he might have chosen to follow but did not.

Commissioner v. National Alfalfa Dehydrating & Milling Co., 417 U.S. 134, 149, 94 S.Ct. 2129, 40 L.Ed.2d 717 (1974).

The doctrine of substance over form can be tricky to apply, *Old Colony Trust* notwithstanding. It is intuitively appealing to state that substance should prevail over form, but the Code often adopts a very formalistic approach: witness the time and geographic conditions imposed for the deduction for moving expenses under § 217, see Chapter 10, and the various requirements for the provision of excludable fringe benefits under §§ 119 and 132. See Chapter 3. It can be difficult for the government to convince a court that the substance of a transaction should trump its form when the Code frequently emphasizes form.

(2) THE STEP TRANSACTION DOCTRINE. Like the doctrine of substance over form, this doctrine tries to determine "what's really going on" in a transaction. As described by the Tax Court, the step transaction doctrine "treats a series of formally separate 'steps' as a single transaction if such steps are in substance integrated, interdependent, and focused toward a particular result." *Penrod v. Commissioner*, 88 T.C. 1415, 1428 (1987). The step transaction doctrine often applies in three situations:

> · *End result*. The step transaction doctrine will apply when it is apparent that each of the separate steps are undertaken specifically to achieve the end result claimed by the taxpayer.
>
> · *Interdependence*. The doctrine can also apply where the facts show that one step would be a meaningless endeavor absent the other step(s).
>
> · *Binding commitment*. Of course, the step transaction doctrine will also apply where, at the time of the first step, the taxpayer is or becomes legally bound to complete the remaining step(s).

Taxpayers can block application of the step transaction doctrine by proving that, when the first step was taken, the remaining steps were not yet planned or contemplated. Historically, the best evidence of the lack of intent to complete the remaining steps is a significant lapse of time between the steps. Some practitioners believe that if Step 1 occurs in Year One and Step 2 occurs in Year Three, a taxpayer is safe from the application of the step transaction doctrine. Though no court has endorsed this "year-between-steps" rule of thumb, it stands to reason that the longer the lapse of time between steps, the better the objective evidence of a lack of intent to complete the steps as part of some overarching plan.

(3) THE BUSINESS PURPOSE DOCTRINE. Courts will disregard a transaction for tax purposes if it appears that the taxpayer was motivated by no business purpose other than to avoid tax or secure some tax benefit. Unlike some of the other doctrines discussed here, the business purpose doctrine is necessarily a subjective inquiry into the taxpayer's intent. If the taxpayer can show some non-tax benefit from (or purpose for) the transaction, then this doctrine loses much of its force. Often taxpayers can meet this challenge, so rarely does the business purpose doctrine alone invalidate a transaction. Of the five doctrines discussed here, then, the business purpose doctrine is Tito while the others are Michael, Janet, LaToya, and Jermaine.

(4) THE SHAM TRANSACTION DOCTRINE. This doctrine singles out those transactions where the purported economic activities giving rise to the claimed tax benefits do not occur. A classic example of the sham transaction doctrine comes from *Knetsch v. United States*, 364 U.S. 361, 81 S.Ct. 132, 5 L.Ed.2d 128 (1960). In *Knetsch*, the taxpayer purchased deferred annuities (rights to regular payments in future years) at a cost of about $4,004,000. The taxpayer paid this cost with $4,000 of cash and the delivery of a $4 million nonrecourse promissory note secured by the annuities. The terms of the promissory note required the taxpayer to pay 3.5 percent interest on the $4 million principal amount (which amounts to $140,000) annually, which the taxpayer did. At the time of the *Knetsch* case, the interest payment was clearly deductible, and the taxpayer used this deduction to offset other ordinary income.

Meanwhile, the taxpayer "borrowed" against the increasing value of the annuities to obtain some current cash flow from the arrangement. To illustrate (using simpler numbers than those in the actual case), assume that the annuities grew at a rate of about 2.5 percent annually, meaning that the $4 million amount was growing at about $100,000 annually. Each year, the taxpayer would borrow about $99,000 (virtually all of the annual growth) from the annuity company. Because the transaction was structured as a loan, each $99,000 loan-slash-withdrawal was not included in the taxpayer's gross income. The taxpayer was obligated to repay these amounts, but the taxpayer satisfied this obligation simply by having the annuity company pay less at the time an annuity contract matured. Thus, the taxpayer took more money now in exchange for less money later.

This arrangement, then, allowed the taxpayer to obtain $99,000 of cash flows annually. But at what cost? The taxpayer had to pay $140,000 of interest annually on the promissory note in order to obtain the benefit of $99,000 annually. That's a loss of $41,000 each year! Why on earth would the taxpayer participate in this complex arrangement only to lose $41,000 annually? The answer, of course, is the tax benefit from the annual $140,000 deduction. At the time of *Knetsch*, the taxpayer's average rate of tax was 80 percent (!). A deduction of $140,000 saved the taxpayer $112,000 of tax ($140,000 x 80% = $112,000). This tax savings more than offsets the $41,000 loss—it actually makes the transaction profitable for the taxpayer! So here is the taxpayer claims a deduction for the payment of $140,000 when in fact the taxpayer's interest "payment" is more than offset by economic benefits provided to the taxpayer.

The Supreme Court held that the entire transaction was a sham entered into solely for the purpose of reducing the taxpayer's taxes. Accordingly, it agreed with the Service that the taxpayer's claimed interest deduction should be disallowed. After all, the interest deduction is premised on there being an actual payment of interest by the taxpayer. Yet in this case, the annuity company each year was "lending" to the taxpayer an amount that reimbursed a substantial portion of the taxpayer's interest payment, and the tax savings more than made up for the difference. There was, ultimately, no real economic outlay by the taxpayer; accordingly, the Court reasoned, no interest deduction should be allowed. Even Congress agreed with this analysis, codifying the denial of an interest deduction in this situation. See § 264(a)(2). But in the absence of a specific disallowance provision in the Code during the years at issue in *Knetsch*, it took the sham transaction doctrine to yield the proper result. For a more detailed and entertaining account of the *Knetsch* case, see Daniel N. Shaviro, *The Story of* Knetsch: *Judicial Doctrines Combating Tax Avoidance*, in Paul L. Caron (ed.), TAX STORIES: AN IN-DEPTH LOOK AT TEN LEADING FEDERAL INCOME TAX CASES 313 (2003).

(5) THE ECONOMIC SUBSTANCE DOCTRINE. Under the economic substance doctrine, courts will deny a tax benefit if the underlying transaction lacks economic substance independent of the tax considerations. As the Tax Court recently observed:

> The tax law * * * requires that the intended transactions have economic substance separate and distinct from economic benefit achieved solely by tax reduction. The doctrine of economic substance becomes applicable, and a judicial remedy is warranted, where a taxpayer seeks to claim tax benefits, unintended by Congress, by means of transactions that serve no economic purpose other than tax savings.

ACM Partnership v. Commissioner, T.C. Memo. 1997–115, aff'd, 157 F.3d 231 (3d Cir. 1998), cert. denied, 526 U.S. 1017, 119 S.Ct. 1251, 143 L.Ed.2d 348 (1999).

Unlike the sham transaction doctrine, the economic substance doctrine does not question whether the purported activity that gave rise to the benefit occurred (such as whether the taxpayer in *Knetsch* really made an interest payment). Instead, it questions whether that activity would have occurred absent the tax benefits claimed by the taxpayer. In this regard, the economic substance doctrine is closely related to the business purpose doctrine. Yet while the business purpose doctrine focuses on the taxpayer's intent for effecting the transaction, the economic substance doctrine requires an objective comparison of the risks and profit potential from a transaction against the transaction's claimed tax benefits.

The economic substance doctrine has proved to be a powerful weapon for the Service in attacking many modern, sophisticated tax shelter transactions, the details of which involve concepts far beyond the scope of this text. The curious (or sleep-deprived) can check out not only the *ACM Partnership* case, *supra*, but also *ASA Investerings Partnership v. Commissioner*, 201 F.3d 505 (D.C. Cir. 2000). For cases in which the taxpayer prevailed on appeal in showing that a transaction had economic substance, see *Compaq Computer Corp. v. Commissioner*, 277 F.3d 778 (5th Cir. 2001) and *IES Industries, Inc. v. United States*, 253 F.3d 350 (8th Cir. 2001).

A. HOBBY ACTIVITIES

Code: IRC §§ 165(d); 183(a)–(d).

Regs: Treas. Reg. §§ 1.183–1(a)–(b); 1.183–2.

Hobby activities, by definition, are activities undertaken not for profit motives but for personal pleasure. In a pure income tax, therefore, expenses incurred with respect to a hobby would not be deductible because they represent personal consumption. Likewise, losses sustained from hobby activities should be disallowed.

So consider now the dentist who works three days a week and escapes to his own cattle ranch every weekend. The expenses of maintaining cattle can be quite significant. But the dentist knows these costs are not deductible unless the ranch qualifies as a business or investment activity. We know that if the dentist works regularly and continuously on the ranch, giving it substantially his full-time efforts, the activity will rise to the level of a trade or business. See *Commissioner v. Groetzinger* at Chapter 4. This would make all of the dentist's ordinary and necessary expenses paid with respect to the cattle ranch deductible under § 162(a). Moreover, any losses from the cattle ranch would be deductible under § 165(c)(1). Most likely, however, the dentist is not devoting substantially all of his full-time efforts to the ranch.

The next best hope for a deduction, then, is to classify the cattle ranch as an investment activity. If it so qualifies, then the expenses can be deducted under § 212. Although the expenses will be miscellaneous itemized deductions, the dentist may itemize already. And *some* deduction beats *no* deduction. More importantly, losses from the ranching activity will be deductible under § 165(c)(2) as losses from a "transaction entered into for profit."

If the cattle ranch is merely a personal hobby, however, then there is no authority to deduct losses under § 165(c) except upon a casualty or theft. Thus, the dentist has an incentive to classify the cattle ranch as a business or investment activity in order to deduct expenses and losses.

Even if the activity is best described as a hobby, however, the lure of a deduction for many is simply too great.

Now consider the proper tax treatment of *income* from hobby activities. If our dentist from the prior example enters his prize bull at the county fair and wins a $500 prize, *Glenshaw Glass* requires the dentist to include the prize in gross income. At this point, the argument for letting the dentist deduct the expenses he incurs to maintain the cattle ranch is more persuasive. After all, if the federal income tax attempts to tax the dentist's net income, allowing the dentist to deduct the costs incurred to win the $500 prize will be the only way to determine whether (and to what extent) the dentist has "income" from the activity.

Section 183 deals with hobby activities in a manner consistent with the foregoing discussion. The general rule in § 183(a) prohibits any deductions attributable to an activity "not engaged in for profit." Section 183(b) then *allows* two types of deductions attributable to a hobby:

TYPE (1) → deductions that would be allowable to the taxpayer no matter whether they relate to a hobby activity (like taxes deductible under § 164); and

TYPE (2) → deductions that would be allowable to the taxpayer if the hobby was instead a for-profit activity, but only to the extent that the income from the hobby exceeds the Type (1) deductions attributable to the hobby.

In effect, losses and expenses attributable to a hobby activity that otherwise may not be deductible *can* be used to offset income from the hobby, but only to that extent.

Defining a Hobby Activity. It almost goes without saying that the threshold determination is whether an activity is one "engaged in for profit." Section 183(c) defines an activity not engaged in for profit simply as one other than a business or investment activity. Section 183(d) creates a presumption of a profit motive where the activity has proven profitable for at least three of the five most recent taxable years including the year at issue. But to determine whether a profit motive exists, one must consider the facts and circumstances at hand. The regulations offer several factors to analyze in making this determination, and the following case makes use of these factors.

PRIETO v. COMMISSIONER

United States Tax Court, 2001.
T.C. Memo. 2001–266.

VASQUEZ, JUDGE. * * *

After concessions, the issues for decision are: (1) Whether petitioners' horse activity was an activity engaged in for profit * * *.

FINDINGS OF FACT

* * * At the time they filed the petition, Victor Prieto (Dr. Prieto) and Marion Prieto (Mrs. Prieto) resided in San Mateo, California.

I. DR. PRIETO'S MEDICAL PRACTICE

Dr. Prieto is an orthopedic surgeon. Since 1984, Dr. Prieto has been in private practice. In 1984, the partnership of Jensen, Watson & Light (JWL) hired him at a salary of $65,000 per year. In 1986, Dr. Prieto made partner at JWL. At this time, his salary increased to between $130,000 and $150,000 per year.

Since 1988, Dr. Prieto has run his own successful medical practice in San Francisco, California. Mrs. Prieto also worked in her husband's medical practice. She spends a considerable amount of time working in the medical practice. Dr. Prieto's medical practice employed Lori Sasaki as a bookkeeper.

From 1991 through 1998, petitioners had no substantial income-producing assets or any other substantial source of income other than Dr. Prieto's medical practice. Petitioners reported the following net profit from Dr. Prieto's Schedule C, Profit or Loss From Business, for his orthopedic medical practice:

YEAR	NET PROFIT
1991	$456,451
1992	548,350
1993	586,073
1994	650,898
1995	695,620
1996	794,424
1997	636,523
1998	737,684
TOTAL	5,106,023

From 1991 through 1998, the net profit of Dr. Prieto's medical practice averaged $638,253.

II. THE HORSE ACTIVITY

A. BACKGROUND

From the age of 4 to 5, Mrs. Prieto rode horses on the farm where she lived. From the age of 16 to 18, Mrs. Prieto owned a horse that was an ex-barrel racer. None of these horses were show jumpers.

Since she was a teenager, Mrs. Prieto had wanted to be involved in the horse field. Mrs. Prieto always enjoyed horses and had a strong interest in horses. Dr. Prieto also enjoyed horses.

Petitioners have two children: Jill and Claire. Jill was born on April 17, 1980, and Claire was born on July 7, 1982. As parents, petitioners were actively involved in their daughters' activities. Some of the activities petitioners' daughters participated in included swimming and dancing. Petitioners would organize dance troops, transport children to events, and arrange for obtaining uniforms. In 1987, when Jill was 7 and Claire was 5, Jill and Claire began riding horses.

Whatever activity petitioners and their family got involved with they did it "110 percent". Petitioners' daughters became interested in horses, so petitioners and their family got deeply involved with horses. Jill and Claire's involvement with horses became a family event where Mrs. Prieto would often be ringside organizing lunches and dinners and Dr. Prieto would do his medical charts and watch Jill and Claire ride the horses. As with swimming and dancing, petitioners' children became deeply involved with horseback riding.

By 1990, petitioners owned three ponies for their daughters to ride. Prior to May 1, 1991, the date the activity in question commenced, Jill and Claire competed in horse shows.

Petitioners became interested in starting the horse activity because of the recreational riding and showing activities that Claire and Jill had participated in since 1987. Prior to 1987, when Jill and Claire got involved with horses, Mrs. Prieto had no experience with show jumpers or showing horses. Petitioners told Jill and Claire if they wanted to participate in horseback riding and perhaps compete on a high level, then petitioners would start the horse activity.

B. STARTUP

Starting in May 1991, petitioners engaged in a horse activity under the name Fordham Farms that included purchasing, training, showing, and selling "hunter", "jumper", and "equitation" horses. None of the horses in the horse activity were held for breeding or bred.

"Hunter" is a category of horse competition that grades each horse on its form, style, and technique as the horse competes on a course of multiple hurdles. "Jumper" is a category of horse competition that grades the horse and rider on their ability to jump fences cleanly and quickly. The courses have tight turns and angled fences making the jumps more difficult than those in the hunter category. "Grand Prix Jumper" is a category of horse competition that also grades each horse on its ability to jump fences cleanly and quickly; however, the courses are of a higher difficulty than in the jumper category (higher fences, multiple hurdles, etc.). "Equitation" is a category of horse competition that grades each <u>rider</u> on his form. Petitioners' daughters mostly competed in equitation events.

Petitioners used the same ponies that their children rode for pleasure to start the horse activity. At the start of the horse activity, petitioners purchased Welsh ponies for the horse activity. They chose Welsh ponies because that was the type of horse their daughters were riding.

When they first started the horse activity, petitioners talked to veterinarians, trainers, and other owners and read periodicals about hunter and jumper horses. Petitioners also owned books about ponies, hunters, and jumpers. Petitioners attended seminars, clinics, and award banquets put on by horse organizations.

C. EMPLOYEES HIRED BY PETITIONERS

Around May 1991, petitioners hired Joe Norick to be the horse activity's trainer. In the middle of 1993, petitioners hired Nicole Shahinian (Nicole) to ride their horses. Shortly thereafter, petitioners decided to replace Mr. Norick with a new trainer. One of the reasons petitioners decided to replace Mr. Norick was because Jill and Claire could not ride the horses petitioners owned. Petitioners replaced Mr. Norick with Nicole.

At this time, Nicole was responsible for training the horses, giving their daughters lessons, and supervising all aspects of the horse activity (including supervising people petitioners hired to clean the stalls and groom, braid, and feed the horses). Nicole's background was as a "junior" rider; she had no experience as a trainer or running a business. At this time, Nicole had just turned 18 years old.

Petitioners hired other people besides Mr. Norick and Nicole to work in the horse activity. Petitioners hired Scott Wilson as an assistant trainer, Bill Nissen as veterinarian, Ms. Sasaki as bookkeeper, Patrick Hurley as accountant for the horse activity, and Carlos Soriano as a groom. At horse shows, when the horse activity needed extra help, petitioners hired people to braid the horses, horseshoers, and a night watchman.

Petitioners sent the horse activity's records to Ms. Sasaki to sort the records into separate file folders, and each year petitioners received a box from Ms. Sasaki with the records sorted. Ms. Sasaki also inputted the financial records of the horse activity onto a computer. Petitioners reviewed the books and records of the horse activity and their tax returns.

D. HOW PETITIONERS CONDUCTED THE ACTIVITY

Petitioners created a logo for the horse activity and had "business cards" and stationery that bore this logo. Petitioners also used envelopes bearing the name Fordham Farms.

Petitioners did not have a written business plan or make a budget for the horse activity. Petitioners did not have bills of sale for every horse they owned. Some of the bills of sale for horses were in petitioners' names rather than the name of the horse activity. Petitioners insured only some of their horses. Petitioners would not force people to pay money owed to them. Jill and Claire advised petitioners which horses to purchase and sell.

The horse activity's opening balance sheet for 1994 listed several horses as assets that had been reported as sold, or as dying, in 1993. This opening balance sheet also listed "Cody Williams" as an asset. Cody Williams is not a horse; he is a person.

Petitioners placed an advertisement in a horse show program that pictured Jill and Claire riding horses, wished them good luck in 1995, and congratulated them on their 1994 equitation medals and participation in the Marshal–Sterling Children's Jumper League. Petitioners also placed one advertisement in a publication called "Horse's International".

Petitioners kept records called "business goals" for 1994 and 1995. Petitioners came up with these goals. These goals were informal ideas that petitioners hoped to implement. Some of the goals for 1994 were: (1) Leasing or selling "Make Believe", (2) selling "Fashion Page", (3) developing "Desire Me" and selling it for either $75,000 as a "pre-green" or $125,000 to $150,000 as a "first year green hunter", and (4) selling "Rising Sun" for $35,000 to $40,000. Other goals were more general such as purchasing and developing a grand prix horse and a junior jumper, increasing the number of horses shown, and increasing the use of trucks to transport horses.

Petitioners did not sell Fashion Page in 1994. Petitioners did sell Make Believe, Desire Me, and Rising Sun in 1994. The sale price and petitioners' original purchase price of each of these horses was as follows:

HORSE	PURCHASE PRICE	SALE PRICE
Make Believe	$22,500	$20,000
Desire Me	22,500	16,000
Rising Sun	1,000	1

Petitioners' goals for 1995 were more general than those for 1994. They included increasing hauling income, increasing their client base, developing their horses, purchasing junior jumper and equitation horses, getting their horses to the shows, and having Nicole stay on as their trainer.

E. BOARDING THE HORSES

The horses and all other items necessary for the horse activity were maintained at the following locations (all located in California):

Dates	Boarding Facility	Location
5/91—12/93	Portola Valley Training Center	Portola Valley
1/94—4/95	Pebble Beach Equestrian Center	Pebble Beach
4/95—8/95	Portola Valley training Center	Portola Valley
8/95—12/95	Hidden Valley Ranch	Hidden Valley

The boarding facility in Portola Valley was a 30–minute drive from petitioners' home in San Mateo, California. The boarding facility in Pebble Beach was a 1.5–to 2–hour drive from petitioners' home. Rather than drive to Pebble Beach, petitioners rented a house near Pebble Beach, California, where petitioners and their children would stay on weekends they visited the boarding facility.

Hidden Valley is in southern California and was not near petitioners home. Nicole recommended to petitioners that they move their horses from northern California to southern California. When petitioners moved their horses to southern California in August 1995, Nicole moved in with her then boyfriend (and future husband), who, at the time, lived in southern California.

F. EXPENSES/LOSSES/AGI

The total entry fees and show costs reported by petitioners for the horse activity were as follows:

Category	1991	1992	1993	1994	1995
Entry fees	$21,831	$37,396	$79,240	$49,057	$56,168
Show costs	4,065	22,792	20,991	21,978	28,030
Reimbursements	(0)	(22,820)	(43,851)	(30,417)	(0)
Total	25,896	37,368	56,380	40,618	84,198

table continued

Category	1996	1997	1998
Entry fees	$882	$91,656	$66,471
Show costs	0	0	0
Reimbursements	(0)	(0)	(0)
Total	882	91,656	66,471

Excluding 1996, the average yearly entry fee and show cost expense of the horse activity was $57,512.

During the years in issue, petitioners showed the horses they owned at least 46 times. In 1996, petitioners' horses that were "serviceable" were "in the ring" at shows petitioners attended. In 1996, petitioners' horse named "Fran's Guy" was in the ring at horse shows one to two times per show attended and was in the ring at least 30 times over the course of the year. This meant that during 1996 petitioners entered their horses in at least 15 shows.

Petitioners reported the following ordinary income and losses from the horse activity:

YEAR	ORDINARY INCOME/(LOSS)
1991	($147,118)
1992	(366,350)
1993	(427,947)
1994	(373,694)
1995	(361,854)
1996	13,703
1997	(455,624)
1998	(437,051)

Petitioners incurred $1,676,963 of losses through 1995 and $2,555,935 of losses through 1998. During these years, the loss from the horse activity averaged $319,492. Excluding 1996, the losses averaged $367,091.

Petitioners reported the following adjusted gross income (AGI):

YEAR	AGI
1991	$343,212
1992	235,390
1993	181,237
1994	290,909
1995	293,567
1996	785,116
1997	157,006
1998	245,474

After excluding the losses (and ordinary income) reported by the horse activity, petitioners' "readjusted" AGI is as follows:

YEAR	READJUSTED AGI
1991	$490,330
1992	601,740
1993	609,184
1994	664,603
1995	665,421
1996	771,413
1997	612,630
1998	682,525

From 1991 through 1998, petitioners' readjusted AGI averaged $635,981.

G. PETITIONERS "ATTEMPTS" TO CUT COSTS

During the years in issue, petitioners spoke with Nicole about cutting the horse activity's costs and increasing its income. Petitioners, however, only discussed with Nicole the fact that the horse activity was losing money; petitioners never informed Nicole of the amount of the losses (which totaled hundreds of thousands of dollars).

H. PERSONAL NATURE OF ACTIVITY/ELEMENTS OF PLEASURE

During the years in issue, petitioners and their children spent almost every weekend with the horses. Dr. Prieto, Mrs. Prieto, Jill, and Claire used the weekends spent with the horses as their time to unwind. Jill and Claire would ride and take lessons on the horses. Jill and Claire enjoyed riding horses. Mrs. Prieto also rode the horses. In addition to watching their daughters compete at the horse shows, petitioners attended hospitality tents located at the horse shows.

In January 1994, petitioners sold a horse named "Browning". In a letter thanking the purchaser of Browning for buying the horse, petitioners wrote that they would be using the money from this transaction to purchase a quality junior jumper for their daughter Jill.

Dr. Prieto only did "simple" tasks for the horse activity. He felt that his college and medical education entitled him not to muck[4] the stalls.

During the years in issue, Mrs. Prieto, Claire, and Jill were members of the following horse organizations: The American Horse Shows Association, the Pacific Horse Show Association, the California Professional Horsemen's Association, the United States Equestrian Team, and the NorCal Hunter Jumper Association. In order for Claire and Jill to compete in horse shows, they had to be members of these organizations.

I. SOURCE OF MONEY FOR THE ACTIVITY

Initially, petitioners had a sufficient amount in savings accumulated to fund the startup of the horse activity. At times, however, the horse activity had cash shortages, and petitioners needed extra money to purchase horses. On these occasions, petitioners borrowed money from Dr. Prieto's medical practice line of credit and transferred funds out of the medical practice bank accounts to provide working capital for the horse activity.

J. END OF THE ACTIVITY

As of October 2000, petitioners were closing up the horse activity. At that time, Jill was 20 and was in Belgium (since February 2000) working with horses, and Claire was 18.

OPINION

The Horse Activity

Section 183(a) provides generally that, if an activity is not engaged in for profit, no deduction attributable to such activity shall be allowed except as provided in section 183(b). Section 183(c) defines an "activity not engaged in for profit" as "any activity other than one with respect to which deductions are allowable for the taxable year under section 162 or under paragraph (1) or (2) of section 212."

The U.S. Court of Appeals for the Ninth Circuit, to which an appeal in this case would lie, has held that for a deduction to be allowed under section 162 or section 212(1) or (2), a taxpayer must establish that he engaged in the activity with the primary, predominant, or principal purpose and intent of realizing an economic profit independent of tax savings. See *Wolf v. Commissioner*, 4 F.3d 709, 713 (9th Cir. 1993), affg. *T.C. Memo. 1991–212*; *Indep. Elec. Supply, Inc. v. Commissioner*, 781 F.2d 724, 726 (9th Cir. 1986), affg. *Lahr v. Commissioner*, *T.C. Memo. 1984–472*.

The expectation of profit need not have been reasonable, but it must be bona fide. See *Golanty v. Commissioner*, 72 T.C. 411, 426 (1979), affd. without published opinion 647 F.2d 170 (9th Cir. 1981); sec. 1.183–2(a), Income Tax Regs. Whether the requisite profit objective exists is determined by looking to all the surrounding facts and circumstances. *Golanty v. Commissioner, supra* at 426; sec. 1.183–2(b), Income Tax Regs. Great-

---

4. To "muck" means "to clear of manure or filth". Merriam Webster's Collegiate Dictionary 762 (10th ed. 1996).

er weight is given to objective facts than to a taxpayer's mere after-the-fact statement of intent. *Indep. Elec. Supply, Inc. v. Commissioner*, *supra*; *Thomas v. Commissioner*, 84 T.C. 1244, 1269 (1985), affd. 792 F.2d 1256 (4th Cir. 1986); sec. 1.183–2(a), Income Tax Regs. Petitioners bear the burden of proof. Rule 142(a).

Section 1.183–2(b), Income Tax Regs., provides a list of factors to be considered in the evaluation of a taxpayer's profit objective: (1) The manner in which the taxpayer carries on the activity; (2) the expertise of the taxpayer or his advisers; (3) the time and effort expended by the taxpayer in carrying on the activity; (4) the expectation that assets used in the activity may appreciate in value; (5) the success of the taxpayer in carrying on other similar or dissimilar activities; (6) the taxpayer's history of income or loss with respect to the activity; (7) the amount of occasional profits, if any, from the activity; (8) the financial status of the taxpayer; and (9) elements of personal pleasure or recreation. This list is nonexclusive, and the number of factors for or against the taxpayer is not necessarily determinative but rather all facts and circumstances must be taken into account, and more weight may be given to some factors than to others. See sec. 1.183–2(b), Income Tax Regs.; cf. *Dunn v. Commissioner*, 70 T.C. 715, 720 (1978), affd. 615 F.2d 578 (2d Cir. 1980).

The evidence submitted to the Court establishes that petitioners' primary, predominant, or principal motive for engaging in the horse activity was not for profit.

A. MANNER IN WHICH THE ACTIVITY IS CONDUCTED

Petitioners hired professionals to keep books and records and to prepare their returns. They also hired professionals to work in the horse activity as grooms, braiders, horseshoers, and veterinarian. While these facts weigh in petitioners favor, they are not the only facts presented to the Court.

While petitioners did keep records, they did not have bills of sale for all their horses, and the records appear to be faulty. Dr. Prieto could not explain why the show costs and entry fees were so low for 1996. Mrs. Prieto testified that they understated the horse activity's show costs for 1996. We agree.[6]

Even though they had records reporting substantial losses, petitioners never developed a written business plan or made a budget. Dr. and Mrs. Prieto testified that the "business plan" of the horse activity was to buy, train (develop), show, and sell horses. This is not a plan; this is merely a statement of what the horse activity did. While petitioners wrote out "business goals" for 1994 and 1995, they never developed a plan to achieve these goals.

Petitioners claimed to have hired other riders, such as Annalee Bennet, to show the horses. The horse show entry forms for 1994 and 1995 list only petitioners' daughters and Nicole as riders of petitioners'

---

6. We note that the likely effect of this understatement was to create the appear-ance of a profit for the horse activity for 1996 when none in fact existed.

horses. Ms. Bennet was not called as a witness. We infer that her testimony would not have been favorable to petitioners.

Petitioners did not attempt to collect debts owed to them. Additionally, when petitioners fired Mr. Norick, they replaced him with Nicole who was 18 years old at the time and, although she had been a junior rider, had no experience as a trainer or running a business. Furthermore, petitioners decided which horses to buy and sell based upon which horses their daughters wanted.

Petitioners further rely on the testimony of Russell Stewart to support the conclusion that they conducted the horse activity in a businesslike manner. Mr. Stewart was qualified as an expert in his knowledge of and in judging grand prix jumper, hunter, and equitation horses. Subsequent to the years in issue, Mr. Stewart rode petitioners' horses and transported petitioners' horses. He did not review petitioners' books and records. Furthermore, all the facts for Mr. Stewart's report were supplied by petitioners or their representatives.

The purpose of expert testimony is to assist the trier of fact to understand evidence that will determine the fact in issue. See *Laureys v. Commissioner, 92 T.C. 101, 127–129 (1989).* We do not find Mr. Stewart's conclusory report to be of any assistance to the Court and accordingly disregard it.

On the whole, we conclude that this factor weighs against petitioners.

B.   EXPERTISE OF PETITIONERS AND THEIR ADVISERS

Dr. Prieto had no significant experience with horses prior to starting the horse activity. Mrs. Prieto's only experience with horses was riding them as a child and a teenager. Petitioners claimed to have talked with many professionals before entering the horse activity. These conversations, however, mainly focused on the fact that a person could make a lot of money or lose a lot of money buying and selling horses. Petitioners did not discuss how to conduct the horse activity to make it profitable, how to train the horses, or how to manage the horse activity. Other than being advised to "get a trainer", petitioners received no useful advice before beginning the horse activity. This factor also weighs against petitioners.

C.   TIME AND EFFORT EXPENDED BY PETITIONERS

Mrs. Prieto claimed to work 40 hours a week, and Dr. Prieto claimed to work 20 to 30 hours a week, in the horse activity. Other than petitioners' self-serving, conclusory statements, there is no evidence to support this assertion. Dr. Prieto is an orthopedic surgeon. Mrs. Prieto works in his office and spends a considerable amount of time doing so. According to Nicole, during the workweek petitioners were not usually with the horses. Accordingly, we do not accept petitioners' testimony. Accordingly, this factor also weighs against petitioners.

D. THE ACTIVITY'S HISTORY OF INCOME OR LOSS

A record of substantial losses over several years may be indicative of the absence of a profit motive. *Golanty v. Commissioner*, 72 T.C. at 426. As was noted by the Court on the record at trial, the losses are large enough to be described as substantial or huge. The only year petitioners did not report a loss is 1996. This appears to be due to the incorrect reporting of expenses for that year, and as we noted *supra* the likely effect of the understatement of expenses was to create the appearance of a profit for the horse activity when none in fact existed. Petitioners' losses from 1991 through 1998 averaged well over $300,000 per year.

Furthermore, petitioners' history of losses belies any notion that it was operated for profit. While a person may start out with a bona fide expectation of profit, even if it is unreasonable, there is a time when, in light of the recurring losses, the bona fides of that expectation must cease. See *Filios v. Commissioner*, 224 F.3d 16 (1st Cir. 2000), affg. *T.C. Memo. 1999–92*. This factor also weighs against petitioners.

E. PETITIONERS' FINANCIAL STATUS

Substantial income from sources other than the activity in question, particularly if the activity's losses generate substantial tax benefits, may indicate that the activity is not engaged in for profit. Sec. 1.183–2(b)(8), Income Tax Regs. From 1991 through 1998, petitioners' net profit from Dr. Prieto's medical practice averaged $638,253. This factor weighs against petitioners.

F. ELEMENTS OF PERSONAL PLEASURE

The absence of personal pleasure or recreation relating to the activity in question may indicate the presence of a profit objective. Sec. 1.183–2(b)(9), Income Tax Regs. Petitioners and their children derived substantial amounts of pleasure from the horse activity. Based on the facts of this case, we find that this factor weighs against petitioners.

G. ADDITIONAL FACTS

The following additional facts also support our conclusion that the horse activity was not entered with the primary, predominant, or principal purpose of making a profit. The evidence established that petitioners' daughters mainly rode the horses in equitation competitions. Equitation competitions grade the <u>rider</u> and not the horse. Dr. Prieto also testified that he went to the horse shows to watch his daughters compete.

Dr. Prieto testified that petitioners never purchased horses for their children and that they never told anyone that the horses were for their children. His testimony, however, was impeached by a letter petitioners wrote in which they state that they were using money specifically to buy a horse for Jill. The fact that petitioners did not purchase horses in their daughters' names is unpersuasive.

Additionally, within months of Jill's leaving the country and Claire's turning 18 petitioners terminated the horse activity.

H. CONCLUSION

After reviewing the entire record, we conclude that petitioners did not engage in the horse activity with the primary, predominant, or principal purpose and intent of making a profit within the meaning of section 183.

* * *

* * *

The following chart summarizes the deduction and loss allowance rules for activities of every kind.

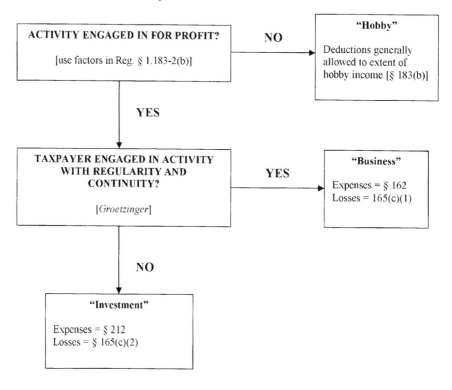

* * *

Deduction Limitations for Hobby Activities. As explained above, § 183(b) classifies all expenses and losses attributable to a hobby as one of two types. Type 1 deductions are those that the taxpayer can claim without regard to whether the activity is operated as a hobby. All other deductions are classified as Type 2 deductions. The distinction between Type 1 deductions and Type 2 deductions is most important: while a taxpayer can claim Type 1 deductions without limitation, Type 2 deductions may be taken only to the extent they do not exceed the excess of hobby income less the Type 1 deductions.

The regulations add a third type—deductions that affect the basis of (and are attributable to) property used in the hobby activity. Treas. Reg.

§ 1.183–1(b)(1)(iii). These deductions include depreciation (§§ 167 and 168), amortization (§ 197), and partially worthless bad debts (§ 166).

For example, suppose Harold, a trainmaster with the Union Pacific Railroad, purchases a five-acre parcel of property in a rural community 20 miles from his urban home. Harold uses the property to raise Christmas trees, and he makes it a point to live on the farm for 15 days each year. While he hopes to earn extra income from the tree operation, he rarely does so. In the current year, Harold harvests the mature trees on his farm and sells a number of them, collecting $10,000 in revenues. Harold incurred the following expenses with respect to the tree operation:

(a)	Interest on the farm mortgage	$5,000
(b)	Property taxes on the farm	$1,000
(c)	Supplies	$1,500
(d)	Depreciation on equipment	$7,000
(e)	Equipment repairs	$500
(f)	Miscellaneous expenses	$800

If the tree operation is an activity not engaged in for profit, then Harold must apply § 183(b) to determine the extent to which these expenses are deductible. He must first categorize the expenses, as follows:

Type (1)—Deductible regardless of whether the activity is operated for profit

· (a)	Interest on the farm mortgage	$5,000 [§ 163(h)(3)]
· (b)	Property taxes on the farm	$1,000 [§ 164(a)]
		$6,000 ← total Type (1) amount

Type (2)—All other expenses except for those that affect basis

· (c)	Supplies	$1,500
· (e)	Equipment repairs	$500
· (f)	Miscellaneous expenses	$800
		$2,800 ← total Type (2) amount

Type (3)—All expenses affecting basis

· (d)	Depreciation on equipment	$7,000 ← total Type (3) amount

Next, Harold applies the categorized expenses against the income from his hobby activity:

Hobby Income	$10,000	
Less Type (1) Deductions	($6,000)	
Limit on Type (2) & (3)	$4,000	
Less Type (2) Deductions	($2,800)	
Limit on Type (3)	$1,200	
Less Type (3) Deductions	($7,000)	← only $1,200 deductible

In this case, then, Harold can deduct all of the Type (2) deductions and $1,200 of the $7,000 in depreciation. Notice that if the mortgage interest expense with respect to Harold's tree farm totals $10,000, none of the Type (2) or Type (3) deductions would be allowed—but Harold would still be able to deduct the $11,000 in mortgage interest and property taxes with respect to the farm.

Self-Assessment Question

(Solutions to Self–Assessment Questions are set forth in Appendix 3.)

SAQ 11–1. Fonzie likes to repair motorcycles as a hobby. Sometimes he charges for his work. In the current year, Fonzie has $1,200 gross income from motorcycle repairs, and he paid the following expenses with respect to the hobby: (a) cost of motorcycle parts, $600; (b) depreciation on equipment, $600; and (c) state *ad valorem* personal property taxes, $200. To what extent can Fonzie deduct these expenses?

* * *

Gambling Losses. Section 165(d) contains a special rule for gambling losses that permits a deduction only to the extent of gains from wagering transactions ("gambling gains"). When a recreational gambler wins a $500 jackpot on a nickel slot machine, the winnings must be included in gross income. To the extent the gambler can document gambling losses (losing lottery tickets, ledgers detailing profits and losses from gambling sessions, and so forth) to offset gambling gains, § 165(d) will allow a deduction.

Given the § 165(d) limitation, taxpayers sometimes argue that various income items constitute gambling gains. In *Technical Advice Memorandum 200417004*, the Service ruled that a taxpayer's winnings in a "no purchase necessary" sweepstakes did not constitute a gambling gain. In order to be a "wagering transaction," said the Service, there must be three elements: a prize, a chance, and consideration. By definition, a "no purchase necessary" sweepstakes does not require the entrant to furnish consideration. Thus, it is not a wagering transaction, and the winnings are not gambling gains.

How does the limitation in § 165(d) apply to professional gamblers, those who make wagering transactions their business activity? The taxpayer in *Bathalter v. Commissioner*, T.C. Memo. 1987–530, was a full-time gambler on horse races. The taxpayer had gambling gains of $91,000 and gambling losses of $87,000. The taxpayer also paid $2,000 in various expenses (racing forms, transportation, and other costs). The taxpayer deducted the expenses under § 162, which the Service challenged. The Service argued that § 165(d) precludes a taxpayer from being engaged in gambling as a "trade or business." The Tax Court held that the taxpayer's gambling was a business activity and allowed the deductions. With respect to § 165(d), the court said:

Respondent misses the point of section 165(d). In the context of the instant case, petitioner's gambling expenses are deducted under the opening flush language of section 162(a), because they are expenses of petitioner's trade or business. *If petitioner had had a loss in his gambling business, rather than the [net] gain the parties stipulated to, then section 165(d) would have served to prevent petitioner from using that loss to offset other income.* Since petitioner did not have a loss in his gambling business, section 165(d) does not operate at all in the instant case. (emphasis added)

This language suggests that § 165(d) applies to gambling losses, and that § 165(d)'s limitation trumps the provisions of §§ 162(a) and 165(c)(1). So while one can deduct *expenses* as a professional gambler under § 162(a), *losses* of the full-time gambler are subject to § 165(d).

This was the result reached in *Valenti v. Commissioner*, T.C. Memo. 1994–483, where the court held that § 165(d) applies to professional gamblers as well as recreational gamblers. As the court notes:

it has been held both by this Court and various courts of appeals that wagering losses cannot be deducted, except to the extent of the taxpayer's gains from wagering activities, *and it has been so held even where such activities were conducted as a trade or business as opposed to a hobby. Boyd v. United States*, 762 F.2d 1369 (9th Cir. 1985); *Estate of Todisco v. Commissioner*, 757 F.2d 1, 6–7 (1st Cir. 1985), affg. T.C. Memo. 1983–247, but remanding for factual recomputation; *Nitzberg v. Commissioner, supra; Skeeles v. United States, supra; Offutt v. Commissioner*, 16 T.C. 1214 (1951); *Kozma v. Commissioner*, T.C. Memo. 1986–177; *Ward v. Commissioner*, T.C. Memo. 1986–237. (emphasis added)

* * *

Problem 11–1

Nearly every weekend, Annie Duke enters a legal poker tournament at the local casino. In Year One, Annie paid total entry fees of $10,000 and had gross winnings of $15,000. After each tournament, Annie logs her entry fee and winnings, if any, in a journal. In addition to spending most every Saturday and Sunday at the casino, Annie devotes several hours each week to reading various treatises on the game or watching tournaments broadcast on television. Annie quit her job three years ago to devote more time to improving her poker skills. She could afford to do so since she received a substantial bequest from her late mother's estate. The results of her efforts are improving: while Annie rarely earned prize money in the early years of her involvement with the game, her winnings have exceeded her entry fees for the past three years. Annie always tells her friends that she would play poker even if she never earned a dime because she derives so much pleasure from the game.

(a) To what extent can Annie deduct the poker tournament entry fees she paid in Year One?

(b) How would the answer to (a) change if Annie's total entry fees for Year One were $20,000?

(c) How would the answer to (a) change if Annie entered bowling tournaments instead of poker tournaments?

B. AT–RISK RULES

Code: IRC § 465(a)(1)–(2), (b)(1)–(2), (b)(4)–(6)(D), (c)(1), (c)(3)(A).

Regs: None.

Eve Uhl earns an annual salary of $200,000. Seeking to minimize her tax liability to the greatest extent possible, Eve borrowed $1 million from Bank on a nonrecourse basis in Year One to purchase depreciable property for use in a new business venture. We learned in Chapter 8 that Eve's basis in the depreciable property, thanks to *Crane v. Commissioner*, started at $1 million. If the property has a five-year recovery period, and if Eve foregoes any bonus depreciation deductions with respect to the property, then Eve can claim a depreciation deduction in Year One of $200,000 under the double-declining balance method and half-year convention available under the accelerated cost recovery system in § 168. That $200,000 deduction will perfectly offset Eve's salary income for the year; if the new business venture generates no income, Eve pays no tax at all!

The problem with this strategy, from a tax policy standpoint at least, is that Eve can simply walk away from the debt to Bank without personal liability. If Eve does not repay the debt, Bank can foreclose against the property but nothing else. Eve loses the building, sure, but she never paid anything out-of-pocket for that asset in the first place. If Eve holds the property throughout its five-year recovery period, she can deduct $1 million over this period without being at risk to lose any actual investment in the property! Congress enacted § 465 in 1976 to address this abuse, as the following excerpt from the legislative history shows.

GENERAL EXPLANATION OF THE TAX REFORM ACT OF 1976

H.R. 10612, 94th Cong., 2d Sess. (December 29, 1976).
JCS–33–76.

* * *

III. GENERAL EXPLANATION OF THE ACT

A. TAX SHELTER PROVISIONS

* * *

2. Limitation of Loss to Amount At–Risk (sec. 204 of the Act and sec. 465 of the Code)

Prior law

Generally, the amount of depreciation or other deductions which a taxpayer has been permitted to take in connection with a property has been limited to the amount of his basis in the property. * * *

The starting point for determining a taxpayer's adjusted basis in a productive activity or enterprise is generally the taxpayer's cost for the assets used in the activity or enterprise (secs. 1011, 1012). * * *

The liabilities of a productive activity may also have an effect upon an investor's adjusted basis in the activity. Thus, a taxpayer's basis in a property includes the portion of the purchase price which is financed even if the taxpayer is not personally liable on the loan and the lender must look solely to the financed property for repayment of the loan. * * *

This approach to nonrecourse * * * liabilities arose from a judicially developed principle known as the *Crane* rule. The *Crane* rule was derived from the Supreme Court's reasoning in *Crane* v. *Commissioner,* 331 U.S. 1 (1947), where it was held that an owner's adjusted basis in a parcel of real property included the amount of a nonrecourse mortgage on the property, under which the mortgagee-lender could seek a recovery of its loan only from the property. (It is because of the *Crane* rule that nonrecourse indebtedness has generally been included in an investor's adjusted basis, as indicated above, in a business or productive property.)

Also, in general, the existence of protection against ultimate loss by reason of a stop-loss order, guarantee, guaranteed repurchase agreement or similar arrangement does not generally impose a limitation on the amount of losses a taxpayer may deduct in the early taxable years of an activity.

Reasons for change

The typical tax shelter has operated as a limited partnership with individual investors participating as limited partners. Virtually all of the equity capital for the activity has been contributed by the limited partners with the major portion of the remaining operating funds (generally 75 percent or more of the total capital) for the partnership financed through nonrecourse loans.

When an investment had been solicited for a tax shelter activity, it had been common practice to promise the prospective investor substantial tax losses which could be used to decrease the tax on his income from other sources. The opportunity to deduct tax losses in excess of the amount of the taxpayer's economic risk had arisen under prior law primarily through the use of nonrecourse financing not only by limited partnerships, but also by individuals and subchapter S corporations. The ability to deduct tax losses in excess of economic risk had also arisen through guarantees, stop-loss agreements, guaranteed repurchase agreements, and other devices used by the partnerships, individuals and subchapter S corporations.

Nonrecourse leveraging of investments and other risk limiting devices which produce tax savings in excess of amounts placed at risk substantially alter the economic substance of the investments and distort the workings of the investment markets. Taxpayers, ignoring the possible tax consequences in later years, can be led into investments which are otherwise economically unsound and which constitute an unproductive use of investment funds.

Congress believed that it was not equitable to allow individual investors to defer tax on income from other sources through losses generated by tax sheltering activities. One of the most significant problems in tax shelters was the use of nonrecourse financing and other risk-limiting devices which enabled investors in these activities to deduct losses from the activities in amounts which exceeded the total investment the investor actually placed at risk in the activity. The Act consequently provides an "at risk" rule to deal directly with this abuse in tax shelters.

Explanation of provision

To prevent a situation where the taxpayer may deduct a loss in excess of his economic investment in certain types of tax shelter activities, the Act provides that the amount of any loss (otherwise allowable for the year) which may be deducted in connection with one of these activities cannot exceed the aggregate amount with respect to which the taxpayer is at risk in each such activity at the close of the taxable year. This "at risk" limitation applies to the following activities: (1) farming; (2) exploring for, or exploiting, oil and gas resources; (3) the holding, producing, or distributing of motion picture films or video tapes; and (4) equipment leasing. The limitation applies to all taxpayers (other than corporations which are not subchapter S corporations or personal holding companies) including individuals and sole proprietorships, estates, trusts, shareholders in subchapter S corporations, and partners in a partnership which conducts an activity described in this provision.

The at risk limitation is to apply on the basis of the facts existing at the end of each taxable year. The at risk limitation applies regardless of the method of accounting used by the taxpayer and regardless of the kind of deductible expenses which contributed to the loss.

The amount of any loss which is allowable in a particular year reduces the taxpayer's at risk amount as of the end of that year and in all succeeding taxable years with respect to that activity.

Losses which are suspended under this provision with respect to a taxpayer because they are greater than the taxpayer's investment which is "at risk" are to be treated as a deduction with respect to the activity in the following year. Consequently, if a taxpayer's amount at risk increases in later years, he will be able to obtain the benefit of previously suspended losses to the extent that such increases in his amount at risk exceed his losses in later years.

The at risk limitation is only intended to limit the extent to which certain losses in connection with the covered activities may be deducted in the year they would otherwise be allowable to the taxpayer. The rules of this provision do not apply for other purposes, such as the determination of basis. * * *

For purposes of this provision, a taxpayer is generally to be considered "at risk" with respect to an activity to the extent of his cash and the adjusted basis of other property contributed to the activity, as well as any amounts borrowed for use in the activity with respect to which the taxpayer has personal liability for payment from his personal assets.

A taxpayer's at risk amount is also generally to include amounts borrowed for use in the activity which are secured by property other than property used in the activity. For example, if the taxpayer acting as a sole proprietor * * * uses personally-owned real estate to secure nonrecourse indebtedness, the proceeds from which are used in an equipment leasing activity, the proceeds may be considered part of the taxpayer's at risk amount. In such a case, the portion of the proceeds which increases the taxpayer's at risk amount is to be limited by the fair market value of the property used as collateral (determined as of the date the property is pledged as security), less any prior (or superior) claims to which the collateral is subject.

* * *

Except where the indebtedness is secured by property not used in the activity, a taxpayer is not to be considered at risk with respect to the proceeds from his share of any nonrecourse loan used to finance the activity or the acquisition of property used in the activity. In addition, if the taxpayer borrows money to contribute to the activity and the lender's only recourse is either the taxpayer's interest in the activity or property used in the activity, the amount of the proceeds of the borrowing are to be considered amounts financed on a nonrecourse basis and do not increase the taxpayer's amount at risk.

Also, under these rules, a taxpayer is not to be "at risk," even as to the equity capital which he has contributed to the activity, to the extent he is protected against economic loss of all or part of such capital by reason of an agreement or arrangement for compensation or reimbursement to him of any loss which he may suffer. Under this concept, a taxpayer is not "at risk" if he arranges to receive insurance or other compensation for an economic loss after the loss is sustained, or if he is entitled to reimbursement for part or all of any loss by reason of a binding agreement between himself and another person.[7]

* * *

7. In livestock feeding operations, for example, some commercial feedlots have offered to reimburse investors against any loss sustained on sales of the fed livestock above a stated dollar amount per head. Under such "stop loss" orders, the investor is to be considered "at risk" (for purposes of this provision) only to the extent of the portion of his capital against which he is not entitled to reimbursement. Similarly, in some livestock breeding investments carried on through a limited partnership, the part-

Similarly, if a taxpayer is personally liable on a mortgage but separately obtains insurance to compensate him for any payments which he must actually make under such personal liability, the taxpayer is at risk only to the extent of the uninsured portion of the personal liability to which he is exposed. The taxpayer will be able to include in the amount which he has at risk any amount of nondeductible premium which he has paid from his personal assets with respect to the insurance. However, a taxpayer who obtains casualty insurance or insurance protecting himself against tort liability will not be considered "not at risk" solely because of such hazard insurance protection.

* * *

In general, in the case of an activity engaged in by an individual, each motion picture film or video tape, item of leased equipment, farm, or oil and gas property is treated as a separate activity. * * *

The at risk limitation applies only to losses produced by deductions which are not disallowed by reason of some other provision of the Code. For example, if a prepaid interest expense is suspended under the prepaid interest limitation (sec. 208 of the Act and sec. 461 of the Code) that expense will not enter into the computation of the loss subject to the at-risk limitation. When the interest accrues and becomes deductible, the expense may at that time be subject to this provision. * * *

The Act specifically requires that a taxpayer not be considered at risk with respect to amounts borrowed for use in an activity (or which are contributed to the activity)[12] where the amounts are borrowed from any person who has an interest in the activity (other than that as a creditor) or who is related to the taxpayer (as described in sec. 267(b)). * * * Those persons considered to be related to the taxpayer include the taxpayer's spouse, ancestors and lineal descendants, brothers and sisters, and corporations and other entities in which the taxpayer has a 50–percent or greater interest.

* * *

Self-Assessment Question

(Solutions to Self–Assessment Questions are set forth in Appendix 3.)

SAQ 11–2. Dr. Quinn, a physician, decided to enter a new line of business. In Year One, she purchased a bus that she leased to Daschund Bus Lines. To facilitate the purchase of the bus, Dr. Quinn paid $20,000 of her own funds and borrowed $180,000 on a nonrecourse basis from

nership agrees with a limited partner that, at the partner's election. it will repurchase his partnership interest at a stated minimum dollar amount (usually less than the investor's original capital contribution). In situations of this kind, the partner is to be considered "at risk" only to the extent of the portion of the amount otherwise at risk over and above the guaranteed repurchase price.

12. The amounts borrowed by the taxpayer and then contributed to the activity (or used to purchase property which is contributed to the activity) are "amounts borrowed with respect to" the activity (as referred to in section 465(b)(1)(B)) and therefore are subject to the rules of section 465(b)(3) even though such amounts (or property) are also described in section 465(b)(1)(A).

Bank (the loan is secured only by the bus). Assume that Dr. Quinn "materially participated" in the new equipment leasing business. In Year One, her expenses related to the new business (depreciation and interest) totaled $50,000, but her rental income totaled only $20,000.

(a) To what extent can Dr. Quinn deduct the expenses incurred in Year One?

(b) How would the answer to (a) change if Dr. Quinn was personally liable for the Bank loan?

(c) In Year Two, the expenses related to the leasing business totaled $40,000 and her rental income from the activity totaled $30,000. What are the federal income tax consequences to Dr. Quinn for Year Two?

(d) Assume the same facts from part (c). In Year Three, the expenses from the leasing business totaled $35,000 and the rental income from the activity totaled $40,000. What are the federal income tax consequences to Dr. Quinn for Year Three?

* * *

Problem 11–2

In Year One, Sofia paid $100,000 of her own funds and borrowed $800,000 from the First National Bank on a nonrecourse basis to produce an independent motion picture film. The terms of the First National Bank loan required no payments of principal until Year Ten. Later in Year One, Sofia contributed an additional $100,000 of her own cash to pay various costs associated with the film. She made another $100,000 cash contribution for similar purposes in Year Two. Sofia's expenses and losses allocable to the motion picture in each of Years One and Two totaled $175,000; she had no revenues from the film in those years since it was not yet completed.

(a) To what extent can Sofia deduct the losses arising in Years One and Two with respect to the motion picture?

(b) Now suppose that Sofia's film is released in Year Three. Although successful with the critics, the film proves to be a modest hit at the box office: her income from the film that year exactly equals her expenses and losses for that year. If Sofia pays $125,000 of the First National Bank debt in Year Three, what consequences result?

(c) How would the answer to (a) change if Sofia paid $50,000 of the First National Bank debt in Year Two?

(d) How would the answer to (a) change if the First National Bank loan was a recourse loan?

C. PASSIVE ACTIVITY LOSSES

Code: IRC § 469(a)–(d)(1), (g)(1), (h)(1), (i)(1)–(i)(3)(A).

Regs: *Skim* Temp. Reg. § 1.469–5T(a).

The at-risk rules enacted in 1976 (the subject of Part B of this Chapter) proved to be an incomplete remedy to prevent many popular tax shelters of the day. While § 465 adequately ensnared those who were claiming deductions beyond the extent to which they bore a risk of loss, it did not address those shelters where wealthy taxpayers could manipulate the realization rule to tremendous advantage.

Consider Uncle Pennybags, a wildly successful attorney in private practice with a bountiful annual salary. Uncle Pennybags would like to generate some deductions to offset the vast amounts of ordinary income he enjoys each year. A loss-producing activity might be just the ticket, but with a large client base he is unwilling to devote much time or energy to it. Uncle Pennybags might choose to invest in an apartment building, borrowing $1 million on a recourse basis from an unrelated bank to purchase the building. Although the building will generate rental income, the expenses from the activity (taxes, insurance, repairs, and the like—not to mention the interest on the bank loan) could easily offset that amount. Then comes depreciation: under § 168, recall, Uncle Pennybags can write off a portion of the $1 million purchase price over 27.5 years. Sure, the building might well appreciate in value over this time, but no portion of that appreciation in value will be realized until Uncle Pennybags sells the property. Between the expenses and the depreciation deductions, the rental activity is almost sure to produce a net loss each year for many years. The gain that results from depreciating the entire cost basis of the building will not be felt until disposition, an event that might not occur for many years.

Section 465 likely will not limit Uncle Pennybags' deductions in these years because he is "at-risk" with respect to the $1 million recourse loan. Thus, this popular device to shelter ordinary income from tax continued even after § 465 came into effect. It took the Tax Reform Act of 1986 and the introduction of § 469 to deal a crippling blow to this and similar tax shelter schemes.

In general, § 469(a) permits taxpayers to deduct losses from "passive activities" only to the extent of the taxpayer's aggregate income from all passive activities. See §§ 469(a); 469(d)(1). Under § 469(b), any disallowed passive losses carry over to the next taxable year. A "passive activity," in general, is any business activity in which the taxpayer does not "materially participate." See § 469(c)(1). A taxpayer is deemed to materially participate in an activity if the taxpayer meets any one of several tests contained in the Regulations. See Temp. Reg. § 1.469–5T. The passive loss rules thus discourage limited participation in activities designed to generate substantial losses.

Going back to Uncle Pennybags, then, the deductions for depreciation and other expenses will be disallowed to the extent they exceed the income from the rental activity each year. When Uncle Pennybags finally sells the building and thus disposes of his entire interest in the rental activity, any losses disallowed under § 469 from prior years can be claimed then. In effect, § 469 postpones the deduction of excessive losses from passive activities until the taxpayer has enough income from that activity or until the taxpayer finally realizes gain or loss on the disposition of the assets used in the activity. This timing limitation makes the tax shelter scheme much less attractive to wealthy taxpayers like Uncle Pennybags.

Keep in mind that Uncle Pennybags' "scheme" was perfectly legal at the time—indeed, it was good "tax planning" prior to 1986. Even today, taxpayers try to accelerate deductions and defer the reporting of income, and that strategy was at the heart of these tax shelter activities. What was so abusive about this particular technique that compelled Congress to shut it down? And why is it targeted at "passive" activities? The following excerpt from the legislative history to § 469 explains Congress' motivation and provides a helpful summary of the major statutory provisions at play.

GENERAL EXPLANATION OF THE TAX REFORM ACT OF 1986

Senate Report 99–313, 99th Cong. 2d Sess. (1986).
1986–3 C.B. 3.

* * *

TITLE XIV—TAX SHELTERS; REAL ESTATE; INTEREST EXPENSE

A. *Limitations on Losses and Credits From Passive Activities (Sec. 1401 of the Bill and Sec. 469 of the Code)*

Present Law

In general, no limitations are placed on the ability of a taxpayer to use deductions from a particular activity to offset income from other activities. Similarly, most tax credits may be used to offset tax attributable to income from any of the taxpayer's activities.

There are some exceptions to this general rule. For example, deductions for capital losses are limited to the extent that there are not offsetting capital gains. * * *

In the absence of more broadly applicable limitations on the use of deductions and credits from one activity to reduce tax liability attributable to other activities, taxpayers with substantial sources of positive income are able to eliminate or sharply reduce tax liability by using deductions and credits from other activities, frequently by investing in tax shelters. Tax shelters commonly offer the opportunity to reduce or avoid tax liability with respect to salary or other positive income, by making available deductions and credits, possibly exceeding real economic costs or losses currently borne by the taxpayer, in excess or in advance of income from the shelters.

Reasons for Change

In recent years, it has become increasingly clear that taxpayers are losing faith in the Federal income tax system. This loss of confidence has resulted in large part from the interaction of two of the system's principal features: its high marginal rates (in 1986, 50 percent for a single individual with taxable income in excess of $88,270), and the opportunities it provides for taxpayers to offset income from one source with tax shelter deductions and credits from another.

The prevalence of tax shelters in recent years—even after the highest marginal rate for individuals was reduced in 1981 from 70 percent to 50 percent—has been well documented. For example, a recent Treasury study revealed that in 1983, out of 260,000 tax returns reporting "total positive income" in excess of $250,000, 11 percent paid taxes equaling 5 percent or less of total positive income, and 21 percent paid taxes equaling 10 percent or less of total positive income. Similarly, in the case of tax returns reporting total positive income in excess of $1 million, 11 percent paid tax equaling less than 5 percent of total positive income, and 19 percent paid tax equaling less than 10 percent of total positive income.

Such patterns give rise to a number of undesirable consequences, even aside from their effect in reducing Federal tax revenues. Extensive shelter activity contributes to public concerns that the tax system is unfair, and to the belief that tax is paid only by the naïve and the unsophisticated. This, in turn, not only undermines compliance, but encourages further expansion of the tax shelter market, in many cases diverting investment capital from productive activities to those principally or exclusively serving tax avoidance goals.

The committee believes that the most important sources of support for the Federal income tax system are the average citizens who simply report their income (typically consisting predominantly of items such as salaries, wages, pensions, interest, and dividends) and pay tax under the general rules. To the extent that these citizens feel that they are bearing a disproportionate burden with regard to the costs of government because of their unwillingness or inability to engage in tax-oriented investment activity, the tax system itself is threatened.

Under these circumstances, the committee believes that decisive action is needed to curb the expansion of tax sheltering and to restore to the tax system the degree of equity that is a necessary precondition to a beneficial and widely desired reduction in rates. So long as tax shelters are permitted to erode the Federal tax base, a low-rate system can provide neither sufficient revenues, nor sufficient progressivity, to satisfy the general public that tax liability bears a fair relationship to the ability to pay. In particular, a provision significantly limiting the use of tax shelter losses is unavoidable if substantial rate reductions are to be provided to high-income taxpayers without disproportionately reducing the share of total liability under the individual income tax that is borne by high-income taxpayers as a group.

The question of how to prevent harmful and excessive tax sheltering is not a simple one. One way to address the problem would be to eliminate substantially all tax preferences in the Internal Revenue Code.

For two reasons, however, the committee believes that this course is inappropriate.

First, while the bill reduces or eliminates some tax preference items that the committee believes do not provide social or economic benefits commensurate with their cost, there are many preferences that the committee believes are socially or economically beneficial. This is especially true when such preferences are used primarily to advance the purposes upon which Congress relied in enacting them, rather than to avoid taxation of income from sources unrelated to the preferred activity.

Second, it would be extremely difficult, perhaps impossible, to design a tax system that measures income perfectly. For example, the statutory allowance for depreciation * * * reflects broad industry averages, as opposed to providing precise item-by-item measurements. Accordingly, taxpayers with assets that depreciate less rapidly than the average, or that appreciate over time (as may be the case with certain real estate), may engage in tax sheltering * * * unless Congress directly addresses the tax shelter problem.

Even to the extent that rules for the accurate measurement of income can theoretically be devised, such rules may involve undue complexity from the perspective of many taxpayers. For example, a system that required all taxpayers to use a theoretically pure accrual method of accounting (e.g., including unrealized appreciation, and allowing only the amount of depreciation actually incurred for each specific asset in each taxable year) would create serious difficulties in both compliance and administration.

However, when the tax system, in order to avoid such complexity, permits simpler rules to be applied (e.g., generally not taxing unrealized gain, and allowing depreciation based on broad industry averages), opportunities for manipulation are created. Taxpayers may structure transactions specifically to take advantage of the situations in which the simpler rules lead to undermeasurement or deferral of income.

The question of what constitutes a tax shelter that should be subject to limitations is closely related to the question of who Congress intends to benefit when it enacts tax preferences. For example, in providing preferential depreciation for real estate or favorable accounting rules for farming, it was not Congress's primary intent to permit outside investors to avoid tax liability with respect to their salaries by investing in limited partnership syndications. Rather, Congress intends to benefit and provide incentives to taxpayers active in the businesses to which the preferences were directed.

In some cases, the availability of tax preferences to nonparticipating investors has even harmed the industries that the preferences were intended to benefit. For example, in the case of farming, credits and favorable deductions have often encouraged investments by wealthy individuals whose principal or only interest in farming is to receive an investment return, largely in the form of tax benefits to offset tax on positive sources of income. Since such investors may not need a positive cash return from farming in order to profit from their investments, they have a substantial competitive advantage in relation to active farmers, who commonly are not in a position to use excess tax benefits to shelter unrelated income. This has significantly contributed to the serious economic difficulties presently being experienced by many active farmers.

The availability of tax benefits to shelter positive sources of income also has harmed the economy generally, by providing a non-economic return on capital for certain investments. This has encouraged a flow of capital away from activities that may provide a higher pre-tax economic return, thus retarding the growth of the sectors of the economy with the greatest potential for expansion.

The committee believes that, in order for tax preferences to function as intended, their benefit must be directed primarily to taxpayers with a substantial and bona fide involvement in the activities to which the preferences relate. The committee also believes that it is appropriate to encourage nonparticipating investors to invest in particular activities, by permitting the use of preferences to reduce the rate of tax on income from those activities; however, such investors should not be permitted to use tax benefits to shelter unrelated income.

There are several reasons why it is appropriate to examine the materiality of a taxpayer's participation in an activity in determining the extent to which such taxpayer should be permitted to use tax benefits from the activity. A taxpayer who materially participates in an activity is more likely than a passive investor to approach the activity with a significant non-tax economic profit motive, and to form a sound judgment as to whether the activity has genuine economic significance and value.

A material participation standard identifies an important distinction between different types of taxpayer activities. In general, the more passive investor is seeking a return on capital invested, including returns in the form of reductions in the taxes owed on unrelated income, rather than an ongoing source of livelihood. A material participation standard reduces the importance, for such investors, of the tax-reduction features of an investment, and thus increases the importance of the economic features in an investor's decision about where to invest his funds.

Moreover, the committee believes that restricting the use of losses from business activities in which the taxpayer does not materially participate against other sources of positive income (such as salary and portfolio income) addresses a fundamental aspect of the tax shelter problem. As discussed above, instances in which the tax system applies simple rules at the expense of economic accuracy encourage the structuring of transactions to take advantage of the situations in which such rules give rise to under-measurement or deferral of income. Such transactions commonly are marketed to investors who do not intend to participate in the transactions, as devices for sheltering unrelated sources of positive income (e.g., salary and portfolio income). Accordingly, by creating a bar against the use of losses from business activities in which the taxpayer does not materially participate to offset positive income sources such as salary and portfolio income, the committee believes that it is possible significantly to reduce the tax shelter problem.

Further, in the case of a nonparticipating investor in a business activity, the committee believes that it is appropriate to treat losses of the activity as not realized by the investor prior to disposition of his interest in the activity. The effort to measure, on an annual basis, real economic losses from passive activities gives rise to distortions, particularly due to the nontaxation of unrealized appreciation and the mismatching of tax deductions and related economic income that may occur, especially where debt financing is used heavily. Only when a taxpayer disposes of his interest in an activity is it possible to determine whether a loss was sustained over the entire time that he held the interest.

The relationship to an activity of an investor who does not materially participate may be little different from the relationship of a shareholder to a corporation. So long as the investor retains an interest in the activity, any reduction in the value of such interest not only may be difficult to measure accurately, but has not been realized by the investor to a greater extent than in the context of a C corporation. In the case of a C corporation, losses and expenses borne by the corporation, and any decline in the value of the corporation's stock, do not give rise to the recognition of any loss on the part of shareholders prior to disposition of their stock.

The distinction that the committee believes should be drawn between activities on the basis of material participation bears no relationship to the question of whether, and to what extent, the taxpayer is at risk with respect to the activities. In general, the fact that a taxpayer has placed a particular amount at risk in an activity does not establish, prior to a disposition of the taxpayer's interest, that the amount invested, or any amount, has as yet been lost. The fact that a taxpayer is potentially liable with respect to future expenses or losses of the activity likewise has no bearing on the question whether any amount has as yet been lost, or otherwise is an appropriate current deduction or credit.

At-risk standards, although important in determining the maximum amount that is subject to being lost, are not a sufficient basis for determining whether or when net losses from an activity should be deductible against other sources of income, or for determining whether an ultimate economic loss has been realized. Congress' goal of making tax preferences available principally to active participants in substantial businesses, rather than to investors seeking to shelter unrelated income, can best be accomplished by examining material participation, as opposed to the financial stake provided by an investor to purchase tax shelter benefits.

In certain situations, however, the committee believes that financial risk or other factors, rather than material participation, should be the relevant standard. * * *

* * * Such activities predominantly involve the production of income from capital. * * * Rental activities generally require less on-going management activity, in proportion to capital invested, than business activities involving the production or sale of goods and services. Thus, for example, an individual who is employed fulltime as a professional could more easily provide all necessary management in his spare time with respect to a rental activity than he could with respect to another type of business activity involving the same capital investment. The extensive use of rental activities for tax shelter purposes under present law, combined with the reduced level of personal involvement necessary to conduct such activities, make clear that the effectiveness of the basic passive loss provision could be seriously compromised if material participation were sufficient to avoid the limitations in the case of rental activities.

* * *

Explanation of Provisions

1. OVERVIEW

The bill provides that deductions from passive trade or business activities, to the extent they exceed income from all such passive activities (exclusive of portfolio income), generally may not be deducted against other income. Similarly, credits from passive activities generally are limited to the tax allocable to the passive activities. Suspended losses and credits are carried forward and treated as deductions and credits from passive trade or business activities in the next year. Suspended losses from an activity are allowed in full when the taxpayer disposes of his entire interest in the activity.

* * *

Losses and credits from a passive activity (taking into account expenses such as interest attributable to acquiring or carrying an interest in the activity) may be applied against income for the taxable year from other passive activities or against income subsequently generated by any passive activity. Such losses (and credits) generally cannot be applied to shelter other income, such as compensation for services or portfolio income (including interest, dividends, royalties, and gains from the sale of property held for investment). For this purpose, property held for investment generally does not include an interest in a passive activity.

Salary and portfolio income are separated from passive activity losses and credits because the former generally are positive income sources that do not bear, at least to the same extent as other items, deductible expenses. Since salary and portfolio income are likely to be positive, they are susceptible to sheltering by means of investments in activities that give rise to tax benefits. The passive loss provision ensures that salary and portfolio income, along with other non-passive income sources, cannot be offset by tax losses from passive activities until the amount of such losses is determined upon disposition.

Under the provision, suspended losses attributable to passive trade or business activities are allowed in full upon a taxable disposition of the taxpayer's entire interest in the activity. The full amount of gain or loss from the activity can then be ascertained. To the extent the taxpayer's basis in the activity has been reduced by suspended deductions, resulting in gain on disposition, the remaining suspended deductions will, in effect, offset such gain. However, the character of any gain or loss is not affected by this provision.

Passive activity

Under the bill, an activity generally is a passive activity if it involves the conduct of any trade or business, and if the taxpayer does not materially participate in the activity. A taxpayer who is an individual materially participates in an activity only if he is involved in the operations of the activity on a regular, continuous, and substantial basis. Regardless of whether an individual directly owns an interest in a trade or business activity (e.g., as a proprietorship), or owns an interest in an activity conducted at the entity level by a pass-through entity such as a general partnership or S corporation, he must be involved in the operations of the activity on a regular, continuous, and substantial basis, in order to be materially participating.

* * *

A passive activity is defined under the bill to include any rental activity, whether or not the taxpayer materially participates. However, operating a hotel or other similar transient lodging, for example, where substantial services are provided, is not a rental activity. An activity as a dealer in real estate is also not generally treated as a rental activity. Long-term rentals or leases of property (e.g., apartments, leased office equipment, or leased cars), on the other hand, generally are considered to be rental activities. Losses from rental activities are allowed against income from other passive activities, but not against other income.

Interest on debt secured by the taxpayer's residence or a second residence is not subject to limitation under the passive loss rule, so long as the debt is secured by a security interest perfected under local law. Thus, if a taxpayer rents out his vacation home and a portion of the mortgage interest is allocable to rental use of the home which would otherwise be treated as a passive activity, it is not subject to limitation under this provision.

* * *

2. TREATMENT OF LOSSES AND CREDITS

In general

Losses. Losses arising from a passive activity generally are deductible only against income from that or another passive activity. Suspended passive activity losses for the year are carried forward indefinitely, but are not carried back, and are allowed in subsequent years against passive activity income. Suspended losses from an activity are allowed in full upon a taxable disposition of the activity, as discussed below.

* * *

* * * A loss that would not be allowed for the year because the taxpayer is not at risk with respect to it is suspended under the at-risk provision, not the passive loss rule. * * * Such amounts may become subject to the passive loss rule in subsequent years when they would be allowable under the at-risk * * * limitations. * * *

Credits. Credits arising with respect to passive activities generally are treated in the same manner as deductions. That is, credits may not be used to offset tax attributable to income other than passive income. The amount of tax attributable to net passive income is determined by comparing (i) the amount that the taxpayer would pay with regard to all income, with (ii) the amount that the taxpayer would pay with regard to taxable income other than net passive income (disregarding, in both cases, the effect of credits).

For example, if a taxpayer would owe $50,000 of tax disregarding net passive income, and $80,000 of tax considering both net passive and other taxable income (in both cases, disregarding the effect of credits), then the amount of tax attributable to passive income is $30,000. In this case, any credits not in excess of $30,000 attributable to the taxpayer's passive activities are allowable. Any passive activity credits not in excess of $30,000 are, in addition, subject to other limitations applicable to the allowance of credits. In the absence of net passive income for a taxable year, no tax is attributable to passive income, and passive credits generally are not allowable for the year.

* * *

Dispositions

In general. When a taxpayer disposes of his entire interest in a passive activity, the actual economic gain or loss on his investment can be finally determined. Thus, under the passive loss rule, upon a fully taxable disposition, any overall loss from the activity realized by the taxpayer is recognized and allowed against income (whether active or passive income). This result is accomplished by triggering suspended losses upon disposition.

The reason for this rule is that, prior to a disposition of the taxpayer's interest, it is difficult to determine whether there has actually been gain or loss with respect to the activity. For example, allowable deductions may exceed actual economic costs, or may be exceeded by untaxed appreciation. Upon a taxable disposition, net appreciation or depreciation with respect to the activity can be finally ascertained. Since the purpose of the disposition rule is to allow real economic losses of the taxpayer to be deducted, credits, which are not related to the measurement of such loss, are not specially allowable by reason of a disposition.

Taxable dispositions of entire interest in activity. The type of disposition that triggers full recognition of any loss from a passive activity is a fully taxable disposition of the taxpayer's entire interest in the activity. A fully taxable disposition generally includes a sale of the property to a third party at arm's length, and thus, presumably, for a price equal to its fair market value. Gain realized upon a transfer of an interest in a passive activity generally is treated as passive, and is first offset by the suspended losses from that activity. This accomplishes the purpose of the rule to recognize net income or loss with respect to the activity when it can be finally determined.

* * *

The taxpayer must dispose of his entire interest in the activity in order to trigger the recognition of loss. If he disposes of less than his entire interest, then the issue of ultimate economic gain or loss on his investment in the activity remains unresolved. * * *

* * *

An installment sale of the taxpayer's entire interest in an activity in a fully taxable transaction triggers the allowance of suspended losses. The losses are allowed in each year of the installment obligation, in the ratio that the gain recognized in each year bears to the total gain on the sale.

A transfer of a taxpayer's interest in an activity by reason of his death causes suspended losses to be allowed to the extent they exceed the amount, if any, by which the basis of the interest in the activity is increased at death under section 1014. Suspended losses are eliminated to the extent of the amount of the basis increase. The losses allowed generally would be reported on the final return of the deceased taxpayer.

Other transfers

A gift of all or part of the taxpayer's interest in a passive activity does not trigger suspended losses. However, if he has given away his entire interest, he cannot make a future taxable disposition of it. Suspended losses are therefore added to the basis of the property (i.e., the interest in the activity) immediately before the gift. Similarly, if the taxpayer gives away less than all of his interest, an allocable portion of any suspended losses are added to the donee's basis. Suspended losses of the donor are eliminated when added to the donee's basis, and the remainder of the losses continue to be suspended in the donor's hands. The treatment of subsequent deductions from the activity, to the extent of the donee's interest in it, depends on whether the activity is treated as passive in the donee's hands.

* * *

Activity no longer treated as passive activity

Other circumstances may arise which do not constitute a disposition, but which terminate the application of the passive loss rule to the taxpayer generally, or to the taxpayer with respect to a particular activity. For example, an individual who previously was passive in relation to a trade or business activity which generates net losses may begin materially participating in the activity. When a taxpayer's participation in an activity is material in any year after a year (or years) during which he was not a material participant, previously suspended losses remain suspended and continue to be treated as passive activity losses. Such previously suspended losses, however, unlike passive activity losses generally, are allowed against income from the activity realized after it ceases to be a passive activity with respect to the taxpayer. * * *

* * *

3. TREATMENT OF PORTFOLIO INCOME

In general

Under the bill, portfolio income is not treated as income from a passive activity, and passive losses and credits generally may not be applied to offset it. Portfolio income generally includes interest, dividends, and royalties. Also included in portfolio income are gain or loss attributable to disposition of (1) property that is held for investment (and that is not a passive activity) and (2) property that normally produces interest, dividend, or royalty income.

Portfolio investments ordinarily give rise to positive income, and are not likely to generate losses which could be applied to shelter other income. Therefore, for purposes of the passive loss rule, portfolio income generally is not treated as derived from a passive activity, but rather is treated like other positive income sources such as salary. To permit portfolio income to be offset by passive losses or credits would create the inequitable result of restricting sheltering by individuals dependent for support on wages or active business income, while permitting sheltering by those whose income is derived from an investment portfolio.

* * *

The rule treating portfolio income as not from a passive activity does not apply to the extent that income, of a type generally regarded as portfolio income, is derived in the ordinary course of a trade or business. For example, the business income of a bank typically is largely interest. Similarly, a securities broker/dealer may earn a substantial portion of the income from the business in the form of dividends and gains on sales of dividend-bearing instruments. Interest income may also arise in the ordinary course of a trade or business with respect to installment sales and interest charges on accounts receivable.

In these cases, the rationale for treating portfolio-type income as not from the passive activity does not apply, since deriving such income is what the business activity actually, in whole or in part, involves. Accordingly, interest, dividend, or royalty income which is derived in the ordinary course of a trade or business is not treated, for purposes of the passive loss provision, as portfolio income. If a taxpayer directly, or through a pass-through entity, owns an interest in an activity deriving such income, such income is treated as part of the activity, which, as a whole, may or may not be treated as passive, depending on whether the taxpayer materially participates in the activity.

* * *

4. MATERIAL PARTICIPATION

General rule

In general, a taxpayer's interest in a trade or business activity is not treated as an interest in a passive activity for a taxable year if the taxpayer materially participates in the activity throughout such year. * * *

Working as an employee, and providing services as part of a personal service business (including professional businesses such as law, accounting, and medicine), intrinsically require personal involvement by the taxpayer. Thus, by their nature, they generally are not passive activities.

Material participation of a taxpayer in an activity is determined separately for each taxable year. In most cases, the material participation (or lack thereof) of a taxpayer in an activity is not expected to change from year to year, although there will be instances n which it does change.

* * *

5. DEFINITION OF ACTIVITY

In applying the passive loss rule, one of the most important determinations that must be made is the scope of a particular activity. This determination is important for several reasons. For example, if two undertakings are part of the same activity, the taxpayer need only establish material participation with respect to the activity as a whole, whereas if they are separate activities he must establish such participation separately for each. In the case of a disposition, knowing the scope of the activity is critical to determining whether the taxpayer has disposed of his entire interest in the activity, or only of a portion thereof.

Defining separate activities either too narrowly or too broadly could lead to evasion of the passive loss rule. For example, an overly narrow definition would permit taxpayers to claim losses against salary, portfolio, or active business income by selectively disposing of portions of their interests in activities with respect to which there has been depreciation or loss of value, while retaining any portions with respect to which there has been appreciation. An overly broad definition would permit taxpayers to amalgamate undertakings that in fact are separate, and thus to use material participation in one undertaking as a basis for claiming without limitation losses and credits from another undertaking.

The determination of what constitutes a separate activity is intended to be made in a realistic economic sense. The question to be answered is what undertakings consist of an integrated and interrelated economic unit, conducted in coordination with or reliance upon each other, and constituting an appropriate unit for the measurement of gain or loss.

Under present law, section 183, relating to hobby losses, involves issues similar to those arising with respect to passive losses. Section 183 requires that separate activities be identified in order to determine whether a specific activity constitutes a hobby. Treasury Regulations interpreting this provision note that all facts and circumstances of a specific case must be taken into account, and then identify as the most significant facts and circumstances: "the degree of organizational and economic interrelationship in various undertakings, the business purpose which is (or might be) served by carrying on the various undertakings separately or together ... and the similarity of the various undertakings." These facts and circumstances likewise are relevant to determining the scope of an activity for purposes of the passive loss rule.

In general, providing two or more substantially different products or services involves engaging in more than one activity (unless customarily or for business reasons provided together—e.g., the appliance and clothing sections of a department store). For example, operating a restaurant and engaging in research and development are objectively so different that they are extremely unlikely to be part of the same activity. In addition, different stages in the production and sale of a particular product that are not carried on in an integrated fashion generally are not part of the same activity. For example, operating a retail gas station and engaging in oil and gas drilling generally are not part of the same activity. In general, normal commercial practices are highly probative in determining whether two or more undertakings are or may be parts of a single activity.

On the other hand, the fact that two undertakings involve providing the same products or services does not establish that they are part of the same activity absent the requisite degree of economic interrelationship or integration. For example, separate real estate rental projects built and managed in different locations by a real estate operator generally will constitute separate activities. Similarly, in the case of farming, each farm generally will constitute a separate activity. On the other hand, an integrated apartment project or shopping center generally will be treated as a single activity.

* * *

6. RENTAL ACTIVITY

In general

Under the passive loss rule, a rental activity is generally treated as a passive activity regardless of whether the taxpayer materially participates in the activity. Deductions and credits from a rental activity generally may be applied to offset only other income from passive activities. In the case of rental real estate activities in which the taxpayer actively participates, a special rule permits the application of losses and credits from the activity against up to $25,000 of nonpassive income of the taxpayer, for taxpayers other than corporations. A taxpayer is not considered to actively participate in the activity if he owns less than a 10 percent interest in it.

In determining what is a rental activity for purposes of these rules, [the intent is to] distinguish between rental activity that is passive in nature and nonrental activity which may not be passive. Thus, under the passive loss rule, a rental activity generally is an activity, the income from which consists of payments principally for the use of tangible property, rather than for the performance of substantial services.

* * *

Notes

1. *Determining Material Participation.* Section 469(c)(1) provides that a "passive activity" is a trade or business activity in which the taxpayer does not "materially participate." Material participation is defined vaguely in § 469(h)(1) as involvement with business operations on a regular, continuous, and substantial basis. The standard harkens to that employed by the Court in *Commissioner v. Groetzinger* in determining whether an activity rises to the level of a business in the first place. See Chapter 4.

Temporary Regulations offer more objective tests for determining whether a taxpayer materially participates in an activity. Regulation § 1.469–5T(a) lists the seven situations where a taxpayer will be deemed to materially participate in an activity:

(1) The taxpayer participates in the activity for more than 500 hours in the taxable year;

(2) The taxpayer participates in the activity for 500 hours or less during the taxable year, but the taxpayer's participation constitutes substantially all of the participation in the activity by all individuals involved in that activity;

(3) The taxpayer participates in the activity for more than 100 hours in the taxable year, and the taxpayer's participation equals or exceeds the hours of participation by any other individual involved in that activity;

(4) The taxpayer participates in the activity for more than 100 hours in the taxable year, and the taxpayer's participation in that activity *and* all other "significant participation activities" (those business activities in which the taxpayer participates for more than 100 hours but no more than 500 hours) in the same year totals more than 500 hours in the taxable year;

(5) The taxpayer materially participated in the activity for any five of the ten taxable years immediately prior to the taxable year at issue;

(6) The activity at issue involves the performance of professional personal services and the taxpayer materially participated in that activity for any three of the five taxable years immediately prior to the taxable year at issue; or

(7) The taxpayer participates in the activity for more than 100 hours in the taxable year and, based on all of the facts and circumstances, the taxpayer participates in the activity on a regular, continuous, and substantial basis.

If the taxpayer's participation satisfies any of these seven tests, the taxpayer materially participates in the activity. Notice that where the taxpayer's participation in an activity totals 100 hours or less, only in rare cases will the taxpayer be considered to "materially participate" in that activity.

2. *There's Something About Renting Real Estate.* Section 469(c)(2) states that rental activities are automatically passive activities, regardless of whether the taxpayer materially participates in the activity. The excerpt from the Senate Report explains the rationale for this rule. While the rule is absolute, it is important to keep in mind two special rules with respect to rental real estate activities that make its application less severe than one might think.

First, a landlord's business of renting real estate will not be considered a passive activity if two tests are met: (a) more than half of the personal services performed by the landlord in all business activities for the year are performed in "active real property businesses" (those in which the landlord materially participates); and (b) the landlord performs more than 750 hours of service in all such active real property businesses. Section 469(c)(7). A qualifying landlord may thus use losses from these active real property businesses to offset (dare we say "shelter?") ordinary income like compensation and interest.

Second, most individuals may nonetheless deduct up to $25,000 of losses (and "deduction equivalents" to passive activity credits) attributable to rental real estate activities against income from other, nonpassive activities. Section 469(i). The only catch here is that the individual must "actively participate" in the rental activity. While "active participation" is not expressly defined in the Code (§ 469(i)(6)(A) simply imposes a requirement that the taxpayer own at least ten percent of all interests in the rental activity at issue), the Senate Report provides some guidance:

> The difference between active participation and material participation is that the former can be satisfied without regular, continuous, and substantial involvement in operations, so long as the taxpayer participates, e.g., in the making of management decisions or arranging for others to provide services (such as repairs), in a significant and bona fide sense. Management decisions that are relevant in this context include approving new tenants, deciding on rental terms, approving capital or repair expenditures, and other similar decisions.

> Thus, for example, a taxpayer who owns and rents out an apartment that formerly was his primary residence, or that he uses as a part-time vacation home, may be treated as actively participating even if he hires a rental agent and others provide services such as repairs. So long as the taxpayer participates in the manner described above, a lack of participation in operations does not lead to the denial of relief.

Sen. Rep. No. 99–313, 99th Cong., 2d Sess. at 737–738 (1986).

* * *

Self-Assessment Question

(Solutions to Self–Assessment Questions are set forth in Appendix 3.)

SAQ 11–3. Dr. Welby, a colleague of Dr. Quinn from SAQ 11–2, also got the entrepreneurial bug. In Year One, Dr. Welby purchased a $500,000 office building that he rented out to customers. To purchase the building, Dr. Welby contributed $100,000 of his own funds and borrowed $400,000 on a nonrecourse basis from Bank, an entity described in § 49(a)(1)(D)(iv) (the loan was secured only by the building). Throughout this Problem, assume that Dr. Welby does not "materially participate" in the leasing activity and that his adjusted gross income in all years exceeds $150,000. In Year One, the expenses from the leasing activity (depreciation and interest) totaled $100,000 but his rental income from the building totaled only $40,000.

(a) To what extent can Dr. Welby deduct the expenses incurred in the leasing activity during Year One?

(b) Assume that Dr. Welby also started a bus leasing business similar to Dr. Quinn's business in Year One. He paid $200,000 of his own funds to buy a bus which he leased to Bulldog Bus Lines. Dr. Welby had rental income of $50,000 from the bus leasing activity, and his expenses allocable to that activity totaled $30,000 for Year One. How do these additional facts change the answer to part (a), assuming Dr. Welby did not "materially participate" in the bus leasing activity?

(c) In Year Two, the rental income from the building activity totaled $100,000 and his expenses for the activity totaled $80,000. What are the federal income tax consequences to Dr. Welby?

(d) Assume the same facts from part (c). On January 1, Year Three, Dr. Welby sold the building to an unrelated purchaser for cash and recognized a total gain of $30,000 on the sale. What additional tax consequences to Dr. Welby stem from this sale?

* * *

Problem 11–3

Grace Van Owen, a partner at a major Los Angeles law firm, earned $300,000 in salary for Year One. In addition to her work as an attorney, Grace owns a bakery business to which she devotes only 50 hours annually. In Year One, the bakery yielded a $30,000 loss. In the same year, Grace received royalty income of $10,000 from a hit song she recorded with her family years earlier.

(a) To what extent may Grace deduct the $30,000 loss from her bakery business in Year One?

(b) In Year Two, Grace sold the bakery to an unrelated buyer at a realized gain of $100,000. What tax consequences arise?

(c) Same as (b), except that instead of selling the bakery, Grace held onto the business and saw it generate some dough: the bakery made a profit of $10,000.

(d) How would the answer to (a) change if Grace worked at the bakery for 300 hours in Year One, an amount in excess of that worked by any other person involved with the bakery?

(e) How would the answer to (a) change if Grace also owned and operated a cinema in which she did not materially participate and that activity yielded a profit in Year One of $20,000?

D. ALTERNATIVE MINIMUM TAX

Code: *Skim* IRC §§ 55–59.

Regs: None.

In this Part, the last stop in our journey through the Internal Revenue Code, we pause briefly to consider the alternative minimum tax ("AMT"). Only about two percent of individual taxpayers are subject to the AMT, but when it applies it can carry quite a sting. The technical application of the statutory provisions here, while clearly fascinating, is perhaps less important than a consideration of the fundamental tax policy implications of the AMT. So, as a reward for trudging through the Code and regulations so carefully throughout the course, this Part takes a more "global" look at the AMT through a policy lens. While you probably should spend some time leafing through the current statutory provisions assigned above, clearly your focus should be on understanding how we got to where we are now, and deciding whether we should be elsewhere. Portions of the text that follows are adapted from Samuel A. Donaldson, *The Easy Case Against Tax Simplification*, 22 Va. Tax Rev. 645 (2003).

The AMT is a backstop measure designed to ensure that wealthy taxpayers pay at least a certain "minimum" amount of income tax. While a complete understanding of the AMT is well beyond the scope of an introductory text, one can learn much from a brief overview of its history, an epic saga spanning over 30 years. As one commentator has observed, the AMT "reflects the worst tendency of incremental policy-making—tinkering with change at the margins rather than confronting the underlying problems." Sheldon D. Pollack, *Tax Complexity, Reform, and the Illusions of Tax Simplification*, 2 Geo. Mason Indep. L. Rev. 319, 346 (1994).

Origins. In the late 1960s, Congress became concerned that some wealthy taxpayers were making what it considered an excessive use of various exclusion and deduction provisions to minimize tax liability. The tax liabilities of taxpayers with equivalent incomes varied significantly because of these "tax preference items."

The first "tax preference items" included the following:

- accelerated depreciation of real property;

- accelerated depreciation of personal property subject to a net lease;

- the difference between the fair market value of a qualified or restricted stock option and its exercise price;

- the depletion deduction for timber, mineral and oil and gas properties; and

- the exclusion then allowed for one-half of an individual taxpayer's net capital gain.

In many cases, wealthier taxpayers exploited tax preference items and thus paid tax at a lower effective rate than taxpayers with substantially less income. In some extreme cases, wealthy individual and corporate taxpayers paid no tax at all. There was thus a crisis of horizontal and vertical equity. Horizontal equity was violated because taxpayers with similar incomes were subjected to differing tax liabilities because some took advantage of tax preference items. Vertical equity was undermined because individuals with high incomes that took advantage of tax preference items paid less tax than those with lower incomes that could not avail themselves of these benefits.

Congress had three options in responding to the crisis: (1) do nothing and accept the disparate tax treatments as a justifiable departure from horizontal and vertical equity; (2) limit the benefit of each tax preference item to wealthier taxpayers (perhaps by phase-out provisions or flat ceilings); or (3) impose an additional tax liability on wealthy taxpayers who claim an excessive amount of tax preference items. Congress opted for the last option, enacting an "add-on minimum tax" as part of the Tax Reform Act of 1969. The add-on minimum tax base was the sum of tax preference items claimed by a taxpayer minus an exemption amount of, in most cases, $30,000. The tax was them computed as ten percent of the tax base. The add-on minimum tax liability was added to the taxpayer's regular tax liability in computing the total tax due.

Of course, the add-on minimum tax made tax computations much more complicated, for wealthy taxpayers were required to perform additional computations and to plan for possible application of an additional tax. But to the extent the add-on minimum tax redressed the violations of horizontal and vertical equity, Congress was apparently happy to make the sacrifice.

Strengthening the Add–On Minimum Tax. Within a few years, however, taxpayers subject to the additional tax found ways to circumvent the add-on minimum tax. In the Tax Reform Act of 1976, Congress strengthened the add-on minimum tax by adding to the list of tax preference items, increasing the tax rate to 15 percent, and reducing the exemption amount. Notice that the 1976 solution was not to repeal the add-on minimum tax as a useless or ineffective technique to restore equity, but to enlarge the scope of the minimum tax, both in the number of tax preference items and the number of taxpayers subject to the tax.

The Shift to the Alternative Minimum Tax. Yet the reforms introduced in 1976 were short lived. By 1978, Congress determined that the add-on minimum tax was adversely affecting market decisions, specifically capital formation. In the Revenue Act of 1978, Congress created a new "alternative minimum tax" for the capital gains deduction (under prior law, individual taxpayers deducted one-half of the net capital gain in determining taxable income; in effect, then, capital gains were always taxed at an effective rate of one-half of the taxpayer's marginal tax rate) and for excess itemized deductions. The add-on minimum tax was preserved for all other tax preference items. Under the first AMT, "alternative minimum taxable income" in excess of $20,000 was subject to marginal tax rates ranging from ten to 25 percent. If the AMT liability exceeded the sum of the taxpayer's regular tax and add-on minimum tax liabilities, the taxpayer was required to pay the AMT liability instead of the other taxes. The first AMT was designed to affect the total tax liability only of those taxpayers with incomes over $50,000. The 1978 Act made a complicated set of rules even more so. Now there were two surcharge taxes, not one. Although the new AMT only taxed wealthier taxpayers who made excessive use of two tax preference items, many had to determine whether either or both the AMT and the leftover add-on minimum tax applied to them.

The two-tax surcharge regime only lasted four years. Congress repealed the add-on minimum tax for individuals in the Tax Equity and Fiscal Responsibility Act of 1982. The tax preference items subject to the add-on minimum tax then became subject to the AMT. Congress also increased the AMT exemption amount to $30,000 (or $40,000 for couples filing a joint return). The intent of the 1982 reforms was to reduce the scope of the AMT. Again, the tax was only supposed to affect those with incomes over $50,000. Congress also hoped to simplify taxpayer computations by consolidating two surcharge taxes into one. Interestingly, the add-on minimum tax was retained for corporate taxpayers, with no explanation as to why the added burden of complexity was acceptable for corporations.

Because the scope of the AMT was reduced, one would expect the AMT to be less effective in preventing taxpayers from making excessive use of exclusions, deductions, and credits. By 1986, the prediction of limited effectiveness had come true. Congress had become concerned that many tax preference items were omitted from the AMT, which allowed many wealthy taxpayers to continue paying less than a "fair" amount of tax. We saw that concern reflected in the legislative history to § 469. See Part C of this Chapter. As part of the Tax Reform Act of 1986, then, Congress added to the list of tax preference items subject to the AMT (including tax-exempt interest and the fair market value deduction for charitable contributions) and substituted a flat AMT rate of 21 percent. Corporate taxpayers were also made subject to the AMT (but at a flat rate of 20 percent) and the add-on minimum tax was fully repealed. So only four years after limiting the scope of the AMT, Congress realized that the desire simplification frustrated the overall purpose of the AMT. It thus deliberately decided to restore complexity in order to advance the equity sought by the AMT.

In the next decade, Congress twice raised the AMT rate for individuals but otherwise left the AMT alone. But with the Taxpayer Relief Act of 1997, Congress made two significant changes to the AMT. First, it modified the adjustment made to depreciation deductions with respect to property placed in service after December 31, 1998. The modification served to curtail AMT liability attributable to the accelerated depreciation deductions available to taxpayers because Congress determined that such liability was impeding capital formation and business operations. Second, Congress repealed the AMT for corporations with average annual gross receipts of less than $7.5 million. Congress cited administrative complexity as the justification for removing small corporations from the reach of the AMT. Considering that about two percent of all taxpayers pay AMT, as discussed more fully below, the degree of simplicity achieved by exempting small corporations is likely minimal. A better justification for the small corporation exemption is that it furthers the original purpose of the AMT. From its inception, the AMT was intended to reach only the wealthy taxpayers, originally defined as those with incomes in excess of $50,000. By relieving small corporations of AMT liability, Congress preserved the limited scope while maintaining an effective deterrent for those taxpayers within its scope. Justifying the exemption as a simplification measure, though, would only serve to open the door to eventual repeal.

Repeal of the AMT? Legislation passed in 1999 but vetoed by President Clinton would have slowly repealed the AMT for individuals altogether. While repeal of the AMT remains a priority item for some policymakers, it has yet to achieve a critical mass of followers in Congress. In 2001, the Joint Committee on Taxation recommended the elimination of both the individual AMT and the corporate AMT. 2 Joint Committee on Taxation, *Study of the Overall State of the Federal Tax System and Recommendations for Simplification Pursuant to Section 8022(3)(B) of the Internal Revenue Code of 1986*, (JCS–3–01) 15 (2001) (the "Joint Committee Report"). It justifies complete repeal on three grounds. First, the Joint Committee Report complains of the significant compliance burden placed on taxpayers, noting Service estimates that taxpayers annually devote over 29 million hours in completing Form 6251, the AMT computation form.

Second, the Joint Committee Report observes that the AMT, if unchanged, will reach an increasing number of taxpayers over the next decade. While the current AMT affects about two percent of all individual taxpayers, the Joint Committee Report estimates that over 11 percent of taxpayers will face AMT liability in 2011—a number far in excess of original intentions. Taxpayers within reach of the AMT will include many middle-income taxpayers with some capital gains who also make use of many personal exemptions and the child tax credit. This threatens horizontal equity. The growing number of taxpayers subject to the AMT is a function of several factors. In general, regular tax rates are lower now than when the AMT was created (in 1969, for instance, the highest marginal tax rate for individuals was 70 percent). The AMT rates, however, have not changed consistently with the regular tax rates. Also, the AMT exemption amount is not subject to inflation adjustments, unlike many aspects of the regular income tax. Finally, miscellaneous itemized deductions are not deductible for purposes of computing the AMT base. By recapturing the deductions, more taxpayers are subject to AMT exposure.

Third, the Joint Committee Report argues that the AMT is no longer necessary now that the regular tax system contains specific provisions that accomplish the same general goal. It cites the enactment of §§ 465 and 469 as evidence that the Code already contains anti-abuse provisions designed to curb tax shelter activities. Consequently, the Joint Committee Report concludes that the regular tax base is too similar to the AMT base to warrant the imposition of a separate tax. As the Joint Committee Report states, "legislative changes since the Tax Reform Act of 1986 ... have had the effect of more closely conforming the regular tax base for individual taxpayers to the alternative minimum tax base." *Id.*

* * *

PRESENT LAW AND ISSUES RELATING TO THE INDIVIDUAL ALTERNATIVE MINIMUM TAX ("AMT")

Joint Committee on Taxation, 1998.
JCX–3–98.

Table 1.—Actual and Projected Individual Income Tax Returns With Tax Liability Under the Individual Alternative Minimum Tax, 1987–2008

Year	Number of returns paying AMT (thousands)	Percentage of returns paying AMT	Excess of AMT liability over regular tax liability ($billions)
1987	140	0.1	1.7
1988	134	0.1	1.0
1989	117	0.1	0.8
1990	132	0.1	0.8
1991	244	0.2	1.2
1992	287	0.3	1.4
1993	335	0.3	2.1
1994	369	0.3	2.2
1995	414	0.4	2.3
1996	data not available		

Year	Number of returns paying AMT (thousands)	Percentage of returns paying AMT	Excess of AMT liability over regular tax liability ($billions)
1997		data not available	
1998	856	0.7	4.3
1999	952	0.8	4.6
2000	1,141	0.9	5.1
2001	1,391	1.1	5.7
2002	1,782	1.4	6.5
2003	2,378	1.9	7.6
2004	2,905	2.2	8.9
2005	3,942	3.0	10.6
2006	5,078	3.8	12.9
2007	6,587	4.9	15.9
2008	8,830	6.5	19.8

Note: These statistics represent taxpayers who actually pay AMT and do not include taxpayers whose regular tax liabilities are affected by the AMT through tax credit limitations. See Tables 5, 6, and 7 for such data.

Source: Internal Revenue Service, *Statistics of Income*, 1987–1995; projections for years 1998–2008 from Joint Committee on Taxation staff estimates.

Table 2.—Distribution of Individual AMT Taxpayers with AMT Liability under Present Law, 1998

Income category(1)	Number of returns (thousands)	AMT taxpayers as a percentage of all taxpayers
Less than $10,000	(2)	(3)
$10,000 to less than 20,000	1	(3)
$20,000 to less than $30,000	(2)	(3)
$30,000 to less than $40,000	9	0.1
$40,000 to less than $50,000	14	0.1
$50,000 to less than $75,000	68	0.3
$75,000 to less than $100,000	97	1.0
$100,000 to less than $200,000	270	3.2
$200,000 and over	388	17.9
Total (all taxpayers)	**848**	**0.8**

(1) The income concept used to place tax returns into income categories is AGI plus: (a) tax-exempt interest; (b) employer contributions to health plans and life insurance; (c) employer share of FICA tax; (d) workers compensation; (e) nontaxable social security benefits; (f) insurance value of Medicare benefits; (g) AMT preference items; and (h) excluded income of U.S. citizens living abroad. Excludes individuals who are dependents of other taxpayers and taxpayers with negative income, resulting in differences with Table 1.
(2) Less than 500
(3) Less than .05 percent
Details may not add due to rounding.

Source: Staff of the Joint Committee on Taxation

Table 3.—Distribution of Individual AMT Taxpayers with AMT Liability under Present Law, 2008

Income category(1)	Number of returns (thousands)	AMT taxpayers as a percentage of all taxpayers
Less than $10,000	(2)	(3)
$10,000 to less than 20,000	(2)	(3)
$20,000 to less than $30,000	9	(3)
$30,000 to less than $40,000	157	0.9
$40,000 to less than $50,000	248	1.8
$50,000 to less than $75,000	1,356	5.8
$75,000 to less than $100,000	2,700	19.7
$100,000 to less than $200,000	3,043	26.6
$200,000 and over	1,310	42.7
Total (all taxpayers)	**8,822**	**7.2**

(1) Same income concept as used in Table 2, measured at 1998 levels.
(2) Less than 500
(3) Less than .05 percent
Details may not add due to rounding.

Source: Staff of the Joint Committee on Taxation

* * *

Problem 11–4

Consider the arguments for repeal of the AMT as made by the Joint Committee on Taxation.

(a) If you had to make the case for retaining the AMT, how would you refute these arguments?

(b) Would you be persuaded by your responses?

(c) How, if at all, should the AMT be reformed?

Appendix 1

Tax Expenditure Estimates by Budget Function, Fiscal Years 2006–2010

Source: Joint Committee on Taxation, Estimates of Federal Tax Expenditures for Fiscal Years 2006–2010 (JCS–2–06), April 25, 2006.

Table 1.--Tax Expenditure Estimates By Budget Function, Fiscal Years 2006-2010
[Billions of dollars]

Function	Corporations					Individuals					Total 2006-10
	2006	2007	2008	2009	2010	2006	2007	2008	2009	2010	
National Defense											
Exclusion of benefits and allowances to Armed Forces personnel						2.8	2.8	2.9	3.0	3.0	14.5
Exclusion of military disability benefits						0.1	0.1	0.1	0.1	0.1	0.4
Deduction for overnight-travel expenses of National Guard and Reserve Members						0.1	0.1	0.1	0.1	0.1	0.3
International Affairs											
Exclusion of income earned abroad by U.S. citizens						3.8	4.0	4.2	4.4	4.6	21.0
Exclusion of certain allowances for Federal employees abroad						0.4	0.5	0.5	0.6	0.6	2.6
Exclusion of extraterritorial income	3.9	1.9				0.1	(1)	(1)	(1)	(1)	6.2
Deferral of active income of controlled foreign corporations	3.4	5.8	6.4	7.0	7.5						30.1
Inventory property sales source rule exception	6.2	6.4	6.6	6.8	7.0						33.0
Deferral of certain active financing income	1.1	1.7									2.8
General Science, Space, and Technology											
Expensing of research and experimental expenditures	2.0	3.7	5.5	6.0	5.8	0.1	0.1	0.1	0.1	0.1	29.4
Energy											
Expensing of exploration and development costs:											
Oil and gas	1.1	1.6	1.2	0.8	0.6	(1)	(1)	(1)	(1)	(1)	5.4
Other fuels	(1)	(1)	(1)	(1)	(1)	(1)	(1)	(1)	(1)	(1)	0.2
Excess of percentage over cost depletion:											
Oil and gas	1.0	1.0	0.9	0.9	0.9	(1)	(1)	(1)	(1)	(1)	4.7
Other fuels	0.1	0.1	0.1	0.1	0.1	(1)	(1)	(1)	(1)	(1)	0.6
Tax credit and deduction for small refiners with capital costs associated with EPA sulfur regulation compliance	(1)	(1)	(1)	(1)	(1)	(1)	(1)	(1)	(1)	(1)	0.1
Tax credit for production of non-conventional fuels	2.7	3.2	1.2	(1)	(1)	1.0	1.0	0.2	(1)	(1)	8.8
Tax credit for alcohol fuels\2\	(1)	(1)	(1)	(1)	(1)						0.2
Tax credit for biodiesel fuels\3\	(1)	0.1	0.1	0.1							0.2
Exclusion of interest on State and local government qualified private activity bonds for energy production facilities	(1)	(1)	(1)	(1)	(1)	0.1	0.1	0.1	0.1	0.1	0.5
Exclusion of energy conservation subsidies provided by public utilities	(1)	(1)	(1)	(1)	(1)	(1)	(1)	(1)	(1)	(1)	0.1
Energy credit (Section 48)	(1)	0.1	0.1	(1)	(1)						0.2
Tax credit for electricity production from renewable resources	2.0	3.7	5.5	6.0	5.8	0.1	0.1	0.1	0.1	0.1	29.4
Deferral of gain from the disposition of electric transmission property to implement Federal Energy Regulatory Commission restructuring policy	0.6	0.5	(4)	-0.3	-0.3	(1)	(1)	(1)	(1)	(1)	0.4
Tax credits for holders of clean renewable energy bonds	(1)	(1)	(1)	(1)	(1)	(1)	(1)	(1)	(1)	(1)	0.2
Tax credits for investments in clean coal power generation facilities	(1)	0.1	0.1	0.2	0.2						0.5
Expensing of the cost of property used in the refining of liquid fuels	(1)	(1)	0.1	0.2	0.3						0.7
Amortization of geological and geophysical costs associated with oil and gas exploration	(4)	0.1	0.2	0.2	0.1	(1)	(1)	(1)	(1)	(1)	0.8

Table 1.--Tax Expenditure Estimates By Budget Function, Fiscal Years 2006-2010
[Billions of dollars]

Function	Corporations					Individuals					Total 2006-10
	2006	2007	2008	2009	2010	2006	2007	2008	2009	2010	
Deduction for expenditures on energy-efficient commercial building property	(1)	0.1	(1)	(4)	(4)	(1)	0.1	(1)	(4)	(4)	0.3
Tax credit for the purchase of qualified energy efficiency improvements to existing homes						0.1	0.3	0.2			0.6
Tax credit for the production of energy-efficient appliances	0.1	0.1									0.2
Tax credits for alternative technology vehicles	0.1	0.1	(1)	(1)	(1)	0.2	0.2	0.1	0.1	(1)	0.8
Tax credit for clean-fuel vehicle refueling property	(1)	(1)	(1)	(1)	(1)	(1)	(1)	(1)	(1)	(1)	0.1
Five-year carryback period for certain net operating losses of electric utility companies	0.1	(1)	(1)	(1)	(4)						0.1
Natural Resources and Environment											
Expensing of exploration and development costs, nonfuel minerals	0.1	0.1	0.1	0.1	0.1	(1)	(1)	(1)	(1)	(1)	0.4
Excess of percentage over cost depletion, nonfuel minerals	0.1	0.1	0.1	0.1	0.1	0.1	0.1	0.1	0.1	0.1	1.0
Expensing of timber-growing costs	0.2	0.2	0.2	0.2	0.2	(1)	(1)	(1)	(1)	(1)	1.1
Exclusion of interest on State and local government qualified private activity bonds for sewage, water, and hazardous waste facilities	0.2	0.2	0.2	0.2	0.2	0.4	0.4	0.5	0.5	0.5	3.3
Special rules for mining reclamation reserves	(1)	(1)	(1)	(1)	(1)	(1)	(1)	(1)	(1)	(1)	0.2
Special tax rate for nuclear decommissioning reserve fund	0.5	0.6	0.7	0.8	0.8						3.4
Exclusion of contributions in aid of construction for water and sewer utilities	(1)	(1)	(1)	(1)	(1)						0.2
Amortization of certified pollution control facilities	(1)	(1)	(1)	0.1	0.1						0.3
Amortization and expensing of reforestation expenditures	(1)	(1)	(1)	(1)	(1)	0.1	0.1	0.1	0.1	0.1	0.6
Agriculture											
Expensing of soil and water conservation expenditures	(1)	(1)	(1)	(1)	(1)	(1)	(1)	(1)	(1)	(1)	0.2
Expensing of fertilizer and soil conditioner costs	(1)	(1)	(1)	(1)	(1)	0.2	0.1	0.1	0.1	0.1	0.7
Expensing of the costs of raising dairy and breeding cattle	(1)	(1)	(4)	(4)	(1)	0.1	0.1	(1)	(1)	(1)	0.2
Exclusion of cost-sharing payments	(1)	(1)	(1)	(1)	(1)	0.1	0.1	0.1	0.1	0.1	0.1
Exclusion of cancellation of indebtedness income of farmers						0.1	0.1	0.1	0.1	0.1	0.4
Income averaging for farmers and fishermen						(1)	(1)	(1)	(1)	(1)	0.1
Five-year carryback period for net operating losses attributable to farming	(1)	(1)	(1)	(1)	(1)	(1)	(1)	(1)	(1)	(1)	0.1
Commerce and Housing											
Financial institutions:											
Exemption of credit union income	1.7	1.8	1.9	2.0	2.1						9.3
Insurance companies:											
Exclusion of investment income on life insurance and annuity contracts	2.5	2.5	2.6	2.7	2.7	25.5	26.1	26.8	27.5	28.2	147.1
Small life insurance company taxable income adjustment	0.1	0.1	0.1	0.1	0.1						0.3
Special treatment of life insurance company reserves	1.9	2.0	2.0	2.1	2.2						10.2

Table 1.--Tax Expenditure Estimates By Budget Function, Fiscal Years 2006-2010

[Billions of dollars]

Function	Corporations					Individuals					Total 2006-10
	2006	2007	2008	2009	2010	2006	2007	2008	2009	2010	
Deduction of unpaid property loss reserves for property and casualty insurance companies	3.4	3.4	3.5	3.6	3.6	......	......	......	......	......	17.5
Special deduction for Blue Cross and Blue Shield companies	0.9	1.0	1.0	1.0	1.0	......	......	......	......	......	5.0
Housing:											
Deduction for mortgage interest on owner-occupied residences	......	......	......	......	......	69.4	75.6	80.7	85.9	91.1	402.7
Deduction for property taxes on owner-occupied residences	......	......	......	......	......	19.9	13.8	13.5	13.4	13.2	73.8
Exclusion of capital gains on sales of principal residences	......	......	......	......	......	24.1	25.2	25.7	26.3	27.1	128.4
Exclusion of interest on State and local government qualified private activity bonds for owner-occupied housing	0.3	0.4	0.4	0.4	0.4	0.9	1.0	1.0	1.1	1.1	7.0
Exclusion of interest on State and local government qualified private activity bonds for rental housing	0.2	0.2	0.2	0.2	0.2	0.5	0.5	0.5	0.6	0.6	3.7
Depreciation of rental housing in excess of alternative depreciation system	0.4	0.5	0.6	0.7	0.8	4.0	4.6	5.3	6.1	7.0	29.9
Tax credit for low-income housing	3.4	3.6	3.8	4.1	4.4	1.4	1.5	1.6	1.7	1.9	27.4
Tax credit for rehabilitation of historic structures	0.3	0.3	0.3	0.3	0.3	0.1	0.1	0.1	0.1	0.1	2.2
Tax credit for rehabilitation of structures, other than historic structures	(1)	(1)	(1)	(1)	(1)	0.1	0.1	0.1	0.1	0.1	0.5
Additional exemption for housing provided to individuals displaced by Hurricane Katrina	......	......	......	......	......	0.1	(1)	......	......	......	0.1
Tax credit for Gulf Opportunity Zone employers providing in-kind lodging for employees and income exclusion for the employees	0.1	(1)	......	......	......	0.1	(1)	......	......	......	0.2
Other business and commerce:											
Reduced rates of tax on dividends and long-term capital gains	......	......	......	......	......	92.2	94.5	101.7	99.6	50.2	438.1
Exclusion of capital gains at death	......	......	......	......	......	50.9	51.9	53.2	69.7	64.5	290.2
Carryover basis of capital gains on gifts	......	......	......	......	......	5.4	5.5	5.7	7.6	56.1	80.3
Deferral of gain on non-dealer installment sales	0.6	0.7	0.7	0.7	0.8	0.5	0.5	0.5	0.6	0.6	6.2
Deferral of gain on like-kind exchanges	2.0	2.1	2.2	2.4	2.5	0.8	0.8	0.9	0.8	1.0	15.5
Depreciation of buildings other than rental housing in excess of alternative depreciation system	0.4	0.6	0.8	1.1	1.4	0.4	0.5	0.7	1.0	1.3	8.3
Depreciation of equipment in excess of alternative depreciation system	5.7	11.0	17.7	23.4	27.7	-2.2	0.1	2.2	4.3	6.1	96.0
Expensing under section 179 of depreciable business property	0.6	0.6	-0.1	-0.4	-0.2	2.8	2.6	0.1	-0.8	-0.4	4.8
Amortization of business startup costs	(1)	(1)	(1)	(1)	(1)	0.7	0.7	0.8	0.8	0.9	3.9
Reduced rates on first $10,000,000 of corporate taxable income	4.3	4.3	4.3	4.3	4.3	......	......	......	......	......	21.6
Permanent exemption from imputed interest rules	(1)	(1)	(1)	(1)	(1)	0.4	0.4	0.4	0.4	0.5	2.1
Expensing of magazine circulation expenditures	(1)	(1)	(1)	(1)	(1)	(1)	(1)	(1)	(1)	(1)	0.1
Special rules for magazine, paperback book, and record returns	(1)	(1)	(1)	(1)	(1)	(1)	(1)	(1)	(1)	(1)	0.2
Completed contract rules	0.3	0.3	0.4	0.4	0.5	(1)	(1)	(1)	(1)	(1)	1.9
Cash accounting, other than agriculture	(1)	(1)	(1)	(1)	(1)	0.8	0.8	0.8	0.9	0.9	4.2

Table 1.--Tax Expenditure Estimates By Budget Function, Fiscal Years 2006-2010
[Billions of dollars]

Function	Corporations					Individuals					Total 2006-10
	2006	2007	2008	2009	2010	2006	2007	2008	2009	2010	
Exclusion of interest on State and local government small-issue qualified private activity bonds	0.1	0.1	0.1	0.1	0.1	0.3	0.3	0.3	0.4	0.4	2.3
Exception from net operating loss limitations for corporations in bankruptcy proceedings	0.6	0.6	0.6	0.6	0.6	...	...	...	...	...	3.0
Tax credit for employer-paid FICA taxes on tips	0.2	0.2	0.2	0.2	0.3	0.3	0.4	0.4	0.4	0.5	3.1
Deduction of certain film and television production costs	0.1	0.1	0.1	(1)	(1)	(1)	(1)	(1)	(1)	(1)	0.3
Production activity deduction	2.7	3.9	5.5	5.9	7.4	0.9	1.3	1.8	2.0	2.6	34.0
Tax credit for the cost of carrying tax-paid distilled spirits in wholesale inventories	(1)	(1)	(1)	(1)	(1)	...	...	...	...	...	0.1
Partial expensing of Gulf Opportunity Zone clean-up costs	(1)	(1)	(1)	(4)	(4)	(1)	(1)	(1)	(4)	(4)	0.1
Additional first-year depreciation for Gulf Opportunity Zone property	0.9	0.9	0.4	-0.1	-0.2	0.4	0.4	0.2	(4)	-0.1	2.9
Ten-year carryback period for casualty losses of public utility property attributable to Hurricane Katrina	0.2	(1)	(4)	(4)	(4)	...	...	...	...	...	0.2
Five-year carryback period for casualty losses of public utility property attributable to Hurricane Katrina	0.1	(1)	(4)	(4)	(4)	...	...	...	...	...	0.1
Five-year carryback period for losses attributable to various expenses related to Hurricane Katrina	1.0	0.3	-0.1	-0.2	-0.2	...	...	...	...	...	0.9
Tax credit for employers for retention of employees affected by Hurricanes Katrina, Rita, and Wilma	(1)	(1)	(1)	(1)	(1)	(1)	(1)	(1)	(1)	(1)	0.2
Transportation											
Exclusion of interest on State and local government qualified private activity bonds for highway projects and rail-truck transfer facilities	(1)	(1)	(1)	(1)	(1)	(1)	(1)	(1)	(1)	(1)	0.1
Provide a 50-percent tax credit for certain expenditures for maintaining railroad tracks	0.1	0.1	0.1	0.1	(1)	...	...	...	...	...	0.4
Deferral of tax on capital construction funds of shipping companies	0.1	0.1	0.1	0.1	0.1	...	...	...	...	...	0.4
Exclusion of employer-paid transportation benefits	...	...	...	...	...	4.2	4.3	4.4	4.5	4.7	22.1
Community and Regional Development											
New York City Liberty Zone tax incentives	0.4	0.2	0.1	(4)	-0.1	-0.1	0.2	0.1	0.1	0.1	1.0
Empowerment zone tax incentives	0.3	0.4	0.4	0.4	0.2	0.4	0.4	0.4	0.5	0.3	3.7
Renewal community tax incentives	0.3	0.2	0.2	0.2	0.3	0.3	0.4	0.4	0.4	0.3	2.9
New markets tax credit	0.2	0.3	0.4	0.3	0.3	...	...	0.5	0.5	0.4	3.7
Exclusion of interest on State and local qualified private activity bonds for green buildings and sustainable design projects	(1)	(1)	(1)	(1)	(1)	(1)	(1)	(1)	(1)	(1)	0.1
Exclusion of interest on State and local government qualified private activity bonds for private airports, docks, and mass-commuting facilities	0.3	0.3	0.3	0.3	0.4	0.7	0.8	0.8	0.9	0.9	5.8

Table 1.--Tax Expenditure Estimates By Budget Function, Fiscal Years 2006-2010

[Billions of dollars]

Function	Corporations					Individuals					Total 2006-10
	2006	2007	2008	2009	2010	2006	2007	2008	2009	2010	
Education, Training, Employment, and Social Services											
Education and training:											
Tax credits for tuition for post-secondary education	......	......	......	......	......	4.9	5.2	5.1	5.0	5.0	25.2
Deduction for interest on student loans	......	......	......	......	......	0.8	0.9	0.9	0.9	1.0	4.5
Exclusion of tax on earnings of Coverdell education savings accounts	......	......	......	......	......	0.1	0.1	0.1	0.2	0.2	0.7
Exclusion of interest on educational savings bonds	......	......	......	......	......	(1)	(1)	(1)	(1)	(1)	0.1
Exclusion of tax on earnings of qualified tuition programs	......	......	......	......	......	0.7	0.8	0.9	1.0	1.0	4.3
Exclusion of scholarship and fellowship income	......	......	......	......	......	1.5	1.6	1.7	1.8	1.9	8.5
Exclusion of income attributable to the discharge of certain student loan debt and NHSC Educational Loan repayments	......	......	......	......	......	(1)	(1)	(1)	(1)	(1)	0.1
Exclusion of employer-provided education assistance benefits	......	......	......	......	......	0.8	0.9	0.9	0.9	0.9	4.4
Exclusion of employer-provided tuition reduction benefits	......	......	......	......	......	0.2	0.2	0.2	0.2	0.2	1.0
Parental personal exemption for students age 19 to 23	......	......	......	......	......	0.5	0.2	0.2	0.1	(1)	1.0
Exclusion of interest on State and local government qualified private activity bonds for student loans	0.1	0.1	0.1	0.1	0.1	0.3	0.3	0.3	0.4	0.4	2.3
Exclusion of interest on State and local government qualified private activity bonds for private nonprofit and qualified public educational facilities	0.4	0.5	0.5	0.5	0.5	1.1	1.2	1.2	1.3	1.3	8.4
Tax credit for holders of qualified zone academy bonds	0.1	0.1	0.1	0.1	0.1	......	......	......	......	......	0.5
Deduction for charitable contributions to educational institutions	0.7	0.7	0.7	0.8	0.8	5.3	5.9	6.3	6.8	7.1	35.1
Employment:											
Exclusion of employee meals and lodging (other than military)	......	......	......	......	......	0.9	0.9	0.9	1.0	1.0	4.9
Exclusion of benefits provided under cafeteria plans\5\	......	......	......	......	......	27.9	30.6	33.4	36.6	40.0	168.5
Exclusion of housing allowances for ministers	......	......	......	......	......	0.5	0.5	0.5	0.6	0.6	2.7
Exclusion of miscellaneous fringe benefits	......	......	......	......	......	6.6	6.8	7.0	7.2	7.7	35.2
Exclusion of employee awards	......	......	......	......	......	0.2	0.2	0.2	0.2	0.2	0.9
Exclusion of income earned by voluntary employees' beneficiary associations	......	......	......	......	......	3.3	3.4	3.5	3.7	3.8	17.6
Special tax provisions for employee stock ownership plans (ESOPs)	0.8	0.9	0.9	1.0	1.1	0.3	0.3	0.3	0.3	0.3	6.2
Work opportunity tax credit	0.2	0.1	0.1	(1)	(1)	(1)	(1)	(1)	(1)	(1)	0.8
Welfare-to-work tax credit	(1)	(1)	(1)	(1)	(1)	(1)	(1)	(1)	(1)	......	0.2
Deferral of taxation and capital gains treatment on spread on acquisition of stock under incentive stock option plans and employee stock purchase plans\6\	......	......	......	......	......	0.4	0.4	0.4	0.2	0.1	1.5
Social services:											
Tax credit for children under age 17\7\	......	......	......	......	......	46.0	45.9	46.1	46.0	46.0	230.0

Table 1.--Tax Expenditure Estimates By Budget Function, Fiscal Years 2006-2010

[Billions of dollars]

Function	Corporations					Individuals					Total 2006-10
	2006	2007	2008	2009	2010	2006	2007	2008	2009	2010	
Tax credit for child and dependent care and exclusion of employer-provided child care\8\	(1)	(1)	(1)	(1)	(1)	3.1	2.7	2.7	2.6	2.5	13.5
Tax credit for employer-provided dependent care	(1)	(1)	(1)	(1)	(1)	(1)	(1)	(1)	(1)	(1)	0.2
Exclusion of certain foster care payments						0.6	0.6	0.7	0.7	0.8	3.4
Adoption credit and employee adoption benefits exclusion						0.4	0.5	0.5	0.5	0.5	2.4
Deduction for charitable contributions, other than for education and health	1.7	1.7	1.7	1.8	1.8	29.1	31.9	34.2	36.8	38.4	179.1
Tax credit for disabled access expenditures	(1)	(1)	(1)	(1)	(1)	0.1	0.1	0.1	0.1	0.1	0.4
Health											
Exclusion of employer contributions for health care, health insurance premiums, and long-term care insurance premiums\9\						90.6	99.7	107.0	114.5	122.2	534.0
Exclusion of medical care and TRICARE medical insurance for military dependents, retirees, and retiree dependents						1.9	2.0	2.1	2.3	2.5	10.9
Deduction for health insurance premiums and long-term care insurance premiums by the self-employed						3.8	4.2	4.5	4.9	5.2	22.6
Deduction for medical expenses and long-term care expenses						7.3	8.2	9.5	10.7	12.1	47.8
Exclusion of workers' compensation benefits (medical benefits)						6.5	6.9	7.4	8.0	8.5	37.3
Health savings accounts						0.1	0.3	0.6	0.9	1.2	3.2
Exclusion of interest on state and local government qualified private activity bonds for private nonprofit hospital facilities	0.6	0.7	0.7	0.8	0.8	1.7	1.8	1.9	2.0	2.1	13.1
Deduction for charitable contributions to health organizations	0.8	0.8	0.9	0.9	0.9	3.7	4.0	4.3	4.7	4.8	25.8
Tax credit for orphan drug research	0.2	0.3	0.3	0.3	0.3						1.4
Tax credit for purchase of health insurance by certain displaced persons						0.2	0.2	0.2	0.2	0.3	1.2
Medicare											
Exclusion of untaxed Medicare benefits:											
Hospital insurance (Part A)						18.5	20.7	22.5	24.5	26.7	112.9
Supplementary medical insurance (Part B)						12.5	14.2	15.4	16.7	18.1	76.9
Prescription drug insurance (Part D)						3.4	6.2	7.5	8.3	9.5	34.9
Exclusion of certain subsidies to employers who maintain prescription drug plans for Medicare enrollees	0.7	1.2	1.4	1.5	1.6						6.3
Income Security											
Exclusion of workers' compensation benefits (disability and survivors payments)						2.5	2.6	2.7	2.7	2.8	13.2
Exclusion of damages on account of personal physical injuries or physical sickness						1.4	1.5	1.5	1.5	1.5	7.4
Exclusion of special benefits for disabled coal miners						0.1	0.1	(1)	(1)	(1)	0.2
Exclusion of cash public assistance benefits						3.4	3.6	3.7	3.9	4.0	18.6
Net exclusion of pension contributions and earnings:											
Employer plans						104.1	110.1	115.2	120.8	126.7	577.1
Individual retirement plans						11.2	14.0	15.5	16.9	18.4	76.0
Plans covering partners and sole proprietors											

Table 1.--Tax Expenditure Estimates By Budget Function, Fiscal Years 2006-2010

[Billions of dollars]

Function	Corporations					Individuals					Total
	2006	2007	2008	2009	2010	2006	2007	2008	2009	2010	2006-10
(sometimes referred to as "Keogh plans")....						9.4	10.3	10.8	11.3	11.6	53.4
Tax credit for certain individuals for elective deferrals and IRA contributions....						0.9	0.6	(\1\)	......	......	1.5
Tax credit for new retirement plan expenses of small businesses....	(\1\)	(\1\)	(\1\)	(\1\)	(\1\)	(\1\)	(\1\)	(\1\)	(\1\)	(\1\)	0.1
Exclusion of other employee benefits:											
Premiums on group term life insurance....						2.5	2.6	2.6	2.7	2.7	13.1
Premiums on accident and disability insurance....						2.6	2.8	2.9	3.0	3.1	14.4
Additional standard deduction for the blind and the elderly....						1.6	1.6	1.7	1.7	1.8	8.4
Tax credit for the elderly and disabled....						(\1\)	(\1\)	(\1\)	(\1\)	(\1\)	0.1
Deduction for casualty and theft losses....						0.7	0.8	0.3	0.3	0.3	2.4
Earned income credit (EIC)....						42.1	42.8	43.5	44.5	45.4	218.3
Social Security and Railroad Retirement											
Exclusion of untaxed social security and railroad retirement benefits....						23.1	24.1	24.8	25.9	27.2	125.1
Veterans' Benefits and Services											
Exclusion of veterans' disability compensation....						3.6	3.8	3.9	4.0	4.0	19.2
Exclusion of veterans' pensions....						0.1	0.1	0.1	0.1	0.1	0.6
Exclusion and veterans' readjustment benefits....						0.2	0.3	0.3	0.3	0.3	1.3
Exclusion of interest on State and local government qualified private activity bonds for veterans' housing....	(\1\)	(\1\)	(\1\)	(\1\)	(\1\)	(\1\)	(\1\)	(\1\)	(\1\)	(\1\)	0.3
General Purpose Fiscal Assistance											
Exclusion of interest on public purpose State and local government bonds....	7.3	7.8	8.2	8.6	9.0	18.7	20.1	21.1	22.1	23.1	146.0
Deduction of nonbusiness State and local government income, sales, and personal property taxes\10\....						36.8	27.3	27.3	28.1	28.9	148.5
Tax credit for Puerto Rico and possession income, and Puerto Rico economic activity....	0.3	......	......	......	......						0.3
Interest											
Deferral of interest on savings bonds....						1.1	1.1	1.2	1.2	1.2	5.8

\1\ Positive tax expenditure of less than $50 million.

\2\ In addition, the exemption from excise tax for alcohol fuels results in a reduction in excise tax receipts, net of income tax effect, of $11.1 billion over the fiscal years 2006 through 2010.

\3\ In addition, the credit from excise tax for biodiesel results in a reduction in excise tax receipts, net of income tax effect, of less than $50 million in each of the fiscal years 2006 through 2010.

\4\ Negative tax expenditure of less than $50 million.

\5\ Estimate includes amounts of employer-provided health insurance purchased through cafeteria plans and employee-provided child care purchased through dependent care flexible spending accounts. These amounts are also included in other line items in this table.

\6\ Tax expenditure estimate does not include offsetting denial of corporate deduction for qualified stock option compensation.

\7\ Tax expenditure estimate includes refundable amounts, amounts used to offset income taxes, and amounts used to offset other taxes. The amount of refundable child tax credit and earned income tax credit used to offset taxes other than income tax or paid out as refunds is: $50.1 billion in 2006, $51.5 billion in 2007, $51.4 billion in 2008, $52.2 billion in 2009, and $53.2 billion in 2010.

\8\ Estimate includes employer-provided child care purchased through dependent care flexible spending accounts.

\9\ Estimate includes employer-provided health insurance purchased through cafeteria plans.

\10\ Deduction for state and local sales taxes expires after December 31, 2005.

Note.--Details may not add to totals due to rounding.
Source: Joint Committee on Taxation.

Appendix 2

Excerpt from

REVENUE PROCEDURE 87–57

1987–2 C.B. 687.

SECTION 1. PURPOSE

.01 This revenue procedure provides guidance to taxpayers and Service personnel in computing depreciation allowances for tangible property under section 168 of the Internal Revenue Code * * *. This revenue procedure describes the applicable depreciation methods, applicable recovery periods, and applicable conventions that must be used in computing depreciation allowances under section 168.

.02 * * * Section 8 of this revenue procedure contains various tables that may be used by certain taxpayers in lieu of computing allowances * * *.

* * *

SECTION 8. OPTIONAL TABLES

.01 This section contains optional depreciation tables that may be used by certain taxpayers in computing annual depreciation allowances under section 168 of the Code. The depreciation tables may be used with respect to any item of property placed in service in a taxable year. * * *

.02 The optional depreciation tables specify schedules of annual depreciation rates to be applied to the *unadjusted basis* of property in each taxable year. If a taxpayer uses a table to compute the annual depreciation allowance for any item of property, the taxpayer must use the table to compute the annual depreciation allowances for the entire recovery period of such property. However, a taxpayer may not continue to use the table if there are any adjustments to the basis of the property for reasons other than (1) depreciation allowed or allowable or (2) an addition or an improvement to such property that is subject to depreciation as a separate item of property. Use of the tables in this revenue procedure to compute depreciation allowances does not require the filing of any notice with the Internal Revenue Service.

Taxpayers use the appropriate table for any property based on the depreciation system, the applicable depreciation method, the applicable recovery period, and the applicable convention. The tables lists the percentage depreciation rates to be applied to the unadjusted basis of property in each taxable year.

In Tables 1–5, for the general depreciation system, the listed depreciation rates reflect the 200 percent declining balance method switching to the straight line method for property with applicable recovery periods of 3, 5, 7 or 10 years and the 150 percent declining balance method switching to straight line method for property with applicable recovery periods of 15 and 20 years.

* * *

Table 1. General Depreciation System
Applicable Depreciation Method: 200 or 150 Percent Declining Balance Switching to Straight Line
Applicable Recovery Periods: 3, 5, 7, 10, 15, 20 years
Applicable Convention: Half-year

If the Recovery Year is:	3–year	5–year	7–year	10–year	15–year	20–year
			the Depreciation Rate is:			
1	33.33	20.00	14.29	10.00	5.00	3.750
2	44.45	32.00	24.49	18.00	9.50	7.219
3	14.81	19.20	17.49	14.40	8.55	6.677
4	7.41	11.52	12.49	11.52	7.70	6.177
5		11.52	8.93	9.22	6.93	5.713
6		5.76	8.92	7.37	6.23	5.285
7			8.93	6.55	5.90	4.888
8			4.46	6.55	5.90	4.522
9				6.56	5.91	4.462
10				6.55	5.90	4.461
11				3.28	5.91	4.462
12					5.90	4.461
13					5.91	4.462
14					5.90	4.461
15					5.91	4.462
16					2.95	4.461
17						4.462
18						4.461
19						4.462
20						4.461
21						2.231

Table 2. General Depreciation System
Applicable Depreciation Method: 200 or 150 Percent Declining Balance Switching to Straight Line
Applicable Recovery Periods: 3, 5, 7, 10, 15, 20 years
Applicable Convention: Mid-quarter (property placed in service in first quarter)

If the Recovery Year is:	3–year	5–year	7–year	10–year	15–year	20–year
			the Depreciation Rate is:			
1	58.33	35.00	25.00	17.50	8.75	6.563
2	27.78	26.00	21.43	16.50	9.13	7.000
3	12.35	15.60	15.31	13.20	8.21	6.482
4	1.54	11.01	10.93	10.56	7.39	5.996

5	11.01	8.75	8.45	6.65	5.546
6	1.38	8.74	6.76	5.99	5.130
7		8.75	6.55	5.90	4.746
8		1.09	6.55	5.91	4.459
9			6.56	5.90	4.459
10			6.55	5.91	4.459
11			0.82	5.90	4.459
12				5.91	4.460
13				5.90	4.459
14				5.91	4.460
15				5.90	4.459
16				0.74	4.460
17					4.459
18					4.460
19					4.459
20					4.460
21					0.557

Table 3. General Depreciation System
Applicable Depreciation Method: 200 or 150 Percent Declining Balance Switching to Straight Line
Applicable Recovery Periods: 3, 5, 7, 10, 15, 20 years
Applicable Convention: Mid-quarter (property placed in service in second quarter)

If the Recovery Year is:			and the Recovery Period is:			
	3–year	5–year	7–year	10–year	15–year	20–year
			the Depreciation Rate is:			
1	41.67	25.00	17.85	12.50	6.25	4.688
2	38.89	30.00	23.47	17.50	9.38	7.148
3	14.14	18.00	16.76	14.00	8.44	6.612
4	5.30	11.37	11.97	11.20	7.59	6.116
5		11.37	8.87	8.96	6.83	5.658
6		4.26	8.87	7.17	6.15	5.233
7			8.87	6.55	5.91	4.841
8			3.33	6.55	5.90	4.478
9				6.56	5.91	4.463
10				6.55	5.90	4.463
11				2.46	5.91	4.463
12					5.90	4.463
13					5.91	4.463
14					5.90	4.463
15					5.91	4.462
16					2.21	4.463
17						4.462
18						4.463
19						4.462
20						4.463
21						1.673

Table 4. General Depreciation System
Applicable Depreciation Method: 200 or 150 Percent Declining Balance Switching to Straight Line
Applicable Recovery Periods: 3, 5, 7, 10, 15, 20 years
Applicable Convention: Mid-quarter (property placed in service in third quarter)

If the Recovery Year is:	3–year	5–year	and the Recovery Period is:			
			7–year	10–year	15–year	20–year
			the Depreciation Rate is:			
1	25.00	15.00	10.71	7.50	3.75	2.813
2	50.00	34.00	25.51	18.50	9.63	7.289
3	16.67	20.40	18.22	14.80	8.66	6.742
4	8.33	12.24	13.02	11.84	7.80	6.237
5		11.30	9.30	9.47	7.02	5.769
6		7.06	8.85	7.58	6.31	5.336
7			8.86	6.55	5.90	4.936
8			5.53	6.55	5.90	4.566
9				6.56	5.91	4.460
10				6.55	5.90	4.460
11				4.10	5.91	4.460
12					5.90	4.460
13					5.91	4.461
14					5.90	4.460
15					5.91	4.461
16					3.69	4.460
17						4.461
18						4.460
19						4.461
20						4.460
21						2.788

Table 5. General Depreciation System
Applicable Depreciation Method: 200 or 150 Percent Declining Balance Switching to Straight Line
Applicable Recovery Periods: 3, 5, 7, 10, 15, 20 years
Applicable Convention: Mid-quarter (property placed in service in fourth quarter)

If the Recovery Year is:	3–year	5–year	and the Recovery Period is:			
			7–year	10–year	15–year	20–year
			the Depreciation Rate is:			
1	8.33	5.00	3.57	2.50	1.25	0.938
2	61.11	38.00	27.55	19.50	9.88	7.430
3	20.37	22.80	19.68	15.60	8.89	6.872
4	10.19	13.68	14.06	12.48	8.00	6.357
5		10.94	10.04	9.98	7.20	5.880
6		9.58	8.73	7.99	6.48	5.439
7			8.73	6.55	5.90	5.031
8			7.64	6.55	5.90	4.654
9				6.56	5.90	4.458
10				6.55	5.91	4.458
11					5.74	4.458
12					5.91	4.458
13					5.90	4.458
14					5.91	4.458
15					5.90	4.458
16					5.17	4.458
17						4.458
18						4.459
19						4.458

20   4.459
21   3.901

* * *

*

Appendix 3

Answers to Self–Assessment Questions

CHAPTER 1

SAQ 1–1. The couple's taxable income is $35,000 under these facts, because we are told to ignore all deductions and exemptions. Using the table in § 1(a), the tax is $5,250, 15 percent of the $35,000.

SAQ 1–2. Alice would not file a return because she has no gross income. Ralph would have taxable income of $35,000, and under the table in § 1(d), his tax liability would be $7,401.50 ($2,767.50 plus 28% of $16,550).

SAQ 1–3. Alice would not file a return, again because she lacks any income. Ralph would have $35,000 of taxable income and would use the table in § 1(c). This produces a tax liability of $6,927 ($3,315 plus 28% of $12,900). Notice that the tax bill here is higher than it is if the couple is married and files a joint return but less than if they were married filing separately.

SAQ 1–4. If they file a joint return, the combined taxable income is $75,000, and the tax due under § 1(a) is $16,203 ($5,535 plus 28% of $38,100).

If they file separate returns, Ralph pays tax of $7,401.50 on his $35,000 of income using the § 1(d) table (see the computation in the solution to SAQ 1–2), and Alice pays tax of $8,801.50 on her $40,000 of income ($2,767.50 plus 28% of $21,550). The combined tax liability is thus $16,203, the same total liability as if they filed a joint return.

If Ralph and Alice were unmarried, Ralph's liability under § 1(c) would still be $6,927 (see the answer to SAQ 1–3), and Alice's tax bill would be $8,327 ($3,315 plus 28% of $17,900). The combined tax liability would thus be $15,254, an amount nearly $1,000 *less* than the joint return liability.

CHAPTER 2

SAQ 2–1. Taxpayers generally prefer above-the-line deductions for two reasons. First, all taxpayers may claim above-the-line deductions, no matter whether they choose to take the standard deduction or to itemize all other deductions. Since above-the-line deductions are available *in addition to* the standard deduction and not *instead of* the standard deduction, above-the-line deductions are preferable. Second, to the extent that the amount of some below-the-line deductions is limited or phased-out if a taxpayer's adjusted gross income is too high, above-the-line deductions are helpful in reducing the amount of adjusted gross income (thus increasing the chance of deductibility for these below-the-line items).

SAQ 2–2. $5,000. An unmarried taxpayer with no dependents can claim a standard deduction of $3,000 and a personal exemption of $2,000, even if that taxpayer had no deductible expenses for the year. See §§ 63(c)(2)(D) and 151(d)(1). Thus, if the taxpayer had $5,000 of gross income or less, there is absolutely no way that the taxpayer would have "taxable income" above zero. If the taxpayer's gross income was $5,001, however, the taxpayer would need at least $1 in deductible expenses to assure no taxable income.

In fact, if the taxpayer's gross income does not exceed $5,000, the taxpayer need not even file a federal income tax return for the year (although he or she will want to file if the taxpayer had wages subject to federal income tax withholding, for the excess tax withheld can only be refunded by the filing of a return). See § 6012(a)(1)(A)(i).

SAQ 2–3. The § 68 limitation on itemized deductions is designed to make the federal income tax more progressive. Suppose, for example, that an unmarried taxpayer has an adjusted gross income of $400,000 and otherwise allowable regular itemized deductions of $50,000. Because the taxpayer's adjusted gross income exceeds $100,000 (ignoring inflation adjustments to the "applicable amount" set forth in the statute), the total itemized deductions will be reduced to $41,000 (since three percent of $300,000 is $9,000). In addition, we will see that the taxpayer's personal exemption would be completely phased-out, as well, but let's ignore that for now.

Thus, the taxpayer's taxable income is $359,000, placing the taxpayer in the highest marginal tax bracket (39.6 percent, ignoring § 1(i) for convenience). If the taxpayer in this example earns an additional $1,000, the taxpayer's itemized deductions will be reduced by another $30, increasing taxable income from $359,000 to $360,030. The extra $1,030 of taxable income will be taxed at 39.6%, resulting in additional tax of $407.88. Thus, the marginal rate of tax on the last $1,000 of gross income is really 40.788 percent, not 39.6 percent as § 1 would imply. The § 68 phase-out alone increased the marginal rate by more than one percent. If the taxpayer in this example was subject to additional phase-outs, it is easy to see how the marginal tax rate can increase even more.

In any event, this example shows how the § 68 limitation can enhance progressivity by increasing the marginal tax rate to a level higher than the highest tax rate in § 1.

Interestingly, one can make the case that § 68 can also, in extreme cases, make the federal income tax *less* progressive. In contrast to the example above, now consider a taxpayer with an adjusted gross income of $1,000,000 and otherwise allowable itemized deductions of $25,000 for the year. Because this taxpayer's adjusted gross income exceeds the "applicable amount" by $900,000, he or she might have to reduce the regular itemized deductions by $27,000 (three percent of the $900,000 excess over the "applicable amount"). Yet the maximum possible reduction to itemized deductions under § 68(a) is $20,000, 80 percent of the otherwise allowable total. Thus, if the taxpayer earns an extra $1,000 of income, there is no further reduction to the regular itemized deductions, meaning that the marginal rate of tax on that extra $1,000 will be capped at 39.6 percent. But that is *less* than the marginal rate applicable to taxpayer in the prior example who had a smaller adjusted gross income figure! The 80–percent cap on the § 68 reduction thus detracts from the progressivity intended from the phase-out.

SAQ 2–4. The two-percent haircut makes above-the-line deductions that much more attractive. Again, above-the-line deductions serve to reduce the taxpayer's adjusted gross income. Since miscellaneous itemized deductions are deductible to the extent they exceed two percent of adjusted gross income, it stands to reason that as adjusted gross income is reduced, the amount of allowable miscellaneous itemized deductions will increase.

For example, suppose a taxpayer has an adjusted gross income of $50,000 and miscellaneous itemized deductions of $1,500. Two percent of adjusted gross income in this case is $1,000, meaning $500 of the total miscellaneous itemized deductions is allowable. If the taxpayer also had a $10,000 above-the-line deduction, then the adjusted gross income would be only $40,000. Two percent of $40,000 is $800, meaning that $700 of the $1,500 in miscellaneous itemized deductions would be allowable.

CHAPTER 3

SAQ 3–1. The taxpayer would have gross income in each of the alternatives. In each case, using the language of *Macomber*, the taxpayer and the other shareholders would be receiving "something out of the company's assets for his (or her) separate use or benefit." The severance of the assets from the corporation is thus sufficient to warrant taxation. This is especially so if the taxpayer receives cash or some other asset from the corporation. It is also true where the taxpayer receives merely a promise for future payment (a promissory note), again because the wealth represented by the promise is severed from the value of the original stock certificates. After a distribution of promissory notes, a shareholder would have both an equity interest in the corporation and an interest as a creditor of the corporation. To the extent these interests have separate legal rights, both the form and substance of the taxpayer's investment in the corporation has changed.

SAQ 3–2. Probably not. Of the eight fringe benefits eligible for exclusion under § 132(a), the only one potentially applicable on these facts would be the *de minimis* fringe in §§ 132(a)(4) and 132(e)(1). Arguably, the value here may be small enough to make accounting for the value more of a pain than it is worth. In *Technical Advice Memorandum 200437030*, the Service ruled on these facts that the holiday coupons were includible in gross income. The Service reasoned that cash and cash equivalent fringe benefits, like gifts certificates, are not administratively difficult to account for and have a readily ascertainable fair market value. Thus, they cannot qualify as *de minimis* fringe benefits.

SAQ 3–3. Recipient can exclude the value of the apartment building from gross income under § 102(a). The rents must be included in gross income under § 102(b)(1).

SAQ 3–4. Recipient can exclude the present value of the life estate interest from gross income under § 102(a). Since the value of the life estate interest is not subject to taxation, it is not important to determine that value with any precision. If the life estate interest was taxable, however, the precise value would have to be determined.

The rents must be included in gross income under § 102(b)(1). Alternatively, one can say that the life estate is really a gift of income itself, since the primary benefit of the life estate is the receipt of rental income. If that is so, then the rents must be included in gross income as they are paid. *See* § 102(b)(2).

SAQ 3–5. Under *Philadelphia Park Amusement Co. v. United States*, Mrs. Davis would acquire the stock with a basis equal to the fair market value of the shares at the time of receipt. If we assume that Mrs. Davis had to include the value of the stock in gross income in the year of receipt, then her "tax cost" basis in the shares is $82,000. A subsequent sale of the shares for $85,000 would thus yield a $3,000 realized and recognized gain ($85,000 amount realized, less $82,000 basis).

If Mrs. Davis was allowed to exclude the value of the shares from gross income, however (as is the case under current law in § 1041), an interesting issue arises with respect to her basis. There is no "tax cost" to Mrs. Davis in this case because she is not required to include any amount in gross income. Yet if we conclude that her basis is zero for lack of cost, then a sale for $85,000 would produce $85,000 of gain, effectively meaning that neither Mr. Davis nor Mrs. Davis would get any tax-free recovery of the $75,000 used to acquire the shares originally. Section 1041 solves this dilemma by requiring Mrs. Davis to take Mr. Davis' basis in the shares, no matter whether the shares had built-in gain (value in excess of basis) or built-in loss (value less than basis) at the time of the transfer.

SAQ 3–6. Most likely, the "security deposit" would be treated as a true deposit, meaning that Mr. Roper would not have gross income unless and until a tenant directed him to apply the deposit toward the last month's rent. As the *Indianapolis Power & Light Co.* case makes clear, a deposit is distinct from an advance payment in that the party making a deposit has the power to get the funds back by fulfilling all of the terms of the contractual agreement. In this case, as long as the tenants remain timely with their rent payments and do not damage the premises, the tenants will get their deposits back. Mr. Roper has no guarantee that he will be allowed to keep the security deposits so long as he performs his obligations under the lease agreement. Because the ultimate treatment of the security deposit is within the discretion of the tenants and not Mr. Roper, the payments should be respected as true deposits. If a tenant defaults in payment or damages the premises, Mr. Roper is entitled to keep the security deposit. At that time, he would have gross income.

CHAPTER 4

SAQ 4–1.

(a) The cost is capitalized. An automobile typically has a useful life that extends beyond the year of purchase, so the cost to acquire an automobile should be capitalized. See Prop. Reg. § 1.263(a)–2(d)(1)(i). By capitalizing the cost, the taxpayer gets no current deduction and instead has a basis in the automobile in an amount equal to its cost.

(b) The cost is an expense. Gasoline and other supplies that are normally consumed within a short period of time following purchase are properly treated as expenses, likely because the benefit from these costs is too "short-term" to warrant capitalization. See Treas. Reg. § 1.162–3. See also Prop. Reg. § 1.263(a)–2(d)(1)(ii), Example 2. Moreover, because the benefit of the gasoline will likely not exceed 12 months, the cost may be treated as an expense under the 12–month rule in the proposed regulations. See Prop. Reg. § 1.263(a)–2(d)(4)(i).

(c) The cost is capitalized. The proposed regulations specifically require capitalization in this case. See Prop. Reg. § 1.263(a)–2(d)(2). Presumably, then, the cost would be added to the taxpayer's basis in the real property.

(d) The cost is capitalized. This is part of the cost of acquiring the building, so it is properly considered to be part of the taxpayer's basis in the building. The proposed regulations see the commissions as a "transaction cost" that facilitates the acquisition of the building and therefore must be capitalized. See Prop. Reg. § 1.263(a)–2(d)(3)(i).

SAQ 4–2.

(a) The cost is capitalized. This cost adapts the vehicle to a new or different use, so the regulations require capitalization. See Prop. Reg. § 1.263(a)–3(e)(1)(iii). The capitalized costs would be added to the taxpayer's basis in the vehicle.

(b) The cost is capitalized. This cost relates to work performed prior to placing the machinery into service, so the cost must be added to the basis of the machinery. See Prop. Reg. § 1.263(a)–3(e)(1)(ii) and 1.263(a)–3(e)(4), Example 4.

(c) The costs are likely expenses. The costs probably do not materially increase the value of the vehicle and likely do not prolong the vehicle's useful life. Holding the vehicle for sale does not constitute a change in use of the property, so the costs do not adapt the vehicle to a different use. See Prop. Reg. § 1.263(a)–3(e)(4), Example 7.

SAQ 4–3.

(a) Under Regulation § 1.263(a)–4(f)(1), amounts paid to create any right or benefit to the taxpayer (like insurance coverage) need not be capitalized if the anticipated benefit does not last beyond the earlier of: (1) 12 months after the date that taxpayer first realizes the right or benefit; or (2) the end of the taxable year following the year of payment. Here, the payment can be deducted in full in Year One because the benefit of the policy does not last beyond either the twelve-month benefit period or the end of Year Two.

(b) Same result. The benefit does not last for more than twelve months nor beyond the end of the taxable year following the year of payment.

(c) The cost of the policy must be capitalized. The benefit lasts only twelve months, but it extends beyond the end of Year Two. Thus, Lucy can deduct $11,000 in Year Two and $1,000 in Year Three; she cannot deduct all $12,000 in Year One, as was the case under parts (a) and (b).

SAQ 4–4. Section 162(a)(1) limits the deduction for compensation to "reasonable" amounts. In order to deduct the salary paid to Ben, therefore, Gary must be prepared to prove that the $60,000 salary is reasonable. To the extent the compensation is excessive, Gary cannot deduct the excess under § 162(a). If any portion of the salary paid to Ben is excessive, the excess might well be considered a gift to Ben from his father, and Gary would get no deduction for the gift portion of the salary. (Likewise, Ben could exclude the excess portion as a gift under § 102.) Here, there are some facts that suggest the compensation is excessive: (1) Ben has no prior experience that would warrant a fixed salary when the other staff members work only on commission; (2) Ben is assured of a salary that no other person with equivalent duties necessarily gets. If Ben's sales would have generated commissions of $60,000 or more, then there should be no problem with the deduction. But to the extent his commissions would have fallen short of $60,000, the excess is probably best treated as a gift.

Because Ben is Gary's employee and not just his son, however, § 102(c) calls into question the use of the § 102(a) exclusion by Ben. By its absolute terms, § 102(c) would seem to deny the exclusion to Ben. Yet in this case, Ben could argue that the reason he received excessive compensation was because of the familial relationship and not because of the employment relationship. Assuming § 102(c) only applies to amounts received from someone acting in the capacity of an employer and not in the capacity of a parent, Ben's argument to exclude the excessive portion of his compensation is persuasive.

Note that Ben's argument directly contradicts Gary's claim for a § 162(a) deduction. Ben's claim is that the compensation was excessive and that the excessive portion is a gift. Gary's claim for a deduction rests on the premise that the entire amount paid was reasonable compensation for services. To the extent Ben successfully claims the § 102(a) exclusion, the deduction to Gary should be disallowed.

SAQ 4–5. YES, it matters (in capital letters, no less). Most § 162(a) deductions are above-the-line deductions. See § 62(a)(1). On the other hand, most § 212 expenses are "miscellaneous itemized deductions." See §§ 62(a); 67(b). This has three adverse impacts. First, while all taxpayers are eligible to claim above-the-line deductions, only those taxpayers who forego the standard deduction may claim itemized deductions. Second, miscellaneous itemized deductions are subject to the two-percent "haircut" limitation in § 67(a). See Chapter 2. This means that the taxpayer will never get to deduct the entire amount otherwise allowed. Finally, though this is a bit premature, miscellaneous itemized deductions are not deductible for purposes of computing liability for alternative minimum tax. See Chapter 11. So, all other things being equal, taxpayers would probably much prefer to shoehorn a deduction into the confines of § 162(a) instead of falling into § 212.

SAQ 4–6.

(a) Depreciable. The summer cabin is held for the production of income and is most likely subject to wear and tear. Accordingly, it meets the eligibility requirements for depreciation in § 167(a).

(b) Not depreciable. The depreciation deduction is available only for tangible property. Since the taxpayer's leasehold interest is an intangible asset, no depreciation deduction under § 167(a) is allowed. Most likely, however, the taxpayer can deduct the costs paid for the lease over the life of the lease. See Treas. Reg. § 1.162–11(a).

(c) Depreciable. The vehicle is held for use in the taxpayer's business and is certainly subject to wear and tear. The fact that the taxpayer uses the car for personal purposes will affect the *amount* of the depreciation deductions over the car's useful life, and it might affect the *method* by which the deduction is taken, but it will not affect the *eligibility* for such deductions assuming that some business use of the vehicle is made.

(d) Not depreciable. *Simon* makes it clear that works of art are not depreciable unless such items are actually subject to wear and tear in the taxpayer's hands. Simply hanging the sculpture in the taxpayer's office is unlikely to subject the artwork to wear and tear, so the cost of the asset would not be depreciable.

(e) Not depreciable. In order to be eligible for depreciation under 167(a), the subject property must be used in the taxpayer business or held for the production of income. A personal residence, by definition, is used for *personal* purposes, not business or productive investment purposes. So no depreciation deductions are allowed on the taxpayer home.

Although it is entirely likely that the taxpayer hopes to make a profit some day on the sale of the home, the dominant motive for holding the home is for the right to occupy it, not for the anticipated production of income many years down the road. Thus, a personal residence is always considered a personal-use asset and not an investment asset. Try as you may to argue otherwise, give it up. As Bruce Hornsby would say, that's just the way it is.

(f) Depreciable. The equipment is used in the taxpayer's business and is almost certainly subject to wear and tear. Equipment represents the quintessential depreciable asset.

SAQ 4–7.

(a) The sale produces a realized loss of $80,000, for the amount realized is only $120,000 but Sakai's adjusted basis is $200,000. The realized loss is not recognized, however, because the loss is not described in § 165(c). The loss does not arise from Sakai's business, nor from a transaction entered into for profit. While Sakai might own the house with the expectation of making a profit, it is accepted that the personal-use benefits from home ownership outweigh the investment aspects. See Treas. Reg. § 1.165–9(a). Section 165(c) does not apply, either, since there is no evidence of a casualty or theft. Thus the loss is not deductible.

(b) Because Kenichi does not make personal use of the home, one can fairly conclude that Kenichi's realized loss of $50,000 (amount realized of $70,000 less basis of $120,000, ignoring any applicable depreciation deductions) is deductible as a loss from a transaction entered into for profit. See § 165(c)(2).

(c) The results make sense if one believes, as most do, that consumption should be part of the tax base. Making personal use of the home is a consumption of the benefit purchased, so the resulting loss should not be deductible. If the $80,000 loss had instead been rental payments totaling $80,000, no deduction would be allowed, so the loss from the sale, likewise, should not be deductible.

Losses from transactions entered into for profit should be deductible as an offset against gains from such transactions in order to get the most accurate reflection of the taxpayer's true income for the taxable year. We will see that Kenichi's loss would be characterized as a capital loss, and since capital losses are more or less limited to the amount of capital gains, it is proper to let the loss from this sale offset gains from the sale of other capital assets in order to determine Kenichi's net capital gain.

SAQ 4–8. No. Section 62(a)(3) only allows losses from the sale of exchange of property to be taken above the line. Since there is no sale or exchange in a casualty loss, the loss is an itemized deduction. At least the deduction is a "regular itemized deduction" that will be spared from the § 67(a) haircut. See § 67(b)(3).

CHAPTER 5

SAQ 5–1.

(a) Because Meade purchased an annuity, the taxation of the annual payments will be governed by § 72. Section 72(a) generally requires inclusion of annuity payments, but § 72(b) permits exclusion of a portion of each payment. The "exclusion ratio" is computed by dividing the "investment in the contract" (here, $100,000) by the "expected return under the contract." Under Treas. Reg. § 1.72–9, Table V, Meade is expected to live for another 25.0 years. Consequently, the expected return on his contract is $250,000 ($10,000 annually for 25 years). The "exclusion ratio" is thus 40 percent ($100,000 ÷ $250,000), meaning Meade can exclude 40 percent of each annual payment. Thus, $4,000 of the first $10,000 installment is excluded, and the remaining $6,000 is included in gross income.

(b) Under § 72(b)(3)(A), any "unrecovered investment in the contract" can be deducted on Meade's final income tax return. Section 72(b)(4) logically defines the "unrecovered investment in the contract" as the excess of Meade's investment in the contract ($100,000) less the annuity payment amounts that have been excluded from gross income. Here, Meade has received four payments, and $4,000 of each payment was excluded from gross income, as computed in part (a). In other words, Meade has recouped $16,000 of his $100,000 investment. He can therefore deduct the remaining $84,000 of his investment on his final income tax return. This will be a regular itemized deduction. See § 67(b)(10).

(c) By this point, Meade's entire investment in the contract has been recovered ($4,000 annually for 25 years). Under § 72(b)(2), each subsequent payment will be fully taxable, as there is no more "unrecovered investment in the contract" immediately before all future payments.

SAQ 5-2.

(a) Wesley can exclude the $100,000 death benefit under § 101(a)(1). The payment is received under a life insurance contract and is paid by reason of Beverly's death. Neither of the exceptions in §§ 101(a)(2) (transfer for value) or 101(d) (installment payments of death benefit) applies.

(b) Wesley can still exclude the $100,000 death benefit, but the $10,000 of interest must be included under § 101(c). As income from gifted property is still includible in gross income, income from excluded death benefits is likewise includible.

(c) If Wesley lives for the entire 25 years, he will receive total payments of $300,000. Presumably, $100,000 of that $300,000 consists of the original death benefit proceeds, and the balance represents gain that should be taxed. Under § 101(d)(1), the $100,000 is to be prorated over the periods with respect to which the payments are to be made. While the exact payment period is not known here, Reg. § 1.101–4(c) instructs us to use Wesley's life expectancy for the proration. Thus, we expect Wesley to receive $4,000 of death benefit each year for 25 years (totaling $100,000). The remaining $8,000 paid to Wesley each year would be included in his gross income, as no exclusion provision applies to that portion of the payment.

SAQ 5-3. The premium payments for a life insurance policy are probably best characterized as part of the cost of the policy. If the coverage acquired by the premium extends substantially beyond the year, then, such payments should be capitalized and, therefore, not deducted. If the taxpayer is acquiring coverage for a period not exceeding one year, as might be the case with a pure "term insurance" policy, a better argument can be made for treating the premium payment as an expense. See also Treas. Reg. § 1.263(a)–4(f)(1). But of course, not all expenses are deductible. Even where the payment is properly classified as an expense, the question becomes whether the benefit secured by the expense is a personal benefit (not deductible) or a benefit to the taxpayer's business or investment activity (generally deductible).

In the vast majority of cases, life insurance policies are secured for personal purposes. Typically the owner-insured designates his or her spouse, partner, children, family members, or other close contacts as the beneficiary of the policy. Because the payment of premiums secures this personal benefit, no deduction is available. See § 262. A business purpose for the payment of life insurance premiums is more common in the context of closely-held corporations, where the taxpayer's business activity will survive the death of the taxpayer. In these cases, it is quite common for the corporation to acquire an insurance policy on the life of the taxpayer because the taxpayer is the "key person" to the continued success of the business. Premiums paid by a corporation toward a policy on the life of a shareholder are expressly made non-deductible. Section 264(a)(1).

If the taxpayer acquires a policy on the life of another, the premium payments will be deductible if: (1) the payment is properly considered an expense and not a capital expenditure; and (2) the expense is paid in carrying on the taxpayer's business. So if the insured is a key employee of the taxpayer, the payment may be deductible if the payment is considered an expense. But again, if the policy is one of permanent insurance and not term insurance, the payment should probably be capitalized and not treated as an expense.

SAQ 5–4. The *Raytheon Production* case stands for the proposition that if the payment represents compensation for lost profits, McDonald has gross income. If the payment compensates for lost capital, then McDonald would have gross income only to the extent that the recovery exceeded McDonalds' basis in his crops. The issue here is whether the damage to the crops represents lost capital or lost profits. In *Estate of Longino v. Commissioner*, 32 T.C. 904 (1959), the Tax Court held that amounts received in settlement for damage to crops were income because they represented lost profits. The court concluded that crops were the taxpayer's inventory, and the sale of the inventory would have represented ordinary income.

Dale can likely deduct the settlement payment because the damages occurred while he was carrying on his extermination business. The payment is properly classified as an expense and not a capital expenditure because the payment does not secure a new asset or a benefit that extends beyond the year of payment. Furthermore, such payments are probably "ordinary and necessary" costs paid by an exterminator. Thus, an above-the-line deduction under § 162(a) is the correct treatment of the payment.

SAQ 5–5. No. These facts are similar to *Lyeth v. Hoey*, 305 U.S. 188 (1938) (and also vaguely similar to a Shakespearean tragedy, for that matter). In *Lyeth*, the Court held that the plaintiff's recovery was excluded under § 102(a) as a substitute for a bequest. The result is logical, for if Lear had made Regan a beneficiary of the will, the bequest received by Regan would have been excluded under § 102(a). A damage award in lieu of an excludable gift should be given the same treatment.

CHAPTER 6

SAQ 6–1. In part (a), where Belinda receives a bill in Year One but pays it in Year Two, Belinda would get a deduction in Year Two, the year of payment.

In part (b), where she pays by credit card in Year One but does not pay off the credit card bill until Year Two, she gets a deduction in Year One. *Revenue Ruling 78–38* states that payment by credit card is deemed to be made when the card is charged, not when the cardholder ultimately pays the bill. In effect, it is as if Belinda borrowed money from the credit card company and used the borrowed funds to make the payment. Since payments with borrowed funds are still "payments," a deduction is proper.

In parts (c) and (d), where Belinda pays $2,000 in Year One and $4,000 in Year Two, Belinda's deduction is likewise split between the two years. Even if Arnie had $6,000 of gross income in Year One (which he did not, but he could have if the contract modification to extend the payment date occurred after the original due date passed), the result would be the same for Belinda. There is no magic matching rule here that allows Belinda to claim a full deduction in Year One if Arnie is saddled with full inclusion that same year.

SAQ 6–2. *Revenue Ruling 74–607* states that "[a]ll the events that fix the right to receive income occur when (1) the required performance occurs, (2) payment therefor is due, or (3) payment therefor is made, whichever happens earliest." In each case, then, we must determine when the earliest of these events occurs.

(a) Here, the "required performance" on Sandy's part took place in Year One, so Sandy should accrue the income from her services for this client in Year One. The fact that the payment is neither due nor paid until Year Two is not controlling.

(b) In this case, the payment for Sandy's services is "due" in Year One, and under the "earlier-of" test described above, Sandy must seemingly accrue the income from these services in Year One. To the extent the establishment of the original due date was within Sandy's control, she should not be able to avoid the "earlier-of" test simply because the client does not pay. Sandy could argue that her decision to perform even though the client had breached the agreement was, in substance, the ratification of a new agreement whereby payment would be due after performance. If the facts and circumstances lend support to this argument, it ought to be persuasive. Given the purpose of the "earlier-of" test is to prevent taxpayers from deferring performance long after receipt of actual payment, the "payment is due" prong of the test perhaps should not be given as much weight.

(c) By getting her hands on the payment in Year One, Sandy must accrue the income in Year One even though she has yet to perform. That is the whole purpose of the ruling: the Service is concerned in cases where accrual method taxpayers receive payment in advance but do not perform until much later. Until the income received is accrued, the accrual method taxpayer enjoys an opportunity to invest the entire income, including the portion that will be used to pay federal income tax. The "earlier-of" test minimizes the incentive to defer income through simple game-playing like this. But as noted in the text, the prevention device effectively places accrual method taxpayers on the cash method if payment precedes performance.

SAQ 6–3.

(a) The business bad debt will enhance Sam's "net operating loss" ("NOL") for Year One. Section 172 will allow Sam to carry the $30,000 loss back up to two taxable years and forward for up to twenty taxable years until the loss is completely recovered. See Chapter 4. Under these facts, Sam can first use the $30,000 NOL carryover in Year Six, as explained further in the answer to part (b).

(b) Yes. Under the inclusionary arm of the tax benefit rule, the recovery of an item previously deducted must be included in gross income. Section 111(a) allows taxpayers to exclude recoveries of deductions that did not have the effect of reducing taxes. But the bad debt deduction in Year One did have the effect of reducing taxes by increasing the NOL amount. See § 111(c). Thus the exclusion does not apply on these facts and Sam must include the recovery in gross income.

SAQ 6–4.

(a) No. The extra deduction will not create an NOL because § 172(d) effectively precludes an NOL from arising out of personal, non-business deductions. Thus, the deduction will not result in any tax savings in Year Six or any other year.

(b) No. Although inclusion of the $5,000 recovery is warranted by the inclusionary arm of the tax benefit rule, § 111(a) will exclude the recovery from gross income because the Year Six deduction did not reduce the amount of income tax imposed.

This result demonstrates that the statute will occasionally disregard the mantra from *Burnet v. Sanford & Brooks* that "every year stands alone." Normally we would tax the $5,000 recovery without regard to what happened from the deduction in Year Six, but in this case the statute expressly asks us to consider whether that deduction had any effect of reducing taxes that year (or any other year, for that matter).

SAQ 6–5. Yes. Since Carla's personal use of the supplies in Year Nine is "fundamentally inconsistent" with the Year Eight deduction (which was premised on a business use of the supplies), Carla must include the amount previously deducted in gross income. *Hillsboro National Bank/ Bliss Dairy.* Section 111(a) does not apply to exclude this amount for two reasons: first, there is no "recovery" of the amount deducted, and the § 111(a) exclusion seems to be limited to actual recoveries, even though *Hillsboro/Bliss* extends the inclusionary arm of the tax benefit rule to include any amount fundamentally inconsistent with a prior deduction; and second, the Year Eight deduction did result in a reduction of Carla's federal income tax liability.

SAQ 6–6.

(a) Yes. This is a DOUBLE DEDUCTION described in § 1312(2). As a result of the Year Eight determination, Alice got to deduct the same expense in Year One and again in Year Eight. The Service will seek to re-open Year One for purposes of eliminating this double deduction.

(b) Yes. This is another DOUBLE DEDUCTION under § 1312(2). The beneficiary and the trustee are "related taxpayers" under § 1313(c)(4), so the fact that the deduction is allowed only once to each party does not prevent application of the mitigation provisions. Section 1312(5) is not the correct provision to cite here because that provision deals with special distribution deductions taken by trusts and estates that are well beyond the scope of our study.

(c) Yes. This is a § 1312(3)(A) DOUBLE EXCLUSION OF AN ITEM PREVIOUSLY INCLUDED. She excluded the income in Year One, then included it in Year Two, then successfully got the Year Two inclusion excluded. See Reg. § 1.1312–3(a)(2), Ex. 1(i).

(d) Yes. This is another § 1312(3)(A) DOUBLE EXCLUSION OF AN ITEM PREVIOUSLY INCLUDED. Although she never "included" the compensation in Year Two's gross income, the statute treats the deficiency payment as if Charlotte included the compensation in Year Two. That's what the "or with respect to which tax was paid" language in § 1312(3)(A) means. See Reg. 1.1312–3(a)(2), Ex. 1(iii).

(e) Yes. This is a § 1312(3)(B) DOUBLE EXCLUSION OF AN ITEM NOT PREVIOUSLY INCLUDED. Charlotte never included the compensation in income, and the court's determination says she can exclude it from income in Year Two. It was, apparently, includible in Year One. See Reg. § 1.1312–3(a)(2), Ex. 1(ii).

BONUS: Although there is a "circumstance" here, there is not a "condition" for adjustment under § 1311(b). Under § 1311(b)(2)(A), when the "circumstance" is described in § 1312(3)(B), the proper year of inclusion (here, Year One) must still be open at the time the Secretary first maintained that the item in question (here, the compensation) should have been included in the year at issue in the determination (here, Year Two). The deficiency notice for Year Two was issued on

September 1, Year Five, at which time Year One was no longer open (the assessment period for Year One closed on April 15, Year Five).

Why have this weird rule and not the usual "maintaining an inconsistent position" condition? Because without it, we effectively eviscerate the statute of limitations. Anytime the Service found improperly excluded income for a closed year, it could simply assess a deficiency for the same item in an open year, get a determination that it should have been included in the closed year, and voila—the Service could always circumvent the statute of limitations because the taxpayer would have maintained an inconsistent position.

(f) Yes. This is an example of a DOUBLE DISALLOWANCE OF A DEDUCTION under § 1312(4). The court disallowed a Year Five deduction that should have been allowed to Dwight in Year One.

Here, too, though, the mitigation provisions will not help because there is no "condition" under § 1311(b). Under 1311(b)(2)(B), when the "circumstance" for adjustment is described in § 1312(4), the proper year of deduction (here, Year One) must not be barred at the time taxpayer first maintained ("in writing") that he was entitled to a deduction. Here, Dwight first maintained his eligibility for the deduction on the Year Five return, filed sometime in Year Six—after Year One had closed. So he is hosed. And this is the right result, too. Imagine how soft the statute of limitations would become if taxpayers could conveniently "remember" or "realize" deductions from closed years and then be able to open them by claiming the deduction in an open year and getting a determination that the deduction was proper in the closed year!

(g) Yes. This is an example of a § 1312(7) BASIS AFTER ERRONEOUS TREATMENT circumstance. For § 1312(7) to apply, the determination (the closing agreement between Frank and the Service) must determine the basis of property (the stock), and in respect of any transaction on which the basis depends (the transfer by Ernestine's father), there occurred, with respect to a § 1312(7)(B) taxpayer, a § 1312(7)(C) error. Here, § 1312(7)(B)(ii) applies—a taxpayer (Ernestine) acquired title to the property in the transaction (she received the stock from her father in the "transaction"), and from whom the taxpayer who got the determination (Frank) derived title (he got it by gift). And as far as Ernestine is concerned, there was an erroneous "omission from" gross income (she did not treat the distribution as taxable). See § 1312(7)(C)(i).

You might have been tempted to use § 1312(7)(B)(iii), seduced by the reference to the gift transfer. But notice that this provision would apply only to property she *already* owned at the time of the "transaction," her father's transfer. See Reg. § 1.1312–7(c), Ex. 2(ii).

CHAPTER 7
SAQ 7–1.

(a) No. Depreciable property used in a trade or business is not a capital asset because it is described in § 1221(a)(2). We will soon see, however, that gains and losses from the disposition of such property will qualify for special treatment under § 1231 if the property was held for more than one year.

(b) Probably not. Assuming the receivables were acquired in exchange for services rendered by the taxpayer or from the sale of inventory property in the ordinary course of the taxpayer's business, accounts receivable are not capital assets because they are described in § 1221(a)(4). This result makes sense. A cash method taxpayer has not yet reported income from the sale of property or services when the receivable is created. If the taxpayer could create a receivable and then sell the receivable as a capital gain, taxpayers might refuse up-front prepayments for services or inventory. If the receivables were acquired by some means other than a sale of services or inventory, however, then they would qualify as capital assets.

(c) Yes, but who cares? Cash is not described in § 1221(a), so it technically would be a capital asset. But the flavoring of capital or ordinary matters only when there is a sale or exchange of the asset that gives rise to gain or loss. By definition, one cannot dispose of cash for a gain or a loss, for cash always has a face-value basis to the holder. So the characterization of cash is only of trivial value. One can realize gains and losses from transactions involving foreign currencies, however. To the extent a taxpayer used United States dollars to purchase cruzeiros that appreciate in value relative to the dollar, gain can result. For the taxation of foreign currency gains and losses, see § 988.

(d) Yes. Although § 1221(a)(3) excludes "copyrights * * * or similar property" from the definition of a capital asset, Regulation § 1.1221–1(c)(1) specifically lists "patents and inventions" as capital assets. Indeed, § 1235 confers automatic long-term capital gain treatment to any transfer of substantially all of the rights to a patent. This confirms the conclusion of the regulation. One might wonder why copyrights are not capital assets when patents are. Perhaps there is a distinction: while a copyright represents one interest in work that is already completed (like an account receivable), a patent represents only the exclusive right to earn future income using the know-how contained in the patent. Thus, one with a copyright has a right to income that can be derived without any future work, while one holding a patent must perform additional work before having a right to income. Then again, maybe the distinction is simply that patent holders have better lobbyists than copyright holders.

(e) Yes. A personal residence is not described in § 1221(a), so it qualifies as a capital asset.

(f) Yes. This is not described in § 1221(a), so it qualifies as a capital asset.

(g) No. For the artist, a completed work is akin to an account receivable in the hands of a service provider—payment received in consideration for the asset represents compensation for services. In the hands of the artist, the painting is much like inventory. Accordingly, § 1221(a)(3)(A) provides that the artwork is not a capital asset in this case.

(h) Maybe. Section 1221(a)(3)(C) states that the classification of the artwork in this case depends upon whether the related party was the creator of the artwork. If so, the artwork is not a capital asset (it keeps its status as faux-inventory or faux-receivable property). If not, then the artwork is a capital asset in the hands of the donee, just as it was in the hands of the donor.

SAQ 7–2.

(a) Long-term capital gain. Under § 1223(2), Jack can tack his father's holding period to his own. This is because Jack received the guitar as a gift, and under § 1015(a) Jack's basis in the guitar is determined with reference to his father's adjusted basis in the guitar. Jack is therefore deemed to have held the guitar for at least 12 years prior to the cash sale. Because there are no facts to suggest that the guitar would be described in § 1221(a), the guitar is a capital asset. Since he sold a capital asset held for more than one year, the gain to Jack is properly characterized as long-term capital gain.

(b) Long-term capital loss. Janet only held the coin collection for a few months, but she acquired the property by bequest, giving her a $1,000 basis under § 1014. Accordingly, under § 1223(11), she automatically takes a long-term holding period in the collection. This would be true even if Jenny only owned the coin collection for a few months herself. Death makes all holding periods long-term.

(c) Chrissy has a short-term capital loss of $20,000 and a short-term capital gain of $2,000, while Larry has a long-term capital loss of $15,000. Both transactions to which Chrissy is a party are taxable exchanges, so no tacking of holding periods under § 1223 is available. In the first transaction, she sells a capital asset for a $20,000 loss. The facts stipulate that the boat was held for investment purposes, so the loss would be recognized under § 165(c)(2). If the boat had been held for personal use, of course, no loss would be allowed under § 165(c) absent a casualty or theft. Chrissy thus took a $10,000 basis in the marketable securities, so her December sale of the securities yields a $2,000 short-term capital gain. Because she only held the stock for one month prior to the sale, and because no part of § 1223 allows for tacking of Larry's holding period, the gain is short-term. Larry's $15,000 realized loss is a long-term capital loss because he held the capital asset (the securities) for three years.

SAQ 7–3.

(a) This is not a sale or exchange. See *Helvering v. William Flaccus Oak Leather Co.*, 313 U.S. 247 (1941). Although the casualty loss is not a sale or exchange, we will soon see that a casualty loss of property used in a business and held for more than one year will often qualify for very favorable characterization under § 1231. But absent the special relief of § 1231, the resulting gain or loss would be ordinary in flavor.

(b) This is a sale or exchange. See *Hawaiian Gas Products, Ltd. v. Commissioner*, 126 F.2d 4 (9th Cir. 1942). Even though a taking is not a voluntary event, the court treated the event as one akin to a sale, at least in the sense that the taxpayer exchanged the property for consideration.

(c) This was held not to be a sale or exchange. *Foote v. Commissioner*, 81 T.C. 930 (1983). The court agreed with the Service that cash payments following termination of employment represent compensation for the loss of employment, not a sale of the right to tenure. The right of tenure, observed the court, is a personal right that is not transferable. When the professor surrenders the right, it is terminated—it does not pass to the university or to any other individual or entity.

SAQ 7–4.

(a) A taxpayer's "net capital gain" is eligible for taxation at preferential rates under § 1(h). Section 1222(11) defines the "net capital gain" as the excess of "net long-term capital gain" for the year over the "net short-term capital loss." Net long-term capital gain, in turn, is defined in § 1222(7) as the excess of long-term capital gains for the year over long-term capital losses for the year. Similarly, § 1222(6) defines net short-term capital loss as the excess of short-term capital losses for the year over net short-term capital gains for the year. One quickly infers that the first task is to net the long-term gains and losses, then to net the short-term gains and losses.

In this case, John has a net long-term capital gain of $7,000, and a net short-term capital loss of $2,000. Therefore, John's "net capital gain" is $5,000. That $5,000 net capital gain will be taxed at the preferential rates of § 1(h). The remaining $10,000 in long-term and short-term capital gains is offset by the $10,000 in long-term and short-term capital losses, so those gains become irrelevant. Do not be troubled by the fact that the $10,000 of deductible losses consists of more short-term losses than long-term losses, for the segregation of long-term and short-term items basically ends once we have the netting complete. Section 1211(b) only limits the deductibility of capital losses to the extent of capital gains plus $3,000—it makes no distinction between long-term and short-term items.

(b) Paul has a net long-term capital gain of $7,000 and a net short-term capital gain of $8,000. Paul's net capital gain is the excess of net long-term capital gain ($7,000) over net short-term capital loss (zero). Thus, his net capital gain is $7,000, and that entire amount will be eligible for the preferential rates of § 1(h). The $8,000 net short-term capital gain is not eligible for preferential rates—it will be taxed as ordinary income. This is because the preferential rates only apply to a "net capital gain," and a net short-term capital gain is not part of the definition of a "net capital gain" in § 1222(11). The moral of the story is that a taxpayer should hold a capital asset for more than one year if that taxpayer seeks the benefit of § 1(h).

(c) George has a net long-term capital loss of $3,000, and a net short-term capital gain of $8,000. Therefore, George has no net capital gain for the year, and nothing is eligible for the preferential rates of § 1(h). The $3,000 net long-term capital loss is deductible since the net short-term capital gain is sufficient to cover it. The remaining $5,000 of net short-term capital gain not offset by capital losses will be taxed as ordinary income.

(d) Ringo has a net long-term capital loss of $3,000 and a net short-term capital loss of $2,000. Preferential rates are not an issue, as all of the gains are more than offset by the losses. The key issue here is the extent to which the net losses are deductible in Year One. Section 1211(b) limits the deduction for capital losses to the extent of capital gains plus up to $3,000. See Chapter 4. There is $20,000 in total capital losses but only $15,000 in total capital gains. The $15,000 in capital gains will allow for a deduction of $18,000 of capital losses ($15,000 gains + $3,000 bonus). Therefore, Ringo can deduct $18,000 of the $20,000 in capital losses in Year One. The remaining $2,000 of capital losses constitutes a "net capital loss" (§ 1222(10)) and will carry over to Year Two under § 1212(b)(1).

But does the $2,000 carry over as short-term capital loss or long-term capital loss? Section 1212(b)(1)(A) says that to the extent that the net short-term capital loss exceeds the net long-term capital gain, the net capital loss carries over as a short-term capital loss. Section 1212(b)(1)(B), on the other hand, says that to the extent that the net long-term capital loss exceeds the net short-term capital gain, the net capital loss carries over as a long-term capital loss. In order to make these determinations, § 1212(b)(2)(A) generally states that the $3,000 bonus deduction in § 1211(b) (or so much of that bonus as was used to offset capital losses for the year) is treated as an additional short-term capital gain. As explained above, Ringo used the entire $3,000 bonus, so for carryover computation purposes we assume that Ringo had an additional $3,000 short-term capital gain. That would cause Ringo to have a net short-term capital gain of $1,000. Thus, since Ringo's net long-term capital loss ($3,000) exceeds his new-and-improved net short-term capital gain ($1,000), by $2,000, we know that the entire $2,000 capital loss carryover to Year Two is long-term capital loss.

(e) This part generally illustrates the same issues as in part (d), but is designed to point out that the carryover amount can consist partly of long-term capital loss and partly of short-term capital loss.

But let's begin at the beginning. Yoko's net long-term capital loss is $3,000, and her net short-term capital loss is $12,000. Again, the gains are not an issue here, as they are offset entirely by the losses. We know that of the $30,000 in total capital losses, $18,000 will be deductible in Year One ($15,000 in capital gains + $3,000 bonus under § 1211(b)). The remaining $12,000 will carry over to Year Two under § 1212(b)(1).

By treating the $3,000 bonus as a short-term capital gain, Yoko's net short-term capital loss for carryover purposes is reduced to $9,000. Thus, $9,000 of the $12,000 carryover capital loss will be characterized as short-term capital loss (see § 1212(b)(1)(A)), and the remaining $3,000 will be characterized as long-term capital loss (see § 1212(b)(1)(B)).

SAQ 7–5. Like Simon, Sally has a net capital gain for Year One. Her net long-term capital gain is $20,000, and her net short-term capital loss is $2,000. Therefore, Sally has a net capital gain of $18,000. Because of this net capital gain, Sally's tax liability under § 1 will be determined under § 1(h)(1).

Section 1(h)(1)(A). The § 1(h)(2)(A)(i) amount is Sally's "taxable income reduced by the net capital gain." Her taxable income is $33,000 ($15,000 salary income plus $18,000 net capital gain, with no deductions), and her net capital gain is $18,000. The § 1(h)(1)(A)(i) amount, therefore, is $15,000.

The § 1(h)(2)(A)(ii) amount is the *lesser* of: (I) her taxable income taxed at a rate below 25 percent ($31,850, if she used the rate table from 2007), or (II) her taxable income reduced by the *adjusted* net capital gain ($15,000, or $33,000 taxable income less $18,000 adjusted net capital gain). As with Simon's situation, Sally has no unrecaptured section 1250 gain nor any 28–percent rate gain, so her adjusted net capital gain equals her net capital gain. The "lesser of" number required for § 1(h)(2)(A)(ii) is $15,000.

In this case, both the § 1(h)(1)(A)(i) amount and the § 1(h)(2)(A)(ii) amount come out to $15,000. Using the 2007 tax table once again, the tax on $15,000 would be $1,408.75. This figure represents the tax on Sally's salary income.

Section 1(h)(1)(B). Sally has not fully utilized her 15–percent bracket (the 15–percent bracket extends up to $31,850, but only $15,000 of ordinary income was taxed). She may thus utilize the five-percent rate on that portion of her adjusted net capital gain equal to the $16,850 excess:

Excess of—

	Taxable income that would be taxed at a rate less than 25% [§ 1(h)(1)(B)(i)]	$31,850
over	*Taxable income minus adjusted net capital gain* [§ 1(h)(1)(B)(ii)]	($15,000)
		$16,850

Therefore, of the $18,000 net capital gain, $16,850 will be taxed at five percent. This produces a total tax of $842.50.

Section 1(h)(1)(C). The remaining adjusted net capital gain, $1,150, is now taxed at a flat rate of 15 percent. The tax on the remaining $1,150 of adjusted net capital gain is $172.50.

Like Simon, Sally had no unrecaptured § 1250 gains, no collectibles gains, and no § 1202 gains, so we can skip the computations in § 1(h)(1)(D) and § 1(h)(1)(E). Sally's maximum income tax liability for Year One can thus be determined:

1(h)(1)(A):	$1,408.75
1(h)(1)(B):	$ 842.50
1(h)(1)(C):	$ 172.50
	$2,423.75 ← total § 1 tax liability

Absent § 1(h), the § 1 tax liability on Sally's $33,000 of taxable income would have been $4,673.75. Even for a relatively low-income taxpayer like Sally, the savings from the preferential rates can be significant.

SAQ 7–6. It is necessary first to characterize each item of gain or loss separately before commencing with any netting of items.

The $5,000 Blackacre gain is a § 1231 gain that goes directly into the hotchpot. The property is not a capital asset (see § 1221(a)(2)), but it is "property used in the trade or business" under § 1231(b)(1). Note specifically that Samantha held Blackacre for more than one year and used the property in her business. Because this § 1231 gain does not arise from casualty or theft, the gain should be assigned to the hotchpot, not the firepot.

The $3,000 Whiteacre gain is an ordinary gain. Again, the property is not a capital asset because it is described in § 1221(a)(2). The gain is not § 1231 gain because the property was not held for more than one year. Thus, the gain is ordinary, meaning it will be included with Samantha's other items of ordinary income and taxed at the regular rates provided in § 1.

The $15,000 stock loss is a long-term capital loss. The stock is not described in § 1221(a), so it is a capital asset. Since there was a "sale or exchange" of a capital asset held for more than one year, the loss qualifies as a long-term capital loss. The loss will not be deductible in full unless Samantha has an offsetting capital gain to absorb it (stay tuned).

The $10,000 computer theft loss is an ordinary loss. Note, first, that the amount of the loss is limited to Samantha's basis. Section 165(b). The computer is not a capital asset because it is described in § 1221(a)(2). But the loss is also not a § 1231 loss because the computer was not held by the taxpayer for more than one year. If Samantha had owned the computer for more than one year, it would have qualified as a "firepot" loss under § 1231(a)(4)(C). But because of the short holding period, the loss retains its flavor as ordinary loss. This is not such a bad result, for an ordinary loss can offset both ordinary income and capital gains.

The $5,000 stock gain is a long-term capital gain. The stock is a capital asset because it is not described in § 1221(a). Because it was held for more than one year, the sale or exchange of this capital asset gives rise to a long-term capital gain.

Putting it all together then, Samantha's hotchpot consists only of the $5,000 § 1231 gain. Because her "§ 1231 gains" exceed her "§ 1231 losses," the single hotchpot item here will be treated as long-term capital gain. Therefore, Samantha has total long-term capital gains of $10,000. By netting the capital gains and losses, we see that Samantha has more capital loss than capital gain:

	LONG–TERM	SHORT–TERM
GAINS	$10,000	0
LOSSES	($15,000)	0
NET	($5,000)	0

Under § 1211(b), Samantha can use $3,000 of the $5,000 net long-term capital loss to offset ordinary income. The remaining $2,000 is considered a "net capital loss" that will carry over to the next taxable year.

In addition to the net capital loss, Samantha has $3,000 of ordinary income and $10,000 of ordinary loss. Again, the net loss can be used to offset other ordinary income that Samantha may have, like business profits, wages, rents, royalties, interest, and the like.

SAQ 7–7.

(a) Kelly's adjusted basis at the end of Year Three is $85,000 ($100,000 cost less $15,000 in depreciation deductions for Years One, Two, and Three). By selling the property for $110,000, she realizes a $25,000 gain. Because she held the property for more than one year, the $25,000 gain is a § 1231 gain that should pass directly into the hotchpot for Year Three. But because the asset was subject to depreciation, we must determine that portion of the gain that will be subject to recapture under § 1245(a).

To determine the recapture amount, we apply the lesser of her "recomputed basis" or the amount realized ($110,000) against her adjusted basis ($85,000). Her recomputed basis under § 1245(a)(2)(A) is her adjusted basis ($85,000) plus all prior depreciation deductions ($15,000). Thus, her recomputed basis is $100,000. That amount is less than her amount realized, so we subtract her adjusted basis from the recomputed basis to conclude that $15,000 of the gain must be treated as ordinary income. The remaining $10,000 of gain will remain § 1231 gain.

This result makes sense because Kelly deducted $15,000 of the cost against ordinary income by the time of the sale. So $15,000 of her gain should be treated as ordinary income in order for the flavors of the deduction and the income to be consistent.

(b) In this case, Kelly's realized gain on the sale of the property is only $10,000 (AR $95,000 less AB $85,000). For § 1245 recapture purposes, the amount realized ($95,000) is less than Kelly's recomputed basis ($100,000, as determined above). Thus, the entire $10,000 gain will be treated as ordinary income. By using the "lower of" rule in § 1245(a)(1), we ensure that the amount of recapture income will never exceed the realized gain from a sale of the property. If you ever have a result where the taxpayer has more depreciation recapture than realized gain, you made a mistake in the calculations.

(c) Section 1245(a)(2)(C) treats the § 179 bonus depreciation amount as "amortization" for purposes of determining recomputed basis. In effect, the bonus depreciation amount is subject to recapture just like regular depreciation deductions.

Here, Kelly's adjusted basis is $65,000 ($100,000 original cost less $20,000 under § 179 and $15,000 in § 168 depreciation deductions in Years One, Two, and Three). A sale of the property for $110,000 yields a realized gain of $45,000. Kelly's recomputed basis is $100,000 (adjusted basis plus all prior depreciation deductions, including the § 179 amount), and that is less than the amount realized. Accordingly, the excess of the recomputed basis ($100,000) over the adjusted basis ($65,000) must be treated as ordinary income. Therefore, Kelly has $35,000 of ordinary income and $10,000 of § 1231 gain from the sale of the property.

CHAPTER 8

SAQ 8–1.

(a) $300,000. The "cost" to Sally in acquiring the building totals $300,000: she pays $50,000 from her own pockets, and she agrees to incur a debt of $250,000. This cost basis is important because depreciation deductions on the building will be determined with reference to that portion of her basis allocable to the building.

If you have trouble adding the debt to Sally's basis in the building, posit the immediate sale of the building for $300,000 cash to an unrelated buyer. Sally will use the proceeds to pay off the Bank loan, so she leaves the transaction with the same $50,000 she started with—clearly the sale should not trigger gain to her. But if the debt is not included in her basis, Sally would have a $250,000 gain:

> AR 300,000
>
> AB <u>50,000</u>
>
> RG 250,000

The gain is recognized, so Sally would pay tax on that gain! Moreover, she gets no deduction for repaying the loan, because the loan was not taxable to her upon receipt. The only way to make sure Sally is not taxed on the loan is to add the debt proceeds to her basis in the underlying property.

(b) Nope. Even though the Bank loan is not secured by the building, Sally is still obligated to repay the loan, so she still incurs a total "cost" of $300,000 to buy the building.

(c) Nope. Again, she still has the legal obligation to repay the loan, even though the Bank could only go after the building (and not her other assets). The *Crane* case makes this clear—acquisition debt is included in basis no matter whether the debt is recourse or nonrecourse, and no matter whether the property securing the debt is worth more or less than the amount of the debt.

SAQ 8–2.

(a) No. In any bona fide loan arrangement, the borrower does not have gross income upon receipt of the loan proceeds because of the simultaneous obligation to repay the loan proceeds at a later date. Sally would have income only if the Bank and Sally did not expect that Sally would repay the loan (or if Sally accepted the loan proceeds with an intent to cheat the Bank and never repay it).

(b) No. *Woodsam Associates* stands for the proposition that a loan is not a realization event, even where the loan is secured only by unrealized appreciation (i.e., equity in excess of basis). As long as the obligation to repay is present, there is never gross income to the borrower upon the receipt of loan proceeds.

(c) No. There is no realization event upon taking out a loan, and that is still the case even where the debt is nonrecourse, for there remains an obligation to repay even though the lender's rights upon default may be limited. In fact, the debt in *Woodsam Associates* was nonrecourse, so the answer here is certain.

(d) Still $250,000. The second debt is not added to the basis of property because: (1) it was not used to acquire the property, so it is not part of the property's "cost;" and (2) no portion of the proceeds were used to improve the property, which would allow for an adjustment to basis under § 1016(a)(1).

(e) Sally's basis increases to $300,000. Here, she used $50,000 of the second loan proceeds to improve the property, so that portion of the loan can be added to the basis of the property under § 1016(a)(1).

SAQ 8–3. No. The statute applies only to the sale of a taxpayer's *principal* residence. In defining a "principal" residence, Regulation § 1.121–1(b)(2) states that "[i]f a taxpayer alternates between 2 properties, using each as a residence for successive periods of time, the property that the taxpayer uses a majority of the time *during the year* ordinarily will be considered the taxpayer's principal residence" (emphasis added). This implies that Bill and Whoopi must have used the Wisconsin home as their principal residence for two of the five years prior to the sale, not merely for a total of 730 days (365 days for two years) in that five-year period. Indeed, in *Guinan v. Commissioner*, 2003–1 U.S. Tax Cas. (CCH) ¶ 50,475; 91 A.F.T.R.2d (RIA) 2174 (D. Ariz. 2003), a summary judgment opinion from the Federal District Court of Arizona, the court agreed that the regulation requires a year-by-year determination of a taxpayer's principal residence, and only where the home at issue was the principal residence for two or more of the five years will the taxpayer be considered to have sold or exchanged the taxpayer's principal residence.

In this case, Wisconsin was Bill and Whoopi's principal residence only for the first year in the five-year period; in each of the other four years, the Wisconsin residence was not their principal residence. Thus, the Wisconsin home ordinarily would not qualify as their principal residence. Indeed, the facts for this question are lifted from the *Guinan* case, where the court concluded that the Wisconsin home was not the taxpayers' principal residence, primarily for this reason.

The court also observed that the number of days spent at a home is but one factor identified in the regulation for determining a taxpayer's principal residence. The regulation also requires examination of various facts including: (1) the taxpayer's place of employment; (2) the principal abode of the taxpayer's family members; (3) the address listed on the taxpayer's federal and state tax returns, driver's license, automobile registration, and voter registration card; (4) the taxpayer's mailing address for bills and correspondence; and (5) the location of the taxpayer's banks. The *Guinan* court determined that the first fact (employment) did not apply in this case, nor did the second fact. But the other facts suggested closer ties to Georgia and Arizona than to Wisconsin. Accordingly, the court saw no reason to deviate from the "number of days" rule based on the facts of this case. Because they did not sell their principal residence, the court ruled that it was proper for the Service to deny the § 121 exclusion on the sale of the Wisconsin home.

SAQ 8–4.

(a) Yes. This is an exchange of real property for real property, and thus qualifies as a like-kind exchange. Regulation § 1.1031(a)–1(b) states that "[t]he fact that any real estate involved is improved or unimproved is not material, for that facts relates only to the grade or quality of the property and not its kind or class." Thus, an exchange of unimproved land for improved land is a like-kind exchange. See Treas. Reg. § 1.1031(a)–1(c)(2).

(b) Yes. Regulation § 1.1031(a)–1(c)(2) provides that an exchange of a real estate leasehold for real property is a like-kind exchange. On these very facts, the Service determined that the like-kind exchange occurred. *Rev. Rul. 68–331*, 1968–1 C.B. 352.

(c) No. In this case, there is an exchange of depreciable personal property for other depreciable personal property. While both are vehicles, they have different General Asset Classes. See Treas. Reg. §§ 1.1031(a)–2(b)(2)(v) (automobiles) and 1.1031(a)–2(b)(2)(viii) (heavy general purpose trucks). Accordingly, because the assets are not of like class, they are not of like kind. See Treas. Reg. § 1.1031(a)–2(b)(1).

(d) Yes. Both items are depreciable personal property, and both have the same General Asset Class. Therefore, they are like-kind. See Treas. Reg. §§ 1.1031(a)–2(b)(1)(ii) and 1.031(a)–2(b)(7), ex. (1).

(e) No. As patents are intangible assets, proper guidance is found at Regulation § 1.1031(a)–2(c)(1), which asks whether the "nature or character of the rights involved" are the same and, if so, whether the "nature or character of the underlying property to which the intangible personal property relates" are the same. While the nature of the rights involved are the same in this case (they are both patent rights), they relate to unlike properties (zippers and hair cutters are not property of the same class or kind). Thus, there is no like-kind exchange here. See Treas. Reg. § 1.1031(a)–2(c)(3), Ex. (1)–(2) (exchange of copyright on one novel for a copyright on a different novel qualifies, but exchange of copyright on a novel for a copyright on a song does not).

SAQ 8–5.

(a) Yes. The condemnation is clearly an involuntary conversion event. Although the taxpayer received cash upon the conversion, all of the proceeds were used to purchase another shopping center. There is no question that the other shopping center is property "similar or related in service or use" ("similar-use property"). Finally, as in all parts of this question, the timing rule in 1033(a)(2)(B) is met. Thus, nonrecognition will be available to the taxpayer.

(b) Yes. This, too, is an involuntary conversion, for any "casualty" (sudden, unexpected, and unusual event) will qualify as the complete or partial destruction of property.

(c) Yes. Although the tavern is not similar-use property under *Revenue Ruling 64–237* because the taxpayer use of the shopping center (rental property) is not the same as the use of the tavern (retail establishment), 1033(g) provides a special rule applicable to the condemnation of business or investment property. Specifically, so long as the replacement property is of like kind, the replacement property will be deemed to be similar-use property. Because the tavern and the shopping center are like-kind properties (two parcels of real property are always like-kind), the special rule in 1033(g) applies and the result is thus the same as in part (a).

(d) No. Here, the shopping center was not subject to condemnation but was lost in a casualty. Section 1033(g) is limited to seizures, requisitions, and condemnations; it does not apply to casualties. Thus, because the tavern is not similar-use property (as described in the answer to part (c) above), the realized gain from the receipt of the condemnation award must be recognized.

(e) No. Section 1033 only applies to realized gains from involuntary conversions. The loss is recognized, likely under 165(c)(2) because the property is likely held for investment purposes. If the condemned property had been personal-use property, the limitations of 165(c)(3) and 165(h) would come into play (the $100 limitation and the adjusted gross income limitation), as discussed in Chapter 4.

(f) No. *Revenue Ruling 64–237* states that for "owner-users" of involuntarily converted property (unlike "owner-investors" who lease out their property), the test for similar-use property is whether the replacement property serves the same functional use to the taxpayer. Here, the taxpayer functional use of the bookstore is different than the functional use of the grocery store. Although both businesses are engaged in retail sales, they are distinctly different activities. Accordingly, the Service would conclude that the bookstore is not similar-use property and would thus require the taxpayer to recognize the gain realized from the conversion.

SAQ 8–6. Thurston's realized gain is $21,000 (amount realized of $50,000 minus his adjusted basis of $29,000). But under the installment method, Thurston recognizes in Year Three that portion of the payments received ($15,000) equal to the amount that the "gross profit" bears to the "total contract price." The fraction produced by dividing gross profit by the total contract price is often called the "gross profit percentage," though the regulations call it the "gross profit ratio." See Reg. § 15A.453–1(b)(2)(i). So first, the elements of the gross profit percentage must be computed.

1. *COMPUTE GROSS PROFIT.* Gross profit means selling price less adjusted basis. Treas. Reg. § 15A.453–1(b)(2)(v). Selling price means gross selling price with no reduction for debt and no reduction for any selling expenses. Treas. Reg. § 15A.453–1(b)(2)(ii). So the selling price here is $50,000. Adjusted basis has the same meaning as always—good old adjusted basis, except that for nondealer sales of real property and for "casual" sales of personal property, basis also includes selling expenses. Treas. Reg. § 15A.453–1(b)(2)(v). So adjusted basis here is $30,000, since it is fair to assume this is a "casual" (isolated, irregular) sale by Thurston. Thus the gross profit is $20,000:

Gross Sales Price	50,000
Adjusted Basis (plus selling expenses)	(30,000)
GROSS PROFIT	20,000

2. *COMPUTE TOTAL CONTRACT PRICE.* Total contract price is the "selling price" minus that portion of "qualifying indebtedness" assumed or taken subject to by the buyer that does not exceed the seller's adjusted basis (as modified in step 1). Treas. Reg. § 15A.453–1(b)(2)(iii). "Qualifying indebtedness" means any debt secured by the property and any other debt incurred in the acquisition or operation of the property. It does not include any debt incurred in disposing of the property. Treas. Reg. § 15A.453–1(b)(2)(iv). There is no debt of any kind here, so the contract price is equal to the selling price, or $50,000.

3. *DETERMINE GROSS PROFIT PERCENTAGE.* Gross profit percentage, again, is gross profit divided by contract price. Here, that totals 40%:

$$\frac{\text{Gross Profit } 20,000}{\text{Contract Price } 50,000} = 40\%$$

4. *APPLY TO PAYMENTS RECEIVED DURING THE YEAR.* Thurston received $15,000 in payments (the $10,000 down plus the first installment payment of $5,000). Thus, he must include $6,000 in gross income for Year Three.

Total Payments	15,000
× GPP	40%
Amount Included	6,000

The flavor of the $6,000 recognized gain in Year Three is long-term capital gain.

SAQ 8–7. Son and Daughter each have a $1 million cost basis in the stock they acquired from Mother. *Crane v. Commissioner* supports the rule that debt is included in basis because of their obligation to pay. Thus, they each have a $1 million capital gain on the sale of the shares. Because the stock was not acquired by gift or in a nonrecognition transaction, however, they cannot tack Mother's holding period to the shares, so the flavor of the gain is ordinary income because they have short-term capital gains.

Under § 453(e)(1), Mother will have to recognize gain from her installment sale in the year of the second disposition by Son and Daughter. Son and Daughter are clearly "related persons" under § 267(b). Section 453(e)(1) generally says to treat the amount realized by Son and Daughter ($4 million) as a payment to Mother, but § 453(e)(3) limits the deemed payment to an amount determined under this formula:

Lesser of: (AR on second disposition) OR (total contract price on first disposition)

Minus: (Payments on first disposition notes this year) + (Prior payments on notes)

Here, since no payments have been made on the first notes, there is no reduction, and the full $2 million "total contract price" is treated as a payment to Mother. Since this is full payment, of course, the consequences to Mother are the inclusion of the full $1,990,000 gain from the first installment sale transactions.

So Son and Daughter have $2 million of ordinary income and Mother has $1.99 million of long-term capital gain from the sale.

SAQ 8–8. Section 453B applies to *T*'s subsequent disposition of the installment note to *Z*. This is because the disposition is not excepted out within the statute.

Under § 453B(a)(1), *T* has gain to the extent the amount realized on the disposition exceeds *T*'s basis in the note. According to § 453B(b), *T*'s basis in the note is the excess of the face value of the note ($150,000) over the amount of income which would be returnable if the note were paid in full. To determine this amount, we have to compute the gross profit percentage and apply it to the unpaid portion of the purchase price. See Treas. Reg. § 1.453–9(b). The gross profit here is $100,000 ($200,000 sales price less $100,000 basis in property). The total contract price is $200,000, so the gross profit percentage is 50% ($100,000 $200,000). Since no portion of the $150,000 face value has been paid, T would have to include $75,000 in income if the note were satisfied in full (50 percent x $150,000). Thus, T's basis in the X note is its $150,000 face value minus the $75,000 that would be included in gross income, or $75,000.

Accordingly, T has $55,000 of gain on the sale of the note for $130,000:

AR	130,000
AB	(75,000)
RG	55,000

This makes sense—T should not have to recognize any portion of the $20,000 realized gain lost in the sale of the note to Z ($150,000 note sold for $130,000). Giving T full basis credit for the note ensures this result.

CHAPTER 9

SAQ 9–1. The § 67 "haircut" only applies to "miscellaneous itemized deductions." See § 67(a) and discussion in Chapter 2. Miscellaneous itemized deductions are defined as itemized deductions *other than* those specifically listed in § 67(b). Sure enough, the § 213 deduction for medical expenses is included in the list. See § 67(b)(5). Therefore, the § 67 haircut will *not* apply to this deduction.

The § 68(a) limitation purports to apply to all itemized deductions, but § 68(c) lists three deductions that are not affected by the limitation. The § 213 medical expense deduction is one of the three exceptions. See § 68(c)(1).

Apparently, Congress thinks the 7.5 percent threshold in § 213 is enough of a hurdle for taxpayers to clear. There is no compelling reason to impose the additional limitations of §§ 67 and 68 on taxpayers who have already surmounted such a large obstacle to deduction.

SAQ 9–2.

(a) No deduction. Federal income taxes are a personal liability, so there is no authority for the deduction under § 162 or § 212. Furthermore, federal income tax is not listed in § 164(a) (logically enough). Thus, there is no authority for the deduction of federal income taxes paid.

(b) Deductible under § 164(a)(3). Because both federal and state income taxes generally tax the same base, the federal income tax graciously gives way to the state income taxes actually paid in the taxable year as a crude way of avoiding double taxation ("crude" because the deduction is an itemized deduction to the extent state income taxes are a personal liability of the taxpayer, so not all taxpayers will get this benefit). Even when one itemizes, a deduction is not the perfect offset that a credit is, and that is why most taxpayers with foreign tax liability claim the § 901 foreign tax credit and not the § 164(a)(3) deduction.

(c) Deductible under § 164(a)(1), assuming the taxes do not represent a special assessment (as discussed below) and also assuming that ownership of the residence did not change hands during the year (also discussed below).

(d) This might be deductible as a "personal property tax" under § 164(a)(2), assuming that the tax is imposed annually based on the value of the property (an "ad valorem" tax). See § 164(b)(1). If the tax is the same for all automobile makes, models, and years, then it is not an ad valorem tax and no deduction would be allowed. If the vehicle was used exclusively in the taxpayer's business, however, a deduction for annual excise taxes would be proper under § 162(a). A one-time excise tax imposed upon acquisition of the car would be a capital expenditure, so no deduction under § 162(a) would be proper (the cost would be added to the basis of the car).

(e) No deduction. Although taxpayers in 2007 may deduct state sales and local general sales taxes by making an election under § 164(b)(5), taxes paid to acquire an asset are part of the "cost" of the asset and should be capitalized. The second sentence in the flush language to § 164(a) confirms this result. So the taxpayer can add the cost to the basis of the asset. If the asset is subject to wear and tear, the tax portion of the cost can be depreciated just like the other portions of the asset's cost.

(f) No deduction. Because the tax is imposed on a "local benefit of a kind tending to increase the value of the property assessed," no deduction is allowed under § 164(a). See § 164(c)(1). Because the tax is paid to improve the property, however, the amount of the tax may be added to the taxpayer's basis in the residence. See § 1016(a)(1). In other words, where a tax is used to provide an improvement to real property, the tax is properly considered a capital expenditure for which no current deduction is allowed.

(g) Deductible under § 164(a)(2). Investment portfolios are personal property, and this tax meets the definition of an ad valorem tax. Thus, any such tax paid is deductible. Even without § 164(a)(2), the tax would likely be deductible under § 212, as the tax does not appear to improve the portfolio in any way.

SAQ 9–3.

(a) No. Babysitting is a purely personal expense. *Smith v. Commissioner*, 40 BTA 1038 (1939), aff'd, 113 F.2d 114 (2d Cir. 1940). Section 21, however, offers a very limited credit of up to $1,050 (at most 35 percent of up to $3,000 in expenses) for child care expenses Alice incurs. This assumes Tommy is under age 13 or unable to care for himself because of physical or mental impairment. If Alice's adjusted gross income exceeds $10,000, the maximum credit amount is reduced until it hits a low of $600 (20 percent of up to $3,000 in expenses). Because Alice can credit only 20–35% of the amounts actually paid, the credit operates as a quasi-deduction (though still better than a deduction in cases of low-income taxpayers in the 10–percent and 15–percent tax brackets).

(b) Under § 45F, Mel gets a credit for up to 25 percent of his "qualified child care expenditures" (up to a maximum credit of $150,000 in any given taxable year) by providing child care for his employees. To the extent he claims this credit, he cannot deduct the costs incurred, for that would be a double benefit. See § 45F(f)(2). But to the extent that the credit does not apply because of the dollar-ceiling rule, Mel should be able to deduct the excess costs as compensation. A deduction should be allowed even though Alice and other employees can exclude up to $5,000 in value from this benefit under § 129. If Alice has less than $5,000 of earned income, the exclusion ceiling is reduced to the amount of her earned income.

SAQ 9–4.

(a) At least a portion of the legal expenses will be deductible. Section 212(1) allows a deduction for ordinary and necessary expenses paid or incurred for the production or collection of income. Because some portion of the attorney fees must be allocable to the negotiation of the amount of alimony to be paid to Tommy, and because Tommy will include the alimony payments in gross income under § 71, that portion of the attorney fee qualifies for the § 212(1) deduction. Moreover, to the extent the legal fees were paid for tax advice, that portion would be deductible under § 212(3).

Before you get too excited for Tommy, however, keep in mind that the deduction will be a miscellaneous itemized deduction subject not only to the two-percent haircut under § 67 but also to the overall limitation on itemized deductions under § 68. So while at least a portion of the expenses will be deductible, all or a portion of the deduction will be lost under § 67 and/or § 68.

(b) Yes. As explained above, attorney fees and other expenses paid in connection with the determination of any tax are deductible under § 212(3). Accordingly, Pam can deduct the fees paid for tax advice (although, as with the Tommy, it will be a miscellaneous itemized deduction). Pam probably cannot deduct the other legal fees she paid for the divorce under *Gilmore*, for the origin of a divorce claim is personal.

Pam's attorney is bright. By separately stating the portion of the total fee attributable to tax advice, the attorney provided Pam with an easy method to compute the proper deduction amount. Attorneys should endeavor to separately state fees owed for tax advice on their bills to assist their clients in this regard.

(c) By making a cash payment on Tommy's behalf, Pam might argue that the payment qualifies as alimony. That would give her an above-the-line deduction for the payment under § 62(a)(10). Cash payments made on behalf of an ex-spouse can qualify as alimony. See Treas.

Reg. § 1.71–1T(b), Q. & A. 6. But if Pam is liable for the payment to Tommy's attorney even if Tommy dies (which is likely the case), then the payment likely cannot qualify as alimony because it flunks the requirement in § 71(b)(1)(D) that there be no liability to make the payment after Tommy's death. Accordingly, Pam's payment to Tommy's attorney is probably not deductible, even if the payment is made while Tommy is still alive. See Treas. Reg. § 1.71–1T(b), Q. & A. 10.

SAQ 9–5.

(a) There are no consequences in Year One, as Ben is not entitled to a deduction for making a loan. Whether Ben can claim a deduction in Year Two under § 166 depends primarily upon whether Ben made a bona fide loan in Year One and not a gift. More facts are required to be sure of the correct answer, but the familial relationship between Ben and Eileen should trigger more scrutiny. If the facts suggest that Ben did not expect repayment, then the Year One transfer is best classified as a gift, not a loan. Section 166 does not apply to gifts, and no authority exists for a deduction in the event the Year One transfer is deemed a gift.

If, on the other hand, the facts suggest that the transfer is a bona fide loan, the next issue for Ben is whether the debt has become "bad" in Year Two. A debt becomes a bad debt when it becomes "worthless" to some extent in the taxable year. Section 166(a). Whether the debt has become worthless depends upon a consideration of all relevant facts. Reg. § 1.166–2(a). Eileen's bankruptcy in Year Two is "generally an indication of the worthlessness of at least a part of an unsecured and unpreferred debt." Reg. § 1.166–2(c)(1). So assuming that Ben's loan was not secured or preferred, it would seem that the debt has gone bad in Year Two.

If so, the final issue is whether the debt is a "business bad debt" or a "nonbusiness bad debt." If Ben made the loan in the course of his business, then his "business bad debt" is deductible as an ordinary loss. Moreover, a deduction would be allowable even if the debt had only become partially worthless.

If the loan was not made in connection with Ben's business, then the deduction for the "nonbusiness bad debt" is automatically treated as a short-term capital loss, which could hinder the immediate deductibility of the loss (since capital losses are limited to the extent of capital gains plus $3,000). Furthermore, a nonbusiness bad debt would be deductible only if it was wholly worthless; there is no deduction for nonbusiness bad debts that have become partially worthless.

Since the facts here suggest that the debt is wholly worthless, the relevance of the distinction between a business bad debt and a nonbusiness bad debt relates entirely to characterization. In either case, Ben's deduction is limited to his basis in the loan, which is $10,000 (the amount extended to Eileen as credit). Section 166(b).

(b) Eileen has no gross income in Year One. If the transfer was really a gift from Ben, then the § 102(a) exclusion applies. Moreover, the cancellation of the "debt" in Year Two is without significance if the transfer was really a gift, because the whole repayment requirement was just a ruse from the start. If the transfer in Year One is in fact a bona fide loan, Eileen has no gross income in Year One because of the obligation of repayment. When she declares bankruptcy in Year Two, the debt is discharged, which at first suggests she has income under § 61(a)(12) (cancellation of debt income). But bankruptcy is one of the grounds for excluding COD income under § 108(a)(1)(A), meaning Eileen can exclude the COD income in Year Two. But the exclusion will affect her other tax attributes under § 108(b). See discussion at Chapter 3.

CHAPTER 10

SAQ 10–1.

(a) Under *Revenue Ruling 99–7*, Tom can deduct expenses incurred in commuting from home to a temporary work location (the trip from Tacoma to Olympia) and between a temporary work location and permanent office (the trip from Olympia to Seattle), but not the commute between his personal residence and his permanent office (the trip from Seattle to Tacoma).

(b) Tom can deduct all of the travel expenses. The first trip (Tacoma to Portland) is one from home to a temporary work location, which is deductible under *Revenue Ruling 99–7*. The second trip (Portland to Seattle) is one from a temporary work location to a regular work location, which of course is deductible. The third trip (Seattle to Olympia) is from a regular work location to another temporary work location, which again is deductible. The last trip (Olympia to Tacoma) involves travel between a temporary work location and home, which (just like the first trip) is deductible.

These answers assume that Tom does not regularly appear in court at Olympia. If so, Olympia might be viewed as another "regular" work location and not a "temporary" one, in which case any transportation between Tacoma and Olympia would not be deductible.

SAQ 10–2.

(a) The job-seeking expenses are deductible under *Revenue Ruling 75–120*. The ruling permits a deduction where an employee seeks new employment in the same trade or business activity. Here, Peggy sought and obtained employment in the same business activity, so her job-seeking expenses are deductible.

(b) The expenses are still deductible. The ruling preserves the rule from the *Cremona* case that the deduction is not contingent upon successfully securing employment in the same trade or business activity.

(c) The deduction is now more questionable. Peggy will be considered to be seeking a job in the same business activity "if no substantial lack of continuity occurred between the time of the past employment and the seeking of new employment." The ruling does not indicate how much time must pass before there is a "substantial lack of continuity," so we cannot with certainty whether Peggy's expenses in this case will be deductible. If Peggy spent the months between her firing in Year One and her job search in Year Two conducting a separate business activity, then the deduction will be lost because she is not seeking employment in her most recent business activity. Conversely, if Peggy spent the interim period recovering from depression or a similar condition that prevented her from seeking work sooner, the deduction probably should not be lost.

(d) No deduction. In this situation, Peggy is seeking employment in a new business activity. She is not "carrying on" the business of employment as a grocery bagger any longer, and her costs in seeking employment as a teacher are incurred prior to the commencement of that business activity.

SAQ 10–3.

(a) No. A deduction may be taken "above the line" (meaning it can be used to compute adjusted gross income) only if it is listed in § 62(a). Section 62(a)(1) generally allows all business-related deductions to be taken above the line, but it specifically excludes business expenses paid or incurred by employees. Section 62(a)(2)(A) permits reimbursed employee expenses to be taken above the line, but job-seeking expenses are not typically included within the reimbursement or allowance arrangements contemplated by § 62(a)(2)(A). The deduction for job-seeking expenses by an employee, therefore, is an itemized deduction. Moreover, because the deduction is not listed in § 67(b), employee job-seeking expenses are miscellaneous itemized deductions that will be subject to the two-percent "haircut" in § 67(a). So while a deduction under *Revenue Ruling 75–120* for employees is better than nothing at all, the limitations imposed on the deductibility of job-seeking expenses certainly undermines the value of the deduction.

(b) The issue here is whether the taxpayer may somehow recover the expenses of job-seeking even though a current deduction is not available under *Revenue Ruling 75–120*. If not, then the expense is forever lost to the taxpayer.

A taxpayer might argue that the expenses of seeking new employment are amortizable under § 195. See Chapter 4. Job-seeking expenses may be seen as amount paid in "creating an active trade or business." See § 195(c)(1)(A)(ii). And we know from *Revenue Ruling 75–120* that if the taxpayer was already engaged in the same trade or business that such job-seeking expenses would be deductible. See § 195(c)(1)(B). Therefore, the costs would qualify as "start-up expenditures." If this argument holds, then the job-seeking expenses can be amortized over a period of no less than 60 months beginning with the month in which the taxpayer commences employment in the new trade or business. If the taxpayer never commences work in the new business activity, then no § 195 election could be made and the costs would never be recovered.

SAQ 10–4.

(a) Section 222(a) allows a deduction for "qualified tuition and related expenses" paid by Dewey during the year. Dewey's adjusted gross income is well beneath the dollar limitations in § 222(b), so he can deduct up to $3,000 or $4,000 under this section (depending upon which year Year One represents).

The tuition paid to Law School in January and September likely meet the test for "qualified tuition and related expenses" in § 222(d)(1) and § 25A(f). But under § 222(c)(1), Dewey cannot claim a deduction under § 222 for a payment that is already deductible under some other provision. Thus, if the tuition paid in Year One is deductible to any extent under § 162 (an issue to be addressed in class), even without § 222, Dewey may not deduct the same payment again under § 222. Any tuition payments not deductible under § 162 will qualify for the § 222 deduction up to the maximum of $3,000 or $4,000, whichever ceiling is applicable to Year One. The deduction is taken above the line, even though it refers to "adjusted gross income" in computing the applicable dollar limitation.

(b) If Dewey's adjusted gross income is $70,000 and his only income comes from a six-week stint as an associate, he should not have left practice.

As for the deduction, if Year One is in 2002 or 2003, Dewey is not entitled to any deduction under § 222 because his adjusted gross income is too high. If Year One is in 2004 or 2005, the maximum amount of the deduction drops from $4,000 to $2,000 under § 222(b)(2)(B)(ii) for tax-payers with adjusted gross incomes between $65,000 and $80,000. Thus, Dewey could deduct up to $2,000 of otherwise non-deductible tuition paid to Law School in Year One.

SAQ 10–5.

(a) If the loan arrangement constitutes a "qualified education loan," then a deduction for the interest payment is allowed under § 221. Otherwise, because the loan was incurred to pay for Ed's education (a personal benefit), no deduction will be allowed. See § 163(h)(1)–(2). Fortunately for Ed, the Bank loan is a qualified education loan. The loan proceeds were used solely to pay Ed's qualified higher education expenses within a reasonable period after the borrowing. The education expenses are attributable to education furnished during a period in which Ed was full-time student at UFO, and Bank is unrelated to Ed.

The amount Ed seeks to deduct, $500, is within the $2,500 limitation imposed by § 221(b)(1). We have no facts to suggest that the limitation should be reduced under § 211(b)(2) because of Ed's modified adjusted gross income. Thus, a full deduction of the $500 interest payment will be allowed, and the deduction may be taken above the line. See § 62(a)(17).

(b) Ed may only deduct $2,500 of the $3,000 interest paid. See § 221(b)(1).

(c) Because Ed's adjusted gross income exceeds $50,000, the $2,500 limitation in § 221(b)(1) is reduced under § 221(b)(2). In this case, the $2,500 limitation is supposed to be reduced by $8,333, computed as follows:

$$\frac{\text{Modified AGI—\$50,000}}{\$15,000} \quad X \quad \$2,500\ \text{limitation} \quad = \quad \text{reduction}$$

$$\frac{\$50,000}{\$15,000} \quad X \quad \$2,500\ \text{limitation} \quad = \quad \$8,333\ \text{reduction}$$

While the reduction cannot reduce the limitation below zero, § 221(b)(2) effectively precludes a deduction for Ed in this case, as his limitation is reduced all the way to zero. Ed can therefore deduct no portion of the interest payment.

(d) Ed can deduct $250 of the interest payment. Although § 221(b)(1) allows a deduction for up to $2,500 in interest on a qualified education loan, the § 221(b)(2) reduction is again triggered:

$$\frac{\text{Modified AGI—\$50,000}}{\$15,000} \quad X \quad \$2,500\ \text{limitation} \quad = \quad \text{reduction}$$

$$\frac{\$13,500}{\$15,000} \quad X \quad \$2,500\ \text{limitation} \quad = \quad \$2,250\ \text{reduction}$$

Reducing the $2,500 limitation by $2,250 leaves a $250 limitation. Ed may thus deduct $250 of the $500 interest paid.

(e) No deduction at all. Loans from related parties cannot constitute qualified education loans. See § 221(d)(1), second sentence. See also Treas. Reg. § 1.221–1(e)(3)(iii).

(f) No change—Ed may still deduct the interest payment. As long as Ed is the person legally obligated to make the payment to Bank, the payment to Bank by Ed's parents will be treated as a gift to Ed (excluded from his gross income under § 102) followed by a payment from Ed to Bank. See Treas. Reg. §§ 1.221–1(b)(4)(i) and 1.221–1(b)(4)(ii), ex. (2).

(g) Ed can deduct no portion of the interest payment. The § 221 deduction is conditioned upon the loan proceeds being used *solely* to pay qualified higher education expenses. Because the proceeds were also used to make a capital expenditure, no deduction for any interest payment on this loan will be allowed under § 221. See Treas. Reg. § 1.221–1(e)(4), ex. (6).

(h) The issue here is whether the qualified higher education expenses were paid "within a reasonable period of time" after the Bank loan was incurred, as required by § 221(d)(1)(B). The Regulations provide that if loan proceeds are used for education expenses for a particular academic term and are paid within the period that begins 90 days prior to the start of the term and ends 90 days after the end of the term, then the taxpayer is deemed to have met the "reasonable period of time" requirement. Treas. Reg. § 1.221–1(e)(3)(ii). We do not know whether that is the case here. If not, then Ed must be prepared to demonstrate that he met the requirement "based on all the relevant facts and circumstances." *Id.*

SAQ 10–6. Hedra can deduct all of the business expenses in full, as they are deductible under § 162(a) without regard to whether she operates the business out of her home. Such expenses are not attributable to the use of her home in the business. Under § 280A(c), Hedra can also deduct the "business percentage" of her home expenses because she uses the basement office regularly and exclusively in her business activity. In this case, because her basement comprises ten percent of the total square footage of her home, she can deduct up to ten percent of the indirect costs of keeping her home as a business expense.

Of course, the property taxes (§ 164) and mortgage interest (§ 163) are likely deductible in full anyway. Section 280A(b) preserves these deductions in full. But the utilities expense and the depreciation expense are only allowed to the extent they come within the deduction limitation of § 280A(c)(5). Applying that limitation in this case, we see that Hedra can deduct only up to $800 of these items:

Gross Income from Business	$5,000
Minus:	
Deductible mortgage interest attributable to office (10%)	($1,000)
Deductible taxes attributable to office (10%)	($200)
Business expenses not related to use of home	($3,000)
Deduction limit	$800

The business percentage of the utilities expense is $100 (ten percent of $1,000) and the business percentage of the depreciation expense is $750 (ten percent of $7,500). The indirect costs attributable to the basement office thus total $850, which exceeds the $800 deduction limit. That means Hedra may deduct $800 of these expenses in Year One. The extra $50 will carry over to Year Two as a deduction allocable to the basement office. If the deduction limit in Year Two is sufficiently high, Hedra may claim the carryover deduction amount in that year.

In summary, Hedra may deduct all of the business expenses, all of the property taxes and mortgage interest, and $800 of the $850 in utilities and depreciation attributable to the basement office.

CHAPTER 11

SAQ 11–1. The facts stipulate that the motorcycle repair activity is Fonzie's hobby, so there is no need to determine whether he has a profit motive sufficient to claim deductions under § 162 or § 212. Generally, § 183(b) allows Fonzie to deduct hobby expenses to the extent of hobby income. Under § 183(b)(1), Fonzie can deduct those expenses for which a deduction is available no matter whether the activity is a hobby, a business, or an investment activity. Under § 183(b)(2), the remaining hobby expenses are deductible to the extent of hobby income. Reg. § 1.183–1(b)(1) thus creates a three-tier structure for hobby expenses. The first tier (Type (1) deduction) consists of deductions that the taxpayer may claim no matter whether the activity is a hobby or business. The second tier (Type (2) deduction) consists of all other items that would be deductible if the activity were engaged in for profit *except* for deductions that would result in an adjustment to the basis of property. The third tier (Type (3) deduction) then consists of all such deductions that give rise to an adjustment in the basis of property.

Under § 164(a)(2), Fonzie can deduct the personal property taxes without regard to whether the motorcycle repair activity is operated with a profit motive. This is a Type (1) deduction. The cost of the motorcycle parts would be a Type (2) deduction, and the depreciation would be a Type (3) deduction. Thus, all of the taxes and all of the parts are deductible, but only $400 of the $600 in depreciation is allowable:

Hobby Income	1,200
Less Type (1) deductions	(200)
Limit on Type (2) & (3)	1,000
Less Type (2) deductions	(600)
Limit on Type (3)	400
Less Type (3) deductions	(600) ← limited to $400
	0

SAQ 11–2.

(a) Dr. Quinn can clearly deduct $20,000 worth of expenses because she has that much income from the activity. Whether she can deduct any of the $30,000 excess depends upon whether she is "at risk" for the activity as of the end of Year One. Section 465(a)(1). Dr. Quinn is "at risk" for only $20,000, as that is the only amount she has contributed to the activity. Section 465(b)(1)(A). Because the loan from Bank is a nonrecourse loan, she is not "at risk" with respect to any portion of the loan. Section 465(b)(2). Thus, she can deduct a total of $40,000 of the expenses (the extent of the income from the activity plus the amount she is "at risk" for) in Year One. The extra $10,000 of loss will carry over to Year Two. Section 465(a)(2).

(b) Dr. Quinn would be considered "at risk" with respect to the entire loan amount. Section 465(b)(2)(A). Thus, she could deduct all of the expenses in Year One since her total "at risk" amount for Year One was $200,000.

(c) As of the end of Year One, her at-risk amount was reduced to zero. Section 465(b)(5). So while Dr. Quinn can deduct $30,000 of the expenses to offset her rental income, she can deduct no portion of the $10,000 loss from the activity in Year Two because she is not "at risk" to any extent as of the end of Year Two. Furthermore, she cannot use any of the $10,000 carryover from Year One. Heading into Year Three, therefore, Dr. Quinn has a total § 465 carryover of $20,000 ($10,000 from Year One plus $10,000 from Year Two).

(d) Now that she is starting to make a profit from the activity, a portion of the § 465 carryover from loss years may be applied. Specifically, Dr. Quinn can use $5,000 of the carryover to offset the $5,000 net income from the activity. This will reduce the carryover to Year Four to $15,000.

SAQ 11–3.

(a) The at-risk rules in § 465 do not apply because Dr. Welby is "at risk" with respect to the entire $500,000 purchase price. That is because the nonrecourse loan is "qualified nonrecourse financing" under § 465(b)(6).

But because Dr. Welby does not "materially participate" in the activity in Year One, the passive activity rules of § 469 will apply to him. Even if Dr. Welby did materially participate in terms of total hours, however, § 469(c)(2) provides that the rental activity will still be classified as a "passive activity" (and Dr. Welby is ineligible for the exception in § 469(c)(7) for those in the regular business of renting). Here, the expenses from the activity exceed the rental income by $60,000. There is thus a "passive activity loss" of $60,000 for the year. Section 469(d)(1). The $25,000 exemption for rental activities in § 469(i)(1) does not apply at all here because Dr. Welby's adjusted gross income is too high (§ 469(i)(3) states that by having an adjusted gross income in excess of $150,000, the $25,000 exemption is completely phased out). Absent any net income from another passive activity, then, the $60,000 passive activity loss is disallowed. Section 469(a)(1). The $60,000 loss will carry over to Year Two under § 469(b).

(b) Dr. Welby still has a $60,000 passive activity loss from the building activity, but now he also has $20,000 of passive activity gross income from the bus leasing business. This reduces the "net" passive activity loss to $40,000, meaning that Dr. Welby can deduct an additional $20,000 from the building activity thanks to the profit from the bus activity. The carryover amount, of course, is reduced to $40,000.

(c) The expenses from Year Two are entirely deductible because there is enough income from the year to offset the expenses. In addition, under § 469(b), $20,000 of the $60,000 disallowed loss from Year One is now deductible, meaning all of the income from the passive activity will be offset by expenses. Heading into Year Three, the carryover amount will be reduced to $40,000.

(d) The $30,000 gain is also passive activity gross income, which would allow Dr. Welby to claim another $30,000 of the $40,000 carryover loss. Moreover, under § 469(g)(1)(A), the excess disallowed loss ($10,000) is also allowed in full because it is not treated as a passive loss anymore.

Index

References are to Pages

References are to Pages

†